Johann Jakob Herzog

Encyclopedia of living divines and Christian workers of all denominations in Europe and America

Johann Jakob Herzog

Encyclopedia of living divines and Christian workers of all denominations in Europe and America

ISBN/EAN: 9783337258733

Printed in Europe, USA, Canada, Australia, Japan

Cover: Foto ©Lupo / pixelio.de

More available books at **www.hansebooks.com**

ENCYCLOPEDIA

OF

LIVING DIVINES

AND

CHRISTIAN WORKERS

OF ALL DENOMINATIONS

IN

EUROPE AND AMERICA

BEING A SUPPLEMENT TO

SCHAFF-HERZOG ENCYCLOPEDIA OF RELIGIOUS KNOWLEDGE.

EDITED BY

REV. PHILIP SCHAFF, D.D., LL.D.,

AND

REV. SAMUEL MACAULEY JACKSON, M.A.

NEW YORK:

FUNK & WAGNALLS, PUBLISHERS,

18 AND 20 ASTOR PLACE.

1887.

PREFACE.

THIS book contains biographical sketches of contemporary divines, celebrated preachers, Christian workers, theological professors, church dignitaries, and editors of prominent religious periodicals. It is intended as a supplement to the *Religious Encyclopædia* published in 1884, in three volumes. The German Encyclopædia of Herzog excludes living authors.

The value of such a book depends on the extent of its authentic information. In this respect we have been highly favored. When the senior editor resolved, somewhat reluctantly, to undertake the delicate task, he issued a circular letter to distinguished divines of Europe and America, requesting them to furnish for publication exact facts and dates concerning their birth, their education, titles, offices, publications, and other noteworthy incidents. To his great encouragement he received prompt and full replies from nearly all, and takes great pleasure in expressing to them publicly his sincere thanks for their kindness. The information thus obtained is presented without note or comment. Where the gentlemen chose to indicate their theological standpoint in a distinctive way, it is given in their own words; if not, it is left to be inferred from their reputation and works.

To secure still greater exactness, proof was sent for revision to each living person named; and their corrections and additions have been inserted as far as possible.

Additional information and corrections received too late for insertion in the proper place have been printed in the appendix.

When no response was received to the circular, the dates and facts desired were derived from the best attainable sources, chiefly the following: HOLTZMANN and ZÖPFFEL'S *Lexikon für Theologie und Kirchenwesen*, for German Protestants; SCHÄFLER'S *Handlexicon der Katholischen Theologie*, for German Roman-Catholics; the thirteenth volume of LICHTENBERGER'S *Encyclopédie des sciences religieuses*, for French authors; CROCKFORD'S *Clerical Directory*, and the latest (eleventh) edition of the *Men of the Times*, for English authors and church dignitaries; denominational cyclopædias, — Baptist, Methodist, Presbyterian, etc., — manuals, year-books, and catalogues of colleges and theological seminaries, for Americans. The articles thus compiled are marked by a star.

Besides living celebrities, the volume includes notices of divines who have died since the completion of the *Religious Encyclopædia* (1884), and a few others who were inadvertently omitted.

Simultaneously with this Supplement will be published a new and revised edition of the *Religious Encyclopædia*, which will embody the corrections made by the authors of the several articles, as well as the editors. Copies were sent to foreign contributors with the request to correct the translation of their articles, and to bring them down to the latest date, which was done.

As to the distribution of labor, the senior editor has procured the material, and written biographical sketches of departed friends (as Drs. Ezra Abbot, Dorner, Lange, Prime, Thiersch), besides aiding in the final revision; while the junior editor has prepared the material for the press, and devoted himself to the work for nearly two years.

The editors have aimed at the greatest possible accuracy and completeness, as well as strict impartiality, in the desire to make a useful and reliable book of reference for readers of all denominations and theological schools.

PHILIP SCHAFF.
SAMUEL M. JACKSON.

NEW YORK, November, 1886.

EXPLANATORY NOTE.

THE general order of arrangement of the sketches is this: Name in full (where initials instead of middle names are given, it is to be understood that the persons had no middle names, but had introduced initials to distinguish their names from others); honorary titles, other than M.A., with their sources and dates in parenthesis; denomination ("Methodist" means Methodist-Episcopal Church North; "Episcopalian" means Protestant-Episcopal Church of the United States; "Presbyterian" means Presbyterian Church in the United States, Northern Assembly; the other divisions which come under these general names are particularly described, e.g., "Methodist-Protestant"); places and dates of study and graduation; positions held in chronological order (except when the person held collegiate and clerical positions simultaneously, in which case it has sometimes seemed better to give each class of positions separately); theological standpoint; publications (the place of publication given with the first book is to be understood as that of all subsequent books until another place is given).

The following information respecting abbreviations used in this work, and the various honors, prizes, etc., mentioned, may be acceptable to American readers.

I.—CONTRACTIONS.

A.B. or **B.A.** Bachelor of Arts (*Artium Baccalaureus*).

A.M. or **M.A.** Master of Arts (*Artium Magister*).

b. born (followed by place and date).

B.D. Bachelor of Divinity.

C.I. Order of the Crown of India, member of.

C.M.G. Companion of the Order of St. Michael and St. George.

d. died (followed by place and date).

D.D. Doctor of divinity.

F.R.G.S. Fellow of the Royal Geographical Society.

F.R.S. Fellow of the Royal Society.

F.R.S.E. Fellow of the Royal Society, Edinburgh.

Lic. Theol. Licentiate of Theology (in Germany, one who has passed the examination for a theological professorship in a university).

LL.D. Doctor of laws.

Lit.D. Doctor of letters.

L.H.D. Doctor of letters.

Ph.D. Doctor of Philosophy.

S.T.D. Doctor of sacred theology (*Sacræ Theologiæ Doctor*).

Ven. Venerable; title of an English archdeacon.

II.—PRIZES AND POSITIONS.

Archdeacon. In the English Church, the assistant of the bishop in the government of his diocese.

Arnold's Historical Prize (Oxford). Open to competition among graduates not older than eight years from matriculation; value £42.

Bampton Lectures (Oxford). Course of eight divinity-lecture sermons, founded by Rev. John Bampton, canon of Salisbury; value £200. See *Encyclopædia*, p. 196.

Battie University Scholarship (Cambridge). Founded by William Battie, M.D., Fellow of King's College, in 1747; competed for by undergraduates, and held for seven years; value £30 to £35.

Bell University Scholarship (Cambridge). Founded by Rev. William Bell, Fellow of Magdalene; competed for by undergraduates, and held four years.

Berkeley Gold Medals (Dublin). Founded by Bp. Berkeley in 1752, for proficiency in Greek language and literature; they are two in number, and are given to the students ranking first and second in the examination.

Boden Sanscrit Scholarship (Oxford). Competed for by students under twenty-five years old; one elected each year; tenable four years; annual value £50.

Boyle Lectures. Course of eight divinity-lecture sermons founded by Robert Boyle. See *Encyclopædia*, p. 315.

Browne Prize (Cambridge). Founded by Sir William Browne, Kt., M.D., who died in 1774; competed for by undergraduates; three prizes, for Greek ode, Latin ode, and Greek and Latin epigrams, respectively.

Burney Prize (Cambridge). Founded in 1845 by Richard Burney, Esq., M.A. of Christ's College, by gift of £3,000 in three per cent consols; open to graduates of the university of not more than three years standing from admission to first degree; for best English essay "on some moral or metaphysical subject, on the existence, nature, and attributes of God, or on the nature and evidences of the Christian religion."

Carus Greek Testament Prize (Cambridge). Founded in 1853, in honor of and by Rev. William Carus, M.A., canon of Winchester, and late senior fellow of Trinity College, his friends and he each giving £500 at three per cent; the prizes are two in number, one for undergraduates and one for graduates.

Chancellor Medal (Cambridge). For classics; instituted by Thomas Hollis, Duke of Westminster, when chancellor 1751, and continued by his successors; two gold medals, senior and junior, open to competition by B.A.'s.

Class (Oxford). A division according to merit, of those who pass an examination.

Classic (senior). A first-class in classics.

Convict. Building in which Roman-Catholic divinity students live at State expense.

Consistorialrath. Counsellor of the Consistory, the governing body in spiritual affairs in German States.

Craven Scholarship (Cambridge). Founded by John, Lord Craven, 1647; open to competition by undergraduates; held seven years; value £80.

Crosse Theological Scholarship (Cambridge). Founded by Rev. John Crosse, vicar of Bradford, Yorkshire, 1816, "for promoting the cause of true religion;" open to competition by B.A.'s; held three years.

Denyer Theological Essay (Oxford). Open to competition among B.A.'s.

Diaconus. The title in Germany of certain assistant clergymen and chaplains of subordinate rank, but equal standing with ordained ministers. See *Encyclopædia*, vol. i. p. 615.

Divinity Testimonium (Dublin). Certificate of attendance on whole divinity course of six terms; graduates arranged in three classes according to merit.

Donnellan Lectures (Dublin). Founded by Miss Anne Donnellan. See *Encyclopædia*, vol. i. p. 661.

Double First (Oxford). To be in the first division in B.A. examination both in classics and mathematics.

Ellerton Theological Essay (Oxford). Open to competition among members of the university, value of prize £21.

Ephorus (German ecclesiastical dignitary). One who presides over and superintends a number of other clergymen.

Evans Prize (Cambridge). Founded in honor of the late Ven. Robert Wilson Evans, B.D., archdeacon of Westmoreland, formerly fellow and tutor of Trinity College; awarded to best student in ecclesiastical history and Greek and Latin Fathers, among the candidates for honors in the second part of the theological tripos.

Fellow. A member of a college who is on the foundation, and receives an income from its revenues.

Gymnasial Professor. Professor in a German gymnasium (college), where students are prepared for the university.

Hall-Houghton Prize (Oxford). Two for work upon the Greek Testament, value £30 and £20 respectively; and two upon the Septuagint, value £25 and £15 respectively.

Houghton Syriac Prize (Oxford). Value £15.

Hulsean Lecturer (Cambridge). See *Encyclopædia*, vol. ii. p. 1037.

Hulsean Prizeman (Cambridge). See *Encyclopædia*, vol. ii. p. 1037.

Hulsean Professor (Cambridge). See *Encyclopædia*, vol. ii. p. 1037.

Inspector (of a *Stift*). Head spiritual officer of a building in which theological students live at State expense. See *Stift*.

Jeremie Septuagint Prize (Cambridge). Founded in 1870, by gift of £1,000 from the Very Rev. James Amiraux Jeremie, D.D., dean of Lincoln, formerly regius professor of divinity; two annual prizes; open to all members of the university of not more than three years standing from their first degree.

Johnson Theological Scholarship (Oxford). Open to B.A.'s; held one year; value £50.

Kennicott Hebrew Scholarship (Oxford). Open to B.A.'s; tenable a year.

Law (Bishop) **Prize** (Dublin). Founded by John, lord bishop of Elphin, in 1796, for proficiency in mathematics; open to competition among undergraduates; there are two prizes.

Le Bas Prize (Cambridge). Founded by Rev. Charles W. Le Bas, M.A., Fellow of Trinity, 1848; subject of essay, general literature, and occasionally some topic connected with the history and prospects of India.

Lloyd Exhibition (Dublin). Founded in memory of Provost Lloyd, by his friends, in 1839; open to competition among undergraduates; subjects, mathematics and physics.

Maitland Prize (Cambridge). Founded in 1844, by gift of £1,000 in honor of Lieut.-Gen. Sir Peregrine Maitland, K.C.B., late commander-in-chief of the forces in South India; for English essay on some subject connected with the propagation of the gospel through missionary exertion in India, and other parts of the heathen world; awarded every three years; open to graduates of not more than ten years standing. The successful essay is published.

Master of the Charterhouse. Principal of the school of that name.

Master of Christ's Hospital. Principal of the school of that name.

Master of Marlborough College. Principal of the school of that name.

Members' Prize (Cambridge). Given by the representatives of the University in Parliament; one for English essay on some subject connected with British history or literature, and one for Latin essay; each prize open to all members of the university not of sufficient standing to be created M.A. or M.L.; value £31. 10*s*. each.

Moderations (Oxford). The second undergraduate examination.

Moderatorship (Dublin). Given at B.A. examination to best students in each of five departments (mathematics, classics, logics and ethics, natural and experimental science, and history); value, a gold medal.

Newdigate Prize Poem (Oxford). Founded by Sir Roger Newdigate; open to competition among members of the university under four years from matriculation; is in English verse; value £21.

Norrisian Prize for Theological Essay (Cambridge). Founded by John Norris in 1777; value £12 (gold medal and books).

Oberkirchenrath. Member of the highest Protestant Church Council in Prussia and Baden.

Optime (Cambridge). One who stands in the second or third class of final honors in mathematics; called Senior and Junior Optime respectively.

Porson Prize (Cambridge). For best translation from any standard English poet into Greek verse, with Latin version of the Greek.

Privat-docent. One who has "habilitated himself," i.e., passed the examination for professor in a German university, and delivers lectures like the professors; but receives, usually, no salary from the State, and therefore depends for support upon lecture-fees or other sources.

Professor Extraordinary. In a German university, has no seat in the faculty or senate, a smaller salary than the regular or ordinary professor, but is in the line of promotion.

Professor Ordinary. In a German university, is a member of the faculty, and salaried by government.

Pusey and Ellerton Hebrew Scholarship (Oxford). Tenable a year; value £55.

Realschule. A school in which modern languages and the arts and sciences are taught; corresponds to a polytechnic.

Repetent. One who in Tübingen and Göttingen conducts weekly examinations in the lectures of the professors, selected from the best graduate students.

Scholefield Prize (Cambridge). Founded by gift of £500 in 1856, in honor of Rev. James Scholefield, M.A., regius professor of Greek; in promotion of the critical study of Holy Scripture; given to that candidate for honors, in the second part of the theological tripos who shows the best knowledge of the Greek Testament and the Septuagint version of the Old Testament.

Seatonian Prize (Cambridge). Founded by Rev. Thomas Seaton, M.A., fellow of Clare College, who died in 1741; given for best English poem on a sacred subject; open to M.A.'s; value £40.

Select Preacher (Oxford). Must be M.A., B.D., D.D., or B.C.L. of Oxford, Cambridge, or Dublin, five chosen yearly, each serves two years; they preach before the university.

Stift (Tübingen and elsewhere in Germany). A building in which theological students live together at the expense of the State.

Smith's Prize (Cambridge). Founded by Rev. Robert Smith, D.D., master of Trinity College, d. 1768; two annual prizes given to the two commencing B.A.'s who are most proficient in mathematics and natural philosophy; value £23 each.

Tripos (Cambridge). One of the honor lists with its three classes, called in mathematics wranglers, senior optimes, junior optimes.

Tyrwhitt Hebrew Scholarship (Cambridge). Founded by Rev. Robert Tyrwhitt, M.A., Fellow of Jesus College, died 1817; open to competition among B.A.'s or students in civil law or medicine; tenable three years; six scholarships, worth together £150.

Whitehall Preachership (Cambridge). Established by George I. in 1724, tenable two years: filled from Oxford and Cambridge (two from each) by appointment of the Bishop of London.

Wrangler (Cambridge). One of the students who pass in the first class of mathematical honors; the first in the list being styled senior wrangler, and the others respectively second wrangler, third wrangler, etc.

DICTIONARY OF CONTEMPORARY DIVINES.

A.

ABBOT, Ezra, S.T.D. (Harvard, 1872), **LL.D.** (Yale, 1869, Bowdoin, 1878), Unitarian layman; b. at Jackson, Waldo County, Me., April 28, 1819; d. at Cambridge, Mass., March 21, 1884, and was buried in Mount Auburn Cemetery, near Boston. He was fitted for college at Phillips Academy, at Exeter (N.H.), and graduated at Bowdoin College, Brunswick (Me.), 1840. He then taught school in Maine until 1847, when he removed to Cambridge (Mass.). He taught the high school at Cambridgeport, and also rendered service in the Harvard University and Boston Athenæum libraries. In 1856 he was appointed assistant librarian of Harvard University. His studies had long been given to the Greek New Testament, and in 1872 he became Bussey professor of New-Testament criticism and interpretation in the Harvard Divinity School, and so remained until his death.

He was the recipient of many testimonials to his scholarship. In 1852 he was elected a member of the American Oriental Society, and since 1853 was its recording secretary; and in 1861 a member of the American Academy of Arts and Sciences. He was University lecturer on the textual criticism of the New Testament, in 1871. He was one of the original members of the American New-Testament Revision Company. In 1880 he aided in organizing the Society of Biblical Literature and Exegesis. He belonged also to the Harvard Biblical Club. He was tendered the degree of D.D. by the University of Edinburgh at its tercentenary (1884), but died shortly before the date of its celebration.

Dr. Abbot, who bore his name Ezra not in vain, was a scholar of rare talents and attainments, who would have done honor to any nation and any university. He was the first textual critic of the Greek Testament in America, and for microscopic accuracy of biblical scholarship he had no superior in the world. His accuracy was proverbial among his friends. He would have accomplished more if he had been less painstaking in minute details. Hence he has hardly done himself justice in his publications; but the results of his labors have gone into other books, to which he was willing to contribute without regard to reward, being satisfied if only the work was done, no matter by whom. He was the very embodiment of the unselfishness of scholarship. His *Literature of the Doctrine of the Future Life*, first published as an Appendix to Alger's *History of the Doctrine of the Future Life* (1864), and afterwards separately, is a model of bibliographical accuracy and completeness, and embraces over fifty-three hundred titles; while Grässe's *Bibliotheca Psychologica* (1845) contains only ten hundred and twenty-five. He enriched Smith's *Bible Dictionary* (Am. ed., 1867-70, 4 vols.) with careful bibliographical lists on the most important topics. His most valuable and independent labors, however, were devoted to textual criticism, and are incorporated in Dr. Gregory's *Prolegomena* to the *Ed. viii. critica major* of Tischendorf's Greek Testament. He followed the preparation of this work with the deepest interest till his last sickness, but died a few months before the first volume appeared (Leipzig, 1884). The chapter *De Versibus* (pp. 167-182) is by him, and he read the MS. and proof of all the rest. Dr. Gregory lost in him, as he says, "a constant and proven guide, counsellor, and support." Oscar von Gebhardt, the editor of Tischendorf's latest text, declares Abbot's loss to biblical science irreparable. "We all feel it who labor in the same field." His services to the American Bible-Revision Committee were invaluable. He attended the monthly meetings from 1871 to 1881 most punctually, and was always thoroughly prepared. The critical papers which he prepared on disputed passages, at the request of the N. T. Company, and which were forwarded from time to time to the British Company, were uncommonly thorough, and had no small influence in determining the text finally accepted. As a Unitarian, he differed on some points from his fellow-revisers; but he had the most delicate regard for their convictions, never obtruded his own, sought only the truth, and as his friend and successor, Dr. Thayer, says in his memorial paper adopted by the Committee, "his Christlike temper rendered him a brother beloved, and lends a heavenly lustre to his memory." His defence of the Johannean *Authorship of the Fourth Gospel* (1880, pp. 104) is an invaluable contribution to the solution of that great question: it is the best within the limits of external evidence, and makes one regret that he did not complete it by the internal evidence, which he thought would require two volumes. Godet (in the third ed. of his *Com. on the Gospel of St. John*, I. 38) says of Abbot's book: "*Ce travail me paraît épuiser la matière. Connaissance complète des discussions modernes, étude approfondie des témoignages du IIe siècle, mesure et netteté dans le jugement, rien n'y manque.*"

Personally, Dr. Abbot was a kind-hearted, modest, courteous, disinterested, amiable, devout, and conscientious Christian gentleman. From the many testimonials to his worth as a scholar and a man, which are published in a memorial volume by the Alumni of the Harvard Divinity School (Cambridge, 1884), we shall select a few. Ex-President Dr. Woolsey, who was associated with him for ten years in the Bible-Revision Committee: "My acquaintance with him during our revision-work gave me profound respect for him as a man as well as a scholar. He was indeed a most admirable man, and one whom it was a great privilege to know. His kindness to everybody who wanted his help was unsurpassed by that of anybody I ever met with. He has had my full confidence, admiration, and respect beyond most men I ever knew." Dr. Sanday of Oxford: "For clearness, accuracy, and precision of detail, I do not think he can have had a rival on either side of the Atlantic; but it was evident that they were qualities which were moral as well as intellectual. My sense of his loss is compounded of gratitude and admiration, and of the deepest regret that such a career should be closed." Dr. Westcott, Canon of Westminster: "It is the simple truth to say that (as far as I know) no scholar in America was superior to him in exactness of knowledge, breadth of reading, perfection of candor, and devotion to truthfulness of judgment. No eye was keener than his, and no one could be more ready to place all his powers at the service of others with spontaneous generosity."

Dr. Abbot's name will ever occupy an honorable place among the few patient and self-denying scholars who have devoted the strength of their lives to the restoration of the pure text of the New Testament of our Lord and Saviour.

Of his writings, besides those already spoken of, may be mentioned, *A Glimpse of Glory* (art. in *Christian Register*, July 27, 1861); edition of *Orme's Memoir of the Controversy respecting the Three Heavenly Witnesses*, New York, 1866; work upon G. R. Noyes's (posthumous) *Translation of the N. T. from the Greek text of Tischendorf*, New York, 1869; work upon C. F. Hudson's *Greek and English Concordance of the N. T.* (furnished appendix and supplementary collation of Tischendorf's ed. VIII., and perfected subsequent editions till 1882); *The Late Professor Tischendorf* (art. in *Unitarian Review*, March, 1875); *On the reading "an only begotten God," or "God only begotten," John i. 18* (art. in the *Unitarian Review*, June, 1875, first privately printed for the American Bible-Revision Committee); *On the reading "Church of God," Acts xx. 28* (art. in *Bibliotheca Sacra*, April, 1876, first privately printed for the American Bible-Revision Committee); *The New-Testament Text* (art. in *Sunday-school World*, October, 1878, repub. in *Anglo-American Bible Revision*, New York, 1879); *The Gospels in the New Revision* (art. in *Sunday-school Times*, May 28, June 4, June 11, 1881); *Bible Text* (art. by Tischendorf and von Gebhardt in Herzog, condensed Eng. translation revised and supplemented for the *Schaff-Herzog Encyclopædia*, New York, 1882); *Recent Discussions of Romans ix. 5* (an exhaustive art. on the punctuation of this passage in *Journal of the Society of Biblical Literature and Exegesis*, June and December, 1883). See *Ezra Abbot* [edited by Rev. S. J. BARROWS], Cambridge, 1884. PHILIP SCHAFF.

ABBOTT, Edwin Abbott, D.D. (by Archbishop of Canterbury, 1872), Church of England; b. in London, Dec. 20, 1838; educated at St. John's College, Cambridge; graduated B.A., 1861 (7th senior optime and senior classic); M.A., 1864; was fellow of his college; assistant master at King Edward's School, Birmingham (1862), then at Clifton College, Bristol, and since 1865 head master of the City of London School. In 1869, and twice subsequently, he was select preacher at Cambridge, and the same at Oxford (1877). In 1876 he was Hulsean lecturer at Cambridge. His theological position is that of the Broad Church School. He goes "beyond many of them in rejecting the miraculous, but does not go with many of them in rejecting what is generally called dualism,—some kind of a recognition of an Evil contending against the Good." His religious publications include *Bible Lessons*, London, 1871; *Good Voices, a Child's Guide to the Bible*, 1872; *Parables for Children*, 1873; *Cambridge Sermons*, 1875; *Through Nature to Christ*, 1877; *Oxford Sermons*, 1879; (in connection with W. G. Rushbrooke, editor of the *Synopticon*), *The Common Tradition of the Synoptic Gospels in the Text of the Revised Version*, 1884. He wrote the article *Gospels* in the 9th ed. of the *Encycl. Brit.* (1879), and the anonymous religious fictions, *Philochristus, Memoirs of a Disciple of Our Lord*, 1878; and *Onesimus, Memoirs of a Disciple of St. Paul*, 1882. Among his other works are, *A Shakespearian Grammar*, 1869, 2d ed., 1871; an edition of Bacon's *Essays*, 1876, 2 vols.; *Bacon and Essex*, 1877; *Hints on Home Teaching*, 1883, 2d ed. same year; *Flatland, a Romance of Many Dimensions*, 1884, 2d ed., 1885, republished, Boston, 1885; *Francis Bacon, an Account of his Life and Works*, 1885; and several instruction-books in English and Latin.

ABBOTT, Lyman, D.D. (New-York University, 1877), Congregationalist; b. at Roxbury, Mass., Dec. 18, 1835; graduated at New-York University, 1853; was for a time partner in his brothers' law-firm, but then studied theology under his uncle, J. S. C. Abbott, and was pastor at Terre Haute, Ind., 1860–65; secretary American Union (Freedmen's) Commission, New York, 1865–68; pastor of the New-England Church, New York, 1866–69; editor of *The Illustrated Christian Weekly*, 1871–76; and since 1876 of *The Christian Union*. He is the author of *The Results of Emancipation in the United States*, New York, 1867; *Jesus of Nazareth*, 1869, new and illus. ed., 1882; *Old-Testament Shadows of New-Testament Truths*, 1870; *Laicus, or the Experiences of a Layman in a Country Parish*, 1872; *Commentary upon Matthew and Mark*, 1875; *Luke*, 1877; *John*, 1879; *Acts*, 1876; (with J. R. Gilmore), *The Gospel History, Complete Life of Christ*, 1881; *For Family Worship*, 1883; *Henry Ward Beecher, a Sketch of his Career*, 1883. He edited Beecher's *Sermons*, 1868, 2 vols.; *Morning and Evening Exercises* (selections from H. W. Beecher), 1871; and (with T. J. Conant) *A Dictionary of Religious Knowledge*, 1873.

ABBOTT, Thomas Kingsmill, Episcopal Church in Ireland; b. in Dublin, March 26, 1829; educated at Trinity College, Dublin; graduated B.A. (senior moderator, large gold medal in mathematics, and senior moderator in ethics and logic), 1851; M.A., 1855; B.D., 1879. He was Lloyd exhibitioner, 1849; Bishop Law's prizeman (first), 1850; elected fellow, 1854. From 1867 to 1872 he was professor of moral philosophy in Trinity College; since 1875 has been professor of Biblical Greek; and since 1879 also of Hebrew. In the ology he is Broad Church. He is the author of *The English Bible, a Plea for Revision*, Dublin, 1857, 2d ed , 1871; *Sight and Touch, an attempt to disprove the Berkeleian theory of vision*, London, 1864; *Kant's Theory of Ethics*, translated with memoir, 1873, 3d ed., 1883; *Collation of Four MSS. of the Gospels, by Ferrar*, edited with introduction, 1877; *Codex rescriptus S. Matthaei Dublinensis (Z)*, Dublin, 1880; *Elements of Logic*, London, 1883, 2d ed., 1885; *Evangelia antehieronymiana ex codice Dublinensi*, Dublin, 1884; *Kant's Introduction to Logic*, translated, London, 1885.

ACHELIS, Ernst Christian, D.D. (*hon.* Halle, 1882), Reformed; b. at Bremen, Jan. 13, 1838; studied theology at Heidelberg and Halle, 1857–60; became successively assistant preacher at Arsten, near Bremen, 1860; pastor at Hastedt, near Bremen, 1862; pastor at Barmen, 1875; ordinary professor of theology at Marburg, 1882. Besides numerous minor publications, he has issued *Die biblischen Thatsachen und die religiöse Bedeutung ihrer Geschichtlichkeit*, Gotha, 1869; *Dr. Richard Rothe*, 1869; *Der Krieg im Lichte der Christlichen Moral*, Bremen, 1871; *Die Bergpredigt nach Matthaeus und Lukas exegetisch und kritisch untersucht*, Bielefeld und Leipzig, 1875; *Parteiwesen und Evangelium*, Barmen, 1878; *Die Entstehungszeit von Luther's geistlichen Liedern*, Marburg, 1884.

ADAMS, Right Rev. William Forbes, D.D. (University of the South, Sewanee, Tenn., 1871), Episcopalian bishop; b. in Ireland, Jan. 2, 1833; came to United States, 1841; ordained priest, 1860; consecrated first missionary bishop of New Mexico and Arizona, 1875; resigned, 1876; became rector at Vicksburg, Miss. *

ADLER, Felix, Ph.D. (Heidelberg, 1873); b. at Alzey, Germany, Aug. 13, 1851; graduated at Columbia College, New-York City, 1870; and at Heidelberg University, 1873. From 1873 to 1876 he was non-resident professor of Oriental languages and literature at Cornell University, Ithaca, N.Y., and since 1876 has been lecturer of the Society for Ethical Culture, New-York City. His "stand-point is not to be classed as theological in a strict sense. His philosophical views are founded on those of Immanuel Kant. He regards ethics as the foundation, and religion as the superstructure. The unity of the world he regards as a necessary idea of the reason, which, however, cannot gather personality about it. Its value consists on the one hand in its regulative application to conduct, on the other hand in its forming the basis for a moral conviction respecting the ultimate good tendencies of the universe." He has published *Creed and Deeds* (lectures), New York, 1878; and single lectures

ADLER, Hermann, Ph.D. (Leipzig, 1861), Hebrew rabbi; b. at Hanover, May 29, 1839; came to London, 1845; studied at University College, London, and graduated at London University, B.A., 1859; studied subsequently at Prague and Leipzig; became principal of the Jews' College, London, 1863, and chief minister of the Bayswater synagogue, 1864; resigned principalship, 1865, and was theological tutor until 1879; since 1879 has been delegate chief rabbi. He is an Orthodox Jew. Besides many sermons and articles in periodicals, he has published, *A Jewish Reply to Colenso*, London, 1865; *Sermons on the Passages in the Bible adduced by Christian Theologians in Support of their Faith*, 1879.

ADLER, Nathan Marcus, Ph.D. (Erlangen, 1826), Orthodox Jew; b. at Hanover, Dec. 14, 1802; graduated at the University of Würzburg; became chief rabbi of the Grand Duchy of Oldenburg, 1829; of the Kingdom of Hanover, 1830; of the United Hebrew congregations of the British Empire, 1845. He was one of the organizers of Jewish schools in London and the provinces; joined Sir Moses Montefiore in appeal for the Holy Land, by which £20,000 were raised; was one of the founders of the "United Synagogue," a federation of the principal synagogues; founder and first president of the Jews' College, London; one of the original members of the committee of the Metropolitan Hospital Sunday Fund. He is the author of many printed sermons in German and English, among which may be mentioned, *Die Liebe zum Vaterlande*, Hanover, 1838; his Installation Sermon, London, 1845; *Sermon on the Day of Humiliation*, 1854 ("pronounced by the English press as the most eloquent of those delivered on that occasion"); *The Jewish Faith*, 1867; *The Claims of Deaf-Mutes* (which led to the founding of the Jews' Deaf and Dumb Home); *The Second Days of the Festivals;* and of *The Nethina Lager* (a Hebrew commentary on the Chaldee paraphrase of the Pentateuch), Wilna, 1874, 2d ed., 1877.

AHLFELD, Johann Friedrich, D.D., Lutheran; b. at Mehringen, Anhalt, Nov. 1, 1810; d. at Leipzig, March 4, 1884. He studied at the University of Halle, 1830–33; became private tutor, 1833; gymnasial teacher at Zerbst, 1834, and rector at Wörlitz, 1837; pastor at Alsleben, 1838; at Halle, 1847; at Leipzig (St. Nicholas' Church), 1851. In early life he was troubled by scepticism; but before beginning his pastoral career he was rid of it, and distinguished himself ever afterwards by the simplicity, clearness, and beauty of his Christian faith. He was one of Germany's most admired preachers, the greatest pulpit orator of the strict Lutherans, and, especially at Leipzig, wielded a powerful influence. To considerable learning he united a knowledge of the human heart, good judgment, ready sympathies, and kindly humor, so that he was the friend and counsellor of all classes, and held by every one in affectionate esteem. His sermons were listened to by throngs, and abounded in apt and beautiful illustration. Besides preaching, he taught in the Leipzig Theological Seminary, and for many years did good service upon the commission to revise the Luther version of the Old Testament. In 1881 he was made pastor emeritus and *Geheimer Kirchenrath*. Of the numerous collections of his discourses may be mentioned, *Predigten über die evangelischen Perikopen*, Halle, 1848, 10th ed., 1880; *Das Leben im Lichte des Worts Gottes*, 1861, 6th ed., 1879; *Predigten über die epistolischen Perikopen*, 1867, 3d ed., 1877; *Confirmationsreden*, Leipzig, 1880, 2 series. See his *Lebensbild*, Halle, 1885. *

AIKEN, Charles Augustus, Ph.D. (Princeton, 1866), **D.D.** (Princeton, 1870), Presbyterian; b. in Manchester, Vt., Oct. 30, 1827; graduated at Dartmouth College, 1846; taught three years in the Lawrence Academy, Groton, Mass., and in Phillips Academy, Andover; entered the Andover

Theological Seminary, graduated 1853, having meanwhile studied at the universities of Halle and Berlin (1851–53). He became successively pastor of the Congregational Church at Yarmouth, Me., 1854; professor of Latin in Dartmouth College, 1859; the same in the College of New Jersey at Princeton, 1866; president of Union College, Schenectady, N.Y., 1869; Archibald Alexander professor of Christian ethics and apologetics in Princeton Theological Seminary, 1871; and since 1882, Archibald Alexander professor of Oriental and Old-Testament literature in the same institution. He was a member of the Old-Testament Revision Company. He translated Zöckler's commentary on *Proverbs* in the Lange series, New York, 1869; and has contributed to the *Presbyterian* and other reviews, etc.

AITKEN, William Hay Macdowall Hunter, Church of England; b. at Liverpool, Sept. 21, 1841; educated at Wadham College, Oxford; graduated B.A. (2d class classics), 1865; M.A., 1867; was curate of St. Jude's, Mildmay Park, 1866–70; incumbent of Christ Church, Everton, Liverpool, 1871–75; has since devoted himself entirely to mission [revival] work, and since 1884 he has been general superintendent of the Church of England Parochial Mission Society, which he founded in 1877, with a view to supply competent mission [revival] preachers. His theology is "eclectic. He desires to be a Churchman pure and simple, to belong to no party, but to comprehend what is good in all. He holds evangelical principles strongly, but without Calvinism, and values highly Church order and the sacraments." He conducted a mission in New-York City in the winter of 1885. He has published *Mission Sermons*, Brighton, 1875–76, 3 series, 2d ed., London, 1877; *Newness of Life*, Brighton, 1877, 2d ed., London, 1878; *Difficulties of the Soul*, London, 1878; *What is your Life?* 1878; *Manual of Parochial Missions*, 1879; *The School of Grace*, 1879; *God's Everlasting "Yea,"* 1880; *The Glory of the Gospel*, 1881; *The Highway of Holiness*, 1883; *Around the Cross*, 1884; *The Revealer revealed*, 1885.

ALDEN, Edmund Kimball, D.D. (Amherst, 1866), Congregationalist; b. at Randolph, Mass., April 11, 1825; graduated at Amherst College, 1844; and at Andover Theological Seminary, 1848; became pastor of First Church, Yarmouth, Me., 1850; at Lenox, Mass., 1854; of Phillips Church, South Boston, Mass., 1859; secretary of the American Board of Commissioners for Foreign Missions, Boston, Mass., 1876. He is the author of various sermons and pamphlets.

ALEXANDER, Right Rev. William, D.D. (by diploma, Oxford, 1867), **D.C.L.** (*hon.*, Oxford, 1876), Lord Bishop of Derry and Raphoe, Episcopalian Church in Ireland; b. at Londonderry, Ireland, April 13, 1824; was a student in Exeter and then in Brasenose College, Oxford University; won the theological prize essay, 1850; graduated B.A., 1854; M.A., 1856; won the sacred prize poem, 1860. He was select preacher, 1870–71, 1882; and Bampton lecturer, 1876. His ministerial life has been spent in Ireland, where he became successively rector of Termonamongan, and of Camus-juxta-Mourne; dean of Emly, 1863; bishop of Derry and Raphoe, 1867. His wife, Cecil Frances Humphreys, is author of many familiar hymns and poems. He has written, besides numerous articles, etc., *Leading Ideas of the Gospels* (Oxford sermons, 1870–71), London, 1872; *The Witness of the Psalms to Christ and Christianity* (Bampton lectures), 1877, 2d ed., 1878, republished, New York; *The Great Question and other Sermons*, 1885; *The New Atlantis and other Poems;* introductions to and comments upon Colossians, Thessalonians, Philemon, and Epistles of John, in *Bible* (Speaker's) *Commentary*, vols. ix., x. (1881).

ALEXANDER, William, D.D. (University of Wooster, O., 1876), Presbyterian; b. near Shirleysburg, Huntingdon County, Penn., Dec. 18, 1831; graduated at Jefferson College, Penn., 1858, and at Princeton Theological Seminary, 1861; was pastor at Lycoming, Penn. (1862–63); stated supply at Waukesha, Wis., while president of Carroll College in that place (1863–64); pastor at Beloit, Wis. (1864–69); and at San José, Cal., 1869–71; president of City College, San Francisco, 1871–74. In October, 1871, he took a leading part in founding the San Francisco Theological Seminary, and was made (1871) its first professor of New-Testament literature. In 1876 he was transferred to the chair of ecclesiastical history and church government. He has published several sermons, *Commentary on International Sunday-school Lessons*, 1881 sqq.; *Letters* (4) *to Gen. George Stoneman on the Sunday Law*, 1881; *Letters* (9) *to Bishop McQuade on Failure of Romanism*, 1883, etc.

ALEXANDER, William Lindsay, D.D., F.R.S.E., Scotch Congregationalist; b. at Edinburgh, Aug. 24, 1808; d. there, Dec. 22, 1884. He was educated in the universities of Edinburgh and St. Andrews; classical tutor in the Lancashire Independent College at Blackburn (now at Manchester) from 1828 to 1835; Congregational pastor in Edinburgh (1835–1854); subsequently professor of theology in the Congregational Theological College, Edinburgh (1854); examiner in philosophy at St. Andrew's University (1861); and member of the Old-Testament Revision Company from its formation (1870). He published *The Connection and Harmony of the Old and New Testament*, London (Congregational lecture for 1840), 2d ed., 1853; *Anglo-Catholicism not Apostolical*, 1843; *Christ and Christianity*, 1854; *The Life and Correspondence of Ralph Wardlaw, D.D.*, 1856; *Christian Thought and Work*, 1862; *St. Paul at Athens*, 1865; *Sermons*, 1875; *Zechariah, his Visions and Warnings*, 1885; and brought out the third edition of Kitto's *Biblical Cyclopædia*, Edinburgh, 1862–66, 3 vols.

ALGER, William Rounseville, Unitarian; b. at Freetown, Mass., Dec. 30, 1822; graduated at Harvard Divinity School, 1847; was pastor at Roxbury, Mass., 1848–55; in Boston, as successor of Theodore Parker, 1855–73; in New York, 1876–79; at Denver, Col. (1880); and Portland, Me. (1881). Since 1882 he has lived without a charge in Boston. He has written *A Symbolic History of the Cross of Christ*, Boston, 1851; *The Poetry of the Orient*, 1856, 5th ed., 1883; *A Critical History of the Doctrine of a Future Life, with a Complete Bibliography of the Subject by Ezra Abbot*, Philadelphia, 1863, 12th ed., Boston, 1885; *The Genius of Solitude*, Boston, 1865, 10th ed., 1884; *Friendships of Women*, 1867, 10th ed., 1884; *Prayers offered in the Massachusetts House of Representatives*, 1868; *Life of Edwin Forrest*, Philadelphia, 1877, 2 vols.; *The School of Life*, Boston, 1881.

ALLEN, Alexander Viets Griswold, D.D. (Kenyon, 1878), Episcopalian; b. at Otis, Berkshire County, Mass., May 4, 1841; graduated at Kenyon College, Gambier, O., 1862, and at Andover Theological Seminary, 1865; became rector of St. John's Church, Lawrence, Mass., 1865, and professor of ecclesiastical history in the Episcopal Theological School in Cambridge, Mass., 1867. He is the author of *The Continuity of Christian Thought, a Study of Modern Theology in the Light of its History*, Boston, 1884.

ALLEN, Joseph Henry, Unitarian; b. at Northborough, Mass., Aug. 21, 1820; graduated at Harvard College (1840), and Divinity School (1843); pastor at Roxbury, Mass., 1843–47; Washington, D.C., 1847–50; Bangor, Me., 1850–57; West Newton, 1858–60; Northborough, 1864–66; and Lincoln, Mass., 1868–74; Ithaca, N.Y., 1883–84; editor (assistant or chief) of the *Christian Examiner*, 1857–69; lecturer upon ecclesiastical history in Harvard University, 1878–82; delegate (1881) of British and Foreign and of American Unitarian Associations to the Supreme Consistory of Transylvania, held in Koloszvár, Hungary. He is the author of *Memoir of Hiram Withington*, Boston, 1849; *Ten Discourses on Orthodoxy*, 1849; *A Manual of Devotions for Families and Sunday Schools*, 1852; *Hebrew Men and Times from the Patriarchs to the Messiah*, 1861, 2d ed., 1879; *Fragments of Christian History*, 1880; *Our Liberal Movement in Theology, chiefly as shown in Recollections of the History of Unitarianism in New England*, 1882; *Christian History in its Three Great Periods*, 1883, 3 vols. (includes *Fragments*); *Outline of Christian History*, 1884, 2d ed., 1885; joint editor of "Allen and Greenough's Classical Series."

ALLIOLI, Joseph Franz, D.D. (Regensburg, 1816), Roman Catholic; b. at Sulzbach, Austria, Aug. 10, 1793; d. at Augsburg, May 22, 1873. After receiving his general training at Sulzbach and Amberg, he studied theology at Landshut, then entered the clerical seminary at Regensburg; was consecrated to the priesthood, Aug. 11, 1816, and shortly afterwards made a Doctor of Divinity. He officiated for short periods as priest, in Grafling, Roding, and Regensburg, but, giving himself up to learned pursuits, studied Oriental languages at Vienna, Rome, and Paris; became successively *privat-docent* (1821), extraordinary (1823) and then ordinary professor (1824) of the Oriental languages and of biblical exegesis and archæology at Landshut. He went with the University to Munich (1826), and became in 1830 member of the Munich Academy of Sciences, and rector of the university. A throat-affection obliging him to give up teaching, he was in 1835 chosen member of the Cathedral Chapter, Munich, and, in 1838, provost of the cathedral at Augsburg. Active in charitable work, he greatly promoted the Franciscan Female Institute of the Star of Mary. Although an invalid, he wrote many academical addresses, sermons, liturgical treatises, and Hebrew and Arabic poems, besides the following important works: *Aphorismen über den Zusammenhang der heiligen Schriften des Alten und Neuen Testaments*, Landshut, 1819; *Häusliche Alterthümer der Hebräer nebst biblische Geographie*, 1821; *Biblische Alterthümer*, 1825; *Leben Jesu*, 1840; *Handbuch der biblischen Alterthumskunde*, 1841–44, 2 vols. (in connection with L. C. Gratz and Haneberg). But by far the greatest of his works was his third edition of H. Braun's annotated German translation from the Vulgate of the entire Bible, Nuremberg, 1830–34, 6 vols. The original work appeared there in 1786, and in a second edition by Michael Feder, 1803, 3 parts. Allioli's edition was such a decided improvement, that his predecessors have been forgotten. It has been repeatedly re-issued, and has the unique honor among German translations of the Bible, of having received the papal sanction. *

ALLISON, James, D.D. (Washington and Jefferson College, Pa., 1868), Presbyterian; b. at Pittsburg, Penn., Sept. 27, 1823; graduated at Jefferson College, 1845, and at Western Theological Seminary, Allegheny, Penn., 1848; became pastor at Sewickley, 1849; editor and proprietor of the *Presbyterian Banner*, Pittsburg, 1864, of which he had been associate editor since 1856. He has been a member of the Presbyterian Board for Freedmen since its organization in 1865, and its treasurer since 1870.

ALLON, Henry, D.D. (Yale College, 1871; St. Andrew's University, 1885), Congregationalist; b. at Welton, near Hull, Yorkshire, Eng., Oct. 13, 1818; graduated at Cheshunt College, Hertfordshire, 1843; and since January, 1844, has been minister of Union Chapel, Islington, London (for the first eight years as associate of the Rev. Thomas Lewis); and in addition, since 1865, editor of the *British Quarterly Review*. In 1864, and again in the Jubilee Year, 1881, he was chairman of the Congregational Union. In December, 1877, his new church in Compton Terrace, Islington, which had cost £41,466, was opened for service. His congregation numbers nearly two thousand. Although so immersed in pastoral labors, he yet has written much for the periodical press, compiled the *Congregational Psalmist*, very generally used in his denomination, and published the following volumes: *The Life of Rev. James Sherman*, London, 1863 (three editions same year); *The Vision of God, and other Sermons*, 1876, 3d ed., 1877; and edited Thomas Binney's sermons, prefacing a critical sketch, 1875.

ANDERSON, Galusha, S.T.D. (University of Rochester, 1866), **LL.D.** (both Rochester and Madison Universities, 1883), Baptist; b. at Bergen, Genesee County, N.Y., March 7, 1832; graduated at University of Rochester (1854), and (Baptist) theological seminary (1856); became pastor at Janesville, Wis., 1856; St. Louis (Second Church), 1858; professor of homiletics, church polity, and pastoral duties in Newton (Mass.) Theological Institution, 1866; pastor in Brooklyn (Strong-place Church), 1873; Chicago (Second Church), 1876; president of University of Chicago, 1878; pastor at Salem, Mass., 1885. From 1880–85 he lectured at Morgan Park (Baptist) Theological Seminary.

ANDERSON, Martin Brewer, LL.D. (Colby University, 1853, New-York Board of Regents, 1880), Baptist; b. at Brunswick, Me., Feb. 12, 1815; graduated at Waterville College (now Colby University), Me., 1840; studied in Newton Theological Seminary, 1840–41; became tutor in Waterville College, 1841; professor of rhetoric, 1843; proprietor and editor-in-chief of the *New-York Recorder*, a denominational weekly, 1850; president of the newly organized University of Rochester, 1853. He was president of the American Baptist Home

Missionary Society, 1864-66; and of the American Baptist Missionary Union, 1870-72; and in the New-York State Board of Charities (1868-81). He has contributed to the periodic press, and written reports, etc. He was an associate editor of Johnson's *Universal Cyclopædia*, New York, 1874-76, 4 vols.

ANDREWS, Edward Gayer, D.D. (Genesee College, 1863), **LL.D.** (Allegheny College, 1881), Methodist bishop; b. at New Hartford, Oneida County, N.Y., Aug. 7, 1825; was licensed to preach, 1844; graduated at Wesleyan University, Conn., 1847; was principal of the Cazenovia Seminary, New York, 1856-64; then a pastor until his election as bishop, 1872. *

ANGUS, Joseph, D.D. (Brown University, U.S.A., 1852), Baptist; b. at Bolam, Northumberland, Eng., Jan. 16, 1816; educated at King's College, London, Stepney Baptist College, and Edinburgh University, whence he was graduated M.A. in 1838 after a brilliant course, having taken the first prize in mathematics, in Greek, in logic, and in *belles-lettres*, the gold medal in ethics and political philosophy, and the students' prize of fifty guineas for the best essay on "The influence of the writings of Lord Bacon." He became successively pastor of the New Park-street Baptist Church, Southwark, London, 1838; co-secretary of the Baptist Missionary Society, 1840; sole secretary, 1842; president of Stepney, now Regent's Park, College, which is affiliated with the University of London, 1849. He has seen the college double in numbers since its removal to Regent's Park, and has recently raised £12,000 for college scholarships, and £30,000 for professors' chairs He was a member of the first London School Board, and of the New-Testament Revision Company from its organization. He is the author of prize essays on *The Voluntary System* (1838); *On the Advantages of a Classical Education as an Auxiliary to a Commercial Education; Christ our Life* (this won the prize for an essay adapted for translation into the vernaculars of India); many articles in the periodical press; of editions of Butler's *Analogy and Sermons*, and Wayland's *Moral Science*, and of *Bible Handbook*, London, 1854; *Christian Churches*, 1862; *Handbook of the English Tongue*, 1862; *Handbook of English Literature* [1865]; *Handbook of Specimens of English Literature* [1866], new ed., 1880; commentary on *Hebrews* in Schaff's *International Commentary on the N. T.*, Edinburgh and New York, vol. 3, 1883.

APPLE, Thomas Gilmore, Ph.D. (Lafayette College, Penn., 1866), **D.D.** (Franklin and Marshall, 1868), Reformed (German); b. near Easton, Penn., Nov. 14, 1829; graduated at Marshall College, Mercersburg, Penn., 1850; after a pastorate in several places, he became in 1865 president of Mercersburg College; in 1871 professor of Church history and New-Testament exegesis in the theological seminary at Lancaster, with which position he has united, since 1877, the presidency of Franklin and Marshall College. He has been a delegate in attendance on every meeting of the General Synod of the Reformed (German) Church since its organization in 1863 (except 1885); a member of the committee that revised the liturgy of the denomination, and of that which restored peace. He was a delegate to the Alliance of the Reformed Churches in 1880 (read paper on *The Theology of the Reformed Church*) and 1884. He has edited the *Reformed Quarterly Review* since 1867, and written much for it.

ARGYLL (Duke of). His Grace, *George Douglas Campbell*, K.T.; b. at Ardencaple Castle, Dumbartonshire, April 30, 1823; succeeded his father April, 1847. He has always been deeply interested in religious questions, and particularly in the affairs of the Church of Scotland. He vindicated that Church's right to legislate for itself, but condemned the Free Church movement. In 1874 he vigorously supported the successful measure in Parliament to transfer patronage in the Church of Scotland from persons to congregations. In politics he has long been numbered among the Liberal peers, and has been a member of the cabinets of the Earl of Aberdeen (1852), Palmerston (1855 and 1859), and Gladstone (1868 and 1880). His publications include, *A Letter to the Peers from a Peer's Son, on the Duty and Necessity of Immediate Legislative Interposition in Behalf of the Church of Scotland, as determined by Considerations of Constitutional Law* (anonymous), Edinburgh, 1842; *A Letter to the Rev. Thomas Chalmers, D.D., on the Present Position of Church Affairs in Scotland, and the Causes which have led to it*, 1842; *Presbytery examined*, London, 1848; *The Reign of Law*, 1866, 18th ed., 1884; *Primeval Man, an Examination of some Recent Speculations*, 1869; *The Patronage Act of 1874 all that was asked for in 1843*, 1874; *The Afghan Question, from 1841 to 1878*, 1879; *The Eastern Question*, 1879, 2 vols.; *Unity of Nature*, 1st and 2d ed., 1884; *Geology and the Deluge*, Glasgow, 1885. *

ARMITAGE, Thomas, D.D. (Georgetown College, Kentucky, 1855), Baptist; b. at Pontefract, Yorkshire, Eng., Aug. 2, 1819; emigrated to America, 1838; from his sixteenth to his twenty-eighth year he was a Methodist preacher, and filled important appointments. Study led him to change his views upon baptism; and he entered the Baptist ministry in 1848, and from that time to this has had one charge in New-York City. He was one of the founders of the American Bible Union (1850), and its president from 1856 to 1875. Besides many miscellaneous issues, he has published, *Preaching, its Ideal and Inner Life* (lectures delivered before Hamilton, Rochester, and Crozer theological seminaries), Philadelphia, 1880. *

ARMSTRONG, George Dodd, D.D. (William and Mary College, Virginia, 1858), Presbyterian (Southern Church); b. at Mendham, Morris County, N.J., Sept. 15, 1813; graduated at College of New Jersey, 1832; and at Union Theological Seminary, Prince Edward County, Va., 1837; became professor of general and agricultural chemistry and geology in Washington College (now Washington and Lee University), Lexington, Va., 1838; pastor of the First Presbyterian Church, Norfolk, Va., 1851, and still retains the position. He is the author of *The Summer of the Pestilence* (a history of the yellow-fever in Norfolk in 1855), Philadelphia, 1856; *The "Doctrine of Baptisms,"* New York, 1857; *The Christian Doctrine of Slavery*, 1858; *The Theology of Christian Experience*, 1860; *The Sacraments of the New Testament*, 1880; *The Books of Nature and Revelation collated*, 1886.

ARNOLD, Edwin, M.A., b. at Rochester, Eng.,

June 10, 1832; educated at University College, Oxford; graduated B.A., 1854; became assistant master of Edward VI. School, Birmingham; later, principal of the government Sanscrit College at Poona, Bombay Presidency; an editor of the London *Daily Telegraph*, 1861. He is a fellow of the Royal Asiatic Society, and of the Royal Geographical Society; 2d class of the imperial order of the Medjidie (Turkish), and companion of the Star of India. He arranged George Smith's first expedition, and Stanley's expedition in search of Livingstone, — both in behalf of the *Daily Telegraph*. He has made numerous poetical translations from Greek and Sanscrit, and has written many poems, of which the most famous are, *The Light of Asia* (the life and teaching of Buddha), London, 1879 (28th ed., 1886, and several reprints: in recognition he was decorated by the King of Siam with the Order of the White Elephant); *Pearls of the Faith, or Islam's Rosary*, 1883, 3d ed., 1884; *The Secret of Death*, 1885. *

ARNOLD, Matthew, D.C.L. (Edinburgh, 1869, Oxford, 1870), son of Thomas Arnold of Rugby; b. at Laleham, near Staines, Dec. 24, 1822; entered Balliol College, Oxford; won the Newdigate prize for English verse (1843); graduated in honors, 1844; became a Fellow of Oriel College (1845); a lay inspector of schools, 1851; was professor of poetry at Oxford from 1857 to 1867. He received the order of Commander of the Crown of India, from the King of Italy, in 1876. In 1883 he was put upon the civil pension list for three hundred pounds, in recognition of his services to literature. In 1884 he visited America on a lecture-tour. Besides poems, and numerous essays upon literary topics, he has published the following bearing on religion: *Culture and Anarchy, an Essay in Political and Social Criticism*, London, 1870; *St. Paul and Protestantism, with an Essay on Puritanism and the Church of England*, 1871; *Literature and Dogma, an Essay towards a Better Apprehension of the Bible*, 1873; *God and the Bible*, 1875; *Last Essays on Church and Religion*, 1877. He has also edited, with prefaces and notes, *The Great Prophecy of Israel's Restoration* (Isa. xl.-lxvi.), 1872, rev. ed., 1875; *Isaiah of Jerusalem* (Isa. i.-xxxix., 1884. *

ARTHUR, William, Methodist; b. at Kells, County Antrim, Ireland, 1819; graduated at Hoxton College, London, 1839; was missionary in India, 1839-41; and in France, 1846-48; secretary of the Wesleyan Missionary Society, 1851-68, and since honorary secretary. He was president of the Wesleyan Conference in 1866; and from 1868 to 1871, of the Belfast Methodist College. He is one of the honorary secretaries of the British Branch of the Evangelical Alliance, and has attended most of the General Conferences of the Alliance. He has written, besides sundry tracts and pamphlets, *A Mission to the Mysore, with Scenes and Facts illustrative of India, its People and its Religion*, London, 1847, 2d ed., 1848; *The Successful Merchant, Sketches of the Life of Mr. Samuel Budgett*, 1852, 95th ed., 1884 (reprinted in New York, and there is also a Welsh trans.); *The Tongue of Fire, or True Power of Christianity*, 1856, 40th ed., 1885; *In America*, 1856 (reprinted, New York); *Italy in Transition, Public Scenes and Private Opinions in the Spring of 1860, illustrated by Official Documents from the Papal Archives of the revolted Legations*, 1860, 7th ed., 1885 (reprinted, New York); *The Pope, the Kings, and the People*, 1877, 2 vols.; *The Difference between Physical and Moral Law*, 1883, 4th ed., 1885; *Religion without God, and God without Religion*, 1885, 2 parts.

ASTIÉ, Jean Frédéric, French Swiss Protestant, b. at Nerac (Lot-et-Garonne), France, Sept. 21, 1822; studied theology at Geneva, Halle, and Berlin; lived for a long time in the United States, and was pastor of a French church in New-York City from 1848 to 1853. From 1856 he has been professor of philosophy and theology in the Free Faculty at Lausanne, and editor of the *Revue de Théologie et de Philosophie*. Besides a history of the United States (Paris, 1865, 2 vols.), and of the revival there of 1857-58 (Lausanne, 1859), and various polemical pamphlets against MM. Scherer, Hornung, and Bersier, he has published an edition of the *Pensées de Pascal*, 1857, 2d ed., 1882; *Esprit d'Alexandre Vinet*, Paris, 1861, 2 vols.; *Les deux théologies nouvelles dans le sein du Protestantisme Français*, 1862; *Explication de l'évangile selon Saint-Jean*. Geneva, 1864, 3 vols. (the first two were anonymous); *Théologie allemande contemporaine*, 1875; *Mélanges de théologie et de philosophie*, Lausanne, 1878.

ATLAY, Right Rev. James, D.D. (Cambridge, 1859), Lord Bishop of Hereford, Church of England; b. at Wakerley, Northamptonshire, Eng., in the year 1817; was scholar of St. John's College, Cambridge; Bell's University scholar, 1837; graduated B.A. (senior optime, 1st class classical tripos), 1840; M.A., 1843; B.D., 1850. He was a fellow of St. John's College, 1842-59; tutor, 1846-59; curate of Warsop, Notts, 1842; vicar of Madingley, Cambridge, 1847-52; Whitehall preacher, 1856-58; vicar of Leeds and rural dean, 1859-68; canon residentiary of Ripon Cathedral, 1861-68; consecrated Lord Bishop of Hereford, 1868. *

ATTERBURY, William Wallace, Presbyterian; b. at Newark, N.J., Aug. 4, 1823; graduated at Yale College, 1843; was resident for a year, then entered Yale Theological Seminary, and graduated, 1847; was ordained, 1848; established Presbyterian Church at Lansing, Mich., 1848; was pastor there until 1854; at Madison, Ind., 1854-66; in Europe and the East; supplied pulpits at Cleveland, O., and elsewhere; became secretary of the New-York Sabbath Committee, 1869. He is an active member of the United-States Branch of the Evangelical Alliance, and was its secretary in 1875. He has written numerous documents, reports, articles for the press, etc., mostly on the various aspects of the Sunday question.

ATWOOD, Isaac Morgan, D.D. (Tufts, 1879), Universalist; b. at Pembroke, Genesee County, N.Y., March 24, 1838; was pastor in the States of New York, Maine, and Massachusetts; editor of the Boston *Universalist*, 1867-72; since and now associate editor of the *Christian Leader;* and since 1879 has been president of the Canton (N.Y.) Theological School, and Dockstader professor of theology and ethics. He has published, *Have we outgrown Christianity?* Boston, 1870; *Latest Word of Universalism*, 1878; *Walks about Zion*, 1882; *Episcopacy*, 1884.

B.

BACH, Joseph, D.D. (University of Munich, 1859), Roman Catholic; b. at Aislingen, near Augsburg, Bavaria, Germany, May 4, 1833; studied philosophy and theology in the University of Munich; became *privat-docent* there, 1865; professor extraordinary of theology, 1867; ordinary professor of philosophy of religion and pedagogics, and university preacher, 1872. He has written *Die Siebenzahl der Sacramente*, Regensburg, 1864; *Meister Eckhart*, Wien, 1864; *Propst Gerhoch von Reichersberg*, 1865; *Die Dogmengeschichte des Mittelalters vom christologischen Standpunkte, oder die mittelalterliche Christologie vom 8. bis 16. Jahr.*, 1873–75, 2 vols.; *Joseph von Görres*, Freiburg, 1876; *Des Albertus Magnus Verhältniss zur Erkenntnisslehre der Griechen, Lateiner, Araber u. Juden*, Wien, 1881; *Vorlesungen über Dante*, 1881; *Ueber das Verhältniss des Système de la Nature zur Wissenschaft der Gegenwart*, Cologne, 1884.

BACHMANN, Johannes Franz Julius, German Lutheran theologian; b. in Berlin, Feb. 24, 1832; became *privat-docent* there, 1856; ordinary professor of theology at Rostock, 1858; and there also university preacher, 1874. Besides sermons, he has issued *Die Festgesetze des Pentateuchs*, Berlin, 1858; *Das Buch der Richter*, vol. i., in 2 parts, 1867–70; *Ernst Wilhelm Hengstenberg, sein Leben und Wirken*, Gütersloh, 1876–80, 2 vols. *

BACON, Leonard Woolsey, M.D. (Yale, 1856), **D.D.** (Yale, 1879), Congregationalist; b. at New Haven, Conn., Jan. 1, 1830; graduated at Yale College, 1850, and at Yale Theological Seminary, 1854; was minister of St. Peter's (Presbyterian) Church, Rochester, N.Y., 1856; of Litchfield (Congregational) Church, Connecticut, 1857–60; missionary at large for Connecticut, 1861–62; minister at Stamford, Conn., 1863–65; Brooklyn, N.Y., 1865–70; Baltimore, Md., 1871; in Europe, 1872–77; minister at Norwich, Conn., 1878–82; stated supply to Woodland Presbyterian Church, Philadelphia, Penn., 1883; chosen pastor of the same, 1885. He has contributed largely in prose and poetry to the press, issued pamphlets and musical compositions, edited *Congregational Hymn and Tune Book*, New Haven, 1857; *The Book of Worship*, New York, 1865; *The Life, Speeches, and Discourses of Father Hyacinthe*, 1872; *The Hymns of Martin Luther set to their Original Melodies, with an English Version*, 1883; *The Church Book: Hymns and Tunes*, 1883; and original books, *Vatican Council*, New York, 1872; *Church Papers: Essays on Subjects Ecclesiastical and Social*, Geneva, London, and New York, 1876; *A Life worth living: Life of Mrs. Emily Bliss Gould*, New York, 1878; *Sunday Observance and Sunday Law* (with six sermons on the sabbath question, by G. B. Bacon), 1882; *The Simplicity that is in Christ* (sermons), 1886.

BAETHGEN, Friedrich Wilhelm Adolf, Lic. Theol. (Kiel, 1877), **Ph.D.** (Leipzig, 1878), Protestant theologian; b. at Lachem, Hannover, Jan. 16, 1849; studied at Göttingen and Kiel; was in the German army in the war against France, 1870–71; was in Russia, 1873–76; in Berlin, 1876–77; in British Museum, London, 1876; became *privat-docent* at Kiel, 1878; professor extraordinary of theology, 1884. From 1881–84 he was also "adjunctus ministerii" in Kiel. He is the author of *Untersuchungen über die Psalmen nach der Peshitâ*, Kiel, 1878; *Sindban oder die sieben weisen Meister. Syrisch und Deutsch*, Leipzig, 1879; *Syrische Grammatik des Mar Elias von Tirhan herausgegeben und übersetzt*, 1880; *Anmuth und Würde in der alttestamentlichen Poesie*, Kiel, 1880 (a lecture); *Fragmente syrischer und arabischer Historiker herausgegeben und übersetzt*, 1884; *Evangelienfragmente: Der griechische Text des Cureton'schen Syrers wiederhergestellt*, 1885. Besides these he has written the following articles: *Ein Melkitischer Hymnus an die Jungfrau Maria* ("Zeitschrift der Deutschen Morgenländischen Gesellschaft," 1879, vol. 33, pp. 666–671 [1879], and in the same the yearly review of matters relating to Syriac, etc., 1879 sqq.); *Kritische Bemerkungen über einige Stellen des Psalmentextes* ("Theolog. Studien und Kritiken," 1880, pp. 751 sqq.); *Philoxenus von Mabug über den Glauben* ("Zeitschrift für Kirchengeschichte," 1881, vol. 5, pp. 122–138); *Der textkritische Werth der alten Uebersetzungen zu den Psalmen* ("Jahrbücher für protestantische Theologie," 1882, vol. 8, pp. 405–459, 593–667); *Nachricht von einer unbekannten Handschrift des Psalterium juxta Hebraeos Hieronymi* ("Zeitschrift für die alttest. Wissenschaft," 1881, vol. 1, pp. 105–112); *Der Psalmencommentar des Theodor von Mopsuestia in syrischer Bearbeitung* (do., 1885, vol. 5, pp. 53–101).

BAIRD, Charles Washington, D.D. (University, New York City, 1876), Presbyterian; b. at Princeton, N.J., Aug. 28, 1828; graduated at the University of the City of New York, 1848, and at Union Theological Seminary, 1852; was chaplain of the American Chapel at Rome, Italy, 1852–54; and pastor of the Reformed Dutch Church on Bergen Hill, Brooklyn, N.Y., 1859–61; but since 1861 has been pastor of the Presbyterian Church of Rye, Westchester County, N.Y. He is the necrologist of Union Theological Seminary. He has written the following books: *Eutaxia, or the Presbyterian Liturgies: Historical Sketches*, New York, 1855 (revised and reprinted under title *A Chapter on Liturgies*, with preface and appendix, *Are Dissenters to have a Liturgy?* both by Thomas Binney, London, 1856); *A Book of Public Prayer, compiled from the Authorized Formularies of Worship of the Presbyterian Church, as prepared by the Reformers Calvin, Knox, Bucer, and others. With Supplementary Forms*, New York, 1857; *Chronicle of a Border Town* [Rye, N.Y.], 1870; *History of Bedford Church* [Westchester County, N.Y.], 1882; *History of the Huguenot Emigration to America* [1885], 2 vols., 2d ed. same year. Besides these he has translated Malan's *Romanism*, New York, 1844; and *Discourses and Essays of J. H. Merle d'Aubigné*, 1846; and written an article in *Magazine of American History* (1879, October) on *Civil Status of Presbyterians in the Province of New York.*

BAIRD, Henry Martyn, Ph.D. (Princeton College, 1867), **D.D.** (Rutgers College, 1877), **LL.D.** (Princeton, 1882), brother of the preceding, Presbyterian; b. in Philadelphia, Penn., Jan. 17, 1832; graduated at the University of the City of New York, 1850; studied in the University of Athens, Greece; in the Union Theological Seminary, New York, 1853-55; graduated at Princeton Theological Seminary, 1856; was tutor in the College of New Jersey, Princeton, N.J., 1855-59; and has been since 1859 professor of the Greek language and literature in the University of the City of New York. He is the author of *Modern Greece: a Narrative of a Residence and Travel in that Country*, New York, 1856; *The Life of the Rev. Robert Baird, D.D.* (his father), 1866; *History of the Rise of the Huguenots of France*, New York, 1879, 2 vols., 2d ed., 1883, London, 1880.

BALAN, Pietro, Roman Catholic; b. at Este, Padua, Italy, Sept. 3, 1840; educated in the seminary at Padua; became ordinary professor in October, 1862, in that institution; director of the Venetian *La Libertà Cattolica*, 1865; of the Modenese *Diritto Cattolico*, 1867; sub-archivist of the Vatican, 1880; retired on account of health, 1883; since 1883 has lived at Pragatto in the province of Bologna. He was nominated chamberlain by Leo XIII., 1881; domestic prelate, 1882; referendary of the Papal "segnatura," 1883; commander of the order of Franz Josef, Emperor of Austria, 1883. He is the author of *Studi sul Papato*, Padua, 1862; *Tommaso Becket*, 1864, 3d ed., Rome, 1866; *Storia di S. Tommaso di Cantobery e dei suoi tempi*, Modena, 1866, 2 vols.; *I precursori del Razionalismo moderno fino a Lutero*, Parma, 1867-68, 2 vols.; *Romani e Longobardi*, Modena, 1868; *Della necessità di ristorare la storia d'Italia*, 1868; *L'Economia, la Chiesa e gli umanitari*, 1869; *Pio IX., la Chiesa e la Rivoluzione*, 1869, 2 vols.; *Dante ed i Papi*, 1870; *Gli assedii della Mirandola nel 1511 e nel 1551*, Mirandola, 1870; *Della preponderanza germanica sull'Occidente dell'Europa*, Modena, 1871; *Chiesa e Stato: lettere a J. I. Doellinger*, 1871; *Sulle legazioni compiute nei paesi nordici da Guglielmo vescovo di Modena nel Secolo XIII.*, 1872; *Il vescovo di Modena Alberto Boschetti*, 1872; *La Chiesa Cattolica ed i Romani Pontefici difesi dalle calunnie del Senatore Siotto Pintor*, Bologna, 1873; *Storia di Gregorio IX. e dei suoi tempi*, Modena, 1873-74, 3 vols.; *Storia d'Italia dai primi tempi fino al 1870*, 1875-86, 7 vols.; *Storia del Pontificato di Papa Giovanni VIII.*, 1876, 3d ed., Rome, 1880; *Storia della Lega Lombarda, con documenti*, Modena, 1876; *Memorie storiche di Tencarola nel Padovano con documenti inediti*, 1876; *Storia della Chiesa Cattolica durante il Pontificato di Pio IX.*, Turin, 1876-86, 3 vols., 4th ed., vols. 1 and 2, 1886 (in continuation of Rohrbacher); *Memorie della B. Beatrice I. di Este*, Modena, 1877, 3d ed., Venice, 1879; *Un giro nei Sette Comuni del Vicentino*, Milan, 1878; *Roberto Boschetti e l'Italia dei suoi tempi*, Modena, 1878-84, 2 vols.; *Discorsi tenuti nel V. Congresso Cattolico in Modena*, Bologna, 1879, 31st ed., Milan, 1885; *Le tombe dei Papi profanate da Ferd. Gregorovius, vendicate dalla storia*, Modena, 1879; *Sull'autenticità del diploma di Enrico II. di Germania a Papa Benedetto VIII.*, Rome, 1880; *S. Catterina da Siena e il Papato*, 1880 (Flemish and French trans., Bruges, 1884); *La politica italiana dal 1863 al 1870, secondo gli ultimi documenti*, 1880; *La storia d'Italia e gli archivi segreti della S. Sede*, 1881; *Le relazioni fra la Chiesa Cattolica e gli slavi meridionali*, 1881 (Slavic trans., Agram, 1882); *I Papi ed i vespri siciliani, con documenti*, 1881 (Spanish trans., Rome, 1881); *Il processo di Bonifazio VIII.*, 1881; *La politica di Clemente VII. fino al sacco di Roma*, 1884; *Roma capitale d'Italia*, 1884 (German trans., 1884); *Monumenta reformationis Lutheranæ ex tabulariis secretioribus s. sedis 1521-25*, Regensburg, 1884; *Monumenta sæculi XVI. historiam illustrantia*, vol. i., Clementis VII. epistolæ per Sadoletum scriptæ, quibus accedunt variorum ad papam et ad alios epistolæ, Innsbruck, 1885; *Clemente VII. e l'Italia del suo tempo*, Milan, 1886.

BALLANTINE, William Gay, Congregationalist; b. at Washington, D.C., Dec. 7, 1848; graduated at Marietta College, Ohio, 1688, and Union Theological Seminary, New York, 1872; professor in Ripon College, 1874-76; in Indiana University, 1876-78; since 1878 connected with the Congregational Theological Seminary of Oberlin, O., first as professor of Greek and Hebrew exegesis (1878-80), and since as professor of Old-Testament language and literature. He studied at the University of Leipzig, 1872-73; was with the American Palestine Exploration Expedition in Palestine, March to August, 1873. Since 1884, he has been one of the editors of the *Bibliotheca Sacra.*

BALOGH, Francis, Reformed; b. at Nagy Várad (*Magnum Varadinum*), Hungary, March 30, 1836; graduated there, 1854; continued theological studies at Debreczen, Hungary, until 1858; resided in the college until 1863, when he went to Paris, London, and Edinburgh for further study; in 1865 he returned to Debreczen as assistant professor, and the next year (1866) became ordinary professor of church history, the history of doctrines, and of Hungarian Protestant church history. His theological standpoint is orthodox and evangelical. He defends the Helvetic Confession of the Hungarian Reformed Church against those who throw away all confessions. He was founder, and editor 1875-78, of the *Evangelical Protestant Gazette* (Debreczen, weekly), which successfully opposed the Budapest "Protestant Union," an imitation of the "Protestanten Verein" of Schenkel. The "Union" has ceased to exist. He was a delegate from his church to the Reformed Alliance Council at Edinburgh, 1877, and made a report; a member of the first general national synod held at Debreczen 1881, again in 1882; and since 1883 has been ecclesiastical assessor of the superintendency (a life office). Besides addresses, translations, articles in Herzog, etc., he has written, all in Hungarian, and published at Debreczen, *Peter Melius, the Hungarian Reformer*, 1866 (German translation, 1867); *The History of the Hungarian Protestant Church*, 1872; *The History of the Christian Church to the 17th Century*, 1872-82, 2 vols.; *Points of Information in the Field of Theology* (against Hungarian "modernism"), 1877; *The Literature of the Hungarian Protestant Church History*, 1879.

BARBOUR, William McLeod, D.D. (Bowdoin

College, 1870). Congregationalist; b. at Fochabers, Morayshire, Scotland, May 29, 1827; graduated at Oberlin College, Ohio, 1859, and at Andover Theological Seminary, 1861; was pastor of South Church, South Danvers (now Peabody), Mass., 1861–68; professor of sacred rhetoric and pastoral duties (1868–75), and of systematic theology (1873–77), in Bangor (Me.) Theological Seminary; since 1877 he has been professor of divinity in Yale College, and college pastor. He is a moderate Calvinist.

BARCLAY, Joseph, D.D. (Dublin University, 1880), **LL.D.** (do., 1865); b. near Strabane, County Tyrone, Ireland, Aug. 12, 1831; d. in Jerusalem, Palestine, Jan. 23, 1880. He was educated at Trinity College, Dublin, but did not distinguish himself; graduated B.A., 1854; M.A., 1857; became curate of Bagnalstown, County Carlow, Ireland, 1854; missionary to the Jews in Constantinople, 1858; minister of Christ Church, Jerusalem, 1861; resigned July 22, 1870; curate of Howe, England, 1871; St. Margaret's, Westminster, 1871–73; rector of Stapleford, near Hertford, 1873; consecrated bishop of Jerusalem, July 25, 1879; arrived in that city Jan. 23, 1880. His attainments were extensive. He preached in Spanish, French, and German, was well read in Hebrew, both biblical and rabbinic, and acquainted with Turkish and Arabic. He is the author of *The Talmud* (select treatises of the Mishna with prolegomena and notes), London, 1877. See his biography (anonymous), London, 1883. *

BARGÈS, Jean Joseph Léandre, Roman Catholic abbé; b. at Auriol (Bouches-du-Rhône), Feb. 27, 1810; studied Arabic and Hebrew at Marseilles; was ordained priest in 1834; has been since 1842 professor of Oriental languages in the faculty of Catholic theology at Paris; and since 1860 honorary canon of Notre Dame. He has written, *Traditions orientales sur les pyramides d'Égypte*, Marseilles, 1841; *Rabbi Yapheth ben Hali Bassorensis Karitæ in librum Psalmorum commentarii arabici edidit et in Latinum convertit*, Paris, 1846, and Yapheth's *Versio*, 1861; *Aperçu historique sur l'Église d'Afrique*, 1848; *Le livre de Ruth*, 1854; *Hébron et le tombeau du patriarche Abraham: Traditions et Légendes musulmanes rapportées par les auteurs arabes*, 1863. *

BARING-GOULD, Sabine, Church of England; b. at Exeter, Jan. 28, 1834; was student in Clare College, Cambridge; graduated B.A., 1854; M.A., 1856; ordained deacon, 1864; priest, 1865; became perpetual curate of Dalton, Yorkshire, 1866; rector of East Mersea, Essex, 1871; and rector of Lew Trenchard, Lew Down, North Devonshire, 1881. He has written, besides volumes of sermons under various titles, in 1872, 1873, 1875, 1879, 1880, 1881, 1884, 1885, and novels, the following: *The Path of the Just*, London, 1856; *Iceland, its Scenes and its Sagas*, 1863; *Post-mediæval Preachers*, 1865; *The Book of Were-wolves*, 1865; *Curious Myths of the Middle Ages*, 1866–68, 2 series, new ed., 1881, 1 vol. (reprinted Boston); *The Silver Store, collected from mediæval Christian and Jewish Mines*, 1868, 2d ed. 1882; *Curiosities of Olden Times*, 1869, 2d ed. 1875; *The Origin and Development of Religious Belief*, 1870–71, 2 vols., 2d ed. 1882 (reprinted New York); *Legends of the Old-Testament Characters*, 1871, 2 vols. (reprinted New York); *Lives of the Saints*, 1872–77, 15 vols.; *The Lost and Hostile Gospels*, 1874; *Yorkshire Oddities*, 1874; *Some Modern Difficulties*, 1875; *The Vicar of Morwenstow* (Rev. Robert Stephen Hawker), 1876 (reprinted New York); *Germany, Past and Present*, 1879. From 1871 to 1873 he edited *The Sacristy*, a quarterly review of ecclesiastical art and literature.

BARNARD, Frederick Augustus Porter, S.T.D. (University of Mississippi, 1861), **LL.D.** (Jefferson College, Miss., 1855, Yale College, 1859), **L.H.D.** (Regents of the University of the State of New York, 1872), Episcopalian; b. at Sheffield, Mass., May 5, 1809; graduated at Yale College, 1828; was tutor there, 1830; teacher in asylums for the deaf and dumb at Hartford, Conn., 1831–33; and New-York City, 1833–37; professor of mathematics and natural philosophy in University of Alabama, 1837–48; of chemistry, 1848–54; professor of mathematics, natural philosophy, and civil engineering in the University of Mississippi, 1854–56; president of the same, 1856–58; chancellor, 1858–61; in charge of chart printing and lithography, United-States Coast Survey, 1863–64; since May, 1864, president of Columbia College, New-York City. He took deacon's orders in the Protestant-Episcopal Church, 1856. He belongs to many scientific societies, and, aside from text-books, has written many educational treatises, of which may be mentioned *Letters on College Government, and the Evils inseparable from the American College in its Present Form*, 1854; *History of the American Coast Survey*, 1857; *University Education*, 1858; *Undulatory Theory of Light*, 1862; *Machinery and Processes of the Industrial Arts, and Apparatus of the Exact Sciences*, New York, 1868; *Metric System of Weights and Measures*, 1871, 3d ed. 1879; *Imaginary Metrological System of the Great Pyramid of Gizeh*, 1884. *

BARRETT, Benjamin Fisk, Swedenborgian; b. at Dresden, Me., June 24, 1808; graduated at Bowdoin College, Brunswick, Me., 1832, and at the Harvard (Unitarian) Divinity School, Cambridge, Mass., 1838; became a Swedenborgian, 1839; was pastor of the New Church Society in New-York City, 1840–48; in Cincinnati, O., 1848–50; retired temporarily from ministerial service because of ill health; was pastor in Philadelphia, Penn., 1864–71; and since has been president and corresponding secretary of the Swedenborg Publishing Association, Philadelphia. He edited *The Swedenborgian*, 1858–60 (when discontinued), and *The New Church Monthly*, 1867–70 (when merged in *The New Church Independent*). He is the author of *Life of Emanuel Swedenborg*, New York, 1841; *Lectures on the Doctrines of the New Church*, 1842 (present title, *Lectures on the New Dispensation*), 11th ed., Philadelphia, 1878; *The Golden Reed*, New York, 1855; *The Question concerning the Visible Church*, 1856 (new edition under title, *The Apocalyptic New Jerusalem*, Philadelphia, 1883); *Beauty for Ashes*, New York, 1856; *Letters to Beecher on the Divine Trinity*, 1860, 4th ed., Philadelphia, 1873; *Catholicity of the New Church*, New York, 1863; *The New View of Hell*, Philadelphia, 1870, 5th ed. 1886; *Prelate and Pastor*, 1871 (title changed to *A Bishop's Gun reversed*, 1882); *Letters to Beecher on the Future Life*, 1872; *The Golden City*, 1874; *The New Church, its Nature and Whereabout*, 1877; *Swedenborg and Chan-*

ning, 1879; *The Question answered* [What are the doctrines of the New Church?], 1883; *Footprints of the New Age*, 1884; *Heaven revealed*, 1885. Compiled and edited *The Swedenborg Library* (giving the substance of Swedenborg's theological teachings), Philadelphia, 1876–81, 12 vols.

BARROWS, John Henry (Lake Forest University, Ill., 1883), Presbyterian; b. at Medina, Mich., July 11, 1847; graduated at Olivet College, 1867; studied at New-Haven (Congregational) Theological Seminary, 1867–68, and at Union (Presbyterian) Theological Seminary, New-York City, 1868–69; was superintendent of public instruction in Osage County, Kansas, 1871–72; stated supply of First Congregational Church of Springfield, Ill., 1872–75; ordained (Congregationalist), April 29, 1875; pastor of the Eliot Congregational Church, Lawrence, Mass., 1875–81; of the Maverick Church, East Boston, 1881–82; since Dec. 8, 1882, he has been pastor of the First Presbyterian Church of Chicago, Ill. *

BARROWS, Samuel June, Unitarian; b. in New-York City, May 26, 1845; graduated B.D. at Harvard Divinity School, 1875, and studied for a year at Leipzig University; became pastor of the First Parish Church, Dorchester (Boston), Mass., 1876; editor of *The Christian Register*, 1881. He edited *Life and Letters of Thomas J. Mumford*, Boston, 1879, and *Ezra Abbot* (memorial volume), Cambridge, 1884; contributed to *Proceedings of the 250th Anniversary of the First Church and Town of Dorchester*, Boston, 1880, and articles on Dorchester in *Memorial History of Boston*, 1880; has published *The Doom of the Majority*, 1883; *A Baptist Meeting-House*, 1885.

BARROWS, Walter Manning, D.D. (Olivet College, 1884), Congregationalist; b. at Franklin, Mich., April 12, 1846; graduated at Olivet College, Mich., 1867, and at Andover Theological Seminary, Mass., 1873; became pastor in Salt Lake City, Utah, 1874; corresponding secretary of the American Home Missionary Society, New-York City, 1881.

BARRY, Most Rev. Alfred, D.D. (Cambridge, 1865), **D.C.L.** (Oxford, 1870), metropolitan, primate of Australia; b. in London, 1826; was student in Trinity College, Cambridge; graduated B.A. (seventh in first class classical tripos, fourth wrangler) and Smith prizeman, 1848; M.A., 1851; B.D., 1858; was elected fellow, 1848; ordained deacon, 1850; priest, 1853; became successively sub-warden of Trinity College, Glenalmond, 1850; head master of the grammar school at Leeds, 1854; principal of Cheltenham College, 1862; principal of King's College, London, 1868; also was canon of Worcester, 1871–81; chaplain in ordinary to the Queen, 1879–83; canon of Westminster, 1881–83; honorary canon of Westminster, 1883–84. He was consecrated lord bishop of Sydney, metropolitan of New South Wales, and primate of Australia, Jan. 1, 1884. His works include five volumes of sermons, London, 1866–81; six lectures on the *Atonement of Christ*, 1871; the Boyle lectures for 1876, entitled, *What is Natural Theology?* (1877) (German trans., *Die natürliche Theologie*, Gotha, 1882), and for 1877–78; *The Manifold Witness for Christ*, 1880; *The Teacher's Prayer Book, being the Book of Common Prayer, with introductions, analyses, notes, and a commentary upon the Psalter*, 1882, 2d ed. 1885; *First Words in Australia*, 1884. He commented upon Ephesians, Philippians, Colossians, and Philemon, in vol. iii. of Bishop Ellicott's *N. T. Commentary for English Readers*, 1879, re-issued in the *Handy Commentary*, 1883. *

BARTLETT, Edward Totterson, Episcopalian; b. at Philadelphia, Penn., July 25, 1843; graduated from the University of Pennsylvania, Philadelphia, 1865, and from Andover Theological Seminary, 1868; became rector at Sharon Springs, N.Y., 1869, and at Matteawan, N.Y., 1874; and since 1884 has been dean of the Divinity School of the Protestant Episcopal Church, Philadelphia, and professor of ecclesiastical history in the same.

BARTLETT, Samuel Colcord, D.D. (Dartmouth College, 1861), **LL.D.** (College of New Jersey, 1878), Congregationalist; b. at Salisbury, N.H., Nov. 25, 1817; graduated at Dartmouth College, 1836, and at Andover Theological Seminary, 1842; became successively pastor at Monson, Mass., 1843; professor of intellectual philosophy in the Western Reserve College, Hudson, O., 1846; pastor at Manchester, N.H., 1852; pastor in Chicago, Ill., and professor of biblical literature in the Congregational Theological Seminary, Chicago, Ill., 1857; resigned pastorate, but retained professorship, 1859; president of Dartmouth College, Hanover, N.H., 1877. He is "in substantial accord with the modified Calvinism of New England, as represented by Andover Seminary in the time of Woods, Stuart, B. B. Edwards, and Park; welcoming all new light, from whatever source, upon the text, composition, or interpretation of the Scriptures, or the doctrines thence legitimately resulting; but resisting all baseless theories, and rash speculations, and, in general, declining to surrender the matured and well-established convictions of the great mass of intelligent evangelical Christians, except on valid evidence." He was the first on the ground to open and organize the Chicago Congregational Theological Seminary, and raised the funds for endowing the chair he occupied. He aided also in the organization of numerous churches in Illinois. He crossed the desert of Et Tih to Palestine (1874) with a view to compare in detail all the circumstances and conditions of the region with the narrative of the journey of the children of Israel. Besides numerous articles in the *Bibliotheca Sacra*, *The New-Englander*, *The North-American Review*, orations at the centennial of the battle of Bennington, the quarter-millennial celebration of Newburyport, and at literary anniversaries, he has written *Life and Death Eternal, a Refutation of the Doctrine of Annihilation*, Boston, 1866, 2d ed. 1878; *Sketches of the Missions of the A. B. C. F. M.*, 1872; *Future Punishment*, 1875; *From Egypt to Palestine, Observations of a Journey*, New York, 1879; *Sources of History in the Pentateuch*, 1883.

BARTOL, Cyrus Augustus, D.D. (Harvard, 1859), Independent Congregationalist; b. at Freeport, Me., April 30, 1813; graduated at Bowdoin College, Maine, 1832, and at the Cambridge Divinity School, 1835; since 1837 he has been pastor of the West Church, Boston. He has written *Discourse on the Christian Spirit and Life*, Boston, 1850; *Discourse on the Christian Body and Form*, 1854; *Pictures of Europe*, 1855; *Church and Congregation*, 1858; *Radical Problems*, 1872; *The*

Rising Faith, 1873; *Principles and Portraits*, 1880.

BASCOM, John, D.D. (Iowa College, 1875), **LL.D.** (Amherst, 1873), Congregationalist; b. at Genoa, N.Y., May 1, 1827; graduated at Williams College, Massachusetts, 1849, and at Andover Theological Seminary, 1855; was professor of rhetoric in Williams College from 1855 to 1874; and ever since has been president of the University of Wisconsin. He is the author of *A Political Economy*, Andover, 1859; *Æsthetics, or the Science of Beauty*, New York, 1862, revised edition 1881; *Rhetoric*, 1865; *The Principles of Psychology*, 1869, revised edition 1877; *Science, Philosophy, and Religion* (Lowell lectures), 1871; *A Philosophy of English Literature*, 1874; *Philosophy of Religion, or the Rational Grounds of Religious Belief*, 1876; *Comparative Psychology, or Growth and Grades of Intelligence*, 1878; *Ethics, or Science of Duty*, 1879; *Natural Theology*, 1880; *Science of Mind*, 1881; *The Words of Christ as Principles of Personal and Social Growth*, 1884; *Problems in Philosophy*, 1885.

BASSERMANN, Heinrich, Lic. Theol. (Jena, 1876), **D.D.** (*hon*, Zürich, 1883), German Protestant; b. at Frankfurt-am-Main, July 12, 1849; studied at Jena, Zürich, and Heidelberg, 1867–72; became assistant preacher at Arolsen, Waldeck, 1873; *privat-docent* at Jena, 1876; professor extraordinary at Heidelberg, 1876; ordinary professor of practical theology, 1880; and *seminar-director* and university preacher, 1884. He is the author of *Dreissig christliche Predigten*, Leipzig, 1875; *De loco Matt. 5, 17-20 commentatio*, Jena, 1876; *Handbuch der geistlichen Beredsamkeit*, Stuttgart, 1885; and since 1881, with Dr. Ehlers, editor of *Zeitschrift für praktische Theologie*. He is announced to furnish the volume on Practical Theology, in the new Freiburg series of theological text-books.

BATES, Cyrus Stearns, D.D. (Western Reserve College, Ohio, 1879), Episcopalian; b. at Chester, O., Dec. 31, 1840; graduated at the Cincinnati Law College, 1865, and at the Gambier Episcopal Theological Seminary, 1873. From 1865 to 1871 he was a lawyer in Cincinnati; became rector at Newark, O., 1873; professor of systematic divinity in the Gambier Theological Seminary, 1878; rector in Cleveland, 1884.

BATTERSON, Hermon Griswold, D.D. (Nebraska College, 1869), Episcopalian; b. at Marbledale, Conn., May 28, 1827; educated privately; was rector at San Antonio, Tex., 1860–61; at Wabasha, Minn., 1862–66; since 1866 in Philadelphia, Penn. (St. Clement's 1869–72, the Annunciation since 1880). He is the author of the *Missionary Tune-Book*, Philadelphia, 1867, 10th ed. 1870; *The Churchman's Hymn-Book*, 1870; *Sketch-Book of the American Episcopate*, 1878, 2d ed. 1883; *Christmas Carols and other Verses*, 1878; *The Pathway of Faith*, New York, 1885, 2d ed. 1886.

BAUDISSIN, Wolf Wilhelm Friedrich, Ph.D. (Leipzig, 1870), Count, German Protestant; b. at Sophienruhe, near Kiel, Sept. 26, 1847; became *privat-docent* at Leipzig, 1874; professor extraordinary at Strassburg, 1876; ordinary professor, 1880; and at Marburg, 1881. He is the author of *Translationis antiquæ libri Jobi quæ supersunt*, Leipzig, 1870; *Jahve et Moloch sive de ratione inter deum Israelitarum et Molochum intercedente*, 1874; *Eulogius und Alvar, ein Abschnitt spanischer Kirchengeschichte aus der Zeit der Maurenherrschaft*, 1872; *Studien zur semitischen Religionsgeschichte*, 1876–78, 2 vols.; *Der heutige Stand der alttestamentlichen Wissenschaft*, Giessen, 1884.

BAUM, Henry Mason. See page 31.

BAUR, Gustav (Adolf Ludwig), D.D., German Protestant; b. at Hammelbach, June 14, 1816; became *privat-docent* at Giessen, 1841; professor extraordinary, 1847; ordinary, 1849; pastor at Hamburg, 1861; ordinary professor of theology at Leipzig, 1870. Besides numerous sermons he has issued *Der Prophet Amos erklärt*, Giessen, 1847; *Grundzüge der Homiletik*, 1848; *Geschichte der alttestamentlichen Weissagung*, first part, 1861; *Grundzüge der Erziehungslehre*, 1st to 3d ed., 1876; *Boëtius und Dante*, Leipzig, 1874.

BAUSMAN, Benjamin, D.D. (Franklin and Marshall College, 1870), Reformed (German); b. at Lancaster, Penn., Jan. 28, 1824; graduated at Marshall College, and the theological seminary, Mercersburg, Penn., 1852; became pastor at Lewisburg, Penn., 1852; editor of *The Reformed Messenger*, published at Chambersburg, Penn., 1858; pastor there, 1861; at Reading, 1863 (First Reformed Church till 1873, since of St. Paul's, which he organized). He was delegate to German Church Diet at Lübeck, 1856, and to Council of Alliance of Reformed Churches held at Belfast, 1884; president of General Synod, Baltimore, Md., 1884. He is the author of *Sinai and Zion* (travels), Philadelphia, 1860, 7th ed. 1883 (German trans., Reading, Penn., 1875, 2d ed. 1885); *Wayside Gleanings in Europe*, Reading, 1876; edited *The Guardian*, 1867–82; Harbaugh's *Harfe* (poems), 1870; founded, and since has edited, *Der Reformirte Hausfreund*, 1867 sqq.

BAYLISS, Jeremiah Henry, D.D. (Ohio Wesleyan University, Delaware, O., 1873), Methodist; b. at Wednesbury, Eng., Dec. 20, 1835; attended Genesee College, Lima, N.Y., 1854–57; was pastor in the Genesee (N.Y.) Conference, 1857–66; in Chicago, Ill., 1866–71; in Indianapolis, Ind., 1871–79; in Detroit, Mich., 1879–82; at Walnut Hills, Cincinnati, O., 1882–84; elected in May, 1884, editor of *The Western Christian Advocate*.

BEARD, Charles, Unitarian; b. at Manchester, Eng., July 27, 1827; studied in the Manchester New College, and University of Berlin; graduated B.A. at London University, 1847; became minister at Gee Cross, near Manchester, 1850; and of Renshaw-st. Chapel, Liverpool, 1867. He was the editor of *The Theological Review* from 1864 to 1879; and is the author of *Outlines of Christian Doctrine*, London, 1859; *Port Royal, a Contribution to the History of Religion and Literature in France*, 1861, 2 vols., cheaper ed. 1873; *The Soul's Way to God*, 1875, 2d ed. 1878; *The Reformation of the XVI. Century in its Relation to Modern Thought and Knowledge* (Hibbert lectures for 1883), 1883, 2d ed. 1885 (German trans. by F. Halverscheid, Berlin, 1884).

BEATTIE, Francis Robert, Ph.D. (Illinois University, U.S.A., 1884), Presbyterian; b. at Guelph, Ontario, Can., March 31, 1848; graduated at the University of Toronto, B.A., 1875 (medallist in philosophy, and prizeman in Oriental literature); M.A., 1876; B.D. at Knox College, Toronto, 1882. He was tutor in the University of Toronto, 1877; examiner, 1877-78, 1882–; tutor in Knox

College, 1877–78; examiner since 1880; since 1878 he has been pastor of the First Presbyterian Church, Brantford, Ontario, Can. He has written, besides numerous articles, *An Examination of the Utilitarian Theory of Morals*, Brantford, 1885; and has in preparation a work covering the whole ground of apologetics.

BEAUDRY, Louis Napoleon, Methodist; b. of Roman-Catholic French-Canadian parentage, at Highgate, Franklin County, Vt., Aug. 11, 1833; entered Troy Conference, 1856; studied in Troy University, but left before graduation, and became chaplain of the 5th regiment of cavalry, N.Y.S.V., Jan. 31, 1863; was in nearly one hundred engagements; in Libby Prison, Richmond, Va., during summer of 1863; and honorably discharged from the service, July 19, 1865. Since 1876 he has been a member of the Montreal Conference, and is now superintendent (presiding elder) of the French District of the conference, and professor of theology in French in the Wesleyan Theological College, Montreal. He was converted from Romanism through the influence of Rev. Joseph Cook, his classmate and room-mate at Keesville, N.Y., 1852–54. He has written, *Army and Prison Experiences with the Fifth New-York Cavalry*, Albany, 1865, 4th ed. 1874; *Spiritual Struggles of a Roman Catholic*, New York, 1875 (6th Canadian ed., Toronto, 1883; French trans., Montreal, 1882; Spanish trans., Mexico, 1884).

BECKWITH, Right Rev. John Watrus, S.T.D. (Trinity College, Hartford, Conn., 1868), **D.D.** (University of Georgia, 1868), Episcopalian, bishop of Georgia; b. at Raleigh, N.C., Feb. 9, 1831; graduated at Trinity College, Hartford, 1852; became rector of Calvary Church, Wadesborough, N.C., 1855; of All Hallows' parish, Anne Arundel County, Md., 1856; chaplain in the Confederate army, 1861; rector of Trinity, New Orleans, 1865; bishop, 1868. He has published addresses, charges, sermons, historical and controversial tracts, etc.

BECKX, Pierre Jean, General of the Society of Jesus (retired), Roman Catholic; b. at Sichem, near Louvain, Belgium, Feb. 8, 1795; entered the novitiate of the Society of Jesus at Hildesheim, Oct. 29, 1819; made his solemn profession, 1830; early distinguished himself; was appointed procurator for the province of Austria, 1847; rector of the Louvain Jesuit College, 1848; secretary to the provincial of Belgium, 1849; to that of Austria, 1852; general of the Jesuit order, July 2, 1853; removed the headquarters of the Society from Rome to Fiesole, near Florence, Italy, 1870; retired from active service, September, 1883, and lives quietly at the Collegio Germanico in Rome. His successor is Vicar-general Anthony M. Anderledy, a native of Switzerland, who was for some years attached to the province of St. Louis, U.S.A., who will on Father Beckx' death become general. Father Beckx has proved himself most efficient in inspiring the Society with new zeal, especially for carrying on missions in Protestant countries. Besides some minor compositions, he wrote the widely circulated and frequently translated *Month of Mary: Scenes from the Life of the Virgin, arranged for the Month of May; with Prayers, etc.*, Vienna, 1843. *

BEDELL, Right Rev. Gregory Thurston, D.D. (Norwich University, Vt., 1856), Episcopalian, bishop of Ohio; b. at Hudson, N.Y., Aug. 27, 1817; graduated at Bristol College, Pennsylvania, 1836, and at the Virginia Theological Seminary, 1840; became successively rector at Westchester, Penn., 1841, and of the Church of the Ascension, in New-York City, 1843; assistant bishop of Ohio, Oct. 13, 1859; and bishop, 1873. Besides sermons and addresses, he has written *Canterbury Pilgrimage to and from the Lambeth Conference and Sheffield Congress*, New York, 1878; *The Pastor, a Text-book on Pastoral Theology*, Philadelphia, 1880. *

BEECHER, Charles, Congregationalist; b. at Litchfield, Conn., Oct. 7, 1815; graduated at Bowdoin College, Maine, 1834; and at Lane Seminary, Cincinnati, O., 1837; was Presbyterian pastor at Fort Wayne, Ind., 1844–50; Congregational pastor at Newark, O., 1851–54; and at Georgetown, Mass., 1857–81; stated supply of Presbyterian church at Wysox, Penn., 1885. He believes that "the resurrection of *The Christ*, both head and members, is a true and proper *Return* to primeval glory in the celestial fatherland, forfeited, but redeemed by the blood of the Lamb slain from the foundation of the world." He is the author of *The Incarnation*, New York, 1849; *Review of the Spiritual Manifestations*, 1853; *David and his Throne*, 1855; *Redeemer and Redeemed*, Boston, 1864; *Spiritual Manifestations*, 1879; *The Eden Tableau*, 1880. He was joint editor with John Zundel of the music of the *Plymouth Collection of Hymns and Tunes*, New York, 1855; and editor of the *Autobiography*, etc., of his father, Lyman Beecher, 1865, 2 vols.

BEECHER, Edward, D.D. (Marietta College, 1831), Congregationalist; b. at East Hampton, Long Island, N.Y., Aug. 27, 1803; graduated at Yale College, 1822; studied for one year (1825) in Andover Theological Seminary, but did not graduate; was tutor in Yale College, 1825–26; pastor of the Park-street Church, Boston, 1826–30; president of Illinois College, 1830–44; pastor of the Salem-street Church, Boston, 1844–56; senior editor of *The Congregationalist*, 1849–53; pastor in Galesburg, Ill., 1856–71; professor extraordinary in Congregational Theological Seminary, Chicago, on the Christian organization of society, for some years after 1860. Since 1871 he has resided, without pastoral charge, in Brooklyn, preaching often in various churches.

He is "an evangelical Calvinist, except as to the nature and cause of original sin, and the question of the suffering of God and its influence in the atonement. He holds that sin did not come through the material system, and of course not through the fall of Adam, but that the material system by its analogies is adapted to regenerate those who have made themselves sinful in a previous state of existence. The doctrine of divine suffering he holds as presenting the character of God in its most affecting and powerful aspects, and as essential to a true view of the atonement.

"He went to Alton, Ill., in 1837, to aid in defending the freedom of the press in the case of E. P. Lovejoy. Resisted by the mob spirit, he aided in forming the Illinois State Anti-slavery Society, drew up its constitution and declaration of principles, and published an address to the people of the State. He was with E. P. Lovejoy and Owen

Lovejoy, his brother, the night before the former's death, Nov. 6, 1837. He aided in landing the second press, and in storing it in the stone store of Godfrey and Gilman, where in defending it E. P. Lovejoy was slain."

Since 1824, he has published in various religious journals articles on questions of theology and practical reform, amounting in all to many volumes. His books are: *On the Kingdom of God*, Boston, 1827; *History of the Alton Riots*, Cincinnati, 1838; *Import and Modes of Baptism*, New York, 1849; *The Conflict of Ages, exposing False Views of the Origin of Sin, False Interpretations on which they are based, the Great Conflict thence originating, and the Means of the Restoration of Harmony*, Boston, 1853, 5th ed. 1855; *The Concord of Ages: A Defence of the Historical Statements and the Interpretations of The Conflict of Ages, and a more Full Discussion of the Doctrine of the Suffering of God, and its Wide Range of Influence in harmonizing the Church*, New York, 1853; *The Papal Conspiracy, exposing the Principles and Plans of the Papacy with respect to this Country*, Boston, 1855; *History of Opinions on the Scriptural Doctrine of Retribution*, New York, 1878.

BEECHER, Henry Ward, Congregationalist; b. at Litchfield, Conn., June 24, 1813; graduated at Amherst College, Mass., 1834; and at Lane Theological Seminary, Cincinnati, O., 1837, where his father was professor; became successively pastor of the Presbyterian Church at Lawrenceburg, Ind., 1837; and at Indianapolis, 1839; and of Plymouth Congregational Church, Brooklyn, N.Y., 1847. The latter building seats nearly 3,000, and the membership is (1885) 2,018. Besides preaching, Mr. Beecher has done much lecturing and political speaking, particularly in behalf of various reform movements. From its start in 1858 to 1861, he was a regular contributor to *The Independent*, a religious weekly of New-York City, and from 1861 to 1863 its editor. From 1870 to 1880, he was editor of the New-York *Christian Union*, a paper of the same tendency. Mr. Beecher visited Europe in 1863, and courageously defended the side of the Northern States in the Civil War then raging.

On Oct. 10, 1882, he withdrew from the Association to which he belonged, because he did not wish to compromise it by his alleged heresies. The chief points of his divergence from the orthodox position relate to the person of Christ, whom he considers to be the Divine Spirit under the limitations of time, space, and flesh; miracles, which he considers divine uses of natural laws; and future punishment, whose endlessness he denies, inclining to a modification of the annihilation theory. He calls his standpoint "evangelical progressive: anti-Calvinistic."

His sermons have been published weekly since 1859, and in book form in numerous volumes. He says he is the author of "swarms of books — of which I know less than any other person — of all sorts, some thirty to forty." Of these books may be mentioned, *Lectures to Young Men*, New York, 1850; *Star Papers*, 1855; *Life Thoughts*, 1858; *Eyes and Ears*, 1863; *Royal Truths*, 1864; *Norwood* (a novel), 1867; *Lecture-room Talks*, 1870; *Life of Christ*, vol. i., 1871; *Yale Lectures on Preaching*, 1872–74, 3 vols.; *A Summer Parish*, 1875; *Evolution and Religion*, 1885. *Cf.* LYMAN ABBOTT: *Henry Ward Beecher*, N.Y., 1883.

BEECHER, Thomas Kennicutt, brother of the preceding, Congregationalist; b. at Litchfield, Conn., Feb. 10, 1824; graduated at Illinois College, 1843, under his brother Edward; became school-principal in Philadelphia, 1846, and in Hartford, Conn., 1848; pastor in Brooklyn, N.Y., 1852; in Elmira, 1854. His theological standpoint is "that of the New Testament, Apostles' Creed, and Catholic faith." He is the author of *Our Seven Churches*, New York, 1870 [a volume of discourses, in a catholic spirit, upon the denominations represented in Elmira], and various articles in periodicals.

BEECHER, Willis Judson, D.D. (Hamilton College, 1875), Presbyterian; b. at Hampden, O., April 29, 1838; graduated at Hamilton College, N.Y., 1858, and at Auburn Theological Seminary, N.Y., 1864; became pastor at Ovid, N.Y., 1864; professor of moral science and belles-lettres in Knox College, Ill., 1865; acting pastor at Galesburg, Ill., 1869; professor of Hebrew language and literature in Auburn Seminary, 1871. He has written *Farmer Tompkins and his Bibles*, Philadelphia, 1874; *General Catalogue of Auburn Theological Seminary*, Auburn, 1883; *Drill Lessons in Hebrew*, 1883; and jointly with Mary A. Beecher, *Index of Presbyterian Ministers, 1706–1881*, Philadelphia, 1883.

BEET, Joseph Agar, Wesleyan Methodist; b. at Sheffield, Eng., Sept. 27, 1840; educated at Wesley College, Sheffield, and Wesleyan Theological College, Richmond, London; for twenty-one years held pastoral charges as a Wesleyan minister; in 1885 entered the faculty of the Wesleyan Theological College at Richmond, as professor of systematic theology. Besides articles, he has published *Commentary on the Epistle to the Romans*, London, 1877, 5th ed. 1885; *Holiness as understood by the Writers of the Bible*, 1880, 3d ed. 1883; *Commentary on the Epistles to the Corinthians*, 1882, 3d ed. 1885; *Commentary on the Epistle to the Galatians*, 1885. (These works have been republished in New York.)

BEHRENDS, Adolphus Julius Frederick, D.D. (Richmond College, 1873), Congregationalist; b. at Nymegen, Holland, Dec. 18, 1839; graduated at Denison University, O., 1862, and at Rochester (Baptist) Theological Seminary, N.Y., 1865; became pastor of the Baptist Church at Yonkers, N.Y., 1865; of the First Baptist Church, Cleveland, O., 1873; of the Union Congregational Church, Providence, R.I., 1876; and of the Central Congregational Church, Brooklyn, N.Y., 1883.

BENDER, Wilhelm (Friedrich), Ph.D. (Göttingen, 1868), **D.D.** (same, *hon.*, 1877), German Protestant; b. at Münzenberg, Hesse, Jan. 15, 1845; studied at Göttingen and Giessen, 1863–66; and at the theological seminary at Friedberg, 1866–67; became teacher of religion and assistant preacher at Worms, 1868; ordinary professor of theology at Bonn, 1876. He is the author of *Schleiermachers philosophische Gotteslehre*, Worms, 1868; *Der Wunderbegriff des Neuen Testaments*, Frankfurt-a.-M., 1871; *Schleiermachers Theologie mit ihren philosophischen Grundlagen*, Nördlingen, 1876–78, 2 vols.; *Friedrich Schleiermacher und die Frage nach dem Wesen der Religion*, Bonn, 1877; *Johann Conrad Dippel. Der Freigeist aus dem Pie-*

tismus, 1882; *Reformation und Kirchenthum*, 1883, 9th ed. 1884; *Das Wesen der Religion und die Grundgesetze der Kirchenbildung*, 1886 (1885), 3d ed. same year.

BENNETT, Charles Wesley, D.D. (Genesee College, N.Y., 1870), Methodist; b. at Bethany, N.Y., July 18, 1828; graduated from Wesleyan University, Middletown, Conn., 1852; studied church history and archæology in Berlin University, and travelled in Europe and the East, 1866–69; was in educational work in connection with schools until 1871, when he became professor of history in Syracuse University; since 1885 he has been professor of historical theology in the Garrett Biblical Institute (Methodist), Evanston, Ill. He edited the "Methodist" department of Appletons' Encyclopædia, revised edition. He has published, besides articles, *History of the Philosophy of Pedagogics*, New York, 1877; *National Education in Italy, France, Germany, England, and Wales*, Syracuse, 1878; *Christian Art and Archæology of the First Six Centuries* (nearly ready).

BENRATH, Karl, German Protestant theologian; b. at Düren, Germany, Aug. 10, 1845; studied at Bonn, Berlin, and Heidelberg, 1863–67; taught in the city school of Düren until 1872; then studied in Italy, principally in Rome (1872–75, 1878–79); became *privat-docent* at Bonn, 1876, and professor extraordinary, 1879. He has written *Bernardino Ochino von Siena*, Leipzig, 1875; *Ueber die Quellen der italienischen Reformationsgeschichte*, Bonn, 1876; *Die Summa der Heiligen Schrift, ein Zeugniss aus dem Zeitalter der Reformation für die Rechtfertigung aus dem Glauben*, Leipzig, 1880.

BENSLY, Robert Lubbock, M.A., layman, Church of England; b. at Eaton, near Norwich, Eng., Aug. 24, 1831; was educated at King's College, London, Gonville and Caius College, Cambridge; studied in University of Halle, Germany; was appointed reader in Hebrew at Gonville and Caius College, 1863; and elected fellow in 1876. He is now (1885) lecturer in Hebrew and Syriac in his college; examiner in the Hebrew text of the Old Testament in the University of London; and was a member of the Old-Testament Revision Company. He has edited *The Missing Fragment of the Latin Translation of the Fourth Book of Ezra, discovered and edited with an Introduction and Notes*, Cambridge, 1875.

BENSON, Right Honorable and Most Reverend Edward White, D.D. (Cambridge, 1867), Lord Archbishop of Canterbury, and Primate of All England, and Metropolitan; b. near Birmingham, July 14, 1829; educated at Trinity College, Cambridge; graduated B.A. (senior optime and first-class classical tripos), and members' prizeman, 1852; M.A., 1855; B.D., 1862; Hon. D.C.L. (Oxford), 1884; was ordained deacon, 1853; priest. 1857. He was also fellow of Trinity College, Cambridge, and senior chancellor medallist. His Grace was assistant master at Rugby School, 1853–59; first head master of Wellington College, 1859–72; examining chaplain to the Bishop of Lincoln, 1869; prebendary of Heydour with Walton in Lincoln Cathedral, 1869–72; chancellor and canon residentiary of Lincoln, 1872–77; select preacher at Cambridge, 1864, 1871, 1875, 1876, 1879, 1882; and same at Oxford, 1875-76; honorary chaplain to the Queen, 1873; chaplain in ordinary to the Queen, 1875–77. In 1877 he was consecrated the first lord bishop of the new see of Truro; in 1882 he was transferred to Canterbury, and enthroned March 29, 1883. His Grace is one of the lords of her Majesty's Most Honorable Privy Council, president of the Corporation of the Sons of the Clergy, of the Society for Promoting Christian Knowledge, and of the Society for the Propagation of the Gospel, an official trustee of the British Museum, and a governor of Wellington College and the Charter House. The population of the diocese of Canterbury is (1885) 653,269; the yearly income of the see is £15,000; there are two residences. Dr. Benson has issued *Sermons preached in Wellington College Chapel*, London, 1859; *Work, Friendship, and Worship* (Cambridge University sermons), 1871; *Boy-life, its Trials, its Strength, its Fulness* (Wellington sermons, 1859–72), 1874, new ed. 1883; *Singleheart*, 1877, 2d ed. 1883; *The Cathedral, its Necessary Place in the Life and Work of the Church*, 1879; *The Seven Gifts*, 1885.

BENTON, Angelo Ames, M.A., Episcopalian; b. at Canea, Crete, July 3, 1837; graduated at Trinity College, Hartford, 1856; served several parishes in North Carolina, 1860–83; became professor of mathematics and modern languages in Delaware College, Newark, Del., 1883; transferred to the chair of ancient languages, 1885. He edited *The Church Cyclopædia*, Philadelphia, 1884.

BENTON, Joseph Augustine, D.D. (Yale College, 1870), Congregationalist; b. at Guilford, Conn., May 7, 1818; graduated at Yale College, 1842, and Yale Theological Seminary, 1846; made the voyage to California *via* Cape Horn with the "Argonauts" in 1849; was pastor of Congregational churches in Sacramento (1849-63) and San Francisco (1863–69); since 1867 editor-in-chief of *The Pacific*, organ of the California Congregational churches; and since 1869 professor in the Pacific Theological Seminary (Congregational), Oakland, Cal. He officiated as chaplain at the inauguration of the Central Pacific Railway, Jan. 8, 1863; and at the completion of the same (on the same spot), May 8, 1869. He has written, besides sermons and addresses, *The California Pilgrim*, Sacramento, 1853.

BERGER, Daniel, D.D. (Westfield College, Ill., 1878), United Brethren in Christ; b. near Reading, Penn., Feb. 14, 1832; studied privately at Springfield, O.; became a school-teacher, 1852; principal of public high school, Springfield, O., 1855; pastor, 1858; editor of publishing house of United Brethren in Christ, Dayton, O., 1864; edited the leading church weekly, *The Religious Telescope*, until 1869, and since, the denominational Sunday-school literature.

BERGER, Samuel, French Lutheran theologian; b. at Beaucourt (Haut-Rhin), May 2, 1843; studied at Strasbourg and Tübingen; in 1867 he became assistant preacher in the Lutheran Church in Paris; in 1877, librarian to the Paris faculty of Protestant theology. He is the author of *F. C. Baur, les origines de l'école de Tubingue et ses principes*, Paris, 1867; *La Bible au seizième siècle; Étude sur les origines de la critique*, 1879; *De glossariis et compendiis biblicis quibusdam medii aevi*, 1879; *Du rôle de la dogmatique* *dans la prédication*, 1881; *La Bible française au moyen âge*, 1884. *

BERNARD, Thomas Dehany, Church of England; b. at Clifton, Bristol, Nov. 11, 1815; entered Exeter College, Oxford; took a second-class in classics, 1837; wrote the Ellerton theological essay, and graduated B.A., 1838; wrote the chancellor's English essay, 1839; graduated M.A., 1840; was ordained deacon, 1840; priest, 1841; became vicar of Great Baddow, Essex, 1841; of Terling, 1848; rector of Walcot, Bath, 1863. In 1868 he became prebendary of Haselbere, and canon residentiary in Wells Cathedral; in 1879, chancellor of Wells Cathedral; and in 1880, proctor for dean and chapter of Wells. He was select preacher at Oxford, 1856, 1862, and 1882; and Bampton lecturer in 1864. He is the author of *The Witness of God* (University sermons), Oxford, 1863; *The Progress of Doctrine in the New Testament* (Bampton lectures), London, 1864, 4th ed. 1878; *Before his Presence with a Song*, 1885.

BERNHEIM, Gotthardt Dellmann, D.D. (North Carolina College, 1877), Lutheran (Old Pennsylvania Ministerium); b. at Iserlohn, Westphalia, Prussia, Nov. 8, 1827; graduated at the Lutheran Seminary of the South Carolina synod, Lexington, S.C., 1849; became successively pastor in Charleston, S.C., 1850; at Mount Pleasant, N.C., and financial secretary of North-Carolina College, 1858; at Charlotte, N.C., 1861; principal of female seminary of the North Carolina Synod, Mount Pleasant, N.C., and pastor of Ebenezer Church in Rowan County, N.C., 1866; pastor of St. Paul's Church, Wilmington, N.C., 1869; an editor and proprietor of *At Home and Abroad*, monthly, published at Wilmington and Charlotte, N.C., 1881; pastor of Grace Evangelical Lutheran Church, Phillipsburg, N.J., 1883. Besides *The Success of God's Work* (sermon), Wilmington, N.C., 1870, and *Localities of the Reformation* (pamphlet), 1877, he has published *History of the German Settlements and of the Lutheran Church in North and South Carolina*, Philadelphia, 1872; *The First Twenty Years* (of the history of St. Paul's Lutheran Church, Wilmington, N.C.), Wilmington, 1879.

BERSIER, Eugene Arthur François, Reformed Church of France; b. of descendants of Huguenot refugees, at Morges, near Geneva, Switzerland, Feb. 5, 1831; pursued his elementary studies at Geneva and Paris; was in America, 1848–50; studied theology at Geneva, Göttingen, and Halle; became pastor in Paris, 1855, where he has been ever since. He was in the Free Church until 1877 (until 1861, over the Faubourg St. Antoine Church; until 1874, assistant of Pressensé in the Taitbout Church; until 1877, over the Etoile Church), when he and his congregation joined the Reformed (established) Church of France. He was made in 1872 a Chevalier of the Legion of Honor, in recognition of his services during the siege of Paris. He is the author of *Sermons*, Paris, 1861-84, 7 vols., several editions apiece (English trans. of selected sermons, *Oneness of the Race in its Fall and its Future*, translated by Annie Harwood, London, 1871); *Sermons*, 1881; *St. Paul's Vision*, translated by Marie Stewart, New York, 1881; *The Gospel in Paris, Sermons, with Personal Sketch of the Author*, by Rev. Frederick Hastings, London, 1884; German trans. of selected sermons, Berlin, 1875, and Bremen, 1881 (also Danish, Swedish, and Russian translations); *Solidarité*, 1869; *Histoire du Synode de 1872*, 1872, 2 vols.; *Liturgie* (now used in the Reformed Church of France), 1874; *Mes actes et mes principes*, 1878; *L'Immutabilité de Jésus Christ*, 1880; *Royauté de Jésus Christ*, 1881; *Coligny avant les Guerres de religion*, 1884, 3d ed. 1885 (Eng. trans., *Coligny: the Earlier Life of the Great Huguenot*, London, 1885); *La Révocation, discours prononcé le 22 Oct., 1885, suivi de notes relatives aux jugements des contemporains sur l'Édit de Révocation*, 1886.

BERTHEAU, Carl, D.D. (*hon.*, Greifswald, 1883), Protestant theologian; b. at Hamburg, Germany, July 6, 1836; studied at Göttingen and Halle; taught in the schools of Hamburg, and has been since 1867 pastor in that city. He has not written any separate works, but has contributed to different periodicals and serials; e.g., to the *Theologische Literaturzeitung* of Harnack and Schürer, and the *Real-encyklopädie* of Herzog, Plitt, and Hauck. He is one of the editors of the Weimar edition of Luther's works, now in course of publication.

BERTHEAU, Ernst, D.D., German Protestant theologian; b. at Hamburg, Nov. 23, 1812; studied in Berlin and Göttingen; in the latter university became ordinary professor of Oriental philology in 1843. He lectures upon the exegesis, archæology, and theology of the Old Testament, and instructs in Arabic, Chaldee, and Syriac. His publications include *De secundo libro Maccabeorum*, Göttingen, 1829; *Comment. Inest carminis Ephraemi Syri textus Syriacus secundum Cod. bib. Angel. denuo editus ac versione et brevi annotatione instructus*, 1837; *Die sieben Gruppen mosaischen Gesetze in den drei mittlern Büchern des Pentateuchs*, 1840; *Zur Geschichte der Israeliten, zwei Abhandlungen*, 1842; an edition of the Syriac grammar of Bar Hebræus, 1843, and the Commentary upon Judges and Ruth (1845, 2d ed. 1883), Chronicles (1854, 2d ed. 1873), Ezra, Nehemiah, and Esther (1862), and Proverbs (1847, 2d ed. 1883), in the *Kurzgefasstes exegetisches Handbuch zum Alten Testament*, Leipzig, 1841–62, 17 parts. *

BERTRAM, Robert Aitkin, Congregationalist; b. at Hanley, Staffordshire, England, Nov. 8, 1836; ended his studies at Owen's College (now Victoria University), Manchester, 1858; since 1859 has been pastor of several Congregational churches; edited *The Christian Age*, 1880–83. He is the author of *The Cavendish Hymnal*, Manchester, 1864; *Parable, or Divine Poesy: Illustrations in Theology and Morals, selected from Great Divines, and systematically arranged*, London, 1866; *The Imprecatory Psalms: Six Lectures, with other Discourses*, 1867; *A Dictionary of Poetical Illustrations*, 1877, 3d ed. 1885; *A Homiletical Encyclopædia of Illustrations in Theology and Morals*, 1878, 7th ed. 1885; *A Homiletical Commentary on the Prophecies of Isaiah*, 1884–86, 2 vols.

BESTMANN, Hugo Johannes, Lic. Theol. (Erlangen, 1877), **Ph.D.** (Halle, 1884), Lutheran, b. at Delve, Holstein, Germany, Feb. 21, 1854; studied at the Universities of Leipzig, Tübingen, Kiel, Berlin, and Erlangen; became *privat-docent* of theology at Erlangen, 1877; teacher in the gymnasium of the Halle orphanage, 1883; in the Missions Seminary, Leipzig, 1884. He is author of *Qua ratione Augustinus notiones philosophiæ græcæ ad dogmata anthropologica describenda adhibuerit*, Erlangen, 1877; (edited) *J. Ch. K. von Hofmanns Encyclopædie der Theologie*, Nördlingen, 1879; *Geschichte der christlichen Sitte*, 1880 sqq., Bud. II. 2te Abt. 1885; *Die theologische Wissenschaft und die Ritschl'sche Schule, eine Streitschrift*, Nördlingen, 1881; *Die Anfänge des Katholischen Christenthums und des Islams*, 1884.

BEVAN, Llewelyn David, D.D. (Princeton, 1879), Congregationalist; b. at Llanelly, Caermarthenshire, South Wales, Sept. 11, 1842; studied at New College, London; graduated at London University, B.A. (an English exhibitioner), 1861; with first-class philosophy honors, 1863; LL.B. (with first-class honors), 1866; became assistant at King's Weigh-house Chapel, London, 1865; minister of Tottenham-court Road Chapel (Whitefield's), London, 1869; of the Brick Presbyterian Church, New-York City, 1876; of Highbury Quadrant Church, London, 1882. He was associated with Rev. F. D. Maurice in the Workingmen's College, London; professor at New College for some years; elected member of the London School Board, 1873. Besides separate sermons and discourses, he has published *Sermons to Students*, New York, 1880; *Christ and the Age*, London, 1885.

BEYSCHLAG, Willibald, D.D., German Protestant theologian; b. at Frankfort-on-the-Main, Sept. 5, 1823; court-preacher at Carlsruhe (1856); appointed in 1860, ordinary professor of theology in Halle, and since 1876 also editor of the *Deutsche Evangelische Blätter*, an organ of the so-called "*Mittelpartei*." Of his numerous writings, besides volumes of sermons and single discourses, may be mentioned, *Die Christologie des Neuen Testaments*, Berlin, 1866; *Die paulinische Theodicee Rom. ix.–xi.*, 1868; *Die Christliche Gemeindeverfassung im Zeitalter des Neuen Testaments* (Von der Teyler'schen *theol. Gesell. gekr. Preiss.*), Haarlem, 1874; *Zur Johanneischen Frage*, Gotha, 1876; the biographies of his brother, F. W. T. Beyschlag (*Aus dem Leben eines Frühvollendeten*, Berlin, 1858–59, 2 parts, 5th ed. 1878), of Carl Ullmann (Gotha, 1867), of Carl Immanuel Nitzsch (Halle, 1872, 2d ed. 1882), and of Albrecht Wolters (1880). His latest work is *Das Leben Jesu*, Halle, 1885–86, 2 vols. He edited Huther's commentary upon *James* in the revised Meyer series (Göttingen, 1882).

BICKELL, Gustav, D.D. (Innsbruck, 1875), Roman-Catholic theologian, the son of a distinguished Protestant jurist; b. in Cassel, July 7, 1838; became in 1862 *privat-docent* at Marburg in Indo-Germanic and Shemitic philology; the same at Giessen, 1863; but in 1865 went over to the Roman Church, was ordained priest in 1866; and after teaching Oriental languages in the Münster Academy from 1867 till 1874 became professor of the Shemitic languages and Christian archæology at Innsbruck. He is the author of *De indole ac ratione versionis Alexandrinæ in interpretando libro Jobi*, Marburg, 1862; *S. Ephraemi Syri carmina Nisibena*, Leipzig, 1866; *Grundriss der hebräischen Grammatik*, 1869–70, 2 parts, English trans. by Prof. S. I. Curtiss, Ph.D., D.D., Leipzig, 1877; *Gründe für die Unfehlbarkeit des Kirchenoberhauptes*, Münster, 1870 (pp. 24); *Conspectus rei Syrorum literariæ*, 1871; *Messa u. Pascha*, 1872; *S. Isaaci Antiocheni opera omnia*, Giessen, 1873; *Metrices biblicæ regulæ exemplis illustratæ*, Innsbruck, 1879; *Synodi Brixinenses sæculi XV. Primus ed.*, 1880; *Carmina V. T. metricæ*, 1882; *Dichtungen der Hebräer*, 1882; *Der Prediger über den Wert des Daseins*, 1884. He is also editor of a theological quarterly, and contributor to the new edition of Wetzer and Welte's *Kirchenlexikon*. *

BICKERSTETH, Very Rev. Edward, D.D. (*hon.* Cambridge, 1864), **F.R.G.S.**, dean of Lichfield, Church of England; b. at Acton, Suffolk, Oct. 23, 1814; was scholar of Sidney Sussex College, Cambridge; graduated **B.A.** (senior optime), 1836; M.A., 1839; wrote the theological prize essay, and became licentiate in theology at Durham University, 1837; was ordained deacon, 1837; priest, 1839; curate of Chetton, 1838; the Abbey, Shrewsbury, 1839; perpetual curate of Pennstreet, Bucks, and rural dean of Amersham, 1849; vicar of Aylesbury, and archdeacon of Buckingham, 1853; dean of Lichfield, 1875. He was select preacher at Cambridge in 1861, 1864, 1873, and 1878, and at Oxford in 1875; prolocutor of the Convocation of Canterbury, 1864–80. He is chairman of the Executive Committee of the Central Council of Diocesan Conferences, and was a New-Testament reviser. He is the author of *Questions illustrating the Thirty-nine Articles of the Church of England*, London, 1844, 6th ed. 1877; *The Mercian Church and St. Chad* (a sermon), 1880, 2d ed. 1881; *My Hereafter*, 1883; *The Revised Version of the New Testament* (a lecture), 1885. He contributed the commentary on St. Mark's Gospel to *The Pulpit Commentary*, 1882, 5th ed. 1885; and in 1877 edited the fifth edition of R. W. Evan's *Bishopric of Souls*, originally published 1842, with a memoir of the author.

BICKERSTETH, Right Rev. Edward Henry, lord bishop of Exeter, Church of England; b. at Islington, Jan. 25, 1825; educated at Trinity College, Cambridge; graduated B.A. (senior optime and third-class classical tripos), 1847; M.A., 1850; Seatonian prize-man, 1854; was ordained deacon, 1848; priest, 1849; became curate of Banningham, Norfolk, 1848; of Christ Church, Tunbridge Wells, 1852; rector of Hinton Martel, Dorset, 1852; vicar of Christ Church, Hampstead, London, 1855; chaplain to the bishop of Ripon (1857–84); rural dean of Highgate, 1878; dean of Gloucester, 1885; and bishop of Exeter, 1885. He is best known as the author of *Yesterday, To-day, and Forever: a Poem in Twelve Books*, London, 1866, 18th ed. 1886; but besides other poems, and the widely used *Hymnal Companion to the Book of Common Prayer*, 1870, revised ed. 1876, he has published a *Practical and Explanatory Commentary on the New Testament*, 1864, and other volumes in prose, of which may be mentioned, *The Spirit of Life, or Scripture Testimony to the Divine Person and Work of the Holy Ghost*, 1870; *Water from the Well-Spring for the Sabbath Hours of Afflicted Believers*, new ed., 1885; *The Reef, and Other Parables*, 1873, 3d ed. 1885; *The Shadowed Home and the Light beyond*, 1874, new ed. 1875; *The Lord's Supper*, 1881; *From Year to Year*, 1883.

BIEDERMANN, Alois Emanuel, D.D., Swiss Protestant; b. at Oberrieden, March 2, 1819;

studied at Basel, 1837–39, and Berlin, 1839–43; became pastor at Mönchenstein, Basselland, 1843; professor extraordinary of theology at Zürich, 1850, and ordinary in 1864; d. at Zürich, Jan. 26, 1885. He was a leading rationalist, a disciple of Hegel, and deeply influenced by the Tübingen School, especially by Strauss. He was a prolific writer for the religious press, published a life of Heinrich Lang (Zürich, 1876), but obtained his greatest repute by his *Christliche Dogmatik* (1869, 2d ed. vol. i., Berlin, 1884, vol. ii. edited by Prof. Dr. Rehmke, 1885), in which he denies the historicity of the Gospels, yet holds to the eternal ideas which the supposed facts of the Gospels embody; denies Christian doctrine, but advocates Christian practice; denies personality to God, and personal immortality to man, yet holds that love to God and man constitutes the essence of religion. In this way he tries to join the speculative and the practical. He was a famous Alpine climber. See his posthumous *Ausgewählte Vorträge und Aufsätze, mit einer biographischen Einleitung* von Kradolfer, Berlin, 1885. *

BINNEY, John, Episcopalian; b. in Philadelphia, Penn., Feb. 23, 1844; graduated at Harvard, B.A., 1864; M.A., 1867; became professor of Hebrew and the literature and interpretation of the Old Testament in the Berkeley Divinity School, Middletown, Conn., 1874.

BINNIE, William, D.D. (Glasgow, 1866), Free Church of Scotland; b. at Glasgow, Aug. 20, 1823; graduated at the University of Glasgow; M.A., 1844; studied theology in Divinity Hall of the Reformed Presbyterian Church, 1843–47 (winter of 1845–46 in Berlin, hearing Neander and Hengstenberg); was minister of the Reformed Presbyterian Church in Stirling, 1849–75; professor of apologetics and systematic theology in Divinity Hall of the Reformed Presbyterian Church, 1863–75; in 1875 became professor of church history and pastoral theology in the Free Church College of Aberdeen. He is the author of *The Psalms: their History, Teachings, and Use*, Edinburgh, 1870, 2d ed. 1886; *The Church*, 1882; besides sermons, lectures, and the pamphlet (pp. 44), *The Proposed Reconstruction of Old-Testament History*, 1880 (3 editions). Died Sept. 22, 1886.

BIRD, Frederic Mayer, Episcopalian; b. in Philadelphia, Penn., June 28, 1838; graduated at the University of Pennsylvania, 1857, and the Union Theological Seminary, New-York City, 1860; became a Lutheran minister, 1860; was an army chaplain, 1862–63; pastor in several places; entered Episcopal ministry, 1868; was rector at Spotswood, N.J., and elsewhere; and since February, 1881, has been chaplain and professor of psychology, Christian evidences, and rhetoric, in the Lehigh University, South Bethlehem, Penn. He has given especial attention to hymnology, and his library on the subject, embracing some 3,500 volumes, is by far the largest in America, and possibly in existence. He has edited *Charles Wesley seen in his Finer and Less Familiar Poems*, New York, 1867; with Rev. Dr. B. M. Schmucker, the Lutheran Pennsylvania Ministerium *Hymns*, Philadelphia, 1865, revised ed. 1868, and now used as Lutheran General Council's *Church-Book*; and, with Bishop Odenheimer, *Songs of the Spirit*, New York, 1871. He has written the department of Hymn Notes in the New-York *Independent* since 1880; wrote most of the hymnological articles in the *Schaff-Herzog Encyclopædia*, and most of the American matter in Julian's *Dictionary of Hymnology*, London and New York, now in course of preparation.

BIRRELL, John, D.D. (Edinburgh, 1878), Established Church of Scotland; b. in the parish of Newburn, near St. Andrews, Oct. 21, 1836; studied four years at the University of St. Andrews, and two years at Halle; was graduated at the former, M.A., 1856. He was examiner in classical literature for degrees in arts in the University of St. Andrews, and minister of Dunino, near St. Andrews (1864–72); but since 1871 has been professor of Hebrew and Oriental languages in the University of St. Andrews. He was for twelve years chairman of the School Board of St. Andrews, has been examiner of many of the secondary schools under its care, and is now chairman of the local examination committee of St. Andrews University. He was an Old-Testament reviser.

BISSELL, Edwin Cone, D.D. (Amherst, 1874), Congregationalist; b. at Schoharie, N.Y., March 2, 1832; graduated at Amherst College, Mass., 1855, and Union Theological Seminary, New York, 1859; was pastor of Congregational churches at Westhampton, Mass. (1859–64); San Francisco, Cal. (1864–69); Winchester, Mass. (1870–73); missionary of the A. B. C. F. M. in Austria, 1873–78; studied the Old Testament in Boston and Leipzig, 1878–81; since 1881 has been professor of Hebrew in the Hartford Theological Seminary. During first pastorate raised and commanded Company K, Fifty-second Regiment Massachusetts Volunteers, which served under Gen. Banks at Port Hudson during 1862–63. For a year (1869–70) he was stated supply at Honolulu, Oahu (Sandwich Islands). He is the author of *The Historic Origin of the Bible*, New York, 1873; *The Apocrypha of the Old Testament* (a revised trans., introduction and notes, forms vol. xv. of the Old Testament in the American Lange series), 1880; *The Pentateuch, its Origin and Structure: an Examination of Recent Theories*, 1885.

BISSELL, Right Rev. William Henry, D.D. (Norwich University, 1852; Hobart College, 1868; Vermont University, 1876), Episcopalian, bishop of the diocese of Vermont; b. at Randolph, Vt., Nov. 10, 1814; graduated at Vermont University, 1836; successively rector of Trinity, West Troy, N.Y., 1841; Grace, Lyons, 1845; Trinity, Geneva, 1848; consecrated, 1868.

BITTNER, Franz Anton, D.D. (Münster, 1835), Roman-Catholic theologian; b. at Appeln, Silesia, Germany, Sept. 17, 1812; was ordained priest, and became professor of theology in the clerical seminary at Posen, 1835; the same in the Lyceum Hosianum at Braunsberg, 1849; ordinary professor of moral theology at Breslau, 1850. He is the author of *De civitate divina commentarii*, Mainz, 1845; *De Ciceronis et Ambrosianis officiorum libris commentatio*, Braunsberg, 1849; *De cathol. theologiæ Romanæ inter præcipua philosophiæ genera salutari ac cœlesti mediocritate*, Breslau, 1850; *Lehrbuch der Kathol. Moraltheologie*, Regensburg, 1855; *Ueber die Geburt, Auferstehung und Himmelfahrt Jesu Christi*, 1859; and the translator of Gousset's *Dogmatik*, Regensburg, 1855–56, 2 vols. *

BJÖRLING, Carl Olof, Swedish theologian; b. at Westerås, Sweden, Sept. 16, 1804; d. there, Jan. 20, 1884. He was graduated at the University of Upsala, Ph.D., 1830; D.D., 1844. He became bishop of Westerås, 1866, having long been connected as teacher and rector with the Gefle gymnasium. He was the author of several learned works, of which should be mentioned *Christian Dogmatics*, 1847 (2d ed. 1866) to 1875, 2 parts, which attracted considerable attention in Germany, and which shows his firm adherence to the Augsburg Confession. *

BLACKBURN, William Maxwell, D.D. (Princeton College, 1870), Presbyterian; b. at Carlisle, Ind., Dec. 31, 1828; graduated at Hanover College, 1850, and at Princeton Theological Seminary, 1854; was pastor of Park (Presbyterian) Church, Erie, Penn., 1856–63; Fourth Church, Trenton, N.J., 1864–68; professor of church history in the Presbyterian Theological Seminary of the Northwest, Chicago, Ill., 1868–81; pastor of the Central Church, Cincinnati, O., 1881–84; president of the Territorial University of North Dakota, 1884–85; since president of Pierre University (Presbyterian), East Pierre, Dak. He has published, besides numerous Sunday-school books, *William Farel*, Philadelphia, 1865; *Aonio Paleario*, 1866; *Ulrich Zwingli*, 1868; *St. Patrick and the early Irish Church*, 1869; *Admiral Coligny*, 1869, 2 vols.; *A History of the Christian Church from its Origin to the Present Time*, New York, 1879.

BLACKWOOD, William, D.D. (Lafayette College, Penn., 1857), **LL.D.** (New-York University, 1871), Presbyterian; b. at Dromara, County Down, Ireland, June 1, 1804; graduated at the Royal College, Belfast, 1832; became pastor successively of the Presbyterian churches of Holywood, near Belfast, 1835; of Trinity Church, Newcastle-on-Tyne, 1843; and of the Ninth Church, Philadelphia, Penn., 1850. He was secretary to the Education Committee of the Irish Presbyterian Church, 1834–40; and mathematical examiner of students under care of the Synod of Ulster, 1839–43; and was moderator of the Presbyterian Church in England, 1846. Besides numerous magazine, review, and newspaper articles, he has written essays on *Missions to the Heathen*, Belfast, 1830; *Atonement, Faith, and Assurance*, Philadelphia, 1856; *Bellarmine's Notes of the Church*, 1858; and edited the papers of the late Rev. Richard Webster (which at his death had been left in a fragmentary state), with introduction and indexes, and published them under the title *Webster's History of the Presbyterian Church*, Philadelphia, 1857; also the *Biblical, Theological, Biographical, and Literary Encyclopædia*, 1873–76, 2 vols. (4to illust.).

BLAIKIE, William Garden, D.D. (Edinburgh, 1864), **LL.D.** (Aberdeen, 1872), **F.R.S.E.** (1861), Free Church of Scotland; b. at Aberdeen, Feb. 5, 1820; graduated at Aberdeen, M.A., 1837; ordained minister of the Established Church of Scotland at Drumblade, Aberdeenshire, 1842; joined the Free Church of Scotland, May, 1843; was translated to Free Church at Pilrig, Edinburgh, 1844; and appointed professor of apologetics and pastoral theology in New College, Edinburgh, by General Assembly of Free Church, in 1868. He was appointed, along with the Rev. William Arnot, delegate from the Free Church to the General Assembly of the Presbyterian Church of the United States at Philadelphia in 1870, to convey congratulations on union. He took a leading part in the formation of the Alliance of the Reformed Churches; convened a private meeting in Edinburgh in its interest in 1874; was one of the clerks of the Conference in London in 1875; from 1875 to 1877 was chairman of the general committee of the Scotch Committee to prepare for the first meeting of the Council; one of the clerks of Council held at Edinburgh, 1877, at Philadelphia, 1880, and at Belfast, 1884. He was editor of the *Free Church Magazine*, 1849–53; *North British Review*, 1860–63; *Sunday Magazine*, 1871–74; *Catholic Presbyterian*, 1879–83. Besides many articles in British and American periodicals, he has written the following books: *David, King of Israel*, London, 1856, 2d ed. 1860; *Bible History in Connection with General History*, 1859, fifth thousand 1868, new revised ed. 1882; *Bible Geography*, 1860; *Better Days for Working People*, 1863, seventy-sixth thousand 1881, new ed. 1882; *Heads and Hands in the World of Labour*, 1865, fifth thousand 1868; *Counsel and Cheer for the Battle of Life*, 1867, sixth thousand 1868; *For the Work of the Ministry*, 1873, 4th ed. 1885; *Glimpses of the Inner Life of our Lord*, 1876, 3d ed. 1878; *Personal Life of David Livingstone*, 1880, 4th ed. 1884; "*My Body*," 1883; *Public Ministry and Pastoral Methods of Our Lord*, 1883; *Leaders in Modern Philanthropy*, 1884; *Present Day Tracts*, 5 nos., 1883–85.

BLAKESLEY, Very Rev. Joseph Williams, dean of Lincoln, Church of England; b. in London, March 6, 1808; d. at Lincoln, April 18, 1885. He studied at Trinity College, Cambridge, and graduated B.A. (twenty-first wrangler, and senior chancellor medallist) 1831; M.A., 1834; B.D., 1850; was fellow of his college, 1831–45; assistant tutor, 1834–39; tutor, 1839–45; select preacher before the university, 1840 and 1843. In 1845, by presentation of his college, he became vicar of Ware; declined, in 1860, the Regius professorship of modern history at Cambridge; was appointed in 1850 a classical examiner, and in 1875 a member of the senate of the University of London; in 1863, a canon of Canterbury; in 1870, a member of the New-Testament Company of the Bible-revision Committee; and in 1872, dean of Lincoln. He was the author of *Thoughts on the Recommendations of the Ecclesiastical Commission*, London, 1837; *Life of Aristotle*, Cambridge, 1839; *Conciones academicæ*, London, 1843; *Four Months in Algeria*, 1859; and edited *Herodotus*, 1852–54, 2 vols. *

BLEDSOE, Albert Taylor, LL.D. (Kenyon College, O., and Mississippi University, both 1854), Methodist; b. at Frankfort, Ky., Nov. 9, 1809; d. at Alexandria, Va., Dec. 8, 1877; graduated at the United States Military Academy, West Point, N.Y., 1830; became lieutenant Seventh Infantry; resigned, 1832; became assistant professor of mathematics, Kenyon College, O., 1834; entered ministry of the Episcopal Church, and was rector at Hamilton, O., and professor of mathematics in Miami University, 1835–36; left the ministry, owing to some theological difficulties, and took up the practice of law in Springfield, Ill., and in the Supreme Court at Washington, D.C., 1840–48; became professor of mathematics in the University of Mississippi, 1848, and in the University of Virginia, 1854. On the breaking-out of the civil war he entered the Confederate service as a colonel, but was soon made assistant secretary of war by Mr. Davis. In 1863 he went to England to prepare a work on the constitutional history of the United States. He returned to America in February, 1866, and in 1867 began, at Baltimore, the publication of *The Southern Review*.

He became a Methodist in 1871, and preached occasionally in Methodist pulpits, but never took charge of a church. His views on theological subjects are difficult to define, as he was not a strict adherent of any church creed. He was a firm believer in, and strenuous advocate of, the doctrine of free-will, — of the responsibility of men for their belief, — a stern opponent of atheism and scepticism. While always friendly towards predestinarians, he fought all his life the doctrine which he believed tarnished the Divine glory, and drove many into unbelief. His views upon these subjects are given in full in his *Review of Edwards on the Will*, in his *Theodicy*, and in the pages of *The Southern Review*. His views on the Constitution are to be found in *Liberty and Slavery*, and *Is Davis a Traitor?*

His literary work was done in a manner somewhat peculiar. He pondered his subject long, revolving it year after year; but when he came to write, the work was done with marvellous rapidity and precision, sometimes thirty or forty pages with scarcely an erasure, and then would come a point where he could not write precisely what he wished to say, and perhaps thirty or forty pages more would be thrown aside, each being an attempt to express one unimportant thought. His memory was prodigious for what he read. Of the six hundred and eighty moral philosophers he had read, he could tell, after the lapse of years, just the precise shade of views each upheld. He was an honest but unsparing controversialist, dealing trenchant blows without mercy, but never once in his long militant career accused of misrepresenting the views of an antagonist: though he made bitter enemies by his pen, they were made in open fair fight.

After the intellectual labor of authorship was over, he lost all interest in the financial success of his books. If a strict profit-and-loss account could be made, he probably made nothing by his books, which reached a number of editions: *An Examination of Edwards on the Will*, Philadelphia, 1845; *A Theodicy, or Vindication of Divine Glory*, New York, 1853; *Liberty and Slavery*, Philadelphia, 1857; *Philosophy of Mathematics*, 1865; *Is Davis a Traitor?* Baltimore (privately published), 1866. MRS. A. T. BLEDSOE.

BLISS, Daniel, D.D. (Amherst College, Mass., 1864), Congregationalist; b. at Georgia, Vt., Aug. 17, 1823; graduated at Amherst College, 1852, and at Andover Theological Seminary, 1855; was missionary of A. B. C. F. M. in Syria, 1855–64; since 1864 president of the Syrian Protestant College, Beirut. He is the author in Arabic of a *Mental Philosophy*, sermons, etc.

BLISS, George Ripley, D.D. (Madison University, 1860), **LL.D.** (Lewisburg University, 1878), Baptist; b. at Sherburne, N.Y., June 20, 1816; graduated at Madison University, Hamilton, N.Y., 1838, and at Hamilton Theological Seminary (Baptist), 1840; became tutor in Madison University, 1840; pastor at New Brunswick, N.J., 1843; professor of Greek in University of Lewisburg, Penn., 1849; professor of biblical exegesis in the Crozer Theological Seminary, 1874; professor of biblical literature and theology in the same institution, 1883. He translated, with additions, Fay's Commentary on Joshua and Kleinert's on Obadiah and Micah in the American Lange series, New York; and is the author of the Commentary on the Gospel of Luke (Philadelphia, 1884), in the "Complete Commentary on the New Testament" edited by Dr. A. Hovey.

BLOMFIELD, Right Rev. Alfred, D.D. (*hon.*, Oxford, 1882), bishop suffragan of Colchester, Church of England; b. at Fulham, Aug. 31, 1833; was scholar of Balliol College, Oxford; won the chancellor's Latin verse prize, 1854; graduated B.A (first-class classics) 1855, M.A. (All Saints' College) 1857; was fellow of All Saints' College, 1856–69; ordained deacon 1857, priest 1858; curate of Kidderminster, 1857–60; perpetual curate of St. Philip's, Stepney, 1862–65; vicar of St. Matthew's, City Road, 1865–71; of Barking, Essex, 1871–82; honorary canon of St Albans, 1875–82; archdeacon of Essex, 1878–82; archdeacon of Colchester and bishop of Colchester, suffragan to the bishop of St. Albans, since 1882. He is the author of *Memoirs of Bishop Blomfield* (his father), London, 1863, 2 vols.; *Sermons in Town and Country*, 1871. *

BLUNT, John Henry, D.D. (Durham University, Eng., 1882), Church of England; b. at Cheyne Walk, Chelsea, Aug. 25, 1823; d. in London, April 11, 1884. He was educated at University College, Durham; graduated M.A., 1855; became licentiate in theology, 1852; was ordained deacon, 1852, and priest, 1855; and filled a number of curacies, until in 1868 he was appointed by the warden and fellows of All Souls' College, Oxford, vicar of Kennington; in 1873 he was presented by Mr. Gladstone with the crown living of Beverston, Gloucestershire, and retained it until his death. He was an industrious and useful literary worker, and a High Churchman of pronounced views. Besides numerous contributions in periodicals, he wrote *The Atonement*, London, 1855; *Three Essays on the Reformation*, 1860; *Miscellaneous Sermons*, 1860; *Directorium pastorale* (English), 1864, 4th ed. 1880; *Key to the Bible*, 1865; *Household Theology*, 1865, 6th ed. 1886; *The Annotated Book of Common Prayer*, 1866, 7th ed. 1883 (a standard work); *The Sacraments and Sacramental Ordinances of the Church*, 1868; *The Reformation of the Church of England*, vol. 1, 1868, 6th ed. 1886, vol. 2, 1882 ("a solid and careful study of a critical period"); *Key to Church History*, 1869; *Union and Disunion*, 1870; *Plain Account of the English Bible*, 1870; *Dictionary of Doctrinal and Historical Theology*, 1870, 2d ed. 1872; *Key to the Prayer-Book*, 1871; *The Condition and Prospects of the Church of England*, 1871; *The Book of Church Law*, 1872, 4th ed., by Sir W. G. F. Phillimore, 1885; *Myroure of Our Lady* (a reprint of a devotional treatise of great rarity, which originally appeared in 1530), 1873; *The Poverty that makes Rich*, 1873; *Dictionary of Sects, Heresies, Ecclesiastical Parties, and Schools of Religious Thought*, 1874; *Historic Memorials of*

Dursley, 1877; *Tewkesbury Cathedral*, 1877; *The Annotated Bible · being a Household Commentary comprehending the Results of Modern Discovery and Criticism*, 1878-81, 3 vols.; *Companion to the New Testament*, 1881; *Key to Christian Doctrine and Practice*, 1882; *A Companion to the Old Testament*, 1883. *

BOARDMAN, George Dana, D.D. (Brown University, 1866), Baptist; b. in Tavoy, Burmah, Aug. 18, 1828 [the son of the missionary to the Karens. His mother married Dr. Judson in 1834. He came to America all alone when only six years of age, and on the voyage experienced harsh treatment]. He was graduated at Brown University, 1852, and at Newton Theological Institution, 1855; pastor at Barnwell Court-house, S.C., December, 1855-May, 1856; of the Second Church, Rochester, N.Y., October, 1856-May, 1864; and since of the First Church, Philadelphia, Penn. He was president of the American Baptist Missionary Union, 1880-84. He delivered before his church, on successive Wednesday evenings from October, 1864, to April, 1882, six hundred and forty-three lectures, going through every word of the New Testament; and is now (1886) engaged on a similar series on the Old Testament. He has written *Studies in the Creative Week*, New York, 1878 (fourteen lectures first delivered on consecutive Tuesday noons); *Studies in the Model Prayer*, 1879; *Epiphanies of the Risen Lord*, 1879; *The Mountain Instruction*, 1880; etc.

BOEHL, Edward, Ph.D. (Erlangen, 1860), **Lic. Theol.** (Basel, 1860), **D.D.** (Vienna, 1865), Reformed; b. at Hamburg, Nov. 18, 1836; educated at Berlin (1855), Halle (1856-58), and Erlangen (1858-60); became *privat-docent* at Basel in 1860; professor of Reformed dogmatics and symbolics, also of pedagogics, philosophy of religion, and apologetics, in the Protestant faculty of theology at Vienna, in 1864. He is the editor of the *Evangelische Sonntagsboten für Oesterreich*; since 1861, member of the German Oriental Society, of the German Palestine Exploration Fund; since 1864, permanent member of the synod of the Reformed Church of Austria; and was in 1883 president of the fourth general synod of the same. He is the author of *De Aramaismis libri Koheleth. Dissertatio historica et philologica, qua librum Salomoni vindicare conatur autor*, Erlangen, 1860; *Vaticinium Jesajæ c. 24-27 commentario illustratum*, Leipzig, 1861; *Zwölf messianische Psalmen erklärt. Nebst einer grundlegenden christologischen Einleitung*, Basel, 1862; *Confessio Helvetica posterior ad I. editionem edendam curavit*, Wien, 1866; *Allgemeine Pädagogik*, 1870; *Forschungen nach einer Volksbibel zur Zeit Jesu und deren Zusammenhang mit der Septuaginta-Uebersetzung*, 1873 (Dutch trans., Amsterdam); *Die alttestamentlichen Citate im Neuen Testament*, 1878; *Alte christliche Inschriften erläutert* (in "Studien und Kritiken," 1881, pp. 692 sqq.); *Christologie des Alten Testaments, oder Auslegung der wichtigsten messianischen Weissagungen*, 1882 (Dutch trans., Amsterdam, 1885); *Zum Gesetz und zum Zeugniss. Eine Abwehr wider die neukritischen Schriftforschungen im Alten Testament*, 1883 (Dutch trans., Amsterdam, 1884); *Von der Incarnation des göttlichen Wortes*, 1884; *Christliche Glaubenslehre*, Amsterdam, 1886.

BOEHRINGER, Georg Friedrich, Swiss Protestant (Tübingen school); b. at Maulbronn, Würtemberg, Germany, Dec. 28, 1812; d. at Basel, blind and crippled, Sept. 16, 1879. He studied at Tübingen, took part in the insurrectionary movements in 1833, and was in consequence compelled to flee to Switzerland; became pastor at Glattfelden, Canton Zürich, 1842; resigned, 1853; removed to Zürich, and then to Basel. He wrote from the sources, and in a scholarly manner, a series of biographies which constituted a church history down to pre-Reformation times, under the general title *Die Kirche Christi und ihre Zeugen*, Zürich, 1842-58, 2d ed. 1860-79, 24 vols.

BOEHRINGER, Paul, Lic. Theol. (*hon.*, Zürich, 1880), son of the preceding, also of the Tübingen school; b. at Glattfelden, Canton Zürich, Switzerland, Sept. 1, 1852; studied at Zürich; became pastor at Niederhasli, near Zürich, 1875; of St. Peter's, Basel, 1879; and *privat-docent* for church history in the University of Basel, 1880. He finished the church history of his father, and, besides numerous articles in different religious journals, has written *Grégoire, Lebensbild aus der französischen Revolution*, Basel, 1878. Since 1881, he has prepared the section upon church history from Constantine to the Reformation, in the *Theologische Jahresbericht*, Leipzig, 1881 sqq.

BOISE, James Robinson, Ph.D. (Tübingen, 1868), **LL.D.** (Michigan, 1868), **D.D.** (Brown, 1879), Baptist; b. at Blandford, Hampden County, Mass., Jan. 27, 1815; graduated at Brown University, 1840; was tutor there for three years, and then professor of the Greek language; resigned in 1850, and for eighteen months pursued his studies in Germany, Greece, Italy, and France. In 1852 he became professor of the Greek language and literature in the University of Michigan at Ann Arbor; in 1868 the same in the University of Chicago; in 1877 professor of New-Testament interpretation in the Baptist Union Theological Seminary at Morgan Park, near Chicago. Besides Greek text-books for school and college use (including *Exercises in Greek Prose Composition*, New York, 1849; *The First Six Books of Homer's Iliad*, Chicago, 1868; *First Lessons in Greek*, Chicago, 1870; *Five Books of Xenophon's Anabasis*, New York, 1878), he has published *Notes* on Paul's Epistle to the *Galatians*, 1871; *Romans*, 1883; and to the *Ephesians*, the *Colossians*, *Philemon*, and the *Philippians*, 1884.

BOMBERGER, John Henry Augustus, D.D. (Franklin and Marshall College, 1854), Reformed (German); b. at Lancaster, Penn., Jan. 13, 1817; graduated from Marshall College, 1837, and Theological Seminary, Mercersburg, Penn., 1838; became tutor in Marshall College, 1836; pastor of the German Reformed Church in Lewistown, Penn., 1838; Waynesborough, Penn., 1840; Easton, Penn., 1845; Philadelphia (Race Street), Penn., 1854; president of Ursinus College and its Theological Department, 1870. From 1856 to 1862 he carried on a condensed translation of the first edition of Herzog's *Encyclopædia*, and published two volumes, embracing six of the original; but the war stopped it. He is the author of *Infant Salvation in its Relation to* [natural] *Depravity, to Regeneration, and to Baptism*, Philadelphia, 1859; *Five Years at the Race-street* [Reformed] *Church, with an Ecclesiastical Appendix*, 1860; a revised translation of Kurtz' *Text-Book of Church History*, 1860;

The Revised Liturgy, a History and Criticism of the Ritualistic Movement in the Reformed Church, 1866; *Reformed not Ritualistic: a Reply to Dr. Nevin's "Vindication,"* 1867. He edited *The Reformed-Church Monthly* (chiefly in opposition to "Mercersburg theology") from 1868–77, 9 vols.

BONAR, Andrew Alexander, D.D. (Edinburgh, 1874), Free Church of Scotland; b. in Edinburgh, May 29, 1810; graduated from the University of Edinburgh, 1838; and until 1856 labored in the parish of Collace, Perthshire, when he removed to his present charge, the Finnieston Church, Glasgow. He left the Established Church in 1843; was moderator of the General Assembly of the Free Church in 1878. He has always sought to identify himself with evangelical and revival movements. He is the author of *Mission of Inquiry to the Jews in Palestine and Other Countries*, Edinburgh, 1842; *Memoir of Rev. R. M. McCheyne*, 1844, many editions, republished and translated; *Commentary on Leviticus*, 1846, 5th ed. 1875; *Redemption Drawing Nigh, a Defence of Pre-millennialism*, 1847; (edited) *Nettleton's Life and Labours*, 1850; *The Gospel pointing to the Person of Christ*, 1852; *Christ and His Church, in the Book of Psalms*, 1859; (edited) *Letters of Samuel Rutherford*, 1862; *Gospel Truths*, 1878; *The Brook Besor*, 1879; *James Scott: A Labourer for God*, 1885; many tracts.

BONAR, Horatius, D.D., Free Church of Scotland; b. in Edinburgh, Dec. 19, 1808; studied at the University of Edinburgh; was pastor at Kelso (1838–66); separated, along with his congregation, from the Kirk, in 1843; since 1866 has been pastor of the Grange Free Church, Edinburgh. His fame mainly rests upon his poems and hymns. He is a diligent student of prophecy, and in 1849 founded the *Quarterly Journal of Prophecy*. His prose publications embrace *Prophetical Landmarks*, London, 1847, 4th ed. 1868; *The Night of Weeping, or Words for the Suffering Family of God*, 1850; *The Morning of Joy*, 1852; *The Desert of Sinai*, 1857, 2d ed. 1858; *The Land of Promise*, 1858; *Light and Truth; or, Bible Thoughts and Themes*, 1868–72, 6 vols.; *The White Fields of France* (a history of the McAll Mission), 1879; *The Life of G. T. Dodds*, 1884. The best-known collections of his poems are *Hymns of Faith and Hope*, 1857–71, 3 vols.; *The Song of the New Creation, and other Pieces*, 1872; *Hymns of the Nativity*, 1878.

BONET-MAURY, Amy Gaston Charles Auguste, D.D. (Paris, 1881), French Protestant; b. in Paris, Jan. 2, 1842; was graduated bachelor in theology at Strassburg, 1867; pastor at Dordrecht, 1869–72; at Beauvais (Oise), 1872–76; and at St Denis (Seine), 1877; licentiate in theology, 1878, and instructor in ecclesiastical history in the Protestant faculty of Paris; professor of the same, 1881. He has written *Les origines de la Réforme à Beauvais*, Paris, 1874; *E quibus Nederlandicis fontibus hauserit scriptor libri de Imitatione Christi*, 1878; *Gérard de Groote, un précurseur de la Réforme au quatorzième siècle*, 1878; *Les origines du christianisme unitaire chez les Anglais*, 1881 (English trans., *Early Sources of English Unitarian Christianity*, London, 1884); *Arnauld de Brescia, un Réformateur au douzième siècle*, 1881; *La doctrine des douze Apôtres. Essai de traduction, avec un commentaire critique et historique*, 1884.

BONNET, Jules, French Protestant, layman; b. at Nîmes, June 30, 1820; educated a lawyer; he has been for many years well known by his works upon Reformation history, and as secretary of the "Société d'histoire du protestantisme français," and editor of its valuable publications. He has published *Olympia Morata: épisode de la renaissance en Italie* (the thesis by which he won the degree of doctor of letters), 1850, 4th ed. 1865, German trans. 1860; *Lettres françaises de Calvin*, 1854 (English trans. of his collection of all Calvin's letters, Edinburgh and Philadelphia, 4 vols.); *Aonio Paleario*, 1863 (English trans. London, 1864); *Récits du seizième siècle*, 1864; *Nouveaux récits du seizième siècle*, 1869; *La Réforme au château de Saint Prevat*, 1873; *Notice sur la vie et les écrits de M. Merle d'Aubigné*, 1874; *Dernier récits du seizième siècle*, 1875; edited *Mémoires de Claude Parthenay Larchevêque, sieur de Soubise*, 1879.

BONWETSCH, Gottlieb Nathanael, D.D. (Bonn, 1881), Evangelical Lutheran; b. at Norka, Russia, Feb. 17 (5), 1848; studied theology at Dorpat, 1866–70; was ordained pastor, 1871; studied at Göttingen, 1874–75; and Bonn, 1877–78; became professor extraordinary of theology at Dorpat, 1882; ordinary professor, 1883. He is the author of *Die Schriften Tertullians untersucht*, Bonn, 1878; *Die Geschichte des Montanismus*, Erlangen, 1881; *Unser Reformator Martin Luther*, Dorpat, 1883; *Kyrill und Methodius, die Lehrer der Slaven*, 1885.

BOONE, Right Rev. William Jones, Episcopalian, missionary bishop of Shanghai, China; b. in China, 1847; graduated at Princeton College, 1865, and at the Theological Seminary, Virginia, 1868; and since 1869 has been a missionary in China; consecrated, 1884. *

BOOTH, William, General of the Salvation Army; b. at Nottingham, Eng, April 10, 1829; became a minister of the Methodist New Connection in 1850; resigned in 1861 rather than settle in ordinary circuit work, for which he did not believe himself to be so well adapted as for the evangelistic services which he had held with great success. It was as an independent evangelist that he started "The Christian Mission," in the East End of London, in July, 1865, and out of it developed the military religious organization to which in 1878 he gave the name of "The Salvation Army" (see *Encyclopædia*, vol. iii. p. 2099). *

BORNEMANN, Friedrich Wilhelm B., Lic. Theol. (Göttingen, 1884), German Protestant theologian; b. at Lüneberg, Hannover, March 2, 1858; studied at Göttingen, 1876–77, 1878–79, and at Leipzig, 1877–78; became private tutor at Bremen, 1879, at Medingen, 1880; *hospes* in the convent at Loccum, 1880; *inspector* of the theological *Stift* in the University of Göttingen, 1882 (fall); and *privat-docent* for church history there in December, 1884. In his special department he calls himself a pupil of Harnack's, but as a theologian he belongs to the school of Ritschl. He has written *Das Taufsymbol Justins des Märtyrers* (in Brieger's *Zeitschrift für Kirchengeschichte*, III., 1 [1878]; *In investiganda monachatus origine quibus de causis ratio habenda sit Origenis*, Göttingen, 1885.

BOUVIER, Ami Auguste Oscar, D.D. (*hon.*,

Bern, 1884), Swiss Protestant (Independent); b. at Geneva, Feb. 16, 1826; educated at the university there, and was ordained 1851; served as missionary and pastor in France, London, and Switzerland; became professor of apologetics and practical theology in the Genevan University, 1861; transferred to chair of dogmatics, 1865. Since 1873 he has also been librarian of the Company of Pastors. He was founder and first president of the committee in Geneva auxiliary to the Evangelical Missionary Society of Paris, 1865, and of the Society of Theological Sciences, 1871; made chevalier of the Legion of Honor, 1885. Among his numerous writings may be mentioned *Étude sur les conditions du développement social du Christianisme*, Geneva, 1851; *Le chrétien, ou l'homme accompli*, 1857; *Sermons*, 1860–62, 2 vols.; *L'Apologétique actuelle*, 1866; *La Révélation*, 1870; *Les sciences théologiques au dix-neuvième siècle*, 1871; *Catholiques libéraux et Protestants*, 1873; *Epoques et charactères bibliques*, 1873; *Les conférenees religieuses à Genève de 1835 à 1875*, 1876; *L'Esprit du Christianisme*, 1877; *La faculté de théologie de Genève pendant le dix-neuvième siècle*, 1878; *L'enseignement supérieur à Genève de 1559 à 1876*, 1878; *La Compagnie des Pasteurs de Genève*, 1878; *Le Pasteur John Bost*, 1881, 5th ed. 1882 (English trans.); *Paroles de foi et de liberté*, 1882; *Le divin d'après les apôtres*, 1883; *Le Protestantisme à Genève*, 1884 (in English in *Modern Review*, January, 1884); *Nouvelles paroles de foi et de liberté*, 1885; *La conscience moderne et la doctrine du péché*, 1886.

BOVET, Eugène Victor Félix, French Swiss Protestant; b. at Neuchâtel, Nov. 7, 1824; in his native city successively librarian, 1848, professor of French literature, and professor of Hebrew, and since 1853 one of the editors of the *Revue Suisse*. He has written *Le Comte de Zinzendorf*, Paris, 1860, 2 vols., 3d ed. 1865 (Dutch trans.; English abridged trans. entitled *The Banished Count*, London, 1865); *Voyage en terre sainte*, Neuchâtel, 1860, 7th ed. Paris, 1881 (Dutch, Swedish, and Italian trans.; German trans. from 4th ed., 1864, Zürich, 1866; English trans., *Egypt, Palestine, and Phœnicia*, London, 1883); *Histoire du Psautier des églises réformées*, Neuchâtel, 1872.

BOWMAN, Thomas, D.D. (Ohio Wesleyan University, 1856), **LL.D.** (Dickinson College, 1872), Methodist bishop; b. near Berwick, Columbia County, Penn., July 15, 1817; graduated as valedictorian at Dickinson College, 1837; licensed, 1838; entered travelling connection, 1839; teacher in the grammar school of the college, 1840–43; supernumerary through ill health until 1848; principal of Dickinson Seminary, Williamsport, Penn., 1848–58; president of Indiana Asbury (now De Pauw) University, Greencastle, Ind., 1858–72; elected bishop, 1872; and in 1884, chancellor of De Pauw University. In 1864–65 he was chaplain of the United-States Senate; and in 1878–79 officially visited his church's missions in Norway, Sweden, Denmark, Germany, Switzerland, Italy, and India; in 1881–82, those in China and Japan. He has written extensively for the denominational press.

BOYCE, James, D.D. (Jefferson College, Penn., and Erskine College, S.C., 1854), Associate Reformed Presbyterian; b. at Sardis, Mecklenburg County, N.C., July 13, 1808; graduated at Jefferson College, Penn., 1829; pastor of New Hope, S C., 1832–69; editor of *Christian Magazine of the South* for nine years; associate editor of *Associate Reformed Presbyterian* since 1870; professor and president of Associate Reformed Presbyterian Theological Seminary, at Due West, S.C., since 1869.

BOYCE, James Petigru, D.D. (Columbian College, Washington, D.C., 1859), **LL.D.** (Union University, Murfreesborough, Tenn., 1872), Baptist; b. at Charleston, S.C., Jan. 11, 1827; graduated at Brown University, 1847; studied theology in Princeton Theological Seminary, 1849–51; became pastor of the Baptist Church, Columbia, S.C., 1851; professor of theology in Furman University, Greenville, S.C., 1855; chairman of the faculty, and professor of systematic theology, 1859, in the Southern Baptist Theological Seminary, then at Greenville, S.C., and of church government and pastoral duties, 1877. In 1877 the seminary was moved to Louisville, Ky. He was chaplain of the Sixteenth South-Carolina Volunteers from 1861 to 1862; member of the South-Carolina Legislature from 1862 to 1865; of the governor's (Magrath) staff and State Council, 1864 and 1865; and of the State convention for reconstruction in 1865; from 1872 to 1879 was annually elected president of the Southern Baptist Convention. He is a trustee of the John F. Slater Fund. Besides speeches, sermons, and articles, he has published *Three Changes in Theological Education*, Greenville, S.C., 1856 (the principles of which address are embodied in the peculiar plan of the Southern Baptist Theological Seminary); *Brief Catechism of Bible Doctrine*, Greenville, S.C., 1863, last ed. Louisville, Ky., 1884; *Abstract of Theology*, Louisville, Ky., 1882.

BOYD, Andrew Kennedy Hutchison, D.D. (Edinburgh, 1864), Church of Scotland; b. in the Auchinleck Manse, Ayrshire, Nov. 3, 1825; educated at King's College, London, and at the University of Glasgow, graduating from the latter as B.A. (taking the highest honors in philosophy and theology), 1846. From November, 1850, to July, 1851, he was assistant in St. George's, Edinburgh; was then minister successively of Newton-on-Ayr, September, 1851–January, 1854; Kirkpatrick-Irongray, January, 1854–April, 1859; St. Bernard's Parish, Edinburgh, April, 1859–September, 1865; and since September, 1865, has been first minister of the city of St. Andrew's. [He is widely known by his signature A. K. H. B., and his *sobriquet* "The Country Parson."] He is the author of *Recreations of a Country Parson*, London, 1859, 1861, 1878, 3 series; *Leisure Hours in Town*, 1861; *Graver Thoughts of a Country Parson*, 1862, 1864, 1875, 3 series; *The Commonplace Philosopher in Town and Country*, 1862; *Counsel and Comfort, spoken from a City Pulpit*, 1863; *The Autumn Holidays of a Country Parson*, 1864; *The Critical Essays of a Country Parson*, 1865; *Sunday Afternoons at the Parish Church of a University City*, 1866; *Lessons of Middle Age*, 1867; *Changed Aspects of Unchanged Truths*, 1869; *Present-day Thoughts*, 1870; *Seaside Musings*, 1872; *A Scotch Communion Sunday*, 1873; *Landscapes, Churches, and Moralities*, 1874; *From a Quiet Place: Some Discourses*, 1879; *Our Little Life*, 1881, 1884, 2 series; *Towards the Sunset: Teachings after Thirty Years*, 1882; *What set him right: with Other Chapters to help*, 1885.

BOYLE, Very Rev. George David, Dean of Salisbury, son of the late Lord Chief Justice-General of Scotland; b. in Scotland, in the year 1828; educated at Exeter College, Oxford; graduated B.A., 1851; M.A., 1853; was curate of Kidderminster (the scene of Baxter's labors), 1853–57; of Hagley, 1857-60; perpetual curate of St. Michael, Handsworth, 1861–67; rural dean of Handsworth, 1866–67; vicar of Kidderminster, and chaplain of Kidderminster Union, 1867–80; honorary canon of Worcester Cathedral, 1872–80; rural dean of Kidderminster, 1877–80; appointed dean of Salisbury, 1880; precentor, 1881. He is the author of *Confession according to the Rule of the Church of England*, London, 1868; *Lessons from a Churchyard*, 1872; *The Trust of the Ministry*, 1882; *My Aids to the Divine Life*, 1883; *Richard Baxter, a Sketch*, 1883. *

BRACE, Charles Loring, Congregationalist; b. at Litchfield, Conn., June 19, 1826; graduated at Yale College, 1846; studied in Yale (1847–48) and in Union Theological Seminaries, New York (1848–49), but did not graduate; went to Europe, 1850; while at Gros Wardein in Hungary, 1851, was tried by court-martial, as an emissary to arouse a revolution against the Austrian government, but released through the efforts of the American *chargé d'affaires* at Vienna, Mr. C. J. McCurdy. On his return, 1852, he became one of the founders of the "Children's Aid Society of New-York City," and its secretary and executive agent the next year, and has ever since held the office. In 1854 he established the first newsboys' lodging-house; in 1855, an Italian industrial school; and in 1856, a German one. He has published *Hungary in 1851*, New York, 1852; *Home Life in Germany*, 1853; *The Norse Folk* (travels in Norway and Sweden), 1857; *Short Sermons to Newsboys*, 1861; *Races of the Old World*, 1863; *The New West*, 1868; *The Dangerous Classes of New York, and Twenty Years Work among them*, 1872, 3d ed. (enlarged) 1880; *Free Trade as promoting Peace and Good Will among Men*, 1879; *Gesta Christi; or, A History of Humane Progress under Christianity*, 1883, 3d ed. 1885.

BRADLEY, Charles Frederic, Methodist; b. in Chicago, Ill., Aug. 1, 1852; graduated at Dartmouth College, 1873; was tutor there, 1874–76; graduated at the Garrett Biblical Institute, Evanston, Ill., 1878; became professor of the Greek language and literature in Hamline University, Hamline, Minn., 1880; adjunct professor of exegetical theology (1883), and professor of New-Testament exegesis (1884), in the Garrett Biblical Institute, Evanston, Ill.

BRADLEY, Very Rev. George Granville, D.D. (Oxford, 1881), **LL.D.** (St. Andrew's, 1873), Dean of Westminster, Church of England; b. at High Wycombe, Dec. 11, 1821; educated at Rugby School, 1837–40; and at University College, Oxford, where he graduated B.A. (first-class in classics), 1844, and M.A., 1847; was fellow of University College, 1844–50; assistant master in Rugby School, 1846-58; head master of Marlborough College, 1858–70; Master of University College, Oxford, 1870–81; since 1881, Dean of Westminster, London, in succession to Dean Stanley. He has also been public examiner in the University of Oxford, 1871–72; select preacher in the same, 1875–76; examining chaplain to the late Archbishop of Canterbury (Dr. Tait), 1874–81; honorary chaplain to the Queen, 1874-76; since, chaplain in ordinary. Besides sermons and papers in periodicals, he has written *Reminiscences of Dean Stanley*, London, 1882; *Lectures on Ecclesiastes*, 1885; and two manuals on Latin writing.

BRASTOW, Lewis Orsmond, D.D. (Bowdoin, 1880), Congregationalist; b. at Brewer, Me., March 23, 1834; graduated at Bowdoin College, Maine, 1857; and Bangor Theological Seminary, 1860; was pastor of the South Congregational Church, St. Johnsbury, Vt., 1861–73; and of the First Congregational Church, Burlington, Vt., 1873–84; professor of homiletics and pastoral theology, Yale Theological Seminary, 1885. He was a chaplain in the Union Army during 1862 and 1863. His publications consist of sermons and review articles.

BREDENKAMP, Conrad Justus, Lic. Theol. (Erlangen, 1880), **D.D.** (*hon.*, Erlangen, 1883), Lutheran; b. at Basbeck, Hannover, June 26, 1847. He studied at the universities of Erlangen, Bonn, and Göttingen; was pastor at Kuppentin in Mecklenburg, 1872–78; without official position, at Göttingen, 1878–79; *privat-docent* at Erlangen, 1880–83; ordinary professor of theology at Greifswald, since 1883. He is the author of *Der Prophet Sacharja erklärt*, Erlangen, 1879; *Vaticinium quod de Immanuele edidit Jesaias* [vii. 1–ix. 6] *explicavit*, 1880; *Gesetz und Propheten. Ein Beitrag zur alttestamentlichen Kritik*, 1881.

BREED, William Pratt, D.D. (New-York University, 1864), Presbyterian; b. at Greenbush, N.Y., Aug. 23, 1816; graduated at the University, New-York City, 1843; and at Princeton Theological Seminary, 1846; pastor of the Second Presbyterian Church, 1847–56; and since, of the West Spruce-street Church, Philadelphia, Penn. He took a leading part in the movement to erect (1877) the monument to Witherspoon, in Fairmount Park, Philadelphia, and delivered *A Historical Discourse on Presbyterians and the Revolution* (subsequently published) in many places in its behalf. He made the address of welcome to the delegates of the Second General Council of the Alliance of the Reformed Churches, September, 1880, and read a paper before them on *The Diffusion of Presbyterian Literature.* He is the author of many volumes for Sunday-school libraries, and others of more permanent value, including *Presbyterianism Three Hundred Years ago*, Philadelphia, 1872; *Handbook for Funerals* [n.d.]; *A Model Christian Worker, John Potter*, 1879; *Aboard and Abroad in 1884*, New York, 1885. *

BREWER, Right Rev. Leigh Richmond, S.T.D. (Hobart College, 1881), Episcopalian, missionary bishop of Montana; b. at Berkshire, Vt., Jan. 20, 1839; graduated at Hobart College, Geneva, N.Y., 1863; and at the General (Episcopalian) Theological Seminary, New-York City, 1866; became rector of Grace Church, Carthage, N.Y., 1866; of Trinity Church, Watertown, N.Y., 1872; was consecrated bishop, 1880.

BRIEGER, Theodor, Ph.D. (Leipzig, 1870), **Lic. Theol.** (Halle, 1870), **D.D.** (*hon.*, Göttingen, 1877), Protestant theologian; b. at Greifswald, June 4, 1842; studied at Greifswald, Erlangen, and Tübingen, 1861–64; became *privat-docent* at Halle, 1870; professor extraordinary, 1873; ordinary professor at Marburg, 1876; at Leipzig, 1886.

Since 1876 he has edited the *Zeitschrift für Kirchengeschichte.* His publications include *De formulæ concordiæ Ratisbonensis origine atque indole,* Halle, 1870; *Gasparo Contarini und das Regensburger Concordienwerk des Jahres 1541,* Gotha, 1870; *Constantin der Grosse als Religionspolitiker,* 1880; *Die angebliche Marburger Kirchenordnung von 1527 und Luther's erster katechetischer Unterricht vom Abendmahl,* 1881; *Neue Mitteilungen über Luther in Worms,* Marburg, 1883; *Luther und sein Werk,* 1883; *Quellen und Forschungen zur Geschichte der Reformation.* 1. Bd. *Aleander u. Luther, 1521. Die vervollständigten Aleander-Depeschen, nebst Untersuchungen über den Wormser Reichstag.* 1 Abthlg., Gotha, 1884.

BRIGGS, Charles Augustus, D.D. (University of Edinburgh, 1884), Presbyterian; b. in New-York City, Jan. 15, 1841; studied in the University of Virginia, 1857–60; in the Union Theological Seminary, New York, 1861–63; and in the University of Berlin, Germany, under Dorner and Rödiger, 1866–69. He marched with the Seventh Regiment (N.Y.V.) to the defence of the capital. From 1863–66 he was in business with his father, in New-York City. He was pastor of the Presbyterian Church, Roselle, N.J., 1870–74; and has been since 1874 professor of Hebrew and the cognate languages in the Union Theological Seminary, New-York City. Since 1880 he has been a managing editor of the *Presbyterian Review,* of which he was a founder. Besides numerous articles in different periodicals, — notably those on biblical theology in the *American Presbyterian Review,* the earliest on the subject in America; and those on the higher criticism, in the *Presbyterian Review,* which beat the way for its study, — he has written *Biblical Study; its Principles, Methods, and History,* New York, 1883, 2d ed. 1885; *American Presbyterianism; its Origin and Growth,* 1885. He was one of the translators of the commentaries on the Psalms and Ezra, in the American Lange series.

BRIGHT, William, D.D. (Oxford, 1869), Church of England; b. at Doncaster, Dec. 14, 1824; educated at University College, Oxford; graduated B.A. (first-class classics), 1846; fellow of his college, 1847; Johnson theological scholar, 1847; Ellerton theological essayist, 1848; M.A., 1849; was theological tutor in Trinity College, Glenalmond, Perthshire, 1851–58; tutor of University College, Oxford, 1862; resigned fellowship on appointment as Regius professor of ecclesiastical history, Oxford University, and canon of Christ Church, 1868; honorary canon of Cathedral of the Isles, Cumbrae, 1865; examining chaplain to the bishop of Lincoln, 1885. He has published *Ancient Collects selected from Various Rituals,* London, 1857, 4th ed. 1869; *A History of the Church from the Edict of Milan, A.D. 315, to the Council of Chalcedon, A.D. 451,* Oxford, 1860, 3d ed. 1875; *Eighteen Sermons of St. Leo the Great on the Incarnation. With the "Tome,"* translated with notes, London, 1862, 2d ed. 1886; *Faith and Life: Readings compiled from Ancient Writers,* 1864, 2d ed. 1866; *Hymns and other Verses,* 1866, 2d ed. 1874; *Chapters of Early English Church History,* 1878; *Later Treatises of St. Athanasius,* translated with notes and appendix (vol. 46, *Library of the Fathers*), 1881; *Private Prayers, for a Week,* 1882; *Notes on the Canons of the First Four General Councils,* 1882; *Family Prayers,* 1885; *Iona, and other Verses,* 1885; edited the original text of Eusebius' *Ecclesiastical History,* 1872, 2d ed. 1882; St. Athanasius' *Orations against the Arians,* 1873, 2d ed. 1883; Socrates' *Ecclesiastical History,* 1878; *Select Anti-Pelagian Treatises of St. Augustine,* 1880; and St. Athanasius' *Historical Writings,* 1881; and with the Rev. P. G. Medd, M.A., edited a Latin translation of the Prayer-Book, 1865, 3d ed. 1877.

BROADUS, John Albert, D.D. (William and Mary, 1859, also Richmond College, 1859), **LL.D.** (Wake Forest College, N.C., 1871), Baptist; b. in Culpeper County, Va., Jan. 24, 1827; graduated at the University of Virginia, Charlottesville, Va., 1850; there assistant professor of Latin and Greek, 1851–53, chaplain, 1855–57; pastor in the Baptist Church, 1851–55, 1857–59. Since its organization in 1859 he has been professor of the interpretation of the New Testament and of homiletics in the Southern Baptist Theological Seminary, then in Greenville, S.C., removed in 1877 to Louisville, Ky. He has for many summers supplied pulpits in New York, Brooklyn, and Orange, N.J. He is a member of the International Sunday-school Lesson Committee. Besides numerous articles in periodicals, he has written *The Preparation and Delivery of Sermons,* Philadelphia, 1870, many editions, latest 1885, republished in London, much of it translated into Chinese, and used for native ministers of all denominations; *Lectures on the History of Preaching,* New York, 1876.

BROOKE, Stopford Augustus, Unitarian; b. at Glendoen rectory, Letter Kenny, County Donegal, Ireland, Nov. 14, 1832; was educated at Trinity College, Dublin, graduated M.A. 1858; since 1857 has preached in London, first as curate of St. Matthew, Marylebone, 1857–59; then of Kensington 1860–63; as minister of St. James's Chapel, York Street, 1866–75; and of Bedford Chapel, Bloomsbury, since 1876. In 1872 he was appointed chaplain in ordinary to the Queen. In 1880 he left the Established Church, and connected himself with the Unitarians. He has published *The Life and Letters of the Late Frederick W. Robertson,* London, 1865 (many subsequent editions and reprints); *Theology in the English Poets,* 1874, 4th ed. 1880; and the following volumes of sermons: *Sermons at St. James's Chapel,* 1868, 11th ed. 1880; 2d series, 1874, 5th ed. 1881; *Christ in Modern Life,* 1872, 14th ed. 1880; *Fight of Faith: Sermons on Various Occasions,* 1877; *Spirit of the Christian Life,* 1881. He also edited the sermons of F. W. Robertson. *

BROOKS, Phillips, D.D. (Harvard, 1877, Oxford, 1885), Episcopalian; b. in Boston, Dec. 13, 1835; graduated at Harvard College, 1855; and at the Protestant Episcopal Theological Seminary of Virginia, near Alexandria, 1859; was from 1859 to 1862 rector of the Church of the Advent, Philadelphia; till 1869, of the Church of the Holy Trinity in the same city; and since, of Trinity Church, Boston. His church was burned in the Boston fire, November, 1872; and the present imposing structure completed in February, 1877. In 1881 Mr. Brooks declined the Plummer professorship of Christian morals and preachership to Harvard College. He has published *Lectures on Preaching delivered before the Divinity School of Yale*

College, January–February, 1877 (Lyman Beecher Foundation), New York, 1877; *Sermons*, 1878; *Influence of Jesus* (the Bohlen Lectures for 1879), 1879; *Candle of the Lord, and other Sermons*, 1881; *Sermons preached in English Churches*, 1883.

BROWN, Charles Rufus, Baptist; b. at East Kingston, N.H., Feb. 22, 1849; educated at Phillips Exeter Academy, N.H., 1863–65; United-States Naval Academy, Annapolis, Md., 1865–69; in the Navy, promoted to master; resigned, and entered Newton Theological Institution in 1874, Harvard College, 1875, and graduated, 1877; studied in Newton Theological Institution, 1877–78, Union Theological Seminary, 1878–79; graduated at Union, May, 1879, and at Newton, June, 1879; studied in Berlin University, 1879–80; in Leipzig, 1880–81; became pastor at Franklin, N.H., 1881; professor of Old-Testament interpretatiou in Newton Theological Institution, 1883. He has published *An Aramaic Method*. Part I., Text, Notes, and Vocabulary. Part II. Grammar. Chicago, 1884–86.

BROWN, David, D.D. (Princeton College, 1852, and Aberdeen University, 1872), Free Church of Scotland; b. at Aberdeen, Aug. 17, 1803; graduated at the University of Aberdeen; was assistant to Edward Irving in London, 1830–32; minister of the Established Church of Scotland in Aberdeenshire, 1836–43; and of the Free Church in Glasgow, 1843–57, when he became principal and professor of divinity in the Free Church College, Aberdeen. He was moderator of the Free Church General Assembly, 1885. He has published *Christ's Second Coming: Will it be Pre-millennial?* Edinburgh, 1843, 6th ed. 1867; *Restoration of the Jews, Literal and Territorial*, 1861; *Crushed Hopes crowned in Death* (memoir of his son Alexander Brown, of the Bengal civil service). London, 1861; *Life of John Duncan, LL.D.* (professor of Hebrew and Oriental languages in New College, Edinburgh), Edinburgh, 1872, 2d ed. same year; *The Rev. John Duncan, LL.D., in the Pulpit and at the Communion-Table*, 1874; *Commentary on the Gospels* and *On the Acts and Romans* (in the Jamieson, Fausset, and Brown series), Glasgow, 1863 and 1869, reprinted Philadelphia, New York, and elsewhere; *On the Epistle to the Romans* (part of the *Portable Commentary*), 1863; *On the Epistles to the Corinthians* (in Schaff's *Popular Commentary*), Edinburgh and New York, 1882.

BROWN, Francis, Ph.D. (Hamilton, 1884), **D.D.** (Dartmouth, 1884), Presbyterian; b. at Hanover, N.H., Dec. 26, 1849; graduated at Dartmouth College, N.H., 1870; taught in Pittsburgh, Penn., 1870–72; was tutor in Greek in Dartmouth College, 1872–74; graduated as prize fellow of his class in Union Theological Seminary, New York, 1877, and as such studied two years in Germany; became instructor in biblical philology in Union Seminary, 1879; associate professor in biblical philology, 1881; full professor, 1885. He edited *The Beginnings of History*, English trans. of *Les origines de l'histoire*, I., by François Lenormant, New York, 1882; and, with President R. D. Hitchcock, *Teaching of the Twelve Apostles*, 1884, 2d ed., revised and greatly enlarged, 1885; independently has published *Assyriology, its Use and Abuse in Old-Testament Study*, 1885.

BROWN, Hugh Stowell, English Baptist; b. at Douglas, Isle of Man, Aug. 10, 1823; d. at Liverpool, Feb. 24, 1886. He learned surveying, then locomotive engineering, but at twenty-one entered King William's College, Castleton, Isle of Man, in order to fit himself for the ministry of the Established Church. But doubts respecting that Church's position toward the State, and on her baptismal teachings, led him ultimately into the Baptist Church; and at the close of 1847 he began his ministry in the Myrtle-street Chapel, Liverpool, being ordained the following January. He soon took a first place in his denomination, and won particular notice by inaugurating the largely attended Sunday-afternoon lectures for working-men, — an idea which was acted upon in many localities. He visited the United States and Canada in 1872; and was elected chairman of the Baptist Union of the United Kingdom. He has published numerous sermons and lectures. *

BROWN, James Baldwin, B.A., Congregationalist; b. in the Inner Temple, London, Aug. 19. 1820; d. in London, June 23, 1884. He was educated at University College, London, and graduated at the University, 1839; studied law for the next two years, but then obeyed an inner call to the ministry; studied theology at Highbury College; became an Independent minister, first of London Road Chapel, Derby, 1843; three years later (1846), of Claylands Chapel, Clapham Road, London. In 1870 he went with his congregation to the new church they had built at Brixton, and remained their pastor until his death. His ministry was faithful and laborious; his influence was consecrated and wide-spread. His distinctive theological peculiarity was his defence of the doctrine of conditional immortality. The esteem in which his brethren held him is shown by his occupancy of the chair of the Congregational Union in 1878. Besides pamphlets, occasional sermons, newspaper articles, sketches of Rev. Drs. Leifchild (1862) and Raffles (1863), he wrote *Studies of First Principles*, London, 1849; *The Divine Life in Man*, 1859, 2d ed. 1860; *The Doctrine of the Divine Fatherhood in relation to the Atonement*, 1860; *The Soul's Exodus and Pilgrimage*, 1862, 3d ed. 1866; *Aids to the Development of the Divine Life*, 1862; *Divine Mystery of Peace*, 1863; *Divine Treatment of Sin*, 1864 (the two together under title *The Divine Mysteries*, 1869); *The Home Life in the Light of its Divine Idea*, 1866, 5th ed. 1870; *Idolatries, Old and New: their Cause and Cure*, 1867; *Misread Passages of Scripture*, 1869, 2d series 1871; *The Christian Policy of Life*, 1870, 2d ed. 1880; *The First Principles of Ecclesiastical Truth: Essays on the Church and Society*, 1871; *The Sunday Afternoon: Fifty-two Brief Sermons*, 1871; *Buying and Selling and Getting Gain*, 1871; *Young Men and Maidens*, 1871 (the two together under title *Our Morals and Manners*, 1872); *The Higher Life: its Reality, Experience, and Destiny*, 1874, 5th ed. 1878; *The Battle and the Burden of Life*, 1875; *The Doctrine of Annihilation in the Light of the Gospel of Love*, 1875, 2d ed. 1878; *Church and State*, 1876; *Home: its Relation to Man and Society*, 1883, 3d ed. 1884. See *In Memoriam: James Baldwin Brown*, by his wife, London, 1884. *

BROWN, Right Rev. John Henry Hobart, S.T.D. (Racine College, Wis., 1874), Episcopalian, bishop of Fond du Lac; b. in New-York City, Dec.

1, 1831; graduated at the General Theological Seminary there, 1854; became assistant minister of Grace Church, Brooklyn Heights, 1854; rector of the Church of the Good Angels, 1855; of the Church of the Evangelists, New-York City, 1856; of St. John's, Cohoes, 1862; consecrated bishop, Dec. 15, 1875. In 1868 he was secretary to the diocesan convention at Albany; in 1870, archdeacon of the Albany convocation. He is "a High Churchman." He has published some sermons and pamphlets.

BROWNE, Right Rev. Edward Harold, D.D. (Cambridge, 1864), **D.C.L.** (Oxford, 1877), lord bishop of Winchester, Church of England; b. at Aylesbury, Buckinghamshire, March 6, 1811; educated at Emmanuel College, Cambridge; graduated B.A. (wrangler) 1832; obtained the Crosse theological scholarship, 1833; the Tyrwhitt Hebrew scholarship, 1834; the Norrisian prize for a theological essay, 1835; M.A., 1835; B.D., 1855. He became fellow and tutor in his college, 1837; curate of Stroud, Gloucestershire, 1840; perpetual curate of St. James, Exeter, 1841; perpetual curate of St. Sidwell, Exeter, 1841; vice-principal and professor of Hebrew in St. David's College, Lampeter, Wales, 1843; vicar of Kenwyn, Cornwall, and prebendary of Exeter, 1849; vicar of Heavitree, 1857; canon of Exeter, 1857. In 1854 he became Norrisian professor of divinity at Cambridge; in 1864, bishop of Ely; and in 1873 was translated to Winchester, and made *ex officio* prelate of the Most Noble Order of the Garter. He has taken great interest in the "Old Catholic" movement, and attended the Old Catholic Congress at Cologne in 1872. He was a member of the Old-Testament Company of Revisers. He is the author of *An Exposition of the XXXIX. Articles*, London, 1850–53, 2 vols., 12th ed. 1882, 1 vol.; three volumes of sermons, — *The Atonement and other Sermons* (1859), *Messiah Foretold and Expected* (1862), *The Strife, the Victory, and the Kingdom* (1872); *The Pentateuch and the Elohistic Psalms, in reply to Bishop Colenso*, 1863; *Position and Parties of the English Church*, 1875. He was a contributor to *Aids to Faith*, to Smith's *Dictionary of the Bible*, and to the *Bible* (Speaker's) *Commentary* (the commentary on Genesis).

BROWNE, John, B.A., Congregationalist; b. at North Walsham, Norfolk, Feb. 6, 1823; studied at Coward College and University College, London, 1839–44; graduated B.A. at London University, 1843; since 1848 he has been pastor at Wrentham, Suffolk. Besides sundry pamphlets he is the author of *History of Congregationalism in Norfolk and Suffolk*, London, 1877.

BRUCE, Alexander Balmain, D.D. (Glasgow, 1876), Free Church of Scotland; b. in the parish of Aberdalgie near Perth, Jan. 30. 1831; educated at Edinburgh, and was minister in Free Church, Cardross, Dumbartonshire, 1859–68; in Broughty Ferry, Forfarshire, 1868–75; since 1875 he has been professor of theology (apologetics and New-Testament exegesis) in the Free Church College, Glasgow. He declares himself to be "in sympathy with modern religious thought, while maintaining solidarity with all that is best in theology of the past; in favor of freedom in critical inquiries on the basis of evangelic faith, and of a simplified and more comprehensive creed." He has written *The Training of the Twelve*, Edinburgh, 1871, 3d ed. 1883; *The Humiliation of Christ* (Cunningham Lecture), 1876, 2d ed., 1881; *The Chief End of Revelation*, London, 1881; *The Parabolic Teaching of Christ*, 1882; *The Galilean Gospel*, Edinburgh, 1882. He delivered the course of Ely Lectures on Miracles in the Union Theological Seminary, New York, 1886.

BRUECKNER, Benno Bruno, D.D., German Protestant theologian and pulpit orator; b. at Rosswein, May 9, 1824; studied at Leipzig, and became afternoon preacher in the University church; pastor at Hohburg, 1850; professor extraordinary and university preacher at Leipzig, 1853; ordinary professor of theology, 1855; university preacher, and director of the seminary for practical theology, 1856; canon of Meissen, and consistorial councillor, 1860; general superintendent and member of the Berlin upper ecclesiastical council; honorary professor of theology at Berlin, 1885. Besides numerous sermons, single or collected in volumes, he is the author of *Epistola ad Philippenses Paulo auctori vindicat contra Baurium*, Leipzig, 1848; *Betrachtungen über die Agende der evangelisch-lutherischen Kirche im Königreich Sachsen*, 1865; with Luthardt and Kahnis he lectured in the course of lectures afterwards published under the title *Die Kirche nach ihrem Ursprung, ihrer Geschichte, ihrer Gegenwart*, 1865, 2d ed. 1866 (English trans. by Sophia Taylor, *The Church: its Origin, its History, and its Present Position*, Edinburgh, 1867). He edited the second and third editions of De Wette's commentary on Peter, Jude, and James, Leipzig, 1853 and 1867; and the fifth edition of his commentary on John, 1863.

BRUSTON, Charles Auguste, French Reformed; b. at Bourdeaux (Drôme) March 6, 1838; graduated at Montauban as bachelor (1859), licentiate (1873), and doctor (1881) of theology, and since 1874 has been professor there of Hebrew and the criticism of the Old Testament. Of his works may be mentioned *Les Psaumes traduits de l'hébreu d'après de nouvelles recherches sur le texte original*, Paris, 1865; and particularly *Histoire critique de la littérature prophétique* (from the beginning to the death of Isaiah), 1881.

BRYCE, George, LL.D. (Toronto University, 1884), Canadian Presbyterian; b. at Mount Pleasant, Brant County, Ont., April 22, 1844; graduated at the University of Toronto (1867), and in theology at King's College, Toronto; professor in Manitoba College since 1871, and one of the founders of Manitoba University, 1878; from 1871–81, secretary of home missions for Manitoba; president of Manitoba historical society, 1884–85; and moderator of the first synod of Manitoba and the North-west territories, 1884. He is *Délégué Regional de l'Institution ethnographique de Paris* (1879), and received a decoration from that body. He is the author of *The Presbyterian Church in Canada*, Toronto, 1875; *Manitoba: its Infancy, Growth, and Present Condition*, London, Eng., 1882; and other articles upon Manitoba.

BRYENNIOS, Philotheos, D.D. (Athens, 1880; Edinburgh, 1884), metropolitan of Nicomedia; b. at Constantinople, March 26 (old style), 1833; graduated in 1856 at the "Theological School in Chalce of the Great Church of Christ," and having distinguished himself was then sent to Germany for further study, and attended lectures in Leipzig, Berlin, and Munich. In 1861 he became professor of ecclesiastical history, exegesis, and other studies, in his *alma mater;* and in 1863, master and director. In December, 1867, he was called to Constantinople to be the head of the "Great School of the Nation" in the Phanar, and so remained until in 1875 he was sent by the Most Holy Synod of Metropolitans and Patriarch to the Bonn Old-Catholic Conference (Aug. 10–16, 1875), and while there received the patriarchal letter announcing his appointment as metropolitan of Serrae in Macedonia, which position he assumed December, 1875. In 1877 he was transferred to the metropolitan see of Nicomedia. In 1880 he went to Bucharest as commissioner of the Eastern Orthodox Patriarchal and other independent churches, to settle the matter of the plundering of Greek monasteries in Moldavia and Wallachia. In 1882, as instructed by the Holy Synod of metropolitans in Constantinople, and the Patriarch Joachim III., he wrote a reply to the encyclical letter of Pope Leo XIII. concerning Cyrillus and Methodius, the Apostles to the Slaves, which was published, with the approbation and at the expense of the Holy Synod, in Constantinople. His fame in the West rests upon his discovery in 1873 of the Jerusalem Manuscript, so called because found in the Jerusalem Monastery of the Most Holy Sepulchre in the Phanar, or Greek portion of Constantinople. This MS. of two hundred and forty small octavo pages contains (1) A Synopsis of the Old and New Testaments in the order of Books by St. Chrysostom; (2) The Epistle of Barnabas; (3) The First Epistle of Clement of Rome to the Corinthians; (4) The Second Epistle of Clement to the Corinthians; (5) The Teaching of the Twelve Apostles; (6) The spurious letter of Mary of Cassoboli; (7) Twelve pseudo-Ignatian Epistles. The Epistles to the Corinthians were published by him with prolegomena and notes in Constantinople, 1875, and at once attracted the attention of scholars, because the text was for the first time entire. "The Teaching of the Twelve Apostles," which Bryennios himself did not at first rightly estimate, is of still greater value both for its age and its contents, being no less than a catechetical church manual from the post-apostolic age. Having discovered its unique importance in 1878, he set to work to prepare a suitable edition of it; and being an erudite patristic scholar he produced it in Constantinople, 1883, with ample notes and prolegomena in Greek. His edition is the basis of the rich literature on the *Didaché* which has grown up in a short time. See his autobiography which he prepared for Schaff's work on the *Didaché*, New York, 1885, rev. ed. 1886, pp. 289–296.

BUCHWALD, Georg Apollo, Ph.D., Lic. Theol. (both Leipzig, 1884), German Protestant; b. at Grossenhain, Saxony, July 16, 1859; studied theology at Leipzig, 1879–82; became provisional upper master in the Mittweida *real-schule*, 1882; teacher of religion in the Zwickau gymnasium, 1883; fourth *diaconus* in the churches of St. Mary and St. Catharine, Zwickau, 1885. In 1883 he discovered in the Zwickau "Ratsschulbibliothek," very important Luther MSS. consisting of lectures, about six hundred sermons, etc. He has written *Ein Nachklang der epistolæ obscurorum virorum*, Dresden, 1882; *Der Logosbegriff des Johannes Scotus Erigena*, Leipzig, 1884; *Literaturbericht fur Kirche, Schule und das christliche Haus*, 1885; and has edited *D. Martini Lutheri scholas ineditas de libro Judicum habitas primum edidit*, Leipzig, 1884; *Ungedruckte Predigten D. Martin Luthers 1530 auf der Coburg gehalten*, Zwickau, 1884; *Andreas Poachs handschriftliche Sammlung ungedruckter Predigten D. Martin Luthers aus den Jahren 1528–46*, Leipzig, 1884 sqq.; *Sechs Predigten Johannes Bugenhagens* (*Osterprogramm* of the university, Halle-Wittenberg), Halle, 1885. He is a collaborator on the Erlangen and on the Weimar editions of Luther's works. He has contributed to the *Theologische Studien und Kritiken, Zeitschrift für kirchliche Wissenschaft und kirchliches Leben, Beiträge für sächsische Kirchengeschichte*.

BUCKLEY, James Monroe, D.D. (Wesleyan University, 1876), **LL.D.** (Emory and Henry College, Virginia, 1882), Methodist; b. at Rahway, N.J., Dec. 16, 1836; entered Wesleyan University, Middletown, Conn., in 1856, but compelled by impaired health to leave in 1858; from then until 1880 he was a Methodist pastor, — in New Hampshire 1858–63, Michigan (Detroit) 1863–66, New York (Brooklyn) 1866–69, 1872–75, 1878–80, and Connecticut (Stamford) 1869–72, 1875–78. In 1880 he was elected to his present position, editor of the *Christian Advocate*, the chief organ of the Methodist Episcopal Church. He is the author of *Appeals to Men of Sense and Reflection to begin a Christian Life*, New York, 1869, 5th ed. 1875; *Two Weeks in Yosemite*, 1873; *Christians and the Theatre*, 1875; *Supposed Miracles*, Boston, 1875; *Oats or Wild Oats? Common Sense for Young Men*, New York, 1885.

BUDDE, Karl (Ferdinand Reinhardt), Lic. Theol. (Bonn, 1873), **D.D.** (*hon.*, Giessen, 1883), German Protestant theologian; b. at Bensberg near Cologne on the Rhine, April 13, 1850; studied at Bonn 1867–68, 1869–70, 1871; at Berlin, 1868–69; Utrecht, 1871–73; became *privat-docent* of Old-Testament theology at Bonn, 1873; professor extraordinary, 1879; was inspector of the evangelical *Stift* of the University of Bonn, September, 1878–April, 1885. He was in the German infantry during the Franco-Prussian war, 1870–71. He is the author of *Beiträge zur Kritik des Buches Hiob*, Bonn, 1876; *Die Biblische Urgeschichte* (*Gen. i–xii. 5*) *untersucht*, Giessen, 1883; and in periodicals has published *Ueber vermeintliche metrische Formen in der hebräischen Poesie*, in *Theol. Studien u. Kritiken*, 1874, pp. 747–764; *Ueber die Capitel 50 und 51 des Buches Jeremia*, in *Jahrb. f. Deutsche Theologie*, 1878, pp. 428–470, 530–562; *Das hebräische Klagelied*, in *Zeitschrift für die alttest. Wissenschaft*, 1882, pp. 1–52; *Die Capitel 27 und 28 des Buches Hiob*, do., pp. 193–274; *Gen. 48 : 7 und die benachbarten Abschnitte*, do., 1883, pp. 56–86; *Ein althebräisches Klagelied*, do., pp. 299–306; *Die hebräische Leichenklage*, in *Zeitschr. d. deutschen Palästina-Vereins*, Bd. VI., pp. 180–194; "*Seth und die Sethiten*," *Berichtigung*, in *Zeitschrift f. d. alttest. Wissenschaft*, 1884, pp. 298–302, 1885, pp. 155–160; *Gen. 3 : 17; 5 : 29; 8 : 21, ein Beitrag zur Quellenkritik der Biblischen Urgeschichte*, do., 1886, pp. 30–43.

BUDER, Paul, D.D. (Tübingen, 1880), German Protestant theologian; b. at Leutkirch, Würtemberg, Feb. 15, 1836; studied at Tübingen, 1851–54; became *repetent* in the Evangelical Theological Seminary at Tübingen, 1861; pastor at Backnang (*Diakonus und Bezirksschul-inspector*), Würtemberg, 1865; second court preacher at Stuttgart, 1868; professor extraordinary of theology, and *ephorus* of the theological seminary, Tübingen, 1872; ordinary professor there, 1877. In 1869 he received the gold medal for saving a child from drowning, at the risk of his own life. He is the author of *Ueber die apologetische Aufgabe der Theologie der Gegenwart*, Tübingen, 1876.

BUEL, Samuel, S.T.D. (Columbia College, N.Y., 1862; *ad eundem* General Theological Seminary of P. E. Church, New-York City, 1884), Episcopalian; b. at Troy, N.Y., June 11, 1815; graduated at Williams College, 1833; was successively rector in Marshall, Mich., Schuylkill Haven, Penn., Cumberland, Md., and Poughkeepsie, N.Y.; professor of ecclesiastical history, subsequently of divinity, in the Seabury Divinity School, Faribault, Minn., 1866; professor of systematic divinity and dogmatic theology in the General Seminary of the Protestant Episcopal Church, New-York City, 1871. He has written, besides numerous articles in periodicals, and a translation from the German of the *Report of the Union Conferences held from Aug. 10 to 16, 1875, at Bonn*, New York, 1876; *The Apostolical System of the Church defended in a Reply to Dr. Whately on the Kingdom of Christ*, Philadelphia, 1844; *Eucharistic Presence, Sacrifice, and Adoration*, New York, 1874.

BUELL, Marcus Darius, Methodist; b. at Wayland, N.Y., Jan. 1, 1851; graduated at New-York University, 1872; and at the School of Theology, Boston University, 1875; held pastorates at King Street, Conn., Great Neck, L.I., in Brooklyn, N.Y., and in Hartford, Conn.; travelled in Europe and the Levant in 1879–80; pursued his studies at the Universities of Cambridge and Berlin, 1884–85; and in 1885 was appointed professor of New-Testament Greek and exegesis in the School of Theology, Boston University.

BURGESS, Right Rev. Alexander, S.T.D. (Brown University, 1866; Racine College, 1882), Episcopalian, bishop of Quincy, Ill.; b. in Providence, R.I., Oct. 31, 1819; graduated at Brown University there, 1838; and at the General Theological Seminary, New-York City, 1841; successively rector of St. Mark's, Augusta, Me., 1843; St. Luke's, Portland, 1854; St. John's, Brooklyn, L.I., 1867; Christ Church, Springfield, Mass., 1869; consecrated, 1878. In 1877 he was president of the House of Deputies. Besides sermons, addresses, carols, and hymns, he has written a memoir of his brother, Bishop George Burgess of Maine (d. April 23, 1866; see *Encyclopædia*, I. 341), Philadelphia, 1869.

BURGESS, Henry, Ph.D. (Göttingen, 1852), **LL.D.** (Glasgow, 1851), Church of England; b. in the parish of St. Mary, Newington, London, Jan. 29, 1808; was educated at the Dissenting College at Stepney, and distinguished himself in Hebrew and the classical languages. After graduation (1830), he became Baptist minister at Suson. But after a time he thought best to alter his church relations (1849), and was ordained deacon 1850, and priest 1851, by the Bishop of Manchester; became curate at Blackburn, 1851; perpetual curate of Clifton Reynes, Buckinghamshire, 1851; vicar of St. Andrew's, Whittlesey, near Peterborough, 1861; d. Tuesday, Feb. 16, 1886. He edited *The Clerical Journal*, 1854–68; *The Journal of Sacred Literature;* the second edition of Kitto's *Cyclopædia of Biblical Literature*, Edinburgh, 1856, 2 vols. He is the translator from the Syriac of *The Festal Letters of St. Athanasius*, London, 1852; and *Metrical Hymns and Homilies of St. Ephrem Syrus*, 1853; and author of *Luther, his Excellences and Defects*, 1857; *The Reformed Church of England in its Principles and their Legitimate Development*, 1869; *Essays, Biblical and Ecclesiastical, relating chiefly to the Authority and Inspiration of the Holy Scriptures*, 1873; *Disestablishment and Disendowment*, 1875; *The Art of Preaching and the Composition of Sermons*, 1881.

BURGON, Very Rev. John William, B.D., dean of Chichester, Church of England; b. at Smyrna, Asia Minor, Aug. 21, 1813; educated at Worcester College, Oxford, graduated B.A. (second-class classics), 1845, M.A. (Oriel), 1848, B.D., 1871; wrote the Newdigate prize poem, 1845, the Ellerton theological essay, 1847, the Denyer theological essay, 1851; was elected a fellow of Oriel College, 1846; ordained deacon, 1848, priest, 1849; Gresham lecturer in divinity, 1868; became vicar of St. Mary the Virgin, Oxford, 1863; dean of Chichester, 1876. He has written *The Life and Times of Sir Thomas Gresham*, London, 1839, 2 vols.; *Petra, a Poem*, 1846; *Oxford Reformers*, 1854; *A Plain Commentary on the Four Holy Gospels*, 1855, 8 vols., new ed. 1877, 4 vols., reprinted Philadelphia, 1868, 2 vols.; *Historical Notices of the Colleges of Oxford*, 1857; *Plain Commentary on the Book of Psalms* (P.B. Version), 1857, 2 vols.; *Inspiration and Interpretation* (answer to *Essays and Reviews*), 1861; *Letters from Rome to Friends in England*, 1862; *A Treatise on the Pastoral Office*, 1864; *Ninety-one Short Sermons*, 1867, 2 vols.; *Disestablishment, the Nation's Formal Rejection of God and Denial of the Faith*, 1868; *England and Rome. Three Letters to a Pervert*, 1869; *The Last Twelve Verses of the Gospel according to St. Mark vindicated against recent Critical Objectors and established*, 1871; *The Athanasian Creed to be retained in its integrity, and why*, 1872; *A Plea for the Study of Divinity in Oxford*, 1875; *The Revision revised. Three Articles from the Quarterly Review*, 1883; *Ten Lives of Good Men*, 1885; *Poems*, 1885

BURNEY, Stanford Guthrie, D.D. (Bethel College, Tenn., 1854), **LL.D.** (Waynesburg College, Penn., 1880), Cumberland Presbyterian; b. in Robinson County, Tenn., April 16, 1814; licensed by the Nashville Presbytery of the Cumberland Presbyterian Church, October, 1834; ordained, March, 1836; pastor at Franklin, Tenn., 1836–38; at Nashville, Tenn., 1841–43; financial agent of Cumberland University, Lebanon, Tenn. (formerly Princeton College, Ky.) 1843; pastor at Memphis, Tenn., 1845; at Oxford, Miss., 1848–73 (president of Union Female College, 1852–62, professor of English literature, Mississippi State University, 1865–73, both at Oxford); has been professor in the theological department of Cumberland University since its re-organization in 1877, — until 1880 professor of biblical literature, since 1880 of systematic theology. He has been a prominent member or chairman of most of the special committees of importance appointed by the General Assembly of the Cumberland Presbyterian Church during the past thirty years, notably these three: on revision of form of government, 1851; on union with Presbyterian Church in the United States, 1867; on revision of Confession of Faith, 1880. He was moderator of the General Assembly at Nashville, 1860, and has repeatedly declined re-election. He is the author of articles in periodicals, and *The Doctrine of Election*, Nashville, Tenn., 1879, and *Baptismal Regeneration*, 1880.

BURNHAM, Sylvester, D.D. (Bowdoin, 1885), Baptist; b. at Exeter, N.H., Feb. 1, 1842; graduated at Bowdoin College, Brunswick, Me., 1862, and from the Newton Theological Institution, Newton Centre, Mass., 1873; and since 1875 has been professor of Hebrew and Old-Testament exegesis in the Baptist Theological Seminary, Hamilton, N.Y.

BURR, Enoch Fitch, D.D. (Amherst, 1868), Congregationalist; b. at Green's Farms, Westport, Conn., Oct. 21, 1818; graduated at Yale College, 1839; carried on for several years in New Haven mingled scientific and theological studies; since 1850 has been pastor in Lyme, Conn.; and since 1868, lecturer in Amherst College on the scientific evidences of religion. In 1874 he delivered by request, in New York and Boston, a course of lectures on "The Latest Astronomy against the Latest Atheism;" and has since lectured on kindred themes at Williams College, the Sheffield Scientific School, and other institutions. He is the author of *The Mathematical Theory of Neptune*, New Haven, 1848; *Spiritualism*, New York, 1859; *Ecce Cœlum*, Boston, 1867; *Pater Mundi*, 1869; *Ad Fidem*, 1871; *Evolution*, 1873; *Sunday Afternoons*, New York, 1874; *Thy Voyage* (poem), 1874; *Toward the Strait Gate*, Boston, 1876; *Work in the Vineyard*, 1876; *From Dark to Day* (poem), 1877; *Dio the Athenian*, New York, 1880; *Tempted to Unbelief*, 1882; *Ecce Terra*, Philadelphia, 1884; *Celestial Empires*, New York, 1885; *Theism as a Canon of Science*, London, 1886.

BURRAGE, Henry Sweetser, D.D. (Brown University, 1883), Baptist; b. at Fitchburg, Mass., Jan. 7, 1837; graduated at Brown University, Providence, R.I., 1861, and at Newton Theological Institution, Newton Centre, Mass., 1867; studied in Halle, Germany, 1868-69; was a Baptist pastor in Waterville, Me., 1869-73; since has been editor and proprietor of *Zion's Advocate*, a Baptist religious paper published at Portland, Me.; since 1876, recording secretary of the American Baptist Missionary Union; and is also chancellor of the Maine Commandery of the Military Order of the Loyal Legion of the United States. While a student of theology at Newton he entered (1862), as private, the Thirty-sixth Massachusetts Volunteer Infantry; was promoted sergeant, sergeant-major, second lieutenant, first lieutenant, captain, brevet major; was wounded at Cold Harbor, June 3, 1864; was assistant adjutant general on the staff of the first brigade, second division, Ninth Army Corps; was a prisoner from Nov. 1, 1864, to Feb. 22, 1865; was mustered out of the service June 8, 1865, and returned to his studies at Newton, — a class having entered and graduated in his absence. He has written, besides numerous articles, *The Act of Baptism in the History of the Christian Church*, Philadelphia, 1879; *A History of the Anabaptists in Switzerland*, Philadelphia, 1882; and has edited *Brown University in the Civil War*, Providence, R.I., 1868; *Henry Wadsworth Longfellow · Seventy-Fifth Birthday. Proceedings of the Maine Historical Society*, Portland, 1882; *History of the Thirty-sixth Regiment Massachusetts Volunteers*, Boston, 1884.

BURROWES, George, D.D. (Washington College, Washington, Penn., 1853), Presbyterian; b. at Trenton, N.J., April 3, 1811; graduated at Nassau Hall (College of New Jersey), Princeton, N.J., 1832, and at Princeton Theological Seminary, 1835; was pastor at West Nottingham, Md., 1836-50; professor of Latin and Greek, Lafayette College, Easton, Penn., 1850-55; pastor of Newtown Presbyterian Church, Penn., 1857-59; built up the City College, San Francisco, Cal., 1859, left it 1865; was principal of the University Mound boarding-school near San Francisco, 1870-73; has been, since its origin in 1872, professor of Hebrew and Greek in the San Francisco Presbyterian Theological Seminary. He is the author of *A Commentary on the Song of Solomon*, Philadelphia, 1853, 3d ed. 1861; *Octorara, a Poem, and other Pieces*, 1856; *Advanced Growth in Grace*, San Francisco, 1885.

BURTON, Ernest De Witt, Baptist; b. at Granville, O., Feb. 4, 1856; graduated at Denison University, Granville, O., 1876; and at Rochester (Baptist) Theological Seminary, N.Y., 1882; was instructor in New-Testament Greek in Rochester Seminary, 1882-83; and since has been associate professor of interpretation of the New Testament, Newton Theological Institution, Newton Centre, Mass.

BURWASH, Nathaniel, S.T.D. (Garrett Biblical Institute, 1876), Methodist; b. at Argenteuil, Quebec, Can., July 25, 1839; graduated at Victoria University, Cobourg, Can., B.A. (valedictorian), 1859; Yale College, 1866; Garrett Biblical Institute, Evanston, Ill., B.D., 1871; was classical tutor in Victoria University, 1860; pastor, 1861-66; professor of natural science, Victoria University, 1867-72; dean of theological faculty, and professor of biblical and systematic theology, Victoria University, since 1873. He is the author of *Genesis, Nature, and Results of Sin*, Toronto, 1878; *Wesley's Doctrinal Standards*, 1881; *Relation of Children to the Fall, the Atonement, and the Church*, 1882.

BUTLER, Clement Moore, D.D. (Kenyon College, O., 1847), Episcopalian; b. at Troy, N.Y., Oct. 16, 1810; graduated at Trinity College, Hartford, 1833: and at the General Theological Seminary, New York, 1836. Between 1837 and 1861 he was rector of Episcopal churches in New York, District of Columbia, Massachusetts, and Ohio; from 1861 to 1864, chaplain to the United-States Embassy at Rome, Italy; from 1864 to 1884, professor of church history in the Protestant Episcopal Divinity School, Philadelphia. While a pastor in Washington, D.C. (1846-54), he was chaplain of the United-States Senate (1849-53), and in that capacity performed the funeral service and preached the sermon upon the death of Mr. Calhoun and Mr. Clay. These sermons were published by the Senate. He is the author of forty published occasional sermons, and of *The Year of the Church: Hymns and Devotional Verse* *for the Sundays and Holy Days of the Ecclesiastical Year. For Young Persons*, Utica, 1839; *The Book of Common Prayer interpreted by its History*, Boston, 2d ed., enlarged, Washington, D.C., 1849; *Old Truths and New Errors*, New York, 1850; *Addresses and Lectures on Public Men and Public Affairs, delivered in Washington City*, Cincinnati, 1856; *Lectures on the Book of Revelation*, New York, 1860; *The Flock Fed: Catechetical Instruction preparatory to Confirmation*, 1862; *St. Paul in Rome* (lectures in Rome), Philadelphia, 1865; *Inner Rome: Political, Religious, and Social*, 1866; *The Ritualism of Law*, 1867; *A Manual of Ecclesiastical History* (from the first to the nineteenth century), 1868–72, 2 vols.; *History of the Book of Common Prayer*, 1880; *History of the Reformation in Sweden*, New York, 1883.

BUTLER, Very Rev. Henry Montagu, D.D. (Cambridge, 1867), dean of Gloucester, Church of England; b. at Harrow in the year 1833; educated at Harrow School (of which his father was then head master, afterward dean of Peterborough), and Trinity College, Cambridge; was elected Bell University scholar, 1852, and Battie University scholar, 1853; won Sir W. Browne's medal for the Greek ode, 1853; the Porson prize, the Greek ode, the Camden medal for Latin hexameters, and the members' prize for a Latin essay, 1854; graduated B.A. (senior classic), 1855; M.A., 1858; was fellow of his college, 1855–59; ordained deacon and priest, 1859; head master of Harrow, 1859–85; honorary chaplain to the Queen, 1875–77; chaplain in ordinary, 1877–85; select preacher at Oxford, 1877, 1878, 1882; at Cambridge, 1879; examining chaplain to Archbishop of Canterbury, 1879–85; appointed dean, 1885. He is the author of *Sermons preached at Harrow*, 1861–69, 2 vols. *

BUTLER, James Glentworth, D.D. (Hamilton College, Clinton, N.Y., 1864), Presbyterian; b. in Brooklyn, N.Y., Aug. 3, 1821; studied in Union Theological Seminary, New-York City, 1846–47, and at the New-Haven (Congregational) Theological Seminary, Conn., 1847–49; was resident licentiate at the latter, 1849–50; Presbyterian pastor in West Philadelphia, Penn., 1852–68; secretary of the American and Foreign Christian Union, New-York City, 1868–71; pastor in Brooklyn (E.D.), N.Y., 1871–73; has been without charge in Brooklyn since 1874. Besides numerous articles, he has issued *The Bible Reader's Commentary, New Testament*, New York, 1879, 2 vols.; in 1883 title changed to *Bible Work* (5 vols. on Old Testament in preparation).

BUTLER, William, D.D. (Dickinson College, Carlisle, Penn., 1862), Methodist; b. in Dublin, Ireland, Jan. 31, 1818; graduated at Didsbury College, near Manchester, Eng., 1844; same year became a member of the Irish Wesleyan Conference; in 1850 joined the New-England Annual Conference; in 1856 went to India to found a mission for the Methodist-Episcopal Church; returned in 1865; succeeded Dr. Mattison as secretary of the American and Foreign Christian Union, 1869; resigned when appointed to found a mission for his denomination in Mexico in 1873; returned, 1879; revisited India, 1883–84. He is the author of *Compendium of Missions*, Boston, 1852; *The Land of the Veda*, New York, 1872; *From Boston to Bareilly, and back*, 1885.

BUTTZ, Henry Anson, D.D. (Princeton, 1875), **LL.D.** (Dickinson, 1885), Methodist; b. at Middle Smithfield, Penn., April 18, 1835; graduated at Princeton, 1858; studied theology in New-Brunswick Seminary; became Methodist-Episcopal minister, 1858; adjunct professor of Greek and Hebrew (1870), and then George T. Cobb professor of New-Testament exegesis, in Drew Theological Seminary, Madison, N.J.; president of the same, 1880. He edited *The Epistle to the Romans in Greek, in which the Text of Robert Stephens, Third Edition, is compared with the Text of the Elzevirs, Lachmann, Alford, Tregelles, Tischendorf, and Westcott, and with the chief uncial and cursive Manuscripts, together with references to the New-Testament Grammars of Winer and Buttmann*, New York, 1876, 3d ed. 1879; and, with a memoir, B. H. Nadal's *Discourses*, New York, 1873.

BAUM, Henry Mason, Episcopalian; b. at East Schuyler, Herkimer County, N.Y., Feb. 24, 1848; educated at Hudson-river Institute, Claverack, Dutchess County, New York; read law for three years; entered the Protestant-Episcopal Divinity School of Philadelphia, 1869; was ordained deacon 1870, priest 1872; was rector of St. Peter's Church, East Bloomfield, N.Y., 1870–71; and missionary to Allen's Hill, Victor, Lima, and Honoye Falls, N.Y.; rector of St. Matthew's Church, Laramie City, Wyoming Territory, 1872–73; in charge of St. James's Church, Paulsborough, N.J., 1873–74; rector of St. Matthew's Church, Lambertville, N.J., 1875–76; and of Trinity Church, Easton, Penn., 1876–80; travelled in Europe, 1879–80; since January, 1881, has been editor and proprietor of *The Church Review*. He is the author of *Rights and Duties of Rectors, Church Wardens, and Vestrymen, in the American Church*, Philadelphia, 1879; *The Law of the Church in the United States*, New York, 1886.

C.

CAIRD, John, D.D. (University of Glasgow, 1860), **LL.D.** (University of St. Andrew's, 1883), Established Church of Scotland; b. at Greenock, Dec. 15, 1820; graduated at the University of Glasgow, M.A., 1845; became minister of Newton-on-Ayr, 1845; of Lady Yester's, Edinburgh, 1847; of the parish of Errol, Perthshire, 1849; of Park Church, Glasgow, 1857; professor of divinity, University of Glasgow, 1862; principal and vice-chancellor of the University of Glasgow, 1873. He is one of her Majesty's chaplains for Scotland. He is the author of *Sermons*, Edinburgh, 1859; *Introduction to the Philosophy of Religion*, Glasgow, 1880; *The Philosophy of Spinoza*, Edinburgh, 1886.

CAIRNS, John, D.D., LL.D. (both of Edinburgh, 1858 and 1884), United Presbyterian; b. near Ayton, Berwickshire, Scotland, Aug. 23, 1818; entered at Edinburgh University, 1834; studied at Berlin, 1843; minister of the United Presbyterian Church, Berwick-on-Tweed, 1845–76. In 1867 he became professor of apologetics in the United Presbyterian Hall, Edinburgh; in 1876 became professor of systematic theology also; and since 1879 has been principal as well. He has written *Life of John Brown, D.D.*, Edinburgh, 1860; *Unbelief in the Eighteenth Century* (Cunningham Lecture for 1880), 1881, New York 1881. He wrote the article *Schottland, kirchliche Statistik*, in the 2d ed. of Herzog's *Real-Encyklopädie*, and the article *Infidelity* in the SCHAFF-HERZOG; also in *Present Day Tracts*, London, 1882–84, those on *Miracles; Christ the Central Evidence of Christianity; Success of Christianity; Argument from Prophecy.*

CALDERWOOD, Henry, LL.D. (Glasgow, 1865), F.R.S.E., United Presbyterian Church of Scotland; b. at Peebles, May 10, 1830; studied in the University of Edinburgh, 1847–53; then in the theological hall of the United Presbyterian Church, Edinburgh; was licensed by the Edinburgh Presbytery, January, 1856, and ordained in Glasgow the same year. He was second in the honor list of Sir William Hamilton's class, Professor John Veitch being first. For a time he taught English and classics in the Southern Institution, Edinburgh, and in the Edinburgh Institution. In 1861, elected examiner in mental philosophy to University of Glasgow. In 1868 he was appointed professor of moral philosophy in the University of Edinburgh. He is the author of *The Philosophy of the Infinite*, London, 1854, 3d ed. 1874; *Handbook of Moral Philosophy*, 1872, 12th ed. 1885; *On Teaching, its Means and Ends*, 1874, 3d ed. 1881; *The Relations of Mind and Brain*, 1879, 2d ed. 1884; *The Parables of our Lord interpreted in View of their Relations to Each Other*, 1880; *The Relations of Science and Religion* (Morse Lectures before Union Theological Seminary, New York, 1880), 1881.

CAMERON, George Gordon, M.A., Free Church of Scotland; b. at Pluscarden, near Elgin, Sept. 13, 1836; graduated with highest classical honors at Aberdeen in 1860; was minister of St. John's Free Church, Glasgow (Dr. Chalmers's congregation) from 1871 to 1882, when he was appointed professor of Hebrew and Oriental languages in the Free Church College, Aberdeen.

CAMPBELL, James Colquhon, D.D. (Cambridge, 1859), lord bishop of Bangor, Church of England; b. at Stonefield, Argyleshire, Scotland, in the year 1813; educated at Trinity College, Cambridge; graduated B.A. (senior optime and second-class classical tripos), 1836; M.A., 1839; was ordained deacon, 1837; priest, 1838; was rector of Merthyr-Tydfil, Glamorganshire, 1844–59; rural dean of the Upper Deanery of Llandaff, Northern Division, 1844-57; honorary canon of Llandaff Cathedral, 1852–57; archdeacon of Llandaff, 1857-59; consecrated bishop, 1859. *

CAMPBELL, John, Presbyterian Church in Canada; b. in Edinburgh, Scotland, June 18, 1840; graduated at the University of Toronto, B.A., 1865; M.A., 1866; studied theology at Knox College, Toronto, and New College, Edinburgh, 1865–68; has been minister of Charles-street Church, Toronto, since 1868; member of the senate and examiner in the University of Toronto since 1871; was lecturer in Knox College, Toronto, and in the Presbyterian College, Montreal, 1872-73; has been professor of church history and apologetics in the latter since 1873. He received the Order of Merit, first class, Roumania; is a member of the Society of Biblical Archæology (London); Canadian Institute; Délégué général de l'Institution ethnographique de Paris (received bronze medal); honorary member della Lega Filellenica di Torino, etc., etc.; and has discussed various ethnographical, philological, and kindred matters in the transactions of these societies since 1869, and in various journals; is now issuing decipherments of Etruscan and other Turanian inscriptions relating to the Canaanite population of Palestine.

CAMPBELL, William Henry, D.D. (Union College, Schenectady, N.Y., 1844), Reformed (Dutch); b. at Baltimore, Md., Sept. 14, 1808; graduated at Dickinson College, Carlisle, Penn., 1828; studied at Princeton Theological Seminary, 1828–29; was pastor of the Reformed Dutch Church at Chittenango, N.Y., 1831–32; principal of Erasmus Hall, Flatbush, Long Island, N.Y., 1833–39; pastor in East New York, 1840-41; of the Third Church, Albany, 1841–48; principal of the Albany Academy, 1848–51; professor of Oriental literature in the Reformed Dutch Theological Seminary, New Brunswick, N.J., 1851–63; in Rutgers College, New Brunswick, professor of belles-lettres, 1851–63; of moral philosophy, 1862–63; president of Rutgers College, and professor of biblical literature, moral philosophy, and evidences of Christianity, 1863–82. His publications consist of occasional sermons and discourses, and articles in periodicals. See list of the chief of these in Corwin's *Manual of the Reformed Church in America*, 3d ed., New York, 1879, p. 206.

CAPEL, Thomas John, D.D., Roman Catholic;

b. at Hastings, Eng., Oct. 28, 1836; ordained priest, 1860; established the English Catholic mission at Pau, and became its chaplain; named private chamberlain to Pope Pius IX., 1868; and domestic prelate with title of Monsignor, 1873. He has been instrumental in the conversion to Romanism of several leading members of the English nobility, and as a proselyter figures in Disraeli's *Lothair*. In January, 1864, he became a founder and vice-principal of St. Mary's Normal College, Hammersmith, but retired in broken health in 1868. In February, 1873, he founded the Catholic Public School at Kensington; the next year was the unanimous choice of the English Roman-Catholic bishops for rector of the College of Higher Studies at Kensington, but resigned the position in 1878. He visited the United States of America in 1884. He is the author of *Catholic: an Essential and Exclusive Attribute of the True Church*, New York, 1884. *

CAPEN, Elmer Hewitt, D.D. (St. Lawrence University, 1879), Universalist; b. at Stoughton, Mass., April 5, 1838; graduated at Tufts College, 1860; admitted to the bar, 1863; was pastor of the Independent (Universalist) Christian Society of Gloucester, Mass., 1865–69; of the First Universalist Church of Providence, R.I., 1870–75; and since 1875 has been president of Tufts College, Mass. He belongs to the school of Universalists who make the final triumph of good over evil a corollary of the nature of God, — a result to be wrought out through those moral processes which are seen in operation around us. He was member of the legislature from Stoughton, 1859–60. His publications consist of sermons, addresses, reports, etc.

CARPENTER, Right Rev. William Boyd, D.D. (*hon.*, Cambridge, 1884), lord bishop of Ripon, Church of England; b. at Liverpool, March 26, 1841; educated at St. Catherine's College, Cambridge; graduated B.A. (senior optime), 1864; M.A., 1867; was ordained deacon 1864, priest 1865; became curate of All Saints, Maidstone, 1864; of St. Paul, Clapham, 1866; of Holy Trinity, Lee, 1867; vicar of St. James, Holloway, 1870; of Christ Church, Lancaster Gate, 1874; chaplain to the bishop of London, 1879; bishop of Ripon, 1884. He was select preacher at Cambridge, 1875, 1877; at Oxford, 1883–84; Hulsean lecturer at Cambridge, 1878; honorary chaplain to the Queen, 1879–83; chaplain in ordinary, 1883–84; canon of Windsor, 1882–84. He is the author of *Thoughts on Prayer*, London, 1871; *Narcissus. a Tale of Early Christian Times*, 1879; *The Witness of the Heart to Christ* (Hulsean Lectures), 1879; *District Visitor's Companion*, 1881; *My Bible*, 1884; *Truth in Tale*, 1885; and the comments on Revelation in Bishop Ellicott's *New-Testament Commentary*, 1879.

CARSON, James Gillespy, D.D. (Monmouth College, Ill., 1875), United Presbyterian; b. at Maryville, Blount County, Tenn., Feb. 11, 1833; graduated at Jefferson College, Canonsburg, Penn., 1849; and at the Associate Presbyterian Seminary there, 1855; became pastor of United Presbyterian churches at South Buffalo, Washington County, Penn., 1856; at Canonsburg, Penn., 1867; and at Xenia, O., 1869. Since 1874 he has been also professor of homiletics and pastoral theology in the United Presbyterian Theological Seminary, Xenia, O.

CARY, George Lovell, A.M., Unitarian, layman; b. at Medway, Mass., May 10, 1830; graduated at Harvard College, 1852; became professor of ancient languages in Antioch College (Yellow Springs, O.), 1857; and professor of New-Testament literature in the Meadville (Penn.) Theological School, 1862. He is "in special sympathy with those who emphasize the doctrine of the immanence of God in nature and the human soul." He has published *An Introduction to the Greek of the New Testament*, Andover, 1878, 2d ed. 1881.

CASPARI, Carl Paul, D.D. (*hon.*, Erlangen, 1860), Lutheran; b. of Jewish parents, at Dessau, Anhalt, Germany, Feb. 8, 1814; studied at Leipzig, 1834–38; and at Berlin, 1839–41; was baptized, 1838; received degree of Ph.D. at Leipzig, 1842. He became professor of theology at Christiania, Norway, 1847; refused calls to Rostock, 1850, and Erlangen, 1857. His theological position is that of a simple evangelical Christian and theologian. Besides very numerous essays on biblical and ecclesiastical topics, in German and Norwegian, he has published an edition of *Borhân-eddîni es Sernudji enchiridion studiosi* (Arabic text, Latin version, notes, etc.), Leipzig, 1838; commentary on *Obadiah* (in Delitzsch and Caspari's *Exegetisches Handbuch zu den Propheten des alten Bundes*), 1842; *Grammatica arabica*, 1844–48, 2 parts, 4th ed. by August Müller, under title *Arabische Grammatik*, Halle, 1876 (English trans. and ed. by William Wright, London, 1862, 2d ed. 1875–76, 2 vols.; French trans. of 4th ed., by E. Uricochea, Brussels, 1879–80, 2 vols.); *Beiträge zur Einleitung in das Buch Jesaia und zur Geschichte der jesaianischen Zeit*, Berlin, 1848 (vol. ii. of Delitzsch and Caspari's *Biblisch-theologische und apologetisch-kritische Studien*, 1846–48, 2 vols.); *Ueber den syrisch-ephraimitischen Krieg unter Jotham und Ahas*, Christiania, 1849; *Ueber Micha den Morasthiten und seine prophetische Schrift*, 1851–52, 2 parts; *Ungedruckte, unbeachtete, und wenig beachtete Quellen zur Geschichte des Taufsymbols und der Glaubensregel*, 1866, 1869, 1875, 3 vols.; *Zur Einführung in das Buch Daniel*, Leipzig, 1869; *Alte und neue Quellen zur Geschichte des Taufsymbols und der Glaubensregel*, 1879; *Martin von Bracara's Schrift "De correctione rusticorum," zum ersten Male vollständig und in verbesserten Text herausgegeben*, 1883; *Kirchenhistorische Anecdota, nebst neuen Ausgaben patristischer und kirchlich-mittelalterlicher Schriften*, 1883; *Eine pseudoaugustinische Homilia "De Sacrilegiis,"* 1886; *Bischof Fastidius' pelagianische Briefe*, 1886. Besides these, he has written in Norwegian a translation of the Book of Concord, Christiania, 1861–66, 2d ed 1862; an essay upon the Wandering Jew, 1862; a commentary upon the first six chapters of Isaiah, 1867; an historical essay on the confession of faith at baptism, 1871; on Abraham's trial, and Jacob's wrestling with God, 1871, 3d ed. 1876; on Abraham's call and meeting with Melchizedek, 1872, 2d ed. 1876; Bible essays, 1884; and since 1857 he has edited the *Theologisk Tidsskrift for den evangelisk-lutherske kirke i Norge*.

CASSEL, Paulus (Stephanus Selig), D.D. (Vienna, 1874), United Evangelical; b. of Jewish parents, at Grossglogau, Silesia, Feb. 27, 1821; educated at the University of Berlin; became a rabbi; was baptized May 28, 1855, at Bussleben, near Erfurt; became licentiate of theology of Erlangen, 1856; professor at Erfurt, the same year; since 1859 public lecturer in Berlin, and gymnasial *Oberlehrer:* and since Jan. 5, 1868, pastor of Christ Church. In early life he was a political journalist, and in 1866-67 was a member of the Prussian parliament. He is a member of the Erfurt Academy and other societies. Since 1875 he has edited the Berlin weekly *Sunem.* His writings are very numerous. Of the theological, may be mentioned article *Geschichte der Juden* in *Ersch u. Gruber,* II., t. 27 (1850); *Der Prophet Elisa,* 1860; *Das Buch der Richter und Ruth,* Bielefeld, 1865 (in Lange's *Commentary,* English trans., ed. Schaff, New York, 1871); *Für ernste Stunden. Betrachtungen und Erinnerungen,* 1868, 2d ed. 1881; *Altkirchlicher Festkalender nach Ursprüngen und Bräuchen,* 1869; *Sunem,* 1. Hft., 1869; *Das Evangelium der Söhne Zebedäi* (holds that the Fourth Gospel was composed by James and John), Berlin, 1870, 2d ed. 1881; *Aus guten Stunden,* Gotha, 1874; *Die Gerechtigkeit aus dem Glauben,* 1874; *Apologetische Briefe,* Berlin, 1875; *Halleluja* (189 hymns), 1878; *Das Buch Esther* (aus d. Hebr. übersetzt, historisch u. theologisch erläutert; 1 Abth. Im Anh. die Uebersetzg. d. 2. Targum), 1878; *Die Symbolik des Blutes und "der arme Heinrich" von Hartmann von Aue,* 1882; *Christliche Sittenlehre. Eine Auslegung des Briefes Pauli an Titus. Mit ein. Schlussbemerkung über Semitismus,* 1882; *Die Hochzeit von Cana, theologisch und historisch, in Symbol, Kunst und Legende ausgelegt. Mit e. Einleitung in das Evangelium Johannis,* 1883; *Fredegunde, Eine Novelle in Briefen,* Leipzig, 1883; *Aus Literatur und Symbolik,* 1884; *Ahasverus, Die Sage vom ewigen Juden,* Berlin, 1885; *Ueber die Probebibel,* 1885 sq.

CATHCART, William, D.D. (Lewisburg University, 1873), Baptist; b. in County Londonderry, Ireland, Nov. 8, 1825; studied in Glasgow University, and at Horton (now Rawdon) Baptist Theological College, Yorkshire, Eng., and graduated 1850; was pastor at Barnsley, near Sheffield, 1850-53; at Mystic River, Conn., 1853-57; in Philadelphia (Second Baptist Church), 1857-84; and is now living at Gwynedd, Penn. He was president of the American Baptist Historical Society, by annual election, from 1876-84. He has published *The Papal System, from its Origin to the Present Time. An Historical Sketch of every Doctrine, Claim, and Practice of the Church of Rome,* Philadelphia, 1872, 4th ed. 1885; *The Baptists and the American Revolution,* 1876; *The Baptism of the Ages and of the Nations,* 1878, 3d ed. 1884. He edited *The Baptist Encyclopædia,* 1881 (1 vol. bound in 2), revised ed. 1883.

CATTELL, William Cassiday, D.D. (College of New Jersey, Princeton, 1864; also Hanover College, Ind., 1864), **LL.D.** (Wooster University, O., 1878), Presbyterian; b. at Salem, N.J., Aug. 30, 1827; graduated at Princeton College, 1848, and at the theological seminary there, 1852; resident licentiate, 1852-53; became professor of Latin and Greek, Lafayette College, Easton, Penn., 1855; pastor at Harrisburg (Pine-street Presbyterian Church), 1859; president of Lafayette College, 1863; resigned, 1883; emeritus professor of mental philosophy, 1883; corresponding secretary of the Presbyterian Board of Ministerial Relief, Philadelphia, Penn., 1883. He has published sermons, addresses, and various articles in reviews, etc., mostly on educational matters, and written the article *Tunkers* in the *Religious Encyclopædia.*

CAVE, Alfred, B.A., Congregationalist; b. in London, Aug. 29, 1847; educated at New College, London; graduated at London University, 1872; was appointed professor of Hebrew and philosophy at Hackney College, London, 1880, and in 1881 principal and professor of theology. He is the author of *The Scriptural Doctrine of Sacrifice,* Edinburgh, 1877; *An Introduction to Theology, its Principles, its Branches, its Results, and its Literature,* 1886; *The Inspiration of the Old Testament, its Data and its Doctrine,* Congregational lecture for 1886. He was co-translator, with Rev. J. S. Banks, of Dorner's *System of Christian Doctrine,* Edinburgh, 1880-82, 4 vols.

CAVEN, William, D.D. (Queen's University, Kingston, Ont., 1875), Presbyterian; b. in parish of Kirkcolm, Wigtownshire, Scotland, Dec. 26, 1830; graduated at Toronto, Ontario, Can., Seminary of United Presbyterian Church, 1852; became minister at St. Mary's, Ont., 1852; professor of exegetical theology and biblical criticism, Knox College, Toronto, 1866; and principal of the college, 1873. He was moderator of the General Assembly of the Canada Presbyterian Church, at the union of the Presbyterian Churches in 1875; president of teachers' association of Ontario, in 1877; and member of the General Councils of the Alliance of the Reformed Churches in Edinburgh (1877), Philadelphia (1880), and Belfast (1884). He has published pamphlets, articles, etc.

CHADWICK, John White, Unitarian; b. at Marblehead, Mass., Oct. 19, 1840; graduated at the Harvard Divinity School, 1864; and ever since has been minister of the Second Unitarian Society, Brooklyn, N.Y. He is a "radical Unitarian." His works are *Life of N. A. Staples,* Boston, 1870; *A Book of Poems,* 1876, 7th ed. 1885; *The Faith of Reason,* 1879, 2d ed. 1880; *The Bible of To-day,* New York, 1879, 3d ed. 1882; *Some Aspects of Religion* (16 discourses), 1879; *Belief and Life* (do.), 1881; *The Man Jesus,* Boston, 1881, 2d ed. 1882; *Origin and Destiny* (16 discourses), 1883; *In Nazareth Town, and other Poems,* 1883; *A Daring Faith* (16 discourses), 1885; *The Good Voices* (poems), Troy, N.Y., 1885.

CHALMERS, William, M.A., D.D. (Aberdeen, 1867), Presbyterian; b. in Malacca, East Indies, April 12, 1812; graduated at Aberdeen, 1829; studied theology in Glasgow and in Edinburgh under Dr. Thomas Chalmers; became minister of the Established Church of Scotland at Aberdour, Fifeshire, 1836, and at Dailly, Ayrshire, 1841; of the Free Church at Dailly, 1843; of Marylebone Presbyterian Church, London, 1845; professor of apologetic and dogmatic theology and church history in the Presbyterian Church of England, 1868; and principal of the Presbyterian Theological College, London, 1880. He has been a frequent contributor to periodicals.

CHAMBERLAIN, Jacob, M.D., D.D. (Rutgers, Western Reserve, and Union, all in 1878), Reformed (Dutch); b. at Sharon, Litchfield County, Conn., April 13, 1835; graduated at Western Reserve College, O., 1856, and at Reformed Theological Seminary (New Brunswick, N.J.) and at the College of Physicians and Surgeons, New York, in 1859; and that December sailed as medical missionary to India; stationed in Madras Presidency, at Palamanair, 1860–63, established new station at Madanapalli, 1863, and since has had charge of both. In 1868 he established a hospital and dispensary at the latter place, and the same in 1872 at the former. In 1873 he was appointed chairman of the committee for bringing out a new translation of the Old Testament from the Hebrew into the Telugu; in 1879, chairman of committee to revise the Telugu New Testament: both works are now (1886) going on. In 1878 he was elected vice-president for India, of the American Tract Society. Broken health compelled a long rest in America, 1874–78; revisited it 1884–86. He translated into Telugu the Reformed Church liturgy, Madras, 1873, 2d ed. 1885; and the "Hymns for Public and Social Worship," 1884, 2d ed. 1885 (in all 3,000 copies); and has published in English, *The Bible tested*, New York, 1878, 7th ed. 1885 (in all 21,000 copies); *Native Churches and Foreign Missionary Societies*, Madras, 1879 (2,000 copies); "*Winding up a Horse," or Christian Giving*, New York, 1879, 2d ed. same year (5,000 copies); "*Break Cocoanuts over the Wheels," or, All pull for Christ*, 1885 (20,000 copies); besides frequent contributions to periodicals.

CHAMBERS, Talbot Wilson, S.T.D. (Columbia College, 1853), **LL.D.** (Rutgers, 1885), Reformed (Dutch); b. at Carlisle, Penn., Feb. 25, 1819; graduated at Rutgers College, New Brunswick, N.J., 1834; studied theology in both the New-Brunswick and Princeton Theological Seminaries; became pastor of the Second Reformed Dutch Church, Somerville, N.J., 1839; and one of the pastors of the Collegiate Dutch Church of New-York City, 1849. He was the Vedder lecturer at New Brunswick in 1875, is chairman of the Committee on Versions of the American Bible Society, and member of the American Bible Revision Committee, Old-Testament Company. He has published, besides numerous articles, addresses, and sermons, *The Noon Prayer Meeting in Fulton Street*, New York, 1857; *Memoir of Theodore Frelinghuysen*, 1863; *Exposition of Zechariah*, in Schaff-Lange Commentary, 1874; *The Psalter a Witness to the Divine Origin of the Bible* (Vedder Lectures), 1875; *Companion to the Revised Version of the Old Testament*, 1885.

CHANCE, Frank, Church of England, layman; b. at Highgate, London, June 22, 1826; graduated in arts and in medicine at Cambridge (B.A. 1854, M.B. 1855, licentiate in medicine 1857); became a member of the Royal College of Surgeons, London, 1856; of the Royal College of Physicians, London, 1859; fellow of the latter, 1863. He paid special attention to Hebrew while at Cambridge, and was Tyrwhitt's University Hebrew scholar in 1854. Since 1864 his health has prevented his continued practice of medicine. He became a member of the Old-Testament Company of Bible Revisers in 1875. He has translated Virchow's *Cellular Pathology*, London, 1860; edited H. H. Bernard's *Commentary on Job*, 1864, re-issued (with appendix), 1884; and written many philological notes in *Notes and Queries*.

CHANNING, William Henry, Unitarian, nephew of William Ellery Channing; b. in Boston, May 25, 1810; d. in London, Dec. 23, 1884. He graduated at Harvard College, 1829, and at the Cambridge Divinity School, 1833; and was ordained at Cincinnati, May 10, 1839. After holding various pastorates in America, he went to England in 1857, and succeeded Rev. Dr. James Martineau as minister of the Hope-street Unitarian Chapel in Liverpool. He returned to America in 1866, and became minister of the Unitarian Church in Washington, D.C.; but for the last fourteen years of his life he lived in England. He was an earnest social reformer and eloquent preacher. Besides numerous contributions to periodical literature, he published a translation of Jouffroy's *Introduction to Ethics*, Boston, 1840, 2 vols.; *Memoirs of William Ellery Channing*, 1848, 3 vols.; *Memoirs of Rev. James H. Perkins*, 1851, 2 vols.; (with R. W. Emerson and J. F. Clarke) *Memoirs of Margaret Fuller Ossoli*, 1851, 2 vols.; *The Christian Church and Social Reform*; (edited) W. E. Channing's *The Perfect Life* (sermons), 1872. *

CHANTRE, Daniel Auguste, Lic. Theol. (Geneva, 1860), French Swiss Protestant; b. at Geneva, Dec. 21, 1836; educated at the university there, 1856–60; pastor in the city, 1862; in charge of the course of historical theology in the university, 1881; ordinary professor, 1882. He is a "liberal theologian." He was one of the founders of *L'Alliance libérale*, 1869, and *Etrenne chrétienne*, 1873; and has written much for them, also a few books and pamphlets.

CHAPONNIÈRE, Jacques François (called **Francis**), **Lic. Theol.** (Geneva, 1867), Swiss Protestant theologian; b. at Geneva, April 6, 1842; graduated M.A. at University of Geneva 1862; studied theology there until 1866; was ordained, 1867; continued his studies in Paris, Germany, England, and Scotland, until 1869; returned to Geneva in 1870, and, while auxiliary pastor in the National Church, lectured in the theological faculty of the university nearly every year upon New-Testament exegesis or ecclesiastical statistics, until in 1880 he became chief editor of the *Semaine Religieuse*, the organ of the evangelical party in the National Church. From 1873 to 1875 he was the Genevan correspondent of the Paris *Christianisme au xixe siècle*. Besides numerous articles, he has written *La question des confessions de foi au sein du protestantisme contemporain*, Geneva, 1867; *Affirmations religieuses de quelques physiciens et naturalistes modernes*, 1874; *Rendez à César ce qui est à César, et à Dieu ce qui est à Dieu* (sermon), 1875; *Quel doit être, dans la crise actuelle, notre programme ecclésiastique?* 1876; *La revision constitutionnelle et la lutte protestante*, 1878; *L'Église nationale évangélique au lendemain de la séparation*, 1880; and has translated Christlieb's *L'incrédulité moderne et les meilleurs moyens de la combattre*, 1874, and Orelli's *L'immutabilité de l'Évangile apostolique*, 1880. *

CHARTERIS, Archibald Hamilton, D.D. (Edinburgh, 1863), Church of Scotland; b. at Wamphray, Dumfriesshire, Dec. 13, 1835; graduated at Edinburgh University, B.A. 1853, M.A. 1854; he became associate and successor minister of St. Quivox, 1858; minister of New Abbey, 1859; of the Park Parish, Glasgow, 1863; professor of biblical criticism, University of Edinburgh, 1868. He was the originator and first convener of the

General Assembly (Church of Scotland) Committee on Christian Life and Work (1868), which established and edited *Life and Work*, a journal of now 100,000 circulation, and which also founded the "Church of Scotland's Young Men's Guild." He is one of her Majesty's chaplains, and a dean of the Chapel Royal. He has written, besides lectures and pamphlets, *Life of Professor James Robertson, D.D.*, Edinburgh, 1863; *Canonicity: a Collection of Early Testimonies to the Canonical Books of the New Testament, based on Kirchhofer's Quellensammlung*, 1881; *The New-Testament Scriptures*, London, 1883.

CHASE, Thomas, LL.D. (Harvard, 1878), **Litt.D.** (Haverford, 1880), Friend; b. at Worcester, Mass., June 16, 1827; graduated at Harvard, 1848; studied at Berlin, 1854, and at Collége de France, Paris, 1855; has been successively tutor and acting professor of Latin at Harvard, 1850–53; professor of Greek and Latin at Haverford College, Penn., 1855, and president since 1875. He was a member of the New-Testament Revision Company. He has edited *Cicero on Immortality*, Cambridge, 1851; *Vergil's Æneid*, Philadelphia, 1868; *Horace*, 1869; *First Six Books of Æneid*, 1870; *Four Books of Livy*, 1872; *Juvenal and Persius*, 1876 (new editions of all these in 1886); and has written besides articles, pamphlets, etc., *Hellas: her Monuments and Scenery*, Cambridge, 1863; *A Latin Grammar*, Philadelphia, 1882, new ed. 1886.

CHASTEL, Étienne (Louis), Litt.D. (Geneva, 1879), **D.D.** (*hon.*, Strasbourg, 1882), French Swiss Protestant; b. in Geneva, July 11, 1801; studied theology, particularly church history, at Geneva, 1819–23; in Paris, 1825, 1830; in Italy, 1826–27; and in England, 1830; became a pastor in Geneva, 1832; professor of church history in the theological faculty of the city's university, 1839; *emeritus*, 1881 (director of the city library, 1845–49); received the cross of the Legion of Honor, 1879. He is the author of *Conférences sur l'histoire du Christianisme*, Geneva, 1839–47, 2 vols.; *Histoire de la destruction du paganisme dans l'empire d'Orient* ("couronné par l'Académie des inscriptions et belles-lettres"), 1850; *Études historiques sur l'influence de la charité durant les premiers siècles chrétiens* ("couronné par l'Académie française"), Paris, 1853 (German trans., *Die christliche Barmherzigkeit*, preface by Dr. Wichern, Leipzig, 1854; English trans. by G. A. Matile, *The Charity of the Primitive Church*, Philadelphia, 1857); *L'Église romaine considérée dans ses rapports avec le développement de l'humanité*, Geneva, 1856; *Destinées de l'école d'Alexandrie*, 1856; *Trois conciles réformateurs au XVe siècle*, 1858; *Le Christianisme et l'Église au moyen âge*, 1859; *Le Christianisme dans l'âge moderne*, 1864; *Le Christianisme dans les six premiers siècles*, 1865; *Le Christianisme au dix-neuvième siècle*, 1874 (English trans. by Rev. John R. Beard, D.D., *Christianity in the Nineteenth Century*, London, 1875); new edition of these volumes chronologically arranged, under the title, *Histoire du Christianisme depuis son origine jusqu'à nos jours*, Paris, 1881–83, 5 vols.; *La France et le pape* (reply to Count de Montalembert), 1860; *Un historien catholique et un critique ultramontain* (De Broglié and Guéranger); *Le martyre dans les premiers siècles de l'Église*, 1861; *Les catacombes et les inscriptions chrétiennes de Rome*, 1867; *Le cimetière de Calliste à Rome*, 1869; *J. James Taylor. Notice biographique*, 1873; *Lettres inédites de Madame de Maintenon au lieutenant de Baville*, 1875; *Fénelon et Bossuet en instance auprès de la cour de Rome*, 1883. Died Feb. 24, 1886.

CHEETHAM, Ven. Samuel, D.D. (Cambridge, 1880), archdeacon of Rochester, Church of England; b. at Hambleton, County of Rutland, March 3, 1827; educated at Christ's College, Cambridge; graduated B.A. (first-class in classics, senior optime in mathematics) 1850, M.A. 1853, B.D. 1880; ordained deacon 1851, priest 1852. He was vice-principal of the Collegiate Institute, Liverpool, 1851–53; fellow (1850–66) and assistant tutor (1853–58) of Christ's College, Cambridge; vice-principal of the Theological College, Chichester, 1861–63; professor of pastoral theology in King's College, London, 1863–82; chaplain of Dulwich College, 1866–84; archdeacon of Southwark 1879–82, and of Rochester since 1882; and since 1883 has been canon of Rochester, and honorary fellow of Christ's College, Cambridge. He is also honorary fellow of King's College, London, and since 1880 examining chaplain to the bishop of Rochester. He has written, besides numerous articles, e.g., on Barrow, Jeremy Taylor, and South, in *The Quarterly Review*, *The Law of the Land and the Law of the Mind*, London, 1866; *Colleges and Tests*, 1871; and edited, with Dr. William Smith, *Dictionary of Christian Antiquities*, 1875–80, 2 vols., for which he wrote largely himself.

CHEEVER, George Barrell, D.D. (New-York University, 1844), Congregationalist; b. at Hallowell, Me., April 17, 1807; graduated at Bowdoin College, Brunswick, Me., 1825, and at Andover Theological Seminary, 1830. He was pastor of the Howard-street (Congregational) Church, Salem, Mass., 1833–36; in Europe, 1836–38; pastor of the Allen-street Presbyterian Church, New-York City, 1839–44; editor of *The New-York Evangelist*, 1845; pastor of the (Congregational) Church of the Puritans, New York, 1846–70; since 1871 has lived in Englewood, N.J., without pastoral charge. He distinguished himself by the advocacy of total abstinence and of the abolition of slavery. Of his numerous writings may be mentioned, *Inquire at Amos Giles's Distillery*, Salem, 1835 (this attack upon drink led to his being tried for libel, and imprisoned for thirty days); *God's Hand in America*, New York, 1841; *Lectures on Hierarchical Despotism*, 1842; *Lectures on The Pilgrim's Progress*, 1843; *Journal and Diary of the Pilgrims of Plymouth*, 1848; *The Hill Difficulty, with other Miscellanies*, 1849; *Punishment by Death: its Authority and Expediency*, 1849; *Windings of the River of the Water of Life*, 1849; *Wanderings of a Pilgrim in the Alps*, 1850; *A Reel in a Bottle, for Jack in the Doldrums*, 1850 (revised ed. under title, *The Log-Book of a Voyage to the Celestial Country*, 1885); *Voices of Nature to her Foster-Child, the Soul of Man*, 1852; *Powers of the World to Come*, 1853, 2d ed. 1856; *Discipline of Time for Life and Immortality*, 1854; *Life, Genius, and Insanity of Cowper*, 1856; *God against Slavery*, 1857; *Right of the Bible in our Public Schools*, 1858; *Guilt of Slavery demonstrated from the Hebrew and Greek Scriptures*, 1860; *Faith, Doubt, and Evidence*, 1881; *God's Timepiece for Man's Eternity*, 1883.

CHENERY, Thomas, b. in Barbadoes in the

year 1826; d. in London, Feb. 11, 1884. He was educated at Eton and at Caius College, Cambridge; practised law for a while; became lord almoner's professor of Arabic at Oxford, 1868; made member of the second class of the Imperial Order of the Medjedie by the Sultan, 1869; appointed an Old-Testament reviser by the Convocation of Canterbury, 1870; resigned his professorship, and became editor of the London *Times*, 1877. He was honorary secretary to the Royal Asiatic Society. He translated *The Assemblies* of Al Hariri, with notes, London, 1867; and edited the *Machberoth Ithiel*, by Yehudah ben Shelomo Alkharizi, 1872.

CHENEY, Charles Edward, D.D. (Iowa College, 1871), Reformed Episcopalian, b. at Canandaigua, Ontario County, N.Y., Feb. 12, 1836; graduated at Hobart College, Geneva, 1857, and at the Protestant-Episcopal Theological Seminary of Virginia, 1859; was assistant minister St. Luke's Church, Rochester, N.Y., 1858–59; in charge St. Paul's Church, Havana, N.Y., 1859–60; since 1860 has been rector of Christ Church, Chicago. He was consecrated a bishop of the Reformed Episcopal Church, Dec. 14, 1873. In theology he is "distinctively evangelical, endeavoring to hold and teach all that was characteristic of the old-fashioned Low-Church element in the Protestant-Episcopal Church." He has published sermons, addresses, etc., and a volume of *Sermons*, Chicago, 1880.

CHEYNE, Thomas Kelly, D.D. (Edinburgh, 1884), Church of England, b. in London, Sept. 18, 1841; educated at Worcester College, Oxford; graduated B.A., 1862; was Kennicott Hebrew scholar 1863, Ellerton theological prizeman 1863, Pusey and Ellerton Hebrew scholar 1864, chancellor's English essayist 1864, M.A., 1865; ordained deacon 1864, priest 1865; and in 1868 gained a fellowship in Balliol College, Oxford, on the ground of Shemitic and biblical attainments. From 1870 to 1881 he was Hebrew and divinity lecturer, also chaplain and librarian, in Balliol College. He was a member of the Old-Testament Revision Company. In January, 1881, he became rector of Tendring, Essex, near London, thus vacating his fellowship; in 1885 was appointed Oriel professor of the interpretation of Holy Scripture at Oxford. He is the author of *Notes and Criticisms on the Hebrew Text of Isaiah*, London, 1869; *The Book of Isaiah, chronologically arranged*, 1870; (with Dr. Driver) *The Variorum Bible*, 1876, 2d ed. 1880 (remarkable for its "minute acquaintance with critical literature"); *The Prophecies of Isaiah* (a new translation with commentary and appendices), 1880-81, 2 vols., 3d ed. 1884; *Micah* (1882) and *Hosea* (1884) in *The Cambridge Bible for Schools and Colleges; Jeremiah* (1883-84), in *The Pulpit Commentary; The Book of Psalms* (1884), a new translation, in *The Parchment Library*. He has also contributed to the ninth edition of the *Encyclopædia Britannica* the articles on *Cosmogony, Daniel, Deluge, Isaiah, Jeremiah*, etc.

CHINIQUY, Charles, Presbyterian, b. of Roman-Catholic parents at Kamoraska, Province of Quebec, Can., July 30, 1809; educated at the college of Nicolet, Can., 1822-29; professor of belles-lettres there till 1833; ordained a Roman-Catholic priest, Sept. 21, 1833; was vicar in Quebec till 1838; curate of Beauport till 1842; curate of Kamoraska till 1846; officially called "apostle of temperance of Canada" till 1851, when called by Bishop Vandevelde of Chicago to direct the tide of Roman-Catholic emigration towards the prairies of Illinois; in 1858 left the Church of Rome, with his entire congregation at St. Anne, Kankakee County, Ill., and joined the Canadian Presbyterian Church. He has been called three times to lecture in England (1860, 1874, 1882), and in Australia (1878–80). He is the author of *Manual of Temperance*, in French, Quebec, 1843 (2d and 3d ed., Montreal, 1849; in English, Montreal, 1849); *The Priest, the Woman, and the Confessional*, in English, St. Anne, Kankakee County, Ill., 1874 (six editions in the United States, five in England, four in Canada, four in Australia; in French, by author, 1876, three editions in Canada, two in Paris, one in Brussels; in Italian, Rome, 1879; in Spanish, 1880; in Danish, 1884); *Fifty Years in the Church of Rome*, Chicago, 1st and 2d ed., 1885; besides minor treatises, all of which have been widely circulated.

CHINNERY-HALDANE, Right Rev. James Robert Alexander, lord bishop of Argyll and the Isles, Episcopal Church of Scotland; b. in the year 1841; educated at Trinity College, Cambridge, where he took the degree of LL.B. 1864; was ordained deacon 1866, priest 1867; curate of Calne, 1866-69; of All Saints, Edinburgh, 1867-76; incumbent of St. Bride's, Nether Lochaber, 1876; of St. John, Ballachulish, and of St. Mary, Glencoe, 1879; honorary canon of the Cathedral of Argyll and the Isles, 1879; dean of Argyll and the Isles, 1881-83; consecrated bishop, 1883.

CHRISTLIEB, Theodor, Ph.D. (Tübingen, 1857), **D.D.** (*hon.*, Berlin, 1870), German Evangelical theologian, b. at Birkenfeld, Würtemberg, March 7, 1833; studied at Tübingen, 1851-55; became pastor of the German congregation in Islington, London, N., 1858, where he built the first German United Church (comprehending Lutherans and Reformed); town-pastor at Friedrichshafen, Lake of Constance, 1865, being called thither by the King of Würtemberg, who resides there during the summer; professor of practical theology and university preacher at Bonn, 1868. He is a Knight of the Red Eagle. In 1873 he attended the Evangelical Alliance Conference in New York, and read a paper (Monday, Oct. 6, 1873) upon *The Best Methods of counteracting Modern Infidelity*, subsequently separately issued in English, New York, 1873; in German, Gütersloh, 1874; in French, Paris, 1874; in Dutch, Swedish, Danish, Italian, and Greek. He has written, tracts, etc., *Leben und Lehre des Johannes Scotus Erigena*, Gotha, 1860; *Moderne Zweifel am christlichen Glauben*, St. Gall, 1868; 2d ed. Bonn, 1870 (English trans., *Modern Doubt and Christian Belief*, Edinburgh and New York, 1874, 4th ed. 1879); *Dr. Karl Bernhard Hundeshagen; eine Lebensskizze*, Gotha, 1873; (editor) *Hundeshagens ausgewählte kleinere Schriften und Abhandlungen*, 1874–75, 2 vols.; *Der Missionsberuf des evangelischen Deutschlands nach Idee und Geschichte*, Gütersloh, 1876; *Der indobritische Opiumhandel und seine Wirkungen*, 1878 (English trans., *The Indo-British Opium Trade and its Effects*, London, 1879, 2d ed. 1881; French trans., Paris, 1879); *Der gegenwärtige Stand der* *evangelischen Heidenmission: eine Weltüberschau*, 1879, 4th ed. 1880 (English trans., *Protestant Foreign Missions, their Present State*, London, 1880, 3d ed. 1881; Boston, 1st and 2d ed. 1880, *Protestant Missions to the Heathen, a General Survey*, Calcutta, 1st to 3d ed. 1882; French trans., Lausanne, 1880; Swedish, Stockholm, 1880; Norwegian, Kristiania, 1881); *Zur methodistischen Frage in Deutschland*, Bonn, 1st and 2d ed., 1882; *Die religiöse Gleichgültigkeit und die besten Mittel zu ihrer Bekämpfung*, Magdeburg, 1st and 2d ed., 1885. Since 1874 he has been co-editor of the *Allgemeine Missionszeitschrift*, Gütersloh. He is president of the West German Branch of the Evangelical Alliance, and attended as delegate the General Conferences of New York (1873), Basel (1879), and Copenhagen (1884).

CHURCH, Pharcellus, D.D. (Madison University, N.Y., 1847), Baptist; b. at Seneca, near Geneva, Ontario County, N.Y., Sept. 11, 1801; educated for the ministry at Hamilton, N.Y.; became pastor at Poultney, Vt., 1825; in Providence, R.I. (Central Church), 1828; in New Orleans, La., 1834; of the First Church, Rochester, N.Y., 1835; of the Bowdoin-square Church, Boston, Mass., 1848; resigned in consequence of disease induced by many years of exciting evangelistic labors, 1852; was occasional supply of destitute churches in Montreal and Williamsburg; from 1855 to 1865 was editor and proprietor of *The New-York Chronicle*, merged in *The Examiner* (1865); since 1870 he has lived in retirement at Tarrytown, N.Y. He was baptized in Lake Ontario, June, 1815. During 1848 he devoted himself to the movement which gave being to the Rochester University and Theological Seminary. In 1846 he attended the Evangelical Alliance meeting in London, and was shipwrecked on his way home, on the coast of Ireland, and compelled to return to Liverpool. He is the author of *The Philosophy of Benevolence*, New York, 1836; *Religious Dissensions, their Cause and Cure* (prize essay of $200), 1838; *Address* at the dedication of Mount Hope Cemetery, Rochester, N.Y., 1838; *Antioch, or the Increase of Moral Power in the Church*, 1842; *Pentecost* (sermon to the Missionary Union at Albany), 1843; *Memoir of Theodosia Dean* (wife of Dr. William Dean, missionary to China), Boston, 1850; *Mapleton, or More Work for the Maine Law* (a temperance tale), Montreal, 1853; *Seed Truths* (written in Bonn on the Rhine), 1870; and of many articles in periodicals.

CHURCH, Very Rev. Richard William, dean of St. Paul's, London, Church of England; b. at Cintra, April 25, 1815; educated at Wadham College, Oxford; graduated B.A. (first-class in classics) 1836, M.A. 1839, Hon. D.C.L. 1875. He was fellow of Oriel College, 1838–53; junior proctor, 1844–45; was ordained deacon 1838, priest 1850; rector of Whatley, near Frome-Selwood, 1853–71; select preacher at Oxford, 1869, 1875, 1881; on Sept. 6, 1871, appointed dean of St. Paul's; elected honorary fellow of Oriel College, 1873. He has published, beside single lectures and sermons, *The Catechetical Lectures of St. Cyril, translated with Notes* (*Library of the Fathers*), London, 1841; *Essays and Reviews*, 1854; *Sermons preached before the University of Oxford*, 1868, 2d ed. 1869; *Life of St. Anselm*, 1871, 2d ed. 1877; *The Beginnings of the Middle Ages*, 1877; *Human Life and its Conditions: Sermons preached before the University of Oxford in 1876–78, with three Ordination Sermons*, 1878; *Dante: an Essay* (with translation of *De Monarchia* by F. J. Church), 1878 (first issued, without the translation, in 1850); *Spenser*, 1879; *Gifts of Civilization, and other Sermons and Lectures*, 1880 (includes the separately published lectures, *Civilization before and after Christianity*, 1872; *On some Influences of Christianity upon National Character*, 1873; *On the Sacred Poetry of Early Religions*, 1874); *Bacon*, 1884; *The Discipline of the Christian Character*, 1885.

CHURCHILL, John Wesley, Congregationalist; b. at Fairlee, Vt., May 26, 1839; graduated at Harvard College, 1865; and at Andover Theological Seminary, 1868, in which he has been since 1869 Jones professor of pulpit delivery, and co-pastor of the chapel church. He is co-editor of *The Andover Review*.

CLAPP, Alexander Huntington, D.D. (Iowa College, 1868), Congregationalist; b. at Worthington, Mass., Sept. 1, 1818; graduated at Yale College, 1842, and at Andover Theological Seminary, 1845 (studied 1842–44 at Yale Theological Seminary); was pastor at Brattleborough, Vt., 1846–53; of the Beneficent Church, Providence, R.I., 1855–65; secretary of the American Home Missionary Society, New-York City, 1865–78; since 1878 its treasurer; and since 1875 New-York editor of *The Congregationalist*, Boston, Mass. He has published occasional sermons, etc.

CLARK, George Whitfield, D.D. (Rochester University, 1872), Baptist; b. at South Orange, N.J., Feb. 15, 1831; graduated at Amherst College 1853, and at Rochester Theological Seminary 1855; became pastor at New Market, N.J., 1855; at Elizabeth, N.J., 1859; at Ballston, N.Y., 1868; at Somerville, N.J., 1873; retired broken in health, 1877; since 1880 has been doing missionary, collecting, and literary work for the American Baptist Publication Society. He is the author of *History of the First Baptist Church, Elizabeth, N.J.*, Newark, N.J., 1863; *New Harmony of the Four Gospels in English*, New York, 1870, Philadelphia, 1873; *Notes on Matthew*, New York, 1870, Philadelphia, 1873; do. *on Mark*, Philadelphia, 1873; do. *on Luke*, 1876; do. *on John*, 1879; *Harmonic Arrangement of the Acts*, 1884; *Brief Notes on the Gospels*, 1884.

CLARK, Joseph Bourne, D.D. (Amherst College, 1881), Congregationalist; b. at Sturbridge, Mass., Oct. 7, 1836; graduated at Amherst College, Mass., 1858, and at Andover Theological Seminary, 1861; became pastor at Yarmouth, Mass., 1861; Newton, 1868; Jamaica Plain (Central Church), Boston, 1872; secretary of the Massachusetts Home Missionary Society, 1879; secretary of the American Home Missionary Society, 1882. He is the author of seven occasional sermons, printed by request while pastor at Yarmouth, Newton, and Boston; twelve sermons in the *Monday Club* volumes, Boston, 1878–80; three papers read before the Annual Meetings of the American Home Missionary Society at Saratoga, 1883, 1884, 1885.

CLARK, Nathaniel George, D.D. (Union College, New York, 1860), **LL.D.** (University of Vermont, 1875), Congregationalist; b. at Calais, Vt.,

Jan. 18, 1825; graduated at University of Vermont 1845, and at Auburn Theological Seminary 1852; studied in Germany, 1852-53; was tutor in the University of Vermont, 1849; became professor of Latin and English literature there, 1853; of logic, rhetoric, and English literature, Union College, Schenectady, N.Y., 1863; one of the secretaries of the American Board of Commissioners for Foreign Missions, 1865. He has written upon *The English Language*, New York, 1864; occasional articles in reviews, papers before the American Board on various missionary themes, etc.

CLARK, Right Rev. Thomas March, D.D. (Union College, 1851), **S.T.D.** (Brown University, 1860), **LL.D.** (Cambridge University, 1867), Episcopalian; b. at Newburyport, Mass., July 4, 1812; graduated at Yale College, 1831; studied two years in Princeton Theological Seminary (1833-35); was licensed by Presbytery at Newburyport, 1835; ordained priest in the Episcopal Church, 1836; became rector of Grace Church, Boston, Mass., 1836; of St. Andrew's Church, Philadelphia, Penn., 1843; assistant minister of Trinity Church, Boston, Mass., 1847; rector of Christ Church, Hartford, Conn., 1851; bishop of Rhode Island, 1854. He has published *Early Discipline and Culture*, Hartford, 1852, Providence, 1855; *Lectures on the Formation of Character*, Hartford, 1853, revised ed. under title *Dew of Youth*, Boston; *Primary Truths of Religion*, New York and London, 1869.

CLARKE, James Freeman, D.D. (Harvard College, 1863), Unitarian; b. at Hanover, N.H., April 4, 1810; graduated at Harvard College 1829, and at the Cambridge Divinity School 1833; pastor at Louisville, Ky., 1833-40; and of the Church of the Disciples, Boston, 1841-50, and from 1853 to the present time. He has published, besides numerous sermons, poems, and articles in periodicals, a translation of De Wette's *Theodore*, Boston, 1840, 2 vols.; and of Hase's *Life of Jesus*, 1881; and also *Service-Book and Hymn-Book for the Church of the Disciples*, 1844, revised ed. 1856; *Life and Military Services of Gen. William Hull*, 1848; *Christian Doctrine of Forgiveness*, 1852; *Eleven Weeks in Europe*, 1852; *Memoir of the Marchioness d'Ossoli*, 1852; *Christian Doctrine of Prayer*, 1854, 2d ed. 1856, new ed. 1874; *The Hour which Cometh and Now Is* (sermons), 1864, 3d ed. 1877; *Orthodoxy: its Truths and its Errors*, 1866, 8th ed. 1885; *The Ten Great Religions*, 1870-83, 2 vols., 1st vol. 22d ed. 1886, 2d vol. 5th ed. 1886; *Steps of Belief*, 1870; *Common Sense in Religion* (essays), 1874; *Exotics, Translations in Verse*, 1876; *Go up Higher, or Religion in Common Life*, 1877; *Essentials and Non-Essentials in Religion*, 1878; *How to Find the Stars*, 1878; *Memorial and Biographical Sketches*, 1878; *Self-Culture, Physical, Intellectual, Moral, and Spiritual*, 1880, 11th ed. 1886; *Events and Epochs in Religious History*, 1881; *Legend of Thomas Didymus, the Jewish Sceptic*, 1881; *Anti-Slavery Days: Sketch of the Struggle which ended in the Abolition of Slavery in the United States*, New York, 1883; *Ideas of the Apostle Paul, translated into their Modern Equivalents*, Boston, 1884; *Manual of Unitarian Belief*, 1884; *Every-day Religion*, 1886.

CLARKE, William Newton, D.D. (Madison University, N.Y., 1878), Baptist; b. at Cazenovia, N.Y., Dec. 2, 1841; graduated at Madison University, N.Y., 1861, and at Hamilton Theological Seminary 1863; became pastor at Keene, N.H., 1863; Newton Centre, Mass., 1869; Montreal, Can., 1880; professor of New-Testament interpretation in the Toronto Baptist (theological) College, Can., 1883. He is the author of the commentary on Mark in *The Complete Commentary on the New Testament*, edited by Dr. Hovey, Philadelphia, 1881 sq.

CLAUGHTON, Right Rev. Thomas Legh, D.D. (Oxford, 1867), lord bishop of St. Albans, Church of England; b. at Haydock Lodge, Lancashire, Nov. 6, 1808; educated at Trinity College, Oxford; won the prize for Latin verse, and the Newdigate prize, 1829; graduated B.A. (first-class classics) 1831, M.A. 1834; was public examiner at Oxford, 1835-36; ordained deacon 1834, priest 1836; vicar of Kidderminster, 1841-67; honorary canon of Worcester, 1845-67; professor of poetry at Oxford, 1852-62; consecrated bishop of Rochester, 1867; translated to St. Albans, 1877. *

CLIFFORD, John, D.D. (Bates College, O., U.S.A., 1883), **F.G.S.** (1875), General Baptist (New Connection); b. at Sawley, near Derby, Eng., Oct. 16, 1836; educated at the Nottingham General Baptist Theological College, 1855-58, and at University College, London, 1858-66, taking the London University degrees of B.Sc. (1862) with honors in geology, logic, and moral philosophy; M.A. (1864) with first honor; LL.B. (1866) with honors in principles of legislation. Since 1858 he has been pastor of the Westbourne-park Church, Paddington, London. He was president of the General Baptist Association, 1872; and secretary, 1876-78, of the London Baptist Association; president, 1879; and from 1870 to 1883 (inclusive), edited *The General Baptist Magazine*. He is the author of *Familiar Talks*, London, 1872; *George Mostyn*, 1874; *Is Life worth Living? an Eightfold Answer*, 1880, 5th ed. 1886; *English Baptists: Who they are, and what they have done* (edited), 1883, 2d ed. 1884; *Daily Strength for Daily Living, Expositions of Old-Testament Themes*, 1885; *The Dawn of Manhood: a Book for Young Men*, 1886.

COBB, Levi Henry, D.D. (Dartmouth College, N.H., 1881), Congregationalist; b. at Cornish, Sullivan County, N.H., June 30, 1827; graduated at Dartmouth College 1854, and at Andover Theological Seminary, Mass., 1857; became pastor at North Andover, Mass., 1857; superintendent of schools, Memphis, Tenn., 1864; instructor in natural sciences and Latin in Kimball Union Academy, Meriden, N.H., 1865; pastor at Springfield, Vt., 1867; superintendent of home missions in Minnesota, 1874; in the Rocky-Mountain district, 1881; secretary of the American Congregational Union, New-York City, 1882. He was invited to the pastorate of Congregational churches at Faribault, Minn., 1873, and Lawrence, Kan., 1876. Besides numerous articles in *The Congregationalist*, *The Advance*, etc., he has written *Biography of E. Adams Knight, M.D.*, Springfield, Vt., 1872; *Biography of Deacon Oren Locke*, 1872; since 1883 has edited *The Church Building Quarterly* of the American Congregational Union.

COE, David Benton, D.D. (Middlebury College, Vt., 1857), Congregationalist; b. at Granville, Mass., Aug. 16, 1814; graduated at Yale College, New Haven, Conn., 1837, and at Yale Divinity School, 1840; was tutor in Yale College, 1839-40; pastor (Congregational) at Milford, Conn., 1840-44; of Allen-street Presbyterian, New-York City, 1844-49; district secretary of the A. B. C. F. M. 1849-51; corresponding secretary of the American Home Missionary Society, 1851-82, and since has been honorary secretary. He is a moderate Calvinist.

COIT, Thomas Winthrop, D.D. (Columbia College, New-York City, 1834), **LL.D.** (Trinity College, Hartford, Conn., 1853), Episcopalian; b. at New London, Conn., June 28, 1803; d. at Middletown, Conn., June 21, 1885. He graduated at Yale College, 1821; was rector of St. Peter's Church, Salem, Mass., 1827-29; of Christ Church, Cambridge, Mass., 1829-34; president and professor of moral philosophy, Transylvania University, Lexington, Ky., 1834-37; rector of Trinity Church, New Rochelle, N.Y., 1837-49; professor of ecclesiastical history in Trinity College, Hartford, Conn., 1849-54; rector of St. Paul's Church, Troy, N.Y., 1854-72; professor of ecclesiastical history in the Berkeley (Episcopalian) Divinity School, Middletown, Conn., 1872 till his death. He edited *The Bible in Paragraphs and Parallelisms*, Boston, 1834; *Townsend's Chronological Bible* (with notes), 1837-38, 2 vols.; and wrote *The Theological Commonplace Book*, Boston, 1832, revised ed. 1857; *Remarks on Norton's "Statement of Reasons,"* 1833; *Puritanism: or, a Churchman's Defence against its Aspersions*, 1844; *Exclusiveness* (a lecture), Troy, 1855, 3d ed. ——; *Lectures on the Early History of Christianity in England, with Sermons on Several Occasions*, 1860; *Necessity of preaching Doctrine: Sermons*, 1860; *Sameness of Words no Hinderance to Devotion* (a sermon), 3d ed. ——. *

COLLIER, Robert Laird, D.D. (Iowa State University, 1865), Unitarian; b. at Salisbury, Md., Aug. 7, 1837; graduated at Boston University, 1858; was pastor of the Church of the Messiah, Chicago, 1861-74; Second Church, Boston, 1876-80; supplied pulpits at Leicester, Bradford, and Birmingham, Eng., 1880-85; and since has been pastor in Kansas City, Mo. He is "a Channing, or conservative, Unitarian, holding to free reasoning in religion and in the use of the evangelical spirit and methods." For the past twenty years has lectured on literary and social topics in the United States and Great Britain, and has written for the press and periodicals of these countries. He is the author of *Every-day Subjects in Sunday Sermons*, Boston, 1874, several editions; *Meditations on the Essence of Christianity*, 1878, several editions; *English Home Life*, 1885.

COLLYER, Robert, Unitarian; b. at Keighly, Yorkshire, Eng., Dec. 8, 1823; educated in the country-school of Fewston, Yorkshire; was a mill-hand at eight years, and a blacksmith at fourteen; emigrated to America in 1850; was a hammer-maker at Shoemakertown, Montgomery, Penn., all the while, however, making good use of his leisure time in study. From 1849 to 1859 he was a Methodist local preacher; but converted to Unitarian views, he went to Chicago, Ill., and took charge of a Unitarian mission among the poor, but soon after was chosen pastor of the Unity Church there, and so remained until in September, 1879, he came to his present charge, the Church of the Messiah, New-York City. He has published *Nature and Life* (sermons), Boston, 1865, 11th ed. 1882; *A Man in Earnest* (a biography of Rev. A. H. Conant), 1868; *The Life that Now Is* (sermons), 1871, 10th ed. 1882; *The Simple Truth*, 1877; *History of Ilkley, Ancient and Modern*, London, 1886.

COMBA, Emilio, D.D. (St. Andrew's, Scotland, 1885), Waldensian; b. at San Germano, Waldensian Valleys, Province of Turin, Italy, Aug. 31, 1839; studied at Torre-Pellice and Geneva (under Merle d'Aubigné); ordained in 1863, and until 1872 was an evangelist, chiefly at Venice. In September, 1872, he entered upon his present position, professor of historical theology and homiletics in the Waldensian College, Florence. He has published, besides an Italian translation from the German of Luthardt's *Fundamental Truths*, and from the English of Killen's *Old Catholic Church*, *Storia della Riforma in Italia*, Florence, vol. i., 1881; and edits *Biblioteca della Riforma Italiana, Sec. XVI.*, 1883 *sqq.* (reprints of books and manuscripts of Italian reformers of the sixteenth century), in which have appeared *Trattatelli di P. P. Vergerio, e sua storia di Francesco Spiera*, 1883, 2 vols.; *Il credo di P. M. Vermigli ed il catechismo di Eidelberga*, 1883; *Istruzione christiana e comparazioni di Giovanni Valdes e trattato della Vera Chiesa di P. M. Vermigli*, 1884; *Dialoghi sette del Rev. Padre Frate Bernardino Occhino Senese, Generale dei Frati Cappuccini*, 1884.

COMPTON, Right Rev. Lord Alwyne Spencer, D.D. (Cambridge, 1879), lord bishop of Ely, Church of England; b. in England in the year 1825; educated at Trinity College, Cambridge, graduated M.A. (wrangler) 1848; ordained deacon 1850, priest 1851; was rector of Castle Ashby, Northamptonshire, 1852-79; honorary canon of Peterborough, 1856-79; proctor of the diocese of Peterborough, 1857-74; rural dean of Preston Deanery, 1874-75; archdeacon of Oakham, 1875-79; dean of Worcester, 1879-85; appointed bishop, 1885. *

CONANT, Thomas Jefferson, D.D. (Middlebury, 1844), Baptist; b at Brandon, Vt., Dec. 13, 1802; studied at Middlebury College, Vt. (Hebrew and German in addition to usual course), graduated 1823; took a post-graduate course of two years in Greek and Hebrew with Professor Robert B. Patton; was tutor in Columbian College (now Columbian University), Washington, D.C., 1825-27; successively professor of the Latin, Greek, and German languages in Waterville College (now Colby University), Waterville, Me., 1827-33; of languages and biblical literature in Hamilton Literary and Theological Institution (now Madison University and Theological Seminary), Hamilton, N.Y., 1835-51; and of the Hebrew language and biblical exegesis in Rochester (N.Y.) Theological Seminary, 1851-57. In 1857 he resigned his professorship in order to revise the English Version of the Bible for the American Bible Union, and in this work was engaged many years. He was a member of the American Old-Testament Revision Company. He is the author of a translation of the eleventh edition of Gesenius' *Hebrew Grammar*, Boston, 1839; and of the seventeenth edition (by Rödiger) with grammatical exercises and a chrestomathy by the translator, New York, 1851, latest and revised edition 1877; *Defence of the Hebrew Grammar of Gesenius against Professor Stuart's Translation, by the Original Translator*, New York, 1847; *Job, Revised Version and Notes* (with and without Hebrew text), 1856; *Matthew, Revised Version* (Greek text with critical and philological notes), 1860; *Baptizein, its Meaning and Use philologically and historically investigated*, 1860 (quarto), 1864 (8vo); *Genesis, Introduction, a Revised Version, and Explanatory Notes*, 1868 and 1873; *The New Testament, Common Version revised*, 1871; *Psalms, Introduction, Common Version revised, with occasional Notes*, 1871; *Proverbs, Introduction, Revised Version, and Notes* (with and without Hebrew text), 1872; *Greek Text of the Apocalypse, as edited by Erasmus*, 1873; *Prophecies of Isaiah, chapters i.-xiii. 22. Translation, Explanatory Notes, and Notes Critical and Philological on the Hebrew Text*, 1874; *Historical Books of the Old Testament, Joshua to 2 Kings; Introduction, Common Version revised, and occasional Notes*, Philadelphia, 1884.

CONRAD, Frederick William, D.D. (Wittenberg College, Springfield. O., 1864), Lutheran; b. at Pinegrove, Schuylkill County, Penn., Jan. 3, 1816; studied at Mount Airy College, Germantown, 1828–31; was collector of tolls on the Union Canal and Railroad at Pinegrove, 1834–41; student of theology at Gettysburg, 1837–39; pulpit supply in and around Pinegrove, 1839–41; pastor at Waynesboro, 1841–44; at Hagerstown, Md. (St. John's), 1844–50; professor of modern languages in Wittenberg College, and of church history and homiletics in the theological department, 1850–55; associate editor, with his brother Professor V. L. Conrad, of *The Evangelical Lutheran*, 1851–55; pastor at Dayton, O. (Zion's English Lutheran Church), 1855–62; at Lancaster, Penn. (Holy Trinity), 1862–64 (joint owner and editor *Lutheran Observer*, Baltimore, Md., 1862–66); at Chambersburg, 1864–66; pastor of Messiah Lutheran Church, Philadelphia, 1866–72; editor-in-chief of *The Lutheran Observer*, Philadelphia, since 1867. Through his exertions he increased the endowments of Pennsylvania College, and of the theological seminary at Gettysburg, and of Wittenberg and Carthage Colleges, by $200,000. He has frequently lectured in these colleges, contributed to *The Evangelical Review* and *The Lutheran Quarterly*. Several of these latter contributions have been republished: e.g., *The Lutheran Doctrine of Baptism*, 1874; *An Analysis of Luther's Small Catechism*, 1875; *The Evangelical Lutheran Church*, 1883; *The Call to the Ministry*, 1883, *The Liturgical Question*, 1884.

CONVERSE, Francis Bartlett, Presbyterian (Southern Church); b. in Richmond, Va., June 23, 1836; graduated at the University of Pennsylvania, Philadelphia, 1856; studied for two years (1859) in Princeton Theological Seminary: was stated supply of Olivet Church, New Kent County, Va., 1861–62; became associate editor of *The Christian Observer*, now published at Louisville, Ky., 1857; since 1873 editor-in-chief.

CONVERSE, Thomas Edwards, Presbyterian (Southern Church); b. in Philadelphia, Penn., Oct. 25, 1841; graduated at Princeton College, 1862, and at Union Theological Seminary, Hampden Sidney, Va., 1868; was missionary at Hangchow, China, 1869–70; pastor at Woodstock, Va., 1871–75; at Bardstown, Ky., 1875–79; since 1879 has been joint editor of *The Christian Observer*, published at Louisville, Ky.

CONWAY, Moncure Daniel, Liberal, b. in Stafford County, Va., March 17, 1832; graduated at Dickinson College, Penn., 1849; studied law, then entered the Baltimore (M.E.) Conference, 1851; became a Unitarian; graduated at Harvard Divinity School, 1854; was pastor in Washington, D.C., 1854–56; Cincinnati, O., 1857–62; London, Eng., 1863–84. He is the author of *Tracts for To-day*, Cincinnati, 1858; *The Rejected Stone*, Boston, 1861; *The Golden Hour*, 1862; *Testimonies concerning Slavery*, London, 1864, 2d ed. 1865; *The Sacred Anthology*, 1870, 5th ed. 1877; *The Earthward Pilgrimage*, 1870, 2d ed. 1877; *Republican Superstitions*, 1872; *Christianity*, 1876; *Idols and Ideals* (with essay on *Christianity*), 1877, 2d ed. 1880; *Demonology and Devil Lore*, 1878, 2 vols.; *A Necklace of Stories*, 1880; *The Wandering Jew*, 1881; *Thomas Carlyle*, 1882; *Emerson at Home and Abroad*, 1882; *Travels in South Kensington*, 1882; *Farewell Discourses*, 1884.

COOK, Frederic Charles, Church of England, b. at Milbrook, Dec. 1, 1804; educated at St. John's College, Cambridge; graduated B.A. (first-class classics) 1828, M.A. 1840; was ordained deacon 1839, priest 1840; one of her Majesty's inspectors of schools; prebendary of St. Paul's Cathedral, 1856–65; preacher at Lincoln's Inn, 1860–80; prebendary in Lincoln Cathedral, 1861–64; became chaplain in ordinary to the Queen, 1857; canon residentiary of Exeter, 1864; chaplain to the bishop of London, 1869; precentor of Exeter, 1872. He is the author of *Acts of the Apostles with Commentary*, London, 1849, new ed. 1866; *Sermons at Lincoln's Inn*, 1863; *Church Doctrine and Spiritual Life* (sermons), 1879; *The Revised Version of the First Three Gospels considered in its Bearings upon the Record of our Lord's Words and of Incidents in his Life*, 1882; *Deliver us from Evil*, 1883; *The Origins of Religion and Language*, 1884; *Letters addressed to Rev. H. Wace and Rev. J. Earle* (relating to *Origins*), 1885; and was the editor of the *Bible* (Speaker's) *Commentary*, 1871–82, 10 vols. (in which he wrote the introductions to *Exodus*, *Psalms*, and *Acts*, and the commentary on *Job*, *Habakkuk*, *Mark*, *Luke*, and *First Peter*, and partly that on *Exodus*, *Psalms*, and *Matthew*).

COOK, Joseph, Congregational licentiate, b. at Ticonderoga, N.Y., Jan. 26, 1838; graduated at Harvard College 1865, and at Andover Theological Seminary 1868; supplied vacant pulpits, and continued studies, 1868–70; acting pastor First (Congregational) Church, Lynn, Mass., 1870–71; not ordained; studied under Tholuck and Müller, and travelled in Europe, 1871–73; began lecturing, 1874; delivered the Monday Lectures upon scientific, philosophic, religious, and social topics, in Boston during the winter of each successive year from 1875 till 1880; in England, Italy, India, Japan, and Australia, as lecturer, 1880–82; resumed his Monday Lectures in 1883. His publications consist of his lectures, and these have been widely circulated: *Biology*, Boston, 1877 (16th ed.); *Transcendentalism*, 1877 (13th ed.); *Orthodoxy*, 1877 (7th ed.); *Conscience*, 1878; *Heredity*, 1878; *Marriage*, 1878; *Labor*, 1879; *Socialism*, 1880; *Occident*, 1884; *Orient*, 1886.

COOPER, Thomas, Baptist, b. at Leicester, Eng., March 28, 1805; was in youth a shoemaker at Gainsborough, Lincolnshire, and employed his leisure time to acquire Latin, Greek, Hebrew, and French. When twenty-three, he taught a school, then was a reporter for several country newspapers. In 1841 he led the Chartists of Leicester, lectured in the Potteries during the "riots" of August, 1842; was convicted of conspiracy and sedition, and for two years was confined in Stafford Jail, where he began his literary career, and on his release became a journalist. In 1848 he first appeared prominently in London as political and historical lecturer; in 1849 edited *The Plain Speaker*, a weekly penny journal of radical politics; and in 1850 started *Cooper's Journal*, a sceptical weekly penny periodical. In 1855 he renounced infidelity, and has since defended and preached Christian truth with the same energy with which he formerly attacked it. In 1859 he was immersed, and ordained as a Baptist preacher. In 1866 he retired in broken health, upon an annuity of one hundred pounds purchased for him by friends. He has published, besides fiction and poetry, *The Triumphs of Perseverance and Enterprise*, London, 1847, new ed. 1879; *The Bridge of History over the Gulf of Time: a Popular View of the Historical Evidence for the Truth of Christianity*, 1871, 3d ed. 1872, reprinted, N.Y. 1876; *Plain Pulpit Talk*, London, 1872, 2d ed. 1873; *Life, written by himself*, 1872, 2d ed. 1880; *God, the Soul, and a Future State*, 1873; *The Verity of Christ's Resurrection from the Dead: an Appeal to the Common Sense of the People*, 1875, new ed. 1884; *The Verity and Value of the Miracles of Christ*, 1877; *Evolution: the Stone Book and the Mosaic Record of Creation*, 1878; *The Atonement*, 1880; *Thoughts at Fourscore and Earlier*, 1885. *

CORNISH, George Henry, Methodist, b. at Exeter, Eng., June 26, 1834; educated at Victoria University, Cobourg, Can., 1855–58; began his ministry June, 1858; was journal secretary of Wesleyan Methodist Conference from 1872 to 1874, and of the London Conference of the Methodist Church of Canada from 1874 to 1877; was elected secretary of London Conference in 1879, and of the Guelph Conference in 1884, in which year he became superintendent of Wingham District; has been twice elected delegate to the General Conference. He is now (1886) pastor of the Central Methodist Church, Stratford, Ontario. He is the author of *Handbook of Canadian Methodism*, Toronto, 1867; *Cyclopædia of Methodism in Canada*, 1881 (supplement preparing); *Pastor's Pocket Record*, 1883; *Pastor's Pocket Ritual*, 1884.

CORRIGAN, Most Rev. Michael Augustine, D.D. (Propaganda College, Rome, 1864), Roman Catholic, archbishop of New York; b. at Newark, N.J., Aug. 13, 1839; graduated at Mount St. Mary's College, Emmittsburg, Md., 1859; was one of thirteen students with whom the American College in Rome was opened (1859); ordained priest by Cardinal Patrizi, Rome, Sept. 19, 1863; appointed by Archbishop Bayley professor of dogmatic theology and Sacred Scripture in the ecclesiastical seminary of Seton Hall College, 1864; succeeded to the presidency, 1868; resigned, 1876; appointed by the Pope bishop of Newark, N.J., 1873; made titular archbishop of Petra, and appointed coadjutor to the archbishop of New York, with the right of succession, 1880; succeeded the late Cardinal McCloskey, 1885.

CORWIN, Edward Tanjore, D.D. (Rutgers College, 1871), Reformed (Dutch); b. in New-York City, July 12, 1834; graduated in the first class of the New-York Free Academy (since 1866, the College of the City of New York) 1853, and at the theological seminary of the Reformed Dutch Church, New Brunswick, N.J., 1856; was resident licentiate, 1856–57; became pastor at Paramus, N.J., 1857, and at Millstone 1863. He is the author of *Manual and Record of Church of Paramus*, New York, 1858, 2d ed. 1859; *Manual of the Reformed Protestant Dutch Church in North America*, 1859, 3d ed. 1879; *Millstone Centennial*, 1866; *Corwin Genealogy*, 1872; and of sundry sermons and articles.

COTTERILL, Right Rev. Henry, D.D. (Cambridge, 1856), lord bishop of Edinburgh, Episcopal Church in Scotland; b. at Ampton, Suffolk, Eng., Jan. 6, 1812; educated at St. John's College, Cambridge; graduated B.A. (first Smith's prize senior wrangler, and first-class classical tripos) 1833, and was elected a fellow; M.A. by royal mandate, 1836; was ordained deacon 1835, priest 1836; was successively chaplain in the Honourable East-India Company's service, in the Madras Presidency, 1836; vice-principal of Brighton College, 1847; principal, 1851; bishop of Grahamstown, South Africa, 1856; bishop coadjutor of Edinburgh, Scotland, 1871; bishop, 1872. He is the author of *The Seven Ages of the Church*, London, 1849; *On Polygamy among Candidates for Baptism*, 1861; *The Epistle to the Galatians, with Explanatory Notes*, 1862; *The Genesis of the Church*, 1872; *Does Science aid Faith in Regard to Creation?* 1883; wrote the introduction to the Pentateuch in *The Pulpit Commentary*, 1880.

COULIN, Frank, French Swiss Protestant; b. in Geneva, Nov. 17, 1828, the son of one of the most distinguished Swiss preachers; was ordained 1851, and since 1853 has been pastor of the parish of Genthod, on the shores of the Lake of Geneva; was delegate to the Evangelical Alliance Conference in New-York City, 1873; made D.D. by the University of St. Andrew's, Scotland, 1862. He is an admired preacher, and has published several volumes of sermons and other edifying works, e.g., *Les Œuvres chrétiennes*, Geneva, 1863; *Le Fils de l'homme*, 1866 (English trans., *Son of Man*, London, 1869); *Homélies*, 1872–74, 2 series, — which have passed through successive editions, and been translated into German, Dutch, Swedish, Russian, and English.

COUSSIRAT, Daniel, Canadian Presbyterian; b. at Nérac, France, March 5, 1841; graduated at Toulouse 1859, and in theology at Montauban 1864; became *suffragant* at Bellocq (Basses-Pyrénées), 1864 (ordained in the Reformed Church of France, 1864); pastor of the Evangelical Church in Philadelphia, Penn., 1865; professor of divinity, Montreal, Can., 1867; pastor of the Reformed Church at Orthez, Basses-Pyrénées, France, 1875; French professor of divinity, Presbyterian College, Montreal, Can., 1880. Since 1882 he has been lecturer in Oriental languages, McGill University, Montreal. He was one of the revisers of the French translation of the Old Testament under the auspices of the Société Biblique de France, Paris, 1881. He published a thesis on *Election*,

Rom. ix.-xi., Toulouse, 1864; and has contributed to the *Revue théologique*, Montauban, and the *Revue chrétienne*, Paris (1870–77). He became an *officier d'Academie*, Paris, 1885.

COWIE, Very Rev. Benjamin Morgan, D.D. (Cambridge, 1880), dean of Exeter, Church of England; b. in England upon June 8, 1816; educated at St. John's College, Cambridge; graduated (senior wrangler) 1839, M.A. 1842, B.D. 1855; ordained deacon 1841, priest 1842; was elected fellow of his college 1839, moderator 1843; principal of the Engineers' College, Putney, 1844–51; select preacher, Cambridge, 1852, 1856; Hulsean lecturer, 1853–54; minor canon of St. Paul's, London, 1856–73; vicar of St. Lawrence-Jewry with St. Mary Magdalene, Milk Street, London, 1857–73; one of her Majesty's inspectors of schools, 1857–72; Warburtonian lecturer, 1866; dean of Manchester, 1872–83; prolocutor of the Lower House of Convocation of York, 1880–82; became chaplain in ordinary to the Queen, 1871; dean of Exeter, 1883. Since 1854 he has been professor of geometry at Gresham College. He is the author of *Catalogue of MSS. and Scarce Books in St. John's College, Cambridge Library*, Cambridge, 1842; *Scripture Difficulties* (Hulsean Lectures), London, 1854, 2 vols.; *Sacrifice and Atonement* (five Cambridge University sermons), 1856; *On "Essays and Reviews,"* 1861; *Reminiscences of a City Church*, 1867; *The Voice of God: Chapters on Foreknowledge, Inspiration, and Prophecy*, 1870; *Ministerial Work*, Manchester, 1872. *

COX, Samuel, D.D. (St. Andrew's, 1882), Baptist theologian; b. in London, Eng., April 19, 1826; graduated at the Stepney Baptist Theological College, London, 1851, and was ordained pastor of St. Paul's Square Baptist Church, Southsea; was pastor at Ryde, 1855–59; and pastor of the General Baptist Church, Mansfield Road, Nottingham, 1863, where he still remains. He was president of the British General Baptist Association in 1873, and the founder and first editor of *The Expositor* (1875 to 1884), a monthly journal devoted to biblical exposition, and in it wrote copiously. His principal separate publications are *The Quest of the Chief Good: Expository Lectures on the Book of Ecclesiastes, with a new translation*, London, 1865; *The Private Letters of St. Paul and St. John*, 1867; *The Resurrection* (expository lectures on 1 Cor. xv.), 1869; *An Expositor's Note-Book*, 1872; *Biblical Expositions*, 1874; *The Pilgrim Psalms* (exposition of the Songs of Degrees), 1874; *The Book of Ruth: a Popular Exposition*, 1875; *A Day with Christ*, 1876; *Salvator Mundi*, 1877; *Expository Essays and Discourses*, 1877; *Commentary on the Book of Job*, 1880; *Genesis of Evil, and other Sermons*, 1880; *The Larger Hope: a sequel to Salvator Mundi*, 1883; *Miracles: an Argument and a Challenge*, 1884; *Balaam*, 1884; *Expositions*, vol. i. 1885, vol. ii. 1886.

COXE, Right Rev. Arthur Cleveland, D.D. (St. James College, Hagerstown, Md., 1856), **S.T.D.** (Trinity College, Hartford, Conn., 1868), **LL.D.** (Kenyon College, Gambier, O., 1868), Episcopalian, bishop of Western New York; b. at Mendham, N.J., May 10, 1818; graduated at the University of the City of New York, 1838, and at the General Theological (Episcopal) Seminary, 1841; became rector at Hartford, Conn., 1842; Baltimore, Md., 1854; and of Calvary Church, New-York City, 1863; bishop of Western New York, 1865. From 1872 to 1874 he was provisional bishop of the church in Haiti, which he visited officially. He was prominent in the formation of the Anglo-Continental Society (1853), and gave it its name. He vigorously and successfully opposed the attempt of the American Bible Society to make slight alterations in the text and punctuation of the Bible issued (see art. BIBLE SOCIETIES, vol. i. p. 263 *sq.*) and, consistently, also the work of the Revision Committee, but was among the first to advocate the revision of the Prayer Book. He has taken great interest in all that concerns Gallicanism and Anglo-Catholicism. He attended the second Lambeth Conference, 1878. He has written much on behalf of the many interests which have claimed his attention. In collaboration with the late Bishop Wilberforce he began in 1873 the issue of a serial in defence of Anglo-Catholicism as against Romanism. Among his separate publications may be mentioned his volumes of poetry, *Advent, a Mystery*, New York, 1837; *Athwold*, 1838; *Christian Ballads*, 1840; *Athanasion, and other Poems*, 1842; *Halloween*, 1844; *Saul, a Mystery*, 1845. In prose, *Sermons on Doctrine and Duty*, 1854; *Impressions of England*, 1856; *The Criterion*, 1866 (in which he defines his position in the Oxford movement); *Moral Reforms*, 1869; *An Open Letter to Pius IX.* (in answer to his brief convoking the Vatican Council), 1869 (widely circulated, and translated into various European languages); *L'Episcopat de l'Occident*, Paris, 1872 (widely circulated by the Anglo-Continental Society); *Apollos, or the Way of God*, New York, 1874; *Covenant Prayers*, 1875; *The Penitential*, 1882. He is the editor of the American reprint of Clark's *Ante-Nicene Library*, Buffalo, 1885–86, 8 vols.

CRAFTS, Wilbur Fisk, B.D., Presbyterian; b. at Fryeburg, Me., Jan. 12, 1850; graduated at Wesleyan University, Middletown, Conn., 1869, and at the School of Theology, Boston (Mass.) University, 1872; was Methodist minister until 1880, his last pastorate in that denomination being Trinity, Chicago, Ill.; became pastor of the Lee Avenue Congregational Church, Brooklyn, N.Y., 1880; and pastor of the First Union Presbyterian Church of New-York City, 1883. He has paid particular attention to Sunday-school work, and conducted the "Sunday-school Parliament" in Thousand Island Park, 1876–77; spoke in many cities of Great Britain in connection with the centennial of Sunday schools (1880). He is a vice-president of the National Temperance Society. Besides numerous articles he has written *Through the Eye to the Heart*, New York, 1873; *Childhood the Textbook of the Age*, Boston, 1875 (Mrs. Crafts joint author of both; the latter appeared in enlarged form as a subscription-book under the title, *The Coming Man is the Present Child*, Chicago, 1879); *The Bible and the Sunday School*, Toronto, 1876, Chicago, 1878; *The Rescue of Child Soul*, London, 1880; *Plain Uses of the Blackboard*, 1880, New York, 1881; *Teachers' Edition of the Revised Version of the New Testament*, New York, 1881; *Talks to Boys and Girls about Jesus*, 1881; *Must the Old Testament go?* Boston, 1883; *Successful Men of To-day*, New York, 1883 (38th thousand, 1885); *Rhetoric made Racy*, Chicago, 1884 (Prof. H. F. Fisk joint author); *The Sabbath for Man*,

New York, 1885 (3d thousand in second month); *What the Temperance Century has made Certain*, 1885; *Pocket Lesson Notes*, 1886 (Mrs. Crafts joint author).

CRAIG, Willis Green, D.D. (Centre College, 1873), Presbyterian; b. near Danville, Ky., Sept. 27, 1834; graduated at Centre College, Danville, 1851, studied at the Danville Theological Seminary until 1861; became pastor at Keokuk, Io., 1862; professor of biblical and ecclesiastical history, of the Presbyterian Theological Seminary of the North-West, Chicago, Ill., 1882.

CRAMER, Michael John, D.D. (Syracuse University, N.Y., 1873), Methodist; b. at Schaffhausen, Switzerland, Feb. 6, 1835; emigrated to the United States of America, 1847; graduated at the Ohio Wesleyan University, 1860; became pastor in Cincinnati, O., 1860; in Nashville, Tenn., 1864; chaplain U.S.A., 1864; consul at Leipzig, 1867; attended lectures in theology and philosophy at Leipzig and Berlin, 1867–70; United-States minister at Copenhagen, Denmark, 1870 (appointed by Gen. Grant, his brother-in-law); at Bern, Switzerland, 1881; professor of systematic theology, School of Theology, Boston University, 1885. He has published a large number of essays of an isogogical, exegetical, and biblico-critical character, in Methodist periodicals.

CRARY, Benjamin Franklin, D.D. (Iowa Wesleyan University, 1858, Indiana State University, 1866), Methodist; b. in Jennings County, Ind., Dec. 12, 1821; educated at Pleasant Hill Academy, Cincinnati, 1839–41; admitted to the bar in Indiana, 1844; was successively pastor in Indiana Conference, 1845; president Hamline University, Minn., 1857; superintendent of public instruction, Minnesota, 1861; chaplain in the army, 1862–63; editor *Central Christian Advocate*, St. Louis, Mo., 1864; presiding elder in Colorado, 1872; editor *California Christian Advocate*, San Francisco, 1880. He was in the campaign against the Sioux Indians after the massacre, 1862; in 1863 visited the soldiers in every hospital from Keokuk, Io., to Memphis, Tenn.; was in every General Conference from 1856–1880. He has written addresses, etc.

CRAVEN, Elijah Richardson, D.D. (Princeton, 1859), Presbyterian; b. at Washington, D.C., March 28, 1824; graduated at the College of New Jersey, Princeton, N.J., 1842; studied law, then theology, and graduated at Princeton Seminary, 1848; was tutor in Princeton College, 1847–49; became Reformed Dutch pastor at Somerville, N.J., 1850; pastor of the Third Presbyterian Church, Newark, N.J., 1854. He was elected a trustee of Princeton College, 1859; a director of Princeton Seminary in 1865; was chairman of the committee of the General Assembly on revision of the Book of Discipline, 1878–84; and moderator of the General Assembly, 1885. He prepared part of the American additions to the commentary on *John* in the American Lange series, and all of those on *The Revelation;* and has written many review articles. He is particularly familiar with Presbyterian Church law, and is an advocate of pre-millenarianism.

CREIGHTON, Mandell, LL.D. (*hon.*, Glasgow, 1881), Church of England; b. at Carlisle, County of Cumberland, Eng., July 5, 1843; educated at Merton College, Oxford; graduated B.A. (first-class classics, second-class law and modern history) 1867, M A. 1870; was fellow and tutor of his college, 1867–75; public examiner in modern history, 1869–70, 1875–76, 1883–84; was ordained deacon 1870, priest 1873; select preacher in the university, 1875–77, 1883; vicar of Embleton, Northumberland, 1875–84; rural dean of Alnwick, 1882–84. In 1884 he became Dixie professor of ecclesiastical history in the University of Cambridge, hon. M.A.; and fellow of Emanuel College; in 1885 canon of Worcester, and hon. D. C. L., Durham. He has published *Primer of Roman History*, London, 1875; *The Age of Elizabeth*, 1876; *Life of Simon de Montfort*, 1876; *The Tudors and the Reformation*, 1876; *Short History of England*, 1879; *History of the Papacy during the Period of the Reformation*, vols. 1 and 2, 1882. He is founder and editor of *The Historical Review*, 1886, *sqq*.

CREMER, August Hermann, Lic. Theol. (Tübingen, 1858), **D.D.** (*hon.*, Berlin, 1873), Lutheran (United Evangelical); b. at Unna, Westphalia, Germany, Oct. 18, 1834; studied at Halle 1853–56, and at Tübingen 1856–59; became pastor at Ostönnen, near Soest, Westphalia, 1859; ordinary professor of systematic theology at Greifswald, and pastor of St. Mary's there, 1870. He is the author of *Die eschatologische Rede Jesu Christi, Matthäi 24. 25. Versuch einer exegetischen Erörterung derselben*, Stuttgart, 1860; *Ueber den biblischen Begriff der Erbauung*, Barmen, 1863; *Ueber die Wunder im Zusammenhang der göttlichen Offenbarung*, 1865; *Biblisch-theologisches Wörterbuch der neutestamentlichen Gräcität*, Gotha, 1866–67, 2d ed. 1872, 3d ed. 1883, 4th ed. 1886 (English trans. by Rev. William Urwick, *Biblico-theological Lexicon of New-Testament Greek*, Edinburgh, 1872, 2d ed. 1878, 3d ed. 1886); *Ueber Luthers Schrift "dass unser Heiland ein geborner Jude sei,"* Cologne, 1867; *Jenseits des Grabes*, Gütersloh, 1868; *Vernunft, Gewissen und Offenbarung*, Gotha, 1869; *Die Auferstehung der Todten*, Barmen, 1870; *Der Gott des Alten Bundes*, 1872; *Die kirchliche Trauung historisch, ethisch und liturgisch*, Berlin, 1875; *Aufgabe und Bedeutung der Predigt in der gegenwärtigen Krisis*, 1876; *Ueber die Befähigung zum geistlichen Amte*, 1878; *Die Bibel im Pfarrhaus und in der Gemeinde*, 1878, 3d ed. 1879; *Die Wurzeln der Anselmischen Satisfactionslehre* (in *Studien u. Kritiken*, 1880); *Unterweisung im Christentum nach der Ordnung des kleinen Katechismus*, Gütersloh, 1883; *Reformation und Wissenschaft* (*Rectoratsrede zur Lutherfeier*), Gotha, 1883; *Ueber den Zustand nach dem Tode, nebst einigen Andeutungen über das Kindersterben und über den Spiritismus*, 1883 (Swedish trans., Jörrköping, 1885; English trans. by Rev. Dr. S. T. Lowrie, *Beyond the Grave*, New York, 1885). He was a delegate to the General Conference of the Evangelical Alliance at Basel, 1879, and read a paper on the state of religion in Germany.

CROOKS, George Richard, D.D. (Dickinson College, 1857), Methodist; b. in Philadelphia, Penn., Feb. 3, 1822; graduated at Dickinson College, Carlisle, Penn., 1840; was teacher and adjunct professor of Latin and Greek in the college, 1841–48; pastor of various Methodist churches in Pennsylvania, Delaware, and New York, 1848–80; editor of *The Methodist*, 1860–75; since 1880 has been professor of church history in Drew Methodist-Episcopal Theological Seminary, Madison, N.J. He published, with Dr. McClintock,

The First Book in Latin, New York, 1846 (numerous editions); with Professor Schem, *Latin-English School Lexicon*, Philadelphia, 1858, last ed. 1882; with Dr. Hurst, an adaptation of Hagenbach's *Theological Encyclopædia and Methodology*, New York, 1884; and separately, an edition of *Butler's Analogy*, with a life of Butler, and Emory's Analysis completed, New York, 1852; *Life and Letters of the Rev. Dr. John McClintock*, 1876; *Sermons of Bishop Matthew Simpson, edited from short-hand Reports*, 1885.

CROSBY, Howard, S.T.D. (Harvard, 1859), **LL.D.** (Columbia College, 1872), Presbyterian; b. in New-York City, Feb. 27, 1826; graduated at the University of the City of New York, 1844; became professor of Greek in this institution, 1851; went in the same capacity to Rutgers College, New Brunswick, N.J., 1859. He was president of the Young Men's Christian Association of the city, 1852–55; licensed by North Berkshire Association, Mass. (Congregational), 1859; received as licentiate by Classis of New Brunswick (Reformed Dutch), Oct. 16, 1860; dismissed to presbytery of New Brunswick, and by it ordained, April 16, 1861; was pastor of the First Presbyterian Church of New Brunswick, in connection with his professorship, 1861–63; since 1863 pastor of the Fourth-avenue Presbyterian Church, New-York City. He was chancellor of the New-York University, 1870–81; member of the American Bible Revision Committee, 1870–81; moderator of the General Assembly at Baltimore, Md., 1873; since 1877 he has been president of the Society for the Prevention of Crime, and takes an active part in temperance and other moral reforms in New-York City. Besides occasional pamphlets, articles, etc., he has written *Lands of the Moslem* (travels), New York, 1851; *Œdipus Tyrannus*, 1852; *New-Testament Scholia*, 1863; *Social Hints for Young Christians*, 1866; *Bible Manual*, 1870; *Jesus, his Life and Work*, 1871; *Healthy Christian*, 1872; *Thoughts on the Decalogue*, Philadelphia, 1873; *Expository Notes on the Book of Joshua*, New York, 1875; *Nehemiah* (in American Lange series), 1877; *The Christian Preacher* (Yale Lectures), 1880; *True Humanity of Christ*, 1880; *Commentary on the New Testament*, 1885.

CROSKERY, Thomas, D.D. (Derry and Belfast Presbyterian Colleges, 1883), Presbyterian; b. at Carrowdore, County Down, Ireland, May 26, 1830; graduated at Belfast College, 1848; became a minister, 1860 (served in various places); professor of logic and rhetoric in Magee College, Londonderry, 1875, and of systematic theology, 1879. He wrote *Treatise on the Doctrines of the Plymouth Brethren*, Belfast, 1880.

CROSS, Joseph, D.D. (Carolina University, Chapel Hill, N.C., 1854), **LL.D.** (North-Western College, Ill., 1875), Episcopalian; b. at East Brent, Somersetshire, Eng., July 4, 1813; studied in Oneida Conference Seminary, Cazenovia, N.Y., 1832–33; entered Methodist ministry, became an Episcopalian, was chaplain in Confederate army; rector at Houston, Tex., 1867; at Buffalo, N.Y., 1868–70; St. Louis, Mo., 1872–73; Jacksonville, Ill., 1874–77; afternoon preacher in the Church of the Heavenly Rest, New-York City, 1884–85. Besides articles in periodicals, he has written *Hebrew Missionary*, Nashville, Tenn., 1855; *Headlands of Faith*, 1856; *A Year in Europe*, 1857; *Knight Banneret*, New York, 1882; *Edens of Italy*, 1882; *Evangel*, 1883; *Coals from the Altar*, 1883; *Pauline Charity*, 1884; *Old Wine and New*, 1884; *Alone with God*, 1884; *Church Reader for Lent*, 1885 (most of these have been republished, London).

CUNITZ, August Eduard, D.D., German Protestant; b. at Strassburg, Aug. 29, 1812; studied in its university; became *privat-docent* in the Protestant Seminary, 1837; professor extraordinary, 1857; ordinary professor, 1864; and since 1872 has held a similar position in the re-organized theological faculty. With Reuss, he edited *Beiträge zu den theologischen Wissenschaften*, Jena, 1847–55, 6 vols.; since 1863, with Baum and Reuss, Calvin's *Opera*, Braunschweig, 1863 *sqq.* (vol. 30, 1885); and with G. Baum, the *Histoire ecclésiastique*, attributed to Beza, Paris, 1883, sqq. He is the author of *De Nicolai II. Decreto de electione pontificum*, Strassburg, 1837; *Considérations historiques sur le développement du droit eccl. prot. en France*, 1840; *Historische Darstellung der Kirchenzucht unter den Protestanten*, 1843; *Ein Katharisches Ritual*, Jena, 1852. *

CURCI, Carlo Maria, Roman Catholic; b. at Naples, Sept. 4, 1809; and was educated at Naples and Rome, among the Jesuits. He entered the company Sept. 14, 1826; was expelled Oct. 17, 1877, for having refused to recognize as a Catholic doctrine the necessity of the temporal power of the popes. He has held no dignity, either within or without his order. He taught literature and philosophy in Naples, and has preached in almost all the great cities of Italy, — permanently for six years in Naples, in Rome for twenty years at different times, and in Florence since 1877. He is strictly Catholic, and peculiarly devoted to the Church of Rome, whose doctrines and interests he has for half a century strenuously defended, deploring at the same time its decadence. Of this decadence he saw a symptom and an effect in the attitude of the Vatican towards United Italy, and publicly invoked a reform on this point. This idea of reform, to which he thought the abolition of the temporal power might be an aid, caused him to be expelled from the order of the Jesuits, and persecuted accordingly. His polemical book, *La nuova Italia e i vecchi zelanti*, 1881, was prohibited by the Congregation of the Index, and to this judgment he submitted himself. His *Il Vaticano Regio, tarlo superstite della Chiesa Cattolica*, 1883, brought upon him an injunction from the Pope, "simply and purely to condemn his book;" and as he, according to the teaching of his conscience, declined to do so, by the order of the Congregation of the Inquisition he was suspended from his sacerdotal functions, and also prohibited from receiving the sacraments. Having declined to obey this order, Leo XIII., in a letter to the archbishop of Florence, lamented his audacity in a general manner, and it was then that Father Curci submitted to the pontiff a general declaration of obedience to the Church, which was sufficient to induce Pope Leo to relieve him from the order of the Inquisition. Notwithstanding this release, Father Curci continues to be persecuted by those of the Catholic clergy who are under the influence of the Jesuits.

In the last half-century there have been few writers among the Catholic clergy who like Father Curci have distinguished themselves by the abundance of their writings. In 1850 he founded, in Naples, the *Civiltà Cattolica*, a religious and political review, which soon became the organ of the Society of Jesus, and of the Vatican. As the *Review* upheld the rights of the Pope over kings and emperors, it soon fell under the ban of Ferdinand II., the despot-king of Naples, and Father Curci was forced to remove it to Rome. But the *Civiltà Cattolica* still pursuing its course, Ferdinand urged upon Pope Pius IX. the necessity of stopping its publication; and as the Pope was reluctant to take this course, the King threatened to expel the Jesuits from his kingdom if his request was not complied with; whereupon the *Review* was suppressed, and Curci went to Bologna, but only for a year (1855–56), and on the death of the King (1859) he returned to Rome to continue his work. With the beginning of the national movement in 1859, Father Curci seemed to have somewhat changed his opinions, and to have taken a more liberal direction; and as his associates continued to hold the old anti-national doctrines of the Church, he gradually separated himself from the *Review*, becoming more reconciled with the progress of the times, so far at least as it involved the reconciliation of the Church with the new Kingdom of Italy. He remains, however, entirely devoted to the interests of the Church; and even when he urges the reconciliation of the papacy with Italy, he does so more as a matter of political necessity than as a moral obligation.

The following are the works of Father Curci: *La questione romana nell'Assemblea francese*, Rome, 1849; *La demagogia italiana et il Papa*, 1849; *La natura e la grazia*, 1865, 2 vols.; *Lezioni esegetiche e morali sopra i quattro Evangeli, dette in Firenze dal 1 Novembre 1873 al 29 Giugno 1874*, Florence, 1874–76, 5 vols. [these lectures attracted a good deal of attention, for in them he expressed his progressive view, e.g., he urged the priests to take part in the elections]; *Le virtù domestiche: il libro di Tobia esposto in lezioni*, 1877; *Il moderno dissidio tra la Chiesa e lo Stato, considerato per occasione di un fatto particolare* ("The modern dissension between Church and State, examined on the occurrence of a personal affair"), December, 1877 [it escaped being put upon the Index, was widely circulated in original and translation, e.g., in German, Vienna, 1878, and brought the author before the world as an enlightened priest]; *Il Nuovo Testamento volgarizzato ed esposto in note esegetiche e morali*, Naples, 1879–80, 3 vols.; *La Nuova Italia ed i vecchi zelanti* ("The New Italy and the old zealots"), Florence, 1881, German trans., Leipzig, 1882, 2 vols. [in this work, promptly put upon the Index, he attempts to mediate between Church and State in Italy, and to re-organize the parliamentary parties]; *Il Salterio volgarizzato dall' Ebreo ed esposto in note esegetiche e morali*, Rome, 1883; *Il Vaticano Regio, tarlo superstite della Chiesa Cattolica*, Florence, 1883; *Lo scandalo del Vaticano Regio*, 1884; *Di un socialismo cristiano nella questione operaia e nel conserto selvaggio degli stati civili*, 1885.

[Advanced in the study of the Scriptures more than the common clergy of Italy, he still moves within the narrow limits of Catholic criticism. His mind, logically trained, is more in sympathy with scholastic theology than with modern philosophy. Hence his writings, which are prolix and heavy in style, lack the strength, freshness, and breadth of truly scholarly compositions, and have neither artistic nor scholarly qualities. His biblical works have no originality, but are substantially only repetitions of mediæval notions; and his polemical books have only a personal interest, simply expressing a conscientious protest against old abuses in the Church, which neither in strength nor in influence can be compared with the protests of Arnaldo da Brescia, of Savonarola, and in more modern times, of Gioberti or Rosmini. Yet as an example of a noble self-sacrifice, renouncing the favors of a powerful association, and condemning himself to poverty, rather than bend his knee before the idol of papal temporal authority, Father Curci deserves to be revered by all who hold in honor truth and independence. — V. B.]

CURREY, George, D.D. (Cambridge, 1862), Church of England; b. in London, April 7, 1816; d. there, April 30, 1885. He was educated at St. John's College, Cambridge; graduated B.A. (wrangler and first-class classical tripos) 1838, M.A. 1841, B.D. 1850. He was elected fellow of his college, 1839; appointed lecturer, 1840; tutor, 1844; Whitehall preacher, 1845; preacher at the Charterhouse, 1849–71; Hulsean lecturer, 1851–52; Boyle lecturer, 1851; master of the Charterhouse, London, 1871, until his death; since 1872, prebendary of Brownswood in St. Paul's Cathedral; and since 1877, examining chaplain to the bishop of Rochester. He edited Tertullian's *De Spectaculis, de idololatria, et de corona militis*, Cambridge, 1854; and prepared the commentary upon *Ezekiel* in the *Bible* (Speaker's) *Commentary*, and that on *Ecclesiastes* and *The Revelation* in the *S. P. C. K. Commentary*. *

CURRIER, Albert Henry, D.D. (Bowdoin College, 1883), Congregationalist; b. at Skowhegan, Me., Nov. 15, 1837; graduated from Bowdoin College, Brunswick, Me., 1857, and from Andover Theological Seminary, 1862; became pastor of Congregational churches of Ashland (1862) and Lynn, Mass. (1865), and professor of homiletics and pastoral theology in Oberlin Theological Seminary, Oberlin, O., 1881. He contributed to the successive volumes of the *Monday Club Sermons* upon the International Sunday-school Lessons (Boston), from 1876 to 1882, and articles to *The Boston Review*, 1865–67.

CURRY, Daniel, D.D. (Wesleyan University, 1852), **LL.D.** (Syracuse University, 1878), Methodist; b. near Peekskill, N.Y., Nov. 26, 1809; graduated from the Wesleyan University, 1837; became principal of the Troy Conference Academy, West Poultney, Vt., 1837; professor in the Georgia Female College at Macon, Ga, 1839; member of the Georgia Conference, and pastor at Athens, Savannah, and Columbus, 1841; in similar work in the New-York Conference, 1844; was president of the Indiana Asbury University, Greencastle, Ind, 1854; member of New-York East Conference, 1857; was editor of the *Christian Advocate*, 1864–76; of the *National Repository*, 1876–80; pastor, 1880–84; since 1884 editor of the *Methodist Review*, New York. He has written *A Life of Wyckliff*, New York, 1846; *The Metropolitan City of America*, 1852; *Life Story of*

Bishop D. W. Clark, 1873; *Fragments, Religious and Theological*, 1880; *Platform Papers*, Cincinnati, 1880. He also edited the works of Rev. Dr. James Floy, New York, 1863, 2 vols.; Southey's *Life of Wesley*, 1852, 2 vols.; and Clark's *Commentary on the New Testament*, 1882–84, 2 vols.

CURRY, Jabez Lamar Monroe, D.D. (Rochester University, 1871), **LL.D.** (Mercer University, 1867), Baptist; b. in Lincoln County, Ga., June 5, 1825; graduated from the University of Georgia, 1843, and the Harvard Law School, Mass., 1845; was representative in Alabama legislature, 1847–48, 1853-54, 1855–56; Buchanan elector, 1856; member of 35th and 36th United-States Congress, and of the Confederate Congress; president of Howard College, Alabama, 1866–68; professor of English and mental philosophy in Richmond College, Va, 1868–81; general agent of Peabody Education Fund, 1881–85. In October, 1885, he was appointed by President Cleveland, envoy extraordinary and minister plenipotentiary of the United States of America to Spain. He never has accepted a pastoral charge, although he has been ordained, and has preached frequently. He has issued numerous addresses on political, educational, literary, and religious topics; and one on the *Evils of a Union of Church and State*, before the General Conference of the Evangelical Alliance in New-York City, 1873 (cf. *Proceedings*, pp. 544 sqq.).

CURTIS, Edward Lewis, A.B., Presbyterian; b. at Ann Arbor, Mich., Oct. 13, 1853; graduated at Yale College, 1874, and at the Union Theological Seminary, New-York City, 1879; was appointed fellow of the seminary; spent two years in study abroad, chiefly at Berlin; in 1881 was appointed instructor, and in 1884 associate professor of Old-Testament literature, in the Presbyterian Seminary of the North-West, Chicago, Ill.

CURTISS, Samuel Ives, Ph.D. (Leipzig, 1876), **Lic. Theol.** (*hon.*, Berlin, 1878), **D.D.** (Iowa College, 1878, Amherst, 1881), Congregationalist; b. at Union, Conn., Feb. 5, 1844; graduated at Amherst College, 1867, and at Union Theological Seminary, New-York City, 1870; was pastor of the Alexander Mission, King Street, New York, connected with the Fifth-avenue Presbyterian Church, 1870-72; and of the American Chapel, Leipzig, 1874–78. In 1872 he went to Germany, studied nine months in Bonn (1872-73), and then at Leipzig (1873-78), and received private instruction from Prof. Franz Delitzsch (four years) and Dr. J. H. R. Biesenthal. From 1878–79 he was New-England professor of biblical literature in Chicago (Congregational) Theological Seminary, and since 1879 has been New-England professor of Old-Testament literature and interpretation. He is the translator of Bickell's *Outlines of Hebrew Grammar*, Leipzig, 1877; and of Delitzsch's *Messianic Prophecies*, Edinburgh, 1880, and *Old-Testament History of Redemption*, 1881; and author of *The Name Machabee*, Leipzig, 1876 (his doctor's thesis); *The Levitical Priests*, Edinburgh, 1877; *De Aaronitici sacerdotii atque thoræ Elohisticæ origine*, Leipzig, 1878 (his licentiate thesis); *Ingersoll and Moses*, Chicago, 1879; and of contributions to *Current Discussions in Theology*, 1883 *sqq.* and in periodicals. He is associate editor of the *Bibliotheca Sacra*.

CUYLER, Theodore Ledyard, D.D. (Princeton, 1866), Presbyterian; b. at Aurora, Cayuga County, N.Y., Jan. 10, 1822; graduated at the College of New Jersey, 1841, and at Princeton Theological Seminary, 1846; became stated supply at Burlington, N.J., 1846; pastor of the Third Presbyterian Church, Trenton, 1849; of the Market-street Reformed Church, New-York City, 1853; and of the Lafayette-avenue Presbyterian Church, Brooklyn, N.Y., 1860. His church reported in 1885 a membership of 2,012. He has contributed 2,700 articles to leading religious papers of America and Europe, and been active in temperance work. He is the author of *Stray Arrows*, New York, 1852, new ed. 1880; *The Cedar Christian*, 1858, new ed. 1881; *The Empty Crib: A Memorial*, 1868; *Heart Life*, 1871; *Thought Hives*, 1872; *Pointed Papers for the Christian Life*, 1879; *From the Nile to Norway*, 1881; *God's Light on Dark Clouds*, 1882; *Wayside Springs from the Fountain of Life*, 1883; *Right to the Point*, 1884; *Lafayette-avenue Church*, 1885 (exercises connected with the celebration of the 25th anniversary of his pastorate, April 5 and 6, 1885).

D.

DABNEY, Robert Lewis, D.D. (Hampden-Sidney College, 1853), **LL.D.** (do., 1872), Presbyterian (Southern); b. in Louisa County, Va., March 5, 1820; after studying in Hampden-Sidney College, Va., to the beginning of senior year, he entered the University of Virginia, Charlottesville, took the whole M.A. course, then the full theological course in Union Theological Seminary, Va., and graduated in 1846; became missionary in Virginia, 1846; pastor of Tinkling-Spring Church, Augusta County, Va., 1847; professor of church history in the Union Theological Seminary, Va., 1853, and of theology in the same institution, 1869; professor of philosophy, mental, moral, and political, in the State University of Texas, Austin, 1883 (his health requiring a milder climate). From 1858 till 1874 he was co-pastor of the Hampden-Sidney College Church. In 1861 he was a chaplain in the Confederate army, with the Virginia troops; in 1862, chief of staff of the Second Corps under Gen. T. J. Jackson. In 1870 he was moderator of the Southern General Assembly. He has published *Memoir of Dr. F. S. Sampson*, Richmond, 1854; *Life of Gen. Thomas J. Jackson*, New York, 1866; *Defence of Virginia and the South*, 1867; *Treatise on Sacred Rhetoric*, Richmond, 1870, 3d ed. 1881; *Sensualistic Philosophy of the Nineteenth Century examined*, New York, 1875; *Theology, Dogmatic and Polemic*, Richmond, 1874, 3d ed. 1885.

DALE, Robert William, D.D. (Yale, 1877), **LL.D.** (Glasgow, 1883), Congregationalist; b. in London, Dec. 1, 1829; educated at Spring Hill College, Birmingham (1847–53), graduated M.A. (with gold medal) at the University of London, 1853; and in June of that year was ordained and installed as co-pastor with John Angell James of the Carr's-lane (Congregational) Church, Birmingham, and since Mr. James's death in 1859 sole pastor. In 1869 he was chairman of the Congregational Union of England and Wales. In 1877 he was lecturer at Yale Seminary on the Lyman Beecher foundation. He is governor of King Edward VI.'s School, Birmingham, on appointment of the Senate of the University of London. He takes an active part in religious, political (radical), and educational matters. As for his theology, he is in "general agreement with evangelical theologians, but claims freedom in relation to inspiration of the Scriptures, and differs widely from the traditional evangelical school in principles of criticism and exegesis." His views are most fully set forth in his *Epistle to the Ephesians*. He "assigns a fundamental position to the relations of the human race to the Eternal Son of God, in whom the race was created. Only by the free consent of the individual man to God's eternal election of him in Christ can he actually realize union with God and the possession of eternal life. The potency of immortality is in the race, and all men survive death and will be judged; but that only those who consent to find the root of their life in Christ will live forever: the rest of the race will sooner or later cease to exist." Besides many articles of importance, addresses separately published, and an edition of Reuss's *History of Christian Theology in the Apostolic Age* (translated by Annie Harwood, London, 1872–74, 2 vols.), he has issued *Life and Letters of the Rev. J. A. James*, London, 1861, 5th ed. 1862; *The Jewish Temple and the Christian Church*, 1865, 7th ed. 1886; *Discourses delivered on Special Occasions*, 1866; *Week-day Sermons*, 1867, 4th ed. 1883; *The Ten Commandments*, 1871, 5th ed. 1885; *Protestantism: its Ultimate Principle*, 1874, 2d ed. 1875; *The Atonement* (the Congregational Union lecture for 1875), 1875, 9th ed. 1883 (German trans. from 7th ed., Gotha, 1880, also French trans. and New-York reprint); *Nine Lectures on Preaching* (Lyman Beecher lectures, referred to above), 1877, 5th ed. 1886; *The Evangelical Revival, and other Sermons*, 1880, 2d ed. 1881; *Epistle to the Ephesians: its Doctrine and Ethics*, 1882, 3d ed. 1884; *The Laws of Christ for Common Life*, 1884, 2d ed. 1885; *Manual of Congregational Principles*, 1884. He edited *The English Hymn-book*, Birmingham, 1875, containing 1,260 hymns. For a time he was joint editor of *The Eclectic Review*, and for seven years sole editor of *The Congregationalist*.

DALES, John Blakely, D.D. (Franklin College, O., 1853), United Presbyterian; b. at Kortright, Delaware County, N.Y., Aug. 6, 1815; graduated at Union College, Schenectady, N.Y., 1835, and at the Associate Reformed Presbyterian Theological Seminary, Newburgh, N.Y., 1839; has been pastor of the First Associate Reformed (now Second United) Presbyterian Church, Philadelphia, Penn., since June 4, 1840, and held the following positions: editor in part of *Christian Instructor* (1846–79); professor of church history and pastoral theology in Newburgh Theological Seminary (1867–76); moderator of the General Assembly (1867); recording secretary of the Presbyterian Historical Society (Philadelphia) since 1851; corresponding secretary of the Board of Foreign Missions of the United Presbyterian Church, since its organization in 1859; stated clerk of the United Presbyterian Synod of New York since 1863. He is the author of *Roman Catholicism*, Philadelphia, 1842; *Introduction to Lectures on Odd Fellowship*, 1851; *The Dangers and Duties of Young Men*, 1857; *History of the Associate Reformed Church and its Missions* (in the *Church Memorial*), Xenia, O., 1859; *A Memorial Discourse* on the fortieth anniversary of his pastorate, Philadelphia, 1882; a *Church Manual*, 1884.

DALTON, Hermann, D.D. (*hon.*, Marburg, 1883), German Reformed; b. at Offenbach, near Frankfurt-am-Main, Aug. 20, 1833 (his father was an Englishman); studied at the universities of Marburg, Berlin, and Heidelberg, 1853–56; has been since 1858 pastor of the German Reformed Church in St. Petersburg, Russia, and member of the ecclesiastical council of the Reformed Church in Russia; since 1876 founder and chairman of the evangelical city mission. He has published, besides minor works, *Nathanael, Vorträge über das Christenthum*, St. Petersburg, 1861, 3d ed. 1886; *Geschichte der reformirten Kirche in Russland*, Gotha, 1865; *Das Gebet des Herrn in den Sprachen Russlands, Linguistische Studie mit Text in 108 Sprachen*, St. Petersburg, 1870; *Immanuel, Der Heidelberger Katechismus als Bekenntniss- u. Erbauungsbuch, der evangel. Gemeinde erklärt und ans Herz gelegt*, Wiesbaden, 1870, 2d ed. 1883 (translated into Dutch); *Reisebilder aus dem Orient*, St. Petersburg, 1871; *Die evangelische Bewegung in Spanien*, Wiesbaden, 1872 (translated into Dutch); *Johannes Gossner*, Berlin, 1874, 2d ed. 1878 (translated into Dutch); *Reisebilder aus London und Holland*, Wiesbaden, 1875; *Johannes von Muralt*, 1876; *Die evangelischen Strömungen in der russischen Kirche der Gegenwart*, Heilbronn, 1881 (translated into Dutch, French, and English); *Johannes a Lasco*, Gotha, 1881 (translated into Dutch and English); *Reisebilder aus Griechenland und Kleinasien*, *Randzeichnungen zu einigen Stellen des Neuen Testamentes*, Bremen, 1884; *Ferienreise eines evangelischen Predigers*, 1885 (with an account of the Belfast Council of the Reformed Churches, and the Copenhagen Conference of the Evangelical Alliance, 1884, which the author attended as a delegate). Besides these may be mentioned his edifying and devotional writings which are all published in Basel, and have been widely circulated: *Der verlorne Sohn, Die Familie* (1865, 2d ed. 1870), *Die sieben Worte am Kreuze* (1871), *Bethanien* (1875), *Die Heilung des Blindgebornen* (1882).

D'ALVIELLA, Count Goblet; b. in Brussels, Aug. 10, 1846; educated at the University of Brussels, 1865–69; became "conseiller provincial" in Brabant, 1872; member of Parliament, 1878; professor of the history of religion in the University of Brussels, 1884. He has received from this university doctorates in political and administrative science 1866, in law 1869, and in philosophy and letters 1884. His theological standpoint is that of "Free Religion." He accompanied the Prince of Wales in India as special correspondent of the *Indépendance Belge* (1875–76). He has written *L'établissement des Cobourg en Portugal*, Brussels, 1869; *Désarmer ou Déchoir* ("ouvrage couronné par la Ligue de la Paix"), Paris, 1871; *Sahara et Laponie*, 1873, 2d ed. 1876 (English trans. by Mrs. Cashel Hoey, *Sahara and Lapland*, London, 1874); *Le catholicisme libéral aujourd'hui et autrefois*, Brussels, 1875; *Inde et Himalaya*, Paris, 1877, 2d ed. 1880; *Partie perdue*, 1877; *Souvenirs d'un voyage dans l'Atlantique*, Verviers, 1881; *De la nécessité d'introduire l'histoire des Religions dans notre enseignement public*, Brussels, 1882; *Harrison contre Spencer, étude sur la valeur religieuse de l'Inconnaissable*, Paris, 1884; *L'évolution religieuse contemporaine chez les Anglais, les Américains et les Hindous*, 1884 (English trans. by Rev. J. Hoden, *The Contemporary Evolution of Religious Thought in England, America, and India*, New York, 1885). Besides these he has written articles upon the history of religion in the *Revue des Deux Mondes*, *Revue de Belgique*, *Revue de l'Histoire des Religions*, etc.

DAVIDSON, Andrew Bruce, D.D., Free Church of Scotland; b. in Scotland about 1840; received a university education; was ordained in 1863, and the same year was appointed professor of Hebrew and Old-Testament exegesis in New College, Edinburgh, which position he still holds. He was a member of the Old-Testament Company of Revisers. He is the author of *A Commentary on Job*, Edinburgh, vol. i., 1862; *An Introductory Hebrew Grammar*, 1874, 4th ed. 1881; *The Epistle to the Hebrews, with Introduction and Notes*, 1882 (in Clark's *Handbooks for Bible Classes*); *Job*, Cambridge, 1884 (in *Cambridge Bible for Schools*, edited by Dean Perowne).

DAVIDSON, Very Rev. Randall Thomas, dean of Windsor, Church of England; b. in Scotland in the year 1848; educated at Trinity College, Oxford; graduated B.A., 1871, M.A. 1875; ordained deacon 1874, priest 1875; was curate of Dartford, Kent, 1874–77; resident chaplain to Archbishop of Canterbury (both Tait and Benson), 1877–83; examining chaplain to the bishop of Durham, 1881–83; sub-almoner and honorary chaplain to the Queen, 1882; one of the six preachers of Canterbury Cathedral; appointed dean, 1883; Queen's domestic chaplain, 1883.

DAVIDSON, Samuel, D.D. (*hon.*, Halle, 1848), **LL.D.** (*hon.*, Marischal College, Aberdeen, 1838); b. at Kellswater, near Ballymena, County Antrim, Ireland, Sept. 23, 1807; educated at the Royal Academical Institution, Belfast, completing the course in 1832. From 1835 to 1841, when he resigned, he was professor of biblical criticism at Belfast to the Presbyterian body called the General Synod of Ulster. In 1842 he became professor of biblical literature and ecclesiastical history in the Lancashire Independent College at Manchester. In 1857 he resigned this position in consequence of an adverse vote of the managing committee, apparently founded upon the view of inspiration expressed in the second volume of the tenth edition of Horne's *Introduction* (see below). Dr. Davidson enjoyed the friendship of Tholuck, Hupfeld, Roediger, Erdmann, Bleek, Lücke, Gieseler, Neander, Ewald, Tischendorf, and other distinguished German theologians. His own theological standpoint is rationalistic. His biblical scholarship is evinced by the following works: (1) *Lectures on Biblical Criticism*, Edinburgh, 1839; (2) *Sacred Hermeneutics*, 1843; (3) *Gieseler's Compendium of Ecclesiastical History*, translated from the German, 1846–47, 2 vols.; (4) *Ecclesiastical Polity of the New Testament*, London, 1848, 2d ed. 1854; (5) *Introduction to the New Testament*, 1848, 1849, 1851, 3 vols.; (6) *A Treatise on Biblical Criticism* (superseding No. 1), Edinburgh, 1852, 2 vols.; (7) *The Hebrew Text of the Old Testament revised from Critical Sources*, London, 1855; *The Text of the Old Testament considered; with a Treatise on Sacred Interpretation, and a brief Introduction to the Old-Testament Books and the Apocrypha* (forming vol. 2 of the tenth edition of Horne's *Introduction to the Scriptures*), 1856, 2d ed. 1859; (9) *An Introduction to the Old Testament, critical, historical, and theological*, 1862–63, 3 vols.; (10) *Fürst's Hebrew and Chaldee Lexicon*, translated from the German, 1865, 4th ed. 1871; (11) *An Introduction to the New Testament* (superseding No. 5), 1868, 2 vols., 2d ed. 1882; (12) *On a Fresh Revision of the English Old Testament*, 1873; (13) *The New Testament, translated from the Critical Text of Von Tischendorf, with an Introduc-*

tion on the Criticism, Translation, and Interpretation of the Book, 1875, 2d ed. 1876; (14) *The Canon of the Bible*, 1876, 3d ed. 1880; (15) *The Doctrine of Last Things contained in the New Testament, compared with the Notions of the Jews and the Statements of the Church Creeds*, 1882.

DAVIES, John Llewelyn, Church of England; b. at Chichester, Feb. 26, 1826; educated at Trinity College, Cambridge; graduated B.A. (senior optime and fifth in first-class classical tripos) 1848, M.A. 1851; elected fellow of his college in 1850; was ordained deacon 1851, priest 1852; from 1853 till 1856, incumbent of St. Mark's, Whitechapel, and since has been rector of Christ Church, Marylebone, London. In 1881 he was appointed a chaplain in ordinary to the Queen, and select preacher at Oxford, and the next year rural dean of St. Marylebone. He was a contributor to Smith's *Dictionary of the Bible*, and to Smith and Wace's *Dictionary of Christian Biography*. Besides five volumes of sermons, he has published (with Rev. D. J. Vaughan) a translation of Plato's *Republic*, London, 3d ed. 1866; *The Epistles to the Ephesians, Colossians, and Philemon, with Introduction and Notes, and an Essay on the Traces of Foreign Elements in the Theology of these Epistles*, London, 1866, 2d ed. 1884; *Theology and Morality*, 1873; *Social Questions from the Point of View of Christian Theology*, 1885.

DAVIS, Peter Seibert, D.D. (Franklin and Marshall College, Penn., 1874), Reformed (German); b. at Funkstown, Md., March 21, 1828; graduated at Marshall College, Mercersburg, 1849; studied in Mercersburg Seminary, and at Princeton; became pastor at Winchester, Va., 1853; teacher at Mount Washington College, 1857; pastor at Norristown, Penn., 1859, and at Chambersburg, Penn., 1864; editor of *The Messenger* (official organ of the Reformed Church), Philadelphia, 1875. He is the author of *The Young Parson*, Philadelphia, 1862, 7th ed. 1885, and of review and magazine articles.

DAWSON, Sir John William, C.M.G. (i.e., Companion of the Order of St. Michael and St. George, 1881), **M.A.** (Edinburgh, 1856), **LL.D.** (McGill 1857, and Edinburgh 1884), **F.R.S.** (1862), **F.G.S.** (1854), etc., Presbyterian layman; b. at Pictou, Nova Scotia, Oct. 13, 1820; studied at the College of Pictou, and at the University of Edinburgh, finishing in 1846; became superintendent of education for Nova Scotia, 1851; principal, and professor of geology, McGill University, 1855. In 1881 he received the Lyell medal of the Geological Society of London for eminent geological discoveries; in 1882 was the first president of the Royal Society of Canada; in 1883, president of the American Association; in 1883 travelled in Egypt and Syria; in 1884 was knighted; in 1885 was president-elect of the British Association for 1886. He became correspondent of the Philadelphia Academy of Natural Sciences, 1846; fellow of Boston Academy Arts and Sciences 1860, of Philadelphia American Philosophical Society 1862; honorary member Boston Natural History Society 1867, and of the New-York Academy of Sciences 1876. He is the author of *Acadian Geology*, London, 1855, 3d ed. 1868; *Archaia, or Studies of Creation in the Bible*, 1860; *Story of the Earth and Man*, 1873; *Nature and the Bible* (Morse lectures before Union Theological Seminary, New-York City), 1875; *Dawn of Life*, 1875; *Origin of the World*, 1877, 4th ed. 1886; *Fossil Man*, 1880; *Chain of Life in Geological Time*, 1883; *Egypt and Syria, Physical Features in Relation to the Bible*, 1885; besides many scientific memoirs in proceedings of societies, etc.

DAY, George Edward, D.D. (Marietta College, 1856), Congregationalist; b. at Pittsfield, Mass., March 19, 1815; graduated at Yale College 1833; was instructor two years in the New-York Institution for the Deaf and Dumb; graduated at the Yale Divinity School 1838, in which he was assistant instructor in sacred literature from 1838 to 1840. For the next ten years he was a Congregational pastor, first in Marlborough, and then Northampton, Mass. From 1851 to 1866 he was professor of biblical literature in Lane (Presbyterian) Theological Seminary, Cincinnati, O.; and since then has been professor of the Hebrew language and biblical theology in the Yale Divinity School (Congregational), New Haven, Conn.; was secretary, from its organization, of the American Bible Revision Committee, in which he served as a member of the Old-Testament Company. He published two extended reports of his personal examination of the condition of deaf-mute instruction in Europe, especially in regard to mechanical articulation, 1845 and 1861; established and edited *The Theological Eclectic*, a repertory of foreign theological literature, 1863-70, for which he translated from the Dutch, and also published separately, Van Oosterzee's *Biblical Theology of the New Testament*, 1871. He also translated, with additions, Van Oosterzee on *Titus*, for Dr. Schaff's edition of Lange's *Commentary*, New York; and edited the American issue of Oehler's *Biblical Theology of the Old Testament*, with an introduction and additional notes, 1883.

DAY, Right Rev. Maurice Fitzgerald, D.D. (Trinity College, Dublin, 1867), Lord Bishop of Cashel, Emly, Waterford, and Lismore, Church of Ireland; b. at Kiltullagh, County Kerry, Ireland, in the year 1816; educated at Trinity College, Dublin; graduated B.A. 1838, M.A. 1858, B.D. 1867; was vicar of St. Matthias, Dublin, 1843-68; dean of Limerick, 1868-72; prebendary of Glankeel in Cashel Cathedral since 1872; consecrated bishop, 1872. He is the author of *The Gospel at Philippi: Sermons preached in St. Matthias Church*, Dublin, 1865, 3d ed. 1876; *The Church: Sermons preached in Limerick Cathedral*, 1870. *

DEANE, Henry, Church of England; b. at Gillingham, Dorset, July 27, 1838; was scholar of Winchester College, 1851; fellow of St. John's College, Oxford, 1856; graduated B.A. (first-class mathematics) 1860, M.A. 1864, B.D. 1869; was ordained deacon 1863, priest 1866; was curate of St. Thomas, Salisbury, 1863-67; of St. Giles, Oxford, 1867-74; mathematical public examiner at Oxford 1868-69, theological 1873-74; senior proctor of the university, 1870-71; vicar of St. Giles, Oxford, since 1874; since 1874 has been assistant lecturer to the regius professor of Hebrew; since 1883, lecturer on Shemitic languages in Wadham College; and since 1885, examiner in theology at the University of Durham. He is a fellow of the Society of Antiquaries. He edited the third book of Irenæus, Oxford, 1874; contributed to Blunt's *Dictionary of Theology*, London, 1868; Cassell's *Bible Educator*, 1875; a commentary on *Jeremiah* (1879) to the S. P. C. K. commentary, and one on *Daniel* (1883) to Bishop Ellicott's.

DEANE, William John, Church of England; b. at Lymington, Hants, Oct. 6, 1823; educated at Oriel College, Oxford; graduated B.A. 1847, M.A. 1872; was ordained deacon 1847, priest 1849; was curate of Rugby 1847–49, of Wyck-Ryssington 1849–52; rector of South Thoresby, Lincolnshire, 1852–53; and since 1853 has been rector of Ashen, Essex. Besides various articles, he has published *Catechism of the Holy Days*, London, 1850, 3d ed. 1886; *Lyra Sanctorum, Lays for the Minor Festivals of the English Church*, 1850; *Manual of Household Prayer*, 1857; *Proper Lessons from the Old Testament, with a Plain Commentary*, 1864; *The Book of Wisdom, with Introduction, Critical Apparatus, and Commentary*, Oxford, 1881.

DE COSTA, Benjamin Franklin, D.D. (William and Mary College, 1881), Episcopalian; b. at Charlestown, Mass., July 10, 1831; graduated at Wilbraham Seminary and Biblical Institute, Concord, N.H. (now part of Boston University), 1856; studied and travelled three years on the Continent; was rector in Massachusetts; chaplain of the 5th and 18th Mass. Vol. Infantry, 1861–62; became rector of St. John Evangelist's, New-York City, 1880. He edited *The Christian Times*, 1863, and *The Magazine of American History*, 1882-83, both published in New-York City. He was first secretary of the Church Temperance Society, 1881; inaugurated the White Cross movement, 1884; and belongs to many learned societies at home and abroad. He is a quite voluminous author, mostly in American history. Among his publications in book form may be mentioned *Pre-Columbian Discovery of America by the Northmen*, Albany, 1869; *The Moabite Stone*, New York, 1870; *The Rector of Roxburgh* (a novel under *nom de plume* of William Hickling), 1873; edited White's *Memoirs of the Protestant-Episcopal Church*, 1881; contributed to Bishop Perry's *History of the American Episcopal Church 1587–1883*, Boston, 1885, 2 vols.; and to *The Narrative and Critical History of America*, 1886, *sqq.*, 8 vols. 8vo.

DEEMS, Charles Force, D.D. (Randolph-Macon College, Ashland, Va., 1850), **LL.D.** (University of North Carolina, Chapel Hill, 1877); b. at Baltimore, Md., Dec. 4, 1820; graduated from Dickinson College, Carlisle, Penn., 1839; entered the ministry of the Methodist Church (South); was general agent of the American Bible Society for North Carolina, 1840–41; professor of logic and rhetoric in the University of North Carolina, 1842–45; and of chemistry in Randolph-Macon College, Va., 1845–46; president of Greensborough Female College, 1850–55; and since 1866 pastor of the Church of the Strangers, an Independent congregation, in New-York City. He edited *The Southern Methodist-Episcopal Pulpit* from 1846–51, and *The Annals of Southern Methodism*, 1849–52; *The Sunday Magazine*, published by Frank Leslie, 1876–79; and since 1883 *Christian Thought*, the organ of the American Institute of Christian Philosophy, of which he was principal founder, and has been from the beginning (1881) president. He has published *Triumph of Peace, and other Poems*, New York, 1840; *Life of Adam Clarke, LL.D.*, 1840; *Devotional Melodies*, Raleigh, N.C., 1842; *Twelve College Sermons*, Philadelphia, 1844; *The Home Altar*, New York, 1850, 3d ed. 1881; *What Now?* New York, 1853; *Hymns for all Christians*, 1869, new ed. 1881; *Forty Sermons preached in the Church of the Strangers*, 1871; *Jesus*, 1872, new ed. (with title, *The Light of the Nations*), 1880; *Weights and Wings*, 1872, new ed. 1878; *Sermons*, 1885.

DE HOOP SCHEFFER. — See HOOP SCHEFFER.

DELITZSCH, Franz, D.D., German Lutheran theologian; b. at Leipzig, Feb. 23, 1813 (of Hebrew descent); studied there, took degree of Ph.D., and became *privat-docent*; went thence as ordinary professor to Rostock 1846, thence to Erlangen 1850, and back to Leipzig in 1867, and has since been of that faculty. By reason of his preeminent attainments in biblical and post-biblical Hebrew, he has been styled "the Christian Talmudist." His writings are of great value, especially his commentaries, — *Der Prophet Habakuk*, Leipzig, 1843; in the Keil and Delitzsch series, *Job*, 1864, 2d ed. 1876 (English trans., Edinburgh, 1866, 2 vols.); *Die Psalmen*, 1869, 3d ed. 1874 (English trans. 1871, 3 vols.); *Das Salomonische Spruchbuch*, 1873 (English trans. 1875, 2 vols.); *Hohelied und Koheleth*, 1875 (English trans. 1877); *Jesaia*, 1866, 3d ed. 1879 (English trans. 1867, 2 vols.); independently, *Genesis*, 1852, 4th ed. 1872; *Hebrews*, 1857 (English trans. 1870, 2 vols.). His other publications include *Zur Gesch. d. jüd. Poesie v. Abschluss d. A. B. bis auf die neuste Zeit*, 1836; *Jesurun sive prolegomenon in Concordantias V. T. a Fuerstio*, Grimma, 1838; *Anekdota zur Geschichte der mittelalterlichen Scholastik unter Juden und Moslemen*, Leipzig, 1841; *Das Sacrament des wahren Leibes und Blutes Jesu Christi*, Dresden, 1844, 7th ed. Leipzig, 1886; *Die biblisch-prophetische Theologie*, Leipzig, 1845; *Vier Bücher von der Kirche*, Dresden, 1847; *Neue Untersuchungen über Entstehung und Anlage der kanonischen Evangelien*, Leipzig, 1853 (only first part, on Matthew, has appeared); *System der biblischen Psychologie*, 1855, 2d ed. 1861 (English trans., *A System of Biblical Psychology*, Edinburgh, 1867); *Jesus und Hillel*, Erlangen, 1867, 3d ed. 1879; *Handwerkerleben zur Zeit Jesu*, 1868, 3d ed. 1878 (English trans. of the two, by Mrs. P. Monkhouse, *Jewish Artisan Life in the Time of our Lord; to which is appended a critical comparison between Jesus and Hillel*, London, 1877, and of the *Artisan Life* alone, from 3d ed. by Croll, Philadelphia, 1883, and by Pick, New York, 1883); *Sehet welch ein Mensch!* Leipzig, 1869, 2d ed. 1872; *System der christlichen Apologetik*, 1869; *Paulus des Apostels Brief an die Römer aus d. Griech. ins Hebr. übersetzt u. aus d. Talmud u. Midrasch erläutert*, 1870; *Ein Tag in Capernaum*, 1871; *Complutensische Varianten zum A. T. Texte*, 1878; *Rohling's Talmudjude beleuchtet*, 1881 (7th ed. same year); *Was D. Aug. Rohling beschworen hat und beschwören will*, 1883 (2d ed. same year); *Schachmatt, den Blutlügnern Rohling u. Justus entboten*, Erlangen, 1883; *Die Bibel und der Wein*, Leipzig, 1885 (pp. 18), cf. *Expositor*, January, 1886. In connection with S. Baer, he has issued revised Hebrew texts of *Genesis*, *Ezra*, *Nehemiah*, *Job*, the *Psalms*, *Proverbs*, *Isaiah*, *Ezekiel*, *Daniel*, and the minor prophets, Leipzig, 1861-84. Dr. Delitzsch's excellent translation of the entire New Testament into Hebrew (1877, 4th ed. 1882) is circulated by the British and Foreign Bible Society. See art. CURTISS, p. 47. His son is *

DELITZSCH, Friedrich, Ph.D. (Leipzig); b. at Erlangen, Sept. 3, 1850; became professor of Assyriology at Leipzig, 1877. He is the author of *Assyrische Studien*, Leipzig, 1874; *Assyrische Lesestücke*, 1878; *Wo lag das Paradies?* 1881; *The Hebrew Language viewed in the Light of Assyrian Research*, London, 1883; *Die Sprache der Kossäer*, 1884; *Studien über indogermanisch-semitische Wurzelverwandtschaft*, 1884. *

DEMAREST, David D., D.D. (College of New Jersey, 1857), Reformed (Dutch); b. in Harrington township, Bergen County, N.J., July 30, 1819; graduated from Rutgers College, New Brunswick, N.J., 1837, and from the Reformed Dutch Theological Seminary there, 1840; became pastor of the Reformed Dutch Church of Flatbush, Ulster County, N.Y., 1841; (the Second) of New Brunswick, N.J., 1843; of Hudson, N.Y., 1852; professor of pastoral theology and sacred rhetoric in the Theological Seminary of New Brunswick, 1865. He has published, besides occasional addresses, *History and Characteristics of the Reformed Dutch Church*, New York, 1856, 3d ed. n. d.; *Practical Catechetics*, 1882.

DEMAREST, John Terheun, D.D. (Rutgers College, N.J., 1851), Reformed (Dutch); b. at Teaneck, near Hackensack, N.J., Feb. 20, 1813; graduated at Rutgers College 1834, and at the New Brunswick Theological Seminary 1837; was pastor at New Prospect, N.Y., 1837-49, 1869-71, 1873-85 (*emeritus*, April 21, 1885); at Minisink, N.J., 1850-52; at Pascack, N.J., 1854-67; principal of Harrisburg Academy, 1852-54. He is a Calvinistic premillenarian. He has written *Exposition of the Efficient Cause of Regeneration, the Duty and Manner of Preaching to the Unrenewed, and the Doctrine of Election*, New Brunswick, N.J., 1842; *Translation and Exposition of the First Epistle of Peter*, New York, 1851; *Commentary on the Second Epistle of Peter*, 1862; (with W. R. Gordon) *Christocracy, or Essays on the Coming and Kingdom of Christ, with Answers to the Principal Objections of Post-Millenarians*, 1867, 2d ed. 1878; *A Commentary on the Catholic Epistles*, 1879.

DENIO, Francis Brigham, Congregationalist; b. at Enosburg, Franklin County, Vt., May 4, 1848; graduated at Middlebury College, Vt., 1871, and at Andover Theological Seminary, 1879; became instructor in New-Testament Greek in Bangor Theological Seminary, Me., 1879, and professor of Old-Testament language and literature in the same institution, 1882.

DENISON, Ven. George Anthony, archdeacon of Taunton, Church of England; b. at Ossington, Nottinghamshire, Eng., Dec. 11, 1805; educated at Christ Church, Oxford; graduated B.A (first-class in classics) 1826; M.A., fellow of Oriel, and Latin essayist (University prize), 1828; English essayist (do.), 1829; was ordained deacon and priest, 1832; from 1832 till 1838 was curate to the bishop of Oxford; in the latter year he resigned his fellowship, and became vicar of Broadwinsor, Dorset, and so remained until 1845, when he became vicar of East Brent, and also examining chaplain to the bishop of Bath and Wells, who in 1851 made him archdeacon of Taunton, and these two positions he has held ever since. The archdeacon is an "English Catholic," or, as such are commonly called, an "ultra High Churchman." From 1839 to 1870 he was prominent as a Church champion in the school controversy as between the Church of England and the civil power, which resulted in the Elementary Education Act, the final and decisive victory of the latter; was from 1854 to 1858 publicly prosecuted for maintaining the real presence, but the prosecution ultimately failed. His publications consist of a large number of pamphlets, sermons, charges, letters, etc., and the following volumes: *Proceedings against the Archdeacon of Taunton*, London, 1854, 1855, 1856; *Defence of the Archdeacon of Taunton*, 1856; *Final Paper put in in Defence*, October, 1856; *Church Rate a National Trust*, 1861; *Notes of my Life, 1805-78*, 1878, 3d ed. 1879. He translated from the manuscript in the British Museum *Saravia on the Holy Eucharist*, 1855.

DENTON, William, Church of England; b. at Carisbrook, Isle of Wight, March 1, 1815; educated at Worcester College, Oxford; graduated B.A. 1844, M.A. 1848; was ordained deacon 1844, priest 1845; curate from 1844-50, and since 1850 vicar of St. Bartholomew, Cripplegate, London. His writings upon the condition of the Christian people of Servia and Montenegro, the result of personal investigations, won him the recognition of the Servian king, who gave him the grand cross of the Order of St. Saba (Servia), and cross of the Saviour of Takova (Servia). He has published *Commentary on the Sunday and Saints'-Day Gospels in the Communion Office*, London, 1861-63, 3 vols., 3d ed. 1875-80; *Servia and the Servians*, 1862; *The Christians under Mussulman Rule*, 1863, 3d ed. 1877; *Commentary on the Lord's Prayer*, 1864; *Commentary on the Sunday and Saints'-Day Epistles in the Communion Office*, 1869-71, 2 vols., 2d ed. 1873-77; *Commentary on the Acts of the Apostles*, 1874-76, 2 vols.; *Montenegro: its People and their History*, 1877; *Records of St. Giles's, Cripplegate*, 1883; *The Antient Church in Egypt*, 1883.

DE PUY, William Harrison, D.D. (Union College, Schenectady, N.Y., 1869), **LL.D.** (Mount Union College, Ohio, 1884), Methodist; b. at Penn Yan, N.Y., Oct. 31, 1821; graduated at Genesee College, Lima, N.Y.; taught in several institutions; was professor of mathematics and natural philosophy in Genesee Wesleyan Seminary 1851-55, being before and after a pastor; was associate editor of *The Christian Advocate*, New York, 1865-84. He edits *The Methodist Year Book*, and has published *Threescore Years and Beyond, or Experiences of the Aged*, New York, 1872; and the valuable *Methodist Centennial Year Book, 1784-1884*, 1884. He is also the author of *Home and Health* and *Home Economics*, 1880 (170,000 copies sold up to 1886); editor of *The People's Cyclopedia of Universal Knowledge*, 3 vols., super royal 8vo, 1882 (100,000 sets sold up to 1886); and *The People's Atlas of the World*, 1886.

DE SCHWEINITZ. — See SCHWEINITZ.

DEUTSCH, Samuel Martin, Lic. Theol. (Jena, 1866), United Evangelical; b. at Warsaw, Feb. 19, 1837; studied at Erlangen 1854-56, Rostock

1856-57; became gymnasial teacher in Berlin, 1857; professor extraordinary of theology in Berlin University, 1885. He is the author of *Des Ambrosius Lehre von der Sünde und der Sündentilgung*, Berlin, 1867; *Drei Actenstücke zur Geschichte des Donatismus*, 1875; *Die Synode zu Sens (1141) und die Verurteilung Abälards*, 1880; *Peter Abälard, ein kritischer Theologe des 12. Jahrhunderts*, Leipzig, 1883; *Luthers These vom Jahre 1519 über die päpstliche Gewalt*, Berlin, 1884.

DE WITT, John, D.D. (Rutgers College, 1860), Reformed (Dutch); b. at Albany, N.Y., Nov. 29, 1821; graduated at Rutgers College 1838, and at the Reformed Dutch Theological Seminary, both in New Brunswick, N.J., 1842; pastor of the Reformed Dutch Church at Ridgeway, Lenawee County, Mich., 1842-44 (he was its first pastor); at Ghent, N.Y., 1844-49; at Canajoharie, N.Y., 1849-50; at Millstone (Hillsborough), N.J., 1850-63; professor of Oriental literature at New Brunswick, 1863-84; and since 1884 of Hellenistic Greek and New-Testament exegesis. He was one of the Old-Testament Revision Company from its formation. He is the author of *The Sure Foundation, and How to Build on it*, New York, 1848, new ed. 1860; *The Praise Songs of Israel, a New Rendering of the Book of Psalms*, 1884, 2d and revised ed. 1885.

DE WITT, John, D.D. (Princeton, 1877), Presbyterian; b. at Harrisburg, Penn., Oct. 10, 1842; graduated at the College of New Jersey, 1861; studied at Princeton and Union Theological Seminaries, 1861-65; became pastor of Presbyterian Church, Irvington, N.Y., 1865; of Congregational Central Church, Boston, 1869; of Tenth Presbyterian Church, Philadelphia, 1876; professor of church history in Lane Theological Seminary (Presbyterian), Cincinnati, O., 1882. He is the author of *Sermons on the Christian Life*, New York, 1885.

DEXTER, Henry Martyn, D.D. (Iowa College, 1865), **S.T.D.** (Yale, 1880), Congregationalist; b. at Plympton, Mass., Aug. 13, 1821; graduated at Yale College 1840, and at Andover Theological Seminary 1844; became pastor at Manchester, N.H., 1844; in Boston, 1849 (also editor of *The Congregationalist* 1851-66, and of *The Congregational Quarterly*, 1859-66); resigned pastoral charge to be editor of *The Congregationalist and Recorder*, 1867. From 1877 to 1880 he was lecturer on Congregationalism at Andover Theological Seminary; since 1869 he has been member of the American Antiquarian and Massachusetts Historical Societies, since 1884 of the American Historical Association. Besides contributions to *The New-Englander*, *The New-England Historic-Genealogical Register*, *The British Quarterly*, the *Memorial History of Boston*, the *Encyclopædia Britannica*, the *Schaff-Herzog*, etc., he has written *The Moral Influence of Manufacturing Towns*, Andover, 1848; *The Temperance Duties of the Temperate*, Boston, 1850; *Our National Condition and its Remedy*, 1856; *The Voice of the Bible the Verdict of Reason*, 1858; *Street Thoughts*, 1859; *Twelve Discourses*, 1860; *What Ought to be Done with the Freedmen and the Rebels?* 1865; *Congregationalism: What it is, Whence it is, How it Works, Why it is better than any other Form of Church Government; and its Consequent Demands*, 1865, 5th ed. 1879; *The Verdict of Reason upon the Question of the Future Punishment of Those who Die Impenitent*, 1865; *Mourt's Relation*, 1865; *Church's Philip's War* (both edited with notes), 1865; *The Spread of the Gospel in the City among the Poor who habitually neglect the Sanctuary*, 1866; *Church's Eastern Expeditions* (edited with notes), 1867; *A Glance at the Ecclesiastical Councils of New England*, 1867; *The Church Polity of the Pilgrims the Polity of the New Testament*, 1870; *Pilgrim Memoranda*, 1870; *As to Roger Williams, and his "Banishment" from the Massachusetts Colony*, 1876, 2d ed. 1877; *The Congregationalism of the last Three Hundred Years, as seen in its Literature: with Special Reference to Certain Recondite, Neglected, or Disputed Passages: with a Bibliographical Appendix*, New York, 1880; *A Handbook of Congregationalism*, Boston, 1880; Roger Williams's *Christenings make not Christians: a Long-lost Tract recovered and exactly reprinted, and edited*, Providence, 1881; *The True Story of John Smyth, the Se-Baptist, as told by himself and his Contemporaries, with an Inquiry whether dipping were a new Mode of Baptism in England in or about 1641; and some consideration of the historical value of certain extracts from the alleged "Ancient Records" of the Baptist Church of Epworth, Crowle and Butterwick, England, lately published, and claimed to suggest important modifications of the history of the seventeenth century; with collections toward a bibliography of the first two generations of the Baptist controversy*, 1881; *Common Sense as to Woman Suffrage*, 1885.

DICKSON, William Purdie, D.D. (St. Andrew's, 1865), **LL.D.** (Edinburgh, 1885), Church of Scotland; b. at Pettinain Manse, Lanarkshire, Scotland, Oct. 22, 1823; graduated at the University of St. Andrew's, 1851; became minister of the parish of Cameron, Fife, 1851; professor in the University of Glasgow, of biblical criticism 1863, and of divinity 1873. Since 1874 he has been convener of the Education Committee of the Church of Scotland, having charge of the training colleges in Edinburgh, Glasgow, and Aberdeen; and since 1866 the curator of the university library of Glasgow, and hence superintendent of the preparation of the new printed catalogue, of which the alphabetic form was completed in 1885, in twenty volumes, and of the seventeen volumes of the subject catalogue already issued. Besides various articles in Fairbairn's *Imperial Bible Dictionary*, Smith's *Dictionary of Christian Biography*, *The Academy*, *The Expositor*, etc., he has published a translation of Mommsen's *History of Rome*, London, 1862-66, 4 vols., revised ed. 1868; and of Meyer's *Commentary on the New Testament*, Edinburgh, 1873-80, 16 vols. (of which ten were revised by him throughout); *St. Paul's Use of the Terms Flesh and Spirit* (Baird lecture for 1883), Glasgow, 1883.

DIECKHOFF, August Wilhelm, Lic. Theol. (Göttingen, 1850), **D.D.** (*hon.*, Greifswald, 1856), a strict Lutheran theologian; b. at Göttingen, Germany, Feb. 5, 1823; studied at Göttingen, where he became ordinary professor of theology, 1854; since 1860 he has held the same position, together with the directorship of the homiletical and catechetical seminary at Rostock; since 1882 he has been *Consistorial-Rath*. From 1860 to 1864 he edited (with Kliefoth) the *Theolog. Zeitschrift*; in Berlin, 1864, he issued Dieterici's *Institutiones* *catecheticæ*. He is the author of *Die Waldenser im Mittelalter*, Göttingen, 1851; *Die evangelische Abendmahlslehre im Reformationszeitalter geschichtlich dargestellt*. 1. Bd. 1854; *Die evangelisch-lutherische Lehre von der heiligen Schrift gegen v. Hofmann's Lehre von der heiligen Schrift und vom kirchlichen Wort Gottes vertheidigt*, Schwerin, 1858; *Der Sieg des Christenthums über das Heidenthum unter Constantin d. Gr.*, 1863; *Luthers Lehre von der kirchlichen Gewalt*, Berlin, 1864; *Schrift und Tradition. Eine Widerlegung der römischen Lehre vom unfehlbaren Lehramte und der römischen Einwürfe gegen das evangel. Schriftprincip, mit besond. Beziehung auf die Schrift des Freiherrn v. Ketteler, Bischop von Mainz: "Das allgemeine Concil und seine Bedeutung für unsere Zeit,"* Rostock, 1870; *Der Schlusssatz der Marburger Artikel und seine Bedeutung für die richtige Beurtheilung des Verhältnisses der Confessionskirchen zu einander*, 1872; *Staat und Kirche. Principielle Betrachtungen über das Verhältniss beider zu einander aus dem Gesichtspunkte des christlichen Staats nebst einer Anhang über das neue preuss-Schulaufsichtsgesetz*, Leipzig, 1872; *Die obligatorische Civilehe*, 1873; *Die kirchliche Trauung, ihre Geschichte im Zusammenhange mit der Entwickelung des Eheschliessungsrechts und ihr Verhältniss zur Civilehe*, Rostock, 1878; *Civilehe und kirchliche Trauung. Das Gegensatzverhältniss zwischen beiden dargelegt*, 1880; *Justin, Augustin, Bernhard und Luther. Der Entwickelungsgang christlicher Wahrheitserfassung in der Kirche als Beweis für die Lehre der Reformation* (five lectures), Leipzig, 1882; *Die Menschwerdung des Sohnes Gottes. Ein Votum über die Theologie Ritschl's*, 1882; *Die Stellung der theologischen Fakultäten zur Kirche*, 1883; *Die Stellung Luthers zur Kirche und ihrer Reformation in der Zeit vor dem Ablassstreit*, Rostock, 1883; *Luthers Recht gegen Rom*, 1883; *Der missourische Prädestinatianismus und die Concordienformel. Eine Entgegnung auf zwei Gegenschriften gegen das Erachten der theologischen Facultät zu Rostock*, 1885; *Der Ablassstreit dogmengeschichtlich dargestellt*, Gotha, 1886.

DIKE, Samuel Fuller, D.D. (Bowdoin, 1872), Swedenborgian; b. at North Bridgewater (now Brockton), Mass., March 17, 1815; graduated at Brown University, Rhode Island, 1838; has been pastor of the Society of the New Jerusalem, Bath, Me., since 1840; is teacher of church history in the Theological School of the General Convention of the New Church, Boston, and has always taken a prominent part in Maine educational interests. He has published *Doctrine of the Lord in the Primitive Christian Church*, Boston, 1870, and various occasional and fugitive pieces.

DIKE, Samuel Warren, Congregationalist; b. at Thompson, Conn., Feb. 13, 1839; graduated at Williams College 1863, and at Andover 1866; was pastor of the Congregational churches at West Randolph (1868-77) and at Royalton, Vt. (1880-83); since 1881 secretary first of the New-England, then of the National Divorce Reform League. He lectured at Andover Theological Seminary in 1885, upon the family and social problems. He is the author of *Some Aspects of the Divorce Question*, in *The Andover Review*, 1884-85; *The Family in the History of Christianity*, N.Y. 1885; and in charge of the department of "Sociological Notes" in the *Andover Review*, 1886, *sqq.*

DILLMANN (Christian Friedrich) August, Ph.D. (Tübingen, 1846), **D.D.** (*hon.*, Leipzig, 1862), Evangelical Lutheran; b. at Illingen, Würtemberg, April 25, 1823; studied in the seminary at Schönthal, 1836-40; at Tübingen, 1840-45; was assistant pastor at Sersheim, Würtemberg, 1845-46; travelled and studied, especially Ethiopic, at Paris, London, and Oxford, 1846-48; became *repetent* (i.e., tutor for three years) at Tübingen, 1848; *privat-docent* for Old-Testament exegesis in the theological faculty, 1852; professor extraordinary of theology, 1853; professor of the Oriental languages in the philosophical faculty at Kiel, 1854; professor of theology at Giessen, 1864; and at Berlin, 1869. He has published *Catalogus codicum orientalium MSS. qui in Museo Britannico asservantur. P. III. Codices Æthiopicos amplectens*, London, 1847; *Catalogus codicum manuscriptorum Bibliothecæ Bodleianæ Oxoniensis. P. VII. Codices Æthiopici, digessit A. Dillmann*, Oxford, 1848; *Liber Henoch, Æthiopice*, Leipzig, 1851; *Das Buch Henoch übersetzt u. erklärt*, 1853; *Das christliche Adambuch des Morgenlandes, aus dem Æthiopischen übersetzt* (reprinted from Ewald's *Jahrbücher*), 1853; *Biblia Veteris Testamenti Æthiopica*, Tomus I. *Octateuchus*. Fasc. 1, *Genesin, Exodum, Leviticum* (1853). Fasc. 2, *Numeros et Deuteronomium* (1854). Fasc. 3, *Josua, Judicum et Ruth* (1855). Tomus II Fasc. 1 et 2, *Libri Regum* (1861 and 1871); *Grammatik der æthiopischen Sprache*, 1857; *Liber Jubilæorum, Æthiopice*, 1859; *Lexicon linguæ Æthiopicæ*, 1865; *Chrestomathia Æthiopica cum glossario*, 1866; *Erklärung des B. Hiob* (1869), *Genesis* (1875, 3d ed. 1886), *Exodus u. Leviticus* (1880), and *Numeri, Deuteronomium u. Josua* (1886), — these commentaries are all in the *Kurzgefassten exegetischen Handbuch* series; *Ascensio Isaiæ, Æthiopice et Latine*, 1877; *Verzeichniss d. abessinischen Hdschr. d. k. Bibliothek zu Berlin*, Berlin, 1878; *Verhandlungen des V.ten internationalen Orientalisten Congresses in Berlin*, 1881; *Das Buch der Jubiläen oder die kleine Genesis, aus dem Aethiopischen übersetzt* (in Ewald's *Jahrbücher der bibl. Wissenschaft*, Göttingen, 1849-51); numerous articles, academical addresses, etc.

DITTRICH, Franz, D.D. (Munich, 1865), Roman Catholic; b. at Thegsten near Heilsberg, East Prussia, Jan. 26, 1839; studied philosophy and theology at Braunsberg; became priest, 1863; continued his theological studies at Rome and Munich; became *privat-docent* at Braunsberg 1866, professor extraordinary 1868, ordinary professor of theology 1873. He is the author of *Dionysius der Grosse von Alexandrien*, Freiburg-im-Breisgau, 1867.

DIX, Morgan, S.T.D. (Columbia, 1862), **D.C.L.** (University of the South, 1885), Episcopalian; b. in New-York City, Nov. 1, 1827; graduated at Columbia College, N.Y., 1848, and at the General Theological Seminary, 1852; became assistant minister of St. Mark's Church, Philadelphia, 1853, and of Trinity Church, New York, 1855; assistant rector of Trinity 1859, and rector 1862. He is president of the Standing Committee of the Diocese of New York; deputy to General Convention; trustee (*ex officio*) of Sailors' Snug Harbor, and of Leake and Watts Orphan House, and president of the board; trustee of General Theological Seminary (and chairman of Standing Committee) of Columbia College, of the Society for promoting Religion and Learning, of House of Mercy, Church Orphan Home, Home for Incurables, St. Stephen's College (Annandale, N.Y.), Hobart College (Geneva, N.Y.), Corporation for Relief of Widows and Orphans of Clergymen, Home for Old Men and Aged Couples; vice-president of N. Y. P. E. Public School; executor of three estates and two private trusts, etc. He has published, besides many single sermons, lectures, and articles, *Manual of the Christian Life*, New York, 1857, new ed. (16th thousand) 1884; *Commentary on Romans*, 1864; *on Galatians and Colossians*, 1866; *Lectures on the Pantheistic Idea of an Impersonal-Substance Deity, as contrasted with the Christian Faith concerning Almighty God*, 1865; *Book of Hours*, 1865, new ed. 1881; *Manual for Confirmation Classes*, 18th thousand, 1885; *Lectures on the Two Estates, that of the Wedded in the Lord, and that of the Single for the Kingdom of Heaven's Sake*, 1872; *Historical Lectures on the First Prayer Book of King Edward VI.*, 1881, 4th ed. 1885; *Sermons*, 1878 (two American and two English editions); *Lectures on the Calling of a Christian Woman, and her Training to fulfil it*, 1883, 6th thousand 1885; *Memoir of John A. Dix* (his father), 1883, 2 vols.

DIXON, Richard Watson, Church of England; b. at Islington, London, May 5, 1833; educated at Pembroke College, Oxford; graduated B.A. (third-class in classics) 1857, M.A. 1860; won the Arnold prize essay, 1858, and the Cramer prize sacred poem, 1863; was ordained deacon 1858, priest 1859; became curate of St. Mary the Less, Lambeth, 1858; of St. Mary, Newington-Butts, 1861; second master of Carlisle high school, 1863; minor canon and honorary librarian of Carlisle Cathedral, 1868; vicar of Hayton with Talkin, Cumberland, 1875; of Warkworth, 1883; since 1874 an honorary canon of Carlisle; and from 1879 to 1883 was rural dean of Brampton; and since 1885 rural dean of Alnwick. He is the grandson of Richard Watson, the famous Wesleyan theologian. At Oxford he associated with William Morris and Edward Burne Jones in issuing *The Oxford and Cambridge Magazine*, in 1856, which advocated pre-Raphaelite principles. He is the author of *Christ's Company, and other Poems*, London, 1861; *Historical Odes, and other Poems*, 1863; *Second Peak Prize Essay on the Maintenance of the Church of England as an Established Church*, 1873; *Life of James Dixon, D.D.* (his father), *Wesleyan Minister*, 1874; *History of the Church of England from the Abolition of the Roman Jurisdiction*, vol. i. (1529-37) 1877, vol. ii. (1538-48) 1880, vol. iii. (1549-53) 1885; *Mano, a Poetical History*, 1883; *Odes and Eclogues*, Oxford, 1884.

DOANE, Right Rev. William Croswell, S.T.D. (Columbia College, New-York City, 1869), **LL.D.** (Union College, New York, 1880), the son of Bishop G. W. Doane of New Jersey, Episcopalian, bishop of Albany; b. in Boston, Mass., March 2, 1832; graduated at Burlington College, N.J., 1850; was professor in the college, 1850-63; rector of St Mary's, Burlington, 1859-63; of St. John's, Hartford, Conn., 1863-67; of St. Peter's, Albany, N.Y., 1867-69; consecrated bishop 1869. Besides many sermons and pamphlets, he has issued *The Life and Writings of Bishop Doane of New Jersey*, New York, 1860, 4 vols.; *Questions on Collects, Epistles, and Gospels of the Church's Year; and their Connection*, Philadelphia, 18—; *Songs by the Way* (poems by Bishop G. W. Doane), Albany, 1875; *Mosaics; or, The Harmony of Collect, Epistle, and Gospel for the Christian Year*, New York, 1882.

DODD, Thomas John, D.D. (Centre College, Danville, Ky., 187-), Methodist; b. at Harper's Ferry, Va., Aug. 4, 1837; graduated at Transylvania University, Lexington, Ky., 1857; became Methodist pastor, 1860; president Kentucky Wesleyan College, 1875; professor of Hebrew, Vanderbilt University, Nashville, Tenn., 1876; resigned in 1885, and took charge of a select high school of collegiate course in that city.

DODGE, Ebenezer, D.D. (Brown University, 1861), **LL.D.** (University of Chicago, 1869), Baptist; b. at Salem, Mass., April 22, 1819; graduated at Brown University, Providence, R.I., 1840, and at Newton Theological Institute, Mass., 1845; became pastor at New London, N.H., 1846; professor of biblical criticism in Hamilton Theological Seminary, 1853, of Christian theology 1861, president since 1871; professor of evidences of Christianity in Madison University, Hamilton, N.Y., 1853-61, president since 1868. He has published *Evidences of Christianity*, Boston, 1869, last ed. 1876; *Christian Theology*, Hamilton, N.Y., last ed. 1884.

DODS, Marcus, D.D. (Edinburgh University, 1872), Free Church of Scotland; b. at Belford, Northumberland, Eng., April 11, 1834; graduated M.A. at Edinburgh University, 1854; studied theology at New College, Edinburgh, 1854-58; was licensed to preach the same year, and for the next six years preached in various places, but was not settled or ordained until he came to his present charge, the Renfield Free Church, Glasgow, August, 1864. He has been nominated for chairs of systematic theology and of apologetics in Free Church College, Edinburgh. He has published *The Prayer that teaches to pray*, Edinburgh, 1863, 5th ed. 1885; *The Epistles to the Seven Churches*, 1865, 2d ed. 1885; *Israel's Iron Age*, London, 1874, 4th ed. 1885; *Mohammed, Buddha, and Christ*, 1877, 4th ed. 1886; *Handbook on Haggai, Zechariah, and Malachi*, Edinburgh, 1879, last ed. 1885; *Isaac, Jacob, and Joseph*, London, 1880, last ed. 1884; *Handbook on Genesis*, Edinburgh, 1882; *Commentary on Thessalonians* (in vol. iii. Schaff's *Popular Commentary*), 1882; *The Parables of our Lord*, 1st series 1883, 2d ed. 1884, 2d series 1885. He edited the English translation of Lange's *Life of Christ*, Edinburgh, 1864 *sq.*, 6 vols., and of Augustin's works, 1872-76; and Clark's series of *Handbooks for Bible Classes*, 1879 *sqq.*; contributed translation of Justin Martyr's *Apologies*, and other portions of Greek writers, to Clark's *Ante-Nicene Christian Library*, and the articles *Pelagius* and *Predestination* to the 9th ed. *Encyclopædia Britannica*.

DOEDES, Jacobus Izaäc, D.D. (Utrecht, 1841), Reformed; b. at Langerak, Zuid Holland, Nederland, Nov. 20, 1817; educated at the Latin school of Amsterdam, 1830-34; and at the University of Utrecht, 1834-41; graduated as doctor of theology, June 16, 1841; became preacher in the Reformed Church at Hall, near Zutfen, 1843; at Rotterdam, 1847; professor of theology in the University of Utrecht, 1859. He teaches New-Testament exegesis, hermeneutics, and encyclopædia. He is a theistic and supernaturalistic theologian; and has vigorously opposed the theological school of Groningen, and the so-called "modern theology." In 1843 he received the prize of the Teyler Society, for his essay upon the textual criticism of the New Testament (see below). With Dr. J. J. Van Oosterzee and two other scholars, he issued the *Jaarboeken voor Wetenschappelijke Theologie*, 1845–57; with Dr. N. Beets and Dr. D. Chantepie de la Saussaye, the *Ernst en Vrede. Maandschrift voor de Nederlandsche Hervormde Kerk*, 1853 *sqq.*; and alone, the *Evangeliebode* (religious weekly), 1849–55; the *Kerklijke Bijdragen* (essays on church law questions), Harderwijk, 1872, two parts. In 1867 he made the report upon the religious condition of Holland, to the Amsterdam (fifth) Conference of the Evangelical Alliance. He is the author of *Diss. theol. Jesu in vitam reditu*, Utrecht, 1841; *Verhandeling over de Tekstkritiek van de Schriften des Nieuwen Verbonds* (the Teyler prize essay), Haarlem, 1844; *De Leer van den Doop en het Avondmaal, op nieuw onderzocht*, 1st part, *Het Avondmaal*, Utrecht, 1847; *Wat dunkt u van uzelven?* 1849; *Avondmaalsgids*, 1850, 4th ed. 1879; *De Groninger School in haren strijd*, 1851; *Drie Brieven aan Dr. L. S. P. Meijboom*, 1852; *De Allocutie van Paus Pius IX. Over de Hiërarchie in de Nederlanden*, 1853; *Hebt gij de kosten berekend? Een woord tot leden der Christ. Kerk*, 1855; *Handleiding bij het onderwijs in de bijbelsche geschiedenis*, 1855, 10th ed. 1880 (German translation by L. M., *Handleitung beim Unterricht in der biblischen Geschichte*, Kaiserslautern, 1861); *De Leer der Zaligheid*, 1858, 9th ed. 1880 (Malay trans. 1860, Javan trans. 1867); *Verkorte Handleiding bij het Onderwijs in de Bijb. Geschiedenis*, 1858, 6th ed. 1880; *Oratio de critica, studiose a Theologis exercenda*, 1859; *Modern of Apostolisch Christendom?* 1860; *De zoogenaamde Moderne Theologie eenigszins toegelicht*, 1861; *Oratio de libertate cum Theologiæ, tum etiam Ecclesiæ Christianæ, strenue vindicanda*, 1865; *De Leer der Zaligheid. Verkorte Leiddraad voor katechetisch onderwijs, ten behoeve van mingeoefenden*, 1865, 4th ed. 1882; *Oud én Nieuw! De leus der Christ. Orthod. Theologie*, 1865; *De gelijktijdige eerbiediging van de welbegrepen vrijheid der Theologie en der Kerk*, 1865; *Hermeneutiek voor de Schr. des N. Verbonds*, 1866, 3d enlarged ed 1878 (English trans., by Stegman, *Manual of Hermeneutics for the Writings of the New Testament*, Edinburgh, 1867); *De Theologische Studiëngang geschetst*, 1866, 2d ed. 1882; *1517–1867, Onze voortzetting van de Kerkhervorming na drie honderd en vijftig jaren*, 1867; *De Heidelbergsche Catechismus in zijne eerste levensjaren (1563–67)*, 1867; *Inleiding tot de Leer van God*, 1870, 2d ed. 1880; *De Leer der Zaligheid volgens het Evangelie in de Schriften des N. Verbonds*, 1870, 2d ed. 1876; *De Leer van God*, 1871; *Geschiedenis van de eerste Uitgaven der Schriften des N. Verbonds in de Nederl. Taal (1522–23)*, 1872; *De toepassing van de ontwikkelingstheorie, niet aantebevelen voor de Geschiedenis der Godsdiensten*, 1874; *De aanval van een Materialist* (Dr. Ludwig Büchner), 1874; *Nieuwe bibliographisch-historische ontdekkingen. Bijdragen tot de kennis v. d. geschiedenis der eerste Uitgaven v. h. N. Testament in de Nederl. Taal; van de eerste lotgevallen des Heidelb. Catechismus in het Nederlandsch, en van de oudste drukken v. h. Doopsgezinde martelaarsboek "Het Offer des Heeren,"* 1876; *Encyclopedie der Christ. Theologie*, 1876, 2d ed. 1883; *De Nederlandsche Geloofsbelijdenis en de Heidelbergsche Catechismus, als Belijdenisschriften der Nederl. Herv. Kerk in de 19de eeuw; getoetst en beoordeeld*, 1880–81, two parts; *Ter Nagedachtenis van Dr. J. J. van Oosterzee*, 1883; *De Heidelb. Catechismus op nieuw overgezet en volgens de vertaling van Datheen* [Heidelberg, 1563] *op nieuw uitgegeven*, 1881; *Eene christelijke samenspreking uit Gods Woord (Over het onderscheid tusschen Wet en Evangelie) door Petrus Dathenus. Op nieuw uitgegeven naar den eersten druk door J. I. D. met een naschrift v. d. uitgever*, 1st and 2d ed. 1884; lectures, sermons, miscellaneous articles.

DOELLINGER, Johann Joseph Ignaz, Ph.D. (*hon.*, Vienna, Marburg, 1873), **D.D.** (Oxford, 1881), **LL.D.** (Oxford and Edinburgh, 1873), Old Catholic; b. at Bamberg, Bavaria, Feb. 28, 1799; became chaplain in the diocese of Bamberg, 1822; teacher in the Lyceum at Aschaffenburg, 1823; and since 1826 has been professor of church history in the University of Munich, except from 1847 to 1849, to which position has been added those of *Propst* of St. Cajetan, *Reichsrath*, member of the Academy of Sciences, 1835 (president since 1873 on nomination of the king, which makes him chief keeper of the Bavarian scientific collections). He represented the University of Munich in the Bavarian Parliament of 1845 and 1849, and a Bavarian election district in the Frankfort Diet in 1848. After 1848 he gradually became an anti-Ultramontane. In 1857 he made a journey to Rome; and what he saw then, and subsequently learned in the Italian war, 1859, had the effect of confirming him in the views to which his historical studies had brought him. In 1861 he delivered three lectures in Munich, in which he advocated the abandonment by the Pope of all temporal power. The lectures were published as an appendix to *Kirche und Kirchen* (see list). He obtained world-wide fame by his vigorous attack, before and during the Vatican Council, upon the infallibility dogma. He, with his fellow-professor Johannes Huber, wrote *Janus*, Leipzig, 1869, and *Römische Briefe vom Concil, von Quirinus*, originally in the Augsburg *Allgemeine Zeitung*. When the dogma was passed, he refused to accept it, and was in consequence excommunicated April 17, 1871. On July 29, 1873, he was elected rector of the University of Munich, by a vote of fifty-four to six, nor has his excommunication decreased his popularity in Bavaria. He presided over the Munich Old-Catholic congress (1871), and was at that of Cologne (1872), but has taken no part in the movement, since he opposes the formation of a separate church. He was president of the Bonn Conferences of 1875 and 1876. Among his numerous books may be mentioned, *Lehrbuch der Kirchengeschichte*, Regensburg, vol. i. 1836, vol. ii. 1st pt. 1838 (English trans. by E. Cox, London, 1839, 2 vols.); *Die Reformation*, 1846–48, 3 vols., vol. i. 2d ed. 1851; *Luther, eine Skizze*, Freiburg-im-Breisgau, 1851; *Hippolytus u. Kallistus*, Regensburg, 1853 (English translation by Alfred Plummer, Edinburgh, 1876); *Heidenthum und Judenthum. Vorhalle zur Geschichte des Christenthums*, 1857 (English translation, *The Gentile and the Jew in the Courts* *of the Temple of Christ*, London, 1862, 2 vols.); *Christenthum und Kirche in der Zeit der Grundlegung*, 1860, 2d ed. 1868 (English trans., *The First Age of Christianity*, London, 1866, 2 vols., 3d ed. 1877); *Kirche u. Kirchen, Papstthum u. Kirchenstaat*, Munich, 1861 (the book referred to above); *Die Papstfabeln des Mittelalters*, 1863 (English trans. by Alfred Plummer, *Fables respecting the Popes in the Middle Ages*, London, 1871; with Döllinger's *Essay on the Prophetic Spirit*, New York, 1872, edited by Prof. H. B. Smith); *Vorträge über die Wiedervereinigung der christlichen Kirch.*, 1872 (English trans., *Lectures on the Reunion of the Churches*, London and New York, 1872); *Sammlung von Urkunden zur Geschichte des Konzils von Trient*, Bd. 1., *Ungedruckte Berichte und Tagebücher*, 1876, 2 parts; and many important essays, addresses, etc. *

DONALDSON, James, LL.D. (Aberdeen University, 1865), layman; b at Aberdeen, April 26, 1831; graduated at Marischal College, Aberdeen, 1849; studied theology at New College, London, 1849–51; and philology at Berlin, 1851; was successively assistant to professor of Greek in the University of Edinburgh, 1852; rector of the grammar school of Stirling, 1854; classical master in the high school of Edinburgh, 1856; rector, 1866; in Aberdeen University, professor of humanity, 1881; principal of the United College of St. Salvator and St. Leonard, 1886. Author of *A Modern Greek Grammar*, Edinburgh, 1853; *Lyra Græca* (Greek anthology), 1854; *Critical History of Christian Literature and Doctrine from the Death of the Apostles to the Nicene Council*, London, 1864–66, 3 vols., 2d ed. of the 1st vol. under title, *The Apostolical Fathers: A Critical Account of their Genuine Writings, and of their Doctrines*, 1874; and in connection with Rev. Prof. Dr. Alexander Roberts, edited *The Ante-Nicene Christian Library*, Edinburgh, 1867–72, 24 vols. reprinted, ed. by Bishop Coxe, Buffalo, 1884–86, 8 vols.; *Lectures on the History of Education in Prussia and England, and on Kindred Topics*, 1874; *Education*, 1874; *On the Expiatory and Substitutionary Sacrifices of the Greeks*, 1875; *Elementary Latin Grammar* (on entirely new plan), 1880.

DORNER, August Johannes, Ph.D., Lic. Theol. (both Berlin, 1867 and 1869), **D.D.** (*hon.*, Halle, 1883), Protestant (son of the late I. A. Dorner); b. at Schiltach, Baden, May 13, 1846; studied at Berlin; was *repetent* in Göttingen, 1870–73; since then has been professor of theology and co-director of the theological seminary at Wittenberg. He is the author of *De Baconis philosophia*, Berlin, 1867; *Augustinus, sein theologisches System und seine religions-philosoph. Anschauung*, 1873; *Predigten vom Reiche Gottes*, 1880; *Kirche u. Reich Gottes*, 1883, besides minor publications and review articles.

DORNER, Isaac August, D.D., one of the greatest modern divines and teachers of Germany; b. at Neuhausen, in the kingdom of Würtemberg, June 20, 1809; d. at Wiesbaden, July 8, 1884; buried, July 27, in the family vault at Neuhausen, where a plain monument is erected to his memory. He was the sixth of twelve children born to the pastor of Neuhausen, and was educated first by a private tutor, then in the Latin school at Tuttlingen. In 1823 he entered the collegiate seminary at Maulbronn; in 1827, the University of Tübingen, where he studied philosophy and theology. He visited England and North Germany. In 1834 he became *repetent* (teaching tutor, or fellow, in the theological department of the university), having two years previous acted as assistant to his father; and in 1837, professor extraordinary of theology in Tübingen. In 1835 David Friedrich Strauss, a colleague of Dorner, published his *Life of Jesus*, and Dorner issued the first pages of his work of directly opposite tendency, *History of the Development of the Doctrine of the Person of Christ*, in which the historical Christ of the Gospels is traced through the ages of the Church as the greatest fact in Christian thought and experience. His teacher, Christian Friedrich Schmid, had incited him to take up the work, into which he put his thought and study until its completion in 1839. This work determined Dorner's place among theologians and doctrinal historians, and was a most effectual, though indirect, answer to Strauss and his mythical theory. The work was afterwards greatly enlarged and improved by an exhaustive study of the sources from the apostolic age down to the recent Kenosis controversy. In 1839 he was called to the University of Kiel as ordinary professor, and there remained until 1843. He formed an intimate friendship with Bishop Martensen, the greatest theologian of Denmark; and even the Schleswig-Holstein difficulty did not disturb it. His principal writing during his Kiel residence is his dogmatic treatise upon the *Foundation Ideas of the Protestant Church*, in which he maintained that the so-called material and formal principles of the Reformation — i.e., justification by faith, and the supreme authority of Scripture, respectively — were to be considered as two pillars inseparably joined, so that each stands with and through the other. This was his word of comfort to those distressed by Strauss: No criticism can alter the fact that the primitive Church did record in the New Testament, by means of the Spirit proceeding from Christ, its impressions and experiences of Christ's salvation. On the other hand, faith holds fast to the written word. For the Christ whom faith experiences is the Christ of Scripture, which alone enables the Christian to understand and assert faith and the mystery of his new personality. Justification, he used to say, is the only completed fact in the Christian: every thing else is growth.

In 1843 he became professor of theology at Königsberg, in 1847 at Bonn, in 1853 at Göttingen, and finally in 1862 at Berlin. Here, besides being professor in the university, he was superior consistorial councillor (*Oberkirchenrath*), and from here for twenty-two years he exerted a quiet but mighty influence on the Evangelical Church of Prussia, and on students from all parts of the world.

In 1873 he visited, with his son August, the United States, as a delegate to the Sixth General Conference of the Evangelical Alliance in New York, and read a thoughtful paper on the *Infallibilism of the Vatican Council*, which is published in the *Proceedings*, New York, pp. 427–436. He travelled in New England, and as far south as Washington, and was deeply impressed with the religious and literary activity of America. He carried back with him the most favorable recollections, and heartily welcomed American students in his hospitable home. The last years of his life were clouded by a painful cancerous affection of his face, and the incurable malady of one of his sons, a promising youth, who lost his mind while studying at college. He bore his trial with meek resignation, and never complained. He continued to work on his *Christian Ethics* till the last weeks of his life, which he spent at Wittenberg, in view of the Luther house. Then, feeble as he was, he set out with his wife on a journey to Switzerland for rest, and proposed visiting, on the way, the national monument of Germania on the Niederwald, by the Rhine; but was seized with a hemorrhage, and died suddenly at Wiesbaden. His wife followed him a few months afterwards to his eternal rest.

Dr. Dorner was one of the profoundest and most learned theologians of the nineteenth century, and ranks with Schleiermacher, Neander, Nitzsch, Julius Müller, and Richard Rothe. He mastered the theology of Schleiermacher and the philosophy of Hegel, appropriated the best elements of both, infused into them a positive evangelical faith and a historical spirit. The central idea of his system was the divine-human personality of Christ, as the highest revealer of God, the perfect ideal of humanity, and the Saviour from sin and death. His theology is pre-eminently christological, and his monumental history of christology will long remain the richest mine of study in that department. He lectured on exegesis, on New-Testament theology, on symbolics, and especially on dogmatics and ethics, in which he excelled all his contemporaries. He was one of the revisers of the Luther Bible, and proposed a correspondence with the Anglo-American Revision Committee, while in New York, 1873, which was carried on for a short time. He was alive to all the practical church questions, and labored in the *Oberkirchenrath* for synodical church government, and the development of the lay agency and the voluntary principle. He had a deep interest in the work of "inner missions," and was one of its directors.

He was, with Wichern and von Bethmann-Hollweg, one of the founders of the German Church Diet, in the revolutionary year 1848, and one of the leading speakers and managers at its annual sessions. His catholicity went beyond the limits of the German churches, and was in full sympathy with the principles and aims of the International Evangelical Alliance. He was a most devoted and conscientious teacher, and a favorite among students. The Johanneum and the Melanchthon House in Berlin are memorials of his active interest in indigent students. The leading traits in his personal character were purity, simplicity, courtesy, gentleness, humility, and love. Decan Jäger and Diaconus Knapp paid noble testimonies to his virtues, at the funeral (*Zur Erinnerung an Dr Isaak August Dorner*, Tuttlingen, 1884); and Dr. Kleinert, as dean of the theological faculty, delivered a eulogy before the University of Berlin, July 26, 1884 (*Zum Gedächtniss I. A. D.'s*, Berlin, 1884), in which he places him next to Schleiermacher, and calls him "a leader and prophet in the highest questions of theology;" adding, that, "great as were his merits in theological science, the noblest thing in him was his personality, which reflected the image of Christ, and impressed itself indelibly on all who knew him." His son has given a good account of his theological system in *Dem Andenken von Dr I. A. Dorner von Dr Dorner, Prof. in Wittenberg*, Gotha, 1885.

The following is a list of Dorner's publications: *Entwicklungsgeschichte der Lehre von der Person Christi von den ältesten Zeiten bis auf die neueste dargestellt*, Stuttgart, 1839; 2d ed., more than doubled in size, 1st part, *Die Lehre von der Person Christi in den ersten vier Jahrhunderten*, Stuttgart, 1845; 2d part, *Die Lehre von der Person Christi vom Ende des vierten Jahrhunderts bis zur Gegenwart*, 3 divisions (*bis zur Reformation*, 1853; *in dem Reformationszeitalter*, 1854; *bis zur Gegenwart*, 1856), Berlin, 1853–56 (English trans., by W. L. Alexander and D. W. Simon, *History of the Development of the Doctrine of the Person of Christ*, Edinburgh, 1861–63, 5 vols.); *Der Pietismus, inbesondere in Würtemberg, und seine speculativen Gegner, Binder und Märklin, mit besonderer Beziehung auf das Verhältniss des Pietismus und der Kirche*, Hamburg, 1840; *Das Princip unserer Kirche nach dem innern Verhältniss seiner zwei Seiten betrachtet*, Kiel, 1841; *De oratione Christi eschatologica Matt. xxiv. 1-36 (Luc. xxi. 5-36, Marc. xiii. 1-32) asservata*, Stuttgart, 1844; *Das Verhältniss zwischen Kirche und Staat, aus dem Gesichtspunkte evangelischer Wissenschaft*, Bonn, 1847; *Sendschreiben über Reform der evangelischen Landeskirchen im Zusammenhang mit der Herstellung einer evangelisch-deutschen Nationalkirche; an Herrn C. I. Nitzsch in Berlin und Herrn Julius Müller in Halle*, Bonn, 1848; *Ueber Jesu sündlose Vollkommenheit*, Gotha, 1862 (translated into English by H. B. Smith, New York); *Geschichte der protestantischen Theologie*, Munich, 1867 (English trans., *History of Protestant Theology, particularly in Germany, viewed according to its fundamental movement, and in connection with the religious, moral, and intellectual life*, Edinburgh, 1871, 2 vols.); *System der christlichen Glaubenslehre*, Berlin, 1879–80, 2d ed. 1886, 2 vols. (English trans., by Rev. Profs. Alfred Cave and J. S. Banks, *A System of Christian Doctrine*, Edinburgh, 1880–82, 4 vols.); *Gesammelte Schriften auf dem Gebiet der systematischen Theologie, Exegese und Geschichte*, Berlin, 1883 (contains his valuable metaphysical essays on the unchangeability of God, and criticism of the Kenosis theory of the incarnation); *System der christlichen Sittenlehre* (560 pp., edited by August Dorner, his son), Berlin, 1885. He founded and edited, with Liebner, the valuable theological quarterly, *Jahrbücher für deutsche Theologie*, Gotha, 1856–1878. PHILIP SCHAFF.

DOUEN, Emmanuel Orentin, Reformed ("Liberal" school); b. at Templeux le Guérard (Somme), France, June 2, 1830; studied theology at Strassburg, 1849–53; was pastor at Quincy-Ségy, near Meaux (Seine et Marne), 1853–61; and since has been agent of the "Société biblique protestante de Paris," and since 1866 a member of the committee of the "Société d'histoire du protestantisme." He is the author of *Histoire de la Société biblique protestante de Paris*, Paris, 1868; *Notes sur les altérations catholiques et protestantes du N. T. traduit en français* (in *Revue de théologie*, Strassburg, 1868); *Intolérance de Fénelon, d'après les documents pour la plupart* *inédits*, 1872, 2d ed. 1875; *Clément Marot et le Psautier huguenot* (published at state expense), Paris, 1878–79, 2 vols.; *Les premiers pasteurs du Désert*, 1879, 2 vols. ("couronné par l'Académie française"); *Etienne Dolet, Ses opinions religieuses*, 1881; *La Révocation de l'Edit de Nantes*, 1886; edited a new edition of Jean Bion's *Relations des tourments qu'on fait souffrir aux Protestants qui sont sur les galères de France*, 1881.

DOUGLAS, Hon. and Right Rev. Arthur Gascoigne, D.D. (Durham, 1883), lord bishop of Aberdeen and Orkney, Episcopal Church of Scotland; son of the nineteenth Earl of Morton; b. in Scotland, Jan. 5, 1827; educated at University College, Durham University; graduated B.A. 1849, Lic. theol. and M.A. 1850; was ordained deacon 1850, priest 1852; curate of Kidderminster, 1850–52; rector of St. Olave, Southwark, 1855–56; of Scaldwell, Northamptonshire, 1856–72; vicar of Shapwick, 1872–83; consecrated bishop, 1883.

DOUGLAS, George, LL.D. (McGill University, Montreal, 1869), **D.D.** (Victoria University, Ontario, 1881), Wesleyan Methodist; b. near Abbotsford, Roxburghshire, Scotland, Oct. 14, 1825; educated in Scotland and Canada; entered the ministry of British Conference, 1848; went as missionary to the West Indies, 1848; entered Methodist Church of Canada, 1854; has been principal of the Wesleyan Theological College, Montreal, since its foundation in 1873. He was president of the General Conference, 1878–82; delegate to Evangelical Alliance Conference in New-York City, 1873, and the Œcumenical Council of Methodism in London, 1881. He has published various sermons and addresses.

DOUGLAS, George Cuningham Monteath, D.D. (University of Glasgow, 1867), Free Church of Scotland; b. at Kilbarchan, Renfrewshire, Scotland, March 2, 1826; graduated B.A. at the University of Glasgow; entered the ministry of the Free Church; and after being pastor at Bridge of Weir, Renfrewshire (1852–57), he was appointed professor of Hebrew and Old-Testament exegesis, later also principal, in the Free Church College, Glasgow. He was one of the Old-Testament revisers, 1870–84. Besides articles in Fairbairn's *Imperial Bible Dictionary* (London, 1866, 2 vols.), and in *The Monthly Interpreter* (Edinburgh, 1885, *sqq*.), and a translation with notes of Keil's *Introduction to the Old Testament*, in Clark's Library (1869–70, 2 vols.), he has published, *Why I still believe that Moses wrote Deuteronomy*, 1878; and notes on *Judges* and *Joshua*, in Dods and Whyte's *Handbook for Bible Classes*, 1881, 1882.

DOW, Neal, layman; b. of Quaker parents at Portland, Me., March 20, 1804; educated at Friends' Academy, New Bedford, Mass.; was chief engineer of the Portland Fire Department 1839–44, mayor of the city 1851–54; and in 1851 drew up the bill "for the suppression of drinking-houses and tippling-shops," since widely known as the "Maine Law." He presented it in a public hearing before the committee of the legislature, "which unanimously adopted it, without change. It was printed during the night; and the next day, Saturday, May 31, 1851, being the last day of the session, it was passed without change through all its stages; and on Monday, June 2, it was approved by the governor, and took effect by special provision from that day." It has since been upheld as the settled policy of the State. He was subsequently, for two terms, a member of the Maine Legislature, 1858–59. "In September, 1884, by a popular vote, the prohibition of the liquor-traffic was incorporated into the Constitution of the State by a very large majority, the affirmative vote being nearly three times larger than the negative." He has been three times in Great Britain as the guest of the United-Kingdom Alliance, the largest and most influential temperance society in the world, and has advocated the cause in all parts of the kingdom. He was commissioned by Gov. Washburn colonel of the Thirteenth Maine Volunteers in September, 1861; went immediately to the Department of the Gulf, where he had three separate commands at different times, having been commissioned brigadier-general by President Lincoln soon after his arrival at the Gulf of Mexico, April, 1862. He was twice wounded at Port Hudson, and, being taken to a plantation-house in the rear of the army, was captured in the night by a detachment of Logan's cavalry (June 30, 1863), and was taken by many successive stages to Richmond, Va., where he was confined six months in Libby Prison. He was also confined two months at Mobile, being exchanged afterwards for Fitz Henry Lee, March 14, 1864. His health was so far broken down by his experiences at Richmond, that he was not able to resume his duties in the field until the war was practically closed. Since the war he has advocated publicly all over the country "the policy of prohibition of the liquor-traffic as a political necessity and a public duty."

DRIVER, Samuel Rolles, D.D. (by decree of Convocation, 1883), Church of England; b. at Southampton, Oct. 2, 1846; was scholar of New College, Oxford; Pusey and Ellerton Hebrew scholar, 1866; graduated B.A. (first-class in classics), 1869; Kennicott Hebrew scholar, 1870; fellow of New College 1870–82, and tutor 1875–82; Hall and Houghton senior Septuagint prizeman, 1871; Houghton Syriac prizeman, and M.A., 1872; ordained deacon 1881, priest 1882; succeeded Dr. Pusey as regius professor of Hebrew and as a canon of Christ Church, Oxford, 1882. In 1884 he was appointed examining chaplain to the bishop of Southwell. In 1875 he became a member of the Old-Testament Revision Company. He has published the following papers: in *The Philological Journal* (Cambridge), *On the Linguistic Affinities of the Elohist* (1882), *On Gen. xlix. 10, an Exegetical Study* (1885); in *Studia Biblica* (Oxford, 1885), *On Recent Theories of the Origin and Nature of the Tetragrammaton*; and the following books: *A Treatise on the Use of the Tenses in Hebrew*, Oxford, 1874, 2d ed. improved and enlarged 1881; (jointly with Ad. Neubauer) *The Fifty-third Chapter of Isaiah according to Jewish Interpreters*, London, vol. ii. 1877 (translations); (jointly with T. K. Cheyne) *The Holy Bible, with Various Readings*, 1876, 2d ed. under title *Variorum Bible* 1880; (as editor) *A Commentary on Jeremiah and Ezekiel by Mosheh ben Shesheth, with Translation and Notes*, 1871; *A Rabbinical Commentary on the Book of Proverbs attributed to Abraham ben Ezra*, Oxford, 1880.

DRUMMOND, Henry, B.Sc., F.G.S., F.R.S.E., Free Church of Scotland; b. at Stirling, Scotland, in the year 1852; educated at Edinburgh and Tübingen; in 1879 appointed professor of natural history and science in the Free Church College, Glasgow. He is the author of *Natural Law in the Spiritual World*, London and New York, 1883, numerous editions.

DRUMMOND, James, LL.D. (University of Dublin, 1882), Liberal Christian; b. in Dublin, May 14, 1835; educated at Trinity College, Dublin; graduated B.A. (first gold medal in classics), 1855; studied theology at Manchester New College, London, under Revs. J. J. Tayler and J. Martineau; became minister of the Cross-street Unitarian Chapel, Manchester, 1860; professor of (chiefly New-Testament) theology in Manchester New College, 1870 (as successor of J. J. Tayler, d. 1869), principal, 1885 (on retirement of James Martineau). He is the author of *Spiritual Religion: Sermons on Christian Faith and Life*, London, 1870; *The Jewish Messiah: a Critical History of the Messianic Idea among the Jews from the rise of the Maccabees to the closing of the Talmud*, 1877; *Introduction to the Study of Theology*, 1884; and articles and addresses, e.g., *Philo and the Principles of the Jewish Alexandrine Philosophy*, 1877; *Religion and Liberty*, 1882; *Retrospect and Prospect*, 1885; *On the reading μονογενὴς Θεός, in John i. 18*, *Justin Martyr and the Fourth Gospel* (in *Theological Review*, October, 1871, and October, 1875, April and July, 1877, respectively).

DRURY, Augustus Waldo, United Brethren in Christ; b. in Madison County, Ind., March 2, 1851; graduated at Western College, 1872, and at Union Biblical Seminary, Dayton, O., 1877; became professor of Latin and Greek, Western College, 1872; pastor, 1877; professor of church history, Union Biblical Seminary, 1880. He has published *Life of Rev. Philip William Otterbein*, Dayton, O., 1884.

DRURY, John Benjamin, D.D. (Rutgers College, 1880), Reformed (Dutch); b. at Rhinebeck, N.Y., Aug. 15, 1838; graduated at Rutgers College, New Brunswick, N.J., 1858, and at the theological seminary there, 1861; was missionary at Davenport, Io., 1861–62; has been since 1864 pastor of First Reformed Church, Ghent, N.Y.; was a superintendent of New-Brunswick Theological Seminary, 1874–76, 1883–85; president particular synod of Albany, 1881; Vedder lecturer, 1883; lecturer in summer school of American Institute of Christian Philosophy, 1885. He has written extensively for the periodical press, and the volumes, *Historical Sketch of the First Church of Ghent*, 1876; *Reformed (Dutch) Church of Rhinebeck, N.Y.*, 1881; *Truths and Untruths of Evolution* (Vedder lectures), New York, 1884.

DUBBS, Joseph Henry, D.D. (Ursinus College, Penn., 1878), Reformed (German); b. at North White Hall, Lehigh County, Penn., Oct. 5, 1838; graduated at Franklin and Marshall College, Penn., 1856, and at the Mercersburg Theological Seminary, 1859; became pastor of Zion Church, Allentown, Penn., 1859; Trinity Church, Pottstown, 1863; and Christ Church, Philadelphia, 1871; professor of history and archæology in Franklin and Marshall College, 1875. In 1872 he was elected an honorary member of the Historical Society of Pennsylvania; in 1879, a corresponding member of the Ethnographic Society of France; in 1885, a fellow of the Royal Historical Society of Great Britain. From 1882 to 1886 he edited *The Guardian*. Besides numerous articles in prose and verse, he has published *Historic Manual of the Reformed Church in the United States*, Lancaster, Penn., 1885 (the fruit of much original research).

DU BOSE, William Porcher, S.T.D. (Columbia College, New-York City, 1875), Episcopalian; b. at Winnsborough, S.C., April 11, 1836; graduated M.A. at the University of Virginia, Charlottesville, Va., 1859; and studied at the theological School, Camden, S.C., 1859–61; was rector at Winnsborough, S.C., 1865–67; at Abbeville, S.C., 1868–71; chaplain of the University of the South, Sewanee, Tenn., 1872–83; and since 1872 professor of moral science and also of New-Testament exegesis in the same institution.

DUCHESNE, Louis, Roman Catholic; b. at St. Servan (Ille-et-Vilaine), Sept. 13, 1843; studied at Paris, and then, devoting himself particularly to church history, continued his studies in the French school at Rome under teachers for three years (1873–76), during which time, however, he made two journeys, — in 1874 to the Epirus, Thessaly, and Macedonia, and for a time lived on Mount Athos; and in 1876 to Asia Minor. In 1877 he was made a doctor of letters by the Faculty of Paris; and has been since professor of ecclesiastical history in the Catholic Institute at Paris; and since 1880 editor of the *Bulletin critique*, which he founded. Besides numerous learned articles, he has published the following important books: *Mission au Mt. Athos et en Macédoine* (with Bayet), Paris, 1875; *De Macario Magnete et scriptis ejus*, 1877; *Etude sur le Liber Pontificalis*, 1877; *De codicibus MSS. græcis Pii II.*, 1880; *Vita S. Polycarpi auctore Pionio*, 1881; *Les origines chrétiennes*, 1882. He is now (1885) issuing an edition of the *Liber Pontificalis*, with introduction and a commentary, in 2 vols. Of his review articles may be mentioned: in *Revue des questions historiques*, *La question de la Pâque au concile de Nicée* (July, 1880), *Virgile et Pélage* (October, 1884); in *Revue des sciences ecclésiastiques*, *Les témoins antenicéens du dogma de la Trinité* (December, 1882); in *Mélanges d'archéologie et d'histoire de l'Ecole française de Rome*, *La succession du pape Félix IV.* (1883), *L'historiographie pontificale au VIIIe siècle* (1884), *Les sources du martyrologe hieronymiers* (1885); in *Bulletin de correspondance hellénique*, *Une inscription chrétienne de Bithynie* (1878), *Les inscriptions chrétiennes de l'Isaurie* (1879–80); in *Mémoire de la société des Antiquaires de France*, t. xliii. (1883), *La civitas Rigomagensium et l'évêché de Nice.*

DUCKWORTH, Robinson, D.D. (Oxford, 1879), Church of England; b. at Liverpool, Eng., in the year 1834; was scholar and exhibitioner of University College, Oxford, where he graduated B.A. (first-class in classics) 1857, M.A. 1859, B.D. 1879; was ordained deacon 1858, priest 1859; assistant master at Marlborough College, 1858–60; fellow of Trinity College, Oxford, 1860–76; tutor of the same, 1860–66; master of the schools, 1860–62; examining chaplain to the bishop of Peterborough, 1864; instructor to his Royal Highness Prince Leopold, 1866–70, and governor to him, 1867–70; since 1870 he has held the crown living of St. Mark's, Marylebone, London, and been chaplain in ordinary to the Queen; since

1875, chaplain to the Prince of Wales, and canon of Westminster (in succession to Charles Kingsley).

DUDLEY, Charles Densmore, Freewill Baptist; b. at Agency, Wakello County, Io., June 14, 1852; graduated at Hillsdale College, Hillsdale, Mich., 1873, and from the Bates Theological School, Lewiston, Me., 1877; was pastor of Freewill Baptist churches at Scituate, R.I., 1877–78; Ashland, N.H., 1878–80; Great Falls, N.H., 1881–83; since June, 1883, has been Burr professor of systematic theology, Hillsdale College, Mich.

DUDLEY, Right Rev. Thomas Underwood, D.D. (St. John's College, Annapolis, Md., 1874, and University of the South, Sewanee, Tenn., 1883), Episcopalian, bishop of Kentucky; b. in Richmond, Va., Sept. 26, 1837; graduated M.A. at the University of Virginia, Charlottesville, 1858; became assistant professor of Latin in it; during the war was major in the commissary department of the Confederate Army; was rector of Christ Church, Baltimore, Md., 1869; consecrated assistant bishop of Kentucky, 1875; became bishop on the death of Bishop Smith, May 31, 1884; was Bohlen lecturer, 1881.

DUFF, David, LL.D. (Glasgow, 1872), United Presbyterian; b. at Greenock, Scotland, Jan. 29, 1824; graduated M.A. at Glasgow, 1843; studied theology, first at Relief, and after the union of Relief and Secession Churches, in United Presbyterian Hall, Edinburgh; became master of grammar school at Greenock, 1847; minister of the United Presbyterian Church, Helensburgh, 1856; professor of church history in the denomination's theological hall, Edinburgh, 1876. He was chairman of the first school board of Row, 1873–76; and since 1882, of that of Edinburgh.

DUFFIELD, George, D.D. (Knox College, Ill., 1872), Presbyterian; b. at Carlisle, Penn., Sept. 12, 1818; graduated at Yale College, 1837, and at the Union Theological Seminary, New-York City, 1840; was successively pastor at Brooklyn, N. Y., 1840; Bloomfield, N.J., 1847; Philadelphia, Penn., 1852; Adrian, Mich., 1861; Galesburg, Ill., 1865; Saginaw City, Mich., 1869; evangelist, Ann Arbor, 1874; pastor at Lansing, 1877–80; since 1884 without charge at Detroit. He is one of the regents of the University of Michigan. He has written many hymns, among them the familiar *Blessed Saviour, thee I love* (1851), and *Stand up, stand up for Jesus* (1858).

DUFFIELD, Samuel (Augustus) Willoughby, Presbyterian; b. at Brooklyn, L.I., N.Y., Sept. 24, 1843; graduated at Yale College, 1863; became pastor of Tioga-street Church, Philadelphia, 1867; Claremont, Jersey City, N.J., 1870; Ann Arbor, Mich., 1871; Chicago (Eighth Church), 1874; (pastor-elect) Auburn (Central Church), N.Y., 1876; Altoona (Second Church), Penn., 1878; Bloomfield, N.J., 1882. He has contributed frequently in prose and verse to the religious press and to magazines, and is the author of *The Heavenly Land* (a translation of Bernard of Cluny's *De contemptu mundi*), New York, 1867; *Warp and Woof: a Book of Verse*, 1868; (with his father, Rev. Dr. George Duffield, jun.) *The Burial of the Dead* (a funeral manual), 1882; *English Hymns: their Authors and History*, 1886; *Latin Hymn-writers and their Hymns*, 1887.

DUHM, Bernhard, German Protestant; b. at Bingum, East Frisia, Oct. 10, 1847; studied at Göttingen, 1867–70; became *repetent* there 1871, *privat-docent* 1873, professor extraordinary 1877. He is the author of *Pauli apostoli de Judæorum lege judicia*, Göttingen, 1873; *Die Theologie der Propheten*, 1875.

DULLES, John Welsh, D.D. (College of New Jersey, 1872), Presbyterian; b. in Philadelphia, Penn., Nov. 4, 1823; graduated at Yale College, 1844, and at Union Theological Seminary, New-York City, 1848; was a missionary of the American Board at Madras, India, 1848–53; secretary American Sunday-school Union, Philadelphia, 1853–57; of the Presbyterian Publication Committee (New School), 1857–70; since 1870 he has been editorial secretary of the Board of Publication of the re-united Presbyterian Church. He has published *Life in India*, Philadelphia, 1854; *Ride through Palestine*, 1881.

DUNLOP, Right Rev. George Kelly, S.T.D. (Racine College, Wis., 1880), Episcopalian, missionary bishop of New Mexico and Arizona; b. in County Tyrone, Ireland, Nov. 10, 1830; graduated at Queen's University, Galway, 1852, taking the second classical scholarship; became rector of Christ Church, Lexington, Mo., 1856; and of Grace Church, Kirkwood, Miss., 1863; was consecrated bishop, 1880.

DUNN, Ransom, D.D. (Bates College, Lewiston, Me., 1873), Freewill Baptist; b. at Bakersfield, Vt., July 7, 1818; was home missionary in Ohio, 1837–43; pastor at Dover and Great Falls, N.H., and in Boston, Mass.; became professor of mental and moral philosophy in Michigan Central College, which was soon after removed to Hillsdale, Mich., 1852; professor of theology in Hillsdale College 1863, and president of the same 1884. He has been corresponding editor of *The Morning Star*, the denominational organ, since 1876.

DUNNING, Albert Elijah, Congregationalist; b. at Brookfield, Conn., Jan. 5, 1844; graduated at Yale College 1867, and at Andover Theological Seminary 1870; became pastor of Highland Church, Boston, 1870; national superintendent of Sunday-school work for Congregational churches, 1881; general secretary of the Congregational Sunday-school and Publishing Society, 1884; also in same year a member of the International Lesson Committee. He is the author of *The Sunday School Library*, Boston, 1883, republished New York, 1884; *Normal Outlines for Sunday-school Teachers*, Boston, 1885; since 1876 has contributed to the *Sermons by the Monday Club;* since 1885 edited the *Pilgrim Teacher* (monthly).

DUNS, John, D.D. (Amherst, U. S. A., 1863), **F.R.S.E., F.S.A.,** Scot. Free Church; b. at Duns, Berwickshire, Scotland, July 11, 1820; educated at Edinburgh University, 1843; became pastor of the Free Church, 1844; professor of natural science, New College, Edinburgh, 1864. He has been editor of the *North British Review* since 1857; was elected a fellow of the Royal Physical Society, Edinburgh, 1864, and president 1868; a fellow of the Royal Society of Antiquaries, Scotland, 1874, and a vice-president 1879; corresponding member of the New-York and of the Philadelphia Academies of Science, 1877. He is the author of *Memoirs* of Rev. Samuel Martin Bathgate and of Professor Fleming, D.D., F.R.S.E. (both

Edinburgh, 1857); *Things New and Old*, London, 1857; *Biblical Natural Science*, 1863-66, 2 vols.; *Science and Christian Thought*, 1866; and of numerous scientific articles and contributions.

DURNFORD, Right Rev. Richard, D.D. (Oxford, 1870), lord bishop of Chichester, Church of England; b. at Sandleford, Berkshire, in the year 1802; educated at Magdalen College, Oxford; graduated B.A. (first-class classics) 1826, M.A. 1829; was elected fellow of his college; ordained deacon 1830, priest 1831; was rector of Middleton, Lancashire, and also rural dean of Manchester, and surrogate of the diocese, 1835-70; honorary canon of Manchester, 1854-68; archdeacon of Manchester, 1867-70; canon residentiary, 1868-70; consecrated bishop, 1870. He is a leader in educational and philanthropic movements in the Church of England.

DURYEA, Joseph Tuthill, D.D. (College of New Jersey, 1866), Congregationalist; b. at Jamaica, L.I., N.Y., Dec. 9, 1832; graduated at the College of New Jersey 1856, and at Princeton Theological Seminary, 1859; became pastor of the Second Presbyterian Church, Troy, N.Y., 1859; of the Collegiate Reformed Dutch Church, New-York City, 1862; of the Classon-avenue Presbyterian Church, Brooklyn, N.Y., 1867; and of the Central Congregational Church, Boston, Mass., 1879. In 1873 he was elected a director of Princeton Theological Seminary. In 1885 he declined the presidency of Union College, Schenectady, N. Y. *

DWIGHT, Timothy, D.D. (Chicago Theological Seminary, Ill., 1869), Congregationalist; b. at Norwich, Conn., Nov. 16, 1828; graduated at Yale College, 1849; studied in the Divinity School of the college; was tutor in the college, 1851-55; studied at Bonn and Berlin, 1856-58; became professor of sacred literature in Yale College, 1858; president of Yale College, 1886. He was a member of the New-Testament Bible Revision Company. He has published a good many articles on various topics; annotated the English translation of Meyer on *Romans* (New York, 1884), *Philippians-Philemon, Timothy-Hebrews*: translated and annotated Godet on the *Gospel of John* (1886, 2 vols.).

DWINELL, Israel Edson, D.D. (University of Vermont, 1864), Congregationalist; b. at East Calais, Vt., Oct. 24, 1820; graduated at the University of Vermont, Burlington, 1843, and at Union Theological Seminary, New-York City, 1848; associate pastor of South (Congregational) Church, Salem, Mass., 1849-63; pastor in Sacramento, Cal., 1863-83; since 1884 has been professor of homiletics and pastoral theology in the Pacific (Congregational) Theological Seminary, Oakland, near San Francisco, Cal. He has published various articles in different reviews.

DYER, Heman, D.D. (Trinity College, Hartford, Conn., 1843), Protestant Episcopal; b. at Shaftesbury, Vt., Sept. 24, 1810; graduated at Kenyon College, Gambier, O., 1833; tutor there, 1832-34; principal of Milnor Hall, 1835-40; professor in the Western University of Pennsylvania 1844-45, and chancellor 1845-49; since 1854 secretary and editor of "The Evangelical Knowledge Society," and since 1865 corresponding secretary of "The American Church Missionary Society," both of which have their headquarters in New-York City. During the war he was actively engaged in the Christian Commission.

DYKES, James Oswald, D.D. (Edinburgh, 1873), Presbyterian; b. at Port Glasgow, near Greenock, Scotland, Aug. 14, 1835; graduated at University of Edinburgh, M.A., 1854; and studied theology at New College, Edinburgh, 1854-58, and at Heidelberg and Erlangen 1856. In 1859 he was ordained, and installed minister of the Free Church at East Kilbride, County Lanark, Scotland. In 1861 he became colleague of the Rev. Dr. R. S. Candlish, in the pastorship of Free St. George's, Edinburgh; but compelled to resign (1864) by reason of his health, he was from 1864 to 1867 in Australia, and in Victoria delivered theological lectures, and filled other temporary posts in the Presbyterian Church. In 1869 he became minister of the Regent-square Presbyterian Church, London, which position he still holds. He is the author of *On the Written Word*, London, 1868; *The Beatitudes of the Kingdom*, 1872; *The Laws of the Kingdom*, 1873; *The Relations of the Kingdom*, 1874 (these three were collected in one vol., under title, *The Manifesto of the King: an Exposition of the Sermon on the Mount*, 1881); *From Jerusalem to Antioch: Sketches of the Primitive Church*, 1875, 2d ed. 1880; *Abraham, the Friend of God: a Study from Old-Testament History*, 1877, 3d ed. 1878; *Sermons*, 1882; *The Law of the Ten Words*, 1884.

E.

EBRARD, (Johannes Heinrich) August, Ph.D., Lic. Theol. (Erlangen, 1841, 1842), **D.D.** (Basel, 1847), Reformed; b. at Erlangen, Jan. 18, 1818; studied at Erlangen and Berlin, 1835–39; became tutor in a family, 1839; *privat-docent* and *repetent* at Erlangen, 1841; professor of theology at Zürich 1844, the same at Erlangen 1847; consistorial councillor at Speyer, 1853; retired at Erlangen, 1861; pastor of the French Reformed Church at Erlangen, 1875. His theological standpoint is "Reformed orthodox, in the sense of the Loudun Synod of 1660, which declared Amyraldism to be 'highly orthodox.'" He has published *Wissenschaftliche Kritik d. evang. Geschichte*, Erlangen, 1842, 3d ed. 1868 (Eng. trans., *The Gospel History*, Edinburgh, 1863); *Das Dogma vom heil. Abendmahl u. s. Geschichte*, Frankfurt-a.-M., 1845–46, 2 vols.; *Christliche Dogmatik*, Königsberg, 1851, 2 vols., 2d ed. 1862; *Vorlesungen über praktische Theologie*, 1864; *Das Buch Hiob als poëtisches Kunstwerk übersetzt u. erklärt*, Landau, 1858; *Handbuch d. christl. Kirchen- u. Dogmengeschichte*, Erlangen, 1865–66, 4 vols.; *Die iroschottische Missionskirche d. 6. 7. u. 8. Jahrh.*, Gütersloh, 1873; *Apologetik*, 1874–75, 2 parts (2d ed., 1st part, 1878; 2d part, 1881); *Bonifatius, der Zerstörer d. columbanischen Kirchentums auf d. Festlande*, 1882; *Christian Ernst*, 1885. Besides these, he has published sermons, edited and completed Olshausen's *Commentary* (Eng. trans., revised by Professor A. C. Kendrick, N.Y., 1856–58, 6 vols.) by writing on *Der Brief an die Hebraeer* (Königsberg, 1850), *Die Offenbarung Johannis* (1853), and *Die Briefe Johannis* (1859), (Eng. trans., Edinburgh, 1860; Swedish trans., Örebro, 1862); and under the pseudonymes, Gottfried Flammberg, Christian Deutsch, Sigmund Sturm, Schliemann d. j., a long series of Christian bellettristic productions.

EDDY, Richard, S.T.D. (Tufts, 1883), Universalist; b. at Providence, R.I., June 21, 1828; was pastor at Rome, N.Y., 1851-54; Buffalo, 1854; Philadelphia, Penn., 1855-56; Canton, N.Y., 1856–61; chaplain of the Sixtieth Regiment, New-York State Volunteers, 1861-63; pastor in Philadelphia, Penn., 1863-68 (librarian State Historical Society 1864-68); Franklin, Mass., 1868-70; Gloucester, Mass., 1870-77; Akron, O., 1880; Melrose, Mass., since 1881. Since 1878 he has been president of the Universalist Historical Society. He is the author of *History of the Sixtieth Regiment New-York State Volunteers from July, 1861, to January, 1864*, Philadelphia, 1864; *Universalism in America, A History*, Boston, 1884–86, 2 vols.

EDDY, Zachary, D.D. (Williams College, Williamstown, Mass., 1858), Congregationalist; b. at Stockbridge, Vt., Dec. 19, 1815; educated privately; ordained by Pennsylvania Presbytery (Cumberland Presbyterian), Pennsylvania, 1835; was missionary in Pennsylvania and Ohio, 1835–38; pastor (Presbyterian), Springville, N.Y., 1838–43; Mineral Point, Wis., 1844–50; Warsaw, N.Y., 1850–56; Birmingham, Conn., 1856–58; Northampton, Mass., 1858–67; Brooklyn Heights (Reformed Dutch Church), Brooklyn, N.Y., 1867–71; First Congregational Church, Detroit, Mich., 1873–84; until 1886 at Atlanta, Ga. (Congregational Church of the Redeemer). He is a Conservative Congregationalist. He is the editor of *Hymns of the Church, compiled for the General Synod of the Reformed Church in America*, New York, 1869; of *Hymns and Songs of Praise* (with Rev. Drs. Roswell Dwight Hitchcock and Philip Schaff), 1874; and of *Carmina Sanctorum* (with Rev. Dr. Roswell Dwight Hitchcock and Lewis Ward Mudge), 1886; author of *Immanuel, or the Life of Christ* (Springfield, Mass., 1868), and several occasional sermons.

EDEN, Right Rev. Robert, D.D. (Oxford, 1851), lord bishop of Moray, Ross, and Caithness, 1851; elected Primus of Scottish Church, 1862; Episcopal Church in Scotland; b. in London, Sept. 2, 1804; educated at Christ Church, Oxford; graduated B.A. 1827, M.A. 1829, B.D. 1851; was ordained deacon and priest, 1828; became successively curate of Weston-sub-Edge 1828; Messing, Essex, 1829; Peldon, 1832; rector of Leigh, 1837; consecrated bishop, 1851. He was appointed rural dean of Rochford, 1837; was justice of the peace for the county of Essex, and inspector of schools. During his episcopate the episcopal residence has been removed from Elgin to Inverness (1853), and an official residence (1879) and new cathedral built (begun 1866, opened 1869, consecrated 1873). He has published various sermons, charges, pamphlets, etc.

EDERSHEIM, Alfred, Ph.D. (Kiel, 1855), **D.D.** (Vienna, Berlin, and New College, Edinburgh), Church of England; b. of Jewish parents at Vienna, March 7, 1825. He studied in the gymnasium and university at Vienna; was baptized in Pesth, Hungary; pursued his studies at Berlin; in 1843 entered New College, Edinburgh; and in 1849 became minister of the Free Church, Old Aberdeen. Being compelled by ill health to seek a warmer climate, he went to Torquay, South-western England, in 1861, where he gathered a congregation, which built him a church (St. Andrew's). His health again obliging him temporarily to give up preaching, he lived for a while in literary retirement at Bournemouth. In 1875 he was ordained deacon and priest of the Church of England, and for a year was the (unsalaried) curate of the Abbey Church, Christchurch, Hants, near Bournemouth. In 1876 he became vicar of Loders, Dorsetshire; resigned in 1883, and removed to Oxford, where he is still living. From 1880 to 1884 he was Warburtonian lecturer at Lincoln's Inn, London. In 1881 he was made honorary M.A. of Christ Church, Oxford; in 1883 M.A. by decree of Convocation of the University of Oxford; and 1884–86 was select preacher to the university. He has also been lecturing in its "Honours School of Theology," upon prophecy. His publications as author, translator, editor, and contributor to dictionaries and serial works, are very numerous (cf. list in Crockford's *Clerical*

Directory for 1885). Perhaps the best-known and most valuable are, *The History of the Jewish Nation from A.D. 70–312*, 2d ed. Edinburgh, 1857; *The Jubilee Rhythm of St. Bernard, and other Hymns, chiefly from the Latin*, London, 1866; *The Golden Diary of Heart-Converse with Jesus in the Psalms*, 1874, 2d ed. 1877; *The Temple: its Ministry and Services as they were in the Time of Jesus Christ*, 1874; *Sketches of Jewish Social Life in the Days of Christ*, 1876; *The Exodus, and the Wandering in the Wilderness*, 1876; *The Life and Times of Jesus the Messiah*, 1883 (November), 2 vols., 3d ed. 1886 (April); *Prophecy and History in relation to the Messiah* (Warburtonian lectures, 1880–84), 1885; *The History of Israel from the Sacrifice on Carmel to the Death of Jehu*, 1885.

EDKINS, Joseph, D.D. (Edinburgh University, 1875), Congregationalist; b. at Nailsworth, Gloucestershire, Eng., Dec. 19, 1823; studied at Coward College and University College, London; graduated at London University, B.A., 1843; was missionary of London Missionary Society in China, 1848–80; translator of scientific and other books into the Chinese language, in the Chinese Imperial Maritime Customs service, 1880–85. He was a member of the committee for translating the New Testament into Chinese. He is the author of the following works in Chinese: *Refutation of the Principal Errors of Buddhism; General View of Western Knowledge*, 1885; sixteen scientific and historical primers rendered into Chinese. In English: *Grammar of the Shanghai Dialect*, Shanghai, 1853; *Grammar of the Mandarin Colloquial Language*, 1857, 2d ed. 1863; *Religious Condition of the Chinese*, London, 1859 (2d ed., entitled *Religion in China*, 1878; 3d ed. 1884); *Progressive Lessons in the Chinese Language*, 1862, 4th ed. 1886; *Vocabulary of the Shanghai Dialect*, Shanghai, 1869; *China's Place in Philology*, London, 1870; *Introduction to the Study of the Chinese Characters*, 1876; *Chinese Buddhism*, 1880.

EDMOND, John, D.D. (Glasgow University, 1861), Presbyterian; b. at Balfron, Stirlingshire, Scotland, Aug. 12, 1816; studied in Glasgow University, 1832–35, and in Anderson's University, Glasgow, 1836; was ordained as colleague of Dr. James Stark, Dennyloanhead, 1841; inducted to Regent Place, Glasgow, 1850; to Islington (now Highbury), London, 1860. He was moderator of the United Presbyterian Synod, 1871; and of the Synod of the Presbyterian Church of England, 1883; with Dr. Norman McLeod, represented the United Presbyterian Synod at the First General Assembly of the reunited Presbyterian Church in the United States, at the General Assembly of the United Presbyterian Church of America, Pittsburgh, and the first General Assembly of the Canada Presbyterian Church, Toronto,—all in 1870. He is a "liberal Calvinist,—a disciple of the Marrow school." He is the author of *The Children's Charter*, Glasgow, 1859; *The Children's Church at Home*, London, 1861–63, 2 vols., 4th ed. 1872, 1 vol.; *Scripture Stories in Verse, with Sacred Songs and Miscellaneous Pieces*, Edinburgh, 1871.

EDWARDS, Lewis, D.D. (Edinburgh, 1865), Welsh Calvinistic Methodist; b. at Pwllcenawon, near Aberystwyth, Wales, Oct. 27, 1809; graduated M.A. at the University of Edinburgh, 1836; has been principal of the Welsh Calvinistic Methodist College, Bala, Wales, since its foundation in 1837; was moderator of the General Assembly of the denomination, 1866 and 1876.

EELLS, James, D.D. (New-York University, 1861), **LL.D.** (Marietta College, O., 1881), Presbyterian; b. at Westmoreland, Oneida County, N.Y., Aug. 27, 1822; graduated from Hamilton College, 1844, and from Auburn Theological Seminary, 1851; pastor (N. S.), Penn Yan, N.Y., 1851–54; Cleveland (Second Church), O., 1855–59, 1870–74; Brooklyn (Reformed Dutch Church, Brooklyn Heights), N.Y., 1859–67; San Francisco, Cal. (Presbyterian Church), 1867–70; Oakland, Cal., 1874–79; professor of practical theology and apologetics in San-Francisco Theological Seminary, 1877–79; and of practical theology and church polity in Lane Theological Seminary, Cincinnati, O., from 1879 till his death, March 9, 1886. He was moderator of the Presbyterian General Assembly in 1877, at Chicago. He has written *Memorial of Samuel Eells*, 1872, occasional sermons, etc.

EGLI, Emil, Lic. Theol. (*hon.*, Zürich, 1884), Swiss Protestant; b. at Flaach, Canton Zürich, Jan. 9, 1848; studied theology at Zürich, 1866–70; was curate at Cappel, 1870–71; pastor at Dynhard, 1871–76; Aussersihl, 1876–85; Mettmenstetten, since 1885 (all these places are in Canton Zürich); since 1880 he has been *privat-docent* of church history in the University of Zürich. Since 1873 he has been a member of the Volkmar Theological and Historical Society at Zürich. He is the author of *Feldzüge in Armenien, Beitrag zur Kritik des Tacitus* (in Büdinger's *Untersuchungen zur Röm. Kaisergeschichte*, Leipzig, 1868); *Schlacht von Cappel*, Zürich, 1873; *Les origines du Nouveau Testament*, Geneva, 1874; *Züricher Wiedertäufer zur Reformationszeit*, Zürich, 1878; *Actensammlung zur Züricher Reformationsgeschichte*, 1879; *Martyrium des Polycarp und seine Zeit* (in Hilgenfeld's *Zeitschrift f. wissenschaftl. Theol.*, 1881); *Lucian und Polycarp* (ib., 1883); (edited) *Zwinglis Lehrbüchlein*, Zürich, 1884; *Luther und Zwingli in Marburg* (in the *Theol. Zeitschrift a. d. Schweiz*, 1884).

EHRENFELD, Charles Lewis, Ph.D. (Wittenberg College, 1877), Evangelical Lutheran; b. near Milroy, Mifflin County, Penn., June 15, 1832; graduated at Wittenberg College (1856) and Seminary (1860), Springfield, O.; was tutor in Wittenberg College, 1857–59; pastor at Altoona, Penn., 1860–63; Shippensburg, 1863–65; Hollidaysburg, 1865–71; principal S.W. Pennsylvania State Normal School, 1871–77; financial secretary State (Penn.) department of public instruction, 1877–78; State librarian, 1878–82; and since has been professor of English literature and Latin at Wittenberg College.

EKMAN, Erik Jakob, Swedish Congregationalist; b. at Strömsbro, a suburb of Gefle, Sweden, Jan. 8, 1842; graduated at Upsala, 1862; ordained minister in the Lutheran State Church, 1864; was promoted to *komminister* at Ogkelbo, 1868; passed pastoral examination at the University of Upsala, 1871; resigned his office in the State Church, Sept. 1, 1879, and became director of the Mission Institute at Kristinehamn, and president of the Swedish Mission Association. He is the author of the following works in Swedish: *The Lord is my Light*, Stockholm, 1877, 3d ed. 1881; *God has done it*, 1878, 3d ed. 1881; *The Obedience of Faith*, Gefle, 1878; *The Suffering and Crucified*

Christ, Stockholm, 1879; *The Living Way*, Gefle, 1880; *Christian Baptism*, 1880; *A Word in Season*, 1880; *The Perfect Prince of our Salvation*, Stockholm, 1881; *The Sin against the Holy Spirit*, 1881; *The Strong and the Stronger*, 1881; *The Work of the Holy Spirit*, 1881; *The Lord's Supper*, 1882; *The Tabernacle*, 1883; *The Trumpet of Peace* (hymn-book), 1883; *A Commentary on Ephesians*, 1884; *The Last Things*, 1886.

ELLICOTT, Right Rev. Charles John, lord bishop of Gloucester and Bristol, Church of England; b. at Whitwell, near Stamford, April 25, 1819; studied at St. John's College, Cambridge; graduated B.A. (senior optime and second-class classical tripos) 1841; became members' prize 1842, and Hulsean prize essayist (see below) 1843; M.A. 1844; fellow of St. John's; was ordained deacon 1846, priest 1847; was rector of Pilton, Rutlandshire, 1841–48; professor of divinity, King's College, London, 1848–60; Hulsean professor of divinity, Cambridge, 1860–61; dean of Exeter, 1861–63; in 1863 consecrated bishop of Gloucester and Bristol. He was chairman of the British New-Testament Revision Company, 1870–81. He has published, besides sermons, lectures, and charges, the following: *The History and Obligation of the Sabbath* (Hulsean prize essay), Cambridge, 1844; *Treatise on Analytical Statics*, 1851; *Critical and Grammatical Commentary on Galatians*, London, 1854, 2d ed. 1859; *Ephesians*, 1855, 5th ed. 1884; *Philippians, Colossians, and Philemon*, 1857, 2d ed. 1861; *Thessalonians*, 1858, 4th ed. 1880; *Pastoral Epistles*, 1858, 5th ed. 1883; *Life of our Lord* (Hulsean lectures for 1859), 1860, 6th ed. 1876; *Considerations on the Revision of the English Version of the New Testament*, 1870, reprinted in volume with Lightfoot and Trench, by Dr. Schaff, New York, 1873; *Modern Unbelief*, 1876; *The Present Dangers of the Church of England*, 1878; *The Being of God*, 1880; *Are we to modify Fundamental Doctrine?* Bristol, 1885. He edited *A New-Testament Commentary for English Readers, by Various Writers*, 1877–82, 3 vols.; *Handy Commentary*, 1883, 13 vols. (revised from preceding); *Old-Testament Commentary for English Readers*, 1882–84, 5 vols. *

ELLINWOOD, Frank Fields, D.D. (University of the City of New York, 1865), Presbyterian; b. at Clinton, N.Y., June 20, 1826; graduated at Hamilton College, 1849; studied theology at Auburn (1851–52) and Princeton (1852–53, graduated) theological seminaries; was pastor of Belvidere, N.J., 1853–54; Central Church, Rochester, N.Y., 1854–65; secretary of the Presbyterian Committee of Church Erection, 1866–70; of the Memorial-Fund Committee, 1870–71; of the Presbyterian Board of Foreign Missions, since 1871. He is the author of *The Great Conquest*, New York, 1876. *

ELLIOT, Very Rev. Gilbert, D.D. (by Archbishop of Canterbury, 1850), dean of Bristol, Church of England; b. in Dresden, Saxony, March 17, 1800; educated at St. John's College, Cambridge; graduated B.A. 1822, M.A. 1824; ordained deacon 1823, priest 1824; became rector of Holy Trinity, Newing-Butts, 1824; of Kirkby Thore, Westmoreland, 1833; of Wivenhoe, Essex, 1845; of Holy Trinity, Marylebone, London, 1846; dean, 1850. He was prolocutor of the Lower House of Convocation, 1857–64; is a member of the Low-Church party. He is the author of *Sermons on Subjects of the Day*, London, 1850.

ELLIOTT, Charles, D.D. (Ohio University, Athens, O., 1861), Presbyterian; b. at Castleton, Roxburghshire, Scotland, March 18, 1815; graduated at Lafayette College, Easton, Penn., 1840; studied for a year at Princeton Theological Seminary; taught in the academy at Xenia, O, 1843–45; became professor of belles-lettres in the Western University of Pennsylvania, Pittsburg, 1847; of Greek, in Miami University, Oxford, O., 1849; of biblical literature and exegesis, in the Presbyterian Theological Seminary of the North-west, Chicago, Ill., 1863; professor of Hebrew in Lafayette College, 1882. He is a member of the American Oriental Society. He translated and edited Kleinert's commentary on Jonah, Nahum, Habakkuk, and Zephaniah, and wrote the introduction to the prophetical writings in the American Lange series, and has published independently, *The Sabbath*, Philadelphia, 1866; *A Treatise on the Inspiration of the Scriptures*, Edinburgh, 1877; (with Rev. W. J. Harsha) *Biblical Hermeneutics* (a translation of Cellérier, *Manuel d'herméneutique*, 1852), New York, 1879; *Mosaic Authorship of the Pentateuch*, Cincinnati, 1884.

ELLIOTT, Right Rev. Robert Woodward Barnwell, D.D. (University of the South, Sewanee, Tenn., 1874), Episcopalian, missionary bishop of Western Texas; b. at Beaufort, S.C., Aug. 16, 1840; graduated at South-Carolina College, Columbia, 1861; was missionary in Georgia, 1868; assistant minister in Church of the Incarnation, New York, 1870; rector of St. Philip's, Atlanta, Ga., 1871; consecrated, 1874. He was aide-de-camp to Gen. A. R. Lawton, C.S.A., 1861–63; wounded at second battle of Manassas, Aug. 28, 1862; promoted to be assistant adjutant-general of division, October, 1863; surrendered at Greensborough, N.C., with Gen. J. E. Johnston's forces, May 10, 1865.

ELLIS, George Edward, D.D. (Harvard University, 1857), **LL.D.** (the same, 1883); b. in Boston, Mass., Aug. 8, 1814; graduated at Harvard College, Cambridge, Mass., 1833, and at the Harvard Divinity School 1836; pastor of the Harvard Church, Charlestown, Mass., 1840–69; professor of doctrinal theology in Harvard Divinity School, 1857–63. He is the president of the Massachusetts Historical Society. He edited for many years the *Christian Register* and *Christian Examiner*. He has delivered several courses of lectures before the Lowell Institute. He has published *The Half-Century of the Unitarian Controversy*, Boston, 1857; *Aims and Purposes of the Founders of Massachusetts*, 1869; *Memoir of Jared Sparks* (1869), of *Count Rumford* (1871), of *Jacob Bigelow, M.D.* (1881), and of *Nathaniel Thayer; History of the Battle of Bunker's Hill*, 1875; *Introduction to the History of the First Church in Boston, 1630–1880*, 1882; *The Red Man and the White Man in North America*, 1882; *Lives of Anne Hutchinson, John Mason*, and *William Penn*, in Sparks's *American Biographies; Address at the Consecration of Woodlawn Cemetery*, 1851; *Oration before the City Government, on the Centennial of the Evacuation of Boston by the British Army*, 1876; *Address at the Unveiling of the Statue of John Harvard*, Cambridge, 1884; *Address on a Memorial of Chief Justice Sewall, in Old South Church*, Boston, 1884; and several chapters in the

Memorial History of Boston, and in the *Narrative and Critical History of America*, etc.

ELMSLIE, William Gray, M.A., English Presbyterian; b. at Insch, Aberdeenshire, Scotland, Oct. 5, 1848; graduated with first-class honors at the University of Aberdeen, 1868; studied theology at New College, Edinburgh, Berlin, and in Paris; became assistant professor of natural philosophy at Aberdeen, 1869; minister of Willesden Church, 1875; and professor of Hebrew in London Presbyterian College, 1883.

EMERTON, Ephraim, Ph.D. (Leipzig, 1876), Unitarian; b. at Salem, Mass., Feb. 18, 1851; graduated at Harvard College, 1871; became instructor in history in Harvard University, 1876; and Winn professor of ecclesiastical history, 1882.

ENDERS, Ernst Ludwig, D.D. (Erlangen, 1883), Lutheran; b. at Frankfurt-am-Main, Germany, Dec. 27, 1833; studied at Heidelberg, Erlangen, and Tübingen, 1852–55; has been pastor at Oberrad, near Frankfurt-am-Main, since 1863. He is the editor of the second edition of the Erlangen edition of Luther's works (1. *Predigten*, 1862–81, 21 vols.; 2. *Reformations- historische und polemische deutsche Schriften*, 1883–85, 3 vols.; 3. *Briefwechsel*, vol. i., 1507–March, 1519), 1884, all published at Frankfurt-am-Main, except the first six vols.

ENGLISH, John Mahan, Baptist; b. at Tullytown, Bucks County, Penn., Oct. 20, 1845; graduated at Brown University, Providence, R.I., 1870, and at Newton Theological Institution, 1875; became pastor in Gloucester, Mass., 1875; in Boston, 1882; and professor of homiletics, pastoral duties, and church polity, in Newton Theological Institution, Mass., 1882.

ERDMANN, (Christian Friedrich) David, D.D., German Protestant theologian; b. at Güstebiese, July 28, 1821; studied at Berlin, 1843–47; became *privat-docent* there of theology 1853, ordinary professor at Königsberg 1856, and general superintendent and honorary professor at Breslau 1864. He is the author of *Lieben und Leiden der ersten Christen*, Berlin, 1854; *Prima Joannis epistolæ argumentum nexus et consilium*, 1855; *Die Reformation und ihre Märtyrer in Italien*, 1855; *Der Brief des Jakobus, erklärt*, 1881; *Luther und die Hohenzollern*, Breslau, 1883, 2d ed. 1884. *

ERRETT, Isaac, M.A. (*hon.*, Bethany College, Bethany, W. Va , 1867), Disciple; b. in New-York City, Jan. 2, 1820; self-educated since his tenth year; has labored as farmer, miller, lumberman, bookseller, printer, school-teacher, pastor, preacher, and editor; became pastor of the Church of the Disciples at Pittsburg, Penn., 1840; New Lisbon, O., 1844; North Bloomfield, 1849; Warren, 1851; Muir and Ionia, Mich., 1856; Detroit, 1863; Muir and Ionia, 1865; Cleveland, 1866; retired, 1868; Chicago, 1870–71. He was corresponding secretary of Ohio Christian Missionary Society 1853–56, and president 1868–71; corresponding secretary of the American Christian Missionary Society 1857–60, and president 1874–76; president of the Foreign Christian Missionary Society since 1875. He was president of Alliance College, Alliance, O., 1868–69; declined elections to the presidency of Agricultural and Mechanical College, Kentucky University, Lexington, Ky. (1869), the professorship of biblical literature in Bethany College, Bethany, W. Va. (1869), and to the professorship of homiletics in the College of the Bible, Kentucky University, Lexington, Ky. (1880). In 1884 he became a member of the International Sunday-school Committee; in 1885, one of the Council of the American Congress of Churches; in 1886, one of the executive committee of the Law and Order League of Cincinnati, O., where he has resided since 1869. He was associated with Alexander Campbell (d. 1866) in editing *The Millennial Harbinger;* since 1866 he has been editor-in-chief of *The Christian Standard*, the denominational organ. He is the author of *Modern Spiritualism compared with Christianity: a Debate between Joel Tiffany, Esq., of Painesville, O., and Rev. Isaac Errett of Warren, O. (a Phonographic Report by J. D. Cox, Esq.)*, Warren, O., 1855; *Brief View of Christian Missions, Ancient and Modern*, Cincinnati, 1857; *First Principles; or, The Elements of the Gospel*, 1867 (twenty thousand copies issued); *Walks about Jerusalem; a Search after the Landmarks of Primitive Christianity*, 1872, 5th ed., St. Louis, Mo., 1884; *Talks to Bereans: a Series of Twenty-three Sermons to Inquirers who acknowledge the Divine Inspiration of the Scriptures*, Cincinnati, 1875, 4th ed., St. Louis, Mo., 1884; *Letters to a Young Christian*, Cincinnati, 1881 (two editions); *Evenings with the Bible*, vol. i., *Studies in the Old Testament*, 1885, 2d ed. 1885; *Life and Writings of George Edward Flower*, 1885; *Our Position: a Brief Statement of the Plea urged by the People known as Disciples of Christ*, 1885 (about seventy-five thousand have been issued).

EVANS, Llewelyn Ioan, D.D. (Wabash College, O., 1872), Presbyterian; b. at Treuddyn, near Mold, North Wales, June 27, 1833; studied at Welsh Presbyterian College, Bala, 1846–49; graduated at Racine College, Wis., B.S. 1854, B.A. 1856, and at Lane Theological Seminary, Cincinnati, O., 1860; became successively pastor of the Seminary Church, 1860; professor of church history, 1863; of biblical literature and exegesis, 1867; of New-Testament Greek and exegesis, 1875. He was a member of the Wisconsin legislature, 1856–57; and corresponding editor of *The Central Christian Herald*, 1863–66. He translated and edited Zöckler's commentary on Job, in the American Lange series, New York, 1874; and has published sermons, pamphlets, etc.

EVANS, Thomas Saunders, D.D. (Edinburgh, 1885), Church of England; b. at Belper, Derbyshire, March 8, 1816; entered St. John's College, Cambridge; received Porson prize 1838; graduated B.A. 1839, M.A. 1845; was ordained deacon 1844, priest 1846; was assistant master of Rugby School; since 1862 canon residentiary of Durham, and professor of Greek and classical literature in the University of Durham. He has contributed to the *Sabrinæ Corolla* and to *The Expositor* (1882–83, on the Revised Version of the New Testament); and published *Tennyson's Œnone translated into Latin Hexameters*, Cambridge, 1873; *Commentary on 1st Corinthians*, in *The Speaker's Commentary*, London, 1881; *The Nihilist in the Hayfield:* a Latin poem, 1882.

EVERETT, Charles Carroll, D.D. (Bowdoin, 1870, Harvard, 1874), Unitarian; b. at Brunswick, Me., June 19, 1829; graduated at Bowdoin College 1850, and at the Harvard Divinity School 1859; tutor (1853–55) and professor of modern languages at Bowdoin (1855–57); minister of Unitarian Church, Bangor, Me., 1859–69; since

1869 has been Bussey professor of theology in Harvard University, and since 1878 dean of the Harvard Divinity School. He has published *The Science of Thought*, Boston, 1869; *Religions before Christianity: a Manual for Sunday Schools*, 1883; *Fichte's Science of Knowledge*, Chicago, 1884.

EWALD, (Heinrich August) Paul, Ph.D. (Leipzig, 1881), **Lic. Theol.** (Leipzig, 1883), German Protestant; b. at Leipzig, Jan. 13, 1857; studied at Leipzig and Erlangen, 1875–79; member of the *Prediger Collegium* of St. Paul's, Leipzig, 1880–82; became *privat-docent* of theology at Leipzig, 1883. He is the author of *Der Einfluss der stoisch ciceronianischen Moral auf die Darstellung der Ethik bei Ambrosius*, Leipzig, 1881; *De vocis συνειδήσεως apud scriptores novi testamenti vi ac potestate, commentatio et biblico-philologica et biblico-theologica*, 1883; edited the 4th ed. of Winer's *Comparative Darstellung des Lehrbegriffs der verschiedenen christlichen Kirchenparteien*, 1882.

EXELL, Joseph Samuel, M.A., Church of England; b. at Melksham, Wilts, May 29, 1849; educated at Taunton and Sheffield Colleges; was ordained deacon 1881, priest 1882; was curate of Weston-super-Mare, 1881–84; and since vicar of Townstall with St. Saviour, Dartmouth, Devonshire. He is, with Canon Spence, joint editor of *The Pulpit Commentary*, London, 1880 sqq., and of *The Homiletical Library*, 1882 sqq.; and, with Canon Spence and Rev. C. Neil, of *Thirty Thousand Thoughts*, 1883 sqq.; sole editor of *The Homiletical Quarterly* since 1880; of *Heart Chords*, 1883 sq.; and of *The Monthly Interpreter*, 1885 sqq. He has independently published *Practical Readings in the Book of Jonah*, and *Homiletical Commentary on the Book of Exodus*, 1879; with T. H. Leate, *Homiletical Commentary on the Book of Genesis*, 1885.

EYRE, Most Rev. Charles, archbishop of Glasgow, Roman Catholic; b. at Askam Bryan Hall, York, in the year 1817; educated at Ushaw College, Durham, and at Rome; was senior priest at St. Mary's Cathedral, Newcastle, 1847–68; appointed in 1868 archbishop for the western district and delegate apostolic for Scotland; consecrated at Rome, Jan. 31, 1869, by the title of Archbishop of Anazarba *in partibus infidelium;* but when the Roman-Catholic hierarchy was restored in Scotland, March 4, 1878, he was appointed archbishop of Glasgow. He published *History of St. Cuthbert*, London, 1849, 3d ed. 1886.

F.

FAIRBAIRN, Andrew Martin, D.D. (Edinburgh, 1878), Congregationalist; b. in the neighborhood of Edinburgh, Nov. 4, 1838; graduated from Edinburgh University, 1860; studied theology at the Evangelical Union Theological Hall, Glasgow, 1856-61, and at Berlin under Dorner, 1866-67; became pastor of Independent Church at Bathgate, Scotland, 1861 (during 1866 and 1867 absent in Berlin to study under Dorner); at Aberdeen, 1872; principal and professor of theology in the Congregational Theological Institution, Airdale College, Bradford, Eng., 1877; principal of Mansfield College, Oxford, 1886. He was Muir lecturer on the science of religion in the University of Edinburgh, 1878-83. He is the author of *Studies in the Philosophy of Religion and History*, London, 1876, New York, 1877; *Studies in the Life of Christ*, 1880, 4th ed. 1885, New York, 1882; *The City of God, a Series of Discussions in Religion*, 1883, 2d ed. 1885; *Religion in History and in Life of To-day*, 1884, 2d ed. 1885; and since 1871 has constantly contributed to the *Contemporary Review* on philosophical and theological subjects, his special field of work being the philosophy and history of religion.

FAIRCHILD, James Harris, D.D. (Hillsdale College, Mich., 1864), Congregationalist; b. at Stockbridge, Mass., Nov. 25, 1817; graduated at Oberlin College, O., 1838, and has been connected with it since 1839,—as professor of languages, 1842-47; of mathematics, 1847-58; of moral philosophy and theology, 1858-66, which chair has since 1866 been held by him along with the presidency. He has published *Moral Philosophy*, New York, 1869; *Oberlin, the College and the Colony, 1833-83*, Oberlin, 1883; and edited *Memoirs of Rev. C. G. Finney*, New York, 1876, and *Finney's Systematic Theology*, Oberlin, 1878.

FALLOWS, Right Rev. Samuel, D.D. (Lawrence University, Wis., 1873), Reformed Episcopalian, bishop; b. at Pendleton, near Manchester, Eng., Dec. 15, 1835; graduated at Lawrence University, Wis., and at the University of Wisconsin, Madison, Wis., graduating as valedictorian at the latter, 1859; was vice-president of Galesville University, Wis., 1859-61; chaplain of the 32d Regiment Wis. Vols., 1862; professor elect of natural sciences, Lawrence University, Wis., 1863; lieutenant-colonel 40th Wis. Vol. Infantry, and colonel 49th, 1864-65; promoted brevet-brigadier-general for meritorious services; was State superintendent of public instruction for the State of Wisconsin, 1870-73; professor elect of logic and rhetoric in the University of Wisconsin, 1873; president of Illinois Wesleyan University, Bloomington, Ill, 1874-75. From 1857 to 1875 he was a minister of the Methodist-Episcopal Church; in 1875 he became rector of St. Paul's Reformed Episcopal Church, Chicago; in 1876 was elected bishop, and given the missionary jurisdiction of the West, and still unites this with his rectorship. While superintendent of public instruction of Wisconsin he devised, and carried out through legislative action, the plan of bringing all the high and common schools of the State into direct connection with the University of Wisconsin. He also perfected the institute plan of instruction for teachers, now in operation in that State. While president of the Illinois Wesleyan University, he inaugurated in America the plan of conferring collegiate degrees, especially the higher ones, upon non-resident students and graduates, based upon a thorough written as well as oral examination on a prescribed course of study, akin to the plan pursued by the London University. He delivered, as the representative of the West, one of the addresses before the American Bible Society in Philadelphia, 1872; as fraternal delegate, addressed the General Conference of the Methodist-Episcopal Church at Cincinnati, O., 1880; delivered the annual oration before the Society of the Army of the Tennessee, at Cleveland, O., 1883. In theology he is an Arminian. He founded in 1876, and for four years edited, *The Appeal*, the first distinctively Reformed Episcopal Church paper, published in Chicago, Ill. (now incorporated with *The Episcopal Recorder*, New York). He is the compiler and editor of *Bright and Happy Homes*, Chicago, Ill., 1881 (several editions); *Synonyms and Autonyms*, 1883; *Abbreviations and Contractions*, 1883; *Briticisms, Americanisms, Colloquial and Provincial Words and Phrases*, 1883 (all three in the *Standard Handbook Series*); *Liberty and Union*, Madison, Wis., 1883; *The Home Beyond*, Chicago, Ill., 1884, last ed. 1886; *The Progressive Dictionary* (a supplement to all the standard dictionaries of the English language), 1885; *Past Noon*, Cincinnati, O., 1886.

FARRAR, Adam Storey, D.D. (Oxford, 1864), **F.C.S., F.R.A.S.,** Church of England; b. in London, April 20, 1826; educated at St. Mary's Hall, Oxford; graduated B.A. (first-class classics and second-class mathematics), 1850; Arnold historical prizeman, Denyer's theological prizeman, 1850; M.A. (Queen's College), 1852; B.D., 1864. He was ordained deacon 1852, and priest 1853; was Michel fellow of Queen's College, Oxford, 1852-63; public examiner in classics and mathematics, 1854-56; tutor of Wadham College, 1855-64; select preacher at Oxford, 1856-57, 1869-70; preacher at Whitehall, 1858-60; Bampton lecturer, 1862; select preacher at Cambridge, 1875 and 1881. Since 1864 he has been professor of divinity and of ecclesiastical history in the University of Durham; since 1868 an examining chaplain to the bishop of Peterborough; since 1878 a canon of Durham. He has published *Science in Theology* (university sermons), London, 1859; *Critical History of Free Thought* (Bampton lectures), 1862; and miscellaneous sermons and lectures.

FARRAR, Ven. Frederic William, D.D. (Cambridge, 1873), **F.R.S.,** archdeacon of Westminster, Church of England; b. in Bombay, India, Aug. 7, 1831; educated at King William's College, Isle of Man, and at King's College, London; graduated B.A. from University of London, and was appointed university scholar, 1852. He went to Cambridge, entered Trinity College, took the chancellor's prize for English verse (see below), 1852; graduated B.A. (fourth in first-class classical tripos, and junior optime in mathematics), 1854; was elected fellow; was Le Bas classical prizeman 1856, and Norrisian prizeman 1857; graduated M.A. 1857, B.D. 1872. He was ordained deacon 1854, and priest 1857; was assistant master in Harrow School, 1854-71; and head master of Marlborough College, 1871-76. He was select preacher at Cambridge, 1868-69, 1872, 1874, and frequently since; honorary chaplain to the Queen, 1869-73, and since 1873 chaplain in ordinary; Hulsean lecturer (Cambridge) 1870, and Bampton lecturer (Oxford) 1885. In 1876 he was installed rector of St. Margaret, Westminster, London, and canon of Westminster; and on April 24, 1883, was appointed archdeacon of Westminster, and rural dean of St. Margaret and St. John the Evangelist, Westminster. Archdeacon Farrar has done much to improve public-school instruction and to promote total abstinence. He is the author of the following works: *The Arctic Regions* (chancellor's prize poem), Cambridge, 1852; *Christian Doctrine of the Atonement* (Norrisian prize), 1857; the three works of fiction for boys: *Eric, or Little by Little*, 1857, 20th ed. 1882; *Julian Home*, 1859, 10th ed. 1882; and *St. Winifred's, or the World of School*, 1863, 13th ed. 1882; *The Origin of Language*, 1860; *The Fall of Man, and other Sermons*, 1865, 3d ed. 1876; *Chapters on Language*, 1865, and *Families of Speech*, 1870 (the two were combined in revised form under title *Language and Languages*, 1878); *Essays on a Liberal Education*, 1866, 2d ed. 1868; *Seekers after God*, 1869, new ed. 1877; *The Witness of History to Christ* (Hulsean lectures), 1871, 3d ed. 1875; *The Silence and Voices of God* (university and other sermons), 1873, 3d ed. 1875; *The Life of Christ*, 1874, 2 vols. (12th ed. same year, 24th ed. 1876, 38th ed. 1880, illustrated ed. 1878, popular ed. in 1 vol. without illustrations 1881, cabinet ed. 5 vols. 32mo 1883); *In the Days of thy Youth* (Marlborough sermons), 1876, 4th ed. 1877; *Eternal Hope* (Westminster sermons on eschatology), 1878, 12th ed. same year; *Saintly Workers* (Lent lectures), 1878; *The Life and Work of St. Paul*, 1879, 2 vols. (18th thousand, 1881; popular ed., 1 vol., 1884); *Gospel according to St. Luke* (*Cambridge Bible for Schools*), 1880, 2d ed. 1884; *Ephphatha, or the Amelioration of the World* (sermons), 1880; *Mercy and Judgment: Last Words on Christian Eschatology*, 1881, 2d ed. 1882; *Early Days of Christianity*, 1882, 2 vols. (new ed. 1883, in 1 vol. 1884); *Hebrews, with Notes and Introduction*, 1883; *My Object in Life* (*Heart-Chords Series*), 1883; *With the Poets: a Selection of English Poetry*, 1883; *Messages of the Books: Discourses and Notes on the New Testament*, 1884; *Sermons and Addresses delivered in America*, 1886; *The History of Interpretation* (Bampton lectures), 1886. For school use he has written, *Greek Grammar Rules* (6th ed. 1865) and *Brief Greek Syntax* (3d ed. 1867). The above list presents only a portion of his literary activity; for he has contributed to Smith's *Dictionaries*, *The Pulpit Commentary*, *Encyclopædia Britannica*, besides to various journals, etc.

FAUSSET, Andrew Robert, Church of England; b. at Silverhill, County Fermanagh, Ireland, Oct. 13, 1821; was scholar of Trinity College, Dublin, 1841; took the vice-chancellor's prize for Latin verse (fourth) and for Greek verse (third), 1841; Berkeley gold medal, 1842; vice-chancellor's prize for Greek verse (second) 1842, and for Latin prose (first) 1843-44; divinity testimonium (second-class), 1845; graduated B.A. (senior moderator classics), 1843, M.A. 1846. He was ordained deacon 1847, priest 1848; became curate of Bishop Middleham, County Durham, 1847; and rector of St. Cuthbert's, York, his present charge, 1859. He was chaplain at Bex, Switzerland, 1870, and at St. Goar on the Rhine, 1873 (both under the Church Colonial and Continental Society). He is evangelical, of the Church-of-England type of orthodoxy. He has edited *Terence*, with notes, Dublin, 1844; *Homer's Iliad, I.-VIII.*, 1846; *Livy, I.-III.*, 1849; *Bengel's Gnomon of the New Testament*, Edinburgh, 1857, 5 vols.; *Vinet's Homiletics, with Notes*, London, 1858; *The Greek Testament* (for the British and Foreign Bible Society), 1877; written, *Scriptures and the Prayer-Book in Harmony*, 1854; *Ireland and the Irish*, 1854; *Faculties of the Lower Animals*, 1858; vols. ii. and iv. of the *Critical and Explanatory Pocket-Bible*, Glasgow, 1862, 4 vols.; vols. iii., iv., and vi. of the *Critical, Experimental, and Practical Commentary* (Jamieson, Fausset, and Brown's), 1868; *Horæ Psalmicæ*, London, 1877, 2d ed. 1885; *The Church and the World*, 1878; *The Englishman's Bible Cyclopædia*, 1879; *The Millennium*, 1880; *The Signs of the Times*, 1881; *Prophecy a Sure Light*, 1882; *The Latter Rain*, 1883; *True Science confirming Genesis*, 1884; *The Personal Antichrist*, 1884; *Spiritualism*, 1885; *Expository Commentary on the Book of Judges*, 1885.

FERGUSON, Right Rev. Samuel D., Episcopalian, missionary bishop of West Africa; b. in Charleston, S.C., Jan. 1, 1842; emigrated to Liberia, 1848; educated in the mission schools; became rector of St. Mark's, Harper, 1868; bishop, 1885. *

FERRIS, John Mason, D.D. (Rutgers College, New Brunswick, N.J., 1867), Reformed (Dutch); b. at Albany, N.Y., Jan. 17, 1825; graduated at the University of the City of New York, 1843, and at the theological seminary of the Reformed Dutch Church, New Brunswick, N.J., 1849; became pastor of Reformed Churches, at Tarrytown, N.Y., 1849; Chicago (Second), Ill., 1854; and at Grand Rapids (First), Mich., 1862; corresponding secretary of the Board of Foreign Missions of the Reformed Church in America, 1865; editor of *The Christian Intelligencer*, New York (the denominational organ), 1883.

FFOULKES, Edmund Salusbury, Church of England; b. at Eriviatt, Denbigh, Jan. 12, 1819; educated at Jesus College, Oxford; graduated B.A. (second-class classics) 1841, M.A. 1844, B.D. 1851; was appointed fellow and tutor of his college; entered the Roman-Catholic Church, 1855; returned to Church of England, 1870; was select preacher at Oxford, 1875-76; became rector of Wigginton, 1876; and then vicar of St. Mary the Virgin, Oxford, 1878. He is the author of *A Manual of Ecclesiastical History*, London, 1851; *Christendom's Divisions*, 1865-67, 2 vols.; *The Athanasian Creed, by whom written and by whom published*, 1871, 2d ed. 1872.

FIELD, Frederick, Church of England; b. in London, in the year 1801; d. at Norwich, April 19, 1885. He was educated at Trinity College, Cambridge, where he graduated B.A. (Tyrwhitt's Hebrew scholar, tenth wrangler, and chancellor's medallist) 1823, M.A. 1826, *hon.* LL.D. 1875; was fellow of Trinity College, Cambridge, 1824-43; rector of Reepham, Norfolk, 1842-63; elected honorary fellow of Trinity College, Cambridge, 1875. He was a member of the Old-Testament Revision Company. He edited the Greek text of Chrysostom's Homilies on Matthew, Cambridge, 1839, 3 vols., and all the Pauline Epistles, 1849-62, 7 vols.; Barrow's *Treatise on the Pope's Supremacy*, London, 1851; Grabe's text of the Septuagint, Oxford; *Otium Norvicense* (I., *Tentamen de reliquiis Aquilæ, Symmachi, Theodotionis e lingua Syriaca in Græcam convertendis;* II., *Tentamen de quibusdam vocabulis Syro-Græcis;* III., *Notes on Select Passages of the Greek Testament*), 3 parts, 1864, 1876, 1881; *Origenis Hexaplorum quæ supersunt*, 1867-74, 2 vols.; *Sermons*, 1878. *

FIELD, Henry Martyn, D.D. (Williams College, 1862), Presbyterian; b. at Stockbridge, Mass., April 3, 1822; graduated at Williams College, Williamstown, Mass., 1838, and at East Windsor Hill (now Hartford) Theological Seminary, Conn., 1841; studied at Yale Divinity School, New Haven, Conn., 1841-42; was pastor in St. Louis, Mo., 1842-47; at West Springfield, Mass., 1850-54; from 1854 has been an editor and proprietor of *The Evangelist*, a Presbyterian denominational weekly, published in New-York City; since 1870, sole editor and proprietor. He has been an extensive traveller, having been five times in Europe, twice in the East, and once round the world. He has written *The Irish Confederates, and the Rebellion of 1798*, New York, 1851; *Summer Pictures from Copenhagen to Venice*, 1859; *History of the Atlantic Telegraph*, 1866; *From the Lakes of Killarney to the Golden Horn*, 1876; *From Egypt to Japan*, 1877 (of the two last named, fifteen editions have been issued); *On the Desert; with Review of Events in Egypt*, 1883; *Among the Holy Hills* (Palestine), 1884; *The Greek Islands and Turkey after the War*, 1885.

FISHER, George Park, D.D. (Brown University, 1866; the same degree was given him by Edinburgh University, 1886), **LL.D.** (College of New Jersey, Princeton, 1879), Congregationalist; b. at Wrentham, Mass., Aug. 10, 1827; graduated at Brown University, Providence, R.I., 1847, and at Andover Theological Seminary, Mass., 1851; became professor of divinity (college preacher) in Yale College, New Haven, Conn., 1854; professor of ecclesiastical history, 1861. He has published *Essays on the Supernatural Origin of Christianity*, New York, 1865, 3d ed. (enlarged) 1877; *Life of Benjamin Silliman*, 1866, 2 vols., new ed., Philadelphia, 1877, 1 vol.; *The Reformation*, New York, 1873; *The Beginnings of Christianity*, 1877; *Faith and Rationalism*, 1879; *Discussions in History and Theology*, 1880; *The Christian Religion*, 1882; *Grounds of Theistic and Christian Belief*, 1883; *Outlines of Universal History*, 1885.

FISK, Franklin Woodbury, D.D. (Olivet College, Mich., 1865), Congregationalist; b. at Hopkinton, N.H., Feb. 16, 1820; graduated at Yale College, New Haven, Conn., 1849, and at the Yale Divinity School, 1852; tutor in Yale College, 1851-1853; became professor of rhetoric and English literature, Beloit College, Wis., 1854; professor of sacred rhetoric in Chicago (Congregational) Theological Seminary, 1859. Besides articles, and contributions to *Current Discussions in Theology* (Chicago, 1884 sqq.), prepared annually by the professors of the seminary, he has published *Manual of Preaching*, New York, 1884.

FITZGERALD, Oscar Penn, D.D. (Southern University, Greensborough, Ala., 1868), Methodist (Southern branch); b. in Caswell County, N.C., Aug. 24, 1829; was missionary in the California mines, 1855-57; editor of *Pacific Methodist, Christian Spectator*, and *California Teacher*, in San Francisco; was superintendent of public instruction of California, 1867-71, and under his administration the State University was founded, and the Normal School fully organized and permanently located; president of Pacific Methodist College, Santa Rosa, Cal., 1872; editor of the Nashville *Christian Advocate*, since 1878. He is the author of *California Sketches*, Nashville, Tenn., 1879, 2 vols., 2d ed. 1879; *The Class Meeting*, 1880, 2d ed. 1880; *Christian Growth*, 1881, 2d ed. 1881; *Glimpses of Truth*, 1883, 2d ed. 1885; *Dr. Summers; a Life-study*, 1884, 2d ed. 1885; *Centenary Cameos*, 1885.

FLICKINGER, Daniel Kumler, D.D. (Otterbein University, Westerville, O., 1875), United Brethren in Christ; b. at Sevenmile, O., May 25, 1824; educated in common schools and Germantown Academy; elected corresponding secretary of the United-Brethren Church Missionary Society, 1857, and quadrennially re-elected until 1885, when he was elected foreign missionary bishop. He has been to Africa eight times, and to Germany five times, on missionary business; has done much work upon the frontiers of the United States, and also among the Chinese. He is the author of *Off-hand Sketches in Africa*, Dayton, O., 1857; *Sermons* (jointly with Rev. W. J. Shuey), 1859; *Ethiopia, or Twenty-six Years of Missionary Life in Western Africa*, 1877, 3d ed. 1885; *The Church's Marching Orders*, 1879.

FLIEDNER, Fritz, German pastor; b. at Kaiserswerth on the Rhine, June 10, 1845; studied at Halle 1864-66, and at Tübingen 1866-67; became professor in the boarding school for young ladies at Hilden, 1868; chaplain to the legation of the German Empire at Madrid, and evangelist in Spain, 1870. Since 1870 he has edited *Leaves from Spain*, a German periodical devoted to evangelization in Spain; has written articles in different reviews, newspapers, and encyclopædias (Herzog and Brockhaus), and *Blätter und Blüten, Gedichte*, Heidelberg, 1885.

FLINT, Robert, D.D., LL.D., Church of Scotland; b. near Dumfries, Scotland, in the year 1838; studied at Glasgow; was pastor from 1859 until 1864, when he became professor of moral philosophy and political economy at the University of St. Andrew's, and in 1876 professor of divinity in the University of Edinburgh. He is the author of *The Philosophy of History in France and Germany*, Edinburgh, 1874; *Theism* (Baird lectures for 1876), 1877, 5th ed. 1886; *Anti-Theistic Theories* (Baird lectures for 1877), 1879, 2d ed. 1880.

FOOTMAN, Henry, M.A., Church of England; b. at Ipswich, Feb. 10, 1831; educated at St. Peter's College, Cambridge, where, after having taken a second-class in the moral science tripos, 1870, he graduated B.A. 1871, M.A. 1874; ordained (both deacon and priest) 1871, standing first in the examination for orders; vicar of Lambourne, Hungerford, 1875–78; in charge of St. George's, Campden Hill, 1878–80; select preacher at Cambridge, 1880–81; vicar of Shoreditch, 1880–81; and since 1881 has been vicar of Nocton Lincoln. Although from early years a student of theology, he pursued a commercial career, and prior to entering Cambridge was partner in a large firm. He is the author of *Life, its Friends and Foes* (Lent lectures), London, 1873; *From Home and Back* (Lenten sermons), 1876; *The Eloquence of the Cross*, 1877; *Nature and Prevalence of Modern Unbelief*, 1880; *Reasonable Apprehensions and Re-assuring Hints*, 1883, 2d ed. 1884, reprinted, New York, 1885.

FORBES, John, LL.D. (King's College, 1837), **D.D.** (Edinburgh, 1873), Church of Scotland; b. at Boharm, Banffshire, July 5, 1802; graduated A.M. at Marischal College, 1819; studied theology for four years at Marischal and King's Colleges, and later at Göttingen, 1828–29; became successively head master and governor of John Watson's Institution, Edinburgh, 1840, and of Donaldson's Hospital, 1850; professor of Oriental languages at Aberdeen University, 1869. He is the author of *Symmetrical Structure of Scripture, or Principles of Scripture Parallelism exemplified in an Analysis of the Decalogue, Sermon on the Mount, etc.*, Edinburgh, 1854; *Analytical Commentary on the Romans, tracing the Train of Thought by the Aid of Parallelism*, 1868; *Predestination and Free Will reconciled; or Calvinism and Arminianism united in the Westminster Confession*, 1878, 2d ed. 1879.

FOSS, Cyrus David, D.D. (Wesleyan University, 1870), **LL.D.** (Cornell College, Iowa, 1879), Methodist-Episcopal bishop; b. at Kingston, N.Y., Jan. 17, 1834; graduated at Wesleyan University, Middletown, Conn., 1854; became teacher 1854, and principal 1856, of Amenia Seminary, N.Y.; pastor (in Chester, N.Y., Brooklyn, and New York), 1857; president of Wesleyan University, 1875; bishop, 1880.

FOSTER, Frank Hugh, Ph.D. (Leipzig, 1882), Congregationalist; b. at Springfield, Mass., June 18, 1851; graduated at Harvard College, Cambridge, Mass., 1873; from 1873 to 1874 was assistant professor of mathematics in the United-States Naval Academy at Annapolis, Md.; graduated at Andover Theological Seminary, Mass., 1877; from 1877 to 1879 was Congregational pastor at North Reading, Mass.; from 1879 to 1882 in Germany, studying at Göttingen (1879–80) under Lotze, and at Leipzig (1880–82) under Luthardt, Delitzsch, and Kahnis; from 1882 to 1884, professor of philosophy at Middlebury College, Vt.; and since 1884 has been professor of church history in Oberlin Theological Seminary. He translated Grotius' *Defence of the Catholic Faith concerning the Satisfaction of Christ*, and has contributed other articles to the *Bibliotheca Sacra*, of which since 1884 he has been one of the editors.

FOSTER, Randolph Sinks, D.D. (Ohio Wesleyan University, Delaware, O., 1853), **LL.D.** (the same, 1858), Methodist-Episcopal bishop; b. at Williamsburg, Claremont County, O., Feb. 22, 1820; studied at Augusta College, Millersburg, Ky., 1835–37, but did not graduate; entered the ministry of the Methodist-Episcopal Church, 1837; served in the Ohio Conference until 1850, when he was transferred to New York; in 1856 became president of the North-western University, Evanston, Ill.; resigned in 1860, and returned to the pastorate; in 1868 became a professor in Drew Theological Seminary, Madison, N.J. (succeeded Dr. McClintock in the presidency of the same, 1870), and in 1872 a bishop. He was delegate to the Wesleyan body in England, 1870; visited the Methodist-Episcopal missions in South America, 1874; Europe (Germany and Scandinavia), 1874; India, 1882; Italy, Germany, and Scandinavia, 1883; Mexico, 1886. He is the author of *Objections to Calvinism as it is* (letters to Rev. Dr. N. L. Rice), Cincinnati, 1848 (many editions to date); *Christian Purity*, New York, 1851 (many editions to date); *Ministry for the Times*, 1852; *Beyond the Grave*, 1879 (many editions); *Centenary Thoughts for the Pew and Pulpit of Methodism in 1884*, 1884; *Studies in Theology*, 1886.

FOSTER, Robert Verrell, D.D. (Trinity University, Texas, 1884), Cumberland Presbyterian; b. in Wilson County, Tenn., Aug. 12, 1845; graduated A.B. and A.M. from Cumberland University, Lebanon, Tenn.; studied theology under Rev. Dr. Richard Beard; graduated from Union Theological Seminary, New-York City, in 1877; and has been ever since professor of Hebrew and biblical theology and exegesis in the theological school of Cumberland University. In 1881 he declined the chief editorship of *The Cumberland Presbyterian*, the principal denominational organ, and later the presidency of Trinity University, Tehuacana, Tex., and the professorship of Greek and Latin in Lincoln University, Ill. He is a frequent contributor to his denominational papers.

FOWLER, Charles Henry, D.D. (Garrett Biblical Institute, 186–), **LL.D.** (Wesleyan University, Middletown, Conn., 1875), Methodist-Episcopal bishop; b. at Burford, Canada, Aug. 11, 1837; graduated at Genesee College, N.Y., 1859, and at the Garrett Biblical Institute, Evanston, Ill., 1861; entered the ministry; became president North-western University, Evanston, Ill., 1872; editor of *The Christian Advocate*, 1876; missionary secretary, 1880; bishop, 1884.

FOX, Norman, Baptist; b. at Glens Falls, N.Y., Feb. 13, 1836; graduated at the University of Rochester, N.Y., 1855, and at Rochester Baptist Theological Seminary 1857; was pastor at Whitehall, N.Y., 1859–62; chaplain of the 77th Regiment N.Y. Vols., 1862–64; professor in the theological department of William Jewell College, Liberty, Mo., 1869–72. He has been editorially connected with the *Central Baptist, National Baptist*, and *Independent*, and also given voluntary service to different churches. He is the author of *George Fox and the Early Friends*, republished from *Baptist Quarterly Review*, 1878; *Rise of the Use of Pouring and Sprinkling for Baptism*, from the same, 1882; *Inspiration of Apostles in Speaking and Writing*, do., 1885; *A Layman's Ministry: Notes on the Life and Services of the Hon. Nathan Bishop, LL.D.*, New York, 1883.

FRANK, Franz Hermann Reinhold, Ph.D., Lic. Theol. (both Leipzig, 1851), **D.D.** (from Erlangen, 1859), German Evangelical Lutheran theologian; b. at Altenburg, March 25, 1827; studied at Leipzig, 1845-51; was sub-rector at Ratzeburg, 1851-53; professor in the gymnasium at Altenburg, 1853-57; extraordinary professor in 1857, and since 1858 ordinary professor of theology in Erlangen. He is the author of *Evangelische Schulreden*, Altenburg, 1856; *Die Theologie der Concordienformel*, Erlangen, 1858-65, 4 vols.; *System der christlichen Gewissheit*, 1870-73, 2 vols., 2d ed. 2d vol. 1881, 2d ed. 1st vol. 1884; *Aus dem Leben christlicher Frauen*, Gütersloh, 1873; *System der christlichen Wahrheit*, 1878-80, 2 vols., 2d ed. 1885-86; *System der christlichen Sittlichkeit*, 1st vol. 1884, and also of many long articles of dogmatic and ethical contents in *Zeitschrift für Protestantismus u. Kirche*, 1869-76, which he edited.

FRANK, Gustav (Wilhelm), Lic. Theol. (*hon.*, Jena, 1858), **D.D.** (*hon.*, Jena, 1867), German theologian; b. at Schleiz, Germany, Sept. 25, 1832; studied at Jena, habilitated himself there 1859; became professor extraordinary of theology, 1864; ordinary professor of dogmatics and symbolics and Christian ethics at Vienna, April 9, 1867, and member of the superior ecclesiastical council, July 31, 1867; received the Austrian order of the Iron Crown, third class, 1882. He is the author of *Memorabilia quædam Flaciana cum brevi annotatione editoris*, Schleiz, 1856; *De Luthero rationalismi præcursore*, Leipzig, 1857; *De Academia Jenensi evangelicæ veritatis altrice*, Schleiz, 1858; *Die Jenaische Theologie in ihrer geschichtlichen Entwickelung*, Leipzig, 1858; *De Matthiæ Flacii Illyrici in libros sacros meritis*, 1859; *Geschichte der protestantischen Theologie*, 1862-75, 3 parts; *Johann Major, der Wittenberger Poet*, Halle, 1863; *Carl Friedrich Bahrdt* (in Raumer's *Historisches Taschenbuch*), 1866; *Die k. k. evangelisch-theologische Facultät in Wien von ihrer Gründung bis zur Gegenwart, Zur Feier ihres fünfzigjährigen Jubiläums*, Vienna, 1871; *Das Toleranzpatent Kaiser Joseph II.*, 1881; numerous articles in periodicals, and in the *Allgemeine deutsche Biographie*; edited E. F. Apelt's *Religionsphilosophie*, Leipzig, 1860.

FRANKE, August Hermann, Lic. Theol. (Bonn, 1878), Lutheran; b. at Gütersloh, Westphalia, Prussia, Aug. 30, 1853; studied at the universities of Leipzig and Bonn, 1872-76; was successively *domcandidat* in Berlin (1878), inspector of Professor Tholuck's "Students' Home" in Halle (1879-84), and also a *privat-docent* in the university there (1881-84), and professor extraordinary, (1881); ordinary professor of theology at Kiel since July 6, 1885. He is the author of *Leben und Wirken des Rev. Charles G. Finney*, Cologne, 1879, Basel, 1880; *Das alte Testament bei Johannes, Ein Beitrag zur Erklärung und Beurtheiligung der johanneischen Schriften*, Göttingen, 1885.

FRASER, Donald, D.D. (Aberdeen University, 1872), English Presbyterian; b. at Inverness, Scotland, Jan. 15, 1826; graduated M.A. at University of Aberdeen, 1842, and pursued theological studies at Knox College, Toronto, and New College, Edinburgh; was Presbyterian minister in Montreal, 1851-59; at Inverness, 1859-70; and since 1870 has been pastor of Marylebone Presbyterian Church, London. He is vice-president of the British and Foreign Bible Society, honorary secretary of the Evangelical Alliance, and is prominent in church courts (twice moderator of the Supreme Court of the English Presbyterian Church) and in public meetings. He is the author of *Synoptical Lectures on the Books of Holy Scripture*, London, 1871-76, 3 vols., 4th ed. 1886, 2 vols. (Italian trans. of lectures on New Testament, Florence, 1878); *Thomas Chalmers, D.D.*, London and New York, 1881; *Speeches of the Holy Apostles*, 1st and 2d ed., 1882; *Metaphors in the Gospels*, 1885; besides minor publications, and various contributions to reviews and magazines.

FRASER, Right Rev. James, D.D. (Oxford, 1870), lord bishop of Manchester, Church of England; b. at Prestbury, near Cheltenham, Aug. 18, 1818; d. at Manchester, Thursday, Oct. 22, 1885. He was scholar of Lincoln College, Oxford, 1836-39; Ireland scholar, and in the first class in classics, 1839; graduated B.A. 1840, M.A. (Oriel) 1842. He was fellow of Oriel College, 1840-60; tutor, 1842-47; ordained deacon 1846, priest 1847; was rector of Cholderton, Wiltshire, 1847-60; select preacher, Oxford, 1854, 1862, 1872, 1877; chancellor of Sarum Cathedral, 1858-60; rector of Ufton-Nervet, Berkshire, 1860-70; prebendary of Bishopton, in Sarum Cathedral, 1861-70. In 1870 he was consecrated bishop of Manchester. He is the author of *Six Sermons preached before the University of Oxford*, London, 1856; and of the special reports presented to Parliament on education (1860), on education in the United States and Canada (1867), and on the employment of children, young persons, and women in agriculture (1868). He was a most faithful prelate, and hastened his death by overwork, for he had not taken adequate rest for several years.

FREMANTLE, Rev. the Honorable William Henry; b. at Swanbourne, Buckinghamshire, Dec. 12, 1831; educated at Eton and at Balliol College, Oxford; graduated B.A. (first-class classics) 1853; gained the prize for the English essay in 1854; M.A. (All Souls' College) 1857; and was fellow of All Souls' College from 1854 to 1864; ordained deacon 1855, priest 1856; was curate of Middle Claydon, 1855-57; vicar of Lewknor, 1857-65; chaplain to Dr. Tait while the bishop of London (1861-68), and archbishop of Canterbury, 1868-82; rector of St. Mary's, Bryanston Square, London, 1866-83; select preacher at Oxford, 1878-80; canon of Canterbury, and fellow and tutor of Balliol College, Oxford, since 1882; Bampton lecturer in 1883. His theological standpoint is in the main similar to that of the late Dr. Arnold, Dean Stanley, and Richard Rothe. He is the author of *Ecclesiastical Judgments of the Privy Council*, London, 1865; *The Doctrine of Reconciliation to God through Jesus Christ*, 1870; *The Gospel of the Secular Life*, 1882; *The World as the Subject of Redemption* (Bampton lectures), 1885; and various separate sermons, pamphlets, and articles in the *Contemporary* and *Edinburgh* Reviews.

FREPPEL, Right Rev. Charles Emile, Roman Catholic; b. at Obernai (Bas Rhin), France, July 1, 1827; studied at Strassburg; was ordained priest, 1849; taught philosophy in Paris, 1850-53; was chaplain of St. Geneviève, 1853; dean, 1867; professor of sacred eloquence in the faculty of Catholic theology at Paris, 1854-70, and greatly distinguished himself by his eloquence. He was called in 1869 to Rome, to assist in the preliminary arrangements for the Vatican Council, and was pronounced in favor of the papal-infallibility dogma. He was consecrated bishop of Angers in 1870, and has made a vigorous prelate, being active in organizing the pilgrimages to Paray-le-Monial, Puy, and elsewhere, in 1872 and 1873, and in founding a Catholic university at Angers. In 1880 he was returned as deputy from Brest, and attracted great notice by the frequency and violence of his opposition to the government, and by his outspoken ultramontanism. His works are numerous. Among them are, *Les Pères apostoliques et leur époque*, Paris, 1859, 2d ed. 1870; *Les apologistes chrétiens au deuxième siècle*, 1860, 3d ed. 1886; *St. Irénée*, 1861; *Examen critique de la vie de Jésus, de M. Renan*, 1863 (numerous editions); *Conférences sur la divinité de Jésus Christ*, 1863; *Tertullien*, 1864, 2 vols.; *St. Cyprien*, 1865, 3d ed. 1875; *Clément d'Alexandrie*, 1865, 2d ed. 1873; *Examen critique des apôtres de M. Renan*, 1866; *Origène*, 1868; *Œuvres pastorales oratoires*, 1869–80, 4 vols.; *Œuvres polémiques*, 1874–80, 2 vols.; *L'Église et les ouvriers*, 1876; *Les devoirs du chrétien dans la vie civile*, 1876; *La vie chrétienne*, 1879 (Lenten sermons delivered in the chapel of the Tuileries, 1862). *

FRICKE, Gustav Adolf, Ph.D. (Leipzig, 1844), **D.D.** (*hon.*, Kiel, 1851), Evangelical Lutheran theologian; b. at Leipzig, Aug. 23, 1822; studied at the university there; habilitated himself in both the theological and philosophical faculties, 1846; became professor extraordinary of theology, 1849; ordinary professor of theology at Kiel, 1851; *obercatechet* in St. Peter's Church, Leipzig, 1865; ordinary professor of theology in the University of Leipzig, 1867. He is also pastor of St. Peter's, *consistorialrath*, member of the synodical committee of the Evangelical Lutheran Church of Saxony. He has received the royal Saxon Albrecht order second class, the Prussian crown order second class, the Swedish Masa order, is a knight of the Prussian Eagle order third class. Besides numerous sermons, of his writings may be mentioned, *Argumenta pro Dei existentia*, Pars 1., Leipzig, 1847; *Die Erhebung zum Herrn im Gebete*, Reichenbach, 1850, 2d ed. 1861; *Lehrbuch der Kirchengeschichte*, 1. Thl., Leipzig, 1850; *Das exegetische Problem im Briefe Pauli an die Galater c. 3, 20, auf Grund v. Gal. 3, 15–25 geprüft*, 1880; *De mente dogmatica loci Paulini ad Rom. 5, 12 sq. Denuo et emendatius typis expressum*, 1880; *Metaphysik und Dogmatik in ihrem gegenseitigen Verhältnisse, unter besond. Bezieh. auf die Ritschl'sche Theologie*, 1882.

FRIEDLAENDER, Michael, Ph.D. (Halle, 1862), Hebrew; b. at Iutroschin, Prussia, April 29, 1833; studied at Berlin under Protestant and Hebrew teachers; was director of the Institute for Talmudic instruction, in Berlin, and since 1865 has been principal of the Jews' College, London; and under the auspices of the Society of Hebrew Literature, he has published *The Commentary of Ibn Ezra on Jesaiah, edited from MSS., and translated, with Notes, Introductions, and Glossary*, London, 1873–77, 3 vols.; *The Guide of the Perplexed of Maimonides, translated from the original text and annotated*, 1882–85, 3 vols.; and a revision of the Authorized Version with the Hebrew text, *The Jewish Family Bible*, 1882.

FRIEDLIEB, Joseph Heinrich, Lic. Theol. (Bonn, 1840), **D.D.** (Breslau, 1848), Roman Catholic; b. at Meisenheim, Germany, Sept. 1, 1810; became priest 1837, *repetent* at Bonn 1839, and *privat-docent* 1840; professor extraordinary of ethics and of New-Testament exegesis at Breslau, 1845; ordinary professor, 1847. He is the author of *Archäologie der Leidensgeschichte unsers Herrn Jesu Christi*, Bonn, 1843; *Synopsis Evangeliorum*, Breslau, 1847; *De codicibus Sibyllinorum manusc. in usum criticum nondum adhibitis*, 1847; *Oracula Sibyllina rec. proleg. illustr. vers. germ. instruxit*, Leipzig, 1852; *Schrift, Tradition und kirchliche Schriftauslegung, oder die katholische Lehre von den Quellen der christlichen Heilswahrheit an den Zeugnissen der fünf ersten christlichen Jahrhunderte geprüft*, Breslau, 1854; *Geschichte des Lebens Jesu Christi mit chronolog. u. andern histor. Untersuchungen*, 1855, 3d ed. Münster, 1886; *Erinnerungen und Kritiken, Sendschreiben an Dr. Sepp*, 1857; *Prolegomena zur bibl. Hermeneutik*, 1868.

FRIEDRICH, Johann, D.D. (Munich, 1862), Old Catholic, b. at Poxdorf, Upper Franconia, Bavaria, May 5, 1836; studied at Bamberg and Munich; was ordained priest, June 4, 1859; became *privat-docent* 1862, and in 1865 professor extraordinary of theology in the University of Munich. In 1869 he accompanied Cardinal Hohenlohe to the Vatican Council, in the capacity of "theologian;" was there severely criticised because he took Döllinger's position of hostility to the infallibility dogma, and left Rome before the council closed. He flatly refused to accept the dogma; and therefore, by archiepiscopal orders, attendance upon his lectures was forbidden, April 13, 1871, and he was excommunicated, April 17. Nevertheless, he continued to exercise priestly functions, kept his academic position, indeed was promoted, for in June, 1872, he became ordinary professor of doctrinal history, symbolics, patrology, Christian archæology, and literature; but in 1882 was removed to the philosophical faculty as professor of history, by request of the Ultramontanes. Although prominent in the organization of the Old Catholic Church, he has kept aloof from it since 1878, because opposed to its abolition of enforced celibacy. His writings embrace *Johann Wessel*, Regensburg, 1862; *Die Lehre des Johann Hus u. ihre Bedeutung für die Entwicklung der neueren Zeit*, 1862; *Astrologie und Reformation*, Munich, 1864; *Das wahre Zeitalter des h. Rupert*, Bamberg, 1866; *Kirchengeschichte Deutschlands*, Bamberg (1867, 1. Bd. 1 Thl., *Die Römerzeit*; 1869, 2. Bd. 1 Thl., *Die Merovingerzeit*); *Drei (bisher unedirte) Concilien aus der Merovingerzeit*, 1867; *Tagebuch während des Vatican. Concils geführt*, Nördlingen, 1871, 2d ed. 1873; *Documenta ad illustrandum concilium Vaticanum anni 1870*, 1871, 2 vols.; *Joannis de Torrecremata, De potestate papæ et concilii generalis tractatus*, Innsbruck, 1871; *Zur Verteidigung meines Tagebuch*, 1872; *Der Mechanismus der Vatican. Religion*, 1st and 2d ed. 1876; *Beiträge zur Kirchengeschichte des 18. Jahrh.*, Munich, 1876; *Geschichte des Vatican. Concils*, Bonn, 1. Bd. 1877, 2. Bd. 1883, 3. Bd. 1886; *Zur ältesten Geschichte des Primates in der Kirche*, 1879; *Beiträge zur Geschichte des Jesuiten-Ordens*, Munich, 1881.

FRITZSCHE, Otto Fridolin, Lic. Theol. (Halle, 1836), **D.D.** (*hon.*, Halle, 1841), Reformed; b. at Dobrilugk, Sept. 23, 1812; studied at the gymnasium and university of Halle, 1826–35; became *privat-docent* at Halle 1836, and then professor extraordinary in 1837, and professor ordinary in 1842, at Zürich. He has also been chief librarian of the cantonal library since 1844. With his father C. F., and his brother K. F. A. Fritzsche, he issued *Fritzschiorum opuscula academica*, Halle, 1838; with C. L. W. Grimm, *Kurzgefasstes exegetisches Handbuch zu den Apokryphen des Alten Testaments*, Leipzig, 1851–60, 6 parts; independently he has written *De Theodori Mopsuesteni vita et scriptis*, Halle, 1836; *Vita J. J. Zimmermann*, Zürich, 1841; *Catalog* of the cantonal library, 1859; edited the works of Lactantius, Leipzig, 1842–44, 2 vols.; of Theodore of Mopsuestia (New-Testament commentary, and fragments of book on the Incarnation), Zürich, 1847, 2 vols.; *Liber judicum secundum LXX. interpretes*, Zürich, 1866; Anselm's *Cur Deus Homo*, 1868, 2d ed. 1886; *Libri apocryphi V. T. Græce, cum commentario critico* (containing also a few pseudepigraphical books), Leipzig, 1871.

FROTHINGHAM, Octavius Brooks, A.M., Rationalist; b. in Boston, Mass., Nov. 26, 1822; graduated at Harvard College, Cambridge, Mass., 1843; became clergyman at Salem, Mass., 1847; Jersey City, N.J., 1855; New-York City, 1859; resigned from ill health, 1879. He is the author of *Stories from the Lips of the Teacher, Retold by a Disciple*, Boston, 1863, 2d ed. New York, 1875; *Stories of the Patriarchs*, Boston, 1864, 2d ed. New York, 1876; *A Child's Book of Religion*, Boston, 1866, 3d ed. New York, 1876; *The Religion of Humanity*, Boston, 1872, 3d ed. New York, 1875; *Life of Theodore Parker*, Boston, 1874; *Safest Creed, and Twelve Other Discourses of Reason*, New York, 1874; *A History of Transcendentalism in New England*, 1876; *Knowledge and Faith, and other Discourses*, 1876; *The Cradle of the Christ*, 1877; *Creed and Conduct, and other Discourses*, 1877; *Spirit of the New Faith*, 1877; *The Rising and the Setting Faith, and other Discourses*, 1878; *Gerrit Smith: a Biography*, 1878; *Visions of the Future, and other Discourses*, 1879; *George Ripley*, Boston, 1882.

FRY, Benjamin St. James, D.D. (Quincy, now Chaddock, College, 1871), Methodist; b. at Rutledge, Granger County, Tenn., June 16, 1824; studied at Woodward College, Cincinnati, three years, but did not graduate; entered the ministry, and the Ohio Conference, 1847; was president of the Worthington Female College, O., 1856–60; chaplain 63d Regiment Ohio Volunteers, 1861–64; in charge of St. Louis branch of the Western Methodist Book Concern, 1865–72; and since has been editor of *The Central Christian Advocate*, St. Louis. He was member of the London Methodist Ecumenical Conference, and of the Centennial Conference at Baltimore, and read an essay on the Methodist press. He is the author of *Property Consecrated* (prize essay on systematic beneficence), New York, 1856, last ed. 1884; *Lives* of Bishops Whatcoat, McKendree, George, and Roberts, 4 vols.; besides articles in reviews, etc.

FULLER, John Mee, Church of England; b. in London, Dec. 4, 1835; entered St. John's College, Cambridge; graduated B.A. and Crosse University scholar, and was elected to a fellowship in his college, 1858; took a first-class in the theological tripos, 1859; was Tyrwhitt's University scholar, 1860; graduated M.A., 1862; took Kaye University prize, 1863; was ordained deacon 1860, priest 1861; curate in Ealing, 1860–62; South Audley Street, London, 1862–63; Pimlico, 1863–70; editorial secretary of the Society for the Promotion of Christian Knowledge (S.P.C.K.), 1870–74; since 1874 he has been vicar of Bexley, Kent; and since 1883 professor of ecclesiastical history in King's College, London. Besides articles in Smith and Wace's *Dict. Eccles. Biography*, he has written or edited the following: *An Essay on the Authenticity of the Book of Daniel* (the Kaye prize essay), Cambridge, 1864; *Harmony of the Gospels*, 1872; *The Book of Daniel*, in *The Speaker's Commentary*, 1875, 2d ed. 1880; *The Student's Commentary* (founded on *The Speaker's Commentary*), 1879 sqq.

FULLONTON, John, D.D. (Dartmouth College, Hanover, N.H., 1862), Free Baptist; b. at Raymond, N.H., Aug. 3, 1812; graduated at Dartmouth College, 1840, and from the Biblical School, Whitestown, N.Y., 1849; became principal of North Parsonsfield Academy, Me., 1840; of the Whitestown Seminary, N.Y., 1843; professor in the Free Baptist Theological School since 1851 (the school, then at Whitestown, in 1854 was removed to New Hampton, N.H., but since 1870 has been a department of Bates College, Lewiston, Me.). He was chaplain of the New-Hampshire Legislature, 1863; a member of the House in that legislature, 1867.

FUNCKE, Otto, German Protestant; b. at Wülfrath, near Elberfeld, Germany, March 9, 1836; studied at Halle, Tübingen, and Bonn; was pastor at Halpe, in the Rhine Mountains, 1862–68; and since 1868 has been pastor of the Friedens Kirche, Bremen. He is the author of *Reisebilder und Heimathklänge*, Bremen, 3 series, 1869 (11th ed. 1886), 1871 (6th ed. 1886), 1872 (5th ed. 1886); *Die Schule des Lebens; oder, christliche Lebensbilder im Lichte des Buches Jonas*, 1871, 6th ed. 1885, reprinted New York (American Tract Society), 1879 (English trans., *The School of Life: Life Pictures from the Book of Jonah*, 1885, 2d ed. 1886); *Christliche Fragezeichen*, 1873, 11th ed. 1885; *Verwandlungen*, 1873, 4th ed. 1885; *Tägliche Andachten*, 1875, 4th ed. 1885; *Gottes Weisheit auf der Kinderstube*, 1876, 5th ed. 1883; *St. Paulus zu Wasser und zu Lande*, 1877, 5th ed. 1884; *Freud, Leid, Arbeit*, 1879, 5th ed. 1886; *Seelenkämpfe und Seelenfrieden*, 1881, 3d ed. 1885; *Willst du gesund werden?* 1882; *Englische Bilder in deutscher Beleuchtung*, 1883, 5th ed. 1886; *Die Welt des Glaubens und die Alltagswelt*, 1885.

FUNK, Franz Xaver, Ph.D., Lic. Theol., D.D. (all Tübingen, 1863, 1871, 1875, respectively), Roman Catholic; b. at Abtsgmünd, Würtemberg, Germany, Oct. 12, 1840; studied theology and philosophy at Tübingen, 1859–63, and theology in the priests' seminary at Rottenburg, 1863–64; was curate at Waldsee, 1864–65; studied political economy in Paris, 1865–66; became *repetent* in Tübingen, 1866; professor extraordinary of church history, patrology, and archæology, 1870; ordinary professor, 1875. He is the author of *Zins und Wucher, eine moraltheologische Abhandlung*, Tübingen, 1868; *Die nationalökonom, Anschauungen der mittelalterlichen Theologen*, 1869; *Geschichte des kirchlichen Zinsverbotes*, 1876; *Die Echtheit der Ignatianischen Briefe aufs neue vertheidigt. Mit e. literar. Beilage: Die alte Lateinische Uebersetzung der Usher'schen Sammlung der Ignatiusbriefe u. d. Polykarpbriefes*, 1883; *Lehrbuch der Kirchengeschichte*, Rottenburg, 1886; and many articles. He edited the 5th ed. of Hefele's *Opera patrum apostolorum*, 1878–81, 2 vols.

FUNK, Isaac Kauffman, D.D. (Wittenberg College, Springfield, O., 1882), Lutheran (General Synod); b. at Clifton, Greene County, O., Sept. 10, 1839; graduated at Wittenberg College, 1860; entered the ministry of the Lutheran Church, 1861; was pastor at Carey, O., 1862-64; in Brooklyn, N.Y. (St. Matthew's Evangelical Lutheran), 1865–72; resigned, and went to Europe, Egypt, and Palestine; on return was associate editor of *Christian Radical*, Pittsburg, Penn., 1872–73; editor of *The Union Advocate*, N.Y., 1873–75; started *The Metropolitan Pulpit*, October, 1876; *Complete Preacher*, 1877; changed the name of the former to *Homiletic Monthly*, and combined it with the second, October, 1878; enlarged the *Monthly*, and called it *Homiletic Review*, January, 1885; began book-publishing in 1877.

FUNKHOUSER, George Absalom, D.D. (Otterbein University, 1879), United Brethren; b. at Mount Jackson, Shenandoah County, Va., June 7, 1841; graduated from Otterbein University, Westerville, O., 1868, and from Western (Presbyterian) Theological Seminary, Alleghany, Penn., 1871; and since has been professor of New-Testament exegesis in Union Biblical Seminary, Dayton, O.

FURMAN, James Clement, D.D., Baptist; b. in Charleston, S.C., Dec. 5, 1809; was educated in Charleston College, ——; studied medicine, but in 1828 was baptized, and began to preach; conducted revival services; was pastor at Society Hill, S.C., ——; in 1843 became professor in Furman Theological Institution, now Furman University, Greenville, S.C., of which he was president many years, and is now professor of intellectual and moral philosophy, logic, and rhetoric.

FURNESS, William Henry, D.D. (Harvard, 1847), Unitarian; b. in Boston, Mass., April 20, 1802; graduated from Harvard College, 1820; studied theology, and was ordained pastor of the First Unitarian Congregational Church, Philadelphia, Penn., Jan. 12, 1825, and held the office until his retirement in 1875. He was a leading abolitionist, and is the author of *Remarks on the Four Gospels*, Philadelphia, 1835, London, 1837; *Jesus and his Biographers*, 1838; *Domestic Worship* (a volume of prayers), 1842, new ed. 1850; *A History of Jesus*, Philadelphia and London, 1850, new ed. 1853; *Discourses*, 1855; *Thoughts on the Life and Character of Jesus of Nazareth*, Boston, 1859; *Veil partly uplifted*, 1864; *The Unconscious Truth of the Four Gospels*, Philadelphia, 1868; *Jesus*, 1871; *The Power of Spirit manifest in Jesus of Nazareth*, 1877; *The Story of the Resurrection told once more*, 1885; *Verses: Translations and Hymns*, Boston, 1886; numerous discourses, mostly on abolition, both in pamphlet form and in the *Pennsylvania Freeman* and *Anti-slavery Standard*. He has also translated from the German Schubert's *Mirror of Nature*, 1849; *Gems of German Verse*, 1851; *Julius, and other Tales*, 1856; and Schenkel's *Character of Jesus portrayed*, Boston, 1866, 2 vols. He edited *The Diadem*, an annual published in Philadelphia, 1845–47.

FURRER, Konrad, D.D. (Bern, 1879), Swiss Protestant theologian; b. at Fluntern, near Zürich, Nov. 5, 1838; studied at Zürich, 1857–62; was ordained, 1862; from 1864 to 1876, pastor in various places of the canton of Zürich; since 1876, pastor of St. Peter's, Zürich. In 1863 he made an exploring tour through Palestine; in 1869 he became *privat-docent* for biblical archæology in the University of Zürich, but did not lecture from 1871 until 1885, when on the death of Biedermann he resumed his position, and now lectures upon the history of religion. He is also a *Kirchenrath* of the canton (since 1885), and teacher of religion in the Zürich female seminary. In theology he is a liberal, right wing. He is the author of *Rudolph Collin, der Freund Zwinglis*, Halle, 1862; *Wanderungen durch Palaestina*, Zürich, 1865 (French trans., Geneva, 1886); *Die Bedeutung der biblischen Geographie für die biblische Exegese*, Zurich, 1870; of the majority of the geographical, zoölogical, and botanical articles in Schenkel's *Bibel-lexicon*, Leipzig, 1869–75; of many essays, e.g., *Die religionsgeschichtliche Bedeutung Jerusalems* (in *Zeitstimmen*, 1866); *Israel als Volk des Morgenlandes* (in the same, 1867); *Die Religion im Jugendalter der Menschheit* (in *Reform*, 1876); *Die allgemeine Religionsgeschichte und die religiöse Bildung* (in Meili's *Theolog. Zeitschrift*, 1884); has in preparation an entire reconstruction of Raumer's *Palaestina*.

G.

GABRIELS, Very Rev. Henry, Lic. Theol. (Louvain, 1864), **D.D.** (*hon.*, Louvain, 1882), Roman Catholic; b. at Wannegem-Lede, Belgium, Oct. 6, 1838; educated at the Episcopal Seminary of Ghent, and the Catholic University of Louvain; became professor of dogmatic theology in St. Joseph's Seminary, Troy, N.Y., 1864; and president and professor of church history, 1871.

GAILEY, Matthew, Reformed Presbyterian; b. at Rathdonnell, near Letterkenny, County Donegal, Ireland, Dec. 16, 1835; graduated at Queen's College, Belfast, 1866; studied theology in Belfast and Edinburgh; has been since 1868 pastor Third Reformed Presbyterian Church, Philadelphia, U.S.A.; and since 1876 professor of biblical literature in the Reformed Presbyterian Seminary, Philadelphia. He was moderator of the General Synod, 1885; and has published *Christian Patriotism* (a sermon), Philadelphia, 1875, 2 editions; *Wreaths and Gems* (poems), 1882.

GAILOR, Thomas Frank, Episcopalian; b. at Jackson, Miss., Sept. 17, 1856; graduated at Racine College, Wis., 1876, and at the General (Episcopal) Theological Seminary, New-York City, 1879; became pastor of the Church of the Messiah, Pulaski, Tenn., 1879; professor of ecclesiastical history in the University of the South, Sewanee, Tenn., 1882, and has been chaplain of the university since 1883. He is in hearty sympathy with the "Oxford movement" in the English Church, as represented by Canon Liddon in England, and Dr. DeKoven in the United States. He is the author of occasional sermons, and articles in reviews; and of *Manual of Devotions for Schoolboys*, New York, 1886.

GALLEHER, Right Rev. John Nicholas, S.T.D. (Columbia College, New-York City, 1875), Episcopalian, bishop of Louisiana; b. at Washington, Ky., Feb. 17, 1839; educated at the University of Virginia, Charlottesville; studied law, and graduated at the Brockenborough Law School at Lexington, Va.; began practice at Louisville, Ky.; was successively rector in New Orleans, La.; Baltimore, Md.; Zion Church, New-York City; consecrated, 1880. He served in the Confederate Army during the war, enlisting as a private in 1861; was captured at Fort Donelson, and imprisoned several months; when exchanged, he was made aide-de-camp to General Buckner, and first lieutenant, afterwards captain and lieutenant-colonel in the Adjutant General's department, and served until the final surrender. He has published occasional sermons, essays, and episcopal charges.

GANDELL, Robert, Church of England; b. in London, Jan. 27, 1818; educated at St. John's and Queen's Colleges, Oxford; graduated B.A. (second-class classics) 1843, Kennicott scholar 1844, Pusey and Ellerton scholar 1845, M.A. 1846; was ordained deacon 1846, priest 1847; Michel fellow of Queen's College, 1845-50; tutor of Magdalen Hall, 1848-72; lecturer in Hebrew for Dr. Pusey, 1848-82; chaplain of Corpus Christi College, 1852-77; select preacher, 1859; Grinfield lecturer on the Septuagint, 1859; senior proctor, 1860-61; examiner in "Rud. Fid. et Relig.," 1881-82; since 1856 he has been one of the four city lecturers at St. Martin Carfax, Oxford; since 1861, Laudian professor of Arabic; since 1870, examining chaplain to the bishop of Bath and Wells; since 1874, fellow of Hertford College, Oxford, and prebendary of Ashill in Wells Cathedral; since 1880 canon of Wells Cathedral, since 1884 precentor. He is the author of *The Prophecy of Joel, in Hebrew, poetically arranged*, London, 1849; *Jehovah Goalenu* (sermon), 1853; *The Greater Glory of the Second Temple* (sermon), 1858; edited Lightfoot's *Horæ Hebraïcæ et Talmudicæ*, 1859, 4 vols.; contributed commentary on *Amos*, *Nahum*, and *Zephaniah* to *The Bible (Speaker's) Commentary*, 1876.

GANSE, Hervey Doddridge, Presbyterian; b. at Fishkill, Dutchess County, N.Y., Feb. 27, 1822; studied at the New-York University, 1835-38; graduated at Columbia College in the same city, 1839, and at the Reformed Dutch Theological Seminary, New Brunswick, N.J., 1843; became pastor of Reformed Dutch Church, Freehold, N.J., 1843; of the North-west (afterwards Madison-avenue) Reformed Church, New-York City, 1856; of the First Presbyterian Church, St. Louis, Mo., 1875; corresponding secretary of the Presbyterian Board for colleges and academies, 1883 (the year of its establishment). He is the author of printed sermons, addresses, review articles; a pamphlet, *Bible Slaveholding*, New York, 1853; a discussion of *The Sabbath's Claim on Christian Consciences* (read before the General Council of the Reformed Churches, Philadelphia, 1880), and of a number of hymns.

GARDINER, Frederic, D.D. (Bowdoin College, Brunswick, Me., 1869), Episcopalian; b. at Gardiner, Me., Sept. 11, 1822; graduated at Bowdoin College, Brunswick, Me., 1842; was rector of Trinity Church, Saco, Me., 1845-47; assistant minister, St. Luke's, Philadelphia, Penn., 1847-48; rector of Grace Church, Bath, Me., 1848-53; and of Trinity Church, Lewiston, Me., 1855-56. In 1865 he became professor of the literature and interpretation of Scripture in Protestant Episcopal Theological Seminary, Gambier, O.; in 1867, assistant rector at Middletown, Conn.; and the next year a professor in the Berkeley (Episcopalian) Divinity School there (1868-82 of Old Testament and literature, and since 1883 of New-Testament literature and interpretation). He is the author of *The Island of Life, an Allegory*, Boston, 1851; *Commentary on the Epistle of St. Jude*, 1856; *Harmony of the Gospels in Greek*, Andover, 1871, 7th ed. 1884; *Harmony of the Gospels in English*, 1871, 3d ed. subsequently; *Diatessaron, The Life of our Lord in the Words of the Gospels*, 1871, 2d ed. subsequently; *The Principles of Textual Criticism*, 1876; *The Old and New Testaments in their Mutual Relations*, New York, 1885. He wrote the commentary on *Leviticus* (incorporating that of

Lange) in the American Lange series, New York, 1876; and that upon Second Samuel (1883) and Ezekiel (1884) in Bishop Ellicott's *Old-Testament Commentary for English Readers*, London and New York.

GARLAND, Landon Cabell, LL.D. (Transylvania University, Lexington, Ky., 1846), Methodist-Episcopal Church South, layman; b. in Nelson County, Va., March 21, 1810; graduated at Hampden-Sidney College, Prince Edward County, Va., 1829; became professor of chemistry and natural philosophy in Washington College, Lexington, Va., 1830; professor of the same in Randolph-Macon College, then in Mecklenburg County (since 1866 at Ashland), Va., 1833; president of the college, 1837; professor of mathematics and physics in the University of Alabama, at Tuscaloosa, 1847; president of the same, 1857; professor of physics and astronomy in the University of Mississippi, at Oxford, 1866; professor of physics and astronomy in Vanderbilt University, Nashville, Tenn., and chancellor, 1875. He is the author of numerous pamphlets, and of a treatise on *Plane and Spherical Trigonometry*.

GARRETT, Right Rev. Alexander Charles, D.D. (Nebraska College, Nebraska City, Neb., 1872, Trinity College, Dublin, 1882), **LL.D.** (University of Mississippi, Oxford, Miss., 1876), Episcopalian, missionary bishop of Northern Texas; b. at Ballymote, County Sligo, Ireland, Nov. 4, 1832; graduated at Trinity College, Dublin, 1855, and took the divinity testimonium, Dec. 19, 1855; was successively curate of East Worldham, Hampshire, Eng., 1857; missionary in British Columbia, 1859; rector in California, 1869; of Trinity Cathedral, Omaha, Neb., 1872; consecrated, 1874. He has published occasional sermons, etc. *

GARRISON, Joseph Fithian, D.D. (College of New Jersey, Princeton, 1879), Episcopalian; b. at Fairton, Cumberland County, N. J., Jan. 20, 1823; graduated from the College of New Jersey at Princeton, 1842, and M.D. from the University of Pennsylvania at Philadelphia, 1845; entered the Episcopal ministry in 1855, and became rector of St. Paul's Church, Camden, N. J.; but since 1884 has been professor of liturgics and canon law in the Episcopal Divinity School in Philadelphia, Penn. He has published numerous sermons, also articles upon ecclesiastical history and canon law. He was a member of the commission for the revision of the Prayer Book.

GARRUCCI, Raffaele, Roman Catholic; b. at Naples, Jan. 23, 1812; d. at Rome, May 5, 1885. He was a Jesuit, and a famous archæologist, especially in iconography. He devoted himself almost entirely to the history of early Christian art, but at the time of his death he had just completed a history of Italian coinage from its origin to the present time. Of his other great works may be mentioned, *Monumenta reipublicæ Ligurum Bæbianorum*, Rome, 1847; *Monumenti del Museo Lateranense*, 1861; *Storia dell'Arte Cristiana nei primi otto secoli della Chiesa*, Prato, 1872–80, 6 vols. He wrote also many dissertations on minor subjects. See *American Journal of Archæology*, i. 309. *

GASS, Friedrich Wilhelm Johann Heinrich, Ph.D. (Berlin, 1838), **Lic. Theol.** (Breslau, 1839), **D.D.** (Greifswald, 1854), German Protestant (United Evangelical Church); b. at Breslau, Nov. 28, 1813; studied at Breslau, Halle, and Berlin, 1832–36; became *privat-docent* of theology at Breslau, 1839; professor extraordinary, 1846; the same at Greifswald, 1847; ordinary professor, 1855; at Giessen, 1861; at Heidelberg, 1868. In 1885 he was made an ecclesiastical councillor. In theology he is a moderate Liberal. Besides numerous articles in reviews, etc., he has written *Gennadius und Pletho, Aristotelismus u. Platonismus in d. griechischen Kirche*, parts 1 and 2, Breslau, 1844; *Georg Calixt u. d. Synkretismus*, 1846; *Die Mystik d. Nikolaus Kabasilas vom Leben in Christo, Erste Ausgabe u. einleitende Darstellung*, Greifswald, 1849; *Schleiermachers Briefwechsel mit J. Chr. Gass herausgegeben*, 1852; *Geschichte d. prot. Dogmatik*, Berlin, 1854–67, 4 vols.; *Zur Geschichte der Athosklöster*, Giessen, 1865; *Die Lehre vom Gewissen*, Berlin, 1869; *Symbolik der griechischen Kirche*, 1872; *Geschichte der christlichen Ethik*, Berlin, Bd. 1. 1881, Bd. 2. 1886. In connection with A. Vial, he edited E. L. T. Henke's posthumous *Neuere Kirchengeschichte* (from the Reformation to 1870), Halle, 1874–80, 3 vols.

GAST, Frederick Augustus, D.D. (Waynesburg College, Waynesburg, Penn., 1877), Reformed (German); b. at Lancaster, Penn., Oct. 17, 1835; graduated from Franklin and Marshall College, in his native town, 1856; studied theology in the Mercersburg (Reformed) Theological Seminary (now at Lancaster), 1856–57; taught for a year, and from 1859 to 1865 was pastor of the New-Holland charge, Penn.; chaplain 45th Penn. Vols., March–July, 1865; pastor of Loudon and St. Thomas charge, Penn., 1865–67; principal of academy of Franklin and Marshall College, 1867–71; assistant professor in the college, 1871–72; tutor in Lancaster Theological Seminary, 1872–74; and since 1874 has been professor of Hebrew and Old-Testament theology. He has written articles upon Old-Testament science, etc.

GAVAZZI, Alessandro, Free Christian Church of Italy; b. of Roman-Catholic parents, March 21, 1809, in Bologna, where his father was professor of law, a famous advocate, noted for his antipathy to the Jesuits; entered the Barnabite Order in the Church of Rome, 1825; made rapid strides in knowledge; became professor of rhetoric and belles-lettres in the public college of Caravaggio, at Naples, 1829; entered the priesthood, and for many years preached in different cities to large and enthusiastic audiences, before whom he appeared both as priest and patriot. None more rejoiced than he when Pius IX., in 1846, began his pontificate; for, in common with many, he hailed him as a liberal and progressive pope. He hastened to Rome, and was welcomed by Pius, who appointed him almoner of the Roman legion which was despatched to Vicenza. The people called him "Peter the Hermit," the leader of the new crusade, the rebellion against Austria, 1848. But the change in the papal policy, through Jesuitical influence, compelled Gavazzi to break with him, and to flee to England when the French reinstated the Pope in Rome, July, 1849. He then renounced Roman Catholicism, and has since in Great Britain and America repeatedly lectured upon the evils of the papal system. In 1860 he went with Garibaldi to Sicily. In 1870 he was again in Italy; in 1881 he made his last visit to America. He was one of the organizers of the Free Italian Church (1870), and of its theological college in Rome (1875), in which he is professor of dogmatics, apologetics, and polemics. He is the author of *Memoirs*, London, 1851; *Orations*, 1852; *Recollections of the last Four Popes*, 1859; *No Union with Rome: an anti-eirenicon*, 1871; *The Priest in Absolution*, 1877. See *Father Gavazzi's Life and Lectures*, New York, 1853.

GEBHARDT, Oscar Leopold von, Ph.D. (Tübingen, 1873), **Lic. Theol.** (*hon.*, Leipzig, 1883), **D.D.** (*hon.*, Marburg, 1883), Lutheran; b. at Wesenberg in Estland, Russia, June 22, 1844; student at Dorpat, 1862–66, Tübingen, Erlangen, Göttingen, and Leipzig, 1867–70; assistant in the library of the University of Leipzig, 1875–76; custos and sub-librarian of the University of Halle, 1876–79; sub-librarian of the University of Göttingen, 1880–84; since 1884 has been librarian of the Royal Library, Berlin. His publications are, *Græcus Venetus* (the Pentateuch, Proverbs, Ruth, Canticles, Ecclesiastes, Lamentations, and Daniel, edited from a Greek MS. discovered in the library of St. Mark's, Venice), Leipzig, 1875; *Novum Testamentum Græce* (the 11th to 14th ed. of Theile), 1875, 1878, 1883, 1885; *Patrum Apostolicorum opera* (in connection with A. Harnack and Zahn), 1875–77, 3 vols.; the same, *editio minor*, 1877; *Evangeliorum codex Græcus purpureus Rossanensis* (Σ). *Seine Entdeckung, sein wissenschaftlicher u. künstlerischer Werth dargestellt* (with A. Harnack), 1880; *Das N. T. griechisch nach Tischendorfs letzter Recension, u. deutsch nach dem revidirten Luthertext*, 1881, 2d (stereotyped) ed. 1884; *N. T. Græce, Recensionis Tischendorfianæ ultimæ textum cum Tregellesiano et Westcottio-Hortiano contulit*, 1881, 2d (stereotyped) ed. 1884; *Texte u. Untersuchungen zur Geschichte der altchristlichen Literatur* (in connection with A. Harnack), since 1882, *Zur handschriftlichen Ueberlieferung der griechischen Apologeten: 1. Der Arethascodex*, Bd. I. Heft 3 (1883); *Die Evangelien d. Matthaeus u. d. Marcus aus d. Codex Ross.* (see above), Bd. I. Heft 4 (1883); *Ein übersehenes Fragment der Διδαχή, in alter lateinischer Uebersetzung mitgetheilt*, Bd. II. Heft 2 (1884); *The Miniatures of the Ashburnham Pentateuch*, London, 1883.

GEDEN, John Dury, D.D. (St. Andrew's, Scotland, 1885), Wesleyan; b. at Hastings, Eng., May 4, 1822; educated at Kingswood School, near Bristol (1830–36), then privately; was probationer for the Wesleyan ministry, 1846; ordained, 1850; was assistant classical tutor in the Wesleyan Theological College, Richmond, Surrey, 1846–51; professor of Hebrew and biblical literature in the Wesleyan Theological College, Didsbury, near Manchester, 1856–83; resigned through failure of health, and died in the month of March, 1886. He was a member of the British Old-Testament Revision Company, 1870–85. He was the author of the Fernley lectures for 1874, *The Doctrine of a Future Life, as contained in the Old-Testament Scriptures*, 2d ed. 1877; and *Didsbury Sermons: Fifteen Discourses preached in the Wesleyan College Chapel*, 1878.

GEIKIE, Cunningham, D.D. (Queen's University, Kingston, Canada, 1871), Church of England; b. in Edinburgh, Scotland, Oct. 26, 1824; educated at Queen's College, Toronto; and was pastor of Argyle-street Presbyterian Church, Halifax, N.S., 1851–54; Argyle-street, Sunderland, Eng., 1860–67; Islington Chapel, London, 1867–73. In 1876 he was ordained deacon in the Church of England, and priest the following year. From 1876 to 1879 he was curate of St. Peter's, Lordship Lane, Dulwich, near London; from 1879 to 1881, rector of Christ Church, Paris; from 1882 to 1885, vicar of St. Mary Magdalene, Barnstaple; and since has been vicar of St. Martin-at-Palace, Norwich. He holds the old "evangelical" views of Christianity, with the right to the fullest investigation in every direction. He is the author of *Entering on Life, a Book for Young Men*, London, 1874, 4th ed. 1884; *The Great and Precious Promises, or Light beyond*, 1875, 4th ed. 1884; *The English Reformation*, 1875, 11th ed. 1883; *The Life and Words of Christ*, 1876, 30th ed. 1885; *Old-Testament Characters*, 1877, 2d ed. 1884; *Hours with the Bible*, 1880–85, 6 vols. (completing the Old Testament).

GERHART, Emanuel Vogel, D.D. (Jefferson College, Canonsburg, Penn., 1857), Reformed (German); b. at Freeburg, Penn., June 13, 1817; graduated from Marshall College, 1838, and from Mercersburg (Penn.) Theological Seminary, 1841; became successively pastor at Gettysburg, Penn., 1843; missionary among foreign Germans at Cincinnati, O., 1849; professor of theology in the theological department, and president, of Heidelberg College, Tiffin, O., 1851; president of Franklin and Marshall College, 1855; vice-president and professor of moral philosophy, 1866; professor of systematic and practical theology in the Reformed Theology Seminary, 1868 (then at Mercersburg, but since 1871 at Lancaster, Penn.). He is the author of *Philosophy and Logic*, Philadelphia, 1858; and many articles in reviews and encyclopædias.

GEROK, Karl (Friedrich), D.D. (*hon.*, Tübingen, 1877), Lutheran; b. at Vaihingen, Würtemberg, Jan. 30, 1815; studied in the Stuttgart gymnasium, under Gustav Schwab; and from 1832 to 1836 in the theological seminary at Tübingen, where he was *repetent* from 1840 to 1843. In 1844 he became *diakonus* at Böblingen; in 1849, *diakonus* at Stuttgart; in 1852, *decan* (superintendent) there; in 1868, chief court preacher, chief councillor of the consistory, and prelate. He is a renowned preacher, and Germany's foremost religious poet. He belongs to the "Positive Union" party in the Church. He has published the following prose volumes: *Gebet des Herrn in Gebeten*, Stuttgart, 1854, 5th ed. 1883; *Evangelienpredigten*, 1855, 7th ed. 1880; *Epistelpredigten*, 1857, 6th ed. 1880; *Pilgerbrot*, 1866, 4th ed. 1882; *Die Apostelgeschichte in Bibelstunden*, 1868, 2 vols., 2d ed. 1882; *Aus ernster Zeit*, 1873; *Jugenderinnerungen* (his autobiography), 1876 (3 editions in six months); *Hirtenstimmen*, 1879, 2d ed. 1882. He furnished the homiletical portion of Lechler's volume on Acts for Lange's *Commentary* (Elberfeld, 1860, 4th ed. 1881, American ed. New York). He also edited Paul Gerhardt's *Geistliche Lieder*, Leipzig, 3d ed. 1883; Matthias Claudius', Gotha, 1878; *Die Wittenberger Nachtigall*, Stuttgart, 1883; and Luther's *Geistliche Lieder*, Stuttgart, 1883. But Karl Gerok's poems have given him his widest fame: *Palmblätter*, Stuttgart, 1857, 51st ed. 1883 (in several editions, plain and illustrated; English trans. by J. E. A. Broom, London, 2d ed. 1885), 2d series 1882, 9th ed. 1885; *Pfingstrosen*, 1866, 9th ed. 1886; *Blumen und Sterne*, 1868, 10th ed. 1882, 2d series, *Der letzte Strauss*, 1884, 3d ed. 1886; *Deutsche Ostern*, 1871, 6th ed. 1883.

GESS, Wolfgang Friedrich, D.D. (Basel, 1864), Lutheran; b. at Kirchheim in Würtemberg, July 27, 1819; studied in Tübingen, 1837–41; was assistant pastor, *repetent*, and pastor in Würtemberg, 1841–50; theological tutor in the Missions House at Basel, and member of the board of directors, 1850–64; ordinary professor of theology at Göttingen, 1864–71; the same at Breslau, and member of the Silesian Consistory, 1871–80; general superintendent of the province of Posen, 1880; *emeritus*, 1885. He is the author of *Christi Person und Werk*, Basel, 1870–86, 3 parts; *Bibelstunden über Joh. xiii.–xvii.*, 1871, 4th ed. 1886; *Bibelstunden über Röm. i.–viii.*, 1885, and minor works.

GIBBONS, His Eminence James, Cardinal, D.D. (St. Mary's University, Baltimore, 1868), Roman Catholic; b. at Baltimore, Md., July 23, 1834; graduated at St. Charles's College, Ellicott City, Md., 1857; studied philosophy and theology at St. Mary's Seminary of St. Sulpice, Baltimore, where he was ordained a priest, June 30, 1861; was successively assistant pastor of St. Patrick's Church, Baltimore, 1861; pastor of St. Bridget's, Canton, fall of 1861; assistant pastor of the cathedral of Baltimore, and secretary to the archbishop (Dr. Spalding), 1865; vicar apostolic of North Carolina, 1866; consecrated bishop, Aug. 16, 1868; translated to see of Richmond, Va., on the death of Dr. McGill, 1872; coadjutor of Dr. Bayley, archbishop of Baltimore, with right of succession, 1877; on Oct. 3, 1877, became archbishop of Baltimore; and in 1886 was created a cardinal. He was present at the Vatican Council, Rome, 1869–70; went to Rome for the preparation of the questions to be treated in the third plenary council of Baltimore, Nov. 9–Dec. 7, 1884, over which he presided as apostolic delegate. Besides various articles in Roman-Catholic magazines, sermons, and lectures, he has written *The Faith of our Fathers*, New York, 1874 (140,000 copies sold up to January, 1886; translated into several languages).

GIBSON, John Monro, D.D. (University of Chicago, Ill., 1875), Presbyterian; b. at Whithorn, Wigtownshire, Scotland, April 24, 1838; went with his father, who was a minister, to Canada, 1855; graduated at Toronto University, Can., B.A. (double first-class honors) 1862, M.A. 1865, and at Knox (Theological) College, Toronto, 1864; was teacher in languages in Knox College, 1863–64; pastor of Erskine Church, Montreal (colleague of Dr. William Taylor), 1864–74; lecturer in Greek and Hebrew exegesis in Montreal Theological College, 1868–74; pastor of Second Presbyterian Church, Chicago, 1874–80; and since, of St. John's Wood Presbyterian Church, London, Eng. He is the author of *The Ages before Moses*, New York and Edinburgh, 1879, 2d ed. in each land; *The Foundations* (lectures on evidences of Christianity), Chicago, 1880, 2d ed.; *The Mosaic Era*, London and New York, 1881, 2d ed. New York; *Rock versus Sand* (revised ed. of *The Foundations*), London, 1883, 2d ed. 1885; *Pomegranates from an English Garden* (selected poems of Browning, with notes), New York, 1885.

GILLESPIE, Right Rev. George De Normandie, S.T.D. (Hobart College, Geneva, N.Y.), 1875, Episcopalian, bishop of Western Michigan; b. at Goshen, Orange County, N.Y., June 14, 1819; graduated at the General Theological Seminary, New-York City, 1840; successively rector at Leroy, N.Y., 1841; Cincinnati, O., 1845; Palmyra, N.Y., 1851; Ann Arbor, Mich., 1861; consecrated, 1875. He has been on the State Board of Corrections and Charities since 1877. He has published occasional sermons, tracts, etc.

GILLETT, Charles Ripley, Presbyterian; b. in New-York City (Harlem), Nov. 29, 1855; prepared for college by his father, Rev. Dr. E. H. Gillett (see *Encyclopædia*, p. 874); graduated B.A. at the University of the City of New York, 1874; B.S. and civil engineer at the same, 1876; practised engineering in the city, 1876–77; entered the Union Theological Seminary, New-York City, 1877; graduated there, 1880; was fellow of the same in the city, 1880–81, and in Berlin, Germany, 1881–83; since 1883 has been librarian of Union Theological Seminary.

GILMAN, Edward Whiting, D.D. (Yale College, New Haven, Conn., 1874), Congregationalist; b. at Norwich, Conn., Feb. 11, 1823; graduated at Yale College, New Haven, Conn., 1843; studied in Union Theological Seminary, New-York City, 1845–47; and graduated at the Yale Theological Seminary, New Haven, Conn., 1848. He was a tutor in Yale College, 1847–49; Congregational pastor at Lockport, N.Y., 1849–56; Cambridgeport, Mass., 1856–58; Bangor, Me., 1859–63; Stonington, Conn., 1864–71. Since 1871 he has been one of the secretaries of the American Bible Society. He is the editor of the *Bible Society Record*, an occasional contributor to various periodicals, and has written articles for Appleton's and Johnson's *Encyclopædias*, etc.

GLADDEN, Washington, D.D. (Roanoke College, Salem, Va., 1884), **LL.D.** (University of Wisconsin, Madison, 1881), Congregationalist; b. at Pottsgrove, Penn., Feb. 11, 1836; graduated at Williams College, Williamstown, Mass., 1859; became successively pastor at Brooklyn, N.Y., 1860; Morrisania, N.Y., 1861; North Adams, Mass., 1866 (until 1871); Springfield, Mass., 1875; Columbus, O., 1883. He was on the editorial staff of the New-York *Independent*, 1871–75; and edited *Sunday Afternoon*, 1878–80. He is the author of *Plain Thoughts on the Art of Living*, Boston, 1868; *From the Hub to the Hudson*, 1869; *Workingmen and their Employers*, 1876, 2d ed. New York, 1885; *Being a Christian*, 1876; *The Christian Way*, New York, 1877; *The Lord's Prayer*, Boston, 1881; *The Christian League of Connecticut*, New York, 1883; *Things New and Old*, Columbus, O., 1884; *The Young Men and the Churches*, Boston, 1885.

GLASGOW, James, D.D. (College of New Jersey, Princeton, 1855), Presbyterian; b. in parish of Dunaghy, near Ballymena, County Antrim, Ireland, May 27, 1805; graduated at Royal Belfast College, 1832; licensed, 1834; ordained in the Congregation of Castledawn, County Londonderry, 1835; was missionary in Bombay, India, 1840–64; since 1866 has been the General-Assembly professor of living Oriental languages in Belfast and in Magee College, Londonderry. He was elected a member of the Bombay branch of the Royal

Asiatic Society (1848), and fellow of the University of Bombay (1862). He was principal translator of the Gujarati Bible, 1850-61; and, besides various papers in religious journals, has written *Exposition of the Apocalypse*, Edinburgh, 1871; *Heart and Voice*, 1873.

GLOAG, Paton James, D.D. (St. Andrew's, 1867), Church of Scotland; b. at Perth, May 17, 1823; attended universities of Edinburgh (1840-43) and of St. Andrew's (1843-44); became minister of Dunning, Perthshire, 1848; Blantyre, Lanarkshire, 1860; Galashiels, Selkirkshire, 1871. He belongs to the positive critical school; is rather an expositor of Scripture than an expounder of doctrine. He was Baird lecturer in 1869. He is the author of *The Assurance of Salvation*, Edinburgh, 1853, 2d ed. Glasgow, 1869; *Justification by Faith*, Edinburgh, 1856; *Primeval World, or Relation of Geology to Revelation*, 1859; *The Resurrection*, London, 1862; translation of Lechler's commentary on Acts, in Lange series, Edinburgh, 1864; *Practical Christianity*, Glasgow, 1866; *Commentary on Acts*, Edinburgh, 1870, 2 vols.; *Introduction to the Pauline Epistles*, 1876; translation of Meyer on Acts, 1877; *The Messianic Prophecies* (Baird lectures), 1879; translation of Lünemann on Thessalonians, 1880, and of Huther on James and Jude, 1881; *Life of Paul (Bible Primer)*, 1881, 10th thousand 1885; *Commentary on James*, in Schaff's *Popular Commentary*, 1883; *Exegetical Studies*, 1884; and articles in reviews and other periodicals.

GLOSSBRENNER, Jacob John, D.D. (Otterbein University, Westerville, O., and Lebanon-Valley College, Annville, Penn., both 1873, and declined; Lebanon-Valley College, 1884), a bishop of the United Brethren in Christ; b. at Hagerstown, Md., July 24, 1813; educated in common schools; apprenticed to a silversmith; converted in 1830, and began reading theological books; was licensed to preach by the Virginia Annual Conference, 1833, and continued to preach as an itinerant missionary, circuit preacher, and presiding elder, till May, 1849, when he was first elected bishop; re-elected for ten quadrennial terms; in May, 1885, elected bishop *emeritus*, and is now senior bishop without any assigned district of labor. Several of his occasional sermons have been published in the denominational organ, *The Religious Telescope*, Dayton, O.

GOADBY, Thomas, D.D. (Central University of Iowa, Pella, Io., 1880; Bates College, Lewiston, Me., 1881), General Baptist; b. at Leicester, Eng., Dec. 23, 1829; studied at the Baptist College, Leicester, and graduated at Glasgow University as B.A. 1856; became minister of churches at Coventry, 1856; Commercial Road, East, London, 1861; Osmaston Road, Derby, 1868; president of Nottingham General Baptist College, 1873. He is evangelical and non-Calvinistic. He has been since 1861 the English correspondent of the Boston (U. S. A.) *Morning Star*, the weekly organ of the Freewill Baptists. He is the author of sermons and addresses published at Leicester in 1865, 1868, 1872; of *The Day of Death, a Poem*, Leicester, 1863; article in *British Quarterly*, April, 1879, on *Christian Theology and the Modern Spirit;* translator of Ewald's *Revelation: its Nature and Record*, Edinburgh, 1881.

GODET, Fréderic (Louis), D.D. (*hon.*, Basel, 1868), Reformed; b. at Neuchâtel, Switzerland, Oct. 25, 1812; educated in his native city, and studied theology at Bonn and Berlin (under Neander); was ordained in 1836; was assistant of the pastor of Valangin, near Neuchâtel, for a year; then preceptor of the Crown Prince of Prussia from 1838 to 1844; from 1845 to 1851 supplied churches in the Val-de-Ruy; from 1851 to 1866 was pastor in Neuchâtel. From 1850 to 1873 he was professor of exegetical and critical theology in the theological school of the National Church of the canton, and since has been in the same capacity in the independent faculty of the Church of Neuchâtel. He is the author of *Histoire de la Réformation et du Refuge dans le Canton de Neuchâtel*, Neuchâtel, 1859; *Commentaire sur l'évangile de Saint Jean*, 1863-65, 2 vols., 3d ed. 1881-85, 3 vols. (Eng. trans. by F. Crombie and M. D. Cusin, Edinburgh, 1877, 3 vols.; translated from 3d ed. by Professor T. Dwight, New York, 1886, 2 vols.; also translated into German, Danish, and Dutch); do. *sur l'évangile de Luc*, 1871, 2d ed. 1872 (Eng. trans. by E. W. Shalders and M. D. Cusin, Edinburgh, 1875, 2 vols., revised by John Hall, D.D., New York, 1881); do. *sur l'épître aux Romains*, 1879-80, 2 vols., 2d ed. 1st vol. 1883 (Eng. trans. by A. Cusin, Edinburgh, 1880-81, 2 vols., revised by T. W. Chambers, D.D., New York, 1883); do. *sur la première épître aux Corinthiens*, 1886, 2 vols.; *Conférences apologétiques*, 1869 (Eng. trans. by W. H. Lyttleton, *Lectures in Defence of the Christian Faith*, Edinburgh, 1881, 2d ed. 1883); *Etudes bibliques*, 1873-74, 2 series, 3d ed. 1876 (Eng. trans. by W. H. Lyttleton, *Old-Testament Studies*, Oxford, 1875, 3d ed. 1885; *New-Testament Studies*, London, 1876, 6th ed. 1885).

GOEBEL, Siegfried Abraham, Reformed; b. at Winningen, near Coblenz, Prussia, March 24, 1844; studied at Erlangen, Halle, and Berlin; from 1868 to 1874 was pastor at Posen; since then he has been court preacher (first preacher in the royal Evangelical Reformed court church) at Halberstadt, Prussia. He is the author of *Die Parabeln Jesu methodisch ausgelegt*, Gotha, 1878-80, 3 parts (Eng. trans. by Professor Banks, *The Parables of Jesus, A Methodical Exposition*, Edinburgh, 1883).

GOLTZ, Baron Hermann von der, D.D., German Protestant; b. at Düsseldorf, March 17, 1835; studied at Erlangen, Berlin, Tübingen, and Bonn, 1853-58; became chaplain to the Prussian embassy at Rome, 1861; professor extraordinary of theology at Basel, 1865; ordinary professor, 1870; at Bonn, 1873; honorary professor at Berlin, superior consistorial councillor and provost of St. Peter's, 1876; ordinary professor, 1883. He is the author of *Die reformirte Kirche Genfs im 19. Jahrhundert*, Basel, 1862; *Gottes Offenbarung durch heilige Geschichte*, 1868; *Die Grenzen der Lehrfreiheit in Theologie u. Kirche*, Bonn, 1873 (pp. 30); *Die christlichen Grundwahrheiten*, Gotha, Bd. 1, 1873; *Tempelbilder aus d. Leben d. Herrn Jesu* (5 sermons), Berlin, 1877, 2d ed. 1879.

GOOD, Jeremiah Haak, D.D. (Franklin and Marshall College, Lancaster, Penn., 1868), Reformed; b. at Rehrersburg, Berks County, Penn., Nov. 22, 1822; graduated at Marshall College, Mercersburg, Penn., 1844; was sub-rector of the preparatory department of the college, 1844-46; pastor of Lancaster charge, Fairfield County, O.,

1846-48; professor of mathematics in Heidelberg College, Tiffin, O., 1850-68; and since 1869 has been professor of dogmatic theology in the theological department. He was founder (1848) and editor of *The Western Missionary*, now called *The Christian World*, Columbus, O. He also was largely instrumental in founding Heidelberg College and Theological Seminary (1850). He is the author of *The Reformed Church Hymnal, with Tunes*, Cleveland, 1878, 20 editions; *The Heidelberg Catechism, newly arranged*, Tiffin, O., 1879, several editions; *The Children's Catechism*, 1881, several editions; *Prayer-book and Aids to Private Devotions*, 1881; *The Church-Member's Handbook*, 1882.

GOODWIN, Daniel Raynes, D.D. (Bowdoin College, Brunswick, Me., 1853), **LL.D.** (University of Pennsylvania, Philadelphia, 1868), Episcopalian; b. at North Berwick, Me., April 12, 1811; graduated from Bowdoin College, Brunswick, Me., 1832; became professor in it of modern languages, 1835; president of Trinity College, Hartford, Conn., 1853; provost of the University of Pennsylvania, Philadelphia, 1860; resigned, 1868. Since 1863 he has been Holy Trinity professor of systematic divinity in the Episcopal Divinity School of Philadelphia. He is the author of *Christianity neither Ascetic nor Fanatic*, New Haven, 1858; *The Christian Ministry*, Middletown, Conn., 1860; *Southern Slavery: A Reply to Bishop Hopkins*, Philadelphia, 1864; *The Perpetuity of the Sabbath*, 1867; *The New Ritualistic Divinity*, 1879, 2d ed. same year; *Memorial Discourse on H. W. Longfellow* (before the alumni of Bowdoin College), Portland, 1882; *Notes on the Late Revision of the New-Testament Version*, New York, 1883; *Christian Eschatology*, Philadelphia, 1885.

GOODWIN, Edward Payson, D.D. (Western Reserve College, Hudson, O., 1867; Amherst College, Amherst, Mass., 1868), Congregationalist; b. at Rome, N.Y., July 31, 1832; graduated from Amherst (Mass.) College, 1856, and the Union (Presbyterian) Theological Seminary, New-York City, 1859; became Congregational minister at Burke, Vt., 1859; Columbus, O., 1860; Chicago, Ill., 1868. *

GOODWIN, Right Rev. Harvey, D.D. (Cambridge, 1858), lord bishop of Carlisle, Church of England; b. at King's Lynn, Norfolk, in the year 1818; entered Caius College, Cambridge; graduated B.A. (second wrangler and Smith's prizeman), 1840, M.A. 1843; was fellow and mathematical lecturer of his college; ordained deacon 1842, priest 1844; was perpetual curate of St. Edward, Cambridge, 1848-58; Hulsean lecturer at Cambridge, 1855-57; dean of Ely, 1858-69; consecrated bishop, 1869. He became visitor of St. Bee's College, 1869; honorary fellow of Caius College, Cambridge, 1881. Besides mathematical works he is the author of *Parish Sermons*, London, 1847-62, 5 vols., several editions; *University Sermons at Oxford and Cambridge*, 1853, 1855, 1876, 3 vols.; *Guide to the Parish Church*, 1855, 4th ed. 1878; *Hulsean Lectures for 1855-56* (1. *Doctrines and Difficulties of the Christian Faith*, etc.; 2. *The Glory of the Only Begotten of the Father seen in the Manhood of Christ*), 1856, 2 vols.; *Short Sermons on the Lord's Supper*, 1856; *Commentary on St. Matthew* (1857), *St. Mark* (1859-60), and *St. Luke* (1864); *Essays on the Pentateuch*, 1867; *Plain Sermons on Ordination and Ministry of the Church*, 1875; *Walks in Regions of Science and Faith*, 1883.

GORDON, Adoniram Judson, D.D. (Brown University, Providence, R.I., 1877), Baptist; b. at New Hampton, N.H., April 19, 1836; graduated at Brown University, Providence, R.I., 1860, and at Newton (Mass.) Theological Seminary, 1863; became pastor at Jamaica Plain, Boston, 1863, of the Clarendon-street Church, Boston, 1869. He is "a prohibitionist in temperance reform; a supporter and co-laborer with Mr. Moody in his evangelistic movement; low church in ecclesiology, and pre-millennial in eschatology." He is the author of *In Christ: or, the Believer's Union with his Lord*, Boston, 1872, 5th ed. 1885; *Congregational Worship*, 1872; *Grace and Glory* (sermons), 1881; *Ministry of Healing*, 1882, 2d ed. 1883; *The Twofold Life*, 1884, 2d ed. 1884.

GORDON, William Robert, D.D. (Columbia College, New-York City, 1859), Reformed (Dutch); b. in New-York City, March 19, 1811; graduated from the University of the City of New York (the first class publicly graduated; the exercises were held in the Middle Dutch Church, subsequently the New-York Post-Office), 1834, and at New Brunswick (N.J.) Theological Seminary, 1837; became pastor at North Hempstead, Long Island, N.Y., 1838; Flushing, L.I., 1843; New York City (Houston Street), 1849; Schraalenburgh, N.J., 1858; and since 1881 has lived in literary retirement. He is the author of *A Rebuke to High Churchism*, New York, 1844; *The Supreme Godhead of Christ*, 1848, 2d ed. 1858; *A Guide to Children in Reading the Scriptures*, 1852; *Particular Providence, illustrated in the Life of Joseph*, 1855, 3d ed. 1863; *A Threefold Test of Modern Spiritualism*, 1856; *Reformation* (a sermon in behalf of domestic missions preached before General Synod, 30,000 copies distributed), 1857; *The Peril of our Ship of State*, 1861; *Christocracy* (with J. T. Demarest), 1867, 2d ed. 1879; *The Reformed Church in America: its History, Doctrines, and Government*, 1869; *Life of Henry Ostrander, D.D.*, 1875; *Revealed Truth impregnable* (Vedder Lectures), 1878.

GOSMAN, Abraham, D.D. (College of New Jersey, Princeton, 1862), Presbyterian; b. at Danby, N.Y., July 25, 1819; graduated from Williams College, Williamstown, Mass., 1843; and from Princeton (N.J.) Theological Seminary, 1847, in which for a year (1850-51) was instructor in Hebrew; since 1851 he has been pastor at Lawrenceville, N.J. He partly translated and edited *Genesis* and *Numbers*; and entirely, with special introduction, *Deuteronomy*, in the American Lange series.

GOTCH, Frederic William, LL.D. (Trinity College, Dublin, 1859), Baptist; b. at Kettering, Northamptonshire, Eng., in the year 1807; studied at Bristol Baptist College, 1832; graduated B.A. at Trinity College, Dublin, 1838; became pastor, Baptist Church at Boxmoor, Hertfordshire, Eng., 1838; philosophical tutor at Stepney College, London, 18—; professor at Bristol College 1845, president 1868; resigned 1883; chairman of the Baptist Union 1868; member of O. T. Revision Company 1870. He edited the *Pentateuch* in a *Revised English Bible*, London, 1877; is author of *Supplement to the Fragments of the Codex Cottonianus*, 1881.

GOTTHEIL, Gustav, Ph.D. (Jena University,

1853), Jewish rabbi; b. at Pinne, Prussia, May 28, 1827; educated at Posen and Berlin, graduated 1853; became rabbi of the Berlin Reformgemeinde, 1853; at Manchester, Eng., 1856; of Temple Emanuel, New-York City, 1873. His theological standpoint is that of Reformed Judaism. He was a delegate to the Leipzig Synod in 1871, and has repeatedly lectured on Jewish topics in Christian pulpits, and has contributed articles to periodicals.

GOTTSCHICK, Johannes, D.D. (*hon.*, Giessen, 1882), Lutheran; b. at Rochau, Prussia, Nov. 23, 1847; studied theology at Erlangen and Halle, 1865–68; became teacher in Halle gymnasium, 1871; at Wernigerode, 1873; *conrector* at Torgau, 1876; religious *inspector* of the *Pädagogium* at Magdeburg, and *vorsteher* of the theological seminary, with title of professor, 1878; professor of practical theology at Giessen, 1882. He is in substantial agreement with the school of Ritschl of Göttingen. He has written *Ueber Schleiermacher's Verhältniss zu Kant*, Wernigerode, 1875; *Kant's Beweis für das Dasein Gottes*, Torgau, 1878; *Luther als Katechet*, Giessen, 1883; *Ueber den evangelischen Religionsunterricht auf den höheren Schulen*, 1884, 2d ed. 1886.

GOUGH, John Bartholomew, Congregationalist, layman, famous temperance orator; b. at Sandgate, Kent, Eng., Aug. 22, 1817; d. in Philadelphia, Penn., Feb. 18, 1886. His father had been a soldier from 1798 to 1823, and had been honorably discharged on a pension of twenty pounds per annum. He was of a stern disposition; yet his heart was tender, and his children loved him. In church connections he was a Methodist. Mr. Gough's mother was a Baptist, an intelligent, sober-minded, gentle, and loving woman, who had been for twenty years the village schoolmistress. He was taken from school at ten, and put to service in a gentleman's family. In his boyhood he enjoyed a village reputation as a good reader. About this time he was struck on the head by a spade, and rendered insensible. His life was for a time despaired of, and then his reason; and indeed he never fully recovered from the blow, for, whenever he was excited from any cause, he felt pricking and darting sensations in his head. One of his earliest amusements was to personate characters, as in amateur Punch-and-Judy shows, and otherwise, showing his rare talent for mimicry and acting. There seeming to be small prospect of his advancement at home, his parents accepted the offer of a Sandgate family about to emigrate to America, who engaged for ten guineas to take him with them, have him taught a trade, and provide for him until he was twenty-one. He sailed from London, June 10, 1829, and arrived in New York, Aug. 3; went with the family to the farm they had purchased in Oneida County, N.Y., and staid with them for two years; and then, having received his father's permission, he left them, and made his way to New-York City, where he arrived in the latter part of December, 1831, friendless, and with only a half-dollar in his pocket. He was then a member of the Methodist-Episcopal Church on probation, and so was induced to lay his case before Mr. Dands, the agent of the *Christian Advocate and Journal*, upon whom he made so favorable an impression, that he secured him a place as errand-boy and apprentice in the book-bindery in the Methodist Book Concern, where he had for a companion John McClintock, who afterwards became the well-known Methodist theologian. Young Gough was taught book-binding, and soon became remarkably skilful. Some of his Methodist friends proposed to educate him for the ministry, but the project was abandoned,—indeed, he withdrew from the denomination. (He later on joined the Congregational Church.) In 1832 he left the Book Concern, and secured elsewhere such good wages by his trade, that he sent for his father, mother, and only sister, who was two years his junior, to join him in New York; and the latter two arrived in August, 1833. His father remained behind, so as not to lose his pension. His sister was a straw-bonnet maker, and worked at her trade in the city. But in November, 1832, he and his sister lost their positions, owing to the hard times, and did not soon get regular employment. Thus the family was reduced to such straits, that when his mother died, July 8, 1834, there was no money for a funeral, and her body was buried in the potter's field. After a brief visit to his former home in Oneida County, he returned to work in the city in September. It was then, when he was about eighteen years old, that he began to drink. His fund of amusing stories, and his wonderful ability to tell them, naturally made him a favorite among the young men he met. Under the name of Gilbert, he sang a comic song entitled "The Water Party" at the Franklin Theatre in Chatham Street, New York. In 1836 he went to Bristol, R.I., and then to Providence. His intemperance was now noticeable, and led to his discharge by successive employers. Once, while out of work, he played low-comedy parts in a theatre in Providence, and then in Boston, where, strangely enough, he personated the keeper of a temperance inn in a play entitled *Departed Spirits, or the Temperance Hoax* (in which Deacon Moses Grant and Dr. Lyman Beecher were ridiculed), but his engagement lasted only a few weeks. He frequently sang comic songs in public. In 1838 he married at Newburyport, Mass.; but his wife and child died at Worcester in 1840. On the last Sunday of October, 1842, at the age of twenty-five, by invitation of Joel Dudley Stratton, who at the time was a waiter in the American Temperance House at Worcester, Mass., but later was a boot-crimper (see sketch of Stratton in Gough's *Autobiog.*, p. 522), he signed the pledge of total abstinence from all intoxicating liquors, at Worcester. The next week he was called upon to relate his experience as a drunkard; and the way in which he told his story of wretchedness, disease, and want, led to frequent requests to repeat it in public, and so he gradually became prominent as a temperance orator. Within five months (April, 1843) he thoughtlessly violated his pledge in Boston, when, almost insane in consequence of a drug taken to relieve his nervous exhaustion, he was offered, by an old companion, a glass of brandy. Again on Friday, Sept. 5, 1845, in New-York City, he was tricked into drinking liquor in a glass of soda-water. On each occasion the single glass aroused his craving, and he drank until intoxicated. His second fall was the more deplorable because he was then a widely known advocate of total abstinence. But he retained the confidence of the public, and showed true repentance. On Nov. 24, 1843, at Worcester, he married Miss Mary Whitcomb, his second wife. In 1853 he was invited by the Scottish Temperance League, and the British Temperance Association, to lecture on temperance in Great Britain for a few weeks; but he staid two years, and returned in 1857, and remained three years. On Nov. 21, 1860, he delivered at New Haven, Conn., his first lecture not directly upon temperance ("Street Life in London"), and thus entered a broader field in which, by his lectures on "London," "Eloquence and Orators," "Peculiar People," "Habit," and other topics, he has delighted thousands on both sides of the ocean. But he never lost interest in temperance work, and introduced the theme prominently in every lecture.

Mr. Gough was one of the most remarkable natural orators of this century. He was endowed with a musical and flexible voice, a winning manner, and a fine presence. He had both laughter and tears at his disposal. No one was superior to him as a story-teller. In proof of his popularity, it may be mentioned, that his receipts per lecture rose from $2.77 in 1843, to $173.39 in 1867. (See *Autobiography*, pp. 247, 248.) His life was that of a humble Christian, nor could he ever forget his years of intemperance. He was remarkably gifted in prayer. He was the author of several volumes, — *Autobiography*, London, 1846 (it was dictated to John Ross Dix, — or, as he then called himself, John Dix Ross, — a short-hand writer, who then was an inmate of his family, and who subsequently claimed the authorship of the book on the strength of a few verbal alterations he had made); *Orations*, 1854; *Autobiography and Personal Recollections*, Springfield, Mass., 1869; *Temperance Lectures*, New York, 1879; *Sunlight and Shadow; or, Gleanings from my Life-work*, London, 1881; *Platform Echoes*, Hartford, 1886. *

GOULBOURN, Very Rev. Edward Meyrick, D.D. (Oxford, 1856), **D.C.L.** (Oxford, 1850), dean of Norwich, Church of England; b. in England in the year 1818; educated at Eton and at Balliol College, Oxford; graduated B.A. (first-class in classics) 1839, M.A. (Merton College) 1842; ordained deacon 1842, priest 1843; was fellow and tutor of Merton College from 1839 to 1841; perpetual curate of Holywell, Oxford, from 1841 to 1850; head master of Rugby from 1850 to 1858; minister of Quebec Chapel, and prebendary of St. Paul's, London, from 1858 to 1859; one of her Majesty's chaplains in ordinary, and incumbent of St. John's, Paddington, London, from 1859 until 1866, when he became dean of Norwich. He was Bampton lecturer in 1850. He is the author of the following volumes, besides numerous other publications: *The Resurrection of the Body* (Bampton Lectures), 1851; *Introduction to the Devotional Study of the Holy Scriptures*, 1854, 10th ed. 1878; *The Idle Word*, 1855, 2d ed. 1864; *Manual of Confirmation*, 1855, 11th ed. 1884; *The Book of Rugby School*, 1856; *Family Prayers*, 1857, 4th ed. 1883; *The Inspiration of the Holy Scriptures*, 1857; *Sermons preached during the last 20 Years*, 1862, 2 vols.; *Thoughts on Personal Religion*, 1862, 2 vols., 17th ed. 1885; *The Office of the Holy Communion in the Book of Common Prayer*, 1863, 2 vols.; *The Acts of the Deacons*, 1866; *The Functions of our Cathedrals*, 1869; *The Pursuit of Holiness*, 1869, 5th ed. 1873; *The Ancient Sculptures in the Roof of Norwich Cathedral; with History of See and Cathedral*, 1872; *The Great Commission: Meditations on Home and Foreign Missions*, 1872; *The Athanasian Creed*, 1872; *The Holy Catholic Church*, 1873, 2d ed. 1875; *The Gospel of Childhood*, 1873; *The Administration of the Lord's Supper*, 1875, 2d ed. 1875; *The Child Samuel*, 1876; *Collects of the Day, Exposition*, 1880, 2 vols., 3d ed. 1883; *Everlasting Punishment*, 1880, 2d ed. same year; *Thoughts on the Liturgical Gospels for the Sundays*, 1883, 2 vols.; *Holy Week in Norwich Cathedral*, 1885. *

GOULD, Sabine Baring. See BARING-GOULD, SABINE.

GRAFE, Eduard, Ph.D. (Tübingen, 1880), **Lic. Theol.** (Berlin, 1882), German Protestant theologian; b. at Elberfeld, March 12, 1855; educated at Bonn (1873–74), Leipzig (1874–76, 1878–79), Tübingen (1876–77), and Berlin (1877–78); became *privat-docent* in Berlin, 1884; professor extraordinary of theology at Halle, 1886. He is the author of *Ueber Veranlassung u. Zweck d. Römerbriefes*, Freiburg-im-Br. and Tübingen, 1881; *Die paulin. Lehre v. Gesetz nach d. 4 Hauptbriefen*, 1884.

GRAHAM, Robert, Disciple; b. in Liverpool, Eng., Aug. 14, 1822; graduated at Bethany College, Bethany, W. Va., A.B. 1847, A.M. 1850; became president of Arkansas College, Fayetteville, Washington County, Ark., in 1852 (the college buildings were burned down during the war by the soldiers, and were never rebuilt); of Kentucky University, Lexington, Ky., in 1866; and since 1875, of the College of the Bible in that university.

GRANBERY, John Cowper, D.D. (Randolph-Macon College, Ashland, Va., 1870), Methodist bishop (Southern Church); b. at Norfolk, Va., Dec. 5, 1829; graduated at Randolph-Macon College, Ashland, Va., 1848; admitted to the Virginia Conference, Methodist-Episcopal Church South, 1848; chaplain in the Confederate Army of Northern Virginia during the war; became professor of moral philosophy and practical theology in Vanderbilt University, Nashville, Tenn., 1875; bishop, 1882. He is the author of *A Bible Dictionary for Sunday Schools and Families*, Nashville, Tenn., 1882.

GRANT, George Monro, D.D. (Glasgow University, 1878), Canadian Presbyterian; b. at East River, Pictou, N.S., Dec. 22, 1835; studied at Glasgow University (letters and theology), 1853–60; graduated M.A. with highest honors in philosophy, 1857; became minister of Georgetown and St. Peter's Road, Prince Edward Island, 1861; of St. Matthew's, Halifax, N.S., 1863; principal of Queen's University, Kingston, Ont., and primarius professor of divinity, 1877. He is the author of *Ocean to Ocean through Canada*, Toronto, 1872, last ed. 1878; and of numerous review articles.

GRAU, Rudolf Friedrich, Lic. Theol. (Marburg, 1859), **Ph.D.** (*hon.*, Rostock, 1870), **D.D.** (*hon.*, Leipzig, 1875), German Lutheran; b. at Heringen-on-the-Werra, Hesse, April 20, 1835; studied at Leipzig, Erlangen, and Marburg, 1854–57; became private tutor at home, *privat-docent* in theology at Marburg, 1860; professor extraordinary, 1865; ordinary professor at Königsberg, 1866. Since its beginning, in 1865, he has been joint editor of the *Beweis des Glaubens*. He is the author of *Semiten und Indogermanen in ihrer Bezie-*

hung zur Religion und Wissenschaft, Stuttgart, 1864, 2d ed. 1867; *Ueber den Glauben als die höchste Vernunft*, Gütersloh, 1865; *Entwickelungsgeschichte des neutestamentlichen Schriftthums*, 1871, 2 vols.; *Ursprünge und Ziele unserer Kulturentwickelung*, 1875; *Bibelwerk für die Gemeinde* (in connection with other theologians), New-Testament part Bielefeld u. Leipzig, 1877–80, 2 vols.; *Der Glaube die wahre Lebensphilosophie*, Gütersloh, 1881 (this lecture and that of 1865 have been widely circulated and translated into English for distribution among the educated Hindus, the earlier in Madras by the Free Church of Scotland, the later by the Church Missionary Society in Bombay); *Biblische Theologie des Neuen Testaments* in Zöckler's *Handbuch der theologischen Wissenschaften*, Nördlingen, 1883, 2d ed. 1885; *Ueber Martin Luthers Glauben*, Gütersloh, 1884.

GRAVES, Right Rev. Charles, D.D. (Trinity College, Dublin, 1851), lord bishop of Limerick, Ardfert and Aghadoe, Church of Ireland; b. in Ireland upon the 6th of November, 1812; was scholar of Trinity College, Dublin, 1832; graduated B.A. (senior moderator in mathematics) 1835, M.A. 1836, B.D. 1851; was fellow of Trinity College, 1836–66; professor of mathematics in the University of Dublin, 1843–62; dean of the chapel royal, Dublin, and chaplain to the lord lieutenant, 1860–66; dean of Clonfert, 1864–66; became bishop and prebendary of Athnett, Limerick Cathedral, 1866; since 1857 he has been a member of the Royal Irish Academy, and president 1860–65.

GRAY, Albert Zabriskie, S.T.D. (Racine College, Racine, Wis., 1882), Episcopalian; b. in New-York City, March 2, 1840; graduated at the University of the City of New York, 1860, and at the General Theological Seminary, New-York City, 1864; was chaplain of the Fourth Massachusetts Cavalry during the war of the Rebellion, 1864–65; rector of Christ Church, Bloomfield, N.J., 1865–68; in Europe, 1868–71; rector of St. Philip's in the Highlands, New York, 1873–82; and was installed warden of Racine (Wis.) College, 1882. His theological standpoint is "Anglo-Catholic." He is the author of *The Land and the Life: Sketches and Studies in Palestine*, New York, 1876; *The Words of the Cross*, 1880; *Jesus Only, and other Sacred Songs*, 1882.

GRAY, George Zabriskie, D.D. (University of the City of New York, 1876), Episcopalian; b. in New-York City, July 14, 1838; graduated at the University of the City of New York, 1858; and after being rector at Vernon, N.J. (1862–63), Kinderhook, N.Y. (1863–65), and at Bergen Point, N.J. (1865–76), he became in 1876 dean of the Episcopal Theological School, and professor of systematic divinity, in Cambridge, Mass. He is the author of *History of the Children's Crusade*, Boston, 1872, 5th ed. 1884; *Scriptural Doctrine of Recognition*, New York, 1875, 4th ed. 1886; *Husband and Wife, or the Theory of Marriage*, Boston, 1885, 2d ed. 1886.

GRAY, William Cunningham, Ph.D. (University of Wooster, O., 1874), Presbyterian, layman; b. at Pleasant Run, Butler County, O., Oct. 17, 1830; graduated at Farmers' College, College Hill, O., 1850; admitted to the bar, 1852; was a political editor, 1853–70; but since 1871, has been editor of the Chicago *Interior*, a Presbyterian journal.

GREEN, Samuel Gosnell, D.D. (University of Chicago, Ill., 1870), Baptist; b. at Falmouth, Cornwall, Eng., Dec. 20, 1822; studied at Stepney College, London, and graduated B.A. at the University of London, 1843; became minister at High Wycombe, Bucks, 1845, and at Taunton, Somerset, 1847. He was classical tutor 1851–63; then president of the Yorkshire Baptist College 1863–76 (first at Bradford, after 1859 at Rawdon); since has been secretary of the Religious Tract Society of London. He is the author of several books for young people, *Addresses*, 1848; *Lectures*, 1853; *Bible Sketches*, 1870–72; *Christian Ministry to the Young*, 1883. Also of books for teachers, *Kings of Israel and Judah*, 1876; *Life and Letters of the Apostle Peter*, 1873; *Notes on the Scripture Lessons* (yearly), from 1872 to 1876. Of a more general character, *Handbook to Grammar of the Greek New Testament*, 1870, 4th revised ed. 1885; *Pen and Pencil Pictures*, 1876–83, 5 vols. He edited the English edition of Hackett on *Acts*, 1862, 2 vols., and new edition of Lorimer's translation of Lechler's *Wiclif*, 1884.

GREEN, William Henry, D.D. (College of New Jersey, Princeton, 1857), **LL.D.** (Rutgers College, New Brunswick, N.J., 1873), Presbyterian; b. at Groveville, near Bordentown, N.J., Jan. 27, 1825; graduated at Lafayette College, Easton, Penn., 1840; was tutor there for two years, then entered Princeton (N.J.) Theological Seminary, and took the full course, interrupted by one year's teaching of mathematics (1843–44) at Lafayette, graduating in 1846. He was appointed instructor in Hebrew in the Seminary from 1846 to 1849, during which time (1847) he was stated supply to the Second Church of Princeton. From 1849 to 1851 he was pastor of the Central Presbyterian Church, Philadelphia; and since 1851 he has been a professor in Princeton Theological Seminary. Until 1859 his chair was styled "Biblical and Oriental literature;" since 1859, "Oriental and Old-Testament literature." He was the chairman of the American Old-Testament Company of the Anglo-American Bible-Revision Committee; and is the author of *A Grammar of the Hebrew Language*, New York, 1861, 4th ed. 1885; *A Hebrew Chrestomathy*, 1863; *The Pentateuch vindicated from the Aspersions of Bishop Colenso*, 1863; *Elementary Hebrew Grammar*, 1866, 2d ed. 1871; *The Argument of the Book of Job unfolded*, 1874; *Moses and the Prophets*, 1883; *The Hebrew Feasts in their Relation to Recent Critical Hypotheses concerning the Pentateuch*, 1885. He edited *The Song of Solomon*, in the American Lange series (1870).

GREEN, Right Rev. William Mercer, D.D. (University of Pennsylvania, Philadelphia, 1845), **LL.D.** (University of North Carolina, Chapel Hill, 1880), Episcopalian, bishop of Mississippi; b. in Wilmington, N.C., May 2, 1798; graduated second in the class at the University of North Carolina, 1818; ordained deacon 1821, priest 1822; became rector of St. John's, Williamsburgh, N.C., 1821; of St. Matthew's, Hillsborough, 1825; chaplain and professor of belles-lettres in his alma mater, 1837; consecrated bishop, Feb. 24, 1850. Since 1866 he has been chancellor of the University of the South. He is "an anti-Calvinist, and a Churchman of the old school." Besides sermons and addresses as chancellor, he has written memoirs of Bishops Ravenscroft (New York, 1870) and Otey (1885).

GREGG, Right Rev. Alexander, D.D. (South Carolina College, Columbia, S.C., 1859), Episcopalian, bishop of Texas; b. at Society Hill, Darlington District, S.C., Oct. 8, 1819; graduated head of his class, South Carolina College, Columbia, 1838; practised law at Cheraw, S.C., until 1843; was rector of St. David's, Cheraw, 1846; consecrated, 1859. He attended the first Lambeth Conference, 1874. He has published, besides sermons, etc., *History of Old Cheraw*, 1867. *

GREGG, Right Rev. Robert Samuel, D.D. (Trinity College, Dublin, 1873), lord bishop of Cork, Cloyne, and Ross, Church of Ireland; son of Bishop Gregg; b. in Dublin, Ireland, in the year 1834; educated at Trinity College, Dublin; graduated B.A. and Divinity Testimonium (second class) 1857, M.A. 1860, B.D. 1873; ordained deacon 1857, priest 1858; rector of Carrigrohane; vicar of St. Fin Barre; dean of Cork, 1874–75; bishop of Ossory, Ferns, and Leighlin, 1875–78; succeeded his father as bishop of Cork, Cloyne, and Ross, 1878. He is a member of the senate of Trinity College. He is the author of *Memorials of the Life of John Gregg, D.D.* (his father), Dublin, 1879; sermons, pamphlets, etc.

GREGG, William, D.D. (Hanover College, Hanover, Ind., 1878), Canadian Presbyterian; b. at Killycreen, near Ramelton, County Donegal, Ireland, July 5, 1817; graduated B.A. at the University of Glasgow, 1843, and M.A. at that of Edinburgh, 1844; studied theology in Free Church College, Edinburgh, 1843–46; became pastor at Belleville, Canada West, 1847; of Cooke's Church, Toronto, 1857; professor of apologetics and church history, Knox College, Toronto, 1872 (having taught apologetics in the college since 1864). He was moderator in 1861, when union was effected between the Presbyterian Church and the United Presbyterian Church in Canada. He edited *Book of Passages for Family Worship*, Toronto, 1878, 3d ed. 1883; wrote *History of Presbyterian Church in Canada from the Earliest Times to 1834* (with chronological tables of subsequent leading events), 1885.

GREGORY, Caspar René, Ph.D. (Leipzig, 1876), **Lic. Theol.** (Leipzig, 1884), Presbyterian; b. in Philadelphia, Penn., Nov. 6, 1846; graduated at the University of Pennsylvania, Philadelphia, 1864, and at Princeton Theological Seminary, 1870; was Dr. Charles Hodge's literary assistant in preparing for and in carrying through the press his *Systematic Theology*, 1870–73 (of which he made the separately printed elaborate *Index*); sub-editor (bibliographer) of Schürer and Harnack, *Theologische Literaturzeitung*, 1876–84; pastor of the American Chapel in Leipzig, 1878–79; *privat-docent* at Leipzig University, May 28, 1884; elected professor of New-Testament Greek, Johns Hopkins University, 1885. Besides several articles, notably upon Tischendorf, and translations of Luthardt's *St. John the Author of the Fourth Gospel* (Edinburgh, 1875, 2d ed. 1885), and *Commentary on St. John's Gospel* (1876–78, 3 vols.), the pamphlet, *Les cahiers des manuscrits grecs*, Paris, 1885, he is the author of the *Prolegomena in N. T. Tischendorfianum ed. viii., maior*, Leipzig, pars prima 1884.

GREGORY, Daniel Seely, D.D. (College of New Jersey, Princeton, 1873), Presbyterian; b. at Carmel, N.Y., Aug. 21, 1832; graduated at the College of New Jersey, 1857, and at Princeton (N.J.) Theological Seminary, 1860; was tutor of rhetoric and belles-lettres in the College of New Jersey, 1858–60; became pastor (elect) of the South Church, Galena, Ill., 1860; of the Second Church, Troy, N.Y., 1863; (elect) of the Third Congregational Church, New Haven, Conn., 1866; pastor there, 1867; at South Salem, N.Y., 1869; professor of metaphysics and logic in Wooster University, Wooster, O., 1871; of mental science and English literature in the same institution, 1875; president of Lake Forest University, Ill., 1878–86. He is the author of *Christian Ethics: or, the True Moral Manhood and Life of Duty*, Philadelphia, 1875, seventh thousand 1886; *Why Four Gospels? or, the Gospel for All the World*, New York, 1876, 3d ed. 1885; *Practical Logic, or the Art of Thinking*, Philadelphia, 1881, third thousand 1886; *The Tests of Philosophic Systems, or a Natural Philosophy, being the L. P. Stone Lectures (enlarged) before Princeton Theological Seminary, 1885*, 1886. He has also written, besides much else, the following review articles: 1. In *The Princeton Review: The Preaching for the Times* (1866), *The Pastorate for the Times*, and *Studies in the Gospels — Matthew the Gospel for the Jew* (1868), *The Novel and Novel-reading* (1869), *The Christian Giving for the Times* (1870), *Mark the Gospel for the Romans* (1871), *Works by Professor March on Anglo-Saxon and English* (1874). 2. In *The Presbyterian Quarterly and Princeton Review: The True Theory and Practice of Education*, and *Studies in the Gospels — Luke the Gospel for the Greek* (1875), *A Grammar of the Hindi Language* (1877). 3. In *The Princeton Review* (new series): *The Eastern Problem*, and *John Stuart Mill and the Destruction of Theism* (1878). 4. In *The Presbyterian Review: A New Principle in Education* (1884).

GRIER, Matthew Blackburne, Presbyterian; b. at Brandywine Manor, Chester County, Penn., July 25, 1820; graduated at Washington and Jefferson College, Washington, Penn., 1838, and at Princeton (N.J.) Theological Seminary, 1844; was pastor at Ellicott's Mills, Md., 1847–52; at Wilmington, N.C., 1852–61; since, has been editor of *The Presbyterian*, Philadelphia, Penn.

GRIER, William Moffatt, D.D. (Monmouth College, Monmouth, Ill., 1873), Associate Reformed Presbyterian; b. near Yorkville, S.C., Feb. 11, 1843; graduated at Erskine College, Due West, S.C., 1860; pastor in Wilcox County, Ala., 1867–71; since 1871 president of Erskine College, and since 1884 professor of pastoral theology in Erskine Theological Seminary. Since 1881 he has been principal editor of *The Associate Reformed Presbyterian*.

GRIFFIS, William Elliot, D.D. (Union College, Schenectady, N.Y., 1884), Congregationalist; b. in Philadelphia, Penn., Sept. 17, 1843; graduated at Rutgers College, New Brunswick, N.J., 1869, and at Union Theological Seminary, New-York City, 1877; became pastor of the First Reformed Church, Schenectady, N.Y., 1877; of the Shawmut Congregational Church, Boston, Mass., 1886. He was in the 44th Penn. Vols. during Lee's invasion of Pennsylvania, 1863; editor of *Our Messenger*, Philadelphia, Penn., 1864; in the educational service of the Japanese Government at Fukui and

Tokio, organizing schools and teaching physical science, 1871–74. He is the author of *The New Japan Series of Reading-Books*, San Francisco and Yokohama, 1872–73, 4 vols.; *The Tokio Guide*, *The Yokohama Guide*, *Map of Tokio with Notes*, Yokohama, 1874; *The Mikado's Empire*, New York, 1876, 4th ed. 1886; *Japanese Fairy World*, Schenectady, 1880; *Schenectady First Church Memorial*, Schenectady, 1880; *Asiatic History, China, Corea, and Japan* (Chautauqua series, No. 34), New York, 1881; *Corea, the Hermit Nation*, New York, 1882, 2d ed. 1885; *Corea, Without and Within*, Philadelphia, 1884, 2d ed. 1885; *Life of Commodore Matthew Calbraith Perry*, New York, 1886.

GRIFFITH, Benjamin, D.D. (University of Lewisburg, Lewisburg, Penn., 1865), Baptist; b. in Juniata County, Penn., Oct. 13, 1821; graduated at Madison University, Hamilton, N.Y., 1846; became pastor at Cumberland, Md., 1846; in Philadelphia, Penn., 1850; corresponding secretary of the American Baptist Publication Society, May, 1857, whose office is in Philadelphia.

GRIMM, Carl Ludwig Wilibald, Ph.D. (Jena, 1832), **Lic. Theol.** (Giessen, 1836), **D.D.** (*hon.*, Giessen, 1838), Lutheran; b. at Jena, Nov. 1, 1807; educated there 1827–32, and has ever since been connected with her university, as *privat-docent*, 1833; professor extraordinary, 1837; honorary ordinary professor, 1844. He became grand ducal ecclesiastical councillor in 1871, and privy ecclesiastical councillor 1885. His theological standpoint is of the "Mittelpartei." His writings embrace, *De joanneæ christologiæ indole paulinæ comparata*, Leipzig, 1833; *De libro sapientiæ*, Jena, 1833; *De Lutheri indole*, 1833; *Oratio de Staupitio*, 1835; *Commentar über das Buch der Weisheit*, Leipzig, 1837; *Die Glaubwürdigkeit der evangelischen Geschichte* (against Strauss), Jena, 1845; *Institutio theologiæ dogmaticæ evangelicæ historico critica*, 1848, 2d ed. 1869; *Die Lutherbibel und ihre Textesrevision*, Berlin, 1874; *Kurzgefasste Geschichte der lutherischen Bibelübersetzung bis zur Gegenwart*, Jena, 1884. He so edited Wilke's *Clavis N. T. philologica* (Leipzig, 1867), that it became a new work which now bears his name, — *Lexicon Græco-Latinum in libros N. T.*, 2d ed. 1879. With O. F. Fritzsche he edited the *Kurzgefasstes exegetisches Handbuch zu den Apokryphen d. A. T.*, Leipzig, 1851–60 (1st Maccabees, 1853; 2d, 3d, 4th Maccabees, 1857; Wisdom, 1860).

GRIMM, Joseph, D.D. (Munich, 1854), Roman Catholic; b. at Freising, Bavaria, Jan. 23, 1827; studied at the University of Munich, 1845–50; became a teacher 1852, chaplain 1854; professor of Old and New Testament exegesis in the royal lyceum at Regensburg, 1856; ordinary professor of New-Testament exegesis at Würzburg, 1874. He is *bischöfl. geistlicher Rath*, and since 1886 knight of the Order of St. Michael. He is the author of *Die Samariter und ihre Stellung in der Weltgeschichte*, Regensburg, 1854; *Der κατέχων des zweiten Thessalonicher-Briefes* (*Programm zum Jahresbericht des Lyceums u. Gymnasiums in Regensburg*), 1861; *Die Einheit des Lukas Evangeliums*, 1863; *Die Einheit der vier Evangelien*, 1868; *Das Leben Jesu*, 1876, sqq. 6 vols. (vol. iv., 1885).

GRISAR, Hermann, Roman Catholic; b. at Coblenz; became a priest at Rome, 1868 (shortly after entered the Society of Jesus); professor of church history at Innsbruck, 1871. He has written essays in his department, in the Innsbruck *Zeitschrift für kathol. Theologie*, and edited from the MS. and annotated Iago Lainez' (1512–1565) *Disputationes Tridentinæ*, Innsbruck, 1886, 2 vols.

GRUBBS, Isaiah Boone, A.M., Disciple; b. near Trenton, Todd County, Ky., May 24, 1833; graduated at Bethany (West Va.) College, 1857; became pastor at Eminence, Ky., 1869; at Louisville, Ky., 1873; editor of *The Apostolic Times*, published in Lexington, Ky., 1876; professor of sacred literature in the College of the Bible, Kentucky University, in that place, 1877. He has written much for denominational journals.

GRUNDEMANN, Peter Reinhold, Ph.D. (Tübingen, 1858), **D.D.** (*hon.*, Berlin, 1885), German Protestant; b. at Bärwalde, Brandenburg, Jan. 9, 1836; studied at the universities of Tübingen, Halle, and Berlin, 1854–58; became assistant preacher at Pouch, near Bitterfeld, 1861; *Gefängnisprediger* in Frankfurt-on-the-Oder, 1863; cartographer at Gotha, 1865; pastor at Mörz, near Belzig, 1869. He was in Greece 1858–59, Norway 1860, Holland 1863, 1865, 1867, England 1865–67, United States 1868. He is a member of the Berlin and Jena Geographical Society, and the author of *Allgemeiner Missionsatlas*, Gotha, 1867–71; *J. F. Riedel, ein Lebensbild*, Gütersloh, 1873; *Kleiner Missionsatlas*, Calw and Stuttgart, 1883, 2d ed. 1886; and edited the second edition of Buckhardt's *Kleine Missionsbibliothek*, Bielefeld, 1876–81, 4 vols.

GRUNERT, Maximilian Eugene, Moravian; b. at Niesky, Silesia, Feb. 26, 1823; educated at Niesky, and in the theological seminary at Gnadenfeld; after being principal of the Female Academy, Salem, N.C., and pastor at Emmaus, Penn., he became in 1879 professor in the Moravian Theological Seminary, Bethlehem, Penn.

GUBELMANN, Jacob Samuel, D.D. (Richmond College, Va., 1885), Baptist; b. in Bern, Switzerland, Nov. 27, 1836; graduated at University of Rochester, N.Y., 1858, and at Rochester Theological Seminary, 1860; became pastor of German Baptist Church at Louisville, Ky., 1860; St. Louis, Mo., 1862; Philadelphia, 1868; professor of systematic theology and homiletics in the German department of the Rochester Theological Seminary, 1884.

GUENTHER, Martin, Lutheran; b. at Dresden, Saxony, Dec. 4, 1831; graduated at Altenburg (Mo.) College, 1849, and at Concordia Theological Seminary, St. Louis, Mo., 1853; held charges in Wisconsin (1853–60), Michigan (1860–72), and in Chicago, Ill. (1872–73); and since 1873 has been professor of theology in the Concordia Theological Seminary, St. Louis, Mo. He is the author of *Populäre Symbolik*, St. Louis, Mo., 1872, 2d ed. 1881; co-editor of *Lutheraner: Magasin für ev. luth. Homiletik*, etc.

GULLIVER, John Putnam, Congregationalist; b. in Boston, Mass., May 12, 1819; graduated from Yale College, New Haven, Conn., 1840, and from Andover (Mass.) Theological Seminary, 1845. He was pastor of churches in Norwich, Conn. (1845–65), Chicago, Ill. (1865–68), Binghamton, N.Y. (1872–78); president of Knox College, Galesburg, Ill., 1868–72; and since 1878 he has been professor of the relations of Christianity and secular science in Andover (Mass.) Theological Seminary.

GUTHE, Hermann, Lic. Theol. (Leipzig, 1876), German Protestant; b. at Westerlinde, Braunschweig, May 10, 1849; studied at Göttingen from 1867 to 1869, and at Erlangen 1869 and 1870; became private tutor in Livonia, 1870; *repetent* of theology at Göttingen, 1873; *privat-docent* at Leipzig, 1877; professor extraordinary there, 1884. As member of the business committee of the German Palestine Exploration Society, he conducted the excavations at Jerusalem in 1881. His theological standpoint is "*Ethischer Supranaturalismus mit völliger Freiheit der historischen Forschung.*" Since 1877 he has edited the *Zeitschrift des Deutschen Palästina Vereins*, Leipzig (1877–85, 8 vols.), and in it written numerous articles upon biblical geography, topography, and archæology. Besides these and articles in Herzog's *Real-Encyklopädie*, 2d ed., and Harnack-Schürer *Theolog. Literaturzeitung*, he has written *De fœderis notione jeremiana* (*Habilitationsschrift*), Leipzig, 1877; *Ausgrabungen bei Jerusalem*, 1883; *Die Siloahinschrift* (Z. D. M. Bd. xxxvi.); *Fragmente einer Lederhandschrift* (Shapira's Deuteronomy) *mitgetheilt und geprüft*, 1883; *Das Zukunftsbild des Jesaia* (*Antrittsvorlesung* enlarged), 1885; and with Georg Ebers made the German edition of *Picturesque Palestine*, London and New York, 1881–84, 2 vols. (*Palästina in Bild u. Wort*, Stuttgart und Leipzig, 1883–84, 2 vols.).

GWYNN, John, D.D. (Dublin, 1880), Church of Ireland; b. at Larne, County Antrim, Ireland, Aug. 28, 1827; graduated at Trinity College, Dublin, B.A. (senior moderator in mathematics) 1850, M.A. 1854, B.D. 1861. He became fellow of Trinity College, 1853; warden of St. Columba's College, Dublin, 1856; was rector of Tullyaughnish, 1863–82; dean of Raphoe, 1873–82; dean of Derry, 1882; and rector of Templemore, Derry, 1882–83; Archbishop King's lecturer in divinity, University of Dublin, 1883, and is a member of the senate. He wrote the commentary (with introduction) on the *Epistle to Philippians*, in *The Bible (Speaker's) Commentary*, London, 1881.

H.

HAERING, Theodor, German theologian; b. in Stuttgart, Würtemburg, April 22, 1848; studied in the Stuttgart gymnasium, and in the evangelical theological seminaries of Urach (1862–66) and of Tübingen (1866–70), and at the University of Berlin (1871); became *repetent* in the Evangelical Theological Seminary at Tübingen, 1873; *diaconus* in Calw 1876, and in Stuttgart, 1881; ordinary professor of theology at Zürich, 1886. His theological position is the biblico-positive, particularly influenced by Ritschl and Kaftan and his deceased teachers Landerer and Beck. He is the author of *Das Bleibende im Glauben an Christus*, Stuttgart, 1880; and since 1880 has edited the *Theologische Studien aus Würtemberg*.

HALE, Charles Reuben, S.T.D. (Hobart College, Geneva, N.Y., 1876), Episcopalian; b. at Lewistown, Mifflin County, Penn.; graduated at the University of Pennsylvania, Philadelphia, 1858; was assistant minister of All Saints' Church, Lower Dublin, Philadelphia, 1861; chaplain in United States Navy, 1863; rector of St. John's Church, Auburn, N.Y., 1870: rector of the Church of St. Mary the Virgin, Baltimore County, Md., 1875; one of the clergy of St. Paul's Church, Baltimore, Md., 1877; since 1886 dean of Davenport, Io. He was secretary to the Italian Church Reformation Commission, 1869; secretary to the Russo-Greek Committee, 1871; clerk to the Commission of the House of Bishops on Correspondence with the Hierarchs of the Eastern Churches, 1874; and with the Old Catholics, 1874; secretary (for America) of the Anglo-Continental Society of England, 1874; secretary to the Commission of the General Convention on Ecclesiastical Relations, 1877. In theology he is an Anglican. His published writings consist of *Reports* (of the Russo-Greek Committee, N.Y., 1872 and 1875; of the Committee on Ecclesiastical Relations, N.Y., 1881 and 1884), a *Paper* on the Russian Church (read before the Church Congress, Leicester, Eng., 1880; republished, Baltimore, 1881), *Speeches and Addresses* (in Baltimore, 1881; two in Church Congress at Carlisle, Eng., 1884, *On Foreign Chaplaincies*, and *England's Duty towards Egypt;* two in Church Congress at Portsmouth, Eng., 1885, *The Prayer Book*, and *The Attitude of the Church towards Movements in Foreign Churches*), *Sermons* (in St. Timothy's Church, N. Y. City, 1874; in Inverness Cathedral, by appointment of the Primus of Scotland, Oct. 5, 1884), and the following: *Report of the Committee appointed by the Philomathean Society of the Univ. of Pennsylvania to translate the Inscription on the Rosetta Stone* (the committee consisted of S. H. Jones, H. Morton, and himself), Philadelphia (privately printed), 1858, 2d ed. 1859; *A List of the Sees and Bishops of the Holy Eastern Church*, 1870; *A List of all the Sees and Bishops of the Holy Orthodox Church of the East*, New York, 1872; *An Eastern View of the Bonn Conference*, Utica, N.Y., 1876; *The Mozarabic Liturgy, and the Mexican Branch of the Catholic Church of our Lord Jesus Christ Militant upon Earth*, New York, 1876; *Innocent of Moscow, the Apostle of Kamchatka and Alaska*, 1877; *The Orthodox Missionary Society of Russia*, 1878; *Russian Missions in China and Japan*, 1878; *An Order for the Holy Communion, arranged from the Mozarabic Liturgy*, Baltimore, 1879 (two supplements to the above, 1879); *An Office for Holy Baptism, arranged from the Mozarabic and Cognate Sources*, 1879; *Mozarabic Collects, translated and arranged from the Ancient Liturgy of the Spanish Church*, New York, 1881; *The Universal Episcopate. A List of the Sees and Bishops in the Holy Catholic Church throughout the World*, Baltimore, 1882; *The Eucharistic Office of the Christian Catholic Church of Switzerland, translated and compared with that in the Missale Romanum*, New York, 1882.

HALE, Edward Everett, S.T.D. (Harvard University, Cambridge, Mass., 1879), Unitarian; b. in Boston, Mass., April 3, 1822; educated at the Boston Latin School, and at Harvard College, Cambridge, Mass., where he graduated in 1839; studied theology privately; was pastor at Worcester from 1846 to 1856, and since that time has been pastor of the South Congregational (Unitarian) Church, Boston. He was chairman of the National Unitarian Council of American Churches, 1882–84; and since 1881 president of the Suffolk Conference of Unitarian Churches. He edited *The Christian Examiner*, the organ of his denomination, 1857–63; *Old and New*, a semi-theological magazine, 1870–75; and since 1886, *Lend a Hand*. Of his many volumes may be mentioned, *Kansas and Nebraska*, Boston, 1856; *Ten Times One is Ten*, 1870; *What Career?* 1878; four volumes of sermons, 1879-81. He was one of the writers of Bryant and Gay's *History of the United States*, New York, 1876–80.

HALEY, John William, Congregationalist; b. at Tuftonborough, N.H., June 8, 1834; graduated at Dartmouth College, Hanover, N.H., 1860, and at Andover Theological Seminary, Mass., 1864; was pastor of the Christian Church, Eastport, Me., 1864–65; professor of metaphysics, Union College, Merom, Ind., 1865; pastor at Somerset, Mass., 1866-69; acting pastor of the Congregational Church, Duxbury, Mass., 1869–70; resident licentiate at Andover, Mass., 1870-71, 1872–74; acting pastor at Dudley, Mass., 1872. Since 1874 has been engaged in literary work at Tyngsborough, Mass. (1874–80), at Lowell, Mass. (1880–84), and since at Amherst; he has also preached in these places and their vicinity. He took an active part in the Lowell Hebrew Club, organized in 1875. He is the author of *Examination of Alleged Discrepancies of the Bible*, Andover, 1874, 3d ed. 1882; *The Hereafter of Sin: What it will be; with Answers to Certain Questions and Objections*, 1881; edited *The Book of Esther, a New Translation, with Notes, Excursuses, Illustrations, and Indexes*, by a Hebrew Club, 1885. He taught Hebrew in 1885, and Hebrew and Greek in 1886, in the Amherst Summer School of Languages. He has also lectured on different topics.

HALL, Isaac Hollister, A.M., LL.B., Ph.D. (Hamilton College, Clinton, N.Y., 1876), Presbyterian layman; b. at Norwalk, Conn., Dec. 12, 1837; graduated at Hamilton College, Clinton, N.Y., 1859, and at Columbia Law School, New-York City, 1865; practised law in the city until 1875; was associate editor of the New-York *Independent*, 1875; professor in the Beirût Protestant College, 1875-77; associate editor of *The Sunday School Times*, Philadelphia, 1877-84; since then has been connected with the Metropolitan Museum of Art, New-York City, and lecturer on New-Testament Greek in Johns Hopkins University, Baltimore, Md. He was an original decipherer of the Cypriote inscriptions; discoverer of the Pre-Harklensian Syriac version in the Beirût MS., and of the Antilegomena Epistles in the Williams MS. of Acts and Epistles. He is the author of *American Greek Testaments, A Critical Bibliography of the Greek New Testament as published in America*, Philadelphia, 1883; *Reproduction in Phototype of 8 Pages of the Beirût MS.*, 1883; *Reproduction in Phototype of 17 Pages of a Syriac MS. containing the Epistles known as Antilegomena*, Baltimore, 1886; *List of Printed Editions of the Greek New Testament*, based upon Reuss' *Bibliotheca N. T. Græci*, in Schaff's *Companion to the Greek Testament and English Version*, New York, 1883; and of articles in the Journals and Transactions of learned societies, particularly of the American Oriental Society (chiefly decipherment of Cypriote and other inscriptions, Syriac MSS., etc.), Society of Biblical Archæology (London), American Philological Association, Society of Biblical Literature and Exegesis, etc.

HALL, John, D.D. (Washington and Jefferson College, Washington, Penn., 1866), **LL.D.** (College of New Jersey, Princeton, 1885, and from Washington and Lee University, Lexington, Va., 1885), Presbyterian; b. in County Armagh, Ireland, July 31, 1829; graduated from the Royal College, and the General Assembly's Theological College, both in Belfast; and was licensed to preach in 1849. For the next three years he labored as the "students' missionary" in the West of Ireland. In 1852 he began his regular ministry as pastor of the First Presbyterian Church at Armagh; in 1858 he went to Dublin as collegiate pastor of Mary's Abbey; and thence in 1867 to the Fifth-avenue Presbyterian Church, New-York City, where he still is. In college he was repeatedly Hebrew prizeman; and in Dublin his interest in education led to his being appointed by the Queen, in 1860, a member of the Board of National Education, upon which he served gratuitously until his departure to America. In 1867 he came as a delegate from the Presbyterian Church in Ireland to the Presbyterian Church in America. In 1882 he was elected chancellor of the University of the City of New York, and in 1885 accepted the position, having meanwhile been chancellor *ad interim*. He receives, however, no salary, and is assisted by a vice-chancellor. In 1874 his congregation removed from the corner of Fifth Avenue and Nineteenth Street to that of Fifth Avenue and Fifty-fifth Street, where they had erected a spacious building at the cost of a million dollars. Dr. Hall is the author of *Family Prayers for Four Weeks*, New York, 1868; *Papers for Home Reading*, 1871; *Familiar Talks to Boys*, n. d.; *Questions of the Day*, 1873; *God's Word through Preaching*, 1875 (Lyman Beecher Lectures at Yale Seminary); *Foundation Stones for Young Builders, New Year's Book for the Boys and Girls of America*, Philadephia, 1880; *A Christian Home, How to make and how to maintain it*, 1883.

HALL, Newman, LL.B. (London University, 1855), Congregationalist; b. at Maidstone, Kent, near London, Eng., May 22, 1816; educated at Totteridge and at Highbury College; and graduated B.A. at the University of London, 1841. From 1842 to 1854 he was minister of the Albion Congregational Church, Hull. In 1854 he went to London, to his present charge. The congregation then worshipped in the Surrey Chapel (Rowland Hill's), Blackfriars Road; but in 1876 they removed to their new building, Christ Church, on the Westminster-Bridge road. Mr. Hall's ministry has been an eventful one, on account of the independence and vigor of his work. He was among the earliest advocates of total abstinence in England, a deprecator of the fears of Roman-Catholic aggression in 1850, and a faithful friend of the North in the late Civil War. After that war he made an extensive tour through the Northern States, with the express design of allaying the popular bitterness against Great Britain, and preached before both houses of Congress assembled in the House of Representatives, on a Sunday in November, 1867. As a memorial of this visit, there was built the Lincoln Tower, as part of his new church, by joint subscription of the British and Americans. This church cost £60,000, and seats two thousand persons. The Church-of-England service is used in a slightly modified form. Mr. Hall is the author of the tract *Come to Jesus*, London, 1846 (of which nearly 3,000,000 copies have been circulated, in upwards of twenty languages); *It is I*, 1848 (139,000 copies of the English ed. up to 1885); *Antidote to Fear*, 1850, new ed. 1869; *The Land of the Forum and the Vatican* (travels), 1852, new ed. 1859; *Sacrifice, or Pardon and Purity through the Cross*, 1857; *Conflict and Victory* (a biography of his father, J. V. Hall), 1865, new ed. 1874; *Homeward Bound, and other Sermons*, 1868; *From Liverpool to St. Louis*, 1868; *Pilgrim Songs in Cloud and Sunshine* (poems), 1871; *Prayer, its Reasonableness and Efficacy*, 1875; *The Lord's Prayer: a Practical Meditation*, 1883; *Songs of Earth and Heaven*, 1885; besides several tracts and minor treatises, of which may be mentioned, *My Friends; Follow Jesus* (246,000 copies of the English ed. up to 1885); *Now; Quench not the Spirit; Memoir of Rowland Hill; Grace and Glory; Scriptural Claims of Teetotalism.*

HALL, Randall Cook, S.T.D. (Racine College, Racine, Wis., 1881; General Theological Seminary, New-York City, 1885), Episcopalian; b. at Wallingford, Conn., Dec. 18, 1842; graduated from Columbia College, 1863, and from the General Theological Seminary (both in New-York City), 1866; and since 1871 has been Clement C. Moore professor of the Hebrew and Greek languages in the latter institution. He is examining chaplain of the diocese of New York.

HALLOCK, Joseph Newton, Congregationalist; b. at Jamesport, N.Y., July 4, 1834; graduated at Yale College, New Haven, Conn., 1857, and at Yale Theological Seminary, 1860; succeeded Rev. Dr. W. M. Taylor as editor-in-chief of *The Christian at Work*, New-York City, 1880. He edited *Tacitus, with Notes*, New Haven, Conn., 1864.

HALSEY, Leroy Jones, D.D. (Hanover College, Ind., 1853), **LL.D.** (South-western University, Clarksville, Tenn., 1880), Presbyterian; b. in Goochland County, Va., Jan. 28, 1812; graduated at Nashville (Tenn.) University in 1834, and at Princeton (N.J.) Theological Seminary in 1840; from 1844 to 1849 was pastor in Jackson, Miss.; until 1859, in Louisville, Ky.; until 1882 professor of pastoral theology, church government, and homiletics, in the Presbyterian Theological Seminary of the North-west, Chicago, Ill. (being one of the four original professors); and since 1882 has been professor emeritus. From 1876 to 1884 he was associate editor of *The Interior*, a religious weekly, published at Chicago; and since, contributing editor. He is the author of *Literary Attractions of the Bible*, New York, 1858 (3 editions); *Life Pictures from the Bible*, Philadelphia, 1859; *Beauty of Immanuel*, 1860; *Life and Works of Philip Lindsley, D.D.*, 1861; *Life and Sermons of Lewis Warner Green, D.D.*, New York, 1867; *Living Christianity*, Philadelphia, 1882; *Scotland's Place in Civilization*, 1885.

HAMBURGER, Jakob, Ph.D. (Leipzig, 1852), Hebrew rabbi; b. at Loslau, Upper Silesia, Nov. 10, 1826; studied philosophy and philology, especially orientalia, at Breslau and Berlin, 1849–52; pursued his Talmud studies at Pressburg, Hungary, and at Nikolsburg, Moravia; since 1859 he has been rabbi of Mecklenburg-Strelitz. He has written *Geist und Ursprung der aramäischen Uebersetzung des Pentateuchs, bekannt unter dem Namen, Targum Onkelos*, Leipzig, 1852 (his doctor's dissertation); *Geist der Hagada*, 1857; *Real-Encyclopädie für Bibel und Talmud*, Strelitz, 1865–83, 2 parts (i. biblical articles, A–Z, 1865–70; ii. articles on the Talmud and Midrash, 1870–83), 2d ed. enlarged and improved, Leipzig, 1884, sqq., supplement preparing. Cf. *Encyclopædia*, p. 635.

HAMILTON, Edward John, D.D. (Wabash College, Crawfordsville, Ind., 1877), **S.T.D.** (Monmouth College, Monmouth, Ill., 1877), Presbyterian; b. in Belfast, Ireland, Nov. 29, 1834; graduated at Hanover (Ind.) College, 1853, and at Princeton (N.J.) Theological Seminary, 1858; was pastor at Oyster Bay, Long Island, N.Y., 1858–61; in charge of congregation at Dromore West, in Ireland, winter of 1862–63; chaplain in the Army of the Potomac, 1863–65; pastor at Hamilton, O., 1866–68; professor of mental philosophy, Hanover College, 1868–79; provisional professor of logic, ethics, and political science, College of New Jersey, Princeton, N.J., 1882; since 1883 professor of intellectual science, Hamilton College, Clinton, N.Y. He is the author of *A New Analysis in Fundamental Morals*, New York, 1872; *The Human Mind*, 1883; *Mental Science*, 1886.

HAMLIN, Cyrus, D.D. (Bowdoin College, Brunswick, Me., 1854; Harvard College, Cambridge, Mass., 1861), **LL.D.** (University of the City of New York, 1870; Bowdoin College, 1880), Congregationalist; b. at Waterford, Me., Jan. 5, 1811; graduated at Bowdoin College, Brunswick, Me., 1834, and at the Congregational Theological Seminary, Bangor, Me., 1837; was commissioned by A. B. C. F. M. missionary to Turkey, Feb. 3, 1837; sailed Dec. 3, 1838 (being delayed by Board's financial straits); opened the Bebek Seminary on the Bosphorus, 1840; became president of Robert College, 1860; foiled Russian, French, and Jesuit plots, and obtained imperial edict committing the college to the United States, — an unexampled favor; resigned presidency in 1876; became professor of dogmatic theology in Bangor Theological Seminary, Me., 1877; president of Middlebury College, 1880; resigned 1885, and retired to Lexington, Mass. His writings are principally in the Armenian language, and include a book on Popery and Protestantism (pp. 350), to counteract Jesuit libels; an *exposé* of the heresies of Archbishop Matteos in his book "True Man and True Christian," a tract on the mediatorship of Christ; and translations of Upham's *Philosophy*, and Wayland's *Moral Science*, etc. He has published in English, *Among the Turks*, New York, 1877, and sermons, lectures, reviews, etc.

HAMMOND, Charles Edward, Church of England; b. at Bath, Somersetshire, Eng., Jan. 24, 1837; was a student in Exeter College, Oxford, took double first-class in moderations (the first public examination at Oxford), 1856; graduated B.A. (third-class classics, first-class mathematics) 1858, M.A. 1861; was fellow of Exeter College 1859–73, tutor 1861–73, lecturer 1873–82, bursar 1869–82; in the university was mathematical moderator 1862–63, junior proctor 1867–68, master of the schools 1875; classical moderator in the pass schools, 1880–81; was ordained deacon 1861, priest 1862; chaplain of the Oxford Female Penitentiary, 1870–82; since 1882 has been rector of Wootton, Northamptonshire, Eng. He is the author of *Outlines of Textual Criticism applied to the New Testament*, Oxford, 1872, 4th ed. 1884; *Liturgies, Eastern and Western*, 1878; (Appendix), *The Ancient Liturgy of Antioch, and other Liturgical Fragments*, 1879.

HAMMOND, Edward Payson, Presbyterian; b. at Ellington, Conn., Sept. 1, 1831; graduated at Williams College, Williamstown, Mass., 1858; studied in Union Theological Seminary, New-York City, 1858–59, and in the Free Church College, Edinburgh, 1860–61; was ordained in 1863, and ever since has been an evangelist and revivalist, in which capacity he has travelled extensively. Among his publications are *Jesus the Way*, London, 1868; *Conversion of Children*, New York, 1878, new ed. 1882; *Gathered Lambs*, 1882; and a volume of verse, *Sketches of Palestine*, Boston, 1868, re-issue 1874. *

HANNE, Johann Wilhelm, D.D., German Protestant theologian; b. at Harber, Lüneburg, Dec. 29, 1813; was pastor at Braunschweig (Brunswick) and Hannover; became ordinary professor of theology, and pastor of St. James at Greifswald, 1861. He is the author of *Rationalismus und speculative Theologie in Braunschweig*, Braunschweig, 1838; *Festreden an Gebildete über das Wesen des christlichen Glaubens, inbesondere über das Verhältniss der geschichtlichen Person Christi zur Idee des Christenthums*, 1839; *Friedrich Schleiermacher als religiöser Genius Deutschlands*, 1840; *Sokrates als Genius der Humanität* (companion volume to the preceding), 1841; *Der moderne Nihilismus und die Strauss'sche Glaubenslehre im Verhältniss zur Idee der christlichen Religion*, Bielefeld,

1842 (this book won him great repute); *Drei Predigten über christliches Glauben und Lieben*, Braunschweig, 1844; *Der ideale Protestantismus*, Bielefeld, 1845; *Anti-orthodox, oder gegen Buchstabendienst und Pfaffenthum und für den freien Geist der Humanität und des Christenthums*, Braunschweig, 1846; *Der freie Glaube im Kampf mit den theologischen Halbheiten unsrer Tage*, 1846; *Religiöse Mahnungen zur Sühne*, 1848; *Vorhöfe zum Glauben oder das Wunder des Christenthums im Einklange mit Vernunft und Natur*, Jena, 1850–51, 3 parts; *Zeitspielgelungen*, Hannover, 1852, 2d ed. 1854; *Bekenntnisse, oder, Drei Bücher vom Glauben. Zum Viaticum auf der Wanderung durch die Wüste dieser Zeit zum reichen Heimathlande des Glaubens. Für werdende Christen*, 1861, 2d ed. 1865; *Die Idee der absoluten Persönlichkeit, oder, Gott und sein Verhältniss zur Welt, insonderheit zur menschlichen Persönlichkeit*, 1861–62, 2 vols., 2d ed. 1865; *Christliche Weihestunden*, Greifswald, 1863; *Die Zeit der deutschen Freiheitskriege in ihrer Bedeutung für die Zukunft des Reiches Gottes und seiner Gerechtigkeit*, 1863; *Anti Hengstenberg*, Elberfeld, 1867; *Der Geist des Christenthums*, 1867; *Die christliche Kirche nach ihrer Stellung und Aufgabe im Reiche der Sittlichkeit*, Berlin, 1868; *Die Kirche im neuen Reiche*, 1871; *Der ideale und der geschichtliche Christus*, Berlin, 1st and 2d ed. 1871.

HAPPER, Andrew Patton, M.D. (University of Pennsylvania, Philadelphia, 1844), **D.D.** (Jefferson College, Canonsburg, Penn., 1864), Presbyterian; b. near Monongahela City, Penn., Oct. 20, 1818; graduated at Jefferson College, Canonsburg, Penn., 1835; taught school, 1835–40; studied in Western Theological Seminary, Alleghany, Penn., 1840–43, and graduated; since 1844 has been a foreign missionary in China. He visited America 1867–68, 1885–86.

HARE, George Emlen, D.D. (Columbia College, New-York City, 1843), **LL.D.** (University of Pennsylvania, Philadelphia, 1873), Episcopalian; b. in Philadelphia, Sept. 4, 1808; graduated at Union College, Schenectady, N.Y., 1826; became rector of St. John's Church, Carlisle, Penn., in 1830; of Trinity Church, Princeton, N.J., in 1834; and of St. Matthew's Church, Philadelphia, Penn., in 1845; professor of biblical learning in the divinity school of the Protestant-Episcopal Church in Philadelphia, Penn., 1852. He is an Old-Testament Reviser, and the author of *Christ to return*, Philadelphia, 1840.

HARE, Right Rev. William Hobart, D.D. (Kenyon College, Gambier, O., 1872), **S.T.D.** (Trinity College, Hartford, Conn., and Columbia College, New-York City, both 1872), Episcopalian, missionary bishop of South Dakota; b. at Princeton, N.J., May 17, 1838; studied at the University of Pennsylvania, Philadelphia, but serious eye-trouble compelled him to withdraw at the close of junior year; was assistant minister at St. Luke's, 1859–62; rector of St. Paul's, Chestnut Hill, 1862–63; in charge of St. Luke's, 1863–64; in charge of, and later rector of, the Church of the Ascension, 1864–70 (all in Philadelphia); secretary and general agent of the Foreign Committee of the Board of Missions, New York, December, 1870–March, 1873; nominated by the House of Bishops missionary bishop of Cape Palmas and parts adjacent in West Africa, 1871, but the nomination was withdrawn in consequence of remonstrance from the House of Deputies, on the ground of his great usefulness as secretary; accepted missionary bishopric of Niobrara, 1872, consecrated Jan. 9, 1873; present diocese defined, 1883. Bishop Hare is classed with the Broad-Church school, but his conservative tendencies are marked.

HARGROVE, Robert Kennon, D.D. (Emory College, Oxford, Ga., 1872), bishop of the Methodist-Episcopal Church South; b. in Pickens County, Ala., Sept. 17, 1829; graduated at the State University of Alabama, at Tuscaloosa, 1852; was itinerant preacher in the Alabama Conference, 1857–67; in the Kentucky Conference, 1868; in the Tennessee Conference, 1868–82; professor of mathematics in the University of Alabama, 1853–57; chaplain in the Confederate army; president of the Centenary Institute, Summerville, Ala., 1865–67; of the Tennessee Female College at Franklin, 1868–73; member of Cape May Commission for adjudicating differences between Methodism North and South, 1876; elected bishop, 1882. He has written articles in periodicals.

HARKAVY, A. (Hebrew name *Abraham Elias*, in ordinary life *Albert*), Hebrew rabbi; b. in St. Petersburg, Russia, Oct. 29, 1839; educated in the Wilna Rabbinical School (1858–63), and at the University of St. Petersburg (1863–67); pursued studies at Berlin (under Rödiger and Dümichen) and at Paris (under Oppert) 1868–70; graduated a rabbi at Wilna, 1863; *magister* (1868) and doctor (1872) of the history of the Orient; was unanimously chosen a *docent* in the Oriental faculty at St. Petersburg in 1870, after delivering test lectures upon the history of the Semitic nations, but prevented by the efforts of a personal enemy from receiving the position; is a member of the Imperial Russian State Council, knight of several orders, librarian of the Imperial Public Library (St. Petersburg), honorary member of the Hellenic Philological Syllogos of Constantinople, member of the Society of the Friends of Natural Science and Anthropology of Moscow, corresponding member of the Geographical Society of Tiflis, and member of the Imperial Russian Archæological Society, etc. He is a moderate conservative in religious matters. His literary activity in Hebrew and Russian dates from 1860. Besides different articles in learned periodicals, he has written in Russian "The Jews and the Slavonic Languages," St. Petersburg, 1867; "Information concerning the Mussulman Writers upon Slavs and Russians," 1870, appendix to same 1871; "The Historical Importance of the Moabite Inscription of King Mesa," 1871; "The Original Home of the Semites, Hamites, and Japhetites," 1872; "Information concerning the Arabs under Thule," 1873; "Information concerning Jewish Writers upon the Chararen and their Kingdom," 1874; "Catalogue of the Samaritan MSS. in the Imperial Public Library," 1874–75; "The Origin of some Geographical Names on the Taurian Peninsula," 1876; "The Information of Abraham of Kertsh on the Embassy of St. Wladimir to the Chararen," 1876; "Biography of Peter Lerch," 1885; "Biography of Caetan Rossowicz, Professor in St. Petersburg University," 1885. In French, *Les mots égyptiens de la Bible*, 1870; *Sur un passage des "Prairies d'or" de Macoudi concernant l'histoire ancienne des Slaves*, 1876. In German, *Catalog der hebräischen Bibel-*

handschriften der kaiserlichen öffentlichen Bibliothek (with H. L. Strack), 1875; *Altjüdische Denkmäler in der Krimm*, 1876; *Meassef Niddachim, Collection zur hebräischen Literatur*, i. 1878–79, ii. 1880; *Studien und Mittheilungen aus der kaiserlichen öffentlichen Bibliothek zu St. Petersburg*, i. 1879, iii. 1880, iv. 1885; *Mittheilungen aus Handschriften der kaiserlichen öffentlichen Bibliothek, Fragment von der arabischen u. hebräischen Vorrede Saadiah's zum* ספר אגרון (in Stade's *Zt. f. Wissensch. d. A. T.*, 1881-82); *Aus dem archäologischen Congress*, 1882; *Neugefundene hebräische Bibelhandschriften*, 1884; *Chadaschim gam Feschanim* (in *Beiträge aus Handschriften zur hebräischen Literatur*, 1885).

HARMAN, Henry Martyn, D.D. (Dickinson College, Carlisle, Penn., 1866), Methodist; b. in Anne Arundel County, Md., March 22, 1822; graduated at Dickinson College, Carlisle, Penn., 1848; was professor in Baltimore (Md.) Female College, 1853–55; professor of languages in West Virginia University, Morgantown, W. Va., 1868–69; since 1870 in Dickinson College (professor of ancient languages and literature, 1870–79; since 1879, of Greek and Hebrew). He is the author of *A Journey to Egypt and the Holy Land*, Philadelphia, 1872; *Introduction to the Study of the Holy Scriptures*, New York, 1878, 4th ed., greatly enlarged, 1884 (this work is part of the course of study for the itinerant ministers of the Methodist-Episcopal Church during the first four years of their ministry).

HARMON, George Milford, Universalist; b. at Thorndike, Waldo County, Me., Nov. 28, 1842; graduated at Tufts College, College Hill, Mass., 1867, and at its divinity school, 1875; was pastor of several churches prior to and subsequent to his theological course; from 1882 to 1883 was professor in Lombard University, Galesburg, Ill.; and since 1883, has been professor of theology in Tufts Divinity School, College Hill, Mass.

HARNACK, (Karl Gustav) Adolf, Ph.D. (Leipzig, February, 1873), **Lic. Theol.** (do., February, 1874), **D.D.** (*hon.*, Marburg, 1879), German Protestant; b. at Dorpat, Livland, May 7, 1851; studied at Dorpat, 1869–72; became *privat-docent* at Leipzig, July, 1874; professor extraordinary, May, 1876; ordinary professor of church history at Giessen, April, 1879; at Marburg, 1886. His theological standpoint is historico-critical. A large part of his literary work is scattered in journals. The following have appeared separately: *Zur Quellenkritik der Geschichte des Gnostizismus*, Leipzig, 1873; *De Apellis gnosi monarchica*, 1874; *Patrum Apostolicorum opera* (ed. with von Gebhardt and Zahn), 1875–77, 3 vols. (vol. 1, 2d ed. 1876–78, 2 parts); *Patrum Apost. opp. ed. minor*, 1877; *Die Zeit des Ignatius und die Chronologie der antiochenischen Bischöfe bis Tyrannus nach Julius Africanus und den späteren Historikern, Nebst ein. Untersuchung über die Verbreitung der Passio S. Polycarp im Abendlande*, 1878; *Das Mönchthum, seine Ideale und seine Geschichte*, Giessen, 1881, 3d ed. 1886; *Texte und Untersuchungen zur Geschichte der altchristlichen Literatur*, 1882, *sqq.* (ed. with von Gebhardt; to the series Harnack has contributed *Die Ueberlieferung der griechischen Apologeten des zweiten Jahrhunderts in der alten Kirche und im Mittelalter*, Bd I., Hft. 1. u. 2., 1882; *Die Altercatio Simonis Judæi et Theophili Christiani nebst Untersuchungen über die antijüdische Polemik in der alten Kirche;* and *Die Acta Archelai und das Diatessaron Tatians*, Bd. I., Hft. 3., 1883; *Der angebliche Evangeliencommentar des Theophilus von Antiochien*, Bd. I., Hft. 4., 1883; *Lehre der zwölf Apostel. Text mit Uebersetzung, Anmerkungen, Einleitung und Prolegomena*, Bd. II., Hft. 1. u. 2., 1884); *Martin Luther in seiner Bedeutung für die Geschichte der Wissenschaft und der Bildung*, Giessen, 1883, 2d ed. 1886; *Lehrbuch der Dogmengeschichte*, Freiburg-im-Br., 1886–88, 2 vols. He edited, with notes and excursus, the German translation of Hatch's *Organization of the Early Christian Churches* (*Die Gesellschaftsverfassung der christlichen Kirchen im Alterthum*), Giessen, 1883; *Tatian's Rede an die Griechen übersetzt und eingeleitet*, 1884. Since 1881 he has edited with Schürer the *Theologische Literaturzeitung*, Leipzig, 1876, sqq.

HARNACK, Theodosius, D.D., Lutheran theologian, father of the preceding; b. at St. Petersburg, Russia, Jan. 3, 1817; studied theology at Dorpat; became *privat-docent* of practical theology there, 1843; professor extraordinary, 1845; ordinary professor, 1848; called to Erlangen, 1853; but returned to Dorpat 1866, and retired 1875. He is the author of *Jesus der Christ*, Elberfeld, 1842; *Die Idee der Predigt entwickelt aus dem Wesen des protestantischen Kultus*, 1844; *Die Grundbekenntnisse der evangelisch-lutherischen Kirche*, Dorpat, 1845; *De theologia practica recte definienda et adornanda*, 1847; *Zwölf Predigten*, 1848; *Der christliche Gemeinde-Gottesdienst im apostolischen und altkatholischen Zeitalter*, Erlangen, 1854; *Der kleine Katechismus Martin Luthers in seiner Urgestalt, Kritisch untersucht und herausgegeben*, Stuttgart, 1856; *Die lutherische Kirche Livlands und die Herrnhutische Brüdergemeinde*, Erlangen, 1860; *Die Kirche, ihr Amt, ihr Regiment*, Nürnberg, 1862; *Luthers Theologie mit besonderer Beziehung auf seine Versöhnungs- u. Erlösungslehre. 1. Abth. Luthers theologische Grundanschauungen*, Erlangen, 1862; edited the 8th and 9th editions of K. Graul's *Die Unterscheidungslehren der verschiedenen christlichen Bekenntnisse im Lichte des göttlichen Worts*, Leipzig, 1868 and 1872; with A. v. Harless wrote, *Die kirchlich-religiöse Bedeutung der reinen Lehre von den Gnadenmitteln*, Erlangen, 1869; *Die freie lutherische Volkskirche*, 1870; *Liturgische Formulare*, Dorpat, 1872–74; *Praktische Theologie*, Erlangen, 1877–78, 2 vols.; *Katechetik*, 1882; *Ueber den Kanon und die Inspiration der heiligen Schrift, Ein Wort zum Frieden*, Dorpat, 1885 (pp. 36). He wrote the sections upon Liturgics and Pastoral Theology in Zöckler's *Handbuch der theologischen Wissenschaften*, Nördlingen, 1883–84, 3 vols., 2d ed. 1884–85, 4 vols.

HARPER, William Rainey, Ph.D. (Yale College, New Haven, Conn., 1875), Baptist layman; b. at New Concord, O., July 26, 1856; graduated at Muskingum College, New Concord, O., 1870; from 1876 to 1879 was principal of the preparatory department of Denison University, Granville, O.; from 1879 to 1886 was professor of Hebrew and the cognate languages, in the Chicago (Morgan Park, Ill.) Baptist Union Theological Seminary; and since 1886 has been professor of Semitic languages in Yale College. He is the author of *Elements of Hebrew by an Inductive Method*, Chicago, 1882, 6th ed. 1885; *Hebrew Vocabularies*, 1883, 3d ed. 1884; *Introductory Hebrew Method*, 1883, 2d ed. 1885; *Intermediate Hebrew Method*, 1883, 2d ed. 1885. He edited *The Hebrew Student* (Chicago, 1882–84), and edits *Hebraica* (Chicago, 1884, sqq.), *Old-Testament Student* (1882, sqq.).

HARRIS, George, D.D. (Amherst College, Amherst, Mass., 1883), Congregationalist; b. at East Machias, Me., April 1, 1844; graduated from Amherst College, Mass., 1866, and from Andover (Mass.) Theological Seminary, 1869; was pastor at Auburn, Me., 1869–72; at Providence, R.I., 1872–83; and since 1883 has been Abbot professor of Christian theology in the Andover Theological Seminary.

HARRIS, Samuel, D.D. (Williams College, Williamstown, Mass., 1855), **LL.D.** (Bowdoin College, Brunswick, Me., 1871), Congregationalist; b. at East Machias, Me., June 14, 1814; graduated at Bowdoin College, Brunswick, Me., 1833, and at Andover (Mass.) Theological Seminary, 1838; was principal of Limerick Academy, Me., 1833–34, and of Washington Academy, East Machias, Me., 1834–35, 1838–41; pastor at Conway, Mass., 1841–51, and at Pittsfield, Mass., 1851–55; professor of systematic theology in the Bangor Theological Seminary, 1855–67 (from 1855 to 1863, jointly with Rev. Prof. George Shepard, D.D., acting pastor of the Center Church in Bangor); president of Bowdoin College, Brunswick, Me., and professor of mental and moral philosophy, 1867–71; since 1871 has been Dwight professor of systematic theology in Yale Theological Seminary, New Haven, Conn. Besides many sermons, pamphlets, and articles in reviews, he has published *Zaccheus, the Scriptural Plan of Beneficence*, Boston, 1844; *Christ's Prayer for the Death of his Redeemed*, 1863; *The Kingdom of Christ on Earth*, Andover, 1874; *The Philosophical Basis of Theism*, New York, 1883.

HARRIS, Right Rev. Samuel Smith, D.D. (William and Mary College, Williamsburg, Va., 1875), **LL.D.** (University of Alabama, at Tuscaloosa, 1879), Episcopalian, bishop of Michigan; b. in Autauga County, Ala., Sept. 14, 1841; graduated at the University of Alabama, at Tuscaloosa, 1859; studied law at the University Law School, Montgomery, Ala., and admitted to the bar in 1860, by special enabling act of the legislature, being a minor; after practising law for some years, was admitted to holy orders in the Protestant-Episcopal Church, at Montgomery, Ala., 1869; became rector of Trinity Church, Columbus, Ga., 1869; of Trinity Church, New Orleans, La., 1871; of St. James's Church, Chicago, Ill., 1875; consecrated bishop, 1879. He is "in sympathy with the liberal school of thought in the Protestant-Episcopal Church." In 1878, with Rev. Dr. John Fulton, he founded *The Living Church* newspaper, and was editor for six months. Besides many occasional sermons, articles in periodicals, etc., he has published *The Relation of Christianity to Civil Society* (Bohlen Lectures for 1882), New York, 1883.

HARRISON, Frederic, Positivist; b. in London, Eng., Oct. 18, 1831; was scholar of Wadham College, Oxford; graduated B.A. (first-class classics) 1853; tutor and fellow of his college; called to the bar, 1858. He was a member of the Royal Commission upon trades-unions, 1867–69; secretary to the Royal Commission for the digest of the law, 1869–70; appointed by the council of legal education, professor of jurisprudence and international law. He was one of the founders of the Positivist School, in 1870; and in 1871, of Newton Hall, London, where the religious services of the Positivists are held. He has in articles, lectures, and addresses advocated his faith. He has been a frequent contributor to *The Westminster Review*, the *Contemporary*, the *Nineteenth Century*, and *Fortnightly* reviews; and in book form have been issued of his writings, *Order and Progress* (Pt. 1, *On Government*; Pt. 2, *Studies of Political Crises*), London, 1875; 2d vol. of English trans. of A. Comte's *Positive Philosophy*, 1875; *Present and Future: a Positivist Address*, 1880; *The Choice of Books, and other Literary Pieces*, 1886. A reprint, unauthorized by him, of his and Herbert Spencer's articles upon *The Nature and Reality of Religion*, appeared in New York, 1885. *

HARTRANFT, Chester David, D.D. (Rutgers College, New Brunswick, N.J., 1876), Congregationalist; b. at Frederick, Montgomery County, Penn., Oct. 15, 1839; graduated at the University of Pennsylvania, Philadelphia, 1861, and at the New Brunswick (N.J.) Theological Seminary, 1864; was pastor of Reformed (Dutch) churches at South Bushwick, Brooklyn, N.Y., 1864–66, and New Brunswick, N.J., 1866–78; and since 1878 has been professor of biblical and ecclesiastical history in the Hartford, Conn. (Congregational) Theological Seminary. He received the degree of Doctor of Music from Rutgers College, New Brunswick, N.J., in 1861.

HARVEY, Hezekiah, D.D. (Colby University, Waterville, Me., 1861), Baptist; b. at Hulver, Suffolk County, Eng., Nov. 27, 1821; came to America, 1830; graduated at Madison University, 1845, and at Hamilton Theological Seminary (both at Hamilton, N.Y.), 1847; was successively tutor of languages in Madison University until 1849; pastor at Homer, N.Y., until 1857, and Hamilton, N.Y., until 1858; professor of ecclesiastical history in Hamilton Theological Seminary until 1861, professor of biblical criticism and interpretation and pastoral theology until 1864; pastor at Dayton, O., until 1869; and since has been professor of New-Testament exegesis and pastoral theology in Hamilton Theological Seminary. He is the author of *Memoir of Rev. Alfred Bennett*, New York, 1852; *The Church: its Polity and Ordinances*, Philadelphia, 1879; *The Pastor: his Qualifications and Duties*, 1879.

HARWOOD, Edwin, D.D. (Trinity College, Hartford, Conn., 1862), Episcopalian; b. in Philadelphia, Aug. 21, 1822; graduated at the University of Pennsylvania, Philadelphia, 1840, and at the General (Episcopal) Theological Seminary, New-York City, 1844; became rector of Christ Church, Oyster Bay, Long Island, N.Y., 1844; of St. Paul's, East Chester, N.Y., 1846; of St. James's, Hamilton Square, New York, 1847; and of the Incarnation, New York, 1850; professor in the Berkeley Divinity School, Middletown, Conn., 1854; and since 1859 rector of Trinity Church, New Haven, Conn. He is a "liberal of the school of Coleridge, perhaps, more than any other." He translated Bähr's commentary on *First Kings*, and Van Oosterzee's on *Second Timothy*, in the American Lange series (both New York, 1872); and is the author of several essays (*Marcion; Was St. Peter ever in Rome? Gnosticism*).

HASE, Karl August, D.D., Lutheran; b. at

Steinbach, Saxony, Aug. 25, 1800; studied first at Leipzig (from which he was expelled for membership in a secret political society of students), and then at Erlangen. In 1823 he became *privat-docent* of theology at Tübingen, but had scarcely begun his instruction before his membership in the Erlangen political society caused his imprisonment for ten months in the fortress of Hohenasperg. In 1829 he became *privat-docent* at Leipzig, and in 1830 he went to Jena as professor of theology. He is now professor emeritus. In 1885 he was raised to the hereditary nobility. His publications embrace *Evangelisch-protestantische Dogmatik*, Leipzig, 1826, 6th ed. 1870; *Gnosis, oder protestantisch-evangelische Glaubenslehre, für die Gebildeten in der Gemeinde, wissenschaftlich dargestellt*, 1827–29, 3 vols., 2d ed. 1869–70; *Libri symbolici ecclesiæ evangelicæ*, 1827, 3d ed. 1845; *Hutterus redivivus, oder Dogmatik d. evangel.-luth. Kirche, Ein dogmatisches Repertorium für Studirende*, 1829, 12th ed. 1883; *Das Leben Jesu*, 1829, 5th ed. 1865 (English trans., by J. F. Clarke, Boston, 1881); *Kirchengeschichte, Lehrbuch zunächst für akademische Vorlesungen*, 1834, 11th ed. 1886 (English trans. from the 7th ed., by Wing and Blumenthal, *A History of the Christian Church*, New York, 1856; French trans. from the 8th ed., by Flobert, Tonneins, 1860–61, 2 vols.); *Theologische Streitschriften*, Leipzig, 1834–37, 3 parts; *Die beiden Erzbischöfe*, 1839; *Neue Propheten* (Maid of Orleans, Savonarola, the Kingdom of the Anabaptists), 1851, 3 vols., 2d ed. 1860–61; *Die Tübinger Schule*, 1855; *Franz von Assisi*, 1856; *Das geistliche Schauspiel*, 1858 (English trans., *Miracle Plays and Sacred Dramas*, London, 1880); *Handbuch der protestantischen Polemik gegen d. röm. kath. Kirche*, 1862, 4th ed. 1878; *Caterina von Siena*, 1864; *Sebastian Franck von Wörd*, 1869; *Ideale und Irrthümer, Jugenderinnerungen*, 1872, 3d ed. 1875 (a sort of autobiography); *Die Bedeutung des Geschichtlichen in der Religion*, 1874; *Geschichte Jesu*, 1875 (semi-rationalistic); *Des Kulturkampfs Ende*, 1879; *Rosenvorlesungen kirchengeschichtlichen Inhalts* (upon Bar Kokhba, Gregory VII., Pius II., Krell, and others), 1880; *Kirchengeschichte auf der Grundlage akademischer Vorlesungen*, 1885 sq., 3 vols. *

HASSELQUIST, Tuvey Nelson, D.D. (Muhlenberg College, Allentown, Penn., 1871), Lutheran; b. at Ousby, Skåne, Sweden, March 2, 1816; ordained at Lund, 1839; came to America 1852, and was one of the founders of the Swedish Lutheran Church in the United States. He was pastor at Galesburg, Ill., 1852–63; president of Augustana College and Theological Seminary when it was located at Paxton, Ill. (1863–75), and since its removal to Rock Island, Ill. (1875–). He has edited the most important religious periodicals published in Swedish in the United States in the interest of the Lutheran Church, for the last thirty years, and is still the editor of *Augustana och Missionären*, the leading religious paper circulated in the Swedish Lutheran Church. He also fills the chair of homiletics and pastoral theology in the institution of which he is president. He has in press a *Commentary on Ephesians*.

HASTINGS, Thomas Samuel, D.D. (University of the City of N.Y., 1865), Presbyterian; b. at Utica, N.Y., Aug. 28, 1827; graduated at Hamilton College, Clinton, N.Y., 1848, and at Union Theological Seminary, New-York City, 1851; was pastor at Mendham, N.J., 1852–56, and of the West Presbyterian Church, New-York City, 1856–81; since 1881, he has been professor of sacred rhetoric in Union Theological Seminary, New York.

HATCH, Edwin, D.D. (University of Edinburgh, 1883), Church of England; b. at Derby, Eng., Sept. 4, 1835; educated at Pembroke College, Oxford; graduated B.A. (second-class classics) 1857, M.A. 1867; won theological prize essay, 1858; was ordained deacon 1858, priest 1859; between 1859 and 1866 was professor of classics in Trinity College, Toronto, Can.; rector of the High School, Quebec; fellow of McGill University, Montreal; became vice-principal of St. Mary Hall, Oxford, Eng., 1867; in addition, since 1883 has been rector of Purleigh, and since 1884 secretary to the boards of faculties, and reader in ecclesiastical history, Oxford. He was master of the schools, 1868, 1869, 1873, 1877; Bampton lecturer, 1880; Grinfield lecturer in the Septuagint, 1882–84. He is the author of *The Student's Handbook to the University and Colleges of Oxford*, London, 1873, 7th ed. 1883; *The Organization of the Early Christian Church* (Bampton Lectures), 1881, 2d ed. 1882 (German trans., *Die Gesellschaftsverfassung der christlichen Kirchen im Alterthum, Vom Verfasser autoris. Uebersetzg. d. 2. durchgesch. Aufl. besorgt u. m. Excursen versehen von D. Adf. Harnack*, Giessen, 1883); *Diversity in Unity, the Law of Spiritual Life* (sermon), 1881; *Progress in Theology* (address to the Edinburgh University Theological Society on Friday, Nov. 14, 1884), Edinburgh, 1885. *

HAUCK, Albert, D.D., Lutheran; b. at Wassertrüdingen, Dec. 9, 1845; studied at Erlangen and Berlin; became pastor in Frankenheim, 1875; professor extraordinary of theology at Erlangen, 1878; ordinary professor, 1882. He has been since 1880 editor of the new edition of Herzog's *Real-Encyklopädie*, which was begun by Professors Herzog and Plitt, 1877. Professor Plitt died in 1880, and Professor Hauck succeeded him as joint editor. Professor Herzog died in 1882, and Professor Hauck has since carried on the work alone. He is the author of *Tertullians Leben und Schriften*, Erlangen, 1877; *Die Bischofswahlen unter den Merovingern*, 1883 (pp. 53).

HAUPT, Erich, D.D. (*hon.*, Greifswald, 1878), German Protestant; b. at Stralsund, July 8, 1841; studied at Berlin, 1858–61; became gymnasial teacher at Colberg 1864, and at Treptow 1866; ordinary professor of theology at Kiel 1878, and at Greifswald 1883. He is a *Consistorialrath*. He is the author of *Der erste Brief des Johannes*, Colberg, 1869; *Die alttestamentlichen Citate in den vier Evangelien*, 1871; *Johannes der Täufer*, Gütersloh, 1874; *Der Sonntag und die Bibel*, Hamburg, 1877; *Die Kirche und die theologische Lehrfreiheit*, Kiel, 1881; *Pilgerschaft und Vaterhaus, Sechs Predigten*, 1881.

HAUPT, Herman, Ph.D. (Würzburg, 1875); b. in Markt-Bibart, Bavaria, June 29, 1854; studied philology and history at Würzburg, 1871–75; became gymnasial teacher in Würzburg, 1874; librarian of the university there, 1876; *Vorstand* (director) of the university library at Giessen, 1885. He is a correspondent of the *Revue historique*, and a contributor to the *Theo-*

logische Literaturzeitung. He is the author of *Die religiösen Sekten in Franken vor der Reformation*, Würzburg, 1882; *Die deutsche Bibelübersetzung der mittelalterlichen Waldenser in dem Codex Teplensis und den ersten gedruckten deutschen Bibeln nachgewiesen*, 1885; *Zur Geschichte des Joachimismus*, Gotha, 1885; *Beiträge zur Geschichte des Beghardenthums und der Sekte vom freien Geiste*, 1885 (both separately printed from the *Zeitschrift für Kirchengeschichte*, Band vii.); *Der waldenische Ursprung der Codex Teplensis und der vorlutherischen deutschen Bibeldrucke gegen die Angriffe des Dr. Franz Jostes vertheidigt*, Würzburg, 1886; and of various articles in the *Zeitschrift für Kirchengeschichte*, Bd. v.–vii. He has in preparation a collection of printed and unprinted sources of the history of the Waldenses in Germany.

HAURÉAU, Jean Barthélemy, Roman Catholic; b. in Paris, Nov. 9, 1812; was first a journalist, sat in the constitutional assembly of 1848; was keeper of the MSS. in the National Library, but resigned when the Empire was re-established; became librarian for the lawyers' corporation of Paris. He is a member of the Academy of Inscriptions and Belles-lettres, and has published many learned works, among which may be mentioned the 14th, 15th, and 16th vols. of *Gallia Christiana; Histoire de la philosophie scolastique*, Paris, 1850, 2 vols., 2d ed. 1881; *Hugo de S. Victor*, 1850; *Bernard Délicieux et l'Inquisition Albigeois*, 1877. *

HAUSRATH, Adolph, Lic. Theol. (Heidelberg, 1861), **D.D.** (*hon.*, Vienna, 1871), Reformed; b. at Carlsruhe, Jan. 13, 1837; studied at Jena, Göttingen, Berlin, and Heidelberg; was *privat-docent* at Heidelberg in 1861; "assessor" of the upper consistory at Carlsruhe in 1864; returned to Heidelberg as professor extraordinary in 1867, and became ordinary professor in 1872. He belongs to the Tübingen school, and is the author of *Der Apostel Paulus*, Heidelberg, 1865, 2d ed. 1872; *Neutestamentliche Zeitgeschichte*, 1868–73, 4 parts, 2d ed. 1873-77, 3d ed. 1st part, *Die Zeit Jesu*, 1879; *Religiöse Reden und Betrachtungen*, Leipzig, 1873, 2d ed. 1882; *David Friedrich Strauss und die Theologie seiner Zeit*, Munich, 1876–78, 2 vols.; *Kleine Schriften religionsgeschichtlichen Inhalts*, Leipzig, 1883. Under the pseudonyme "George Taylor" he has written several historical romances: *Antinous* (from the time of the Roman emperors), Leipzig, 1880, 5th ed. 1884; *Klytia* (from the 16th century), 1883, 5th ed. 1884; *Jetta* (from the time of the great immigrations), 1884, 3d ed. same year.

HAWEIS, Hugh Reginald, Church of England; b. at Egham, Surrey, April 3, 1838; educated at Trinity College, Cambridge; graduated B.A. 1859, M.A. 1864; was curate of St. Peter's, Bethnal Green, 1860–63; of St. James the Less, Westminster, 1863–66; and since 1866 has been incumbent of St. James, Marylebone, — all London. He is an ardent friend of the humbler classes; and for their benefit he organized the penny readings, and holds Sunday-evening services in which by means of orchestral music, oratorios, pictures of sacred scenes, he seeks to impress religious truth. He is a voluminous writer, and has published in book form *Music and Morals*, London, 1871, 14th ed. 1886; *Thoughts for the Times*, London, 1872, 14th ed. 1886; *Pet* (a child's book), 1873; *Unsectarian Family Prayers*, 1874, 4th ed. 1886; *Speech in Season*, 1874, 6th ed. 1886; *Ashes to Ashes* (an argument for cremation), 1874; *New Pet*, 1875; *Current Coin*, 1876, 4th ed. 1881; *Arrows in the Air*, 1878, 4th ed. 1881; *Shakspeare and the Stage*, 1878; *American Humourists*, 1882; *Poets in the Pulpit*, 1883; *Key of Doctrine and Practice*, 1884, 15th thousand same year; *My Musical Life*, 1884; *Winged Words; or, Truths re-told*, 1885.

HAY, Charles Augustus, D.D. (Pennsylvania College, Gettysburg, Penn., 1859), Lutheran (General Synod); b. at York, Penn., Feb. 11, 1821; graduated at Pennsylvania College, Gettysburg, Penn., and studied in Germany at Berlin and Halle. After a nine-months' pastorate at Middletown, Md., he became in 1845 professor of Hebrew, German, and New-Testament exegesis, in the Gettysburg Theological Seminary, and served until 1848, and again from 1865 to the present time. From 1848 to 1849 he was pastor at Hanover, Penn.; and from 1850 to 1865, at Harrisburg. He is the author of *Life of Captain Sees*, Harrisburg, 1867; and, with Prof. Dr. H. E. Jacobs, translated Schmid's *Doctrinal Theology of the Evangelical Lutheran Church*, Philadelphia, 1875.

HAYES, Benjamin Francis, D.D. (Hillsdale College, Hillsdale, Mich., 1871), Free Baptist; b. at New Gloucester, Me., March 28, 1830; graduated at Bowdoin College, Brunswick, Me., 1855, and from the Freewill Baptist Theological Seminary, New Hampton, N.H. (now at Lewiston, Me.), 1858; was teacher of sciences and German in New Hampton Literary Institution, 1855–59; pastor of Free Baptist Church at Olneyville., R.I., 1859–63; principal of Lapham Institute, North Scituate, R I., 1863–65; since 1865 has been professor in Bates College, Lewiston, Me. (professor of modern languages, 1865–69; of intellectual and moral philosophy since 1869); and since 1873 professor of exegetical theology in the Free Baptist Theological Seminary at Lewiston, Me. He studied at Halle, Germany, with Ulrici, 1873–74. He has published since 1860 various articles in the *Freewill Baptist Quarterly*, *Centennial Record*, etc., Dover, N.H.; also *Questions and Notes, with an Analysis of Butler's Analogy*, Lewiston, Me.

HAYGOOD, Atticus Greene, D.D. (Emory College, Oxford, Ga., 1870), **LL.D.** (South-Western University, Georgetown, Tex., 1884), Methodist (Southern Church); b. at Watkinsville, Ga., Nov. 19, 1839; graduated at Emory College, Oxford, Ga., 1859; entered the ministry, was Sunday-school secretary M. E. Church South, 1870–75; president of Emory College, 1876–84; agent of the "John F. Slater Fund" since 1885. He declined election as bishop in 1882; was member of General Conference in 1870, 1874, 1878, and 1882. He is the author of *Our Children*, New York, 1876; *Our Brother in Black*, 1881; *Sermons and Speeches*, Nashville, Tenn., 1883.

HEARD, John Bickford, Church of England; b. in Dublin, Ireland, Oct. 26, 1828; entered Caius College, Cambridge, obtained a scholarship, wrote the Hulsean theological prize essay, took the Whewell prize in moral philosophy, and graduated B.A. (first class in moral science tripos) 1853, M.A. 1862. He was ordained deacon and priest, 1852; vicar of Bilton, Harrogate, 1864–68; editor

Religious Tract Society, 1866-73; curate of St. Andrew's, Westminster, London, 1878-80; and since 1880 has been vicar of St. John's, Caterham, Surrey. His standpoint is that of Tholuck and the German "Vermittelung" school. He holds firmly the *historical* faith as summed up in the Apostles' Creed, but classes inspiration, as he does that of church authority, among the *inquirenda* rather than *credenda*. His principal aim as a writer has been to trace the lines of a Christian psychology which should form a support and not a conflict with theology as at present. The reigning Cartesianism of body and soul seems to him to be a defective draught of human nature; and the error being a root one has affected the whole of theology, at least of the Western Church and since Augustine. To this extent he describes himself as *anti-Augustinus*, not as opposing Augustine's doctrines of grace, but as showing that Paulinism is a much deeper, truer, and broader draught of the purposes of God than the theology of the fifth century. He is the author of *The Pastor and Parish* (a £100 prize essay on pastoral theology), London, 1865; *The Tripartite Nature of Man*, Edinburgh, 1870, 5th ed. 1883; *Old and New Theology: a Constructive Critique*, 1885.

HECKER, Isaac Thomas, Roman Catholic; b. in New-York City, Dec. 18, 1819; brought up a Protestant; in 1843 joined the community at Brook Farm, West Roxbury, Mass., and some months later that at Fruitlands, Worcester County, Mass. For a time he lived with Thoreau in his hermitage. In 1845, on returning to New York, he became a Roman Catholic, and entered the Society of the Redemptorist Fathers in 1847, having passed a novitiate of two years at St. Trond, Belgium. Until 1851 he did mission work in England. He returned to America in 1851, and continued his labors there. In 1857 he was at Rome released from his Redemptorist vows, and allowed to organize a new society, "The Congregation of St. Paul the Apostle," of which he has ever been the chief. The Paulist Fathers, as they are called, are almost entirely Americans and converts from Protestantism, and have proved themselves most efficient. Since 1865 they have carried on *The Catholic World*, a monthly of ability and honesty. Father Hecker attended the Vatican Council as procurator of Bishop Rosecrans, Columbus, O. He is the author of *Questions of the Soul*, 1855; *Aspirations of Nature*, 1857; *Catholicity in the United States*, 1879; *Catholics and Protestants agreeing on the School Question*, 1881 (the last two are pamphlets). *

HEDGE, Frederic Henry, D.D. (Harvard College, Cambridge, Mass., 1852), Unitarian; b. at Cambridge, Mass., Dec. 12, 1805; graduated at Harvard College, Cambridge, Mass., 1825, and at its divinity school, 1828; became pastor at West Cambridge (now Arlington), 1829; at Bangor, Me., 1835; at Providence, R.I., 1850; and at Brookline, Mass., 1856; retired, 1872. He was teacher of ecclesiastical history (1857-77), and professor of German (1872-81), in Harvard University. "As a preacher he is connected with the Unitarian communion into which he was born, attached to it rather by the absence in that body of any compulsory creed, than by sympathy with its distinctive doctrine. His view of Christ is essentially that of the two natures, as defined by the Council of Chalcedon (A.D. 451)." He was for some years president of the American Unitarian Association. He is the author of *Prose Writers of Germany*, Philadelphia, 1848, 3d ed. 1871; *Christian Liturgy for the Use of the Church*, Boston, 1853; *Reason in Religion*, 1865, 2d ed. 1875 (repub., London); *The Primeval World of Hebrew Tradition*, 1870; *The Ways of the Spirit, and other Essays*, 1877; *Atheism in Philosophy, and other Essays*, 1884; *Hours with German Classics*, 1886.

HEFELE, Right Rev. Carl Joseph von, Ph.D. (*hon.*, Bonn, 1868), **D.D.** (Tübingen, 1838), Roman-Catholic bishop; b. at Unterkochen, Würtemberg, March 16, 1809; studied philosophy and theology at Tübingen from 1827 to 1832, and then for a year in theological seminary at Rottenburg; was ordained a priest, Aug. 14, 1833; was *repetent* at Tübingen in 1834; taught in the Rottweil gymnasium in 1835; in 1836 became tutor for Möhler, at Tübingen; there in 1837 professor extraordinary, and in 1840 professor ordinary, of church history and patrology, in the Roman-Catholic faculty. He was ennobled in 1853; was a member of the Würtemberg House of Representatives from 1842-45; in 1868 and 1869 was one of the council to prepare for the Vatican Council, which he attended, and in which he opposed the infallibility dogma. On Dec. 29, 1869, he was at Rottenburg enthroned bishop of Rottenburg; and on April 21, 1871, he promulgated the new dogma in his diocese, and in 1872 publicly announced his acceptance of it. He is the author of *Geschichte der Einführung des Christenthums im südwestlichen Deutschland, besonders in Würtemberg*, Tübingen, 1837; *Patrum Apostolicorum Opera*, 1839, 4th ed. 1855; *Das Sendschreiben des Apostels Barnabas*, 1840; *Der Cardinal Ximenes und die kirchlichen Zustände Spaniens am Ende des 15. u. Anfang des 16. Jahrh.*, 1844, 2d ed. 1851; *S. Bonaventuræ breviloquium et itinerarium mentis ad Deum*, 1845, 3d ed. 1861; *Chrysostomus-Postille*, 1845, 3d ed. 1857; *Beiträge zur Kirchengeschichte, Archäologie und Liturgik*, 1864-65, 2 vols.; *Causa Honorii papæ*, Naples, 1870 (German trans. by Rump, *Die Honorius-frage*, Münster, 1870 (pp. 28); *Honorius und das sechste allgemeine Concil* (also from the Latin), Tübingen, 1870. But his great work, and one of the greatest books in modern times, is his *Conciliengeschichte* (from the first council to that of Ferrara Florence; the work is to be continued by other hands), Freiburg, 1855-74, 7 vols., 2d ed. 1873 sqq., vol. 5, 1886 (Eng. trans., *History of the Councils of the Church*, Edinburgh, 1871, sqq.; vol. 3 [*To 451*], 1882.

HEINRICI, Karl Friedrich Georg, Ph.D. (Halle, 1866), **Lic. Theol.** (Berlin, 1868), **D.D.** (Marburg, 1875), Protestant; b. at Karkeln, East Prussia, March 14, 1844; studied at Halle and Berlin; became inspector of the *Domkandidatenstift* at Berlin, 1870; *privat-docent* in the university, 1871; professor extraordinary at Marburg, 1873; ordinary professor of New-Testament exegesis, 1874. In 1881 he became a member of the royal consistory at Cassel. He is the author of *Die Valentinianische Gnosis und die Heilige Schrift*, Berlin, 1871; *Erklärung der Korintherbriefe*, 1880-86, 2 vols.; edited the 6th ed. of Meyer's *Commentar zu d. Korintherbriefen*, Göttingen, 1881-83, 2 vols.

HEMAN, Carl Friedrich, Ph.D. (Tübingen, 1870), **Lic. Theol.** (Basel, 1883), Swiss Protestant theologian; b. at Grunstadt, Rheinpfalz, Aug. 30, 1839; studied at Basel, Erlangen, and Tübingen; became pastor in the Rheinpfalz, 1872; agent of the *Verein der Freunde Israels* at Basel, 1874, and *privat-docent* in the university. His theological standpoint is *positiv offenbarungsglaubig*. He is the author of *Ed. von Hartmann's Religion der Zukunft in ihrer Selbstzersetzung nachgewiesen*, Leipzig, 1875; *Die Erscheinung der Dinge in der Wahrnehmung*, 1881; *Die religiöse Weltstellung des jüdischen Volkes*, 1882 (these two were translated into Norwegian and Swedish, 1882); *Die wissenschaftlichen Versuche neuer Religionsbildungen*, Basel, 1884; *Der Ursprung der Religion*, 1886.

HEMPHILL, Charles Robert, Presbyterian, Southern Church; b. at Chester Court House, S.C., April 18, 1852; was educated at the University of South Carolina (1868), and at the University of Virginia, Charlottesville, Va. (1869–70); graduated at Columbia (S.C.) Theological Seminary, 1874; tutor in Hebrew there, 1874–78; fellow in Greek, Johns Hopkins University, Baltimore, Md., 1878; professor of ancient languages, Southwestern Presbyterian University, Clarksville, Tenn., 1879–81; since 1881, has been professor of biblical literature in the Columbia (S.C.) Theological Seminary. *

HENDRIX, Eugene Russell, D.D. (Emory College, Oxford, Ga., 1878), Methodist-Episcopal Church South; b. at Fayette, Mo., May 17, 1847; graduated at Wesleyan University, Middletown, Conn., 1867, and at Union Theological Seminary (Presbyterian), New-York City, 1869; was Methodist (Southern Church) stated supply at Leavenworth, Kan., 1869–70; pastor at Macon, Mo., 1870–72; St. Joseph, 1872–76; Glasgow, 1877; became president of Central College, Fayette, Mo., 1878; bishop, 1886. In 1876–77 he made a missionary tour of the world, with Bishop Marvin of St. Louis. In 1885 he declined the vice-chancellorship of Vanderbilt University, and also the presidency of the University of Missouri. He is the author of *Around the World*, Nashville, Tenn., 1878, 5th ed. 1882.

HENSON, Poindexter Smith, D.D. (Lewisburg University, Lewisburg, Penn., 1867), Baptist; b. in Fluvanna County, Va., Dec. 7, 1831; graduated at Richmond (Va.) College, 1849, and the University of Virginia, at Charlottesville, 1851; became principal of the Milton (N.C.) Classical Institute, 1851; professor of natural science in the Chowan Female College, Murfreesborough, N.C., 1853; pastor of Fluvanna Baptist Church, Va., 1855; Broad-street Church, Philadelphia, 1860; Memorial Church, Philadelphia, 1867 (which he organized); First Church, Chicago, 1882. Since 1870 he has been editor of *The Baptist Teacher* (American Baptist Publication Society, Philadelphia), and published numerous articles, occasional sermons, etc.

HERGENROETHER, His Eminence Joseph, Cardinal, D.D. (Munich, 1850), Roman Catholic; b. at Würzburg, Bavaria, Sept. 15, 1824; studied at Würzburg and in Rome, there ordained priest in 1848; became, in the University of Munich, successively *privat-docent* (1851), professor extraordinary (1852), and ordinary professor of ecclesiastical law and history (1855). In 1868–69 he was one of the committee to prepare for the Vatican Council. He has been a consistent defender of the infallibility dogma. Pius IX. made him one of his domestic prelates; and Leo XIII., on May 12, 1879, a cardinal deacon, with the title of S. Nicola in Carcere, and residence in Rome, where he is prefect of the apostolic archives. His publications are numerous: of especial interest are, *Der Kirchenstaat seit der französischen Revolution*, Freiburg-im-Br., 1860; *Photius, Patriarch von Constantinople*, Regensburg, 1867–69, 3 vols. (this is one of the great monographs of modern times; in vol. 3 is *Monumenta Græca ad Photium ejusque historiam spectantia*, also separately issued, 1869); *Anti-janus*, Freiburg-im-Br., 1870 (English trans., Dublin, 1870, a reply to Döllinger's *Janus*); *Katholische Kirche und christlicher Staat in ihrer geschichtlichen Entwicklung und in Beziehung auf die Fragen der Gegenwart*, 1872, abridged ed. 1873 (English trans., *Catholic Church and Christian State*, London, 1876, 2 vols.); *Literaturbelege und Nachträge dazu*, 1876; *Piemonts Unterhandlungen mit dem heiligen Stuhl im 18. Jahrh.*, Würzburg, 1876; *Handbuch der allgemeinen Kirchengeschichte*, Freiburg-im-Br., 1876–80, 3 vols., 3d ed. 1884–85; *Cardinal Maury*, Würzburg, 1878. *

HERING, Hermann, D.D., German Protestant theologian; b. at Dallmin in the Westpriegnitz, Feb. 26, 1838; studied at Halle, 1858–61; became *diakonus* at Weissensee, 1863; *archi-diakonus* at Weissenfels-a.-d.-S., 1869; chief pastor at Lützen, 1874; superintendent of the diocese of Lützen, 1875; ordinary professor of practical theology at Halle, 1878. He is the author of *Die Mystik Luthers im Zusammenhange seiner Theologie und in ihrem Verhältniss zur älteren Mystik*, Leipzig, 1879.

HERMINYARD, Aimé Louis, Reformed; b. at Vevey, Switzerland, Nov. 7, 1817; studied at Lausanne; for many years was a teacher in Russia, France, and Germany, but latterly has lived at Lausanne. After thirty years' labor, he began the publication, with full annotations, of the correspondence of the French Reformers, in a series of volumes of unique and priceless value, for which he has the profoundest gratitude of all students of the period: *Correspondance des réformateurs dans les pays de langue française*, Geneva, 1866 *sqq.* (vol. 6, 1883).

HERRMANN, Johann Georg Wilhelm, Lic. Theol. (Halle, 1874), **Ph.D., D.D.** (both Marburg, 1880), German Protestant; b. at Melkow, Magdeburg, Dec. 6, 1846; studied at Halle, 1866–70; became *privat-docent* there, 1874; ordinary professor of theology at Marburg, 1879. He is the author of *Die Metaphysik in der Theologie*, Halle, 1774; *Die Religion im Verhältniss zum Welterkennen und zur Sittlichkeit*, 1879; *Die Bedeutung der Inspirationslehre für die evangelische Kirche*, 1882; *Warum bedarf unser Glaube geschichtlicher Thatsachen?* 1884.

HERSHON, Paul Isaac, Nonconformist; b. of Jewish parents, at Buczacz (pronounced *boochurch*), Galicia, Austrian Poland, in May (8th day of the Jewish month Iyyar), 1818; studied at the then Hebrew College in Jerusalem, under the auspices of the "London Society for promoting Christianity amongst the Jews," 1842–46; was superintendent of the society's house of industry in that city, 1847; resigned, was reinstated 1848 after visit to England, retained position till 1855, resigned again; became the society's missionary to the Jews at Manchester, Eng.; was superintendent of the Palestine model farm at Jaffa, started by a committee of Hebrew Christians; resigned through ill health, and returned to England, 1859. He has published *Extracts from the Talmud, Being Specimens of Wit, Wisdom, Learning, etc., of the Wise and Learned Rabbis*, London, 1860; *Pentateuch according to the Talmud, Genesis*, 1874 (Hebrew; in English, 1883); an improved edition of the New Testament, in Judæo-Polish, published by the British and Foreign Bible Society, 1874; *A Talmudic Miscellany*, 1880; *Treasures of the Talmud*, 1882; *A Rabbinical Commentary on Genesis*, 1885; and has in manuscript *Exodus according to the Talmud; Key to the Babylonian Talmud* (references to 1,400 classified subjects); *Modern Orthodox Judaism, and what it teaches about God, Man, and the World to come*, etc.

HERVEY, Right Rev. Lord Arthur Charles, D.D. (Cambridge, 1869), lord bishop of Bath and Wells, Church of England; b. in London, Aug. 20, 1808; entered Trinity College, Cambridge; graduated M.A. (first-class classical tripos), 1830; ordained deacon and priest, 1832. He is the son of the first Marquis of Bristol, and after a short service as curate was appointed by his father rector of Ickworth in 1832, to which Horringer, the adjacent living (both in Suffolk), was united in 1853; and the united living was held by him until 1869. In 1862 he was promoted to the archdeaconry of Sudbury, and in 1869 was consecrated bishop of Bath and Wells. He is visitor of Wadham College, Oxford. He was a member of the Old-Testament Revision Company. He contributed to Smith's *Dictionary of the Bible*, to *The Bible (Speaker's) Commentary* (*Ruth* and *Samuel*), to *The Pulpit Commentary* (*Judges, Ruth*, and *Acts*), and *The Brief Commentary* of the S. P. C. K.; and has also published various single sermons and charges, and three volumes of collected discourses, — *Parochial Sermons*, London, 1850, 2 vols.; *The Inspiration of Holy Scripture* (four Cambridge University sermons), 1855. His most important publication is *The Genealogies of our Lord and Saviour Jesus Christ, as contained in the Gospels of Matthew and Luke, reconciled with each other, and with the Genealogy of the House of David, from Adam to the Close of the Canon of the Old Testament, and shown to be in harmony with the True Chronology of the Times*, 1853.

HERZOG, Right Rev. Eduard, D.D. (*hon.*, Bern, 1876), Christian Catholic (Old Catholic); b. at Schongau, Canton Luzern, Switzerland, Aug. 1, 1841; studied theology at Tübingen, Freiburg, and Bonn, 1865–68; became teacher of religion in the teachers' institute of the Canton Luzern, and of exegesis in the theological (Roman-Catholic) seminary at Luzern, 1868; Old-Catholic pastor at Crefeld, Prussia, 1872; at Olten, 1873; Bern, 1876–84; chosen bishop of the Christian Catholic Church of Switzerland, June 7, 1876; consecrated, Sept. 18, 1876. Since 1874 he has been professor of theology at Bern, and was rector of the university 1884–85. He has written *Ueber die Abfassungszeit der Pastoralbriefe*, Luzern, 1870; *Christ-kath. Gebetbuch*, Bern, 1879, 2d ed. 1884; *Gemeinschaft mit der Anglo-Americ. Kirche*, 1881; *Religionsfreiheit in der helvet. Republik*, 1884; about twenty episcopal charges, relative to excommunication, confession, the three Peter-passages, etc., essays and sermons. He edited the *Katholische Stimme*, Luzern, 1870–71 (a weekly newspaper against papal infallibility); *Katholische Blätter*, Olten, 1873–76 (weekly, Old Catholic); is joint editor of *Katholik*, Bern, 1878, sqq. (weekly, organ of the Christian Catholic Church of Switzerland).

HESSEY, Ven. James Augustus, D.C.L. (Oxford, Eng., 1846), **D.D.** (University of the South, Sewanee, Tenn., U.S.A., 1884), Church of England; b. in London, July 17, 1814; became probationary fellow of St. John's College, Oxford, 1832, fellow 1835; graduated B.A. (first-class classics) 1836, M.A. 1840, B.D. 1845, B.C.L. 1846; ordained deacon 1837, priest 1838; was vicar of Helidon, 1839, resigned; college logic lecturer, 1839–42; examiner for the Hertford Latin scholarship at Oxford, 1842–43; public examiner in the university, 1842–44; head master of Merchant Taylors' School, London, 1845–70; select preacher in the University of Oxford, 1849; preacher of Gray's Inn, London, 1850–79; Bampton lecturer, Oxford, 1860; prebendary of St. Paul's, London, 1860–75; Grinfield lecturer in the Septuagint in the University of Oxford, 1865–69; examining chaplain of the bishop of London since 1870; Boyle lecturer, 1871–73; classical examiner, Indian Civil Service, 1872–74; governor of Repton School, 1874; of Aldenham School, 1875; of St. Paul's School, 1876; of Highgate School, 1876; became archdeacon of Middlesex, 1875; was select preacher in the University of Cambridge, 1878–79. He is an active member of the great Church societies; one of the three permanent chairmen of the general meetings of the Society for Promoting Christian Knowledge; chief mover in the establishment of the diocesan conference for London, 1883; chairman of committees of the Lower House of Convocation of Canterbury, on duties of archdeacons and on resolutions of diocesan conferences; particularly active in the "Marriage Law Defence Union" (i.e., against legalizing marriage with a deceased wife's sister). He is a moderate High Churchman, with great sympathy with all that is earnest and true in every school of the Church of England. He is the author of *Schemata rhetorica, or Tables Illustrative of the Enthymeme of Aristotle*, Oxford, 1845; *Sermons*, London, 1859 and 1873; *Sunday* (Bampton Lectures), 1860, 4th ed. 1880; *Biographies of the Kings of Judah*, 1864; *Moral Difficulties connected with the Bible* (Boyle Lectures), 1871; *Imprecatory Psalms* (do., 2d series), 1872; *The Recent Controversies about Prayer* (do., 3d series), 1873; various sermons on public occasions, articles in Smith's *Dictionary of the Bible*, charges as archdeacon; reports, etc.; pamphlets, *Clergyman's Letter to a Friend* (against marriage with deceased wife's sister), 1849, revised ed. 1883; and *Six Grand Reasons for not allowing Marriage with a Deceased Wife's Sister*, 1883.

HETTINGER, Franz, D.D. (Collegium Germanicum, Rome, Italy, 1845), **Ph.D.** (*hon.*, Würzburg, Germany, 1859), Roman Catholic; b. at Aschaffenburg, Germany, Jan. 13, 1819; studied at Würzburg, then in the Collegium Germanicum at Rome, Italy; became priest there, 1843; chaplain at Alzenau, Lower Franconia, 1845; *assistent* in the clerical seminary at Würzburg, 1847, *subregens* 1852; professor extraordinary of theological encyclopædia and patrology in the University of Würzburg, 1856; ordinary professor of the same, 1857; ordinary professor of apologetics and homiletics, 1867; in 1862 and 1867, rector of the University of Würzburg; in 1865 he was made honorary member of the Vienna theological faculty; in 1868, summoned to Rome to assist in preparing for the Vatican Council; in 1870, papal domestic prelate. He is the author of *Das Priesterthum der katholischen Kirche*, Regensburg, 1851; *Die kirchl. und socialen Zustände von Paris*, Mainz, 1852; *Die Idee der geistlichen Uebungen*, Regensburg, 1853; *Herr, den du liebst der ist krank* Würzburg, 1854, 3d ed. 1878; *Die Liturgie der Kirche und der latein. Sprache*, 1856; *Das Recht und die Freiheit der Kirche*, 1860; *Der Organismus der Universitätswissenschaften und die Stellung der Theologie in demselben*, 1862; *Apologie des Christenthums*, Freiburg-im-Br., 1862–67, 2 vols., 6th ed. 1885; *Die Kunst im Christenthum*, Würzburg, 1867; *Die kirchl. Vollgewalt des apostol. Stuhles*, Freiburg-im-Br., 1873, 5th ed. 1879; *D. F. Strauss*, 1875; *Lehrbuch der Fundamental-theologie oder Apologetik*, 1879, 2 vols.; *Die Theologie der göttlichen Komödie d. Dante Alighieri in ihren Grundzügen*, Köln, 1879; *Die göttl. Komödie d. Dante nach ihrem wesentl. Inhalt u. Character*, Freib.-im-Br., 1880; *Die "Krisis des Christenthums," Protestantismus u. katholische Kirche*, 1881; *Aus Welt u. Kirche*, 1885, 2 vols.

HEURTLEY, Charles Abel, D.D. (Oxford, 1853), Church of England; b. in England, about the year 1806; was scholar, and later fellow (1832–41), of Corpus Christi College, Oxford; graduated B.A. (first-class in mathematics), 1827; Ellerton theological prizeman, 1828; M.A. 1831, B.D. 1838; was ordained deacon 1831, priest 1832; was curate of Wardington and Claydon, Oxford, 1831–40; rector of Fenny Compton, Warwickshire, 1840–72. In 1834, 1838, and 1851 he was select preacher to the university; in 1845 the Bampton lecturer; from 1848 to 1853 honorary canon of Worcester Cathedral. In 1853 he became Margaret professor of divinity, and canon of Christ Church, Oxford. From 1864 to 1872 he was a member of the hebdomadal council of the university. His publications include numerous sermons (single and collected), pamphlets, and essays; his Bampton lectures on *Justification*, 1845; *Harmonia symbolica*, Oxford, 1858; *Essay on Miracles*, 1862; *The Doctrine of the Eucharist*, 1867; *Inquiry into the Scriptural Warrant for addressing Prayer to Christ*, 1867; *The Doctrine of the Church of England touching the Real Objective Presence*, 1867; *De fide et symbolo: documenta SS. Patrum tractatus*, 1869, 3d ed. 1884; *The Athanasian Creed: Reasons for rejecting Mr. Ffoulkes' Theory of its Age and Author*, 1872.

HEWIT, Augustine Francis, Roman Catholic; b. at Fairfield, Conn., Nov. 27, 1820; graduated at Amherst College, Amherst, Mass., 1839; was ordained in the Roman-Catholic Church, March 25, 1847; vice-principal of Cathedral Collegiate Institute, Charleston, S. C., 1847–49; missionary (i.e., engaged in preaching missions at large in parochial churches), 1851–65; since 1865 has been professor in the Paulist Seminary, New-York City. He is the author of *Memoir of Rev. Francis A. Baker*, New York, 1865; *Problems of the Age. With Studies in St. Augustine, and on Kindred Topics*, 1868; *Light on Darkness, a Treatise on the Obscure Night of the Soul*, 1871; *The King's Highway, or the Catholic Church the Way of Salvation as revealed in the Holy Scriptures*, 1874, 2d ed. 1879.

HICKOCK, Laurens Perseus, D.D. (Hamilton College, Clinton, N.Y., 1843), **LL.D.** (Amherst College, Amherst, Mass., 1866), Presbyterian; b. at Bethel, Conn., Dec. 29, 1798; graduated from Union College, Schenectady, N.Y., 1820; and after studying theology under Rev. William Andrews and Bennet Tyler, D.D., from 1821 to 1823, was pastor (Congregational) at Kent, Conn., 1824–29, and at Litchfield, 1829–36. From 1836 to 1844 he was professor of theology in Western Reserve College, Ohio; until 1852 in Auburn (Presbyterian) Theological Seminary, N.Y.; until 1866 was professor of mental and moral science, and vice-president, of Union College; until 1868 president. He then resigned, and has since lived in literary retirement at Amherst, Mass. He is the author of *Rational Psychology*, New York, 1849; *A System of Moral Science*, 1853, revised ed. 1880; *Empirical Psychology*, 1854, revised ed. 1882; *Rational Cosmology*, 1858; *Creator and Creation*, 1872; *Humanity Immortal*, 1872; *Logic of Reason*, 1875.

HILGENFELD, Adolf (Bernhard Christoph Christian), Ph.D. (Halle, 1846), **Lic. Theol.** (Jena, 1847), **D.D.** (*hon.*, Jena, 1858), German Protestant theologian; b. at Stappenbeck, near Salzwedel, June 2, 1823; studied theology at Berlin 1841–43, and at Halle 1843–45; became *privat-docent* of theology at Jena, 1847; professor extraordinary, 1850; honorary ordinary professor, 1869; ecclesiastical councillor, 1873. He is a liberal theologian. Since 1858 he has edited the *Zeitschrift für wissenschaftliche Theologie*. He is the author of *Die clementinischen Recognitionen und Homilien*, Jena, 1848; *Das Evangelium und die Briefe Johannis nach ihrem Lehrbegriff*, Halle, 1849; *Kritische Untersuchungen über die Evangelien Justins, der clementinischen Homilien und Marcions*, 1850; *Die Glossolalie in der alten Kirche*, Leipzig, 1850; *Das Markusevangelium*, 1850; *Die Göttingische Polemik gegen meine Forschungen*, 1851; *Der Apostel Paulus, ein Vortrag*, Jena, 1851; *Der Galaterbrief*, Leipzig, 1852; *Die apostolischen Väter*, Halle, 1853; *Die Evangelien nach ihrer Entstehung und geschichtlichen Bedeutung*, Leipzig, 1854; *Das Urchristenthum in den Hauptwendepunkten seines Entwickelungsganges*, Jena, 1855; *Die jüdische Apokalyptik*, 1857; *Der Paschastreit der alten Kirche*, Halle, 1860; *Die Propheten Esra und Daniel und ihre neuste Bearbeitung*, 1863; *Novum Testamentum extra canonem receptum* (containing Clement, Barnabas, Hermas, Gospel according to the Hebrews, etc.), Leipzig, 1866 in 4 parts, 2d ed. 1876–84 (the last part of the 2d ed. contains *The Teaching of the Apostles*); *Messias Judæorum, libris eorum paulo ante et paulo post Christum natum conscriptis illustratus*, 1869; *Hermæ Pastor, veterem latinam interpretationem, e codicibus*, 1873; *Historisch-kritische Einleitung in das Neue Testament*, 1875; *Die Lehninische Weissagung über die Mark Brandenburg*, 1875; *Die Ketzergeschichte des Urchristenthums, urkundlich dargestellt*, 1884.

HILL, David Jayne, LL.D. (Madison University, Hamilton, N.Y., 1883), Baptist; b. at Plainfield, N.J., June 10, 1850; graduated at the University of Lewisburg, Penn., 1874; became professor of rhetoric there, 1877, and president, 1879. He is the author of *The Science of Rhetoric*, New York, 1877; *Elements of Rhetoric and Composition*, 1878; *Biography of Washington Irving*, 1878; *Biography of William Cullen Bryant*, 1879; *The Ultimate*

Ground of Knowing and Being, Philadelphia, 1882; *The Executive Faculty in Man*, 1883; *Lecture Notes on Economics*, Lewisburg, 1884; *Lecture Notes on Anthropology*, 1885. He edited Jevons's *Logic*, New York, 1883.

HILL, Right Rev. Rowley, D.D. (*hon.*, Cambridge, 1877), lord bishop of Sodor and Man, Church of England; b. at St. Colombs, County Derry, Ireland, in the year 1836; educated at Trinity College, Cambridge; graduated B.A. 1859, M.A. 1863; was ordained deacon 1860, priest 1861; became curate of Christ Church, Dover, 1860; of St. Mary's, Marylebone, 1861; vicar of St. Luke's, Nutford Place, London, 1863; rector of Frant, Sussex, 1868; vicar of St. Michael's, Chester Square, London, 1871; of Sheffield, and rural dean, 1873; bishop, 1877. He was prebendary of Strensall in York Cathedral, 1876-77, and chaplain to the Marquis of Abergavenny. He is the author of *Sunday Lessons on the Collects*, London, 1865, 7th ed. 18—; do. *on the Gospels*, 1866, 4th ed. 18—; do. *on the Titles of Our Lord*, 1870; do. *on the Church Catechism*, 1875, 2d ed. 1880; *The Church at Home*, 1881. *

HILL, Thomas, S.T.D. (Harvard College, Cambridge, Mass., 1860), **LL.D.** (Yale College, New Haven, Conn., 1863), Unitarian; b. at New Brunswick, N.J., Jan. 7, 1818; graduated at Harvard College, Cambridge, Mass., 1843, and at the Cambridge Divinity School, 1845; was pastor at Waltham, Mass., 1845-59; president of Antioch College, Yellow Springs, O., 1859-62, and of Harvard College, 1862-68; has been since 1873 pastor at Portland, Me. He took the Scott premium of the Franklin Institute, for an instrument which calculates eclipses and occultations; and also invented the nautrigon for solving spherical triangles. He accompanied Agassiz around South America in 1871 and 1872. He is the author of *Christmas, and Poems upon Slavery*, Boston, 1843; *Elementary Treatise on Arithmetic*, 1845; *On Curvature*, 1850; *Geometry and Faith*, New York, 1849, enlarged ed. 1874, greatly enlarged ed., Boston, 1882; *First Lessons in Geometry*, Boston, 1855, revised and enlarged 1878; *Jesus the Interpreter of Nature*, 1860; *Second Book of Geometry*, 1862; *The True Order of Studies*, New York, 1876; *The Natural Sources of Theology*, Andover, 1877; and sundry sermons, orations, and lectures; also numerous communications in reviews, magazines, and scientific journals.

HILLER, Alfred, D.D. (Wittenberg College, Springfield, O., 1882), Lutheran (General Synod); b. at Sharon, N.Y., April 22, 1831; graduated at Hartwick Seminary, N.Y., 1857; became pastor at Fayette, Seneca County, N.Y., 1857; at German Valley, N.J., 1858; Dr. G. B. Miller professor of systematic theology in Hartwick Seminary, Otsego County, N.Y., 1881.

HIMPEL, Felix von, D.D. (*hon.*, Tübingen, 1857), Roman Catholic; b. at Ravensburg, Würtemberg, Germany, Feb. 28, 1821; studied philosophy and theology; became priest 1845; upper teacher in the Latin school at Rottenburg; *convictsvorstand* and professor in the upper gymnasium at Ehingen, 1849; professor of Old-Testament exegesis and of the Oriental languages at Tübingen, as Welte's successor, 1857. He is the author of *Untersuchungen über die Siegfriedssage*, Ehingen, 1850; *Die Unsterblichkeitslehre des A. T.*, 1857; contributions to the Tübingen *Theol. Quartalschrift*. *

HINCKS, Edward Young, Congregationalist; b. at Bucksport, Me., Aug. 13, 1844; graduated at Yale College, New Haven, Conn., 1866, and at Andover Theological Seminary, Mass., 1870; was pastor of State-street Church, Portland, Me., 1870-81; since 1882 has been Smith professor of biblical theology in Andover Theological Seminary.

HITCHCOCK, Roswell Dwight, D.D. (Bowdoin College, 1855, Edinburgh, 1884), **LL.D.** (Williams College, Williamstown, Mass., 1873), Presbyterian; b. at East Machias, Me., Aug. 15, 1817; graduated at Amherst College, Amherst, Mass., 1836; studied theology in Andover Theological Seminary, Mass., 1838-39, and in Germany; was tutor in Amherst College, 1839-42; pastor of the First (Congregational) Church, Exeter, N.H., 1845-52; professor of natural and revealed religion in Bowdoin College, Brunswick, Me., 1852-55; and of church history in Union Theological Seminary (Presbyterian), New-York City, since 1855, and president of the same since 1880. He is the author of *Life of Edward Robinson*, New York, 1863; *Complete Analysis of the Bible*, 1869; *Hymns and Songs of Praise* (with Drs. Schaff and Eddy), 1878; *Socialism*, 1879; *Teaching of the Twelve Apostles* (translator and editor with Dr. Francis Brown), 1884, 2d ed., revised and greatly enlarged, 1885; *Carmina Sanctorum* (with Dr. Eddy and Rev. L. W. Mudge), 1885.

HODGE, Archibald Alexander, D.D. (College of New Jersey, Princeton, 1862), **LL.D.** (Wooster University, Wooster, O., 1876), oldest son of the late Dr. Charles Hodge, Presbyterian; b. at Princeton, N.J., July 18, 1823; graduated from the College of New Jersey, Princeton (1841), and Princeton Theological Seminary (1847); was missionary of the Presbyterian Board of Foreign Missions (Old-school) at Allahabad, India, 1847-50; pastor at Lower West Nottingham, Md., 1851-55; Fredericksburg, Va., 1855-61; and at Wilkesbarre (First Church), Penn., 1861-64. In 1864 he became professor of didactic and polemic theology in the Western (Presbyterian) Theological Seminary, Alleghany, Penn. In connection with his professorship he held the pastorate of the North Church, Alleghany, from 1866 to 1877. In 1877 he removed to Princeton, first as associate professor, but since 1878 he has been full professor, of didactic and polemic theology. He is the author of *Outlines of Theology*, New York, 1860, rewritten and enlarged ed. 1878 (translated into Welsh, modern Greek, and Hindustani); *The Atonement*, Philadelphia, 1868; *Commentary on Confession of Faith*, 1869; *Presbyterian Forms*, Philadelphia, 1876, 2d ed. (rewritten) 1882; *Life of Charles Hodge*, New York, 1880.

HODGE, Caspar Wistar, D.D. (College of New Jersey, Princeton, 1865), son of the late Dr. Charles Hodge, Presbyterian; b. at Princeton, N.J., Feb. 21, 1830; graduated from the College of New Jersey, Princeton, 1848, and from the theological seminary 1853; tutor in the college, 1850-51; teacher in Princeton, 1852-53; stated supply of Ainslie-street Church, Williamsburg, N.Y., 1853-54; pastor, 1854-56; at Oxford, Penn., 1856-60. Since 1860 he has been professor of New-Testament literature and biblical Greek in Princeton Theological Seminary. *

HODGSON, Telfair, D.D. (University of the South, Sewanee, Tenn., 1878), Episcopalian; b. at Columbia, Va., March 14, 1840; graduated at College of New Jersey, Princeton, 1859; chaplain in the Confederate Army, 1863–65; rector of Keyport, N.J., 1866–71; professor in the University of Alabama, Tuscaloosa, 1871–73; assistant at Christ Church, Baltimore, Md., 1873–74; rector of Trinity Church, Hoboken, N.J., 1874–78; since 1878 vice-chancellor of the University of the South, Sewanee, Tenn. He has published occasional sermons, addresses, and reports.

HOELEMANN, Hermann Gustav, D.D., German Protestant theologian; b. at Bauda, Saxony, Aug. 8, 1809; studied at Leipzig, 1829-34; became *privat-docent* in the philosophical faculty there 1834, changed to the theological faculty 1844; professor extraordinary of theology, 1853; ordinary honorary professor of New-Testament exegesis, 1867. He is the author of *Die trostreiche Ueberzeugung, dass Gott über die Schicksale gebietet, bei trüben Aussichten in eine kriegerische Zukunft* (*Eine gekrönte Preispredigt über Ps. lxvi. 9, 10, 11*), Leipzig, 1831 (pp. 16); *De Bibliorum Dinteri ingenio exegetico sive interpretationis epistolæ ad Philippenses Paulinæ specimina ac symbolæ*, 1834 (pp. 32); *Commentarius in epistolam divi Pauli ad Philippenses*, 1839; *De evangelii Joannei introitu introitus geneseos augustiore effigie*, 1855; *Die Krone des Hohen Liedes, Einheitliche Erklärung seines Schlussactes*, 1856; *Die Stellung St. Pauli zu der Frage um die Zeit der Wiederkunft Christi*, 1858 (pp. 38); *Bibelstudien*, 1859-60, 2 parts; *Die Einheit der beiden Schöpfungsberichte Genesis i.–ii.*, 1862; *Neue Bibelstudien*, 1866; *De justitiæ ex fide ambabus in vetere testamento sedibus ter in novo testamento memoratis commentatio exegetica*, 1867; *Die Reden des Satan in der heiligen Schrift*, 1875; *Letzte Bibelstudien*, 1885.

HOERSCHELMANN, Ferdinand, D.D., Lutheran theologian; b. at St. Martens, Esthonia (a Baltic province of Russia), Jan. 2, 1834; studied at Dorpat, 1851–55; became pastor at Fellin, 1858; ordinary professor of theology at Dorpat, 1875.

HOFFMAN, Eugene Augustus, D.D. (Rutgers College, New Brunswick, N.J., 1864), **S.T.D.** (General Theological Seminary, New-York City, 1885), Episcopalian; b. in New-York City, March 21, 1829; graduated from Rutgers College, New Brunswick, N.J., 1847; from Harvard College, Cambridge, Mass., 1848; and from General Theological Seminary, New-York City, 1851. He became rector successively at Elizabeth Port, N.J., 1851; Elizabeth, 1853; Burlington, 1863; Brooklyn, N.Y., 1864; Philadelphia, 1869; dean of the General Theological Seminary, New-York City, 1879. He is the author of *Free Churches*, New York, 1856; *The Eucharistic Week*, 1859; and various sermons and addresses.

HOFMANN, Rudolf Hugo, Ph.D. (Leipzig, 1847), **Lic. Theol.** (*hon.*, Leipzig, 1851), **D.D.** (*hon.*, Leipzig, 1860), Lutheran; b. at Kreischa, near Dresden, Jan. 3, 1825; studied at Leipzig, 1843–47; became pastor at Strönthal, near Leipzig, 1851; professor at Meissen, 1854; professor of theology, and second university preacher, at Leipzig, 1862. He is an Evangelical Lutheran, of the *Mittelpartei*. He is the author of *Das Zeichen des Menschensohns* ("*gekrönte Preisschrift*"), Leipzig, 1848; *Das Leben Jesu nach den Apokryphen*, 1851; *Symbolik*, 1856; *Die Lehre vom Gewissen*, 1866; *Predigten gehalten in der Universitätskirche zu Leipzig*, 1869; *Zum System der praktischen Theologie*, 1874; *Schulbibel*, Dresden, 1875, 2d ed. 1878; *Die practische Vorbildung der Candidaten des höheren Schulamts auf der Universität*, Leipzig, 1881; *Predigten über das Vaterunser*, 1881; *Die freien christlichen Liebesthätigkeiten und die Gemeinde*, 1884; and of numerous articles in Herzog's *Real-Encyclopädie*, etc.

HOGE, Moses Drury, D.D. (Hampden-Sidney College, Va., 1858), Presbyterian; b. on College Hill, Hampden-Sidney, Sept. 17, 1819; graduated from Hampden-Sidney College, Prince Edward County, Va., 1839, and from the Union Theological Seminary there, 1843; was assistant pastor of the First Presbyterian Church, Richmond, Va., 1843-45; and since 1845 (the year of its organization) has been pastor of the Second Presbyterian Church in the same city. He was moderator of the General Assembly (Southern Church) at St. Louis, 1874; and a delegate to the General Conferences of the Evangelical Alliance, New York, 1873, and Copenhagen, 1884, and to the Council of the Reformed Churches in Edinburgh, 1877.

HOLE, Charles, Church of England; b. at Newport, near Barnstaple, Devonshire, Eng., March 23, 1823; educated at Trinity College, Cambridge; graduated B.A. (wrangler in the mathematical tripos), 1846; was ordained deacon 1846, priest 1847; became curate of St. Mary's Chapel, Reading, 1846; of Shanklin, Isle of Wight, 1858; rector of Loxbeare, Devonshire, 1868; resigned, 1876; lecturer in ecclesiastical history since 1879, and in English history since 1884, at King's College, London; since 1883 chaplain to Lord Sackville. He is the author of *A Brief Biographical Dictionary*, London, 1865, 2d ed. 1866; *Life of Archdeacon Phelps*, 1871, 2 vols.; *Maintenance of the Church of England as an Established Church* (first Peek prize essay), 1874; editor of *The Christian Observer*, 1877; contributor to Smith and Wace's *Dictionary of Christian Biography*, 1877–86, 4 vols., and Smith and Cheetham's *Dictionary of Christian Antiquities*, 1877–80, 2 vols.

HOLLAND, Henry Scott, Church of England; b. at Underdown, Ledbury, Herefordshire, Jan. 26, 1847; educated at Eton College, and Balliol College, Oxford; graduated B.A. (first-class in classics) 1870, M.A. (Christ Church) 1873; was elected a senior student (i e., fellow) of Christ Church College, Oxford, 1870; tutor, 1872–84; ordained deacon 1872, priest 1874; select preacher at the university, 1880–81; senior proctor, 1882; honorary canon of Truro, 1883-84; appointed examining chaplain to the bishop of Truro, 1883; canon residentiary of St. Paul's Cathedral, London, 1884, whereupon he resigned his tutorship. He is the author of *The Apostolic Fathers*, London, 1878; *Four Addresses on the Sacrifice of the Cross*, 1879; *Logic and Life*, 1882, 3d ed. 1885, reprinted, New York, 1882; *Good-Friday Addresses in St. Paul's Cathedral*, 1884. He wrote the article on *Justin Martyr* in Smith and Wace's *Dictionary of Christian Biography*, vol. ii.

HOLSTEN, Karl Johann, Lutheran; b. at Güstrow, Mecklenburg, March 31, 1825; studied at Leipzig, Berlin, and Rostock; became teacher in the Rostock Gymnasium, 1848; professor extraordinary of theology at Bern, 1870; ordinary professor, 1871; at Heidelberg, 1876. He is the author of *Zum Evangelium d. Paulus u. d. Petrus*, Rostock, 1867; *Das Evangelium des Paulus dargestellt*, Berlin, 1880, *sqq*. *

HOLT, Levi Herbert, Baptist; b. at Topsham, Me., Aug. 14, 1849; graduated at University of Chicago, Ill., 1874, and at Morgan-Park Baptist Theological Seminary, Ill., 1877; became pastor at De Kalb, Ill., 1877; at Clay Center, Kan., 1881; editor *Western Baptist*, Topeka, Kan., 1884.

HOLTZMANN, Heinrich Julius, Lic. Theol. (Heidelberg, 1858), **D.D.** (*hon.*, Vienna, 1862), German Protestant; b. at Carlsruhe, May 17, 1832; studied theology at Heidelberg and Berlin; was in the service of the Baden Church, 1854–57; became *privat-docent* at Heidelberg, 1858; professor extraordinary, 1861; ordinary professor, 1865; at Strassburg, 1874. He is the author of *Kanon und Tradition*, Ludwigsburg, 1859; *Die synoptischen Evangelien, ihr Ursprung und geschichtlicher Character*, Leipzig, 1863; *Christenthum und Judenthum im Zeitalter der neutest. und apokryphischen Literatur*, 1867 (vol. 2 of Weber's *Geschichte des Volks Israel u. der Entstehung des Christenthums*, 1867, 2 vols.); *Kritik der Epheser und Colosserbriefe*, 1872; *Die Pastoralbriefe*, 1880; (with R. O. Zöpffel) *Lexikon für Theologie u. Kirchenwesen*, 1882; *Hist. kritische Einleitung in das N. T.*, Freiburg, 1885.

HOOD, Edward Paxton, English Congregationalist; b. in Westminster, London, Dec. 18, 1820, and educated privately; began his ministry in 1852; was for many years a preacher in London, and, at the time of his death, was pastor of Falcon-square Independent Chapel. He died in Paris, France, Saturday, June 13, 1885. He was for many years the editor of *The Eclectic Review*, and of *The Preacher's Lantern* from 1871 to 1875. He lectured on social, literary, and religious subjects in Great Britain, and also on his visit to the United States in 1881. He was rather an industrious collector of anecdotes and curious and miscellaneous information and extracts, than an original author; still his works are instructive, and his *Lamps, Pitchers, and Trumpets*, his best-known work, is a valuable history of homiletics. He is the author of *The Age and its Architects*, London, 1850; *Dark Days of Queen Mary*, 1851; *Genius and Industry*, 1851; *Golden Days of Queen Bess*, 1851; *John Milton, the Patriot and Poet*, 1851; *Literature of Labour*, 1851; *Mental and Moral Philosophy of Laughter*, 1851; *Old England's Historic Pictures*, 1851; *Self-education*, 1851; *Common-sense Arguments*, 1852; *Hammers and Ploughshares, a Book for the Labourer*, 1852; *Uses of Biography*, 1852; *Dreamland and Ghostland*, 1852; *Swedenborg, a Biography*, 1856; *Wordsworth, a Biography*, 1856; *An Earnest Ministry: Record of Life and Writings of B. Parsons*, 1856; *Havelock, the Broad Stone of Honour*, 1858; *Book of Temperance Melody*, 185–, new ed. 1858; *Self-formation*, 185–, 4th ed. 1883; *Blind Amos and his Velvet Principles*, 185–, 6th ed. (enlarged) 1884; *Peerage of Poverty*, 1st and 2d series 1859, 5th ed. 1870; *Sermons*, 1859; *Lamps, Pitchers, and Trumpets*, 1867; *World of Anecdote*, 1869, 3d ed. 1886; *Dark Sayings on a Harp: Sermons*, 186–, 2d ed. 1870; *World of Moral and Religious Anecdote*, 1870, 4th ed. 1885; *Bye-path Meadow*, 1870, 2d ed. 1885; *Villages of the Bible*, 1874; *Thomas Carlyle*, 1875; *Romance of Biography*, 1876; *Robert Raikes of Gloucester*, 1880; *Vignettes of the Great Revival of the 18th Century*, 1880; *The Day, the Book, and the Teacher*, 1880; *Christmas Evans, the Preacher of Wild Wales*, 1881; *Oliver Cromwell*, 1882; *Scotch Characteristics*, 1883; *The World of Proverb and Fable*, 1884; *The King's Windows, or Glimpses of the Wonderful Works of God*, 1885; *The Throne of Eloquence: Great Preachers, Ancient and Modern*, 1885. *

HOOP-SCHEFFER, Jacob Gysbert de, Dutch philologist and historian; b. at The Hague, Sept. 28, 1819. Having lost his father at an early age, he was brought up in Amsterdam by his uncle de Hoop, whose name he took; studied in the Mennonite Theological Seminary at Amsterdam, and graduated at the University of Utrecht. During this period he employed his leisure time in the study of the mediæval literature of the Netherlands, and was one of the founders (1842) of the society for the publication of Dutch texts of the thirteenth, fourteenth, and fifteenth centuries. He was pastor successively at Hoorn (1843-46), Groningen (1846-49), Amsterdam (1849-60); has been professor in the Mennonite Seminary since 1860; and professor of Old-Testament exegesis, and the Christian literature of the first two centuries, in the Municipal University of Amsterdam, since 1877. Besides a number of articles in the *Navorscher*, *Studien en Bijdragen*, etc., he has written in Dutch, "A Brief History of the Mennonites," Amsterdam, 1860; "A History of the Reformation in the Netherlands before 1531," 1873; "A History of the Brownists of Amsterdam," 1881; and contributed the article upon the Mennonites in the "Pictures of the History of the Christian Church in the Netherlands," 1869.

HOOYKAAS, Isaac, D.D. (Leiden, 1862), Dutch theologian; b. at Nieuwe Tonge, Holland, Oct. 21, 1837; studied at the University of Leiden; became pastor of the Reformed Church at Nieuw Helvoet 1862, and at Schiedam 1867, and is now Remonstrant Gereformeerd pastor at Rotterdam. He was joint author with Oort of *The Bible for Young People*, English trans. London, 1873–79, 6 vols.; republished (under title "*The Bible for Learners*"), Boston, 1878–79, 3 vols.

HOPKINS, John Henry, S.T.D. (Racine College, Racine, Wis., 1873), Episcopalian; b. at Pittsburg, Penn., Oct. 28, 1820; graduated at the University of Vermont, Burlington, 1839, and at the General Theological Seminary, New-York City, 1850; ordained deacon, 1850; was assistant in Zion Church, Greensburg, in St. George the Martyr, and then in St. Timothy's Church, New-York City; in charge of St. Paul's Church, Vergennes, Vt., and of St. John's Church, Essex, N.Y.; ordained priest, 1872; became rector of Trinity Church, Plattsburg, N.Y., 1872; of Christ Church, Williamsport, Penn., 1876. He founded the New-York *Church Journal*, February, 1853, and edited it until May, 1868. Besides many review articles, etc., he has written *Carols, Hymns, and Songs*, New York, 1863, 3d ed. (enlarged) 1882; *Gregorian Canticles*, etc., 1866; *Life of Bishop Hopkins of Vermont*, 1873, 2d ed. 1875; *Poems by the Wayside*, 1883; edited *Collected Works of Rev. Milo Mahan, D.D., with Memoir*, 1872–75, 3 vols.

HOPKINS, Mark, D.D. (Dartmouth College, Hanover, N.H., 1837; Harvard College, Cambridge, Mass., 1841), **LL.D.** (University of State of New York, 1857), Congregationalist; b. at Stockbridge, Mass., Feb. 4, 1802; graduated from Williams College, Williamstown, Mass., 1824; was tutor for two years; studied medicine, and graduated M.D. at the Berkshire Medical College, 1828, and began (1829) practice in New-York City; but in 1830 accepted the call to the professorship of moral philosophy and rhetoric in Williams, and has ever since been connected with the college, as professor, 1830–36; as president, 1836–72; since, as professor of intellectual and moral philosophy. From 1836 until 1883 he was the pastor of the college church. Since 1857 he has been president of the American Board of Commissioners for Foreign Missions. Besides many occasional sermons and addresses, he has published *The Evidences of Christianity* (Lowell Lectures of 1844), Boston, 1846, 3d ed. (revised) 1875; *Miscellaneous Essays and Reviews*, 1847; *Moral Science* (Lowell Lectures), 1862; *The Law of Love, and Love as a Law*, New York, 1869, rev. ed. 1881; *An Outline Study of Man*, 1873, new ed. 1876; *Strength and Beauty*, 1874 (re-issued with modifications and additions, under title *Teachings and Counsels*, 1884); *Scriptural Idea of Man*, 1883.

HOPKINS, Samuel Miles, D.D. (Amherst College, Amherst, Mass., 1854), Presbyterian; b. at Geneseo, N.Y., Aug. 8, 1813; graduated from Amherst College, Amherst, Mass., 1832; studied theology at Auburn (N.Y.) Theological Seminary, 1834–36, and at Princeton (N.J.) Theological Seminary, 1836–37; pastor at Corning, N.Y., 1839–43; at Fredonia, 1843–46; and at Avon, 1846–47; since 1847 he has been professor of church history in Auburn Theological Seminary. He was moderator of General Assembly (N. S.) at St. Louis, Mo., 1866. He is the author of *A Manual of Church Polity*, Auburn, 1878; *A Liturgy and Book of Common Prayer for the Presbyterian Church*, New York, 1883, 2d ed. 1886.

HOPPIN, James Mason, D.D. (Knox College, Galesburg, Ill., 1870), Congregationalist; b. at Providence, R.I., Jan. 17, 1820; graduated at Yale College, New Haven, Conn., 1840; studied at law school, Cambridge, Mass., 1840–42; Union Theological Seminary, New-York City, 1842–44; at Andover Theological Seminary, 1844–45 (graduated); at Berlin University, 1846–47; was pastor at Salem, Mass., 1850–59; professor of homiletics and pastoral theology in Yale College, 1861–79 (acting pastor of the college, 1861–63; lecturer on forensic eloquence in its law school, 1872–75); since 1879 has been professor of the history of art in Yale College. He taught homiletics in Union Theological Seminary, New York, in 1880. He is the author of *Notes of a Theological Student*, New York, 1854; *Old England: its Art, Scenery, and People*, Boston, 1867, 8th ed. 1886; *Office and Work of the Christian Ministry*, New York, 1869; *Life of Rear-Admiral Andrew Hull Foote*, 1874; *Memoir of Henry Armitt Brown*, Philadelphia, 1880; *Homiletics*, New York, 1881, 2d ed. 1883; *Pastoral Theology*, 1884 (these two books are re-written divisions of the *Office and Work*, etc.).

HORT, Fenton John Anthony, D.D. (Cambridge, 1875), Church of England; b. in Dublin, April 23, 1828; educated at Trinity College, Cambridge; graduated B.A. (first-class in classics), 1850; took first-class in the moral science and natural science triposes, 1851; proceeded M.A. 1853, B.D. 1875; was ordained deacon 1854, priest 1856; was fellow of Trinity College, 1852–57; since 1872, fellow of Emmanuel College; vicar of St. Ippolyts with Great Wymondley, Herts (a college living), 1857–72; examining chaplain to the bishop of Ely (Dr. Browne), 1871–73; and when Dr. Browne was translated to the see of Winchester, he retained him in that capacity. In 1871 he was Hulsean lecturer. From 1872 to 1878 he was divinity lecturer of Emmanuel College, and in 1878 elected Hulsean professor of divinity. He has several times been examiner for the moral science and natural science triposes, a select preacher before the university, and is a member of the council of the senate of the university. He was one of the original members of the New-Testament Company of Anglo-American Bible-revision Committee. Besides various articles in *The Journal of Philology*, and Smith and Wace's *Dictionary of Christian Biography*, he has published *Two Dissertations* (i. On μονογενὴς θεός in Scripture and tradition. ii. On the Constantinopolitan and other Eastern creeds of the fourth century), London, 1876. He was joint editor with Canon Westcott of *The New Testament in the Original Greek. A Revised Text, with Introduction and Appendix* (May–Oct. 1881, 2 vols., corrected issue, Dec. 1881–April, 1882, smaller edition of text 1885, repub. New York); These eminent biblical scholars worked together upon the text from 1853 to 1881. The second volume was written by Dr. Hort, and includes an elaborate statement and defence of their principles of textual criticism, with various illustrative matter. [See SCHAFF, *Companion to Greek Testament*, New York, 1883, 2d ed. 1885, pp. 268–282.]

HOTT, James William, D.D. (Avalon College, Avalon, Mo., and Western College, Toledo, Io., both 1882), United Brethren in Christ; b. at Winchester, Va., Nov. 15, 1844; self-educated; became pastor (in Virginia and Maryland), 1861; treasurer of the Home Frontier and Foreign Missionary Society of his denomination, 1873; editor of *The Religious Telescope* (the denominational organ), Dayton, O., 1877. He was a member of the Pan Methodist Congress, London, 1881; and of each General Conference of his denomination since 1869, representing the Virginia Conference, to which he belongs. He is the author of *Journeyings in the Old World; or, Europe, Palestine, and Egypt*, Dayton, O., 1884, 4th ed. 1886.

HOVEY, Alvah, D.D. (Brown University, Providence, R.I., 1856), **LL.D.** (Denison University, Granville, O., and Richmond (Va.) College, 1876), Baptist; b. at Greene, Chenango County, N.Y., March 5, 1820; graduated from Dartmouth College, Hanover, N.H., 1844, and from Newton Theological Institution, Newton Centre, Mass., 1848; with the latter has been connected since 1849, as assistant teacher of Hebrew (1849–55), and as professor, first of church history (1853–55), and then of theology and Christian ethics since 1855, president since 1868. For one year (1848–49) he preached at New Gloucester, Me.; for a year (1861–62) was in Europe. From 1868 to 1883, was member of the executive committee of the American Baptist Missionary Union. With Rev. D. B. Ford, he translated F. M. Perthes' *Life of Chrysostom*, Boston, 1854. He is author of *Life* *of Rev. Isaac Backus*, Boston, 1858; *The State of the Impenitent Dead*, 1859; *The Miracles of Christ as attested by the Evangelists*, 1864; *The Scriptural Law of Divorce*, 1866; *God with us, or the Person and Work of Christ*, 1872; *Normal Class Manual*, Part I., *What to Teach*, 1873; *Religion and the State*, 1874; *The Doctrine of the Higher Christian Life compared with the Teachings of the Holy Scriptures*, 1876; *Manual of Systematic Theology and Christian Ethics*, 1877, re-issued, Philadelphia, 1880. He is general editor of *The Complete Commentary on the New Testament*, Philadelphia, 1881 sqq., in which series he contributed the commentary on *The Gospel of John*, 1885.

HOW, Right Rev. William Walsham, D.D. (by Archbishop of Canterbury, 1879), bishop suffragan of Bedford (for East London), Church of England; b. at Shrewsbury, Dec. 13, 1823; educated at Wadham College, Oxford; graduated B.A. (third-class classics) 1845, M.A. 1847; was ordained deacon 1846, priest 1847; was curate of St. George, Kidderminster, 1846; Holy Cross, Shrewsbury, 1848; rector of Whittington, 1851-79; diocesan inspector of schools, 1852-70; rural dean of Oswestry, 1853-79; select preacher at Oxford, 1868-69; proctor of diocese of St. Asaph, 1869-79; examining chaplain to bishop of Lichfield, 1878-79; became bishop, 1879; since 1859 has been prebendary of Llanefydd and chancellor of St. Asaph Cathedral; since 1879, prebendary of Brondesbury in St. Paul's Cathedral, and rector of St. Andrew's Untershaft with St. Mary Axe, City and Diocese of London. He is the author of *Daily Family Prayers for Churchmen*, London, 1859, 5th ed. 1879; *Collect Lyrical Pieces*, 1860; *Plain Words*, 1860-80, 4 series; *Psalm li.*, 1861, 7th ed. 1874; *Twenty-four Practical Sermons*, 1861, 2d ed. 1870; *Pastor in Parochia*, 187–, 8th ed. 1883; *Private Life and Ministrations of a Parish Priest*, 1873; *Plain Words to Children*, 1876; *Revision of the Rubrics*, 1878; *Holy Communion*, 1878, 2d ed. 1882; *Gospel according to St. John, with Commentary*, 1879; *Notes on the Church Service*, 1884; *Boy Hero*, 1884; "*Was lost and is found:*" *A Tale of the London Mission of 1874* (poem), 1885; *Poems*, 187–, new and enlarged ed. 1885; *Words of Good Cheer*, 1885, 2d ed. 1886; *Hymns*, 1886; sermons and minor works. *

HOWARD, His Eminence Edward, Roman Catholic; b. at Nottingham, Eng., Feb. 13, 1829; was an officer of the 2d Life Guards when he left the army to become a priest. In 1855 he entered the personal service of Pius IX. In 1872 he was appointed archbishop of Neocæsaria *in partibus infidelium:* and on March 12, 1877, a cardinal priest, with the "title" of SS. John and Paul on the Cœlian Hill, Rome. On March 24, 1878, he became protector of the English College at Rome; and in December, 1881, arch-priest of the Basilica of St. Peter's, and prefect of the congregation in charge of the building. His Eminence is an extraordinary linguist. *

HOWE, James Albert, D.D. (Hillsdale College, Hillsdale, Mich., 1876), Freewill Baptist; b. at Dracut, Mass., Oct. 10, 1834; graduated at Bowdoin College, Brunswick, Me., 1859, and at Andover Theological Seminary, Mass., 1862; became Freewill Baptist pastor at Blackstone, Mass., 1862; at Olneyville, R.I., 1863; professor of systematic theology and homiletics in the Freewill Baptist Theological School of Bates College, Lewiston, Me., 1872.

HOWE, Right Rev. Mark Antony DeWolfe, D.D. (Brown University, Providence, R.I., 1848), **LL.D.** (University of Pennsylvania, Philadelphia, 1875), Episcopalian, bishop of Central Pennsylvania; b. at Bristol, R.I., April 5, 1809; graduated at Brown University, Providence, R.I., 1828; taught in Boston public schools, 1829-30; was classical tutor in Brown University, 1831-32; entered the ministry, and after three months service in St. Matthew's, South Boston, became rector of St. James's, Roxbury, 1832; editor of *The Christian Witness*, and rector of Christ Church, Cambridge, 1835-36; of St. James's again, 1837-46; of St. Luke's, Philadelphia, Penn., 1846-72; consecrated bishop, Dec. 28, 1871. He had declined his election as missionary bishop of Nevada in 1865. He stands "on the doctrines of God's Word, as recognized in the Catholic creeds, and in the Articles and Liturgy of the Protestant-Episcopal Church." He is author of *A Critique on the Annual Report of the Boston School Committee*, Boston, 1846; an *Introduction* to Butler's edition of the poetical works of Bishop Reginald Heber, 1858; *Memoirs of Bishop Alonzo Potter*, 1871; and of various occasional sermons, essays, and controversial pamphlets.

HOWE, Right Rev. William Bell White, D.D. (University of the South, Sewanee, Tenn., 1871), **S.T.D.** (Columbia Coll., N. Y. City, 1872), Episcopalian, bishop of South Carolina; b. at Claremont, N.H., March 31, 1823; graduated at the University of Vermont, Burlington, 1844; was successively rector of St. John's, Berkeley, S.C., 1848-60; of St. Philip's, Charleston, 1863-71; bishop, 1871.

HOWSON, Very Rev. John Saul, D.D. (Cambridge, 1861), dean of Chester, Church of England; b. at Giggleswick, Yorkshire, Eng., May 5, 1816; d. at Bournemouth, Dec. 15, 1885. He was a student in Trinity College, Cambridge, and graduated B.A. (wrangler and first-class classical tripos) 1837, M.A. 1841; won the member's prize in 1837 and 1838, and wrote the Norrisian prize essay in 1840. He was ordained deacon in 1845, and priest in 1846; from 1845 to 1865 he was connected with the Liverpool Collegiate Institute, first as senior classical master, and from 1849 as principal. In 1862 he was Hulsean lecturer at Cambridge. From 1866 to 1867 he was vicar of Wisbech St. Peter; and examining chaplain to the bishop of Ely from 1867 to 1873. In 1867 he was made dean of Chester. He was the joint author, with the late Rev. W. J. Conybeare, of *The Life and Epistles of St. Paul*, London, 1852, 2 vols. 4to, 8vo. ed. 1856, people's ed. 1862 (widely circulated, several reprints in America). Besides numerous lectures, sermons, articles in periodicals and Smith's *Dictionary of the Bible*, he published *Sunday Evenings* (short sermons for family reading), 1849, new ed. 1857; *Deaconesses, or the Official Help of Women in Parochial Work and in Charitable Institutions*, 1862; *Sermons to Schoolboys*, 1850, 2d ed. 1858, 2d series 1866; *The Character of St. Paul* (Hulsean Lectures), 1864, 4th ed. 1884; *Scenes from the Life of St. Paul, and their Religious Lessons*, 1866; *The Metaphors of St. Paul*, 1868, 2d ed. 1883; *The Companions of St. Paul*, 1871, 2d ed 1883; *Meditations on the Miracles of Christ*, 1871-77, 2 series; *Chester as it was*, 1872; *Sacramental Confession*, 1874; *The River Dee, its Aspect and His-*

tory, 1875; "*Before the Table:" an Inquiry into the True Meaning*, 1875; *Homely Hints in Sermons suggested by Experience*, 1876; *Position during Consecration at the Communion*, 1877; *Evidential Value of the Acts of the Apostles* (Bohlen Lectures, 1880), New York and London, 1880; *Horæ Petrinæ: Studies in the Life of St. Peter*, 1883; *Thoughts for Saints' Days*, 1886. He contributed to Schaff's *Popular Commentary*, New York and Edinburgh, 1879–83, 4 vols. (*Acts*, with Canon Spence, in vol. ii., 1880); to *The Bible Commentary*, London and New York, 1871–82, 10 vols. (*Galatians*, in vol. ix., 1881); and to *The Pulpit Commentary*, London and New York, 1880 sqq. (*Titus*, 1886). *

HOYT, Wayland, D.D. (University of Rochester, N.Y., 1877), Baptist; b. at Cleveland, O., Feb. 18, 1838; graduated at Brown University, Providence, R.I., 1860, and at Rochester (N.Y.) Theological Seminary, 1863; became pastor at Pittsfield, Mass., 1863; Cincinnati, O., 1864; Brooklyn, N.Y. (Strong Place), 1867; New York (Tabernacle), 1873; Boston, Mass., 1874; Brooklyn (Strong Place), 1876; Philadelphia, Penn. (Memorial Church), 1882. Besides numerous articles, he has written *Hints and Helps in the Christian Life*, New York, 1880; *Present Lessons from Distant Days*, 1881; *Gleams from Paul's Prison*, 1882; *Along the Pilgrimage*, Philadelphia, 1885.

HUGHES, John, D.D. (Washington and Jefferson College, Washington, Penn., 1876), Welsh Presbyterian; b. at Llanerchymedd, Anglesea, North Wales, Sept. 27, 1827; educated at the Welsh Presbyterian College, Bala, North Wales, 1848–51; ordained, 1854; since 1857 has been pastor in Liverpool. He was moderator of the Association of North Wales 1871, and of the General Assembly 1880. He has written, in Welsh, "On the Unity of the Scriptures," Liverpool, 1866; "The Christian Ministry" (lectures delivered to the students of Bala College), Dolgelley, 1879; "History of Christian Doctrine" (first period), Holywell, 1883.

HUGHES, Right Rev. Joshua, D.D. (by Archbishop of Canterbury, 1870), lord bishop of St. Asaph, Church of England; b. at Newport, Pembrokeshire, in the year 1807; educated at St. David's College, Lampeter, Wales; took first-class in final examination, B.D.; was ordained deacon and priest, 1831; became vicar of Abergwili, 1839; of Llandovery, 1846; also rural dean, surrogate, and proctor in convocation for the diocese of St. David's; bishop, 1870. *

HUIDEKOPER, Frederic, Unitarian minister; b. at Meadville, Penn., April 7, 1817; entered Harvard University, Cambridge, Mass., in 1834, but in 1835 was forced by his failing sight to abandon study, to which during the next four years he devoted ten minutes a day. From 1839 to 1841 he travelled in Europe, and then studied theology privately for two years. In 1844 he aided in organizing the Meadville Theological School, in which institution he had charge of the New-Testament department 1844–49, and of ecclesiastical history 1845–77, besides being for many years librarian, as also treasurer. His eyesight has since boyhood been diminishing; total blindness of one eye and approximate blindness of the other has since 1883 caused need of an attendant when in the street. The disease is painless, and the eyes apparently clear. He is the author of *Belief of the First Three Centuries concerning Christ's Mission to the Underworld*, Boston, 1854, 5th ed., New York, 1883; *Judaism at Rome, B.C. 76–A.D. 140*, New York, 1876, 6th ed. 1885; *Indirect Testimony of History to the Genuineness of the Gospels*, 1878, 4th ed. 1883.

HULBERT, Eri Baker, D.D. (Baptist Union Theological Seminary, Morgan Park, Ill., 1880), Baptist; b. in Chicago, Ill., July 16, 1841; graduated at Union College, Schenectady, N.Y., 1863, and at Hamilton (N.Y.) Theological Seminary, 1865. After holding several pastorates (Manchester, Vt., 1865–68; Chicago, Ill., 1868–70; St. Paul, Minn., 1870–74; San Francisco, Cal., 1874–78; Fourth Church, Chicago, Ill., 1878–81), he became in 1881 professor of church history in the Baptist Union Theological Seminary, Morgan Park, near Chicago, Ill.

HUMPHRY, William Gilson, Church of England; b. at Sudbury, Suffolk, Jan. 30, 1815; educated at Trinity College, Cambridge; graduated B.A. (twenty-seventh wrangler, senior classic, second chancellor medallist) 1837, M.A. 1840, B.D. 1850; ordained deacon 1842, priest 1843; was elected fellow of his college (1837), and assistant tutor. From 1847 to 1856 he was examining chaplain to the bishop of London; in 1849 and 1850, Hulsean lecturer; in 1857 and 1858, Boyle lecturer; and from 1852 to 1855 he was vicar of Northholt, Middlesex. In 1852 he became prebendary of Twyford in St. Paul's Cathedral, and in 1855 vicar of St. Martin-in-the-Fields, London, and was rural dean of St. Martin-in-the-Fields deanery. He sat upon the Clerical Subscription Commission in 1865, and upon the Ritual Commission in 1869. He was a member of the New-Testament Company of the Bible-revision Committee; and the thanksgiving service of the company was held in his church, Nov. 11, 1880. He is the author of *A Commentary on Acts*, London, 1847, 2d ed. 1854; *The Doctrine of a Future State* (Hulsean Lecture for 1849), 1850; *The Early Progress of the Gospel* (Hulsean Lecture for 1851), 1851; *An Historical and Explanatory Treatise on the Book of Common Prayer*, 1853, 5th ed. 1874; *The Miracles* (Boyle Lectures for 1857), 1858; *The Character of St. Paul* (Boyle Lectures for 1858), 1859; *A Commentary on the Revised Version of the N.T., for English Readers*, 1882; edited *Theophilus of Antioch*, 1852, and *Theophylact on St. Matthew*, 1854; one of the authors of *A Revised Version of St. John's Gospel and the Epistles to the Romans and Corinthians*, 1857–58. Died Jan. 10, 1885. *

HUNT, Albert Sandford, D.D. (Wesleyan University, Middletown, Conn., 1873), Methodist; b. at Amenia, N.Y., July 3, 1827; graduated at Wesleyan University, Middletown, Conn., 1851; was tutor (1851–53) and adjunct professor of moral science there (1853–55); joined the New-York Conference of the Methodist-Episcopal Church, 1859; was pastor in Brooklyn, N.Y., 1859–78; since, has been corresponding secretary of the American Bible Society, New-York City. In 1874 he was chairman of fraternal delegation from General Conference of the Methodist-Episcopal Church, to General Conference of Methodist-Episcopal Church South; in 1886, fraternal delegate from the General Conference of the Methodist-Episcopal Church to British Wesleyan Conference. He has published several occasional sermons.

HUNT, John, D.D. (University of St. Andrew's, Scotland, 1878), Church of England; b. at Bridgend, parish of Kinnoul, Perth, Scotland, Jan. 21, 1827; matriculated at St. Andrew's. 1847; was ordained deacon 1855, and priest 1857; was curate of Deptford, Sunderland, Eng., 1855–59; and in churches in and about London until 1877, when, on nomination of Dean Stanley, he was appointed vicar of Otford, in Kent. In theology he is "liberal." He was on the staff of *The Contemporary Review*, 1867–77, and has been contributor to other periodicals. He is the author of *Poems from the German*, London, 1852; *Luther's Spiritual Songs translated*, 1853; *Essay on Pantheism*, 1866; *Religious Thought in England*, 1870–73, 3 vols.; *Contemporary Essays in Theology*, 1873; *Pantheism and Christianity*, 1884 (the *Essay on Pantheism* revised, and the argument brought to a more definite issue).

HUNT, Sandford, D.D. (Alleghany College, Meadville, Penn., 1871), Methodist; b. in Erie County, N.Y., April 1, 1825; graduated at Alleghany College, Meadville, Penn., 1847; became pastor in Genesee Conference, presiding elder, and since 1879 has been agent of the Methodist Book Concern. He is the author of *Handbook for Trustees of Religious Corporations in the State of New York*, New York, 1872, 2d ed. 1873; *Laws relating to Religious Corporations in the United States*, 1876, revised ed. 1882.

HUNTINGTON, Right Rev. Frederic Dan, S.T.D. (Amherst College, Amherst, Mass., 1855), Episcopalian; b. at Hadley, Mass., May 28, 1819; graduated as valedictorian from Amherst College, Mass., 1839, and at the divinity school of Harvard University, 1842; was Unitarian minister in Boston until 1855; professor of Christian morals and preacher to Harvard University until 1860; was chaplain and preacher to the Massachusetts State Legislature; was ordered deacon in the Episcopal Church, Sept. 12, 1860; ordained priest, March 19, 1861; and was rector in Boston of Emmanuel Church, which he organized, until he was consecrated bishop of Central New York, April 8, 1869. He was editor of *The Church Monthly*, Boston, 1861 sqq., and of *The Christian Register* and *The Monthly Religious Magazine*, both Boston. He is the author of *Lessons on the Parables of our Saviour*, Boston, 1856; *Sermons for the People*, Boston, 1856, 11th ed. New York, 1879; *Christian Believing and Living* (sermons), 1860, 7th ed. New York, 1867; *Elim* (a collection of ancient and modern sacred poems), Boston, 1865; *Divine Aspects of Human Society* (Lowell and Graham Lectures), N.Y., 1860; *Helps to a Holy Lent*, 1872; *New Helps to a Holy Lent*, 1876; *Christ in the Christian Year, and in the Life of Man*, 1878; *The Fitness of Christianity to Man* (Bohlen Lectures for 1878), 1878; *Sermons on the Christian Year*, 1881, 2 vols.; numerous articles in periodicals, minor works, etc.

HUNTINGTON, William Reed, D.D. (Columbia College, New-York City, 1873), Episcopalian; b. at Lowell, Mass., Sept. 20, 1838; graduated at Harvard College, Cambridge, Mass., 1859; instructor there in chemistry, 1859–60; assistant at Emmanuel Church, Boston, 1861–62; rector of All Saints', Worcester, Mass., 1862–83; since 1884 rector of Grace Church, New York. He was the class poet (1859) and Φ.B.K. poet at Harvard (1870); and secretary of the joint committee of the General Convention of the Episcopal Church, on the enrichment and better adaptation to American needs of the Book of Common Prayer. Besides various Sunday-school text-books and manuals, he has published *The Church Idea: an Essay towards Unity*, New York, 1870, 3d ed. 1884; *Conditional Immortality*, 1876.

HURST, John Fletcher, D.D., LL.D. (both from Dickinson College, Carlisle, Penn., 1866 and 1877 respectively), Methodist; b. at Salem, Md., Aug. 17, 1834; graduated at Dickinson College, Carlisle, Penn., 1854; taught ancient languages in New York, 1854–56; then studied theology at Halle and Heidelberg, 1856–57; was a Methodist pastor in New Jersey and on Staten Island, N.Y., 1858–66; professor of theology in the Mission Institute of the Methodist-Episcopal Church (for the training of ministers for the German Methodist Church) at Bremen, 1866–69; institute removed to Frankfort-on-the-Main, and re-endowed as the Martin Mission Institute; was professor there, 1869–71; professor of historical theology in Drew Theological Seminary, Madison, N.Y., 1871–80, and president from 1873; elected a bishop of the Methodist-Episcopal Church, 1880. Besides translations of Hagenbach's *History of the Church in the 18th and 19th Centuries* (New York, 1869, 2 vols.), Van Oosterzee's *Apologetical Lectures on John's Gospel* (Edinburgh, 1869), and of Lange's *Commentary on Romans* (New York, 1870), he has written *Why Americans love Shakespeare*, Catskill, N.Y., 1855; *History of Rationalism*, New York, 1866, London, 1867; *Martyrs to the Tract Cause*, New York, 1872; *Outlines of Bible History*, 1873; *Outlines of Church History*, 1874, 3d ed. 1880; *Life and Literature in the Fatherland*, 1876; *Our Theological Century*, 1877; *Bibliotheca theologica* (a bibliography of theology), 1883; *Short History of the Reformation*, 1884; (jointly with Prof. Dr. G. R. Crooks) an adaptation of Hagenbach's *Theological Encyclopædia and Methodology*, 1884, as part of *The Library of Theological and Biblical Literature* begun in 1879.

HURTER, Hugo, Ph.D. (Rome, 1851), **D.D.** (do., 1855), Roman Catholic; b. at Schaffhausen, Switzerland, Jan. 11, 1832; studied in Rome, partly in the Propaganda and partly in the German College; and since 1858 has been professor of dogmatic theology in the University of Innsbruck. On Oct. 30, 1845, entered the Roman-Catholic Church, and on June 15, 1857, the Jesuit Order. He is the author of *Ueber die Rechte der Vernunft und des Glaubens*, Innsbruck, 1863; *Opuscula selecta SS. Patrum ad usum præsertim studiosorum theologiæ*, 1868–85, 48 vols., 2d series 1884 sqq.; *Leonardi Lessii S. J. de summo bono et æterna beatitudine hominis, libri 4*, newly edited, Freiburg-im-Br., 1869; *Nomenclator literarius recentioris theologiæ catholicæ*, Innsbruck, 1871–86; *D. Thomas Aq. sermones*, newly edited, 1874; *Theologiæ dogmaticæ compendium*, 1876, 3 vols. 5th ed. 1885; *Medulla theologiæ dogmaticæ*, 1880, 2d ed. 1885.

HYACINTHE, Father (whose full name is *Charles Jean Marie Augustin Hyacinthe Loyson*); b. at Orleans, France, March 10, 1827, and educated privately under care of his father, who was rector of the University of France, attached to the Academy of Pau. After taking his degree of B.A. he entered (1845) the Seminary of St. Sulpice, Paris, and there studied philosophy and theology under the first masters of religious science. He was ordained a priest at Notre Dame de Paris, June 14, 1851, and for the next five years was a professor, first of philosophy at the Grand Seminary of Avignon (1851–54), then of dogmatic theology at the Seminary of Nantes (1854–56). In 1856–57 he was curate of St. Sulpice, Paris, being member of the company of the priests of St. Sulpice, and was made honorary canon of Troy. In 1858 he decided upon a monastic life, and made a six-months' novitiate in the Dominican Order (as reformed by Lacordaire); but preferring a more austere order, on April 22, 1862, he entered that of the Barefooted Carmelites (as reformed by St. Theresa and St. John of the Cross in the sixteenth century); rose to be superior of his order in Paris and second definator of the province of Avignon, and remained in it until September, 1869. From 1864 to 1869 he was metropolitan preacher of Notre Dame de Paris; but refused to be court preacher under Napoleon III., and also to be archbishop of Lyons, always maintaining that his vocation of preacher was preferable to all social or ecclesiastical "preferment." He has preached in the large cities of France (sometimes under great difficulties), England, Holland, Belgium, Germany, Switzerland, Italy, and the United States. On Sept. 20, 1869, he published a manifesto against the usurpations of Rome, protesting against the lack of œcumenity in the convocation of the Vatican Council. At the same time he quitted his convent; and then, to avoid importunity, he went to America for a few months, awaiting the deliberations of the council. When the decree of infallibility was pronounced (July 18, 1870), he found it was impossible for him longer to submit to Rome; and since then he has devoted himself to preaching Catholic reform (the Bible to be read by all, vernacular worship, the cup to be given to the laity, liberty of marriage for priests, freedom of confession), and as far as possible carrying it out in practice. On Sept. 3, 1872, he married in London, Mrs. Emilie Jane (Butterfield) Meriman of New York, N.Y., U.S.A., who had been previously engaged in Catholic reform in Rome. In 1873 he began reformed public worship in Geneva, Switzerland, whither he was called by the disaffected Roman Catholics, who elected him their vicar. There he remained five years, but separated himself from the Old Catholics there, because of their too radical tendencies in politics and religion. In 1877 and 1878 he gave a series of conferences in the Cirque d'Hiver in Paris, on the necessity of religious reform in Catholic countries, which was a political event feared by the French Republic. In 1879 he returned to live in Paris, and opened a free church, known as the Catholic Gallican Church, with the episcopal aid of Bishop Herzog of Bern of the Old Catholic Church, and the bishops of the Anglican Church, with which churches his own is in communion. His church was legalized in December, 1883, by a decree of the French Government, signed by President Grévy. It has therefore the right to exist; but it is free, and unsubsidized by the government. In July, 1885, it numbered over a thousand members and six clergy.

In philosophy M. Loyson is a disciple of Plato, Descartes, Malebranche, and Leibnitz. An assiduous investigator of the Holy Scriptures from earliest childhood, his theology is that of the Bible and of the Fathers. Always a devoted, liberal, and evangelical Catholic, he accepts the Primacy of the early Church, but rejects the Papacy. He holds to the faith of the undivided church, i.e., the Episcopate, as expressed in the Nicene Creed, which he believes to be the broad yet firm basis of all social and scientific progress, as well as the adaptation of all spiritual truth; and his aim is the unity (not uniformity) of all Christians.

Among his numerous publications are the following: *Poëmes*, Pau, 1841-45; *La société civile dans ses rapports avec le Christianisme* (*Conférences de Notre Dame*), *Paris*, 1867, 5th ed. ——; *La famille* (*Conférences de Notre Dame*), 1867, 2d ed. ——; *Education des classes ouvrières*, 1867; *Profession de la foi Catholique d'une protestante convertie*, 1868; *De la Réforme Catholique: lettres, fragments, discours*, 1869–72, 2d ed (English trans., *Catholic reform: Letters, Fragments, etc.*, by Madame Loyson, introd. by Dean Stanley, London, 1874); *L'Eglise Catholique en Suisse*, Geneva, 1875; *Réforme Catholique, II. Catholicisme et Protestantisme*, Paris, 1873; *L'Ultramontanisme et la Révolution*, 1873; *Trois conférences au Cirque d'Hiver* (April 15, 22, and 29, 1877), 1877; *Les principes de la Réforme Catholique* (*Conférences au Cirque d'Hiver*, 1878), 1878 (English trans., London, 1879); *Programme de la Réforme Catholique*, 1879; *Liturgie Gallicane*, 1879, 5th ed. 1883; *L'Inquisition*, 1882. In 1880 Madame Hyacinthe Loyson translated into French, and he published, Döllinger's *Réunion des Eglises*. His son, Paul Emmanuel Hyacinthe Loyson, was born at Geneva, Oct. 19, 1873.

HYDE, James Thomas, D.D. (Yale, New Haven, Conn., and Beloit College, Mich., 1870), Congregationalist; b. at Norwich, Conn., Jan. 28, 1827; graduated at Yale College, New Haven, Conn., 1847, and at Yale Divinity School 1850; tutor in Yale College, 1849-52; became colleague of Rev. Dr. John Fiske at New Braintree, Mass., 1853; acting pastor of North Church (Rev. Dr. Horace Bushnell's), Hartford, Conn., 1855; pastor at Middlebury, Vt., 1857; inaugurated Iowa professor of pastoral theology and special studies in the Chicago (Congregational) Theological Seminary, Ill., 1870; transferred to the chair of New-Testament literature and interpretation, 1879. He is the author of *New-Testament Introduction*, Chicago, 1881; *A New Catechism, or Manual of Instruction for Students and other Thoughtful Inquirers*, 1884.

J.

JACKSON, George Anson, Congregationalist; b. at North Adams, Mass., March 17, 1846; graduated from Yale (New Haven, Conn.) scientific department Ph.B. 1868, and from Andover (Mass.) Theological Seminary 1871; was pastor at Leavenworth, Kan., from 1871 to 73; Southbridge, Mass., 1874-78; since at Swampscott, Mass. He is the author of *The Christian Faith: a Manual for Catechumens*, Boston, 1875; *The Apostolic Fathers*, New York, 1879; *The Fathers of the Third Century*, 1881; *The Post-Nicene Greek Fathers*, 1883; *The Post-Nicene Latin Fathers*, 1883 (these volumes were revised for London reprint and Gotha German translation in 1884, when *The Teaching of the Apostles* was embodied in *The Apostolic Fathers*).

JACKSON, Right Rev. and Right Hon. John, D.D. (Oxford, 1853), lord bishop of London; b. in London, Feb. 22, 1811; d. there Jan. 6, 1885. He was educated at Pembroke College, Oxford; graduated B.A. (first-class classics) 1833, M.A. 1836, B.D. 1853; was Ellerton theological prize essayist, 1834; ordained deacon 1835, priest 1836; was head master of the proprietary school at Islington, 1836-46; select preacher to the University of Oxford, 1845, 1850, 1862, 1866; Boyle lecturer in London, 1853; rector of St. James, Westminster, London, 1846-53; bishop of Lincoln, 1853-69; translated to London, 1869. He was one of her Majesty's Most Honorable Privy Council; dean of her Majesty's Chapels Royal; provincial dean of Canterbury; official trustee of the British Museum; official governor of King's College, London; visitor of Harrow and Highgate schools, and of Balliol College; a governor of the Charterhouse. He was the author of *The Leading Points of the Christian Character* (six sermons), London, 1844; *Sanctifying Grace, and the Grace of the Ministry*, 1847; *The Day of Prayer and the Day of Thanksgiving* (two sermons), 1849; *The Sinfulness of Little Sins*, 1849, 20th ed. 1875; *Rome and her Claims* (a sermon), 1850; *The Spirit of the World, and the Spirit which is of God*, 1850; *Repentance, its Necessity, Nature, and Aids* (a course of Lent sermons), 1851, 9th ed. 1866; *An Address to the Newly Confirmed, preparatory to the Holy Communion*, 1852; *Sunday a Day of Rest or a Day of Work* (a few words to workingmen), 1853; *War, its Evils and Duties* (a sermon), 1854; *The Witness of the Spirit*, 1854, 3d ed. 1870; *God's Word and Man's Heart*, 1864 (the latter two volumes consist of sermons preached before the University of Oxford); *The Parochial System* (a charge), 1871; *Five Years in the Diocese of London*, 1884; commentary on *Timothy* and *Titus* in *Bible (Speaker's) Commentary*, 1881. *

JACKSON, Lewis Evens, Presbyterian layman; b. on Staten Island, Richmond County, N.Y., Aug. 31, 1822; educated in the common schools of New-York City; has been identified with Christian and charitable work in the city since 1846, having been first a city missionary, and since 1863 corresponding secretary and treasurer of the New-York City Missionary and Tract Society. He is the author of *Gospel Work, a Semi-centennial of City Missions*, New York, 1878; and of *Christian Work in New York: being the Annual Report of the New-York City Missionary and Tract Society, with Brief Notices of the Operations of other Societies, Church Directory, List of Benevolent Societies, and Statistics of Population, etc.* (since 1863).

JACKSON, Samuel Macauley, Presbyterian; b. in New-York City, June 19, 1851; graduated at the College of the City of New York, 1870, and at Union Theological Seminary, in the same city, 1873; studied and travelled, 1873-76; pastor at Norwood, N.J., 1876-80; since in literary work; contributor to Schaff's *Bible Dictionary*, 1878-80; associate editor of the *Schaff-Herzog Encyclopædia*, 1880-84.

JACKSON, Sheldon, D.D. (Hanover College, Hanover, Ind., 1874), Presbyterian; b. at Minaville, N.Y., May 18, 1834; graduated at Union College, Schenectady, N.Y., 1855, and at Princeton (N.J.) Theological Seminary, 1858; became missionary to the Choctaws, Indian Territory; home missionary for Western Wisconsin and Southern Minnesota, with headquarters at Crescent, Minn., 1859; pastor at Rochester, Minn., with oversight of mission-work in Southern Minnesota, 1864; superintendent of missions for Northern and Western Iowa, Dakota, Nebraska, and other Western territories, 1869; superintendent of missions for the Rocky-Mountain territories, 1870 (the first under commission of the presbyteries of Fort Dodge, Des Moines, and Council Bluffs, the second under that of the Board of Home Missions); business manager of *The Presbyterian Home Missionary*, New-York City, 1882 (which had grown out of *The Rocky-Mountain Presbyterian*, which he established at Denver, 1872). In 1879 and 1880 he brought Indian children from New Mexico and Arizona to the Indian training-schools at Carlisle, Penn., and Hampton, Va., under commission of the U. S. Government. He organized the first Presbyterian churches and missions in Wyoming, Montana, Idaho, Utah, Arizona, and Alaska.

JACOB, George Andrew, D.D. (Oxford, 1852), Church of England; b. at Exmouth, Dec. 16, 1807; was scholar of Worcester College, Oxford; graduated B.A. (first-class classics) 1829, M.A. 1832, B.D. 1852; was tutor of his college; ordained deacon 1831, priest 1832; head master of King Edward's Grammar School, Bromsgrove, 1832-43; principal of Sheffield College School, 1843-53; head master of Christ's Hospital [School], London, 1853-68, when he resigned. He is the author of (besides Greek and Latin grammars for schools) *A Letter to Sir Robert Peel on National Education*, London, 1839; *Tirocinium Gallicum*, 1849; *Four Sermons before the University of Oxford*, 1858; *The Ecclesiastical Polity of the New Testament, a Study for the Present Crisis of the Church of England*, 1871, 3d ed. 1884, reprinted, New York, 1872, 4th ed. 1874; *Reply on Eucharistic Doctrine* *of Romanists and Ritualists*, 1874; *Sabbath made for Man*, 1880; *The Lord's Supper historically considered*, 1884.

JACOBI, Justus Ludwig, Lic. Theol., D.D. (Berlin, 1841 and 1851), United Evangelical; b. at Burg, near Magdeburg, Aug. 12, 1815; studied in Halle and Berlin, in the latter university became *privat-docent*, 1841; professor extraordinary, 1847; ordinary professor of theology at Königsberg, 1851; at Halle, 1855. He is the author of *Die Lehre des Pelagius*, Berlin, 1842; *Die kirchliche Lehre von der Tradition u. heiligen Schrift in ihr. Entwickelung dargestellt*, Berlin, 1. Abth., 1847; *Lehrbuch der Kirchengeschichte*, 1. Theil, 1850; *Die Lehre der Irvingiten verglichen mit der heiligen Schrift*, 1853, 2d ed. 1868; *Erinnerung. an D. Aug. Neander*, Halle, 1882; do. *an Baron von Kottwitz*, 1882.

JACOBS, Henry Eyster, D.D. (Thiel College, Carthage, Ill., 1877), Lutheran; b. at Gettysburg, Penn., Nov. 10, 1844; graduated at Pennsylvania College, Gettysburg, Penn., 1862, and at the Gettysburg Theological Seminary, 1865; was tutor in Pennsylvania College, 1864–67; home missionary at Pittsburg, Penn., 1867–68; pastor and principal of Thiel Hall, Phillipsburg, Penn. (now Thiel College, Greenville, Penn.), 1868–70; professor in Pennsylvania College, of Latin 1870–80, of Latin and Greek 1880–81, of Greek 1881–83; and since 1883 has been professor of systematic theology in the Evangelical Lutheran Seminary, Philadelphia, Penn. He has published many articles and the following books: *Hutter's Compend of Lutheran Theology* (trans. with Rev. G. F. Spieker), Philadelphia, 1867, 4th ed. 1882; *Schmid's Doctrinal Theology of the Evangelical Lutheran Church* (trans. with Rev. Dr. C. A. Hay), 1875; *Proceedings of the First Lutheran Diet* (edited), 1878; *The Book of Concord, or the Symbolical Books of the Evangelical Lutheran Church* (trans. with notes), vol. 1, 1882, vol. 2, historical introduction, appendices, and indexes, 1883; Meyer's *Commentary on Galatians and Ephesians* (American ed., with translation of references and supplementary notes), New York, 1884. Since 1883 has been editor of *Lutheran Church Review*.

JACOBSON, Right Rev. William, D.D. (by Convocation of Canterbury, 1848), lord bishop of Chester, Church of England; b. at Great Yarmouth, Norfolk, in the year 1803; d. at Chester, July 13, 1884. He was educated at the Dissenting College, Homerton, Middlesex, and afterwards at Lincoln College, Oxford; graduated B.A. (second-class classics) 1827, M.A. 1829; won Ellerton theological prize for essay: "*What were the Causes of the Persecution to which the Christians were subject in the First Centuries of Christianity?*" elected fellow of Exeter College, 1829; was curate of St. Mary Magdalen, Oxford, 1830–32; perpetual curate of Iffley, 1839–40; vice-principal of Magdalen Hall, Oxford, 1832–48; public orator of the university, 1842–48; regius professor of divinity, canon of Christ Church, and rector of Ewelme, Oxford, 1848–65; bishop of Chester, 1865 till his death. He was select preacher to the university, 1833, 1842, and 1869; elected honorary fellow of Hertford College, Oxford, 1874. He was on the Royal Commission of 1864, to consider the terms of clerical subscription. He edited Dean Rowell's *Catechismus, sive prima institutio disciplinaque pietatis Christianæ, Latine explicata*, Oxford, 1835, 2d ed. 1844; *Patres Apostolici* (Clemens Romanus, Ignatius, Polycarp, martyrdoms of Ignatius and Polycarp), 1838, 2 vols., 4th ed. 1863; *The Oxford Paraphrase and Annotations upon all the Epistles of St. Paul*, 1852; *The Collected Works of Bishop Sanderson*, 1854, 6 vols.; *Fragmentary Illustrations of the History of the Book of Common Prayer, from MS. Sources* (Bishops Sanderson and Wren), 1874; was the author of *Sermons preached in the Parish Church of Iffley, Oxon.*, 1840, 2d ed. 1846; *On the Athanasian Creed* (a speech in the Convocation of York), 1872; the commentary on the *Acts* in *The Bible (Speaker's) Commentary*, London and New York, 1880; and a number of charges and single sermons. *

JACOBY, Carl Johannes Hermann, D.D. (*hon.*, Halle, 1873), German Protestant theologian; b. in Berlin, Dec. 30, 1836; studied at Berlin 1854–57, and in the *Königl. Prediger-Seminar* at Wittenberg 1858–59; was gymnasial teacher at Landsberg-a.-W. 1859–63, and at Stendal 1863–64; *diakonus* in Schloss Heldrungen, 1866–68; became ordinary professor of practical theology at Königsberg, 1868; and since 1871 has also been university preacher. He holds to the "*Vermittelnde Theologie, wie sie in der evangel. Vereinigung vertreten ist.*" He is the author of *Zwei evangelische Lebensbilder aus der katholischen Kirche* (Princess Galitzin and Bishop Sailer), Bielefield, 1864; *Beiträge zu christlicher Erkenntniss* (sermons), Gütersloh, 1870; *Liturgik der Reformatoren*, Gotha, 1871–76, 2 vols.; *Staatskirche, Freikirche, Landeskirche*, Leipzig, 1875; *Die Gestalt des evangelischen Hauptgottesdienst*, Gotha, 1879; *Allgemeine Pädagogik auf Grund der christlichen Ethik*, 1883; *Christliche Tugenden* (sermons), 1883.

JAEGER, Abraham, D.D. (University of the South, Sewanee, Tenn., 1880), Episcopalian; b. at Stanislaw, Austria, March 25, 1839; educated at rabbinical schools, and was rabbi at Selma and Mobile, Ala., 1870–72. In the spring of 1872 he was converted from Judaism, and in May joined the Baptist Church, and studied Christian theology in the Southern Baptist Seminary, Greenville, S.C. (now at Louisville, Ky.), and was there honorary professor 1875–76. In 1877 he joined the Episcopal Church; was ordered deacon, 1878; and ordained priest, 1880. From 1878 to 1880 he was professor in the University of the South, Sewanee, Tenn.; and since has been professor in the theological seminary of the Protestant-Episcopal diocese of Ohio, at Gambier. He is the author of *Mind and Heart in Religion, or Judaism and Christianity*, Chicago, 1873; *Infant Baptism versus Converted Membership* (announced); *Modern Conception of the Development of the Religion of Israel* (in preparation).

JAGGAR, Right Rev. Thomas Augustus, D.D. (University of Pennsylvania, Philadelphia, 1874), Episcopalian, bishop of Southern Ohio; b. in New-York City, June 2, 1839; studied at General Theological Seminary in New-York City, 1859; became rector of Anthon Memorial (now All Souls') Church, New-York City, 1864; St. John's, Yonkers, 1868; Holy Trinity, Philadelphia, 1870; bishop, 1875. He is the author of occasional sermons, addresses, etc. *

JAMES, Fleming, D.D. (Protestant-Episcopal Seminary of Ohio, Gambier, 1876); b. at Richmond, Va., Dec. 7, 1835; graduated M.A. at University of Virginia at Charlottesville, 1856, and at General Theological Seminary, New-York City, 1868; was assistant minister in New-York City, and Baltimore, Md., 1868–70; rector of St. Mark's, Baltimore, 1870–75, and of Calvary, Louisville, Ky., 1875–76; and since 1876 has been professor in the theological seminary of the Protestant-Episcopal diocese of Ohio, and pastor of Harcourt parish, both at Gambier.

JANSSEN, Johannes, Ph.D. (Bonn, 1853), **D.D.** (*hon.*, Würzburg, 1882, Louvain, 1884), Roman Catholic; b. at Xanten, Germany, April 10, 1829; studied at the universities of Louvain, Belgium (1850–51), and Bonn, Germany (1851–53); became *privat-docent* in the academy at Münster, 1854; the same year, professor of history in the gymnasium at Frankfurt-am-Main, and so remains. He is now papal domestic prelate, apostolical protonotar, and archiepiscopal ecclesiastical councillor of Freiburg. His literary work has been often interrupted by illness. He is the author of *Wibald von Stablo und Corvey*, Münster, 1854; vol. 3 of *Geschichtsquellen des Bisthums Münster*, 1856; *Frankreichs Rheingelüste*, Frankfurt, 1861, 2d ed. Freiburg, 1883; *Frankfurts Reichscorrespondenz von 1476 bis 1519*, Freiburg, 1863–66, 2 vols.; *Schiller als Historiker*, 1863, 2d ed. 1879; *Joh. Friedr. Böhmer's Leben, Briefe und kleine Schriften*, 1868, 3 vols.; *Zur Genesis der ersten Theilung Polens*, 1869; *Zeit- und Lebensbilder*, 1875, 3d ed. 1879; *Friedrich Leopold Graf zu Stolberg*, 1875–76, 2 vols. (in 1 vol. 1882, 3d ed. 1883); *Geschichte des deutschen Volkes seit dem Ausgang des Mittelalters*, 1876, sqq., vols. i.-iv. (12th ed. of the first 4 vols. 1884–85, 13th ed. vol. ii. 1885). In defence of his history, which has been vigorously attacked by Protestant scholars, he has published *An meine Kritiker, Nebst Ergänzungen und Erläuterungen zu den 3 ersten Bänd. meiner Geschichte*, 1882, 16th thousand 1884; *Ein zweites Wort an meine Kritiker*, 1883, 16th thousand 1884.

JEBB, John, D.D. (Trinity College, Dublin, 1860), Episcopal Church in Ireland; b. in Dublin, Ireland, in the year 1805; d. at Peterstow, Eng., January, 1886; graduated at Trinity College, Dublin, B.A. 1827, M.A. 1829, B.D. 1860; ordained deacon 1828, priest 1829; was rector of Dunurlin, Ireland, 1831–32; prebendary of Donoughmore in Limerick Cathedral, 1832–43; proctor of the diocese of Hereford, Eng., 1857–80; *prælector* of Hereford Cathedral, 1863–70. Since 1843 he was the rector of Peterstow; since 1858, prebendary of Preston Wynne; since 1870, canon residentiary; since 1878, chancellor of the choir of Hereford Cathedral. He was one of the revisers of the Old Testament, and the author of *Three Lectures on the Cathedral Service*, London, 1841; *The Choral Service of the United Church of England and Ireland*, 1843; *A Literal Translation of the Book of Psalms, with Dissertations*, 1846, 2 vols.; *The Choral Responses and Litanies of the United Churches of England and Ireland*, 1847–57, 2 vols.; *The Principle of Ritualism defended*, 1856; *The Ritual Law and Custom of the Church Universal*, 1866; *The Rights of the Irish Branch of the United Church of England and Ireland considered*, 1868. *

JEFFERS, Eliakim Tupper, D.D. (Washington and Jefferson College, Washington, Penn., 1872), Presbyterian; b. at Stewiacke, N.S., April 6, 1841; graduated at Jefferson College, Canonsburg, Penn., 1862, and at Princeton (N.J.) Theological Seminary, 1865; became pastor of the United-Presbyterian Church, Oxford, Penn., 1865; president of Westminster College, Penn., 1872; professor of theology in Lincoln University, Oxford, Penn., 1883. He was moderator of the United-Presbyterian Church, 1880.

JEFFERS, William Hamilton, D.D. (Western Reserve College, Hudson, O., 1874), **LL.D.** (University of Wooster, Wooster, O., 1879), Presbyterian; b. near Cadiz, O., May 1, 1838; graduated at Geneva College, Northwood, Penn. (now Beaver Falls, O.), 1855; and at Xenia (United-Presbyterian) Theological Seminary, O., 1859. From 1862 to 1866 he was pastor of the United-Presbyterian united churches of Bellefontaine and Northwood, O.; in 1866 became professor of Latin and Hebrew in Westminster College, New Wilmington, Penn.; in 1869, professor of Greek in the University of Wooster, O.; in 1875, pastor of the Euclid-avenue Presbyterian Church, Cleveland, O.; and since 1877 has been professor of Old-Testament literature and exegesis in the Western (Presbyterian) Theological Seminary, Allegheny, Penn. While pastor at Bellefontaine, he was put on the committee to revise the United-Presbyterian metrical version of the Psalms.

JENNINGS, Arthur Charles, Church of England; b. in London, Dec. 19, 1847; educated at Eton and Radley; entered Jesus College, Cambridge; took the Carus prize in 1869; graduated B.A. 1872; Carus Bachelor's prizeman, and Jeremie Septuagint prizeman, and Crosse scholar, 1872; took a first-class in the theological tripos, the university Hebrew prize, Evan's prize, and Scholefield's prize; was Tyrwhitt's scholar and Fry's scholar (St. John's), 1873; M.A. 1875. He was ordained deacon 1873, priest 1874; was curate of St. Edward, Cambridge, 1873–74; became vicar of Whittlesford, near Cambridge, 1877. He is broad on doctrinal points; inclined to the view that the English Church may retain her position, if she accommodates herself to the modern views on such points as the inspiration of the Scriptures, doctrinal development, etc. He advocates a limitization of episcopal authority by the revival of a truly representative Convocation. He is a moderate High Churchman in his view of public worship, but desires a revision of the Prayer Book. He is the author of *Commentary on the Psalms* (jointly with W. H. Lowe), published in parts, London, 1875–77, 2 vols., 2d ed. 1884; *Ecclesia Anglicana, A History of the Church of Christ in England, from the Earliest to the Present Times*, 1882; *Synopsis of Ancient Chronology*, 1886. He contributed the comments on *Nahum*, *Haggai*, *Habakkuk*, and *Zephaniah*, in Ellicott's *Old-Testament Commentary* (vol. v., 1884).

JERMYN, Right Rev. Hugh Willoughby, D.D. (Cambridge, 1871), lord bishop of Brechin, Episcopal Church of Scotland; b. about the year 1820; educated at Trinity Hall, Cambridge; graduated B.A. 1841, M.A. 1847; was ordained deacon 1843, priest 1845; archdeacon of St. Christopher's, West Indies, 1854–58; rector of Nettlecombe, near Taunton, 1858–70; vicar of Barking, Essex, 1870–71; lord bishop of Colombo, 1871–75; elected to Brechin, 1875. *

JESSUP, Henry Harris, D.D. (University of New-York City, and College of New Jersey, Princeton, 1865), Presbyterian; b. at Montrose, Penn., April 19, 1832; graduated at Yale College, New Haven, Conn., 1851, and Union Theological Seminary, New-York City, 1855. In 1856 he went as a missionary to Tripoli, Syria, and there remained until 1860, when he removed to Beirut, which has ever since been the centre of his operations. He has several times made brief home visits, and during one of these in 1879 was elected moderator of the General Assembly at Saratoga, N.Y. He is the author of *The Mohammedan Missionary Problem*, Philadelphia, 1879.

JOHNSON, Elias Henry, D.D. (University of Rochester, N.Y., 1878), Baptist; b. at Troy, N.Y., Oct. 15, 1841; graduated at the University of Rochester, N.Y., 1862, and at the Rochester Theological Seminary, 1871; was pastor at Le Sueur, Minn., 1866–68; Ballston Spa, N.Y., 1873–75; and at Providence, R.I., 1875–82; in 1882 became professor of systematic theology in Crozer Theological Seminary, Chester, Penn. He published (jointly with W. H. Doane, Mus. D.) *Baptist Hymnal*, Philadelphia, 1883; (alone) *Songs of Praise for Sunday Schools*, 1882; *Select Sunday-school Songs*, 1885; articles in reviews and other periodicals.

JOHNSON, Herrick, D.D. (Western Reserve College, Hudson, O., 1867), **LL.D.** (Wooster University, Wooster, O., 1880), Presbyterian; b. near Fonda, Montgomery County, N.Y., Sept. 21, 1832; graduated from Hamilton College, Clinton, N.Y., 1857, and from Auburn (N.Y.) Theological Seminary, 1860. He was colleague pastor of the First Church, Troy, N.Y., 1860–62; pastor of the Third Church, Pittsburg, Penn., 1862–68; and of the First Church, Philadelphia, Penn., 1868–74. In 1874 he went to Auburn as professor of homiletics and pastoral theology; in 1880 he removed to Chicago, where he is pastor of the Fourth Church, and professor of sacred rhetoric in the Theological Seminary of the North-west. He was moderator of the General Assembly at Springfield, Ill., 1882. He is president of the Presbyterian Church Board of Aid for Colleges and Academies, and of the board of trustees of Lake Forest University, Ill. He was chairman of the committee on higher education, which reported to the General Assembly of 1883 a plan for the organization of the former. The report was unanimously adopted. Besides many sermons, articles, etc., he has published *Christianity's Challenge*, Chicago, Ill., 1882, 4th ed. 1884; *Plain Talks about the Theater*, 1883; *Revivals, their Place and Power*, 1883.

JOHNSON, William Allen, Episcopalian; b. at Hyde Park, Dutchess County, N.Y., Aug. 4, 1833; graduated at Columbia College, New-York City, 1853, and at the General Theological Seminary, New-York City, 1857. He was successively rector at Bainbridge, N.Y., 1857–62; missionary in Upper Michigan, 1862–64; rector at Burlington, N.J., 1864–70, and at Salisbury, Conn., 1871–82. On Jan. 1, 1883, he went to his present position, the professorship of Christian evidences and homiletics in the Berkeley Divinity School, Middletown, Conn.

JONES, Samuel P, the "Mountain Evangelist," Methodist Church South; b. in Chambers County, Ala., Oct. 16, 1847; received a good academic education; entered the legal profession, to which his father belonged, in 1870, and practised law for three years in his native county, with indifferent success, owing to his bad habits. He was, however, converted, joined the Methodist Church, and became a preacher under the sanction of the North Georgia Conference. At first he did not go outside of his State; but in 1881 he went into Alabama, and has since been not only all over the South, but also through the North, and has always labored with remarkable success. He uses the plainest speech, and abounds in witty and pregnant sayings. Some of his sermons have been printed, New York, 1885. *

JONES, Right Rev. William Basil, D.D. (University of Oxford, 1874), lord bishop of St. David's, Church of England; b. at Cheltenham, Gloucestershire, Eng., in the year 1822; was scholar of Trinity College, Oxford, 1840; Ireland scholar, 1842; graduated B.A. (second-class classics) 1844, M.A. (Queen's College) 1847; was ordained deacon 1848, priest 1853; was Michel fellow of Queen's College, Oxford, 1848–51; fellow of University College, 1851–57; master of the schools, 1848; tutor of University College, 1854–65; classical moderator, 1856 and 1860; select preacher at Oxford, 1860–62, 1866–67, 1876–78; at Cambridge, 1881; senior proctor, Oxford, 1861–62; examining chaplain to the archbishop of York, 1861–74; public examiner in theology, 1870; cursal prebendary of St. David's Cathedral, 1859–65; prebendary of Grindal in York Cathedral, 1863–71; perpetual curate of Haxby, Yorkshire, 1863–65; vicar of Bishopthorpe with Middlethorpe, 1865–74; archdeacon of York, 1867–74; rural dean of Bishopthorpe, 1869–74, and of the city of York, 1873–74; chancellor of York Cathedral, and prebendary of Laughton-en-le-Morthen, 1871–74; canon residentiary of York, 1873–74; consecrated bishop, 1874. He is the author of *Vestiges of the Gael in Gwynedd*, London, 1851; *Christ College, Brecon, its History and Capabilities considered with Reference to a Measure now before Parliament*, 1853; *The History and Antiquities of St. David's* (conjointly with E. A. Freeman, LL.D.), 1856; *Notes on the Œdipus Tyrannus of Sophocles, adapted to the Text of Dindorf*, 1862, 2d ed. 1869; *The Clergyman's Office* (a sermon), 1864; *The New Testament illustrated with a Plain Explanatory Commentary for Private Reading* (with Archdeacon Churton), 1865; *Judgment, Mercy, and Faith* (University sermon), 1866; *The Mystery of Iniquity* (University sermons), 1867; *The Peace of God, Sermons on the Reconciliation of God and Man*, 1869, 2d ed. 1885; Commentary on *St. Luke* in *The Bible (Speaker's) Commentary*, 1878; visitation charges; papers in literary and antiquarian journals; contributions to Smith's *Dictionary of the Bible.*

JOSTES, Franz (Ludwig), Ph.D. (Leipzig, 1882), Roman Catholic; b. at Glandorf, Hannover, Germany, July 12, 1858; studied history and German at Freiburg (where he first, however, studied medicine), Berlin, Strassburg, and Leipzig, 1878–82; became *privat-docent* of the German language and literature in the Royal Academy of Münster, in Westphalia, 1884. He is the author of *Johannes Veghe*, Halle, 1882; *Johannes Veghe, ein deutsche Städte-Prediger des 15. Jahrhunderts, Zum ersten Male herausgegeben*, 1883; *Drei unbekannte deutsche Schriften von Johannes Veghe* (in *Histor. Jahrbuch*, 1885, pp. 345–412); *Beiträge zur Kenntniss der* *niederdeutschen Mystik* (in *Germania*, 1885); *Westfälische Predigten* (in *Jahrbuch des Vereins für niederdeutsche Sprachforschung*, 1884); *Schriftsprache und Volksdialecte, Bemerkungen zu einer historischen Grammatik der niederdeutschen Sprache* (in the same, 1885); *Zur Geschichte der mittelalterlichen Predigt in Westfalen* (in *Zeitschrift für vaterländische Geschichte und Alterthumskunde*, Band 44); *Die Waldenser und die vorlutherische Bibelübersetzung, Eine Kritik der neuesten Hypothese*, Münster, 1885; *Die Satiren des (pseudonymen) Daniel von Soest*, 1886 (in the *Deutschen Städtechroniken*, published by the historical commission of the Bavarian Academy of Sciences).

JOWETT, Benjamin, LL.D. (University of Leiden, 1875), Church of England; b. at Camberwell, Eng., in the year 1817; scholar of Balliol College, Oxford, 1835; Hertford university scholar, 1837; graduated B.A. (first-class in classics) 1839, M.A. 1842; was ordained deacon 1842, priest 1845. In 1838 he was elected to a fellowship at Balliol College; was tutor from 1842 to 1870; public examiner in classics, 1849-50, 1853-54; classical moderator, 1859-60. In 1854 he was a member of the commission appointed to arrange the examinations for admission to the East-Indian Civil Service; and in 1855, on the recommendation of Lord Palmerston, he was appointed regius professor of Greek. In 1870 he resigned his fellowship, and took the mastership of Balliol College, which he still holds along with his professorship. In 1875 he became a member of the Hebdomadal Council of the university, and in 1882 was vice-chancellor. He is the author of *St. Paul's Epistles to the Thessalonians, Galatians, and Romans*; *Critical Notes and Dissertations*, London, 1855, 2d ed. 1859; *On the Interpretation of Scripture* (an essay in *Essays and Reviews*), 1860; *The Dialogues of Plato translated into English, with Analyses and Essays*, 1871, 4 vols., 2d ed. 1875, 5 vols.; *Thucydides translated into English, with Introduction, Marginal Analysis, Notes, and Indices*, 1881, 2 vols. (American reprint, preface by Rev. A. P. Peabody, Boston, 1883, 1 vol.); *The Politics of Aristotle* (trans. with notes, etc.), 1885, 2 vols.

JUNGMANN, Joseph, Roman Catholic; b. at Münster, Germany, Nov. 11, 1830; d. at Innsbruck, Nov. 25, 1885. He studied theology there, and in the Collegium Germanicum at Rome, Italy, 1850-56; became priest there, 1855; Jesuit, 1857; ordinary professor of sacred rhetoric and catechetics in the University of Innsbruck, and professor of liturgics in the theological *convict* there. He was the author of *Die Schönheit und ihre schöne Kunst*, Innsbruck, 1866, 2 parts; *Das Gemüth und das Gefühlsvermögen der neueren Psychologie*, 1868, 2d ed. Freiburg-im-Br., 1885; *Theorie der geistlichen Beredsamkeit*, Freiburg-im-Br., 1877-78, 4 parts, 2d ed. 1884; *Die Andacht zum heiligsten Herzen Jesu und die Bedenken gegen dieselbe*, 1885 (pp. 51). *

K.

KAEHLER, (Carl) Martin (August), Lic. Theol. (Halle, 1860), **D.D.** (*hon.*, Halle, 1878), German Protestant theologian; b. at Neuhausen, near Königsberg, East Prussia, Jan. 6, 1835; studied law at Königsberg, 1853–54; theology at Heidelberg 1854–55, Halle 1855–58, Tübingen 1858–59; became *privat-docent* at Halle, 1860; professor extraordinary of theology at Bonn, 1864; at Halle, 1867, and at the same time *Inspector des Schlesischen Convicts;* ordinary professor there 1879. He is the author of *Paulus, der Jünger und Bote Jesu Christi*, Halle, 1862; *Die schriftgemässe Lehre vom Gewissen in ihrer Bedeutung für das christliche Lehren und Leben*, 1864; *Die starken Wurzeln unserer Kraft*, Gotha, 1872; *Bedeutung und Erfolge des kirchlichen Octoberversammlung in Berlin*, Gotha, 1872; *August Tholuck, Ein Lebensabriss*, Halle, 1877; *Das Gewissen, Ethische Untersuchung; 1. geschichtliches Teil, 1. Hälfte, Alterthum u. neues Testament*, 1877; *D. Julius Müller*, 1878; *Der Hebräerbrief in genauer Wiedergabe seines Gedankenganges*, 1880; *Die Wissenschaft der christlichen Lehre, von dem evangel. Grundartikel aus im Abrisse dargestellt*, Erlangen, 1883, *sqq.* (1. Heft, *Einleitung u. Apologetik;* 2. Heft, *Dogmatik*, 1884; 3. Heft follows); *Der Brief des Paulus an die Galater in genauer Wiedergabe seines Gedankenganges durch sich selbst ausgelegt und übersichtlich erörtet*, Halle, 1884.

KAFTAN, Julius Wilhelm Martin, Ph.D. (Leipzig, 1872), **Lic. Theol.** (do., 1873), **D.D.** (*hon.*, Basel, 1883), German Protestant; b. at Loit near Apenrade in Schleswig-Holstein, Sept. 30, 1848; studied at Erlangen, Berlin, and Kiel, 1866–70; became professor extraordinary of theology at Basel, 1873; ordinary professor there, 1881; at Berlin, 1883. He is the author of *Die Predigt des Evangeliums im modernen Geistesleben*, Basel, 1879; *Das Evangelium des Apostels Paulus, in Predigten der Gemeinde dargelegt*, 1879; *Das Wesen der christlichen Religion*, 1881; *Das Leben in Christo: Predigten*, 1883.

KAHNIS, Karl Friedrich August, D.D., Lutheran; b. at Greiz, Dec. 22, 1814; studied in Halle; was *privat-docent* at Berlin in 1842; professor extraordinary at Breslau in 1844; became ordinary professor at Leipzig in 1850; retired in 1886. He was a leader of the "Old Lutherans," but since 1861 has been more liberal. Besides numerous sermons, he has published *Die Lehre vom Heiligen Geiste*, Halle, 1st part 1847; *Die Lehre vom Abendmahle*, Leipzig, 1851; *Der innere Gang des deutschen Protestantismus seit Mitte des vorigen Jahrhunderts*, 1854, 3d ed. 1874, 2 parts (English trans., *Internal History of German Protestantism from the middle of Last Century*, Edinburgh, 1856); *Die lutherische Dogmatik historisch-genetisch dargestellt*, 1861–68, 3 vols., 2d ed. 1874–75, 2 vols.; (with Luthardt and Brückner) *Die Kirche nach ihrem Ursprung, ihrer Geschichte, ihrer Gegenwart*, 1865, 2d ed. 1866 (English trans., *The Church*, Edinburgh, 1867); *Christenthum und Lutherthum*, 1871; *Die deutsche Reformation*, vol. i. 1872; *Der Gang der Kirche in Lebensbildern*, 1881; *Ueber das Verhältniss der alten Philosophie zum Christenthum*, 1884 (pp. 84). *

KALKAR, Christian Andreas Herman, Ph.D. (Kiel, 1833), **D.D.** (Copenhagen, 1836), Lutheran; b. at Stockholm, Nov. 27, 1802; d. at Copenhagen, Feb. 2, 1886. His father was a Jewish rabbi. He went with the family to Cassel, Germany; then in 1812, immediately after his father's death, to Copenhagen, in whose university he studied law; when converted to Christianity he studied theology in the same university. On March 27, 1827, he became adjunct in the cathedral school in Odense; and on Aug. 23 of the same year, head master. In 1842 he visited most of Western Europe; and on March 27, 1843, became pastor in Gladsaxe (six miles from Copenhagen) and Herliv; resigned, July 2, 1868. He received the gold medal of the Haager Society (see title in *Encyclopædia*), 1840; was knight of the Danish Order (gold and silver crosses); member of the Leiden Society of Literature, of the theological examining board of the University of Copenhagen (since 1871), of the Danish Bible Society; was president of the Danish Missionary Society (1860–73), member of the royal commission to revise the Danish Bible (1866–74); president of the Danish branch of the Evangelical Alliance, and presided over the Copenhagen Conference (1884). He published in Danish a commentary on the Old Testament, Copenhagen, 1836–38, 2 vols.; a Bible history, Odense, 1836–39, 2 vols. (German trans., Kiel, 1839, 2 vols.; also in Dutch); documents of Danish Reformation's history, Copenhagen, 1845; a Danish version of the Bible, 1847, 3 vols. (with Helweg, Levensen, and Hermansen); a history of evangelical (1857) and of Roman-Catholic missions (1862; German trans. of both 1867, 2 vols.), and of missions among the Jews (1868, German trans.); a history of Christian missions (1879, 2 vols.; German trans., Gütersloh, 1879–81, 2 vols.); *Israel and the Church*, 1881; and *The Activity of the Church among the Mohammedans, to the Fall of Constantinople*, 1884. Cf. notice in *Evangelical Christendom* (London) for March, 1886, pp. 92, 93.

KALISCH, Marcus, M.A., Ph.D., Hebrew; b. at Trepton, Pomerania, Prussia, May 16, 1828; d. at Rowsley, Derbyshire, Eng., Aug. 23, 1885. He studied classical philology and Semitic languages at Berlin University, and at the same time Talmudic literature under Jewish teachers. In 1849 political causes drove him out of the country; and he settled in London, where he soon came into intimate relations with the Rothschild family, by whose liberality he was able to devote himself since 1850 to the preparation of a critical commentary upon the Old Testament, of which he published *Exodus* (London, 1855), *Genesis* (1858), *Leviticus* (1867–72, 2 parts); besides *Prophecies of Balaam*, 1877; *Jonah*, 1878; *Path and Goal, a Discussion on the Elements of Civilization and the Conditions of Happiness*, 1880. His best work was, however, his *Hebrew Grammar*, London, 1863. His commentaries are rationalistic. *

KAMPHAUSEN, Adolf (Hermann Heinrich), D.D. (*hon.*, Halle, 1867), German Protestant theologian; b. at Solingen, Rhenish Prussia, Sept. 10, 1829; studied at Bonn, 1849–55; became there *privat-docent*, August, 1855; in October went to Heidelberg to be Bunsen's private secretary, and to work on his *Bibelwerk*, and taught as *privat-docent* in the university there; removed with Bunsen to Bonn in 1859, and there became professor extraordinary of theology in 1863, and ordinary professor in 1868. He has taken prominent part in the revision of the German Bible, 1871, sqq. He is the author of *Das Lied Moses*, Leipzig, 1862; *Das Gebet des Herrn*, Elberfeld, 1866; *Die Hagiographen des Alten Bundes nach den überlieferten Grundtexten übersetzt und mit erklärenden Anmerkungen versehen*, Leipzig, 1868; *Die Chronologie der hebräischen Könige*, Bonn, 1883. He contributed to Riehm's *Handwörterbuch des biblischen Alterthums* (Bielefeld, 1885); and edited Bleek's *Einleitung ins Alte Testament*, Berlin, 1860, 3d ed. 1870.

KARR, William Stevens, D.D. (Amherst College, Amherst, Mass., 1876), Congregationalist; b. at Newark, N.J., Jan. 9, 1829; graduated at Amherst (Mass.) College, 1851, and at Union Theological Seminary, New-York City, 1854; was Presbyterian pastor at Brooklyn, N.Y. (1854–67), and Congregational pastor at Chicopee, Mass. (1867–68), Keene, N.H. (1868–72), Cambridge, Mass. (1873–76); and since 1876 has been professor of systematic theology in the Hartford (Conn.) Theological Seminary. He edited Dr. H. B. Smith's *Apologetics* (New York, 1882), *Introduction to Christian Theology* (1883), and *System of Christian Theology*, 1884.

KATTENBUSCH, (Friedrich Wilhelm) Ferdinand, Lic. Theol. (Göttingen, 1875), **D.D.** (*hon.*, Göttingen, 1879), German Protestant; b. at Kettwig-on-the-Ruhr, Rhenish Prussia, Oct. 3, 1851; studied at Bonn, Berlin, and Halle; became *repetent* at Göttingen 1873, *privat-docent* there 1876; professor of systematic theology at Giessen, 1878. He belongs to the school of A. Ritschl of Göttingen. He is the author of *Luthers Lehre vom unfreien Willen und von der Prædestination*, Göttingen, 1875; *Der christliche Unsterblichkeitsglaube*, Darmstadt, 1881; *Luthers Stellung zu den oecumenischen Symbolen*, Giessen, 1883; *Die oecumenischen Symbole, Geschichte ihrer Entstehung und Geltung in der christlichen Kirche*, 1886.

KAULEN, Franz Philipp, D.D. (Würzburg, 1862), Roman Catholic; b. at Düsseldorf, Germany, March 20, 1827; studied theology and philosophy at Bonn, 1846–49; in the theological seminary at Cologne, 1849; became priest, 1850; chaplain at Duisdorf, 1850; at Dottendorf, 1852; rector and prison chaplain at Pützchen, near Bonn, 1853; tutor in Count Mirbach's family at Harff; *repetitor* in the theological *convict* at Bonn, 1859; *privat-docent* for Old-Testament exegesis at Bonn, 1863; professor extraordinary of the same, 1880; ordinary professor of Catholic theology, 1883. He succeeded Dr. Hergenröther as editor of the 2d edition of Wetzer and Welte's *Kirchenlexicon*, Freiburg-im-Br., 1880, sqq., when the latter was made cardinal and called to Rome, 1879. He translated from the Spanish Vieira's *Ausgew. Reden auf d. Festtage U. L. Frau*, Paderborn, 1856; from the Italian, *St. Francisci Blüthengärtlein*, Mainz, 1860, 2d ed. 1880; from the Latin, St. Thomas of Villanova's *Ein Büchlein von der Liebe*, Freiburg-im-Br., 1872; edited the fifth and succeeding editions of C. H. Vosen's *Rudimenta linguæ hebraicæ*, Freiburg, 1872, sqq. (now in German). He is the author of *Linguæ Mandshuricæ Institutiones*, Regensburg, 1856; *Die Sprachverwirrung zu Babel*, Mainz, 1861; *Librum Jonæ Prophetæ exposuit*, 1862; *Legende des sel. Hermann Joseph*, 1862, 2d ed. 1880; *Geschichte der Vulgata*, 1869; *Handbuch zur Vulgata*, 1870; *Einleitung in die hl. Schriften des A. u. N. T.*, Freiburg, 1876, sqq.; *Assyrien und Babylonien nach den neuesten Entdeckungen*, Cologne, 1877, 3d ed. Freiburg, 1885; and numerous theological and linguistic essays.

KAUTZSCH, Emil Friedrich, Ph.D. (Leipzig, 1863), **D.D.** (*hon.*, Basel, 1873), German Protestant; b. at Plauen, Saxony, Sept. 4, 1841; studied at Leipzig, 1859–63; was adjunct of the Nicolai-gymnasium, 1863–66; head master, 1866–72; *privat-docent* in the university, 1869–71; professor extraordinary, 1871; ordinary professor at Basel, 1872–80; since 1880 at Tübingen. In 1877 he founded, with A. Socin and Zimmermann, the German Palestine Exploration Society. He prepared, with F. Mühlau, an edition of the unpointed text of Genesis, Leipzig, 1868, 2d ed. 1885; brought out the second edition of H. Scholz's *Abriss der Hebr. Laut und Formenlehre*, 1874, 5th ed. 1885; the 22d to the 24th editions of Gesenius' *Hebräischer Grammatik*, 1876–85, to which he added an *Übungsbuch*, 1881, 2d ed. 1884; and the 10th and 11th editions of Hagenbach's *Encyklopädie und Methodologie*, 1880, 1884; and has written *De Veteris Testamenti locis a Paulo apostolo allegatis*, 1869; (with Socin) *Die Aechtheit der moabitischen Alterthümer geprüft*, 1876; *Johannes Buxtorf der Aeltere*, Basel, 1879; *Ueber die Derivate des Stammes צדק im alttestamentlichen Sprachgebrauch*, Tübingen, 1881 (pp. 59); *Grammatik des Biblisch-Aramäischen. Mit einer kritischen Erörterung der aramäischen Wörter im N. T.*, Leipzig, 1884.

KAWERAU, Gustav, D.D. (*hon.*, Halle and Tübingen, 1883), German theologian; b. at Bunzlau, Silesia, Feb. 25, 1847; studied at Berlin, 1863–66; became assistant preacher in St. Lucas', Berlin, 1870; pastor at Langheinersdorf, Brandenburg, 1871; at Klemzig, 1876; professor and *geistlicher Inspector am Kloster U. l. Frauen*, and president of the theological seminary, Magdeburg, 1882; ordinary professor of pastoral theology, Kiel, 1886. In 1883 he participated with the archivist Jacobs and Prof. Dr. Koestlin in founding the *Verein für Reformations Geschichte*, of which he has since been the editor. He is the author of *Johann Agricola von Eisleben*, Berlin, 1881; *Caspar Güttel. Ein Lebensbild aus Luther's Freundeskreise*, Halle, 1882; five articles against Janssen in *Zeitschrift für kirchl. Wissenschaft und kirchl. Leben*, 1882 and 1883; the introduction to the reprint of *Von der Winckelmesse und Pfaffen Weihe. D. Martin Luther*, Halle, 1883; and that of *Passional Christi und Antichristi*, Berlin, 1885; edited the *Briefwechsel des Justus Jonas*, 1884–85, 2 parts; the third (1885) and fourth (1886) volumes of the Weimar edition of Luther's works.

KAY, William, D.D. (Oxford, 1885), Church of England; b. at Pickering, Yorkshire, April 8,

1820; educated at Lincoln College, Oxford; graduated B.A. (first-class in classics, second-class in mathematics), 1839; Pusey and Ellerton Hebrew scholar and M.A. 1842, B.D. 1849; ordained deacon 1843, priest 1844; was fellow of Lincoln College, 1840–66; tutor, 1842–49; principal of Bishop's College, Calcutta, 1849–65; and since 1866 has been rector of Great Leghs, and since 1877 chaplain to the bishop of St. Alban's, and honorary canon of St. Alban's. He is the author of *On Pantheism*, Calcutta, 1853, 2d ed., Madras, 1879; *Promises of Christianity*, Oxford, 1855; *The Psalms, translated with Notes*, Calcutta, 1863, 2d ed., London, 1871, 4th ed. 1877; *Crisis Hupfeldiana*, Oxford, 1865; contributed commentary on *Isaiah* and *Hebrews* to *The Bible (Speaker's) Commentary*, and on *Ezekiel* in *S. P. C. K. Commentary*.

KAYSER, August, Lic. Theol. (Strassburg, 1850), German theologian; b. at Strassburg, Feb. 14, 1821; d. there, June 17, 1885. He was educated in his native city; became pastor at Stossweier 1858, at Neuhof-in-Alsace 1868; professor extraordinary of theology at the newly organized University of Strassburg, 1873; ordinary professor, 1879. He was the author of *De Justini Martyris doctrina*, Strassburg, 1850; *Das vorexilische Buch der Urgeschichte Israels und seine Erweiterungen. Ein Beitrag zur Pentateuch-Kritik*, 1874; *Die Theologie des Alten Testaments, in ihrer geschichtlichen Entwickelung dargestellt* (posthumous, ed. by E. Reuss), 1886. *

KEENER, John Christian, D.D. (Florence College, Ala., 1855), **LL.D.** (Southern University, Greensborough, Ala., 1880), Methodist bishop (Southern Church); b. in Baltimore, Md., Feb. 7, 1819; educated at Wesleyan University, Middletown, Conn., 1836; went into business, but became a preacher in 1843, and was a preacher in charge until 1852, when he became a presiding elder; was in the war, 1861–65; editor *New-Orleans Christian Advocate*, 1865–70, when he was elected a bishop. He visited the City of Mexico in 1873, bought property there, and established a mission of the Methodist-Episcopal Church South. He is the author of *Post-Oak Circuit*, Nashville, 1857, 13th thousand 1860, many since; edited William Elbert Munsey's *Sermons and Lectures*, Macon, Ga., 1878, 3d ed. 1879; 4th to 9th thousand 1885, Nashville, Tenn.

KEIL, Johann Carl Friedrich, Lic. Theol., Ph.D., D.D. (all Berlin, 1832, 1834, and 1838, respectively), Lutheran; b. at Oelnitz, Saxony, Feb. 26, 1807; studied at Dorpat (1827–30) and at Berlin (1831–33); became *privat-docent* at Dorpat, 1833; professor extraordinary, 1838; ordinary professor, 1839; since 1859 has been professor emeritus, and has lived at Leipzig. He is the author of *Apologetischer Versuch üb. d. BB. d. Chronik u. üb. d. Integrität d. B. Esra*, Berlin, 1833; *Ueber d. Hiram-Salomonische Schiffart n. Ophir u. Tarsis*, Dorpat, 1834; *Der Tempel Salomo's*, 1839; *Commentar üb. d. BB. d. Könige*, Leipzig, 1845; *Josua*, Erlangen, 1847; 3d part of Hävernick's *Einleitung A. T.*, 1849; *Biblische Archaeologie*, Frankfort, 1857, 2d ed. 1875; *Einleitung in d. kanon. Schriften A. T.*, 1853, 3d ed. 1873; in the series edited jointly with Delitzsch, has contributed commentaries upon *Genesis* and *Exodus*, Leipzig, 1861, 3d ed. 1878; *Leviticus, Numbers*, and *Deuteronomy*, 1862, 2d ed. 1870; *Joshua, Judges*, and *Ruth*, 1863, 2d ed. 1874; *Samuel*, 1865, 2d ed. 1875; *Kings*, 1866, 2d ed. 1876; *Chronicles, Ezra, Nehemiah*, and *Esther*, 1870; *Jeremiah* and *Lamentations*, 1872; *Ezekiel*, 1868, 2d ed. 1881; *Daniel*, 1869; *Minor Prophets*, 1867, 2d ed. 1873 (these are all translated in Clark's Library); separately, commentaries on *Maccabees*, 1875; *Matthew*, 1877; *Mark* and *Luke*, 1879; *John*, 1881; *Peter* and *Jude*, 1883; *Hebrews*, 1885.

KELLER, Ludwig, Ph.D. (Marburg, 1873), Reformed (layman); b. at Fritzlar, Hesse-Nassau, March 28, 1849; studied at Leipzig and Marburg, 1868–72; is director of the state archives at Münster. He is the author of the following books: *Geschichte der Wiedertäufer u. ihres Reichs zu Münster*, Münster, 1880; *Die Gegenreformation in Westfalen und am Niederrhein, Actenstücke und Erläuterungen*, Leipzig, vol. i. 1880; *Ein Apostel der Wiedertäufer* (Hans Denck), 1882; *Die Reformation und die älteren Reformparteien*, 1885; and of the following historical articles: *Hermann von Kerssenbroick, Ein Beitrag zur Quellenkunde des 16. Jahrh.* (in the *Zeits. f. Preuss. Geschichte u. Landeskunde*, Berlin, Jahrg., 1878); *Zur Kirchengeschichte Nordwest-deutschlands im 16. Jahrh.* (in the *Zeits. d. Berg. Gesch.-Vereins*, Elberfeld, 1880); *Zur Geschichte der Wiedertäufer* (in the *Zts. f. Kirchengeschichte*, Gotha, 1881); *Herzog Alba u. d. Wiederherstellung d. kath. Kirche am Rhein* (in the *Preuss. Jahrbücher*, December, 1881); *Zur Geschichte der kathol. Reformation im nordwestlichen Deutschland, 1530–34* (in the *Historisches Taschenbuch*, VI. Folge, Bd. 1., 1881); *Die Wiederherstellung d. kathol. Kirche nach den Wiedertäufer-Unruhen in Münster, 1535–37* (in Sybel's *Hist. Zts.*, Neue Folge, Bd. XI., 1881); *Zur Geschichte der Wiedertäufer nach dem Untergang des Münsterschen Königsreichs* (in the *West-deutsche Zts. für Gesch. u. Kunst*, 1882, Hft. 4.); *Johann von Staupitz und das Waldenserthum* (in the *Historisches Taschenbuch*, VI. Folge, Bd. IV. 1885).

KELLNER, Karl Adam Heinrich, D.D. (Munich, 1862), Roman Catholic; b. at Heiligenstadt, Thuringia, Germany, Aug. 26, 1837; studied at Münster, Tübingen, and Trier; became chaplain at Trier; pastor at Bitburg; professor of church law in the theological seminary at Hildesheim, Hanover, 1867; professor of church history in the University of Bonn, 1882. He is the author of *Das Buss- und Strafverfahren gegen Kleriker in den sechs ersten christlichen Jahrhunderten*, Trier, 1863; *Hellenismus und Christenthum, oder die geistl. Reaktion des antiken Heidenthums gegen das Christenthum*, Köln, 1866; *Verfassung, Lehramt und Unfehlbarkeit der Kirche*, Kempten, 1873, 2d ed. 1784; *Tertullians sämmtliche Schriften, übersetzt*, Köln, 1882, 2 vols.

KELLOGG, Samuel Henry, D.D. (College of New Jersey, Princeton, 1877), Presbyterian; b. at Quiogue, Long Island, N.Y., Sept. 6, 1839; graduated at the College of New Jersey, Princeton, 1861, and at Princeton (N.J.) Theological Seminary, 1864; was missionary in India, 1864–76 (1872–76, theological instructor in synod's school at Allahabad); pastor of the Third Presbyterian Church, Pittsburg, Penn.; and professor of systematic theology, and lecturer on comparative religion, in Western Theological Seminary, Allegheny, Penn., 1877–85; since 1886 pastor in Toronto, Ontario, Can. He is the author of *A Grammar of the Hindi Language*, London, 1876;

The Jews, New York, 1883; *The Light of Asia and the Light of the World*, London and N.Y., 1885.

KENDALL, Henry, D.D. (Hamilton College, Clinton, N.Y., 1858), Presbyterian; b. at Volney, N.Y., Aug. 24, 1815; graduated at Hamilton College, Clinton, N.Y., 1840, and at the theological seminary, Auburn, N.Y., 1844; became pastor at Verona, N.Y., 1844; East Bloomfield, 1848; Pittsburg, Penn. (Third Church), 1858; secretary of the Board of Home Missions, New-York City, 1861. He was a trustee of Auburn Theological Seminary, 1855-58, and since 1871 of Hamilton College.

KENDRICK, Asahel Clark, D.D. (Union College, Schenectady, N.Y., 1845), **LL.D.** (Lewisburg University, Lewisburg, Penn., 1870), Baptist; b. at Poultney, Vt., Dec. 7, 1809; graduated at Hamilton College, Clinton, N.Y., 1831; professor of Greek in Madison University, Hamilton, N.Y., 1832-50; and since 1850 has held similar position in Rochester (N.Y.) University, and taught at intervals Hebrew and New-Testament Greek in Rochester (Baptist) Theological Seminary. He was a member of the New-Testament Company of the Anglo-American Bible-revision Committee (1871-81). He is the author of a *Greek Introduction*, New York, 1833; *Greek Ollendorff*, 1851; *Echoes, or Leisure Hours with the German Poets*, Rochester, 1855; *Life and Letters of Mrs. Emily C. Judson*, New York, 1860; *Our Poetical Favorites* (selected poems), 1873, 2 series, new ed. Boston, 1883; *The Anabasis of Xenophon, with Notes and Vocabulary*, New York, 1873; revised and in part translated Olshausen's *Commentary*, New York, 1856-58, 6 vols.; trans. Moll on *Hebrews* in American ed. of Lange's *Commentary*, 1868; revised and edited trans. of Meyer's *Commentary on John*, 1884; besides has written various magazine articles, a series of exegetical articles under the title of *Biblical Hours*, and aided in several publications of the American Bible Union.

KENNEDY, Benjamin Hall, D.D. (Cambridge, 1836), Church of England; b. at Summer Hill, near Birmingham, Nov. 6, 1804; entered St. John's College, Cambridge; gained the Porson prize, and Browne's medal for Latin ode, in 1823; the Pitt University scholarship, Browne's medals for Greek and Latin odes, and the Porson prize, in 1824; Browne's medal for epigrams in 1825, the Porson prize in 1826; graduated B.A. (senior optime, and first in the first class of the classical tripos, and senior chancellor's medallist) 1827, M.A. 1830; gained the member's prize for a Latin essay, *De origine scripturæ alphabeticæ;* was fellow of his college, and classical lecturer, 1828-36; assistant master at Harrow, 1830-36; head master of Shrewsbury School, 1836-66; was ordained deacon 1829, priest 1830; was prebendary of Gaia Major in Lichfield Cathedral, 1843-67; select preacher to the university, 1860; rector of West Felton, Salop, 1865-67; became regius professor of Greek in the University of Cambridge, and canon of Ely, 1867. In 1870 he was elected a member of the council of the university; appointed Lady Margaret's preacher for 1873; elected honorary fellow of St. John's College in 1880. He was a member of the New-Testament Company of Bible Revisers (1870-81). His works are mostly Latin school-books or translations of classic authors: e.g., *Birds* of Aristophanes (London, 1874), *Agamemnon* of Æschylus (1878, 2d ed. 1882), *Œdipus Tyrannus* of Sophocles: but he has also published *Between Whiles: Wayside Amusements of a Working Life*, 1877; *Occasional Sermons*, 1877; and *Ely Lectures on the Revised Translation of the New Testament*, 1882. *

KENRICK, Most Rev. Peter Richard, D.D., Roman Catholic; b. in Dublin, Ireland, in the year 1806; educated at Maynooth, and ordained; he came to Philadelphia, U.S.A., where his brother, F. P. Kenrick (see title in *Encyclopædia*), was coadjutor bishop; there he edited *The Catholic Herald*, and was made vicar-general. From 1841 to 1843 he was bishop of Drasa, and coadjutor bishop of St. Louis; and since 1843 bishop, and since 1847 the first archbishop. He sat in the Vatican Council, and vigorously opposed the infallibility dogma, but acquiesced. He is author of numerous translations, and of *The Holy House of Loretto*, Philadelphia, and *Anglican Ordinations*.

KEPHART, Ezekiel Boring, D.D. (Otterbein University, Westerville, O., 1881), bishop of the United Brethren in Christ; b. at Decatur, Penn., Nov. 6, 1834; graduated at Otterbein University, Westerville, O., in the English scientific course, 1865; in the regular classical course, 1870; was licensed to preach, 1857; received as a minister into the Allegheny Conference, Penn., January, 1859; became principal of Michigan Collegiate Institute, Leoni, Mich., 1865; a pastor in Pennsylvania, 1866; president of Western College (now at Toledo, Io.), 1868; bishop, 1881. He was State senator of Iowa, 1871-75.

KESSELRING, Heinrich, D.D., Swiss Protestant theologian; b. at Frauenfeld, Canton Thurgau, Switzerland, July 15, 1832; studied theology at Zürich, Tübingen, and Berlin, 1850-56; was *vicar* at Horgen, Switzerland, 1856-57; pastor at Wipkingen, near Zürich, 1859-64; became *privat-docent* at Zürich, 1858; professor extraordinary of theology there, 1864; ordinary professor of New Testament and practical theology, 1874. He is author of contributions to different periodicals, sermons, etc.

KIDDER, Daniel Parish, D.D. (McKendree College, Lebanon, Ill., 1851), Methodist; b. at Darien, N.Y., Oct. 18, 1815; graduated at Wesleyan University, Middletown, Conn., 1836; was missionary in Brazil, 1837-40; pastor at home, 1840-44; was Sunday-school editor and secretary, 1844-56; professor of practical theology in Garrett Biblical Institute, Evanston, Ill., 1856-71; held the same chair in Drew Theological Seminary, Madison, N. J., 1871-80, when he was elected secretary of the M. E. Board of Education, New-York City. He is author of *Mormonism and Mormons*, N.Y., 1841; *Sketches of Residence in Brazil*, 1845, 2 vols.; *The Christian Pastorate*, Cincinnati, 1871; *A Treatise on Homiletics*, New York, 1864; *Helps to Prayer*, 1874; with Rev. J. C. Fletcher, of the standard work, *Brazil and the Brazilians*, Philadelphia, 1857, 9th ed. Boston, 1880; translated from the Portuguese, Feijo's *Necessity of abolishing a Constrained Clerical Celibacy*, New York, 1844.

KIHN, Heinrich, D.D. (Würzburg, 1866), Roman Catholic; b. at Michelbach, Bavaria, April 30, 1833; studied at the lyceum at Aschaffenburg, and at the University of Würzburg, philology and theology, 1846-54; entered the Episcopal Seminary at Würzburg, 1855; won the prize for the best essay on *Die Bedeutung der Antiochenischen Schule auf dem exegetischen Gebiete*, 1857; was ordained priest, 1857, and became city chaplain at Hammelburg; sub-rector and *Studienlehrer* in the Latin school at Hammelburg, 1858; teacher in the arts-gymnasium at Eichstätt, 1864; professor extraordinary of theology at Würzburg, 1874; ordinary professor of canon law, patrology, encyclopædia, and biblical hermeneutics, 1879. In 1884 and 1885 he was rector of the university. He is the author of *Ueber die Nutzbarkeit unserer Lateinschule* (*Programm*), Würzburg, 1860; *Die Bedeutung der antiochenischen Schule auf dem exegetischen Gebiete, nebst einer Abhandlung über die ältesten christlichen Schulen*, Weissenburg, 1866; *Weg zur Weisheit, Andachtsbuch für Studierende und Gebildete*, Eichstätt, 1870, 4th ed., Würzburg, 1886; *Theodor von Mopsuestia und Junilius Africanus als Exegeten*, Freiburg-im-Br., 1880; *Junilii Africani Instituta regularia divinæ legis*, 1880; *Der Ursprung des Briefes an Diognet*, 1882; *Prof. Dr. J. A. Moehler, Ein Lebensbild* (rectoral address), Würzburg, 1884, 2d ed. 1885; *Praktische Methode zur Erlernung der hebräischen Sprache* (with Gymnas. Prof. D. Schilling), Tübingen, 1885.

KILLEN, William Dool, D.D. (Glasgow, 1843), Irish Presbyterian; b. at Ballymena, County Antrim, Ireland, April 5, 1806; educated at Royal Academical Institution, Belfast; became minister of Raphoe, County Donegal, 1829; professor of ecclesiastical history in Belfast, 1841; president of the faculty, 1869. He is the author of *Plea of Presbytery*, Belfast, 1837 (with others); *Ancient Church*, London, 1859, 4th ed. New York, 1883; *Life of Rev. Dr. Edgar*, Belfast, 1867; *Old Catholic Church*, 1871 (Italian trans., Florence, 1877); *Ecclesiastical History of Ireland*, London, 1875, 2 vols.; various minor works.

KING, John Mark, D.D. (Knox College, Toronto, 1882), Canadian Presbyterian; b. at Yetholm, Roxburghshire, Scotland, May 25, 1829; graduated at Edinburgh University, 1854 (April), and at the United Presbyterian Church Divinity Hall, Edinburgh, 1854 (September); studied at Halle, 1855–56; became minister of Columbus and Brooklin, Ontario, Can., 1857; of Gould-street (now St. James's Square) Presbyterian Church, Toronto, 1863; principal of Manitoba College, Winnipeg, Man., 1883. He was moderator of the General Assembly of the Presbyterian Church in Canada, 1883. He has published occasional sermons.

KIP, Right Rev. William Ingraham, S.T.D. (Columbia College, New-York City, 1847), **LL.D.** (Yale College, New Haven, Conn., 1872), Episcopalian, bishop of California; b. in New-York City, Oct. 3, 1811; graduated at Yale College, New Haven, Conn., 1831, and at the General Theological Seminary, New-York City, 1835; became rector of St. Peter's, Morristown, N.J., 1835; assistant minister of Grace Church, New-York City, 1836; rector of St. Paul's, Albany, N.Y., 1837; missionary bishop of California, 1853; diocesan bishop, 1857. He was by appointment of the President a member of the Board of Examiners in the Naval Academy at Annapolis, Md. (1880), and in the Military Academy at West Point, N.Y. (1883). He is the author of *Lenten Fast*, New York, 1843, 12th ed. 1881; *Double Witness of the Church*, 1844, 23d ed. 1884 (reprinted in London, Eng., 1884, and has been introduced as a text-book in several of the English colleges); *Christmas Holy-days at Rome*, 1845, 10th ed. 1884 (in England, 10th ed. 1884); *Early Jesuit Missions in North America*, 1846), 5th ed. 188–; *Early Conflicts of Christianity*, 1850, 4th ed. 187–; *Catacombs of Rome*, 1854, 4th ed. 1881; *The Unnoticed Things of Scripture*, 1868, 3d ed. 1879; *Olden Time in New York*, 1872; *Historical Scenes from Old Jesuit Missions*, 1875; *Church of the Apostles*, 1877.

KIRKPATRICK, Alexander Francis, Church of England; b. in England, in the year 1849; was late scholar of Trinity College, Cambridge; Porson and Bell university scholar 1868, Craven scholar 1870; graduated B.A. (second classic), 1871; first-class theological examination, 1872; M.A. and Tyrwhitt scholar 1874; ordained deacon 1874, priest 1875; was university preacher, 1875 and 1878; examiner for classical tripos 1878–79, for theological tripos 1881–82; Cambridge Whitehall preacher, 1878–80; junior proctor, 1881–82; Lady Margaret preacher, 1882. Since 1871 he has been fellow of Trinity College, Cambridge; since 1878, examining chaplain to the bishop of Winchester; since 1882, regius professor of Hebrew in the University of Cambridge, and canon of Ely. He is the author of the commentary on *First* and *Second Samuel*, in *The Cambridge Bible for Schools*, London, 1880–81.

KIRKPATRICK, John Dillard, D.D. (Bethel College, McKinzie, Tenn., 1884), Cumberland Presbyterian; b. in Wilson County, Tenn., July 8, 1838; educated at Cumberland University, Lebanon, Tenn.; licensed, 1859; ordained, 1861; pastor in East Nashville, Tenn., 1861–65; and has since 1865 been a professor of practical theology and church history in Cumberland University; and since 1880, editor of *The Cumberland Presbyterian Review*, Lebanon, Tenn. He is the author of essays, reviews, etc.

KISTLER, John Luther, Lutheran (General Synod); b. at Ickesburg, Penn., Sept. 25, 1849; educated at Pennsylvania College and Theological Seminary, both at Gettysburg, Penn.; since 1876 has been professor of Greek and mathematics in the classical department, and of New-Testament exegesis in the theological department, of Hartwick Seminary, Otsego County, N.Y.

KITCHIN, Very Rev. George William, D.D. (by decree of Convocation, 1883), dean of Winchester, Church of England; b. at Naughton Rectory, Suffolk, Eng., Dec. 7, 1827; student of Christ Church, Oxford, 1846; graduated B.A. (double first-class) 1850, M.A. 1853; was ordained deacon 1852, priest 1859; tutor of Christ Church (classical), 1853; public examiner for honors in mathematics (1855), in classics (1862–63), and in modern history (twice); select preacher, Oxford, 1863–64; censor of Christ Church, 1863; Oxford Whitehall preacher, 1866–67; lecturer and tutor in history, Christ Church, 1870–83; examining chaplain to the late bishop (Jacobson) of Chester, 1865–84; censor of non-collegiate students, Oxford, 1868–83; became dean, 1883. In theology he is "moderate and liberal." He has edited Bacon's *Novum Organon* (Latin text and English translation, with notes), Oxford, 1855, 2 vols.; Bacon's *Advancement of Learning*, London, 1860; Spenser's *Faerie Queene*, Books 1 and 2, Oxford, 1867–69; compiled *Catalogue of MSS. in the Library of Christ Church*, Oxford, 1867; translated Brachet's *Grammar of the French Tongue*, 1869, 5th ed. 1884; Brachet's *Etymological Dictionary of the French*

Tongue, 1873, 3d ed. 1883; is author of *A History of France down to the Year 1789*, 1873–77, 3 vols., 3d ed. 1884; *A Memoir of Pope Pius II.* (written for the Arundel Society, to accompany their issue of the frescos by Pinturicchio in the library at Siena), 1881.

KITTREDGE, Abbott Eliot, D.D. (Williams College, Williamstown, Mass., 1878), Presbyterian; b. at Roxbury, Mass., July 20, 1834; graduated at Williams College, Williamstown, Mass., 1854, and at Andover (Mass.) Theological Seminary, 1859; pastor of Winthrop Congregational Church, Charlestown, Mass., 1859–64; Eleventh Presbyterian Church, New-York City, 1865–70; Third Presbyterian Church, Chicago, Ill., 1870–86; since of Madison-ave. Reformed Church, N.Y. City. *

KLEINERT, (Hugo Wilhelm) Paul, Ph.D. (Halle, 1857), **Lic. Theol.** (do., 1860), **D.D.** (*hon.*, Halle, 1874), German Protestant; b. at Vielguth, Silesia, Sept. 25, 1837; studied at Breslau and Halle, 1854–57; became *diakonus* and teacher of religion in the Oppeln gymnasium, 1861; in the Berlin Friedrich-Wilhelm gymnasium, 1863; *privat-docent* of theology (Old-Testament) in the Berlin University, 1864; professor extraordinary, 1868; ordinary professor (of Old-Testament and practical theology), 1877. On Nov. 22, 1873, he became a *consistorialrath* for Brandenburg; in 1885–86, was rector of the university. As a student he was influenced by Hupfeld and Julius Müller, later by Oehler and Dorner. In theology he is evangelical, although of the critical school. He contributed the commentaries upon *Obadiah–Zephaniah* to Lange's *Bibelwerk*, Bielefeld, 1869 (English trans. in American Lange series, New York, 1874); *Untersuchungen zur alttestamentlichen Rechts- und Literatur-geschichte*, Part 1, 1872; *Abriss der Einleitung zum A. T. in Tabellenform*, Berlin, 1878. Since 1862 he has contributed to *Studien und Kritiken*, upon Old-Testament exegesis and theology, practical theology, and ecclesiastical history (especially of worship) in the seventeenth century, to Herzog[2] and to Riehm's *Bibl. Handwörterbuch*, etc.

KLIEFOTH, Theodor Friedrich Detlev, D.D., Lutheran; b. at Körchow, Mecklenburg, Jan. 18, 1810; was the tutor of Duke Wilhelm of Mecklenburg, 1833, and of the Grand Duke Friedrich Franz of Mecklenburg-Schwerin; preacher at *Ludwigslust, and superintendent of the diocese of Schwerin, 1840; and since 1850 has been chief ecclesiastical councillor, and member of the ecclesiastical upper court of Mecklenburg-Schwerin. He is the leader of the strict confessional Lutherans, and has written much upon liturgics and church government, and published many sermons. Among his works may be mentioned, *Liturgische Abhandlungen*, Schwerin, 1854–61, 8 vols., 2d ed. 1858–69; and commentaries upon *Zechariah* (1861), *Ezekiel* (1864–65, 2 parts), *Daniel* (1868), and *Revelation* (1874). *

KLOEPPER, Albert Heinrich Ernst, Lic. Theol. (Greifswald, 1853), **D.D.**, Protestant theologian; b. at Weitenhagen, near Greifswald, March 20, 1828; studied at Greifswald and Berlin, 1847–51; passed the examination for a teacher of theology at Greifswald, 1858; became curator of the royal library at Königsberg, 1866; professor extraordinary of theology there, 1875. He is the author of *De origine epistolarum ad Ephesios et Colossenses, a criticis Tubingensibus e gnosi Valentiniana deducta*, Greifswald, 1853; *Exegetisch-kritische Untersuchungen über den zweiten Brief des Paulus an die Gemeinde zu Korinth*, Göttingen, 1870; *Kommentar über das 2. Sendschreiben des Apostel Paulus an die Gemeinde zu Korinth*, Berlin, 1874; *Der Brief an die Colosser*, 1882.

KLOSTERMANN, (Heinrich) August, Lic. Theol. (Göttingen, 1865), **D.D.** (Göttingen, 1868), Lutheran; b. at Steinhude, Schaumburg-Lippe, May 16, 1837; studied at Erlangen and Berlin, 1855–58; became gymnasial and seminary teacher at Bückeburg, 1859; *privat-docent* at Göttingen, 1864; ordinary professor at Kiel, 1868. He is the author of *Vindiciæ Lucanæ*, Göttingen, 1865; *Das Markus Evangelium*, 1867; *Untersuchungen zur A. T. Theologie*, Gotha, 1868; *Korrekturen zur bisherigen Erklärung des Römerbriefes*, 1881; *Probleme im Aposteltexte, neu erörtet*, 1883; *Ueber deutsche Art bei Martin Luther*, Kiel, 1884; *Die Gottesfurcht als Hauptstück der Weisheit*, 1885.

KNEUCKER, Johann Jakob, Lic. Theol. (Heidelberg, 1873), **D.D.** (*hon.*, Bern, 1884), German Protestant; b. at Wenkheim, Baden, Feb. 12, 1840; studied at Heidelberg; became *privat-docent* there, 1873; professor extraordinary, 1879; and also, since Oct. 31, 1883, pastor of Eppelheim, near Heidelberg. As the pupil of Ferdinand Hitzig and Richard Rothe, he adopts a "*streng wissenschaftliche Richtung.*" He is the author of *Siloah: Quell, Teich und Thal in Jerusalem, Eine Dissertation*, Heidelberg, 1873; *Das Buch Baruch, Geschichte und Kritik, Uebersetzung und Erklärung auf Grund des wiederhergestellten hebräischen Urtextes, Mit einem Anhang über den pseudepigraphischen Baruch*, Leipzig, 1879; *Die Anfänge des Römischen Christenthums, Ein Vortrag*, Karlsruhe, 1881; (edited) Dr. Ferdinand Hitzig's *Vorlesungen über Biblische Theologie und Messianische Weissagungen des Alten Testaments, Mit einer Lebens- und Character-Skizze*, Karlsruhe, 1880.

KNICKERBACKER, Right Rev. David Buel, D.D. (Trinity College, Hartford, Conn., 1873), Episcopalian, bishop of Indiana; b. at Schaghticoke, N.Y., Feb. 24, 1833; graduated at Trinity College, Hartford, Conn., 1853, and at the General Theological Seminary, New-York City, 1856; became rector of Gethsemane Church, Minneapolis, Minn., 1857; bishop, 1883. He is a High Churchman. He has published occasional sermons and addresses, annual reports, etc.

KNIGHT, George Thomson, Universalist; b. at Windham, Me., Oct. 29, 1850; graduated at Tufts College, College Hill, Mass., 1872, and at Tufts Divinity School (B.D.) 1875; in the latter was instructor in rhetoric and church history from 1875 to 1882, when he became professor of church history.

KNOX, Charles Eugene, D.D. (College of New Jersey, Princeton, 1874), Presbyterian; b. at Knoxboro, N.Y., Dec. 27, 1833; graduated at Hamilton College, Clinton, N.Y., 1856, and at Union Theological Seminary, New-York City, 1859; was tutor in Hamilton College, 1859–60; pastor elect (Reformed Dutch Church), Utica, 1860–62; pastor (Presbyterian), Bloomfield, N.J., 1864–73; president of the German Theological School, Newark, N.J., since 1873. He is the author of *A Year with St. Paul*, New York, 1863; a series of graded Sunday-school text-books, 1864–70; *Love to the End*, 1866; *David the King*, 1874.

KNOX, Right Rev. Robert Bent, D.D. (Trinity College, Dublin, 1849), lord bishop of Down, Connor, and Dromore, Church of Ireland; b. in Ireland, in the year 1808; educated at Trinity College, Dublin; graduated B.A. 1829, M.A. 1834, D.D. 1849; was chancellor of Ardfert, 1834–41; prebendary of St. Munchin, in Limerick Cathedral, 1841–49; became bishop, 1849; primate, and archbishop of Armagh, 1886.

KOBER, Franz, Lic. Theol. (Tübingen, 1856), **D.D.** (Tübingen, 1857), Roman Catholic; b. at Warthausen, near Biberach, Germany, March 6, 1821; studied theology and philosophy at Tübingen; became priest there, 1845; and successively in its university, *repetent* to the *Wilhelmsstift* (1846), *privat-docent* of pedagogics, didactics, and the exegesis of the N. T. Epistles (1851), professor extraordinary (1853), ordinary professor of church law, pedagogics, and the exegesis of the Epistles (1857). He is the author of *Der Kirchenbann nach den Grundsätzen des kanonischen Rechts*, Tübingen, 1857, 2d ed. 1863; *Die Suspension der Kirchendiener*, 1862; *Die Deposition und Degradation*, 1867. *

KOEGEL, Rudolf, D.D., German Protestant theologian; b. at Birnbaum, Posen, Feb. 18, 1829; pastor at The Hague, 1857–63, and since court preacher at Berlin; and since 1880 general superintendent of the Kurmark. He is the author of commentaries on *First Peter* (Mainz, 1863, 2d ed. Berlin, 1872) and *Romans* (1876, 2d ed. 1883); *Aus dem Vorhof ins Heiligthum* (sermons), Bremen, 1875–76, 2 vols., 2d ed. 1878–80. Since 1880 he has, with W. Baur and E. Frommel, edited *Neue Christoterpe*. *

KOEHLER, August, Ph.D. (Jena, 1856), **Lic. Theol.** (Erlangen, 1857), **D.D.** (Erlangen, 1864), Lutheran theologian; b. at Schmalenberg, Rheinpfalz, Germany, Feb. 8, 1835; educated at Bonn, Erlangen, and Utrecht, 1851–55; made a scientific journey in Holland, 1856; became *privat-docent* at Erlangen, 1857; professor extraordinary of theology, 1862; ordinary professor at Jena 1864, at Bonn 1866, at Erlangen 1868. He is the author of *Die niederländische reformirte Kirche*, Erlangen, 1856 (Dutch trans., *De nederlandsche hervormde Kerk*, Amsterdam, 1857); *Principia doctrinæ de regeneratione in novo testamento obviæ*, 1857; *Die nachexilischen Propheten erklärt*, 1860–65, 4 parts; *Commentatio de vi ac pronunciatione sacrosancti Tetragrammatis*, 1857; *Lehrbuch der biblischen Geschichte alten Testamentes* (down to the disruption of the kingdom), 1st vol., 2d vol. 1st pt., 1875–84; *Ueber die Grundanschauungen des Buch Koheleth*, 1885; *Ueber die Berichtigung der Luther'schen Bibelübersetzung*, 1886; numerous articles in theological periodicals, etc.

KOENIG, Arthur, D.D. (Breslau, Germany, 1873), Roman Catholic; b. at Neisse, Germany, June 4, 1843; studied at Breslau 1861–65, and in the episcopal priests' seminary there 1866–67; became priest, 1867; teacher of religion in the Gross Glogau gymnasium, soon after in the Realschule at Neisse (1868); chief teacher in the latter, 1880; ordinary professor of dogmatics in the university of Breslau, Germany, 1882. He is the author of *Das Kalendarium des Breslauer Kreuzstiftes* (in the *Zeitschrift des Vereins für Geschichte u. Alterthümer Schlesiens*, 1866); *Die Echtheit der Apostelgeschichte*, Breslau, 1867; *Das Zeugniss der Natur für Gottes Dasein*, Freiburg-im-Br., 1870 (Hungarian trans., Calocsa, 1871, 2d ed. Pesth, 1872); *Die Bibel und die Sklaverei* (*Programm der Neisser Realschule*, 1874); *Lehrbuch für den katholischen Religionsunterricht in den oberen Klassen der Gymnasien und Realschulen*, Freiburg-im-Br., 1879, 4th ed. 1885; *Handbuch für den katholischen Religionsunterricht in den mittelren Klassen der Gymnasien und Realschulen*, 1881; articles in the homiletical monthly, *St. Hedwigsblatt*, Breslau, etc.

KOENIG, Friedrich Eduard, Ph.D., Lic. Theol. (both Leipzig, 1872 and 1879), German Protestant; b. at Reichenbach, Saxony, Nov. 15, 1846; studied at Leipzig, 1867–71; became *privat-docent* there, 1879; professor extraordinary of theology, 1885. His theological standpoint is that of a be, liever in revelation. He is the author of *Gedanke-Laut und Accent, als die drei Factoren der Sprachbildung, comparativ und physiologisch am Hebräischen dargestellt*, Weimar, 1874; *Neue Studien über Schrift, Aussprache und allgemeine Formenlehre des Aethiopischen*, Leipzig, 1877; *De criticæ sacræ argumento e linguæ legibus repetito*, 1879; *Historisch-kritisches Lehrgebäude der Hebräischen Sprache*, I. Theil, 1881; *Der Offenbarungsbegriff des Alten Testaments*, 1882; *Die Hauptprobleme der altisraelitischen Religionsgeschichte*, 1884 (English trans., *The Religious History of Israel*, Edinburgh, 1885); *Falsche Extreme in der neueren Kritik des Alten Testaments*, 1885.

KOENIG, Joseph, D.D. (Freiburg-im-Br., 1846), Roman Catholic; b. at Hausen-on-the-Aach, Germany, Sept. 7, 1819; studied philosophy and theology at Freiburg-im-Br.; became priest and *repetitor* in the theological *convict* there, 1845; and successively in this university, *privat-docent* (1847), professor extraordinary (1854), ordinary professor of Old-Testament literature (1857). He is the author of *Die Theologie der Psalmen*, Freiburg-im-Br., 1857; *Das alttestamentl. Königthum*, 1863; *Das Alter u. die Entstehungsweise des Pentateuchs*, 1884; *Beiträge zur Geschichte der theologischen Facultät in Freiburg am Schlusse des vorigen und im Beginne des jetzigen Jahrhunderts*, 1884. *

KOESSING, Friedrich, Roman Catholic; b. at Mimmenhausen, Germany, Feb. 15, 1825; became spiritual instructor at Donaueschingen, 1851; in the lyceum at Heidelberg, 1853; professor of moral theology and theological encyclopædia at Freiburg-im-Br., 1863. He is the author of *De suprema Christi cœna*, Heidelberg, 1858; *Das christl. Gesetz*, 1862.

KOESTLIN, Julius Theodor, Ph.D., Lic. Theol. (both Tübingen, 1855), **D.D.** (*hon.*, Göttingen, 1860), **LL.D.** (*hon.*, Marburg, 1883); b. at Stuttgart, May 17, 1826; studied in Tübingen 1844–48, and Berlin 1849–50; became *repetent* in the evangelical seminary in Tübingen, 1850; professor extraordinary, especially of New-Testament theology, and university preacher, in Göttingen, 1855; ordinary professor, especially of systematic theology, at Breslau 1860, at Halle 1870; since 1865 consistorial councillor, and since 1877 member of the Magdeburg consistory. His theological standpoint is that of the so-called orthodox new German theology, with critical reference to the biblical revelation and the facts of the moral and religious Christian consciousness, and effort after the union of the Lutheran and Reformed confessions. He studied Presbyterianism in Scotland in 1849, and took an active part in organizing the new consistorial constitution, which has Presbyterian features. Since 1873 he has, with Professor Riehm, edited the *Theologische Studien und Kritiken.* He is the author of *Die schottische Kirche, ihr inneres Leben und ihr Verhältniss zum Staat*, Hamburg u. Gotha, 1852; *Luthers Lehre von der Kirche*, Stuttgart, 1853; *Das Wesen der Kirche nach Lehre u. Geschichte d. N.T.*, 1854, 2d ed. Gotha, 1872; *Der Glaube, sein Wesen, Grund u. Gegenstand, seine Bedeutung für Erkennen, Leben u. Kirche*, Gotha, 1859; *De miraculorum, quæ Christus et primi ejus discipuli fecerunt, natura et ratione*, Breslau, 1860; *Luthers Theologie*, Stuttgart, 1863, 2 vols.; *Martin Luther, sein Leben und seine Schriften*, Elberfeld, 1875, 2 vols., 3d ed. 1883; *Luthers Leben*, Leipzig, 1882, 3d ed. 1883 (English trans., London and New York, 1883, and Philadelphia, 1883); *Martin Luther (Festschrift)*, Halle, 1883, 22d ed. 1884 (English trans., London, 1883).

KOLDE, Theodor (Hermann Friedrich), Ph.D. (Halle, 1874), **Lic. Theol.** (Marburg, 1876), **D.D.** (*hon.*, Marburg, 1881), German Protestant theologian; b. at Friedland, Upper Silesia, May 6, 1850; studied at Breslau 1869–70, and at Leipzig 1871–72; became *privat-docent* in church history at Marburg, 1876; professor extraordinary, 1879; ordinary professor of historical theology at Erlangen, 1881. He is a pupil of Hermann Reuter's. He is author of *Der Kanzler Brück u. seine Bedeutung für die Entwicklung der Reformation*, Halle, 1874 (Prof. Kolde is one of Brück's descendants); *Luthers Stellung zu Conzil und Kirche bis zum Wormser Reichstag*, Gütersloh, 1876; *Walther von der Vogelweide in seiner Stellung zu Kaiserthum und Hierarchie*, 1877; *Die deutsche Augustiner-Congregation und Johann von Staupitz*, Gotha, 1879; *Friedrich der Weise und die Anfänge der Reformation*, Erlangen, 1881; *Analecta Lutherana, Briefe und Actenstücke*, Gotha, 1883; *Luther und der Reichstag zu Worms*, 1883, 2d ed. same year; *Martin Luther, eine Biographie*, vol. i. 1884; *Die Heilsarmee* ("The Salvation Army") *nach eigener Anschauung und nach ihren Schriften*, Erlangen, 1885.

KRAFFT, Wilhelm Ludwig, D.D., Reformed; b. at Cologne, Sept. 8, 1821; studied at Bonn and Berlin, 1839–44; made a scientific journey in the East, 1844; *privat-docent* at Bonn, 1846; professor extraordinary, 1850; ordinary professor since 1859, and member of the Rhenish Consistory since 1881. Among his publications may be mentioned *Die Topographie Jerusalems*, Bonn, 1846; *Die Kirchengeschichte der germanischen Völker*, Berlin, vol. i. 1854; *Briefe und Documente aus der Zeit der Reformation*, Elberfeld, 1876.

KRAUS, Franz Xaver, Ph.D., D.D. (both Freiburg-im-Br., 1862 and 1865), Roman Catholic; b. at Treves, Rhenish Prussia, Sept. 18, 1840; studied at Freiburg, Paris, and Bonn; was ordained priest, 1865; held a beneficiary at Pfalzel, near Treves, 1865–72; became professor extraordinary of art, archæology, and history, at Strassburg, 1872; ordinary professor of church history at Freiburg-im-Breisgau, 1878. He is archducal conservator of antiquities. He advocates, in the Roman-Catholic Church, religious catholicism in opposition to political ultramontanism. His principal writings are *Observationes criticæ in Synesii Cyrenæi epistulas*, Regensburg, 1863; *Studien über Synesios von Kyrene*, Tübingen, 1866; *Die Kunst bei den alten Christen*, Frankfurt-a.-M., 1868; *Beiträge zur Trierischen Archäologie und Geschichte*, I., Trier, 1868; *Die Blutampullen der röm. Katacomben*, Freiburg, 1868; *Die christliche Kunst in ihren frühesten Anfängen*, Leipzig, 1872; *Das Spottcrucifix vom Palatin*, Freiburg, 1872; *Lehrbuch der Kirchengeschichte*, Trier, 1872–75, 3 parts, 3d ed. 1886; *Roma sotterranea*, Freiburg, 1873, 2d ed. 1879; *Synchronistische Tabellen zur christlichen Kirchengeschichte*, Trier, 1876; *Ueber Begriff, Umfang und Geschichte der christlichen Archäologie*, Freiburg, 1879; *Kunst und Alterthum in Elsass-Lothringen*, Strassburg, 1876–87, 3 vols.; *Gedächtnissrede auf Joh. Alzog*, Freiburg, 1879; *Synchronistiche Tabellen zur christlichen Kunstgeschichte*, 1880; *Real-encyclopädie der christlichen Alterthümer*, 1880–86, 2 vols.; *Ludwig Spach*, Strassburg, 1880; *Miniaturen des Codex Egberts zu Trier*, Freiburg, 1884; *Die Wandgemälde in Oberzell auf der Reichenau*, 1884; *Die Kunstdenkmäler des Grossherzogthum Baden*, Bd I., 1887. He edited the 10th edition of Alzog's *Handbuch der Allgemeinen Kirchengeschichte*, Mainz, 1882, 2 vols.; and *Lettere di Benedetto XIV.*, 1884; and has contributed to numerous periodicals.

KRAUSS, Alfred (Eduard), Lic. Theol. (Basel, 1866), **D.D.** (*hon.*, Basel, 1868), Reformed; b. at Rheineck, Canton St. Gallen, Switzerland, March 19, 1836; studied at Heidelberg (1855–56), Halle (1856–57), and Zürich (1857–58); passed the state theological examination at St. Gallen, 1859; became pastor of Stettfurt, Canton Thurgau, Switzerland, 1859; professor extraordinary at Marburg, 1870; ordinary professor, 1871; at Strassburg, 1873. He belongs to the school of Schleiermacher. He lectures upon comparative symbolics, dogmatics, ethics, homiletics, catechetics, pastoral theology, liturgics, practical exegesis, and conducts a homiletical and catechetical *seminar*. He is the author of *Bedeutung des Glaubens für die Schriftauslegung*, Frauenfeld, 1862; *Theologischer Commentar zu I. Korinther xv.*, 1864; *Die Lehre von der Offenbarung, ein Beitrag zur Philosophie des Christenthums*, Gotha, 1868; *Predigten für alle Sonn- und Festtage des Jahres*, Strassburg, 1874; *Das protestantische Dogma von der unsichtbaren Kirche*, Gotha, 1876; *Lehrbuch der Homiletik*, 1883; various articles upon doctrinal and practical theology in different Swiss and German periodicals.

KRAWUTZCKY, Adam, D.D. (Munich, 1865), Roman Catholic; b. at Neustadt, Upper Silesia, March 2, 1842; studied in the universities of Breslau (1860–62), Tübingen (1863–64), and Munich (1864), and in the priest-seminary in Breslau (1864–65), and was ordained priest in 1865. He became *sub-regens* in the seminary, and *privat-docent* in the university of Breslau, 1868; on April 1, 1885, he was appointed professor extraordinary of theology. He is the author of *Zählung u. Ordnung d. hl. Sacramente in ihrer geschichtl. Entwickelung*, Breslau, 1865 (pp. 66); *De visione beatifica in Benedicti XII. constitutionem "Benedictus Deus" commentatio historica*, 1868 (pp. 40); *Petrinische Studien*, 1872–73, 2 parts; *Des Bellarmin kleiner Katechismus mit Kommentar*, 1873; essays in periodicals, especially *Ueber die Bedeutung d. neutest. Ausdrucks Menschensohn* (in *Tübinger Theol. Quartalschrift*, 1869, pp. 600–652); *Ueber das altkirchliche Unterrichtsbuch "Die zwei Wege"* (do.,

1882, pp. 359–445); *Ueber die sog. Zwölfapostellehre* (do., 1884, pp. 542–606).

KROTEL, Gottlob Frederick, D.D. (University of Pennsylvania, Philadelphia, 1865), Lutheran (General Council); b. at Ilsfeld, Würtemberg, Germany, Feb. 4, 1826; graduated from the University of Pennsylvania, Philadelphia, 1846; studied theology, was licensed 1848; pastor at Passyunk (Philadelphia), Lebanon, Lancaster (1853–62), Philadelphia (1862–68); professor in Evangelical Lutheran Theological Seminary there (1864–68); and since 1868 has been pastor of Holy Trinity, New-York City. He edited *Der Lutherische Herold*, 1872–75, and *The Lutheran*, 1881–83. He was president of the Ministerium of Pennsylvania 1866–68, and since 1884; and of that of New York, 1869–76, and of the General Council in 1869. He is the author of translations of Ledderhose's *Life of Melanchthon*, Philadelphia, 1854, and of Uhlhorn's *Luther and the Swiss*, 1876; *Who are the Blessed? Meditations on the Beatitudes*, 1855; (with Rev. Prof. Dr. Mann) *Explanation of Luther's Small Catechism*, 1863.

KUEBEL, Robert Benjamin, Lic. Theol. (Tübingen, 1867), **D.D.** (*hon.*, Leipzig, 1879), Lutheran; b. at Kirchheim, Würtemberg, Feb. 12, 1838; studied at Tübingen, 1856–60; became *repetent* there, 1865; *diakonus* at Balingen, 1867; professor and director in Herborn preachers' seminary, 1870; city pastor and professor at Ellwangen, 1874; ordinary professor of theology at Tübingen, 1879. His theological standpoint is the positive biblical. He is the author of *Bibelkunde*, Stuttgart, 1870, 2 vols., 3d ed. 1881; *Das christliche Lehrsystem nach der heiligen Schrift*, 1873; *Umriss der Pastoraltheologie*, 1st ed. as *Seminarprogramm* at Herborn, 1873, 2d ed. Stuttgart, 1873; *Predigten und Schriftbetrachtungen*, Barmen, 1874; *Katechetik*, Stuttgart, 1877; *Ueber den Unterschied zwischen der positiven u. der liberalen Richtung in der modernen Theologie*, Nördlingen, 1881; lectures, etc.; contributed to Grau's *Bibelwerk* (Bielefeld, 1876–80); to the 2d ed. of Herzog, and *Apologetik* in Zöckler's *Handbuch*, Nördlingen, 1884, 2d ed. 1885.

KUENEN, Abraham, D.D. (Leiden, 1851); b. at Haarlem, North Holland, Sept. 16, 1828; studied at the gymnasium of Haarlem, and at the University of Leiden, 1846–51; and since March 12, 1853, has been professor of theology there. He is a member of the Teyler Theological Society of Haarlem, and of the Royal Academy of Sciences and Literature at Amsterdam; secretary of The Hague Society for the Defence of the Christian Religion; and September, 1883, was president of the Sixth International Congress of Orientalists, held at Leiden. In theology he is "liberal," belongs to what is called in Holland "the modern school," advocates the application of historical criticism to the Bible, especially to the Old Testament. Since 1866 he has been one of the editors of the *Theologisch Tydschrift*. Besides numerous articles he has written *Historisch-kritisch Onderzoek naar het onstaan en de verzameling van de boeken des Ouden Verbonds* (*Historico-critical Investigation into the Origin and Collection of the Books of the Old Testament*), Leiden, 1861–65, 3 vols., 2d ed. revised and enlarged, 1885, sqq. (French trans. by Dr. A. Pierson, of the first two volumes, on the historical and prophetical books, Paris, 1866–79; English trans. of the first two chapters by Bishop J. W. Colenso, in his *Pentateuch and Book of Joshua critically examined*, London, 1865; German trans. of the 2d ed. by Dr. Th. Weber, Leipzig, 1885, sqq.); *De godsdienst van Israël tot den ondergang van den Joodschen Staat*, Haarlem, 1869–70, 2 vols. (English trans. by A. W. May, *The Religion of Israel to the Fall of the Jewish State*, London, 1874–75, 3 vols.); *De profeten en de profetie onder Israël*, Leiden, 1875, 2 vols. (English trans. by A. Milroy, *Prophets and Prophecy in Israel*, 1877); *National Religions and Universal Religion* (Hibbert Lectures for 1882), London, 1882 (Dutch edition, *Volksgodsdienst en Wereldgodsdienst*, Leiden, 1882; French trans. by Vernes, Paris, 1883; German trans., Berlin, 1883); minor pamphlets, university orations, etc.

KURTZ, Johann Heinrich, Lic. Theol. (*hon.*, Königsberg, 1844), **D.D.** (*hon.*, Rostock, 1849), Lutheran (moderately confessional); b. at Montjoie, near Aachen, Prussia, Dec. 13, 1809; studied at Halle 1830, and at Bonn 1831–33; became head master in religion at the Mitau gymnasium, 1835; ordinary professor of theology in Dorpat University, 1850; professor emeritus, 1870. Since 1871 he has lived at Marburg. His books are, *Das Mosaische Opfer*, Mitau, 1842; *Die Astronomie und die Bibel*, 1842 (5th ed. under title *Bibel und Astronomie*, Berlin, 1865; English trans., *The Bible and Astronomy*, Philadelphia, 1857); *Lehrbuch der heiligen Geschichte*, Königsberg, 1843, 16th ed. 1884 (English trans., *Manual of Sacred History*, Philadelphia, 1855); *Beiträge zur Verteidigung und Begründung des Pentateuchs*, 1844; *Christliche Religionslehre*, Mitau, 1844, 13th ed. Leipzig, 1883; *Die Einheit der Genesis*, Berlin, 1846; *Biblische Geschichte mit Erläuterungen*, 1847, 34th ed. 1882 (English trans. by A. Melville, *Bible History*, Edinburgh, 1867); *Geschichte des Alten Bundes* (*bis zum Tode Mosis*), 1848–55, 2 vols., 3d ed. vol. i. 1864, 2d ed. vol. ii. 1858 (English annotated trans. by Dr. A. Edersheim, *History of the Old Covenant*, Edinburgh, 1860, 3 vols.); *Lehrbuch der Kirchengeschichte*, Mitau, 1849, 9th ed. Leipzig, 1885, 2 vols. in 4 parts (English trans., *Text-book of Church History*, Philadelphia, 1860, 2 vols.; new ed. revised, 1875); *Leitfaden* (now called *Abriss*) *der Kirchengeschichte*, Mitau, 1852, 11th ed. Leipzig, 1886; *Handbuch der allgemeinen Kirchengeschichte*, Mitau, vol. i. 1853–54, 3 parts, 2d ed. 1856–68, vol. ii. 1st part (to the end of the Carolingian age), 1856 (English trans., *History of the Christian Church*, Edinburgh, 1863); *Die Ehen der Söhne Gottes mit den Töchtern der Menschen in 1. Mos. vi. 1–4*, Berlin, 1857; *Die Söhne Gottes in 1. Mos. vi. 1–4 und die sündigenden Engel in 2. Petri ii. 4, 5 und Judäi, 6, 7*, Mitau, 1858; *Die Ehe des Propheten Hosea*, Dorpat, 1859; *Der alttestamentliche Opferkultus nach seiner gesetzlichen Begründung und Anwendung*, Mitau, 1862 (English trans., *Sacrificial Worship of the Old Testament*, Edinburgh, 1863); *Zur Theologie der Psalmen*, Dorpat, 1865; *Der Brief an die Hebräer erklärt*, Mitau, 1869.

L.

LADD, George Trumbull, D.D. (Western Reserve College, Hudson, O., 1880), Congregationalist; b. at Painesville, O., Jan. 19, 1842; graduated at Western Reserve College, Hudson, O., 1864, and at Andover (Mass.) Theological Seminary 1869; pastor Spring-street Church, Milwaukee, Wis., 1871–79; professor of intellectual and moral philosophy in Bowdoin College, Brunswick, Me., 1879–81; and since 1881 has filled the corresponding chair in Yale College. He is the author of *Principles of Church Polity*, New York, 1882; *Doctrine of Sacred Scripture: Critical, Historical, and Dogmatic Inquiry into the Origin and Nature of the Old and New Testaments*, 1883, 2 vols. (the product of many years of labor and of wide research).

LAEMMER, Hugo, Ph.D. (Berlin, 1855), **Lic. Theol.** (Berlin, 1856), **D.D.** (*hon.*, Breslau, 1859), Roman-Catholic convert; b. at Allenstein, East Prussia, Jan. 25, 1835; studied at Königsberg, Leipzig, and Berlin, 1852–56; became *privat-docent* for historical theology at Berlin, 1857; made a scientific journey through Italy, and on his return went formally over to Catholicism at Braunsberg, Nov. 21, 1858. He then entered the clerical seminary there; was ordained a priest 1859; immediately thereafter went to Rome, and was appointed *missionarius apostolicus*, 1861. On his return to Braunsberg that year, he was made *sub-regens* of the seminary; was called to Rome by the Pope in 1863, as *consultor* of the *Congregatio de Propaganda Fide*. In 1864 he became professor of moral theology at Braunsberg, and later in the year, in spite of the protest of the Protestant faculty, professor of dogmatics in the Roman-Catholic theological faculty at Breslau, and soon after *Consistorialrath*, *Prosynodalexaminator*, and episcopal *Pönitentiar*. In 1865 he became honorary member of the *Doktorencollegium* of the Vienna theological faculty. He is the author of *Clementis Alexandrini de λόγῳ doctrina*, Leipzig, 1855 (an academical prize essay, whose preparation gave him his first impulse towards Roman Catholicism); *De theologia romano-catholica, quæ reformatorum ætate viguit, antetridentina* (another prize essay, Berlin, 1857; translated by him into German under the title, *Die vortridentinisch-katholische Theologie des Reformations-Zeitalters aus den Quellen dargestellt*, Berlin, 1858); *Papst Nikolaus der Erste u. d. Byzantinische Staats-Kirche seiner Zeit*, 1857 (his *habilitationsrede*); (ed.) *Eusebii Pamphili hist. eccles. libri x.*, Schaffhausen, 1859–62; *Analecta Romana. Kirchengeschichtliche Forschungen in Römischen Bibliotheken u. Archiven. Eine Denkschrift*, Schaffhausen, 1860; *Misericordias Domini*, Freiburg-im-Br., 1861 (his autobiography, in which he relates the history of his conversion, and attributes it to his work upon Anselm's *Cur Deus Homo*, which he edited, Berlin, 1857, his study of Hermann von Kappenberg's *De conversione sua*, the reading of Roman-Catholic books, a severe illness, and the Jesuit revival meetings in Berlin); *Monumenta Vaticana historiam ecclesiasticam sæculi XVI. illustrantia*, 1861; *Zur Kirchengeschichte des 16. und 17. Jahrh.*, 1863; (edited) *Scriptorum Græciæ orthod. bibliotheca selecta*, 1864–66; *In decreta concilii Ruthenorum Zamosciensis animadversiones theologico-canonicæ*, 1865; *Cœlestis Urbs Jerusalem*, 1866; *Meletematum romanorum mantissa*, 1876; *De martyrologio Romano, Parergon historico-criticum*, Regensburg, 1878.

LAGARDE, Paul Anthony de, Ph.D. (Berlin, 1849), **Lic. Theol.** (*hon.*, Erlangen, 1851), **D.D.** (*hon.*, Halle, 1868), German Protestant; b. in Berlin, Nov. 2, 1827; studied in Berlin University from Easter, 1844, to Easter, 1846, and in Halle from Easter, 1846, to Easter, 1847; taught in schools in Berlin from Easter, 1855, to Easter, 1866; and since Easter, 1869, has been professor of Oriental languages at Göttingen. "He accepts nothing but what is proved, but accepts every thing that has been proved." He is the author of the following works: *Didascalia apostolorum syriace*, 1854; *Zur urgeschichte der Armenier*, 1854; *Reliquiæ iuris ecclesiastici antiquissimæ syriace*, 1856, *græce*, 1856; *Analecta Syriaca*, 1858; *Appendix arabica*, 1858; *Hippolyti romani quæ feruntur omnia græce*, 1858; *Titi bostreni contra Manichæos libri quatuor syriace*, 1859; *Titi bostreni quæ ex opere contra Manichæos in cod. hamburgensi servata sunt græce accedunt Iulii romani epistulæ et Gregorii Thaumaturgi κατὰ μέρος πίστις*, 1859; *Geoponicon in sermonem syriacum versorum quæ supersunt*, 1860; *Clementis romani recognitiones syriace*, 1861; *Libri V. T. apocryphi syriace*, 1861; *Constitutiones apostolorum græce*, 1862; *Anmerkungen zur griechischen übersetzung der Proverbien*, 1863; *Die vier evangelien arabisch aus der Wiener handschrift herausgegeben*, 1864; *Iosephi Scaligeri poemata omnia ex museio Petri Scriverii*, 1864; *Clementina*, 1865; *Gesammelte abhandlungen*, 1866; *Der pentateuch koptisch*, 1867; *V. T. ab Origene recensiti fragmenta*, *Materialien zur geschichte und kritik des Pentateuch*, I., II., 1867; *Genesis græce*, 1868; *Hieronymi quæstiones hebraicæ in libro Geneseos*, 1868; *Beiträge zur baktrischen lexicographie*, 1868; *Onomastica sacra*, 1870; *Prophetæ chaldaice*, 1872; *Hagiographa chaldaice*, 1874; *Psalterium iuxta Hebræos Hieronymi*, 1874; *Psalmi 1–49 in usum scholarum arab.*, 1875; *Psalterii versio memphitica, etc.*, 1875; *Psalterium Iob Proverbia arabice*, 1876; *Armenische studien*, 1877; *Symmicta*, I. 1877, II. 1880; *Semitica*, I. 1878, II. 1879; *Deutsche Schriften*, 1878–86; *Prætermissorum libri duo syriace*, 1879; *Orientalia*, I. 1879, II. 1880; *Aus dem deutschen gelehrtenleben*, 1881; *Die lateinischen übersetzungen des Ignatius*, 1882; *Ankündigung einer neuen ausgabe der griechischen übersetzung des alten testaments*, 1882; *Ignatii antiocheni quæ feruntur græce. Sapientii utraque et Psalterium latine. Beschreibung des in Granada üblich gewesen dialekts der arabischen sprache. Iohannis Euchaitorum metropolitæ quæ in codice vaticano græco 676 supersunt Iohannes Bollig descripsit*, 1882; *Iudæ Harizii macamæ hebraice*, 1883; *Ægyptiaca*, 1883; *Librorum V. T. P. I. græce*, 1883; *Isaias persicæ*, 1883; *Programm für die konservative Partei Preussens*, 1884; *Persische Studien*, 1884; *Mittheilungen*, 1884; *Probe einer neuen Ausgabe der lateinischen Uebersetzungen des alten Tes-*

taments, 1885; *Die revidierte Lutherbibel des Halleschen Waisenhauses, besprochen*, 1885; *Catenæ in Evangelia Ægyptiacæ, quæ supersunt*, 1886.

LAIDLAW, John, D.D. (Edinburgh, 1880), Free Church of Scotland; b. in Edinburgh, April 7, 1832; graduated as M.A. at Edinburgh University, 1855; studied theology in Reformed Presbyterian Divinity Hall, Glasgow, and then in New College (the Free Church College), Edinburgh; became Free Church minister at Bannockburn, 1859; Perth, 1863; Aberdeen, 1872; professor of systematic theology, New College, Edinburgh, 1881. He is the author of *The Bible Doctrine of Man* (Cunningham Lectures), Edinburgh, 1879; and editor of *Memorials of the Late Rev. John Hamilton*, Glasgow, 1881.

LAKE, Very Rev. William Charles, D.D. (Durham, 1882), dean of Durham, Church of England; b. in England, in January of the year 1817; was scholar at Balliol College, Oxford, 1834; graduated B.A. (first-class classics) 1838, M.A. 1841; obtained the Latin essay, 1840; was ordained deacon 1842, priest 1844; fellow and tutor of his college; proctor and university preacher, public examiner in classics and in modern history, 1853–54; preacher at the Chapel Royal, Whitehall; commissioner of army education 1856, and of popular education 1858; rector of Huntspill, Somerset, 1858–69; prebendary of Combe the 10th in Wells Cathedral, 1860–69; became dean of Durham, 1869. *

LANG, John Marshall, D.D. (Glasgow, 1874), Church of Scotland; b. in the manse of Glasford, Lanarkshire, May 14, 1834; graduated at the University of Glasgow (prizeman in theology and philosophy, and historical medallist), 1856; was successively minister of the East Parish, Aberdeen, 1856; Fyvie Parish, Aberdeenshire, 1858; Anderston Church, Glasgow, 1865; Morningside Parish, Edinburgh, 1868; and since January, 1873, of the Barony Parish, Glasgow. He was associated with the earlier movements in the Church of Scotland, for improvement in modes of worship; was appointed in 1871 convener (chairman) of the Church of Scotland committee on correspondence with foreign churches; along with Professor Milligan, was deputy to the General Assembly of the Presbyterian Church of the United States in 1872; was member of the Councils of the Reformed Churches at Edinburgh, Philadelphia, and Belfast. He was the successor of Norman Macleod in the care of the Barony Parish, the largest in Scotland. He is the author of *Heaven and Home*, Edinburgh, 1879, 3d ed. 1881; *The Last Supper of Our Lord*, 1881, 2 editions; *Life: is it Worth Living?* London, 1883, 2 editions; and contributed to St. Giles' Lectures for 1881 (*The Religions of Central America*), and for 1883 (*A Historical Sketch of the Church of Scotland*); and has published sermons, review articles, lectures, etc.

LANGE, Carl Heinrich Rudolf, Lutheran (Missouri Synod); b. at Polnisch Wartenberg, Silesia, Jan. 8, 1825; graduated at Breslau 1846, and licensed in St. Louis, Mo., 1848; since 1878 has been professor of theology in Concordia Seminary, St. Louis, Mo. He is the author of *Lehrbuch der Englischen Sprache*, Fort Wayne, Ind., 1870; *Kleines Lehrbuch der Englischen Sprache*, Chicago, Ill., 1873, 8th ed. St. Louis, 1883; *Athanasius, De decretis Nic. Syn.*, Greek text, St. Louis, 1879; *Justinus, Apologiæ*, Greek text, 1882.

LANGE, Johann Peter, D.D., United Evangelical; b. on the Bier, a small farm in the parish of Sonnborn, near Elberfeld, Prussia, April 10, 1802; d. at Bonn, July 8, 1884. His father was a farmer and wagoner, and brought his son up in the same occupations, but allowed him at the same time to indulge his passion for reading. He was instructed in the Heidelberg Catechism, which is still used in the Reformed congregations of Prussia, although they are since 1817 united with the Lutheran under the name of the United Evangelical Church. His Latin teacher, the Rev. Hermann Kalthof, who discovered in him unusual talents, induced him to study theology. He attended the gymnasium at Düsseldorf, from Easter, 1821, till autumn, 1822; and the University of Bonn, where he was particularly influenced by Professor Nitzsch, from 1822 till 1825. For a year after leaving the university he was at Langenberg, near Elberfeld, as assistant minister to the Rev. Emil Krummacher (brother of the celebrated Rev. Dr. Frederick William Krummacher), 1825–26; then became successively Reformed pastor of Wald, near Solingen, 1826; of Langenberg, 1828; and of Duisburg, 1832. While at Duisburg, he attracted attention by his brilliant articles in Hengstenberg's *Evangelische Kirchenzeitung* and other periodicals, by his poems, and by his able work upon the history of the Saviour's infancy (see below) in refutation of Strauss. In 1841, after Strauss had been prevented from taking his professorship of theology in the University of Zürich, Dr. Lange was called to the position. Here he elaborated his *Life of Jesus* (1844–47, see below), which is a positive refutation of the famous work of Strauss, and had a wide circulation in German and English, and a marked effect upon the large subsequent literature on the subject. He remained in Zürich until 1854, when he was called to a professorial chair in the University of Bonn. In 1860 he became *consistorialrath.* He labored incessantly as academic teacher and writer, and retained his faculties to the end. He ceased to lecture five days before his death. An American student (Bossard) to whom he showed great kindness, and who informed me of the fact, called, and found him suffering from a cold, but reading and writing as usual, and full of animation and pleasant humor. Even a day before his death, he spoke of the beautiful summer and the beautiful Rhine, and hoped to resume his lectures shortly. "I never saw Lange appear happier than on this day; his eyes were brighter than ever, his countenance was serene, he was all kindness and friendliness, and seemed at peace with the whole world." On the 8th of July he arose as usual, spent the morning among his books, and after dinner, while his daughter went down-stairs to get him his cup of coffee, he quietly fell asleep in his arm-chair, to awake no more on earth.

Dr. Lange was small of stature, had a strong constitution, a benignant face, and bright eye which retained its strength to the last. He was twice happily married, lived in comfortable circumstances, and left a large and interesting family. He was simple in his tastes and habits, of unblemished character, genial, agreeable, full of kindness, wit, and humor, and even in his old age fully alive to all the religious, literary, and social questions of the day. He was at once a poet and a theologian, teeming with new ideas, often fanciful, but always interesting and suggestive. He indulged in poetico-philosophical speculations, and sometimes soared high above the clouds. He was one of the most original and fertile theological authors of the nineteenth century. His theology is biblical and evangelical catholic. His most useful publication is his *Bibelwerk*, which has probably a larger circulation in Germany and America than any commentary of the same size, and is especially helpful to ministers. He organized the plan, engaged about twenty contributors, and commented himself on Matthew, Mark, John, Romans, Revelation, Genesis, Exodus, Leviticus, Numbers, Haggai, Zechariah, and Malachi, giving original and brilliant homiletical hints.

He was the author of *Die Lehre der heiligen Schrift von der freien und allgemeinen Gnade Gottes*, Elberfeld, 1831; *Biblische Dichtungen*, 1832–34, 2 vols.; *Zehn Predigten*, 1833; *Kleine polemische Gedichte*, Duisburg, 1835; *Gedichte und Sprüche aus dem Gebiete christlicher Naturbetrachtung*, 1835; *Die Welt des Herrn in didaktischen Gesängen*, Essen, 1835; *Ueber den geschichtlichen Character der kanonischen Evangelien, inbesondere der Kindheitsgeschichte Jesu, mit Beziehung auf das Leben Jesu von D. F. Strauss*, Duisburg, 1836; *Das Land der Herrlichkeit, oder die christliche Lehre vom Himmel* Meurs, 1838; *Die Verfinsterung der Welt, dargestellt in einem Cyklus von Lehrgedichten und Liedern*, Berlin, 1838; *Grundzüge der urchristlichen frohen Botschaft*, Duisburg, 1839; *Homilien über Col. iii. 1–17. Eine praktische Auslegung dieses apostolischen Aufrufs zum neuen Leben*, Barmen, 1839, 4th ed. 1844; *Vermischte Schriften*, Meurs, 1840-41, 4 vols., new series, Bielefeld, 1860–64, 3 vols.; *Christliche Betrachtungen über zusammenhängende biblische Abschnitte, für die häusliche Erbauung*, Duisburg, 1841; *Welche Geltung gebührt der Eigenthümlichkeit der reformirten Kirche immer noch in der wissenschaftlichen Glaubenslehre unserer Zeit? Eine Abhandlung als freie Ueberarbeitung seiner Antrittsrede*, Zürich, 1841; *Deutsches Kirchenliederbuch oder die Lehre vom Kirchengesang, practische Abtheilung*, 1843; *Die kirchliche Hymnologie, oder die Lehre vom Kirchengesang, theoretische Abtheilung, im Grundriss. Einleitung in das deutsche Kirchenliederbuch*, 1843 (these two books were reprinted in the form of one work, under the title *Geistliches Liederbuch*, 1854); *Gedichte*, Essen, 1843; *Das Leben Jesu nach den Evangelien*, Heidelberg (Book 1, 1844; Book 2, 3 parts, 1844–46; Book 3, 1847; English translation, Edinburgh, 1864, in 6 vols., new ed. Philadelphia, 1872); *Worte der Abwehr (in Beziehung auf das Leben Jesu)*, Zürich, 1846; *Ueber die Neugestaltung des Verhältnisses zwischen Staat und Kirche*, Heidelberg, 1848; *Christliche Dogmatik*, Heidelberg, 1849–52, 3 parts (i. Philosophical Dogmatics; ii. Positive Dogmatics; iii. Polemics and Irenics); *Neutestamentliche Zeitgedichte*, Frankfurt-am-Main, 1849; *Briefe eines communistischen Propheten*, Breslau, 1850; *Goethes religiöse Poesie*, 1850; *Die Geschichte der Kirche*, Brunswick, 1853-54 (1. Theil, *Das apostolische Zeitalter*, 2 vols.); *Vom Oelberge. Geistliche Dichtungen*, Frankfurt-am-Main, 1853, 2d ed. 1858; *Auswahl von Gast- und Gelegenheits-Predigten aus meinen Zürcherischen Lebensjahren*, Bonn, 1855, 2d ed. 1857; edited (and contributed commentaries on Matthew, Mark, John, Romans, James [critical and exegetical notes, introduction, and translation], Revelation, Genesis, Exodus, Leviticus, Haggai, Zechariah, Malachi), *Theologisch-homiletisches Bibelwerk*, Bielefeld, 1857–76 (New Testament, 1857–71, 16 parts; Old Testament, 1865–76, 20), American trans., enlarged and adapted, edited by Schaff in connection with different American scholars, New York, 1864–74, 24 vols. (in the American series is included Bissell's *Commentary on the Apocrypha*, 1880); *Das Sic et Non, oder die Ja- u. Nein-Theologie der modernen Theologen*, 1869, pp. 18; *Zur Psychologie in der Theologie, Abhandlungen und Vorträge*, Heidelberg, 1873; *Ueber die Risse und Zerklüftungen in der heutigen Gesellschaft*, 1876, pp. 26; *Grundriss der theologischen Encyklopädie mit Einschluss der Methodologie*, 1877; *Grundriss der biblischen Hermeneutik*, 1878; *Grundriss der christlichen Ethik*, 1878; *Grundlinien einer kirchlichen Anstandslehre*, 1879; *Die Menschen- u. Selbstverachtung als Grundschaden unserer Zeit. Eine Folge der Verwahrlosung der Lehre von der Gottverwandtschaft des Menschen*, 1879; *Grundriss der Bibelkunde*, 1881; *Meine Verwickelung mit dem Methodismus der sogenannten Albrechtsleute*, Bonn, 1881; *Entweder Mysterien oder Absurdum. Zur Festnagelungen haltloser Geister*, 1882 (pp. 29); *Gegen d. Erklärung d. Organ f. positive Union zu Gunsten e. bedingten Anerkennung d. Missionirens der Methodisten in der evangelischen Kirche Deutschlands*, 1883 (pp. 34); *Die biblische Lehre von der Erwählung, Zur Apologie der Geistesaristokratie*, 1883 (pp. 48). PHILIP SCHAFF.

LANGEN, Joseph, D.D. (Freiburg, 1861), Old Catholic; b. at Cologne, June 3, 1837; studied at Bonn; was ordained priest, 1859; *privat-docent* at Bonn, 1861; professor extraordinary, 1864; ordinary professor, 1867; excommunicated for refusing to accept the infallibility dogma, 1872. He is the author of *Die deuterokanonischen Stücke des Buches Esther*, Freiburg, 1862; *Die letzten Lebenstage Jesu*, 1864; *Das Judenthum in Palästina zur Zeit Christi*, 1866; *Einleitung ins N. T.*, 1868, 2d ed. Bonn, 1873; *Die Kirchenväter u. d. N. T.*, Bonn, 1874; *Die Trinitarische Lehrdifferenz*, 1876; *Das Vaticanische Dogma in seinen Verhältniss zum N. T. u. der Überlieferung*, 1876; *Johannes von Damaskus*, Gotha, 1879; *Geschichte der römischen Kirche*, Bonn, vol. i. 1881, vol. ii. 1885 (to Nicholas I.).

LANGHANS, Eduard, D.D., Swiss Protestant theologian; b. at Guttannen, Berner Oberland, April 20, 1832; studied at Bern, Basel, Berlin, and Montauban; was pastor and teacher of religion at Münchenbuchsee, from 1876–80, and, at the same time *privat-docent* of the theological faculty at Bern, where in 1880 he became ordinary professor. He is the author of *Handbuch der biblischen Geschichte und Literatur*, Bern, 1875–81, 2 vols.

LANGWORTHY, Isaac Pendleton, D.D. (Iowa College, Grinnell, Io., 1878), Congregationalist; b. at Stonington (now North Stonington), Conn., Jan. 19, 1806; graduated at Yale College, New Haven, Conn., 1839, and at Yale Theological Seminary 1841; became pastor at Chelsea, Mass., 1841; corresponding secretary of the American Congregational Union, New York, 1858; corresponding secretary of the American Congregational Association, Boston, 1868 He inaugurated the church-building work of the American Congregational

Union. The Congregational House, with its library of over thirty thousand books and more than a hundred thousand pamphlets, is largely the result of his energy. He has published several sermons, many reports and newspaper articles.

LANSDELL, Henry, D.D. (by Archbishop of Canterbury and Queen's letters patent, 1882), Church of England; b. at Tenterden, Kent, Jan. 10, 1841; educated in the London College of Divinity, 1865–67; was ordained deacon 1867, priest 1868, curate of Greenwich 1868–69; secretary to the Irish Church Missions, 1869–79; founder and honorary secretary of the Church Homiletical Society, 1874–86; originator and editor of *The Clergyman's Magazine*, 1875; curate in charge of St. Peter's, Eltham, Kent, 1885. He is a member of the Royal Asiatic Society, and of the General Committee of the British Association for the Advancement of Science (life member, 1880); fellow of the Royal Geographical Society, 1876. He has not only since 1870 journeyed round the world, and with two exceptions throughout every country of Europe; but he has visited parts of Siberia, Central Asia, Bokhara, and Khiva, where no Englishman had preceded him. Since 1874 he has gone not only as traveller, but as amateur missionary, distributing tracts through Denmark, Sweden, Finland, and Russia, 1874; Norway and Sweden, 1876; Hungary and Transylvania, 1877; tracts and Scriptures through Russia, 1878; Siberia, 1879; Armenia, 1880; Russian Central Asia, 1882. He is the author of *Through Siberia*, London, 1882, 2 vols. 5th ed. 1883; *Russian Central Asia, including Kuldja, Bokhara, Khiva, and Merv*, 1885, 2 vols.

LANSING, John Gulian, D.D. (Union College, Schenectady, N Y., 1885), Reformed (Dutch); b. in Damascus, Syria, Nov. 27, 1851; graduated at Union College, Schenectady, N.Y., 1875, and at New Brunswick (N.J.) Theological Seminary, 1877; became minister at Mohawk, N.Y., 1877; at West Troy, N.Y., 1880; professor of Old-Testament languages and exegesis in the New Brunswick Theological Seminary, 1884. He is the author of the *American Revised Version of the Book of Psalms*, New York, 1885; *An Arabic Manual* (in press).

LASHER, George William, D.D. (Madison University, Hamilton, N.Y., 1874), Baptist; b. at Duanesburg, Schenectady County, N.Y., June 24, 1831; graduated at Madison University, Hamilton, N.Y., 1857, and at Hamilton Theological Seminary in the same place, 1859; became pastor of First Baptist Church, Norwalk, Conn., 1859; chaplain of Fifth Connecticut Regiment Volunteers, 1861; pastor of First Baptist Church, Newburgh, N.Y., 1862; of the Portland-street Church, Haverhill, Mass., 1864; of the First Baptist Church, Trenton, N.J., 1868; secretary of the Baptist Education Society of the State of New York, 1872; was in Europe and the East, 1875; since 1876 has been editor of the *Journal and Messenger*, Cincinnati, O. He is the author of occasional sermons, articles in *Baptist Quarterly Review*, etc.

LATIMER, James Elijah, D.D. (Wesleyan University, Middletown, Conn., 1868), Methodist; b. at Hartford, Conn., Oct. 7, 1826; d. in Boston, Mass., Nov. 25, 1884; graduated at Wesleyan University, Middletown, Conn., 1848; became teacher of languages at Newbury (Vt.) Seminary, 1848; teacher of Latin and geology in the Genesee Wesleyan Seminary, Lima, N.Y., 1849; principal of seminary, Northfield, N.H., 1851; principal of Fort Plain Seminary, N.Y., 1854; teacher of languages in Elmira (N.Y.) Female College, 1859; pastor of the First Methodist-Episcopal Church, Elmira, 1861–62; of the Asbury Church, Rochester, N.Y., 1863–64; of the First Church, Rochester, 1865–67; in Europe, 1868; pastor at Penn Yan, N.Y., 1869; professor of historic theology in the school of theology of Boston University, Mass., 1870–74; dean and professor of systematic theology in said school, 1874–84. He published only review articles and occasional sermons.

LAWRENCE, William, Episcopalian; b. in Boston, May 30, 1850; graduated from Harvard University, Cambridge, Mass., 1871, and from the Episcopal Theological School of Cambridge, Mass.; rector in Lawrence, Mass., 1876–83; and since then professor of homiletics and pastoral care in the Episcopal Theological School, Cambridge, Mass.

LAWSON, Albert Gallatin, D.D. (Madison University, Hamilton, N.Y., 1883), Baptist; b. at Poughkeepsie, N.Y., June 5, 1842; studied in New-York Free Academy (now College of the City of New York), 1856–59, and in Madison University, Hamilton, N.Y., 1859–60, but did not graduate; became pastor of First Baptist Church, Perth Amboy, N.J., 1862; at Poughkeepsie, N.Y., 1866; of the Greenwood Church, Brooklyn, N.Y., 1867; secretary of the American Baptist Missionary Union, Boston, Mass., 1884. He was clerk of the Long-Island Baptist Association, 1870–84; was active on the boards of the Brooklyn Young Men's Christian Association, and of the National Temperance and Publication Society. Besides addresses and sermons, he has written for the National Temperance Society a number of widely circulated temperance leaflets, principal of which are *The Threefold Cord* (1874), and *Methods of Church Temperance Work* (1877).

LEATHES, Stanley, D.D. (Edinburgh, 1878), Church of England; b. at Ellesborough, Bucks, March 21, 1830; educated at Jesus College, Cambridge; graduated B.A. 1852, first Tyrwhitt scholar 1853, M.A. 1855; was ordained deacon 1856, priest 1857; was curate in London, 1856–69; minister of St. Philip's, Regent Street, 1869–80; has been prebendary of Caddington Major, in St. Paul's Cathedral, since 1876; and rector of Cliffe-at-Hoo, diocese of Rochester, since 1880. Since 1863 he has been professor of Hebrew, King's College, London. He was Boyle lecturer 1868–70, Hulsean lecturer 1873, Bampton lecturer 1874, Warburtonian lecturer 1876–80; also member of the Old-Testament Company of the Bible-revision Committee. He is the author of *The Witness of the Old Testament to Christ* (Boyle Lectures, 1868), London, 1868; *The Witness of Paul to Christ* (same, 1869), 1869; *The Witness of St. John to Christ* (same, 1870), 1870; *The Structure of the Old Testament*, 1873; *The Gospel its own Witness* (Hulsean Lectures), 1874; *The Religion of the Christ* (Bampton Lectures), 1874, 2d ed. 1876; *The Grounds of Christian Hope*, 1877; *The Christian Creed: its Theory and Practice*, 1877; *Old-Testament Prophecy: its Witness as a Record of Divine Foreknowledge* (Warburton Lectures), 1880; *The Foundations of Morality: Discourses* *upon the Ten Commandments*, 1882; *The Characteristics of Christianity*, 1883; *Christ and the Bible*, 1885. He also contributed the comments upon *Daniel*, the *Minor Prophets*, and the *New Testament*, to the commentary published by Eyre and Spottiswoode. *

LECHLER, Gotthard Victor, Ph.D. (Tübingen, 1840), **D.D.** (*hon.*, Göttingen, 1858), German Lutheran theologian; b. at Kloster Reichenbach, Würtemberg, April 18, 1811; studied at Tübingen, 1829–34; became *diakonus* at Waiblingen, Würtemberg, 1841; *decan* and city pastor at Knittlingen, Würtemberg, 1853; pastor of St. Thomas's and superintendent at Leipzig, 1858; emeritus, 1883; has been since 1858 professor of theology in the University of Leipzig, and since 1880 *Geheimer Kirchenrath*. He is the author of *Geschichte des Englischen Deismus*, Stuttgart, 1841; *Das apostolische und das nachapostolische Zeitalter, Mit Rücksicht auf Unterschied und Einheit in Lehre und Leben dargestellt* (the Teyler prize essay), Haarlem, 1851 (3d ed., thoroughly revised and re-written, Karlsruhe and Leipzig, 1885; Eng. trans., *The Apostolic and Post-apostolic Times: their Diversity and Unity in Life and Doctrine*, Edinburgh, 1886); *Geschichte der Presbyterial- und Synodalverfassung seit der Reformation* (crowned by The Hague Society), Leiden, 1854; *De Thoma Bradwardino*, Leipzig, 1862 (pp. 19); *Robert Grosseteste, bischof von Lincoln*, 1867; *Der Kirchenstaat und die Opposition gegen den päpstlichen Absolutismus im Anfange des 14. Jahrhunderts*, 1870; *Johann von Wiclif und die Vorgeschichte der Reformation*, 1873, 2 vols. (Eng. trans. of vol. i. by Principal Lorimer, *John Wiclif and his English Precursors*, London, 1878, 2 vols. in 1 vol. 1881; new ed. by Rev. Dr. S. G. Green, 1884, 1 vol.); contributor of commentary on *Acts* in Lange's *Bibelwerk*, Bielefeld, 1859, 4th ed. 1881 (Eng. trans. by C. F. Schaeffer, D.D., in the American Lange series, N.Y., 1866); editor of Wiclif's *Tractatus de officio pastorali* (Leipzig, 1863), *Trialogus*, and *Supplementum Trialogi sive de dotatione ecclesiæ* (Oxford, 1869); and, with Dibelius, of *Beiträge zur sächsischen Kirchengeschichte*, Leipzig (part 1, 1882; part 2, 1883; part 3, 1885).

LEE, Right Rev. Alfred, S.T.D. (Trinity College, Hartford, Conn., and Hobart College, Geneva, N.Y., 1841; Harvard College, Cambridge, Mass., 1860), **LL.D.** (Delaware College, Newark, Del., 1877), Episcopalian, bishop of Delaware and presiding bishop; b. at Cambridge, Mass., Sept. 9, 1807; graduated at Harvard College, Cambridge, Mass., 1827; studied law, and practised two years in Norwich, Conn.; graduated at the General Theological Seminary, New-York City, 1837; was rector of Calvary, Rockdale, Penn., until his elevation to the episcopate, Oct. 12, 1841; became presiding bishop on death of Bishop B. B. Smith, May 31, 1884. He is a moderate Episcopalian. He was a member of the New-Testament Revision Company, 1870–81. Besides charges, addresses, etc., he has written *Life of the Apostle Peter*, New York, 1852; *The Beloved Disciple*, 1854; *Life of Susan Allibone*, Philadelphia, 1855; *The Voice in the Wilderness*, New York, 1857; *Co-operative Revision of the New Testament*, 1881; *Eventful Nights in Bible History*, 1886.

LEE, Frederick George, D.C.L. (Oxford, 1864), **D.D.** (Washington and Lee University, Lexington, Va., 1879), Church of England; b. at Thame Vicarage, Oxfordshire, Jan. 6, 1832; educated at St. Edmund's Hall, Oxford; graduated S.C.L., 1854; wrote the Newdigate prize poem for 1854; was elected fellow of the Society of Antiquaries in 1857. He was honorary secretary of the Association for the Promotion of the Unity of Christendom, 1857–69; one of the originators and officers of the Order of Corporate Re-union, established in 1877: was ordained deacon 1854, priest 1856; curate of Sunningwell, Berks, 1854–56. Since 1867 he has been vicar of All Saints', Lambeth, London. Of his numerous works, which include volumes of poetry and of sermons, may be mentioned, *Petronilla and other Poems*, 1858, 2d ed. 1869; *The Beauty of Holiness*, 1859, 4th ed. 1869; *The Christian Doctrine of Prayer for the Departed*, 1874, 2d ed. 1875; *Glimpses of the Supernatural*, 1875, 2 vols.; *Memorials of R. S. Hawker*, 1876; *Glossary of Liturgical and Ecclesiastical Terms*, 1876; *Historical Sketches of the Reformation*, 1878; *More Glimpses of the World Unseen*, 1878; *Prayers for Re-union*, 3d ed. 1878; *The Church under Queen Elizabeth*, 1879–80, 2 vols.; *History and Antiquities of the Church of Thame*, 1883; *Glimpses in the Twilight*, 1884. *

LEE, William, D.D. (Edinburgh, 1868), Church of Scotland; b. in Edinburgh, Nov. 6, 1817; graduated from Edinburgh University, 1839; was minister of the parish of Roxburgh, Scotland, 1843–74; and since has been professor of ecclesiastical history in the University of Glasgow. His father was John Lee, D.D., LL.D. (d. 1859), principal and professor of divinity in the University of Edinburgh, dean of the Chapel Royal in Scotland, one of the Queen's chaplains for Scotland, and an authority in Scottish church history. He is the editor of Dr. John Lee's *Lectures on the History of the Church of Scotland*, 1860, 2 vols.; Thomas Somerville's *My Own Life and Times*, 1861; and the author of *National Education in Scotland*, Edinburgh, 1848, 2d ed. 1851; *The Increase of Faith*, 1867, 2d ed. 1868; *The Days of the Son of Man: a History of the Church in the Time of Christ*, 1874; and various contributions to the *Bible Educator*, the *Schaff-Herzog Encyclopædia*, etc. D. at Glasgow, Oct. 10, 1886.

LEFFINGWELL, Charles Wesley, D.D. (Knox College, Galesburg, Ill., 1875), Episcopalian; b. at Ellington, Conn., Dec. 5, 1840; studied at Union College, Schenectady, N.Y., 1857–59; was principal of Galveston Academy, Tex., 1859–60; graduated at Knox College, Galesburg, 1862; was vice-principal of Poughkeepsie (N.Y.) Military Institute, 1862–65; graduated B.D. at Nashotah Theological Seminary, 1867; was tutor in Nashotah Seminary, and assistant at St. James's Church, Chicago, 1867–68; founder and rector of St. Mary's School, Knoxville, Ill., since 1868; president of the standing committee of the diocese of Quincy; editor of the diocese and province, 1875–79; editor of *The Living Church*, 1879, sqq. He is a High Churchman. He is the compiler of *Reading Book of English Classics for Young Pupils*, New York, 1879.

LEGGE, James, LL.D. (Aberdeen, and Edinburgh, 1884), **D.D.** (University of New-York City, 1842), Congregationalist; b. at Huntly, Aberdeenshire, Scotland, Dec. 20, 1815; educated at King's College, Old Aberdeen; graduated M.A., 1835; studied at Highbury Theol. Seminary, London;

was missionary of the London Missionary Society, and in charge of the Anglo-Chinese College, Malacca, 1839–43; missionary, and in charge of the theological seminary of the London Missionary Society, and pastor of the Union Church, Hongkong, 1843–73; since 1876 has been professor of the Chinese language and literature at Oxford, where he is also fellow of Corpus Christi College, and received an honorary M.A. 1876. He is the author of *Notions of the Chinese concerning God and Spirits*, Hongkong, 1852; *Confucian Analects, Doctrine of the Mean, and Great Learning*, 1861; *Works of Mencius*, 1861; *The Shu King, or Book of Historical Documents*, 1865; *The Shi King, or Book of Poetry*, 1871; *The Ch'un Ch'iu, with the Tso Chwan*, 1872 (the last five works contain the Chinese text, translation, prolegomena, and notes); *The Life and Teachings of Confucius*, 1866, 4th ed. 1875; *The Life and Works of Mencius*, 1875; *The Book of Ancient Chinese Poetry in English Verse*, 1876; *The Religions of China: Confucianism and Tâoism described and compared with Christianity*, London 1880, New York 1881, Utrecht (Dutch trans.) 1882. In Max Muller's series, *Sacred Books of the East*, he has published *The Shu King: Religious Portions of the Shi King and the Hsiao King* (Oxford, 1879), *The Yi King* (1882), *The Li Ki, Book of Ceremonial Usages*, 2 vols. (1886); and *The Travels of the Buddhist Pilgrim Fa-hsien in India* (1886); author of other smaller works and sermons.

LEO XIII., His Holiness the Pope, the two hundred and fifty-eighth successor of St. Peter, **Vincenzo Gioacchino Pecci,** son of Count Ludovico Pecci; b. at Carpineto, Anagni, States of the Church, March 2, 1810; educated at the Jesuit colleges of Viterbo (1818–24) and Rome (Collegio Romano, 1824–31), and graduated D.D. 1831. He then entered the College of Noble Ecclesiastics, attended lectures on canonical and civil law in the Roman University, and graduated D.C.L. 1837. His college course was very brilliant. In 1837 he was appointed by Gregory XVI. a domestic prelate, and refendary of the segnatura, March 16, 1837; ordained priest, Dec. 23, 1837; was made successively prothonotary apostolic, and apostolic delegate at Benevento (where he put down brigandage), Perugia, and Spoleto; archbishop of Damietta, *in partibus infidelium*, Jan. 17, 1843; papal *nuncio* to Belgium, 1843–46; archbishop of Perugia, Jan. 19, 1846, and so remained until his elevation to the papacy. On Dec. 19, 1853, he was proclaimed cardinal by Pius IX., and Sept. 21, 1877, created Cardinal Camerlengo of the Holy Roman Church. On the death of Pius IX., Feb. 7, 1878, he acted as pope *ad tempore*, and superintended all the arrangements for the papal obsequies and conclave. The conclave (Feb. 18–20, 1878) to choose a new pope was attended by sixty-two cardinals. He received nineteen votes on the first ballot, thirty-four on the second, forty-four on the third; his election was then made unanimous, and he accepted the position, and chose the name Leo. On March 3 he was crowned in the Sistine Chapel. He retains the prefectship of the following sacred congregations: the Holy Roman and Universal Inquisition or Holy Office, the Apostolic Visitation, the Consistorial Congregation. On March 4, 1878, he restored the papal hierarchy in Scotland. He has proved himself to be much more liberally inclined than Pius IX. was in the latter part of his life; and has shown his scholarly tastes by opening the Vatican to scholars, within certain limits, and by recommending the study of Aquinas. The following are the encyclicals he has issued: (1) *Inscrutabili Dei consilio*, the inaugural encyclical (April 21, 1878), which shows from history how the Roman Church has been the protectress of all true civilization; (2) *Quod Apostolici muneris* (Dec. 28, 1878), on the dangers which threaten civilization from communism and socialism, and how they should be met; (3) *Æterni Patris* (Aug. 4, 1879), on the necessity of a restoration of science upon the foundation of the philosophical principles of Thomas Aquinas; (4) *Arcanum divinæ sapientiæ consilium* (Feb. 10, 1880), on the holiness and indissolubleness of Christian marriage; (5) *Grande munus* (Sept. 30, 1880), on the canonization of Cyril and Methodius; (6) *Sancta Dei civitas* (Dec. 5, 1880), on Roman-Catholic missions; (7) *Diuturnum* (June 29, 1881), on the origin of the civil power; (8) *Auspicato concessum* (Sept. 17, 1882), on the third order of St. Francis; (9) *Misericors Dei Filius* (May 30, 1883), on the rule of the third Seraphic order; (10) *Supremi Apostolatus* (Sept. 1, 1883), on the rosary of Mary; (11) *Nobilissima* (Feb. 8, 1884), on the religious affairs of France; (12) *Humanum genus* (April 20, 1884), on the Masonic "sect;" (13) *Immortale Dei* (Nov. 1, 1885), on the position of the Roman Church towards modern governments. He has also issued two briefs, (1) *Cum hoc sit* (Aug. 4, 1880), on St. Thomas Aquinas, the patron of scholars; (2) *Sæpenumero considerantes* (Aug. 13, 1883), on historical studies; and one apostolic letter, *Militans Christi* (March 12, 1881), appointing an extraordinary jubilee. The complete Latin text of all these is found in the *Papæ Acta Leonis XIII.*, Paris, 1885.

LEWIS, Abram Herbert, D.D. (Alfred University, Alfred Centre, N.Y., 1881), Seventh-day Baptist; b. at Scott, Cortland County, N.Y., Nov. 17, 1836; graduated at Milton College, Milton, Wis., 1861, and at Alfred University, Alfred Centre, N.Y., 1863; took post-graduate lectures at Union Theological Seminary, New-York City, 1868; was pastor of the Seventh-day Baptist Church, Westerly, R.I., 1864–67; in New-York City, 1867–68; since 1868 professor of church history and homiletics in Alfred University; general agent of the American Sabbath Tract Society, 1869–72; pastor at Plainfield, N.J., since 1880. He was president of the New-Jersey State Sunday-school Association, 1881–82. He is the author of *Sabbath and Sunday*, Alfred Centre, N.Y., 1870; *Biblical Teachings concerning the Sabbath and the Sunday*, 1884; *A Critical History of the Sabbath and the Sunday in the Christian Church*, 1886, 2 vols.

LEWIS, Right Rev. Richard, D.D. (by diploma, 1883), lord bishop of Llandaff, Church of England; b. in Wales, in the year 1821; was scholar of Worcester College, Oxford; honorary fourth-class classics, 1842; graduated B.A. 1843, M.A. 1846; was ordained deacon 1844, priest 1846; rector of Lampeter Velfry, 1851–83; prebendary of Caerlarchell in St. David's Cathedral, 1867–75; archdeacon of St. David's; prebendary of Mydrim in St. David's Cathedral, and chaplain to the bishop of St. David's, 1875–83; became bishop, 1883.

LIAS, John James, Church of England; b. in London, Nov. 30, 1834; studied at King's College, London, 1850–53, and was scholar of Emmanuel College, Cambridge, where he graduated as B.A. 1857, M.A. 1861; was ordained deacon 1858, priest 1860; was curate of Shaftesbury 1858–60, of Folkestone 1865–67; vicar of Eastbury, Berks, 1867–68; minor canon of Llandaff, 1868–71; professor of modern literature, and lecturer in theology and Hebrew, at St. David's College, Lampeter, 1871–80; select preacher at Cambridge, 1876 and 1880; Hulsean lecturer there, 1884; Lady Margaret's preacher, 1884; Whitehall preacher, 1884–86; since 1880 has been vicar of St. Edmund's, Cambridge. He is the author of *The Rector and his Friends: Dialogues on the Religious Questions of the Day*, London, 1869; *The Doctrinal System of St. John considered as Evidence for the Date of his Gospel*, 1875; *Commentary on First Corinthians* (in *Cambridge Bible for Schools*), Cambridge, 1878; do. on *Second Corinthians*, 1879; *Sermons preached at Lampeter, St. David's College*, London, 1880; *Commentary on Joshua* (in *Pulpit Commentary*), 1881; *Commentary on Judges* (in *Cambridge Bible for Schools*), Cambridge, 1882; *The Atonement in the Light of Certain Modern Difficulties* (Hulsean Lectures for 1883–84), 1884; papers read before the Victoria Institute: 1. *On the Moral Influence of Christianity;* 2. *Is it Possible to know God?* (considerations on the "Unknown and Unknowable" of modern thought); *The Benefactors of To-day* (sermon preached before the University of Cambridge at the annual commemoration of Benefactors), 1884; sundry single sermons, lectures, and addresses.

LICHTENBERGER, Frédéric Auguste, Lic. Theol., D.D. (both Strassburg, 1857 and 1860); b. at Strassburg, March 21, 1832; studied at Strassburg, Paris, and in Germany, and since 1864 has been member of the French Protestant theological faculty, first at Strassburg, and since 1877 in Paris. On the re-organization of the faculty, necessitated by its removal, he became its dean. He edited the *Encyclopédie des sciences religieuses*, (Paris, 1877–82, 13 vols.), and contributed twenty important articles to it. Among his works are, *La théologie de G. E. Lessing*, 1854; *Etude sur le principe du protestantisme d'après la théologie allemande contemporaine*, 1857; *Sermons*, 1867; *L'Alsace en deuil*, 1871, 10 editions; *Histoire des idées religieuses en Allemagne depuis le milieu du dix-huitième siècle jusqu'à nos jours*, 1873, 3 vols. *

LIDDON, Henry Parry, D.D. and **Hon. D.C.L.** (both Oxford, 1870), Church of England; b. at Stoneham, Hants, Aug. 20, 1829: was student of Christ Church College, Oxford; graduated B.A. (second-class in classics) 1851, M.A. 1853, and was Johnson theological scholar 1851; ordained deacon 1852, priest 1853; was vice-principal of the theological college of Cuddesdon, 1852–59; prebendary of Major Pars Altaris in Salisbury Cathedral, 1864–70; examining chaplain to the late bishop (Hamilton) of Salisbury; member of the hebdomadal council of the University of Oxford, 1866–75; Ireland professor of exegesis of Scripture at Oxford, 1870–October, 1882; became a canon residentiary in St. Paul's Cathedral, London, 1870; was Bampton lecturer in 1866; and select preacher at Oxford, 1863–65, 1870–72, 1877–79, 1884, and in 1884 filled a similar position at Cambridge. He is one of the greatest preachers of the Church of England. Among his publications may be mentioned, *Lenten Sermons*, London, 1858; *The Divinity of our Lord and Saviour Jesus Christ* (Bampton Lectures), 1867, 11th ed. 1885; *Sermons preached before the University of Oxford*, 1st series (1863–68) 1869, 8th ed. 1884, 2d series (1868–79) 1880, 3d ed. 1882; *Walter Ken Hamilton, Bishop of Salisbury: a Sketch*, 1869, 2d ed. 18—; *Some Elements of Religion*, 1871, 5th ed. 1885; *Sermons on Various Subjects*, 1872, 1876, 1879; *Report of Proceedings at the Bonn Re-union Conference in 1875*; *Thoughts on Present Church Troubles*, 1881, 2d ed. same year; *Easter in St. Paul's: Sermons on the Resurrection*, 1885, 2 vols. He has edited Bishop Andrews' *Manual for the Sick*, 1869, 4th ed. 1883; Pusey's *Prayers for a Young Schoolboy* (1883, 2d ed. 1884), and *Private Prayers* (1883, 2d ed. 1884); Antonio Rosmini's *Of the Five Wounds of the Church* (trans. from Italian), 1883. *

LIGHTFOOT, Right Rev. Joseph Barber, D.D. (Cambridge, 1864; Durham, 1879), **D.C.L.** (Oxford, 1879), **LL.D.** (Glasgow, 1879), lord bishop of Durham, Church of England; b. at Liverpool, April 13, 1828; entered Trinity College, Cambridge; obtained a scholarship in 1849; graduated B.A. (wrangler, senior classic, and senior medallist) 1851, M.A. 1854; elected fellow of his college, 1852; in 1853 he was Norrisian prizeman. He was ordained deacon in 1854, and priest in 1858. In 1857 he was appointed tutor in his college; in 1858 was select preacher to the University of Cambridge; in 1861 became chaplain to the late Prince Consort, and Hulsean professor of divinity at Cambridge; in 1862, examining chaplain to the bishop of London (Dr. Tait), and honorary chaplain in ordinary to the Queen; in 1866 and 1867 was Whitehall preacher. In 1869, Dr. Tait being elevated to the see of Canterbury, he became one of his examining chaplains, and remained so until 1879. From 1871 to 1879 he was canon residentiary of St. Paul's Cathedral, London; in 1874 and 1875 he was select preacher at Oxford. In 1875 he resigned his Hulsean professorship, and became Lady Margaret professor of divinity, Cambridge, and in the same year deputy clerk of the closet to her Majesty. In 1879 he was recommended by the Earl of Beaconsfield to the then vacant see of Durham, and was consecrated bishop in Westminster Abbey. His remarkable scholarship is shown in his commentaries on *Galatians* (London, 1865, 8th ed. 1884), *Philippians* (1868, 7th ed. 1883), *Colossians*, and *Philemon* (1875, 8th ed. 1886), and on the Apostolic Fathers, *S. Clement of Rome* (1869; appendix volume, containing the complete second epistle discovered by Bryennios, 1877), *S. Ignatius*, and *S. Polycarp* (1885, 2 vols.). Each of these commentaries contains a revised Greek text, introduction, notes, and dissertations. The last is a peculiar feature of great interest and value. Dr. Lightfoot was one of the original members of the New-Testament Company of Bible Revisers, and wrote *On a Fresh Revision of the English New Testament*, 1871, 2d ed. 1872 (republished, with permission, by Dr. Schaff, New York, 1873).

LINCOLN, Heman, D.D. (Rochester University, Rochester, N.Y., 1865), Baptist; b. in Boston, Mass., April 14, 1821; graduated at Brown University, Providence, R.I., 1840, and at Newton (Mass) Theological Institution, 1845; became pastor in Pennsylvania, 1845: at Jamaica Plain, Mass., 1853; Providence, R.I., 1860; professor of church history in Newton Theological Institution, 1868. He was one of the editors of *The Christian Chronicle*, 1848–53, and of *The Watchman and Reflector*, 1854–67. He has written *Outline Lectures in Church History*, Boston, 1884; do. *in History of Doctrine*, 1886, etc.

LINSENMANN, Franz Xaver, Lic. Theol. (Tübingen, 1867), **D.D.** (*hon.*, Tübingen, 1872), Roman Catholic; b. at Rottweil, Nov. 28, 1835; studied philosophy and theology at Tübingen, 1854–58; was ordained priest at Rottenburg, 1859, and the same year curate at Oberndorf; became *repetent* of dogmatics at Tübingen, 1861; professor extraordinary of moral theology, 1867; ordinary professor of moral and pastoral theology, 1872. He is the author of *Mich. Bajus u. die Grundlegung des Jansenismus*, Tübingen, 1867; *Der ethische Character der Lehre Meister Eckhardt's* (*program*), 1873; and these articles in the *Tübinger Theolog. Quartalschrift: Gabriel Biel*, 1865; *Albertus Pighius*, 1866; *Das Verhältniss d. heidn. zur christl. Moral*, 1868; *Ueber populäre Predigtweise*, 1873; *Ueber apologetische Predigtweise*, 1874 and 1875.

LIPSCOMB, Andrew Adgate, D.D. (University of Alabama, Tuscaloosa, 1850; Emory College, Oxford, Ga., 1870), Methodist Protestant; b. at Georgetown, D.C., Sept. 6, 1816; licensed to preach, 1834; united with the Maryland Conference of the Methodist Protestant Church, 1835; removed to Montgomery, Ala., 1842; became president of the Alabama Conference; founded the Metropolitan Institute for Young Ladies, at Montgomery, 1849; president of Tuskegee Female College, Methodist-Episcopal Church South, 1856-59; chancellor of the University of Georgia, at Athens, 1860-74; professor of philosophy and criticism in Vanderbilt University, Nashville, Tenn., 1875-84. He is the author of *Our Country: its Danger and Duty* (a prize essay), N. Y., 1844; *The Social Spirit of Christianity*, Phila., 1846; *Christian Heroism illustrated in the Life and Character of St. Paul*, Macon, Ga., 1880, 4th ed. 1881; *Studies in the Forty Days between Christ's Resurrection and Ascension*, Nashville, Tenn., 1884; *Lessons from the Life of St. Peter*, Athens, Ga., 1884; *Supplementary Studies*, 1885.

LIPSIUS, Richard Adelbert, Ph.D., Lic. Theol. (both Leipzig, 1853 and 1854), **D.D.** (*hon.*, Jena, 1858); b. at Gera, Feb. 14, 1830; studied at Leipzig, 1848–51; became *privat-docent* there, 1855; professor extraordinary, 1859; ordinary professor at Vienna 1861, at Kiel 1865, and at Jena 1871, where he is also *Geheimer Kirchenrath*. As a philosophical adherent of Kant's, and as a theological follower of Schleiermacher's, he seeks, while relegating metaphysical doctrines to the background, to build up a system of dogmatics upon the religious experience of the Christian communion and of the individual believer. In 1875 he founded, and has ever since edited, the *Jahrbücher für protestantische Theologie*, and since 1885 has edited the *Theologischer Jahresbericht*. Besides his numerous writings in periodicals and encyclopædias, including that of Smith and Wace, he has published *Die paulinische Rechtfertigungslehre*, Leipzig, 1853; *De Clementis Romani epistola ad Corinthios priore disquisitio*, 1855; *Ueber das Verhältniss der drei syrischen Briefe des Ignatios zu den übrigen Recensionen der Ignatianischen Literatur*, 1859; *Der Gnosticismus, sein Wesen, Ursprung und Entwickelungsgang*, 1860; *Zur Quellen-kritik des Epiphanios*, Wien, 1865; *Die Papstverzeichnisse des Eusebios und der von ihm abhängigen Chronisten kritisch untersucht*, Kiel, 1868 (pp. 29); *Chronologie der römischen Bischöfe bis zur Mitte des 4. Jahrh.*, 1869; *Die Pilatus-Acten kritisch untersucht*, 1871; *Die Quellen der römischen Petrus-sage kritisch untersucht*, 1871; *Glaube und Lehre, Theologische Streitschriften*, 1871; *Ueber den Ursprung des Christennamens*, 1873; *Die Quellen der ältesten Ketzergeschichte*, 1875; *Lehrbuch der evangelisch-protestantischen Dogmatik*, Braunschweig, 1876, 2d ed. 1879; *Dogmatische Beiträge zur Vertheidigung und Erläuterung meines Lehrbuch*. Leipzig, 1878; *Die edessenische Abgar-sage kritisch untersucht*, Braunschweig, 1880; *Die apokryphen Apostelgeschichten und Apostellegenden*, vol. i. 1883, vol. ii. 2d half 1884, 1st half 1886; *Philosophie u. Religion*, Leipzig, 1885.

LITTLE, Charles Eugene, Methodist; b. at Waterbury, Vt, April 7, 1838; graduated in the School of Theology, Boston University, Boston, Mass., 1860, and has since been a pastor in various towns of New York, Vermont, and New Jersey. He is the author of *Biblical Lights and Side Lights*, New York, 1883, 2d ed. 1884 (each two thousand copies); *Historical Lights*, 1886.

LITTLEDALE, Richard Frederick, LL.D. (Dublin, 1862), **D.C.L.** (Oxford, 1862), Church of England; b. in Dublin, Sept. 14, 1833; graduated at Trinity College, Dublin, B.A. (first-class in classics) 1854, M.A. 1858, LL.D. 1862. In 1855 he won the second biblical Greek prize, and the first Berkeley gold medal, and a first divinity testimonium in 1856. He was a London curate from 1856 to 1861; but, being compelled by ill health to abandon parochial work, he has devoted himself to religious literature, and been a voluminous writer. As an opponent of the Church of Rome, he has attracted much attention. Among his works may be mentioned, *Religious Communities of Women in the Early Church*, London, 1862, 2 editions; *Offices of the Holy Eastern Church*, 1863; *The Mixed Chalice*, 1863, 4th ed. 1867; *The North Side of the Altar*, 1864, 5 editions; *Catholic Ritual in the Church of England*, 1865, 13 editions; *The Elevation of the Host*, 1865, 2 editions; *Early Christian Ritual*, 1867, 2 editions; *The Children's Bread: a Communion Office for the Young*, 1868, 4 editions: *Commentary on the Psalms* (in continuation of Dr. Neale's), vols. ii.-iv., 1868–74; *Commentary on the Song of Songs*, 1869; *Religious Education of Women*, 1872; *At the Old Catholic Congress*, 1872; *Papers on Sisterhoods*, 1874–78; *Last Attempt to reform the Church of Rome from within*, 1875; *Ultramontane Popular Literature*, 1876; *An Inner View of the Vatican Council*, 1877; *Why Ritualists do not become Roman Catholics*, 1878; *Plain Reasons against joining the Church of Rome*, 1879, 40th thousand 1886. He is contributor to the *Encyclopædia Britannica* (9th ed.); edited Anselm's *Cur Deus Homo?* (1863); and shared in editing *The Priests' Prayer-Book*, 1864, 6th ed. 1884; *The People's Hymnal*, 1867, 6 editions; *Primitive Liturgies and Translations*, 1868–69; *The Altar Manual*, 1877 (45th thousand).

LITTLEJOHN, Right Rev. Abram Newkirk, D.D. (University of Pennsylvania, Philadelphia, 1855), **LL.D.** (University of Cambridge, Eng.,

1880), Episcopalian, bishop of Long Island; b. at Florida, Montgomery County, N.Y., Dec. 13, 1824; graduated at Union College, Schenectady, N.Y., 1845; studied at Princeton (N.J.) Theological Seminary, 1845–46; became rector of Christ Church, Springfield, Mass., 1850; of St. Paul's, New Haven, Conn., 1851; of Holy Trinity, Brooklyn, N.Y., 1860; bishop, 1869. He lectured on pastoral theology in the Berkeley Divinity School, Middletown, Conn., 1853–58; declined presidency of Hobart College, Geneva, N.Y., 1858, and bishopric of Central New York, 1868. In 1874 he was appointed by the presiding bishop to take charge of the American Episcopal churches on the Continent of Europe. Besides charges, addresses, and occasional sermons, his contributions to current literature embrace critiques, essays, etc., on *Philosophy of Religion; The Metaphysics of Cousin; The Life and Writings of S. T. Coleridge; The Poetry of George Herbert; Sir James Stephens's Lectures on the History of France; Rogers's Eclipse of Faith; The Bible and Common Sense; The Outwardness of Popular Religion; Human Progress dependent on Tradition rather than Invention; Thoughts and Enquiries on the Alt-Catholic Movement; Discourse at the Consecration of St. Paul's Church within the Walls, Rome, Italy; Essay before the Church Congress*, New York, 1877; *Conciones ad Clerum, 1879–80*, 1881; *Individualism: its Growth and Tendencies, with some Suggestions as to the Remedy for its Evils, being Sermons preached before the University of Cambridge, Eng., November, 1880*, 1881; *The Christian Ministry at the Close of the Nineteenth Century, being Lectures before the General Theological Seminary, New York, on the "Bishop Paddock Foundation,"* 1884.

LIVERMORE, Abiel Abbot, A.M., Unitarian; b. at Wilton, N.H., Oct. 30, 1811; graduated at Harvard College, Cambridge, Mass., 1833, and at the Harvard Divinity School, 1836; was pastor in Keene, N.H. (1836–50), Cincinnati, O. (1850–56), Yonkers, N.Y. (1856–63); editor of *The Christian Inquirer*, New-York City, 1856–63; and since 1863 has been president of the Meadville (Penn.) Theological School. He is a Channing Unitarian. Besides reviews and occasional sermons, he is the author of *Priestley's Corruptions of Christianity, abridged*, Keene, N.H., 1838; *Christian Hymns, compiled*, Boston, 1840, 59th ed. 1861; *Commentary on the New Testament*, 1842–82, 6 vols., many editions; *Lectures to Young Men*, Keene, N.H., 1846; *The Marriage Offering*, Boston, 1848, 16th ed. 1862; *The Mexican War reviewed*, 1852; *Sermons*, 1857; *Syllabus on Ethics*, 1870; *Syllabus on Systematic Theology*, 1874; *Syllabus on Creeds*, 1878; *Anti-Tobacco*, 1883.

LOBSTEIN, Paul, D.D. (Göttingen, 1884), German Protestant; b. at Epinal (Département des Vosges), July 28, 1850; studied at Strassburg, Tübingen, and Göttingen; became *privat-docent* at Strassburg, 1876; professor extraordinary, 1877; ordinary professor, 1884. He belongs to the school of Ritschl. He has written *Die Ethik Calvins in ihren Grundzügen entworfen*, Strassburg, 1877; *Petrus Ramus als Theologe*, 1878; *La notion de la préexistence du Fils de Dieu*, Paris, 1883; and articles in Lichtenberger's *Encyclopédie des sciences religieuses*, etc.

LOESCHE, Georg (Carl David), Ph.D. (Jena, 1880), **Lic. Theol.** (Berlin, 1883), German Protestant theologian; b. in Berlin, Aug. 22, 1855; educated at Bonn, Tübingen, and Berlin; became preacher to the German Church in Florence, Italy, 1880; *privat-docent* in the University of Berlin, 1885. He is an adherent of the critical school in theology. He is the author of *De Augustino Plotinizante in doctrina de deo disserenda*, Halle, 1880; *Florenzer Predigten*, 1884; *Ernst Moritz Arndt, der deutsche Reichsherold*, Gotha, 1884; *Haben die späteren neuplatonischen Polemiker gegen das Christenthum das Werk des Celsus benutzt?* (in Hilgenfeld's *Zeitschrift f. w. Theologie*, 1884, xxvii. 3).

LONG, Albert Limerick, D.D. (Alleghany College, Meadville, Penn., 1867), Methodist; b. at Washington, Penn., Dec. 4, 1832; studied in the Western University of Pennsylvania, Pittsburg, Penn., and at Alleghany College, Meadville, Penn.; graduated from the latter institution, 1852; studied theology in what is now the theological department of the Boston University, 1857; went to Bulgaria as missionary in 1857; was transferred to Constantinople in 1863, to assist in the translation of the Scriptures into Bulgarian; edited a Bulgarian periodical, and various other publications, and acted as superintendent of the Bulgarian Mission of the Methodist-Episcopal Church until 1872, when he became professor in Robert College, Constantinople. The National Assembly of Bulgaria at their first meeting (1879) accorded him a vote of thanks in recognition of his services to the Bulgarian cause. In 1883 he was elected a corresponding member of the National Literary Society of Bulgaria; in 1884 Prince Alexander of Bulgaria, as a mark of personal appreciation, conferred upon him the Cross of Commander of the Order of St. Alexander. He is a corresponding member of the American Oriental Society, of the Numismatic Society of Philadelphia, and other associations. His contributions to literature have been chiefly in the Bulgarian language; but he has written upon subjects connected with Bulgaria, for English and American journals.

LOOFS, (Armin) Friedrich, Ph.D., Lic. Theol. (both Leipzig, 1881 and 1882), Lutheran; b. at Hildesheim, Hannover, Germany, June 19, 1858; studied at Leipzig, Tübingen, and Göttingen, 1877–81; became *privat-docent* of church history in the University of Leipzig, 1882. He is the author of *Zur Chronologie der auf die fränkischen Synoden des hl. Bonifaz bezüglichen Briefe der bonifazischen Briefsammlung*, Leipzig, 1881; *Antiquæ Britonum Scotorumque ecclesiæ quales fuerint mores, quæ ratio credendi et vivendi, quæ controversiæ cum Romana ecclesia causa atque vis*, 1882.

LOOMIS, Augustus Ward, D.D. (Hamilton College, Clinton, N.Y., 1873), Presbyterian; b. at Andover, Conn., Sept. 4, 1816; graduated at Hamilton College, Clinton, N.Y., 1841, and at Princeton (N.J.) Theological Seminary, 1844; was missionary in China, at Macao, Chusan, and Ningpo, from 1844 to 1850, when his health failed; and missionary among the Creek Indians at Kowetah, 1852–53; stated supply at St. Charles, Mo., 1853–54; at Edgington, Ill., 1854–59; but since 1859 has been missionary to the Chinese in San Francisco, Cal. He is the author of *Learn to say No*, Philadelphia, 1856; *Scenes in Chusan*, 1857; *How to die Happy*, 1858; *Scenes in the Indian Country*, 1859; *A Child a Hundred Years Old*, 1859; *Profits* *of Godliness*, 1859; *Confucius and the Chinese Classics*, San Francisco, Cal., 1867, 2d ed. Boston, 1882; *Chinese and English Lessons*, New York, 1872, 2d ed. 1882.

LORD, Willis, D.D. (Lafayette College, Easton, Penn., 1846), **LL.D.** (University of Wooster, Wooster, O., 1874), Presbyterian; b. at Bridgeport, Conn., Sept. 15, 1809; graduated at Williams College, Williamstown, Mass., 1833; studied theology in Princeton (N.J.) Theological Seminary, 1833-34; became pastor of the Congregational Church of New Hartford, Conn., 1834; of the Richmond-street Congregational Church, Providence, R.I., 1838; of the Penn-square Presbyterian Church, Philadelphia, Penn., 1840; of the Broadway Presbyterian Church, Cincinnati, O., and professor of biblical literature and pastoral theology in the theological seminary there, 1850; pastor of the Second Presbyterian Church, Brooklyn, N.Y., 1854; professor of biblical and ecclesiastical history, and then of didactic and polemic theology, in the Theological Seminary of the North-West, Chicago, Ill., 1859; president of the University of Wooster, 1870; retired in impaired health, 1874, and since then has been prevented by this cause from holding permanent public office, although acting as pastor elect of Central Church, Denver, Col., 1875-76; and of the First Church, Columbus, O., 1878-79; and during 1884 and 1885 giving assistance in building up the "Presbyterian College of the North-West" at Del Norte, Col. He is the author of *Men and Scenes before the Flood*, Philadelphia, 1816; *Christian Theology for the People*, New York, 1873, 2d ed. 1875; *The Blessed Hope*, Chicago, 1876, 2d ed. 1884; and of numerous sermons, addresses, articles, etc.

LOWE, William Henry, Church of England; b. at Whaplode Drove, Lincolnshire, England, April 10, 1848; educated at Christ College, Cambridge; graduated B.A. (senior optime) 1871, Tyrwhitt Hebrew scholar 1872, M.A. 1874, when he was appointed Hebrew lecturer in his college, and so remains. He was chaplain of his college from 1874 to 1881. He belongs to the critical school, and is the author of *The Psalms, with Introductions and Critical Notes*, London, 1875-77 (edited jointly with A. C. Jennings, and issued in parts), 2 vols., 2d ed. 1884-85; *Twelve Odes of Hafiz, translated from the Persian, with Sudi's Commentary from the Turkish*, Cambridge, 1877; *The Fragment of Talmud Babli, Pesachim, of ix.-x. cent., with Notes illustrative of the New Testament*, London, 1879; *The Memorbuch of Nürnberg, in Connection with the Persecution of the Jews in 1349*, 1881; *The Hebrew Student's Commentary on Zechariah*, 1882; *The Palestinian Mishnah* (from the unique MS. preserved in the University Library, edited for the syndics of the University Press), Cambridge, 1883; *Al-Badáúní's Reign of Akbar* (translated from the Persian for the Asiatic Society of Bengal), Calcutta, 1884-86; comments on *Zechariah* and *Malachi* in Bishop Ellicott's *Bible for English Readers*, London, 1884.

LOWRIE, John Cameron, D.D. (Miami University, Oxford, O., 1852), Presbyterian; b. at Butler, Penn., Dec. 16, 1808; graduated at Jefferson College, Canonsburg, Penn., 1829; was at Western Theological Seminary, Allegheny, Penn., 1829-32, at Princeton Theological Seminary, N.J., 1832-33; missionary in Upper India 1833-36, when, his health failing, he returned to America, and since 1838 has been connected with the Board of Foreign Missions, until 1850 as assistant secretary, and since as secretary. From 1845 to 1850 he was minister of the Forty-second-street Church, New York; moderator of the O. S. General Assembly at Pittsburg, Penn., 1865. He is the author of *Two Years in Upper India*, New York, 1850; *The Foreign Missions of the Presbyterian Church in the United States of America*, 1855, 3d ed. 1868; *Missionary Papers*, 1882.

LOWRIE, Samuel Thompson, D.D. (Washington and Jefferson College, Washington, Penn., 1874), Presbyterian; b. at Pittsburgh, Penn., Feb. 8, 1835; graduated at Miami University, Oxford, O., 1852, and at Western (Presbyterian) Theological Seminary, Allegheny, Penn., 1855; took a fourth year; studied two semesters at Heidelberg, Germany; was pastor of the Presbyterian Church at Alexandria, Penn., December, 1858, to April, 1863; then nine months in Europe; pastor of the Bethany Church, Philadelphia, 1865-69, and of the Abington Church, 1869-74; professor of New-Testament exegesis and literature in Western Theological Seminary, 1874-78; from April, 1879, to October, 1885, he was pastor of the Ewing Presbyterian Church, near Trenton, N.J. He assisted Rev. Dr. D. Moore upon *Isaiah* in the American Lange series (New York, 1878), and Rev. Dr. A. Gosman upon *Numbers* in the same series (1879); wrote *An Explanation of the Epistle to the Hebrews*, 1884; and translated Cremer's (of Greifswald) *Ueber den Zustand nach dem Tode*, Gütersloh, 1883, under the title *Beyond the Grave*, 1885.

LOWRY, Robert, D.D. (Lewisburg University, Lewisburg, Penn., 1875), Baptist; b. in Philadelphia, Penn., March 12, 1826; graduated at the head of his class at Lewisburg University, Lewisburg, Penn., 1854; was pastor at West Chester, Penn., 1854-58; in New-York City, 1858-61; in Brooklyn, 1861-69; at Lewisburg, Penn., and professor of belles-lettres in the university there, 1869-75; pastor at Plainfield, N.J., 1876-85; president of the New-Jersey Baptist Sunday-school Union, 1880-86. He participated in the Robert Raikes centennial, London, 1880; travelled in Europe 1880, in Mexico 1885; was poet before the Grand Arch Council of the Phi Kappa Psi Fraternity, 1885. He is a composer and hymn-writer, and has edited *Chapel Melodies*, N.Y., 1868; *Bright Jewels*, 1869; *Pure Gold*, 1871; *Hymn Service*, 1871; *Royal Diadem*, 1873; *Temple Anthems*, 1873; *Tidal Wave*, 1874; *Brightest and Best*, 1875; *Welcome Tidings*, 1877; *Fountain of Song*, 1877; *Chautauqua Carols*, 1878; *Gospel Hymn and Tune Book*, 1879; *Good as Gold*, 1880; *Our Glad Hosanna*, 1882; *Joyful Lays*, 1884; *Glad Refrains*, 1886; with Christmas and Easter services annually, and numerous single songs; over 3,000,000 of these books have been issued.

LOY, Matthias, Confessional Lutheran; b. in Cumberland County, Penn., March 17, 1828; studied in Columbus (O.) Theological Seminary, and was pastor at Delaware, O., 1849-65; since 1864 has edited *Lutheran Standard*; since 1865 has been professor of theology in the Evangelical Lutheran Theological Seminary, Columbus, O.; and since 1880 been president of Capital University. He established the Columbus (O.) *Theological Maga-*

zine in 1881. Since 1860, with the exception of 1878–80, when out of health, he has been yearly president of the Evangelical Lutheran Joint Synod of Ohio and other States. He edited the translation of Luther's *House-postils*, Columbus, 1864, 3 vols.; translated *Life and Deeds of Dr. M. Luther*, 1869; *The Doctrine of Justification*, 1869, 2d ed. 1880; *Essay on the Ministerial Office* 1870.

LUARD, Henry Richards, D.D. (Cambridge, 1878); Church of England; b. in London, Aug. 17, 1825; studied at Trinity College, Cambridge (1843–47), where he graduated B.A. (fourteenth wrangler) 1847, M.A. 1850, B.D. 1875; became fellow of Trinity College, 1849; was assistant tutor, 1855–65; ordained deacon and priest, 1855; became vicar of St. Mary the Great, Cambridge, 1860; registrary of the University of Cambridge, 1862; honorary canon of Ely, 1884. He is the author of *Catalogue of the MSS. in the Cambridge University Library* (the theological portion and the index), 1856–67; *Life of Richard Porson* (in *Cambridge Essays*), Cambridge, 1857; editor of *Lives of Edward the Confessor* (in the Master of the Rolls series of Chronicles and Memorials), 1858; *Bartholomæi de Cotton Historia Anglicana* (same series), 1859; *Diary of Edward Rud*, 1860; *Epistolæ Roberti Grosseteste* (Rolls series), 1861; *Annales Monastici* (the same), 1864–69, 5 vols.; *The Correspondence of Porson*, 1867; *List of Documents, etc., concerning the Cambridge University Library*, 1870; *Matthæi Parisiensis Chronica Majora* (Rolls series), 1872–83, 7 vols.; *Graduati Cantabrigienses, 1800–72*, 1873, *1800–84*, 1884; author of *On the Relations between England and Rome during the Earlier Portion of the Reign of Henry III.*, 1878; occasional pamphlets, reviews, sermons, etc.

LUCIUS, Paul Ernst, Lic. Theol. (Strassburg, 1879), German Protestant; b. at Ernolsheim, Elsass, Oct. 16, 1852; studied theology at Strassburg, 1871–76; afterwards at Zürich (1876), Paris (1877), Jena (1877), Berlin (1878); became assistant at Sessenheim, 1878; assistant pastor in Strassburg, 1879; *privat-docent* there, 1880; professor extraordinary, 1883. He is the author of *Die Therapeuten und ihre Stellung in der Geschichte der Askese, Eine kritische Untersuchung der Schrift "De vita contemplativa,"* Strassburg, 1879; *Der Essenismus in seinem Verhältniss zum Judenthum*, 1881; *Die Quellen der älteren Geschichte des aegyptischen Mönchthums* (in *Zeitschrift für Kgsch.*, 1884); *Die Kräftigung des Missionssinnes in der Gemeinde*, 1885.

LUCKOCK, Herbert Mortimer, D.D. (Cambridge, 1879), Church of England; b. at Great Barr, Staffordshire, July 11, 1833; educated at Jesus College, Cambridge; graduated as B.A. (second-class classical tripos, and first-class theological tripos) 1858, M.A. 1862; was fellow of Jesus College, Crosse divinity scholar, Tyrwhitt Hebrew scholar; took Carus and Scholefield prizes 1860, member's prize 1860–61–62; was ordained deacon 1860, priest 1862; chaplain to Lord Carrington, examining chaplain to bishop of Ely since 1873; honorary canon of Ely, 1874–75; canon of Ely since 1875; principal of Ely Theological College since 1876; select preacher in the University of Cambridge, 1865, 1874–75, 1883; vicar of All Saints', Cambridge, 1862–63, and again 1865–75; rector of Gayhurst with Stoke-Golding-ton, 1863–65. His theological standpoint is Anglo-Catholic. He is the author of *Tables of Stone: a Course of Sermons*, London, 1867; *After Death, the State of the Faithful Dead, and their Relationship to the Living*, 1879, 5th ed. 1885; *Studies in the History of the Prayer-book*, 1881, 2d ed. 1882; *An Appeal to the Church not to withdraw her Clergy from the Universities*, 1882; *Footprints of the Son of Man as traced by St. Mark, being Eighty Portions for Private Study, Family Reading, and Instruction in Church*, 1884, 2 vols., 2d ed. 1885.

LUDLOW, James Meeker, D.D. (Williams College, Williamstown, Mass., 1872), Presbyterian; b. at Elizabeth, N.J., March 15, 1841; graduated at College of New Jersey, Princeton, 1861, and at Princeton Theological Seminary, 1864; was pastor First Church, Albany, N.Y., 1864–68; Collegiate Reformed Dutch Church, New-York City, 1868–77; Westminster Presbyterian Church, Brooklyn, N.Y., 1877–85; East Orange since 1886. He is the inventor and compiler of the *Concentric Chart of History*, New York, 1885; author of *The Captain of the Janizaries*, 1886; and contributor to periodicals, secular and religious. *

LUEDEMANN, Hermann, Ph.D., Lic. Theol. (both Kiel, 1870 and 1871), **D.D.** (Heidelberg, 1883), German Protestant theologian; b. (son of the succeeding) at Kiel, Prussia, Sept. 15, 1842; studied at Kiel, Heidelberg, and Berlin, 1861–67; became *privat-docent* at Kiel, and teacher in a private school, 1872; professor extraordinary of the New Testament at Kiel, 1878; ordinary professor of church history at Bern, Switzerland, 1884. He is a critical and liberal theologian, in sympathy with the Jena school. He is the author of *Die Anthropologie des Apostel Paulus und ihre Stellung innerhalb seiner Heilslehre, Nach den vier Hauptbriefen dargestellt*, Kiel, 1872; *Zur Erklärung des Papiasfragments Euseb. H. E. iii. 39* (in *Jahrb. f. prot. Theol.*, 1879); *Die "Eidbrüchigkeit" unserer neukirchlichen (freisinnigen) Geistlichen*, Kiel, 1881, 3d ed. 1884; *Die neuere Entwicklung der protestantischen Theologie*, Bremen, 1884; from 1873 to 1883 he contributed to the *Literarisches Centralblatt*, *Jenaer Literaturzeitung*, *Protestantische Kirchenzeitung*, and political journals; since 1881 he has contributed the section on church history down to the Council of Nicæa, in Pünjer's *Theologischer Jahresbericht*.

LUEDEMANN, Karl, D.D., German Protestant theologian; b. at Kiel, July 6, 1805; studied there, 1823–28; became preacher in St. Nicholas' Church there, 1831; convent and garrison preacher, and *privat-docent*, 1834; professor extraordinary, 1839; ordinary professor, 1841. In 1855 he was made *Kirchenrath*. He is the author of *Die sittlichen Motive des Christenthums*, Kiel, 1841; *Ueber das Wesen des protestantischen Cultus*, 1846; *Das Wort des Lebens* (sermons), 1863; *Erinnerung an Claus Harms und seine Zeit*, 1878. *

LUENEMANN, Georg Conrad Gottlieb, Lic. Theol. (Göttingen, 1847), **D.D.** (*hon.*, Göttingen, 1860), German Protestant theologian; b. at Göttingen, April 17, 1819; studied at its university; became *repetent* there, 1844; *privat-docent*, 1847; professor extraordinary of theology, 1851. He is the author of *De epistolæ, quam Paulus ad Ephesios dedisse perhibetur, authentia, primis lectoribus, argumento summo ac consilio* (*Preisschrift*), Göttingen, 1842; *Pauli ad Philippenses epistola, Contra F. Chr. Baurium*, 1847; *Kritisch exegetisches Handbuch über die Briefe an die Thessalonicher* (*Abtheil X. des Meyer'schen Kommentars*), 1850, 4th ed. 1878 (English trans. by Gloag, Edinburgh, 1880); do. *über den Hebräerbrief* (*Abth. XIII. des M'schen Kommentars*), 1855, 4th ed. 1878 (English trans. by Evans, Edinburgh, 1882); *Disputatio de literarum, quæ ad Hebræos inscribuntur, primis lectoribus*, 1853; edited (with H. Messner) the 6th ed. of De Wette's *Einleitung in die kanonischen Bücher des N. T.*, Berlin, 1860; and the 7th ed. of Winer's *Grammatik des neutestamentlichen Sprachidioms*, Leipzig, 1867 (English trans. by J. Henry Thayer, Andover, 1869; 6th by W. F. Moulton, Edinburgh, 1870).

LUTHARDT, Christoph Ernst, Lic. Theol., Ph.D., D.D. (all Erlangen, 1852, 1854, and 1856 respectively), Lutheran; b. at Maroldsweisach, Bavaria, March 22, 1823; studied at Erlangen and Berlin, 1841–45; was ordained at Münden, 1846; from 1846 till 1851 was teacher in the Munich gymnasium; until 1854 *repetent* at Erlangen, and *privat-docent* 1853-54; for the next two years professor extraordinary at Marburg; since 1856 has been professor of systematic theology and New-Testament exegesis at Leipzig; and since 1865 a consistorial councillor. In theology he is orthodox, and in general belongs to the Erlangen school. He is renowned as a university lecturer and pulpit orator. Since 1868 he has edited the *Allgemeine evang. luth. Kirchenzeitung*, and since 1880 *Das Theologisch-Literaturblatt* and *Die Zeitschrift für Kirchl. Wissenschaft und Kirchl. Leben*. Of his very numerous publications, which include nine volumes of collected sermons (1861–86), and lectures and articles upon many topics, may be mentioned, *De compositione evangelii Joannei*, Nuremberg, 1852; *Das johanneische Evangelium nach seiner Eigenthümlichkeit geschildert u. erklärt*, 1852–53, 2 vols., 2d ed. 1875–76 (Eng. trans. by C. R. Gregory, *St. John's Gospel described and explained according to its Peculiar Character*, Edinburgh, 1878, 3 vols.); *De primæ Joannis epistolæ compositione*, Leipzig, 1860; *De compositione evangelii Matthæi*, 1861; *Die Offenbarung Johannis übersetzt u. kurz erklärt für die Gemeinde*, 1861; *Die Lehre von den letzten Dingen in Abhandlungen und Schriftauslegungen dargestellt*, 1861, 3d ed. 1885; *Die Lehre vom freien Willen u. sein Verhältniss zur Gnade*, 1863; *Apologetische Vorträge über die Grundwahrheiten des Christenthums*, 1864, 10th ed. 1883 (Eng. trans., *The Fundamental Truths of Christianity*, Edinb., 1865, 3d ed. 1873); *Kompendium der Dogmatik*, 1865, 7th ed. 1886; *Die Ethik Luthers in ihren Grundzügen*, 1867, 2d ed. 1875; *Apologetische Vorträge über die Heilswahrheiten des Christenthums*, 1867, 5th ed. 1883 (Eng. trans., *The Saving Truths of Christianity*, Edinburgh, 1868); *Die Ethik d. Aristoteles in ihr. Unterschied von der Moral des Christenthums*, 1869–76, 3 parts; *Vorträge über die Moral des Christenthums*, 1872, 3d ed. 1882 (Eng. trans., *The Moral Truths of Christianity*, Edinburgh, 1873); *Der johanneische Ursprung des vierten Evangeliums*, 1874 (Eng. trans., with enlarged literature, by C. R. Gregory, *St. John the Author of the Fourth Gospel*, Edinburgh, 1875, 2d ed. 1885); *Gesammelte Vorträge verschiedenen Inhalts*, 1876; *Die modernen Weltanschauungen u. ihre praktischen Konsequenzen*, 1880, 2d ed. same year; *Licht und Leben* (sermons), 1885.

LYMAN, Right Rev. Theodore Benedict, S.T.D. (College of St. James, Washington County, Md., 1856), Episcopalian, bishop of North Carolina; b. at Brighton, near Boston, Mass., Nov. 27, 1815; graduated at Hamilton College, Clinton, N.Y., 1837, and at the General Theological Seminary, New-York City, 1840; became rector of St. John's Parish, Hagerstown, Md., 1840; of Trinity Church, Pittsburgh, Penn., 1850; was in Europe 1860–70, during which time he was chaplain to the American embassy (1865), organized what is now St. Paul's Church, Rome, Italy (1866), and continued in charge four years; became rector of Trinity Church, San Francisco, Cal., 1870; assistant bishop of North Carolina, 1873; bishop, on the death of Bishop Atkinson, 1881. He declined the deanery of the General Theological Seminary, New-York City, to which office he was elected during his residence in Europe; appointed to the care and jurisdiction of the American Episcopal Churches, which have been established on the Continent of Europe, 1886. He is the author of several sermons and addresses.

LYON, David Gordon, Ph.D. (Leipzig, 1882), Baptist; b. at Benton, Ala., May 24, 1852; graduated at Howard College, Marion, Ala., 1875; studied at the Southern Baptist Theological Seminary, Louisville, Ky., 1876–79, and at Leipzig, 1879–82, and in the latter year became Hollis professor of divinity in Harvard University, Cambridge, Mass. His specialty is Assyrian. He has issued *Keilschrifttexte Sargon's Königs von Assyrien (722–705 v. Chr.) nach den Originalien neu herausgegeben, umschrieben, übersetzt und erklärt*, Leipzig, 1883.

M.

MABON, William Augustus Van Vranken, D.D. (Rutgers College, New Brunswick, N.J., 1861), **LL.D.** (Union College, Schenectady, N.Y., 1882), b. at New Brunswick, N.J., Jan. 24, 1822; graduated at Union College, Schenectady, N.Y., 1840, and at New Brunswick Theological Seminary, N.J., 1844; became home missionary at Buffalo, N.Y., 1844; pastor at New Durham, Hudson Co., N.J., and superintendent of the county schools, 1846; professor of didactic and polemic theology in the Reformed (Dutch) Theological Seminary at New Brunswick, N.J., 1881. He edited *The Sower*, New York, 1878-79. See Appendix.

McALL, Robert Whitaker, F.L.S., Congregationalist; b. at Macclesfield, Cheshire, Eng., Dec. 17, 1821; studied architecture under Mr. Walters, architect of the Free Trade Hall, Manchester, and Sir Gilbert Scott, R.A.; afterwards turned his attention to theology, and studied in the Lancashire Independent (Congregational and theological) College, Manchester; graduated B.A. at London University in 1847; and for twenty-four years was a Congregational pastor in England, during which time he ministered to four churches. In 1871, while pastor at Hadleigh, Suffolk, he and his wife made a brief holiday visit to Paris, and were so struck with the spiritual destitution of the working classes there, that they resolved to devote themselves to the effort to evangelize them. Accordingly he left his charge, much to its regret, and single-handed they began their mission. Their success has been beyond their hopes. In 1885 there were a hundred stations in Paris and throughout France. The money required to carry on their operations comes from France, Great Britain, and America. See article *McAll Mission*, in *Encyclopædia*.

MacARTHUR, Robert Stuart, D.D. (University of Rochester, N.Y., 1880), Baptist; b. at Dalesville, Argenteuil County, Province of Quebec, Can., Aug. 31, 1841; graduated from the University of Rochester, N.Y., 1867, and from the Rochester Theological Seminary, N.Y., 1870; and since June, 1870, has been pastor of Calvary Baptist Church, New-York City, which in 1883 erected a new church at an expense of nearly five hundred thousand dollars. He is the regular weekly New-York correspondent of the Chicago *Standard*, one of the editors of *The Baptist Quarterly Review* (since 1885), and with Rev. Dr. C. S. Robinson of the *Calvary Selection of Hymns and Spiritual Songs*, New York, 1879.

McAULEY, Jeremiah (better known as "Jerry McAuley"), layman; b. in Ireland, in the year 1839; d. in New-York City, Sept. 18, 1884. His father was a counterfeiter, who fled the country to escape arrest while his son was an infant. Jerry was brought up by his grandmother, who was a devout Romanist; but he never received any schooling. At the age of thirteen he came to New-York City, and lived with a married sister for a time. Soon he became as great a rogue as one of his years could be. On leaving his sister he boarded in Water Street, and supported himself by stealing from vessels lying in the river. The money procured by selling the articles stolen was spent in all sorts of wickedness. He became a prize-fighter, and a terror and a nuisance in the Fourth Ward. When nineteen years old he was arrested for highway robbery, an offence he had not committed. But he had no one to defend him; and so bad was his character, that he was condemned, in January, 1857, on circumstantial evidence, to fifteen years imprisonment at Sing-Sing. On his way thither he determined to be obedient to prison rules, do the best he could under the circumstances, and trust that somebody would be raised up to help him. He was set at carpet-weaving, and for two years had the approbation of his keepers. For the next three years he was, in consequence of illness, uneasy and intractable, and hence often severely punished, without being anywise improved. On one Sunday, when he had been some five years in prison, Orville Gardner (known as "Awful" Gardner), a former confederate in sin, addressed the convicts, and made a profound impression upon Jerry. On returning to his cell he took down the Bible, with which each cell is supplied, to find a verse which Gardner had quoted. He soon became a constant Bible-reader; and so, although he never found the verse he sought, he stored his mind with the Word of God. A great desire to be saved was awakened within him. But weeks of anxiety and struggle passed before the "words were distinctly spoken to his soul" which assured him that he was forgiven. Then the Lord began to use him in the prison among his fellow-convicts, and several were led to Christ by him. On March 8, 1864, he was pardoned. Like many another one, he had no one to help him to an honest living on leaving prison, so fell back into his former evil courses. He went into the bounty business, and made a great deal of money, which he spent freely. He became a sporting man, and often attended the races. After the war he dealt in stolen and smuggled goods, which he paid for in counterfeit money, until, being found out, no one would steal for him. He then became once more a river thief. But he could not shake off the religious impressions received in prison, although he tried to deaden conscience by drink. This wretched life continued until 1872, when he found Christian friends who manfully stood by him, notwithstanding his frequent falls, until he was confirmed in the Christian life. In October, 1872, he opened his "Helping Hand for Men," at 316 Water Street, as a resort for the forlorn wayfarers, sailors, and others who frequented the locality. From the start the work was remarkably blessed. He manifested extraordinary aptitude for dealing with the degraded. His kindly ways drew them to him; while his simple-minded, whole-hearted piety, and his burning zeal, deeply impressed them. The result was, that many were converted. In 1876 the old building was replaced by a far better one, and the mission incorporated under the title of "The McAuley Water-street Mission." In 1882, feeling that his work in Water Street was done, he began a similar work at 104 West Thirty-second Street, called "The Cremorne Mission," from its contiguity to the notorious Cremorne Garden. In June, 1883, he began the publication of *Jerry McAuley's Newspaper*, which is still issued every other Thursday. Some time before his death his health began to fail, but he continued his work. His end came suddenly. On Wednesday, Sept 17, 1884, he had a hemorrhage of the lungs, and on Thursday afternoon at four o'clock another, and in a few minutes he was dead. On Sunday, Sept. 21, at half-past two P.M., he was buried from the Broadway Tabernacle, Thirty-fourth Street and Sixth Avenue. The spacious church was crowded in every part long before the services began, and a great multitude stood all around the building. For nearly two hours after the conclusion of the services, the procession of mourners filed past the coffin. In the throng were many of the very classes among whom and for whom his life had been spent, — the criminal, the vicious, the immoral.

By competent testimony and common acknowledgment Jerry McAuley was one of the most useful, remarkable, and indeed wonderful men in the city of New York. Himself for many years a criminal and an outcast, he knew from bitter experience that the way of transgressors is hard. Himself the subject of the Saviour's infinite love, he knew that God had mercy for even the vilest. When, therefore, he spoke to those who had fallen, it was with a thorough knowledge which they could not fail to recognize. His work was, however, not carried on without many hinderances and difficulties; but he triumphed over all. Liberal and wealthy friends supported his enterprises, and in his wife he found a devoted and efficient helper. See *Jerry McAuley, His Life and Work*, ed. Rev. R. M. Offord, New York, 1885. *

McCABE, Charles Cardwell, D.D. (Central Tennessee College, Nashville, Tenn., 1875), Methodist; b. at Athens, O., Oct. 11, 1836; studied at Ohio Wesleyan University, Delaware, O., but did not graduate; was pastor in the Ohio Conference, 1860–61; chaplain of the 122d Ohio Infantry, 1862–63; was taken prisoner at the battle of Winchester, Va., and was in Libby Prison, Richmond, Va , for four months; on his release rejoined his regiment; agent of the Christian Commission, 1864–65; Centenary agent in Ohio, 1866–67; assistant secretary of the Church Extension Society, 1868–84; missionary secretary since 1884.

McCLELLAN, John Brown, Church of England; b. in Glasgow, Scotland, March 7, 1836; educated at Trinity College, Cambridge, 1855–58 (elected scholar 1857); graduated B.A. (Wrangham gold medallist, and the only double first classical and mathematical honors of his year) 1858, M.A. 1861; was elected fellow of Trinity College, 1859; ordained deacon 1860, priest 1861; was vicar of Bottisham, diocese of Ely, 1861–79; rural dean of first division of Camp's deanery, 1871–77; since 1880 he has been principal of the Royal Agricultural College, Cirencester. He is a moderate High Churchman, in favor of disestablishment and of freedom of the Church. He is the author of *Fourth Nicene Canon, and Election and Consecration of Bishops*, London, 1870; *A New Translation of the New Testament, from a critically revised Greek Text, a Contribution to Christian Evidence*, vol. i. (the Four Gospels, with notes and dissertations, and a new chronological harmony) 1875.

McCLOSKEY, His Eminence John, Cardinal, D.D., Roman Catholic; b. in Brooklyn, N.Y., March 10, 1810; d. in New York, Oct. 10, 1885. He was graduated with the highest honors at St. Mary's College, Emmittsburg, Md., 1828; ordained priest at New York, Jan. 9, 1834; studied for two years at the Collegium Romanum in Rome, and a year in France. Returning to America in 1837, he was appointed pastor of St. Joseph's Church, New-York City. On March 10, 1844, he was consecrated bishop of Axiere *in partibus*, and co-adjutor to the bishop (later archbishop) of New York (John Hughes); translated to the new see of Albany, May 21, 1847; after the death of Archbishop Hughes (Jan. 3, 1864) he was appointed his successor, May 6, 1864. He attended the Vatican Council (1869-70), and was on the Committee on Discipline. He was by Pius IX. created cardinal priest of the Most Holy Roman Church, March 15, 1875, under the title of "*Sancta Maria sopra Minervam.*" He was the first American cardinal. He received the red hat from Leo XIII. in the consistory held in Rome on March 28, 1878. He enjoyed the respect of Protestant and Roman Catholic alike; and did much for his Church, as by buildings (e.g., the Fifth-avenue Cathedral) and new institutions, and by the introduction of the Capuchins, Franciscans, Sisters and Little Sisters of the Poor, who had previously no houses in his diocese. Under him the number of churches in New York increased from seventy to a hundred and seventy, and the number of clergy from a hundred and fifty to four hundred. Archbishop Gibbons, in his funeral oration, said of him: "He [the cardinal] has left you . . . the legacy of a pure and unsullied life, as priest, bishop, archbishop, and cardinal. He never tarnished the surplice of the priest, nor the rochet of the bishop, nor the pallium of the archbishop, nor the scarlet robes of the cardinal. After spending upwards of half a century in the exercise of the ministry, he goes down to his honored grave without a stain upon his moral character."

McCOOK, Henry Christopher, D.D. (Lafayette College, Easton, Penn., 1880), Presbyterian; b. at New Lisbon, O., July 3, 1837; graduated at Jefferson College, Canonsburg, Penn., 1859; studied at the Western Theological Seminary, Allegheny, Penn., 1859-61; was first lieutenant Company F, Forty-first Regiment Illinois Volunteers, 1861; chaplain of the regiment, 1861–62; acting pastor, Clinton, Ill., 1861, 1862–63; home missionary, St. Louis, Mo., 1863–70; since 1870 has been pastor of the Tabernacle Presbyterian Church, Philadelphia. He is vice-president of the Academy of Natural Sciences of Philadelphia (in whose proceedings he has published numerous papers upon the habits and industry of American ants and spiders), and vice-director of the American Entomological Society. He is the author of *Object and Outline Teaching*, St. Louis, 1871; *The Last Year of Christ's Ministry*, Philadelphia, 1871; *The Last Days of Jesus*, 1872; *The Tercentenary Book* (edited), 1873; *The Mound-making Ants of the Alleghenies*, 1877; *The Natural History of the Agricultural Ant of Texas*, 1880; *Historic Decorations at Pan-Presbyterian Council*, 1880; *Garfield Memorial Sermons* (four discourses), 1881; *Honey Ants and Occident Ants*, 1882; *Tenants of an Old Farm, Leaves from the Note-Book of a Naturalist*, N.Y., 1884; *The Women Friends of Jesus*, 1885.

McCOSH, James, S.T.D. (Brown University, Providence, R.I., 1868), **LL.D.** (Harvard College, Cambridge, Mass., 1868; Washington and Jefferson College, Washington, Penn., 1868), **D.Lit.** (Queen's University, Ireland), Presbyterian; b. at Carskeoch, Banks of the Doon, Ayrshire, Scotland, April 1, 1811; was educated at the universities of Glasgow (1824-29), and Edinburgh (1829-34), and from the latter received, while a student, the honorary degree of M.A. in recognition of the ability of his essay upon the Stoic philosophy. He was licensed as probationer in 1833, and in 1835 was ordained and appointed minister of Arbroath, Scotland, and belonged to the so-called non-intrusion party, whose leader was Thomas Guthrie. In 1839 he became minister in first charge in his district, Brechin; and in 1843, when the disruption came, he entered the Free Church. In 1851 was appointed professor of logic and metaphysics in Queen's College, Belfast, Ireland, and entered his labors there the next year. In the spring of 1868 he was elected president of the College of New Jersey, at Princeton, and in the autumn was inaugurated. He has greatly increased the resources of the institution. He has been a voluminous writer. Besides contributions to various periodicals, and other minor papers, he has published *The Method of the Divine Government, Physical and Moral*, Edinburgh, 1850, 5th ed. revised, London, 1856; (with George Dickie, M.D., professor of natural history in the Queen's University, Ireland) *Typical Forms and Special Ends in Creation*, 1855; *The Intuitions of the Mind inductively investigated*, 1860; *The Supernatural in Relation to the Natural*, 1862; *Examination of Mill's Philosophy, being a Defence of Fundamental Truth*, 1866; *The Laws of Discursive Thought, being a Treatise on Formal Logic*, New York, 1869; *Christianity and Positivism*, 1871; *The Scottish Philosophy, Biographical, Expository, Critical; from Hutcheson to Hamilton*, 1874; *The Emotions*, 1880; and completed in 1886 the "Philosophical Series" (1882, sqq.), in which he has short papers upon *Criteria of Diverse Kinds of Truth as opposed to Agnosticism* (1882); *Energy, Efficient and Final Cause* (1883); *Development: what it can do, and what it can not do* (1883); *Certitude, Providence, and Prayer* (1883); *Locke's Theory of Knowledge, with Notice of Berkeley* (1884); *Agnosticism of Hume and Huxley, with Notice of the Scottish School* (1884); *Criticism of the Critical Philosophy* (1884); *Herbert Spencer's Philosophy as Culminating in his Ethics* (1885); *Psychology, The Cognitive Powers* (1886).

MacCRACKEN, Henry Mitchell, D.D. (Wittenberg College, Springfield, O., 1877), Presbyterian; b. at Oxford, O., Sept. 28, 1840; graduated at Miami University, Oxford, O., 1857; was teacher of classics, and school principal, 1857-60; studied at United Presbyterian Theological Seminary, Xenia, O., 1860-62; at Princeton (N.J.) Presbyterian Theological Seminary, 1863 (graduated); and at Tübingen and Berlin universities, 1867-68; was pastor of the Westminster Presbyterian Church, Columbus, O., 1863-67; of the First Presbyterian Church, Toledo, O., 1868-81; chancellor of Western University, Pittsburgh, Penn., 1881-84; since 1884 has been professor of philosophy, and also vice-chancellor of the University of the City of New York. He was deputy to the Free Church Assembly of Scotland, and to the Irish Presbyterian General Assembly, 1867; proposer of the observance of 1872 as tercentenary year of Presbyterianism, 1870 (see *Minutes* of General Assembly, 1870, p. 29, 1871, p. 568); delivered historical oration at re-union of the Scotch-Irish race in Belfast, Ireland, July 4, 1884. He is the editor, translator, and author of *Leaders of the Church Universal*, 1879 (published by Presbyterian Board, Philadelphia, by the official publication boards of ten other denominations, and by T. & T. Clark, Edinburgh), from the German of Piper's *Evangelische Calender*, Berlin, 1875.

McCURDY, James Frederick, Ph.D. (College of New Jersey, Princeton, N.J., 1878), Canadian Presbyterian; b. at Chatham, New Brunswick, Can., Feb. 18, 1847; graduated at University of New Brunswick, Fredericton, N.B., 1866, and at Princeton (N.J.) Theological Seminary, 1871; in the latter was instructor in Hebrew and cognate languages, 1873-82; studied in Germany, 1882-84; lectured on the Stone foundation, Princeton, N.J., 1885-86; became professor of Oriental languages in University College, Toronto, Can., 1886. Besides review of Gesenius' *Handwörterbuch*, 9th ed. (*Am. Jour. Philology*, July, 1883); a paper on *The Semitic Perfect in Assyrian*, in *Transactions* of the Sixth Congress of Orientalists, Leyden, September, 1883; *Ayro-Semitic Speech, a Study in Linguistic Archæology*, Andover and London, 1881; *The Assyrian and Babylonian Inscriptions, with Special Reference to the Old Testament*, N.Y., 1886; he has also written the exposition of *Haggai* (N.Y., 1876), and translated, edited, and enlarged Moll's exposition of *Ps. lxxiii.-cl.* (1872), and Schmoller's of *Hosea* (1876); all three in the American Lange series.

MACDUFF, John Ross, D.D. (University of City of New York, 1857; Glasgow, 1859), Church of Scotland; b. at Bonhard, Perthshire, May 23, 1818; studied at the University of Edinburgh, 1835-42; was minister of parishes of Kettins, Forfarshire, 1843-49, and of St. Madoes, 1849-55; of Sandyford church and parish, Glasgow, 1855-70. He now resides in England. He is the author of *Morning and Night Watches*, London, 1852; *Mind and Words of Jesus*, 1855; *Memories of Bethany* (1857), *of Gennesaret* (1858), *of Olivet* (1867), and *of Patmos* (1870); *Grapes of Eshcol*, 1860; *Sunsets on Hebrew Mountains*, 1862; *Prophet of Fire*, 1863; *Noontide at Sychar*, 1868; *Comfort Ye*, 1872; *Brighter than the Sun*, 1877, 4th ed. 1886; *Eventide at Bethel*, 1878; *Palms of Elim*, 1879; *In Christo*, 1880; *Parish of Taxwood*, 1883; *Communion Memories*, 1885; *Parables of the Lake*, 1885; and numerous other books, all of which have passed through several, many through numerous, editions, been promptly reprinted in America, and widely circulated.

McFERRIN, John Berry, D.D. (LaGrange College, Ala., and Randolph Macon College, Ashland, Va., both in 1851), Methodist (Southern Church); b. in Rutherford County, Tenn., June 15, 1807; entered Tennessee Conference, 1825; edited *Christian Advocate*, Nashville, Tenn., 1840-48; was book-agent of the Southern Church, 1858–66; secretary of Board of Missions, 1866–78; since 1878 has been book-agent at Nashville, Tenn. He is the author of *Methodism in Tennessee*, Nashville, 1870–72, 3 vols. (several later editions).

McGARVEY, John William, Christian; b. at Hopkinsville, Ky., March 1, 1829; graduated at Bethany (W. Va.) College; preached at Dover, Mo., and Lexington, Ky. (1862-65), and since 1865 has been professor of sacred history and evidences in the College of the Bible, Kentucky University, Lexington, Ky. He is the author of a commentary on *Acts* (Cincinnati, O., 1863), and on *Matthew* and *Mark* (1875); *Lands of the Bible* (visited 1879), Philadelphia, 1881 (16th thousand, 1882); *Evidences of Christianity*, Cincinnati, 1886.

McGILL, Alexander Taggart, D.D. (Marshall College, Lancaster, Penn., 1842), **LL.D.** (College of New Jersey, Princeton, 1868), Presbyterian; b. at Canonsburg, Penn., Feb. 24, 1807; graduated at Jefferson College, Canonsburg, Penn., 1826; was admitted to the bar in Georgia, and elected by her Legislature a surveyor for the State, to trace inter-State lines, and divide into sections the Cherokee lands within her chartered limits. In 1831 he turned to theology, took the full course of four years in the theological seminary of the Associate (now United) Presbyterian Church, at Canonsburg; was ordained at Carlisle, Penn., in 1835, and until 1838 ministered to three small Associate Presbyterian churches in Cumberland, Perry, and York counties. In 1838 he entered the Old-School branch of the Presbyterian Church, and until 1842 was pastor of the Second Church, Carlisle, Penn. From 1842 till 1854 (except 1852–53, when professor in Columbia Theological Seminary, S.C.), he was professor in the Western Theological Seminary, Allegheny, Penn., when he was transferred by the General Assembly to Princeton, and remained as professor of ecclesiastical, homiletic, and pastoral theology, until in 1883 he resigned from active service, and became professor emeritus. His publications consist of numerous articles, and occasional sermons and addresses.

McILVAINE, Joshua Hall, S.T.D. (University of Rochester, N.Y., 1854), Presbyterian; b. at Lewes, Del., March 4, 1815; graduated at the College of New Jersey, Princeton, N.J., 1837, and at Princeton Theological Seminary, 1840; became pastor at Little Falls, N.Y., 1841; of Westminster Church, Utica, N.Y., 1843; of First Church, Rochester, N.Y., 1848; professor of belles-lettres in the College of New Jersey, Princeton, N.J., 1860; pastor of the High-street Church, Newark, N.J., 1870. He introduced the name "Westminster" for churches, in founding the Westminster Church, Utica, 1845, which also, it is believed, was the first Presbyterian church in the United States with a rotary eldership. He was the first in America, it is believed, to explain (at the meeting of the Association for the Advancement of Science, in Montreal, 1850) the method by which Sir Henry Rawlinson deciphered the Persian cuneiform inscriptions. He was long a fellow of the American Oriental Society. In 1859 he delivered a course of six lectures on comparative philology in relation to ethnology (including an analysis of the structure of the Sanscrit language, and the process of deciphering the cuneiform inscriptions), before the Smithsonian Institution; and in 1869 a similar course on social science in Philadelphia, under the auspices of the University of Pennsylvania, in which institution he was subsequently chosen professor of that science. He is the author of *The Tree of the Knowledge of Good and Evil*, New York, 1845; *Elocution, the Sources and Elements of its Power*, New York, 1870, 2d ed. 1874; *The Wisdom of Holy Scripture, with reference to Sceptical Objections*, 1883; *The Wisdom of the Apocalypse*, 1886; and articles in reviews on religious and scientific subjects, etc.

MACKARNESS, John Fielder, D.D. (Oxford, 1870), lord bishop of Oxford, Church of England; b. in London, Dec. 3, 1820; was educated at Merton College, Oxford, of which he was postmaster; graduated B.A. (second-class classics) 1844, M.A. (Exeter College) 1847; was ordained deacon 1844, priest 1845; fellow of Exeter College, 1844–46; vicar of Tardebigge, Worcestershire, 1845–55; honorary canon of Worcester Cathedral, 1854; rector of Honiton, 1855–69; prebendary of Exeter, 1858–69; consecrated bishop, 1870. He is chancellor of the Most Noble Order of the Garter; visitor of Cuddesdon, Bradfield, and Radley Colleges

McKENZIE, Alexander, D.D. (Amherst College, Amherst, Mass., 1879), Congregationalist; b. at New Bedford, Mass., Dec. 14, 1830; graduated at Harvard College, Cambridge, Mass., 1859, and at Andover (Mass.) Theological Seminary, 1861; pastor of South Church, Augusta, Me., 1861-67; since, pastor of First Church, Cambridge, Mass.: since 1886, preacher to Harvard University. In 1882 he was lecturer on theology of the New Testament, in Andover Theological Seminary (of which he became trustee in 1876) and in Harvard Divinity School. He has published *Hist. First Church, Cambridge*, Boston, 1873; *Cambridge Sermons*, 1883.

McKNIGHT, Harvey Washington, D.D. (Monmouth College, Monmouth, Ill., 1883), Lutheran (General Synod); b. at McKnightstown, Adams County, Penn., April 3, 1843; graduated at Pennsylvania College, 1865, and at the Lutheran Theological Seminary (both at Gettysburg, Penn.), 1867; became pastor of Zion's Lutheran Church, Newville, Penn., 1867; of St. Paul's, Easton, 1872; of the First English, Cincinnati, O., 1880; president of Pennsylvania College, 1884. He was second lieutenant Company B, 138th Regiment Pennsylvania Volunteers, Aug. 16 to Dec. 17, 1862; adjutant 26th Regiment during Lee's invasion of Pennsylvania; captain Company D, 210th Regiment Pennsylvania Volunteers, Sept. 24, 1864, to June 9, 1865. He delivered an address before the alumni of the Gettysburg Theological Seminary, June, 1878, and an historical address at the semi-centennial of Pennsylvania College, June, 1882.

MACLAGAN, Right Rev. William Dalrymple, D.D. (*jure dignitatis*, Cambridge, 1878), lord bishop of Lichfield, Church of England; b. at Edinburgh in the year 1826; educated at St. Peter's College, Cambridge; graduated B.A. (junior optime) 1856, M.A. 1860; was ordained deacon 1856, priest 1857; curate of St. Saviour, Paddington, London, 1856-58; of St Stephen, Marylebone, London, 1858–60; secretary of the London Diocesan Church Building Society, 1860–65; curate in charge of Enfield, 1865–69; rector of Newington, 1869–75; vicar of Kensington, 1875–78; honorary chaplain in ordinary to the Queen, 1877–78; prebendary of Reculverland in St. Paul's Cathedral, 1878; consecrated bishop, 1878. He edited, with Dr. Archibald Weir, *The Church and the Age, Essays on the Principles and Present Position of the Anglican Church*, London, 1870; and has published sermons, etc. *

McLAREN, Alexander, D.D. (Edinburgh, 1875), Baptist; b. at Glasgow, Feb. 11, 1826; educated at Stepney (now Regent's Park) College, and graduated B.A. in London University; was minister of Portland Chapel, Southampton, from 1846 to 1858; since which time he has been minister of Union Chapel, Manchester. He was chairman of the Baptist Union of England in 1875. He has published *Sermons preached in Manchester*, (1st series 1864, 10th ed. 1883; 2d series 1869, 7th ed. 1883; 3d series 1873, 6th ed. 1883); *A Spring Holiday in Italy*, 1865. 2d ed. 1866; *Week-day Evening Addresses*, 1877, 5th ed. 1885; *Life of David as reflected in his Psalms*, 1880, 6th ed. 1885; *Secret of Power, and other Sermons*, 1882, 2d ed. 1883; *A Year's Ministry*, 1884, 2 series, 2d ed. 1885.

McLAREN, Right Rev. William Edward, S.T.D. (Racine College, Racine, Wis., 1875), **D.C.L.** (University of the South, Sewanee, Tenn., 1884), Episcopalian, bishop of Chicago; b. at Geneva, N.Y., Dec. 13, 1831; graduated at Jefferson College, Canonsburg, Penn., 1851; was an editor until 1857, when he entered the Western (Presbyterian) Theological Seminary, Allegheny, Penn.; graduated there 1860, and became a Presbyterian minister; entered the Protestant-Episcopal ministry, 1872; and became rector of Trinity Church, Cleveland, O., 1872; bishop of Illinois, 1875; diocese divided into that of Illinois, Quincy, and Springfield, he retaining that of Illinois, which included Chicago and the northern part of the State, 1877; in 1883 the name of this diocese was changed to that of Chicago. He is the author of *Catholic Dogma the Antidote of Doubt*, 1883; and numerous sermons, addresses, articles, etc. *

McLEAN, Alexander, D.D. (Hamilton College, Clinton, N.Y., 1874), Presbyterian; b. in Glasgow, Scotland, Oct. 1, 1833; graduated at Hamilton College, Clinton, N.Y., 1853, and at Union Theological (Presbyterian) Seminary, New-York City, 1856; became pastor of the Congregational Church, Fairfield, Conn., 1857; of the Calvary Presbyterian Church, Buffalo, N.Y., 1866; corresponding secretary of the American Bible Society, 1874.

MACLEAR, George Frederick, D.D. (Cambridge, 1872), Church of England; b. at Bedford, Eng., Feb. 3, 1833; was scholar of Trinity College, Cambridge; graduated B.A. (second-class classical tripos, first-class theological tripos) 1855, M.A. 1860, B.D. 1867; won the Carus (1854 and 1855), Burney University (1857), Hulsean (1857), Maitland University (1858 and 1860), and Norrisian (1863) prizes (see below); was ordained deacon 1856, priest 1857; was assistant minister of Curzon Chapel, Mayfair, and of St Mark, Notting-hill, London; assistant preacher at the Temple Church, 1865-70; head master of King's College School, 1868-80; Boyle lecturer, 1879-80; select preacher at Cambridge, 1868 and 1880; examiner for the Lightfoot scholarships there, 1876-77; select preacher at Oxford, 1881-82; since 1880 he has been warden of St. Augustine's College, Canterbury. He is the author of the following prize essays: *Incentives to Virtue, Natural and Revealed* (Burney), 1855; *The Cross and the Nations* (Hulsean), 1857; *The Christian Statesman and our Indian Empire* (Maitland), 1858, 2d ed. 1859; *Missions of the Middle Ages* (Maitland), 1861; *The Witness of the Eucharist* (Norrisian), 1863; also of *Class Books of Old and New Testament History*, 1861, 2 vols., 15th ed. 1880; *Class Book of the Catechism*, 1868, 6th ed. 1878; *Class Book of the Confirmation*, 1869, many editions; *Apostles of Mediæval Europe*, 1869, 2d ed. 18—; *The Gospel according to St. Mark* (English), 1877; *The Book of Joshua*, 1878 (both in *Cambridge Bible for Schools* series); *The Greek Gospel of St. Mark*, 1878 (in *Cambridge Greek Testament for Schools*); *The Conversion of the Celts, the English, the Northmen, and the Slavs*, 1878-79 (S. P. C. K.), 4 vols.; *The Evidential Value of the Holy Eucharist* (Boyle Lectures), 1883; articles in Smith and Cheetham's *Dictionary of Christian Antiquities*, and in Smith and Wace's *Dictionary of Christian Biography*, *The Bible Educator*, and *Encyclopædia Britannica*.

MACLEOD, Donald, D.D. (Glasgow, 1876), Church of Scotland; b. in the manse of Campsie, March 18, 1831; the son of the late Norman Macleod, sen. (dean of the Chapel Royal, Celtic scholar, and writer of Celtic literature), and the brother of Norman Macleod, D.D., late of Barony Parish, Glasgow (dean of Chapel Royal, dean of the Thistle, etc.); educated at the University of Glasgow; and was minister of Lauder, Berwickshire, 1858-62; Linlithgow, 1862-69; and since 1869 of the parish of the Park, Glasgow. He is one of her Majesty's chaplains for Scotland, and since 1873 has edited *Good Words*, a monthly magazine. He is the author of *Memoir of Norman Macleod*, London, 1872, 2 vols., 2d ed. 1876, 1 vol.; *The Sunday Home Service*, 1885.

MACMILLAN, Hugh, D.D. (Edinburgh, 1879), **LL.D.** (St. Andrew's, 1871), **F.R.S.E.** (1871), Free Church of Scotland; b. at Aberfeldy, Perthshire, Sept. 17, 1833; educated at Edinburgh University; was minister of Kirkmichael, Perthshire, 1859-64; of Free St. Peter's, Glasgow, 1864-78; and since 1878 has been minister of Free West Church, Greenock. He is the author of numerous contributions to periodicals, and the following books: *Bible Teachings in Nature*, 1866, 24th ed. 1886 (translated into Danish, Swedish, German, and other Continental languages); *Holidays in High Lands, Search of Alpine Plants*, 1869, 2d ed. 1875; *The True Vine: or, The Analogies of our Lord's Allegory*, 1871, 5th ed. 1886; *First Forms of Vegetation*, 1861, 2d ed. 1874; *The Ministry of Nature*, 1872, 5th ed. 1886; *The Garden and the City, with other Contrasts and Parallels of Scripture*, 1872, 2d ed. 1873; *Sun-glints in the Wilderness*, 1872; *Our Lord's Three Raisings from the Dead*, 1875; *Sabbath of the Fields* (Danish and Norwegian translations), 1875. 5th ed. 1886; *Two Worlds are Ours*, 1880, 4th ed. 1880; *The Marriage in Cana of Galilee*, 1882, 2d ed. 1886; *The Riviera*, 1885.

McTYEIRE, Holland Nimmons, D.D. (Emory College, Oxford, Ga., 1858), Methodist-Episcopal bishop (Southern Church); b. in Barnwell District, S.C., July 28, 1824; graduated at Randolph-Macon College, Ashland, Va., 1844; was tutor, 1844-45; entered the Methodist ministry, 1845; was stationed at Mobile and New Orleans; was first editor of the New Orleans *Christian Advocate* (1851); editor of *Christian Advocate*, Nashville,

Tenn., 1858; elected bishop in 1866; through him Commodore Vanderbilt presented the million dollars which founded Vanderbilt University, Nashville, Tenn. (1873). He is the author of *The Duties of Christian Masters*, Nashville, 1851 (a prize essay); *A Catechism on Church Government*, 1869; *A Catechism on Bible History*, 1869; *Manual of the Discipline*, 1870; *A History of Methodism*, 1884.

MacVICAR, Donald Harvey, D.D. (Knox College, Toronto, 1883), **LL.D.** (McGill University, Montreal, 1870), Presbyterian; b. at Dunglass, south end of Cantyre, Argyleshire, Scotland, Nov. 29, 1831; graduated at Knox College, Toronto, Can., 1858; became pastor of Knox Church, Guelph, 1859; of Coté-street (now Crescent-street) Free Church, Montreal, 1861 (during his pastorate the annual increase averaged over one hundred members); principal and professor of divinity in the Presbyterian College, Montreal, 1868. When he began his work, the institution existed only in its charter. For four years he was the only professor; but now (1886) the seminary has extensive and costly buildings, a large and valuable library, a staff of four professors and four lecturers, with over seventy students in attendance. He lectures on dogmatics, church government, and homiletics. He is at the head of the work of French evangelization in Canada, and was for many years on the Protestant board of school commissioners of Montreal. In 1871 he was lecturer upon logic in McGill University, Montreal; in 1876 and 1884 he delivered courses of lectures upon applied logic, and in 1878 a course on ethics before the Ladies' Educational Association of Montreal. In 1881 he was chosen moderator of the General Assembly of the Presbyterian Church in Canada; was delegate to the councils of the Reformed churches held in Edinburgh (1877), Philadelphia (1880), and Belfast (1884). In 1881 he received the diploma of membership of the Athénée Oriental of Paris. He is the author of a primary and an advanced text-book on arithmetic; of numerous review articles, etc.

MacVICAR, Malcolm, Ph.D. (University of the State of New York, 1870), **LL.D.** (University of Rochester, N.Y., 1870), Baptist; b. in Argyleshire, Scotland, Sept. 30, 1829; graduated at the University of Rochester, N.Y., 1859; became professor of mathematics, Brockport Collegiate Institute, N.Y., 1859; principal of the same, 1863; principal of the State Normal School, Brockport, 1867; superintendent of public schools, Leavenworth, Kan., 1868; principal of State Normal School, Potsdam, N.Y., 1869; principal of the State Normal School, Ypsilanti, Mich., 1880; professor of apologetics and biblical interpretation in English, in the Baptist College, Toronto, Ontario, Can., 1881. He was the principal mover in securing a law to establish four new normal schools in the State of New York, 1866. He is the inventor of the MacVicar tellurian globe, and of various devices to illustrate principles in arithmetic, geography, and astronomy; and author of text-books in arithmetic.

MAGEE, Right Rev. William Connor, D.D. (Trinity College, Dublin, 1860), **D.C.L.**, lord bishop of Peterborough, Church of England; b. at Cork, Dec. 17, 1821; graduated at Trinity College, Dublin, B.A. 1842, B.D. 1854. He was first a curate of St. Thomas's, Dublin; then of St. Saviour's, Bath, 1848; then minister of the Octagon Chapel, Bath, 1850; of Quebec Chapel, London, 1860; rector of Enniskillen, Ireland, 1861; dean of Cork, 1864; lord bishop of Peterborough, 1868. He was Donellan lecturer, Trinity College, Dublin, 1865–66; dean of the Vice-Regal Chapel, Dublin, 1866–69; select preacher at Oxford, 1880-82. He is the author of *Sermons at St. Saviour's Church, Bath*, London, 1852, 2d ed. 1852; *Sermons at the Octagon Chapel, Bath*, 1853, 2d ed. 1853; *The Voluntary System and the Established Church*, 1861 (a lecture in defence of the Established Church, which attracted wide attention).

MAHAN, Asa, D.D., LL.D. (Adrian College, Adrian, Mich., 1877), Congregationalist; b. at Vernon, N.Y., Nov. 9, 1800; graduated at Hamilton College, Clinton, N.Y., 1824, and at Andover Theological Seminary, Mass., 1827; pastor at Pittsford, N.Y., 1829–31; in Cincinnati (Pres.), 1831–35; president of Oberlin College, O., 1835–50; of Cleveland University, Jackson, Mich., 1850–54; pastor (Cong.) there, 1855–57, and at Adrian, Mich., 1857–60; president of Adrian College, 1860–71; since then has resided in England. He is the author of *System of Intellectual Philosophy*, New York, 1845; *Election, and the Influence of the Holy Spirit*, 1851; *Modern Mysteries explained and exposed*, Boston, 1855; *The Science of Logic*, New York, 1857; *Science of Natural Theology*, Boston, 1867; *Phenomena of Spiritualism scientifically explained and exposed*, New York, 1876; *Critical History of the late American War*, 1877; *System of Mental Philosophy*, Chicago, 1882; *Crit. Hist. of Philosophy*, N.Y., 1883, 2 vols.

MAIER, Adalbert, D.D. (Freiburg-im-Br., 1836), Roman Catholic; b. at Villingen, Baden, Germany, April 26, 1811; studied philosophy and theology at Freiburg-im-Br.; became priest there, and provisional teacher in the theological faculty, 1836; professor extraordinary of theology, 1840; ordinary professor, 1841; since 1846 has lectured especially upon the literature of the New Testament; since 1848 has been a grand-ducal ecclesiastical councillor. He is the author of *Exeget.-dogmat. Entwicklung der neutestamentlichen Begriffe von Zoë, Anastasis und Krisis*, Freiburg-im-Br., 1839; *Commentar über das Evangelium des Johannes*, 1843–45, 2 vols.; *Commentar über den Brief Pauli an die Römer*, 1847; *Gedächtnissrede auf Joh. Leonh. Hug*, 1847; *Einleitung in die Schriften des N.T.*, 1852; *Commentar über den ersten Brief Pauli an die Korinther*, 1857; do. *über den zweiten Brief*, 1865; do. *über den Brief an die Hebräer*, 1861.

MALAN, Solomon Cæsar, D.D. (University of Edinburgh, 1880), Church of England; b. in Geneva, Switzerland, April 22, 1812; educated at St. Edmund Hall, Oxford; Boden Sanscrit scholar, 1834; Pusey and Ellerton Hebrew scholar, B.A. (second-class classics), 1837; M.A., and member of Balliol College, 1843; ordained deacon 1838, priest 1843; was senior classical professor at Bishop's College, Calcutta, 1838–40, and secretary to the Asiatic Society of Bengal, 1839; from 1845 to 1886 he was vicar of Broadwindsor, Dorsetshire, and from 1870–75 he was prebendary of Ruscombe-Southbury in Sarum Cathedral. He is the son of the late Rev. Cæsar Malan, D.D., of Geneva, and is the author of *Persomache Herodotica, a Tabular Analysis of Herodotus*, Oxford, 1837; *An Outline of Bishop's College and its Missions*, London, 1843;

Family Prayers, 1844; *A Plain Exposition of the Apostles' Creed*, 1847; *A Systematic Catalogue of the Eggs of British Birds*, 1848; *List of British Birds*, 1849; *Who is God in China — Shin or Shang-Te? Remarks on the Etymology of Elohim and of Theos, and on the rendering of those terms into Chinese*, 1855; *A Vindication of the Authorised Version*, 1856; *A Letter to the Earl of Shaftesbury on the Buddhistic and Pantheistic Tendency of the Chinese and Mongolian Versions of the Bible published by the British and Foreign Bible Society*, 1856; *The Threefold San-tsze King, or Triliteral Classic of China*, translated into English, with notes, 1856; *Aphorisms on Drawing*, 1856; *Magdala and Bethany, a Pilgrimage*, 1857; *The Coast of Tyre and Sidon*, 1858; *Letters to a Young Missionary*, 1858; *Prayers and Thanksgivings for the Holy Communion*, translated from Armenian, Coptic, and other Eastern rituals, for the use of the clergy, 1859; *Meditations on a Prayer of S. Ephrem*, translated from the Russian, 1859; *The Gospel according to S. John*, translated from the eleven oldest versions, except the Latin (viz., Syriac, Ethiopic, Armenian, Sahidic, Memphitic, Gothic, Georgian, Slavonic, Anglo-Saxon, Arabic, and Persian), 1862; *Preparation for the Holy Communion*, translated from Coptic, Armenian, and other Eastern originals, for the use of the laity, 1863; *Meditations on our Lord's Passion*, translated from the Armenian of Matthew Vartabed, 1863; *A Manual of Daily Prayers*, translated from Armenian and other Eastern originals, 1863; *Philosophy, or Truth? Remarks on the First Five Lectures by the Dean of Westminster on the Jewish Church, with Plain Words on Questions of the Day, regarding Faith, the Bible, and the Church*, 1865; *History of the Georgian Church*, translated from the Russian of P. Joselian, 1866; *Sermons by Gabriel, Bishop of Imereth*, translated from the Georgian, 1867; *Repentance*, translated from the Syriac of S. Ephrem, 1867; *On Ritualism*, 1867; *The Life and Times of St. Gregory the Illuminator*, translated from the Armenian, 1868; *The Holy Sacrament of the Lord's Supper according to Scripture, Grammar, and the Faith*, 1868; *A Plea for the Authorised Version and for the Received Text in Answer to the Dean of Canterbury*, 1869; *Instruction in the Christian Faith*, translated from the Armenian, 1869; *The Liturgy of the Orthodox Armenian Church*, translated from the Armenian, 1870; *Differences between the Armenian and the Greek Churches*, translated from the Russian, 1871; *The Conflicts of the Holy Apostles, an Apocryphal Book of the Early Eastern Church*, translated from an Ethiopic MS., together with *The Epistle of S. Dionysius the Areopagite to Timothy, on the Death of S. Paul*, also translated from an Ethiopic MS., and *The Assumption of S. John*, translated from the Armenian, 1871; *Misawo, the Japanese Girl*, translated from the Japanese, 1871; *Our Lord's Parables explained to Country Children*, 2 vols., 1871; *A Form of Prayer for the Use of Sunday Schools*, 1871; *Bishop Ellicott's New Translation of the Athanasian Creed*, 1872; *The Confession of Faith of the Orthodox Armenian Church, together with the Rite of Holy Baptism, as it is administered in that Church*, translated from the Armenian, 1872; *The Divine Liturgy of S. Mark the Evangelist*, translated from an old Coptic MS., and compared with the same liturgy as arranged by S. Cyril, 1872; *The Coptic Calendar*, translated from an Arabic MS., with notes, 1873; *A History of the Copts, and of their Church*, translated from the Arabic of Tāqi ed-Dīn El-Maqrīzī, with notes, 1873; *The Holy Gospel and Versicles, for every Sunday and other Feast Day in the Year, as used in the Coptic Church*, translated from a Coptic MS., 1874; *The Divine Εὐχολόγιον and the Divine Liturgy of S. Gregory the Theologian*, translated from an old Coptic MS., together with the additions found in the Roman ed. of 1737, 1875; *Prayers and Thanksgivings for the Use of my Parishioners*, Beaminster, 1878; *The Two Holy Sacraments of Baptism and of the Lord's Supper according to Scripture, Grammar, and the Faith*, London, 1880; *The Miracles of our Lord and Saviour Jesus Christ explained to Country Children*, 1881; *Seven Chapters* (St. Matt. i.-vi., St. Luke xi.) *of the Revision of 1881 revised*, 1881; *Select Readings in the Greek Text of S. Matthew, lately published by the Rev. Drs. Westcott and Hort, revised, with a Postscript on the Pamphlet, "The Revisers and the Greek Text of the New Testament," by two members of the Revision Company*, 1882; *The Book of Adam and Eve, also called The Conflict of Adam and Eve with Satan, a Book of the Early Eastern Church*, translated from the Ethiopic, with notes from the Kufale, Talmud, Midrashim, and other Eastern works, 1882; *Morning and Evening Prayers for Day and Sunday Schools in the Parish of Broadwindsor*, 1884.

MALLALIEU, Willard Francis, D.D. (East Tennessee Wesleyan University, Athens, Tenn., 1874), Methodist bishop; b. at Sutton, Worcester County, Mass., Dec. 11, 1828; graduated at Wesleyan University, Middletown, Conn., 1857; joined the New-England Conference of the Methodist-Episcopal Church, 1858; became presiding elder, Boston district, 1882; bishop, 1884.

MALLORY, George Scovill, D.D. (Hobart College, Geneva, N.Y., 1874), Episcopalian; b. at Watertown, Conn., June 5, 1838; graduated head of his class at Trinity College, Hartford, Conn., 1858; travelled in Europe, 1858; entered the Berkeley Divinity School, Middletown, Conn., 1859, and graduated 1862; was assistant professor of ancient languages in Trinity College, Hartford, Conn., 1862–64; Brownell professor of literature and oratory in the same, 1864–72; trustee of the same since 1872; editor of *The Churchman*, New York, since 1866.

MANGOLD, Wilhelm Julius, Lic. Theol. (Marburg, 1852), **D.D.** (*hon.*, Vienna, 1852); b. at Cassel, Nov. 20, 1825; studied at Halle (1845–47), Marburg (1847–48), and Göttingen (1848–49); became *repetent* at Marburg, 1851; *privat-docent* there, 1852; professor extraordinary, 1857; ordinary professor of theology, 1863; at Bonn, 1872. He declined calls to professorships at Vienna (1863) and Basel (1866); was member for Marburg of the Prussian *Landtag*, 1871-72. He became *consistorialrath*, 1882. He belongs to the critical school. He is the author of *De monachatus originibus et causis*, Marburg, 1852; *Die Irrlehrer der Pastoralbriefe*, 1856; *Jean Calas und Voltaire*, 1861; *Julian der Abtrünnige*, 1862; *Drei Predigten über Johanneische Texte*, 1864; *Der Römerbrief u. die Anfänge der römischen Gemeinde*, 1866; *Andreæ Hyperii de methodo in conserribenda historia ecclesiastica consilium*, 1866; *Humanität und Christenthum*, Bonn, 1876; *Wider Strauss*, 1877; *Ernst Ludwig*

Henke, Ein Gedenkblatt, Marburg, 1879; *De ecclesia primæva pro Cæsaribus ac magistratibus romanis preces fundente,* Bonn, 1881; *Der Römerbrief u. seine geschichtlichen Voraussetzungen, Neu untersucht,* Marburg, 1884. He edited the 3d ed. of Bleek's *Einleitung in d. N.T.*, Berlin, 1875, and the 4th ed., 1886.

MANLY, Basil, D.D. (University of Alabama, Tuscaloosa, Ala., 1859), **LL.D.** (Agricultural College, Auburn, Ala., 1874), Baptist; b. in Edgefield County, S.C., Dec. 19, 1825; graduated at University of Alabama (at Tuscaloosa), 1843, and at Princeton (N.J.) Theological Seminary, 1847; became pastor at Providence, Ala., 1848; Richmond, Va., 1850; president Richmond Female Institute, 1854; professor of biblical introduction and Old-Testament interpretation in the Southern Baptist Theological Seminary, 1859; president of Georgetown College, Ky., 1871; professor in Southern Baptist Theological Seminary, 1879. He compiled, with his father, *The Baptist Psalmody, a Selection of Hymns* (about twenty original), Charleston, S.C., 1850 (some forty thousand copies sold); and has, in addition to pamphlets and occasional sermons, issued *A Call to the Ministry,* Philadelphia, 1867.

MANN, William Julius, D.D. (Pennsylvania College, Gettysburg, Penn., 1857), Lutheran (General Council); b. at Stuttgart, Germany, May 29, 1819; graduated at Tübingen, 1841; was from 1850 to 1884 pastor of Zion Evangelical Lutheran Church, Philadelphia; now pastor emeritus; since 1864 has been professor of Hebrew, ethics, and symbolics in the Philadelphia Theological Seminary of the Lutheran Church. He edited the *Kirchenfreund,* Philadelphia, 1851–60; and is the author of *Lutheranism in America,* 1857; *General Principles of Christian Ethics,* 1872 (abridgment of Dr. Ch. Fr. Schmid's *Ethic*); *Heilsbotschaft* (sermons), 1881; *Leben und Wirken William Penn's,* Reading, Penn., 1882; *Ein Aufgang im Abendland* (evangelical missions in America), 1883; *Das Buch der Bücher und seine Geschichte,* 1884; *Halle Reports* (new and enlarged ed.), Allentown, Penn., vol. 1, 1885.

MANNING, His Eminence Henry Edward, Cardinal, D.D. (Rome, Italy, 1854), Roman Catholic; b. at Totteridge, Hertfordshire, Eng., July 15, 1808; educated at Harrow and at Balliol College, Oxford; graduated B.A. (first-class in classics), 1830, and was elected fellow of Merton College, and for some time a select preacher to the university. In 1834 he became rector of Lavington and Graffham, Sussex, and married. In 1840 he was appointed archdeacon of Chichester. He was a leader in the so-called "Oxford movement," and in 1851 resigned his ecclesiastical preferments. On April 20, 1851, entered the Roman-Catholic Church, and (his wife having died some time previously), a little later, the priesthood. He then repaired to Rome, where he studied theology until 1854, when he received the degree of D.D. Returning to England, he entered upon a career of great activity. In 1857 he founded at Bayswater a congregation of the "Oblates of St. Charles Borromeo," and became its first superior; summoned Zion Sisters from Paris to teach the girls' schools; erected a protectory; founded a Roman-Catholic university at Kensington (Oct. 15, 1874), and in other ways greatly increased the influence of his Church. In recognition of his eminent services, Pius IX. appointed him successively provost of the Roman-Catholic archdiocese of Westminster (1857), prothonotary apostolic and his domestic prelate (1860), archbishop of Westminster (consecrated June 8, 1865), and cardinal priest, with the title of SS. Andrew and Gregory on the Cœlian Hill, March 15, 1875; received his hat in a consistory held at the Vatican, Dec. 31, 1877. Cardinal Manning sat in the Vatican Council, 1869–70. Of his publications may be mentioned, *The Grounds of Faith,* London, 1852; *Temporal Sovereignty of the Popes,* 1860; *The Present Crisis of the Holy See tested by Prophecy,* 1861; *The Temporal Power of the Vicar of Jesus Christ,* 1862, 2d ed. 1862; *Sermons on Ecclesiastical Subjects,* 1863–73, 3 vols.; *The Temporal Mission of the Holy Ghost,* 1865, 3d ed. 1877; *The Vatican Council and its Definitions,* 1870; *The Four Great Evils of the Day,* 1871, 2d ed. 1871; *Cæsarism and Ultramontanism,* 1874; *The Internal Mission of the Holy Ghost,* 1875; *Vatican Decrees in their Bearing on Civil Allegiance,* 1875; *True Story of the Vatican Council,* 1877; *Miscellanies,* 1877, 2 vols.; *The Catholic Church and Modern Society,* 1880; *The Eternal Priesthood,* 1883. See W. S. Lilly's *Cardinal Manning's Characteristics, Political, Philosophical, and Religious,* 1885. *

MARQUIS, David Calhoun, D.D. (Washington and Jefferson College, Washington, Penn., 1875), Presbyterian; b. in Lawrence County, Penn., Nov. 15, 1834; graduated at Jefferson College, Canonsburg, Penn., 1857, and at the Theological Seminary of the North-west, Chicago, Ill., 1863; and after pastorates in Decatur, Ill. (1863), Chicago (1866), Baltimore, Md. (1870), and St. Louis, Mo. (1878), was in 1883 called to the Theological Seminary of the North-west, Chicago, Ill. (since 1886 called the McCormick Theological Seminary of the Presbyterian Church), as professor of New-Testament literature and exegesis.

MARTIGNY, Joseph Alexandre, Roman Catholic; b. at Sauverny (Ain), in the year 1808; ordained priest in 1832; served at a village near Belley; then was arch-priest of Bagé-le-Châtel in 1849, and later titular canon of the cathedral of Belley. He was a member of a great number of learned societies, and noted for archæological researches. He died in 1880. His greatest work is *Dictionnaire des antiquités chrétiennes,* Paris, 1865 (270 engravings), 2d ed. 1877 (675 engravings). *

MARTIN, William Alexander Parsons, D.D. (Lafayette College, Easton, Penn., 1860), **LL.D.** (University of the City of New York, 1870), Presbyterian; b. at Livonia, Ind., April 10, 1827; graduated at the State University at Bloomington, Ind., and at the Presbyterian Theological Seminary of New Albany (now removed to Chicago); from 1850–60 was a missionary at Ningpo, China; from 1863–68 was missionary at Peking; in 1869 became president of the Imperial Tungwen College of Peking, and professor of international law. He visited the United States in 1860, 1868, and 1879. He is a member of the European Institute of International Law, and of other learned societies. His position in China is of the highest importance. During his long life there he has had several unusual experiences. In 1855 he was captured by Chinese pirates; in 1858 he served as interpreter to the United-States minister in negotiating the treaty of Tientsin; in 1859 he accompanied the United-States minister to Peking, and to Yedo, Japan; in 1866 he visited a colony of Jews in Honan, visiting also the tomb of Confucius, and was the first foreigner in recent times to make the journey from Peking to Shanghai by the grand canal (for account of this journey, see *Journal* North China Branch Royal Asiatic Society, 1866); in the conflict with France, 1884-85, as well as in former disputes, acted as adviser to the Chinese Government on questions of international law, and in 1885 was made a mandarin of the third rank, by imperial decree. In February, 1885, he was elected first president of the newly organized Oriental Society of Peking. Dr. Martin edited *The Peking Scientific Magazine* from 1875 to 1878 (printed in Chinese); and has written in Chinese, *Evidences of Christianity*, 1855, 10th ed. 1885 (translated into Japanese, and widely circulated in Japan); *The Three Principles* (1856), and *Religious Allegories* (1857), and numerous small tracts which have been widely distributed. In English, besides his correspondence with the learned societies to which he belongs, and his contributions to reviews and other periodicals, he has published *The Education and Philosophy of the Chinese*, Shanghai and London, 1880, new ed. under title, *The Chinese: their Education, Philosophy, and Letters*, New York, 1881. In French he has written much. But his largest works have been his translations into Chinese, of Wheaton (1863) and of Woolsey (1875) and Bluntschli (1879) on *International Law*, De Marten's *Guide diplomatique* (1874), and the compilation in Chinese of courses of natural philosophy (1866) and mathematical physics (1885).

MARTINEAU, James, LL.D. (Harvard College, Cambridge, Mass., U.S.A., 1872), **Th.D.** (Leiden, Holland, 1875), **D.D.** (Edinburgh, Scotland, 1884), Unitarian; b. at Norwich, Eng., April 21, 1805; educated at Norwich grammar school until 1819; Dr. Lant Carpenter's, Bristol, 1819-21; studied civil engineering, 1821-22; took course in Manchester New College, York, 1822-27 (degrees in England were then inaccessible to Non-conformists); 1827-28, master of Dr. Lant Carpenter's school, Bristol, during his absence from illness; 1828-32, junior minister of Eustace-street Presbyterian Meeting-house, Dublin; 1832-57, minister (at first junior, then sole) of congregation of Protestant Non-conformists worshipping in Paradise-street Chapel, and since 1849 in Hope-street Church, Liverpool; with simultaneous professorship in philosophy in Manchester New College, first in Manchester, then in London, from 1840; 1857-85, professor of philosophy in said college, London, and principal 1869-85; with ministry of Little Portland-street Chapel (two years with Rev J. J. Tayler) from 1859-72. He was the younger brother of Harriet Martineau. He is the author of *The Rationale of Religious Enquiry, or the Question Stated of Reason, The Bible, and the Church*, London, 1836, 4th ed. 1853; *Unitarianism Defended* (five lectures of thirteen in the Liverpool controversy, delivered in connection with J. H. Thom and H. Giles), 1839; *Hymns for the Christian Church and Home*, 1840, 23d ed. 1885; *Endeavours after the Christian Life*, 1843-47, 2 vols., in 1 vol. 1866, 8th ed. 1886; *Hours of Thought on Sacred Things*, 1876-80, 2 vols.; *A Study of Spinoza*, 1882, 2d ed. 1883; *Types of Ethical Theory*, 1885, 2 vols., 2d ed. 1886; numerous separate sermons, academic addresses, and articles in reviews, some of which have been collected by American editors, and published in the following volumes: *Miscellanies* (edited by Rev. T. Starr King), Boston, 1852; *Studies of Christianity* (ed. by Rev. W. R. Alger), 1858; *Essays, Philosophical and Theological*, 1866-69, 2 vols.,—*Religion as affected by Modern Materialism*, London, 1874; *Modern Materialism, its Attitude towards Theology*, 1876,—combined by the author and repub. 1878.

MATHESON, George, D.D. (Edinburgh, 1879), Church of Scotland; b. at Glasgow, March 27, 1842; lost his sight in youth, but after a brilliant course at the University of Edinburgh, taking the first prize in senior division of logic (1860) and in moral philosophy (1861), graduated M.A. 1862, B.D. 1866; minister at Innellan, 1868-86; since of St. Bernard's, Edinburgh. In 1880 he declined a unanimous call to succeed Dr. Cumming of London. In 1881 he was Baird lecturer, and in 1882 a St. Giles lecturer (*Confucianism*, in *Faiths of the World*). He is the author of many articles and the following books: *Aids to the Study of German Theology*, Edinburgh, 1874, 2d ed. 1876; *Growth of the Spirit of Christianity*, 1877, 2 vols.; *Natural Elements of Revealed Theology* (Baird Lectures, 1881); *My Aspirations* (Heart-Chord series), London, 1883; *Moments on the Mount, a Series of Devotional Meditations*, 1884, 2d ed. 1886; *Can the Old Faith live with the New? or, The Problem of Evolution and Revelation*, 1885, 2d ed. 1886.

MATTOON, Stephen, D.D. (Union College, Schenectady, N.Y., 1870), Presbyterian; b. at Champion, N.Y., May 5, 1816; graduated at Union College, Schenectady, N.Y., 1842, and at Princeton Theological Seminary, N.J., 1846; was missionary of the Presbyterian Board of Foreign Missions in Siam, 1846-66; pastor at Ballston Spa, N. Y., 1867-69; from 1870 till 1884 was president of Biddle Memorial Institute (now Biddle University), Charlotte, N.C., and since 1877 professor of systematic theology in its theological department. He completed the translation of the New Testament into Siamese in 1865, and it was printed that year complete at the Presbyterian Mission Press at Bangkok, Siam: portions had been printed earlier as they were finished.

MEAD, Charles Marsh, Ph.D. (Tübingen, 1866), **D.D.** (Middlebury College, Vt., 1881), Congregationalist; b. at Cornwall, Vt., Jan. 28, 1836; graduated at Middlebury (Vt.) College, 1856, and at Andover (Mass.) Theological Seminary, 1862; studied at Halle and Berlin, 1863-66; was professor of Hebrew in Andover Theological Seminary, 1866-82; since he has lived in Germany. He was a member of the Old-Testament Revision Company. He translated *Exodus*, in the American Lange series (N.Y., 1876), and wrote *The Soul Here and Hereafter, a Biblical Study*, Boston, 1879.

MEDD, Peter Goldsmith, Church of England; b. at Leyburn in Wensleydale, Yorkshire, July 18, 1829; was scholar of University College, Oxford; graduated B.A. (first-class classics) 1852, M.A. 1855; fellow of his college, 1852-77; resident fellow, lecturer, tutor, bursar, and dean of same, 1853-70; ordained deacon 1853, priest 1859; was curate of St. John Baptist, Oxford, 1858-67; rector of Barnes, 1870-76; since 1876 has been rector of North Cerney, Gloucestershire, and since 1883 proctor in convocation for diocese of Gloucester and Bristol; since 1871, examining chaplain to bishop of Rochester (afterwards St. Alban's); since 1870, member of governing council of Keble College, Oxford. He was select preacher to the University of Oxford, 1881–82; Bampton lecturer, 1882; examiner in theology at Oxford, 1877–79, 1884–86. He is an "English Catholic." He is the author of *Christian Meaning of the Psalms, and Supernatural Character of Christian Truth*, Oxford, 1862; *Fundamental Principle of the Christian Ministry*, 1867 (two volumes of university sermons); *Household Prayer*, London, 1864; *Parish Sermons*, 1877; *The One Mediator* (Bampton Lectures), 1884. With Dr. William Bright he edited *Latin Version of the Prayer-Book*, 1865, 3d ed. 1877.

MEINHOLD, Johannes, Lic. Theol. (Greifswald, 1884), Lutheran; b. at Cammin, Pomerania, Germany, Aug. 12, 1861; studied at the universities of Leipzig, Berlin, Tübingen, and Greifswald; became *privat-docent* of theology at Greifswald, Dec. 17, 1884. He is the author of *Die Composition des Buches Daniel* (*Habilitationsschrift*), 1884.

MENZEL, Andreas, Lic. Theol. (Breslau, 1843), **D.D.** (Breslau, 1857), Old Catholic; b. at Mehlsack, East Prussia, Nov. 25, 1815; studied theology at Braunsberg, 1837–41; was ordained priest, 1841; became *vikar* at Braunsberg, 1841; *stipendiat* in Rome, 1844; *sub-regens* of the Episcopal seminary at Braunsberg, 1845; professor extraordinary of theology in the university there, 1850; ordinary professor of systematic theology, 1853; at Bonn, 1874. In 1849–51 and 1862–63 he was member of the House of Deputies in Berlin. Since 1870, although an ordinary professor of theology, he has had no students, because he was excommunicated for refusing to accept the Vatican decrees. He has always striven to make Catholicism, in the spirit of the New Testament, accord with the requirements and conceptions of our time. He is the author of *De natura conscientiæ*, Braunsberg, 1852; *Traducianismus an Creationismus?* 1856; and other Latin academical dissertations. He died at Bonn, Aug. 5, 1886.

MERIVALE, Very Rev. Charles, D.D. (Cambridge, 1870; Durham, *ad eund.*, 1883), **D.C.L.** (*hon.*, Oxford, 1866), **LL.D.** (*hon.*, Edinburgh, 1884), dean of Ely, Church of England; b. in Bloomsbury, London, March 8, 1808; entered St. John's College, Cambridge, 1826; was Browne's medallist, 1829; graduated B.A. (senior optime and first-class classical tripos) 1830, M.A. 1833, B.D. 1840; was fellow and tutor of St. John's College, 1833–48; ordained deacon 1833, priest 1834; select preacher 1838, and Whitehall preacher 1839–41; Hulsean lecturer 1862, and Boyle lecturer 1864–65; chaplain to the speaker of the House of Commons, 1863–69. From 1848 to 1870 he was rector of Lawford, Essex. On Dec. 29, 1869, he was installed dean of Ely. His theological standpoint is that of "the Church of the Revolution,—the platform of Tillotson and Burnet." He is the author of *History of the Romans under the Empire*, London, 1850–62, 7 vols., new ed. 1865, 8 vols. (with re-issues); *Sallust's Catiline and Jugurtha*, 1854; *Keats's Hyperion in Latin Verse*, 1862; *The Conversion of the Roman Empire* (Boyle Lectures for 1864), 1864; *The Conversion of the Northern Nations* (do. for 1865), 1865; *Homer's Iliad in English Rhymed Verse*, 1869; *General History of Rome*, 1875; *St. Paul at Rome*, 1877; *Conversion of the West*, 1878; *Four Lectures on Epochs of Early Church History*, 1879.

MERRILL, Selah, D.D. (Iowa College, Grinnell, Io., 1875), **LL.D.** (Union College, Schenectady, N.Y., 1884), Congregationalist; b. at Canton Centre, Hartford County, Conn., May 2, 1837; entered Yale College, New Haven, Conn., 1859; left the class, but later received honorary A.M. from the college "for special services in biblical learning;" studied theology in New Haven (Conn.) Theological Seminary; preached at Chester (Mass.), Le Roy (N.Y.), San Francisco (Cal.), and Salmon Falls (N.H.); was chaplain of the Forty-ninth U.S. Colored Infantry at Vicksburg, Miss., 1864–65; student in Germany, 1868–70; archæologist of the American Palestine Exploration Society, 1874–77, working in Moab, Gilead, and Bashan, east of the Jordan; United-States consul in Jerusalem from 1882 to 1886. In 1872, and again in 1879, taught Hebrew in Andover Theological Seminary. He is a member of the American Oriental Society, of the Society of Biblical Literature and Exegesis, and of the Society of Biblical Archæology (British). He is the author of several articles in the *Bibliotheca Sacra* and other periodicals, on biblical geography, the cuneiform inscriptions, and other Oriental topics; and of *East of the Jordan*, New York, 1881, 2d ed. 1883, reprinted London, 1881; *Galilee in the Time of Christ*, Boston 1881, London 1885; several parts of *Picturesque Palestine*, New York and London, 1882–83; he published *Greek Inscriptions collected in the Years 1875–77, in the Country East of the Jordan*, 1885 (these were revised by Professor F. W. Allen of Cambridge, Mass.).

MERX, (Ernst Otto) Adalbert, D.D., German Protestant theologian and Orientalist; b. at Bleicherode, Nov. 2, 1838; studied at Marburg, Halle, and Berlin, 1857–64; became *privat-docent* of theology at Jena, 1865; professor extraordinary there, 1869; ordinary professor in the philosophical faculty at Tübingen, 1869; ordinary professor of theology at Giessen, 1873; at Heidelberg, 1875. He is the author of *Meletemata Ignatiana, Critica de epistolarum Ignatianarum versione Syriaca commentatio*, Halle, 1861; *Bardesanes von Edessa*, 1863; *Cur in libro Danielis juxta hebræam aramæa adhibita sit dialectus explicatur*, 1865; *Das Gedicht vom Hiob, Hebräischer Text, kritisch bearbeitet und übersetzt, nebst sachlicher und kritischer Einleitung*, Jena, 1871; *Die Prophetie des Joel und ihre Ausleger von den ältesten Zeiten bis zu den Reformatoren*, Halle, 1879; *Eine Rede vom Auslegen ins Besondere des Alten Testaments*, 1879.

MESSNER, (Karl Ferdinand) Hermann, Lic. Theol. (Göttingen, 1856), **D.D.** (*hon.*, Wien, 1871), German theologian; b. at Öbisfelde (Altmark), Prussia, Oct. 25, 1824; studied at Halle and Berlin, 1844–50; was *repetent* at Göttingen, 1850; adjunct, 1856; later inspector of the *Domkandidatenstift* in Berlin; and since 1860 has been professor extraordinary of theology in her university. From 1860 to 1876 he was a member of the Royal *Wissenschaftlichen Prüfungs Commission* in Berlin. His theological standpoint is the positive evangelical. Since 1859 he has edited the *Neue evangelische Kirchenzeitung*. He is the author of *Die "Lehre der Apostel,"* Leipzig, 1856; and edited the third edition of De Wette's *Corinthians* (1855), the fourth edition of his *Matthew* (1857), and, with Prof. Dr. Lünemann of Göttingen, the sixth edition of De Wette's *Lehrbuch der historisch kritischen Einleitung in's Neue Testament*, Berlin, 1860.

MEUSS, Eduard, Lic. Theol. (Berlin, 1854), **D.D.** (Berlin, 1860), Protestant theologian; b. at Rathenow (Province of Brandenburg), Prussia, Jan. 19, 1817; studied at Leipzig, Göttingen, Berlin, and Halle, 1836–41; became member of the Wittenberg theological seminary, 1844; assistant preacher in Berlin, 1847; court preacher at Köpenick, 1852; university preacher, and professor extraordinary of theology, in Breslau, 1854; was ordinary professor, 1863–July 1, 1885; and since 1880 has been member of the consistorium. He is the author of *In parabolam Jesu Christi de œconomo injusto denuo inquiritur*, Breslau, 1856; *Μακαρισμῶν Jesu Christi usu ecclesiæ publico receptum historia*, 1863; *Das Weihnachtsfest und die Kunst*, 1866, 2d ed. Gera, 1876; *Leben und Frucht des evangelischen Pfarrhauses vornehmlich in Deutschland*, Bielefeld, 1876, 2d ed. 1883.

MEYRICK, Frederick, Church of England; b. at Ramsbury Vicarage, Wiltshire, Jan. 28, 1827; entered Trinity College, Oxford; graduated B.A. (second-class in classics) 1847, M.A. 1850; ordained deacon 1850, priest 1852; was a fellow of Trinity College, Oxford, 1847–60, and tutor in it, 1851–59; in 1856 public examiner in classics; preacher at the Chapel Royal, Whitehall, 1856; select preacher before the University of Oxford, 1855–56, 1865–66, 1875–76; examiner for the Johnson theological scholarship at Oxford, 1859; one of her Majesty's inspectors of schools from 1859 to 1869; examining chaplain to Bishop Christopher Wordsworth, 1869–85; since 1868 rector of Blickling, Norfolk; and since 1869 non-residentiary canon of Lincoln. He was tutor to the late and the present Marquis of Lothian from 1847–53, when the rest of the family, with their exception, joined the Church of Rome. In 1853 he founded the Anglo-Continental Society (now numbering six hundred, with two hundred publications), for making known upon the Continent the principles of the Anglican Church, and promoting the principles of the English Reformation abroad. As secretary of this society he has edited many dogmatic and controversial treatises in Latin, Italian, Spanish, etc. He attended the Bonn Conference of 1875, and formed one of the Committee on the Doctrine of the Procession of the Holy Spirit. His theological standpoint is "that of the historical school of Anglican divines, commencing with Bishop Andrewes, and ending with Dean Hook and Bishop Christopher Wordsworth." Since 1877 he has edited *The Foreign Church Chronicle and Review*. His writings are very numerous (see list in Crockford's *Clerical Directory for 1886*), and include contributions to Smith's Dictionaries of the Bible and of Christian Antiquities, *The Bible (Speaker's) Commentary* (*Joel* and *Obadiah*, 1876; *Ephesians*, 1880), *The Pulpit Commentary* (*Leviticus*, 1882), *The Theological Library* (*Is Dogma a Necessity?* 1883), etc. Of general interest may be mentioned, *The Practical Working of the Church of Spain*, London, 1850–51; *Clerical Tenure of Fellowships*, Oxford, 1854; *Moral and Devotional Theology of the Church of Rome*, London, 1856; *Correspondence with Old Catholics and Orientals*, 1877–78, 4 series; *The Old Catholic Movement*, 1877; Sketches of *Döllinger* (1879) and of *Hyacinthe* (1880); *The Doctrine of the Church of England on the Holy Communion*, 1885; editions of works of Bishop Cosin, Andrewes, Hall, etc.

MICHAUD, Philibert Eugène, Christian Catholic; b. at Pouilly-sur-Saône, Côte d'Or, France, March 13, 1839; studied theology in the seminary at Dijon and at the Dominican College of St. Maximin in Provence; became curate of St. Roch, and then of the Madeleine, Paris; refused to accept the infallibility dogma, and so was dismissed; was Old-Catholic minister at Paris, but since 1876 has been professor of theology at Bern, Switzerland. He is the author of *Guillaume de Champeaux et les écoles de Paris au XIIe siècle, d'après des documents inédits*, Paris, 1867, 2d ed. 1867; *L'Esprit et la Lettre dans la morale religieuse*, 2 series, 1869 and 1870; *Guignol et la Révolution dans l'Eglise romaine, M. Veuillot et son parti condamnés par les archevêques et évêques de Paris, Tours, Viviers, Orléans, Marseille, Verdun, Chartres, Moulins*, etc., 1872, 2d ed. 1872; *Plutôt la mort que le déshonneur, Appel aux anciens-catholiques de France, contre les révolutionnaires romanistes*, 1872; *Comment l'Eglise romaine n'est plus une Eglise catholique*, 1872; *Programme de réforme de l'Eglise d'Occident, proposé aux anciens-catholiques et aux autres communions chrétiennes*, 1872; *Les faux libéraux de l'Eglise romaine, Réponse au R. P. Perraud (depuis évêque d'Autun), et Lettres de polémique*, 1872; *De la falsification des catéchismes français et des manuels de théologie par le parti romaniste, de 1670 à 1868*, 1872; *La Papauté antichrétienne*, 1873; *Le mouvement contemporain des Eglises, Etudes religieuses et politiques: I. La nouvelle Eglise romaine; II. Devoirs des gouvernements et des peuples envers la nouvelle Eglise romaine; III. Les anciens-catholiques et la réunion des Eglises; IV. La situation morale et religieuse en France*, 1874; *De l'état présent de l'Eglise catholique-romaine en France, ouvrage interdit en France sous le ministère de M. Buffet (de l'Ordre moral)*, 1875, 2d ed. Bonn, 1876; *Etude stratégique contre Rome*, Paris, 1876; *Catéchisme catholique*, Bern, 1876; *Discussion sur les sept conciles œcuméniques, étudiés au point de vue traditionnel et libéral*, 1878; *Louis XIV. et Innocent XI.*, Paris, 1882–83, 4 vols.; *Quelques Réformes scolaires*, Chaux-de-fonds, 1884; *Mme. Steck et ses Poésies*, Bern, 1885; numerous critical, literary, historical, and philosophical articles in Swiss periodicals.

MICHELSEN, Alexander, Ph.D., Lutheran; b. in the year 1802; pastor at Lübeck; d. at Schwartau, June 3, 1885. He was the brother-in-law of the poet Geibel, and noted as the translator of the writings of Bishop Martensen and other Danish authors into German. *

MILLIGAN, William, D.D. (St. Andrew's, 1862), Church of Scotland; b. at Edinburgh, March 15, 1821; graduated at St. Andrew's University, April, 1839; was settled at Cameron, Fifeshire, 1844; at Kilconquhar, 1850; and appointed professor of divinity and biblical criticism in the University of Aberdeen, 1860. He was moderator of the General Assembly in 1882, and is now principal clerk of the Assembly. Besides many articles in theological reviews and other periodicals, he has published *Words of the New Testament as altered by Transmission and ascertained by Modern Criticism* (with Dr. Roberts), Edinburgh, 1873; *Resurrection* *of our Lord*, London, 1881, 3d thousand 1884; *The Revelation of St. John* (Baird Lecture, 1885), 1886; and commentaries on the Gospel (with Dr. Moulton, 1880) and on the Revelation of John (1883), in Schaff's *Popular Commentary*, New York and Edinburgh.

MINER, Alonzo Ames, S.T.D. (Harvard College, Cambridge, Mass., 1863), **LL.D.** (Tufts College, College Hill, Mass., 1875), Universalist; b. at Lempster, N.H., Aug. 14, 1814; was public-school teacher at intervals, 1830–35; became principal of Unity (N.H.) scientific and military academy, 1835; pastor at Methuen, Mass., 1839; Lowell, 1842; Boston, since 1848. He was president of Tufts College, College Hill, Mass., 1862–75; since 1869 has been a member of the State Board of Education; since 1873, chairman of the board of visitors of the State Normal Art School; is president of the State Temperance Alliance; was Prohibition candidate for governor, 1878; was original projector of the Universalist Publishing House, Boston. He delivered the Fourth-of-July oration before the municipal authorities of Boston, 1855; was elected by the Legislature an overseer of Harvard College, 1863; was chaplain of the Massachusetts Senate, 1864. Besides numerous pamphlets, he has published *Bible Exercises*, Boston, 1854, last ed. 1885; *Old Forts taken*, 1878, last ed. 1885.

MITCHELL, Alexander Ferrier, D.D. (St. Andrew's, 1862), Church of Scotland; b. at Brechin, Sept. 10, 1822; studied literature, philosophy, and theology at University of St. Andrew's, 1837–41; graduated M.A., 1841; became minister of the parish of Dunnichen, in the presbytery and county of Forfar, 1847; professor of Hebrew and Oriental languages in the College of St. Mary in the University of St. Andrew's, 1848; transferred to the chair of ecclesiastical history and divinity in the same college, 1868. From 1856 to 1874 he was convener (chairman) of the Church of Scotland's Jewish Mission; visited the stations of the mission in Turkey, and recommended the occupation of Alexandria, Beyrout, and Constantinople; has been convener of the Assembly's committee on the minutes of the Westminster Assembly since its institution; has been one of the Church of Scotland's representatives at all the General Councils of the Reformed Churches, and is the convener of its committee on the *desiderata* of Presbyterian history. He is the author of *The Westminster Confession of Faith, a Contribution to the Study of its History and the Defence of its Teaching*, Edinburgh, 1866, 3d ed. 1867; *The Wedderburns and their Work, or the Sacred Poetry of the Scottish Reformation in its Relation to that of Germany*, 1867; *Minutes of the Westminster Assembly from November, 1644, to March, 1649, with Historical Introduction*, 1874; *Historical Notice of Archbishop Hamilton's Catechism* (prefixed to black-letter reprint of the same), 1882; *The Westminster Assembly, its History and Standards* (Baird Lecture for 1882), London, 1883; *The Catechisms of the Second Reformation*, 1886. He edited in 1860 the *Sum of Saving Knowledge, translated into Modern Greek* by the late Professor Edward Masson, and in 1876 the late Professor Crawford's *The Preaching of the Cross, and other Sermons*; and has contributed to journals and encyclopædias articles on historical topics.

MITCHELL, Arthur, D.D. (Williams College, Williamstown, Mass., 1876), Presbyterian; b. at Hudson, N.Y., Aug. 13, 1835; graduated at Williams College, Williamstown, Mass., 1853, and at Union Theological Seminary, New-York City, 1859; was tutor in Lafayette College, Easton, Penn., 1853–54; became pastor of Third Church, Richmond, Va., 1859; of Second Church, Morristown, N.J., 1861; of First Church, Chicago, Ill., 1868; of First Church, Cleveland, O., 1880; secretary of Board of Foreign Missions, New-York City, 1884. He has published many discourses in pamphlet form.

MITCHELL, Edward Cushing, D.D. (Colby University, Waterville, Me., 1870), Baptist; b. at East Bridgewater, Mass., Sept. 20, 1829; graduated at Waterville College (now Colby University), Me., 1849, and at Newton (Mass.) Theological Institution, 1853; was resident graduate for a year; pastor at Calais, Me., 1854–56; Brockport, N.Y., 1857–58; Rockford, Ill., 1858–63; professor of biblical interpretation, Alton, Ill., 1863–70; of Hebrew and Old-Testament literature, Baptist Union Seminary, Chicago, 1870–77; of Hebrew, Regent's Park College, London, Eng., 1877; president Baptist Theological School, Paris, France, 1878–82; president Roger Williams University, Nashville, Tenn., 1884–85. He edited *The Present Age*, Chicago, 1883–84; delivered the Lowell Institute lectures for 1884, upon *Biblical Science and Modern Discovery*; during the same year, courses at the Hebrew school in Morgan Park, Ill., and Worcester, Mass.; and during 1885 in Brooklyn, N.Y. He edited and enlarged Benjamin Davies' *Hebrew Lexicon*, Andover, 1880; and revised and re-edited Davies' Gesenius' *Hebrew Grammar* (from ed. of Kautzsch), 1881; and has written *A Critical Handbook. A Guide to the Authenticity, Canon, and Text of the New Testament*, Andover, 1881; *Les sources du Nouveau Testament, Recherches sur l'authenticité, le canon, et le texte du Nouveau Testament*, Paris, 1882; *Hebrew Introduction, An Elementary Hebrew Grammar and Reading Book*, Andover, 1883.

MITCHELL, Hinckley Gilbert, Ph.D. (Leipzig University, 1879), Methodist; b. at Lee, Oneida County, N.Y., Feb 22, 1846; graduated at Wesleyan University, Middletown, Conn., 1873, and B.D. at Boston (Mass.) Theological Seminary, 1876; studied in Germany, 1876–79; joined Central New-York Conference, 1879; became pastor at Fayette, N.Y., 1879; tutor of Latin, and instructor in Hebrew, Wesleyan University, 1880; instructor of Hebrew and Old-Testament exegesis in Boston University, 1883; professor of the same, 1884. He is the secretary of the Society of Biblical Literature and Exegesis; and is the author of *Final Constructions of Biblical Hebrew*, Leipzig, 1879; *Hebrew Lessons*, Boston, 1884, 2d ed. 1885.

MITCHELL, Samuel Thomas, African Methodist-Episcopalian layman; b. at Toledo, O., Sept. 24, 1851; graduated at Wilberforce University, Xenia, O., 1873; was principal of Pleasant-street School, Springfield, O., 1875–78; principal of Lincoln Institute, State Normal School, Jefferson City, Mo., 1879–84; since June 20, 1884, has been president of Wilberforce University. He presided over the Missouri State Teachers' Association at Jefferson City, 1875; was member of General Conference of the African Methodist-Episcopal Church in 1884; is founder of the present educational system in that denomination.

MOBERLY, Right Rev. George, D.C.L. (Oxford, 1836), lord bishop of Salisbury (Sarum), Church of England; b. in St. Petersburg, Russia, Oct. 10, 1803; d. at Salisbury, July 6, 1885. He was educated at Balliol College, Oxford; graduated B.A. (first-class classics) 1825, M.A. 1828; won English essay prize, 1826; was ordained deacon 1826, priest 1828; was fellow and tutor of Balliol College; public examiner in the university, 1830 and 1833–35; select preacher, 1833, 1858, 1863; head master of Winchester College, 1835–66; rector of Brightstone, Isle of Wight, 1866–69; fellow of Winchester College, 1866–70; Bampton lecturer, 1868; canon of Chester, 1868–69; consecrated bishop, 1869. He was the author of *Practical Sermons*, London, 1838; *Sermons preached at Winchester College*, 1844, 2d series (with a preface on fagging) 1848; *The Sayings of the Great Forty Days between the Resurrection and Ascension, regarded as Outlines of the Kingdom of God* (five sermons) 1844, 2d ed. (with *An Examination of Mr. Newman's Theory of Development*) 1846; *The Proposed Degradation and Declaration considered* (a letter addressed to the master of Balliol), Oxford, 1845; *All Saints, Kings, and Priests* (two sermons on papal aggression, preached at Winchester), London, 1850; *The Law of the Love of God* (an essay), 1854; *Sermons on the Beatitudes*, Oxford, 1860; *Five Short Letters to Sir William Heathcote, on the Studies and Discipline of Public Schools*, London, 1861; *The Administration of the Holy Spirit in the Body of Christ* (Bampton Lectures), 1868; *Sermons at Brighstone*, 1869, 3d ed. 1874. He was one of the "five clergymen" (Henry Alford, John Barrow, Charles John Ellicott, William Gilson Humphry), who published a revised version of *John, Romans, Corinthians, Galatians*, and *James;* and a member of the New-Testament Revision Company. *

MOELLER, Ernst Wilhelm, Lic. Theol. (Halle, 1854), **D.D.** (*hon.*, Greifswald, 1863), **Ph.D.** (*hon.*, Halle, 1883), German theologian; b. at Erfurt, Oct. 1, 1827; studied at Berlin, Halle, and Bonn, 1847–51; became *privat-docent* at Halle, 1854; pastor near Halle, 1863; ordinary professor of church history at Kiel, 1873. He holds to the *Vermittlungstheologie*. He is the author of *Gregorii Nysseni doctrin. de hominis natura et illustravit et cum Origeniana comparavit*, Halle, 1854; *Geschichte der Kosmologie in der griechischen Kirche bis auf Origenes*, 1860; *Andreas Osiander, Leben und ausgewählte Schriften*, Elberfeld, 1870; *Ueber die Religion Plutarchs*, Kiel, 1881 (pp. 14); edited the 3d ed. of De Wette's commentaries on *Galatians* and *Thessalonians* (Leipzig, 1864), and the *Pastoral Epistles* and *Hebrews* (1867).

MOFFAT, James Clement, D.D. (Miami University, Oxford, O., 1853), Presbyterian; b. at Glencree, in the South of Scotland, May 30, 1811; graduated at the College of New Jersey, Princeton, N.J., 1835; tutor in Greek there, 1837; professor of Greek and Latin, Lafayette College, Easton, Penn., 1839; of Latin and modern history, Miami University, Oxford, Butler County, O., 1841; of Greek and Hebrew in a theological seminary, Cincinnati, O., 1852; of Latin and history, College of New Jersey (Princeton), 1853; and of Greek and church history there, 1854; since 1861 has been professor of church history in the Princeton (N.J.) Theological Seminary, retaining Greek literary history until 1877. He is the author of *Life of Dr. Chalmers*, Cincinnati, 1853; *Introduction to the Study of Æsthetics*, 1856, new ed. 1860; *Comparative History of Religions*, New York, 1871–73, 2 vols.; *Song and Scenery, or a Summer Ramble in Scotland*, 1874; *Alwyn, a Romance of Study* (a poem), 1875; *The Church in Scotland: History . . . to the First Assembly of the Reformed Church*, Philadelphia, 1882; *Church History in Brief*, 1885.

MOFFAT, James David, D.D. (Hanover College, Ind., 1882; College of New Jersey, Princeton, 1883), Presbyterian; b. at New Lisbon, O., March 15, 1846; graduated at Washington and Jefferson College, Washington, Penn., 1869; studied at Princeton Theological Seminary, N.J., 1869–71; was stated supply of the Second Presbyterian Church, Wheeling, Va., 1871–73; pastor of the same, 1873–82; since has been president of Washington and Jefferson College.

MONOD, Guillaume, the son of Jean Monod, Reformed; b. at Copenhagen, March 10, 1800; studied theology at Geneva; began his ministry at St. Quentin; in 1846 went to Lausanne; in 1849 to Alger; in 1853 to Rouen; in 1856 to Paris, and preached there as his brother Adolph's successor until 1874, when he opened a free church where he still preaches. Of his numerous publications may be mentioned, *Vues nouvelles sur le christianisme*, 1874; *Mémoires de l'auteur des Vues nouvelles: Suite des mémoires du même*, 1874.

MONOD, Jean Paul Férdéric, Reformed; b. at Paris, the son of preceding, Nov. 23, 1822; pastor at Marseilles, 1848–56; Nîmes, 1856–64; since 1864, professor of dogmatic theology at Montauban. He was made chevalier of the Legion of Honor, July 14, 1880. He has written many articles, and translated Neander's commentaries upon the Epistles of *James* and *John*, 1851 and 1854.

MONOD, Theodore, Reformed; b. in Paris, the son of Frederick Monod, Nov. 6, 1836; studied law, 1855–58; but, converted in New York, April, 1858, he turned to the ministry, and studied theology in the Western Theological Seminary, Allegheny, Penn., 1858–60; until 1863 he preached among the French Canadians in Illinois; from 1864 till 1875 he was his father's successor in Paris; from 1875 till 1878 he was travelling agent of the Inner Mission work in France; but since 1878 he has been the successor of M. Montandon in Paris. From 1875 to 1879 he edited *Le Libérateur*, now absorbed in the *Bulletin de la mission intérieure*. His writings embrace *Regardant à Jésus*, 1862 (English trans., *Looking unto Jesus*, New York, 1864); *The Gift of God* (published in English), London, 1876 (in French, Paris, 1877); *Life more Abundant*, 1881.

MONRAD, Ditlev Gothard, Danish Lutheran; b. at Copenhagen, Nov. 24, 1811; graduated in theology from its university; studied also in Paris; went into politics, and had a successful career; was from March 22 to Nov. 10, 1848, minister of public worship; bishop of Lolland-Falster, 1849; again minister of public education and worship, 1859 (May 6 to Dec. 2), recalled to form a new cabinet; two months after his dismission he took the portfolio of worship. After the Schleswig-Holstein war, he emigrated to New Zealand, but returned in 1869, and since 1871 has been bishop of Lolland. His writings are numerous, but very many are of political, temporary, or local interest. He is widest known by his *World of Prayer*, 1851 (English trans., Edinburgh, 1879). Of his later writings may be mentioned *Laurentius Valla und das Konzil zu Florence*, German trans., Gotha, 1882; *Festklänge*, Ger. trans., 1883.

MOOAR, George, D.D. (Williams College, Williamstown, Mass., 1868), Congregationalist; b. in Andover, Mass., May 27, 1830; graduated at Williams College, Williamstown, Mass., 1851, and at Andover (Mass.) Theological Seminary, 1855; was pastor at Andover, Mass., 1855–61; at Oakland, Cal., 1861–72, and since 1874; professor of systematic theology and church history in the Pacific Theological Seminary, Oakland, since 1870; associate editor of *The Pacific* since 1863. He was one of the commission of twenty-five appointed by the National Council of Congregational Churches to prepare a statement of doctrine and a catechism (1881–84). He is the author of *Historical Manual of the South Church*, Andover, 1859; *Handbook of the Congregational Churches of California*, 1863, 4th ed. 1882; *The Religion of Loyalty*, Oakland, 1865; *The Prominent Characteristics of the Congregational Churches*, San Francisco, 1866.

MOODY, Dwight Lyman, Congregational layman; b. at Northfield, Feb. 5, 1837; worked on a farm until seventeen years old, then became clerk in a shoe-store in Boston; joined a Congregational church; in 1856 went to Chicago; during the Civil War was employed by the Christian Commission, and after by the Young Men's Christian Association of Chicago as lay missionary. A church was the result of his efforts. This was burned in the great Chicago fire in 1871; but a new one, accommodating twenty-five hundred persons, has since been erected. From 1873 to 1875 he and Mr. I. D. Sankey (see title) held revival meetings in Great Britain, and they have since been associated in revival work upon an extensive scale there (again in 1883) and in America. Mr. Moody has published *The Second Coming of Christ*, Chicago, 1877; *The Way and the Word*, 1877; *Secret Power; or, The Secret of Success in Christian Life and Work*, 1881; *The Way to God, and how to find it*, 1884. Several collections of his sermons have been published; e.g., *Glad Tidings* (New York, 1876), *Great Joy* (1877), *To all People* (1877); *Best Thoughts and Discourses* (with sketch of his life and Sankey's), 1876; also *Arrows and Anecdotes* (with sketch of life), 1877. *

MOORE, Dunlop, D.D. (Washington and Jefferson College, Washington, Penn., 1877), Presbyterian; b. at Lurgan, County Armagh, Ireland, July 25, 1830; studied at Edinburgh and Belfast, graduated 1854; was missionary of the Irish Presbyterian Church to Gujurât, India, 1855-67; to the Jews, Vienna, 1869-74; since 1875 has been pastor of the First Presbyterian Church, New Brighton, Penn. He assisted in translating the Scriptures into the Gujurâti language; composed treatises on Mohammedanism and Jainism, and edited a monthly periodical, *The Gnyandipaka*, in the same tongue; translated with Dr. S. T. Lowrie Nägelsbach's *Isaiah*, in the American Lange series (New York, 1878); and has contributed to various reviews.

MOORE, George Foot, D.D. (Marietta College, Marietta, O., 1885), Presbyterian; b. at West Chester, Penn., Oct. 15, 1851; graduated at Yale College, New Haven, Conn., 1872, and at Union (Presbyterian) Theological Seminary, New-York City, 1877; became pastor of the Putnam Presbyterian Church, Zanesville, O., 1878; Hitchcock professor of the Hebrew language and literature, Andover (Mass.) Theological Seminary, 1883.

MOORE, William Eves, D.D. (Marietta College, Marietta, O., 1873), Presbyterian; b. at Strasburgh, Penn., April 1, 1823; graduated at Yale College, New Haven, Conn., 1847; studied theology with Rev. Dr. Lyman H. Atwater at Fairfield, Conn.; became pastor at West Chester, Penn., 1850, and at Columbus, O., 1872. Since 1884 he has been permanent clerk of the General Assembly of the Presbyterian Church. He is the author of the *New Digest of the Acts and Deliverances of the Presbyterian Church* (New School), Philadelphia, 1861; *Presbyterian Digest* (United Church), 1873, new ed. 1886.

MOORE, William Walter, Presbyterian (Southern Church); b. at Charlotte, N.C., June 14, 1857; graduated at Davidson College, N.C., 1878, and at Union Theological Seminary, Hampden-Sidney, Va., 1881; became evangelist of Mecklenburg Presbytery, N.C., 1881; pastor at Millersburg, Ky., 1882; associate professor of Oriental literature in that seminary, 1883.

MOORHOUSE, Right Rev. James, D.D. (*jure dignitatis*, Cambridge, 1876), lord bishop of Manchester, Church of England; b. at Sheffield, Eng., in the year 1826; educated at St. John's College, Cambridge; graduated B.A. (senior optime) 1853, M.A. 1860; was ordained deacon 1853, priest 1854; became curate of St. Neots, 1853; of Sheffield, 1855; and Hornsey, Middlesex, 1859; perpetual curate of St. John's, Fitzroy Square, London, 1861; vicar of Paddington, and rural dean, 1867; bishop of Melbourne, Australia, 1876; translated to the see of Manchester, in succession to Dr. Fraser, 1886. He was Hulsean lecturer at Cambridge, 1865; Warburtonian lecturer, London, 1874; chaplain to the queen, and prebendary of Caddington Major in St. Paul's Cathedral, London, 1874–76. He is the author of *Nature and Revelation* (four sermons before University of Cambridge), London, 1861; *Our Lord Jesus Christ the Subject of Growth in Wisdom* (Hulsean Lectures), 1866; *Jacob* (three sermons before University of Cambridge), 1870; *The Expectation of the Christ*, 1879.

MORAN, Most Rev. Patrick Francis, D.D., Roman Catholic; b. at Leighlinbridge, County Carlow, Ireland, Sept. 16, 1830; was graduated at the Irish College of St. Agatha, Rome, and made vice-president of it, and professor of Hebrew in the College of the Propaganda, 1856; became private secretary to Cardinal Cullen at Dublin, 1866, and bishop of Ossory, 1872. He is the author of *Memoir of the Most Rev. Oliver Plunkett*, Dublin, 1861; *Essays on the Origin . . . of the Early Irish Church*, 1864; *History of the Catholic Archbishops of Dublin*, 1864; *Historical Sketch of the Persecutions . . . under Cromwell and the Puritans*, 1865; *Acta S. Brendani*, 1872; *Monasticon Hibernicum*, 1873; *Spicilegium Ossoriense, being a Collection of Documents to illustrate the History of the Irish Church from the Reformation to the Year 1800*, 1874–78, 2 vols. *

MOREHOUSE, Henry Lyman, D.D. (University of Rochester, N.Y., 1879), Baptist; b. at Stanford, Dutchess County, N.Y., Oct. 2, 1834; graduated at the University of Rochester, N.Y., 1858, and at Rochester (N.Y.) Theological Seminary, 1864; became pastor of the First Baptist Church, East Saginaw, Mich., 1864; of East Avenue Baptist Church, Rochester, N.Y., 1873; corresponding secretary of the American Baptist Home Mission Society, and editor of the *Baptist Home Mission Monthly*, New York, 1879.

MORISON, James, D.D. (Adrian College, Adrian, Mich., 1862; University of Glasgow, 1882), Evangelical Union; b. at Bathgate, Linlithgowshire, Scotland, Feb. 14, 1816; graduated in arts at the University of Edinburgh, and studied theology at the United Presbyterian Halls of Glasgow and Edinburgh; was pastor in Kilmarnock, 1840–51, and in Glasgow, 1851-84. From the first year of his pastorate he had a hard battle to fight for the doctrine of the universality of Christ's atonement. The battle continued for more than twenty years. The ecclesiastical outcome is a group of about a hundred churches in Scotland, called the Evangelical Union. Since 1843 he has been principal and professor of New-Testament exegesis in Evangelical Union Hall, Glasgow. He holds to "the three great universalities: (1) God's love to 'all,' (2) Christ's atonement for 'all,' (3) the Holy Spirit's influence shed forth on 'all.'" He is the author of *The Extent of the Atonement*, London, 1842; *Saving Faith*, 1842; *An Exposition of the Ninth Chapter of the Epistle to the Romans*, 1849; *Vindication of the Universality of the Atonement*, 1861; *Apology for Evangelical Doctrines*, 1863; *A Critical Exposition of the Third Chapter of the Epistle to the Romans*, 1866; *A Practical Commentary on the Gospel of St. Matthew*, 1870, 5th ed. 1883; do. *on St. Mark*, 1873, 3d ed. 1882 (the last two republished from last edition, Boston, *Mark* 1882, *Matthew* 1883).

MORRIS, Right Rev. Benjamin Wistar, D.D. (University of Pennsylvania, Philadelphia, 1868), **S.T.D.** (Columbia College, New-York City, 1868), Episcopalian, missionary bishop of Oregon; b. at Wellsboro', Penn., May 30, 1819; graduated from the General Theological Seminary, New-York City, 1846; became rector of St. Matthew's, Sunbury, Penn., 1847; of St. David's, Manayunk, 1851; of St. Luke's, Germantown (both suburbs of the city of Philadelphia), 1857; bishop of Oregon and Washington Territory, 1868; his diocese limited to the former, 1880.

MORRIS, Edward Dafydd, D.D. (Hamilton College, Clinton, N.Y., 1863), **LL.D.** (Maryville College, Maryville, Tenn., 1885), Presbyterian; b. at Utica, N.Y., Oct. 31, 1825; graduated at Yale College, New Haven, Conn., 1849, and at Auburn (N.Y.) Theological Seminary, 1852; was pastor of the Second Presbyterian Church, Auburn, N.Y., 1852–55; of the Second Church, Columbus, O., 1855–67; professor of church history, Lane Theological Seminary, Cincinnati, O., 1867–74, and since of theology. He was moderator of the Presbyterian General Assembly at Cleveland, O., in 1875. Besides review articles, he has published *Outlines of Christian Doctrine*, Cincinnati, 1880 (only for students' use); *Ecclesiology, Treatise on the Church*, New York, 1885.

MORRIS, John Gottlieb, D.D. (Pennsylvania College, Gettysburg, Penn., 1839), **LL.D.** (do., 1875), Lutheran; b. at York, Penn., Nov. 14, 1803; graduated at Dickinson College, Carlisle, Penn., 1823, and at Princeton (N.J.) Theological Seminary, 1826; was pastor of the First English Lutheran Church, Baltimore, Md., 1827–60; librarian of the Peabody Institute in that city, 1860–63; since has been non-resident professor of pulpit elocution and relations of science and revelation, in the theological seminary, Gettysburg, Penn.; lecturer on natural history in Pennsylvania College. He was president of the Maryland State Bible Society, and vice-president of the Maryland Historical Society; has received diplomas from the Ante-Columbian Society of Northern Antiquaries of Denmark, from the *Natur historische Gesellschaft* of Nuremberg, and from the Royal Historical Society of London; and is a corresponding and honorary member of ten or twelve scientific and historical societies in the United States. He is the author or translator of *Henry and Antonio* (translated from Bretschneider), Philadelphia, 1831 (2d ed. under title *To Rome and Back again*, 1833); *Von Leonard's Geology* (trans.), Baltimore, 1840; *Life of John Arndt*, 1853; *Martin Behaim, the German Cosmographer*, 1853; *Life of Catharine von Bora*, 1856; *The Blind Girl of Wittenberg*, Philadelphia, 1856; *Quaint Sayings and Doings concerning Luther*, 1859; *Catalogue of Lepidoptera of North America*, 1860, and *Synopsis of the Diurnal Lepidoptera of the United States*, Smithsonian Institute (both Washington), 1862; *The Lords Baltimore*, Baltimore, 1874; *Bibliotheca Lutherana*, Philadelphia, 1876; *Fifty Years in the Lutheran Ministry*, 1878; *A Day in Capernaum* (trans. from Delitzsch), 1879; *The Diet of Augsburg*, 1879; *Augsburg Confession and the Thirty-nine Articles*, 1879; *Journeys of Luther: their Relation to the Work of the Reformation*, 1880; *Luther at Wartburg and Coburg*, 1882; *Life of Luther* (trans. from Köstlin), 1882; *Lutheran Doctrine of the Lord's Supper*, 1883; *Memoirs of the Stork Family*, 1886; etc.

MORSE, Richard Cary, Presbyterian; b. at Hudson, N.Y., Sept. 19, 1841; graduated at Yale College, 1862; studied at Union Theological Seminary, New-York City, 1865–66, '67 (graduated), and at Princeton Theological Seminary, N.J., 1866–67; was ordained Dec. 21, 1868; was editor in New-York City, 1867–71; has been secretary of the executive committee of the Young Men's Christian Association of the United States and Canada since 1873. *

MOULTON, William Feddian, D.D. (Edinburgh, 1874), Wesleyan; b. at Leek, Staffordshire, Eng., March 14, 1835; graduated at London University, 1856, and gained the gold medal for mathematics, and prizes for scriptural examination and biblical criticism. In 1858 he was appointed classical tutor in the Wesleyan Theological College, Richmond; and in 1874 head master of the Leys School, Cambridge, a Wesleyan institution. In 1872 he was elected a member of the Legal Hundred; made an honorary M.A. by Cambridge, 1877; and was a member of the New-Testament Company of Bible-revisers (1870–81). He translated and edited Winer's *Grammar of New-Testament Greek*, Edinburgh, 1870, 2d ed. 1876; and wrote *History of the English Bible*, London, 1878. *

MUDGE, Elisha, Christian; b. at Blenheim, Canada West, April 17, 1834; was principal of Union School, Edwardsburg, Mich.; minister at Maple Rapids, Mich., twenty years; county superintendent of schools, Clinton County, Mich., six years; in 1882 became president of the Union Christian College, Merom, Ind.

MUEHLAU, (Heinrich) Ferdinand, Ph.D. (Leipzig, 1862), **Lic. Theol.** (do., 1869), **D.D.** (*hon.*, Leipzig, 1885), Lutheran; b. at Dresden, Saxony, June 20, 1839; studied at Erlangen and Leipzig, 1857–62; was *privat-docent* at Leipzig, 1869; professor extraordinary at Dorpat, 1870, and ordinary professor there of exegetical theology in 1871. He is the author of *De Proverbiorum quæ dicuntur Aguri et Lemuelis, origine atque indole*, Leipzig, 1869; *Besitzen wir den ursprünglichen Text der Heiligen Schrift?* Dorpat, 1884 (pp. 24). With Volck he edited the eighth, ninth, and tenth editions of Gesenius' *Hebräisch und Chaldäisches Handwörterbuch über das Alte Testament*, Leipzig, 1878, 1883, and 1886; with Kautzsch, *Liber Genesis sine punctis exscriptus*, ed. ii. 1885; alone, Fr. Böttcher's *Neue exegetisch-kritische Aehrenlese zum Alten Testament*, 1863–65, 3 vols.; and his *Lehrbuch der hebräischen Sprache*, 1866–68, 2 vols. Besides *Geschichte der hebräischen Synonymik* in *J. D. M. G.* (1863, pp. 316 sqq.), he has written numerous geographical articles in Riehm's *Handwörterbuch des Biblischen Alterthums*.

MUELLER, George (originally **Georg Friedrich**), Plymouth Brother, founder of the Bristol Orphanage; b. at Kroppenstädt, near Halberstadt, Prussia, Sept. 27, 1805. After preliminary training at the Cathedral classical school at Halberstadt, at Heimersleben, under a classical tutor, and at the Nordhausen gymnasium, he entered the University of Halle, 1825. His early life had been careless, even profligate, and his reckless course involved him in pecuniary embarrassments. Once (during the Christmas holidays of 1821) he was imprisoned for debt contracted at a hotel in Wolfenbüttel. He often told deliberate lies. But shortly after entering the university he was converted, and, declining to receive any further support from his father, entered upon that life of faith in the Lord to supply his needs, which has been so remarkable. He determined to become a missionary, and meanwhile manifested his Christian zeal in visiting the sick, distributing tracts, and in conversing upon the subject of religion with persons whom he casually met. In August, 1826, he began to preach, having obtained license to do so in consequence of the very honorable testimonials he brought with him to the university. For two months he lived in Francke's Orphan House at Halle, in the free lodgings provided for poor divinity students. In March, 1829, having through ill health obtained release from military duty, — an obligation which he had feared would prevent him from accepting the society's appointment received June, 1828, — he went to London to prepare himself for missionary work among the Jews, in the service of the London Society for Promoting Christianity among the Jews. But after some months of the prescribed study of Hebrew, Chaldee, and German Jewish, he left the society, January, 1830; joined the Plymouth Brethren; became minister at Teignmouth; and married Mary Groves, the daughter of Kitto's friend. Of his own accord he declined to receive any stated salary, abolished pew-rents, and from October, 1830, lived upon voluntary offerings put in the box provided for them in the chapel. This course often reduced himself and wife to great straits; but by prayer and simple faith their wants were always ultimately relieved. In 1832 he became pastor of Gideon Chapel, Bristol. Impressed by the number of destitute children he found in Bristol, he prayed for divine guidance in doing something for them. Being led thereto, as he believed, he collected the children at 8 A.M., gave them a piece of bread for breakfast, then taught them to read, and read the Bible to them for about an hour and a half. But the plan not working well, he abandoned it, and in 1834 started "The Scriptural Knowledge Institution for Home and Abroad," which was designed to assist day-schools, Sunday schools, and adult-schools; to circulate the Holy Scriptures; to aid missionary work; to board, clothe, and educate scripturally, whole orphan children. The institution, he decided, should have no patron but the Lord, no workers but believers, and no debts. Up to 1884 it had provided for the education of 95,143 children and grown persons in its schools; circulated over 1,000,000 copies or portions of the Bible; spent £196,633. 12*s.* 5*d.* on missionary work; and trained up 6,892 orphans at a cost of £661,186. 9*s.* 2*d.* It is still flourishing. He then asked the Lord to give him a suitable house for the orphan children, assistants for the work, and a thousand pounds in money. And he was heard. Provided with assistants and money, he hired a house on Wilson Street, Bristol, and opened his orphanage on April 11, 1836. A second house was opened about eight months after the first By June, 1837, he had received the asked-for thousand pounds. He then opened a third house; a fourth, March, 1844. He then bought a site on Ashley Down, near Bristol, and put up the first building, 1846. There are now there five immense orphan-houses, containing over two thousand inmates. The last one was opened in 1869. In February, 1870, his wife, who had so faithfully joined him in all his enterprises, died. After a time he re-married. Besides managing his orphanages and the institution, and preaching to his congregation, he has also taken missionary tours through the British Isles, the United States (going across the continent) and Canada (1877). In 1881 he visited the East, and in 1882 India. As is well known, he does not in the ordinary way advertise any of his enterprises. But the circulation of his *Life of Trust: Narrative of the Lord's Dealings with George Müller*, first issued in 1837, and continued in 1841, 1844, and 1856, which has been reprinted in repeated editions in New York, translated into German (Stuttgart, 1844, 2 parts), and into French (Paris, 1848), and other books and pamphlets published under his auspices, secures public attention to them. It remains true, however, that the Orphanage has no endowment, and none of the usual machinery of support. Mr. Müller looks to God to supply the daily food of the thousands of children therein gathered, and to pay all the expenses of their care. Results have justified his confidence. Money comes in, sometimes at very critical moments, and the work is sustained. Besides the *Narrative* above referred to, Mr. Müller has published *Jehovah Magnified: Addresses*, London, 1876; *Preaching Tours*, 1883, etc. Cf. Mrs. E. R. Pitman, *George Müller*, London, 1885. *

MUELLER, Karl (Ferdinand Friedrich), Ph.D.

Lic. Theol. (both Tübingen, 1876 and 1878), **D.D.** (*hon.*, Giessen, 1883), German Protestant; b. at Langenberg, Würtemberg, Sept. 3, 1852; studied at Tübingen and Göttingen; became *vikar*, 1875; *repetent* at Tübingen, 1878; *privat-docent* at Berlin, 1880; professor, 1882; at Halle, 1884; at Giessen, 1886. He is the author of *Der Kampf Ludwigs des Baiern mit der römischen Kurie*, Tübingen, 1879–80, 2 vols.; *Die Anfänge des Minoritenordens und der Bussbrüderschaften*, Freiburg-im-Br., 1885.

MULFORD, Elisha, LL.D. (Yale College, New Haven, Conn., 1872), Episcopalian; b. at Montrose, Susquehanna County, Penn., Nov. 19, 1833; d. at Cambridge, Mass., Dec. 9, 1885. He graduated from Yale College, New Haven, Conn., 1855; studied theology at Union Theological Seminary, New-York City, at Andover, Mass., and in Halle and Heidelberg; was ordained deacon 1859, priest 1862; had charges at Darien, Conn., 1861; South Orange, N.J., 1861–64; Friendsville, Penn., 1877–81. From 1864 to 1877 he was without charge at Montrose, Penn.; after 1881 he resided at Cambridge, where he lectured in the Episcopal Divinity School. He wrote *The Nation, the Foundation of Civil Order and Political Life in the United States*, New York, 1870, 9th ed. 1884; *The Republic of God, an Institute of Theology*, 1881, 7th ed. 1884.

The main feature of Dr. Mulford's theology, as presented in his *Republic of God*, is the union of the utmost liberty of philosophic thought with Christian dogmas. He urges the personality of God as the central principle of the universe, but in a form so comprehensive and elevated as to seem no longer incompatible with that conception of Deity, to which modern thought is approximating, of an infinite energy diffused throughout the universe, from whom all things proceed, and in whom they consist. The nature as well as the possibility of a revelation is based upon the postulate, that humanity is endowed potentially with personality as it exists in God. Revelation is the manifestation of the Divine personality in history, finding its highest and absolute expression in Christ. The organic relation of Christ to humanity involves the principle of the solidarity of the human race. Individualism, which has been a ruling idea in Protestant theology, is subordinated to the conception of man as essentially and primarily a member of the race from which in his history and fortunes he cannot be detached. The redemption in Christ extends to humanity as a whole, and is emphasized as an accomplished fact, as constituting a great objective epoch in man's spiritual history. It consist in ransoming man from bondage to the order of nature, and elevating him into the life of the spirit. While Dr. Mulford's thought is monistic, every trace of dualism or root of evil stronger than the love of God being disowned in virtue of the efficacy of the Incarnation, yet he affirms the reality and the deep significance of the conflict in human experience, finding its origin in the opposition between *nature* and *spirit*, not between *matter* and *spirit* as it is sometimes popularly represented. The Incarnation witnesses that the law of the course and constitution of nature has no dominion in the sphere of the spiritual; death, which reigns supreme in nature, is not the law of the spirit; the suffering in the kingdom of nature is transmuted by Christ into the principle of self-sacrifice, the essential condition of spiritual life and growth. In this struggle between the natural and the spiritual, humanity is supported by the indwelling Spirit of God, so that the course of human history becomes a process in which humanity is increasingly convicted of sin and of righteousness and of judgment. The judgment is interpreted, with the prophets of the Old Testament, as a constituent factor of life, whose result is purification and restoration. And this result is a necessary consequence of all judgment, whether here or hereafter, whether temporary or final; for death does not break the continuity of the spiritual order, and resurrection is not postponed to a distant future, but is immediate. But the "last things" naturally find no extensive treatment in a theology whose object is to enforce the reality of the life of the spirit in humanity, in this present world. To this life of the spirit, the Bible, the church, and the sacraments bear witness, by this also becoming divine agencies in the education of the race; but they are the symbols of a spiritual order, and not to be identified with the order itself. The Bible witnesses to a revelation, but is not the revelation; sacraments witness to a divine process of purification and feeding, but are not themselves the process; the church bears witness to a life of the spirit in humanity, which goes beyond its boundaries as an organization. So strong is the emphasis laid upon this point, — the reality of the life of the spirit, — that Dr. Mulford has devoted to it a chapter which he regarded as the most important in his book, entitled *Christianity not a Religion and not a Philosophy*, in which he disclaims the formalism of the one, and the tendency to abstraction of the other. It was the burden of his teaching and conversation, that revelation was co-efficient with the reason; that it was *through* experience, but not *from* experience; that theology was the interpretation of life, — an appeal to life closing every theological argument; that the true centre of theology must be the living, present God, not theories about him, not covenants or attributes or doctrines of anthropology. His thought has much that resembles Erskine and Maurice; and, as in the case of the latter, the difficulty in understanding him springs mainly from what is distinctive in his theology, rather than from obscurity of style. Among German theologians he was most indebted to Rothe, with whom he asserts the continuousness of the Incarnation, the abiding presence of the spiritual or essential Christ as distinguished from the historical Christ. With Hegel he maintains that principle of realism, which was also characteristic of the great theologians of the scholastic age, that the highest and necessary thought of man is identical with reality; as in the condensed expression which sums up his argument for the existence of God, — "the idea of God is in, with, and through the being of God." But apart from his kinship with these and other thinkers, his work in theology has a character of its own. It was meditated and conceived in that inspiring epoch in American history which drew from him his first book, *The Nation*. As in that treatise he carried theology into statesmanship, finding in the solidarity of the state a divine personality, so in his later work he carried the national principle into theology, expanding the idea of the nation into the Republic of God, — the solidarity of mankind in the incarnate Christ. A. V. G. ALLEN.

MUNGER, Theodore Thornton, D.D. (Illinois College, Jacksonville, Ill., 1883), Congregationalist; b. at Bainbridge, Chenango County, N.Y., March 5, 1830; graduated from Yale College, New Haven, Conn., 1851, and the theological seminary there, 1855; was pastor at Dorchester, Mass., 1856–60; Haverhill, 1862-70; Lawrence, 1871–75; lived in San José, Cal., and established a Congregational church, 1875-76; pastor at North Adams, Mass., 1877–85; since, pastor of United Church, New Haven, Conn. He is the author of *On the Threshold*, Boston, 1881, 20th ed. 1885 (reprinted London, Eng.); *The Freedom of Faith*, 1883, 15th ed. 1885 (two English reprints); *Lamps and Paths*, 1885; besides numerous sermons and contributions to literary magazines and religious newspapers.

MURPHY, James Gracey, LL.D., D.D. (both from Trinity College, Dublin, 1842 and 1880 respectively), Presbyterian; b. at Ballyaltikilikan, parish of Comber, County Down, Ireland, Jan. 12, 1808; entered Trinity College, Dublin, as sizar, 1827, became scholar 1830, graduated A.B. 1833; was minister at Ballyshannon, 1836; classical head master at the Royal Belfast Academical Institution, 1841; professor of Hebrew, Presbyterian College, Belfast, 1847. He is the author of *A Latin Grammar*, London, 1847; *A Hebrew Grammar*, 1857; *Nineteen Impossibilities of Part First of Colenso on the Pentateuch shown to be Possible*, Belfast, 1863; *The Human Mind*, 1873; and of the well-known commentaries upon *Genesis* (Edinburgh, 1864), *Exodus* (1866), *Leviticus* (1872), *The Psalms* (1875), *Revelation* (London, 1882), *Daniel* (1884), all reprinted in United States except *Revelation.*

MUSTON, Alexis, Lic. Theol., D.D. (both Strassburg, 1834), Reformed Church of France; b. at La Tour (Vallées Vaudoises), Feb. 11, 1810; educated at Lausanne and at Strassburg; ordained at La Tour, 1833; exiled from Piedmont (1835), he went to Nîmes, France, where he was naturalized; since 1836 has lived at Bourdeaux, first as assistant (1836–40), then as pastor. He is the author of *Histoire des Vaudois*, vol. i. Paris, 1834 (the occasion of his exile, it having been put by the Roman-Catholic hierarchy upon the Index); *L'Israël des Alpes*, Paris, 1851, 4 vols. (a complete history of the Waldenses, English trans. last ed. London, 1875, 2 vols.; German trans. Duisburg, 1857); articles in the Strassburg *Revue de théologie*, the *Revue du protestantisme*, etc. Cf. article *Waldenses* in *Schaff-Herzog Encyclopædia*, vol. iii., p. 2476. *

MYRBERG, Otto Ferdinand, Ph.D. (Upsala, 1849), **Lic. Theol.** (Upsala, 1851), **D.D.** (by the King of Sweden, 1868), Lutheran; b. at Gothenburg, Sweden, April 26, 1824; studied theology at Upsala, and received holy orders in 1859; became dean of the Trinity Church of Upsala, and professor of exegetical theology at the University of Upsala, 1866. He is the author of *In librum qui Joëlis inscribitur brevis commentatio academica*, Upsala, 1851; *De schismate Donatistarum, dissertatio academ.*, 1856; *Commentarius in epistolam Johanneam, diss. acad.*, 1859; *Om aposteln Petrus och den äldsta kyrkans falska gnosis* ("On the Apostle Peter and the False Gnosis of the Early Church"), 1865; *Den hel. skrifts lära om försoningen* ("The Doctrine of the Holy Scriptures on the Atonement"), 1870; *Pauli bref till Romarne i ny öfversättning med textkritiska noter* ("The Epistle to the Romans, new translation with Textual Critical Notes"), 1871; *Salomos ordspråk, Från grundtexten öfversatt* ("The Proverbs, translated from the Hebrew"), 1875; and several pamphlets.

N.

NAVILLE, Jules Ernst, Swiss religious philosopher; b. at Chancy, near Geneva, Dec. 13, 1816; studied at the University of Geneva; became licentiate in theology, and was ordained in 1839; was professor of philosophy in the university, 1844; removed (1846) in consequence of the Genevan revolution, and has since held no official position, except during 1860–61 when he was professor of apologetics in the theological faculty; but he lectures in the department of letters, and is an admired preacher. He has written many books (see Lichtenberger, vol. xiii., pp. 146, 147). The following have been translated: *Modern Atheism; or, The Heavenly Father*, Boston, 1867, 2d ed. 1882; *The Problem of Evil*, New York, 1871; *The Theory and Practice of Representative Elections*, London, 1872; *The Christ*, Edinburgh, 1880; *Modern Physics: Studies Historical and Philosophical*, 1883. *

NEELY, Right Rev. Henry Adams, D.D. (Hobart College, Geneva, N.Y., 1866; Bishops' College, Quebec, Can., 1875), Episcopalian, bishop of the diocese of Maine; b. at Fayetteville, Onondaga County, N.Y., May 14, 1830; graduated at Hobart College, Geneva, N.Y., 1849; was tutor in the college 1850–52, while studying theology under Bishop De Lancey; became rector of Calvary Church, Utica, N.Y., 1852; of Christ Church, Rochester, 1855; chaplain of Hobart College, 1862; assistant minister of Trinity Church, with charge of Trinity Chapel, New-York City, 1864; consecrated bishop, 1867. He is a "conservative Anglican." He is the author of occasional sermons, review articles, etc.

NEIL, Charles, Church of England; b. in St. John's Wood, London, May 14, 1841; educated at Trinity Hall, Cambridge; graduated B.A. 1862, M.A. 1866; was ordained deacon 1865, priest 1866; became curate of Bradford Abbas, near Sherborne, Dorset, 1865; vicar of St. Paul's, Bethnal Green, 1866; incumbent of St. Matthias, Poplar, London, 1875. He was called to the bar (Inner Temple), 1864. He is a liberal Evangelical Churchman. He is joint editor of *The Clergyman's Magazine*, London, 1876, sqq. He is the author of *Eleven Diagrams illustrating the Lord's Prayer*, London, 1867; *Holy Teaching* (key to preceding), 1867; *The Expositor's Commentary* (vol. i. *Romans*, 1877, 2d ed. 1882); *A Classified List of Subjects proposed for Discussion at the Meeting of Ruridecanal Chapters*, 1881; *The Christian Visitor's Handbook*, 1882; edited John Todd's *Index Rerum*, London, 1881; with Canon Spence and J. S. Exell, *Thirty Thousand Thoughts*, 1883, sqq. (to be completed in 6 vols.). Some of his tracts and pamphlets are, *Am I answerable for my Belief?* 1871; *Parochial Reason Why*, 1872; *Cecilia, or Near the Museum*, 1873; *The Divine Aspects of Redemption*, 1875; *The Preaching and Value of the Doctrine of Christ crucified*, 1875; *Open-air Preaching, or a Common-sense Answer to the Common Cry of the Church, "How to reach the Masses,"* 1881; *The Courier Bible Aid and Reading-marker* (No. 1, key to *Chronicles* and *Kings*, historical and geographical card), 1884.

NESTLE, (Christoph) Eberhard, Ph.D. (Tübingen, 1874), **Lic. Theol.** (*hon.*, Tübingen, 1883), Evangelical; b. at Stuttgart, Würtemberg, May 1, 1851; studied in Stuttgart, at the evangelical theological seminaries at Blaubeuren and Tübingen, and at Leipzig (1874–75), and in England (1875–77); was tutor at the evangelical theological seminary at Tübingen, 1877–80; *diaconus* at Münsingen, Würtemberg, 1880–83; and since has been gymnasial professor at Ulm. He is an adherent of the *Vermittlungstheologie*. He has published *Die israelitischen Eigennamen nach ihrer religionsgeschichtlichen Bedeutung* (prize essay of the Tyler Society), Haarlem, 1876; *Conradi Pellicani de modo legendi atque intelligendi Hebræum*, Tübingen, 1877; *Psalterium tetraglottum* (Græce, Syriace, Chaldaice, Latine), Tübingen, London, Leiden, Paris, 1879; Tischendorf's *Septuaginta*, 6th ed. Leipzig, 1880 (with appendix, *Veteris Testamenti græci codices Vaticanus et Sinaiticus cum textu recepto collati*); *Brevis linguæ Syriacæ grammatica, litteratura, chrestomathia, cum glossario*, Carlsruhe and Leipzig, 1881.

NEVIN, Alfred, D.D. (Lafayette College, Easton, Penn.), **LL.D.** (Western University of Pennsylvania, Pittsburgh, Penn.), Presbyterian; b. at Shippensburg, Penn., March 14, 1816; graduated at Jefferson College, Canonsburg, Penn., 1834; admitted to the bar at Carlisle, Penn., 1837; studied theology at the Western (Presbyterian) Theological Seminary, Allegheny, Penn., 1837–40 (graduated); was licensed by the presbytery of Carlisle, 1840; became pastor of the Cedar-Grove Church, Lancaster County, Penn., 1840; of the German Reformed Church, Chambersburg, 1845; of the Second Presbyterian Church, Lancaster, Penn., 1852; of the Alexander Church (which he organized), Philadelphia, 1857; resigned 1861; was editor (and proprietor) of *The Standard*, Philadelphia (now *The North-western Presbyterian*, Chicago), 1860–63; of *The Presbyterian Weekly*, Philadelphia (now *The Baltimore Observer*), 1872–74; and of *The Presbyterian Journal*, Philadelphia, 1875–80; stated supply of the Union Presbyterian Church, Philadelphia, from September, 1885, to January, 1886. He addressed the alumni of Jefferson College, 1858; was lecturer in the National School of Oratory, Philadelphia, 1878–80; was one of the original members of the Presbyterian Historical Society, Philadelphia (organized 1852, incorporated 1857), and trustee 1853–60; member of the Presbyterian Board of Publication, 1858–61; trustee of Lafayette College, 1858–61, and of the Presbyterian Hospital in Philadelphia, 1871–78; has been a number of times a commissioner to the General Assembly, and by its appointment has represented the Presbyterian Church in the Massachusetts Congregational Association (1855), in the synod of the Reformed Dutch Church (1875), and in the General Assembly of the Presbyterian Church of Canada (1878). He was moderator of the synod of Philadelphia, 1856. He was elected member of the Pennsylvania (1865) and Wisconsin (1858) historical societies, and of the literary societies of several prominent colleges in the United States. He is the author of *Christian's Rest*, Lancaster, Penn., 1843; *Spiritual Progression*, Chambersburg, Penn., 1848; *Churches of the Valley*, Philadelphia, 1852; *Guide to the Oracles*, Lancaster, 1857 (title changed to *The Book Opened: Analysis of the Bible*, 1869 2d ed. Cincinnati, O., 1873, 3d ed. Danville, Ind., 1882); *Words of Comfort*, New York, 1867; *The Age Question, A Plea for Christian Union*, Philadelphia, 1868; *Popular Expositor of the Gospels and Acts*, Philadelphia, 1872, 4 vols.; *The Voice of God*, 1873; *The Sabbath-school Help*, 1873, 3d ed. 1874; *Notes on Exodus*, 1873, 3d ed. 1874; *Men of Mark in Cumberland Valley, Penn.*, 1876; *Notes on the Shorter Catechism*, 1878; *Prayer-meeting Manual*, 1880; *Glimpses of the Coming World*, 1880; *Prayer-meeting Talks*, 1880; *Parables of Jesus*, 1881; *Triumph of Truth; or, Jesus the Light and Life of the World*, 1881; *Letters to Col. Robert G. Ingersoll, Infidelity Rebuked*, 1882; *How they Died, or Last Words of Presbyterian Ministers*, 1883; *Encyclopædia of the Presbyterian Church in the United States of America*, 1884; *Folded Lambs*, 1885; *Twelve Revival Sermons*, 1885.

NEVIN, Edwin Henry, D.D. (Franklin College, New Athens, O., 1870), Presbyterian; b. at Shippensburg, Cumberland County, Penn., May 9, 1814; graduated at Jefferson College, Canonsburg, Penn., 1833, and at Princeton Theological Seminary, N.J., 1836; became pastor at Portsmouth, O., 1837; president of Franklin College, New Athens, O., 1841; pastor at Mount Vernon, O., 1845; at Cleveland, O., 1851; Lancaster, Penn., 1865; in Philadelphia (First Reformed), 1870; retired from the pastorate 1875, and joined the Central Presbytery of Philadelphia. He is the author of numerous hymns, which are found in nearly all the evangelical hymn-books in the United States; of several pamphlets; and of *Man of Faith*, Boston, 1858; *The City of God*, Lancaster, Penn., 1868; *The Minister's Handbook*, Philadelphia, 1872; *Thoughts about Christ*, 1882; one of the editors of *History of all Religious Denominations*, Philadelphia, 1872.

NEVIN, John Williamson, D.D. (Jefferson College, Canonsburg, Penn., 1839), **LL.D.** (Union College, Schenectady, N.Y., 1873), Reformed (German); b. in Franklin County, Penn., Feb. 20, 1803; graduated at Union College, Schenectady, N.Y., in 1821, and at Princeton (N.J.) Theological Seminary in 1826, where from 1826 to 1828 he taught Hebrew as substitute for Dr. Charles Hodge, who had gone to Europe to study. During the following year he was stated supply at Big Spring, Penn. From 1829 to 1840 he was professor at Allegheny in the Western Theological Seminary. He then followed a call to the theological seminary of the Reformed (German) Church at Mercersburg, in which he taught theology from that time (1840) until 1851. He was also president of Marshall College, Mercersburg, Penn., from 1841 to 1853, and of Franklin and Marshall College, Lancaster, 1866 to 1876, when he retired to Caernarvon Place, near Lancaster, Penn., where he died June 7, 1886. He was one of the founders of the "Mercersburg theology," for which see the *Schaff-Herzog Encyclopædia*, ii., 1473 sqq. He edited *The Mercersburg Review* from 1849 to 1853, and wrote the largest part of its contents himself. Of the articles contributed by him to the *Review* then and subsequently, especially noteworthy are the following: *Doctrine of the Reformed Church on the Lord's Supper, in Reply to Dr. Charles Hodge of Princeton*, 1848; *The Apostles' Creed: Origin, Constitution, and Plan*, 1849; *Early Christianity*, 1851; *Cyprian*, 1852; *Dutch Crusade*, 1854; *Review of Dr. Hodge's Commentary on Ephesians*, 1857; *Introduction to the Tercentenary Edition of the Heidelberg Catechism*, 1863; *The Liturgical Question*, 1863; *Vindication of the Revised Liturgy*, 18—; *Answer to Professor Dorner*, 1865; *Revelation and Redemption*, 18—. In book form have appeared from him, *Biblical Antiquities*, Philadelphia, 1828, 2 vols., revised ed. 1849, reprinted Edinburgh, 1853; *The Anxious Bench*, Chambersburg, Penn., 1842; Dr. Schaff's *The Principle of Protestantism*, translated with introduction and appendage, 1845; *The Mystical Presence*, Philadelphia, 1846; *History and Genius of the Heidelberg Catechism*, Chambersburg, 1847; *Antichrist, or the Spirit of Sect and Schism*, New York, 1848.

NEWMAN, Albert Henry, D.D. (Mercer University, Macon, Ga., 1885), **LL.D.** (South-Western Baptist University, Jackson, Tenn., 1883), Baptist; b. in Edgefield County, S.C., Aug. 25, 1852; graduated at Mercer University, Macon, Ga., 1871, and Rochester (N.Y.) Theological Seminary, 1875; studied Oriental languages in the Southern Baptist Theological Seminary, Greenville, S.C. (now Louisville, Ky.), 1875–76; became acting professor of church history in Rochester (N.Y.) Theological Seminary, 1877, and professor 1880; professor of church history and comparative religion in the Baptist (Theological) College, Toronto, Ontario, Can., 1881 His theological position is conservative. He translated (with additional notes) Immer's *Hermeneutics of the New Testament*, Andover, 1877; and has written numerous newspaper and review articles.

NEWMAN, Francis William, LL.D., layman; b. in London, June 27, 1805; educated at Worcester College, Oxford; graduated B.A. (double first-class), 1826; was fellow of Balliol, 1826–30, but resigned because unable conscientiously to subscribe to the Thirty-nine Articles, which was then requisite before obtaining a master's degree. From 1830 to 1834 he lived and travelled in the East; became classical tutor at Bristol College, 1834, and in Manchester New College, 1840; professor of Latin in University College, London, 1846. He resigned in 1863, and has since devoted himself to literature. He is the brother of Cardinal Newman, and, like him, has left the Church of England, in which he was born; but, unlike him, he has thrown away all religious belief. His writings are numerous. Of theological interest are, *History of Hebrew Monarchy*, London, 1847; *The Soul, its Sorrows and Aspirations*, 1849; *Phases of Faith, Passages from my own Creed*, 1850; *Catholic Union, Essay toward a Church of the Future*, 1854; *Theism, Doctrinal and Practical*, 1858. *

NEWMAN, His Eminence John Henry, cardinal deacon of the Roman-Catholic Church; b. in London, Feb. 21, 1801; educated at Trinity College, Oxford; graduated B.A. (second-class in classics), 1820; in 1822, fellow of Oriel College; in 1825, vice-principal of St Alban's Hall; in 1826, tutor of his college; in 1828 became incumbent of St. Mary's, Oxford, and chaplain of Littlemore in the neighborhood. He resigned his tutorship in 1832, but retained his incumbency until 1843, standing in the highest esteem for his noble mental and moral qualities, and wielding a great influence upon the undergraduates. He stood with Pusey as recognized leader of the High Church party. He engaged in the production of the *Tracts for the Times*, and wrote No. 90 (the last of the series), which appeared March, 1841, in which he endeavored to show how the Thirty-nine Articles may be interpreted in the Roman-Catholic sense. In 1842 he established at Littlemore a kind of monastery, of which he was head for three years. At length, in 1845, he took the step to which his avowed principles logically led him: seceded to the Church of Rome, and entered her priesthood. He was in 1847 appointed to found the Oratory of St. Philip Neri, in England; in 1854, rector of the newly founded Catholic University at Dublin; resigned in 1858, and returned to Birmingham to take charge of a school for the sons of Roman-Catholic gentry at Edgbaston, near that city. On May 12, 1879, Pope Leo XIII. created him a cardinal deacon of the Holy Roman Church. A collected edition of his writings appeared in London, 1870-79, 36 vols.; these include *Parochial and Plain Sermons*, 8 vols.; and three other volumes of sermons; five volumes of miscellanies; two religious novels, *Loss and Gain, or The Story of a Convert*, 1848; *Callista, a Sketch of the Third Century*, 1855; his autobiography, *Apologia pro vita sua*, 1864; *Arians of the Fourth Century*, 1833; *Lectures on Justification*, 1838; *Two Essays on Biblical and on Ecclesiastical Miracles*, 1843; *Essay on the Development of Christian Doctrine*, 1845; *Difficulties of Anglicans*, 1850, 2 vols.; *Essay in Aid of the Grammar of Assent*, 1870. He wrote "Lead, kindly Light," and other hymns. Cf. JENNINGS: *Story of Cardinal Newman's Life*, London, 1882.

NEWMAN, John Philip, D.D. (Rochester Seminary, N.Y., 1864), **LL.D.** (Wesleyan University, Athens, Tenn., 1882); b. in New-York City, Sept. 1, 1826; graduated at Cazenovia Seminary, 1848; entered the ministry of the Methodist-Episcopal Church, 1848; was editor of *The New-Orleans Advocate*, 1866-69; pastor of the Metropolitan Methodist-Episcopal Church, Washington, D.C., 1869-72, 1875-78; and chaplain to the United-States Senate, 1869-75. He visited Greenland in 1870. In December, 1873, he was appointed by President Grant inspector of United-States consulates, and in this capacity made a tour of the world, 1873-74. From 1882 to 1884 he preached in the Madison-ave. Congregational Church, New-York City. He was Gen. Grant's pastor, 1869-85. He is a member of the British Society of Biblical Archæology. He is the author of *From Dan to Beersheba, or The Land of Promise as it now appears*, New York, 1864; *The Thrones and Palaces of Babylon and Nineveh, from the Persian Gulf to the Mediterranean*, 1876; *Sermons preached in the Metropolitan Church, Washington, D.C.*, 1876; *Christianity Triumphant*, New York, 1884.

NEWTH, Samuel, D.D. (Glasgow, 1875), Congregationalist; b. in London, Feb. 15, 1821; graduated at London University, B.A. 1841, M.A. 1842; was pastor at Broseley, Salop, 1842; professor of classics and mathematics, Western College, Plymouth, 1845; of mathematics and ecclesiastical history, New College, London, 1854; and since 1872 has been principal and professor of New-Testament exegesis and ecclesiastical history. He was a member of the New-Testament Revision Company, 1870-81; and chairman of the Congregational Union of England and Wales, 1880. He is the author of *Elements of Mechanics*, London, 1850, 6th ed. 1879; *First Book of Natural Philosophy*, 1854, 40th thousand 1885; *Mathematical Examples*, 1859, 3d ed. 1871; *Memoir of Rev. Alfred Newth*, 1876; *Lectures on Bible Revision*, 1881.

NEWTON, Richard, D.D. (Kenyon College, Gambier, O., 1845), Episcopalian (Low Church); b. in Liverpool, Eng., July 25, 1813; graduated at the University of Pennsylvania, Philadelphia, 1836, and at General Theological Seminary, New-York City, 1839; became rector of St. Paul's Church, Philadelphia, 1840; of Church of Epiphany, 1862; of Church of the Covenant, 1882. He has published twenty-three volumes in all; some of these have been translated into more than twenty different languages; they are mostly discourses to children and youth. Of those recently issued may be mentioned, *Pearls from the East, Stories and Incidents from Bible History*, Philadelphia, 1881; *Covenant Names and Privileges*, New York, 1882; *A Bible Portrait-Gallery*, Philadelphia, 1885; *Heroes of the Reformation*, 1885.

NEWTON, Richard Heber, D.D. (Union College, Schenectady, N.Y., 1881), Episcopalian (Broad Churchman); b. in Philadelphia, Oct. 31, 1840; studied in the University of Pennsylvania, Philadelphia, and Episcopal Divinity School, Philadelphia; was assistant to his father; became minister in charge, Trinity Church, Sharon Springs, N.Y., 1864; rector of St. Paul's, Philadelphia, 1866; and rector of All Souls' Church, New York, 1869. He is the author of *Children's Church* (a Sunday-school hymn-book and service-book), New York, 1872; *The Morals of Trade*, 1876; *Womanhood*, 1879; *Studies of Jesus*, 1881; *Right and Wrong Uses of the Bible*, 1883 (1st ed. 25,000 copies), 2d ed. 1884; *Book of the Beginnings*, 1884; *Philistinism*, 1885; *Problems*, 1886.

NICCOLLS, Samuel Jack, D.D. (Centre College, Danville, Ky., 1867), **LL.D.** (Hanover College, Hanover, Ind., 1865), Presbyterian; b. in Westmoreland County, Penn., Aug. 3, 1838; graduated at Jefferson College, Canonsburg, Penn., 1857, and at Western Theological Seminary, Allegheny, Penn., 1860; became pastor at Chambersburg, Penn., 1860; of the Second Presbyterian Church, St. Louis, Mo., 1864. He was moderator of the General Assembly of 1872, at St. Louis; in 1883 declined election to professorship of pastoral theology in Western Theological Seminary. Besides many published sermons, he has written *The Eastern Question in Prophecy*, St. Louis, 1878.

NICHOLSON, Right Rev. William Rufus, D.D. (Theological Seminary of the Diocese of Ohio, Gambier, 1857), Reformed Episcopalian; b. in Green County, Miss., Jan. 8, 1822; graduated at La Grange College, North Ala., 1840; became pastor of the Poydras-street Methodist-Episcopal Church, New Orleans, La., 1842; entered the Protestant-Episcopal Church, and became rector of St. John's, Cincinnati, O., 1849; of St. Paul's, Boston, 1850; of Trinity Church, Newark, N.J., 1872; of Second

Reformed Episcopal Church, Philadelphia, 1874; was consecrated bishop in February, 1876. He is the author of some pamphlets and essays, of which may be mentioned, *James the Lord's Brother, and Jesus, were equally the Sons of Mary* (in *Protestant-Episcopal Quarterly Review*, New York, 1860); *Reasons why I became a Reformed Episcopalian*, Philadelphia, 1875; *Concerning Sanctification*, 1875; *The Priesthood of the Church of God*, 1876; *The Real Presence in the Lord's Supper*, 1877; *A Call to the Ministry*, 1877.

NICOLL, William Robertson, Free Church; b. in Free Church manse, Auchindoir, Aberdeenshire, Oct. 10, 1851; graduated at University of Aberdeen, M.A., 1870; completed curriculum at Free Church College, Aberdeen, and became minister at Mortlach, Banffshire, 1874; at Kelso, 1877. Since 1880 he has edited *The Household Library of Exposition;* since January, 1885, *The Expositor*, in succession to Dr. Cox; and since 1886 three new series, — *The Foreign Biblical Library, The Theological Educator*, and *The Expositor's Bible.* He has published *Calls to Christ*, London, 1877, 2d ed. 1878; *Songs of Rest*, Edinburgh, 1879, 5th ed. London, 1885 (2d series, 1885); *The Incarnate Saviour, A Life of Jesus Christ*, Edinburgh, 1881 (reprinted, New York, 1881); *The Lamb of God*, 1883, 2d ed. London, 1884; *English Theology in the Victorian Era, a Biographical and Critical History* (announced).

NIELSEN, Fredrik Kristian, D.D. (Copenhagen, 1879), Danish Lutheran; b. at Aalborg, North Jutland, Denmark, Oct. 30, 1846; graduated at the University of Copenhagen; was catechist at the Church of Our Saviour from 1873 to 1877, and has since been professor of divinity in the university. He is orthodox in the faith, a liberal Lutheran in theology, and a Presbyterian in matters of church government. Of his works (all in Danish) may be mentioned, *The Christian Faith and Free Thought*, Copenhagen, 1872; *The Roman Church in the Nineteenth Century*, 1876–81, 2 vols. (German trans., Gotha, 1878–82, 2 vols.; vol. 1, 2d ed., 1880); *The Waldensians in Italy* (German trans., Gotha, 1880, pp. 40); *Free Church and Established Church*, 1882; *Christianity and Free-Masonry* (opposed), 1882, 3d ed. 1882 (German trans., Leipzig, 1882, 3d ed. 1884); *Characteristics and Critics* (a collection of essays and reviews), 1883; *Handbook of Church History* (Part 1, *The Ancient Church*), 1884–85.

NILES, Right Rev. William Woodruff, S.T.D. (Trinity College, Hartford, Conn., 1870; Dartmouth College, Hanover, N.H., 1879), Episcopalian, bishop of New Hampshire; b. at Hatley, Province of Lower Canada (now Quebec), May 24, 1832; graduated at Trinity College, Hartford, Conn., 1857, and at the Berkeley Divinity School, Middletown, Conn., 1861; tutor in his alma mater, 1857–58; rector of St. Philip's, Wiscasset, Me., 1862–64; professor of the Latin language and literature in his alma mater, 1864–70; rector of St. John's, Warehouse Point, Conn., 1868–70; bishop, 1870. At the time of his consecration he was a British subject, and was not naturalized until December, 1873. He edited *The Churchman*, Hartford, Conn., 1866–67. He is the author of addresses, essays, etc.

NILLES, Nikolaus, Roman Catholic; b. at Rüppweiler, Luxemburg, Germany, June 21, 1828; studied at the Collegium Germanicum at Rome, 1847–52; became priest there, 1852; pastor at Tüntingen, Luxemburg, 1855; Jesuit, 1858; acting professor at Innsbruck, Austria, 1859; ordinary professor of church law there, 1860, and at the same time *regens* of the theological *convict;* and since 1861 member of the Luxemburg Archæological Society. Besides numerous popular religious works, he has written, *Maria, die mächtige Patronin zur Eiche, oder die gräfliche Kirche und Schule bei Ansenburg*, Luxemburg, 1857; *Commentarius in proœmium breviarii et missalis de computo ecclesiastico*, Arras and Innsbruck, 1864; *Commentarius de rationibus festi ss. cordis Jesu e fontibus juris canon. erutis*, Innsbruck, 1867, 5th ed. 1885; *De rationibus festorum mobilium utriusque ecclesiæ occidentalis atque orientalis commentarius usui clericorum accommodatus*, Wien, 1868; *Selecta pietatis exercita erga ss. cor Jesu et puriss. cor Mariæ*, Innsbruck, 1869; *Kalendarium manuale utriusque ecclesiæ orientalis et occidentalis academiis clericorum accommodatum*, 1879–85, 2 vols.

NINDE, William Xavier, D.D. (Wesleyan University, Middletown, Conn., 1874), Methodist bishop; b. at Cortland, N.Y., June 21, 1832; graduated at the Wesleyan University, Middletown, Conn., 1855; became pastor, 1856; professor of practical theology, Garrett Biblical Institute, Evanston, Ill., 1873; president of same, 1879; bishop of the Methodist-Episcopal Church, 1884.

NIPPOLD, Friedrich Wilhelm Franz, Ph.D. (Tübingen, 1860), **Lic. Theol.** (Heidelberg, 1865), **D.D.** *hon.*, Leiden, 1870), German theologian; b. at Emmerich, Sept. 15, 1838; studied at Halle and Bonn; travelled in the East, 1860; became *privat-docent* at Heidelberg, 1865; professor extraordinary there, 1867; ordinary professor at Bern 1871, and at Jena 1884. He belongs to the school of Rothe, and is in friendly relations with the Old Catholics. He is the author of *Handbuch der neuesten Kirchengeschichte seit der Restauration von 1814*, Elberfeld, vol. i. 1867, 3d ed. 1880, vol. ii. 1883; *Welche Wege führen nach Rom? Geschichtliche Beleuchtung der römischen Illusionen über die Erfolge der Propaganda*, Heidelberg, 1869; *Richard Rothe, Ein Lebensbild*, Wittenberg, 1873–74, 2 vols., 2d ed. 1877–78; *Berner Beiträge zur Geschichte der schweizerischen Reformationskirchen* (edited with original contributions), Bern, 1884; *Zur geschichtlichen Würdigung der Religion Jesu, Vorträge, Predigten, Abhandlungen*, 1884; edits the new edition of Hagenbach's *Kirchengeschichte*, Leipzig, 1885, sqq.

NITZSCH, Friedrich August Berthold, Lic. Theol. (Berlin, 1858), **D.D.** (*hon.*, Greifswald, 1866), German theologian; b. at Bonn, Feb. 19, 1832; studied at Berlin, Halle, and Bonn, 1850–55; was *Collaborator* in the gymnasium of the "Grauen Kloster" in Berlin, 1857–58; became *privat-docent* at Berlin, 1859; ordinary professor ot theology at Giessen, 1868; at Kiel, 1872. He is the author of *Das System des Boëthius und die ihm zugeschriebenen theologischen Schriften*, Berlin, 1860; *Augustinus Lehre vom Wunder*, 1865; *Grundriss der christlichen Dogmengeschichte*, 1. Thl. (all published) 1870; *Luther und Aristoteles*, Kiel, 1883.

NORMAN, Richard Whitmore, D.C.L. (Bishops' College, Lennoxville, Can., 1878), Episcopal Church of Canada; b. at Southborough, near Bromley, Kent, Eng., April 24, 1829; educated at King's College, London, and Exeter College,

Oxford, where he graduated B.A. 1851, M.A. 1854; was ordained deacon 1852, and priest 1853; curate of St. Thomas, Oxford, 1852; fellow of St. Peter's College, Radley, 1853–57; head master of St. Michael's College, Tenbury, 1857–61; warden of St. Peter's College, Radley, 1861–66; assistant minister of St. John the Evangelist, Montreal, Can., 1867–72; of St. James the Apostle, Montreal, 1872–83; rector of St. Matthias, Montreal, since 1883. He has been honorary fellow of St. Michael's College, Tenbury, since 1856; honorary canon of Montreal, and vice-chancellor of Bishops' College, Lennoxville, Can., since 1878; fellow of McGill College, Montreal, since 1884; chairman of Protestant school board since 1880; honorary clerical secretary of the Provincial Synod, 1880; vice-president of the Montreal Philharmonic Society, 1880, and of the Art Association, Montreal, 1884; chairman of Montreal Botanic Garden Association, 1885; member of the executive committee and many other important diocesan committees. He is a moderate but decided Anglican. He is the author of *Manual of Prayers for the Use of Schools*, Oxford, 1856, 3d ed. 1862; *Occasional Sermons*, 1860; *Sermons preached in Radley College Chapel*, 1861; and the following pamphlets, etc.: *Ritualism*, Montreal, 1867; *Thoughts on the Conversion of the Heathen*, 1867; *St. John our Example*, 1867; *Gallio* (sermon), 1868; *Harvest* (two sermons), 1868–69; *Anniversary Sermon* (Port Hope School, 1869; Dunham Ladies' College, 1884); *Confession* (three sermons), 1873; *Considerations on the Revised New Testament*, 1881; *Sermon to Young Men*, 1882; *Sermon to Young Women*, 1882; *Lecture on Hymnology*, 1885.

NORTHRUP, George Washington, D.D. (University of Rochester, N.Y., 1864), **LL.D.** (Kalamazoo College, Kalamazoo, Mich., 1879), Baptist; b. at Antwerp, Jefferson County, N.Y., Oct. 15, 1825; graduated from Williams College, Williamstown, Mass., 1854, and from Rochester (N.Y.) Theological Seminary, 1857; became professor of church history in the latter institution, 1857, and president of the Baptist Union Theological Seminary, Morgan Park, Chicago, Ill., 1867.

NOWACK, Wilhelm Gustav Hermann, Ph.D. (Halle, 1872), **Lic. Theol.** (Berlin, 1873), **D.D.** (Berlin, 1883), German Protestant; b. in Berlin, March 3, 1850; studied at Berlin, 1869–73; became inspector in the Berlin Johanneum, 1872; temporary *Divisionspfarrer*, 1875; *Pfarrverweser* at St. Gertrud's in Berlin, 1876, and in the orphanage of Rummelsburg, near Berlin, 1877; *privat-docent* at Berlin, 1875; professor extraordinary of theology, 1880; ordinary professor at Strassburg, 1881. He belongs to the historico-critical school of Ewald-Dillmann. He is the author of *Die Bedeutung des Hieronymus für die alttestamentliche Textkritik*, Göttingen, 1875; *Die assyrisch-babylonischen Keilinschriften und das Alte Testament*, Berlin, 1878; *Der Prophet Hosea erklärt*, 1880; edited second edition of E. Bertheau on *Proverbs*, and of F. Hitzig on *Ecclesiastes*, in the *Kurzgefasst. exegetisches Handbuch zum Alten Testament*, Leipzig, 1883.

NYSTRÖM, Johan Erik, Ph.D. (Upsala, 1866), General Baptist; b. in Stockholm, Sweden, Sept. 8, 1842; graduated at University of Upsala, 1866; was teacher of languages in the New Elementary School of Stockholm, 1867; in Greek and Hebrew in the Baptist Seminary there, 1867–72; secretary of the Swedish Evangelical Alliance, 1872–78; missionary to the Jews at Beirût, Syria, 1878–81. In 1871 he was a member of the Evangelical Alliance deputation to the Russian Emperor on account of the persecuted Lutherans in the Baltic provinces; in 1872 travelled in aid of the Baptist building-fund, through Germany, England, and Scotland; in 1884 was deputy of the Swedish Baptists to the Evangelical Alliance Conference in Copenhagen; in 1885 was elected a member of the Swedish Parliament for three years. He is the translator into Swedish of Sophocles' *Antigone*, I. verses 1–383, with commentary (Ph.D. dissertation), Stockholm, 1866; Nicholl's *Help to the Reading of the Bible*, 1866; Dr. Rudelbach on *Civil Marriage*, 1868; Lyon's *Homo contra Darwin*, 1873; Merle d'Aubigné's *History of the Reformation in the Time of Calvin*, 1874–77; Sankey's *Gospel Hymns*, 1876; Spurgeon's *John Ploughman's Talks*, 1880; Spurgeon's *Clue of the Maze*, 1884; and of other works; and is the author (in Swedish) of *Bible Dictionary*, 1868, 2d ed. 1883; *Four Letters on Religious Liberty*, 1868; *Christian Hymns from Ancient and Modern Times*, 1870; *Lecture on the "Läseri"* (i.e., "reading," a nickname for living Christianity), 1872; *Library of Biblical Antiquities*, 1874; *Letters to Brother Olof upon the Doctrine of Atonement*, 1876; *What is wanting in our Church*, 1876; *Spiritual Songs for Young Men's Christian Associations, Sunday Schools, and Prayer-meetings*, 1877; *Illustrated Missionary News*, 1877.

O.

OETTINGEN, Alexander von, Magister Theol., D.D. (both Dorpat, 1854 and 1856 respectively), Lutheran theologian; b. at Wissust, near Dorpat, Russia (Livonia), Dec. 24, 1827; studied theology at Dorpat, 1845-49, then at Erlangen and Berlin; became *privat-docent* at Dorpat, 1854; declined call to Erlangen; became professor extraordinary at Dorpat, 1856, and the same year ordinary professor of systematic theology, history of doctrines, and ethics. During 1861 and 1862 he was at Meran on account of the illness of his wife, a daughter of Professor Karl von Raumer of Erlangen; and, as pastor of the Evangelical Diaspora Congregation, there built its first Protestant chapel. He is the author of *Die synagogale Elegik des Volkes Israel insbesondere die Zion-Elegie Judah ha Levi's als Ausdruck der Hoffnung Israels im Lichte der heiligen Schrift dargestellt* (his *Magister* dissertation), Dorpat, 1854; *De peccato in spiritum sanctum, qua cum eschatologia christiana contineatur ratione disputatio* (his *Doctor* dissertation), 1856; *Durch Kreuz zum Licht, Predigten gehalten in Meran im Winter 1861-62*, Erlangen, 1862; *Die Moralstatistik in ihrer Bedeutung für eine Socialethik*, 1868-69, 2 vols., 3d ed. 1882; *Die Moralstatistik und die christliche Sittenlehre, Versuch einer Socialethik auf empir. Grundlage*, 1874; *Antiultramontana, Kritische Beleuchtung der Unfehlbarkeitsdoctrin vom Standpunkt evangelischer Glaubensgewissheit*, 1876; *Vorlesungen über Goethe's Faust*, 1879-80, 2 vols.; *Obligatorische und fakultative Civilehe nach den Ergebnissen der Moralstatistik*, Leipzig, 1881; *Ueber akuten und chronischen Selbstmord, Ein Zeitbild*, Dorpat, 1882; *Christliche Religionslehre auf reichsgeschichtlicher Grundlage*, Erlangen, 1885-86, 2 vols. He was joint editor of the *Dorpater Zeitschrift für Theologie und Kirche*, 1859-72, 14 vols.; and editor of Hippel's *Lebensläufe*, jubilee ed. Leipzig, 1878, 3 vols., 2d cheap ed. 1879.

OLSSON, Olof, b. at Karlskoga, Vermland, Sweden, March 31, 1841; studied at Leipzig, and graduated at the University of Upsala; pastor at Persberg, 1864-67, and at Sunnemo, 1867-69, in Sweden; came to America, 1869; pastor at Lindsborg, Kan., 1869-76; professor of Theology in Augustana College and Theological Seminary, 1876-83; professor of church history, symbolics, and catechetics in Augustana Theological Seminary (Swedish Lutheran) at Rock Island, Ill., 1883-; editor of various Swedish papers and periodicals, 1873-83. Published in Swedish, *Reminiscences of Travel*, 1880 (translated into Norwegian, Christiania, 1882); also in Swedish, *At the Cross*, 1878 (reprinted in Sweden, 4th ed. 1882); author of many tracts in Swedish, some of which have had a very large circulation.

OLTRAMARE, Marc Jean Hugues, Swiss Protestant theologian; b. at Geneva, Dec. 27, 1813; studied arts and theology at Geneva; was ordained 1838; continued his studies at Tübingen and Berlin, 1841-42; returned home; was a city pastor, 1845-54. Since 1854 he has been professor of New-Testament exegesis in the university. He was a member of the National Consistory, 1851-59; and, under commission of the Venerable Company of Pastors, prepared a new French version of the New Testament, which appeared, Geneva, 1872 (many subsequent editions). He is the author of *Commentaire sur l'Epître aux Romains*, Geneva, 1843, 2d ed. 1881-82; *Instruction évangélique sur trois questions: Qui est Jésus Christ? Qu'est-il venu faire? Que faire pour être sauvé?* 1845; *Catéchisme à l'usage des chrétiens réformés*, 1859, 4th ed. 1877; *Le Salut, les Sacrements* (in *Conférence ssur les principes de la foi réformée*, 1853-54, 2 vols.); *Calvin* (in *Calvin: cinq discours*, 1864); and sermons, etc.

OORT, Henricus, Dutch Orientalist; b. at Eemnes, Utrecht, Dec. 27, 1836; studied theology at Leiden, and graduated doctor in 1860; was successively pastor of the Reformed Church at Zandpoort 1860, at Harlingen 1867; professor of Oriental literature at the Athenæum, Amsterdam, 1873; and since 1875 has been professor of Hebrew and Jewish antiquities at Leiden. He is the author (in Dutch) of *The Religion of the Baalim among the Israelites*, 1864 (English trans. by Bishop Colenso, 1865); *The Last Centuries of Israel*, 1877-78, 2 vols.; *The Gospel and the Talmud compared in their Morality*, 1881. With Hooykaas he wrote *The Bible for Young People*, 1871-73, 6 vols. (English trans. by P. H. Wicksteed, London, 1873-79, 6 vols.; reprinted Boston, 1878-79, 3 vols., under title *The Bible for Learners*).

ORELLI, (Hans) Conrad von, Ph.D. (Leipzig, 1871), **D.D.** (*hon.*, Greifswald, 1885), Swiss Protestant; b. at Zürich, Jan. 25, 1846; studied at Zürich, Lausanne, Erlangen, Tübingen, and Leipzig; became orphan-house preacher at Zürich, 1869; *privat-docent*, 1871; professor extraordinary of theology at Basel, 1873; ordinary professor at Basel, 1881. He is the author of *Die hebräischen Synonyma der Zeit und Ewigkeit*, Leipzig, 1871; *Durchs Heilige Land, Tagebuchblätter*, Basel, 1878, 3d ed. 1884; *Die Unwandelbarkeit des apostolischen Evangeliums* (address before the Evangelical Alliance), Basel, 1879; *Die alttestamentliche Weissagung von der Vollendung d. Gottesreiches*, Wien, 1882 (English trans., *The Old-Testament Prophecy of the Consummation of God's Kingdom traced in its Historical Development*, Edinburgh, 1885); many articles in Herzog[2] and in the Calw *Bibellexicon*, 1885.

ORMISTON, William, D.D. (University of the City of New York, 1865), **LL.D.** (University of Victoria College, Cobourg, Can., 1881), Reformed (Dutch); b. in the parish of Symington, Lanarkshire, Scotland, April 23, 1821; went to Canada in 1834; graduated at the University of Victoria College, Cobourg, Can., B.A. 1848, M.A. 1856; was classical tutor in Victoria College, 1845-47, and professor of moral philosophy in the same, 1847-48; pastor of Presbyterian church at Clarke, County of Durham, Can., 1849-53; mathematical master, and lecturer in natural philosophy and chemistry, in the normal school, Toronto, 1853-57; examiner in Toronto University 1854-57; superintendent of grammar (classical) schools in the Province of Ontario, 1853-63; pastor of Central Presbyterian Church at Hamilton, 1857-70; and since 1870 has been a pastor of the Collegiate Reformed Dutch Church, New-York City. He assisted in preparing a full series of school-books, 1866-68; edited the American edition of the English translation of Meyer on *Acts*, New York, 1883; has contributed to various periodicals, and published a few sermons and addresses.

OSBORN, Henry Stafford, LL.D. (Lafayette College, Easton, Penn., 1864), Presbyterian; b. in Philadelphia, Penn., Aug. 17, 1823; graduated at the University of Pennsylvania, Philadelphia, 1841, and at Union Theological Seminary, New-York City, 1845; was stated supply at Coventry, R.I., 1845-46; pastor at Hanover Court House, Va., 1846-49; Richmond, Va., 1849-53; Liberty, Va., 1853-58; stated supply at Salem, Va., 1858-59; pastor at Belvidere, N.J., 1859-66; professor in Lafayette College, Easton, Penn., 1866-70; since 1870 has been at Oxford, O., stated supply, 1870-71, 1873 to date; professor in Miami University, Oxford, O., 1871-73. He is the author of *Biblical Tables*, Philadelphia, 18—; *Palestine, Past and Present*, 1858; *Little Pilgrims in the Holy Land*, 1859; *Teachers' Guide to Palestine*, 1868; *New Descriptive Geography of Palestine*, Oxford, O., 1877; *Ancient Egypt in the Light of Modern Discoveries*, Chicago, 1883. *

OSGOOD, Howard, Baptist; b. on Magnolia Plantation, parish of Plaquemines, La., Jan. 4, 1831; graduated at Harvard College, Cambridge, Mass., 1850; was pastor at Flushing, N.Y., 1856-58; New York, 1860-65; professor in Crozer Theological Seminary, Chester, Penn., 1868-74, and in Rochester (N.Y.) Theological Seminary since 1875. He has been since 1874 a member of the Old-Testament Revision Company. He translated Lange's general and special Introduction to *Exodus*, *Leviticus*, and *Numbers*, in the American Lange series, New York, 1876.

OSWALD, Johann Heinrich, Lic. Theol., D.D. (both Münster, 1843 and 1855), Roman Catholic; b. at Dorsten, Westphalia, Germany, June 3, 1817; studied theology in the seminary at Münster, and in the University of Bonn; became *privat-docent* at Münster, then professor in the Semin. Theodorianum at Paderborn; then went to his present professorship at Braunsberg. He is the author of *Die dogmatische Lehre von den heiligen Sacramenten der katholischen Kirche*, Münster, 1856, 2 vols., 4th ed. 1877; *Eschatologie*, Paderborn, 1868, 4th ed. 1879; *Die Lehre von der Heiligung*, 1873, 3d ed. 1885; *Die Erlösung in Christo Jesu*, 1878, 2 vols., 2d ed. 1886; *Die religiöse Urgeschichte der Menschheit, das ist der Urstand des Menschen, der Sündenfall im Paradiese und die Erbsünde, nach der Lehre der katholischen Kirche*, 1881; *Angelologie*, 1883; *Schöpfungslehre im allgemeinen und in besonderer Beziehung auf den Menschen*, 1885; besides other minor treatises.

OTTO, (Johann) Karl (Theodor), Ritter von Otto (by the Emperor Franz Joseph I. at Vienna, July 18, 1871, raised to the hereditary nobility), **Ph.D.** (Jena, 1841), **Lic. Theol.** (*hon.*, Königsberg, 1844), **D.D.** (*hon.*, Königsberg, 1848), German Protestant; b. Oct. 4, 1816; studied philosophy and theology at Jena, 1838-41; became *privat-docent* of historical theology and exegesis of the New Testament at Jena, 1844; professor extraordinary of theology there, 1848; since 1851 has been ordinary professor of church history in the evangelical theological faculty at Vienna. From 1852-61 he was ordinary professor of New-Testament exegesis; from 1863-67 was member of the imperial educational council. Since 1841 he has been a member of the Societas Latina Jenensis, since 1848 of the Societas Hagana, since 1879 of the Society for the History of Protestantism in Austria. He is a knight of the Greek Order of the Saviour (1858), of the Austrian Order of the Iron Crown, third class (1871), of the Grand Duke of Saxony Order of the White Hawk, first division (1872), of the Prussian Order of the Red Eagle, third class (1873), received the Austrian (1862) and the Grand Duke of Saxony's (1857) gold *Verdienst-Medaille für W. u. K.* Since 1869 he has been an Austrian Imperial *Regierungsrath*; since 1876 has been president of the examining commission for Protestant ministers at Vienna. He is the author of *De Justini Martyris scriptis et doctrina*, Jena, 1841; *De Victorino Strigelio liberioris mentis in ecclesia lutherica vindice*, 1843; *De epistola ad Diognetum S. Justini philosophi et martyris nomen præ se ferente*, 1845, 2d ed. Leipzig, 1852; *Zur Charakteristik des heiligen Justinus, Philosophen und Märtyrers*, Wien, 1852; *Des Patriarchen Gennadios von Constantinopel Confession, kritisch untersucht u. herausgegeben, Nebst einem Excurs über Arethas' Zeitalter*, 1864; *De gradibus in theologia*, 1874. He edited the posthumous commentaries of Baumgarten Crusius upon *Matthew* (Jena, 1844), *Mark* and *Luke* (1845). But his chief work is his edition of the works of the Christian apologists of the second century, *Corpus apologetarum Christianorum sæculi secundi*, Jena, 1842-72, 9 vols. (vols. i.-v., *Justin Martyr*, 1842-48, 3d ed. 1876-81; vol. vi., *Tatian*, 1851; vol. vii., *Athenagoras*, 1857; vol. viii., *Theophilus of Antioch*, 1861; vol. ix., *Hermias, Quadratus, Aristides, Aristo, Miltiades, Melito, Apollinaris*, 1872). He shares in editing *Jahrbuch der Gesellschaft für die Geschichte des Protestantismus in Oesterreich*, Wien and Leipzig, 1880, sqq.: and contributed to it the article, *Die Anfänge der Reformation im Erzherzogthum Oesterreich* (1880, 1883). His principal other articles are: *Beziehungen auf die Johanneischen und Paulinischen Schriften bei Justinus Martyr und dem Verfasser des Briefes an Diognetos* (in Illgen's *Ztsch. f. d. hist. Theol.*, 1841, 1842, 1843, 1844, 1859); *Der dem Patriarchen Gennadios von Constantinopel beigelegte Dialog über die Hauptstücke des christl. Glaubens* (in same, 1850, 1864); *Justinus der Apologet* (in *Ersch. u. Gruber* sect. ii., Th. 30); *De inscriptione et ætate Apologiæ Athenagoricæ* (in *Ztsch. f. d. hist. Theol.*, 1856); *Florianus*, etc. (in Piper's *Die Zeugen der Wahrheit*); *Ueber den apostol. Gruss* (in *Jahrb. f. deutsche Theol.*, 1867); *Haben Barnabas, Justinus und Irenæus den zweiten Petrusbrief* (3, 8) *benutzt?* (in *Ztsch. f. wiss. Theol.*, 1877); *Ueber das Zeitalter des Erzbischofs Arethas* (in same, 1878).

OVERBECK, Franz Camillo, Ph.D. (Leipzig, 1860), **D.D.** (*hon.*, Jena, 1870), Swiss Protestant; b. in St. Petersburg, Nov. 4 (16), 1837; studied at Leipzig and Göttingen, 1856-60; became *privat-docent* at Jena, 1864; professor extraordinary of theology at Basel, 1870; ordinary professor, Basel, 1871. He edited the fourth edition of De Wette on *Acts* (Leipzig, 1870), and has written *Quæstionum*

Hippolytearum specimen, Jena, 1864; *Ueber Entstehung und Recht einer rein historischen Betrachtung der Neutestam. Schriften in der Theologie*, Basel, 1871, 2d ed. 1874; *Ueber die Christlichkeit unserer heutigen Theologie, Eine Streit- und Friedensschrift*, Leipzig, 1873; *Studien zur Geschichte der alten Kirche*, 1st part, Schloss-Chemnitz, 1875; *Zur Geschichte des Kanons*, 1880.

OXENDEN, Right Rev. Ashton, D.D. (by decree of Convocation, 1869), Church of England; b. at Broome, near Canterbury, Sept. 25, 1808; educated at University College, Oxford; graduated B.A. 1833; was ordained deacon 1833, priest 1834; was rector of Pluckley, Kent, 1848-69; lord bishop of Montreal and metropolitan of Canada, 1869-78; rural dean of Canterbury, 1879-84; since 1879, vicar of Hackington (or St. Stephen's), near Canterbury. He is the author of numerous devotional works, many of which have had large sales on both sides of the Atlantic. The following may be mentioned; *Cottage Sermons*, 1853; *The Earnest Communicant*, 1856; *The Pathway of Safety*, 1856; *The Christian Life*, new ed. 1870; *Our Church and its Services*, new ed. 1868; *The Parables of our Lord*, new ed. 1868; *Portraits from the Bible*, 1872, 2 vols.; *The Earnest Churchman*, 1878; *Short Comments on the Gospels, for Family Worship*, 1885.

OXENHAM, Henry Nutcombe, Roman Catholic; b. at Harrow, Eng., Nov. 15, 1829; educated at Balliol College, Oxford; graduated B.A. (second-class in classics) 1850, M.A. 1854; held curacies from 1854 to 1857; joined the Roman-Catholic Church in 1857, and was successively in the London Oratory (1859-60), professor at St. Edmund's College, Ware (1860), and master at the Oratory School, Birmingham, 1861; resigned at Christmas of that year. He is the author of numerous review articles, of the English translation of Döllinger's *First Age of the Church* (London, 1866, 3d ed. 1877) and *Lectures on Re-union of the Churches* (1872), and of vol. 2 of Hefele's *History of the Councils of the Church* (1876); and of the following original works: *Poems*, 1854, 3d ed. 1871; *Church Parties*, 1857; *Catholic Doctrine of the Atonement*, 1865, 3d ed. 1881; *Recollections of Oberammergau*, 1872, 2d ed. 1880; *Catholic Eschatology and Universalism*, 1876, 2d ed. 1878; *Short Studies in Ecclesiastical History and Biography*, 1884; *Short Studies, Ethical and Religious*, 1885.

P.

PACKARD, Joseph, D.D. (Kenyon College, Gambier, O., 1847), Episcopalian; b. at Wiscasset, Me., Dec. 23, 1812; graduated at Bowdoin College, Brunswick, Me., 1831, and studied (1833) in Andover (Mass.) Theological Seminary; since 1836 has been professor of biblical learning in the Protestant-Episcopal Seminary of Virginia, near Alexandria, and is now dean. He contributed the commentary on *Malachi* to the American edition of Lange, and was one of the American revisers of the Old Testament (1870–85).

PADDOCK, Right Rev. Benjamin Henry, S.T.D. (Trinity College, Hartford, Conn., 1867), Episcopalian, bishop of Massachusetts; b. at Norwich, Conn., Feb. 29, 1828; graduated at Trinity College, Hartford, Conn., 1848, and at the General Theological Seminary, New-York City, 1852; was assistant teacher in the Episcopal Academy of Connecticut, Cheshire, 1848–49; assistant minister at the Church of the Epiphany, New-York City, while deacon, 1852–53; rector of St. Luke's, Portland, Me., 1853, but withdrew after three months on account of climate; was rector of Trinity, Norwich, Conn., 1853–60; of Christ Church, Detroit, Mich., 1860–69; of Grace Church, Brooklyn Heights, Long Island, N.Y., 1869–73; consecrated bishop, 1873. He is the author of sundry articles in reviews and periodicals, canonical digests, sermons, charges (1876, 1879, 1880), etc.: among which may be mentioned, *Ten Years in the Episcopate*, 1883; *The First Century of the Diocese of Massachusetts*, 1885; *The Pastoral Relation*, etc.

PADDOCK, Right Rev. John Adams, S.T.D. (Trinity College, Hartford, Conn., 1870), Episcopalian, missionary bishop of Washington Territory; b. at Norwich, Conn., Jan. 19, 1825; graduated at Trinity College, Hartford, Conn., 1845, and at the General Theological Seminary, New-York City, 1849; was rector of Christ Church, Stratford, Conn., 1849–55; of St. Peter's, Brooklyn, N.Y., 1855–80; consecrated bishop, 1880. Since his work began, the number of churches in his diocese has doubled; a Church hospital has been erected; and two Church schools built, costing about sixty thousand dollars, and endowed with one hundred thousand dollars. He is the author of *History of Christ Church, Stratford, Conn.*, 185–; occasional sermons and addresses.

PAINE, Levi Leonard, D.D. (Yale College, New Haven, Conn., 1875), Congregationalist; b. at Holbrook (formerly East Randolph), Mass., Oct. 10, 1832; graduated at Yale College, New Haven, Conn., 1856; was tutor there, 1859–61; pastor at Farmington, Conn., 1861–70; and since 1871 has been professor of ecclesiastical history in Bangor (Me.) Theological Seminary; has published some addresses and sermons.

PAINE, Timothy Otis, LL.D. (Colby University, Waterville, Me., 1875), New-Jerusalem Church (Swedenborgian); b. at Winslow, Kennebec County, Me., Oct. 13, 1824; graduated at Waterville College (now Colby University), Me., 1847. Since 1856 he has been pastor of the Swedenborgian Church at Elmwood, Plymouth County, Mass.; since July 3, 1866 (the date of its organization), teacher of Hebrew in the theological school of the General Convention of the New Jerusalem Church in the United States, now located at Boston, Mass. "In all these thirty years he can hardly be said to have taken vacations, or made exchanges with ministers; working through summer, autumn, winter, and spring, again and again, with only one end never for a day out of view, trying to answer the one question: How did the holy forms described in the Scriptures look? He began his study before 1847, but received the first leading thought on the sabbath afternoon of Dec. 26, 1852." He is the author of *Solomon's Temple, or the Tabernacle; The First Temple; House of the King, or House of the Forest of Lebanon; Idolatrous High Places; The City on the Mountain* (*Rev. xxi.*); *The Oblation of the Holy Portion; and The Last Temple* (with 21 plates of 61 figures, accurately copied by the lithographer from careful drawings made by the author), Boston, 1861; *Solomon's Temple and Capitol, Ark of the Flood and Tabernacle, or The Holy Houses of the Hebrew, Chaldee, Syriac, Samaritan, Septuagint, Coptic, and Itala Scriptures* (with 42 full plates and 120 text-cuts, being photographic reproductions of the original drawings made by the author), Boston and New York, 1885.

PALMER, Benjamin Morgan, D.D. (Oglethorpe University, Milledgeville, Ga., 1852), **LL.D.** (Westminster College, Fulton, Mo., 1870), Presbyterian (Southern Church); b. in Charleston, S.C., Jan. 25, 1818; graduated at the University of Georgia, 1838, and at the Theological Seminary, Columbia, S.C., 1841; became pastor of the First Presbyterian Church, Savannah, Ga., 1841; of the First Presbyterian Church, Columbia, S.C., 1843; of the First Presbyterian Church, New Orleans, La., December, 1856. His church seats fourteen hundred persons, and numbered in 1886 six hundred communicants. He was professor of church history and polity in the Columbia (S.C.) Theological Seminary, 1853–56; was moderator of the First Southern Assembly, Augusta, Ga., 1861. He has declined elections to professorships in three theological seminaries; viz., of Hebrew at Danville, Ky. (1853), of pastoral theology at Princeton, N.J. (1860), of the same at Columbia, S.C. (1881); also the chancellorship of the South-Western Presbyterian University, Clarksville, Tenn. (1874); and calls at different times to churches in Macon (Ga.), Charleston (S.C.), Philadelphia, Baltimore, and New York. He was a director of the Columbia Theological Seminary, S.C., 1842–56, and has been a director in the South-Western Presbyterian University, Clarksville, Tenn., since 1873, and in Tulane University, New Orleans, La., since its organization in 1882. He has been commissioner to ten General Assemblies (three of them before the Civil War); since 1847 one of the editors and contributors of *The Southern Presbyterian Review*, Columbia, S.C., of which he was one of the founders. He is the author of *The Life and Letters of Rev. James Henley Thornwell, D.D., LL.D.*, Richmond, 1875; *Sermons*, New Orleans, La., 1875-76, 2 vols.; *The Family in its Civil and Churchly Aspects*, New York, 1876; and addresses, sermons, pamphlets, etc.

PALMER, Ven. Edwin, D.D. (Oxford, 1878), archdeacon of Oxford, Church of England; b. at Mixbury, Oxfordshire, July 18, 1824; entered Balliol College, Oxford, 1842; obtained the Hertford and Ireland scholarships, 1843; the chancellor's prize for Latin verse, 1844, and for the Latin essay, 1847; graduated B.A. (first-class classics) 1845, M.A. 1850; in Balliol College was fellow, 1845-67; philological lecturer, 1858-66; tutor, 1866-70; was Corpus professor of the Latin language and literature in the University of Oxford, 1870-78; ordained deacon 1854, priest 1868; was select preacher to the University of Oxford, 1865-66, 1873-74; became archdeacon of Oxford, and canon of Christ Church, 1878. He was a member of the New-Testament Company of Revisers of the Authorized Version, 1873-81; and edited the Greek Testament with the Revisers' Readings, published by the Clarendon Press, Oxford, 1881.

PALMER, Ray, D.D. (Union College, Schenectady, N.Y., 1852), Congregationalist; b. at Little Compton, R.I., Nov. 12, 1808; fitted for college at Phillips Academy, Andover, Mass.; graduated at Yale College, New Haven, Conn., 1830; taught the higher classes in a private seminary for young ladies in New-York City, 1830-31; was associated with Professor E. A. Andrews in the New Haven (Conn.) Young Ladies' Institute (which was one of the earliest attempts in this country to furnish young ladies advantages as nearly as possible equal to those of the other sex), 1831; licensed to preach by the New Haven West Association, 1832; was pastor of the Central Congregational Church, Bath, Me., 1835-50; during this period was on the board of overseers of Bowdoin College, Brunswick, Me., and took an active interest in education and literature; in 1847 he made a tour through Europe, notes of which were published in *The Christian Mirror* of Portland, Me.; was pastor of the First Congregational Church, Albany, N.Y., 1850-66; secretary of the American Congregational Union at New York, 1866-78, during which time more than six hundred church edifices were erected by the aid of the society. He was on the board of visitors of the Andover (Mass.) Theological Seminary, 1865-78, and regularly attended its examinations and business meetings. He has of late years lived in literary retirement at Newark, N.J. His printed discourses and other publications in pamphlet form are quite numerous. He has often written for the higher periodicals articles critical, philosophical, and miscellaneous, and very widely for the leading religious papers. His hymns are familiar to the whole English-speaking world, and some of them have been translated into many languages; his best known hymn, "My faith looks up to Thee," into twenty or more. Not to mention some smaller early volumes, he has written: *Spiritual Growth, or Aid to Growth in Grace*, Boston and Philadelphia, 1839, republished and entitled *Closet Hours*, Albany, 1851; *Remember Me, or The Holy Communion*, Boston, 1855, new ed. New York, 1873; *Hints on the Formation of Religious Opinions*, New York, 1860, new ed. 1877, republished in London and Edinburgh; *Hymns and Sacred Pieces*, New York, 1865; *Hymns of my Holy Hours*, 1868; *Home, or the Unlost Paradise*, 1868; *Earnest Words on True Success in Life*, 1873; *Complete Poetical Works*, 1876; *Voices of Hope and Gladness*, New York and London, 1880.

PARET, Right Rev. William, D.D. (Hobart College, Geneva, N.Y., 1867), Episcopalian, bishop of Maryland; b. in New-York City, Sept. 23, 1826; graduated at Hobart College, Geneva, N.Y., 1849; studied theology under Bishop De Lancey; became successively rector of St. John's Church, Clyde, N.Y., 1852; of Zion Church, Pierrepont Manor, N.Y., 1854; of St. Paul's, East Saginaw, Mich., 1864; of Trinity Church, Elmira, N.Y., 1866; of Christ Church, Williamsport, Penn., 1868; of Church of the Epiphany, Washington, D.C., 1876; bishop of Maryland, 1885.

PARK, Edwards Amasa, D.D. (Harvard University, Cambridge, Mass., 1844); b. at Providence, R.I., Dec. 29, 1808; graduated at Brown University, Providence, R.I., 1826; at Andover (Mass.) Theological Seminary, 1831; was pastor at Braintree, Mass., 1831-33; professor of mental and moral philosophy at Amherst College, Mass., 1835-36; professor of sacred rhetoric at Andover (Mass.) Theological Seminary, 1836-47; professor of Christian theology at Andover, 1847-81. He held a professorship at Andover forty-five years. In theology he has adopted the tenets set forth in the creed of Andover Theological Seminary (see article "Andover Theological Seminary," *Schaff-Herzog Encyclopædia*, vol. i., pp. 81, 82). These articles are often called "New-England Theology" (see *Encyclopædia*, vol. ii., pp. 1634-1638). In 1842-43 he spent sixteen months in Switzerland and Germany. In 1862-63 he spent the larger part of sixteen months in Germany. In 1869-70 he spent about sixteen months in England, Italy, Egypt, Palestine, and Greece. He began to write for the religious periodicals in 1828. Since that time he has written for *The American Quarterly Register, The Spirit of the Pilgrims, American Quarterly Observer, American Biblical Repository, The Congregational Quarterly, Christian Review, Bibliotheca Sacra*, Smith's *Dictionary of the Bible* (American edition), McClintock and Strong's *Cyclopædia, Schaff-Herzog Encyclopædia*. In 1844 Professor B. B. Edwards and Professor Park founded the *Bibliotheca Sacra*: Professor Edwards was editor-in-chief from 1844 to 1851; Professor Park was editor-in-chief from 1851 till 1884. Thus he was an editor of the work for forty years, and was concerned in the publication of forty volumes. He has published sixteen pamphlets. Among these are: a *Memorial* of Rev. Charles B. Storrs, D.D., president of Western Reserve College (Boston, 1833); of Professor Moses Stuart (Andover, 1852); Professor B. B. Edwards (Andover, 1852); Rev. Joseph S. Clark, D.D. (Boston, 1861); Rev. Richard S. Storrs, D.D., pastor at Braintree, Mass. (Boston, 1874); Rev. Samuel C. Jackson, D.D. (Andover, 1878); Rev. Leonard Woods, D.D., LL.D., president of Bowdoin College (Andover, 1880). His last pamphlet was on *The Associate Creed of Andover Theological Seminary* (Boston, 1883, pp. 98). He was one of the editors and translators of *Selections from German Literature*, Andover, 1839; edited *The Writings of Rev. William Bradford*

Homer, 1842, 2d ed. with an introductory essay of forty-nine pages, 1849; *The Preacher and Pastor* (to which he wrote an introduction of thirty-six pages), 1845; *The Writings of Professor B. B. Edwards* (to which was prefixed a memoir of 370 pages), Boston, 1853; published a *Memoir of the Life and Character of Samuel Hopkins, D.D.*, 1852, 2d ed. 1854 (which was also prefixed to the works of Dr. Hopkins). In connection with Professor Austin Phelps, D.D., and Dr. Lowell Mason, he compiled and edited *The Sabbath Hymn-Book*, New York, 1858 (between the years 1858 and 1866, with the appendages of tunes for congregational worship, it reached a circulation of about 120,000); in connection with the *Hymn Book* he, with Drs. Austin Phelps and Daniel L. Furber, published a volume entitled *Hymns and Choirs*, Andover, 1860 (of this work, an essay of sixty-one pages on *The Text of Hymns* was written by Professor Park). He edited *The Atonement, Discourses and Treatises by Edwards, Smalley, Maxcy, Emmons, Griffin, Burge, and Weeks, With an Introductory Essay* [of eighty pages], Boston, 1860; wrote a *Memoir of Nathanael Emmons*, 1861 (which was prefixed to the theological works of Dr. Emmons in 6 vols. 8vo.). His last publication is a volume of fourteen *Discourses on some Theological Doctrines as related to the Religious Character*, Andover, 1885.

PARKER, Edwin Pond, S.T.D. (Yale College, New Haven, Conn., 1872), Congregationalist; b. at Castine, Me., Jan. 13, 1836; graduated at Bowdoin College, Brunswick, Me., 1856, and at Bangor Theological Seminary, Me., 1859; since Jan. 11, 1860, has been pastor of the Second Church in Hartford, Conn.

PARKER, Joseph, D.D., Congregationalist; b. at Hexham, Northumberland, Eng., April 9, 1830; educated at University College, London, and privately; entered the Congregational ministry, and became successively pastor at Banbury (Oxfordshire), 1853; Manchester (Cavendish Chapel), 1858; and of the City Temple, London, 1869. In 1884 he was chairman of the Congregational Union. His church seats more than two thousand persons, and is largely attended. His sermons are taken down in short-hand. He has published *Emmanuel*, Lond., 1859; *Hidden Springs*, 1864; *Wednesday Evenings at Cavendish Chapel*, *Homiletic Hints*, 1865; *Ecce Deus, Essays on the Life and Doctrine of Jesus Christ*, 1868, 5th ed. 1875; *Springdale Abbey, Extracts from the Letters and Diaries of an English Preacher*, 1869; *The Paraclete*, 1874, new ed. 1876; *The Gospel by Matthew* (homiletic analysis), 1869; *Ad Clerum*, 1870; *Pulpit Notes, with Introductory Essay on the Preaching of Jesus Christ*, 1873; *The Priesthood of Christ*, 1876; *Adam, Noah, and Abraham*, 1880; *The Inner Life of Christ, as revealed in the Gospel of Matthew*, 1881-82, 3 vols.; *Apostolic Life*, 1882-84, 3 vols.; *The People's Bible: Discourses on Holy Scripture*, 1885 sqq., to be completed in 25 vols.; *Tyne Chylde, my Life and Ministry, partly in the Daylight of Fact, partly in the Limelight of Fancy*, 1883, 2d ed. 1885; *Weaver Stephen, Odds and Evens in English Religion*, 1885. Almost all these works have been republished in America.

PARKHURST, Charles Henry, D.D. (Amherst College, Mass., 1880), Presbyterian; b. at Framingham, Mass., April 17, 1842; graduated at Amherst College, Mass., 1866; studied theology in Halle (1869) and Leipzig (1872-73); was principal of high school, Amherst, 1867; professor in Williston Seminary, Easthampton, Mass., 1870-71; pastor (Congregational) at Lenox, Mass., 1874-80; and since 1880 has been pastor of the Madison-square Presbyterian Church, New-York City. He is the author of articles in different periodicals; and *Forms of the Latin Verb illustrated by the Sanscrit*, Boston, 1870; *The Blind Man's Creed, and other Sermons*, New York, 1883; *Pattern in the Mount, and other Sermons*, 1885.

PARRY, Right Rev. Edward, D.D. (Oxford, 1870), bishop suffragan of Dover (suffragan to the archbishop of Canterbury), Church of England; b. at Government House, Sydney, New South Wales, in the year 1830; entered Balliol College, Oxford, 1849; graduated B.A. (first-class classics) 1852, M.A. 1855; ordained deacon 1854, priest 1855; was tutor of the University of Durham, 1853-56; curate of Sonning, Berkshire, 1856; domestic chaplain to the bishop of London, 1857-59; rector of Acton, Middlesex, and rural dean, 1856-69; bishop suffragan, 1870 (one of the first two suffragan bishops consecrated in the Anglican Church for three hundred years). Since 1870 he has been commissary to the bishop of Madras; since 1874, same to the bishop of Gibraltar. He is the author of *A Memoir of Rear-Admiral Sir W. Edward Parry* (his father), London, 1856; *An Ordination Sermon preached in Whitehall Chapel*, 1857; *Memorials of Commander Parry, R.N.* (his brother), 1870, 2d ed. 1879; *A Sermon preached in Canterbury Cathedral after Dean Alford's Funeral*, 1871. *

PASSAGLIA, the Abbé Carlo, D.D., Roman Catholic; b. at Prive de San Paolo, near Lucca, Italy, in the year 1814; educated at Rome; became a Jesuit, and professor of theology in the Roman University. He edited the dogmatic theology of Petavius; wrote *A Commentary on the Prerogatives of St. Peter*, Ratisbon, 1850; *On the Eternity of Future Punishment;* in defence of the immaculate conception; but particularly a Latin pamphlet urging the Pope to renounce the temporal power (Rome, 1861), which was put upon the Index, and obliged him to leave Rome. He was made by Victor Emmanuel a theological professor at Turin; in 1863 sat in the Italian Parliament. In November, 1882, he made his peace with the Holy See, and resumed his priestly functions. *

PATERSON, Hugh Sinclair, M.D. (Glasgow, 1862), Presbyterian; b. at Campbelltown, Argyllshire, Feb. 26, 1832; educated at the University of Glasgow; entered the ministry of the Free Church, 1854; became minister of Free St. Mark's, Glasgow, 1854; removed to London in 1872 as minister of Belgrave Presbyterian Church; in 1880 came to his present charge, Trinity Presbyterian Church, Notting Hill, London. He has edited *Dickinson's Quarterly* (1878-81); since January, 1880, *The British and Foreign Evangelical Review* (quarterly); and since Nov. 3, 1881, *Word and Work* (weekly). He is the author of *Studies in Life, The Human Body and its Functions*, and *Health Studies* (all in 1880, several thousands sold, republished in 1 vol., *Life, Function, and Health*, 1884); *"In defence:" The Earlier Scriptures*, 1883; *The Fourfold Life*, 1884; *Crosses and Crowns*, 1884; *Christ and Criticism*, 1884; *Faith and Unfaith, their Claims and Conflicts*, 1885.

PATON, John Brown, D.D. (University of Glasgow, 1882), Congregationalist; b. in Loudon Parish, Ayrshire, Scotland, Dec. 17, 1830; educated at Springhill Theological College, affiliated with London University, where he graduated B.A. 1849 (Old-Testament honors examination, 1850); won Dr. Williams divinity scholarship, 1851; graduated M.A. (both in classics and philosophy), and gold medal in philosophy, 1853; became pastor of Congregational Church at Sheffield, 1854; principal of the Congregational Institute, Nottingham, 1863. He was editor of *The Eclectic Review*, 1859–62; and consulting editor of *Contemporary Review* since 1882. In theology, especially in apologetic tendencies, he is allied to Dorner; in his doctrine of the Church, an Independent. He is the author of *Evangelization of Town and Country*, London, 1861; "*Inspiration,*" *Criticism of Theories of J. D. Morell and Professor F. Newman*, 1862, *A Review of the "Vie de Jésus:" containing Discussions on the Doctrine of Miracle, the Mythical Theory, and the Authenticity of the Gospels*, 1864; *The Origin of the Priesthood in the Church*, 1875; *Supernatural Religion: a Criticism*, 1878; *The Inner Mission of Germany, and its Lessons to us*, 1885; *The Inner Mission of the Church* (in one volume with *Women's Work in the Church* and *The Present State of Europe in Relation to the Spread of the Gospel*), 1885; *The Twofold Alternative* (containing *Religion or Atheism* and *A Priesthood or a Brotherhood*), 1885; *Evening Schools under Healthy Conditions*, 1886; *Contemporary Controversies on the Doctrine of the Church and the Relations of Church and State*, 1886.

PATTERSON, Robert Mayne, D.D. (College of New Jersey, Princeton, 1880), Presbyterian; b. in Philadelphia, Penn., July 17, 1832; graduated from the Philadelphia High School, 1849, and (after five years' reporting in United-States Senate, and special study) from Princeton (N.J.) Theological Seminary, 1859; pastor at Great Valley, Penn., 1859; South Church, Philadelphia, 1867; editor of Philadelphia Pan-Presbyterian Council in 1880; member of the Philadelphia and Belfast Councils; editor of *Presbyterian Journal*, 1881; author of several volumes and of review articles, and of papers read to Philadelphia and Belfast Councils.

PATTISON, Thomas Harwood, D.D. (Madison University, Hamilton, N.Y., 1880), Baptist; b. at Launceston, Cornwall, Eng., Dec. 14, 1838; graduated at Regent's Park Baptist College, London, 1862; pastor at Newcastle-on-Tyne and Rochdale, Eng., 1865; New Haven, Conn., 1875; Albany, N.Y., 1879; professor of homiletics and pastoral theology in Rochester (N.Y.) Theological Seminary, 1881. He contributed to *Religious Republics*, London, 1869; published *Present-Day Lectures*, 1872; and is the American correspondent of *The Freeman*, a London Baptist journal.

PATTON, Alfred Spencer, D.D. (Madison University, Hamilton, N.Y., 1865), Baptist; b. in Suffolk, Eng., Dec. 12, 1825; came to America when a child; graduated at Columbian University, Washington, D.C., 1848; became pastor at West Chester, Penn., 1848; Haddonfield, N.J., 1852; Hoboken, N.J., 1854; Roxbury, Mass., 1859; Utica, N.Y., 1863; retired from pastorate, 1872, and has ever since been editor and proprietor of *The Baptist Weekly*, New-York City. In 1862 and 1863 he was chaplain of the Massachusetts Senate.

PATTON, Francis Landey, D.D. (Hanover College, Ind., 1872), **LL.D.** (Wooster University, O., 1878), Presbyterian; b. at Warwick, Island of Bermuda, Jan. 22, 1843; graduated at Princeton (N.J.) Theological Seminary, 1865; pastor Eighty-fourth-Street Church, New-York City, 1865; at Nyack, 1867; pastor South Church, Brooklyn, 1871; professor of theology in the Presbyterian Theological Seminary, Chicago, Ill., 1871; and of relations of philosophy and science to religion, Theological Seminary, Princeton, 1881. He is also professor of ethics in the College of New Jersey, Princeton. He was pastor elect of the Jefferson-Park Church, Chicago, 1874, and pastor 1879–81; editor of *The Interior*, 1873–6; and moderator of the General Assembly at Pittsburgh, Penn., in 1878. Besides numerous articles in periodicals, he has published *Inspiration of the Scriptures*, Philadelphia, 1869; *Summary of Christian Doctrine;* and is one of the editors of *The Presbyterian Review*.

PATTON, William Weston, D.D. (Indiana Asbury University, Greencastle, Ind., 1863), **LL.D.** (University of the City of New York, 1882), Congregationalist; b. in New-York City, Oct. 19, 1821; graduated at the University of the City of New York, 1839, and at Union Theological Seminary, New-York City, 1842; became pastor of Phillips Congregational Church, Boston, Mass., 1843; of the Fourth Church, Hartford, Conn., 1846; of the First Church, Chicago, Ill., 1857; was editor of *The Advance*, Chicago, Ill., 1867–72; lecturer on modern scepticism at Oberlin (O.) and Chicago (Ill.) Congregational theological seminaries, 1874–77; since 1877, president of Howard University, Washington, D.C., and in its theological department professor of natural theology and evidences of Christianity. He took an earnest part in the anti-slavery movement; was chairman of the committee which presented to President Lincoln, Sept. 13, 1862, the famous memorial from Chicago asking for a proclamation of emancipation; was vice-president of the North-Western Sanitary Commission during the Civil War, and as such made repeated visitations of the Eastern and Western armies, and published various pamphlet reports; visited Great Britain and the Continent on behalf of the freed men in 1866. He is the author of *The Young Man*, Hartford, Conn., 1847 (republished as *The Young Man's Friend*, Auburn, N.Y., 1850); *Conscience and Law*, New York, 1850; *Slavery and Infidelity*, Cincinnati, 1856; *Spiritual Victory*, Boston, 1874; *Prayer and its Remarkable Answers*, Chicago, 1875, 20th ed. New York, 1885; and numerous articles in the various theological magazines.

PAXTON, John R., D.D. (Union College, Schenectady, N.Y., 1882), Presbyterian; b. at Canonsburg, Penn., Sept. 18, 1843; graduated at Washington and Jefferson College, Washington, Penn., 1866, and at Western Theological Seminary, Allegheny, Penn., 1869; became pastor at Churchville, Md., 1871; of Pine-street Church, Harrisburg, Penn., 1874; of New-York-avenue Church, Washington, D.C., 1878; of West Church, New-York City, 1882.

PAXTON, William Miller, D.D. (Jefferson College, Canonsburg, Penn., 1860), **LL.D.** (Washington and Jefferson College, Washington, Penn., 1883), Presbyterian; b. in Adams County, Penn., July 7, 1824; graduated at Pennsylvania College,

Gettysburg, 1843, and at Princeton (N.J.) Theological Seminary, 1848 (having studied law after leaving college); was pastor at Greencastle, Penn., 1848–50; of First Church, Pittsburgh, Penn., 1851–65; professor of sacred rhetoric in the Western Theological Seminary, Allegheny, Penn., 1860–67; pastor of First Church, New-York City, 1866–83; and since has been professor of ecclesiastical, homiletical, and pastoral theology in the Princeton (N.J.) Theological Seminary. From 1872 to 1875 he was lecturer on sacred rhetoric in Union Theological Seminary, New-York City. He was moderator of the General Assembly of the Presbyterian Church at Madison, Wis., in 1880. He has published a *Memorial of Rev. Francis Herron, D.D.*, Pittsburgh, 1861.

PAYNE, Charles Henry, D.D. (Dickinson College, Carlisle, Penn., 1870), **LL.D.** (Ohio State University, Athens, O., 1876), Methodist; b. at Taunton, Mass., Oct. 24, 1830; graduated at Wesleyan University, Middletown, Conn., 1856; studied theology in the Biblical Institute, Concord, N.H. (now the Boston School of Theology); was pastor from 1857 until 1876, when he became president of Ohio Wesleyan University, Delaware, O. He was a member of the committee to revise the hymn-book of the Methodist-Episcopal Church, 1876; of the Œcumenical Methodist Conference, London, September, 1881; and of the General Conference of the Methodist-Episcopal Church, 1880 and 1884. He is the author of *Guides and Guards in Character Building*, New York, 1883, 6th ed. 1886, republished London, 1884; and of the pamphlets, *The Social Glass and Christian Obligation*, 1868; *Shall our American Sabbath be a Holiday, or a Holy-day?* Philadelphia, 1872; *Daniel, the Uncompromising Young Man*, New York, 1872.

PAYNE-SMITH, Very Rev. Robert, Dean of Canterbury, Church of England; b. in Gloucestershire, in November, 1818; educated at Pembroke College, Oxford; graduated B.A. (second-class in classics) 1841, M.A. 1843; Boden Sanscrit scholar, 1840; Pusey and Ellerton Hebrew scholar, 1843; was ordained deacon 1843, priest 1844; and became successively head master of the Kensington proprietary school (1853), sub-librarian of the Bodleian Library, Oxford (1857), canon of Christ Church, Oxford, and regius professor of divinity, and rector of Ewelme (1865), and dean of Canterbury (1871). He was Bampton lecturer in 1869, and an Old-Testament reviser (1870–84). He is the author, translator, and editor of *S. Cyrilli Alex. comment. in Lucæ evangel. quæ supersunt Syriace*, Oxford, 1858; *St. Cyril's Commentary on St. Luke's Gospel*, in English, 1859, 2 vols.; *Ecclesiastical History of John, Bishop of Ephesus* (translated), 1860; *The Authenticity and Messianic Interpretation of the Prophecies of Isaiah vindicated*, 1862; *Catalogus codicum Syriacorum et Carshunicorum in bibliotheca Bodleiana*, 1864; *Thesaurus Syriacus*, 1868 sqq.; *Prophecy a Preparation for Christ* (Bampton Lecture), 1869; commentary on *Jeremiah*, in *Bible* (*Speaker's*) *Commentary;* on *Isaiah*, in *S. P. G. Commentary;* and on *Genesis*, in Bishop Ellicott's *Commentary*. *

PEABODY, Andrew Preston, D.D. (Harvard College, Cambridge, Mass., 1852), **LL.D.** (University of Rochester, N.Y., 1863), Unitarian; b. at Beverly, Mass., March 19, 1811; graduated at Harvard College, Cambridge, Mass., 1826, and at the theological seminary in connection with it, 1832; was pastor at Portsmouth, N.H., 1833–60; professor of Christian morals, and preacher to Harvard University, 1860–81. He edited *The North-American Review*, 1852–61; and has published, besides articles, sermons, etc., *Lectures on Christian Doctrine*, Boston, 1844, 3d ed. 1857; *Christian Consolations*, 1846, 6th ed. 1872; *Conversation, its Faults and Graces*, 1856, 3d ed. 1882; *Christianity the Religion of Nature* (Lowell Lectures), 1864; *Sermons for Children*, 1866, 2d ed. 1867; *Reminiscences of European Travel*, New York, 1868; *Manual of Moral Philosophy*, 1873; *Christianity and Science* (Union Seminary Lectures), 1874; *Christian Belief and Life*, Boston, 1875; *Baccalaureate Sermons*, 1885; and translations of Cicero's *De officiis* (1883) and *De senectute* (1884); *De Amicitia* and *Scipio's Dream*, 1884; *Plutarch on the Delay of the Divine Justice*, 1885; A translation of Cicero's *Tusculan Disputations* (On the contempt of death, On bearing pain, etc.), 1886.

PECK, Thomas Ephraim, D.D. (Hampden-Sidney College, Prince-Edward County, Va., 1867), **LL.D.** (Washington and Lee University, Lexington, Va., 1883), Presbyterian; b. at Columbia, S.C., Jan. 29, 1822; graduated at South-Carolina College, Columbia, 1840; pastor in Baltimore, 1846–60; professor of church history and polity in Union Theological Seminary, Hampden-Sidney, Va., 1860–83, and since of systematic and pastoral theology. He has published review articles and sermons.

PEIRCE, Bradford Kinney, D.D. (Wesleyan University, Middletown, Conn., 1868), Methodist; b. at Royalton, Windsor County, Vt., Feb. 3, 1819; graduated at Wesleyan University, Middletown, Conn., 1841; received into New-England Conference, Methodist-Episcopal Church, 1843; was editor *Sunday-school Messenger* and *Sunday-school Teacher*, Boston, 1844–45; agent of American Sunday-School Union, 1854–56; senator from Norfolk County in Massachusetts Legislature, 1855–56; superintendent and chaplain of State Industrial School for Girls, Lancaster, Mass., 1856–62; chaplain of House of Refuge, New-York City, 1863–72; and since has been editor of *Zion's Herald*, Boston. He is a trustee of Boston University (since 1874), of Wellesley College (since 1876), and of Cushing Academy, Ashburnham, Mass. (since 1877), and was of Wesleyan University, Middletown, Conn., from 1870 to 1881. He is the author of *Temptation*, Boston, 1840, 2d ed. New York, 1844; *One Talent improved*, New York, 1845; *The Eminent Dead*, Boston, 1846 (second and subsequent editions at Nashville, Tenn.); *Bible Scholar's Manual*, New York, 1847; *Notes on the Acts*, 1848; *Questions upon Acts, Genesis, and Exodus*, 1848; *The Token of Friendship*, Boston, 1850; a series of reports upon Juvenile Reform and Industrial School, Lancaster, Mass., 1856–61; edited, by order of Legislature of Massachusetts, in 1856, a new edition, with additional notes and newspaper articles published at the time, of the debates and proceedings of the convention of the Commonwealth of Massachusetts, held in the year 1788, which ratified the Constitution of the United States, octavo, printed by the State; a series of chaplain's reports of House of Refuge, 1862–72; *Life in Woods, or Adventures of Audubon*, N.Y.,

1863; collection of hymns and ritual for House of Refuge, New York, 1864; *Trials of an Inventor: Life and Discoveries of Charles Goodyear*, 1866; *Stories from Life which the Chaplain Told*, Boston, 1866; *Sequel to Stories from Life*, 1867; *The Word of God Opened*, New York, 1868, 2d ed. 1874; *A Half-Century with Juvenile Offenders*, New York, 1869; *Under the Cross*, Boston, 1869; *The Young Shetlander and his Home: Biographical Sketch of Thomas Edmondston*, New York, 1870; *The Chaplain with the Children*, 1870; *Hymns of the Higher Life*, 1871; various articles.

PELHAM, Hon. and Right Rev. John Thomas, D.D. (*per Literas Regias*, 1857), lord bishop of Norwich; b. in London, June 21, 1811; educated at Christ Church, Oxford; graduated B.A. 1832, M.A. 1857; ordained deacon 1834, priest 1835; was rector of Berg Apton, Norfolk, 1837–52; perpetual curate of Christ Church, Hampstead, 1852–55; rector of St. Marylebone, London, 1855–57; consecrated bishop, 1857

PELOUBET, Francis Nathan, D.D. (University of East Tennessee, Knoxville, Tenn., 1884), Congregationalist; b. in New-York City, Dec. 2, 1831; graduated at Williams College, Williamstown, Mass., 1853, and from the theological seminary, Bangor, Me., 1857; was pastor of Congregational church at Lanesville (1857–60), Oakham (1861–66), Attleboro' (1866–71), and Natick (1871–83), all in Massachusetts. He is the author (with Mrs. Mary A. Peloubet) of *Select Notes on the International Sunday-school Lessons*, Boston, 1875 sqq. (12 vols. to 1886 inclusive, circulation over 230,000 vols.); *International Question Book*, 1874 sqq. (two grades, senior and intermediate, 26 vols.); *Sunday-school Quarterly*, 1880 sqq; *Intermediate Quarterly*, 1881 sqq. (circulation of question-books and quarterlies over 1,370,000); *Smith-Peloubet Bible Dictionary* (a revision, with additions to date, of Smith's condensed *Bible Dictionary*), Philadelphia, 1884; *Select Songs for the Sunday School and Social Meetings*, New York, 1884; occasional discourses, and temperance lesson-leaves.

PENDLETON, James Madison, D.D. (Denison University, Granville, O., 1865), Baptist; b. in Spottsylvania County, Va., Nov. 20, 1811; was pastor at Bowling Green, Ky., 1837–57, professor of theology, Union University, Murfreesboro', Tenn., 1857–61; pastor at Hamilton, O., 1862–65, and at Upland, Penn., 1865–83. He has never had a collegiate education, but received an honorary A.M. from Georgetown College, Ky., 1841. He is the author of *Three Reasons why I am a Baptist*, Cincinnati, O., 1853, last ed. St. Louis, Mo., 1884; *Sermons*, Nashville, Tenn., 1859; *Church Manual*, Philadelphia, 1868 (40 editions of 500 copies each); *Christian Doctrines*, 1878, 13th ed. 1885 (each edition 500 copies); *Distinctive Principles of Baptists*, 1881, 3d ed. 1885 (each edition 500 copies); with Rev. Dr. G. W. Clark, *Brief Notes on the New Testament*, 1884; *The Atonement of Christ*, 1885. His *Three Reasons* was translated into Welsh.

PENICK, Right Rev. Charles Clifton, D.D. (Kenyon College, Gambier, O., 1877), Episcopalian, retired bishop; b. in Charlotte County, Va., Dec. 9, 1843; studied in Hampden-Sidney College, Va., and graduated at the Theological Seminary of Virginia, near Alexandria, 1869; was rector of Emmanuel Church, Goodson, Va., 1869–70; of St. George's Church, Mount Savage, Md., 1870–73; of the Church of the Messiah, Baltimore, Md., 1873–77; bishop of Cape Palmas and parts adjacent, Africa, 1877–83; since 1883 has been rector of St. Andrew's Church, Louisville, Ky. He entered the Confederate army in 1861, and served through the war. He founded Cape Mount Station, Liberia, West Africa. He is the author of *More than a Prophet*, New York, 1880.

PENTECOST, George Frederick, D.D. (Lafayette College, Easton, Penn., 1884), Congregationalist; b. at Albion, Ill., Sept. 23, 1842; apprenticed to a printer at fifteen; went to Kansas Territory at seventeen, was there as printer for a year; then became private secretary to Govs. Denver and Walsh, then clerk in United-States District Court and in Supreme Court of the Territory; studied law; entered Georgetown College, Ky., but left it in 1862, and joined the Eighth Kentucky Union Cavalry under Col. Bristow (subsequently general, and secretary of the treasury under President Grant). He left the service in 1864, with the rank of captain. Since 1864 he has held the following pastorates: First Baptist Church, Greencastle, Ind., 1864–66; First Baptist Church, Evansville, Ind., 1866–68; First Baptist Church, Covington, Ky., 1868–69; Hanson-place Baptist Church, Brooklyn, N.Y., 1869–72; Warren-avenue Baptist Church, Boston, Mass., 1872–77; evangelist, 1877–81; since 1881 has been pastor of Tompkins-avenue Congregational Church, Brooklyn, N.Y. He has been three times abroad, always on invitation to preach and do evangelistic work, twice with Mr. Moody. He is the author of *Angel in Marble*, Boston, 1876, 3d ed. 1884, London 1884; *In the Volume of the Book*, New York, 1879, 3d ed. 1880, London, 1884; *Out of Egypt*, London, 1884, New York, 1885 (the last two books have had a joint circulation of 40,000 copies), many tracts and pamphlets; since 1885, editor of *Words and Weapons for Christian Workers* (monthly), New York, 1885 sqq.

PEROWNE, Very Rev. John James Stewart, D.D. (Cambridge, 1873), Church of England; b. at Burdwan, Bengal, India, March 13, 1823; was Crosse scholar, and educated at Corpus Christi College, Cambridge; graduated B.A. 1845, M.A. 1848, B.D. 1856; was members' prizeman (Latin essay) in 1844, 1846, 1847, and Tyrwhitt's Hebrew scholar in 1848; ordained deacon 1847, priest 1848; was examiner for classical tripos, 1851–52; select preacher to the university, 1853, 1861, 1873, 1876, 1879, and 1882; vice-principal of St. David's College, Lampeter, 1862–72; examining chaplain to the bishop of Norwich, 1865–78; prebendary of St. Andrew's, and canon of Llandaff Cathedral, 1869–78; prælector in theology in Trinity College, Cambridge, 1872–78; fellow of Trinity College, 1873–75; Hulsean professor of divinity, 1875–78. In 1868 he was Hulsean lecturer; in 1874–75, Margaret preacher; in 1874–76, Whitehall preacher. He was a member of the Old-Testament company of Bible-revisers, 1870–84, and of the royal commission on ecclesiastical courts, 1881–83. In 1875 he was appointed honorary chaplain to the Queen; and in 1878, dean of Peterborough. He is the author of *The Book of Psalms, a New Translation, with Notes, Critical and Exegetical*, London, 1864–68, 2 vols. 6th ed. 1886; *Immortality* (Hulsean Lectures), 1869; *Sermons*, 1873. He is the editor of *The Cambridge Bible for Schools*, 1877 sqq., to which series he contributed the notes on *Jonah*, 1878.

PERRIN, Lavalette, D.D. (Yale College, New Haven, Conn., 1869), Congregationalist; b. at Vernon, Conn., May 15, 1816; graduated at Yale College, New Haven, Conn., 1840, and at Yale Theological Seminary, 1843; was pastor at Goshen, Conn., 1843-57; of First Church, New Britain, Conn., 1858-70; since 1872, pastor of the Third Church, Torrington, Conn.; since 1876, annalist of General Conference of Congregational Churches of Connecticut; since 1880, treasurer of National Council of Congregational Churches; since 1882, member of corporation of Yale College. He took the initiatory steps in organizing the State Conference in 1867, and the Connecticut Congregational Club, Dec. 18, 1876; projected and is agent of the Memorial Hall estate in Hartford, Conn. He is conservative in doctrinal, and progressive in practical, theology; accepting the old creeds, and favoring such new measures as accord with them. He has published several sermons on various subjects.

PERRY, George Gresley, Church of England; b. at Churchill, Somerset, Dec. 21, 1820; scholar of Corpus Christi College, Oxford, 1837; graduated B.A. (second-class classics) 1840, M.A. (Lincoln College) 1843; was fellow of Lincoln College, 1842-52, in which was tutor, 1847-52; master of the schools, 1847-48; ordained deacon 1844, priest 1845; has been rector of Waddington, Lincolnshire, since 1852; rural dean of Longoboby; canon and prebendary of Milton Manor in Lincoln Cathedral since 1861; proctor for diocese of Lincoln, 1867-81; proctor in the Convocation of Canterbury. He is a moderate Anglican. He is the author of *History of the Church of England from the Death of Elizabeth to the Present Century*, London, 1861-64, 3 vols.; *Victor: a Tale of the Great Persecution*, 1864; *Life of Bishop Grosseteste*, 1865; *History of the Crusades*, 1865, 3d ed. 1872; *Croyland Abbey*, 1867; *Christian Fathers*, 1870; *Vox ecclesiæ Anglicanæ*, 1870; *Student's Manual of English Church History*, part i. 1881, part ii. 1877, 3d ed 1885; *Life of St. Hugh, Bishop of Lincoln*, 1879; *The Reformation in England*, 1886.

PERRY, Right Rev. William Stevens, S.T.D. (Trinity College, Hartford, Conn., 1869); **LL.D.** (William and Mary College, Williamsburg, Va., 1876), **D.C.L.** (University of Bishops' College, Lennoxville, Can., 1885), Episcopalian, bishop of Iowa; b. at Providence, R.I., Jan. 22, 1832; graduated at Harvard College, Cambridge, Mass., 1854; studied theology first at the Alexandria Theological Seminary, Va., then privately with Rev. Drs. A. H. Vinton, Boston, and J. S. Stone, Brookline, Mass.; became assistant minister at St. Paul's, Boston, Mass., 1857; rector of St. Luke's, Nashua, N.H., 1858; of St. Stephen's, Portland, Me., 1861; of St. Michael's, Litchfield, Conn., 1864; of Trinity, Geneva, N.Y., 1869; president of Hobart College, Geneva, N.Y., April, 1876; bishop, Sept. 10, 1876 He was deputy from New Hampshire to the General Convention, 1859; from the diocese of Maine, 1862, at which convention he was made assistant secretary; succeeded to the secretaryship, 1865; was elected secretary to the House of Clerical and Lay Deputies in the General Convention, 1868, 1871, and 1874; historiographer of the American Church, 1868; professor of history in Hobart College, 1871-73. With Dr. J. Cotton Smith he edited *The Church Monthly*, Boston, 1864. A full list of his numerous and valuable writings down to date is given in Batterson's *Sketch-book of the American Episcopate*, Philadelphia, 2d ed. 1885. Leaving out sermons, charges, and minor publications, of these may be mentioned, *Historical Sketch of the Church Missionary Association of the Eastern District of Massachusetts*, Boston, 1859; *Journals of the General Convention of the Protestant-Episcopal Church of the United States of America* (with illustrative historical notes and appendices by the Rev. Francis L. Hawks and the Rev. William Stevens Perry), vol. i. (all published), Philadelphia, 1861; *Bishop Seabury and Bishop Provoost: an Historical Fragment*, privately printed, 1862: *Documentary History of the Protestant-Episcopal Church in South Carolina*, Francis L. Hawks and William Stevens Perry editors, No. 1 (all published), 1862; *The Collects of the Church*, privately printed, 1863, 2d ed. 1878; *The Connection of the Church of England with Early American Colonization*, Portland, 1863; *Bishop Seabury and the "Episcopal Recorder" a Vindication*, privately printed, 1863; *A Century of Episcopacy in Portland* (a sketch of the history of the Episcopal Church in Portland, Me., from the organization of St. Paul's, Falmouth, Nov. 4, 1763, to the year 1883), Portland, 1863; *Documentary History of the Protestant-Episcopal Church in the United States of America* (containing numerous hitherto unpublished documents concerning the Church in Connecticut), Francis L. Hawks and William Stevens Perry editors, New York, 1863-64, 2 vols.; *Liturgic Worship. Sermons on the Book of Common Prayer, by Bishops and Clergy of the Protestant-Episcopal Church*, New York, 1864 (edited, the course planned, and one of the sermons delivered, by William Stevens Perry); *A Memorial of the Rev. Thomas Mather Smith, D.D.*, privately printed, 1866; *A History of the Book of Common Prayer, with a Rationale of its Offices*, by Francis Proctor (with an introductory chapter on the *History of the American Liturgy*, by William Stevens Perry), New York, 1868, new ed. London and New York, 1881; *Questions on the Life and Labors of the Great Apostle*, 1869; *The Churchman's Year-Book*, Hartford, 1870; do., 1871; *Historical Collections of the American Colonial Church*, vol. i., Virginia, 1871; do., vol. ii., Pennsylvania, 1872; do., vol iii., Massachusetts, 1873; do., vol. iv., Maryland, 1878; do., vol. v., Delaware, 1878; *Life Lessons from the Book of Proverbs*, New York, 1872, 4th ed. 1885; *A Sunday-school Experiment*, 1874, 3d ed. 1877; *Handbook of the General Convention*, 1874, 4th ed. 1881; *Journals of the General Convention, 1785 to 1835*, 3 vols.: *Historical Notes and Documents illustrating the Organization of the Protestant-Episcopal Church in the United States of America*, 1874; *The Re-union Conference at Bonn, 1875. A Personal Narrative*, 1876; *The American Cathedral*, 1877; *Missions and Missionary Bishoprics in the American Church* (a paper read before the Church Congress held at Stoke-upon-Trent, Eng., October, 1875), privately printed, 1877; *Scriptural Reasons for the Use of Forms of Prayer*, Davenport, 1878; *The Second Lambeth Conference: a Personal Narrative*, 1879; *A Brief Account of the Proceedings of the*

General Convention held in the City of Boston 1877, New York, 1880; *Some Summer Days Abroad*, Davenport, 1880; *Ober-Ammergau in 1875 and 1880*, privately printed, 1881; *Easter with the Poets*, Davenport, 1881; *The Church's Year*, Davenport, 1881; *Catechetical Instruction*, with an introduction, 1882; *The Church's Growth and the Church's Needs in Iowa*, 1882; *Griswold College: Shall it be built up?* a few words to Churchmen, 1883; *A Pastoral* about the Lenten fast, 1883; *Historical Sketch of the Protestant-Episcopal Church, 1784–1884*, New York, 1884; *A Discourse on the Centenary of the Consecration of Bishop Seabury*, 1884; *The Election of the First Bishop of Connecticut*, an historical review, 1885; *The Men and Measures of the Massachusetts Conventions of 1784–85*, a centenary discourse, Boston, 1885; *The History of the American Episcopal Church, 1587–1883*, vol. i., *The Planting and Growth of the American Colonial Church, 1587–1783*, Boston, 1885; do., vol. ii., *The Organization and Progress of the American Church, 1783–1883*, Boston, 1885; Ten Episcopal Addresses, 1877–86.

PETERKIN, Right Rev. George William, D.D. (Kenyon College, Gambier, O., and Washington and Lee University, Lexington, Va., both 1878), Episcopalian, first bishop of West Virginia; b. at Clear Spring, Md., March 21, 1841; studied at the University of Virginia, Charlottesville, 1858–59; graduated at the Theological Seminary of Virginia, near Alexandria, 1868; ordained deacon 1868, priest 1869; became rector of St. Stephen's Church, Culpepper, Va., 1869; of Memorial Church, Baltimore, Md., 1873; consecrated bishop, 1878.

PETERS, George Nathaniel Henry, Lutheran (Wittenberg Synod); b. at New Berlin, Union County, Penn., Nov. 30, 1825; graduated at Wittenberg College, Springfield, O., 1850; pastor at Woodbury, Springfield, Xenia, and Plymouth, O., but long since retired. He is a conservative premillenarian; and, besides numerous articles, has published, as the result of thirty years' labor, *The Theocratic Kingdom of our Lord Jesus Christ*, New York, 1884, 3 vols.

PETERS, John Punnett, Ph.D. (Yale College, New Haven, Conn., 1876), Episcopalian; b. in New-York City, Dec. 16, 1852; graduated at Yale College, New Haven, Conn., A.B., 1873; studied theology at Yale Divinity School, and Oriental languages at Berlin (1879–81) and Leipzig (1882–83); was tutor in Yale, 1876–79; ordained priest, 1877; chaplain of American Episcopal Church at Dresden, 1881–82; assistant minister at St. Michael's Church, New-York City, 1883–84; and since September, 1884, has been professor of Old-Testament languages and literature in the Protestant-Episcopal Divinity School, Philadelphia, Penn. He translated Müller's *Political History of Recent Times*, New York, 1883; and edited, with Rev. E. T. Bartlett, *The Scriptures for Young People*, 1886.

PFLEIDERER, Otto, D.D. (*honoris causa*, Jena, 1870), German Protestant; b. at Stetten, near Cannstatt, Würtemberg, Sept. 1, 1839; studied under Baur at Tübingen, 1857–61; became pastor at Heilbronn, 1868; superintendent at Jena 1870, and the same year ordinary professor of theology, and *Kirchenrath*; went to Berlin as professor of theology, 1875. He belongs to the historical, critical, dogmatic, and liberal school of Baur. He is the author of *Die Religion, ihr Wesen und ihre Geschichte*, Leipzig, 1869, 2 vols., 2d ed. 1878; *Moral und Religion, gekrönte Preisschrift*, Haarlem, 1870; *Der Paulinismus*, Leipzig, 1873; *F. G. Fichte. Lebensbild eines deutschen Denkers und Patrioten*, Stuttgart, 1877; *Religionsphilosophie auf geschichtlicher Grundlage*, Berlin, 1878, 2d ed. 1883–84, 2 vols.; *Zur religiösen Verständigung*, 1879; *Grundriss der christlichen Glaubens- und Sittenlehre*, 1880, 3d ed. 1886; *Lectures on the Influence of the Apostle Paul on the Development of Christianity* (Hibbert Lectures for 1885), London, 1885.

PHELPS, Austin, D.D. (Amherst College, Mass., 1856), Congregationalist; b. in West Brookfield, Mass., Jan. 7, 1820; graduated at the University of Pennsylvania, Philadelphia, 1837; was pastor of Pine-street Church, Boston, Mass., 1842–48; and professor of sacred rhetoric in Andover (Mass.) Theological Seminary, 1848–79. He has published *The Still Hour*, Boston, 1859; *Hymns and Choirs*, Andover, 1860; *The New Birth*, Boston, 1867; *Sabbath Hours*, 1870; *Studies of the Old Testament*, 1879; *The Theory of Preaching*, 1881; *Men and Books*, 1882; *My Portfolio*, 1882; *English Style*, 1883; *My Study*, 1885; and numerous articles.

PHELPS, Sylvanus Dryden, D.D. (Madison University, Hamilton, N.Y., 1854), Baptist; b. at Suffield, Conn., May 15, 1816; graduated at Brown University, Providence, R.I., 1844; at Yale Divinity School, New Haven, Conn., 1847; was pastor of First Baptist Church, New Haven, Conn., 1846–74; of Jefferson-street Church, Providence, R.I., 1874–76; and since has been proprietor and editor of *The Christian Secretary*, Hartford, Conn. He has published *Eloquence of Nature, and other Poems*, Hartford, 1842; *Sunlight and Hearthlight* (poems), New York, 1856; *Holy Land: a Year's Tour*, 1863, republished under title, *Bible Lands*, Chicago, 1869, 11th ed. 1877; *The Poet's Song for the Heart and the Home*, 1867; *Rest Days in a Journey to Bible Lands: Sermons preached in the Four Quarters of the Globe*, 1886.

PHILLIPS, Philip, Methodist layman; b. in Chautauqua County, N.Y., Aug. 13, 1834; brought up on the farm of a neighbor; early attracted attention by his singing, received his first musical education at the country singing-school, and later from Dr. Lowell Mason; began his first singing-school at Alleghany, N.Y., in 1853; conducted such schools subsequently in adjacent towns and cities. His parents were Baptists, and he was one himself from 1852 to 1860; but in 1860 he and his wife (whom he had married that year) joined the Methodist Church at Marion, O., and have ever since been in that denomination. He brought out his first musical publication, *Early Blossoms*, in 1860, and sold twenty thousand copies of it. In 1861 he moved to Cincinnati, and opened a music-store. His next book, *Musical Leaves*, Cincinnati, 1862, sold to the extent of seven hundred thousand copies. During the war he entered vigorously into the work of the Christian Commission, and raised much money for it by his *Home Songs*, and his personally conducted "services of song" in different parts of the country. He then issued *The Singing Pilgrim*, and since other books. In 1866 his music-store in Cincinnati was burned, and he moved his business to New York. In 1868 he first visited England, and successfully held services of song in all parts of the United Kingdom. He prepared *The American Sacred Songster* for the British Sunday-school Union, of which eleven hundred thousand copies have been sold. He has since held his praise and Bible-reading services in all parts of the world. He is the only man who has belted the entire globe with his voice in song, conducting 571 services during the journey. See PHILIP PHILLIPS: *Song Pilgrimage around and throughout the World*, with biographical sketch by Alexander Clark, Chicago, 1880, London, 1883.

PHILPOTT, Right Rev. Henry, D.D. (Cambridge, 1847), lord bishop of Worcester, Church of England; b. at Chichester, Nov. 17, 1807; educated at St. Catharine's College, Cambridge; graduated B.A. (senior wrangler, and Smith's prizeman, and first-class classical tripos) 1829, M.A. 1832; ordained deacon 1831, priest 1833; was fellow of his college, assistant tutor, then tutor, and then was master with a canonry of Norwich annexed, 1845-60; chaplain to his late Royal Highness the Prince Consort, 1854-60; vice-chancellor of the University of Cambridge, 1856-58; consecrated bishop, 1861; has been since 1861 clerk of the closet to the Queen, and is also provincial chaplain of Canterbury. *

PICK, Bernhard, Ph.D. (University of New-York City, 1877), Lutheran; b. at Kempen, Prussia, Dec. 19, 1842; educated at Breslau and Berlin; graduated at Union Theological Seminary, New-York City, 1868; became pastor at New York, 1868; North Buffalo, N.Y., 1869; Syracuse, N.Y., 1870; Rochester, N.Y., 1874; Allegheny, Penn., 1881. He became member of the German Oriental Society of Halle-Leipzig, 1877, and of the Society of Biblical Literature and Exegesis (U.S.A.), 1881. Since 1872 he has been a constant contributor to McClintock and Strong's *Cyclopædia*, translated Delitzsch's *Jewish Artisan Life in the Time of Jesus*, New York, 1883; is author of *Luther as a Hymnist*, Philadelphia, 1875; *Jüdisches Volksleben zur Zeit Jesu*, Rochester, N.Y., 1880; *Luther's "Ein feste Burg" in Nineteen Languages*, 1880, 2d ed. (in twenty-one languages) Chicago, 1883; *Index to Lange's Commentary on the Old Testament*, New York, 1882; and of articles in reviews, etc.

PIEPER, Franz Augustus Otto, Lutheran (Missouri Synod); b. at Carwitz, Pommerania, Germany, June 27, 1852; graduated at North-western University, Watertown, Wis., 1872, and at Concordia Seminary, St. Louis, Mo., 1875; was pastor at Manitowoc, Wis., 1875-78; and since has been professor of theology in Concordia Seminary. He is the author of *Das Grundbekenntniss der evangelisch-lutherischen Kirche*, St. Louis, Mo., 1880.

PIERCE, George Foster, D.D., bishop of the Methodist-Episcopal Church South; b. in Greene County, Ga., Feb. 3, 1811; d. near Sparta, Ga., Sept. 3, 1884; he was the son of the famous Lovick Pierce; studied law, but abandoned it for the ministry, and in 1831 was received into the Georgia Conference of the Methodist-Episcopal Church. After filling various important appointments in South Carolina and Georgia, he became in 1848 president of Emory College, Ga., and so remained until 1854, when he was elected a bishop. He was a very influential man in his denomination. He was the author of *Incidents of Western Travel*, edited by T. O. Summers, Nashville, 1857; and numerous sermons. *

PIERCE, Right Rev. Henry Niles, D.D. (University of Alabama, Tuscaloosa, 1863), **LL.D.** (William and Mary College, Williamsburg, Va., 1869), Episcopalian, bishop of Arkansas; b. at Pawtucket, R.I., Oct. 19, 1820; graduated at Brown University, Providence, R.I., 1842; was rector of St. John's, Mobile, Ala., 1857-68; of St. Paul's, Springfield, Ill., 1868-70; consecrated bishop, 1870. Besides occasional sermons, essays, addresses, etc., he has written *The Agnostic, and other Poems*, New York, 1884.

PIERSON, Arthur Tappan, D.D. (Knox College, Galesburg, Ill., 1874), Presbyterian; b. in New-York City, March 6, 1837; graduated at Hamilton College, Clinton, N.Y., 1857, and at Union Theological Seminary, New-York City, 1860; pastor at Binghamton, N.Y., 1860; Waterford, N.Y., 1863; Detroit, Mich., 1869; Indianapolis, 1882; and Philadelphia (Bethany Church), 1883. He is a frequent contributor to periodicals.

PIGOU, Francis, D.D. (Trinity College, Dublin, 1878), Church of England; b. at Baden-Baden, Germany, Jan. 8, 1832; educated at Trinity College, Dublin; graduated B.A. 1853, divinity testimonium 1854, M.A. 1857, B.D. 1878; was ordained deacon 1855, priest 1856; curate of Stoke Talmage, Oxfordshire, 1855-56; chaplain to Bishop Spencer at Marbœuf Chapel, Paris, 1856-58; curate of St. Philip, Regent Street, and of St. Mary, Kensington, London, 1858-60; perpetual curate of St. Philip, Regent Street, London, 1860-69; vicar of Doncaster, 1869-75; rural dean of Doncaster, 1870-75; honorary chaplain in ordinary to the Queen, 1871-74; became chaplain in ordinary, 1874; vicar and rural dean of Halifax, 1875; canon of Ripon Cathedral, 1885. He has held "missions" in England and America (1885), and many "retreats." He is the author of *Faith and Practice* (sermons), London, 1865; *Early Communion*, 1877; *Addresses to District Visitors and Sunday-school Teachers*, 1880; *Addresses delivered on Various Occasions*, 1883.

PIPER, Karl Wilhelm Ferdinand, German Protestant; b. at Stralsund, May 7, 1811; studied at Berlin and Göttingen, 1829-33; was *repetent* at Göttingen, 1833; *privat-docent* at Berlin, 1840; professor extraordinary, 1842; and since 1849 director of the Christian Archæological Museum, which he had himself founded. From 1850 to 1870 he edited the *Evangelischer Kalender* (Berlin); and has written much upon Christian archæology, of which may be mentioned, *Geschichte des Osterfestes*, Berlin, 1845; *Mythologie der christlichen Kirche*, Weimar, 1847-51, 2 vols.; *Einleitung in die monumentale Theologie*, Gotha, 1867; *Evangelischer Kalender*, Berlin, 1875. *

PIRIE, Very Rev. William Robinson, D.D. (King's College and University of Aberdeen, 1846), principal of Aberdeen University, Church of Scotland; b. in the manse of Slains, Aberdeenshire, July 26, 1804; d. at Chanonry, Old Aberdeen, Nov. 3, 1885. He matriculated at King's College and University of Aberdeen, 1816, and attended all the classes, but did not graduate, it being unusual and almost useless at that time to do so; became minister of Dyce, Aberdeenshire, 1830; professor of divinity at Marischal College and University of Aberdeen, 1843; professor of divinity and church history in Aberdeen University, 1860; principal of the university, 1877.

He was moderator of the General Assembly of the Church of Scotland, 1864; author of the Patronage Abolition Act in Church of Scotland; first chairman of school board of Aberdeen under Education Act of 1872. He was a conservative in politics. He was the author of *Inquiry into the Constitution of the Human Mind*, Aberdeen, 1858; *Natural Theology*, Edinburgh, 1868; *Philosophy of Christianity*, 1872; pamphlets upon *Position, Principles, and Prospects of the Church of Scotland* (Edinburgh, 1884), and upon other church questions, which went through many editions.

PITCHER, James, Lutheran; b. at Knox, Albany County, N.Y., Oct. 11, 1845; graduated at Hartwick Seminary, N.Y., 1869, and since 1872 has been president.

PITRA, His Eminence Jean Baptiste, D.D., cardinal of the Roman-Catholic Church; b. at Champforgueil, near Autun, Aug. 31, 1812; was early consecrated; taught rhetoric in the seminary at Autun; entered the order of St. Benedict, and lived in the abbey of Solesme. There he devoted himself to historical research. In 1858 he was sent by the Pope to Russia to study the Slavic liturgy, and on his return was in the service of the Propaganda. On March 16, 1863, he was created a cardinal priest of the Holy Roman Church; in 1869 he became librarian of the Vatican; and in 1879 he was raised to the rank of cardinal bishop of Frascati. He is the author of *Histoire de Saint Leger*, Paris, 1846; *Vie du R. P. Libermann*, 1855, 2d ed. 1873; *Spicilegium Solesmense*, 1852-60, 5 vols. (a monumental work of immense value, as it is a treasure-house of hitherto unprinted documents relating to ecclesiastical history, the result of a visit to nearly all the great European libraries); *Juris ecclesiastici Græcorum historia et monumenta*, Rome, 1864; *Triodion katanacticon*, 1879 (these two volumes are the result of four years journeys and of special study since 1858, when he was directed by the Pope to devote his attention to the ancient and modern canons of the Oriental churches); *Hymnographie de l'Eglise grecque*, 1867.

PITZER, Alexander White, D.D. (Arkansas College, Ark., 1876), Presbyterian (Southern Church); b. at Salem, Roanoke County, Va., Sept. 14, 1834; studied at Virginia Collegiate Institute (now Roanoke College), 1848-51; graduated at Hampden-Sidney College, Prince Edward County, Va., 1854; studied at Union Theological Seminary, Prince Edward County, Va., 1854-55, and at Danville Theological Seminary, Ky., 1855-57, and graduated 1857; was pastor at Leavenworth, Kan., 1857-61; Sparta, Ga., 1862-65; Liberty, Va., 1866-67; organized Central Presbyterian Church, Washington, D.C., in 1868, and has since been its pastor; since 1875 has been professor of biblical history and literature in Howard University in the same city. Since 1865 he has been a trustee of Hampden-Sidney College; since 1872, stated clerk of presbytery of Chesapeake; since 1873, president of the Washington-City Bible Society by annual unanimous re-election (was chairman of special committee of the society to report on the Canterbury revision, and reported favorably; under his presidency the city has been twice canvassed); since 1874, secretary of the Washington-City branch of the Evangelical Alliance. He was a member of the Prophetic Conference in New York, 1878, and suggested and aided in preparing the Doctrinal Basis, which was unanimously adopted. He introduced in the Southern General Assembly held at Atlanta, Ga., in 1882, resolutions to establish fraternity with the Northern Assembly, and aided in passage of the same. He favors the union of American Presbyterians on the basis of consensus of Presbyterian creeds. He is the author of *Ecce Deus Homo* (published anonymously), Philadelphia, 1867; *Christ, Teacher of Men*, 1877, *The New Life not the Higher Life*, 1878; contributions to reviews (*North-American, Presbyterian, Southern Presbyterian, Southern, Homiletic*), magazines (*Catholic Presbyterian, Pulpit Treasury*), and newspapers (*New-York Observer, Christian Observer, Presbyterian, New-York Evangelist*); *Journal*, Philadelphia.

PLATH, Karl Heinrich Christian, Lic. Theol. (Berlin, 1869), Lutheran; b. at Bromberg, Sept. 8, 1829; educated at Halle (1849-52), Bonn (1852-53), and at Wittenberg Theological Seminary (1854-56); was preacher at Halle, and gymnasial teacher, 1856-63; third secretary of the Berlin Mission, 1863-71; first secretary of Gossner's Mission, Berlin, since 1871; *privat-docent* in University, 1869; titular professor, 1883. He visited India in winter of 1877-78 on behalf of Gossner's Mission. He is author of *Leben des Freiherrn von Canstein*, Halle, 1861; *Sieben Zeugen des Herren aus allerlei Volk*, Berlin, 1867; *Die Erwählung der Völker im Lichte der Missionsgeschichte*, 1867; *Drei Neue Missionsfragen*, 1868; *Die Missionsgedanken des Freiherrn von Leibnitz*, 1869; *Missions-Studien*, 1870; *Die Bedeutung der Atlantik-Pacifik Eisenbahn für das Reich Gottes*, 1871; *Die Kulturhistorische Bedeutung der Kolhsmission in Ostindien*, 1876; *Gossner's Mission unter Hindus und Kolhs um Neujahr 1878*, 1879; *Nordindische Missionseindrucke*, 1879, 2d ed. 1881; *Eine Reise nach Indien für kleine und grosse Leute beschrieben*, 1880; *Welche Stellung haben die Glieder der christlichen Kirche dem modernen Judenthum gegenüber einzunehmen?* 1881; *Was machen wir Christen mit unsern Juden?* Nördlingen, 1881; *Shakespeares Kaufmann von Venedig. Ein Beitrag zum Verständnisse der Judenfrage*, Greifswald, 1883.

PLUMB, Albert Hale, D.D. (Brown University, Providence, R.I., 1882), Congregationalist; b. at Gowanda, Erie County, N.Y., Aug. 23, 1829; graduated at Brown University, Providence, R.I., 1855, and at Andover Theological Seminary, Mass., 1858; became pastor of First Church, Chelsea, Mass., 1858; and of Walnut-avenue Church, Boston Highlands, Mass., 1872.

PLUMMER, Alfred, D.D. (Durham, 1882), Church of England; b. at Heworth parsonage, on the Tyne, Feb. 17, 1841; was Gifford exhibitioner of Exeter College, Oxford; first-class in moderations in 1861; graduated B.A. (second-class classics) 1863, M.A. (of Trinity College) 1866; ordained deacon, 1866; fellow of Trinity College, 1864-74; tutor and dean, 1867-74; master of the schools, 1868; pro-proctor, 1873; master of University College, Durham, 1874; senior proctor, 1877. In June, 1871, he bore the degree of D.D. by diploma sent by the University of Oxford to Dr. von Döllinger, one of whose last students he had been (1870 and 1872), and whom he had met at the Bonn re-union conferences of 1874 and 1875. Dr. Plummer translated Döllinger's *Fables respecting the Popes*, London, 1871; *Prophecies and* *the Prophetic Spirit*, 1873; and *Hippolytus and Callistus*, Edinburgh, 1876 (each with additional original matter); and has also published *Intemperate Criticism*, Durham, 1879; and written on *SS. Peter* and *Jude*, in Ellicott's *Commentary*, London, 1879; on *St. John's Gospel* (1880, 2d ed. 1884) and *Epistles* (1883), in *The Cambridge Bible;* on *St. John's Gospel*, in *Cambridge Greek Testament*, 1882; and the *Historical Introduction* in *The Pulpit Commentary*, London, 1880.

PLUMPTRE, Very Rev. Edward Hayes, D.D. (Glasgow, 1875), Church of England; b. in London, Aug. 6, 1821; was scholar of University College, Oxford; graduated B.A. (double first-class) 1844, M.A. 1847. He was fellow of Brasenose College. 1844-47; assistant preacher at Lincoln's Inn, 1851-58; select preacher at Oxford, 1851-53, 1864-66, 1872-73; chaplain of King's College, London, 1847-68; professor of pastoral theology there, 1853-63; dean of Queen's College, London, 1855-75; prebendary of Portpool, in St. Paul's Cathedral, 1863-81; professor of exegesis in King's College, London, 1863-81; examining chaplain to the bishop of Gloucester and Bristol, 1865-67; Boyle lecturer, 1866-67; rector of Pluckley, Kent, 1869-73; Grinfield lecturer on the Septuagint at Oxford, 1872-74; examiner in school of theology at Oxford, 1872-73; vicar of Bickley, Kent, 1873-81; principal of Queen's College, London, 1875-77; examining chaplain to the late archbishop of Canterbury, 1879-82. On Dec. 21, 1881, he was installed dean of Wells. He was a member of the Old-Testament company of revisers, 1870-74. He has been a frequent contributor to theological and literary journals. In Smith's *Dictionaries* he wrote many articles; for *The Bible* (*Speaker's*) *Commentary* he wrote the comments on *The Book of Proverbs* (1873); for Bishop Ellicott's *New-Testament Commentary for English Readers*, those on the first three Gospels, the *Acts*, and *Second Corinthians* (1877); for the same's *Old-Testament Commentary*, those on *Isaiah*, *Jeremiah*, and *Lamentations* (1883-84); for *The Cambridge Bible*, those on *Ecclesiastes, James, Peter*, and *Jude*, and for Dr. Schaff's *Popular Commentary on the New Testament*, those on *First* and *Second Timothy* (1883). He edited *The Bible Educator*, 1875. He has likewise published *The Calling of a Medical Student* (4 sermons), 1849; *The Study of Theology and the Ministry of Souls* (3 sermons), 1853; *King's College Sermons*, 1860; *Dangers Past and Present*, 1862; *Sophocles* (translation), 1865, 2d ed. 1867; *Æschylus* (translation), 1868; *St. Paul in Asia Minor and the Syrian Antioch*, 1877; *The Epistles to the Seven Churches*, 1877, 2d ed. 1879; *Movements in Religious Thought*, 1879; *Biblical Studies*, 1870, 4th ed. 1884; *Introduction to the New Testament*, 1883; *Things New and Old*, 1884; *Theology and Life* (sermons), 1884; *Spirits in Prison, and other Studies on Life after Death*, 1884, 3d thousand 1885; *Life and Letters of Thomas Kerr, Bishop of Bath and Wells*, 1886.

PLUNKET, Right Hon. and Most Rev. William Conyngham, Lord, D.D. (Trinity College, Dublin, 1876), lord archbishop of Dublin, Glendalough, and Kildare, Church of Ireland, second son of Lord Plunket; b. in Dublin, Ireland, in the year 1828; succeeded to the title on the death of his father in 1871; graduated B.A. at Trinity College, Dublin, 1853, M.A. 1864; was ordained deacon 1857, priest 1858; was rector of Kilmoylan and Cummer, Tuam, 1858-64; chaplain and private secretary to the bishop of Tuam, and treasurer of St. Patrick's Cathedral, Dublin, 1864-67; precentor of St. Patrick's, 1869-77; consecrated lord bishop of Meath, 1876; translated to archbishopric of Dublin, 1884.

POOR, Daniel Warren, D.D. (College of New Jersey, Princeton, 1857), Presbyterian; b. at Tillipally, Ceylon, Aug. 21, 1818; graduated at Amherst (Mass.) College, 1837; studied the next two years in Andover (Mass.) Theological Seminary; was pastor (Congregational) at Fairhaven, Mass., 1843-49; Newark, N.J. (Presbyterian), 1849-69; and at Oakland, Cal., 1869-71; professor of church history in the San Francisco (Cal.) Theological Seminary, 1871-76; and since has been corresponding secretary of the Presbyterian Board of Education, Philadelphia. He translated and edited, in connection with Dr. Wing, Kling's commentary on *Corinthians* in the American edition of Lange, New York, 1868.

POPE, William Burt, D.D. (Edinburgh, 1876), Methodist; b. at Horton, N.S., Feb. 19, 1822; studied theology at Richmond College, Eng.; from 1841 to 1867 was a Methodist pastor; and since 1867 has been professor of theology in Didsbury College, Manchester. In 1877 he was president of the British Wesleyan Conference. He is the author of a translation of Stier's *Words of the Lord Jesus, and of the Risen Saviour*, Edinburgh, 10 vols.; also of *Discourses on the Kingdom and Reign of Christ*, London, 1869; *Person of Christ* (Fernley Lecture), 1st and 2d ed. 1875; *A Compendium of Christian Theology*, 1875-76, 3 vols.; *The Prayers of St. Paul*, 1876; *Discourses, chiefly on Lordship of the Incarnate Redeemer*, 1st to 3d ed. 1880; *Sermons, Addresses, and Charges of a Year*, 1878; *A Higher Catechism of Theology*, 1883, 2d ed. 1884.

PORTER, Josias Leslie, D.D. (Edinburgh, 1864), **LL.D.** (Glasgow, 1864), **D.Litt.** (Queen's University, Ireland, 1881), Presbyterian; b. at Burt, County Donegal, Ireland, Oct. 4, 1823; graduated at Glasgow, B.A. 1842, M.A. 1843; studied theology at the Free Church College and University, both Edinburgh, 1843-45; in the Presbyterian Church of England, pastor at Newcastle-on-Tyne, 1846-49; missionary of the Presbyterian Church of Ireland in Damascus, 1849-59; professor of biblical criticism in the Assembly's College, Belfast, Ireland, 1860-77; appointed by the British Parliament commissioner of education in Ireland, 1878; and by the Queen, president of Queen's College, Belfast, and senator of the Queen's University, 1879; and in 1880 senator of the Royal University of Ireland. He was moderator of the Irish General Assembly, 1875; was largely engaged in preparing the great scheme of intermediate education in Ireland, 1878-79, and in framing the constitution and the educational courses of the Royal University, 1881-84. He has travelled very extensively in Palestine, Syria, Arabia, Asia Minor, Turkey, Egypt, North Africa, Europe, and America, 1849-80. He is the author of *Five Years in Damascus, with Travels and Researches in Lebanon, Palmyra, and Hauran*, London, 1855, 2 vols., 2d ed. 1870; *Hand-book for Syria and Palestine* (Murray's), 1858, 2 vols., 3d ed. 1875; *The Pentateuch and the Gospels*, Edinburgh, 1864; *The Giant Cities of Bashan, and Holy Places of*

Syria, 1865; *The Life and Times of Henry Cooke, D.D., LL.D.* (his father-in-law), London, 1871, 3d ed. Belfast, 1877; *The Pew and Study Bible*, 1876; numerous articles in the *Bibliotheca Sacra*, Andover, U.S.A.; *Journal of Sacred Literature*, London; Smith's *Dictionary of the Bible;* Kitto's *Cyclopædia of Biblical Literature*, ed. W. L. Alexander; *Encyclopædia Britannica*, 8th ed.; numerous pamphlets, reviews, and lectures. He edited *Kitto's Bible Readings*, Edinburgh, 1866; and *Brown's Bible*, London. 1873.

PORTER, Noah, D.D. (University of New-York City 1858, Edinb. 1886), **LL.D.** (Western Reserve College, O., 1870; Trinity College, Hartford, Conn., 1871), Congregationalist; b. at Farmington, Conn., Dec. 14, 1811; graduated at Yale College, New Haven, Conn., 1831; was master of Hopkins Grammar School, New Haven, 1831–33; tutor at Yale, 1833–35; pastor at New Milford, Conn., 1836–43; at Springfield, Mass., 1843–46; Clark professor of metaphysics and moral philosophy at Yale College, 1846–71; president of Yale College, 1871–86. He is the author of *Historical Discourse at Farmington, Nov. 4, 1840* (commemorating two-hundredth anniversary of its settlement), Hartford, 1841; *The Educational Systems of the Puritans and Jesuits compared*, New York, 1851; *The Human Intellect*, 1868, 3d ed. 1876; *Books and Reading*, 1870, 6th ed. 1881; *American Colleges and the American Public*, 1870, 2d ed. 1878; *Elements of Intellectual Science*, 1871, 2d ed. 1876; *Sciences of Nature versus the Science of Man*, 1871; *Evangeline: the Place, the Story, and the Poem*, 1882; *Science and Sentiment*, 1882; *The Elements of Moral Science, Theoretical and Practical*, 1885; *Bishop Berkeley*, 1885; *Kant's Ethics, a Critical Exposition*, Chicago, 1886. He was the principal editor of the revised editions of Webster's *Unabridged Dictionary*, Springfield, Mass., 1864 and 1880.

POST, George Edward, M.D. (University of New-York City, 1860), Presbyterian; b. in New-York City, Dec. 17, 1838; graduated at the New-York Free Academy (now the College of the City of New York), 1854; studied medicine; graduated at the Union Theological Seminary, New-York City, 1861; was chaplain in the United-States Army, 1861–63; from 1863 till 1868 was a missionary at Tripoli, Syria; and since has been professor of surgery in the Protestant College at Beirut. He contributed to the American edition of Smith's *Dictionary of the Bible*, and is an authority in biblical natural history.

POTTER, Right Rev. Henry Codman, D.D. (Union College, Schenectady, N.Y., 1865; Trinity College, Hartford, Conn., 1883), **LL.D.** (Union College, Schenectady, N.Y., 1881), Episcopalian, assistant bishop of New York; b. at Schenectady, N.Y., May 25, 1835; graduated from the Protestant-Episcopal Theological Seminary of Virginia, 1857; became rector of Christ Church, Greensburgh, Penn., 1857; St. John's Church, Troy, N.Y., 1859; assistant minister of Trinity Church, Boston, 1866; rector of Grace Church, New-York City, 1868; assistant bishop of New York (with the right of succession), October, 1883. He has published *Sisterhoods and Deaconesses at Home and Abroad*, New York, 1871; *Gates of the East, a Winter in Egypt and Syria*, 1876; *Sermons of the City*, 1881.

POTTER, Right Rev. Horatio, D.D. (Trinity College, Hartford, Conn., 1838), **LL.D.** (Hobart College, Geneva, N.Y., 1856), **D.C.L.** (Oxford, 1860), Episcopalian, bishop of New York; b. at Beekman (now Lagrange), Dutchess County, N.Y., Feb. 9, 1802; graduated at Union College, Schenectady, N.Y., 1820; was rector at Saco, Me., 1828–33; at St. Peter's, Albany, 1833–54; provisional bishop of New York 1854–61, bishop 1861. He has published numerous sermons, charges, etc. *

POWER, Frederick Dunglison, Disciple; b. near Yorktown, York County, Va., Jan. 23, 1851; graduated at Bethany College, Bethany, W. Va., 1871; became pastor at Charlottesville, Va., 1874; adjunct professor of ancient languages, Bethany College, 1874; pastor Vermont-avenue Christian Church, Washington, D.C. (the late President Garfield's church), 1875. He was chaplain of the Forty-seventh Congress.

PRATT, Lewellyn, D.D. (Williams College, Williamstown, Mass., 1877), Congregationalist; b. in Essex, Conn., Aug. 8, 1832; graduated at Williams College, Williamstown, Mass., 1852; became professor of natural science, National College, Washington, D.C., 1865; of Latin, Knox College, Galesburg, Ill., 1869; pastor at North Adams, Mass., 1871; professor of rhetoric at Williams College, 1876; professor of practical theology at Hartford (Conn.) Theological Seminary, 1880. He has published various magazine and review articles.

PREGER, Johann Wilhelm, D.D. (Erlangen, 1874), German Protestant; b. at Schweinfurt, Aug. 25, 1827; studied at Erlangen and Berlin; became professor in the Munich Protestant preachers' seminary, 1850; and since 1851 has been professor of religion and history in the Munich gymnasium. In 1868 he was elected a member of the Bavarian Academy of Sciences. He is the author of *Die Geschichte der Lehre vom geistlichen Amte auf Grund der Geschichte der Rechtfertigungslehre*, Nördlingen, 1857; *Matthias Flacius Illyricus und seine Zeit*, Erlangen, 1859–61, 2 vols.; *Die Briefe Heinrich Suso's nach ein. Handschrift des XV. Jahrh.*, Leipzig, 1867; *Dantes Matelda*, 1873; *Das Evangelium æternum und Joachim von Floris*, 1874; *Geschichte der deutschen Mystik im Mittelalter*, 1874–81, 2 vols.; *Beiträge zur Geschichte der Waldesier*, München, 1875; *Tractat des David von Augsburg über die Waldesier*, 1878; *Beiträge u. Erörterungen zur Geschichte des Deutschen Reiches in den Jahren 1330–34*, 1880; *Ueber die Anfänge d. kirchenpolitischen Kampfes unter Ludwig dem Baier*, 1882.

PRENTISS, George Lewis, D.D. (Bowdoin College, Brunswick, Me., 1854), Presbyterian; b. at Gorham, Me., May 12, 1816; graduated at Bowdoin College, Brunswick, Me., 1835, and was assistant in Gorham Academy, 1836–37. He studied theology at the universities of Halle and Berlin (1839–41), enjoying the friendship of Tholuck in the former place; and became pastor of the South Trinitarian Church, New Bedford., Mass., April, 1845. In April, 1851, he was installed pastor of the Mercer-street Presbyterian Church, New-York City; resigned on account of ill health in the spring of 1858, and sought rest in Europe for the next two years. On his return, the "Church of the Covenant," Murray Hill, New-York City, was gathered by him; and he remained its pastor from the spring of 1862 until April, 1873, when he resigned to become Skinner and McAlpin professor of pastoral theology, church polity, and mission-work, in Union Theological Seminary, New-York City; and this position he now occupies. Besides numerous sermons, addresses, and articles in periodicals, he has published *A Memoir of Seargent S. Prentiss* (his brother), New York, 1855, 2 vols., new ed. 1879; *A Discourse in Memory of Thomas Harvey Skinner, D.D., LL.D.*, 1871; *The Life and Letters of Elizabeth Prentiss* (his wife), 1882.

PRESSENSÉ, Edmond (Dehault) de, D.D. (*hon.*, Breslau 1869, Montauban 1876, Edinburgh 1884), French Protestant; b. in Paris, Jan. 21, 1824; studied arts at the University of Paris; theology under Vinet at Lausanne (1842–45), and under Tholuck and Neander at Halle and Berlin (1846–47); was pastor of the Free Evangelical Congregation of the Taitbout at Paris, 1847–70; deputy to the National Assembly from the Department of the Seine, 1871–76; elected a life senator of France, 1883. He is president of the Synodical Commission of the Free Church of France, in whose organization he took a prominent part, and active in the Evangelical Alliance and in the evangelization of France. He is a chevalier of the Legion of Honor. Since 1854 he has edited the *Revue chrétienne*, Paris, which he founded. Of his numerous publications may be mentioned, *Conférences sur le christianisme dans son application aux questions sociales*, Paris, 1849; *Du catholicisme en France*, 1851; *Le Rédempteur*, 1854, 2d ed. 186– (English trans., *The Redeemer, Discourses*, Edinburgh, 1864, Boston, 1867; German trans., *Der Erlöser*, Gotha, 1883; also in Swedish and Dutch); *La Famille chrétienne*, 1856, 2d ed. 18— (German trans., Leipzig, 1864); *Histoire des trois premiers siècles de l'Eglise chrétienne*, 1858–77, 4 vols. (German trans. by Ed. Fabarius, Leipzig, 1862–78, 6 parts; English trans. by Annie Harwood, London and New York, 1869–78, 4 vols.); *Discours religieux*, 1859; *L'Ecole critique et Jésus Christ*, 1863; *Le pays de l'Evangile*, 1864, 3d ed. 187– (English trans., *The Land of the Gospel, Notes of a Journey in the East*, London, 1865); *L'Eglise et la Révolution française*, 1864, 2d ed. 1867 (English trans., *Religion and the Reign of Terror; or, The Church during the French Revolution*, trans. by J. P. Lacroix, New York, 1868; by T. Stroyan, London, 1869); *Jésus Christ, son temps, sa vie, son œuvre*, 1866, 7th ed. 1884 (English trans. by Annie Harwood, London, 1866, 4th ed. 1871; German trans. by Ed. Fabarius, Halle, 1866); *Etudes évangéliques*, 1867–68, 2 series (English trans. by Annie Harwood, *Mystery of Suffering, and other Discourses*, London, 1868; German trans., *Evangelische Studien*, Halle, 1869, 2d ed. 1884); *La vraie Liberté* (four discourses), 1869; *Rome and Italy at the Opening of the Œcumenical Council* (trans. from the French), New York, 1870; *Le Concile du Vatican, son histoire et ses conséquences politiques et religieuses*, 1872 (German trans. by Ed. Fabarius, *Das Vaticanische Concil*, Nördlingen, 1872); *La liberté religieuse en Europe depuis 1870*, 1874; *Le devoir*, 1875; *La question ecclésiastique en 1877*, 1878; *L'apostolat missionnaire*, 1879; *Etudes contemporaines*, 1880 (English trans. by A. H. Holmden, *Contemporary Portraits*, New York, 1880); *Les origines*, 1882 (English trans., *Study of Origins; Problems of Being and Duty*, London, 1883; German trans. by Ed. Fabarius, *Die Ursprünge*, Halle, 1884).

PRESTON, Thomas Scott, Roman Catholic; b. at Hartford, Conn., July 23, 1824; graduated at Trinity College, Hartford, Conn., 1843; entered the Protestant-Episcopal ministry, 1846; became a Roman Catholic, 1849, and priest 1850; domestic prelate of his Holiness, 1881; and is now vicar-general and chancellor of the diocese of New York, and parish priest of St. Ann's. He is the author of *Ark of the Covenant, Discourses upon the Joys, Sorrows, and Glories of the Mother of God*, New York, 1860; *Life of Mary Magdalen*, 1861; *Sermons for the Seasons*, 1864; *Lectures on Christian Unity*, 1866; *Purgatorian Manual*, 1867; *Reason and Revelation*, 1868; *Christ and the Church*, 1870; *Lectures upon the Devotion to the Sacred Heart of Jesus Christ*, 18—; *The Vicar of Christ*, 18—; *The Divine Sanctuary: Series of Meditation upon the Most Sacred Heart of Jesus*, 1878; *Divine Paraclete*, 1880; *Protestantism and the Bible*, 1880; *Protestantism and the Church*, 1882; *God and Reason*, 1884; *Watch on Calvary*, 1885. *

PRIME, Edward Dorr Griffin, D.D. (Jefferson College, Canonsburg, Penn., 1857), Presbyterian; b. at Cambridge, N.Y., Nov. 2, 1814; graduated at Union College, Schenectady, N.Y., 1832, and at Princeton (N.J.) Theological Seminary, 1838; was pastor at Scotchtown, N.Y., 1839–51; American chaplain at Rome, winter of 1854–55; since 1853 has been co-editor of *The New-York Observer*. He has published *Around the World*, New York, 1872 (several editions); *Forty Years in the Turkish Empire* (memoirs of Dr. William Goodell), 1875, 6th ed. 1883.

PRIME, Samuel Irenæus, D.D. (Hampden Sidney College, Va., 1854) Presbyterian; b. at Ballston, Saratoga County, N.Y., Nov. 4, 1812; d. while on a vacation trip, at Manchester, Vt., Saturday, July 18, 1885. He was educated in the academy at Cambridge, N.Y., and at Williams College, Williamstown, Mass.; graduated from the latter, 1829; and studied theology at Princeton (N.J.) Theological Seminary, 1832–33. He ever afterwards remained a firm friend and active supporter of his literary and of his theological alma mater. He was pastor at Ballston Spa 1833–35, and at Matteawan, N.J., 1837–40. He became editor of *The New-York Observer* in 1840, and continued to occupy this position till his death, being at the same time the chief proprietor of this old and influential family paper, which is read in all parts of the United States, as well as in many reading-rooms of Europe. He was for some time corresponding secretary and one of the directors of the American Bible Society, corresponding secretary of the Evangelical Alliance, president of Wells College, and a trustee of Williams College. He took an active and leading part in all the affairs of the Presbyterian Church, and in the Christian and philanthropic enterprises of the age. He repeatedly visited Europe. He wrote a number of books which had an extraordinary circulation at home and abroad (see list below). Among these we mention *Travels in Europe and the East; The Bible in the Levant; The Alhambra and the Kremlin; Life of Samuel F. B. Morse*; the *Irenæus Letters* (from *The New-York Observer*); and especially the *Power of Prayer* (1859, enlarged 1873), and *Prayer and its Answer* (1882). The *Irenæus Letters* are unique, and show an extraordinary faculty of clothing every-day topics and experiences with a fresh interest, and extracting from them lessons of practical wisdom. He left a third series, of an autobiographical character, which were published after his death (in *The New-York Observer*, 1886).

Dr. Prime was an indefatigable worker till within a few days of his death; and hardly a week passed without one of his *Irenæus Letters*, so highly prized by the readers of the *Observer*. His health, however, began to fail some years before his death.

With the Evangelical Alliance of America, founded in 1866, he was closely identified almost from the beginning. He attended the fifth General Conference at Amsterdam in 1867, read there the report on Religion in America, prepared by the late Dr. Henry B. Smith, and extended an invitation to the European Alliances to hold the sixth General Conference in the city of New York. The invitation was cordially accepted. On his return from Europe, he was elected one of the corresponding secretaries of the American Alliance, and served it in that capacity without any compensation till Jan. 28, 1884. He took a very prominent share in the preparations for the great New-York Conference, which, after two vexatious postponements, was held in the autumn of 1873. It is still well remembered as the first international and inter-continental religious meeting in America, and its influence for good reached every country on the globe. He advocated the cause of the Alliance, — which is the cause of Christian union and religious liberty, — in *The Observer*, and at many public meetings. He was very active in the anti-Romish controversy.

Dr. Prime was a wise counsellor, a man of an uncommon amount of common-sense, executive ability, and sound judgment, of quick wit, rich humor, and a hopeful temperament. He was eloquent in speech, and had a fluent, easy, and racy pen. Possessed of a generous heart, strong convictions, and large catholicity, he was one of the leaders of public opinion, and, altogether, one of the most untiring and useful writers and workers of his age and country. His genial humor, generous sympathy, and inexhaustible fund of illustrations and anecdotes, made him one of the most agreeable of friends and companions; and his company will long be missed in the social circles which he used to grace and delight with his presence.

On account of growing infirmities, he resigned his active secretaryship of the Evangelical Alliance, Jan. 28, 1884; but continued to attend the meetings regularly, and accepted the appointment of honorary corresponding secretary, which was offered him unanimously at the seventeenth annual meeting, Jan. 26, 1885. After his death a special meeting was called on Monday, July 27, where a suitable paper, prepared by Dr. King, was presented, adopted, and entered on the minutes. And on Tuesday, Jan. 5, 1886, an interesting memorial service in his honor was held at Association Hall, New-York City, in which Rev. Drs. R. S. Storrs (Congregationalist), E. Bright (Baptist), and J. M. Buckley (Methodist) made appreciative addresses to a large representative audience. See report in *The New-York Observer*, Jan. 14, 1886.

Many of his publications were anonymous; but he was the acknowledged author of the following volumes, most if not all of which have passed through several editions: *The Old White Meeting-house, or Reminiscences of a Country Congregation*, New York, 1845; *Life in New York*, 1845; *Annals of the English Bible, abridged from Anderson, and continued to the Present Time*, 1849; *Thoughts on the Death of Little Children*, 1850; *Travels in Europe and the East*, 1885; *Power of Prayer* (history of the Fulton-street prayer-meeting, New-York City), 1859; *The Bible in the Levant; or, the Life and Letters of the Rev. C. N. Righter, Agent of the American Bible Society in the Levant*, 1859; *Letters from Switzerland*, 1860; *Memoirs of the Rev. Nicholas Murray, D.D.* (Kirwan), Boston, 1862; *Five Years of Prayer* [in the Fulton-street prayer-meeting] *with the Answers*, New York, 1864; *Walking with God, Life hid with Christ*, 1872; *Songs of the Soul, gathered out of many Lands and Ages*, 1873; *Alhambra and the Kremlin, Journey from Madrid to Moscow*, 1873; *Fifteen Years of Prayer in the Fulton-street Prayer-meeting*, New York, 1873; *Under the Trees*, 1874; *Life of Samuel F. B. Morse*, 1875; *Prayer and its Answer illustrated in the first Twenty-five Years of the Fulton-street Prayer-meetimg*, 1882; *Irenæus Letters*, 3 series 1882 (with portrait), 1885 (with sketch of Dr. Prime's life), 1886 (containing his autobiography in the form of letters). PHILIP SCHAFF.

PRINS, Johannes Jacobus, D.D. (Leiden, 1838), Dutch theologian; b. at Langezwaag, in the year 1814; studied in Amsterdam and at Leiden; was Reformed pastor at Eemnes-Binnendyks (Utrecht), 1838; Alkmaar and Rotterdam, 1843–55; professor of exegetical and practical theology at Leiden, 1855–76, till 1885 (retired) of N. T. criticism and hermeneutics, and of history of primitive Christian literature, in the same university. He was a member of the synod, university preacher, and is one of the directors of The Hague Society for the Defence of the Christian Religion. He was one of the synodical translators of the New Testament. He is the author of *Disputatio theologica inauguralis de locis Euangelistrarum, in quibus Jesus baptismi ritum subiisse traditur* (his D.D. dissertation), Amsterdam, 1838; and in Dutch of "Manual of Elementary Religious Instruction," 1842; "Manual of Bible Knowledge," 1851, 2 parts; "The Reality of the Resurrection," 1861; "The Lord's Supper in the Corinthian Church of St. Paul's Day," 1868; "Ecclesiastical Law of the Reformed Church of the Netherlands," 1870; "The Epistle to the Galatians," 1878, etc.

PUAUX, François, French Protestant; b. at Vallon Ardèche, Dec. 24, 1806; practised law for a while, but turned to theology, and was pastor successively at Luneray, Rochefort, and Mulhouse. He has been a voluminous author. Among his works may be mentioned, *Anatomie du papisme*, Paris, 1845; *Histoire de la Réformation française*, 1857–64, 7 vols. *

PUENJER, (Georg Christian) Bernhard, Ph.D. (Jena, 1874), **D.D.** (*hon.*, Heidelb., 1883), Protestant theologian; b. at Friedrichsgabekoog, Schleswig-Holstein, June 7, 1850; d. at Jena, May 13, 1885. He was educated at Jena, Erlangen, Zürich, and Kiel, 1870–74; became *privat-docent* in the theological faculty of Jena, 1878; professor extraordinary, 1880. He was the author of *De M. Serveti doctrina*, Jena, 1876; *Geschichte der christlichen Religionsphilosophie seit der Reformation*, Braunschweig, 1880–83, 2 vols.; *Die Aufgaben des heutigen Prot-*

estantismus, Jena, 1885 (pp. 23); and founder and editor of the *Theologischer Jahresbericht*, Leipzig, 1882-85 (now conducted by Professor R. L. Lipsius). *

PULLMAN, James Minton, D.D. (St. Lawrence University, Canton, N.Y., 1879), Universalist; b. at Portland, Chautauqua County, N.Y., Aug. 21, 1836; graduated at St. Lawrence Divinity School, Canton, N.Y., 1860; was pastor First Universalist Church, Troy, N.Y., 1861-68; of Sixth Universalist Church (Our Saviour), New-York City, 1868-85; since 1885 of First Universalist Church, Lynn, Mass. He organized and was first president of the Young Men's Universalist Association of New-York City, 1869; was secretary of the Universalist General Convention, 1868-77, and chairman of the publication board of the New-York State Convention, 1869-74; trustee of St. Lawrence University, Canton, N.Y., 1870-85; president "Children's Country Week," 1883-85; president of the Alumni Association of St. Lawrence University, 1885-86; since 1885, trustee of New-England Conservatory of Music, and president of the Associated Charities of Lynn, Mass. Under him the new Church of Our Saviour, New-York City (dedicated 1874), was built. His theological standpoint is "the ethical interpretation of Christianity, as opposed to the magical interpretation; belief in the perfectibility of man (no evil is remediless); the inexorableness of the Divine love; the complete success of Jesus Christ (here and elsewhere), and the final moral harmony of the universe (evil completely eradicated and overcome)." His publications are sermons, lectures, pamphlets, and review articles.

PUREY-CUST, Very Rev. Arthur Perceval, D.D. (Oxford, 1880), dean of York, Church of England; b. in England, in the month of February, 1828. educated at Brasenose College, Oxford; graduated B.A. 1850, M.A. (All Souls' College) 1854, B.D. 1880; ordained deacon 1851, priest 1852; was fellow of All Souls' College, 1850-54; curate of Northchurch, 1851-53; rector of Cheddington, 1853-62; rural dean of Mursley, 1858-62; vicar of St. Mary, and rural dean of Reading, 1862-75; vicar of Aylesbury, 1875-76; archdeacon of Buckingham, 1875-80; since 1874 he has been honorary canon of Christ Church, Oxford; and since 1880, dean of York.

Q.

QUINTARD, Right Rev. Charles Todd, M.D. (University of the City of New York, 1846), **S.T.D.** (Columbia College, New-York City, 1866), **LL.D.** (Cambridge, Eng., 1867), Episcopalian, bishop of Tennessee; b. at Stamford, Conn., Dec. 22, 1824; appointed physician in New-York Dispensary, 1847; professor of physiology and pathological anatomy in the Medical College, Memphis, Tenn., 1851; ordained deacon 1854, priest 1855; became rector of the Church of the Advent, Nashville, Tenn., 1858; was chaplain in the Confederate army during the civil war; consecrated bishop, 1865; was vice-chancellor of the University of the South, 1866-72. He is the author of occasional sermons, charges, tracts, and letters, and of *Preparation for Confirmation*, New York, 187-.

R.

RADSTOCK, Granville A. W. Waldegrave, lord, Irish peer, lay evangelist, Church of England; b. in England in the year 1833; succeeded to his title in 1857. After graduating from Oxford (Balliol College), he planned a political career for himself; but, being converted, he consecrated his talents and his property to gospel work, and for the past quarter of a century has been a lay evangelist at home and abroad. He carried on an important work among the Russian nobility until his expulsion from the country. He has also labored in Scandinavia. A volume of his addresses was published, London, 1872.

RAEBIGER, Julius Ferdinand, German Protestant; b. at Lohsa, April 20, 1811; studied at Leipzig and Breslau, 1829–34; became *privat-docent* at Breslau, 1838; professor extraordinary, 1847; ordinary professor, 1859. Among his publications may be mentioned, *Ethice librorum apocryphorum V. T.*, Breslau, 1838; *Kritische Untersuchungen über den Inhalt der korinther Briefe*, 1847; *De christologia Paulina contra Baurium commentatio*, 1852; *Theologik oder Encyklopädie der Theologie*, Leipzig, 1880 (English trans., *Encyclopædia of Theology*, Edinburgh, 1885, 2 vols.).

RAINY, Robert, D.D. (Glasgow, 18—, Edinburgh, 18—), Free Church of Scotland; b. in Glasgow, Jan. 1, 1826; graduated at its university, 1843; and studied theology at New College, Edinburgh, completing the course in 1848; became minister of the Free Church at Huntly, 1851; of the Free High Church, Edinburgh, 1854; professor of church history in New College, Edinburgh, 1862; principal, 1874. He is the author of *Three Lectures on the Church of Scotland*, Edinburgh, 1872, 5th ed. 1884; *The Delivery and Development of Christian Doctrine* (Cunningham Lectures), 1874; *The Bible and Criticism*, London, 1878; various pamphlets, and occasional publications.

RALSTON, Thomas Neely, D.D. (Wesleyan University, Florence, Ala., 1857), Methodist Church South; b. in Bourbon County, Ky., March 21, 1806; studied at the Baptist College of Georgetown, Ky., but did not graduate; was received into the Kentucky Conference in 1827; was a member of the General Conference of the Methodist-Episcopal Church at Baltimore in 1840, before the division; member of the Convention at Louisville, Ky., in 1845, which organized the Methodist-Episcopal Church South, and of the general conferences of that church at Petersburg, Va., in 1846 (was secretary), at St. Louis, Mo., in 1850, and at Columbus, Ga., in 1854. He was chairman of the committee to revise the Discipline of the Methodist-Episcopal Church South; was principal of the Methodist Female Collegiate High School at Lexington, Ky., 1843–47. He edited *The Methodist Monthly* (Lexington, Ky.), for 1851. He is the author of *Elements of Divinity*, Louisville, Ky., 1847, several later editions, republished, revised and enlarged by addition of *Evidences, Morals, and Institutions of Christianity* (also published separately, 18—), Nashville, Tenn., 1871, 3d ed. 1875 (the book in its first form was translated into Norwegian, 1858, in its enlarged form into Chinese, 1886); (under pseudonym, "Eureka") *Ecce Unitas; or, A Plea for Christian Unity*, Cincinnati, O., 1875; *Bible Truths*, Nashville, Tenn., 1884.

RAND, William Wilberforce, D.D. (University of the City of New York, 1883), Reformed (Dutch); b. at Gorham, Me., Dec. 8, 1816; graduated at Bowdoin College, Brunswick, Me., 1837, and at Bangor Theological Seminary, Me., 1840; licensed by Waldo Congregational Association, Me., 1840; pastor of the Reformed Dutch Church of Canastota, N.Y., 1841–44; editor of the American Tract Society, New-York City, 1848–72; publishing secretary of the same since 1872. He is the author of *Songs of Zion*, New York, 1851 (88,000 copies printed), revised and enlarged, 1865 (86,000 copies printed); *Dictionary of the Bible for General Use*, 1860 (206,000 copies have been printed), enlarged and largely re-written, 1886; other smaller books.

RANDOLPH, Right Rev. Alfred Magill, D.D. (William and Mary College, Williamsburg, Va., 1875), Episcopalian, assistant bishop of Virginia; b. at Winchester, Frederick County, Va., Aug. 31, 1836; graduated at William and Mary College, Williamsburg, Va., 1855, and at the Theological Seminary of Virginia, 1858; became rector of St. George's, Fredericksburg, Va., 1860; of Emmanuel Church, Baltimore, Md., 1867; bishop, 1875.

RANKE, Ernst, D.D. (*hon.*, Marburg, 1851), **Ph.D.** (Erlangen, 1846), Evangelical German theologian; b. at Wiehe, Thuringia, Sept. 10, 1814; studied at Leipzig (1834), Berlin (1835–36), and Bonn (1836–37); was private tutor in his brother's family, 1837–39; pastor at Buchau, 1840–50; and professor of theology at Marburg, 1850 to date. He is a Lutheran, but favors the union of the Lutheran and Reformed churches. He is *consistorialrath*. He is the author of *Das kirchliche Perikopensystem aus den ältesten Urkunden der römischen Liturgie*, Berlin, 1847; *Das Buch Tobias metrisch übersetzt*, Bayreuth, 1847; *Kritische Zusammenstellung der . . . neuen Pericopenkreise*, 1850; *Der Fortbestand d. herköm. Pericopenkreises*, Gotha, 1859; and editor of *Fragmenta versionis Latinæ antihieronymianæ Prophetarum Hoseæ, Amosi, Michæ, aliorum e cod. mscr. eruit. atque adnotat. crit. instruxit*, Marburg, 1856–58, 2 parts; *Marburger Gesangbuch von 1549 mit verwandten Liederdnecken hrsg. u. historisch-kritisch erläutert*, 1862; *Codex Fuldensis. N. T. lat. . . . prolegomenis introduxit, commentariis adornavit*, 1868; *Par palimpsestorum Wirceburgensium*, Vienna, 1871; *Fragmenta antiq. ev. Lucani ver. Lat.*, 1874; *Chorgesänge zum Preis der h. Elizabeth, aus mittelalterl. Antiphonarien hrsg.*, Leipzig, 1883–84, 2 parts. He has also written poems: *Gedichte*, Erlangen, 1848; *Zuruf au das deutsche Volk*, 1849; *Carmina academica*, Marburg, 1866; *Lieder aus grosser Zeit*, 1870, 2d ed. 1875; *Horæ Lyricæ*, Vienna, 1874; *Die Schlacht im Teutoburger*

Wald, Marburg, 1876; *Rhythmica*, Vienna, 1881; *De Laude Nivis* (a Latin poem), Marburg, 1886.

RANKE, Leopold von, b. at Wiehe, Thuringia, Dec. 21, 1795; d. in Berlin, Sunday, May 23, 1886; studied at Leipzig; was appointed head teacher in the Frankfort (on the Oder) gymnasium in 1818; and since 1825 has been professor of history at the University of Berlin. In 1827 he was sent by the Prussian government to Vienna, Venice, and Rome, to conduct historical researches. In 1841 he was appointed historiographer of Prussia; in 1848, elected a member of the Frankfort National Assembly; and in 1866, ennobled. He was an historian of the first rank, and continued his labors till his ninety-first year. Of those more immediately relating to theological study, which have been translated, may be mentioned, *The History of the Roman and Germanic Peoples, from 1494 to 1535; The Popes of Rome, their Church and their State, especially of the Conflict with Protestantism in the Sixteenth and Seventeenth Century*, 3 vols.; *German History in the Times of the Reformation; A History of England, principally in the Seventeenth Century; French History; Universal History*, vol. 1, trans. 1884 (the sixth part of the *Weltgeschichte*, extending to the death of Otto the Great, appeared in 1885). *

RAUSCHENBUSCH, Augustus, Baptist; b. at Altena, Southern Westphalia, Germany, Feb. 13, 1816; studied at Berlin and Bonn; in 1841 was installed pastor of the Lutheran Church at Altena; in 1850 joined the Baptists in America, and was assistant secretary (for the Germans) of the American Tract Society; then pastor of a German Baptist Church in Gasconade County, Mo.; and in 1858 professor of the German department of the Rochester Theological Seminary. From 1848 to 1866 he was editor of the German monthly paper and the German Almanac of the American Tract Society, and prepared numerous German books and tracts for the society. Since he has largely contributed to the German Baptist weekly paper, *Der Sendbote*, and to several other Baptist periodicals.

RAUWENHOFF, Lodewijk Willem Ernst, D.D. (Leiden, 1852), Dutch theologian; b. at Amsterdam, July 27, 1828; studied theology at Amsterdam and Leiden, 1846-52; became pastor at Mydrecht (Utrecht) 1852, Dordrecht 1856, Leiden 1859; professor in the University of Leiden, 1860; of church history, history of doctrine, and patristics, 1860-81; of theological encyclopædia and philosophy of religion, 1881 to date. With A. Kuenen and A. D. Loman he has, since 1867, edited the *Theologisch Tijdschrift*, Leiden, 1867 sqq. He is the author of *De loco Paulino qui est de Δικαίωσει* (his D.D. dissertation), Leiden, 1852; and in Dutch of "Christian Independence," Dordrecht, 1857; "The Heroes of History," 1862; "History of Protestantism," 1865-71, 3 vols.; "The Old Faith and the New" (against Strauss), 1873 (German trans. by F. Nippold, Leipzig, 1873); "State and Church," 1875; and numerous articles in different periodicals.

RAWLINSON, George, Church of England; b. at Chadlington, Oxfordshire, Eng., Nov. 23, 1815; entered Trinity College, Oxford; wrote the Denyer theological prize essay in 1842 and 1843; graduated B.A. (first-class in classics) 1838, M.A. (Exeter College) 1841; ordained deacon 1841, priest 1842; was fellow of Exeter College, 1840-46; tutor, 1842-46; sub-rector, 1844-45; curate of Merton, Oxfordshire, 1846-47; classical moderator at Oxford, 1852-54; public examiner, 1855-57, 1868-79, 1875-79; Bampton lecturer, 1859. Since 1861 he has been Camden professor of ancient history to the university; since 1872, a canon of Canterbury; since 1873, proctor in convocation. Canon Rawlinson is a moderate High Churchman, but anxious in no way to narrow the liberty of opinion which has historically been claimed and allowed within the Anglican communion. In politics he is a moderate (or Conservative) Liberal. He supported Mr. Gladstone in all his Oxford contests, and received his canonry from the Crown on the recommendation of Mr. Gladstone as prime minister. In the elections of 1885, however, he found himself unable to support the (advanced) Liberal candidates. He is well known as a speaker in the Convocation of Canterbury, at church congresses, and elsewhere. Besides numerous articles in reviews and magazines (*Contemporary, Princeton*, etc), in Smith's *Dictionary of the Bible*, Cassell's *Bible Educator*, and in ninth edition *Encyclopædia Britannica*, commentaries on *Kings, Ezra, Nehemiah*, and *Esther* in *The Bible (Speaker's) Commentary* (1872-73), on *Exodus* in Bishop Ellicott's *Commentary* (1882), and on *Exodus, Ezra, Nehemiah*, and *Esther* in *The Pulpit Commentary* (1880-82), he is the author of *The History of Herodotus*, a new English version with copious notes (in conjunction with Sir Henry Rawlinson and Sir Gardner Wilkinson), London, 1858-60, 4 vols., 5th ed. 1881; *The Historical Evidences of the Truth of the Scripture Records* (Bampton lectures), 1859, 2d ed. 1860; *The Contrasts of Christianity with Heathen and Jewish Systems* (in nine sermons), 1861; *The Five Great Monarchies of the Ancient Eastern World*, 1862-67, 4 vols., 2d ed. 1870; *A Manual of Ancient History*, Oxford, 1870, 2d ed. 1880; *Historical Illustrations of the Old Testament*, London, 1871; *The Sixth Great Oriental Monarchy* (Parthia), 1873; *The Seventh* (the Sassanians), 1876; *St. Paul in Damascus and Arabia*, 1877; *The Origin of Nations*, 1878; *A History of Egypt*, 1881, 2 vols.; *The Religions of the Ancient World*, 1882; *Egypt and Babylon from Scripture and Profane Sources*, 1884.

RAYMOND, Miner, D.D. (Wesleyan University, Middletown, Conn., 1854), **LL.D.** (North-western University, Evanston, Ill., 1884), Methodist; b. in New-York City, Aug. 29, 1811; educated at the Wesleyan Academy, Wilbraham, Mass.; became teacher in the same, 1834; received honorary M.A. from Wesleyan University, 1840; pastor in Massachusetts (Worcester, Boston, and Westfield), 1841; principal of the Wesleyan Academy, 1848; professor of systematic theology in Garrett Biblical Institute, Evanston, Ill., 1864. He has been a member of six general conferences. He published a *Systematic Theology*, Cincinnati, O., 1877, 3 vols.

REDFORD, Robert Ainslie, Congregationalist; b. at Worcester, Eng., March 21, 1828; studied at Glasgow University, Spring Hill College, Birmingham; and graduated at London University, M.A. 1852, LL.B. 1862; was pastor of Congregational Church at Newcastle-on-Tyne, 1853-55; Hull, 1855-73; Streatham Hill, London, 1873-76; since 1876, of Union Church, Putney, London;

since 1873 he has been professor of systematic theology and apologetics in New College, London. He is the author of *Sermons*, London, 1869; *The Christian's Plea against Modern Unbelief, a Handbook of Christian Evidence*, 1881, 2d ed. 1882; *Prophecy, its Nature and Evidence*, 1882; *The Authority of Scripture*, 1883; *Studies in the Book of Jonah*, 1883; *Primer of Christian Evidence*, 1884; *Four Centuries of Silence, or from Malachi to Christ*, 1885; has contributed to commentaries upon *Genesis, Leviticus, Nehemiah*, and *Acts*, in *Pulpit Commentary*, 1881 sqq.

REED, Villeroy Dibble, D.D. (Union College, Schenectady, N.Y., 1858), Presbyterian; b. at Granville, Washington County, N.Y., April 27, 1815; graduated at Union College, Schenectady, N.Y., 1835; studied at Auburn (N.Y.) and Princeton (N.J.) Theological Seminaries, 1835–36; was pastor at Stillwater, N.Y., 1839–44; Lansingburgh, N.Y., 1844–58; president of Alexander College, Dubuque, Io., 1858; stated supply at Buffalo, N.Y., 1858–60; Cohoes, N.Y., 1860–61; pastor at Camden, N.J., 1861–84. He was appointed in 1866 one of the Old School Assembly's Committee of fifteen on Re-union, and was its secretary. He has been president of the Presbyterian Board of Ministerial Relief from its organization in 1876. He has published only occasional sermons.

REICHEL, Right Rev. Charles Parsons, D.D. (Trinity College, Dublin, 1858), lord bishop of Meath, Church of Ireland; b. at Fulnec, near Leeds, Yorkshire, Eng., in the year 1816; was scholar of Trinity College, Dublin, Ireland, 1841; graduated B.A. (senior moderator classics) 1843, divinity testimonium (first-class) 1844, M.A. 1847, B.D. 1853; was ordained deacon and priest, 1846; was professor of Latin, Queen's College, Belfast, 1850–64; Donellan lecturer at Trinity College, Dublin, 1854; vicar of Mullingar, 1864–75; rector of Trim, and archdeacon of Meath, 1875–85; select preacher at Cambridge, Eng., 1876 and 1883, and at Oxford 1880–82; professor of ecclesiastical history, Trinity College, Dublin, 1878; prebendary of Tipper, and canon of St. Patrick's Cathedral, Dublin; dean of Clonmacnois, 1882–85; consecrated bishop, 1885. He is a member of the Senate of Trinity College, Dublin. He is the author of *The Nature and Offices of the Church* (Donellan Lectures), London, 1856; *Sermons on the Lord's Prayer; Lectures on the Prayer-book; Sermons on Modern Infidelity*, London, 1864; *The Resurrection, God or Baal* (two sermons), 1878; *Origins of Christianity*, etc., *Sermons before the Universities of Oxford and Dublin*, 1882; *Short Treatises on the Ordinal;* and a number of occasional discourses.

REID, John Morrison, D.D. (University of the City of New York, 1858), **LL.D.** (Syracuse University, N.Y., 1883), Methodist; b. in New-York City, May 30, 1820; graduated at the University of the City of New York, 1839; became principal of Mechanics Institute School of the city, 1839–44; Methodist pastor, 1844; president of Genesee College, Lima, N.Y., 1858; editor of *Western Christian Advocate*, Cincinnati, O., 1864; of *Northwestern Christian Advocate*, Chicago, 1868; corresponding secretary of the Missionary Society of the Methodist-Episcopal Church, New-York City, 1872. He is the author of *Missions and Missionary Societies of the Methodist-Episcopal Church*, New York, 1879, 2 vols.; (editor of) *Doomed Religions*, 1884; multitudinous tracts, magazine and other articles.

REID, William James, D.D. (Monmouth College, Ill., 1874), United Presbyterian; b. at South Argyle, Washington County, N.Y., Aug. 17, 1834; graduated at Union College, Schenectady, N.Y., 1855, and at Allegheny (U.P.) Theological Seminary, Penn., 1862; has been pastor of the First United Presbyterian Church, Pittsburg, Penn., since 1862; principal clerk of the General Assembly of the United Presbyterian Church since 1875; was corresponding secretary of the United Presbyterian Board of Home Missions, 1868–72. He is the author of *Lectures on the Revelation*, Pittsburg, Penn., 1878; *United Presbyterianism*, 1881, 2d ed. 1883; various sermons and pamphlets.

REIMENSNYDER, Junius Benjamin, D.D. (Newberry College, Newberry, S.C., 1880), Lutheran (General Synod); b. at Staunton, Va., Feb. 24, 1842; graduated at Pennsylvania College, Gettysburg, Penn., 1861, and at the Gettysburg Theological Seminary, 1865; became pastor at Lewistown, Penn., 1865; Philadelphia (St. Luke's), 1867; Savannah, Ga. (Ascension), 1874; New-York City (St. James), 1881. He was delegate to General Council of the Lutheran Church, Jamestown, N.Y., 1874; to General Synod (South), Staunton, Va., 1876, and Newberry, S.C., 1878; to General Council (North) from General Synod (South), bearing fraternal greetings, Bethlehem, Penn., 1876; to General Synod (North), Springfield, O., 1883, and Harrisburg, Penn., 1885. He is the author of *Heavenward, or the Race for the Crown of Life*, Philadelphia, 1874, 4th ed. 1877; *Christian Unity* (sermon), Savannah, Ga., 1875; *Duelling* (sermon), 1878; *Doom Eternal, the Bible and Church Doctrine of Everlasting Punishment*, Philadelphia, 1880; *Spiritualism* (sermon), New York, 1882; *Lutheran Literature, Distinctive Traits and Excellencies*, 1883; *Luther, Work and Personality of, Biographical Sketch*, 1883; *Usefulness after Death* (sermon), New York, 1885; *Six Days of Creation, Lectures on the Mosaic Account of the Creation, Fall, and Deluge*, Philadelphia, 1886.

REINKENS, Joseph Hubert, D.D. (Munich, 1850), Old-Catholic bishop; b. at Burtscheid, near Aachen, Prussia, March 1, 1821; became priest, 1848; *privat-docent* at Breslau, 1850; professor extraordinary, 1853; ordinary professor, 1857. He joined Döllinger in the Nuremburg declaration (Aug. 26, 27, 1870) against the infallibility dogma; and on Aug. 11, 1873, was ordained an Old-Catholic bishop, with his residence at Bonn. He is the author of *De Clemente presbytero Alexandrino*, Breslau, 1851; *Hilarius von Poitiers*, Schaffhausen, 1864; *Martin von Tours*, 1866; *Die Geschichtsphilosophie des h. Augustinus*, 1866; *Papst und Papstthum*, Münster, 1870; *Die päpstlichen Dekrete vom 18 Juli, 1870*, 1871; *Revolution und Kirche*, Bonn, 1876 (3 editions); *Ueber Einheit der katholischen Kirche*, Würzburg, 1877; *Melchior von Diepenbrock*, Leipzig, 1881; *Lessing über Toleranz*, 1883.

REISCHLE, Max Wilhelm Theodor, German Protestant; b. in Vienna, June 18, 1858; educated at the theological seminary ("Stift") at Tübingen, 1876–80, and at Berlin and Göttingen, 1882–83; was vicar at Gmünd, 1881–82; *repetent* at Tübingen since 1883. He belongs to the school of Ritschl.

RENAN, Joseph Ernst, b. at Tréguier, Côtes du Nord, Feb. 27, 1823; was educated at the Seminary of St. Sulpice, Paris, where he studied with avidity Hebrew, Arabic, and Syriac, but abandoned the intention of becoming a priest. In 1845 his *Étude de la langue grecque au moyen âge*, was crowned by the institute. In 1848 he gained the Volney prize for a memoir upon the Shemitic languages by his *Histoire générale et systèmes comparés des langues Sémitiques*, 1855, 2d ed. 1858, 2 vols. In 1848 he was sent by the Académie des Inscriptions to Italy; in 1856, elected a member; in 1860, sent on a mission to Syria; in 1862, appointed professor of Hebrew at the College of France; in 1863, published his *Life of Jesus*; was in consequence dismissed from his professorship, and not re-instated until 1870. In 1860 he was appointed to the Legion of Honor; in July, 1884, made a commander. In 1878 he was elected a member of the French Academy; in April, 1881, director; in June, 1883, vice-rector (manager) of the College of France. Of his works may be mentioned, translations of *Job* (1859), *Song of Songs* (1860), *Ecclesiastes* (1882); essays, *Essais de morale et de critique*, 1853, 3d ed. 1867; *Études d'histoire religieuse*, 1857, 7th ed. 1864 (English trans. by O. B. Frothingham, *Studies of Religious History and Criticism*, New York, 1864); his collaboration on vol. xxiv. of *Histoire littéraire de la France*, Orientalia, *Mission en Phénice*, 1865-74, *Rapport sur les progrès de la littérature orientale et sur les ouvrages relatifs à l'Orient*, 1868; *Corpus inscriptionum semiticarum*, 1881 sqq. Of more general interest are his *Averroès et l'averroïsme*, 1852, 2d ed. 1860; *Les dialogues philosophiques*, 1876; *Caliban*, 1878; and especially the remarkable series upon the "Histoire des origines du christianisme," *Vie de Jésus* (1863), *Les Apôtres* (1866), *Saint Paul et sa mission* (1869), *L'Antéchrist* (1871), *Les évangiles et la seconde génération chrétienne* (1877), *L'Église chrétienne* (1879), *Marc Aurèle et la fin du monde antique* (1881); the Hibbert lectures for 1880: *The Influence of the Institutions, Thought, and Culture of Rome on Christianity and the Development of the Catholic Church* (English trans., London, 1880, 3d ed. 1885); and his semi-autobiography, *Souvenirs d'Enfance et de jeunesse*, 1883 (English trans., *Recollections of my Youth*, London and New York, 1883). *

RENOUF, Peter Le Page, Roman-Catholic layman; b. in the isle of Guernsey, 1824; educated at Pembroke College, Oxford; entered the Church of Rome, 1842; became professor of ancient history and Eastern languages on the opening of the Catholic University of Ireland, 1855, but in 1864 one of her Majesty's inspectors of schools. He is the author of several works in Egyptology, and of *The Condemnation of Pope Honorius*, London, 1868 ("furiously attacked by the Roman-Catholic press, and placed on the Index"); *The Case of Honorius reconsidered with Reference to Recent Apologies*, 1869; *Lectures on the Origin and Growth of Religion as illustrated by the Religion of Ancient Egypt* (Hibbert lectures for 1879), 1880, 2d ed. 1885. *

REUSCH, Franz Heinrich, Lic. Theol. (Münster, 1849), **D.D.** (Münster, 1859), Old Catholic; b. at Brilon in Westphalia, Germany, Dec. 4, 1825; student at Bonn, Tübingen, and Munich, 1843-47; consecrated priest at Cologne, 1849; chaplain in Cologne, 1849-53; became *repetent* in the theological "convictorium," and *privat-docent* at Bonn, 1854; professor extraordinary of theology there, 1858; ordinary professor, 1861. He was suspended, then excommunicated (March, 1872), by the archbishop of Cologne for refusing acceptance to the Vatican Decrees (1871). He played a prominent part in the organization of the Old-Catholic movement, 1871. He was rector of the Bonn University in 1873. From 1866 to 1877 he edited the *Theologische Litteraturblatt*. He is the author of *Erklärung des Buches Baruch*, Freiburg, 1853; *Das Buch Tobias*, 1857; *Liber Sapientiæ græce secundum exemplar Vaticanum*, 1858; *Lehrbuch der Einleitung in das Alte Testament*, 1859, 4th ed. 1870; *Observationes criticæ in Librum Sapientiæ*, 1861; *Bibel und Natur*, 1862, 4th ed. 1876 (English trans., *Nature and the Bible*, Edinburgh, 1886, 2 vols.); *Libellus Tobit e Codice Sinaitico editus et recensitus*, Bonn, 1870; *Luis de Leon und die spanische Inquisition*, 1873; *Berichte über die Unions-Conferenzen zu Bonn*, 1874, 1875; *Predigten*, 1876; *Gebetbuch*, 1877; *Die biblische Schöpfungsgeschichte*, 1877; *Die deutschen Bischöfe und der Aberglaube*, 1879; *Der Process Galilei's und die Jesuiten*, 1879; *Der Index der verbotenen Bücher*, 1883-85, 2 vols.; minor writings, articles in periodicals, etc.

REUSS, Eduard (Wilhelm Eugen), Lic. Theol. (Strassburg, 1829), **D.D.** (*hon.*, Jena, 1843), **Ph.D.** (*hon.*, Halle, 1875), **LL.D.** (Georgetown College, Georgetown, Ky.), Protestant theologian; b. at Strassburg, July 18, 1804 (29 Messidor XII.); studied at Strassburg, first philology 1819-22, then theology there and at Göttingen and Halle 1822-26, and Oriental literature at Paris under De Sacy 1827-28; became *privat-docent* in the theological faculty at Strassburg, 1828; professor extraordinary, 1834; ordinary professor, 1836, and so remains. Of his numerous works may be mentioned, *De statu literarum theologicarum per sæcula VII. et VIII.*, Strassburg, 1825; *De libris Veteris Testamenti apocryphis plebi non negandis*, 1829; *Ideen zur Einleitung in das Evangelium Johannis*, 1840; *Geschichte der heiligen Schriften, Neues Testament*, Halle, 1842, 5th ed. Braunschweig, 1874 (Eng. trans. by Edward L. Houghton, Boston, 1884, 2 vols.); *Altes Testament*, Braunschweig, 1881; *Die johanneische Theologie*, Jena, 1847; *Fragments littéraires et critiques relatifs à l'histoire de la bible française I.-VIII.*, Strassburg, 1851-67; *Histoire de la théologie chrétienne au siècle apostolique*, 1852, 2 vols., 3d ed. 1864 (trans. into Dutch, Haarlem, 1854; Swedish, Stockholm, 1866; English, London, 1872); *Die deutsche Historienbibel vor Erfindung d. Bücherdrucks*, Jena, 1859; *L'Epître aux Hébreux*, Strassburg, 1860; *Ruth*, 1861; *Les Sibylles chrétiennes*, 1861; *Histoire du canon des saintes Écritures dans l'Église chrétienne*, 1862, 2d ed. 1863 (English trans., Edinburgh, 1884); *Das Buch Hiob*, 1869; *Bibliotheca N. T. græci*, Braunschweig, 1872; *La Bible, Traduction nouvelle avec commentaire*, Paris, 1874-80, 13 parts in 17 vols.; *Reden an Theologie-Studirende*, Leipzig, 1878, 2d ed. Braunschweig, 1879. With Professors Baum and Cunitz, he edited the first twenty volumes of the monumental edition of Calvin's *Opera*, Braunschweig, 1863 sqq. (since alone), but he furnished throughout the Prolegomena. It is to be completed in about forty-five volumes (vol. xxxi., 1886).

REUTER, Hermann Ferdinand, Lic. Theol. (Berlin, 1843), **Ph.D.** (*hon.*, Greifswald, 1865), Lutheran; b. at Hildesheim, Aug. 30, 1817; studied at Göttingen and Berlin; became *privat-docent* at Berlin, 1843; professor extraordinary of church history at Breslau, 1852; D.D. from Kiel, 1853; ordinary professor at Greifswald, 1855; professor at Breslau 1866, and at Göttingen 1876. In 1869 he became a royal consistorial councillor, and in 1881 abbot of Bursfeld. He is the author of *Johannes von Salisbury*, Berlin, 1842; *Abhandlungen zur systematischen Theologie*, 1855; *Geschichte Alexanders III. und der Kirche seiner Zeit*, 1846, 1 vol., 2d ed. 1860–64, 3 vols.; *Geschichte der religiösen Aufklärung im Mittelalter*, 1875–77, 2 vols.

REVEL, Albert, Waldensian; b. at Torre Pellice, Waldensian Valley, Italy, Jan. 2, 1837; educated in the Waldensian college of his native place, in the Waldensian theological school at Florence, and in the New College (Free Church), Edinburgh; was ordained in 1861; became professor of Latin and Greek literature in the Waldensian college at Torre Pellice, 1861, and professor of biblical literature and exegesis to the Waldensian Church, Florence, 1870. Since 1880 he has been a member of the Oriental Academy of the Royal Institute of Florence. He is the author of *L'Epistola di S. Jacobo*, Florence, 1868; *L'Epistola di S. Clemente Romano á Corinti*, 1869; *Antichita bibliche*, 1872; *Teoria del culto*, 1875; *Le origini del Papato*, 1875; *Cento lezioni sulla vita di Gesu*, 1875; *Storia letteraria dell' antico Testamento*, Poggibonsi, 1879; *Manuale par lo studio della lingua ebraica*, Florence, 1879; *I Salmi; verzione e commento sopra i Salmi i.–xl.*, 1880; *Il Nuovo Testamento, tradotto sul testo originale*, 1881.

RÉVILLE, Albert, D.D. (Leyden, 1862), French Protestant; b. at Dieppe, Seine-Inférieure, Nov. 4, 1826; studied at Dieppe, Geneva, and Strassburg, and in 1848 became a bachelor in theology; was pastor of the Walloon Church at Rotterdam, 1851–72, and then resided near Dieppe, engaged in philosophical studies, until, in 1880, he was called to the chair of the history of religions in the College of France, Paris. He is the author of *Manuel d'histoire comparée de la philosophie et de la religion* (after Scholten), 1859 (English trans., *Manual of Religious Instruction*, London, 1864); *De la rédemption*, Paris, 1860; *Essais de critique religieuse*, 1860; *Études critiques sur l'Évangile selon Saint Matthieu*, 1862; *Théodore Parker, sa vie et ses œuvres*, 1869; *Manuel d'instruction religieuse*, 1863, 2d ed. 1866; *Apollonius*, English trans., London, 1866; *Histoire du dogme de la divinité de Jésus Christ*, 1869, 2d ed. 1876 (English trans., *History of the Doctrine of the Deity of Jesus Christ*, London, 1870); *The Devil, his origin, greatness, and decadence*, English trans., 1871, 2d ed. 1877; *The Song of Songs*, English trans., 1873; *Prolégomènes de l'histoire des religions*, 1881 (English trans., 1884); *The Native Religions of Mexico and Peru*, English trans., 1884 (Hibbert lectures for 1884).

REYNOLDS, Henry Robert, D.D. (Edinburgh University, 1869), Congregationalist; b. at Romsey, Hampshire, Eng., Feb. 26, 1825; educated at Coward College and University College; graduated at London University B.A. 1848; became pastor at Halsted, Essex, 1846; at Leeds, 1849; president of Countess of Huntingdon's College, Cheshunt, Herts, 1860. He is the author of *Beginnings of the Divine Life*, London, 1858, 3d ed. 1860; *Notes of the Christian Life*, 1865; *John the Baptist* (Congregational Union lecture for 1874), 1874, 2d ed. 1876; *Philosophy of Prayer, and other Essays*, 1882; joint author of *Yes and No, Glimpses of the Great Conflict*, 1860, and of commentary on *Hosea* and *Amos* in Bishop Ellicott's *Old-Testament Commentary*, 1884; author of commentary on the *Pastoral Epistles* in *Expositor* (first series), and of exposition, commentary, and introduction to the *Gospel of John* in the *Pulpit Commentary;* joint editor and compiler of *Psalms, Hymns, and Passages of Scripture for Christian Worship*, 1853; editor of *Ecclesia, Church Problems considered in a Series of Essays*, 1870, 2d ed. 1871 (contributed essay on "*The Forgiveness and Absolution of Sins*"); second series, 1871 (essay, *The Holy Catholic Church*); for eight years (1866–74) edited with Rev. Dr. Allon *The British Quarterly Review;* for five years, *The Evangelical Magazine.* Besides his contributions to periodicals, he has written for Kitto's *Cyclopædia* and Smith and Wace's *Dictionary of Christian Biography.*

RICE, Edwin Wilbur, D.D. (Union College, Schenectady, N.Y., 1884), Congregationalist; b. at Kingsborough, N.Y., July 24, 1831; graduated at Union College, Schenectady, N.Y., 1854; and studied in Union Theological Seminary, New-York City, 1855–57; taught, 1857–58; was missionary of American Sunday-school Union, 1859–64; ordained in 1860; superintendent of its missions, 1864–70; assistant secretary of missions, and assistant editor of periodicals, Philadelphia, 1871–78; editor, 1878, and of periodicals and publications since 1879. He planned and prepared the lesson papers of the American Sunday-school Union, 1872 sqq.; the *Scholar's Handbook on the International Lessons*, 1874 sqq.; wrote the geographical and topographical articles in Schaff's *Bible Dictionary*, Philadelphia, 1880, 3d ed. 1885; edited Paxton Hood's *Great Revival of the Eighteenth Century*, 1882; Kennedy's *Four Gospels*, 1881; and has independently produced, *Pictorial Commentary on St. Mark*, 1881, 2d ed. 1882; *Historical Sketch of Sunday Schools*, 1886.

RICHARDSON, Ernest Cushing, Congregationalist; b. at Woburn, Mass., Feb. 9, 1860; graduated at Amherst College, Mass., 1880, and at the Hartford Theological Seminary, Conn., 1883; was assistant librarian of Amherst College, 1879–80; assistant librarian of Hartford Theological Seminary, 1882–84; since 1884 librarian, and since 1885 assistant secretary, of the American Library Association. He is the author of several papers in the *Proceedings* of the American Library Association (1885 and 1886), one in the *Journal of the Society of Biblical Exegesis* (1886), and various notes, articles, or reviews in the *Library Journal*, New York, and *Bibliotheca Sacra*, Oberlin, O.

RIDDLE, Matthew Brown, D.D. (Franklin and Marshall College, Lancaster, Penn., 1870), Congregationalist; b. in Pittsburg, Penn., Oct. 17, 1836; graduated at Jefferson College, Canonsburgh, Penn., 1852, and from New Brunswick (N.J.) Theological Seminary, 1859; was chaplain Second New-Jersey Regiment, 1861; Reformed (Dutch) pastor at Hoboken, N.J., 1862–65; at Newark, 1865–69; in Europe, 1869–71; since 1871 has been professor of New-Testament exegesis in Hartford (Conn.) Theological Seminary. He was a member of the New-Testament Revision Company. He translated and edited *Galatians, Ephesians*, and *Colossians*, in the American edition of Lange's *Commentary;* wrote (with Dr. Schaff) upon *Matthew, Mark*, and *Luke* (1879), *Romans* (1882), alone upon *Ephesians* and *Colossians* (1882), in Schaff's *Illustrated Popular Commentary;* upon *Mark* (1881), *Luke* (1883), and *Romans* (1884) in Schaff's *International Revision Commentary;* edited *Mark* and *Luke* (1884) in American edition of Meyer's *Commentary;* revised and edited Robinson's *Greek Harmony of the Gospels* (Boston, 1885), and Robinson's *English Harmony* (1886); edited portions of vols. vii., viii. of Bishop Coxe's edition *Ante-Nicene Fathers*, contributing the *Teaching of the Twelve Apostles* and *Second Clement*. With Rev. Dr. J. E. Todd he prepared the notes on the International Sunday-school Lessons (New Testament), 1877 to 1881, for the Congregational Publishing Society, Boston.

RIDGAWAY, Henry Bascom, D.D. (Dickinson College, Carlisle, Penn., 1869), Methodist; b. in Talbot County, Maryland, Sept. 7, 1830; graduated at Dickinson College, Carlisle, Penn., 1849; was successively pastor in Virginia, Baltimore (Md.), Portland (Me.), New-York City, and Cincinnati (O.); professor of historical theology in Garrett Biblical Institute, Evanston, Ill., 1882–84, and since of practical theology. He was fraternal delegate to the Methodist-Episcopal Church South, 1882; and one of the regular speakers in the Methodist Centennial Conference at Baltimore, 1884. He is the author of *The Life of Alfred Cookman*, New York, 1871; *The Lord's Land, a Narrative of Travels in Sinai and Palestine* (1873, 1874), 1876; *The Life of Bishop Edward S. Janes*, 1882; *Bishop Beverly Waugh*, 1883; *Bishop Matthew Simpson*, 1885.

RIEHM, Eduard (Carl August), Lic. Theol. (Heidelberg, 1853), **D.D.** (*hon.*, Halle, 1864), German Protestant theologian; b. at Diersburg, in Baden, Dec. 20, 1830; studied at Heidelberg and Halle; became city curate at Durlach, 1853; garrison preacher at Mannheim, 1854; *privat-docent* at Heidelberg, 1858; professor extraordinary there, 1861; the same at Halle, 1862; ordinary professor there, 1866. A believer in revelation, he claims freedom for critical study of the Bible. He was a member of the Luther Bible Revision Commission, 1865–81; rector of the University of Halle-Wittenberg, 1881–82. He is the author of *Die Gesetzgebung Mosis im Lande Moab*, Gotha, 1854; *Der Lehrbegriff des Hebräerbriefes*, Basel and Ludwigsburg, 1858–59, 2 parts, 2d ed. 1867; *De natura et notione symbolica Cheruborum*, 1864; *Die besondere Bedeutung des A. T. für die religiöse Erkenntniss und das religiöse Leben der christlichen Gemeinde*, Halle, 1864; *Hermann Hupfeld*, 1867; *Das erste Buch Mose nach der deutschen Uebersetzung D. Martin Luthers in revidirten Text, mit Erläuterungen*, 1873; *Initium Theologiæ Lutheri S. exempla scholiorum quibus D. Lutherus Psalterium interpretari cœpit* (part 1, Septem Psalmi pœnitentiales, Textum originalem nunc primum de Lutheri autographo exprimendum curavit), 1874; *Zur Erinnerung an D. Carl Bernhard Hundeshagen*, Gotha, 1874; *Die Messianischen Weissagungen*, 1875, second edition 1885; *Der Begriff der Sühne im Alten Testament*, 1877; *Kirche und Theologie*, Halle, 1880; *Religion und Wissenchaft* (rector's oration), Gotha, 1881; *Der biblische Schöpfungsbericht*, Halle, 1881; *Zur Revision der Lutherbibel, ueber die messianischen Stellen des Alten Testaments*, 1882; *Luther als Bibelübersetzer*, Gotha, 1884. He edited the second edition of Hupfeld, *Die Psalmen*, Gotha, 1867–71, 4 vols.; and a *Handwörterbuch des biblischen Alterthums*, Bielefeld, 1875–84, pp. 1,849, 1 vol.; and (1865) has been joint editor of the quarterly *Theologische Studien und Kritiken*.

RIGG, James Harrison, D.D. (Dickinson College, Carlisle, Penn., 1864), Wesleyan; b. at Newcastle-on-Tyne, Eng., Jan. 16, 1821; educated at Old Kingswood School; taught there and in other schools, 1835–45; entered the Wesleyan ministry in 1845; in 1866 was elected a member of the "Hundred," and in 1868 principal of the Wesleyan Training College, Westminster, London. In 1878 he was chosen president of the Wesleyan Conference. His name is associated with the admission of laymen into the conference that year, and with the Thanksgiving Fund initiated at the same time, which has realized over three hundred thousand pounds for Methodist work. He was one of the original members of the London school board, and is now a member of the Royal Commission on Education. He was English correspondent of *The New Orleans Christian Advocate*, 1851–52, and of *The Christian Advocate*, New York, for many years. He is the editor of *The London Quarterly Review*. He is the author of *The Principles of Wesleyan Methodism*, London, 1850; *Connexionalism and Congregational Independency*, 1851; *Modern Anglican Theology*, 1857, 3d ed. 1879; *The Churchmanship of John Wesley*, 1868, 2d ed. 1879; *Essays for the Times on Ecclesiastical and Social Subjects*, 1866; *National Education*, 1873; *The Living Wesley as he was in his Youth and in his Prime*, 1875; *Connexional Economy of Wesleyan Methodism*, 1879; *Discourses and Addresses on Leading Truths of Religion and Philosophy*, 1880; *The Sabbath and the Sabbath Law before Christ*, 1881 (2 editions); *The Character and Life-Work of Dr. Pusey*, 1883; *Was Wesley a High Churchman? and Is Modern Methodism Wesleyan Methodism? or, John Wesley, the Church of England, and Wesleyan Methodism*, 1883.

RIGGENBACH, Bernhard Emil, Ph.D. (Tübingen, 1874), **Lic. Theol.** (Basel, 1876), Swiss Reformed; b. at Karlsruhe, Oct. 25, 1848; studied at Basel and Tübingen, 1867–71; was ordained 1871; pastor at Arisdorf, Baselland, 1872–81; in the penitentiary, Basel, since 1885; *privat-docent* of New Testament and practical theology at Basel since 1882. His theological standpoint is positive biblical. He is the author of *Johann Eberlin von Gunzburg und sein Reformprogramm. Ein Beitrag zur Geschichte des xvi. Jahrhunderts*, Tübingen, 1874; *Taschenbuch für die schweizerischen reformierten Geistlichen*, Basel, 1876 sqq. (xi. Jahrgang, 1886); *Das Chronikon des Konrad Pellikan, zur vierten Säkularfeier der Universität Tübingen herausgegeben*, 1877; *Das Armenwesen der Reformation*, 1882; *Frauengestalten aus der Geschichte des Reiches Gottes*, 1st and 2d ed. 1884 (Danish trans., 1885); numerous articles in *Herzog* and the *Allg.-Deutsche Biographie*.

RIGGENBACH, Christoph Johannes, Swiss Protestant theologian; b. at Basel, Oct. 8, 1818; studied at Basel, Berlin, and Bonn, 1836–41; became pastor in Bennevil, Baselland, 1843; ordinary professor of theology at Basel, 1851; and, in 1878, president of the missions committee. Besides many sermons, he has published *Vorlesungen über das Leben Jesu*, Basel, 1858; *Der Kirchengesang in Basel seit der Reformation*, 1870; *Der sogenannte Brief des Barnabas*, 1873; and the comments upon *Thessalonians* in Lange's *Commentary*.

RIGGS, Elias, D.D. (Hanover College, Ind., 1853), **LL.D.** (Amherst College, Mass., 1871), Presbyterian; b. at New Providence, N.J., Nov. 19, 1810; graduated at Amherst College, Mass., 1829, and at Andover Theological Seminary, Mass., 1832; was missionary of the A. B. C. F. M. in Greece (at Athens and Argos), 1832–38; in Smyrna, Asia Minor, 1838–53; since that in Constantinople. He has made but one visit to the United States (in 1856). Being detained in New York for electrotyping an Armenian Bible, he taught Hebrew in the Union Theological Seminary (1857–58), and was invited to become professor in that department. The translation of the Scriptures into the Turkish language, after having engaged the labors of many others, was in 1873 placed by the British and Foreign Bible Society and the American Bible Society in the hands of a committee consisting at first of the Revs. W. G. Schauffler, D.D. (of the American Bible Society, formerly of the A. B. C. F. M.), George T. Herrick, Elias Riggs, D.D. (of the A. B. C. F. M.), and Robert H. Weakley (of the Church Missionary Society), as a result of whose labors, and those of native Turkish scholars, the entire Bible was published in both Arabic and Armenian characters in 1878. Experience having shown the need of retouching this version in a way to render it more intelligible to common readers, the same Bible societies, in 1883, consented to the organization of a larger committee (comprising so far as practicable the members of the former committee), and placed this work in their hands. The revised Turkish version, the work of this large committee, was issued 1886. Dr. Riggs is the author of *A Manual of the Chaldee Language, containing a Grammar* (chiefly translation of Winer), *Chrestomathy, and a Vocabulary*, Andover, Mass., 1832 (revised edition, New York, 1858, and since several editions); *The Young Forester, a Brief Memoir of the Early Life of the Swedish Missionary Fjelstedt* (Massachusetts Sabbath-school Society); *Grammatical Notes on the Bulgarian Language*, Smyrna, 1844; *Grammar of the Modern Armenian Language, with a Vocabulary*, Smyrna, 1847, second edition, Constantinople, 1856; *Grammar of the Turkish Language as written in the Armenian Character*, Constantinople, 1856; *Translation of the Scriptures into the Modern Armenian Language*, completed with the aid of native scholars, Smyrna, 1853 (reprinted in many editions in Constantinople and New York); *Translation of the Scriptures into the Bulgarian Language*, completed with the aid of native scholars throughout, and on the New Testament of the Rev. Dr. Albert L. Long (now professor in Robert College), Constantinople, 1871 (several editions, Constantinople and Vienna); *A Harmony of the Gospels* (in Bulgarian), Constantinople, 1880; *A Bible Dictionary* (in Bulgarian), 1884; minor publications, such as tracts, hymns, and collections of hymns, in Greek, Armenian, and Bulgarian.

RIGGS, James Stevenson, Presbyterian; b. in New-York City, July 16, 1853; graduated at the College of New Jersey, Princeton, 1874; studied at Leipzig, 1875; graduated at Auburn Theological Seminary, N.Y., 1880; became pastor at Fulton, N.Y., 1880; adjunct professor of biblical Greek in Auburn Theological Seminary, 1884.

RITSCHL, Albrecht, Ph.D. (Halle, 1843), **Lic. Theol.** (Bonn, 1846), **D.D.** (*hon.*, Bonn, 1855), **LL.D.** (Göttingen, 1881); b. in Berlin, March 25, 1822; studied at Bonn and Halle; became *privat-docent* at Bonn, 1846; professor extraordinary there, 1852; ordinary professor, 1859; professor at Göttingen, 1864; consistorial councillor, 1874. He thus describes his theological standpoint: "In strictest recognition of the revelation of God through Christ; most accurate use of the Holy Scripture as the fountain of knowledge of the Christian religion; view of Jesus Christ as the ground of knowledge for all parts of the theological system; in accord with the original documents of the Lutheran Reformation respecting those peculiarities which differentiate its type of doctrine from that of the middle ages."[1] He is a determined opponent of Protestant scholasticism, is the only living German theologian who has a "school;" but since 1881, he says, he has been in the position of the prophet Jeremiah (Jer. xviii. 18). He is the author of *Doctrina Augustini de creatione mundi, peccato, gratia* (*Diss. inauguralis*), Halle, 1843; *Das Evangelium Marcions und das kanonische Evangelium des Lucas*, Tübingen, 1846; *Die Entstehung der altkatholischen Kirche*, Bonn, 1850, 2d ed. (entirely worked over; standpoint of the Tübingen school, adopted in the first, abandoned), 1857; *Ueber das Verhältniss des Bekenntnisses zur Kirche, Ein Votum gegen die neulutherische. Doctrin*, 1854; *Die christliche Lehre von der Rechtfertigung und Versöhnung*, 1870–74, 3 vols., 2d ed. 1882–83 (English trans., vol. i., *A Critical History of the Christian Doctrine of Justification and Reconciliation*); *Die christliche Vollkommenheit*, Göttingen, 1874; *Schleiermachers Reden über die Religion und ihre Nachwirkungen auf die evang. Kirche Deutschlands*, Bonn, 1874; *Unterricht in der christlichen Religion*, 1875, 3d ed. 1886; *Ueber das Gewissen*, 1876; *Theologie u. Metaphysik. Zur Verständigung u. Abwehr*, 1881; *Geschichte des Pietismus*, 1880 sqq., 3d and last vol. 1886.

RITSCHL, Otto, Lic. Theol. (Halle, 1885), German Protestant theologian, son of the preceding; b. at Bonn, June 26, 1860; studied at Bonn, Göttingen, and Giessen, 1878–84; became *privat-docent* of theology at Halle, 1885. He is the author of *De epistulis Cyprianicis, dissertatio inauguralis*, Halle, 1885; *Cyprian von Karthago und die Verfassung der Kirche, eine kirchengeschichtliche und kirchenrechtliche Untersuchung*, Göttingen, 1885.

ROBERTS, William, D.D. (University of the city of New York, 1863), Welsh Calvinistic Methodist; b. at Llanerchymedd, Wales, Sept. 25, 1809; after education at Presbyterian Collegiate Institute, Dublin, Ireland, was pastor and

[1] "In strengster Anerkennung der Offenbarung Gottes durch Christus, genauster Benützung der heiligen Schrift als Erkenntnissgrund der christlichen Religion, Verwendung Jesu Christi als des Erkenntnissgrundes für alle Glieder des Systems, im Einklang mit den Urkunden der lutherischen Reformation in Hinsicht des eigenthümlichen von der Theologie des Mittelalters abweichenden Lehrtypus."

principal of academy, Holyhead, Wales; preacher of Countess of Huntingdon's chapel, Runcorn, Eng., 1848–55; pastor of Welsh Presbyterian Church, New-York City, 1855–68; Welsh pastor at Scranton, Penn., 1869–75; and since at Utica, N.Y. He has been several times moderator of the United-States Welsh Presbyterian General Assembly, and representative in councils of the Alliance of Reformed Churches. He edited the *Traethodydd*, New York, 1857–61, and since 1871 the *Cyfaill* (denominational organ), Scranton and Utica; and has written, *The Abrahamic Covenant*, New York, 1858; *The Election of Grace*, 1859 (both in Welsh).

ROBERTS, William Charles, D.D. (Union College, Schenectady, N.Y., 1872), Presbyterian; b. at Alltmai, near Aberystwith, Wales, Sept. 23, 1832; graduated at the College of New Jersey, Princeton, 1855, and at Princeton Theological Seminary 1858; became pastor of First Church, Wilmington, Del., 1858; First Church, Columbus, O., 1862; Second Church, Elizabeth, N.J., 1864; Westminster Church, Elizabeth, N.J., 1866; elected corresponding secretary of the Board of Home Missions, New-York City, 1881. He was chairman of the committee which laid the foundations of the Wooster University, O.; declined the presidency of Rutgers College, New Brunswick, N.J., 1882; declined a professorship in Western Theological Seminary, Allegheny, Penn., and accepted the presidency of Lake Forest University, Ill., 1886; was moderator of synods of Ohio (1864) and New Jersey (1875); member of the first (Edinburgh, 1877) and third (Belfast, 1884) councils of the Reformed Churches, and read paper on American colleges; was trustee of Lafayette College, Easton, Penn., from 1859 to 1863, and has been trustee of College of New Jersey, Princeton, since 1866. He is the author of a series of letters on the great preachers of Wales, translation of the *Shorter Catechism* into Welsh, and a number of occasional sermons.

ROBERTS, William Henry, D.D. (Western University of Pennsylvania, Pittsburgh, 1883), Presbyterian, son of William Roberts; b. at Holyhead, Wales, Jan. 31, 1844; graduated at the College of the City of New York, 1863; was statistician United-States Treasury Department, Washington, D.C., 1863–65; assistant librarian of Congress, 1866–72; graduated at Princeton (N.J.) Theological Seminary, 1873; pastor at Cranford, N.J., 1873–77; from 1877 to 1886 was librarian of Princeton Theological Seminary; became in 1886 professor in Lane Theological Seminary, Cincinnati, O.; from 1880 to 1884, permanent clerk of the General Assembly; since 1884, stated clerk. With Rev. Dr. W. E. Schenck, he prepared *General Catalogue of Princeton Theological Seminary*, 1881, and has published sermons, articles, etc.

ROBERTSON, Right Rev. Charles Franklin, S.T.D. (Columbia College, New-York City, 1868), **D.D.** (University of the South, Sewanee, Tenn., 1883), **LL.D.** (University of Missouri, Columbia, Mo., 1883), Episcopalian, bishop of Missouri; b. in New-York City, March 2, 1835; graduated at Yale College, New Haven, Conn., 1859, and at the General Theological Seminary, New-York City, 1862; became rector of St. Mark's, Malone, N.Y., 1862; of St. James, Batavia, 1868; bishop, 1868; died in St. Louis, Mo., May 1, 1886. He was vice-president of the St. Louis Social Science Association, of the National Conference of Charities and Corrections; member of historical associations and societies. He was the author of papers on *Historical Societies in Relation to Local Historical Effort*, St. Louis, 1883; *The American Revolution and the Mississippi Valley*, 1884; *The Attempt to separate the West from the American Union*, 1885; *The Purchase of the Louisiana Territory in its Influence on the American System*, 1885; pamphlets, sermons, charges, etc.

ROBINS, Henry Ephraim, D.D. (University of Rochester, N.Y., 1868), Baptist; b. at Hartford, Conn., Sept. 30, 1827; graduated at Newton (Mass.) Theological Institution, 1861; pastor at Newport, R.I., 1862–67; Rochester, N.Y., 1867–73; president of Colby University, Waterville, Me., 1873–82; since 1882 has been professor of Christian ethics in Rochester (N.Y.) Theological Seminary.

ROBINSON, Charles Seymour, D.D. (Hamilton College, Clinton, N.Y., 1866), **LL.D.** (Lafayette College, Easton, Penn., 1885), Presbyterian; b. at Bennington, Vt., March 31, 1829; graduated at Williams College, Williamstown, Mass., 1849; studied at Union (New-York City) and Princeton (N.J.) Theological Seminaries; was pastor in Troy and Brooklyn, N.Y.; Paris, France; and since 1870 of Memorial Church, New-York City. He has published *Songs of the Church*, New York, 1862; *Songs for the Sanctuary*, 1865; *Songs for Christian Worship*, 1866; *Short Studies for Sunday-school Teachers*, 1868; *Chapel Songs*, 1872; *Psalms, Hymns, and Spiritual Songs*, 1874; *Christian Work* (sermons), *Bethel and Penuel* (do., both 1874); *Spiritual Songs*, 1878; *Spiritual Songs for Social Worship*, 1880; *Studies in the New Testament*, 1880; *Spiritual Songs for Sunday School*, 1881; *Studies of Neglected Texts*, 1883; *Laudes Domini* (hymn-book), 1884; *Simon Peter: Early Life and Times*, 1887; *Sermons in Songs*, 1885. His hymn and tune books sell between seventy-five and eighty thousand a year. His sermons have passed through several editions.

ROBINSON, Ezekiel Gilman, D.D., LL.D. (both Brown University, Providence, R.I., 1853 and 1872), Baptist; b. at Attleborough, Mass., March 23, 1815; graduated at Brown University, Providence, R.I., 1838, and at Newton (Mass.) Theological Institution, 1842; pastor at Norfolk, Va., 1842–45; professor of Hebrew in Covington (Ky.) Theological Seminary, 1846–49; pastor in Cincinnati, O., 1849–52; professor of theology in Rochester (N.Y.) Theological Seminary, 1852–72; president, 1864–72; and since 1872 has been president of Brown University. He edited *Christian Review*, 1859–64; revised Neander's *Planting and Training of the Christian Church*, 1864; published *Yale Lectures*, 1883.

ROBINSON, Thomas Hastings, D.D. (Hamilton College, Clinton, N.Y., 1868), Presbyterian; b. at North-East, Erie County, Penn., Jan. 30, 1828; graduated at Oberlin College, O., 1850, and at Western Theological Seminary, Allegheny, Penn., 1854; pastor in Harrisburg, Penn., 1854–84; and since has been professor of sacred rhetoric, church government, and pastoral theology in the Western Theological Seminary, Allegheny, Penn.

ROHLING, Johann Francis Bernard Augustin, Lic. Theol. (Münster, 1865), **Ph.D.** (Jena, 1867), **D.D.** (Münster, 1871), Roman Catholic; b. at Neuenkirchen, near Münster, Westphalia, Germany, Feb. 15, 1839; studied theology in the University of Münster; was instituteur du comte de Merode en Belgique et en France, 1863–64; chaplain and con-rector at Rheinberg, near Wesel, 1865; *repetent* of dogmatics and ethics at Münster; vicar of St. Martin's Church, and *privat-docent* of biblical literature, 1866–70; professor extraordinary of exegesis of the Old and New Testament, 1870–74; professor of theology at St. Francis' Seminary, near Milwaukee, Wis., U.S.A., 1874–75; since April, 1876, ordinary professor of biblical studies and exegesis at the University of Prague, Bohemia. In 1883 he was prohibited by the Austrian Government from writing against the Jews, on account of the so-called "excited times." He is the author of the German translation of Lamy's book against Renan, Münster, 1864; *Hosea's Ehe*, Tübingen, 1865; *Der Jehova-Engel*, 1866; *Mose's letztes Lied*, Jena, 1867; *Erklärung der Psalmen*, Münster, 1871; *Isaias*, 1872; *Evangelien, Acta, Römer-Corinther-Galaterbr.*, 1873; *Daniel*, Mainz, 1876; *Sprüche Salomo's*, 1880; *Der Talmudjude*, Münster, 1871, 6th ed. 1876; *Louise Lateau*, Paderborn, 1873, 9 editions; *Der Antichrist*, St. Louis, 1875; *Medulla theologiæ moralis*, 1875; *Katechismus des 19. Jahrhunderts für Juden, Protestanten und Katholiken*, Mainz, 1878; *Fünf Briefe über den Talmudismus und das Blutritual der Juden*, Paderborn, 1st to 3d eds. 1883; *Die Polemik und das Menschenopfer des Rabbinismus*, 1st to 5th thousand 1883.

ROLLER, Théophile, French Protestant; b. at Aubusson (Creuse), April 5, 1830; educated at Paris and Montauban; Reformed pastor at Bolbec (Seine-Inféricure), 1853–57; at Naples, Italy, 1857–63; in different parts of France and Italy, 1864–66; at Rome, 1867–73; in 1874 he retired, because of his health, to Tocqueville (Seine-Inférieure), and devoted himself entirely to the composition of his great work, *Les catacombes de Rome: histoire de l'art et des croyances religieuses pendant les premiers siècles du christianisme*, Paris, 1879–80, 2 vols. folio, with a hundred plates.

ROMESTIN, Augustus Henry Eugene de, Church of England; b. in Paris, France, May 9, 1830; scholar of Winchester College, Eng., 1843–48, of St. John's College, Oxford; graduated B.A. 1852, M.A. 1854; was ordained deacon 1852, priest 1854; was curate of Mells, Somerset, 1853; of St. Thomas Martyr, Oxford, 1853–54; English chaplain at Freiburg-im-Breisgau 1863-65, and at Baden-Baden 1865–68; chaplain of Woolland, Dorset, 1868–69; perpetual curate of Freeland, Oxford, 1874–85: rural dean of Woodstock, 1879–85; vicar of Stony Stratford, Buckinghamshire, 1885; warden of House of Mercy, Great Maplestead, Essex, since 1885. His theological standpoint is that of the school of Dr. Pusey. He is the author of *Sketch of Primary Education in Germany*, London, 1866; *Last Hours of Jesus*, 1866; *Teaching of the Twelve Apostles*, 1884, 2d ed. 1885; *St. Augustine, On instructing the Unlearned, Concerning Faith of Things not seen, On the Advantages of Believing, The Enchiridion to Laurentius, and Concerning Faith, Hope, and Charity*, Latin and English, 1885; articles in newspapers, magazines, etc., on various subjects, 1856–86.

ROPES, Charles Joseph Hardy, Congregationalist; b. in St. Petersburg, Russia, Dec. 7, 1851; graduated at Yale College, New Haven, Conn., 1872, and at Andover Theological Seminary, Mass., 1875; pastor at Ellsworth, Me., 1877–81; and since 1881 professor of New-Testament language and literature in Bangor Theological Seminary, Me. He translated and edited (with Professor Dr. E. C. Smyth) Uhlhorn's *Conflict of Christianity with Heathenism*, New York, 1879.

ROPES, William Ladd, Congregationalist; b. at Newton, Mass., July 19, 1825; graduated at Harvard College, Cambridge, Mass., 1846, and at Andover Theological Seminary, Mass., 1852; was pastor at Wrentham, Mass., 1853–62; acting pastor of Crombie-street Church, Salem (residence at Cambridge, Mass.), 1862–63; acting pastor at South Hadley, Mass., and Windsor Locks, Conn., 1865–66; since 1866 has been librarian of Andover Theological Seminary.

ROSSI, Giovanni Battista de, Italian archæologist, Roman Catholic; b. in Rome, Feb. 23, 1822; educated at the Collegium Romanum; under the Jesuit Marchi's impulse devoted himself to archæology, particularly to the Catacombs, and in this department is the universally acknowledged chief. In 1886 the emperor of Germany conferred upon him the cross of the Order of Merit. His two monumental works are *Inscriptiones christianae urbis Romanæ*, Rome, 1857–61; *La Roma sotterranea christiana*, 1869–77, 3 vols. Since 1863 he has issued *Bulletino di archæologia christiana*. *

RUDIN (Eric Georg) Waldemar (Napoleon), Ph.D. (Upsala, 1857), **D.D.** (by the king's appointment, 1877, in consequence of a theological examination before the faculty of Upsala, 1871), Swedish Lutheran theologian; b. at Ö. Ryd, Ostrogothia, Sweden, July 20, 1833; studied at the University of Upsala; ended the course in philosophy 1857, in theology 1859; was sec'y of the National Evangelical Society at Stockholm, 1859–62; director of the Foreign Missionary Institute there, 1862–69; vice-chaplain of the parish of St. Clara, Stockholm, 1869–72; *privat-docent* in the University of Upsala, 1872 (appointed 1871)–75; *adjunct* in theology, 1875–77; professor extraordinary of exegetical theology, 1877 to date. He was appointed a court preacher 1873. Since 1884 he has been a member of the committee for the revision of the Swedish translation of the Old Testament. He is a moderate Lutheran, friendly to the biblical theology of Beck, and to the mystics. He is the author in Swedish of "Intimations of Eternity" (sermons on the texts of the Church Year), Stockholm, 1872–73, 2d ed. 1878; "Biblical Psychology," Upsala, 1st part 1875; "Sören Kierkegaard," 1880; "Synopsis of the Gospels," 1881; "Gospel of Mark," translated, with notes, 1883; "Introduction to Old-Testament Prophecy," 1884; "Commentary on the Minor Prophets," 1884 sqq.; "Discussions on Theological and Ecclesiastical Subjects (1. Is it worth while to Instruct our Children in the Old Testament? 2. On the Influence of Personality in Preaching"), 1885–86; several sermons, addresses, tracts, etc.

RÜETSCHI, Albert Rodolph, D.D. (*hon.*, Zürich,

1864), Swiss Reformed; b. in Bern, Dec. 3, 1820; studied at Bern, Berlin (1844–45), and Tübingen (1845); became *privat-docent* at Bern, 1845; pastor at Trub 1848, at Kirchberg 1853; rector of Bern Cathedral since 1867; honorary professor at the University of Bern since 1878. He was president of the Synod, 1864–72; of the Synodal rath, 1878–82. He edited Lutz's *Biblische Dogmatik*, Pforzheim, 1847; and has written numerous articles in Herzog's *Real-Encyclopädie*, and in *Studien und Kritiken* and other theological periodicals.

RÜETSCHI, Rudolf, Lic. Theol. (*hon.*, Bern, 1882), Swiss Reformed; b. at Trub, Canton Bern, Jan. 13, 1851; studied at Bern 1870–74, Berlin 1874–75, Tübingen 1875; became pastor at Reutigen, Canton Bern, 1875; at Münchenbuchsee, 1880; *privat-docent* at the University of Bern, 1883. He has been since 1880 teacher of religion in the normal school at Hofwyl. He is the author of *Welches ist das Prinzip des evangelischen Protestantismus?* Bern, 1880; *Geschichte und Kritik der kirchlichen Lehre von der ursprünglichen Vollkommenheit und vom Sündenfall* (prize essay of the Hague Association), Leiden, 1881.

RULISON, Right Rev. Nelson Somerville, D.D. (Kenyon College, Gambier, O., 1879), Episcoplian, assistant bishop of Central Pennsylvania; b. at Carthage, Jefferson County, N.Y., April 24, 1843; graduated at the General Theological Seminary, New-York City, 1866; became assistant minister at the Church of the Annunciation, New-York City, 1866; rector of Zion Church, Morris, N.Y., 1867; of St. John's Church, Jersey City, N.J., 1870; of St. Paul's Church, Cleveland, O., 1877; bishop, 1885. He has published a few sermons in pamphlet form, etc.

RUNZE, Georg August Wilhelm, Ph.D. (Königsberg, 1876), **Lic. Theol.** (Berlin, 1879), German Protestant; b. at Woltersdorf, Pomerania, Feb. 13, 1852; studied theology and philosophy at Greifswald and Berlin, 1870–74; was tutor in a noble family in Curland, 1874–76; adjunct of the *Domkandidatenstift* in Berlin, 1876–77; in the army, 1877–78; *inspector des Studentenkonvikt* "Johanneum" in Berlin, 1878–80; *privat-docent* of speculative and philosophical theology in Berlin University since 1880. He holds to Dorner's *Vermittelungs* theology in general. He is the author of *Schleiermachers Glaubenslehre in ihrer Abhängigkeit von seiner Philosophie kritisch dargelegt und an einer Speziallehre erläutert*, Berlin, 1877; *Der ontologische Gottesbeweis, Kritische Darstellung seiner Geschichte seit Anselm bis auf die Gegenwart*, Halle, 1882; *Grundriss der evangelischen Glaubens- und Sittenlehre*, Berlin (1. Theil; *Allgemeine Dogmatik mit Einschluss der Religionsphilosophie*, 1883; II. Theil; *Spezielle Dogmatik*, 1884); arts. *Unsterblichkeit* and *Willensfreiheit*, in *Herzog;* and articles in periodicals, etc.

RUST, Herman, D.D. (Franklin and Marshall College, Lancaster, Penn., 1872), Reformed (German); b. in Bremen, Germany, Dec. 8, 1816; graduated at Marshall College (1848) and Theological Seminary (1850), Mercersburg, Penn.; pastor in Cincinnati, O., 1851–62, and since has been professor of church history and exegesis in Heidelberg Theological Seminary, Tiffin, O.

RYAN, Most Rev. Patrick John, LL.D. (University of the State of New York, through Manhattanville College of Christian Brothers, 1860), Roman Catholic, archbishop of Philadelphia; b. at Thurles, Ireland, Feb. 20, 1831; completed the ecclesiastical course at Carlow College, Ireland, 1852; was professor in Theological Seminary, St. Louis, Mo., 1852–54; rector of the Cathedral in that city, 1855–60; pastor of the Church of the Annunciation, 1860–68, and of St. John's, 1868; vicar-general of the diocese, 1868–84; coadjutor bishop of St. Louis, 1872; archbishop of Philadelphia, Penn., 1884. He preached the English Lenten course in Rome (1868), the dedication sermon of the Cathedral, New-York City (1879), and lectured before the Legislature and University of Missouri. He is the author of published lectures on *What Catholics do not believe*, St. Louis, 1877; *Some of the Causes of Modern Religious Scepticism*, 1883; and of occasional sermons.

RYDBERG, Abraham Viktor, D.D. (Upsala, 1876); b. at Jönköping, Province of Småland, Sweden, Dec. 18, 1829; studied philosophy at the University of Lund, 1848–52; was literary editor of *Göteborgs Handelstidning* ("The Gothenburg Daily Commercial"), 1855–76; lay representative at the Church Congress of the Swedish State Church, 1868; member of the lower house of the Swedish Parliament as representative of the city of Gothenburg, 1870–72; has been professor at the high school of Stockholm since 1884. He was elected as member of the Swedish Academy in 1877; made knight of the Order of the North Star in 1879. Nominally a Lutheran, he is in reality Unitarian. He is the author (in Swedish) of "Romantic Stories," Gothenburg, 1856, 2d ed. Gefle, 1865; "The Freebooter on the Baltic," Gothenburg, 1857, 2d ed. Gefle, 1866; "The Last Athenian," Gothenburg, 1859, 2d ed. Stockholm, 1866, 3d ed. 1876 (trans. into English [Philadelphia, 1879] Danish, and German); "The Doctrine of the Bible on Christ," Gothenburg," 1862, 4th ed. 1880; "The Jehovah Worship among the Hebrews before the Babylonian Captivity," Gothenburg, 1864, 2d ed. Gefle, 1869; "Magic of the Middle Ages," Stockholm, 1865 (English trans., New York, 1879); "On the Pre-existence of Man," Stockholm, 1868; "Genealogy of the Patriarchs in Genesis and the Chronology of the LXX." Gothenburg, 1873; "Adventure of Little Vigg on Christmas Eve," Gothenburg, 1874, 2d ed. 1875; "Roman Legends about St. Paul and St. Peter," Stockholm, 1874; "Roman Days," Stockholm, 1875 (English trans., London, 1879); "Translation of Goethe's Faust," Stockholm, 1876; "On Eschatology," Stockholm, 1880; numerous pamphlets.

RYLANCE, Joseph Hine, D.D. (Western Reserve College, Hudson, O., 1867), Episcopalian; b. near Manchester, Eng., June 16, 1826; educated at King's College, London University; graduated, 1861; curate in London, 1861–63; rector in Cleveland, O., 1863–67; Chicago, Ill., 1867–71; and since 1871 has been rector of St. Mark's, New-York City. His theological standpoint is that of Christian rationalism. He is the author of *Preachers and Preaching*, London, 1862; *Social Questions*, New York, 1880.

RYLE, Right Rev. John Charles, D.D. (by diploma, 1880), lord bishop of Liverpool, Church of England; b. at Macclesfield, May 10, 1816; entered Christ Church, Oxford; took Craven University scholarship in 1836; graduated B.A. (first-class in classics) 1837, M.A. 1871; became successively curate of Exbury, Hants, 1841; rector of St. Thomas, Winchester, 1843; of Helmingham, Suffolk, 1844; vicar of Stradbroke, Suffolk, 1861 (rural dean, 1870; honorary canon of Norwich Cathedral, 1872; select preacher at Cambridge 1873-74, at Oxford 1874-76); dean designate of Salisbury, 1880 (never took possession, because within a short time after nomination he became bishop of Liverpool, upon the formation of the diocese, 1880). He has written about one hundred theological tracts on doctrinal and practical subjects, of which more than two millions have been circulated, and many have been translated into foreign languages (they are now published in six volumes); *Coming Events and Present Duties*, 1867, 2d ed. 1879; *Bishops and Clergy of Other Days*, London, 1868; *The Christian Leaders of the Last Century* (in England), 1869; *Expository Thoughts on the Gospels*, 1856-69, 7 vols., 11th ed. 1873-79.

S.

SABINE, William Tufnell, Reformed Episcopalian; b. in New-York City, Oct. 16, 1838; graduated at Columbia College 1859, and at the General Theological Seminary 1862, both in New-York City; became rector in Philadelphia, Penn., 1863; in New-York City, 1866; pastor of the First Reformed Episcopal Church, New-York City, 1874. He has published various pamphlets.

SAGE, Adoniram Judson, D.D. (Rochester University, N.Y., 1872), Baptist; b. at Massillon, O., March 29, 1836; graduated at the University of Rochester, N.Y., 1860, and at Rochester Theological Seminary, 1863; became pastor at Shelburne Falls, Mass., 1863–67; in Philadelphia, Penn., 1868–69; Hartford, Conn., 1872–81; professor of Latin, University of Rochester, N.Y., 1870–71; since 1884 has been professor of homiletics in the Baptist Union Theological Seminary, Morgan Park, near Chicago, Ill.

SALMON, George, D.D. (Dublin, 1859; Edinburgh, 1884), **D.C.L.** (Oxford, 1868), **LL.D.** (Cambridge, 1874), Church of Ireland; b. in Dublin, Sept. 25, 1819; educated at Trinity College, Dublin; graduated B.A. (senior moderator in mathematics) 1839, M.A. 1843, B.D. 1859; was fellow from 1841 to 1866; and has been regius professor of divinity since 1866. He was ordained deacon in 1844, priest in 1845. He is fellow of the Royal Societies of London and Edinburgh, corresponding member of the Institute of France, and honorary member of the Royal Academies of Berlin, Göttingen, and Copenhagen. Besides mathematical works, he has issued *College Sermons*, 1st series, London, 1861; 2d series (*Reign of Law*), 1873; 3d series (*Non-miraculous Christianity*), 1881; *Introduction to the New Testament*, 1885; 2d ed. 1886.

SALMOND, Stewart Dingwall Fordyce, D.D. (Aberdeen University, 1881), Free Church of Scotland; b. at Aberdeen, June 22, 1838; educated at King's College and University, Aberdeen; graduated, 1858; was assistant professor, 1861–64; classical examiner, 1864–67; minister at Barry, Forfarshire, 1865–76; since 1876 professor of systematic theology and New-Testament exegesis in the Free Church College, Aberdeen. He translated with notes the works of *Hyppolytus* (except the "Refutation of the Heresies") in the Ante-Nicene Library, vols. v. and ix., Edinburgh, 1868–69; *Julius Africanus*, etc., in vol. ix.; *Theognostus*, etc. (fragments), vol. xiv., 1869; *Gregory Thaumaturgus*, etc., vol. xx., 1871; Augustine's *Harmony*, etc., in vols. viii. and ix. Augustine's works, 1873; wrote the notes on *Epistles of Peter* in Schaff's *Popular Commentary on the New Testament*, vol. iv., 1883; *The Life of the Apostle Peter*, 1884; edited *Bible-class Primers*, 1881 sqq., and *Commentary on the Epistle of Jude*, London (in press). He has besides written numerous articles in periodicals.

SAMSON, George Whitefield, D.D. (Columbian University, Washington, D.C., 1858), Baptist; b. at Harvard, Mass., Sept. 29, 1819; graduated at Brown University, 1839, and at Newton Theological Institution, Newton Centre, Mass., 1843; was pastor E-street Church, Washington, D.C., 1843–50; Jamaica Plain, Boston, Mass., 1850–52; E-street, Washington, D.C., 1853–59; president of Columbian College, Washington, D.C., 1859–71; of Rutgers Female Seminary, New-York City, 1871–75; pastor of First (Mount Morris) Church, Harlem, New-York City, 1873–81; since 1883 has been secretary in charge of Liberia College; since 1884 has conducted private collegiate instruction; since 1886 has been acting president of Rutgers Female College, New-York City. He is the author of *To daimonión, or the Spiritual Medium*, Boston, 1852, 2d ed. (under title *Spiritualism Tested*) 1860; *Thanksgiving Discourse*, 1853; *Memoir of M. J. Graham* (prefaced to ed. of Graham's *Test of Truth*), 1859; *Outlines of the History of Ethics*, 1860; *Elements of Art Criticism*, Philadelphia, 1867, abridged ed. 1868; *Physical Media in Spiritual Manifestations, illustrated from Ancient and Modern Testimony*, 1869; *The Atonement, viewed as Assumed Divine Responsibility*, 1878; *Divine Law as to Wines, established by the Testimony of Sages, Physicians, and Legislators against the Use of Fermented and Intoxicating Wines, confirmed by Egyptian, Greek, and Roman Methods of preparing Unfermented Wines for Festal, Medicinal, and Sacramental Uses*, New York, 1880, 2d ed. 1885; *English Revisers' Greek Text shown to be Unauthorized except by Egyptian Copies discarded by the Greeks*, 1882; *Guide to Self Education*, 1886.

SANDAY, William, D.D. (Durham, 1882; Edinburgh, 1877), Church of England; b. at Holme Pierrepont, Nottingham, Aug. 1, 1843; educated at Corpus Christi College, Oxford; graduated B.A. (first-class in classics) 1865, M.A. (Trinity College) 1868; was fellow of Trinity College, Oxford, 1866–73; ordained deacon 1867, priest 1869; lecturer of St. Nicholas, Abingdon, 1871–72; vicar of Great Waltham, Essex, 1872–73; of Barton-on-the-Heath, Warwickshire, 1873–76; public examiner in the Honors School of Theology at Oxford, 1876–77; principal of Bishop Hatfield's Hall, Durham, 1876–83; examining chaplain to the bishop of Durham, 1879–81; select preacher at Cambridge, 1880; became Dean Ireland's professor of exegesis of Holy Scripture, Oxford, 1882; and tutorial fellow of Exeter College, Oxford, 1883. He is the author of *Authorship and Historical Character of the Fourth Gospel*, London, 1872; *The Gospels in the Second Century*, 1876; commentary on *Romans* and *Galatians* in Bishop Ellicott's *Commentary*, 1878; (joint editor of) *Variorum Bible*, 1880; *Inaugural Lecture*, Oxford, 1883.

SANDERSON, Joseph, D.D. (University of Kittanning, Penn., 1868), Presbyterian; b. at Ballibay, County Monaghan, Ireland, May 23, 1823; graduated at the Royal College, Belfast, 1845; went to America, 1846; was classical teacher in the Washington Institute, New-York City, 1847–49; studied theology under care of the Associate Presbytery of New York, by which licensed, 1849;

became pastor of Associate Presbyterian Church, Providence, R.I., 1849, and of Stanton-street Presbyterian Church, New-York City, 1853; removed with his congregation to their new church, Lexington Avenue and Forty-sixth Street, 1860; resigned, 1869; was prevented from preaching by partial aphonia until 1871; was acting pastor of Saugatuck Congregational Church, Conn , 1872–78; assistant editor of the *Homiletic Monthly*, New York, 1881–83; editor of the *Pulpit Treasury*, New York, since 1883. He is the author of *Jesus on the Holy Mount*, New York, 1869, last ed. 1884; *Memorial Tributes*, 1883, last ed. 1885.

SANKEY, Ira David, Methodist lay evangelist; b. at Edinburgh, Lawrence County, Penn., Aug. 28, 1840; in business at New Castle, Penn., 1855–71; joined Mr. Moody in evangelical work in Chicago in the latter year, and has been with him ever since. He leads the singing in the revival meetings, and sings alone, and is a worker in the inquiry-rooms. He has edited several collections of hymns, which have had an enormous circulation, and has written and adapted numerous tunes. *

SAPHIR, Adolph, D.D. (Edinburgh, 1878), Presbyterian; b. at Pesth, Hungary, Sept. 26, 1831; received his elementary education at Pesth until 1844; attended the gymnasium of the Graue Kloster, Berlin, till 1848; studied in Glasgow University and Marischal College, 1848–49, 1850–51; in Theological College of the Free Church, Edinburgh, 1851–54; graduated B.A. at University of Glasgow, 1854; became missionary to the Jews in Hamburg, Germany, 1854; German preacher in Glasgow, 1855; minister of English Presbyterian Church, South Shields, 1856; Greenwich, London, 1861; Notting Hill, London, 1872; of Belgrave Presbyterian Church, London, 1881. He was the first convert of the Scotch Jewish mission at Pesth; was baptized in 1843, with father, mother, brother, and three sisters; has devoted himself to promoting interest in Jewish missions by addresses, pamphlets, and in other ways. He holds to the Old Reformation theology, but gives prominence to the historical and prophetical elements of Scripture. He is the author of *Diaries of Philipp Saphir, by his Brother*, Edinburgh, 1852; *Conversion*, 1861, 10th ed. (under title *Found by the Good Shepherd*) London [1880]; *Christ and the Scriptures*, London, 1864, 28th thousand, 1884 (trans. into Dutch, German, 3d ed. Leipzig, 1882, prefaces by Kogel and Delitzsch; Italian, Hungarian, Swedish, Norse, Hindi, Slavonian); *Lectures on the Lord's Prayer*, 1869, 9th ed. 1884; *Christ Crucified* (lectures on 1 Cor. ii.), 1872, 4th ed. 18—; *Christ and the Church, Lectures on the Apostolic Commission*, 1874, 2d ed. 1884; *Expository Lectures on Epistle to the Hebrews*, 1875–76, 2 vols., several later editions; *The Hidden Life, Thoughts on Communion with God*, 1877, later editions; *Our Life-Day, Thoughts on John xix. 4*, 1878, reprinted, New York, 1879; *The Compassion of Jesus*, 1880, 2d ed. 1882 (trans. into German); *Martin Luther, a Witness for Christ and the Scriptures*, 1884, 3d ed.; translation of Auberlen, *The Prophet Daniel and Book of Revelation*, Edinburgh, 1856; German tracts for the Jews (*Der Weihnachtsbaum, Wer ist der Jude? Wer ist der Apostat?*), which have passed through many editions since 1854, and been translated into Italian and into Jewish German. *Who is the Apostate?* into English (1878) and Dutch; *All Israel shall be saved*, 188–, 3d thousand, 1885 (translated into German, Leipzig, 1884, 2d ed. 1885, and Danish); *The Everlasting Nation*, 3d ed. 1885; eight tracts for children, *Christian Perfection*, 1885; many other expository and devotional pamphlets.

SAUSSAYE, Pierre Daniel Chantepie de la, D.D. (Utrecht, 1871), Dutch Protestant; b. at Leeuwarden, April 9, 1848; educated at Leiden and Rotterdam. Since 1878 he has been professor of the history of religions at the University of Amsterdam. From 1874 to 1882 he was, with Drs. J. J. P. Valeton, jun., and Is Van Dyk, editor of *Studien*, a theological review, and wrote many papers, mostly in the field of biblical theology and history of religion. He has since contributed to other periodicals. His separate publications are, *Methodologische bydrage tot het onderzoek naar den oorsprong van den godsdienst* (his D.D. dissertation), Utrecht, 1871; *Vier Schetsen uit de Godsdienstgeschiedenis*, 1883 (German trans. preparing); expects to issue in 1888, at Freiburg-im-Br., in German, a compendious history of religions for the *Theologische Lehrbücher* series.

SAVAGE, George Slocum Folger, D.D. (Iowa College, Grinnell, Io., 1870), Congregationalist; b. at Upper Middletown (now Cromwell), Conn., June 29, 1817; graduated at Yale College, New Haven, Conn., 1844; studied at Andover (Mass.) Theological Seminary 1844–45, and at Yale Theological Seminary 1845–47, and graduated; was pastor at St. Charles, Ill., 1847; Western secretary of the American Tract Society, Chicago, Ill., 1860; Western secretary of the Congregational Publishing Society, Chicago, 1870; secretary and treasurer of the Chicago Theological Seminary, 1872; since 1885, secretary. He has been trustee of Beloit College, Wis., since 1850; director of Chicago Theological Seminary since 1854. He was corresponding editor of *The Prairie Herald*, 1849-52, and of *The Congregational Herald*, 1852–55; editor and publisher of *The Bi-Monthly Congregational Review*, 1868–71, — all published in Chicago; and is author of sermons, addresses, etc.

SAVAGE, Minot Judson, Unitarian; b. at Norridgewock, Me., June 10, 1841; graduated at Bangor (Me.) Theological Seminary, 1864; became American home (Congregational) missionary in California, 1864; was at Framingham, Mass., 1867; became pastor at Hannibal, Mo., 1869; Unitarian pastor in Chicago, 1873; of the "Church of the Unity," Boston, 1874. He is the author of *Christianity the Science of Manhood*, Boston, 1873, 2d ed. 1874; *The Religion of Evolution*, 1876; *Light on the Cloud*, 1876; *Bluffton, a Story of To-Day*, 1878; *Life Questions*, 1879; *The Morals of Evolution*, 1880; *Talks about Jesus*, 1880; *Minister's Hand-book*, 1880, 2d ed. 1882; *Belief in God*, 1881; *Beliefs about Man*, 1882; *Poems*, 1882; *Beliefs about the Bible*, 1883; *The Modern Sphinx*, 1883; *Sacred Songs for Public Worship* (edited with H. M. Dow), 1883; *Man, Woman, and Child*, 1884; *The Religious Life*, 1886; *Social Problems*, 1886.

SAYCE, Archibald Henry, LL.D. (*hon.*, Trinity College, Dublin, 1881), Church of England; b. at Shirehampton, near Bristol, Sept. 25, 1846; was a scholar and taberdar of Queen's College, Oxford (1865), where he took a first-class in moderations (1866) and again in final classical schools (1868);

graduated B.A. (first-class in classics) 1869, M.A. 1871; ordained deacon 1870, priest 1871; became fellow of his college 1869, tutor 1870, and later senior tutor, deputy professor of comparative philology 1876, and was public examiner 1877-79. In 1874 he joined the Old-Testament Revision Company. He is an honorary member of the Royal Academy of Spain, the Asiatic Society of Bengal, and the Anthropological Society of Washington. He edited George Smith's *History of Babylonia*, London, 1877, 2d ed. 1884; *Sennacherib*, 1878; and *Chaldean Genesis*, 1880; and has written, *Assyrian Grammar for Comparative Purposes*, 1872; *Principles of Comparative Philology*, 1873, 3d ed. 1884 (French trans. 1884); *Astronomy and Astrology of the Babylonians*, 1874; *Elementary Assyrian Grammar*, 1875, 2d ed. 1877; *Lectures on the Assyrian Syllabary and Grammar*, 1877; *Babylonian Literature*, 1877; *Introduction to the Science of Language*, 1880, 2d ed. 1883; *The Monuments of the Hittites*, 1881; *The Cuneiform Inscriptions of Van deciphered and translated*, 1882; *The First Three Books of Herodotus, edited with Notes and Appendices*, 1883; *The Ancient Empires of the East*, 1884; *Fresh Light from the Monuments*, 1884; *Introduction to the Books of Ezra, Nehemiah, and Esther*, 1885.

SCARBOROUGH, Right Rev. John, D.D. (Trinity College, Hartford, Conn., 1872), Episcopalian, bishop of New Jersey; b. in Castle Wellan, Ireland, April 25, 1831; graduated at Trinity College, Hartford, Conn., 1854, and at the General Theological Seminary, New-York City, 1857; became assistant minister of St. Paul's Church, Troy, N.Y., 1857; rector of the Church of the Holy Comforter, Poughkeepsie, N.Y., 1860; and of Trinity Church, Pittsburg, Penn., 1867; bishop, 1875. *

SCHAEFER, Aloys, D.D. (Würzburg, 1879), Roman Catholic; b. at Dingelstädt, Saxony, May 2, 1853; studied philosophy and theology at Prague and Würzburg, 1873-79; became chaplain in the Court Church at Dresden, 1879; professor in the royal lyceum at Dillingen, Bavaria, 1881; professor extraordinary of New-Testament exegesis at Münster, 1885. He is the author of *Die biblische Chronologie vom Auszug aus Ægypten bis zum Beginn des babylonischen Exils, mit Berücksichtigung der Resultate der Ægyptologie und Assyriologie* (prize essay at Würzburg), Münster, 1879; essays on biblico-mariology in the *Theol. prakt. Quartalsschrift*, Linz, 1885 sqq.

SCHAEFFER, Charles William, D.D. (University of Pennsylvania, Philadelphia, 1879), Lutheran (General Council); b. at Hagerstown, Md., May 5, 1813; graduated at University of Pennsylvania, Philadelphia, 1832; was pastor in Montgomery County, Penn., 1835-41; at Harrisburg, Penn., 1841-49; at Germantown, Penn., 1849-75; has been professor in the theological seminary of the Lutheran Church, Philadelphia, since 1864; and a member of the Board of Trustees in the University of Pennsylvania since 1857. He is the author of *Early History of the Lutheran Church in America*, Philadelphia, 1857, 2d ed. 1864; *Bogatzky's Golden Treasury*, translated 1858, several later editions; *Family Prayer, a Book of Devotions*, 1859, 5th ed. 1885; *Halle Reports*, translated from the German, with extensive historical, critical, and literary annotations, vol. i., 1880; *Wackernagel's Life of Luther*, translated 1883; *Hans Sachs' Wittenberg Nightingale*, translated 1883; numerous articles for reviews, etc.

SCHAEFFER, Hermann Moritz, Baptist; b. at Lage, Lippe-Detmold, Germany, Aug. 22, 1839; emigrated in 1854; studied in the German department of Rochester (N.Y.) Theological Seminary, 1861-64; graduated from the English department, 1867; became pastor of the First German Baptist Church, New-York City, 1867; professor of biblical literature in the German department, Rochester Baptist Seminary, 1872. *

SCHAFF, David Schley, Presbyterian; b. at Mercersburg, Penn., Octob. 17, 1852; graduated at Yale College, New Haven, Conn., 1873, and at Union Theol. Seminary, N. Y. City, 1876; pastor at Hastings, Neb., 1877-81; associate editor of *Schaff-Herzog Encyclopædia*, N. Y. City, 1881-83; pastor of First Presbyterian Church, Kansas City, Mo., 1883 to date. He contributed to Schaff's (his father's) *Bible Dictionary*, Phila., 1880; edited, abridged, and adapted to the Revised Version, Howson and Spence's commentary on *Acts* (originally published in Schaff's *Popular Commentary*) for the *International Revision Commentary*, N.Y., 1882.

SCHAFF, Philip, Lic. Theol. (Berlin, 1841), **D.D.** (*hon.*, Berlin, 1854), **LL.D.** (Amherst College, Mass., 1874), Presbyterian; b. at Coire, Switzerland, Jan. 1, 1819; studied at Coire, in the gymnasium at Stuttgart, and in the universities of Tübingen, Halle, and Berlin; travelled as tutor of a Prussian nobleman, through Italy and other countries of Europe, 1841; returned to Berlin, and lectured in the university there as *privat-docent*, on exegesis and church history, 1842-44; was called in 1843 (upon the recommendation of Neander, Tholuck, Julius Müller, and others) to a professorship in the theological seminary of the German Reformed Church of the United States, then located at Mercersburg, Penn., and held the position until 1863 (including eleven months spent in Europe, 1851). He was charged with heresy, but acquitted by the synod at York, 1845. He lectured on all departments of theology, and was chairman of two committees which prepared a new liturgy (1857) and a new hymn-book (1859). During the Civil War, when the seminary at Mercersburg (on the borders of the scene of conflict) was turned into a military hospital, he removed to New-York City, December, 1863; was secretary of the New-York Sabbath Committee, 1864-69; and delivered courses of lectures on church history in the theological seminaries at Andover, Hartford, and New York (Union); made a second visit to Europe (1865), in behalf of Sunday observance and Sunday schools; was called to a professorship in the Union Theological Seminary, New-York City, 1869; was professor of theological encyclopædia and Christian symbolics, 1870-72; of Hebrew, 1872-74; since 1875, of sacred literature. He is one of the founders and honorary secretaries of the American branch of the Evangelical Alliance; and was sent three times (1869, 1872, 1873) as commissioner to Europe to make arrangements for the sixth General Conference of the Alliance, which, after a second postponement in consequence of the Franco-German war, was held in New York, October, 1873. He was also one of the Alliance delegates to the emperor of Russia in 1871, to intercede with him in behalf of the religious liberty of his subjects in the Baltic provinces, and prepared the official report. He was sent as a delegate to the General Conferences of the Alliance at Basel (1879), and at Copenhagen (1884). He attended, as a delegate, the meeting in London which organized the Alliance of the Reformed Churches in 1875, and its first General Council in Edinburgh, 1877; and was chairman of the programme committee for its second General Council in Philadelphia, 1880 (in behalf of which he made the arrangements in Europe). He is president of the American Bible-revision Committee, which he organized in 1871 at the request of the British Committee; and he was sent to England in 1875 to negotiate with the British revisers and university presses about the terms of co-operation and publication of the Anglo-American Revision. He attended several meetings of the British Committee in the Jerusalem Chamber, London, the last in July, 1884. In 1877 he made a tour through Bible lands, in 1884 through Scandinavia and Russia, in 1886 through Spain, France, and Germany.

His books are mostly historical and exegetical.

I. His principal works are: *History of the Apostolic Church*, Mercersburg, 1851, in German (Eng. trans., by Dr. Yeomans, New York, 1853, Edinburgh, 1854, several editions without change; 2d German revised ed., Leipzig, 1854; Dutch trans., Tiel, 1857); *History of the Christian Church*, New York, 1858 sqq., *A.D. 1-600*, 3 vols. (German ed., Leipzig, 1867, 2d ed. 1869, 3 vols.); entirely rewritten in English, and more than doubled in size, New York and Edinburgh, 1882-84, 3 vols., vol. iv., *A.D. 590-1073*, New York and Edinburgh, 1885; 3d revision of the entire set, 1886 (to be continued); *Bibliotheca Symbolica Ecclesiæ Universalis: The Creeds of Christendom, with a History and Critical Notes*, New York and London, 1877, 3 vols., 4th ed. 1884; *A Companion to the Greek Testament and the English Version*, New York and London, 1883, revised ed. 1885; *The Oldest Church Manual, called the Teaching of the Twelve Apostles* (an independent supplement to the second volume of his revised *Church History*) New York, 1885, revised ed. 1886; *The Person of Christ*, Boston, 1865, 12th ed., New York and London, 1882 (translated into German, French, Dutch, Greek, Russian, Japanese, etc.); *Through Bible Lands: Notes of Travel in Egypt, the Desert, and Palestine*, New York and London, 1878, several editions; *Bible Dictionary*, with illustrations, Philadelphia (American Sunday-school Union, 1880, 3d ed. revised, 1885, translated into several languages); *Commentaries* on *Matthew* and on *Galatians* (in his *Popular Commentary*), and large additions to the American edition of Lange on *Matthew, Luke* (the first 3 chs.) *John*, and *Romans* (especially in the textual and critical department); *Christ and Christianity*, New York and London, 1885; *St. Augustin, Melanchthon, and Neander*, N.Y. and Lond., 1886; *August Neander*, Gotha, 1886.

II. His earliest books were written and published in Germany; viz., *Die Sünde wider den heiligen Geist*, Halle, 1841; and *Das Verhältniss des Jakobus, Bruders des Herrn, zu Jakobus Alphäi*, Berlin, 1842.

III. His other publications, German and English, including those which he edited in connection with other American scholars, are as follows: *Das Princip des Protestantismus* (his inaugural address, German and English, translated by Dr. Nevin), Chambersburg, 1845; *What is Church History? A Vindication of the Idea of Historical Development*, Philadelphia, 1846; *Der heilige Augustinus*, Berlin, 1854 (trans. by Th. C. Porter, N.Y. and Lond.); *Amerika* (lectures delivered in Berlin on a visit in 1854), Berlin, 1854, 2d ed. 1858, enlarged ed. 1865 (in English, New York, 1866, also in Dutch); *German Universities*, Philadelphia, 1857 (translated into Dutch, Utrecht, 1858); *Christlicher Katechismus*, Philadelphia, 1863, many editions in German and English (*Christian Catechism for Sunday Schools and Families*, Philadelphia, 1863; new ed. by the American Sunday-school Union, Philadelphia, 1881, etc.; translated into Syriac, Arabic, Chinese, and Japanese); *Der Bürgerkrieg u. d. christl. Leben in America* (lectures delivered in Berlin on a visit in 1865), Berlin, 1865, 3d ed. 1866. He edited, with hymnological introduction and notes, *Deutsches Gesangbuch*, Philadelphia and Berlin, 1859, new ed. with tunes and appendix, 1874; *Deutsches Sonntagsschulgesangbuch*, Philadelphia, 1864; *Der Heidelb. Katechismus* (with its history to the tercentenary celebration in 1863), Philadelphia, 1863, revised ed. 1866; *Christ in Song*, New York 1868, London 1869 and 1876; Lightfoot, Trench, and Ellicott, *On the Revision of the English Version of the New Testament* (3 essays in 1 vol., with introductory essay on Bible revision), New York, 1873; *Proceedings of the General Conference of the Evangelical Alliance in New York*, 1874; W. E. Gladstone's *Rome and the Newest Fashions in Religion* (with introduction on the Vatican Council), New York, 1875. He prepared, with the co-operation of many scholars from various denominations, the Anglo-American edition of Lange's *Commentary on the Old and New Testaments* (with supplementary volume on the Apocrypha by E. C. Bissell), New York and Edinburgh, 1864-80, 25 vols., a new ed. 1886; *Popular Illustrated Commentary on the New Testament*, New York and Edinburgh, 1878-83, 4 vols. (re-issued in revised form, on basis of Revised Version, under title, *International Revision Commentary on the New Testament*, New York, 1882 sqq.). He edited, in connection with Professor Henry B. Smith, *The Philosophical and Theological Library*, New York and London, 1872-79 (in which appeared Ueberweg's *History of Philosophy*, 1872-74, 2 vols.; Van Oosterzee's *Christian Dogmatics*, 1874, 2 vols.; and *Practical Theology*, 1879); with Rev. Drs. Hitchcock and Zachary Eddy, *Hymns and Songs of Praise*, New York, 1874; with Mr. Arthur Gilman, *Library of Religious Poetry*, New York, 1881, new ed. 1886; with Rev. Samuel M. Jackson and Rev. D. S. Schaff, *The Religious Encyclopædia*, based on Herzog, New York and Edinburgh, 1884, 3 vols., revised ed. 1887; and with Rev. Samuel M. Jackson, the *Dictionary of Contemporary Divines*, N.Y., 1887. He founded and edited the *Deutsche Kirchenfreund* (the first German theological monthly in America), Mercersburg, Penn., 6 vols., 1848-53; and *Evangelische Zeugnisse*, Phila., 1863-66. He was one of the associate editors of Johnson's *Univ. Cyclopædia*, N.Y., 1875, rev. 1886. He assumed in 1886 the editorship of *A Select Library of the Nicene and Post-Nicene Fathers*, to be published by the "Christian Literature Company" at Buffalo, N.Y., in about 25 volumes, with the aid of a number of patristic scholars in England and America. The first volume appeared October, 1886. Besides the above, he has written documents, reports, addresses, review and encyclopædia articles, etc.

SCHANZ, Paul, Ph.D. (Tübingen, 1867), **D.D.** (Tübingen, 1876), Roman Catholic; b. at Horb, Würtemberg, March 4, 1841; studied at Tübingen, 1861–65; in Rottenburg Seminary, 1865–66; became professor of mathematics and the natural sciences in the Rottweil gymnasium, 1870; of New-Testament exegesis in the Roman-Catholic theological faculty at Tübingen, 1876; of dogmatics and apologetics in the same, 1883. He is the author of *Cardinal Nicolaus von Cusa als Mathematiker* (program), Rottweil, 1872; *Die astronomischen Anschauungen des Nicolaus von Cusa und seiner Zeit*, 1873; *Die christliche Weltanschauung und die modernen Naturwissenschaften* (academical lecture), Tübingen, 1876; *Die Composition des Matthaeusevangeliums* (program), 1877; *Einleitung in das N.T. von Prof. Dr. Aberle* (edited), 1877; *Galileo Galilei und sein Process*, Würzburg, 1878.

SCHÉELE, Knut Henning Gezelius von, D.D. (Upsala, 1877), Lutheran; b. in Stockholm, Sweden, May 31, 1838; graduated at Upsala; became *privat-docent*, 1865; provost, 1877; ordinary member of consistory, 1878; professor, 1879, and inspector of the teachers' seminary (1880), and censor of the demission examinations in the Swedish upper schools (1884); in 1885 appointed bishop of Visby. He was member of the House of Nobility in the Swedish parliament, 1865–66; president of the General Seminary Meeting in Stockholm, 1880 and 1884; member of the Basel Alliance Conference, 1879, and reported on Scandinavia; also of the General Swedish Clergy Conferences in Stockholm, 1881 and 1884. He is the author in Swedish of *The Ontological Evidence of the Existence of God*, Upsala, 1863; *The Preparations of the Theological Rationalism*, 1868, 2d ed. Stockholm, 1877; *The Church Catechising*, Upsala, 1869, 4th ed. Stockholm, 1881; *The Christmas Cycle of the Second Series of the New Evangelical Pericops* (in the Swedish Church), Upsala, 1874; *Theological Symbolic*, 1877–79, 2 parts (German trans., Gotha, 1881); *From the Court into the Sanctuary, Apologetic Essays*, Stockholm, 1879 (Norwegian trans., Christiania, 1880); *The Fight for the Peace, Apologetic Essays*, 1881; *Compendium of Theological Symbolic*, Upsala, 1885; sermons, and review articles.

SCHEGG, Peter, Roman Catholic; b. at Kaufbeuren, June 6, 1815; d. at Munich, July 9, 1885. He was professor of biblical hermeneutics and New-Testament exegesis at the University of Munich; founded, with three hundred thousand marks (fifteen thousand pounds), a Roman-Catholic orphan-asylum in his native place; and wrote commentaries on the *Psalms* (Munich, 2d ed. 1857, 3 vols.), *Minor Prophets* (1854, 2 vols., 2d ed. 1862), *Matthew, Mark, Luke* (1856–70, 8 vols., 2d ed. 1863 sqq.); *Geschichte der letzten Propheten*, Regensburg, 1853–54, 2 parts; *Sechs Bücher des Lebens Jesu*, Freiburg-im-Br., 1874–75, 2 vols.; *Erinnerungen an Dr. Bonifacius, Bischof von Speyer*, Munich, 1877; *Das Todesjahr des Königs Herodes u. das Todesjahr Jesu Christi*, 1882; *Jakobus, der Bruder des Herrn, und sein Brief*, 1883; *Das hohe Lied Salomos*, 1885 (derived almost entirely from Delitzsch; cf. notice by V. Ryssel, in Schürer's *Literaturzeitung*, No. 17, Aug. 22, 1885).

SCHELL, Herman, Ph.D. (Freiburg, 1872), **D.D.** (Tübingen, 1883); Roman Catholic; b. at Freiburg-im-Breisgau, Feb. 28, 1850; educated at Freiburg, 1868–70; at Würzburg, 1870–73; in the College of Anima, Rome, 1879–81; became professor extraordinary of apologetics at Würzburg, 1884. He is the author of *Die Einheit des Seelenlebens aus den Principien der aristotelischen Philosophie entwickelt*, Freiburg, 1873; *Das Wirken des dreieinigen Gottes*, Mainz, 1885, 2 vols.

SCHENCK, William Edward, D.D. (Jefferson College, Canonsburg, Penn., 1861), Presbyterian; b. at Princeton, N.J., March 29, 1819; graduated at the College of New Jersey, Princeton, 1838, and at Princeton Theological Seminary, 1841; became pastor at Manchester, N.J., 1842; of Hammond-street Church, New-York City, 1845; of First Church at Princeton, N.J., 1848; superintendent of church extension in Presbytery of Philadelphia, Penn., 1852; corresponding secretary of the Presbyterian board of publication, Philadelphia, 1854. He was editor of the board of publication, 1862–70; permanent clerk of the General Assembly (Old School), 1862–70; has been trustee of the General Assembly (and vice-president of the board of trustees) since 1864; director of Princeton Theological Seminary since 1866. He is the author of *A Historical Account of the First Presbyterian Church of Princeton, N.J.*, Princeton, 1851; *Aunt Fanny's Home*, Philadelphia, 1865; *Children in Heaven*, 1866; *Nearing Home*, 1867; *General Catalogue of Princeton Theological Seminary*, Trenton, 1881; sermons, tracts (*God our Guide*, 1867; *The Fountain for Sin*, 1868 [in German], etc.); necrological reports of the Princeton Theological Seminary, 1875–85; minor works.

SCHENKEL, Daniel, D.D., German Protestant theologian; b. at Dägerlen, Canton Zürich, Switzerland, Dec. 21, 1813; d. at Heidelberg, Germany, May 19, 1885. He studied at Basel and Göttingen; became *privat-docent* at Basel, 1838; pastor in the minster at Schaffhausen, in succession to F. E. von Hurter (see *Encyclopædia*), 1841, and *kirchenrath*, 1842; ordinary professor of theology at Basel, 1849; professor, *seminardirector*, and university preacher at Heidelberg, 1851; later also a *kirchenrath*. At twenty-five he was editor of the *Basler Zeitung*, in which he vigorously opposed Swiss radicalism. He was at first nearly orthodox, but became the head of the *Protestantenverein*, and from 1860 to 1872 edited in its interest the *Allgemeine kirchliche Zeitschrift*, published at Elberfeld. He was the author of *Johannes Schenkel, Pfarrer zu Unterhallau*, Hamburg, 1837; *De ecclesia Corinthia primæva factionibus turbata*, Basel, 1838; *Die Wissenschaft und die Kirche*, 1839; *Vier und zwanzig Predigten über Grund und Ziel unseres Glaubens*, Zürich, 1843, 2 vols.; *Die confessionellen Zerwürfnisse in Schaffhausen und Friedrich Hurter's Uebertritt zur römisch-katholischen Kirche*, Basel, 1844; *Die protestantische Geistlichkeit und die Deutsch-Katholiken*, Zürich, 1846; *Das Wesen des Protestantismus aus den Quellen des Reformationszeitalters beleuchtet*, Schaffhausen, 1846–51, 3 vols., 2d ed. 1862; *Die religiösen Zeitkämpfe in ihrem Zusammenhange mit dem Wesen der Religion und der religiösen Gesammtentwicklung des Protestantismus*, Hamburg, 1847; *Das Kommen des Herrn in unserer Zeit*, Schaffhausen, 1849; *W. M. L. de Wette und die Bedeutung seiner Theologie für unsere Zeit*, 1849; *Predigten*, 1850–51, 2 vols.; *Das Princip des Protestantismus*, 1852;

Gespräche über Protestantismus und Katholicismus, Heidelberg, 1852–53, 2 parts; *Evangelische Zeugnisse von Christo* (sermons on texts from the *Gospel of John*), 1853–54, 2 vols.; *Das Wesen des evangelischen Glaubens* (lectures on behalf of the Inner Mission), Frankfurt-am-Main, 1854; *Der Unionsberuf des evangelischen Protestantismus*, Heidelberg, 1855; *Die Reformatoren und die Reformation*, Wiesbaden, 1856; *Die christliche Dogmatik vom Standpunkte des Gewissens*, 1858–59, 2 vols.; *Die Erneuerung der deutschen evangelischen Kirche nach den Grundsätzen der Reformation*, Gotha, 1860; *Die kirchliche Frage und ihre protestantische Lösung*, Elberfeld, 1862; *Die Bildung der evangelischen Theologen für den praktischen Kirchendienst*, Heidelberg, 1863; *Das Charakterbild Jesu*, Wiesbaden, 1864, 4th ed. 1873 (English trans. by W. H. Furness, *Character of Jesus portrayed*, Boston, 1866, 2 vols.); *Zur Orientirung über meine Schrift, "Das Charakterbild Jesu,"* 1864; *Die protestantische Freiheit in ihrem gegenwärtigen Kampfe mit der kirchlichen Reaktion*, 1865; *Christenthum und Kirche im Einklange mit der Culturentwicklung*, 1867, 2 parts, 2d ed. 1872; *Der deutsche Protestantenverein und seine Bedeutung in der Gegenwart, nach den Akten dargestellt*, 1868, 2d ed. 1871; *Luther und seine Kampfgenossen*, Lahr, 1868; *Bibel-Lexikon* (edited, with Dillmann, Hausrath, Holtzmann, Keim, Lipsius, Reuss, Schrader, and others), Leipzig, 1868–75, 5 vols.; *Brennende Fragen in der Kirche der Gegenwart*, Wiesbaden, 1869, 2d ed. 1871; *Luther in Worms und in Wittenberg und die Erneuerung der Kirche in der Gegenwart*, Elberfeld, 1870; *Die Grundlehren des Christenthums aus dem Bewusstsein des Glaubens im Zusammenhange dargestellt*, Leipzig, 1877; *Das Christusbild der Apostel und der nachapostolischen Zeit*, 1879; numerous sermons, essays, and minor works. *

SCHERER, Edmond Henri Adolphe, B. Theol., Lic. Theol., D.D. (all Strassburg, 1839, 1841, 1843, respectively), French Protestant; b. in Paris, April 8, 1815; studied theology at Strassburg; became professor of exegesis at the Genevan School of Theology, where he had Gaussen for his colleague (1845), and where he edited the *Réformation au dix-neuvième siècle* (1845–48). In 1849 he resigned because of a change of views, and became a leader among the Liberals, and a prolific writer for the religious press. In 1860 he removed to Versailles; has since written many critical and political articles for *Le Temps;* represented Seine et Oise in the National Assembly, 1871; and on Dec. 15, 1875, was appointed a senator for life. Of his religious works may be mentioned, *Prolégomènes à la dogmatique de l'Église réformée*, Paris, 1843; *Alexandre Vinet*, 1853; *Lettres à mon curé*, 1853, 2d ed. 1859; *Mélanges d'histoire religieuse*, Paris, 1864; *Diderot*, 1884; besides these he has published several volumes of literary and critical essays.

SCHERESCHEWSKY, Right Rev. Samuel Isaac, D.D. (Kenyon College, Gambier, O., 1876), **S.T.D.** (Columbia College, New-York City, 1877); b. at Tanroggen, Russian Lithuania, May 6, 1831; educated at the rabbinical college at Zhitomer (Russia), the University of Breslau (Germany), and the General Theological Seminary (New-York City); elected missionary bishop of China, 1875 (declined) and 1877; resigned on account of serious and prolonged illness, 1883. He has translated the Old Testament from Hebrew into Mandarin Chinese, Mark into Mongolian, with Bishop Burdon of Hong Kong the Prayer-Book into Mandarin Chinese, and was one of the committee to translate the New Testament into it. *

SCHLOTTMANN, Konstantin, D.D. (——————), German Protestant theologian; b. at Minden, March 7, 1819; became *privat-docent* at Berlin, 1847; Prussian embassy preacher at Constantinople, 1850; ordinary professor of theology at Zürich 1855, at Bonn 1859, and at Halle 1866. He is one of the revisers of the German Bible. Among his writings may be mentioned, *Das Buch Hiob verdeutscht und erläutert*, Berlin, 1851; *De Philippo Melanchthone reipublicæ litterariaê reformatore*, Bonn, 1860; *De reipublicæ litterariæ originibus*, 1861; *David Strauss als Romantiker des Heidenthums*, Halle, 1878; *Erasmus redivivus sive de curia hucusque romana insanabili*, 1883; *Wider Kliefoth und Luthardt. In Sachen der Luther-Bibel*, 1885. *

SCHMID, Aloys, D.D. (Munich, 1850), Roman Catholic; b. at Zaumberg, Bavaria, Dec. 22, 1825; studied at Munich, 1844–50; was professor in the Zweibrücken gymnasium, 1852–54; professor of philosophy in the royal lyceum at Dillingen, 1852–66; has been professor of apologetics and dogmatics in the University of Munich since 1866. He is an archiepiscopal ecclesiastical councillor. He is the author of *Die Bisthumsynode*, Regensburg, 1850–51, 2 vols.; *Entwicklungsgeschichte der Hegel'schen Logik*, 1858; *Thomistische und Scotistische Gewissheitslehre*, Dillingen, 1859; *Wissenschaftliche Richtungen auf dem Gebiete des Katholicismus in neuester und in gegenwärtiger Zeit*, Munich, 1862; *Wissenschaft und Auctorität*, 1868; *Untersuchungen über den letzten Grund des Offenbarungsglaubens*, 1879.

SCHMID, Andreas, D.D. (Munich, 1866), Roman Catholic; b. at Zaumberg, Bavaria, Jan. 9, 1840; studied theology at Munich, 1860–63; was ordained priest, 1863; became *subregens* of the Georgianum priests' seminary at Munich, 1865; director of the same, and professor of pastoral theology in the University of Munich, 1877. He is the author of *Der christliche Altar und sein Schmuck*, Regensburg, 1871.

SCHMID, Heinrich, German Lutheran theologian; b. at Harburg, near Nördlingen, July 31, 1811; studied at Halle, Berlin, and Erlangen; became at the latter *repetent* 1837, *privat-docent* 1846, professor extraordinary 1848, and ordinary 1854, and retired in 1881. He has written, *Die Dogmatik der evangelisch-lutherischen Kirche dargestellt und aus den Quellen belegt*, Erlangen, 1843, 6th ed. Frankfurt-am-Main, 1876 (English trans., *The Doctrinal Theology of the Lutheran Church*, Philadelphia, 1876); *Geschichte der synkretitistischen Streitigkeiten in der Zeit des Georg Calixt*, Erlangen, 1846; *Lehrbuch der Kirchengeschichte*, Nördlingen, 1851, 2d ed. 1856; *Die Theologie Semlers*, 1858; *Lehrbuch der Dogmengeschichte*, 1859, 3d ed. 1877; *Geschichte des Pietismus*, 1863; *Der Kampf der lutherischen Kirche um Luthers Lehre vom Abendmahl im Reformationszeitalter*, Leipzig, 1867, 2d ed. 1873; *Handbuch der Kirchengeschichte*, Erlangen, 1880–81, 2 parts. D. 1885. *

SCHMIDT, Charles Guillaume Adolphe, Lic. Theol., D.D. (both Strassburg, 1835 and 1836), Lutheran; b. at Strassburg, Alsace, June 20, 1812; studied theology in its university, 1828–33;

became *privat-docent*, 1837; professor of practical theology in its Protestant seminary, 1839; of the same in the university, 1843; of ecclesiastical history, 1863; professor *emeritus*, 1877. He is the author of *Études sur Farel*, Strassburg, 1834; *Vie de Pierre Martyr Vermigli* (thesis for his degree of licentiate in theology), 1835; *Essai sur les mystiques du XIVe siècle* (thesis for his degree of D.D.), 1836; *Essai sur Jean Gerson*, 1839; *Meister Eckart* (in *Theol. Studien u. Kritiken*), 1839; *Plaintes d'un laique allemand du XIVe siècle sur la décadence de la chrétienté*, 1840; *Ueber die Sekten zu Strassburg im Mittelalter*, 1840; *Johannes Tauler von Strassburg*, Hamburg, 1841; *Heinrich Suso* (in *Theol. Studien u. Kritiken*), 1842; *Claudius von Turin*, 1843; *Gérard Roussel prédicateur de la reine Marguérite de Navarre*, Strassburg, 1845; *Étude sur le mysticisme allemand au XIVe siècle* (in *Mémoires de l'académie des sciences morales*), 1847; *Histoire et doctrine de la secte des Cathares ou Albigeois*, Paris, 1849, 2 vols.; *Essai historique sur la société civile dans le monde romain et sur sa transformation par le christianisme*, Strassburg, 1853 (German trans., Leipzig, 1857; Dutch trans., Amsterdam, 1862; English trans., *The Social Results of Early Christianity*, London, 1885); *Die Gottesfreunde im vierzehnten Jahrhundert* (in *Beiträge zu den theologischen Wissenschaften von Reuss u. Cunitz*), Jena, 1854; *La vie et les travaux de Jean Sturm, fondateur du gymnase de Strasbourg*, Strassburg, 1855; *Peter Martyr Vermiglis Leben und Schriften*, Elberfeld, 1858; *Rulman Merswin, Die neun Felsen, nach dem Autograph herausgegeben*, Leipzig, 1859; *Girolamo Zanchi* (in *Theol. Studien u. Kritiken*), 1859; *Histoire du chapitre de Saint Thomas de Strasbourg pendant le moyen âge*, Strassburg, 1860; *Calio Secundo Curioni* (in *Zeitschrift für hist. Theologie*), 1860; *Wilhelm Farel und Peter Viret*, Elberfeld, 1860; *Melanchthons Leben*, 1860; *Berthold von Regensburg* (in *Theol. Studien und Kritiken*), 1864; *Nicolaus von Basel, Leben und Schriften*, Wien, 1866; *Traités mystiques écrits en 1547–1549*, Basel, 1876; *Histoire littéraire de l'Alsace à la fin du 15. siècle et au commencement du 16.*, Paris, 1878, 2 vols.; *Poésies huguénotes du 16. siècle*, Strassburg, 1881; *Zur Geschichte der ältesten Bibliotheken und der ersten Buchdrucker zu Strassburg*, 1882; *Précis de l'histoire de l'Église d'Occident au moyen âge*, Paris, 1885.

SCHMIDT, Christoph Hermann, D.D. (*hon.*, Halle, 1881), Protestant theologian; b. at Frickenhofen, Würtemberg, Feb. 23, 1832; studied at Tübingen, 1850–54; was there *repetent*, 1858–61; *diakonus* in Kalw, 1863–69, and at Stuttgart, 1869–81; became ordinary professor of theology at Breslau, 1881. He has written *Geschichte der inneren Mission in Württemberg*, Hamburg, 1879; *Das Verhältniss der christlichen Glaubenslehre zu den anderen Aufgaben akademischer Wissenschaft*, Gotha, 1881; *Die Kirche, ihre biblische Idee und die Formen ihrer Erscheinung*, Leipzig, 1884.

SCHMIDT, Paul (Wilhelm), Ph.D. (Halle, 1865), **Lic. Theol.** (Berlin, 1867), **D.D.** (*hon.*, Strassburg, 1885), Protestant theologian; b. in Berlin, Dec. 25, 1845; educated at Berlin; was *privat-docent* there, 1869–76; editor of the *Protestantische Kirchenzeitung*, 1870–76; general secretary of the German Protestant Union, 1874–76; became ordinary professor of theology at Basel, 1876; since 1880 has been a member of the Basel *Kirchenrath*. He was a contributor to the *Protestanten-Bibel, Neuen Testaments*, Leipzig, 1873, 3d ed. 1879 (English trans. by Francis Henry Jones, B.A., *A Short Protestant Commentary on the Books of the New Testament*, London, 1882–84, 3 vols.); and has written independently, *Spinoza u. Schleiermacher*, Berlin, 1868; *Neutestamentliche Hyperkritik, an dem jüngsten Angriff gegen die Æchtheit des Philipperbriefes auf ihre Methode hin untersucht. Nebst e. Erklärg. d. Briefes*, 1880; *Der erste Thessalonicherbrief, neu erklärt, Nebst e. Excurs üb. d. zweiten gleichnam. Brief*, 1885; numerous articles and pamphlets upon theological and ecclesiastical subjects, e.g., as in F. von Holtzendorff's *Zeit u. Streit fragen*.

SCHMIDT, Woldemar Gottlob, D.D. (*hon.*, Göttingen, 187–), Protestant theologian; b. at St. Afra in Meissen, Saxony, June 2, 1836; studied at Leipzig and Göttingen, 1854–57; was "teacher of religion" at Plauen, Zwickau, and St. Afra gymnasiums, 1858–66; became professor extraordinary at Leipzig 1866, and ordinary professor 1876. He is the author of *Der Lehrgehalt des Jakobusbriefes*, Leipzig, 1869; *Der Bericht der Apostelgeschichte über Stephanus* (*Program*), 1882; articles and reviews in *Jahrbücher für deutsche Theologie*, 1866 sqq.; book-notices in Harnack and Schürer's *Theolog. Lit-Zeitung*, 1876 sqq.; articles "Hermeneutik," "Kanon d. N. T.," "Paulus," etc., in the 2d ed. of Herzog's *Real Encyklopädie*; editor of 5th ed. Meyer's *Commentary on Ephesians*, Göttingen, 1878.

SCHMIEDEL, Paul Wilhelm, Lic. Theol. (Jena, 1878), Protestant theologian; b. at Zaukeroda, near Dresden, Saxony, Dec. 22, 1851; studied at Leipzig 1871–74, at Jena 1874–75; became *privat-docent* of theology at Jena, 1878. He is a moderate liberal. He is the author of *Quæ intercedat ratio inter doctrinam epistolæ ad Hebræos missæ et Pauli apostoli doctrinam*, Jena, 1878; articles upon "Kanon (A. u. N. T.)," "Katholische Briefe," "Kolossæ, Briefe an die Kolosser und an die Epheser," "Korintherbriefe," in Ersch u. Gruber, *Allgemeine Encyclopädie der Wissenschaften und Künste*, Leipzig.

SCHMUCKER, Beale Melancthon, D.D. (University of Pennsylvania, Philadelphia, 1870), Lutheran (General Council); b. at Gettysburg, Penn., Aug. 26, 1827; graduated at Pennsylvania College, Gettysburg, Penn., 1844, and at the Theological Seminary there 1847; was pastor at Martinsburg, Va., 1848–51; Allentown, Penn., 1852–62; Easton, Penn., 1862–67; Reading, Penn., 1867–81; since at Pottstown, Penn. He has been corresponding secretary of the General Council of the Lutheran Church since 1867, secretary of Committee for Foreign Missions of the General Council since 1869. He edited *Liturgy of Pennsylvania Synod*, Philadelphia, 1860; *Church-Book for the Use of Evangelical Lutheran Congregations*, 1868, 2d ed. 1870; *Halle Reports, Reprinted with Historical and Explanatory Notes* (with Drs. W. J. Mann and W. Germann), vol. i. 1886; pamphlets, etc.

SCHNEDERMANN, Georg Hermann, Ph.D. (Leipzig, 1878), **Lic. Theol.** (Leipzig, 1880), Lutheran theologian; b. at Chemnitz, Saxony, July 3, 1852; studied at Leipzig 1872–75, at Erlangen 1874; was teacher in Switzerland and Westphalia, 1875–77; member of the Theological Seminary at Leipzig, 1877–79; became *privat-docent* of theology there 1880; at Basel, 1883. He belongs to the school of Frank of Erlangen. He is the author of *Die Controverse des Ludovicus Cappellus mit den Buxtorfen über das Alter der hebr. Punctation* (doctor's dissertation, 1878), Leipzig, 1879; *De fidei notione ethica Paulina* (*Habilitationsschrift*), 1880; *Der christliche Glaube und die heilige Schrift* (lecture), Basel, 1884; *Das Judenthum und die christliche Verkündigung in den Evangelien. Ein Beitrag zur Grundlegung der bibl. Theologie und Geschichte*, Leipzig, 1884; editor (with Delitzsch) of Weber's *System der altsynagogalen palästinischen Theologie*, 1880; has written essays on phases of Pharisaical Judaism for Luthardt's jubilee, 1881, in Luthardt's *Zt. f. K. Wiss.*, 1882–84, and in the Basel *Kirchenfreund*, 1885-86.

SCHODDE, George Henry, Ph.D. (Leipzig, 1876), Lutheran (General Council); b. at Allegheny City, Penn., April 15, 1854; graduated at Capital University, Columbus, O. (at college 1872, theological seminary 1874); studied at Tübingen 1874-75, Leipzig 1876; became pastor at Wheeling, W. Va., 1877; professor of Greek in the college of Capital University, 1881 (also has taught in the Hebrew department of the theological seminary). He is the author of *The Book of Enoch, translated from the Ethiopic*, Andover, 1882; and of numerous contributions to the *Journal of the German Oriental Society*, *Bibliotheca Sacra*, *Lutheran Quarterly*, *Independent*, etc.

SCHOELL, Carl Wilhelm, Ph.D. (Tübingen, 1851), Lutheran; b. at Güglingen, Würtemberg, Aug. 4, 1820; educated at Tübingen; became in 1846 assistant minister, and in 1859 pastor of the German Lutheran Church in the Savoy, now Cleveland Street, London. He has been examiner in the German language and literature to the Military Education Division, War Office, London, since 1858; to the Civil Service Commission, London, since 1864; and in the University of London since 1882 (as from 1872-75). He is the author of *De ecclesiasticæ Britonum Scotorumque historiae fontibus*, Berlin, 1851; and contributor to Herzog's *Real Encyklopädie*, 1st and 2d editions.

SCHOENFELDER, Josephus Maria, D.D. (Munich, 1860), Roman Catholic; b. at Forchheim, Bavaria, June 8, 1838; educated at Bamberg, Erlangen, and Munich; was *sacellanus* at Bamberg, 1861-65; professor of theology at Hildesheim, 1866; *chorvicar* of St. Cajetan in Munich, 1867-71; court preacher at St. Michael's, Munich, 1871-74; *privat-docent* in the University of Munich, 1869-73; professor extraordinary of theology, 1873-74; since 1874 ordinary professor; since 1886 canon of St. Cajetan's. He is also senator. He is the author of *Die Kirchengeschichte des Johannes von Ephesus*, Munich, 1862; *Salomonis Episcopi Bassorensis Liber Apis*, Bamberg, 1866; *Onkelos und Peschittho*, Munich, 1869; treatises and articles in theological periodicals.

SCHOLTEN, Jan Hendrik, Ph.D., D.D. (both Utrecht, 1835 and 1836, respectively), Dutch Protestant theologian; b. at Vleuten, near Utrecht, Aug. 17, 1811; d. at Leiden, April 10, 1885. He studied at the University of Utrecht; became pastor at Meerkerk, 1836; professor of theology in the Athenæum at Franeker, 1840; the same in the University of Leiden, 1843; retired in 1881. He was rector of the university in 1847, 1857, and 1877. He was the head of the critical school of Dutch theologians, and the author of the so-called "modern theology," which arose about 1858, and which rejects the supernatural; looks upon Christianity as the religion of Jesus, rather than as founded upon Jesus; and God as a transcendent entity, devoid of all anthropomorphic attributes which would limit his infinitude, but the source of all force and all life. Among his numerous writings may be mentioned his theses for his doctorates, *De Demosthenis eloquentiæ charactere*, Utrecht, 1835, and *De Dei erga hominem amore, principe religionis christianæ loco*, 1836; his inaugural address at Leiden, *De Religione christiana, suæ ipsa divinitatis in animo humano vindice*, Leiden, 1843; his three rectoral addresses, *De pugna theologiam inter ac philosophiam recto utriusque studio tollenda*, 1847; *De sacris literis, theologiæ nostra ætate libere excultæ, fontibus*, 1857; and (in Dutch), "The *rôle* of Theology in the Dutch Universities as affected by the Law of 1876," 1877. His principal works, in Dutch and Latin, are, "Principles of the Theology of the Reformed Church," Leiden, 1848–50, 2 vols., 4th ed. 1861 (French trans. by C. B. Huet in the *Revue de théologie* of Strassburg, German trans. by F. Nippold in the *Zts. f. hist. Theologie*, 1865); *Dogmatices christianæ initia*, 1853–54, 2d ed. 1858; *Geschiedenis der godsdienst en wijsbegeerte*, 1853, 3d ed. 1863 (French trans. by A. Réville, Paris, 1861, 2d ed. 1864; German trans. by Redepenning, Elberfeld, 1868; English trans., London, 1870); "Historical and Critical Introduction to the New Testatment," 1853, 2d ed. 1856 (German trans., Leipzig, 1856); "The Freedom of the Will," 1859 (French trans. in the *Revue de théologie et philosophie*, Lausanne, 1875); "The Causes of Contemporary Materialism," 1859 (French trans. by A. Réville in the *Revue*, Strassburg, 1860); "A Critical Study of the Gospel of John," 1864 (German trans. by Lang, Berlin, 1867); "The Oldest Witnesses to the Writings of the New Testament," 1866 (German trans. by C. Manchot, Bremen, 1867); "Supernaturalism *en rapport* with the Bible, Christianity, and Protestantism," 1867; "The Oldest Gospel: Critical Examination of the Relations of the Gospels of Matthew and Mark," 1868 (German trans. by Redepenning, Elberfeld, 1869); "The Formula of Baptism," 1869 (German trans. by Max Gubalke, Gotha, 1885); "The Pauline Gospel: a Critical Examination of the Gospel of Luke, and its Relation to Mark, Matthew, and the Acts," 1870 (German trans. by Redepenning, Elberfeld, 1881); "The Apostle John in Asia Minor," 1871 (German trans. by B. Spiegel, Berlin, 1872); "Did the Third Evangelist write the Acts?" 1873; *Afscheidsrede bij het neerleggen van het hoogleeraarsambt*, 1881 (his address on retiring from his professorship, in which he reviews his theological development); *Historisch-critische Bijdragen naar Aanleiding van de nieuwste Hypothese aangaande Jezus en den Paulus der vier Hoofdbrieven*, 1882. *

SCHOLZ, Anton, Th.D. (Würzburg, 1856), Roman Catholic; b. at Schmachtenberg, Bavaria, Feb. 25, 1829; educated at Munich and Würzburg; became *co-operator* at Zell, 1853; secretary of the late Bishop Anton von Stahl in Würzburg, 1854; pastor at Eisingen, near Würzburg, 1861; professor of Old-Testament exegesis and biblical Oriental languages at Würzburg, 1872. He made an extensive scientific journey through Palestine in 1870. He is the author of *De inhabilitatione spiritus Sancti* (inaugural dissertation), Würzburg, 1872; *Der Masoreth. Text u. d. LXX. Übersetzung d. Buch. Jeremias*, Regensburg, 1875; *Commentar zu Jeremias*, Würzburg, 1880; *Die alexandrinische Uebersetzung des Buch Iesaias*, 1880; *Commentar zu Hoseas*, 1882; do., *Joel*, 1884; *Das Buch Judith, eine Prophetie*, 1885.

SCHOLZ, Paul, Lic. Theol. (Breslau, 1852), **D.D.** (*hon.*, Münster, 1862), Roman Catholic; b. at Breslau, Germany, June 29, 1828; was educated at Breslau; became priest and chaplain at Guhrau, 1852; *repetent* of theology in the University of Breslau, and teacher of religion in the Matthias gymnasium in the same city, 1853; *privat-docent* of theology in the university, 1857; professor extraordinary, 1864; ordinary professor, 1868. He is the author of *Handbuch der Theologie des Alten Bundes im Lichte des Neuen*, Regensburg, 1861–62, 2 vols.; *Commentarium de caritate christiana intra familiæ, civitatis ecclesiæ fines* (4th and last part of Diekhoff's *Compend. ethicæ christ. cath.*), Paderborn, 1864; *Die Ehen der Söhne Gottes mit den Töchtern der Menschen*, Regensburg, 1865; *Die heiligen Alterthümer des Volkes Israel*, 1868–69, 2 vols.; *Götzendienst und Zauberwesen bei den alten Hebraeern und den benachbarten Völkern*, 1877.

SCHRADER, Eberhard, Ph.D. (Göttingen, 1860), **D.D.** (*hon.*, Zürich, 1870), German Protestant (critical school of Ewald and De Wette); b. at Brunswick, Jan. 5, 1836; studied at Göttingen; became ordinary professor of theology at Zürich 1863, at Giessen 1870, at Jena 1873; professor of Oriental languages at Berlin, 1875. He is a member of the Royal Prussian Academy. He is the author of *De linguâ Æthiopicâ*, Göttingen, 1860; *Studien zur Kritik u. Erklärung der biblischen Urgeschichte. Gen. i.–xi.*, Zürich, 1863; (edited 8th ed. of De Wette's) *Lehrbuch der historisch-kritischen Einleitung in die kanonischen u. apokryphischen Bücher des A. T.*, Berlin, 1869; *Die assyrisch-babylonischen Keilinschriften, Kritische Untersuchung der Grundlagen ihrer Entzifferung*, Leipzig, 1872; *Die Keilinschriften u. d. Alte Testament*, Giessen, 1872, 2d ed. 1883 (English trans., *The Cuneiform Inscriptions and the Old Testament*, London, 1885–86, 2 vols.); *Die Höllenfahrt der Istar*, Giessen, 1874; *Keilinschriften und Geschichtsforschung*, 1878.

SCHROERS, Johann Heinrich, D.D. (Würzburg, 1880), Roman Catholic; b. at Krefeld, Prussia, Nov. 26, 1852; studied theology, history, and jurisprudence at Bonn, Würzburg, Innsbruck, and Münster; became *privat-docent* of canon law and historical theology at Freiburg, 1885; ordinary professor at Bonn, 1886. Author of *Der Streit über die Prädestination im 9. Jahrhundert*, Freiburg-im-Breisgau, 1884; *Hinkmar, Erzbischof von Reims, sein Leben und seine Schriften*. 1884.

SCHUERER, Emil, Ph.D. (Leipzig, 1868), **D.D.** (Tübingen, *honoris causa*, 1877), Lutheran; b. at Augsburg, May 2, 1844; studied at Erlangen, Berlin, and Heidelberg, 1862–66; became *privat-docent* at Leipzig 1869, professor extraordinary 1873; ordinary professor at Giessen, 1878. He has edited *Theologische Literaturzeitung* from its foundation in 1876 (with Harnack since 1881), and is the author of *Schleiermacher's Religionsbegriff und die philosophischen Voraussetzungen desselben*, Leipzig, 1868; *De controversiis paschalibus secundo post Chr. nat. sæculo exortis*, 1869; *Lehrbuch der neutestamentlich. Zeitgeschichte*, 1874, 2d edition under title, *Geschichte des jüdischen Volkes*, 1886–87, 2 vols. (English trans., Edinb., 1886 sqq.); *Die Gemeindeverfassung der Juden in Rom in der Kaiserzeit nach den Inschriften dargestellt*, 1879; *Ueber φαγεῖν τὸ πάσχα Joh. 18: 28*, Giessen, 1883.

SCHUETTE, Conrad Herman Louis, Lutheran; b. at Varrel, Hanover, Germany, June 17, 1843; graduated at Capital University, Columbus, O., 1863, in theology 1865; became pastor at Delaware, O., 1865; professor of mathematics and natural philosophy, Capital University, 1873, and of theology 1881. He has written *Church-member's Manual*, Columbus, 1873; *The State, the Church, and the School*, 1883.

SCHULTZ, Friedrich Wilhelm, Protestant theologian; b. at Friesack (Mark Brandenburg), Sept. 24, 1828; studied at Berlin, 1847–51; became *privat-docent* there, 1853; professor extraordinary, 1856; and ordinary professor, 1864, at Breslau. He has written *Das Deuteromium erklärt*, Berlin, 1859; *Die Schöpfungsgeschichte nach Naturwissenschaft und Bibel*, Gotha, 1865; and the comments on *Ezra*, *Nehemiah*, and *Esther*, in Lange's *Commentary*, Bielefeld, 1875. See App. *

SCHULTZ, Hermann, Lic. Theol., D.D. (both Göttingen, 1861 and 1865), Protestant theologian; b. at Lüchow, Hanover, Dec. 30, 1836; studied at Göttingen and Erlangen, 1853–56; became teacher in Hamburg, 1857; *repetent* 1859, and *privat-docent* 1861, at Göttingen; ordinary professor at Basel 1864, at Strassburg 1872, at Heidelberg 1874, at Göttingen 1876, and in 1881 consistorial councillor. He is also university preacher. He has written *Die Voraussetzungen der christlichen Lehre von der Unsterblichkeit*, Göttingen, 1861; *Alttestamentliche Theologie*, Frankfurt-a.-M., 1869, 3d ed. Göttingen, 1885; *Zu den kirchlichen Fragen der Gegenwart*, Frankfurt, 1869; *Die Stellung des christlichen Glaubens zur heiligen Schrift*, Karlsruhe, 1872, 2d ed. 1878; *Die Lehre von der Gottheit Christi*, Gotha, 1881; *Predigten gehalten in der Universitätskirche zu Göttingen*, 1883.

SCHULTZE, Augustus, Moravian; b. at Nowawes, near Potsdam, Prussia, Feb. 3, 1840; graduated at Moravian College at Niesky, and theological seminary at Gnadenfeld, Silesia, 1861; became professor at Niesky, 1862; assistant principal, 1869; professor of exegesis and dogmatics in Moravian College and Theological Seminary at Bethlehem, Penn., 1870, president, 1885; also editor of *Der Brüder Botschafter*, and a member of the "Provincial Elders' Conference" of the American Moravian Church, 1881. He has published pamphlets, etc.

SCHULTZE, Maximilian Victor, Lic. Theol. (Leipzig, 1879), Lutheran theologian; b. at Fürstenberg, Germany, Dec. 13, 1851; studied at Basel, Jena, Strassburg, and Göttingen; became *privat-docent* at Leipzig, 1879; professor extraordinary of theology at Greifswald, 1884. He is the author of *Die Katakomben von S. Gennaro dei Poveri in Neapel*, Jena, 1877; *Archäologische Studien über altchristliche Monumente*, Vienna, 1880; *Die Katakomben, ihre Geschichte und ihre Monumente*, Leipzig, 1882.

SCHULZE, Ludwig Theodor, Lic. Theol. (Berlin, 1856), **Ph.D.** (Berlin, 1858), **D.D.** (*hon.*, Rostock, 1874), Lutheran theologian; b. in Berlin, Feb. 27, 1833; studied philosophy and theology there, 1851–56; became *privat-docent* of New-Testament exegesis and biblical theology there, 1859; professor extraordinary at Königsberg, 1863; inspector and director at Magdeburg, 1866; ordinary professor of theology at Rostock, 1874. He is the author of *De fontibus ex quibus historia Hycsosorum haurienda sit*, Berlin, 1858; *Ueber die Gottesoffenbarungen (Engel des Herrn) im alten Bunde* (in *Studien u. Kritiken*, 1859); *Ueber die Wunder des Herrn, mit Beziehung auf das Leben Jesu von Renan*, Königsberg, 1864; *Martha u. Maria*, Gotha, 1866; *Ueber die Auferstehung Jesu Christi* (in *Beweis des Glaubens*, 1867); *Das Wunder im Verhältniss zur Sündenvergebung* (do., 1868); *Ueber die assyrisch-babylonischen Ausgrabungen in ihrer Beziehung auf das A. T.* (do., 1880); *Passions-Osterfeier* (sermons), Gotha, 1866; *Vom Menschensohn u. vom Logos*, 1867; *Friede im Herrn* (sermons), 1871; *anweisung zum planmässigen Lesen der heiligen Schrift*, Leipzig, 1875; *Philipp Wackernagel nach seinem Leben u. Wirken*, 1879; *Friedrich Adolf Philippi, ein Lebensbild*, Nördlingen, 1883; *Luther und die evangelische Kirche* (Luther jubilee address), Rostock, 1883; editor of 3d ed. Wuttke's *Christl. Sittenlehre*, Leipzig, 1874-75, 2 vols. 2d ed. (with latest literature), 1886; contributed "Einleitung ins N.T." "Neutestamentliche Zeitgeschichte," "Leben Jesu u. apostolisch. Zeitalter" in Zöckler's *Handbuch der theologischen Wissenschaften*, Nördlingen, 1883, 2d ed. 1885; and has published numerous sermons, articles, etc., in different periodicals and separately.

SCHWANE, Josephus, Lic. Theol. (Münster, 1851), **D.D.** (Münster, 1860), Roman Catholic; b. at Dorsten, Westphalia, Germany, April 2, 1824; studied at Münster 1843-48, at Bonn and Tübingen 1848-50; became *privat-docent* in the theological faculty at Münster, 1853; professor extraordinary there, 1859; ordinary professor, 1867. He is the author of *Ueber die scientia media* in the *Tübinger-Quartalschrift*, Tübingen, 1850; *Das göttliche Vorherwissen*, Münster, 1855; *De controversia inter S. Staphanum et S. Cyprianum*, 1859; *Dogmengeschichte der vornicänischen Zeit* 1862, *der patristischen Zeit* 1869, *der mittleren Zeit* 1882, *De operibus supererogatoriis*, 1868; *Specielle Moraltheologie*, Freiburg, I., II. 1878, III. 1875, 2d ed. 1885; *Allgemeine Moraltheologie*, 1885.

SCHWARZ, Karl Heinrich Wilhelm, Protestant theologian; b. at Wiek auf Rügen, Nov. 19, 1812; became *privat-docent* 1842, and professor extraordinary at Halle 1849; superior consistorial councillor and court preacher at Gotha, 1856; first court preacher, 1858; superintendent, 1876. He was one of the founders of the *Protestant Verein:* and among other works has written, *Das Wesen der Religion*, Halle, 1847; *Lessing als Theologe*, 1854; *Zur Geschichte der neuesten Theologie*, Leipzig, 1856, 4th ed. 1869. Died March 25, 1885. *

SCHWEINITZ, Edmund de, S.T.D. (Columbia College, New-York City, 1871), Moravian bishop; b. at Bethlehem, Penn., March 20, 1825; graduated at the Moravian Theological Seminary there, 1844; studied at Berlin, 1845; pastor at Canal Dover, O., 1850; Lebanon, Penn., 1851-53; Philadelphia (First Church), 1853-60; Lititz, Penn., 1860-64; and Bethlehem, Penn., 1864-80; consecrated bishop, 1870. He is president of the provincial board — i.e., the governing board — of the American Province of the Unitas Fratrum, and of the theological seminary. He belongs to a family that for more than a hundred years has furnished ministers in an unbroken line to the American branch of the Moravian Church, and is a great-great-grandson of Count Zinzendorf. He is the author of *The Moravian Manual*, Philadelphia, 1859, 2d ed. Bethlehem, 1869; *The Moravian Episcopate*, Bethlehem, 1865, 2d ed. London, 1874; *The Life and Times of David Zeisberger*, Philadelphia, 1870; *Some of the Fathers of the Moravian Church*, Bethlehem, 1881; *The History of the Unitas Fratrum*, Bethlehem, 1885.

SCHWEIZER, Alexander, D.D., Reformed theologian; b. at Murten, March 14, 1808; studied at Zürich and Berlin; became professor of practical theology at Zürich 1835, and in 1845 also pastor. He is a member of the church and school council, and of the Great Council. Besides numerous sermons and essays, he has published *Die Glaubenslehre der evangelisch-reformirten Kirche, aus den Quellen*, Zürich, 1844-47, 2 vols.; *Homiletik der evangelisch-protestantischen Kirche*, Leipzig, 1848; *Die protestant. Centraldogmen in ihre Entwicklung innerhalb der reformirten Kirche*, Zürich, 1854-56, 2 parts; *Die christliche Glaubenslehre nach protestantischen Grundsätzen dargestellt*, Leipzig, 1863-72, 2 vols., 2d ed. 1877; *Pastoraltheologie*, 1875; *Nach Rechts und nach Links. Besprechungen über Zeichen d. Zeit*, 1876; *Die Zukunft der Religion*, 1878; *Zwingli's Bedeutung neben Luther*, Zürich, 1884.

SCOTT, Hugh McDonald, Congregationalist; b. at Guysborough, N.S., March 31, 1848; graduated at Dalhousie College, Halifax, 1870, and B.D. at Edinburgh 1873; Presbyterian pastor at Merigomish, N.S., 1874-78; studied theology in Germany, 1878-81; has been since 1881 professor of ecclesiastical history in Chicago Congregational Theological Seminary. He has contributed to *Current Discussions in Theology* (department of history), Chicago, vols. i. and ii., 1883 and 1884.

SCOTT, John, D.D. (Washington College, Washington, Penn., 1860), Methodist-Protestant; b. in Washington County, Penn., Oct. 27, 1820; educated in the common schools, and afterwards privately; joined the Pittsburg Conference of the Methodist-Protestant Church in 1842, and was president of it 1858, 1878; has been a member of every General Conference, with perhaps two exceptions, since 1854, and president 1866; was editor of *The Methodist Recorder*, official organ of the Church, 1864-70, and has held the position since 1879, and while such was, except since 1884, editor of the Sunday-school publications of the denomination. He is the author of *Pulpit Echoes, or Brief Miscellaneous Discourses*, Cincinnati, 1873; *The Land of Sojourn, or Sketches of Patriarchal Life and Times*, Pittsburg, 1880.

SCOTT, Very Rev. Robert, D.D. (Oxford, 1854), Church of England; b. at Bondleigh, Devonshire, Jan. 26, 1811; student of Christ Church, Oxford, 1830; was Craven scholar, 1830; Ireland scholar and B.A. (first-class in classics), 1833; Latin essayist, 1834; M.A. (Balliol College), 1836; Denyer theological essayist, 1838; B.D., 1854. He was fellow and tutor of Balliol College, 1835-40; rector of Duloe, Cornwall, 1840-50; prebendary of Exeter Cathedral, 1845-66; rector of S. Luffenham, Rutland, 1850-54; select preacher at Oxford, 1853-54, 1874-75; master of Balliol College and member of Hebdomadal Council, 1854-70; University press delegate, 1855-70; became professor of Scripture exegesis, 1861; dean of Rochester, 1870;

member of the N.T. Revision Company. Author of *Twelve Sermons*, 1851; *University Sermons*, 1860; commentary on *Epis. of St. James*, in *Bible (Speaker's) Commentary*, 1882; and, with Dean Liddell, of *A Greek-English Lexicon*, 1843, 7th ed. 1883.

SCOTT, William Anderson, D.D. (University of Alabama, Tuscaloosa, Ala., 1844), **LL.D.** (University of New-York City, 1872), Presbyterian; b. at Rock Creek, Bedford County, Tenn., Jan. 31, 1813; d. in San Francisco, Cal., Jan. 14, 1885. He was graduated at Cumberland College, Princeton, Ky., 1833; studied in Princeton (N.J.) Theological Seminary, 1833–34; was missionary in Louisiana and Arkansas, 1835–36; principal of academies in Tennessee, 1836–40; became pastor at Tuscaloosa, Ala., 1840, and in New Orleans, La. (first church), 1843; pastor-elect of Calvary Church, San Francisco, Cal., 1854–61; in Europe, and for a while in charge of the new John-street Presbyterian Church of Birmingham, Eng.; pastor of Forty-second-street Church, New-York City, 1863–70; of St. John's Church, San Francisco, 1870 till his death. He held his latter position along with that of professor of mental and moral philosophy and systematic theology in the San Francisco Theological Seminary from its establishment in 1871. In 1858 he was moderator of the General Assembly (old school). He published *Daniel, a Model for Young Men*, New York, 1854; *Achan in El Dorado*, San Francisco, 1855; *Trade and Letters*, New York, 1856; *The Giant Judge*, San Francisco, 1858; *The Church in the Army, or the Four Centurions of the Gospels*, New York, 1862, 2d ed. 1868; *The Christ of the Apostles' Creed: the Voice of the Church against Arianism, Strauss, and Renan*, New York, 1867. *

SCOULLER, James Brown, D.D. (Muskingum College, New Concord, O., 1880), United Presbyterian; b. near Newville, Cumberland County, Penn., July 12, 1820; graduated at Dickinson College, Carlisle, Penn., 1839, and at the Associate Reformed Theological Seminary, Allegheny, Penn., 1842; was pastor of United Presbyterian Churches in Philadelphia (fourth), Penn., 1844–46; Cuylerville, N.Y., 1847–52; Argyle, N.Y., 1852–62; editor of *The Christian Instructor*, Philadelphia, Penn., 1862–63. He has since 1863 lived as an invalid at Newville, Penn. He is the author of "Forty Letters from Abroad, principally Italy and Egypt," published in *The Christian Instructor*, 1860–61; *History of the Big Spring Presbytery* (U. P.), Harrisburg, Penn., 1879; *History of the Presbytery of Argyle* (U. P.), 1880; *A Manual of the United Presbyterian Church*, 1881; *Calvinism: its History and Influences*, 1885 (pp. 29); a number of pamphlets, lectures, and sermons, and a large amount of miscellaneous matter published in the columns of *The Christian Instructor*, *The United Presbyterian*, and *The Evangelical Repository*, since 1844.

SCRIMGER, John, Canadian Presbyterian; b. at Galt, Ontario, Can., Feb. 10, 1849; graduated at the University of Toronto, B.A. 1869, M.A. 1871, and at Knox College, Toronto, 1873; was pastor of St. Joseph-street Presbyterian Church, Montreal, 1873–82; lecturer on Hebrew and Greek exegesis in the Presbyterian College, Montreal, 1874–82; since 1882 has been professor there of the same. Since 1873 he has been member of the General Assembly's board of French evangelization; is convener of General Assembly's committee on religious instruction in the public schools of the Province of Quebec, and of the General Assembly's committee on co-operation with other Protestant churches in sparsely settled districts.

SCRIVENER, Frederick Henry Ambrose, LL.D. (St. Andrew's, 1872), **D.C.L.** (Oxford, 1876), Church of England; b. at Bermondsey, Surrey, Sept. 29, 1813; educated at Trinity College, Cambridge; graduated B.A. (third in second-class classical tripos) 1835, M.A. 1838; became assistant master of King's School, Sherborne, 1835; curate of Sandford Orcas, Somerset, 1838; perpetual curate of Penwerris, Cornwall, 1846; rector of St. Gerrans, Cornwall, 1861; vicar of Hendon, Middlesex, 1876. He was a member of the New-Testament Revision Company, received a pension of a hundred pounds in 1872 in recognition of his eminent biblical services, and is the author of *Notes on the Authorized Version of the New Testament*, London, 1845; *Collation of Twenty Greek Manuscripts of the Holy Gospel*, 1853; *Codex Augiensis, and Fifty other Manuscripts*, 1859; *Novum Testamentum Textus Stephanici*, 1860, 6th ed. 1873; *Plain Introduction to the Criticism of the New Testament*, 1861, 3d ed. much enlarged, 1883; *Collation of the Codex Sinaiticus*, 1863, 2d ed. revised, 1867; *Bezæ Codex Cantabrigiensis*, 1864; *Six Popular Lectures on the Text of the New Testament*, 1875; edited *The Cambridge Paragraph Bible*, 1873 (Introduction, revised separate edition, 1884); *Greek Testament*, 7th ed. 1877; *Greek Testament with Changes of New-Testament Revisers*, 1881. *

SCUDDER, Henry Martyn, M.D. (University of the City of New York, 1853), **D.D.** (Rutgers College, New Brunswick, N.J., 1859), Congregationalist; b. at Panditeripo, Jaffna District, Island of Ceylon, Feb. 5, 1822; studied at New York University and Williams College; graduated at the University 1840, and at Union Theological Seminary 1843; was a foreign missionary under American Board at Madras, India, 1844–51, and at Arcot, India, 1851–63; resigned on account of ill-health; was pastor of the Grand-street Reformed Church, Jersey City, N.J., for six months, 1864–65; of the Howard Presbyterian Church, San Francisco, Cal., 1865–71; of the Central Congregational Church, Brooklyn, N.Y., 1871–82; since has been pastor of Plymouth Congregational Church, Chicago, Ill.

SEABURY, William Jones, D.D. (Hobart College, Geneva, N.Y., 1876; General Theological Seminary, New-York City, 1885), Episcopalian; b. in New-York City, Jan. 25, 1837; graduated there at Columbia College, 1856; admitted to the bar, 1858; graduated from General Theological Seminary, New-York City, 1866; rector of the Church of the Annunciation, New York, since 1868; in 1873 became professor of ecclesiastical polity and law in the General Theological Seminary. He edited Dr. Samuel Seabury's *Memorial*, New York, 1873, and *Discourses on the Nature and Work of the Holy Spirit*, 1874; and, besides occasional pamphlets, has published *Suggestions in Aid of Devotion and Godliness*, 1878.

SEEBERG, Reinhold, Lutheran theologian; b. at Pernau, Livonia, 1859; studied at Dorpat (1878–82) and at Erlangen; became *privat-docent* of theology at Dorpat, 1884; *etatmässiger-docent*, 1885; since 1884, second pastor of the University Church. He is the author of *Der Begriff der christlichen Kirche*, vol. i., Erlangen, 1885; *Vom Lebensideal* (lecture), Dorpat, 1886.

SEELEY, John Robert, M.A., layman; b. in London, Eng., in 1834; graduated at Cambridge, B.A. (first-class in classical tripos), 1857, and was senior chancellor's medallist; became fellow of Christ's College, 1858; a master in City of London School, 1861; professor of Latin, University College, London, 1863; professor of modern history at Cambridge, 1869. He is the author of *Ecce Homo, a Survey of the Life and Work of Jesus Christ*, London, 1865, 15th ed. 1885, reprinted in U.S.A.; *Lectures and Essays*, 1870; *Life and Times of Stein*, 1879, 3 vols.; *Natural Religion*, 1882, 2d ed. 1885; *The Expansion of England*, 1883; *A Short History of Napoleon the First*, 1886.

SEELYE, Julius Hawley, D.D. (Union College, Schenectady, N.Y., 1862), **LL.D.** (Columbia College, New-York City, 1876), Congregationalist; b. at Bethel, Conn., Sept. 14, 1824; graduated from Amherst (Mass.) College 1849, and from Auburn Theological Seminary (Presbyterian), N.Y., 1852; became professor of moral philosophy and metaphysics, Amherst College, 1858; member of Congress, 1875; president of Amherst College, 1877. He is the author of a translation of Schwegler's *History of Philosophy*, New York, 1856; *The Way, the Truth, and the Life, Lectures to Educated Hindus*, Bombay and Boston, 1873; *Christian Missions*, New York, 1875; sermons, addresses, and reviews. *

SECOND, Jacques Jean Louis, B.D., Lic. Theol., D.D. (all Strassburg, 1834, 1835, and 1836, respectively), Swiss Protestant theologian; b. at Plainpalais, near Geneva, Oct. 4, 1810; d. in Geneva, June 18, 1885. He was educated at the University of Strassburg and at Bonn, where he studied Oriental languages under Freytag. On his return to Geneva he founded (1836) a society for the exegetical study of the New Testament, which lasted until 1841; and gave free lectures upon Old-Testament exegesis in the university. From 1840 to 1864 he was pastor at Chênes-Bougeries; from 1862 to 1864 lectured upon Old-Testament introduction in Geneva University, where, from 1872 to his death, he was professor of Old-Testament exegesis. He made a trip through Palestine in 1873. His fame rests upon his translation of the entire Bible (Old Testament, Geneva, 1874, 2 vols.; New Testament, 1880, many subsequent editions), which he prepared at the request of the Venerable Company of Pastors of Geneva. It is a remarkably successful work. It was reprinted by the Oxford University Press, first edition fifty thousand copies. His other works are, *Ruth*, Geneva, 1834; *l'Ecclésiaste*, 1835; *De voce Scheol et notione Orci apud Hebræos*, 1835; *De la nature de l'inspiration chez les auteurs et dans les écrits du Nouveau Testament*, 1836; *Monologues* (trans. from Schleiermacher), 1837, 2d ed. 1864; *A. M. l'abbé de Baudry sur son dernier opuscule*, 1838; *Traité élémentaire des accents hébreux*, 1841, 2d ed. 1874; *Soirées chrétiennes*, 2d series 1850, 3d series 1871; *Géographie de la Terre Sainte*, 1851; *Catéchisme, ou Manuel d'instruction chrétienne*, 1858, 2d ed. 1863; *Récits bibliques à l'usage de la jeunesse*, 1862 (twenty-four thousand copies sold); *Souvenir pour mes anciens catéchumènes* (four discourses), 1864; *Chrestomathie biblique*, 1864; *Le prophète Esaie*, 1866; *Les réalités du saint ministère* (ordination sermon), 1866. *

SEISS, Joseph Augustus, D.D. (Pennsylvania College, Gettysburg, Penn., 1860), **LL.D.** (Roanoke College, Salem, Va., 1874), Lutheran (General Council); b. near Graceham, Md., March 18, 1823; was student in Pennsylvania College, Gettysburg, 1839-41, but left without graduating; theological study mostly private; became pastor at Martinsburg and Shepherdstown, Va., 1843; Cumberland, Md., 1847; Baltimore, Md., 1852; of St. John's, Philadelphia, 1858; of Holy Communion, Philadelphia, 1874. He was one of the founders of the General Council, and one of the committee which made its *Church Book*. He edited *Prophetic Times*, a monthly devoted to prophecy, 1863-75; also *The Lutheran*, Philadelphia, 1873-79 (was associate editor 1868-73 and 1879-80); travelled in Europe and the East, 1864-65. He is the author of *Lectures on Epistle to the Hebrews*, Baltimore, 1846; *Baptist System examined*, 1854, 3d enlarged ed. Philadelphia, 1882; *Digest of Christian Doctrine*, Baltimore, 1855; *Last Times*, 1856, 7th ed. Philadelphia, 1880, republished London; *Holy Types* (Gospel in Leviticus), 1860, Philadelphia and London, 1875; *Book of Forms* (liturgical), Philadelphia, 1860; *Evangelical Psalmist*, 1860, 2d ed. 1870; *Parable of the Ten Virgins*, 1862, 2d ed. 1873, also London; *Child's Catechism*, 1865, 2d ed. 1880; *Ecclesia Lutherana*, 1867, 2d ed. 1871; *A Question in Eschatology*, 1868; *How shall we Order our Worship?* 1869; *Plain Words* (sermons), 1869; *Lectures on the Apocalypse*, 1870-84, 3 vols., also London and Basel; *The Javelin, by a Lutheran*, 1871; *Uriel, Occasional Discourses*, 1874; *Church Song* (musical), 1875-81; *Lectures on the Gospels*, 1876, 2 vols.; *A Miracle in Stone* (Great Pyramid), 1877, new ed. 1882, also London; *Recreation Songs* (poetical), 1878; *Thirty-three Practical Sermons*, 1879; *Voices from Babylon* (lectures on Daniel), 1879, 2d ed. 1881, also London; *Blossoms of Faith* (sermons), 1880; *The Golden Altar* (manual of private devotions), New York, 1882; *Gospel in the Stars* (primeval astronomy), Philadelphia, 1882, 2d ed. 1885; *Luther and the Reformation*, 1883; *Lectures on the Epistles*, 1885, 2 vols.; *Right Life*, Philadelphia, 1886; also numerous special sermons, addresses, pamphlets, review articles, etc., since 1845.

SELBORNE, The Right Hon. Roundell Palmer, Earl of, D.C.L. (*hon.*, Oxford, 1863); b. at Mixbury, Nov. 27, 1812; educated at Trinity College, Oxford; graduated B.A. (first-class in classics) 1834, M.A. 1837; called to the bar, 1837; became a queen's counsel, 1849; M.P., 1847-52, 1853-57, 1861-72; solicitor-general, 1861; attorney-general, 1863-66; lord chancellor of England, 1872-74, 1880-85. He was elected lord rector of the University of St. Andrew's, 1877; and president of the first house of laymen of the Church of England, Westminster, February, 1886. He edited the *Book of Praise, from the Best English Hymn-Writers*, London, 1862.

SEMISCH, Karl Aenotheus, Protestant theologian; b. at Prettin, Saxony, Dec. 31, 1810; studied at Leipzig, 1829-32; became professor at Greifswald 1844, at Breslau 1855, at Berlin 1866; and is the author of *Justin der Märtyrer*, Breslau, 1840-42, 2 parts; *Die apostolischen Denkwürdigkeiten des Märtyrers Justinus*, Hamburg, 1848; *Julian der Abtrünnige*, Breslau, 1862. *

SEPP, Johann Nepomuk, Roman Catholic; b. at Tölz, Bavaria, Aug. 7, 1816; studied at Munich; travelled in the East, 1845-46; became professor of history at Munich, 1846; deposed and expelled from the city 1847, for his political opinions; re-instated, 1850; retired, 1867. He has been prominent in politics. He is the author of *Das Leben Jesu*, Regensburg, 1842–46, 5 vols., 2d ed. 1853–62, 6 vols.; *Das Heidenthum und dessen Bedeutung für das Christenthum*, 1853, 3 parts; *Jerusalem und das Heilige Land*, Schaffhausen, 1862–63, 2 vols., 2d ed. 1872–74; *Thaten und Lehren Jesu mit ihrer weltgeschichtlichen Beglaubigung*, 1864; *Geschichte des Apostel vom Tod Jesu bis zur Zerstörung Jerusalems*, 1865, 2d ed. 1866; *Kritische Reformentwürfe beginnend mit der Revision des Bibelkanons*, Munich, 1870; *Das Hebräer Evangelium*, 1870; *Deutschland und der Vatikan*, 1872; *Görres u. seine Zeitgenossen*, Nördlingen, 1877; *Meerfahrt nach Tyrus zur Ausgrabung der Kathedrale mit Barbarossas Grab*, 1878.

SERVICE, John, D.D. (Glasgow, 1877), Church of Scotland; b. at Campsie, Feb. 26, 1833; d. in Glasgow, March 15, 1884. He studied at the University of Glasgow irregularly from 1858 to 1862, but did not take a degree; was sub-editor of Mackenzie's *Imperial Dictionary of Universal Biography*, under P. E. Dove; married in 1859; became minister at Hamilton 1862, and there remained for ten months, when he resigned on account of ill-health, and went to Melbourne, Australia, where he spent two years (1864–66), leaving it for Hobart Town, Tasmania, where he was minister four years (1866–70). In both these colonial charges he exercised a considerable influence. In 1870 he returned home, and in 1872 was appointed to the parish of Inch, Wigtownshire, which he left in 1879 for Hyndland Established Church, Glasgow, of which he was incumbent when he died. His first literary work of mark was a novel, known as *Novantia* when it was published in *Good Words*, and afterwards as *Lady Hetty*, London, 1875, 3 vols. It is full of interesting pictures of Scotch village and rural life, in vivid contrast with wider colonial experiences. The hero is a Scotch clergyman; and the charm of the book lies, not so much in its plot, as in the fresh views of life under the varied conditions which had fallen to the author's lot. His volume *Salvation, here and hereafter: Sermons and Essays* (1876, 4th ed. 1885) gave him at once a foremost place among the leaders of what is known as the "Broad Church" in Scotland. Occasional magazine articles, journalistic contributions, and sermons appeared from his pen from time to time; but *Salvation, here and hereafter*, has only been followed by two posthumous volumes, — *Sermons* (1884) and *Prayers* (1885), — in both of which there is the same note of vigorous unconventionalism of opinion, and of deep spiritual life, which has arrested attention in his previous volumes. His personal influence was one element of his power, and the secret of its charm is easily understood from his books. WILLIAM JACK.

SEWALL, John Smith, D.D. (Bowdoin College, Brunswick, Me., 1878), Congregationalist; b. at Newcastle, Me., March 20, 1830; graduated at Bowdoin College, Brunswick, Me., 1850; was commander's clerk, United-States Navy, in China, and in Commodore Perry's expedition (1853–54), 1850–54; graduated at Bangor (Me.) Theological Seminary, 1858; pastor at Wenham, Mass., 1859–67; professor of rhetoric and oratory in Bowdoin College, 1867–75; and since 1875 has been professor of sacred rhetoric and oratory in Bangor Theological Seminary. He has contributed to various periodicals.

SEYERLEN, Karl Rudolf, Ph.D. (Tübingen, 1854), **D.D.** (*hon.*, Jena, 1875), Protestant theologian; b. at Stuttgart, Nov. 18, 1831; studied at Tübingen, 1849–53; was curate at Giengen, 1854–55; student of scholastic theology and philosophy at Paris, 1855–56; teacher of religion in Ulm Gymnasium, 1857–59; *repetent* at Tübingen, 1859–61; *diakonus* at Crailsheim 1862–69, at Tübingen 1869–72; archdeacon there, 1872–75; became ordinary professor of practical and systematic theology at Jena, 1875. In theology he belongs to the school of Baur, in philosophy to that of Friedrich Rohmer. He is the author of *Avicebron, de materia universali (Fons Vitæ)*, *Ein Beitrag zur Geschichte der Philosophie des Mittelalters* (in Baur and Zeller's *Theologische Jahrbücher*, 1856–57); *Entstehung und erste Schicksale der Christengemeinde in Rom*, Tübingen, 1874; *Ueber Bedeutung und Aufgabe der Predigt der Gegenwart* (*Antrittsrede* at Jena), 1876; *Der christliche Cultus im apostolischen Zeitalter* (in Bassermann's *Zeitschrift für praktische Theologie*, 1881); *Das System der praktischen Theologie in seinen Grundzügen* (do. 1883); editor of *Johann Caspar Bluntschli* (autobiography), Nördlingen, 1884, 3 vols.; *Friedrich Rohmer's Wissenschaft vom Menschen*, 1885, 2 vols.; author of numerous articles upon church polity and church law in the *Protestantische Kirchenzeitung*, Berlin, 1880–83.

SEYMOUR, Right Rev. George Franklin, S.T.D. (Racine College, Wis., 1867), **LL.D.** (Columbia College, New-York City, 1878), Episcopalian, bishop of Springfield, Ill.; b. in New-York City, Jan. 5, 1829; graduated head of his class at Columbia College, New-York City, 1850, and from the General Theological Seminary, New-York City, 1854; was founder and first warden of St. Stephen's College, Annandale, N.Y., 1855–61; rector of St. Mary's Church, Manhattanville, 1861–62; of Christ Church, Hudson, N.Y., 1862–63; of St. John's, Brooklyn, N.Y., 1863–67; professor of ecclesiastical history in the General Theological Seminary, New-York City, 1865–79; dean of the same, 1875–79; consecrated first bishop of Springfield, Ill., June 11, 1878. In 1868 he was chosen by the clergy of Missouri several times as their bishop, and was elected bishop of Illinois in 1874, and twice bishop of Springfield in 1878 and 1879. He supervised the Greek text, and translated a portion never before rendered into English, of Fulton's *Index Canonum*, New York, 1871; *Introduction to Papal Claims*, 1882; many sermons, addresses, essays, and charges.

SHAFTESBURY, the Right Hon. Anthony Ashley-Cooper, Seventh Earl of, K.G., D.C.L. (Oxford, 1841), Church of England, layman; b. in London, April 28, 1801; d. at Folkestone, Oct. 1, 1885. He was educated at Christ Church, Oxford; graduated B.A. (first-class in classics) 1822, M.A. 1832; sat as Lord Ashley in the House of Commons, as member for Woodstock 1828–30, Dorchester 1830, Dorsetshire 1831–46, Bath 1847–51, when he succeeded his father in the peerage, and took his seat in the House of Lords. He supported the governments of Liverpool and Canning; was commissioner of the board of control under Wellington; was Lord of the Admiralty in Sir Robert Peel's administration of 1834–35, but declined to join it in 1841 because Peel would not support the Ten-hours Bill. It was not, however, as a statesman and politician that Lord Shaftesbury distinguished himself, but as a leader in philanthropy and religion. Throughout his long lifetime he labored assiduously for the benefit of the working-classes, among whom he was a great favorite; visiting them in their homes, and planning measures for their relief and elevation by reducing their hours of labor, improving their workshops, factories, and lodging-houses, caring for their children, and guarding them against vice. He was a consistent opponent of slavery, and a firm friend of the United States during the late civil war. In religious affairs he was a pronounced Evangelical, and the leader of that party in the Church of England. He was called upon to preside at innumerable meetings in Exeter Hall, and elsewhere, on behalf of all sorts of enterprises. His name was synonymous with every virtue, and a household word in Great Britain. He was president of many religious and philanthropic societies. Among them may be mentioned, The Church Pastoral Aid Society, The Surgical Aid Society, Field Lane Refuges and Ragged Schools for the Destitute and Homeless Poor, Ragged-school Union, The Victoria Institute, Society for the Conversion of the Jews, Society for the Relief of Persecuted Jews, The British and Foreign Bible Society. His funeral was held on Thursday, Oct. 8, in Westminster Abbey, and was attended by enormous crowds. Thousands stood outside in the drenching rain, unable to enter. Delegations came from the different societies which owed to him their prosperity, if not their existence. Noticeable among them was that of the Shoe-black Brigade. Upon his coffin the wreath from the Crown Princess of Germany lay side by side with one from the poor flower-girls of London. He was buried at the family seat of St. Giles, Dorsetshire. *

SHAW, William Isaac, Methodist; b. at Kingston, Can., April 6, 1841; graduated at Victoria University, Cobourg, Can., A.B. 1861, LL.B. 1864, at McGill University, Montreal, M.A. 1880; entered the ministry of the Wesleyan Methodist Church of Canada 1864, and after thirteen years' pastoral work became (1877) professor of exegesis and church history in the Wesleyan Theological College, Montreal. He is the author of *Discussion on Retribution*, Toronto, 1884; and various contributions to reviews.

SHEDD, William Greenough Thayer, D.D. (University of Vermont, Burlington, 1857), **LL.D.** (University of the City of New York, 1876), Presbyterian; b. at Acton, Mass., June 21, 1820; graduated at the University of Vermont, Burlington, 1839, and at Andover Theological Seminary 1843: became Congregational pastor at Brandon, Vt., 1844; professor of English literature, University of Vermont, 1845; of sacred rhetoric in Auburn Presbyterian Theological Seminary, 1852; of ecclesiastical history in Andover Congregational Theological Seminary, 1853; co-pastor of the Brick (Presbyterian) Church, New-York City, 1862; but since 1863 has been professor in Union Theological Seminary, New-York City, of biblical literature until 1874, and since of systematic theology. He translated from the German of Theremin, *Eloquence a Virtue*, New York, 1850, 2d ed. Andover, 1859; and Guericke's *Manual of Church History*, Andover, 1860–70, 2 vols.; and has written *A History of Christian Doctrine*, New York and Edinburgh, 1865, 2 vols., 8th ed. 1884; *Homiletics and Pastoral Theology*, 1867, 8th ed. 1881; *Sermons to the Natural Man*, 1871, 3d ed. 1884; *Theological Essays*, 1877; *Literary Essays*, 1878; *Commentary on Romans*, 1879; *Sermons to the Spiritual Man*, 1884; *The Doctrine of Endless Punishment*, 1886.

SHELDON, Henry Clay, Methodist; b. at Martinsburg, N.Y., March 12, 1845; graduated at Yale College, New Haven, Conn., 1867, and at the Theological School of Boston University, Mass., 1871; studied at Leipzig, 1874–75; since 1875 has been professor of historical theology in Boston University. He is anti-Romish, but not anti-Catholic, with a leaning to evangelical Arminianism, as opposed both to strict Calvinism and to Liberalism. He is the author of *History of Christian Doctrine*, New York, 1886, 2 vols.

SHEPHERD, Thomas James, D.D. (Columbian College, now Columbian University, Washington, D.C., 1865), Presbyterian; b. in the vicinity of Berryville, Clarke County, Va., April 25, 1818; graduated at Columbian College, Washington, D.C., 1839, and at the Union Theological Seminary, New-York City, 1843; was pastor of the Harmony Presbyterian Church, Lisbon, Md., 1843–52; of the First Presbyterian Church, Northern Liberties, Philadelphia, Penn., 1852–81, since *pastor emeritus*. He was associate editor of the *American Presbyterian* (new school newspaper), Philadelphia, 1856–61. He is the author of *History of First Presbyterian Church, Northern Liberties, Philadelphia*, Philadelphia, 1864, new ed. (supplemented by an account of his pastorate) 1881; *Social Hymn and Tune Book*, 1865; *Westminster Bible Dictionary*, 1880, 2d ed. 1885.

SHERATON, James Paterson, D.D. (Queen's University, Ontario, Can., 1882), Episcopal Church in Canada; b. at St. John, N.B., Nov. 29, 1841; graduated at the University of New Brunswick, B.A. (with honors, gold medallist) 1862; studied theology in the University of King's College, Windsor, N.S., privately with the bishop of Fredericton; was ordained deacon 1864, priest 1865; became rector of Shediac, N.B., 1865; of Pictou, N.S., 1874; principal and professor of exegetical and systematic theology in Wycliffe College, Toronto, 1877. He became a member of the senate of the University of Toronto in 1885. He was editor of *The Evangelical Churchman* from 1877–82, since 1882 principal editorial contributor. He is the author of numerous essays on education, the church, the ministry, Christian unity, etc.

SHERWOOD, James Manning, Presbyterian; b. at Fishkill, N.Y., Sept. 29, 1814; educated mainly through private tutors; studied theology under Rev. George Armstrong at Fishkill, N.Y.; was pastor at New Windsor on the Hudson, N.Y., 1835–40; Mendon, N.Y., 1840–45; Bloomfield, N.J., 1852–58; editor of *National Preacher* and *Biblical Repository*, New York, 1846–51; *Eclectic Magazine*, 1864–71; founder and editor of *Hours at Home* (monthly), 1865–69; editor *Presbyterian Review*, 1863–71; *Presbyterian Quarterly and Princeton Review*, 1877–78; *Homiletic Review*, since September, 1883. During his thirty years of editorial life he has been extensively engaged as a "reader" of manuscripts for publishing-houses, and has critically noticed for the press several thousand volumes, chiefly in the reviews of the country. He is the author of *Plea for the Old Foundations*, New York, 1856; *The Lamb in the midst of the Throne, or the History of the Cross*, 1883, 2d ed. 1884; editor of *Memoirs*, and two volumes of *Sermons* of Rev. Ichabod Spencer, D.D., 1855; Brainerd's *Memoirs*, with new preface, notes, and lengthy introduction on his life and character, 1884. He has in press, 1886, a book entitled *Books and Authors, and how to use them*.

SHIELDS, Charles Woodruff, D.D. (College of New Jersey, Princeton, 1861), **LL.D.** (Columbian University, Washington, D.C., 1877). Presbyterian; b. at New Albany, Ind., April 4, 1825; graduated at the College of New Jersey, Princeton, 1844, and at Princeton Theological Seminary, N.J., 1847; became pastor at Hempstead, Long Island, N.Y., 1849; of Second Church, Philadelphia, Penn., 1850; professor of harmony of science and revealed religion in the College of New Jersey, Princeton, 1866 (he projected the first such college professorship). His theological standpoint is Presbyterian, but (1) advocating the restoration of the Presbyterian Prayer Book of 1661 for optional use by any ministers or congregations which desire a liturgy; and (2) also advocating church unity on a liturgical basis, with the hope of an ultimate organic re-union of Presbyterianism with Congregationalism and Episcopacy in the American Protestant Catholic Church of the future. He has published *Philosophia ultima*, Philadelphia, 1861; *The Book of Common Prayer as amended by the Presbyterian Divines of 1661*, 1864, 2d ed. New York, 1883; *Liturgia expurgata*, Philadelphia, 1864, 3d ed. New York, 1884; *The Final Philosophy as issuing from the Harmony of Science and Religion*, New York, 1877, 2d ed. 1879; *Order of the Sciences*, 1884.

SHIPP, Albert Micajah, D.D. (Randolph-Macon College, Ashland, Va., 1859), **LL.D.** (University of North Carolina, 1883), Southern Methodist; b. in Stokes County, N.C., Jan 15, 1819; graduated at the University of North Carolina, Chapel Hill, 1840; entered the ministry; became president of Greenborough Female College, N.C., 1847; professor of history and French in University of North Carolina, 1849; president of Wofford College, Spartanburg Court-House, S.C., 1859; professor of exegetical and biblical theology in Vanderbilt University, Nashville, Tenn., 1874; and dean of the theological faculty, and vice-chancellor of the university, 1882. He originated the policy of biblical chairs for teaching the Bible to the whole body of students in all Methodist institutions of learning, and was one of the first advocates of biblical institutes for the proper education of preachers for the Methodist-Episcopal Church South. He wrote *The History of Methodism in South Carolina*, Nashville, Tenn., 1882, 2d ed. 1884.

SHONE, Right Rev. Samuel, lord bishop of Kilmore, Elphin, and Ardagh, Church of Ireland; b. in Ireland about the year 1822; educated at Trinity College, Dublin; graduated B.A. and divinity testimonium (second-class) 1843, M.A. 1857; ordained deacon 1843, priest 1844; became curate of Rathlin Island, County Antrim, 1843; of St. John's, Sligo, County Sligo, 1846; incumbent of Calry, County Sligo, 1856; rector of Urney and Annegelliff, County Cavan, 1866; bishop, 1884. *

SHORE, Thomas Teignmouth, F.R.G.S., Church of England; b. in Dublin, Ireland, Dec. 28, 1841; graduated at Trinity College, Dublin, B.A. 1861, divinity honors 1863, M.A. (Oxford) 1865; became curate at Chelsea 1865, and at Kensington 1867; vicar of St. Mildred's, Lee, 1870; incumbent of Berkeley Chapel, Mayfair, London, 1873. He was honorary chaplain to the Queen from 1878 to 1881, and since has been chaplain in ordinary. He was the religious instructor of the three daughters of the Prince of Wales, and prepared them for confirmation. [He is a noted preacher to children.] He is a moderate High Churchman. He is the author of *Some Difficulties of Belief*, London, 1878, 8th ed. 1884; *The Life of the World to come, and other Subjects*, 1879, 4th ed. 1883; *The First Epistle to the Corinthians*, 1870, 5th ed. 1885 (in Bishop Ellicott's commentary); "*St. George for England*," *and other Sermons preached to Children*, 1882, 5th ed. 1885; and *Shortened Church Services as used at Children's Services*, 1883, 2d ed. 1885; *Prayer (a Helpful Manual for Believers)*, 1886; since 1886 editor of *Helps to Belief* (a series).

SHORT, Charles, A.M. (Harvard College, Cambridge, Mass., 1849), **LL.D.** (Kenyon College, Gambier, O., 1868), Episcopalian, layman; b. at Haverhill, Mass., May 28, 1821; graduated at Harvard College, Cambridge, Mass., 1846; taught classical schools in Roxbury, Mass., and Philadelphia; was president of Kenyon College, Gambier, O., and professor of intellectual and moral philosophy, 1863–67; and since 1868 has been professor of Latin in Columbia College, New-York City. He is a director of the American Oriental Society, and was a member of the New-Testament Revision Company. He has made numerous contributions of a critical character to reviews and other periodicals, including a series of elaborate articles in *The American Journal of Philology* on the revision of *St. Matthew's Gospel*; and the essay "on the order of words in Attic-Greek prose" prefixed to the American edition of C. D. Yonge's *English-Greek Lexicon*, New York. With Dr. C. T. Lewis he edited and enlarged E. A. Andrews-Freund's *Latin Dictionary*, 1879.

SHUEY, William John, D.D. (Hartsville University, Ind., 1880, but declined), United Brethren in Christ; b. at Miamisburg, O., Feb. 9, 1827; educated in the common schools and at the academy, Springfield, O.; was pastor at Lewisburg, O., 1849–51, Cincinnati 1851–55; missionary to the West Coast of Africa, between Liberia and Sierra Leone, 1855; pastor at Cincinnati, O., 1855–58; Dayton, O., 1860–62; presiding elder, 1862–64; became general manager of the United Brethren in Christ Publishing House at Dayton, O., 1864. He has been a member of the United Brethren Board of Missions since 1861, and member of six General Conferences.

SIEFFERT, Friedrich Anton Emil, Protestant Reformed theologian; b. at Königsberg, Prussia, Dec. 24, 1843; studied at Königsberg, Halle, and Berlin; became *privat-docent* at Bonn 1871, and professor extraordinary 1873; ordinary professor at Erlangen (Reformed theology), 1878. He is the author of *Nonnulla ad apocryph. libri Henochi* *originem, etc., pertinentia*, 1867; *Galatien und seine ersten Christengemeinden*, 1871; and of *Friedrich Ludwig Sieffert*, 1881; and editor of the sixth and seventh editions of Meyer's commentary on *Galatians*, Göttingen, 1880 and 1886. He is a Ph.D. and Lic. Theol.

SIEGFRIED, Carl (Gustav Adolf), Ph.D. (Halle, 1859), **D.D.** (*hon.*, Jena, 1875), Protestant theologian; b. at Magdeburg, Jan. 22, 1830; studied philology and theology at Halle and Bonn, 1849–53; became teacher in gymnasium at Magdeburg 1857, and at Guben 1860; professor and second minister at Pforta, 1865; ordinary professor of theology at Jena, 1875; appointed ecclesiastical councillor, 1885. He is a Knight of the Red Eagle, fourth class. He is the author of *De inscriptione Gerbitana* (Program), Magdeburg, 1863; *Die hebräischen Worterklärungen des Philo und die Spuren ihrer Einwirkung auf die Kirchenväter*, 1863; *Spinoza als Kritiker und Ausleger des Alten Testaments*, Berlin, 1867; *Philo von Alexandrien als Ausleger des A. T.*, Jena, 1875; (with H. Gelzer) *Eusebii canonum epitome ex Dionysii Telmaharensis Chronico petita* (translated and annotated his Latin translation of the Syriac), Leipzig, 1884; (with H. L. Strack) *Lehrbuch der neuhebräischen Sprache und Litteratur* (wrote the grammar of the new Hebrew), Carlsruhe, 1884; since 1881 has furnished the Old-Testament division in the *Theologischer Jahresbericht* (Punjer's, now edited by Lipsius), and has written numerous articles upon Old-Testament subjects.

SIMON, David Worthington, Ph.D. (Tübingen, 1863), Congregationalist; b. at Hazelgrove, Cheshire, Eng., April 28, 1830; educated in the Lancashire Independent College, Manchester, 1848–54, and at Halle, Germany, 1854–55 and 1857–58; was pastor at Royston, Hertfordshire, for nine months of 1856; travelled on the Continent, 1857; was pastor at Rusholme, Manchester, 1858; returned to Germany for study, 1859; was agent of the British and Foreign Bible Society, 1863–69; professor of general theology and philosophy at Springfield College, Birmingham, 1869–84; since 1884 principal and professor of systematic theology and church history in Congregational Theological Hall, Edinburgh. He translated Hengstenberg's *Commentary on Ecclesiastes*, Edinburgh, 1860; (with W. L. Alexander) Dorner's *History of the Development of the Doctrine of the Person of Christ*, Edinburgh, 1861–63, 5 vols., etc.; and is the author of *The Bible an Outgrowth of Theocratic Life*, Edinburgh, 1885, and articles in *British Quarterly Review*, *Bibliotheca Sacra*, *Expositor*, and other publications.

SIMPSON, Matthew, D.D., LL.D., bishop of the Methodist-Episcopal Church; b. at Cadiz, O., June 21, 1811; d. in Philadelphia, Penn., June 17, 1884. He was educated at Madison College (subsequently merged into Alleghany College, Meadville, Penn.), where he was tutor in 1829. He then studied medicine, and commenced its practice in 1833, but abandoned it in 1835, when he was ordained deacon by the Pittsburg Conference of the Methodist Episcopal Church, and in 1837 elder. He was vice-president and professor of natural science in Alleghany College, 1837–39; president of Indiana Asbury University, Greencastle, Ind., 1839–48; editor of *The Western Christian Advocate*, Cincinnati, O., 1848–52; bishop, 1852 till death. He was delegate of the General Conference to the Irish and British Conference 1857, and to the Evangelical Alliance Conference, Berlin, the same year; and during this year and next travelled over Europe and the East. He visited Europe again officially in 1870, 1875, and 1881. He changed his residence in 1859 from Pittsburg, Penn., to Evanston, Ill., and was president of the Garrett Biblical Institute in the latter place. He visited Mexico in 1874. As bishop he held conferences in all the States and in most of the Territories. He was the acknowledged prince of Methodist preachers. By his eloquent addresses he did good service to the Union cause during the Civil War. He enjoyed the personal friendship of President Lincoln. He was the author of *Hundred Years of Methodism*, New York, 1876; *Cyclopædia of Methodism*, Philadelphia, 1878, 5th rev. ed. 1882; *Lectures on Preaching*, New York, 1879; *Sermons* (posthumous, ed. by Rev. Dr. G. R. Crooks, 1885).

SINKER, Robert, Church of England; b. in Liverpool, July 17, 1838; graduated at Trinity College, Cambridge, B.A. (wrangler and second-class classical tripos), 1862; first-class theological tripos, Scholefield prizeman, and Crosse scholar, 1863; Tyrwhitt Hebrew scholar and Hulsean prizeman, 1864; M.A., 1865; Norrisian prizeman, 1868; B.D., 1880; chaplain of Trinity College, 1865; librarian, 1871. He edited *Testamenta xii. Patriarcharum* (Cambridge and Oxford MSS.), Camb., 1869, Appendix (collation of Roman and Patmos manuscripts), 1879; *Catalogue of Fifteenth-Century Books in Library of Trinity College*, 1876; *Pearson on the Creed*, 1881; *Catalogue of English Books printed before 1601 in Library of Trinity College*, 1885; and, besides numerous articles in Smith and Cheetham's *Dictionary of Christian Antiquities*, has published *The Characteristic Differences between the Books of the New Testament and the Immediately Preceding Jewish and the Immediately Succeeding Christian Literature, considered as an Evidence of the Divine Authority of the New Testament*, 1865; and the translation of the "Testaments of the Twelve Patriarchs," in Clark's Ante-Nicene Library, 1872.

SKINNER, Thomas Harvey, D.D. (College of New Jersey, Princeton, 1867), Presbyterian; b. in Philadelphia, Penn., Oct. 6, 1820; graduated at the University of the City of New York, 1840, and Union Theological Seminary, 1843; was (Presbyterian) pastor at Patterson, N.J., 1843–46; New-York City, 1846–55; Honesdale, Penn., 1856–59; (Reformed) Stapleton, Staten Island, N.Y., 1859–68; (Presbyterian) Fort Wayne, Ind., 1868–71; Cincinnati, O., 1871–81; has been professor of didactic and polemic theology, North-western (now McCormick) Theological Seminary, Chicago, Ill., since 1881.

SLOANE, James Renwick Wilson, D.D. (Westminster College, New Wilmington, Penn., 1869), Reformed Presbyterian; b. at Topsham, Orange County, Vt., May 29, 1833; d. at Allegheny, Saturday, March 6, 1886. He graduated at Jefferson College, Canonsburg, Penn., 1847; was president of Richmond College, Richmond, Jefferson County, O., 1848–50, of Geneva College, Geneva, O., 1851–56; pastor in New-York City, 1856–68; and since was professor of systematic theology and homiletics in Allegheny Theological Seminary, Penn. He published various sermons, etc.

SMEND, Rudolf, Ph.D. (Bonn, 1874), **Lic. Theol.** (Halle, 1875), **D.D.** (Giessen, 1885), Swiss theologian; b. at Lengerich, Westphalia, Germany, Nov. 5, 1851; educated at Göttingen, Berlin, and Bonn; became *privat-docent* of theology at Halle, 1875; professor extraordinary at Basel, 1880; ordinary professor of theology there, 1881. He is the author of *Der Prophet Ezechiel erklärt*, Leipzig, 1880.

SMITH, Benjamin Mosby, D.D., LL.D. (Hampden-Sidney College, Prince Edward County, Va., 1854 and 1880, respectively), Presbyterian (Southern Church); b at Montrose, Powhatan County, Va., June 30, 1811; graduated at Hampden-Sidney College, Prince Edward County, Va., 1829, and at the Union Theological Seminary, Va., 1834; tutor there, 1834-36; pastor at Danville, Va., 1838-40; at Tinkling Spring and Waynesborough, 1840-45; and at Staunton, 1845-54; and ever since has been professor of Oriental and biblical literature in Union Seminary. From 1858 to 1874 he was with Dr. Dabney pastor of the Hampden-Sidney College Church. Since 1842 he has been trustee of Washington College (now Washington and Lee University). He has published *A Commentary on the Psalms and Proverbs*, Glasgow, Scotland, 1859, 3d ed. Knoxville, Tenn., 1883; *Family Religion*, Philadelphia, 1859; *Questions on the Gospels*, Richmond, vol. i., 1868; and articles in *Southern Presbyterian Review*.

SMITH, Charles Strong, Congregationalist; b. at Hardwick, Vt., July 21, 1824; graduated at the University of Vermont, at Burlington, 1848; taught academy at Craftsbury, Vt., 1848-50; studied for a year (1851) at Andover Theological Seminary, Mass., but completed the course at East Windsor (now Hartford) Theological Institute, Conn., and graduated 1853; was pastor at New Preston, Conn., 1853-55; North Walton, N.Y., 1855-57; out of health five years; represented the town of Hardwick, Vt., in State legislature in 1863; since 1863 has been secretary of the Vermont Domestic Missionary Society, and written the annual reports; was associate editor of *Vermont Chronicle*, Montpelier (denominational weekly), 1875-77; since 1885 editor. He is the author of an essay, *Systematic Beneficence*, Montpelier, Vt., 1877.

SMITH, Charles William, Methodist; b. in Fayette County, Penn., Jan. 30, 1840; entered the ministry of the Methodist-Episcopal Church, 1859; was pastor until 1880; presiding elder, 1880-84; since May, 1884, has been editor of *The Pittsburg Christian Advocate*, Penn. In the autumn of 1864 he served one term in the Christian Commission in the Army of the Potomac.

SMITH, George Vance, Ph.D. (Tübingen, 1858), **D.D.** (Jena, 1873), Unitarian; b. at Portarlington, Ireland, June 13, 1816; educated in Manchester New College, York and Manchester, 1836-41; graduated B.A. at London University, 1841; was minister at Bradford, Yorkshire, 1841-43, Macclesfield, 1843-46; theological tutor in Manchester New College, Manchester and London, 1846-57; minister at York, 1858-75; at the Upper Chapel, Sheffield, 1875-76; since 1876 has been principal of Carmarthen Presbyterian College, Wales. He was one of the New Testament revisers from the formation of the committee in 1870. He is a Liberal Christian, unfettered by subscription to theological creeds. He is the author of *The Prophecies relating to Nineveh and the Assyrians, from the Hebrew, with Introductions and Commentary*, London, 1857; *The Bible and Popular Theology, in Reply to Mr. Gladstone, Dr. Liddon, etc.*, 1871, 3d ed. 1871; *The Spirit and the Word of Christ, and their Permanent Lessons*, 1875; *The Prophets and their Interpreters*, 1878; *Texts and Margins of the Revised New Testament*, 1881; joint author of *The Holy Scriptures of the Old Covenant, a Revised Translation from the Hebrew*, 1865, 3 vols.; has written many minor publications (sermons, lectures, tracts, etc.).

SMITH, Henry Preserved, D.D. (Maryville College, Tenn., 1883), Presbyterian; b. at Troy, O., Oct. 23, 1847; graduated at Amherst College, Mass., 1869, and at Lane Theological Seminary, Cincinnati, O., 1872; was student at Berlin (1873-74) and Leipzig (1876-77); instructor in Lane Theological Seminary, 1874-76; and since 1877 has been professor of Hebrew and Old Testament exegesis there.

SMITH, Judson, D.D. (Amherst College, Mass., 1877), Congregationalist; b. at Middlefield, Hampshire County, Mass., June 28, 1837; graduated at Amherst College, Amherst, Mass., 1859; and at the Oberlin Theological Seminary, Oberlin, O., 1863; was tutor in Latin and Greek in Oberlin College, O., 1862-64; instructor in mathematics and metaphysics, Williston Seminary, Easthampton, Mass. (where he had fitted for college), 1864-66; professor of the Latin language and literature, Oberlin College, 1866-70; professor of ecclesiastical history and positive institutions, and dean of the faculty, Oberlin Theological Seminary, 1870-84; lecturer on modern history, Oberlin College, 1875-84; lecturer on history, Lake Erie Female Seminary, Painesville, O., 1879-84; acting pastor Second Congregational Church, Oberlin, O., 1874-75, 1882-84; editor of *Bibliotheca Sacra*, Oberlin, O., 1883-84; since associate editor; foreign secretary A.B.C.F.M., Boston, Mass., since 1884. He was president of the board of education, Oberlin, O., 1871-84. His theological standpoint is that of New-England theology; holds fast to the historic faith of Christendom, with hospitality to all new light that breaks forth from the Word of God. He is the author of *Lectures in Church History and the History of Doctrine, from the beginning of the Christian Era to 1648*, Oberlin, O., 1881; *Lectures on Modern History*, 1881 (both privately printed); articles in *Bibliotheca Sacra*, *New Englander*, and religious journals, etc.

SMITH, Justin Almerin, D.D. (Shurtleff College, Upper Alton, Ill., 1858), Baptist; b. at Ticonderoga, N.Y., Dec. 29, 1819; graduated at Union College, Schenectady, N.Y., 1843; became pastor at North Bennington, Vt., 1844; at Rochester, N.Y., 1849; editor of *The Christian Times*, now *The Standard*, Chicago, Ill., since 1853. From 1863 to 1868 he was pastor of the Indiana Avenue Baptist Church; was from 1877 to 1885 lecturer in Baptist Union Theological Seminary, Morgan Park, Chicago, of which institution he has been a trustee from its foundation. He was present at the opening of the Vatican Council, Dec. 8, 1869, and for some time afterwards. He is the author of *Memoir of Nathaniel Colver, D.D.*, Chicago, 1873; *Patmos, or the Kingdom and the Patience*, 1874; *Memoir of Rev. John Bates*, Toronto, 1877; *A Commentary on the Revelation*, Philadelphia, 1884; *The*

New Age, or Studies in Modern Church History, Chicago, 1886.

SMITH, Lucius Edwin, D.D. (Williams College, Williamstown, Mass., 1869), Baptist; b. at Williamstown, Mass., Jan. 29, 1822; graduated at Williams College, in his native town, 1843, and at Newton Theological Institution, Mass., 1857; was admitted to the bar, 1845; associate editor *Hartford* (Conn.) *Daily Courant*, 1847–48; editor *Free-soil Advocate*, Hartford, Conn., 1848; associate editor *Boston Republican*, 1849; was assistant Secretary of the American Baptist Missionary Union, editing the *Baptist Missionary Magazine* 1849–54; pastor at Groton, Mass., 1858–65; professor of rhetoric and pastoral theology, University of Lewisburg, Penn., 1865–68; editor of *The Baptist Quarterly*, New York, 1867–69; literary editor of the New York *Examiner*, 1868–76; editor of *The Watchman*, Boston, Mass., 1877–81, and since associate editor. He is the author of *Heroes and Martyrs of Modern Missionary Enterprise, with an Historical Review of Earlier Missions*, Boston, 1852 (some 10,000 copies sold); articles in *Baptist Quarterly, Baptist Quarterly Review, Knickerbocker Magazine* (1845–49), *North-American Review* (1860), *Bibliotheca Sacra* (1880), McClintock and Strong's *Cyclopædia, Encyclopædia Americana* (Philadelphia, 1886), etc.

SMITH, Matson Meier, S.T.D. (Columbia College, New-York City, 1863), Episcopalian; b. in New-York City, April 4, 1826; graduated from Columbia College, 1843, and from Union Theological Seminary, New-York City, 1847; pastor (Congregational) at Brookline, Mass., 1851–58; at Bridgeport, Conn., 1858–65; rector (Episcopal) at Newark, N.J., 1866–71, and at Hartford, Conn., 1872–76, has been since 1876 professor of homiletics and pastoral theology in the divinity school of the Protestant-Episcopal Church, Philadelphia, Penn. He contributed many sermons during our civil war, and articles to the religious journals.

SMITH, Robert Payne.—See PAYNE-SMITH, ROBERT.

SMITH, Samuel Francis, D.D. (Waterville College, now Colby University, Waterville, Me., 1854), Baptist; b. in Boston, Mass., Oct. 21, 1808; educated at Boston Latin School, 1820–25; graduated at Harvard University, Cambridge, Mass., 1829, and at Andover Theological Seminary, Mass., 1832; was pastor of the First Baptist Church, Waterville, Me., 1834–42, and during the same period professor of modern languages in Waterville College; pastor of First Baptist Church, Newton, Mass., January, 1842, to July 1, 1854; editor of *The Christian Review*, Boston, January, 1842–48, and of the publications of the American Baptist Missionary Union, 1854–69. He spent a year in Europe, from July, 1875, to July, 1876; also over two years in Europe and Asia, visiting missionary stations of various denominations, from September, 1880, to October, 1882. He resides at Newton Centre, Mass. He is the author of the national hymn, *My country, 'tis of thee* (written at Andover, Mass., in February, 1832, while a student in the theological seminary), and the missionary hymn, *The morning light is breaking* (in same year and place), and many others. Most of the pieces included in Lowell Mason's *Juvenile Lyre* (Boston, 1832), the first book of children's music, were his translations from the German; about one entire volume of the *Encyclopædia Americana*, edited by Francis Lieber (Philadelphia, 1828–32, 13 vols.), is composed of his translations from the German *Conversations-Lexicon* of Brockhaus. He was editor of *Lyric Gems* (selections of poetry, with several original pieces), Boston, 1843; *The Psalmist* (chiefly his work, with twenty-seven of his hymns, the hymn-book of the Baptist Churches of the United States for thirty years), 1843; *Rock of Ages* (selections of poetry, with several original pieces), 1866, new ed. 1877; several volumes for D. Lothrop & Co., Boston; etc.; author of *Life of Rev. Joseph Grafton*, 1848; *Missionary Sketches*, 1879, last ed. 1883; *History of Newton, Mass.*, 1880; *Rambles in Mission-fields*, 1884; contributions to many periodicals. See *America: our National Hymn*, Boston [1880].

SMITH, William, LL.D., D.C.L. (Oxford, 1870), layman, Church of England; b. in London, 1813; graduated at London University, in which from 1853 to 1869 he was classical examiner, and since has been a member of the senate, and since 1867 editor of *The Quarterly Review.* He is famous for his dictionaries of biblical and classical literature, upon which he secured the labor of many eminent and learned men, and for his Greek and Latin text-books. The following are his principal editorial labors: *Dictionary of Greek and Roman Antiquities*, London, 1840–42; *Dictionary of Greek and Roman Biography and Mythology*, 1843–49; *Dictionary of Greek and Roman Geography*, 1852–57; *Dictionary of the Bible*, 1860–63, 3 vols (American ed. by Hackett and Abbot, Boston, 1869–70, 4 vols.); *Atlas of Biblical and Classical Geography*, 1875 (with George Grove); *Dictionary of Christian Antiquities*, 1875–80, 2 vols. (with Professor Cheetham); *Dictionary of Christian Biography*, 1877–86, 4 vols. (with Dr. Wace): the last two comprise only the first eight centuries.

SMITH, William Robertson, LL.D. (Aberdeen, 1882), Free Church of Scotland; b. at Keig, Aberdeenshire, Nov. 8, 1846; educated at Aberdeen University (M.A., 1865), New College Edinburgh, and at Bonn and Göttingen; was assistant to the chair of physics at Edinburgh, 1868–70; professor of Hebrew in the Free-church College, Aberdeen, 1870–81, when he was removed by the General Assembly on account of his alleged heretical teaching; and has been since associate editor of the ninth edition of the *Encyclopædia Britannica*, and was (1883–86) Lord Almoner's professor of Arabic at Cambridge; since 1886, librarian to the university. He is the author of *The Old Testament in the Jewish Church*, London, 1881; *The Prophets of Israel, and their Place in History to the Close of the Eighth Century B.C.*, 1882 (both reprinted, N.Y.); *Kinship and Marriage in Early Arabia*, 1885. *

SMYTH, Egbert Coffin, D.D. (Bowdoin College, Brunswick, Me., 1866), Congregationalist; b. at Brunswick, Me., Aug. 24, 1829; graduated at Bowdoin College, Brunswick, Me., 1848, and Bangor (Me.) Theological Seminary, 1853; became professor of rhetoric at Bowdoin College, 1856; of ecclesiastical history in Andover Theological Seminary, 1863; and has also been president of the faculty since 1878. Besides *Value of the Study of Church History in Ministerial Education* (lecture), Andover, 1874, pamphlet sermons, etc., he has since its foundation (1884) edited the *Andover Review*, and with Professor Ropes has published a translation of Uhlhorn's *Conflict of Christianity with Heathenism*, New York, 1879. *

SMYTH, (Samuel Phillips) Newman, D.D. (University of the City of New York, 1881), Congregationalist; b. at Brunswick, Me., June 25, 1843; graduated at Bowdoin College, Brunswick, Me., 1863, and at Andover Theological Seminary, Mass., 1867; was acting pastor of Harrison-street Chapel (now Pilgrim Church), Providence, R.I., 1868; in Europe, 1868–69; pastor of the First Church, Bangor, Me., 1870–75; of the First Presbyterian Church, Quincy, Ill., 1876–82; since of the First Congregational Church, New Haven, Conn. He is the author of *The Religious Feeling: a Study for Faith*, New York, 1877; *Old Faiths in New Light*, 1879; *The Orthodox Theology of To-day*, 1881: *The Reality of Faith* (sermons), 1884. *

SOUTHGATE, Right Rev. Horatio, S.T.D. (Columbia College, New York, 1846), Episcopalian; b. in Portland, Me., July 5, 1812; graduated at Bowdoin College, Brunswick, Me., 1832, and at Andover (Congregational) Theological Seminary, 1835; was engaged, under appointment by the Episcopal Church, in investigating the state of Mohammedanism in Turkey and Persia, 1836–38; ordained priest, 1839; missionary in Constantinople, as delegate to the Oriental churches, 1840–44; consecrated Episcopalian missionary bishop for the dominions and dependencies of the Sultan of Turkey, Oct. 26, 1844; at Constantinople, 1844–50; resigned his jurisdiction, 1850; was rector of St. Luke's Church, Portland, Me., 1851–52; of the Church of the Advent, Boston, Mass., 1852–58; and of Zion Church, New-York City, 1859–72; retired, 1872; and has since lived at Ravenswood, Long Island, N.Y. He was elected bishop of California 1850, and of Hayti 1870, but declined both elections. He is the author of *Narrative of a Tour through Armenia, Kurdistan, Persia, and Mesopotamia*, New York, 1840, 2 vols. (republished in England); *Narrative of a Visit to the Syrian (Jacobite) Church of Mesopotamia*, 1844; *A Treatise on the Antiquity, Doctrine, Ministry, and Worship of the Anglican Church* (in Greek), Constantinople, 1849; *Practical Directions for the Observance of Lent*, New York, 1850; *The War in the East*, 1855 (republished in England); *Parochial Sermons*, 1860; *The Cross above the Crescent, a Romance of Constantinople*, Philadelphia, 1877.

SPAETH, Adolf, D.D. (University of Pennsylvania, Philadelphia, 1875), Lutheran (General Council); b. at Esslingen, Würtemberg, Oct. 29, 1839; graduated at the University of Tübingen, 1861; was tutor in the family of the Duke of Argyle, 1863; collegiate pastor of St. Michael's and Zion's German Lutheran congregation, Philadelphia, 1864–67; and since 1867 has been pastor of St. Johannis' Church, Philadelphia; since 1872 professor at the Lutheran Theological Seminary, Philadelphia; and since 1880 president of the General Council of the Evangelical Lutheran Church in North America. He has published *Brosamen von des Herrn Tische*, Philadelphia, 1869; *Die Evangelien des Kirchenjahrs*, 1870; *Americanische Beleuchtung des americanischen Reisebilder des Herrn Prof. Dr. Pfleiderer*, 1882; *The General Council of the Evangelical Lutheran Church in North America*, 1885; *Phœbe, the Deaconess*, 1885. He prepared the appendix to the American edition of Büchner's *Concordanz*, 1871; and edited the General Council's German Sunday-school Book 1875, and Church Book 1877.

SPALDING, Right Rev. John Franklin, D.D. (Trinity College, Hartford, Conn., 1874), Episcopalian, missionary bishop of Colorado, with jurisdiction in New Mexico and Wyoming; b. at Belgrade, Me., Aug. 25, 1828; graduated at Bowdoin College, Brunswick, Me., 1853, and at the General Theological Seminary, New-York City, 1857; was missionary at Old Town, Me., 1857–59; rector of St. George's Church, Lee, Mass., 1859–60; assistant minister at Grace Church, Providence, R.I., 1860, to December, 1861; rector of St. Paul's Church, Erie, Penn., April, 1862, to March 1, 1874; elected bishop, October, 1873; consecrated, Dec. 31, 1873. He is the author of *Lay Co-operation* (in Western Massachusetts), New York, 1860; *Christianity and Modern Infidelity, an Essay*, Erie, Penn., 1863; *Manual of Mothers' Meetings*, 1871; *Hymns from the Hymnal, with Tunes and Notes*, 1872; *Congregationalism in the Church, an Essay*, New York, 1875; *The Cathedral and Cathedral System* (a sermon), Denver, Col., 1880; *Commemorative Address of Ten Years' Episcopal Work in Colorado*, 1885; Episcopal charges, addresses, reports, review articles, tracts, etc.

SPALDING, Right Rev. John Lancaster, Roman Catholic; b. at Lebanon, Ky., June 2, 1840; studied at Mount St. Mary's College, Emmitsburg, Md., and at Cincinnati, O.; became secretary and chancellor of the diocese of Louisville, Ky., 1865; pastor of the congregation for colored Catholics, Louisville, 1869; bishop of Peoria, Ill., 1877. He is president of the Irish Catholic Colonization Society, and of the Roman Catholic State Temperance Union of Illinois. He is the author of *Life of Archbishop Spalding of Baltimore*, New York, 1872; *Essays and Reviews*, 1876; *Religious Mission of the Irish People*, 1880; *Lectures and Discourses*, 1882.

SPALDING, Right Rev. Martin John, D.D., Roman Catholic; b. in Marion County, Ky., May 23, 1810; d. at Baltimore, Md., Feb. 7, 1872. He graduated at St. Mary's College, Lebanon, Ky., 1826; studied theology, and completed his course in the Propaganda College in Rome, where he was ordained priest Aug. 13, 1834. He was pastor of the cathedral at Bardstown, Ky., 1834–38, 1841–48; president of St. Joseph's Theological Seminary, Bardstown, 1838–40; pastor of St. Peter's Church, Lexington, Ky., 1840–41; coadjutor bishop of Louisville, Ky., 1848–50; bishop, 1850–54; archbishop of Baltimore from 1864 till his death. He founded *The Catholic Advocate*, Louisville, in February, 1835, and was connected with it until 1858; *The Louisville Guardian* in 1858; was main promoter of the Catholic Publication Society and *Catholic World*, both New-York City. While coadjutor bishop, he established a colony of Trappist monks at Gethsemane, near Bardstown, Ky., and a house of Magdalens in connection with the Convent of the Good Shepherd. While bishop of Louisville he built a magnificent cathedral in that city. He was at the First Plenary Council of Baltimore, May, 1852, and successfully advocated the erection of the see of Covington. In November, 1852, he obtained in Belgium Xaverian Brothers for the parochial schools of Louisville, Ky., and from Archbishop Zurysen of Utrecht several priests and sisters to instruct deaf-mutes. In 1855 he had a famous debate with George D. Prentice of the *Louisville Journal*, upon the Know-nothing Movement. Bishop Spalding was the author of *D'Aubigné's History of the Reformation reviewed*, Baltimore, 1844, 2d ed. London, 1846, Dublin, 1848 (subsequently enlarged and re-issued as *History of the Protestant Reformation in Germany and Switzerland, and in England, Ireland, Scotland, the Netherlands, France, and Northern Europe*, Louisville, 1860, 2 vols., 8th ed. Baltimore, 1875); *Sketches of the Early Catholic Missions in Kentucky, 1787–1827*, Louisville, 1846; *Lectures on the General Evidences of Catholicity*, 1847, 6th ed. Baltimore, 1866; *Life, Times, and Character of the Right Rev. B. J. Flaget*, Louisville, 1852; *Miscellanea: comprising Reviews, Lectures, and Essays on Historical, Theological, and Miscellaneous Subjects*, Louisville, 1855, London, 1855, 6th ed. Baltimore, 1866; *Papal Infallibility*, Baltimore, 1870; edited, with introduction and notes, Abbé J. E. Dana's, *General History of the Catholic Church*, New York, 1865–66, 4 vols.; and was a frequent contributor to religious periodicals. *

SPENCE, Henry Donald Maurice, Church of England; b. in London in the year 1836; educated at Corpus Christi College, Cambridge; took Carus undergraduate university prize, 1862; B.A., 1864; first-class in the theological tripos, 1865; Carus and Scholefield university prize, 1865, 1866; M.A., 1866; ordained deacon 1865, priest 1866; became professor of English literature and modern languages, and Hebrew lecturer, at St. David's College, Lampeter, 1865; rector of St. Mary-de-Crypt, with All Saints and St. Owen, Gloucester, 1870; and principal of Gloucester College, 1875; resigned the two latter positions, and became vicar of St. Pancras and rural dean, 1877. In 1870 he was appointed examining chaplain to the bishop of Gloucester and Bristol; in 1875 honorary canon of Gloucester. He is editor of *The Pulpit Commentary*, London, 1880 sqq.; and has contributed to Bishop Ellicott's *Commentary* (*First Samuel* and *Pastoral Epistles*), and to Dr. Schaff's *Popular Commentary on the New Testament* (on *Acts*, with Dean Howson). He wrote an essay on *The Babylonian Talmud*, 1882; on *The Teaching of the Twelve Apostles*, 1884. *

SPENCER, Herbert; b. at Derby, Eng., April 27, 1820; began work as a civil engineer, 1837; but since 1850 has been a literary man, and has won recognition as the author of a system of philosophy, in which the doctrine of evolution is applied to the different departments of thought and life. He began the series with his *First Principles*, London, 1862; then came *Principles of Biology*, 1867; *Principles of Psychology*, 1872; *Principles of Sociology*, 1877 sqq., part 6 1885; *Principles of Morality*, 18 ; *Ecclesiastical Institutions*, 1885. *

SPITTA, Friedrich (Adolph Wilhelm), Lic. Theol. (Leipzig, 1879), German theologian; b. at Wittingen, Hanover, Jan. 10, 1852; studied at Göttingen and Erlangen, 1871–75; became teacher in the high school at Hanover, 1876; inspector of the Tholuck *convict* at Halle, 1877; assistant preacher at Bonn, 1879; pastor of Obercassel, near Bonn, 1881; and has also been since 1880 *privatdocent* of evangelical theology in Bonn University. He is the author of *Der Brief des Julius Africanus an Aristides, Kritisch untersucht und hergestellt*, Halle, 1877; *Die liturgische Andacht am Luther Jubiläum*, Halle, 1883; *Der Knabe Jesus, eine biblische Geschichte und ihre apokryphischen Entstellungen*, 1883; *Luther und der evangelische Gottesdienst*, 1884; *Haendel und Bach, zwei Festreden*, Bonn, 1885; *Der zweite Brief des Petrus und der Brief des Judas. Eine geschichtliche Untersuchung*, Halle, 1885; *Die Passionen nach den vier Evangelisten von Heinrich Schütz*, 1886; *Heinrich Schütz, sein Leben und seine Kunst*, 1886; numerous articles, popular and scientific, in various periodicals.

SPRECHER, Samuel, D.D. (Washington College, Penn., 1850), **LL.D.** (Pennsylvania College, Gettysburg, 1874), Lutheran (General Synod); b. near Hagerstown, Md., Dec. 28, 1810; studied in Pennsylvania College and Theological Seminary, Gettysburg, Penn., 1830–36; was pastor at Harrisburg, Penn., Martinsburg, Va., and Chambersburg, Penn., 1836–49; president of Wittenberg College, Springfield, O., 1849–74; and since 1874 has been professor of systematic theology there. He is the author of *Groundwork of a System of Evangelical Lutheran Theology*, Philadelphia, 1879; and various addresses, etc.

SPRINZL, Josef, D.D. (Vienna, 1864), Roman Catholic; b. at Linz, Austria, March 9, 1839; studied in the priests' seminary at Linz, 1857–61; ordained priest, 1861; studied in the priests' institute at Vienna, 1861–64; became professor of theology in the Linz Seminary, 1864; professor of dogmatics at Salzburg University, 1875; ordinary professor of the same at Prague, 1881. He became *geistlicher Rath* of bishop of Linz, Feb. 23, 1873, and of the prince bishop of Salzburg, Jan. 28, 1880. From 1865 to 1875 he edited the Linz *Theolog. praktische Quartalschrift*; in 1868, the Linz *Katholisch. Blätter* (a tri-weekly). He is the author of *Handbuch der Fundamentaltheologie*, Vienna, 1876; *Die Theologie der apostolischen Väter*, 1880 (trans. into Hungarian); *Compendium summarium theologiæ dogmaticæ in usum prælectionum academicarum concinnatum*, 1882; several minor theological works.

SPROULL, Thomas, D.D. (Westminster College, New Wilmington, Penn., 1857), Reformed Presbyterian (Old School); b. near Freeport, Penn., Sept. 15, 1803; graduated at the Western University of Pennsylvania, Pittsburg, 1829; pastor of the Reformed Presbyterian Congregation of Allegheny and Pittsburg, 1834–68; professor in Reformed Presbyterian Western Theological Seminary, 1838–40; in Eastern and Western Seminaries united, 1840–45; again since 1856; professor *emeritus* since 1875. He edited *The Reformed Presbyterian*, 1855–62, and *The Reformed Presbyterian and Covenanter*, 1862–74, both published in Pittsburg, Penn. Besides sermons, etc., is the author of *Prelections on Theology*, Pittsburg, 1882.

SPURGEON, Charles Haddon, Baptist; b. at Kelvedon, Essex, Eng., June 19, 1834. He is the grandson of Rev. James Spurgeon, for many years pastor of the Independent Church at Stambourne, Essex, and son of Rev. John Spurgeon, who was also an Independent minister, and who until 1876 was pastor of the Independent Church, Upper Street, Islington, London. When just old enough to leave home, he was removed to his grandfather's, and there remained until 1841, when his father placed him in a school at Colchester, where he acquired a fair acquaintance with Latin, Greek, and French, and led his class at every examination. In 1848 he spent a few months in an agricultural college at Maidstone, conducted by a relative. In 1849 he became usher in a school at Newmarket kept by a Baptist. He then began to attend the Baptist Church. On Dec. 15, 1850, when home for a holiday, he was converted in the Colchester Primitive Methodist Chapel, under the preaching of an individual unknown, who chose for his text Isa. xlv. 22, emphasizing the words "Look . . . and be saved;" which words were exactly suited to relieve the mind of young Spurgeon, who had been for some time under profound conviction of sin, and who looked and was saved. He was immersed at Isleham, on Friday, May 3, 1851, and thus formally left the Independent connection in which he had been brought up. His works at once attested his faith. He commenced distributing tracts and visiting the poor in Newmarket. He addressed the Sunday-school children in the vestry of the Independent chapel. He wrote *Antichrist and her Brood*, in competition for a prize for an essay on popery. No prize was awarded, but he received a handsome gift from Samuel Morley as an encouragement. In 1851 he became usher in a school at Cambridge, entered the "Lay-preachers Association" in connection with the Baptist Church meeting in St. Andrew's Street, Cambridge, and the same year preached his first sermon from 1 Pet. ii. 7, at Teversham, a village four miles from Cambridge. He was then a boy of sixteen years, and wore a round jacket and broad turn-down collar. His success was so great that he was encouraged to hold evening services, after his school duties were over, in villages around Cambridge and Waterbeach; and this he did in thirteen stations, preaching sometimes in a chapel, sometimes in a cottage, or in the open air. In 1852 he became pastor at Waterbeach, and during the two years he was there the membership increased from forty to nearly a hundred. His father and others strongly advised him to enter Stepney (now Regent's Park) College to prepare more fully for the ministry. A meeting with Dr. Angus, the tutor, was arranged at the house of Mr. Macmillan, the publisher, at Cambridge; but although the two parties were in the house at the same time, through the failure of the servant to announce Mr. Spurgeon, Dr. Angus was not aware of his presence, and returned to London without seeing him. The college scheme was then given up. His address at the anniversary of the Cambridge Union of Sunday Schools, in 1853, greatly impressed a gentleman, who on the strength of it recommended him as a candidate for the then vacant Baptist Church of New Park Street, Southwark, London; and, after preaching for three months on probation, the small opposition to him when he first came had entirely vanished, and he accepted, April 28, 1854, a unanimous call to become their pastor. The church had been very prosperous, but had so dwindled down that only one hundred persons attended Mr. Spurgeon's first service, while the building seated twelve hundred. Before three months had passed, the chapel was crowded; within a year, it was necessary to enlarge it, and he preached in Exeter Hall during the progress of the alterations. But the enlarged building could not accommodate the crowds; and in 1856 he preached at the Royal Surrey Gardens Music Hall, which seated seven thousand persons. On Aug. 16, 1859, the corner-stone of the new Metropolitan Tabernacle was laid, and the building opened for service March 25, 1861. It seats about five thousand persons, with standing room for a thousand more; cost thirty-one thousand pounds, and was entirely paid for by the end of the opening five weeks' services. When the church removed from New Park Street, in 1861, it numbered eleven hundred and seventy-eight members; there were in 1885 upwards of fifty-five hundred. Mr. Spurgeon's only children, twin sons, are both preachers, — one in England, the other in New Zealand.

Besides preaching, not only in his own church twice every Sunday and on Thursday evening, and discharging the other duties of his pastorate, Mr. Spurgeon manages two important enterprises, the Pastors' College and the Stockwell Orphanage. Shortly after the commencement of his London pastorate, he gave his personal attention to the theological education of Thomas William Medhurst, a man of his own age, now a pastor at Landport; but finding that his time was too fully occupied to undertake the extra labor, he put Mr. Medhurst under the care of Rev. George Rogers, an Independent minister, who was long the principal and theological tutor of the Pastors' College. Other students soon presented themselves. These were at first assembled every week in Mr. Spurgeon's house for instruction in theology, pastoral duty, and other practical matters. From 1856 to 1861 the other lectures were delivered by Mr. Rogers in his own house; from 1861 to 1874, in the class-rooms under the Tabernacle; since 1874 in the New College buildings. Mr. Spurgeon lectures to the students every week.

The Stockwell Orphanage was incorporated in 1867, with an endowment of twenty thousand pounds, given by Mrs. Hillyard; and fifty orphan boys were taken in the following year. It now consists of twelve houses, and accommodates nearly five hundred children of both sexes, from six to fourteen years old. [Stockwell was formerly a suburb of London, but is now included in its limits.]

In connection with the church there are a Colportage Association (started in 1866, which through paid colporteurs sells religious books in neglected villages), and Mrs. Spurgeon's Book Fund (1876), the latter to supply poor ministers with free gifts of valuable books.

Mr. Spurgeon's remarkable constitution yielded, at length, to the tremendous strain of his manifold and multifarious duties and burdens, and since 1867 he has had frequent attacks of illness. In order that the interests of the church might not suffer, his brother, the Rev. James Archer Spurgeon, has been since 1868 co-pastor.

Mr. Spurgeon's pen has been very busy. Aside from his private correspondence, and that arising out of his various enterprises, he has each year since 1857 issued *Spurgeon's Illustrated Almanac* (containing short articles by him and others); in 1861 and 1862 was joint editor with Revs. D. Katterns and W. G. Lewis of *The Baptist Magazine*, has personally conducted since Jan. 1, 1865, *The Sword and the Trowel*, a monthly magazine, in which he writes copiously, and which is in the interest of his church and of religion generally; since 1872, *John Ploughman's Almanac*, and has written the works mentioned below, and done much literary work besides. His first printed sermon, entitled *Harvest Time*, appeared in the *Penny Pulpit*, October, 1854; the second, *God's Providence*, shortly afterwards, and so a dozen before the end of the year. From the first week of 1855 one has been issued every week. Each of these receives his revision. The average sale is twenty-five thousand copies weekly. A few have approached a hundred thousand copies; two have exceeded it; and one on *Baptismal Regeneration*, preached in the summer of 1864, sold to the extent of a hundred and ninety-eight thousand copies, and was the occasion of a great controversy on the subject. The sermon *Pictures of Life, and Birthday Reflections*, in relation to his twenty-first birthday, is accompanied by his portrait, the first issued, and shows that he was then pale and thin.

His *works* embrace a great number of published sermons, more than nineteen hundred; e.g., in *The Metropolitan Tabernacle Pulpit* (containing his sermons which have been published weekly since the close of 1854), London, 1855 sqq., vol. i. 1855, vol. xxxi. 1885; *The Pulpit Library*, 1856-58, 3 vols.; *Types and Emblems*, 1875; *Trumpet Calls to Christian Energy*, 1875; *The Present Truth*, 1883 (these three volumes are made up of his Sunday and Thursday evening sermons); *Farm Sermons*, (nineteen discourses on farming), 1882; and the following, which together with the above have been reprinted in New York, translated into different languages, and circulated in thousands of copies; *The Saint and his Saviour*, 1857; *Smooth Stones taken from Ancient Brooks* (sentences from Thomas Brooks), 1859; *Morning by Morning, or Daily Readings for the Family or the Closet*, 1866, 100th thousand 1885; *Our Own Hymn Book* (used in many churches, has several original hymns and paraphrases of Psalms), 1866; *Evening by Evening, or Readings at Eventide for the Family or the Closet*, 1868, 75th thousand 1885; *John Ploughman's Talks, or Plain Advice for Plain People*, 1869, 340th thousand; *The Treasury of David* (containing an original exposition of the book of *Psalms*, a collection of illustrative extracts from the whole range of literature, a series of homiletical hints upon almost every verse, and lists of writers upon each psalm; in the preface to each successive volume, he acknowledges fully and heartily the important assistance rendered him by several persons in the researches necessary to carry out his plan), 1870-85, 7 vols. (thousands of copies sold, reprinted in United States); *Feathers for Arrows, or Illustrations for Preachers and Teachers, from my Note-Book*, 1870, 26th thousand 1885; *The Interpreter, or Scripture for Family Worship* (with running comments and suitable hymns), 1872; *Lectures to my Students* (a selection from addresses delivered to the students of the Pastors' College, Metropolitan Tabernacle), 1st series 1875, 30th thousand 1885; 2d series 1877, 16th thousand 1885; *Commenting and Commentaries* (two lectures to his students, with a catalogue of Bible commentaries and expositions), 1876; *The Metropolitan Tabernacle: its History and Work* (with thirty-two illustrations), 1876; *John Ploughman's Pictures, or More of his Plain Talk for Plain People*, 1880, 110th thousand 1885; *Illustrations and Meditations, or Flowers from a Puritan's Garden, distilled and dispensed*, 1883; *The Clue of the Maze*, 1884; *My Sermon Notes* (a selection from outlines of discourses delivered at the Metropolitan Tabernacle), 1884-87, 4 vols. (covering the whole Bible); *Storm Signals* (sermons), 1886; many minor works, articles, etc. Revised by MR. SPURGEON.

STADE, Bernhard, Ph.D., Lic. Theol. (Leipzig, 1871 and 1873), **D.D.** (*hon.*, Giessen, 1875), German Lutheran, critical school; b. at Arnstadt, Thuringia, May 11, 1848; studied at Leipzig (1867-69) and at Berlin (1869-70); became assistant librarian at Leipzig, 1871; *privat-docent* there, 1873; ordinary professor of theology at Giessen, 1875. Since 1881 he has edited *Die Zeitschrift für A. T. Wissenschaft*. He is the author of *Ueber die mehrlautigen Thatwörter der Ge'ezsprache*, Leipzig, 1871; *De Isaiæ vaticiniis æthiopicis diatribe*, 1873; *Ueber die alttestamentlichen Vorstellungen vom Zustande nach dem Tode*, 1877; *Lehrbuch der hebräischen Grammatik*, 1st part (*Schriftlehre, Lautlehre, Formenlehre*), 1879; *De populo Javan parergon*, Giessen, 1880; *Geschichte des Volkes Israel*, parts 1-4, Berlin, 1881-85; *Ueber die Lage der evangelischen Kirche Deutschlands*, Giessen, 1883 (2 eds.).

STAEHELIN, Rudolf, Swiss Protestant; b. at Basel, Sept. 22, 1841; studied at Berlin and Tübingen, 1859-65; became *privat-docent* at Basel 1873, professor extraordinary 1875, and ordinary professor 1876. He has published *Erasmus Stellung zur Reformation hauptsächlich von seinen Beziehungen zu Basel aus beleuchtet*, Basel, 1873; *W. M. L. de Wette nach seiner theologischen Wirksamkeit und Bedeutung geschildert*, 1880; *Die ersten Märtyrer des evangelischen Glaubens in der Schweiz*, Heidelberg, 1883; *Huldreich Zwingli und sein Reformationswerk*, Halle, 1883. *

STALKER, James, Free Church of Scotland; b. at Crieff, Perthshire, Scotland, Feb. 21, 1848; graduated at Edinburgh University and New College; and since 1874 has been minister of St. Brycedale Free Church, Kirkealdy. He was Cunningham fellow in 1874; declined principalship of Presbyterian College, Melbourne, 1883, and Edinburgh churches, 1883 and 1884. He is the author of *The Life of Jesus Christ*, Edinburgh, 1879, 3d ed. 1884; *The New Song: Sermons for Children*, 1883; *The Life of St. Paul*, 1884, 2d ed. same year.

STALL, Sylvanus, Lutheran (General Synod); b. at Elizaville, Columbia County, N.Y., Oct. 18, 1847; graduated from Pennsylvania College, Gettysburg, Penn., 1872; studied theology at Union Theological Seminary, New-York City, and at Gettysburg, Penn.; became pastor at Cobleskill, N.Y., 1874; Martin's Creek, Penn., 1877; Lancaster, Penn., 1880. He is statistical secretary of the General Synod of the Lutheran Church. He is the author of *Pastor's Pocket Record*, Albany, N.Y., 1875, 5th thousand Lancaster, Penn., 1885; *Ministers' Handbook to Lutheran Hymns in the Book of Worship*, Philadelphia, 1879; *How to pay Church Debts, and how to keep Churches out of Debt*, New York, 1880; since 1884 has published annually, through different Lutheran publishing houses, *Stall's Lutheran Year-Book*, which represents all branches of the Lutheran Church in the United States and in Europe; circulation, fifteen thousand copies.

STANFORD, Charles, D.D. (Brown University, Providence, R.I., 1878), Baptist; b. at Northampton, Eng., March 9, 1823; d. in London, March 18, 1886. He studied at Bristol College; became minister at Loughborough, 1845; Deviges, 1847; London (Denmark-place Church, Camberwell), 1858. He was president of the London Baptist Association in 1882. He is the author of *Friendship with God*, London, 1850, last ed. 1882; *Power in Weakness: Memorial of Rev. William Rhodes*, 1858, 2d ed. 1870; *Central Truths*, 1858, 12th ed. 1870; *Joseph Alleine, his Companions and Times*, 1861, 2d ed. 1862; *Instrumental Strength*, 1862; *Symbols of Christ*, 1865, 3d ed. 1882; *Home and Church*, 1870; *Homilies on Christian Work*, 1878; *Philip Doddridge*, 1880; *Voices from Calvary*, 1880; *From Calvary to Olivet*, 1885; *Alternations of Faith and Unbelief*, 1885; *Homilies on the Lord's Prayer*, 1882; and many smaller works.

STARKEY, Right Rev. Thomas Alfred, S.T.D. (Hobart College, Geneva, N.Y., 1864), Episcopalian, bishop of Northern New Jersey; b. in Philadelphia, Penn., in the year 1824; educated for and practised as a civil engineer, 1839–45; studied theology under Rev. Dr. F. Ogilby, Bishop Odenheimer, and Rev. W. C. Cooley; ordained deacon 1847, priest 1848; was missionary in Schuylkill County, Penn., 1847–50, where he founded the Church of the Holy Apostles, St. Clair; was rector of Christ Church, Troy, N.Y., 1850–54; St. Paul's, Albany, N.Y., 1854–58; Trinity, Cleveland, O., 1858–69; the Epiphany, Washington, D.C., 1869–72; resigned because compelled to take a rest, which he did until 1875, when he filled Rev. Dr. Irving's place in the Mission Rooms in New-York City (autumn, 1875, to spring, 1876); became rector of St. Paul's, Paterson, N.J., 1877; bishop of Northern New Jersey, 1880. The name of his diocese was changed to that of Newark, 1886.

STEARNS, Lewis French, D.D. (College of New Jersey, Princeton, N.J., 1881), Congregationalist; b. at Newburyport, Mass., March 10, 1847; graduated at the College of New Jersey, Princeton, N.J., 1867; studied at Princeton Theological Seminary, 1869–70; in the universities of Berlin and Leipzig, 1870–71; at Union Theological Seminary, New-York City, 1871–72 (graduated); was pastor of the Presbyterian Church of Norwood, N.J, 1873–76; professor of history and *belles-lettres*, Albion College, Albion, Mich., 1876–79; has been since 1880 professor of systematic theology in the Bangor (Me.) Theological Seminary. He has written articles in the *Andover Review*, *New Englander*, etc.

STEARNS, Oakman Sprague, D.D. (Colby University, Waterville, Me., 1863), Baptist; b. at Bath, Me., Oct. 20, 1817; graduated at Waterville College (Me.), 1840, and at Newton Theological Institution (Mass.), 1846; was instructor in Hebrew there, 1846–47; pastor at Southbridge, Mass., 1847–54; Newark, N.J., 1854–55; Newton Centre, Mass., 1855–68; and since 1868 has been professor of biblical interpretation of the Old Testament in Newton Theological Institution. He translated Sartorius' *The Person and Word of Christ*, Boston, 1848; is author of *A Syllabus of the Messianic Passages in the Old Testament*, 1881.

STEELE, David, D.D. (Rutgers' College, New Brunswick, N.J., 1866), Reformed Presbyterian (General Synod); b. near Londonderry, Ireland, Oct. 20, 1827; graduated at Miami University, O., 1857; professor of Greek there, 1858–59; has been pastor of Fourth Reformed Presbyterian Church, Philadelphia, Penn., since 1861; and since 1863 professor in the Reformed Presbyterian Theological Seminary, Philadelphia, Penn., of biblical literature 1863–75, and since of doctrinal theology. He served in the Christian commission, 1862; was moderator of General Synod 1868, and delegate to the Council of Reformed Churches, Philadelphia, 1880. He edited *The Reformed Presbyterian Advocate* from 1867 to 1877, and has published several discourses.

STEENSTRA, Peter Henry, D.D. (Shurtleff College, Upper Alton, Ill., 1882), Episcopalian; b. near Franeker, Friesland, Netherlands, Jan. 24, 1833; graduated from Shurtleff College, Upper Alton, Ill., 1858; entered the Baptist ministry; but in 1864 became rector of Grace Church, Newton, Mass.; and in 1868 professor of Hebrew and Old and New Testament exegesis, in the then newly founded Episcopal Theological School at Cambridge, Mass.; since 1883 he has been professor of Hebrew literature and interpretation of the Old Testament. He translated and edited *Judges* and *Ruth* in the American edition of Lange's *Commentary*, New York, 1872.

STEINER, Heinrich, Ph.D. (Heidelberg, 1864), **Lic. Theol.** (Heidelberg, 1866), **D.D.** (*hon.*, Bern, 1875), Swiss Protestant; b. at Zürich, Jan. 10, 1841; studied theology there and at Heidelberg, orientalia at Leipzig; became *privat-docent* at Heidelberg, in the philosophical (1865) and then in the theological (1866) faculties; professor extraordinary in the latter, 1869; ordinary professor at Zürich, 1870. In 1882–84 he was rector of the university. He is in theology a free critic. He is the author of *Die Mu'taziliten oder die Freidenker im Islam*, Leipzig, 1865; *Ueber hebräische Poesie* (lecture), Basel, 1873; *Ferdinand Hitzig* (rector's address), Zürich, 1882; *Zur fünfzigjährigen Stiftungsfeier der Hochschule Zürich* (address), 1883; editor of 4th ed. Hitzig, *Die Zwölf kleinen Propheten*, Leipzig, 1881; contributor of many articles in Schenkel's *Bibel Lexikon*, Leipzig, 1869–75.

STEINMEYER, Franz Ludwig, German Protestant; b. at Beeskow-in-der-Mittelmark, Nov. 15, 1812; became ordinary professor at Berlin, 1852; at Bonn, 1854; again at Berlin, 1858. He published *Zeugnisse von der Herrlichkeit Jesu Christi*, Berlin, 1847; *Beiträge zum Schriftverständiss in Predigten*, Berlin, 1850–57, 4 vols., 2d ed. 1859–66; *Apologetische Beiträge*, 1866–74, 4 vols. (English trans. of 1st vol., *Miracles of Our Lord*, Edinburgh, 1875; of the 2d and 3d vols. together, *Passion and Resurrection of our Lord*, 1879); *Beiträge zur practischen Theologie*, 1874–79, 5 vols.; *Beiträge zur Christologie*, 1880–82, 3 vols.; *Die Geschichte der Passion des Herrn in Abwehr des kritischen Angriffs betrachtet*, 1st and 2d ed. 1882; *Die Wunderthaten des Herrn*, 1884; *Die Parabeln des Herrn*, 1884. *

STELLHORN, Frederick William, Lutheran (Synod of Ohio); b. at Brueninghorstedt, Hanover, Germany, Oct. 2, 1841; graduated at Concordia College, Fort Wayne, Ind., and Concordia Seminary, St. Louis, Mo.; became pastor at St. Louis 1865, Fairfield Centre, Ind., 1867; professor at North-western University, Watertown, Wis.

(1869), at Concordia College, Fort Wayne, Ind. (1874), and at Capital University, Columbus, O. (1881). Since 1881 he has been chief editor of the *Lutherische Kirchenzeitung* and the *Theologische Zeitblätter*, Columbus, O. He is the author of a Greek New-Testament lexicon, 1886.

STEPHENS, David Stubert, D.D. (Western Maryland College, 1885), Methodist Protestant; b. at Springfield, O., May 12, 1847; attended Wittenberg College in his native place, 1864–67; left there in junior year, and graduated at Adrian College, Adrian, Mich., 1868; attended the University of Edinburgh, 1869–70, and took M.A. degree in philosophy 1870, obtaining a prize for his English essay from Professor Masson, also in moral philosophy under Professor Henry Calderwood, and in metaphysics under Professor Fraser; attended Harvard University, 1873–74; was instructor in natural sciences in Adrian College, 1870–73; became professor of mental science and logic in Adrian College, 1874; president of the college, and professor of mental science and natural theology, 1882. He edited *The Methodist Protestant Magazine*, published at Adrian, Mich., 1877–81; wrote three pamphlets, published in 1884, bearing on certain changes proposed in the constitution of the Methodist Protestant Church; and has written numerous fugitive pieces.

STEVENS, Abel, LL.D. (Indiana State University, Bloomington, 1856), Methodist; b. in Philadelphia, Penn., Jan. 19, 1815; educated at Wesleyan Academy, Wilbraham, Mass., and at Wesleyan University, Middletown, Conn.; completed a course of study at the latter institution, 1834; joined the New-England Conference, 1834; was appointed to churches in Boston, Mass., and Providence, R.I.; became editor of *Zion's Herald*, Boston, 1840; of *The National Magazine*, New York, 1852; of *The Christian Advocate*, New York, 1856; was joint editor, with Drs. McClintock and Crooks, of *The Methodist*, 1860–74; and pastor of churches in New-York City and Mamaroneck, N.Y. On retiring from the editorial life, he travelled extensively in the United States, and then in Europe, where located at last at Geneva, Switzerland, took charge of the American Union Church there, and became correspondent of American journals. He is the author of *Sketches and Incidents*, New York, 1843; *Tales from the Parsonage*, 184–, new ed. 1855; *Introduction of Methodism into the Eastern States*, 1848; *Progress of Methodism in the Eastern States*, 1851 (the 2d series of the preceding); *Church Polity*, 1847; *Preaching required by the Times*, 1855; *The Great Reform*, 1856; *History of Methodism*, 1858–61, 3 vols.; *Life of Nathan Bangs*, 1863; *History of the Methodist Episcopal Church*, 1864–67, 4 vols. (abridgment 1867, 1 vol.); *Centenary of American Methodism*, 1865; *Women of Methodism*, 1866; *Madame de Staël*, 1881, 2 vols.; *Character Sketches*, 1882; *Christian Work*, 1882; many articles in reviews, magazines, and other periodicals.

STEVENS, George Barker, D.D. (Jena University, after examination, 1886), Presbyterian; b. at Spencer, N.Y., July 13, 1854; graduated from the University of Rochester, N.Y., 1877; and from the Yale Divinity School, New Haven, Conn., 1880; became pastor of the First Congregational Church, Buffalo, N.Y., 1880; of the First Presbyterian Church, Watertown, N.Y., 1883; professor of sacred literature, Yale Divinity School, New Haven, Conn., 1886. He is the author of numerous essays, reviews, and articles in the religious press. *

STEVENS, William Arnold, D.D. (Denison University, 1882), **LL.D.** (Rochester University, 1862), Baptist; b. at Granville, O., Feb. 5, 1839; graduated at Denison University, Granville, O., 1862; studied philology and theology at Rochester Theological Seminary (N.Y.), Harvard College, Leipzig, and Berlin, 1862–68; became professor of Greek at Denison University, 1868, and of New Testament exegesis in Rochester Theological Seminary, N.Y., 1877. He published *Select Orations of Lysias*, Chicago, 1876, 4th ed. 1882.

STEVENS, Right Rev. William Bacon, D.D. (University of Pennsylvania, Philadelphia, 1848), **LL.D.** (Union College, Schenectady, N.Y., 1862), Episcopalian, bishop of Pennsylvania; b. at Bath, Me., July 13, 1815; educated at Phillips Academy, Andover, Mass., but was obliged, through the failure of his health, to give up his studies; travelled two years around the world, and on his return graduated M.D. at Dartmouth, Hanover, N.H., 1837; was ordained deacon 1843, priest 1844; was historian of the State of Georgia, 1841; professor of *belles-lettres* and moral philosophy in the University of Georgia, Athens, Ga., 1844–48; became rector of St. Andrew's, Philadelphia, Penn., 1848; assistant bishop of Pennsylvania, 1862; bishop, 1865. He was in 1868 appointed by the presiding bishop to take charge of the American Episcopal churches on the continent of Europe, and held the position for six years. He edited with prefaces and notes the *Georgia Historical Collections*, Savannah, vols. i. and ii., 1841, 1842; and is the author of *Discourse delivered before the Georgia Historical Society, Savannah, Feb. 12, 1841* (on the history of silk culture in that State), Boston, 1841; *A History of Georgia from its First Discovery by Europeans to the Adoption of the Present Constitution in 1797*, vol. i., New York, 1847, vol. ii., Philadelphia, 1859; *The Parables of the New Testament Practically Unfolded*, Philadelphia, 1855; *Consolation: the Bow in the Cloud*, 1855, 2d ed. 1871; *Sunday at Home: Manual of Home Service*, 1856; *The Lord's Day, its Obligations and Blessings*, 1857; *The Past and Present of St. Andrew's* [*Church*], 1858; *Sabbaths of our Lord*, 1872; *Sermons*, New York, 1879; many addresses, charges, essays, sermons, etc.

STEVENSON, John Frederic, D.D. (Queen's University, Kingston, Ontario, Can., 1880), Congregationalist; b. at Loughborough, Eng., March 9, 1833; educated at University College, London, 1849–50; Regent's Park College, London, 1850–54; graduated B.A. London University 1853, LL.B. 1866; became pastor at Long Sutton, 1854; Nottingham, 1858; Reading, 1863; of Emmanuel Church, Montreal, Can., 1874; since 1882 he has also been principal of the Congregational College of British North America, at Montreal. He is the author of occasional literary and theological articles.

STEWART, William, D.D. (Glasgow, 1874), Church of Scotland; b. at Annan, Dumfriesshire, Aug. 15, 1835; graduated at Glasgow University, B.A. 1861, M.A. 1862, B.D. 1867; was examiner in the same in mental philosophy for degrees in arts, 1867–70; minister of the parish of St. George'sin-the-Fields, Glasgow, 1868–75; since 1873 has been professor of divinity and biblical criticism in the University of Glasgow; since 1876 has been secretary to the university. He is the author of *Plan of St. Luke's Gospel*, Glasgow, 1873.

STIFLER, James Madison, D.D. (Shurtleff College, 1875), Baptist; b. at Hollidaysburg, Penn., Dec. 8, 1839; graduated at Shurtleff College, Upper Alton, Ill., 1866; completed theological course there, 1869; became pastor at Nokomis, Ill., 1868; professor of biblical exegesis in Shurtleff College, 1871; pastor at Hamilton, N.Y., 1875; at New Haven, Conn., 1879; professor of the New Testament in Crozer Theological Seminary, Penn., 1882.

STOCKMEYER, Immanuel, Swiss Protestant; b. at Basel, July 28, 1814; studied at Erlangen and Berlin, 1832–36; became pastor at Oltingen, Baselland, 1841; at Basel, 1846 (Antistes, 1871); and ordinary professor of theology at Basel, 1876. He published a volume of sermons, *Jesus Christus Gestern und Heute und derselbe in Ewigkeit*, Basel, 1860; *Der Brief des Jacobus*, 1874; *Die Structur des ersten Johannesbriefes*, 1875; *Rede bei der Lutherfeier*, 1884.

STODDARD, Charles Augustus, D.D. (Williams College, Williamstown, Mass., 1871), Presbyterian; b. in Boston, Mass., May 28, 1833; graduated at Williams College, Williamstown, Mass., 1854; and at Union Theological Seminary, New-York City, 1859; was pastor of Washington Heights Presbyterian Church, New-York City, from 1859 to 1883, and since 1873 an editor of the New-York *Observer*.

STOECKER, Adolf, United Evangelical; b. at Halberstadt, Germany, Dec. 11, 1835; studied at the Halberstadt gymnasium; at the universities of Halle and Berlin, 1854–57; passed his first clerical examination at Berlin 1858, his second 1859; became pastor at Seggerde and Hamersleben, 1863; chaplain to the division of the German army at Metz, 1871; court and cathedral preacher at Berlin, 1874. He is first assessor in the Brandenburg provincial synod, member of the synodical council of the Prussian Church. He is the author of *Christlich-Sozial*, Bielefeld, 1884; *Eins ist noth, ein Jahrgang Volkspredigten über freie Texte*, Berlin, 1884, 3d ed. 1885; *O Land, höre des Herrn Wort, ein Jahrgang Volkspredigten über die Episteln*, 1885, 2d ed. 1886; many addresses and minor publications.

STOKES, George Thomas, Church of England and Ireland; b. at Athlone, County Westmeath, Ireland, Dec. 28, 1843; graduated B.A. Trinity College, Dublin, 1864; 2d class divinity testimonium, 1865; M.A., 1871; D.D., 1886; became vicar of All Saints, Blackrock, Dublin, 1869; assistant to the regius professor of divinity, 1880; and professor of ecclesiastical history in the University of Dublin, 1883; besides articles in Smith and Wace's *Dictionary of Christian Biography*, and in the *Contemporary Review* and *Expositor*, he has published *Scriptural Authority for a Liturgy*, Dublin, 1868; *Work of the Laity in the Church of Ireland*, 1869; *Ecclesiastical History and Scientific Research*, 1883.

STOLZ, Alban, Roman Catholic; b. at Bühl, Baden, Feb. 8, 1808; ordained priest, 1833; was professor of pastoral theology and pedagogik at Freiburg, 1848–80; d. there, Oct. 16, 1883. He was a very popular and prolific writer. His collected works make 13 vols. (Freiburg, 1871–77). The most widely circulated were his *Kalender für Zeit und Ewigkeit*, which appeared yearly from 1843 to 1884.

STORRS, Richard Salter, D.D. (Union College, Schenectady, N.Y., 1853; Harvard College, 1859), **LL.D.** (College of New Jersey, Princeton, 1874), Congregationalist; b. at Braintree, Mass., Aug. 21, 1821; graduated at Amherst College, 1839; entered the law-office of Hon. Rufus Choate, and spent two years in a course of legal study; then studied at Andover Theological Seminary, and graduated there 1845; became pastor of the Harvard Congregational Church, Brookline, Mass., 1845; and of the Church of the Pilgrims, Brooklyn, N.Y., 1846, then recently organized, and in this position has ever since remained. He was one of the editors of *The Independent*, from 1848 to 1861. Besides numerous occasional discourses and articles in periodicals, he is the author of *The Constitution of the Human Soul*, New York, 1857; *Conditions of Success in Preaching without Notes*, 1875; *Early American Spirit, and the Genesis of it*, 1875; *Declaration of Independence, and the Effects of it*, 1876; *John Wycliffe and the First English Bible*, 1880; *Recognition of the Supernatural in Letters and in Life*, 1881; *Manliness in the Scholar*, 1883; *The Divine Origin of Christianity indicated by its Historical Effects*, 1884. *

STORY, Robert Herbert, D.D. (Edinburgh, 1874), Church of Scotland; b. at Rosneath, Dunbartonshire, Jan. 28, 1835; studied at the universities of Edinburgh (1849–55), and St. Andrew's (1856–57); ordained assistant in St. Andrew's Church, Montreal, Can., Sept. 20, 1859; inducted minister of Rosneath, Scotland, in succession to his father, February, 1860, and so remains. He belongs to the "Broad Church." Since 1865 he has been convener of the editorial committee of the "Church Service Society" of Scotland; and since its foundation in 1885, editor of *The Scottish Church* (monthly magazine). He was appointed in 1885 the first lecturer under the trust by which the "Lee lectureship" was founded, in memory of Dr. Robert Lee, and in that capacity delivered the first lecture in St. Giles, Edinburgh, on April 11, 1886. He is the author of *Robert Story of Rosneath, a Memoir*, London, 1862; *Christ the Consoler*, Edinburgh, 1865; *Life and Remains of Robert Lee, D.D.*, London, 1870; *William Carstares*, 1874; *On Fast Days* (a pamphlet), Glasgow, 1876; *Creed and Conduct, Sermons preached in Rosneath Church*, 1878; *Health Haunts of the Riviera*, Paisley, 1881; *Nugæ Ecclesiasticæ*, Edinburgh, 1884; many sermons, addresses, articles, etc., published in *Good Words*, *Scottish Church*, *Sunday Talk*, *Glasgow Herald*, *Saturday Review*, etc.

STOUGHTON, John, D.D. (Edinburgh, 1869), Congregationalist; b. in Norwich, Eng., Nov. 15, 1807; educated at Highbury College, Islington, and University College, London; pastor at Windsor 1832–43, at Kensington 1843–75; professor of historical theology and homiletics in New College, St. John's Woods, London, 1872–84; was Congregational lecturer 1855, and chairman of Congregational Union 1856. He edited *The Evangelical Magazine* for many years; was delegate and speaker in Evangelical Alliance Conferences in New York 1873, and Basel 1879; lectured on missions in Westminster Abbey, 1877;

received a testimonial of three thousand pounds on retiring from his pastorate at Kensington, 1875. He is the author of the following works, many of which have passed through several editions: *Tractarian Theology*, London, 1843; *Windsor in the Olden Time*, 1844; *Spiritual Heroes*, 1845; *Philip Doddridge*, 1851; *The Lights of the World*, 1852; *Ages of Christendom*, 1856; *The Pen, the Palm, and the Pulpit*, 1858; *The Song of Christ's Flock in the Twenty-third Psalm*, 1860; *Church and State 200 Years ago*, 1862; *Shades and Echoes of Old London*, 1864; *Ecclesiastical History of England*, 1867–74, 5 vols.; *Religion in England during the Reign of Queen Anne and the Georges*, 1878: (the two works revised and republished together, 1881, 6 vols.); *Haunts and Homes of Martin Luther*, 1875; *Lights of the World*, 1876; *Progress of Divine Revelation*, 1878; *Our English Bible*, 1878; *Worthies of Science*, 1879; *Historical Theology*, 1880; *William Wilberforce*, 1880; *Footprints of Italian Reformers*, 1881; *William Penn*, 1882; *The Spanish Reformers*, 1883; *Congregationalism in the Court Suburb* (Kensington), 1883; *John Howard the Philanthropist*, 1884; *Religion in England 1800–1850*, 1884; *Golden Legends of the Olden Time*, 1885

STOWE, Calvin Ellis, D.D. (Indiana University, Bloomington, Ind., and Dartmouth College, Hanover, N.H., both 1839), Congregationalist; b. at Natick, Mass., April 26, 1802; graduated at Bowdoin College, Brunswick, Me., 1824, and at Andover Theological Seminary, Mass., 1828; became assistant teacher of sacred literature in the seminary, 1828; professor of Latin and Greek, Dartmouth College, Hanover, N.H., 1831; of biblical literature, Lane Theological Seminary, Cincinnati, O., 1833; of natural and revealed religion, Bowdoin College, 1850; of sacred literature, Andover Theological Seminary, 1852; retired, 1864; d. Aug. 22, 1886. His wife was Harriet Beecher Stowe, author of *Uncle Tom's Cabin*. He translated Jahn's *History of the Hebrew Commonwealth*, Andover, 1828, 2d ed. 1871, Lond. 1829, 2 vols., 3d ed. 1840; and from the Latin, Lowth's *Lectures on Hebrew Poetry*, Andover, 1829 (both with additions); *Introduction to the Criticism and Interpretation of the Bible*, Cincinnati, O., vol. i. 1835 (all published); *On Elementary Public Instruction in Europe* (a report to the General Assembly, Harrisburg, O., 1838; and published by Ohio, Pennsylvania, Virginia, North Carolina, Michigan, etc.); *Essay* (on the same), Boston, 1839; *The Religious Element in Education* (lecture at Portland, Me.), 1844; *The Right Interpretation of the Sacred Scriptures* (inaugural address), Andover, 1853; *Origin and History of the Books of the Bible, both Canonical and Apocryphal*, Hartford, 1867. *

STRACK, Hermann Lebrecht, Ph.D. (Leipzig, 1872), **Lic. Theol.** (do., 1877), **D.D.** (do., 1884), Protestant theologian; b. in Berlin, May 6, 1848; studied at Berlin and Leipzig, 1865–70; taught in Kaiser Wilhelm Gymnasium, 1872–73; worked in the Imperial Library, St. Petersburg, Russia, 1873–76 (see below); became professor extraordinary of theology at Berlin, 1877; spent six weeks with Abr. Harkavy, on request of the Russian Government, at Tschufutkale (in the Crimea), examining Firkowitsch's third great collection of manuscripts. (For his monumental labors upon the *Codex Babylonicus Petropolitanus*, see below.) "One of the tasks of his life is to make the Christians acquainted with the history and literature of the Jews, and to promote Christianity amongst the Jews." He edited Max Strack's *Aus Süd und Ost, Reisefrüchte aus drei Weltteilen*, Leipzig, 1885–86, 2 parts; and edits "*Nathanael, Zeitschrift der berliner Gesellschaft zur Beförderung des Christenthums unter der Juden*," Berlin, 1885 sqq.; and is the author of *Vollständiges Wörterbuch zu Xenophon's Anabasis*, Leipzig, 1871, 4th ed. 1884; *Prolegomena critica in V.T. Hebraicum*, 1873; *Katalog der hebräischen Bibelhandschriften der kaiserlichen öffentlichen Bibliothek in St. Petersburg* (with A. Harkavy), St. Petersburg u. Leipzig, 1875; *Prophetarum posteriorum codex Babylonicus Petropolitanus*, 1876 (edited at an expense of three years' labor, photolithographed and published at the expense of the Emperor Alexander II. of Russia. This codex is dated A.D. 916; the text has the "Babylonian" or "Assyrian" system of vocalization, whose peculiarities consist in having signs of a different shape to represent the vowels, and in putting the vowels in all cases above the letters. The text occupies four hundred and forty-nine folio pages, and is surrounded with Massoretic notes. The Codex occupies the same place in the determination of text for the portion of the Old Testament which it covers, as the Codex Sinaiticus does for the whole New Testament); *A. Firkowitsch und seine Entdeckungen*, Leipzig, 1876; *Die Dikduke hateamim des Ahron ben Moscheh ben Ascher und andere alte grammatisch-massoretische Lehrstücke* (with S. Baer), 1879; *Vollständiges Wörterbuch zu Xenophon's Kyropädie* 1881; *Pirke Aboth, Die Sprüche der Väter*, Karlsruhe u. Leipzig, 1882; *Lehrbuch der neuhebräischen Sprache u. Litteratur* (with C. Siegfried) 1882 (various parts of the Mishnah in preparation); *Hebräische Grammatik*, 1883, 2d ed. 1885 (English trans. New York and London, 1886).

STRONG, Augustus Hopkins, D.D. (Brown University, Providence, R.I., 1870), Baptist; b. at Rochester, N.Y., Aug. 3, 1836; graduated from Yale College, New Haven, Conn., 1857; and at Rochester Theological Seminary, N.Y., 1859; studied at German universities, 1859–60; became pastor at Haverhill, Mass., 1861, and at Cleveland, O., 1865; and president and professor of theology in Rochester Theological Seminary, 1872. He has contributed much to the denominational press, and is the author of a *Systematic Theology*, Rochester, 1886.

STRONG, James, S.T.D., LL.D. (both Wesleyan University, Middletown, Conn., 1856 and 1881), Methodist layman; b. in New-York City, Aug. 14, 1822; graduated at Wesleyan University, Middletown, Conn., 1844; teacher of ancient languages in Troy Conference Academy, West Poultney, Vt., 1844–46; professor of biblical literature, and acting president of Troy University, 1858–61; and since 1868 has been professor of exegetical theology in Drew Theological Seminary, Madison, N.J. In 1874 he travelled in Egypt and Palestine. He is a member of the Old-Testament Company of Bible revisers; and is the author of *Harmony and Exposition of the Gospels*, New York, 1852; *Harmony in Greek*, 1854; *Scripture History delineated from the Biblical Records and all Other Accessible Sources*, Madison, N.J., 1878; *Irenics*, *a Series of Essays showing the Virtual Agreement between Science and the Bible*, New York, 1883; editor of translation of the commentary on *Daniel* (1876), and *Esther* (1877), in the American edition of Lange; and (with Dr. McClintock for 3 vols.; afterwards alone) of a *Cyclopædia of Biblical, Theological, and Ecclesiastical Literature*, 1867–81, 10 vols., supplement in 2 vols., vol. i. 1885 (the work was begun in 1853). He published a literal translation of *Ecclesiastes*, 1877.

STROSSMAYER, Right Rev. Joseph Georg, D.D., Roman Catholic; b. at Essek, Sclavonia, Feb. 4, 1815; studied at Pesth, and was ordained priest in 1838; became professor at the Seminary of Diakovar, and bishop of Bosnia and Sirmia, May 20, 1850. He earnestly opposed the infallibility dogma in the Vatican Council, and quitted Rome without accepting it, but afterwards submitted. *

STUART, George Hay, Presbyterian layman; b. at Rose Hall, County Down, Ireland, April 2, 1816; educated at Banbridge, Ireland; took up his residence in Philadelphia, Penn., went into business; is now president of the Merchants' National Bank of that city. He was the president of the United-States Christian Commission during the civil war (see art. *Christian Commission* in *Schaff-Herzog Encyclopædia*, i. 449); is president of the Philadelphia Branch of the United-States Evangelical Alliance; vice president of the American Bible Society, of the American Tract Society, of the National Temperance Society; and is prominently connected with other religious and philanthropic associations. See sketch of his life by Rev. Dr. Wylie in A. S Billingsley's, *From the Flag to the Cross, Scenes and Incidents of Christianity in the War*, Philadelphia, 1872.

STUBBS, Right Rev. William, D.D. (by decree of convocation, 1879), **LL.D.** (*hon.*, Cambridge, 1879; Edinburgh, 1880), Church of England; b. at Knaresborough, June 21, 1825; graduated at Christ Church College, Oxford, B.A. (first-class classics, third-class mathematics) 1848, M.A. (Trinity College) 1851; was fellow of Trinity College, Oxford, 1848–51; of Oriel, 1867–84; honorary fellow of Balliol, 1876–84; honorary student of Christ Church, 1878-84; vicar of Navestock, Essex, 1850–67; librarian to the archbishop of Canterbury, and keeper of the manuscripts at Lambeth, 1862–67; examiner in the schools of law and modern history, Oxford, 1865–66; regius professor of modern history, 1866–84; select preacher, 1870; examiner in the school of theology, 1871-72; and of modern history, 1873, 1876, 1881; rector of Cholderton, Wilts, 1875–79; canon of St. Paul's, London, 1879–84; member of royal commission on ecclesiastical courts, 1881. In 1884 he was appointed bishop of Chester. He is the editor or author of *Registrum sacrum Anglicanum*, Oxford, 1858; *Mosheim's Church History*, 1863; *Chronicles and Memorials of the Reign of Richard I.*, London, 1864–65, 2 vols.; *Benedictus Abbas*, 1867, 2 vols.; *Roger Hoveden*, 1868–71, 4 vols.; *Select Charters*, 1871; *Councils and Ecclesiastical Documents* (vol. iii.), 1871; *Walter of Coventry*, 1872-73, 2 vols.; *Constitutional History of England*, 1874-78, 3 vols.; *Memorials of St. Dunstan*, 1874; *The Early Plantagenets*, 1876; *The Historical Works of Ralph de Diceto*, 1876, 2 vols.; *Works of Gervase of Canterbury*, 1879, 2 vols.; *Chronicles of Edward I. and II.*, 1882–83, 2 vols. *

STUCKENBERG, John Henry Wilburn, D.D. (Wooster University, O., 1874), Lutheran (General Synod); b. at Bramsche, Germany, Jan. 6, 1835; graduated at Wittenberg College, Springfield, O., 1857; studied at Halle, Göttingen, Berlin, and Tübingen; pastor in Iowa and Pennsylvania; chaplain One Hundred and Forty-fifth Pennsylvania Volunteers, September, 1862, to October, 1863; theological professor in Wittenberg College, 1873–80; in charge of American Chapel, Berlin, Germany, since 1881, and contributor to magazines. He belongs to the Philosophical Society of Berlin; translated (with Dr. W. L. Gage) from Hagenbach *German Rationalism*, Edinburgh, 1866; and is author of *Ninety-five Theses*, Baltimore, 1867; *The History of the Augsburg Confession*, Philadelphia, 1869; *Christian Sociology*, New York, 1880 (reprinted, London, 1881); *The Life of Immanuel Kant*, London, 1882; *Introduction to the Study of Philosophy* (in preparation).

STUDER, Gottlieb Ludwig, Swiss Protestant; b. at Bern, Jan. 18, 1801; became professor extraordinary of theology at Bern, 1850; ordinary professor, 1863, and was retired 1878. He has published *Das Buch der Richter erklärt*, Bern, 1835; *Matthiæ Neoburgensis chronica*, 1866; *Die berner Chronik von Konrad Justinger*, 1870; *Thüring Frickharts Twingherren-Streit und Bend. Tschachlans berner Chronik*, 1877; *Das Buch Hiob erläutert*, Bremen, 1881.

SUPER, Henry William, D.D. (Heidelberg College, Tiffin, O., 1874), Reformed (German); b. in Baltimore, Md., Dec. 31, 1824; graduated at Marshall College, Mercersburg, Penn., 1849; pastor at Waynesboro', Penn., 1851–61; Greensborough, 1861–75; professor of mathematics in State Normal School (1867–70), and of church history and biblical literature in Ursinus College, Freeland, Penn., since 1870. He has written various articles.

SWAINSON, Charles Anthony, D.D. (Cambridge, 1864), Church of England; b. in Liverpool, May 29, 1820; educated at Trinity College, Cambridge; graduated B.A. (sixth wrangler) 1841, M.A. (Christ's College) 1844; was ordained deacon 1843, priest 1844; was fellow (1841–52) and tutor of Christ's College, Cambridge (1847–51); Whitehall preacher, 1849–51; Hulsean Lecturer, 1857–58; principal of Chichester Theological College, 1854–64; Norrisian professor of divinity in the University of Cambridge, 1864–79; canon residentiary of Chichester, 1863–82; proctor for diocese and chapter of Chichester, 1874–83; became prebendary of Firle in Chichester Cathedral, 1856; Lady Margaret professor of divinity in University of Cambridge, 1879; examining chaplain to the bishop of Chichester, 1870; master of Christ's College, Cambridge, 1881; vice-chancellor of the University of Cambridge, 1886. He is the author of *Commonplaces, read in Christ's College Chapel*, London, 1848; *Creeds of the Church in their Relation to the Word of God and the Conscience of the Christian* (Hulsean Lecture), 1858; *The Authority of the New Testament, the Conviction of Righteousness, and the Ministry of Reconciliation*, 1859 (Hulsean Lecture); *Essay on the History of Article xxix.*, 1856; *Letter to the Dean of Chichester on the Original Object of the Athanasian Creed*, 1870; *A*

Plea for Time in dealing with the Athanasian Creed (a Letter to the Abp. of Cant., with Postscripts), 1873; *The Nicene and Apostles' Creeds, their Literary History, together with an Account of the Growth and Reception of the Sermon on the Faith commonly called the Creed of St. Athanasius*, 1875; *The Parliamentary History of the Act of Uniformity, with Documents not hitherto published*, 1875; *The Advertisement of 1566, an Historical Enquiry*, 1880; *Constitution and History of a Cathedral of the Old Foundation, illustrated by Documents in the Muniment-room at Chichester*, Part 1, 1880; *Greek Liturgies, chiefly from Original Sources*, 1884.

SWETE, Henry Barclay, D.D. (Cambridge, 1880), Church of England; b. at Bristol, Eng., March 14, 1835; educated at Gonville and Caius College, Cambridge (senior fellow), Carus Greek Testament prizeman, 1855; member's prizeman, 1857; first-class classical tripos, 1858; graduated B.A. (first-class classical tripos) 1859, M.A. 1862, B.D. 1874; was fellow of Gonville and Caius College, 1858-71; tutor of the same, 1872-75; ordained deacon 1858, priest 1859; curate of Blagdon, 1858-65; of All Saints, Cambridge, 1866-68; divinity lecturer, Cambridge, 1875-77; since 1877 rector of Ashdon, Essex; since 1881 examining chaplain to bishop of St. Albans; since 1882 professor of pastoral theology, King's College, London. He is the author of *England versus Rome, a Brief Handbook of the Roman Catholic Controversy*, London, 1868 (Italian trans., entitled *Paragone dottrinale*, Rome, 1872); *On the Early History of the Doctrine of the Holy Spirit*, Cambridge, 1873; *Theodorus Lascaris Junior: De Processione Spiritus Sancti oratio apologetica*, London, 1875; *On the History of the Doctrine of the Procession of the Holy Spirit, from the Apostolic Age to the Death of Charlemagne*, Cambridge, 1876; *Theodori Episcopi Mopsuesteni in Epistolas B. Pauli Commentarii: The Latin Version, with the Greek Fragments*, vol. i., Cambridge University Press, 1880, vol. ii. 1882. Contributor to Smith and Wace's *Dictionary of Christian Biography*, 1877-86, 4 vols.; is preparing an edition of the Septuagint for the Cambridge University Press, the text of the Vatican manuscript, with an *apparatus criticus*.

SYDOW, (Karl Leopold) Adolph, Ph.D., German Protestant; b. at Charlottenburg, Nov. 23, 1800; d. in Berlin, Oct. 22, 1882. He studied at Berlin from 1819 to 1823, and became an ardent disciple of Schleiermacher. In 1824 he became *repetent*; in 1828, preacher and ordinary teacher of the cadet corps at Berlin. In 1836 he was called by Frederick William III. to Potsdam as court preacher, and enjoyed also the friendship of Frederick William IV., who sent him in 1841, with others, to Great Britain, to study in London and elsewhere the ecclesiastical arrangements. In consequence he became a defender of the free church system; thus forfeited the king's favor, gave up his position at court, went in 1846 to Berlin as preacher of the New Church, and so remained until he was made emeritus in 1876. In 1872 he was deposed by the Brandenburg consistory, because in a public lecture he declared that Jesus was the legitimate son of Joseph and Mary. He appealed to the upper church council: twenty-six ministers of the province of Brandenburg and twelve of Berlin protested against his deposition; the theological faculty at Jena declared to Dr. Falk, the minister of religious affairs, that his deposition would "endanger the liberty of teaching;" and the council, while sharply rebuking him, ordered his reinstatement on the ground that the objectionable statement was extra-official. See Sydow's *Aktenstücke*, Berlin, 1873. He made, with F. A. Schulze, a translation of Channing's works, Berlin, 1850-55, 12 vols. His other publications consist of sermons, etc. See M. SYDOW: *Dr. A. Sydow. Ein Lebensbild*, Berlin, 1885. *

T.

TALCOTT, Daniel Smith, D.D. (Waterville College, Me., 1853; Bowdoin College, Brunswick, Me., 1858), Congregationalist; b. at Newburyport, Mass., March 7, 1813; graduated at Amherst College, Mass., 1831, and at Andover Theological Seminary, Mass., 1834; became teacher of Hebrew in Andover Theological Seminary, 1833; pastor at Sherborn, Mass., 1836; professor of sacred literature in Bangor Theological Seminary, Me., 1839; retired in 1881. His name, originally Daniel Talcott Smith, was changed in 1863. He is the author of sundry addresses, etc., and of articles in the American edition of Smith's *Dictionary of the Bible.*

TALMAGE, Thomas DeWitt, D.D., Presbyterian; b. near Bound Brook, N.J., Jan. 7, 1832; graduated at the University of the City of New York 1853, and at the New Brunswick (Reformed Dutch) Theological Seminary, N.J., 1856; became pastor of the Reformed Dutch Church at Belleville, N.J., 1856; Syracuse, N.Y., 1859; Second Church, Philadelphia, Penn., 1862; Central Presbyterian Church, Schermerhorn Street, Brooklyn, N.Y., 1869. In 1870 the congregation erected, on the same street near the old site, a new and much larger church, known as the "Tabernacle." It was burnt Dec. 22, 1872; rebuilt, 1873; dedicated, Feb. 22, 1874. The old church is now used for the Free Lay College, a training-school for Christian workers, of which Dr. Talmage is president; also for reading-rooms and general purposes. The new tabernacle seats some five thousand persons; the church reported in 1886 thirty-three hundred and eleven communicants. Dr. Talmage edited *The Christian-at-Work*, New York, 1873–76, now edits *Frank Leslie's Sunday Magazine.* His sermons are published every week, either in synopsis or fully, and many of them have appeared in separate volumes. Of the volumes made up of his sermons, lectures, etc., may be mentioned *Crumbs swept up*, Philadelphia, 186–; *Abominations of Modern Society*, New York, 1872, new ed. 1876; *Sermons*, 1872–75, 4 series; *Around the Tea-Table*, Philadelphia, 1874; *Night Sides of City Life*, 1878; *Masque torn off*, 1879; *The Brooklyn Tabernacle: a Collection of 104 Sermons*, 1884; *The Marriage Ring*, 1886. (See Appendix.) *

TARBOX, Increase Niles, D.D. (Iowa College, Grinnell, Io.; Yale College, New Haven, Conn., both 1869), Congregationalist; b. at East Windsor, Conn., Feb. 11, 1815; graduated at Yale College, New Haven, Conn., 1839, and at Yale Theological Seminary, 1844; was tutor in Yale College, 1842–44; pastor of Plymouth Congregational Church, Framingham, Mass., 1844–51; secretary of the American Educational Society and American College and Educational Society, Boston, 1851–84. He is the author of *Winnie and Walter Stories* (juveniles), Boston, 1860, 4 vols.; *When I was a Boy* (juvenile), 1862; *The Curse, or the Position occupied in History by the Race of Ham*, 1864; *Nineveh, or the Buried City*, 1864; *Tyre and Alexandria: Chief Commercial Cities of the Early World*, 1865; *Missionary Patriots, James H. and Edward M. Schneider*, 1867; *Uncle George's Stories* (juveniles), 1868, 4 vols.; *Life of Israel Putnam ("Old Put"), Major-General in the Continental Army*, 1876; *Sir Walter Raleigh and his Colony in America*, 1884; *Songs and Hymns for Common Life*, 1885; *Diary of Thomas Robbins, D.D.*, 1886.

TAYLOR, Barnard Cook, A.M., Baptist; b. at Holmdel, N.J., May 20, 1850; graduated at Brown University, Providence, R.I., 1874, and at Crozer Theological Seminary, Chester, Penn., 1877; became in the latter institution assistant instructor of Hebrew (1877), assistant professor of biblical interpretation (1880), and professor of Old-Testament exegesis (1883).

TAYLOR, Charles, D.D. (Cambridge, 1881), Church of England; b. in London, May 27, 1840; educated in King's College School, London, and at St. John's College, Cambridge; graduated B.A. (ninth wrangler and second-class classical tripos) 1862, M.A. 1865; was first-class in theology, 1863; Crosse scholar and Tyrwhitt scholar, 1864; Kaye prize, 1867; ordained deacon 1866, priest 1867; was fellow of St. John's College, 1864–81; examiner at Lampeter, 1874–77; lecturer in theology, Cambridge, 1873–81; became honorary fellow of King's College, London, 1876; master of St. John's College, Cambridge, 1881. He is the author of *Geometrical Conics*, London, 1863; *The Gospel in the Law: a Critical Examination of the Citations from the Old Testament in the New*, 1869; *Elementary Geometry of Conics*, 1872, 4th ed. 1883; *The Dirge of Coheleth* (in Eccles. xii.) *discussed and literally interpreted*, 1874; *The Sayings of the Jewish Fathers, including Pirke Aboth, etc., in Hebrew and English, with Critical and Illustrative Notes*, 1877; *An Introduction to the Ancient and Modern Geometry of Conics, with Historical Notes and Prolegomena*, 1881; *The Teaching of the Twelve Apostles, with Illustrations from the Talmud* (two lectures delivered at the Royal Institution of Great Britain, May 29 and June 6, 1885), Cambridge, 1886.

TAYLOR, George Lansing, D.D. (Syracuse University, N.Y., 1876), Methodist; b. at Skaneateles, N.Y., Feb. 13, 1835; was freshman and sophomore at Ohio Wesleyan University, Delaware, O., and junior and senior at Columbia College, New-York City; graduated, 1861; was assistant editor of the *Christian Advocate*, New York, 1861; entered itinerant ministry of the Methodist-Episcopal Church in New-York East Conference in April, 1862, and has ever since been in its pastorates. Since 1870 a trustee of Syracuse University, N.Y. He served in the Christian Commission during the war, in Maryland and Virginia; has always been an ardent temperance laborer, was for years in the National Society's Board, and delivered on the subject many speeches and lectures. He built the Simpson Methodist-Episcopal Church, Brooklyn, N.Y., and the Jesse Lee Memorial Church, Ridgefield, Conn.; and has preached about a hundred camp-meeting sermons. He is the author of *Six Centennial Hymns* (for the centenary of 1866, pamphlet),

New York, 1866; many pamphlets, sermons, speeches, and tracts; many contributions to the religious and secular press, including several hundred occasional poems and hymns; latest books are, *Ulysses S. Grant, Conqueror, Patriot, Hero: an Elegy, and other Grant Poems*, 1885; *Elijah the Reformer, and other Poems*, 1885. See *Alumni Record of Wesleyan University* and *Allibone*.

TAYLOR, John Phelps, Congregationalist; b. at Andover, Mass., April 6, 1841; graduated at Yale College, New Haven, Conn., 1862, and at Andover Theological Seminary, Mass., 1868; was pastor at Middletown, Conn., 1868–74; at Newport, R.I., 1874–76; at New London, Conn., 1878–83; and since has been professor of biblical history and oriental archæology in Andover Theological Seminary.

TAYLOR, Marshall William, D.D. (Central Tennessee College, Nashville, Tenn., 1878), Methodist; b. of free parents at Lexington, Fayette County, Ky., July 1, 1846; taught by white children at Ghent, Ky., 1851–53; by colored and white Methodist preachers, 1853–55; in school for free negroes at Louisville, Ky., 1855–58; was messenger for a law-firm in Louisville, Ky., 1853–55; steamboat cook, 1858–61; in the Army of the Cumberland, 1862–65; teacher at Hardinsburg, Ky., 1866–70; at Midway and Wittsburg, Ark., 1870–71; entered the ministry of the Methodist-Episcopal Church in the Lexington (Ky.) Conference, 1872; was supply at Litchfield, Ky. (1871), pastor at Louisville (1872–74), at Indianapolis, Ind. (1875–76), at Cincinnati, O. (1877–78); presiding elder, O., 1878–83; at Louisville, Ky., 1883–84; since 1884, editor of the *South-western Christian Advocate*, New Orleans, La. He was appointed a delegate to the Pan Methodist Conference in London, Eng., and to the Centennial Conference in Baltimore, Md.; and is a founder of the Colored Secret Society of United Brothers of Friendship at Louisville, Ky., 1861. He is the author of *Handbook for Schools in South-western Kentucky*, Louisville, Ky., 1871; *Life of Rev. George W. Downing*, 1878, 3d ed. 18—; *Plantation Melodies and Revival Songs of the Negroes*, 1882, 4th ed. 18—; *The Universal Reign of Jesus* (a sermon), 1872; numerous pamphlets, etc.

TAYLOR, William, D.D. (Mount Union College, O., and Abbington Hedding College, Ill.), bishop of the Methodist-Episcopal Church; b. at Rockbridge County, Va., May 2, 1821; went from his father's farm and tan-yard into the ministry; was regular itinerant, 1842–49; missionary in California, 1849–56; evangelist in the Eastern States and Canada until 1862, when he went to Australia, thence to Africa, thence to India. In Bombay he founded in 1872 an independent, self-supporting mission, of which the South-India Conference is the result. In 1878 he visited Chili and Peru. He was elected a bishop in 1884. He is the author of *Seven Years' Street Preaching in San Francisco*, New York, 1856, 27th thousand, London, 1863; *California Life illustrated*, New York, 1858, 24th thousand, London, 1863; *The Model Preacher*, Cincinnati, 1860, 16th thousand, London, 1865; *Reconciliation, or How to be Saved*, 1867; *Infancy and Manhood of Christian Life*, 1867; *The Election of Grace*, Cincinnati, 1868; *Christian Adventures in South Africa*, 1867; *Four Years' Campaign in India*, 1875; *Our South American Cousins*, 1878; *Letters to a Quaker on Baptism*, 188–; *Ten Years of Self-supporting Missions in India*, 1882; *Pauline Methods of Missionary Work*, 188–.

TAYLOR, William James Romeyn, D.D. (Rutgers College, New Brunswick, N.J., 1860), Reformed (Dutch); b. at Schodack, Rensselaer County, N.Y., July 31, 1823; graduated at Rutgers College, New Brunswick, N.J., 1841; and at the theological seminary of the Reformed Church in America, in the same place, 1844; became pastor at New Durham, N.J., 1844; Jersey City, N.J. (Second Church), 1846; Schenectady, N.Y. (First Church), 1849; Jersey City, N.J. (Third Church), 1852; Philadelphia, Penn. (Third Church), 1854; corresponding secretary of the American Bible Society, 1862; pastor of the Clinton-avenue Reformed Church, Newark, N.J., 1869. He edited *The Christian Intelligencer* (the denominational organ), New York, 1872–76; was president of the General Synod of the denomination, 1871; has been trustee of Rutgers College since 1878. He is the author of *Louisa, a Pastor's Memorial*, Philadelphia, 1860; many occasional sermons and addresses in pamphlet form; tracts; about two hundred columns, chiefly biographical and historical, in McClintock and Strong's *Cyclopædia*; *The Bible in the Last Hundred Years: a Historical Discourse for the American Bible Society in the United States Centennial*, 1876; *Church Extension in Large Cities* (1880), and *On Co-operation in Foreign Missions* (1884), papers in the second and third councils, respectively, of the Alliance of Reformed Churches, etc. See list in Corwin's *Manual of Reformed Church*, 3d ed. New York, 1879, pp. 480, 481.

TAYLOR, William Mackergo, D.D. (Yale College, New Haven, Conn., and Amherst College, Mass., both 1872), **LL.D.** (College of New Jersey, Princeton, 1883), Congregationalist; b. at Kilmarnock, Scotland, Oct. 23, 1829; graduated at University of Glasgow 1849, and at the United Presbyterian Theological Seminary, Edinburgh, 1852; became pastor (United Presbyterian) at Kilmaurs, Scotland, 1853; of Derby-road Church, Liverpool, Eng., 1855; and of the Broadway Tabernacle Church (Congregationalist), New-York City, 1872. He was Lyman Beecher lecturer in Yale Seminary, 1876 and 1886; L. P. Stone lecturer in Princeton Seminary, 1880; and editor of the *Christian at Work*, 1876–80. He is the author of *Life Truths* (sermons), Liverpool, Eng., 1862, 2d ed. 1863; *The Miracles: Helps to Faith, not Hindrances*, Edinburgh, 1865; *The Lost found, and the Wanderer welcomed*, 1870, last ed. New York, 1884; *Memoir of the Rev. Matthew Dickie*, Bristol, 1872; *Prayer and Business*, New York, 1873; *David, King of Israel*, 1875; *Elijah the Prophet*, 1876; *The Ministry of the Word* (Yale Lectures), 1876; *Songs in the Night*, 1877, last ed. 1884; *Peter the Apostle*, 1877; *Daniel the Beloved*, 1878; *Moses the Lawgiver*, 1879; *The Gospel Miracles in their Relation to Christ and Christianity* (Princeton Lectures), 1880; *The Limitations of Life, and other Sermons*, 1880; *Paul the Missionary*, 1882; *Contrary Winds, and other Sermons*, 1883; *Jesus at the Well*, 1884; *John Knox, a Biography*, 1885; *Joseph, the Prime Minister*, 1886.

TEMPLE, Right Rev. Frederick, D.D. (Oxford, 1858), lord bishop of London, Church of England; b. at Santa Maura Nov. 30, 1821; educated at

Balliol College, Oxford; graduated B.A. (double first class) 1842, M.A. 1846, B.D. 1858; was elected fellow and mathematical tutor of his college, 1842; ordained deacon 1846, priest 1847; was principal of Kneller Hall Training College, near Twickenham, 1848–55; head master of Rugby School, 1858–69; chaplain-in-ordinary to the Queen; bishop of Exeter, 1869-85; select preacher at Oxford 1873–74, and Bampton lecturer 1884; translated to London, 1885. He is the author of the essay on *The Education of the World*, in *Essays and Reviews*, London, 1860; *Sermons preached in the chapel of Rugby School* (1858–69), London, 1862–71, 3 series; *Relations between Religion and Science* (Bampton Lectures), 1884, 2d ed. 1885.

TERRY, Milton Spenser, S.T.D. (Wesleyan University, Middletown, Conn., 1879), Methodist; b. at Coeymans, N.Y., Feb. 22, 1840; graduated at Charlotteville (N.Y.) Seminary 1859, and Yale Theological Seminary, New Haven, Conn., 1862; was pastor, 1863-84; and since professor of Old-Testament exegesis in Garrett Biblical Institution, Evanston, Ill. He is the author of commentary on *Joshua* to *Samuel*, New York, 1873, 5th ed. 1884; and on *Kings* to *Esther*, 1875; *Biblical Hermeneutics*, 1883, 2d ed. 1885.

THAYER, Joseph Henry, D.D. (Yale College, New Haven, Conn., 1883; Harvard University, Cambridge, Mass., 1884), Congregationalist; b. in Boston, Mass., Nov. 7, 1828; graduated at Harvard College, Cambridge, Mass., 1850, and at Andover Theological Seminary, Mass., 1857; was pastor at Salem, Mass., 1859-62; chaplain Fortieth Massachusetts Volunteers, 1862-63; professor of sacred literature in Andover Theological Seminary, 1864–82; and since 1884 professor of New-Testament criticism and interpretation in the theological department of Harvard University. He translated the 7th ed. (Lünemann's) of *Winer's Grammar of the New-Testament Greek*, Andover, 1869, last ed. 1884; *A. Buttmann's Grammar of the New-Testament Greek*, 1873, last ed. 1883; and with revision and enlargement the 2d ed. of Grimm's Wilke's *Clavis Novi Testamenti*, under title, *A Greek-English Lexicon of the New Testament*, New York, 1886.

THIERSCH, Heinrich Wilhelm Josias, D.D., Irvingite; b. in Munich, Bavaria, Nov. 5, 1817; d. at Basel, Dec. 3, 1885. He studied philology at Munich, chiefly with his father, an eminent Greek scholar; and theology at Erlangen and Tübingen; became *privat-docent* at Erlangen, 1839; professor of theology at Marburg, 1843; resigned in 1850, in order to labor in the interest of the "Catholic Apostolic Church," which then began to be organized in Germany by "Evangelists" from England. He had charge of a small Irvingite congregation at Augsburg, and afterwards at Basel. He was connected by marriage with the Zeller family of Beuggen, and with Bishop Gobat of Jerusalem, who married a sister of his wife.

Dr. Thiersch was a man of sincere and profound piety, of rare classical, theological, and general culture, an enthusiastic teacher, and might have become the successor of Neander in Berlin; but, in obedience to what he believed to be a divine call, he sacrificed a brilliant academic career to his religious convictions. He lived in poverty and isolation. He was lame; but had a very striking, highly intellectual and spiritual countenance, and an impressive voice and manner. He was the most distinguished German convert to Irvingism. He sincerely believed that the Lord had restored the offices and gifts of the Apostolic Church in the Irvingite community; and, notwithstanding the apparent failure of the movement, he adhered to it till his death.

His chief writings are, *Versuch zur Herstellung des historischen Standpunkts für die Kritik der neutestamentlichen Schriften*, Erlangen, 1845 (a very able book against the Tübingen school of Baur, who answered in *Der Kritiker und der Fanatiker, in der Person des Herrn Heinrich W. J. Thiersch. Zur Charakteristik der neuesten Theologie*, Stuttgart, 1846); *Vorlesungen über Katholicismus und Protestantismus*, Erlangen, 1846, 2 vols. (very able, written in an irenic spirit, and in elegant style); *Die Kirche im apostolischen Zeitalter*, Frankfurt-am-Main, 1852, 3d ed. 1879 (English trans. by Carlyle the Irvingite, London, 1852); *Ueber christliches Familienleben*, 1854, 7th ed. 1877; *Döllinger's Auffassung des Urchristenthums beleuchtet*, 1861; *Die Gleichnisse Christi*, Frankfurt-am-Main, 1867, 2d ed. 1875; *Die Bergpredigt Christi*, Basel, 1867, 2d ed., Augsburg, 1878; *Die Strafgesetze in Bayern zum Schutz der Sittlichkeit*, 1868; *Luther, Gustav Adolf und Max I. von Bayern*, Nördlingen, 1868; *Das Verbot der Ehe innerhalb der nahen Verwandtschaft nach der heiligen Schrift und nach den Grundsätzen der christlichen Kirche*, 1869; *Die Genesis*, Basel, 1869 (English trans., *The Book of Genesis*, London, 1878); *Ueber den christlichen Staat*, 1875; *Christian Heinrich Zeller's Leben*, Basel, 1876, 2 vols.; *Die Anfänge der heiligen Geschichte, nach dem 1. Buche Mosis betrachtet*, 1877; *Ueber die Gefahren und die Hoffnungen der christlichen Kirche*, 1877, 2d ed. 1878; *Blicke in die Lebensgeschichte des Propheten Daniel*, 1884; *Inbegriff der christlichen Lehre*, 1886 (his last work, which was published after his death, and contains a manual of Christian doctrine and Christian life which he used in his catechetical instruction). PHILIP SCHAFF.

THOMAS, David, D.D. (Waynesburg College, Penn., 1862), Congregationalist; b. at Hollybush-Vatson, near Tenby, Pembrokeshire, South Wales, Feb. 1, 1813; educated at Newport Pagnel, now Cheshunt College, Buckingham, under the Rev. T. Bull, the friend and neighbor of Cowper the poet; entered the Independent ministry, 1841; was minister of Stockwell Independent Church, London, 1845–74. He founded in 1855 the National Newspaper League Company, for cheapening and improving the daily press, which numbered ten thousand members, and of which he was chairman; also the Working Men's Club and Institute Unions, 1861; originated the University for Wales in 1862, when the first letters and resolutions were sent out; the University College was opened at Aberystwith, March 11, 1877. He comes of an old family who have resided upon the same property for upwards of three hundred and fifty years. His grandfather lived to a hundred years; great-grandfather to a hundred and twenty years; great-uncle to a hundred and twelve years. He is a Broad Churchman, in close theological sympathy with Horace Bushnell of United States of America, Dean Stanley of Westminster, F. W. Robertson of Brighton, and Bishop Fraser of Manchester. In all his writings he recognizes the fact, that as Christ is the only revealer of absolute truth, he is not to be interpreted by the Old-Testament writers or by the apostles, but they are all to be interpreted by him. He is the author of *The Crisis of Being*, London, 1849; *The Core of Creeds*, 1851; *The Progress of Being*, 1854; *The Biblical Liturgy*, 1855; *Journalism and the Pulpit*, 1857; *Unreasonableness of People in Relation to the Pulpit*, 1857; *Resurrections: Thoughts on Duty and Destiny*, 1863; *The Genius of the Gospel: a Homiletical Commentary on St. Matthew*, 1864; *The Augustine Hymn-Book*, 1865; *The Minister, the Parent, and the Church: Inaugural Addresses*, Bristol, 1866; *The Philosophy of Happiness* (including *Crisis* and *Progress of Being*), London, 1869; *Homiletic Commentary on Acts of the Apostles*, 1869; *The Practical Philosopher: a Daily Monitor*, 1873; *Problemata Mundi, the Book of Job considered*, 1878; editor of *The Homilist*, 1851–82; 50 vols.; and since of *The Homilistic Library*, in which have appeared his *Book of the Psalms, exegetically and practically considered*, 1882–83, 3 vols.; *The Genius of the Fourth Gospel*, 1884.

THOMAS, Jesse Burgess, D.D. (University of Chicago, 1866), Baptist; b. at Edwardsville, Ill., July 29, 1832; graduated at Kenyon College, Gambier, O., 1850; was admitted to the bar in Illinois, 1852; studied in Rochester Theological Seminary, N.Y., 1853–54; obliged to abandon his studies through ill health, he engaged in mercantile pursuits at Chicago, Ill.; in 1862 he entered the Baptist ministry, and was pastor at Waukegan, Ill., 1862–64; of the Pierrepont-street Church, Brooklyn, N.Y., 1864–68; of the First Church, San Francisco, Cal., 1868–69; of the Michigan-avenue Church, Chicago, 1869–74; has been pastor of the First Baptist Church of Brooklyn, N.Y., since 1874. He is the author of *The Old Bible and the New Science*, New York, 1877; *The Mould of Doctrine*, Philadelphia, 1883.

THOMPSON, Augustus Charles, D.D. (Amherst College, Mass., 1860), Congregationalist; b. at Goshen, Litchfield County, Conn., April 30, 1812; educated at Yale College, New Haven, Conn., with the class of 1835, but did not graduate; graduated from the Theological Seminary, Hartford, Conn., 1838; studied at the University of Berlin, 1838–39; ordained at Eliot Church, Roxbury, Mass., July 27, 1842; now senior pastor. He was associated with Rev. Dr. Rufus Anderson in a deputation to the missions of the A. B. C. F. M. in India, 1854–55; with Rev. Dr. N. G. Clark, as a delegate to the Missionary Conference in London, Eng., 1878; lecturer on foreign missions at Andover Theological Seminary (Mass.), 1877–80; at the Boston University (Mass.), 1882; and at Hartford Theological Seminary (Conn.), 1885–86. He is the author of *Songs in the Night*, Boston, 1845; *Young Martyrs*, 2d ed. 1848; *Lambs Fed*, 1849 (translated into Mahrathi, Bombay, 1853); *Last Hours*, 1851; *Poor Widow*, 1854 (translated into Tamil, Jaffna, Ceylon, 1855); *The Better Land*, 1854 (republished Edinburgh 1865, new ed. 1869); *The Yoke in Youth*, 1856; *Gathered Lilies*, 1858; *Eliot Sabbath-school Memorial*, 1859; *Morning Hours in Patmos*, 1860; *Lyra Cœlestis*, 1863; *The Mercy Seat*, 1863 (republished London, 1864); *Our Little Ones*, 1867; *Christus Consolator*, 1867; *Seeds and Sheaves*, 1868; *Discourse Commemorative of Rev. Rufus Anderson, DD.*, 1880; *Moravian Missions*, New York, 1882; *Happy New Year*, 1883; *Future Probation and Foreign Missions*, 1886; various sermons, addresses, and articles in sundry periodicals.

THOMPSON, Right Rev. Hugh Miller, S.T.D. (Hobart College, Geneva, N.Y., 1863), **LL.D.** (University of Alabama, Tuscaloosa, 1885), Episcopalian, assistant bishop of Mississippi; b. in County Londonderry, Ireland, June 5, 1830; graduated B.D. from Nashotah Theological Seminary, Wis., 1852; was missionary and minister in Wisconsin, Illinois, and Kentucky, 1852–60; professor of church history at Nashotah, 1860–71, and during the same period editor of *The American Churchman*; rector of Christ Church, New-York City, 1872–76; editor of *The Church Journal*, 1871–79; rector of Trinity Church, New Orleans, 1876–83; consecrated assistant bishop of Mississippi, 1883. He is the author of *Unity and its Restoration*, New York, 1860, 15th thousand 1885; *Sin and Penalty*, 1862, 15th thousand 1885; *First Principles*, 1868, 20th thousand 1885; *Absolution*, 1872, last ed. 1885; *Copy*, 1872, 3d ed. 1885; *The Kingdom of God*, 1873, 15th thousand 1885; *The World and the Logos* (Bedell Lectures for 1885), 1885.

THOMPSON, William, D.D. (Union College, Schenectady, N.Y., 1847), Congregationalist; b. at Goshen, Conn., Feb. 17, 1806; graduated at Union College, Schenectady, N.Y., 1827; since 1834 has been professor of Hebrew in Hartford Theological Seminary, Conn.; since 1881 *emeritus* and dean of the faculty.

THOMSON, Right Hon. and Most Rev. William, D.D. (Oxford, 1856), **F.R.S., F.R.G.S.**, archbishop of York, primate of England, and Metropolitan, Church of England; b. at Whitehaven, Cumberland, Feb. 11, 1819; educated at Queen's College, Oxford; graduated B.A. (third-class classics) 1840, M.A. 1843, B.D. 1856; was ordained deacon 1842, priest 1843; was fellow, dean, bursar, tutor, and provost of his college, 1855–62; preacher to the Honorable Society of Lincoln's Inn, London, 1858–61; rector of All Saints, Marylebone, 1855–61; in 1861 was consecrated bishop of Gloucester and Bristol, and 1863 translated to York. He was select preacher at Oxford 1848 and 1856, and Bampton lecturer 1853. He is visitor of Queen's College, Oxford; elector of St. Augustine's College, Cambridge, and one of the lords of her Majesty's Most Honorable Privy Council. He is the author of *The Atoning Work of Christ* (Bampton Lectures), London, 1854; *Sermons preached in Lincoln's Inn Chapel*, 1860; *Life in the Light of God's Word* (sermons), 1868; *Word, Work, and Will*, 1879; *Outline of the Laws of Thought*, 1883.

THOMSON, William McClure, D.D. (Wabash College, Crawfordsville, Ind., 1858), Presbyterian; b. at Springfield (now Spring Dale), near Cincinnati, O., Dec. 31, 1806; graduated at Miami University, Oxford, O., 1826; studied at Princeton Theological Seminary, N.J., 1826–27; ordained an evangelist by Presbytery of Cincinnati, O., Oct. 12, 1831; was missionary in Syria and Palestine under A. B. C. F. M. and Presbyterian Board of Foreign Missions, 1833–49, 1850–57, 1859–76. He now resides in New-York City. He is the author of *The Land and the Book, or Biblical Illustrations Drawn from the Manners and Customs, the Scenes and Scenery, of the Holy Land*, New York, 1859, 2 vols. later editions; new ed. thoroughly revised and re-written, with numerous illustrations,

3 vols. (vol. i., *Southern Palestine and Jerusalem*, New York and London, 1880; vol. ii., *Central Palestine and Phœnicia*, 1882; vol. iii., *Lebanon, Damascus, and Beyond Jordan*, 1886).

THOROLD, Right Rev. Anthony Wilson, D.D. (by diploma, 1877), lord bishop of Rochester, Church of England; b. at Hougham, June 13, 1825; educated at Queen's College, Oxford; graduated B.A. 1847, M.A. 1850; ordained deacon 1849, priest 1850; became rector of St. Giles-in-the-Fields, London, 1857; minister of Curzon Chapel, Mayfair, 1868; vicar and rural dean of St. Pancras, Middlesex, 1869; lord bishop of Rochester, 1877. He was examining chaplain to the archbishop of York, 1874–77; and select preacher at Oxford, 1878–80. He is the author of *The Presence of Christ*, London, 1869, 16th ed. 1884; *The Gospel of Christ*, 1881, 5th ed. 1884; *The Claim of Christ on the Young*, 1882, 2d ed. 1883; *The Yoke of Christ*, 1883, 7th ed. 1887.

TIELE, Cornelis Petrus, D.D. (*hon.*, Leiden, 1853), Dutch theologian; b. at Leiden, Dec. 16, 1830; studied at the Remonstrants' Seminary and at the Athenæum of Amsterdam; became Remonstrant pastor at Moordrecht, 1853; Rotterdam, 1856; professor in the Remonstrants' Seminary, translated to Leiden, 1873; professor of the history of religions, in the University of Leiden, 1877 (for his inaugural addresses, see below). He edited for a time "The Signs of the Times" (in Dutch), the organ of the so-called "modern theology;" and assisted upon *Gids;* and since its foundation, in 1867, has been joint editor with A. Kuenen, A. D. Loman, and L. W. Rauwenhoff of the *Theologisch Tijdschrift*, Leiden. He is the author of *Specimen theologicum sistens annotationem in locos nonnullos evangelii Joannei, ad vindicandam hujus evangelii authentiam* (publicly defended, Amsterdam), 1853; and in Dutch of "The Gospel of John considered as a source of the Life of Jesus," 1855; "The Religion of Zarathustra," 1864; *Vergelijkende Geschiedenis der Egyptische en Mesopotamische Godsdiensten* ("Comparative History of the Egyptian and Mesopotamian Religions"), 1869–72, 2 parts (French trans., Paris, 1882; English authorized trans. by James Ballingal, part 1, *History of the Egyptian Religion*, London, 1882); *De plaats van de Godsdiensten der Natuurvolken in de Godsdienst-geschiedenis* ("The Place of the Religions of the Savages in the History of Religion," inaugural), 1873; *Geschiedenis van den Godsdienst tot aan de heerschappij der Wereldgodsdiensten*, 1876 (English trans. by J. E. Carpenter, *Outlines of the History of Religion to the Spread of the Universal Religions*, London, 1878, 3d ed. 1884; French trans., Paris, 1880; German trans., Berlin, 1880); *De vrucht der Assyriologie voor de vergelijkende geschiedenis der Godsdiensten* ("The Results of Assyriology for the Comparative History of Religion," inaugural), 1877 (German trans. by K. Friederici, Leipzig, 1878); *De Gelijkenis van het Vaderhuis* ("The Parable of the Father's House"), 1861, later eds.; *Twaalf Preken* ("Twelve Sermons"), 1873; *Huldreich Zwingli* (an address at the Zwingli Festival in the Remonstrants' Church at Rotterdam, Dec. 30, 1883), 1884; contributions in the *Revue de l'histoire des Religions*, Paris, —— etc.

TILLETT, Wilbur Fisk, A.M., Methodist (Southern Church); b. at Henderson, N.C., Aug. 25, 1854; graduated at Randolph Macon College, Ashland, Va., 1877, and at Princeton Theological Seminary, N.J., 1880; became member of Virginia Conference, Methodist-Episcopal, South; and pastor at Danville, Va., 1880; chaplain of Vanderbilt University, Nashville, Tenn., 1882; adjunct professor of systematic theology in the same 1883, and full professor 1884. He is the author of various review articles.

TITCOMB, Right Rev. Jonathan Holt, D.D. (Cambridge, 1877), Church of England; b. in London, in the year 1819; educated at St. Peter's College, Cambridge; graduated B.A. (junior optime) 1841, M.A. 1844; ordained deacon 1842, priest 1843; was perpetual curate of St. Andrew the Less, Cambridge, 1845–59; secretary to the Christian Vernacular Education Society for India, 1859–61; vicar of St. Stephen, South Lambeth, London, 1861–76; rural dean of Clapham, 1870–76; vicar of Woking, 1876–77; consecrated first lord bishop of Rangoon, British Burmah, 1877; resigned his bishopric, 1882; became bishop coadjutor of the English Church for Northern and Central Europe, 1884. Since 1874 he has been honorary canon of Winchester. He is the author of *Bible Studies as to Divine Teaching*, London, 1857; *Baptism: its Institution, Privileges, and Responsibilities*, 1866; *Revelation from Adam to Malachi: Bible Studies*, 1871; *Church Lessons for Young Churchmen*, 1873; *Anglo-Israel Post-bag*, 1878; *Before the Cross*, 1878; *British Burmah, and its Church Mission Work in 1878–79*, 1880; *Cautions for Doubters*, 1880; *Short Chapters on Buddhism Past and Present*, 1883. *

TOLLIN, Henri Guillaume Nathanael, Lic. Theol. (Berlin, 1857), **M.D.** (*hon.*, Bern, 1884), Reformed theologian; b. at Berlin, May 5, 1833; educated at Berlin and Bonn; was teacher in the French gymnasium in Berlin, 1859–62; preacher to the Reformed Church at Frankfort-on-the-Oder, 1862; afterwards at Schulzendorf, near Lindow; since 1876 he has been preacher to the French Reformed Church at Magdeburg. He established at Frankfort-on-the-Oder and at Schulzendorf a fund for poor people, and at Magdeburg an educational union. He is the author of *Biographische Beiträge zur Geschichte der Toleranz*, Frankfort-on-the-Oder, 1866; *Ein Ahnherr der Hohenzollern*, 1866; *Geistliche Reden von Havenstein, nebst Biographie*, 1866; *Geschichte der französichen Colonie in Frankfurt a. d. Oder*, 1868; *H. W. Beecher's Geistliche Reden, nebst Biographie*, Berlin, 1870; *Luther und Servet*, 1875; *Melanchthon und Servet*, 1876; *Characterbild Michael Servet's*, 1876 (translated into English, Hungarian, French, Italian, and Danish); *Die Entdeckung des Blutkreislaufs*, Jena, 1876; *Das Lehrsystem Michael Servet's*, Gütersloh, vols. i.–iii., 1876–78; *Mi. Villanovani Apologetica disceptatio*, Berlin, 1880; *Mi. Servet und Martin Butzer*, 1880; *William Harvey*, 1880; *Mateo Realdo Colombo*, 1880; *Harvey und seine Vorgänger*, Erlangen, 1883; *Cassiodore de Reina*, Paris, 1883–84; *Andreas Caesalpin*, Bonn, 1884; *Andreas Vesal*, Erlangen, 1885; *Geschichte der französisch reformirten Gemeinde zu Magdeburg*, Halle, 1886–87; numerous articles in the *Zeitschriften* of Kahnis, Hilgenfeld, Hase, Köstlin, Guericke, Zöckler, Lehmann, von Raumer, Virchow, von Holtzendoff, etc.; many on Servetus.

TOORENENBERGEN, Johan Justus van, theologian; b. at Utrecht, Feb. 12, 1822; studied at the University of Utrecht; became Reformed pastor at Elspeet 1844, Flessingen 1848; director of studies and secretary of the Mission Institute of Utrecht, 1864; pastor at Rotterdam, 1869; professor of ecclesiastical history in the University of Amsterdam, 1880. He is the author (in Dutch) of two volumes of sermons, minor works, and "A Page of the History of the Confession of the Reformed Church of the Netherlands," Amsterdam, 1861; "Dogmatic Theses relating to the Doctrine of the Reformed Church," 1852–65; "The Symbolical Books of the Reformed Church of the Netherlands" (critical text), 1869; "The Religious and Ecclesiastical Works of Ph. Marnix de Sainte Aldegonde," 1871–78, 3 vols.; editor of the Marnix Society ("Documents relating to the History of the Reformed Church of the Netherlands prior to 1618") 1870–85, 10 vols.; *Monumenta reformationis Belgicæ*, tom. i., 1882.

TOUSEY, William George, Universalist; b. at Portage, N.Y., Sept. 22, 1842; graduated A.B. at Tufts College, College Hill, Mass., 1869, and divinity school 1871; since 1873 has been professor of psychology and natural theology there.

TOWNSEND, Luther Tracy, D.D. (Dartmouth College, Hanover, N.H., 1871), Methodist; b. at Orono, Me., Sept. 27, 1838; graduated at Dartmouth College, Hanover, N.H., 1859, and Andover Theological Seminary, Mass., 1862; was professor of exegetical theology, Boston University, Mass., 1867–68, of historical theology 1869–73, and since of practical theology. He was adjutant of Sixteenth New-Hampshire Volunteers, 1863–64. Of his works may be mentioned, *True and Pretended Christianity*, Boston, 1869; *Sword and Garment*, 1871; *God-Man*, 1872; *Credo*, 1873; *Outlines of Theology*, New York, 1873; *Arena and Throne*, Boston, 1874; *Lost Forever*, 1875; *The Chinese Problem*, 1876; *The Supernatural Factor in Revivals*, 1877; *The Intermediate World*, 1878; *Elements of General and Christian Theology*, New York, 1879; *Fate of Republics*, Boston, 1880; *Art of Speech*, vol. i., *Studies in Poetry and Prose* (1880), vol. ii., *Studies in Eloquence and Logic* (1881); *Mosaic Record and Modern Science*, 1881; *Bible Theology and Modern Thought*, 1883; *Faith Work, Christian Science, and other Cures*, 1885; *Handbook upon Church Trials*, New York, 1885.

TOY, Crawford Howell, A.M., Baptist; b. at Norfolk, Va., March 23, 1836; graduated A.M. at University of Virginia, Charlottesville, Va., 1856; studied at Berlin, 1866–68; was professor of Old Testament interpretation in Southern Baptist Theological Seminary, Greenville, S.C. (now Louisville, Ky.), 1869–79, and since 1880 of Hebrew in Harvard University, Cambridge, Mass. He is a "liberal conservative." He is the author of *History of the Religion of Israel*, Boston, 1882, 3d ed. 1884; *Quotations in the New Testament*, New York, 1884.

TRECHSEL, Friedrich, D.D., Swiss theologian; b. at Bern, Nov. 30, 1805; d. there Jan. 30, 1885. He studied in the university of his native city, then in Paris, Göttingen, Halle, and Berlin. Of his teachers, Lücke of Göttingen and Neander of Berlin had the most influence upon his intellectual development. In 1829 he became chaplain of the city hospital at Bern, and *privat-docent* in the academy; pastor at Vechigen, 1837; of the Minster at Bern, 1859; retired on a pension, 1876. He was the author of *Ueber den Kanon, die Kritik und Exegese*, Bern, 1832; *Johannes Philoponus* (in *Theologische Studien und Kritiken*, 1835); *Die protestantischen Antitrinitarier vor Faustus Socin., Nach Quellen und Urkunden geschichtlich dargestellt* (his chief work), Heidelberg, 1839–44, 2 vols. (vol. i., *Michael Servet und seine Vorgänger;* vol. ii., *Lelio Sozini und die Antitrinitarier seiner Zeit*); *Beiträge zur Geschichte der schweizerisch-reformirten Kirche, zunächst derjenigen des Kantons Bern*, Bern, 1844; valuable articles in Herzog's *Real-Encyklopädie*, in the *Berner Taschenbuch*, etc. Cf. obituary notice by R. Ruetschi in Meile's *Theologische Zeitschrift aus der Schweiz*, vol. ii. (Zürich, 1885), pp. 312–314.

TRENCH, Francis Chenevix, Church of England; b. in Dublin, Ireland, July, 1806; d. at Bursleden, Hants, April 3, 1886. He was educated at Harrow and at Oriel College, Oxford (two second-class classics), 1828; B.A. 1834, M.A. 1839; ordained deacon 1835, priest 1836; curate of St. Giles, Reading, 1836; perpetual curate of St. John, Reading, 1837–57; rector of Islip, Oxfordshire, 1857–75. He was the author of *Sermons at Reading*, London, 1843; *Travels in France and Spain*, 1845; *Scotland: its Faith and Features*, 1846; *Portrait of Charity* (exposition of 1 Cor. xiii.), 1846; *Walk around Mt. Blanc*, 1848; *Life and Character of St. John the Evangelist*, 1850; *Job's Testimony to Jesus, and the Resurrection of the Body*, 1853; *Theological Works* (collected edition), 1857, 3 vols.; *Few Notes from Past Life*, 1862; *Notes on the Greek of the New Testament, chiefly for English Readers*, 1864; *Four Assize Sermons* (preached in York Minster and Leeds' Parish Church), 1865; *Islipiana* (miscellanies), 1869–70, 2 series. *

TRENCH, Most Rev. Richard Chenevix, D.D. (Cambridge, 1856; Trinity College, Dublin, 1864), lord archbishop of Dublin, Church of Ireland; b. in Dublin, Ireland, Sept. 9, 1807; d. in London, March 28, 1886. He was educated at Trinity College, Cambridge; graduated B.A. 1829, M.A. 1833, B.D. 1850; was ordained deacon 1832, priest 1833; became curate of Curdridge 1835, and Alverstoke 1840; rector of Itchinstoke, Hants, 1845; dean of Westminster, 1856; archbishop of Dublin, Glandelagh, and Kildare, 1864; retired, 1884. He was Hulsean lecturer at Cambridge, 1845–46; chaplain to the bishop of Oxford (Wilberforce), 1847–64; professor of divinity in King's College, London, 1847–58. He was a devout and conservative High Churchman of the best type, but his theological writings are free from sectional bias. He had no special administrative ability, and therefore was only moderately successful as archbishop. He threw the weight of his influence against disestablishment. As a writer, he showed choice biblical, patristic, and modern Anglo-German learning, original thought, and a reverential and truly Christian spirit. He is one of the chief authorities on the English language. He was the author of *The Story of Justin Martyr, and other Poems*, London, 1835, 5th ed. 1862; *Sabbaton, Honor Neale, and other Poems*, 1838; *Elegiac Poems*, 1841; *Notes on the Parables of our Lord*, 1841, 15th ed. 1886; *Poems from Eastern Sources*, 1842; *Genoveva and other Poems*, 1842; *Sermons*, Cambridge, 1843; *Exposition of the Sermon on the Mount, from St. Augustine*, London, 1844, 4th ed. 1881; *The Fitness of Holy Scripture for unfolding* *the Spiritual Life of Men* (Hulsean Lectures for 1845), Cambridge, 1846; *Christ the Desire of all Nations, or the Unconscious Prophecies of Heathendom* (Hulsean Lectures for 1846), 1846; together, 5th ed. 1880; *Sacred Poems for Mourners*, London, 1846; *Notes on the Miracles of our Lord*, 1846, 13th ed. 1886; *Sacred Latin Poetry*, 1849, 3d ed. 1874; *The Star of the Wise Men*, 1850; *On the Study of Words*, 1851, 18th ed. 1882; *On the Lessons in Proverbs*, 1853, 7th ed. 1879; *Synonymes of the New Testament*, Cambridge, 1854, 2d series 1863: together, 10th ed. 1886; *Alma and other Poems*, 1854; *English, Past and Present*, London, 1855, 11th ed. 1881; *Life's a Dream: the Great Theatre of the World, from the Spanish of Calderon, with an Essay on his Life and Genius*, 1856, 2d ed. 1880; *Sermons*, 1856; *On the Authorized Version of the New Testament, in Connection with some Recent Proposals for its Revision*, 1858 (reprinted by Dr. Schaff, with Ellicott and Lightfoot's treatises, New York, 1873); *A Select Glossary of English Words used formerly in Senses differing from their Present*, 1859, 5th ed. 1879; *Sermons preached in Westminster Abbey*, 1860; *Commentary on the Epistles to the Seven Churches in Asia*, 1861, 4th ed. 1883; *Subjection of the Creature to Vanity* (sermons), Cambridge, 1863; *Two Sermons*, 1864; *Gustavus Adolphus: Social Aspects of the Thirty Years' War*, 1865, 2d ed. 1872; *Poems, collected and arranged anew*, 1865, 9th ed. 1886, 1 vol.; *Studies on the Gospels*, 1867, 4th ed. 1878; *Shipwrecks of Faith* (3 sermons), 1867; *A Household Book of English Poetry*, selected and arranged, 1868; *Plutarch: his life, Lives and Morals*, 1873, 2d ed. 1874; *Lectures on Mediæval Church History*, 1877, 2d ed. 1879. *

TRISTRAM, Henry Baker, D.D. (Durham, 1882), **LL.D.** (Edinburgh, 1868), F.R.S., Church of England; b. at Eglingham, Northumberland, May 11, 1822; educated at Lincoln College, Oxford; graduated B.A. (second-class classics) 1844, M.A. 1846; was ordained deacon 1845, priest 1846; was chaplain in Bermuda, 1847–49; rector of Castle-Eden, County Durham, Eng., 1849–60; master of Greatham Hospital and vicar of Greatham, 1860–73; honorary canon of Durham, 1870–74; rural dean of Stockton, 1872–76; of Chester-le-Street, Western Division, 1876–80; and since 1880 of Durham; since 1874 he has been canon of Durham. He is (1885) proctor in convocation for the archdeaconry of Durham, and honorary association secretary of Church Missionary Society for Durham and Northumberland. He has travelled long and frequently in the East, especially in Syria and Palestine, to which he has made five expeditions. He was offered the bishopric of Jerusalem in 1879. He is the author of *The Great Sahara*, London, 1860; *The Land of Israel*, 1865, 4th ed. 1882; *Natural History of the Bible*, 1867, 5th ed. 1880; *Ornithology of Palestine*, 1867; *Daughters of Syria*, 1869, 3d ed. 1874; *Seven Golden Candlesticks*, 1871; *Bible Places*, 1872, 11th thousand, 1884; *The Land of Moab*, 1873, 2d ed. 1874; *Pathways of Palestine*, 1882, 2 vols.; *Fauna and Flora of Palestine*, 1884.

TROLLOPE, Right Rev. Edward, D.D. (Oxford, 1877), **F.S.A.**, bishop suffragan of Nottingham, Church of England; b. at Caswick, Eng., April 15, 1817; educated at Christ Church, Oxford; graduated B.A. 1839, M.A. 1855; was ordained deacon 1840, priest 1841; was prebendary of Liddington in Lincoln Cathedral, 1867–74; since 1843 has been rector of Leasingham, with Roxholm, diocese of Lincoln; and bishop suffragan of Nottingham since 1877. He is the author of *Illustrations of Ancient Art*, London, 1854; *Life of Pope Adrian IV.*, 1856; *The Captivity of John, King of France*, 1857; *A Handbook of Lincoln*, 1857; *Temple Bruer and the Templars*, 1857; *The Introduction of Christianity into Lincolnshire*, 1857; *Labyrinths, Ancient and Mediæval*, 1858; *Sepulchral Memorials*, 1858; *Fens and Submarine Forests*, 1859; *The Danes in Lincolnshire*, 1859; *Memorabilia of Grimsby*, 1859; *The Use and Abuse of Red Bricks*, 1859; *The Roman House at Apethorpe*, 1859; *The History of Workshop Priory*, 1860; *Monastic Gate-Houses*, 1860; *The Life of the Saxon Hereward*, 1861; *History of Anne Askewe*, 1862; *Battle of Bosworth Field*, 1862; *Shadows of the Past*, 1863; *The Raising of the Royal Standard at Nottingham*, 1864; *Spilsby and other Churches*, 1865; *Gainsborough and other Churches*, 1866; *The Norman Sculptures of Lincoln Cathedral*, 1866; *Grantham and other Churches*, 1867; *The Roman Ermine Street*, 1868; *The Norman and Early English Styles of Gothic Architecture*, 1869; *Boston and other Churches*, 1870; *Newark and other Churches*, 1870; *Newark Castle*, 1871; *The Battle of Stoke*, 1871; *Sleaford and the Wapentakes of Flaxwell and Aswardham*, 1872; *Holbeach and other Churches*, 1872; *South Park Abbey, South and other Churches*, 1873; *Churches in the Neighbourhood of Grantham* (1875), *of Newark* (1876), *of Southwell* (1877), *of Grimsby* (1878), *of Stamford* (1879); *Church Spires*, 1875; *Little St. Hugh of Lincoln*, 1880; various sermons and charges.

TROUTBECK, John, D.D. (by archbishop of Canterbury, 1883), Church of England; b. at Blencowe, Cumberland, Eng., Nov. 12, 1832; educated at University College, Oxford; graduated B.A. 1856, M.A. 1858; was ordained deacon 1855, priest 1857; curate of St. Cuthbert, Wells, Somerset, 1855–58; vicar of Dacre, Cumberland, 1859–64; precentor and minor canon of Manchester, 1864–69; Sunday-evening lecturer of St Matthew, Westminster, 1870–72; secretary of the New-Testament Revision Company, 1870–81; has been since 1869 minor canon of Westminster, and since 1883 honorary chaplain to the Queen. He edited *The Manchester Psalter and Chant-Book*, London, 1867; *Westminster Abbey Hymn-Book*, 1883.

TRUE, Benjamin Osgood, Baptist; b. at Plainfield, N.H., Dec. 17, 1845; graduated at Dartmouth College, Hanover, N.H., 1866, and at Rochester (N.Y.) Theological Seminary, 1870; was pastor at Baldwinsville, N.Y., 1870–72; in Europe, 1872; pastor of First Baptist Church, Meriden, Conn., 1873–79; in Europe and the East, 1879–80; pastor of Central Baptist Church, Providence, R.I., 1880–81; since 1881 has been professor of ecclesiastical history in Rochester (N.Y.) Theological Seminary. He is the author of miscellaneous reviews, articles, etc.

TRUMBULL, Henry Clay, D.D. (Lafayette College, Easton, Penn., 1881; University of the City of New York, 1882); Congregationalist; b. at Stonington, Conn., June 8, 1830; was at Williston Seminary, Easthampton, Mass., 1844; education chiefly private; received honorary M.A. from Yale College, New Haven, Conn., 1866; was

State missionary of the American Sunday-school Union for Connecticut, 1858-62; ordained as Congregational clergyman, Sept. 10, 1862, in order to go as chaplain to the Tenth Regiment Connecticut Volunteers; in army service until September, 1865 (prisoner of war in South Carolina and Virginia in 1863); missionary secretary for New England of American Sunday-school Union, 1865-71; normal secretary of the American Sunday-school Union, 1871-75; has been editor of the *Sunday-school Times*, Philadelphia, since 1875. He travelled in Egypt, Arabia, and Syria, in 1881. He is the author of *The Sunday-school Concert*, Boston, 1861; *The Knightly Soldier*, 1865; *Memorial of E. B. Preston*, Hartford, Conn., 1866; *Falling in Harness*, Philadelphia, 1867; *Childhood Conversion*, Boston, 1868; *The Captured Scout of the Army of the James*, 1869; *Children in the Temple*, Springfield, Mass., 1869; *The Worth of a Historic Consciousness*, Hartford, Conn., 1870; *Review Exercises in the Sunday-school*, Philadelphia, 1873; *The Model Superintendent: Sketch of the Life, Character, and Methods of Work of Henry P. Haven*, New York, 1880; *Kadesh Barnea*, 1884, republished London, 1884; *Teaching and Teachers*, Philadelphia, 1885, republished London, 1885; *The Blood Covenant*, New York, 1885.

TSCHACKERT, Paul (Moritz Robert), Lic. Theol. (Breslau, 1875), **Ph.D.** (Leipzig, 1875), **D.D.** (*hon.*, Halle, 1883), German Protestant; b. at Freystadt, Lower Silesia, Prussia, Jan. 10, 1848; studied at Breslau, Halle, and Göttingen, 1868-74; became *privat-docent* of historical theology at Breslau, 1875; professor extraordinary of church history at Halle, 1877; ordinary professor of church history at Königsberg, 1884. He belongs to the school of Tholuck and Julius Müller. He is the author of *Anna Maria von Schürmann*, Gotha, 1876; *Peter von Ailli. (Petrus de Alliaco), Anhang: Petri de Alliaco anecdotorum partes selectae*, 1877; *Die Päpste der Renaissance*, Heidelberg, 1879; *Ueber evangelischen Kirchenbaustil*, Berlin, 1881; *Evangelische Polemik gegen die römische Kirche*, Gotha, 1885, 2d ed. 1887 (Dutch trans., Utrecht, 1886).

TUCKER, Henry Holcombe, D.D. (Columbian College, Washington, D.C., 1860), Baptist; b. in Warren County, Ga., May 10, 1819; graduated at Columbian College (now Columbian University), Washington, D.C., 1838; was professor of *belles-lettres* in Mercer University, Macon, Ga., 1856-62; president, 1866-71; chancellor of the University of Georgia, Athens, Ga., 1874-78; at present, editor of *The Christian Index*, Atlanta, Ga. He is the author of *The Gospel in Enoch*, Philadelphia, 1868; *The Old Theology restated in Sermons*, 1884. One of his sermons, *The Position of Baptism in the Christian System* (Philadelphia, 1882), has had an immense circulation in the United States and Canada, and has been translated into Swedish, German, Turkish, Greek, Armenian, and Spanish.

TUCKER, William Jewett, D.D. (Dartmouth College, Hanover, N.H., 1875), Congregationalist; b. at Griswold, Conn., July 13, 1839; graduated at Dartmouth College, Hanover, N.H., 1861, and at Andover (Mass.) Theological Seminary 1866; became pastor of the Franklin-street Church, Manchester, N.H., 1867; of Madison-square Presbyterian Church, New-York City, 1875; professor of sacred rhetoric, Andover (Mass.) Theological Seminary, 1880.

TULLOCH, Very Rev. Principal John, D.D. (St. Andrew's, 1854), **LL.D.** (Glasgow and Edinburgh, 1884), Church of Scotland; b. near Tibbermuir, Perthshire, June 1, 1823; d. at Torquay, Eng., Feb. 13, 1885. He was educated at St. Andrew's and Edinburgh; became parish minister at Dundee 1845, and at Keltins, Forfarshire, 1849; principal and primarius professor of divinity in St. Mary's College, St. Andrew's University, 1854; and senior principal of the university, 1860. His theological standpoint was thus defined by himself: "Broad evangelical. The aim is to see all Christian truth first in its pure historical form, — the mind of Christ, the thought of St. Paul, the teaching of St. James; then its living relation to the Christian consciousness, — what man needs, what God gives. The historic method, rightly applied, is the primary key to all Christian truth; and the renovation of theology is through this method bringing all Christian ideas freshly into the light of consciousness." He studied theology in Germany in 1847-48 and 1863-64. He was "especially attracted by Neander, and much interested by the problems raised by the Tübingen school and the writings of F. C. Baur, and greatly attracted in later years by Dean Stanley's historical writings and Bishop Lightfoot's critico-historical essays." He was an ardent student of literature and philosophy, and his writings are very highly prized. He first came into notice when in Dundee, by his frequent contributions in the *Dundee Advertiser*; but later by his elaborate articles in *The North-British Review*, *The British Quarterly*, and *Kitto's Journal of Sacred Literature*. Two of his articles — one on *Carlyle's Life of Sterling* (*North-British Review*, vol. iv., 1845), the other on *Bunsen's Hippolytus* (the same, vol. xix., 1853) — attracted wide attention; and the latter so pleased Baron Busen that he successfully exerted his influence to press the claim of Mr. Tulloch to the then vacant principalship in St. Mary's College. His appointment when barely thirty years old to this position, one of the most dignified and responsible connected with the Established Church of Scotland, was naturally a great surprise and occasion of unfavorable remark. But he soon proved his superior fitness for the office. In 1856 he was appointed one of the examiners of the Dick bequest, and so continued until his death. In 1858 he was deputed by the General Assembly of the Church to formally open the Scotch Presbyterian Church in Paris, and preached there during the summer. In 1859 he was appointed one of her Majesty's chaplains for Scotland, and often preached before the Queen at Crathie. In 1862 he became deputy clerk of the General Assembly, in 1875 succeeded Rev. Dr. Cook of Haddington as clerk, and in 1878 was elected moderator. The regard in which he was held, and the position he occupied, are authoritatively expressed in the following memorial passed by the senatus of the University of St. Andrew's immediately after his death: —

"The senatus record their deep sense of the severe loss the university has sustained in the death of its honored and revered head, — the Very Rev. Principal Tulloch, who for thirty-two years held the offices of principal and primarius professor of divinity in St. Mary's College, and for twenty-six years the office of senior principal in the university. During the whole of this period,

Principal Tulloch devoted himself to the interests of the colleges and university with unwearied zeal and energy; and the successful management of university affairs under critical circumstances was largely due to his wisdom and tact, his sound public judgment, commanding influence, and great executive ability. As chairman of the university council, Principal Tulloch's thorough knowledge of academic questions, and capacity for directing their discussion into useful channels, were equally conspicuous. As vice-chancellor, Principal Tulloch represented the university on public occasions with unfailing dignity and distinction. As a permanent member of the university court, his knowledge of official procedure, and scrupulous care and impartiality in dealing with judicial questions, were, in its early years, of the greatest service in helping to define the powers, and develop the functions, of the newly established tribunal; while to the end they constituted an important element in guiding the deliberations of the court, and giving weight to its decisions. As a university reformer, Principal Tulloch combined an enlightened regard for the past with the keenest perception of the newest forces and requirements of social and national life. Having carefully studied the university system of the country, and been familiar with its working for nearly half a century, he was supremely anxious that any changes initiated by the universities, or undertaken by the legislature, should be fully considered in the interest of the public, so as to extend the usefulness, and strengthen the national position, of the universities. While keeping up the standard of attainment, he felt that it was desirable to give greater elasticity to the curriculum, and thus make the whole system more widely fruitful in solid educational results. As a member of the Central Board of Education, Principal Tulloch was engaged for several years in the re-organization and extension of primary schools, and in various efforts for the multiplication of good secondary schools. The removal of so able, earnest, and experienced an adviser and authority is a heavy loss, alike to the universities of which Principal Tulloch was the senior representative, and to the educational interests of the country at large. The senatus cannot but feel, indeed, that the calamity they mourn affects every department of the nation's higher life.

"The Church of Scotland has lost in Principal Tulloch her most eloquent and courageous leader; her wisest and most far-sighted statesman; her most accomplished, large-hearted, and generous-minded representative. The loss falls with almost equal weight on Scottish thought, Scottish literature, and Scottish public life, — in all of which Principal Tulloch was deeply interested, and in all of which he took so active and so influential a part. But it is in relation to the higher and more distinctive work of his life as a Christian thinker and constructive theologian, that Principal Tulloch's death will be most widely felt and deeply mourned. His profound religious convictions, the spiritual elevation of his thought, his living sympathy with the past as affording light and guidance for the present, his powers of luminous insight and interpretation, the breadth of his literary culture, and his command of a graceful and impressive style — all conspired to give Principal Tulloch's matured studies in Church history and Christian philosophy a unique character, a high and permanent value. This has been widely recognized on both sides of the Atlantic, — wherever, indeed, the English language is spoken. Critics and thinkers of widely different schools have felt and acknowledged how much Principal Tulloch's writings have done to harmonize the principles of religious life with the movements of modern thought, and thus to bring the spirit of Christianity into closer relation with the spirit of the age. In this aspect of his work, Principal Tulloch's death in the plenitude of his powers cannot but be regarded as a serious national loss. Alike, therefore, in the variety and extent, the high character and lasting value, of his labors, the senatus feel that Principal Tulloch will occupy a foremost place in the history of the time, and has shed an undying lustre on the university he adorned. In placing on record this slight tribute to his worth, the members of the senatus cherish with pride and gratitude the inspiring example of their late principal's noble character and life, and will ever hold in affectionate regard the memory of his generous nature, his goodness of heart, the warmth and fidelity of his attachments, his loyal and kindly qualities as a colleague and a friend."

Principal Tulloch was the author of *Theism* (second Burnett prize essay), Edinburgh, 1855; *Leaders of Reformation*, 1859, 3d ed. 1883; *English Protestants and their Leaders*, 1861; *Beginning Life*, 1862, 15th thousand 1880; *The Christ of the Gospels, and the Christ of Modern Criticism* (against Renan), 1864; *Rational Theology and Christian Philosophy*, 1872, 2 vols., 2d ed. 1873; *Facts of Religion and Life* (sermons preached before the Queen), 1876; *Pascal*, 1876, 2d ed. 1882; *The Christian Doctrine of Sin*, 1877; *Modern Theories in Philosophy and Religion*, 1884; *Movements of Religious Thought in Britain during the Nineteenth Century*, 1885; numerous contributions to the newspaper-press and to the reviews.

TUTTLE, Right Rev. Daniel Sylvester, D.D. (Columbia College, New-York City, 1857), Episcopalian, diocesan bishop of Missouri; b. at Windham, Greene County, N.Y., Jan. 26, 1837; fitted for college in Delaware Academy, Delhi, N.Y.; taught in a boys' boarding-school at Scarsdale, N.Y., 1853-54; entered the sophomore class, and graduated at Columbia College, New-York City, 1857; was special private tutor to many boys preparing for Columbia College, 1857-59; entered the General Theological Seminary in the same city 1859, and graduated 1862; was assistant minister of Zion Church, Morris, N.Y., 1862-63; rector of the same, 1863-67; consecrated missionary bishop of Montana, with jurisdiction in Utah and Idaho, May 1, 1867; lived at Virginia City (1867-68) and Helena (1868-69), both in Montana; since September, 1869, has resided in Salt Lake City; in October, 1880, by the setting apart of Montana for a separate missionary district, became missionary bishop of Utah with jurisdiction in Idaho. In 1868, was elected bishop of Missouri, but declined; in 1886 re-elected and accepted. He is an "old-fashioned High Churchman, of the Bishop Hobart school."

TYERMAN, Luke, Wesleyan; b. at Osmotherley, North Riding of Yorkshire, Feb. 26, 1820;

educated at the Didsbury Wesleyan Methodist Theological Institution, near Manchester, 1842-45, and since has been in the ministry. He is the author of *Life and Times of Rev. Samuel Wesley*, London, 1866; *Life and Times of Rev. John Wesley*, 1870-71, 3 vols.; *The Oxford Methodists*, 1873; *Life of Rev. George Whitefield*, 1876, 2 vols.; *Wesley's Designated Successor: the Life, Letters, and Literary Labours of Rev. John W. Fletcher, Vicar of Madeley*, 1882.

TYLER, William Seymour, D.D. (Harvard College, Cambridge, 1857), **LL.D.** (Amherst College, Mass., 1871), Congregationalist; b. at Harford, Penn., Sept. 2, 1810; graduated (second honor) at Amherst College, Mass., 1830; studied theology at Andover, 1831-32, 1834-35; spent winter of 1835-36 with Rev. Dr. Skinner, in the class out of which Union Theological Seminary, New-York City, was developed; was teacher in Amherst Academy, 1830-31; tutor in Amherst College, 1832-34; licensed to preach by the Third Presbytery of New York, Feb. 29, 1836; ordained without charge by a Congregational Council held at Amherst, Oct. 6, 1859. He was professor of Latin and Greek in Amherst College, 1836-47; and since has been professor of Greek only. He was never a pastor, but has preached in his turn with the president and other professors in college, and often as supply in churches. He is the author of *Germania and Agricola of Tacitus, with Notes for Colleges*, New York, 1847, carefully revised 1852, revised and enlarged 1878; *Histories of Tacitus*, 1848; *Prayer for Colleges* (premium essay), 1854, revised and enlarged repeatedly; *Plato's Apology and Crito*, 1859, re-written and reprinted 1886; *Memoir of Lobdell, Missionary to Assyria*, Boston, 1859; *Theology of the Greek Poets*, 1867; *Plutarch on the Delay of the Deity*, etc. (with Prof. Hackett), N. Y., 1867; *Address at Semi-Centennial of Amherst College, with other Addresses on that Occasion*, 1871; *History of Amherst College*, 1873; *Demosthenes, De Corona*, Boston, 1874, numerous editions; *Demosthenes, Philippics and Olynthiacs*, 1875, numerous editions; *Homer's Iliad*, books xvi.-xxiv., New York, 1886; many articles, discourses, etc.

TYNG, Stephen Higginson, D.D. (Jefferson College, Canonsburg, Penn., 1832; Harvard College, Cambridge, Mass., 1851), Episcopalian; b. at Newburyport, Mass., March 1, 1800; d. at Irvington on the Hudson, Sept. 4, 1885. He graduated at Harvard College, Cambridge, Mass., 1817; was in business, 1817-19; studied theology from 1819-21; and then was successively rector at Georgetown, D.C., 1821-23; in Queen Anne Parish, Prince George's County, Md., 1823-29; of St. Paul's, Philadelphia, 1829-33; of the Church of the Epiphany, in the same city, 1833-45; of St. George's, New-York City, 1845-78, when he retired as pastor emeritus. He was for years one of the leaders of the Low Church party in his denomination, and was famous for eloquence and Christian zeal. He was prominent in the organization of the Evangelical Knowledge Society, the American Church Missionary Society, and the Evangelical Education Society. His temperance and patriotic addresses were memorable. He was a ready and polished platform-speaker, and much in demand. He edited for several years *The Episcopal Recorder* and *The Protestant Churchman*. He was the author of *Lectures on the Law and the Gospel*, Philadelphia, 1832, 6th thousand New York, 1854; *Memoir of Rev. G. T. Bedell*, Philadelphia, 1835, 2d ed. 1836; *Sermons*, 1839, republished as *The Israel of God*, 6th thousand New York, 1854; *Recollections of England*, New York, 1847; *Christ is All* (sermons), 1852, 4th ed. 1864; *A Lamb from the Flock*, 1852; *Christian Titles, a Series of Practical Meditations*, 1853; *Fellowship with Christ*, 1854; *The Rich Kinsman, or the History of Ruth*, 1855; *Memoir of Rev. E. P. J Messenger*, 1857; *The Captive Orphan, Esther, Queen of Persia*, 1859; *Forty Years' Experience in Sunday Schools*, 1860; *The Prayer-Book illustrated by Scripture*, 1865-67, 8 vols.; *The Child of Prayer: a Father's Memorial of D. A. Tyng*, 1866; *The Reward of Meekness*, 1867; *The Feast Enjoyed*, 1868; *The Spencers*, 1870; *The Office and Duty of a Christian Pastor*, 1874; many minor works, articles in periodicals, etc. *

U.

UHLHORN, Johann Gerhard Wilhelm, German Lutheran; b. at Osnabrück, Feb. 17, 1826; became *repetent* and *privat-docent* at Göttingen, 1852; consistorial councillor and court-preacher in Hanover, 1855; member of the consistory 1866, and abbot of Lokkum 1878. He is the author of *Exponuntur librorum symbolicorum*, Göttingen, 1848; *Fundamenta chronologiæ Tertullianeæ*, 1852; *Ein Sendbrief von Antonius Corvinus an den Adel von Göttingen . . . mit einer biographischen Einleitung*, 1853; *Die Homilien und Recognitionen des Clemens Romanus*, 1854; *Das basilidianische System mit besonderer Rücksicht auf die Angaben des Hippolytus*, 1855; *Urbanus Rhegius*, Elberfeld, 1861; *Zwei Bilder aus dem kirchlichen Leben der Stadt Hannover*, Hanover, 1867; *Das Weinachtsfest, seine Sitten und Bräuche*, 1869; *Das römische Concil*, 1870; *Der Kampf des Christenthums mit dem Heidenthum*, Stuttgart, 1874, 3d ed. 1879 (English trans. by Profs. E. Smith and C. J. H. Ropes, *The Conflict of Christianity with Heathenism*, N.Y., 1879); *Vermischte Vorträge über kirchliches Leben der Vergangenheit und der Gegenwart*, 1875; *Gnade und Wahrheit* (sermons), 1876, 2 vols.; *Die christliche Liebesthätigkeit:* 1 Bd. *Die alte Kirche*, 1881 (Eng. tr., Edinb., 1883); 2 Bd. *Das Mittelalter*, 1884. *

UPHAM, Francis William, LL.D. (Union College, Schenectady, N.Y., 1868), layman; b. at Rochester, Stafford County, N.H., Sept. 10, 1817; educated at Phillips Exeter Academy; graduated at Bowdoin College, Brunswick, Me., 1837; admitted to the bar of Massachusetts, on motion of Hon. Rufus Choate, 1844; was professor of mental and moral philosophy in Rutgers Female College, New-York City, 1867–70. He is the author of *The Debate between the Church and Science, or the Ancient Hebraic Idea of the Six Days of Creation; with an Essay on the Literary Character of Tayler Lewis* (published anonymously), Andover, 1860; *The Wise Men: who they were, and how they came to Jerusalem*, New York, 1869, 4th ed. 1872, London, 1873; *The Star of our Lord, or Christ Jesus King of all Worlds, both of Time and Space; with Thoughts on Inspiration, and the Astronomic Doubt as to Christianity*, 1873; *Thoughts on the Holy Gospels: how they came to be in Manner and Form as they are*, 1881.

UPHAM, Samuel Foster, D.D. (Mount Union College, O., 1872); Methodist; b. at Duxbury, Plymouth County, Mass., May 19, 1834; graduated at Wesleyan University, Middletown, Conn., 1856; pastor of the leading Methodist-Episcopal churches in New England from 1856 to 1881, when he became professor of practical theology in Drew Theological Seminary, Madison, N.J.

UPSON, Anson Judd, D.D. (Hamilton College, Clinton, N.Y., 1870), **LL.D.** (Union College, Schenectady, N.Y., 1880), Presbyterian; b. in Philadelphia, Penn., Nov. 7, 1823; graduated at Hamilton College, Clinton, N.Y., 1843, where he was tutor 1845–49; professor of rhetoric, 1849–70; from 1870 to 1880 he was pastor of Second Presbyterian Church, Albany, N.Y.; but since has been professor of sacred rhetoric and pastoral theology in Auburn Theological Seminary, N.Y; since 1874 he has been a regent in the University of the State of New York. He has published many addresses, sermons, and articles.

V.

VAIL, Right Rev. Thomas Hubbard, D.D. (Brown University, Providence, R.I., 1858), **LL.D.** (University of Kansas, Lawrence, Kan., 1875), Episcopalian; b. in Richmond, Va., Oct. 21, 1812; graduated at Washington (now Trinity) College, Hartford, Conn., 1831, and at the General Theological Seminary, New-York City, 1835; and after ministerial service in St. James's Church, Philadelphia, and Trinity Church, Boston, he organized All Saints' Church, Worcester, Mass., 1836; became rector of Christ Church, Cambridge, Mass., 1837; of St. John's Church, Essex, Conn., 1839; of Christ Church, Westerly, R.I., 1844; of St. Thomas's Church, Taunton, Mass., 1857; of Trinity Church, Muscatine, Io., 1863; first bishop of Kansas, 1864. As a Churchman he is evangelical, liberal, conservative. He edited, with memoir, Rev. Augustus Foster Lyte's *Buds of Spring* (poems, with additional poems of his own), Boston, 1838; and is the author of *Plan and Outline, with Selection of Books under Many Heads, of a Public Library in Rhode Island*, 1838; *Hannah: a Sacred Drama* (published anonymously), Boston, 1839; *The Comprehensive Church*, 1841, 3d ed. New York, 1883; *Reports* (of school committees in Massachusetts); sermons, charges, addresses, pastoral letters, etc.

VALENTINE, Milton, D.D. (Pennsylvania College, Gettysburg, Penn., 1866), Lutheran (General Synod); b. near Uniontown, Carroll County, Md., Jan. 1, 1825; graduated at Pennsylvania College, Gettysburg, Penn., 1850; became tutor in the college, 1850; pastoral supply, Winchester, Va., 1852; missionary at Allegheny, Penn., 1853; pastor at Greensburg, Penn., 1854; principal of Emmaus Institute, Middletown, Penn., 1855; pastor of St. Matthew's, Reading, Penn., 1859; professor of ecclesiastical history and church polity in the theological seminary of the Lutheran Church, Gettysburg, Penn., 1866; president of Pennsylvania College, 1868; has been president and professor of systematic theology in the Gettysburg Theological Seminary since 1884. He edited *The Lutheran Quarterly*, 1871-75, 1880-86. He is the author of *Natural Theology, or Rational Theism*, Chicago, 1885; numerous pamphlets and addresses; since 1855, frequent contributions in *The Evangelical Review* and in *The Lutheran Quarterly*.

VAN DYCK, Cornelius Van Alen, M.D. (Jefferson Medical College, Philadelphia, 1839), **D.D.** (Rutgers College, New Brunswick, N.J., 1865), Reformed (Dutch); b. at Kinderhook, N.Y., Aug. 13, 1818; educated at Kinderhook Academy, and in medicine at Jefferson Medical College, Philadelphia; appointed missionary of the A. B. C. F. M. for Syria, 1839; sailed from Boston, January, 1840; arrived at Beirut, April 2, 1840; was ordained by Syrian Mission in council, Jan. 14, 1846; principal of Missionary Seminary, 1848-52; then missionary in the Sidon field till 1857; translator of the Bible into Arabic from 1857, and manager of the Mission Press 1857-80; physician to St. John's Hospital, and professor of pathology in the Syrian Protestant College, Beirut, till 1882; since then physician to St. George's Hospital. He is "broad Calvinistic" in his theology. He taught Hebrew in Union Theological Seminary, New-York City, while superintending the printing of his translation of the Arabic Bible at the American Bible Society, 1866-67. He translated into Arabic, the *Westminster Assembly's Shorter Catechism*, Beirut, 1843, last ed. 1884; *Schönberg-Cotta Family*, 1885; and is the author in Arabic of *School Geography*, Beirut, 1850, 3d ed. 1886; *Algebra*, 1853, 2d ed. 1877; *Elements of Euclid*, 1857; *Treatise on Arabic Versification*, 1857; *Chemistry, Organic and Inorganic*, 1869; *Trigonometry and Logarithms* (with tables), 1873; *Mensuration, Surveying and Navigation*, 1873; *Astronomy*, 1874; *Physical Diagnosis*, 1874; *Pathology*, 1878; various tracts, etc.

VAN DYKE, Henry Jackson, D.D. (Westminster College, Mo., 1860), Presbyterian; b. at Abington, Montgomery County, Penn., March 2, 1822; graduated at University of Pennsylvania, Philadelphia, 1843; studied at Princeton Theological Seminary, N.J., 1843-44; became pastor at Bridgeton, N.J., 1845; at Germantown, Penn., 1852; and in Brooklyn, N.Y., 1853. In 1876 he was moderator of the General Assembly at Brooklyn. *

VAN DYKE, Henry Jackson, Jun., D.D. (College of New Jersey, Princeton, 1884), Presbyterian; b. at Germantown, Penn., Nov. 10, 1852; graduated at the College of New Jersey, Princeton, 1873, and at Princeton Theological Seminary 1877, of which latter institution, since 1884, he has been a director. He studied in Berlin University; became pastor of the United Congregational Church, Newport, R.I., 1879, and of the Brick Presbyterian Church, New-York City, 1882. Besides contributions to various periodicals, he has published *The Reality of Religion*, N.Y., 1884, 2d ed. 1885.

VAN VLECK, Henry Jacob, bishop of the Unity (Moravian); b. in Philadelphia, Jan. 29, 1822; graduated at Moravian Theological Seminary, Bethlehem, Penn., 1841; was teacher in Nazareth Hall, Northampton County, Penn., 1841-44; in the Moravian Parochial School, Salem, N.C., 1845-48; in Nazareth Hall, 1849-50; principal of the Moravian Parochial School at Nazareth, Penn., 1850-66; was ordained deacon at Nazareth, Penn., 1865; presbyter at Lititz, Penn., 1867; pastor at South Bethlehem, Penn., 1866-74; at Gnadenhütten, Fry's Valley, and at Ross, O., 1874-82; at Fry's Valley, O., since 1882; consecrated a bishop, Sept. 18, 1881, being appointed by the Provincial Synod of 1881, and the Unity Elders' Conference in Berthelsdorf, Germany, both appointments being sanctioned by "the Lot." Both his grandfather and father were bishops; a fact unprecedented in the Moravian Church.

VAUGHAN, Very Rev. Charles John, D.D. (Cambridge, 1845), dean of Llandaff, Church of England; b. at Leicester, Aug. 6, 1816; became scholar of Trinity College, Cambridge; Craven University scholar; Porson prizeman, 1836-37; Browne's medallist for Greek ode and epigrams, and Member's prizeman for Latin essay, 1837; chancellor medallist and B.A. (senior classic) 1838, M.A. 1841; was ordained deacon and priest 1841; was fellow of Trinity College, 1839-42; vicar of St. Martin, Leicester, 1841-44; head master of Harrow School, 1844-59; chaplain in ordinary to the Queen, 1851-79; vicar of Doncaster, and rural dean, 1860-69; chancellor of York Cathedral, 1860-71; select preacher at Cambridge 1861-82, and at Oxford 1875 and 1878. Since 1869 he has been master of the Temple, London; since 1879, dean of Llandaff; and since 1882, deputy clerk of the Closet. He was a member of the Cambridge University Commission 1858-62, and of the New Testament Revision Company 1870-81. He is the author of a number of volumes of sermons, parochial, academical, etc., and of *St. Paul's Epistle to the Romans*, London, 1859, 3d ed. 18—; *Memorials of Harrow Sundays*, 1859, 4th ed. 1885; *Lectures on Philippians*, 1862 (4th ed. 1883); *Revelation of St. John*, 1863, 5th ed. 1882; *Church of the First Days: Lectures upon the Acts of the Apostles*, 1863-65, 3 vols., 3d ed. 1878; *Temple Sermons*, 1881; *Authorized or Revised? Lectures on Texts differing in the Two Versions*, 1882; *Philippians* (translation, paraphrase, notes, etc.), 1885.

VENABLES, Edmund, Church of England; b. in London, July 5, 1819; educated at Merchant Taylors School, London (1830-38), and Pembroke College, Cambridge; graduated B.A. (wrangler and second-class classical tripos) 1842, M.A. 1845; ordained deacon 1844, priest 1846; was curate to Archdeacon Julius C. Hare, at Herstmonceux, 1844-53; curate of Bonechurch, Isle of Wight, 1853-55; examining chaplain to John Jackson, D.D. (d. 1885), while bishop of Lincoln, and chaplain while bishop of London; since 1867 has been canon residentiary and precentor of Lincoln Cathedral; since 1881, diocesan representative in the Society for the Propagation of the Gospel. He is an Evangelical High Churchman. From childhood he has been devoted to architectural and archæological pursuits: was one of the founders of the Cambridge Camden Society; one of the first members of the Archæological Institute. He edited his brother's translation of Bleek's *Introduction to the Old Testament*, London, 1869, 2 vols.; translated and edited Wieseler's *Chronological Synopsis of the Four Gospels*, 1876; edited, in the Clarendon Press series of English classics, Bunyan's *Pilgrim's Progress, Grace Abounding, Relation of the Imprisonment of Mr. John Bunyan*, Oxford, 1879; contributed articles *Luke, Matthew, Mark*, etc., to vols. ii. and iii. of W. L. Alexander's edition of Kitto's *Cyclopædia of Biblical Literature*, Edinburgh, 1862-66, 3 vols.; articles *Jude*, etc., to Smith's *Dictionary of the Bible*, London, 1863; articles *Catacombs, Coronation, Ecclesiastical Painting and Sculpture*, etc., to Smith and Cheetham's *Dictionary of Christian Antiquities*, 1875-80, 2 vols.; articles *Basil, Chrysostom, Gregorius Nyssenus, Theodoret*, etc., to Smith and Wace's *Dictionary of Christian Biography*, 1877-86, 4 vols.; article on *Teaching of the Twelve Apostles*, in *British Quarterly*, 1885; etc.

VINCENT, John Heyl, S.T.D. (Ohio Wesleyan University, Delaware, O., 1870), **LL.D.** (Washington and Jefferson College, Washington, Penn., 1885), Methodist; b. at Tuscaloosa, Ala., Feb. 23, 1832; received thorough early training in academies at Lewisburg and Milton, Penn., and in Newark (N.J.) Wesleyan Institute; was pastor at Newark, N.J., 1852; Franklin, N.J., 1853-54; Irvington, N.J., 1855-56; Joliet, Ill., 1857-58; Mt. Morris, Ill., 1858; Galena, Ill., 1859-61; Rockford, Ill., 1862-64; Chicago, Ill., 1865; Sunday-school agent, 1866-67; has been corresponding secretary of Sunday-School Union of Methodist-Episcopal Church, New-York City, since 1868; was superintendent of instruction at Chautauqua, N.Y., 1874-84; since then, chancellor of Chautauqua University. He is the author of *Sunday-school Institutes and Normal Classes*, New York, 1866, 2d ed. 1868; *The Church School and its Officers*, 1868; *The Chautauqua Movement*, 1886; *The Home Book*, 1886; many small manuals, lesson-helps, tracts, etc., e.g., *The Lesson Commentary on the International Sunday-school Lessons*.

VINCENT, Marvin Richardson, D.D. (Union College, Schenectady, N.Y., 1868), Presbyterian; b. at Poughkeepsie, N.Y., Sept. 11, 1834; graduated at Columbia College, 1854; became professor of Latin in Troy University, N.Y., 1858; pastor of First Presbyterian Church, Troy, 1863, and of the Church of the Covenant, New-York City, 1873. With Dr. Charlton T. Lewis he translated Bengel's *Gnomon of the New Testament*, Philadelphia, 1862; and has since written, besides tracts, articles, and the minor volumes, *Amusement a Force in Christian Training* (1867), *The Two Prodigals* (1876), and *The Expositor in the Pulpit* (1884), *Gates into the Psalm-country* (expository discourses), 1878, last ed. 1883; *Stranger and Guest* (five tracts), New York, 1879; *The Minister's Handbook*, 1882; *In the Shadow of the Pyrenees* (travels), 1883; *God and Bread* (sermons), 1884.

VOGEL, (Karl) Albrecht, German Protestant; b. in Dresden, Saxony, March 10, 1822; studied at Leipzig and at Berlin; became *privat-docent* at Jena 1850, and later professor extraordinary; ordinary professor at Vienna, 1861. He is the author of *Ratherius von Verona und das 10. Jahrhundert*, Jena, 1854, 2 parts; *Peter Damiani*, 1856; *Der Kaiser Diokletian*, Gotha, 1857; *Beiträge zur Herstellung der alten lateinischen Bibel-Uebersetzung*, Vienna, 1867; *Die Semi-säcularfeier d. k.k. evangelisch-theologisch. Facultät in Wien*, 1872. *

VOIGT, Heinrich Johann Matthias, German Protestant; b. at Oldenburg, Aug. 2, 1821; studied at Halle, Berlin, and Göttingen; became a pastor, and then in 1864 ordinary professor of theology, at Königsburg. He is the author of *Die Lehre des Athanasius von Alexandrien*, Bremen, 1861; *Fundamentaldogmatik*, Gotha, 1874. *

VOLCK, Wilhelm, Ph.D., Lic. Theol., D.D. (all Erlangen; 1859, 1861, 1870, respectively), German Lutheran; b. at Nuremberg, Nov. 18, 1835; studied at Erlangen and Leipzig, 1853-58; became *privat-docent* at Erlangen, 1861; professor extraordinary of the Semitic languages in the theological faculty at Dorpat, 1862; ordinary professor, 1864. He is the author of *Kalendarium syriacum auctore Cazwinio*, Leipzig, 1859; *Mosis canticum cygneum* (Deut. xxxii.), Nördlingen, 1861; *Ibn Mâliks Lamiyat al af'âl. Arabischer Text*, Leipzig, 1865; *Vindiciæ Danielicæ*, Dorpat, 1866; *Der Chiliasmus seiner neuesten Bekämpfung gegenüber*, 1869; *De summa carminis Iobi sententia*, 1869; *Der Segen Mosis untersucht und ausgelegt*, Erlangen,

1873; *In wie weit ist der h. Schrift Irrthumslosigkeit zuzuschreiben?* 1884, 2d ed. same year; *Festrede, zur Jahresfeier der Stiftung der Universität Dorpat*, 1884; *Die Bibel als Kanon*, 1885. He contributed sections *Kanonik* and *Hermeneutik*, to Zöckler's *Handbuch*, Nördlingen, 1883 sqq.; edited the ninth volume of Hofmann's *Die heilige Schrift N. T.* (Nördlingen, 1881), and with Mühlau the eighth to tenth editions of Gesenius' *Heb. u. chald. Handwb.*, Leipzig, 1878, 1882, 1886.

VOLKMAR, Gustav, Swiss Protestant; b. at Hersfeld, Hessia, Jan. 11, 1809; studied at Marburg, 1829–32; taught in various places; became *privat-docent* at Zürich 1853, professor extraordinary 1858, and ordinary professor 1863. He is the author of *Das Evangelium Marcions*, Leipzig, 1852; *Ueber Justin den Märtyrer und Sein Verhältniss zu unsern Evangelien*, Zürich, 1853; *Die Quellen der Ketzergeschichte bis zum Nicänum, kritisch untersucht*, 1855 (1st vol.); *Die Religion Jesu und ihre Entwickelung*, Leipzig, 1857; *Das vierte Buch Esra und apokalyptische Geheimnisse überhaupt*, Zürich, 1858; *Handbuch der Einleitung in die Apokryphen*, Tübingen, 1860–63 (1st part); *Commentar zur Offenbarung Johannis*, Zürich, 1862; *Der Ursprung unserer Evangelien*, 1866; *Mose Prophetie und Himmelfahrt*, Leipzig, 1867; *Die Evangelien des Marcus und die Synopses d. kan. u. ausserkan. Evangelien, mit Com.*, 1869, 2d ed. 1876; *Zwingli, sein Leben und Wirken*, Zürich, 1870; *Die römische Papstmythe*, 1873; *Die Herkunft Jesu Christi nach der Bibel selbst*, 1874; *Die neutestamentlichen Briefe erklärt*, 1. Bd. 1875; *Die Kanon. Synoptiker . . . u. das Geschichtliche vom Leben Jesu*, 1876; *Jesus Nazarenus und die erste christliche Zeit*, 1882; *Die neuentdeckte urchristliche Schrift "Lehre der Zwölf Apostel,"* 1st and 2d ed. 1885; edited *Polycarpi Smyrnæi epistola genuina*, 1885. *

VOYSEY, Charles, theist; b. in London, March 18, 1828; educated at St. Edmund Hall, Oxford; graduated B.A., 1851; held various curacies; was vicar of Healaugh, Yorkshire, 1864–71; deprived Feb. 11, 1871, in consequence of rationalistic views upon the Bible; and has since lectured and preached independently in London. His sermons are published weekly, and in several volumes under title, *The Sling and the Stone*, London, 1868, sqq., vol. viii., 1881; *Mystery of Pain, Death, and Sin*, 1879; also *Fragments from Reimarus*, vol. i., 1879.

W.

WACE, Henry, D.D. (Oxford, 1883; Edinburgh, 1882), Church of England; b. in London, Dec. 10, 1836; educated at Brasenose College, Oxford; graduated B.A. (second class in classics and mathematics) 1860, M.A. 1873, B.D. 1882; was ordained deacon 1861, priest 1862; was curate of St. Luke's (1861-63), and of St. James's (1863-69), London; lecturer of Grosvenor Chapel, 1870-72; chaplain of Lincoln's Inn, 1872-80; Boyle lecturer, 1874-75; professor of ecclesiastical history in King's College, 1875-83; select preacher at Cambridge, 1878; Bampton lecturer at Oxford 1879, and select preacher 1880-82. Since 1880 he has been preacher at Lincoln's Inn; since 1881, prebendary in St. Paul's Cathedral; since 1883, chaplain to the archbishop of Canterbury, and principal of King's College; and since 1884, honorary chaplain in ordinary to the Queen. He is the author of *Introduction to the Pastoral Epistles*, in the *Bible Commentary;* and of *Christianity and Morality* (Boyle Lectures), London, 1876, 7th ed. 1886; *The Foundations of Faith* (Bampton Lectures), 1880, 2d ed. 1881; *The Gospel and its Witnesses: some of the Chief Facts in the Life of our Lord*, 1883, 2d ed. 1884; *The Student's Manual of the Evidences of Christianity*, 1886; joint editor with Dr. William Smith of *A Dictionary of Christian Biography, Literature, Sects, and Doctrines, from the Time of the Apostles to the Age of Charlemagne*, 1880-86, 4 vols.; with Professor Buchheim, of *The First Principles of the Reformation, or the Primary Works of Luther*, 1884; and alone of *The Bible* (Speaker's) *Commentary on the Apocrypha*, 1886, 2 vols.

WADDINGTON, Charles, French Reformed; b. in Paris, June 19, 1819; became doctor of letters in Paris, 1818; taught philosophy in the Sorbonne, 1850-56; at Strassburg, 1856-64; and since in the Paris faculty. Among his works may be mentioned *Ramus, sa vie, ses écrits, et ses opinions*, Paris, 1855; *Essais de logique* (crowned by the Academy), 1857; *De l'âme humaine*, 1862; *De la philosophie de la Renaissance*, 1872; *De l'autorité d'Aristote au moyen âge*, 1877. He is a founder of the Société de l'histoire du protestantisme français (1852), and a chevalier of the Legion of Honor (1866). *

WAGENMANN, Julius August, German Protestant; b. at Berneck, Würtemberg, Nov. 23, 1823; studied at Tübingen, 1841-45; became *repetent* at Blaubeuren 1846, and at Tübingen 1849; *diakonus* at Göppingen 1852, *archidiakonus* 1857; ordinary professor of theology at Göttingen 1861, and there became consistorial councillor 1878.

WALDEN, John Morgan, D.D. (Farmers' College, Belmont, O., 1865), **LL.D.** (McKendree College, Ill., 1878), Methodist; b. at Lebanon, Warren County, O., Feb. 11, 1831; graduated at Farmers' (now Belmont) College, Hamilton County, O., 1852; was principal of the preparatory department of the same, 1852-54; editor, 1854-58; entered the ministry in the Cincinnati Conference, 1858; was pastor 1858-64 (in Cincinnati, O., 1860-64); corresponding secretary of the Western Freedmen's Aid Committee, 1863-66; corresponding secretary of the Freedmen's Aid Committee of the Methodist-Episcopal Church, 1866-67; presiding elder of the East Cincinnati district, 1867-68; agent of the Western Methodist Book Concern, Cincinnati, O., 1868-84; elected bishop, May 15, 1884. Since 1847 he has been identified with temperance reform. He was a prominent antislavery man; established in 1857 at Quindaro, Kan., a paper to promote Free State principles; was a member of the Topeka (Kan.) Legislature, and of the Leavenworth Constitutional Convention, and author of its address to the country; member of the Board of Education, Cincinnati; chairman of the Library Board after re-organization of the Public Library, in which he was active; sent teachers to the contrabands in the Mississippi Valley, early in 1863, and has been ever since officially connected with educational work in the South. He was a delegate to the General (Methodist-Episcopal) Conferences of 1868, 1872, and 1876; and to the Methodist Œcumenical Council, London, Eng., 1881.

WALDENSTRÖM, Paul Petter, Swedish Lutheran Church; b. at Luleå, a town in the northern part of Sweden, July 20, 1838; graduated as Ph.D. at the University of Upsala 1863; ordained 1864; became head master of gymnasium at Umeå 1864, and of that at Gefle 1874. He came into conflict with Lutheran Orthodoxy in 1872, upon the doctrine of the atonement, in regard to which he holds that the reconciliation through Christ is of us to God, not of God to us; not *per gratiam propter Christum salvatio*, but *propter gratiam per Christum*. The *subject* is God, the Father of Christ; the *source* is the love of God; the *object* is the whole world; the *mediator* is Christ, the only begotten God, the Son of God; the end is the restitution of men to God, not the redemption of God to men. His subsequent writings in defence of his position have excited great interest, and stirred up a great controversy. He is also a leader in the Free-Church movement in Sweden, and in consequence frequently prosecuted by the Upsala Consistory. He resigned his clerical position in the State Church in 1880. For baptizing two children in September, 1884, he was prosecuted by the Consistory, but by appeal to the king he was cleared. He is a member of the Swedish Parliament. [His eloquence renders him an attractive and powerful preacher, and the Free-Church movement owes much to him. See M. W. MONTGOMERY, *A Wind from the Holy Spirit in Sweden and Norway*, New York, 1884.] Of his numerous and highly popular writings, all in Swedish, may be mentioned, *Sermons over the New Pericopes of the Swedish Church*, Stockholm, 1868-80, 4 vols.; *The Lord is Holy*, 1875 (reprinted in Chicago, Ill.), and translated into German (Leipzig, 1877); *The Eternal Decree of Election*, 1880 sqq., 3 vols.; *The History of Infant-Baptism; The New Testament, newly translated, with Notes*, 1883 sqq.

WALKER, Right Rev. William David, S.T.D. (Racine College, Wis., 1883; Columbia College, New-York City, 1884), Episcopalian, missionary bishop of North Dakota; b. in the city of New York, June 29, 1839; graduated at Columbia College, New-York City, 1855, and at the General Theological Seminary there 1862; as deacon, took charge of Calvary Chapel, New-York City, October, 1862; ordained priest, June 29, 1863; remained in charge of Calvary Chapel until Feb. 1, 1884, when he resigned to enter upon his episcopate to which he was elected October, 1883; consecrated bishop, Dec. 20, 1883. He is the author of *Funeral Address*, New York, 1868; *Convocation Address*, 1884.

WALSH, Right Rev. William Pakenham, D.D. (Trinity College, Dublin, 1873), lord bishop of Ossory, Ferns, and Leighlin; b. in Ireland, about the year 1820; educated at Trinity College, Dublin; graduated B.A. 1841, M.A. 1853, B.D. 1873; ordained deacon 1843, priest 1844; became curate of Avoca, 1843; of Rathdrum, 1845; chaplain of Sandford, 1858; dean of Cashel, 1873; bishop, 1878. He is the author of *Christian Missions* (Donellan Lectures for 1861), Dublin, 1862; *The Moabite Stone*, 1872, 2d ed. 1873; *"Put me in Remembrance:" Prayers*, 1872; *The Forty Days of the Bible, and their Teachings*, 1874; *The Angel of the Lord, or Manifestations of Christ*, 1875; *Daily Readings for Holy Seasons, Advent to Epiphany*, 1875; *Ancient Monuments and Holy Writ*, 1878, 2d ed. 1878; *Heroes of the Mission-Field*, 1879, 2d ed. 1882; *The Decalogue of Charity*, 1882. *

WALTHER, Carl Ferdinand Wilhelm, D.D. (Capital University, Columbus, O., 1877), Lutheran (Missouri Synod); b. at Langenchursdorf, Saxony, Oct. 25, 1811; graduated at the University of Leipzig 1833; emigrated in 1838; and since 1849 has been professor of theology, and president of Concordia Seminary, and pastor of the Evangelical Lutheran joint congregation, St. Louis, Mo. [He is the founder and leader of the Missouri Synod, the most orthodox branch of the Lutheran Church in America, and which has grown very rapidly.] He is the author of *Die Stimme unserer Kirche in der Frage von Kirche und Amt*, Erlangen, 1852, 3d ed. 1875; *Die rechte Gestalt einer vom Staate unabhängigen ev. luth. Ortsgemeinde*, St. Louis, 1863, 2d ed. 1880; *Die ev. luth. Kirche die wahre sichtbare Kirche Gottes auf Erden*, 1867; *Americanisch-Luth. Evangelien-Postille*, 1871, 9th ed. 1883 (Norwegian trans., Bergen, 1878); *Americanisch-Lutherische Pastoraltheologie*, 1872, 3d ed. 1885; *Lutherische Brosamen* (sermons and speeches), 1876; *Der Concordienformel Kern und Stern. Mit einer geschichtl. Einleitung*, 1877, Norwegian ed. Decorah, Io., 1877; *Joh. Guil. Baieri Compendium Theologiæ positivæ* (edited), 1879, 3 vols.; *Americanisch-Luther. Epistel-Postille*, 1882; *Goldkörner*, Zwickau, 1882.

WARD, James Thomas, D.D. (Adrian College, Mich., 1871), Methodist Protestant; b. at Georgetown, D.C., Aug. 21, 1820; studied at Columbian Academy, Washington, D.C., and at Brookeville Academy, Md., 1836-38; entered the ministry, August, 1840; served charge at East Washington, D.C., 1840-41; united with the Maryland Annual Conference; appointed to Pipe Creek Circuit, Frederick County, Md., 1841; Williamsport Circuit, Washington County, Md., and Berkeley County, Va., 1842; and to Cumberland City, Md., 1845; edited *The Columbian Fountain*, a daily and weekly temperance journal, at Washington, D.C., 1846-47; was pastor in Philadelphia, 1848-56; Uniontown, Md., 1857-59; Alexandria, Va., 1860-62; Libertytown, Md., 1863-64; Washington, D.C., 1865-66; president of Western Maryland College, Westminster, Carroll County, Md., 1867-86; since, president of the Westminster Theological Seminary in the same place. He is the author of *A Tribute to the Memory of George Alexander Johnson*, Philadelphia, 1853; *Thanksgiving Day and Christmas* (sermon and poem), Baltimore, 1885; several pamphlets; many contributions to church periodicals, including a series of sketches and reminiscences of ministers in *The Methodist Recorder*, 1884, etc.

WARD, Julius Hammond, Episcopalian; b. at Charlton, Worcester County, Mass., Oct. 12, 1837; graduated at Yale College, New Haven, Conn., 1860; educated at Berkeley Divinity School, Middletown, Conn.; was rector of Christ Church, Ansonia, Conn., 1862-65; of St. Peter's, Cheshire, Conn., 1865-67; missionary at Rockland and Thomaston, Me., 1867-75; rector of St. Michael's, Marblehead, Mass., 1875-78; since then has been a constant writer on religious subjects in the secular and religious press. He is the author of *Life and Letters of James Gates Percival*, Boston, 1866; *The Modern Church*, and *The Bible in Modern Thought* (both preparing); and numerous articles, etc.

WARD, William Hayes, D.D. (University of New-York City, and College of New Jersey, Princeton, both 1873), **LL.D.** (Amherst College, Mass., 1885), Congregationalist; b. at Abington, Mass., June 25, 1835; educated at Phillips Academy, Andover, Mass., and at Amherst College, Mass.; graduated B.A., 1856; studied in Union Theological Seminary, New-York City, 1856-57; in the Sheffield Scientific School, New Haven, Conn., 1857; was tutor in Beloit College, Wis., 1857-58; in Andover Theological Seminary, Mass., 1858-59 (graduated); was pastor at Oskaloosa and Grasshopper Falls, Kan., 1859-61; teacher in Williston Seminary, Easthampton, Mass., 1861; at Utica, N.Y., 1862-64; professor of Latin, Ripon College, Wis., 1865-67; associate editor *New-York Independent*, 1868-71; has been superintending editor since 1871. He was director of the Wolfe Exploration to Babylonia, 1884-85. He edited (with Mrs. Lanier) Sidney Lanier's *Poems*, New York, 1884; has contributed to *Bibliotheca Sacra, Journal American Oriental Society, Proceedings Palestine Exploration Society*, etc.

WARFIELD, Benjamin Breckinridge, D.D. (College of New Jersey, Princeton, 1880); Presbyterian; b. at Lexington, Ky., Nov. 5, 1851; graduated at Princeton College 1871, and Theological Seminary 1876; since 1879 has been professor of New-Testament language and literature at Western Theological Seminary, Allegheny, Penn. He has written several review articles.

WARNECK, Gustav, Ph.D. (Jena, 1870), **D.D.** (*hon.*, Halle, 1883), German Protestant; b. at Naumburg, Germany, March 6, 1834; studied at the University of Halle, 1855-58; became *hilfsprediger* at Roitzsch, 1862; *archidiaconus* at Dommitzsch, 1863; *missionsinspector* at Barmen, 1871; pastor at Rothenschirmbach, near Eisleben, 1874.

He has edited the *Allgemeine Missions Zeitschrift*, Gütersloh, since 1874. He is the author of *Pontius Pilatus, der Richter Jesu Christi*, Gotha, 1867; *Nacht und Morgen auf Sumatra*, Barmen, 1872, 2d ed. 1873; *Christiane Kähler, Eine Diakonissin auf dem Missionsfelde*, 1873, 3d ed. 1882 (translated into Dutch); *Briefe über die Versammlungen in Brighton*, Hamburg, 1876; *Die apostolische und die moderne Mission*, Gütersloh, 1876 (translated into Dutch); *Das Studium der Mission auf der Universität*, 1877; *Die Belebung des Missionssins in der Heim* ·. 1878 (translated into Swedish); *Missionsstunden*, I. 1878, 2d ed. 1883 (translated into Dutch and Swedish), II. 1884, 2d ed. 1886 (translated into Swedish); *Die gegenseitigen Beziehungen zwischen der modernen Mission und Kultur*, 1879 (translated into Dutch; into English by Thomas Smith, *Modern Missions and Culture*, Edinburgh, 1883); *Warum ist das 19. Jahrhundert ein Missionsjahrhundert?* Halle, 1880; *Warum hat unsere Predigt nicht mehr Erfolg?* Gütersloh, 1880, 5th ed. 1882 (translated into Dutch, French, Swedish, Danish); *Abriss einer Geschichte der protestantischen Missionen*, Leipzig, 1882, 2d ed. 1883 (translated into Dutch, French, and Swedish; into English, *Outline of the History of Protestant Missions*, Edinburgh, 1884); *Protestantische Beleuchtung der römischen Angriffe auf die evangelische Heidenmission: Ein Beitrag zur Charakteristik ultramontaner Geschichtschreibung*, Gütersloh, 1884–85, 2 parts; *Welche Pflichten legen uns unsere Colonien auf?* Heilbronn, 1885; and of many articles and pamphlets upon foreign missions.

WARNER, Zebedee, D.D. (Otterbein University, Westerville, O., 1878), United Brethren in Christ; b. in Pendleton County, Va. (now in West Virginia), Feb. 28, 1833; studied at Clarksburg (Va.) Academy, left in 1852; graduated in Chautauqua Sunday-School Normal Course, 1879; entered on pastoral work, 1854; was presiding elder, 1862–69; in charge of church at Parkersburg, W. Va., 1869–80; presiding elder of the district, 1880–85; elected corresponding secretary of the General Missionary Society, 1885. He has been elected seven times to the General Conference; was for two years president of the Eastern Sunday-School Assembly; was for eight years teacher of theology in Parkersburg Conference; has been since 1858 a trustee of Otterbein University. He is the author of *Christian Baptism*, Parkersburg, W. Va., 1864; *Rise and Progress of the United Brethren Church*, 1865; *Life and Times of Rev. Jacob Bachtel*, Dayton, O., 1867; *The Roman Catholic not a True Christian Church*, Parkersburg, W. Va., 1868.

WARREN, Henry White, D.D. (Dickinson College, Carlisle, Penn., 1872), bishop of the Methodist-Episcopal Church; b. at Massachusetts, 18—; graduated at Wesleyan University, Middletown, Conn., 1853; taught natural science at Amenia, N.Y., and ancient languages at Wilbraham, Mass., ——; joined the New-England Conference in 1855; was stationed at Westfield, Lynn, Worcester, Charlestown, Cambridge, twice in Boston, all Mass.; was transferred to Philadelphia Conference, 1871; to New-York East, 1874; to Philadelphia, 1877; elected bishop, 1880. He was in evangelical work in the South, 1880–84; was delegate to Pan-Methodist Council in London, 1881. He is the author of *Sights and Insights* (travels in Europe and the East), New York, 1874; *Recreations in Astronomy*, 1879.

WARREN, Israel Perkins, D.D. (Iowa College, Grinnell, Io., 1868), Congregationalist; b. at Bethany, Conn., April 8, 1814; graduated at Yale College, New Haven, Conn., 1838; principal of Cromwell (Conn.) Academy, 1838-39; studied at Yale Theological Seminary, 1839–40; became pastor at Granby, Conn., 1842; Mt. Carmel, Conn., 1846; Plymouth, Conn., 1851; corresponding secretary of American Seamen's Friend Society, New-York City, 1856; secretary and editor of the American Tract Society, Boston, 1859; editor and book publisher in Boston, 1870; editor of *The Christian Mirror*, of Maine, October, 1875; editor and proprietor of the same, Portland, Me., April 1, 1877. In 1859, when the controversies on slavery, which at length eventuated in the civil war, were at their height, the American Tract Society of Boston withdrew from its connection with the society of the same name at New York, and commenced a distinct publication work of its own. Mr. Warren, who had had some editorial experience in connection with his work for seamen, was chosen secretary of the Boston society, in charge of its publication department. In this capacity he served eleven years, until May, 1870, when the causes which led to the separation of the two societies having disappeared, it was deemed advisable to re-unite them, and transfer the publishing work and material of the Boston society to that of New York. During this period a very large number of tracts, books, and periodicals, were issued under his editorial care. *The Tract Journal* and *Child at Home* were published for families, and for several years *The Sabbath at Home*, an illustrated monthly magazine. *The Christian Banner* was distributed in great numbers in the army and navy. *The Freedman* and *The Freedman's Journal* were small monthly sheets for the use of the emancipated blacks. About five hundred different tracts and pamphlets were issued, and five hundred and twenty-five volumes of various sizes, making an aggregate, including periodicals, of 55,672,276 copies. In addition to the ordinary uses of this class of publications, there was a very wide distribution among the soldiers and sailors in service; and another, of matter provided specially for them, among the freedmen, to aid in the incipient stages of their education. The entire cost of these publications, from May 1, 1859 to May 1, 1870, was $1,002,997.06. Dr. Warren is the author of the following publications: Sermons, *On Female Education* (Hartford, 1852), *On the Death of Mrs. Mary Langdon of Plymouth* (June, 1853), *On Finished Work: Pastoral Valedictory* (January, 1856). Tracts and pamphlets, *A Corpse in a Ball-dress* (Boston, 1859), *The Pemberton Mill* (1860), *How to Begin to be a Christian* (1861), *A Happy New Year* (1864), *The Flag of our Country* (1864), *The Death of the Soul* (1867, pp. 28), *How to Repent* (1867, pp. 31), *How to Believe* (1867, pp. 32). Bound volumes, *The Seamen's Cause: embracing the History, Results, and Present Condition of the Efforts for the Moral Improvement of Seamen*, New York, 1858; *The Sisters, a Memoir of Elizabeth H., Abbie A., and Sarah F. Dickerman*, Boston, 1859 (often reprinted); *Sadduceeism, a Refutation of the Doctrine of the Annihilation of the Wicked*, 1860, pp. 66 (the same work re-written and republished under the title, *The Wicked not Annihilated*, 1866, pp. 76); *The Cross-Bearer, a Vision*, 1861; *The Picture Lesson-Book*, 1861 (designed for the use of the refugee slaves in the camps, and believed to be the first book ever printed for the special benefit of that class), pp. 32; *Life of Governor Briggs* (for distribution among the soldiers), 1861, pp. 48; *Snow-Flakes: A Chapter from the Book of Nature*, 1863; *The Freedman's Primer, or First Reader*, 1864, pp. 64; *The Freedman's Second Reader*, 1864, pp. 160; *The Christian Armor*, 1864; *The Cup-Bearer*, 1865; *The Freedman's Third Reader*, 1865, pp. 264; *The Freedman's Spelling-Book*, 1865, pp. 160; *The Sabbath at Home: An Illustrated Religious Magazine for the Family*, 1867–69, 3 vols.; *The New Testament, with Notes, Pictorial Illustrations, and References*; vol. i., *The Four Gospels, with a Chronological Harmony*, 1867; the same work, enlarged by the addition of the *Acts of the Apostles*, 1871; *Jerusalem, Ancient and Modern, a Descriptive Book of Selous' two Pictures of that City, containing a detailed account of nearly two hundred points of interest in the pictures, a résumé of the recent explorations in the city, and outlines of its topography, history, and antiquities*, 1873, pp. 64; *The Three Judges, Story of the Men who beheaded their King* (with an introduction by Rev. Leonard Bacon, D.D., New York, 1873; *Chauncey Judd, or The Stolen Boy of the Revolution*, 1874; *The Parousia, A Critical Study of the Scripture Doctrines of Christ's Second Coming, his Reign as King, the Resurrection of the Dead, and the General Judgment*, Portland, Me., 1879, 2d ed. (re-written and enlarged) 1884; *Our Father's Book, or The Divine Authority and Origin of the Bible*, Boston, 1885; *The Book of Revelation, a Study*, New York, 1886; *The Stanley Families in America*, 8vo., Portland (in press).

WARREN, William Fairfield, D.D. (Ohio Wesleyan University, Delaware, 1862), **LL.D.** (Wesleyan University, Middletown, Conn., 1874), Methodist; b. at Williamsburg, Mass., March 13, 1833; graduated at Wesleyan University, Middletown, Conn., 1853; entered the Methodist ministry, 1854; studied at Berlin and Halle, and travelled in Europe and the East, 1856–58; was professor of systematic theology in the Methodist Missionary Institute at Bremen, 1861–66; acting president of Boston Theological Seminary, and professor of systematic theology, 1866–71; dean of the School of Theology, Boston University, 1871–73; since 1873 has been president of Boston University, and professor of comparative history of religions, comparative theology, and philosophy of religion. He is the author of *Anfangsgründe der Logik*, Bremen, 1863; *Systematische Theologie*, 1 Theil., 1865; *Paradise Found; the Cradle of the Human Race at the North Pole: a Study of the Prehistoric World*, Boston, 1885, 5th ed. same year; and many reports, pamphlets, articles, etc. See list in *Wesleyan University Alumni Record*. *

WASHBURN, George, D.D. (Amherst College, Mass., 1874), Congregationalist; b. at Middleborough, Mass., March 1, 1833; graduated at Amherst College, Mass., 1855; studied in Andover Theological Seminary, 1855–56; from 1858 to 1868 was missionary of A.B.C.F.M. in Turkey, and since 1869 has been president of Robert College, and professor of philosophy and political economy, Constantinople. Circumstances brought him into very intimate relations with the political events in Europe connected with the last Russo-Turkish war, and secured him the personal friendship of many English statesmen. The first Bulgarian parliament passed a resolution thanking him for what he had done to secure liberty for Bulgaria and for the elevation of the Bulgarian people. He is a commander of the Order of St. Alexander (Bulgaria). He has written much for American periodicals under his own name, and also much for English reviews under assumed names.

WATSON, Right Rev. Alfred Augustin, D.D. (University of North Carolina, Chapel Hill, N.C., 1868; University of the South, Sewanee, Tenn., 1884), Episcopalian, bishop of East Carolina; b. in New-York City, Aug. 21, 1818; graduated at the University of the City of New York, 1857; admitted to the bar of the Supreme Court of the State of New York, 1841; ordered deacon in the diocese of New York, 1844; ordained priest in the diocese of North Carolina, 1845; in charge of Grace Church, Plymouth, N C., and St. Luke's, Washington County, N.C., 1844–58; rector of Christ Church, New Berne, N.C., 1858–65; chaplain in the Confederate Army, 1861–62; in charge of St. James's Parish, Wilmington, N.C., 1863–84; consecrated bishop, 1884. He is the author of occasional sermons.

WATSON, Frederick, Church of England; b. in York, Oct. 13, 1844; educated at St. John's College, Cambridge; graduated B.A. (twelfth wrangler) 1868, M.A. 1871, B.D. 1884; was ordained deacon 1871, priest 1872; was first-class theological and Hulsean prizeman, 1869; Carus Greek Testament prizeman and Crosse scholar, 1870; first Tyrwhitt scholar, 1871; fellow of St. John's College, 1871–78; theological lecturer, 1874–78; Hulsean lecturer, 1882; since 1878 he has been rector of Starston, Norfolk. He is the author of *The Ante-Nicene Apologies*, Cambridge, 1870; *Defenders of the Faith*, 1878; *The Law and the Prophets* (Hulsean Lectures), 1883.

WATTS, Robert, D.D. (Westminster College, Missouri, 1865), Irish Presbyterian; b. at Moneylane, County Down, Ireland, July 10, 1820; graduated at Washington College, Lexington, Va., 1849, and at Princeton Theological Seminary, N.J., 1852; became pastor in Philadelphia, Penn., 1853, and in Dublin, Ireland, 1863; and in 1866, professor of systematic theology, Assembly's College, Belfast, Ireland. He is the author of *Calvin and Calvinism*, Edinburgh, 1866; *Utilitarianism*, Belfast, 1868; *What is Presbyterianism?* 1870; *Prelatic Departures from Reformation Principles*, Edinburgh, 1871; *Arminian Departures from Reformation Principles*, 1871; *Atomism*, Belfast, 1874; *Herbert Spencer's Biological Hypothesis*, 1875; *Atomism*, London, 1875; *The Doctrine of Eternal Punishment*, Belfast, 1877; *The New Apologetic*, Edinburgh, 1879; *The Newer Criticism*, 1881; *The Rule of Faith and the Doctrine of Inspiration*, London, 1885.

WAYLAND, Heman Lincoln, D.D. (Brown University, Providence, R.I., 1869), Baptist; b. (son of President Francis Wayland) at Providence, R.I., April 23, 1830; graduated in Brown University there, 1849; studied at Newton Theological Institution, Mass., 1849–50; taught the academy at Townshend, Vt., 1850–51; was resident graduate at Brown University, 1851-52; tutor at University of Rochester, N.Y., 1852-54; pastor of the Third Baptist Church, Worcester, Mass., 1854-61; chaplain of the Seventh Connecticut Volunteers, 1861-64; home missionary at Nashville, Tenn., 1864-65; professor of rhetoric and logic in Kalamazoo College, Mich., 1865-70; president of Franklin College, Ind., 1870-72; editor of *The National Baptist*, Philadelphia, since 1872. He is the author of *Life and Labors of Francis Wayland* (with his brother Francis Wayland), New York, 1867, 2 vols.; and of numerous contributions to periodicals.

WEAVER, Jonathan, D.D. (Otterbein University, Westerville, 1873), bishop of the United Brethren in Christ; b. in Carroll County, O., Feb. 23, 1824; raised on a farm; educated in common schools and Hagerston Academy, O.; began preaching when twenty-one; was pastor, 1847-52; presiding elder, 1852-57; general agent for Otterbein University, 1857-65; bishop since 1865, re-elected five times; now in Ohio diocese. He is the author of *Discourses on the Resurrection*, Dayton, O., 1871, two editions; *Ministerial Salary*, 1873, two editions; *Divine Providence*, 1873, three editions; *Universal Restoration not sustained by the Word of God*, 1878, two editions.

WEIDNER, Revere Franklin, b. at Centre Valley, Lehigh County, Penn., Nov. 22, 1851; graduated at Muhlenberg College, Allentown, Penn., and at the Evangelical Lutheran Theological Seminary at Philadelphia; pastor at Phillipsburg, N.J., 1873-78; also professor of English and history at Muhlenberg College, 1875-77; pastor at Philadelphia, 1878-82; and since 1882 professor of dogmatics and exegesis at Augustana Theological Seminary (Swedish Lutheran), Philadelphia. He is a member of the American Philological Association, of the American Oriental Society, and of the Society of Biblical Literature and Exegesis; author of a *Commentary on Mark* (Philadelphia, 1881), and of a *Theological Encyclopædia* (Part I., *Introduction, and exegetical Theology*, Philadelphia, Penn.; 1885, Part II., *Biblical theology of the Old Testament*, Chicago, 1886), and a frequent contributor to reviews and the religious press.

WEIFFENBACH, Ernst Wilhelm, German Protestant; b. at Bornheim, Rhenish Hesse, May 25, 1842; studied at Giessen, Utrecht, and Heidelberg, 1859-65; became *privat-docent* at Giessen, 1868; professor extraordinary, 1871; professor in the *Prediger-seminar* of Hesse Darmstadt, 1882. He is the author of *Exegetisch-theologische Studie über Jacobus ii. 14-26*, Giessen, 1871; *Der Wiederkunftsgedanke Jesu*, Leipzig, 1873; *Das Papias-Fragment bei Eusebius*, Giessen, 1874; *Die Papias-Fragmente über Marcus u. Matthäus*, Berlin, 1878; *Zur Auslegung der Stelle Phil. ii. 5-11*, Carlsruhe, 1884. *

WEINGARTEN, Hermann, German Protestant; b. in Berlin, March 12, 1834; studied at Jena and Berlin; became *privat-docent* at Berlin, 1862; professor extraordinary, 1862; ordinary professor at Marburg 1873, and at Breslau 1876. He is the author of *Pascal als Apologet des Christenthums*, Leipzig, 1863; *Die Revolutionskirchen Englands*, 1868; *Zeittafeln zur Kirchengeschichte*, Berlin, 1870, 2d ed. Leipzig, 1874; *Der Ursprung des Mönchthums im nachconstantinischen Zeitalter*, Gotha, 1877; and editor of Richard Rothe's *Vorlesungen über Kirchengeschichte*, Tübingen, 1875, 2 parts. *

WEISS, Bernhard, D.D., German Protestant; b. at Königsberg, June 20, 1827; studied there and at Halle and Berlin; became *privat-docent* at Königsberg, 1852; professor extraordinary, 1857; ordinary professor at Kiel 1863, and at Berlin 1877, where, since 1880, he has been superior consistorial councillor, and councillor to the department of spiritual affairs. He is the author of *Der petrinische Lehrbegriff*, Berlin, 1855; *Der Philipperbrief*, 1859; *Der johanneische Lehrbegriff*, 1862; *Lehrbuch der biblischen Theologie des N.T.*, 1868, 4th ed. 1884; *Das Marcusevangelium u. seine synoptischen Parallelen*, 1872; *Das Matthäusevangelium und seine Lucas-Parallelen*, Halle, 1876; *Ueber die Bedeutung der geschichtlichen Betrachtung für die neuere Theologie*, Kiel, 1876 (pp. 21); *Das Leben Jesu*, Berlin, 1882, 2 vols., 2d ed. 1884 (English trans. Edinburgh, 1883-84, 3 vols.). Dr. Weiss has revised and rewritten Meyer's Commentary on Matthew (Göttingen, 1883), Mark and Luke (1878), John (1880), and Romans (1881), Timothy and Titus (1885).

WEISS, Hermann, D.D. (*hon.*, Tübingen, 1877), German Protestant; b. at Rottenburg, Würtemberg, Sept. 29, 1833; studied at the Maulbronn Evangelical Seminary 1847-51, and at Tübingen 1851-55; was *repetent* at Tübingen, 1858-61; *diaconus* and *bezirkschulinspector* at Vaihingen and Nürtingen, 1863-75; since 1875 has been ordinary professor of theology at Tübingen. He was a member of the first Würtemberg evangelical *Landessynode*, 1878. He is the author of *Sechs Vorträge über die Persone Christi*, Ingolstadt, 1863; *Ueber die hauptsächlichsten Bildungsideale der Gegenwart*, Tübingen, 1876 (pp. 35); *Die christliche Idee des Guten und ihre modernen Gegensätze*, Gotha, 1877; essays and critical articles in *Theol. Studien und Kritiken* since 1861.

WEIZSÄCKER, Karl (Heinrich) von, German Protestant; b. at Öhringen, Würtemberg, Dec. 11, 1822; became *privat-docent* of theology 1847, preacher 1848, and court chaplain 1851, at Stuttgart; superior consistorial councillor, 1857; and in 1861 Baur's successor in the theological faculty at Tübingen. From 1856 to 1878 he edited the *Jahrbücher für deutsche Theologie*, and in it wrote numerous articles. He is also the author of *Zur Kritik des Barnabasbriefes aus dem Codex Sinaiticus*, Tübingen, 1863; *Untersuchungen über die evangelische Geschichte*, Gotha, 1864; *Lehrer und Unterricht an der evangelisch-theologischen Facultät der Universität Tübingen von der Reformation bis zur Gegenwart*, Tübingen, 1877. *

WELCH, Ransom Bethune, D.D. (University of City of N.Y., and Rutgers College, 1868), **LL.D.** (Maryville College, Tenn., 1872), Presbyterian; b. at Greenville, N.Y.; graduated from Union College 1846, and from Auburn Theological Seminary 1852; was (Reformed Dutch) pastor at Gilboa 1854-56, and at Catskill, N.Y., 1856-59; professor of rhetoric, logic, and English literature in Union College, New York, 1866-76, and since 1876 of theology in Auburn Theological Seminary. He is the author of *Faith and Modern Thought*, New York, 1876, 2d ed. 1880; *Outlines of Christian Theology*, 1881; and numerous articles in periodicals.

WELLES, Right Rev. Edward Randolph, S.T.D. (Racine College, Wis., 1874), Episcopalian, bishop of Wisconsin; b. at Waterloo, Seneca County, N.Y., Jan. 10, 1830; graduated at Hobart College, Geneva, N.Y., 1850; studied theology with Rev. Dr. Wilson of Geneva, under direction of Bishop De Lancey, by whom he was ordered deacon, and ordained priest; was tutor of De Veaux College, Suspension Bridge, N.Y., with Sunday services at Lewiston, Lockport, and this town, 1857–58; rector of Christ Church, Red Wing, Minn., 1858–74; dean of the Southern Convocation in Minnesota; member of standing committee; trustee of Bishop Seabury University, Minnesota; deputy to General Convention from diocese of Minnesota; consecrated bishop, 1874.

WELLHAUSEN, Julius, b. at Hameln-on-the-Weser, May 17, 1844; studied at Göttingen under Heinrich Ewald, 1862–65; became there *privat-docent* of theology, 1870; ordinary professor at Greifswald, 1872; professor in the philosophical faculty at Halle, 1882; at Marburg, 1885. His theological position is "*Polytheismus und Monotheismus zugleich.*" He says that he left the theological faculty at Greifswald in 1882 of his accord ("*freiwillig*") "*in dem Bewusstsein, durchaus nicht mehr auf dem Boden der evangelichen Kirche oder des Protestantismus zu stehen.*" He is the author of *Text der Bücher Samuels*, Göttingen, 1871; *Pharisaeer und Sadducaeer*, Greifswald, 1874; *Prolegomena zur Geschichte Israels*, Berlin, 1878, 3d ed. 1886; *Skizzen und Vorarbeiten*, I. 1884, II. 1885.

WELTON, Daniel Morse, Ph.D. (Leipzig, 1878), **D.D.** (Acadia College, Nova Scotia, 1884), Baptist; b. at Aylesford, Kings County, Nova Scotia, July 20, 1831; graduated at Acadia College, N.S., 1855; studied as resident graduate there, 1855–56; at Newton Theological Institution, 1856–57; at Leipzig, Germany, 1876–78; was pastor of the Baptist Church at Windsor, N.S., 1857–74; professor of theology, University of Acadia College, 1874–83; of Semitic languages and Old-Testament interpretation, Toronto Baptist College, Can., 1883 to date. He is the author of *John Lightfoot, or the History of Hebrew Learning in England*, Leipzig, 1878 (doctor's dissertation).

WENDT, Hans Hinrich, Ph.D. (Tübingen, 1875), **D.D.** (Göttingen, 1883), German Protestant; b. in Hamburg, June 18, 1853; studied at Tübingen; became *privat-docent* of theology at Göttingen, 1877; professor extraordinary, 1881; ordinary professor at Kiel, 1883, at Heidelberg, 1885. He is the author of *Die Begriffe Fleisch und Geist im biblischen Sprachgebrauch*, Gotha, 1878; (edited 5th edition of Meyer's) *Commentar über die Apostelgeschichte*, Göttingen, 1880; *Die christliche Lehre von der menschlichen Vollkommenheit*, 1882; *Die Lehre Jesu*, first part (*Die evangelischen Quellenberichte über die Lehre Jesu*), 1886.

WERNER, Karl, D.D. (Vienna, 1845), Roman Catholic; b. at Hafnerbach, Lower Austria, March 8, 1821; graduated at the University of Vienna; taught theology and philosophy in the Episcopal Seminary at St. Pölten, 1847–70, and New-Testament theology in the University of Vienna, 1871–82. He is *k.k. Ministerialrath*, and member of the Vienna Imperial Academy of Sciences. Besides numerous articles upon mediæval scholasticism and recent Italian philosophy, he has written *System der christlichen Ethik*, Regensburg, 1850–52, 3 vols.; *Grundlinien der Philosophie*, 1855; *Der heilige Thomas von Aquino*, 1858–59, 3 vols.; *Grundriss einer Geschichte der Moralphilosophie*, Vienna, 1859; *Franz Suarez u. die Scholastik der letzten Jahrhunderte*, Regensburg, 1860–61, 2 vols.; *Geschichte der apologetischen und polemischen Literatur der christlichen Theologie*, Schaffhausen, 1862–67, 5 vols.; *Enchiridion theol. moral.*, Vienna, 1863; *Ueber Wesen und Begriff der Menschenseele*, Brixen, 1865, 3d ed. Schaffhausen, 1867; *Geschichte der katholischen Theologie Deutschlands seit dem Trienter Concil*, Munich, 1866; *Speculative Anthropologie*, 1870; *Religionen u. Culte des vorchristlichen Heidenthums*, Schaffhausen, 1871; *Beda der Ehrwürdige und seine Zeit*, Vienna, 1875, 2d ed. 1881; *Alcuin und sein Jahrhundert*, 1876, 2d ed. 1881; *Gerbert von Aurillac, die Kirche und Wissenschaft seiner Zeit*, 1878, 2d ed. 1881; *Giambattista Vico als Philosoph und gelehrter Forscher*, 1879, 2d ed. 1881; *Die Scholastik des späteren Mittelalters*, 1881 sqq., vol. iii. 1883; *Die italienische Philosophie d. XIX. Jahrhunderts*, 1884 sqq., vol. v. 1886.

WEST, Robert, Congregationalist; b. at Coal Run, Washington County, O., Sept. 14, 1845; graduated at Lane Theological Seminary, Cincinnati, O., 1870; became pastor of the First Cong. Church, Alton, Ill., 1872; superintendent of home missions in the South-West for the American Home Missionary Society, 1876–81; pulpit supply in Boston, 1881–82; editor-in-chief of *The Advance* (Congregational organ), Chicago, July, 1882.

WESTCOTT, Brooke Foss, D.D. (Cambridge, 1870; *hon.*, Edinburgh, 1884), **D.C.L.** (*hon.*, Oxford, 1881), Church of England; b. near Birmingham, Jan. 12, 1825; was educated at Trinity College, Cambridge; Battie University scholar, 1846; Browne medallist for Greek ode, 1846–47; Latin essay (Undergraduate Bach.), 1847, 1849; B.A. (equal senior classic, twenty-second wrangler, and chancellor's medallist) 1848, M.A. 1851, B.D. 1864; was ordained deacon and priest, 1851; was elected fellow of Trinity College, 1849; was Norrisian prizeman, 1850; assistant master at Harrow School, 1852–69; examining chaplain to the bishop of Peterborough, 1868–83; canon residentiary, 1869–83; rector of Somersham with Pidley and Colne, Hunts, 1870–82; honorary chaplain to the Queen, 1875–79; select preacher at Oxford, 1877–80. Since 1870 he has been regius professor of divinity, Cambridge; since 1879, chaplain in ordinary to the Queen; since 1882, fellow of King's College, Cambridge; since 1883, examining chaplain to the archbishop of Canterbury; and since 1884, canon of Westminster. In May, 1885, he declined the deanery of Lincoln. He was a member of the New-Testament Revision Company (1870–81), is a contributor to the *Bible* (Speaker's) *Commentary* (Gospel of John), to Smith's *Dictionary of the Bible* and *of Christian Biography*; and is the author of *Elements of Gospel Harmony*, Cambridge, 1851 (Norrisian essay); *A General Survey of the History of the Canon of the New Testament during the first four centuries*, London, 1855, 5th ed. 1881; *Characteristics of the Gospel Miracles*, 1859; *Introduction to the Study of the Gospels*, 1860, 6th ed. 1882; *The Bible in the Church*, 1864, 9th ed. 1885; *The Gospel of the Resurrection*, 1866, 5th ed. 1884; *A General View of the History of the English Bible*, 1868; *Christian Life Manifold and One* (sermons), 1872; *Some Points in the Religious Office of the Universities*, 1873; *The Paragraph Psalter, arranged for the use of choirs*, Cambridge, 1879, 2d ed. 1881; *The Revelation of the Risen Lord*, London, 1882; *The Gospel according *to St. John* (from *Bible Comm.*), 1882, 2d ed. 1884; *The Historic Faith* (lectures on the Apostles' Creed), 1883, 3d ed. 1885; *Epistles of St. John, Greek Text, Notes, and Essays*, 1883, 2d ed. 1886; *Revelation of the Father: titles of the Lord*, 1884. Conjointly with Rev. Prof. Dr. Hort, he edited *The New Testament in the Original Greek*, 1st and 2d ed. 1881, 2 vols.: school edition of text alone, 1885. [See HORT.]

WESTON, Henry Griggs, D.D. (University of Rochester, N.Y., 1859), Baptist; b. at Lynn, Mass., Sept. 11, 1820; graduated at Brown University, Providence, R.I., 1840, and at Newton Theological Institution, Mass, 1843; after serving as pastor from 1843 to 1868, he became president of Crozer Theological Seminary, Pennsylvania.

WHEDON, Daniel Denison, D.D. (Emory and Henry College, 1847), **LL.D.** (Wesleyan University, 1868); b. at Onondaga, N.Y., March 20, 1808; d. at Atlantic Highlands, N.J., June 8, 1885. He graduated at Hamilton College, Clinton, N.Y., 1828; studied law at Rochester, N.Y.; became a teacher in Oneida (N.Y.) Conference Seminary; a tutor in Hamilton College, 1831; professor of ancient languages and literature in Wesleyan University, Middletown, Conn., 1833; Methodist pastor, 1843; professor of rhetoric, logic, and history, in the University of Michigan, Ann Arbor, 1845; again in the pastorate, at Jamaica, L.I., N.Y., 1855; elected by General Conference of the Methodist-Episcopal Church, editor of *The Methodist Quarterly Review*, 1856, and re-elected quadrennially until May, 1884, when his health, which had long been feeble, forbade his continued holding of the position. He was a man of learning, literary ability, and great industry. He was the author of *Public Addresses, Collegiate and Popular*, Boston, 1856; *Commentary on Matthew and Mark*, New York, 1860; *The Freedom of the Will, as a Basis of Human Responsibility, elucidated and maintained in its Issue with the Necessitarian Theories of Hobbes, Edwards, the Princeton Essayists, and other Leading Advocates*, 1864, 3d ed. same year; *Commentary on the New Testament: intended for popular use*, 1860–75, 5 vols.; and editor of a *Commentary on the Old Testament*, 1880 sqq., of which the seventh vol. (Jeremiah) appeared in 1886; published many single sermons and addresses, contributions in the *Bibliotheca Sacra*, and other periodicals, etc. *

WHEELER, David Hilton, D.D. (Cornell College, Mount Vernon, Io., 1867), **LL.D.** (North-western University, Evanston, Ill., 1881), Methodist; b. at Ithaca, N.Y., Nov. 18, 1829; graduated at Rock-River Seminary, Mount Morris, Ill., 1851; tutor in same, 1851–53; professor of ancient languages, Cornell College, Mount Vernon, Io., 1853–55; editor of *Carroll County Republican*, 1855–57; superintendent of Carroll County schools, 1855–57; professor of Greek, Cornell College, 1857–61; United-States consul, Genoa, Italy, 1861–66; war correspondent in Austro-Italian war, 1866; commissioner of correspondence of *New-York Tribune*, 1866–67; professor of English literature, North-western University, Evanston, Ill., 1867–75; editor of *The Methodist*, New York, 1875–82; president of Allegheny College, Meadville, Penn., 1883 to date. He has written extensively for the periodical press since 1855. He is the author of *Brigandage in South Italy*, London, 1864, 2 vols.; *Celesia's Conspiracy of Fieschi* (translation), 1866; *By-Ways of Literature*, New York, 1883.

WHIPPLE, Right Rev. Henry Benjamin, A.M. (*hon.*, Hobart College, Geneva, N.Y., 18—), **D.D.** Racine College, Wis., 1859), Episcopalian; b. at Adams, Jefferson County, N.Y., Feb. 15, 1822; educated at private schools, but prevented by ill health from entering college; engaged in business; became a candidate for orders, 1847; rector of Zion Church, Rome, N.Y., 1849; of the Church of the Holy Communion, Chicago, Ill., 1857; bishop, 1859. He has written tracts and letters on the Indian policy of the United States.

WHITAKER, Right Rev. Ozi William, D.D. (Kenyon College, Gambier, O., 1869), Episcopalian, assistant bishop of Pennsylvania; b. at New Salem, Mass., May 10, 1830; studied in Amherst College, Mass., 1851–52; graduated from Middlebury College, Vt., 1856, and from the General Theological Seminary, New-York City, 1863; became missionary in Nevada, 1863; rector of St. Paul's Church, Englewood, N.J., 1865; of St. Paul's Church, Virginia City, Nev., 1867 to 1886; missionary bishop of Nevada, 1869; assistant bishop of Penn., 1886. Author of *Occasional Sermons*.

WHITE, Erskine Norman, S.T.D. (University of the City of New York, 1874), Presbyterian; b. in New-York City, May 31, 1833; graduated at Yale College, New Haven, Conn., 1854, and at Union Theological Seminary, N. Y. City, 1857; became pastor at Richmond, Staten Island, N.Y., 1859; New Rochelle, 1862; Buffalo, 1868; New York (W. 23d St.), 1874. In 1886 he became corresponding secretary of the Board of Church Erection of the Presbyterian Church. He has written several review articles, etc., and a history of the West Twenty-third Street Church.

WHITEHEAD, Right Rev. Cortlandt, D.D. (Union College, Schenectady, N.Y., 1880), Episcopalian, bishop of Pittsburgh; b. in New-York City, Oct. 30, 1842; graduated at Phillips Academy, Andover, Mass., 1859; at Yale College, New Haven, Conn., 1863; and at Philadelphia Divinity School, 1867; became missionary at Black Hawk and Georgetown, Col., 1867; rector of the Church of the Nativity, South Bethlehem, Penn., 1870; bishop, 1882. He was assistant secretary of Diocesan Convention of Central Pennsylvania, 1872–82; deputy to General Convention, 1877–80; trustee of St. Luke's Hospital, Lehigh University, and Bishopthorpe School, South Bethlehem; trustee of Western University, Pittsburgh, Penn.

WHITON, James Morris, Ph.D. (Yale College, New Haven, Conn., 1861), Congregationalist; b. in Boston, Mass., April 11, 1833; educated in Boston Latin School, and graduated at Yale College 1853; was rector of Hopkins Grammar School, New Haven, Conn., 1854–64; pastor of the First Congregational Church, Lynn, Mass., 1865–69; of the North Congregational Church, Lynn, 1869–75; principal of Williston Seminary, Easthampton, Mass., 1876–78; pastor of First Congregational Church, Newark, N.J., 1879–85; acting pastor of the Trinity Congregational Church, Tremont, New-York City, 1886. His theological standpoint is that of a Trinitarian Christian evolutionist; regarding the Trinity, interpreted through the principle of the Divine immanency as the biblical symbol which sets forth the being and the relation of God to the world, as the fundamental and comprehensive article of faith. Creation, revelation, and judgment are eternal Divine processes, all manifested in the world of the past, present, and future. Redemption is essentially a constructive rather than a reconstructive process. Atonement is the Divine process of the reconciliation of man to God, by an expiatory satisfaction — mediated through the historical experience of the Christ, producing an adequate repentance — to that which is of God in conscience. The norm of conscience for faith, duty, and hope, is in the Holy Scriptures, whose authority as a divine revelation centres in the living Word of God, the Christ, speaking therein. The promised advent of the Christ is now being progressively realized in the life of the world that now is, and the resurrection likewise in the life of the world to come. He is the author of *Latin Lessons*, Boston, 1860; *Greek Lessons*, New York, 1861; *Select Orations of Lysias*, Boston, 1875, 2d ed. 1881; "*Is Eternal Punishment Endless?*" 1876, 2d ed. 1877 (maintaining that endless punishment is not decisively revealed in the New Testament: it raised a question as to his further fellowship in the Congregational body, which was decided in his favor by a council at Newark, 1879, — twenty-eight to three, cf. stenographic report in *The Congregationalist*, April 12, 1879); *Six Weeks' Preparation for Reading Cæsar*, 1877, 3d ed. 1886; *Auxilia Vergiliana* (pamphlet), 1878, 2d ed. 1886; *Essay on the Gospel according to Matthew*, 1880; *The Gospel of the Resurrection*, 1881, reprinted in London, Eng., under title *Beyond the Shadow*, 1884; *Early Pupils of the Spirit* (pamphlet), Lond., 1884; *Three Months' Preparation for Reading Xenophon* (published in conjunction with his daughter Mary B. Whiton), N. Y., 1885; *The Evolution of Revelation* (pamphlet), 1885; *The Divine Satisfaction*, London, 1886; frequent contributions to the religious journals, occasional articles in *The New-Englander*, etc.

WHITSITT, William Heth, D.D. (Mercer University, Macon, Ga., 1874), Baptist; b. near Nashville, Tenn., Nov. 25, 1841; studied at Union University, 1857-60); was first private, then chaplain, in the Confederate Army, 1861-65; studied at the University of Virginia, Charlottesville, Va., 1866, and at the Southern Baptist Seminary (then at Greenville, S.C., since 1877, at Louisville, Ky.), 1867-69; at Leipzig, 1869-70; and at Berlin, 1870-71; was pastor at Albany, Ga., February-July, 1872; professor of biblical introduction and ecclesiastical history in the Southern Baptist Theological Seminary, 1872 to date. He has published *The Relation of Baptists to Culture* (his inaugural address, published in *The Baptist Quarterly*, 1872); *History of the Rise of Infant Baptism*, Louisville, Ky., 1878; *History of Communion among Baptists*, 1880.

WHITTLE, Right Rev. Francis McNeece, D.D. (Theological Seminary of Ohio, Gambier, O., 1867), **LL.D.** (College of William and Mary, Williamsburg, Va., 1873), Episcopalian, bishop of Virginia; b. in Mecklenburg County, Va., July 7, 1823; graduated at the Theological Seminary of Virginia, near Alexandria, 1847; became rector of Kanawha Parish, Kanawha County, Va., 1847; St. James's, Northern Parish, Goochland County, 1849; Grace, Berryville, 1852; St. Paul's, Louisville, Ky., 1857; assistant bishop of Virginia, 1868; bishop, 1876.

WIBERG, Andreas, Baptist; b. in the parish of Tuna, province of Helsingland, in the North of Sweden, July 17, 1816; graduated at the University of Upsala, 1843, and received holy orders the same year at the same place; took the S.C. "pastoral degree" at Upsala in 1847; received the degree of M.A. from the University of Lewisburg, Penn., U.S.A., in 1854; was minister in the Lutheran State Church of Sweden, 1843-1851; colporter evangelist in the service of the American Baptist Publication Society among sailors in New York, and immigrants in the West of the U.S.A., 1852-1853; Baptist missionary in Sweden, 1855 to date. He is the author, in Swedish, of "Who is to be baptized?" Upsala, 1852; "Christian Baptism as set forth in the Holy Scriptures" (published both in English and Swedish), Philadelphia, U.S.A., 1854, 3d ed. Philadelphia, 1873; "Translation of the Gospel according to St. Matthew, with Commentary," Stockholm, 1858; "The Evangelist" (bi-monthly), 1856-73; "The Doctrine of the Holy Scripture on Sanctification," 1868; "The Doctrine of Justification," 1869; "Come to Jesus," 1869; "Unity of Christians," 1878; "Reply to Prof. P. Waldenstrom's Book, History of Infant Baptism," 1880; "The Victorious Reign of Christ," Kristianen, 1883; "The Church," Kristianen, 1884.

WIESELER, Karl, Lic. Theol. (Göttingen, 1839), **D.D.** (*hon.*, Kiel, 1846), German theologian; b. at Altenzelle, near Celle, Hannover, Feb. 28, 1813; d. at Greifswald, March 11, 1883. He was the second son of Pastor Christian Christoph Wieseler, and younger brother of the well-known Friedrich Wieseler, professor of philology and archæology at Göttingen. In his seventh year both his parents died; and he was brought up by near relatives, who first thought to make him a forester. He attended the gymnasium at Salzwedel from 1826 to 1831; then the university of Göttingen, where he was especially influenced by Lücke, from 1831 to 1835. In the latter he became *repetent*, 1836; *privat-docent* of Old and New Testament exegesis, 1839; professor extraordinary there, 1843; ordinary professor at Kiel, 1851; at Greifswald, 1863. In 1870 he was made *Consistorialrath* and member of the Pommeranian Consistory at Stettin, and discharged these latter duties, in connection with those of his professorship, until his death. He was the author of *De christiano capitis pœnæ vel admittendæ vel repudiandæ fundamento* (prize essay), Göttingen, 1835; *Num loci Mk. xvi. 9-20 et Jo. 21 genuini sint nec ne indogatur eo fine, ut aditus ad historiam apparitionum J. Christi site conscribendam aperiatur*, 1839; *Auslegung und Kritik der apokalyptischen Literatur des A. u. N. T.*, 1 Beitrag. *Die 70 Wochen und die 63 Jahrwochen des Propheten Daniel, erörtert und erläutert mit steter Rücksicht auf die biblischen Parallelen sowie Geschichte und Chronologie, nebst einer historisch-kritisch Untersuchung über den Sinn, etc., der Worte Jesu von s. Parusie in den Evang.*, 1839; *Chronologische Synopse der vier Evangelien, ein Beitrag zur Apologie der Evangelien und evangelischen Geschichte vom Standpunkte der Voraussetzunglosigkeit*, Hamburg, 1843 (English trans., *Chronology of the Four Gospels*, London, 1864; another trans. by E. Venables, *A Chronological Synopsis of the Four Gospels*, London, 1876, 2d ed. 1878. His chief results are: birth of Jesus, 750 A.U.C.; imprisonment of the Baptist, Purim 782 A.U.C.; day of Jesus' death, April 7, 783 A.U.C., or 30 A.D.); *Chronologie des apostolischen Zeitalters bis zum Tode* *der Apostel Paulus and Petrus*, Göttingen, 1848 (chief results: stoning of Stephen, about 39 A.D.; conversion of Paul, 40 A.D.; apostolic council at Jerusalem, about 50 A.D.; beginning of the third Pauline missionary journey, 54 A.D.; duration of the Cæsarean and Roman imprisonment, 58–64 A.D. He rejects the theory of the second Roman imprisonment of Paul, and dates the pastoral epistles partly from the third missionary journey, especially in the Ephesian residence of the apostle, and partly from the end of his Roman imprisonment); *Exercitationum criticarum in Clementis Romani quæ feruntur homilias*, 1857; *Commentar über den Brief Pauli an die Galater*, 1859; *Eine Untersuchung über den Hebräerbrief, namentlich seinen Verfasser und seine Leser*, Kiel, 1860–61, 2 halves; *Beiträge zur richtigen Würdigung der Evangelien und der evangelischen Geschichte*, Gotha, 1869 (a reproduction of the principal contents of his *Chronolog. Synopse*); *Geschichte des Bekenntnissstandes der lutherischen Kirche Pommerns bis zur Einführung der Union*, Stettin, 1870; *Der Abschnitt Röm. vii. 7–25 exegetisch und biblisch-theologisch erörtert*, Greifswald, 1875 (pp. 16); *Die deutsche Nationalität der kleinasiatischen Galater*, Gütersloh, 1877; *Die Christenverfolgungen der Cäsaren bis zum 3. Jahrhundert historisch und chronologisch untersucht*, 1878; *Zur Geschichte der neutestamentlichen Schrift und des Urchristenthums*, Leipzig, 1880 (contains three essays: 1. The Corinthian parties, and their relation to the false teachers mentioned in Galatians, Romans, and Revelation; 2. The teaching and structure of the Epistle to the Romans; 3. The author, date, and mode of interpretation, of the Johannean revelation); *Untersuchungen zur Geschichte und Religion der alten Germanen in Asien und Europa, mit religionsgeschichtl. Parallelen*, 1881. Articles in periodicals, of especial value, may be mentioned, *Die Lehre des Hebräerbriefs und der Tempel von Leontopolis* (in *Theol. Studien und Kritiken*, 1867, IV.), in which he defends his book on *Hebrews*, although on some points presenting a different opinion; *Das 4 Buch Ezra* (do., 1870), *Das Todesjar Polykarps* (do., 1880), *Die Assumptio Mosis* (in *Jahrb. f. d. Theologie*, 1868), *Der Barnabasbrief* (do., 1870), *Der Clemensbrief an die Korinther* (do., 1877), *Ueber einige Data aus dem Leben Luthers* (in Kahnis' *Zeitschrift für historische Theologie*, 1874, IV.), discussing the dates of his birth, entrance into the convent, and journey to Rome; articles in Herzog, etc. Cf. art. *Wieseler*, by Zöckler, in Herzog [2], xvii. 100–104. *

WIKNER, Carl Pontus, Ph.D. (Upsala, 1883), Lutheran; b. in the parish of Ryr, province of Dal, Sweden, May 19, 1837; educated at the University of Upsala; became *Lektor* in theology and Hebrew at the Elementary School of Upsala, 1873; vice-professor of theoretical philosophy at the University of Upsala, 1869; professor of philosophy at the University of Christiania, Norway, 1884. He has received the prize of King Charles Johan XIV., "for literary merits." Nominally Lutheran, he is an independent religious philosopher of strong caliber. He is the author (in Swedish) of "Investigations on Unity and Diversity," Upsala, 1863; *De imagine Dei, dissert. theol.*, 1873; "Can Philosophy confer any Blessing on Mankind?" 1864, 2d ed. same year; "What we Need," 1865; "Can we get any Knowledge of God?" 1865; "The Curse of Nature," 1866; "Sketch of Anthropology," 1867; "Culture and Philosophy," 1869; "Manual of Anthropology," 1870; "Investigations on the Materialistic Views of the Universe," 1870; "Essays on Religious Subjects," 1871; "On Authority and Independence," 1872; "Thoughts and Questions before the Son of man," 1872; "Religious Meditations and Sermons" (vols. i.–iii.), 1873–75.

WILBERFORCE, Right Rev. Ernest Roland, D.D. (by diploma 1882, *hon.*, Durham, 1882), lord bishop of Newcastle-on-Tyne, Church of England, the third son of the late bishop of Winchester; b. at Brigstone (Brixton), Isle of Wight, Jan. 22, 1840; educated at Exeter College, Oxford; graduated B.A. 1864, M.A. 1865; ordained deacon 1864, priest 1865; was curate of Cuddesdon, 1864–66; chaplain to late bishop (Wilberforce) of Oxford, 1864–69; curate of Lea, Lincolnshire, 1866; rector of Middleton Stony, Oxford, 1866–69; domestic chaplain to late bishop (Wilberforce) of Winchester, 1869–73; sub-almoner to the Queen, 1871–82; canon of Winchester, and warden of the Wilberforce Missionary College, Winchester, 1878–82; consecrated bishop, 1882. *

WILKES, Henry, D.D. (University of Vermont, Burlington, 1850), **LL.D.** (McGill University, Montreal, Can., 1870), Congregationalist; b. at Birmingham, Eng., June 21, 1805; studied at Glasgow University and Glasgow Theological Academy (Congregational), 1829–33; graduated at the University, M.A., 1833; was pastor of Congregational Church, Albany Street, Edinburgh, 1833–36; in Montreal, Can., 1836–71; principal and professor of theology in the Congregational College of British North America, 1870–83; since 1883, professor of theology and church history in the same. He represented the Colonial Missionary Society, London, Eng., 1836–83. He became member of the University Institute, University of Vermont, Burlington, 1850; Φ Β Κ, Dartmouth College (Hanover, N.H.), Chapter 1862; Cliosophic Society, College of New Jersey, Princeton, 1873; He is the author of *The Internal Administration of the (Congregational) Churches*, Montreal, 1858, 3 editions; numerous sermons, college addresses, etc.

WILKINSON, William Cleaver, D.D. (University of Rochester, N.Y., 1873), Baptist; b. at Westford, Vt., Oct. 19, 1833; graduated at the University of Rochester, N.Y., 1857, and at the Rochester Theological Seminary, 1859; was pastor of Second Baptist Church, New Haven, Conn., 1859–61; professor *ad interim* of modern languages in University of Rochester, N.Y., 1863–64; Mt. Auburn Church, Cincinnati, 1865–66; professor of homiletics and pastoral theology, Rochester Theological Seminary, New York, 1872–81. He was offered the chair of the German language and literature in University of Michigan, Ann Arbor, 1871; also of English literature there, 1873. He has been from the beginning (1878) one of the "counsellors" of the Chautauqua Literary and Scientific Circle, and is "dean" of the department of literature and art in the Chautauqua School of Theology. He is the author of *The Dance of Modern Society*, 1868, last ed. 1884; *A Free Lance in the Field of Life and Letters* (essays), 1874, last ed. 1882; *Preparatory Greek Course in English*, 1882; *Preparatory Latin Course in English*, 1883; *College Greek Course in English*,

1884; *College Latin Course in English*, 1885 (the four books constitute "The After-school Series," of which, up to 1886, more than a hundred thousand volumes had been sold); *Poems*, 1883; *Edwin Arnold as Poetizer and as Paganizer*, 1885.

WILLCOX, Giles Buckingham, D.D. (University of the City of New York, 1881), Congregationalist; b. in New-York City, Aug. 7, 1826; graduated at Yale College, New Haven, Conn., 1848, and Andover Theological Seminary, Mass., 1851; became pastor at Fitchburg, Mass., 1853; Lawrence, 1856; New London, Conn., 1859; Jersey City, N.J., 1869; Stamford, Conn., 1875; professor of pastoral theology and special studies in Chicago Theological Seminary, 1879. He has contributed frequently to religious periodicals.

WILLIAMS, Right Rev. Channing Moore, S.T.D. (Columbia College, New-York City, 1867), Episcopalian, missionary bishop of Yedo, Japan; b. at Richmond, Va., July 18, 1829; graduated from the College of William and Mary, Virginia, 1853, and from the Theological Seminary of Virginia, near Alexandria, 1855; became missionary bishop of China (with jurisdiction in Japan), 1866; relieved by the General Convention of 1874 of the China mission, and his title changed to that of missionary bishop of Yedo, with jurisdiction in Japan. *

WILLIAMS, George, Church of England, layman, the founder of the Young Men's Christian Association; b. at a farmhouse in the parish of Dulverton, Somersetshire, Eng., Oct. 11, 1821. Having completed his education, he began his business-life at Bridgewater. There he was converted in 1837, and immediately endeavored to lead his associates to Christ. In this he was so successful that a considerable number professed religion. In 1841 he became a junior assistant in the dry-goods establishment of Messrs. George Hitchcock & Co., 72 St. Paul's Churchyard, London. Finding that the majority of his fellows (there were some 120 in all) were indifferent to religion, while many were licentious, in 1843 he induced a few of the spiritually minded assistants to hold with him, at regular intervals, a prayer-meeting in a bedroom of the establishment, — it being then customary for clerks to occupy rooms in the business houses where they were employed, — for the conversion of their fellow-clerks; and out of that meeting originated the Young Men's Christian Association movement. Mr. George Hitchcock, their principal, who had been converted since Mr. Williams came, having mentioned these meetings to his friend Mr. W. D. Owen, proprietor of a large drapery establishment in the West End, the latter spoke of them to Mr. James Smith, his principal assistant, who immediately commenced similar meetings amongst the young men. In the spring of 1844, Mr. Williams was impressed with the importance of introducing similar meetings in all the large establishments of London. He broached the subject, first of all, to his most intimate friend and fellow-assistant, the late Mr. Edward Beaumont, on a Sunday evening in the latter part of May, 1844. The following week, after the prayer-meeting, three or four of the most zealous remained behind for conversation upon the subject; and it was then resolved to call a meeting of all the religious young men of the establishment, to meet on Thursday, June 6, 1844, to consider the importance and practicability of establishing a society for improving the spiritual condition of young men engaged in the drapery and other trades. At this meeting the following persons were present: Messrs. George Williams, C. W. Smith, James Smith (from Mr. Owen's, by invitation of Mr. Williams), Norton Smith, Edward Valentine, Edward Beaumont, —— Glasson, Francis John Cockett, Edward Rogers, John Harvey, John C. Symons, William Creese. Mr. James Smith was chosen chairman; Mr. Valentine, treasurer; and Messrs. Symons and Creese, secretaries. It was decided to form the projected society; and Mr. C. W. Smith, being delegated to choose a name for it, suggested among others that of *The Young Men's Christian Association*, which was afterwards adopted, Thursday, July 4. Mr. Williams being a young man, and merely a draper's assistant, modestly kept himself in the background in the early meetings of the Association, yet in the absence of the first chairman was always asked to preside; but to him, under God, belongs the credit of being the founder of that organization which has spread all over the world, and to it he has freely given his time and his means. He was the treasurer of the parent association from 1863 to 1885, succeeding Mr. Hitchcock; and is now president, succeeding the late Earl of Shaftesbury. He was taken by Mr. Hitchcock into partnership, and now is the head of the firm of Hitchcock, Williams, & Co., in which establishment he was a clerk. Besides the Young Men's Christian Association, Mr. Williams is the president of the Commercial Travellers' Christian Association, the Christian Community, the Young Men's Foreign Missionary, and of several other societies. He takes an active interest in the British and Foreign Bible Society, the London City Mission, the Sunday-school Union, the Bishop of London's Diocesan Council for Young Men, the Young Women's Christian Association, and many others.

The success of the Young Men's Christian Association was assured from the start. Its membership was twelve on June 6; in five months the association numbered seventy, each of whom had been carefully examined as to his Christian zeal before admittance, and religious services had been founded by it in ten drapers' establishments. On March 6, 1845, the membership was 160; on Nov. 5, 1846, the second annual meeting, branch associations in different places in London and in other cities were reported. In 1848, 480 members in London, and 1,000 in all, were reported. In 1849 the Earl of Shaftesbury became president, and so continued until his death, Oct. 1, 1885, when he was succeeded by Mr. Williams. In September, 1886, it was reported that there were 3,376 branch associations throughout the world, with nearly 200,000 members and associates. For an interesting and trustworthy history of the parent association, see George J. Stevenson's *Historical Records of the Young Men's Christian Association from 1844 to 1884*, London, 1884; for a brief account of the movement in general, see article, *Young Men's Christian Association*, in the *Schaff-Herzog Encyclopædia*, vol. iii. 2564-2566.

WILLIAMS, Right Rev. John, D.D. (Union College, Schenectady, N.Y., 1847; Trinity College, Hartford, Conn., 1849; Columbia College, New-

York City, 1851; Yale College, New Haven, Conn., 1883), **LL.D.** (Hobart College, Geneva, N.Y., 1870), Episcopalian, bishop of Connecticut; b. at Deerfield, Mass., Aug. 30, 1817; studied in Harvard College, Cambridge, Mass., 1831-33, and at Trinity College, Hartford, Conn., 1833-35; graduated at the latter, 1835; was tutor in the college, 1837-40; assistant in Christ Church, Middletown, Conn., 1841-42; rector of St. George's, Schenectady, N.Y., 1842-48; president of Trinity College, 1848-53; assistant bishop of Connecticut 1851-65, bishop since 1865. He is the author of *Ancient Hymns of Holy Church*, Hartford, 1845; *Thoughts on the Gospel Miracles*, New York, 1848; *The English Reformation* (Paddock Lectures), 1881; *The World's Witness to Jesus Christ* (Bedell Lectures), 1882; editor of Bishop Harold Browne's *Exposition of the Thirty-nine Articles*, 1865; many sermons and review articles.

WILLIAMS, Samuel Welles, LL.D. (Union College, Schenectady, N.Y., 1850), Congregationalist, layman; b. at Utica, September, 1812; d. at New Haven, Conn., Feb. 17, 1884. He studied at the Rensselaer School, Troy, N.Y.; went to China in 1833 as a printer for the A.B.C.F.M. Missionary Board at Canton; printed at Macao, Medhurst's *Hokkeen Dictionary* (Chinese), 1835; visited Japan, 1837, and translated into Japanese Genesis and Matthew; assisted in editing *The Chinese Repository*, Canton, 1838-51; was interpreter to Commodore Perry's Japan expedition, 1853-54; became secretary and interpreter of the American Legation, Peking, 1855; assisted Minister Reed in negotiating the treaty with China, 1856. He visited the United States in 1845, where he staid three years, teaching; again in 1860; returned to live there in 1876, and was appointed lecturer in Chinese in Yale College, New Haven, Conn. He was president of the American Bible Society, 1881-83. He was one of the most eminent of sinologues. He was the author of *Easy Lessons in Chinese*, Macao, 1842; *A Chinese Commercial Guide*, 1843, 5th ed. Hong-Kong, 1863; *An English and Chinese Vocabulary in the Court Dialect*, Macao, 1844; *The Middle Kingdom: a Survey of the Geography, Government, Education, Social Life, Arts, Religion, etc., of the Chinese Empire and its Inhabitants*, New York, 1848, 3d ed. 1857, new ed. rev. 1883, 2 vols. (a standard work); *Tonic Dictionary of the Chinese Language*, Canton, 1856; *Syllabic Dictionary of the Chinese Language*, Shanghai, 1874 (this was the great work of his life); *Chinese Immigration*, New York, 1879. *

WILLIAMS, William R., LL.D. (Union, 1859), **S.T.D.** (Columbia College, New-York City, 1837); b. in New-York City, Oct. 14, 1804; d. there, April 1, 1885. He graduated, head of his class, at Columbia College, New-York City, 1822; studied law for three years in the office of Peter A. Jay, and, on being admitted to the bar, became his partner, and practised law for two years, when the failure of his health compelled him to break off, and go to Europe. On his return he was converted, and, abandoning the law, entered the Baptist ministry, and from 1832 till his death was pastor of the Amity Church (at first in Amity Street, about 1865 transferred to West Fifty-fourth Street). He was a trustee of Columbia College, 1838-48. He was a man of great learning, and famous for his eloquence, although his congregation was latterly very small, for his voice was too weak to fill a large church. He had a library of some twenty thousand volumes. He was the author of *Miscellanies*, New York, 1850, 3d ed. Boston, 1860; *Religious Progress: Discourses on the Development of Christian Character*, New York, 1850; *Lectures on the Lord's Prayer*, 1851, new ed. 1878; *God's Rescues: or, the Lost Sheep, the Lost Coin, and the Lost Son*, 1871; *Lectures on Baptist History*, Philadelphia, 1877; *Eras and Characters of History*, 1882; numerous discourses (among them the memorable address upon *The Conservative Principle in Our Literature*, delivered at Hamilton, N.Y., June 13, 1833, reprinted in Glasgow, and pronounced the greatest of his productions); articles, etc. *

WILLSON, David Burt, Reformed Presbyterian (O.S.); b. at Philadelphia, Penn., Sept. 27, 1842; graduated at the University of Pennsylvania, Philadelphia, 1860; at the Jefferson Medical College, 1863; and at the Reformed Presbyterian Theological Seminary, Allegheny, Penn., 1869. He was in the medical service, United-States Army, 1863-65, and pastor in Allegheny, Penn., 1870-75; and has been since 1875 professor of biblical literature, Theological Seminary of the Reformed Presbyterian Church (O.S.), Allegheny, Penn. Since 1874 he has been an editor of *The Reformed Presbyterian and Covenanter* (monthly), Pittsburgh, and author of occasional addresses.

WILMER, Right Rev. Richard Hooker, D.D. (William and Mary College, Va., 1860), **LL.D.** (University of Oxford, Eng., 1867; University of Alabama, Tuscaloosa, Ala., 1880), Episcopalian, bishop of Alabama; b. at Alexandria, Va., March 15, 1816; graduated at Yale College, New Haven, Conn., 1836, and from the Theological Seminary of Virginia, near Alexandria, 1839; became rector of St. Paul's, Goochland County, and St. John's, Fluvanna County, Va., 1839; St. James's, Wilmington, N.C., 1843; Grace and Wickliffe Churches, Clarke County, Va., 1844; Emmanuel, Loudoun County, and Trinity, Fauquier County, Va., 1850; St. Stephen's and Trinity Churches, Bedford County, Va., 1853; Emmanuel Church, Henrico County, Va., 1859; bishop, 1862.

WILSON, Henry Rowan, M.D. (University of Pennsylvania, Philadelphia, 1832), **D.D.** (Washington College, Washington, Penn., 1850), Presbyterian; b. at Bellefonte, Penn., June 10, 1808; graduated at Jefferson College, Canonsburg, Penn., 1828; studied at Princeton Theological Seminary, N.Y., 1830-32; was missionary to the Cherokee and Choctaw Indians, 1832-37; missionary of A.B.C.F.M. to India, stationed at Futteghur, 1837-42; agent of the Presbyterian Board of Foreign Missions at Philadelphia and Pittsburgh, 1842-43; pastor of Neshaminy Church, Penn., 1843-48; principal Presbyterian Academy at Attleborough, and stated supply Pleasant Valley, Penn., 1848-55; pastor of Fairmount Church, Sewicklyville, Penn., 1855-60; stated supply Bensalem Church, 1860-66; president of the Springfield (O.) Female College, 1861-6-; district secretary of the Board of Domestic Missions, St. Louis, Mo., 186--68; corresponding secretary of the Board of Church Extension, St. Louis, Mo., 1868-70; corresponding secretary of the Board of Church Erection, N.Y. City, from its organization, 1871, to his death, June 8, 1886. He wrote many articles on home and foreign missions and church erection.

WILSON, John Leighton, D.D. (Lafayette College, Easton, Penn., 1854), Presbyterian (Southern Church); b. in Sumter County, S.C., March 25, 1809; d. near Marysville, S.C., July 13, 1886; graduated at Union College, Schenectady, N.Y., 1829, and at Theological Seminary, Columbia, S.C., 1833; was foreign missionary in Western Africa, 1834–53; secretary of Foreign Missions for the Presbyterian Church, New-York City, 1853–61; the same for the Southern Presbyterian Church, Columbia, S.C. (now Baltimore, Md.,) since 1861. He edited *The Foreign* (Missionary) *Record*, New York, 1853–61, and *The Missionary*, Baltimore, since 1868. He is the author of *Western Africa: Its History, Condition, and Prospects*, New York, 1857; between thirty and forty articles in reviews of United States and England, notably one on the slave-trade, written about 1852, in which the proposed withdrawal of the British squadron from the coast of Africa, under the impression that the slave-trade could not be broken up, was opposed. Of the article, Lord Palmerston had many thousand copies printed and circulated to prevent the withdrawal.

WILSON, Joseph Ruggles, D.D. (Oglethorpe University, Milledgeville, Ga., 1857), Presbyterian; b. at Steubenville, O., Feb. 28, 1828; graduated at Jefferson College, Canonsburg, Penn., 1844; studied at Western Theological Seminary, Allegheny, Penn., 1845, and at Princeton Theological Seminary, N.J., 1846–48; was pastor at Chartiers, Penn., 1849–51; professor of natural sciences at Hampden-Sidney College, Va., 1851–55; pastor at Staunton, Va., 1856–58; Augusta, Ga., 1858–70; professor of pastoral theology and homiletics in Columbia Theological Seminary, S.C., 1870–74; pastor at Wilmington, N.C., 1874–85; professor of theology in South-western Presbyterian University, Clarkesville, Tenn., 1885 to date. He has been stated clerk of the Southern General Assembly since 1861, and has represented it in other ecclesiastical bodies; was a member of the second general council of the Alliance of the Reformed Churches, Philadelphia, 1880, and read a paper on *Evangelism;* is a contributor to *The South. Presbyterian Review*, etc.

WILSON, Robert Dick, Presbyterian; b. at Indiana, Penn., Feb. 4, 1856; graduated at College of New Jersey, Princeton, N.J., 1876, and at Western Theological Seminary, Allegheny, Penn., 1879; became instructor in the latter institution, 1880; professor of Hebrew, Chaldee, and Old-Testament literature in the same, 1886. *

WILSON, Right Rev. William Scot, LL.D. (*speciali gratia* Trinity College, Dublin, 1859), lord bishop of Glasgow and Galloway; b. in Scotland, about the year 1807; graduated at King's College and University of Aberdeen, M.A., 1827; ordained deacon 1827, priest 1829; was chaplain to the bishop of Ross and Argyle, 1827–32; incumbent of Holy Trinity, Ayr, 1839–84; synodical clerk of the united diocese of Glasgow and Galloway, 1840–45; dean, 1845–59; became bishop, 1859. *

WING, Conway Phelps, D.D. (Dickinson College, Carlisle, Penn., 1857), Presbyterian; b. at Marietta, O., Feb. 12, 1809; graduated from Hamilton College, Clinton, N.Y., 1828, and at Auburn Theological Seminary, N.Y., 1831; was pastor at Sodus, N.Y., 1831–36; Ogden, N.Y., 1836–38; Monroe, Mich., 1838–41; Columbia, Tenn., 1841–42; Huntsville, Ala., 1842–48; Carlisle, Penn. (First Church), 1848–76. He was active in the revivals of 1832–35, in the anti-slavery agitation in Western New York, zealous in opposition to slavery in Tennessee and Alabama, a member of the Joint Committee of Reconstruction for the Presbyterian Church in 1870. He was an adherent of the New-School branch of the Presbyterian Church, but a warm supporter of the re-union in 1869 and 1870. He translated *Hase's Manual of Ecclesiastical History* (with Professor Blumenthal), New York, 1856; Kling's *Commentary on Second Corinthians* (with large additions) in Schaff's edition of Lange's *Commentary*, 1868; wrote *History of the Presbyteries of Donegal and Carlisle*, Carlisle, 1876; *A History of the First Presbyterian Church of Carlisle*, 1877; *A History of Cumberland County, Penn.*, 1879; *Historical and Genealogical Register of the Descendants of John Wing of Sandwich*, New York, 1885, 2d ed. 1886; eleven elaborate articles in *Presbyterian* and *Methodist Quarterly Reviews;* two extensive articles in McClintock and Strong's *Cyclopædia*, vols. iv., v. (1870 and 1872); many articles in *New-York Evangelist* and in *The Christian Observer*, etc.

WINGFIELD, Right Rev. John Henry Ducachet, D.D. (William and Mary College, Williamsburg, Va., 1869), **LL.D.** (do., 1874), Episcopalian, missionary bishop of Northern California; b. at Portsmouth, Va., Sept. 24, 1833; graduated from St. Timothy's College, Md., 1850, and from William and Mary College, Williamsburg, Va. (with gold medal for prize essay), 1853; was tutor at former college, 1850–52, 1853–54; at the Churchill Military Academy, New York, 1854-55; studied at the Theological Seminary of Virginia, Alexandria, 1855–56; was principal of the Ashley Institute, Little Rock, Ark., 1856–58; ordered deacon 1858, priest 1859; assistant minister in Christ Church, Little Rock, 1858; the same in Trinity Church, Portsmouth, Va. (of which his father was rector), 1858–64; rector of Christ Church, Rockspring, Harford County, Md., 1864–66; assistant minister in Trinity Church, Portsmouth, Va., 1866–68; rector of St. Paul's Church, Petersburg, Va., 1868–74; of Trinity Church, San Francisco, Cal., 1874; returned to Petersburg, Va., 1874; consecrated bishop there, Dec. 2, 1874; had charge of his parish until April 1, 1875, when he removed to his jurisdiction, and now resides at Benicia, Cal. He founded St. Paul's School for Young Ladies, Petersburg, Va., and became rector and professor, 1871; became president of the missionary College of St. Augustine, 1875; rector of St. Paul's Church, and rector of St. Mary's of the Pacific, a girls' school, 1876, — the three at Benicia, Cal.; declined election to the bishopric of Louisiana, 1879, and to the assistant bishopric of Mississippi, and to the rectorship of Grace Church, San Francisco, Cal., both in 1882. He has published sermons, addresses, pastoral letters, articles, etc.

WIRTHMUELLER, Johann Baptist, D.D. (Munich, 1859), Roman Catholic; b. at Haarpaint, Bavaria, June 20, 1834; taught philosophy and theology at Regensburg Lyceum 1853–57, and in

University of Munich 1857–60; became *privat-docent* of theology at Munich, 1864; professor of theology at Würzburg, 1867; at Munich, 1874. He is the author of *Die Nazoräer*, Regensburg, 1864; *Die Lehre des heiligen Hilarius von Poitiers über die Selbstentäusserung Christi*, 1865; *Encyclopädie der katholischen Theologie*, Landshut, 1874; *Ueber das Sittengesetz*, Würzburg, 1878; *Die moralische Tugend der Religion*, Freiburg, 1881; *Ueber das kathol. Priesterthum*, Straubing, 1882.

WISE, Daniel, A.M., D.D. (both *hon.*, Wesleyan University, Middletown, Conn., 1849, 1859, respectively), Methodist; b. at Portsmouth, Eng., Jan. 10, 1813; educated in Portsmouth Grammar School; removed to the United States, 1833; was pastor of various churches, 1837–52; editor of *Zion's Herald*, Boston, 1852–56; editor of the Sunday-school publications of the Methodist-Episcopal Church (including editorship of *Sunday-school Advocate* and *Sunday-school Teacher's Journal*), and corresponding secretary of the Sunday-school Union 1856–72, and of the Tract Society of said church, and editor of tract publications, including *Good News*, a tract periodical, New-York City, 1860–72; supernumerary preacher, disabled through disease of the throat from much pulpit work, but engaged in authorship, 1872 to date. He published and edited the first Sunday-school *paper* ever issued for the Sunday schools of the Methodist-Episcopal Church. It was originally a magazine published by D. S. King in Boston in 1836. He purchased it in 1838, changed it into a *paper*, and continued his connection with it, either as publisher or editor, until 1844. It was subsequently merged into *The Sunday-school Advocate*, published in New York by the book-agents of the Methodist-Episcopal Church. He is the author of *Life of Lorenzo Dow*, Lowell, Mass., 1840 (one edition of four thousand copies); *History of London for Boys and Girls*, 1841 (one edition of four thousand copies); *Personal Effort*, Boston, 1841, last ed. 1880; *Questions on Romans*, Lowell, 1843, last ed. 1869; *Cottage on the Moor*, New York, 1845, last ed. 1870; *McGregor Family*, 1845, last ed. 1864; *Infant Teacher's Manual*, 1845, last ed. 1880; *Benevolent Traveller*, 1846, last ed. 1867; *Lovest Thou Me?* Boston, 1846, last ed. 1862; *Guide to the Saviour*, New York, 1847, last ed. 1868; *The Path of Life*, Boston, 1847, last ed. 1885; *Bridal Greetings*, New York, 1850, last ed. 1884; *Life of Ulric Zwingle*, 1850, last ed. 1882; *Young Man's Counsellor*, Boston, 1850, last ed. 1883; *Young Lady's Counsellor*, 1851, last ed. 1883; *Aunt Effie*, New York, 1852, last ed. 1885; *My Uncle Toby's Library*, 12 vols., *nom de plume* of Francis Forrester, Esq., Boston, 1853; *Precious Lessons from the Lips of Jesus*, 1854, last ed. 1862; *Living Streams from the Fountain of Life*, 1854, last ed. 1862; *Sacred Echoes from the Harp of David*, 1855, last ed. 1862; *Popular Objections to Methodism Considered and Answered*, 1856, last ed. 1858; *Glen-Morris Stories*, 5 vols., *nom de plume* of Francis Forrester, Esq., New York, 1859, last ed. 1883; *Pleasant Pathways*, 1859, last ed. 1879; *Lindendale Stories*, 5 v., *nom de plume* of Lawrence Lancewood, Boston, 1865, last ed. 1883; *Hollywood Stories*, 6 vols., *nom de plume* of Francis Forrester, Esq., Philadelphia, 1872, last ed. 1885; *Little Peach Blossom*, New York, 1873, last ed. 1877; *The Squire of Walton Hall: a Life of Waterton the Naturalist*, 1874, last ed. 1885; *The Story of a Wonderful Life: Pen Pictures from Life of John Wesley*, Cincinnati, 1874, last ed. 1883; *Summer Days on the Hudson*, New York, 1875, last ed. 1876; *Uncrowned Kings*, Cincinnati, 1875, last ed. 1886; *Our King and Saviour* (a Life of Christ for the young), New York, 1875, last ed. 1883; *Vanquished Victors*, Cincinnati, 1876, last ed. 1885; *Winwood Cliff Stories*, 4 vols., Boston, 1876, last ed. 1883; *Lights and Shadows of Human Life*, New York, 1878, last ed. 1882; *Saintly and Successful Worker: A Life of William Carvosso*, Cincinnati, 1879, last ed. 1883; *Heroic Methodists*, N.Y., 1882, last ed. 1884; *Sketches and Anecdotes of American Methodists*, 1883; *Our Missionary Heroes and Heroines*, 1884; *Boy Travellers in Arabia*, 1885; *Men of Renown* (for young men), Cincinnati, O., 1886; *Some Remarkable Women* (for young ladies), in press; aggregate sale of these volumes exceeds a half-million copies; frequent contributions to *The Ladies' Repository*, *The National Repository*, *The Methodist Review*, and the weekly periodicals of the Methodist-Episcopal Church.

WITHEROW, Thomas, D.D. (Presbyterian Theological Faculty of Ireland, 1883), **LL.D.** (Royal University of Ireland, 1885), Irish Presbyterian; b. at Ballycastle, County Londonderry, May 29, 1824; educated at Belfast College 1839–43, and at Free Church College, Edinburgh, under Dr. Chalmers, 1843–44; became pastor at Maghera, 1845; and professor of ecclesiastical history, Magee College, Londonderry, 1865. He was moderator of the Irish General Assembly, 1878; became editor of *The Londonderry Standard* (tri-weekly), 1878; and senator of the Royal University, 1884. He is the author of *Three Prophets of our Own*, Belfast, 1855, 2d ed. Derry, 1880; *Which is the Apostolic Church? an Inquiry*, Belfast, 1856 (reprinted Edinburgh, 1884; London, 1869; and Philadelphia, n.d.); *The Scriptural Baptism*, Belfast 1854 (reprinted, Edinburgh, 1884; Italian trans. Florence); *Derry and Enniskillen in 1689*, Belfast, 1873, 3d ed. 1885; *The Boyne and Aghrim: Story of Famous Battlefields in Ireland*, 1879; *Historical and Literary Memorials of Irish Presbyterianism*, London, 1879, 2 vols.; and various smaller works and review articles.

WITHERSPOON, Thomas Dwight, D.D. (University of Mississippi, Oxford, Miss., 1867), **LL.D** (the same, 1885), Presbyterian (Southern Church); b. at Greensborough, Hale County, Ala., Jan. 17, 1836; graduated at University of Mississippi, 1856, and at the Columbia Theological Seminary, S.C., 1859; was post-graduate student in the University of Virginia, Charlottesville, 1871–73; pastor at Oxford, Miss., 1859–65; chaplain in the Confederate Army, 1861–65; pastor of the Second Church, Memphis, Tenn., 1865–70; chaplain of the University of Virginia, 1871–73; pastor of Tabb-street Church, Petersburg, Va., 1873–82; of First Church, Louisville, Ky., 1882 to date. He has declined elections to professorships in Columbia Theological Seminary, to the presidency of Davidson College, Mecklenburgh County, N.C., and of other literary institutions. He is the author of *Children of the Covenant*, Richmond, Va., 1873, 2d ed. 1874, later editions; *Letters on Romanism*, 1882.

WITHROW, John Lindsay, D.D. (Lafayette College, Easton, Penn., 1872), Congregationalist; b. at Coatesville, Chester County, Penn., March

19, 1837; graduated at the College of New Jersey, Princeton, 1860, and at Princeton Theological Seminary, 1863; became pastor of the Presbyterian Church, Abington, Penn., 1863; of the Arch-street Presbyterian Church, Philadelphia, Penn., 1868; of the Second Presbyterian Church, Indianapolis, Ind., 1873; of the Park-street Congregational Church, Boston, Mass., 1876. He is consistently conservative, and thoroughly wanting in sympathy with so-called progressive theology.

WITHROW, William Henry, D.D. (University of Victoria College, Cobourg, Can., 1882), Methodist; b. at Toronto, Can., Aug. 6, 1839; educated at Toronto Academy, Victoria College, Cobourg, and Toronto University; graduated at the last, B.A. 1863, M.A. 1864; was in the Methodist ministry at Montreal, Hamilton, Toronto, and Niagara, 1864–73; professor of ethics and metaphysics in Wesleyan Ladies' College, Hamilton, 1873–74; since has been editor of *Methodist Magazine* and Sunday-school periodicals, Toronto, being re-elected 1878, 1882, 1883, 1886. He is the author of *The Catacombs of Rome, and their Testimony relative to Primitive Christianity*, New York, 1874, London, Eng., 1876, two later editions; *School History of Canada*, Toronto, 1875; *History of Canada*, Boston, 1877, Toronto, 1883, 7th ed. 1886; *Worthies of Methodism*, Toronto, 1878; *Romance of Missions*, 1879; *Lawrence Temple's Probation* (story), 1879, 3d ed. 1884; *Barbara Heck* (story), 1880; *Great Preachers, Ancient and Modern*, 1880; *Neville Truman* (story), 1880; *Canadian in Europe* (travels), 1881; *Valeria, the Martyr of the Catacombs* (story), 1882, London, 1883, New York, 1885; *Men worth Knowing*, Toronto, 1883; *Life in a Parsonage; or, Lights and Shadows of Itinerancy*, 1885.

WOERTER, Friedrich, D.D. (Freiburg, 1855), Roman Catholic; b. at Offenburg, Baden, Germany, Dec. 6, 1819; studied at Freiburg-im-Br. 1841–44, Tübingen 1844–45, Munich 1845; became lyceum teacher at Freiburg, 1852; professor extraordinary of theology at Freiburg, 1856; ordinary professor of apologetics and dogmatics, 1860. He is the author of *Die christliche Lehre über das Verhältniss von Gnade und Freiheit v. d. apostol. Zeiten bis auf Augustin*, Freiburg-im-Br., vol. i. 1856–60, 2 parts; *Der Pelagianismus nach seinem Ursprung und seiner Lehre*, 1866, 2d ed. 1874; *Gedächtnissrede auf J. B. von Hirscher*, 1867; *Zurückweisung der jüngsten Angriffe auf die dermalige Vertretung der katholischen Dogmatik an der Universität zu Freiburg*, 1867; *Prosper von Aquitanien über Gnade und Freiheit*, 1867; *Die Unsterblichkeitslehre in den philosophischen Schriften Augustins*, 1880.

WOLF, Edmund Jacob, D.D. (Franklin and Marshall College, Lancaster, Penn., 1876), Lutheran (General Synod); b. near Rebersburg, Centre County, Penn., Dec. 8, 1840; graduated at Pennsylvania College, Gettysburg, Penn., 1863; studied theology at Gettysburg, Tübingen, and Erlangen; became pastor of Paradise Charge, Northumberland County, Penn., 1866, and of Second English Lutheran Church, Baltimore, Md.; professor of church history and New-Testament exegesis in the Theological Seminary at Gettysburg, Penn., 1873. He served a while in the army of the Union during college course; declined presidency of Roanoke College, Va., 1877. He has written numerous articles in the religious press, and separately issued *The Church's Future*, Gettysburg, 1882; *The Drama of Providence on the Eve of the Reformation*, 1884.

WOOD, John George, Church of England; b. in London, July 21, 1827; educated at Ashbourne Grammar School; entered Merton College, Oxford, 1844; elected Jackson's scholar, 1845; graduated B.A. 1848, M.A. 1851; attached to anatomical museum for two years; ordained deacon 1852, priest 1854; was curate of St. Thomas's, Oxford, 1852–54; assistant chaplain to St. Bartholomew's Hospital, London, 1856–62; reader at Christ Church, Newgate Street, London, 1858–62; elector precentor of the Canterbury Diocesan Choral Union, 1858; resigned, 1876. He was associate commissioner (educational department) International Exhibition, Paris, 1867. In 1880 he began to deliver sketch-lectures on natural history, illustrated by colored pastel drawings, executed before the audience, upon a large sheet of canvas; in October or November, 1883, delivered the opening course of the Lowell Lectures in Boston, Mass.; subsequently delivered many sketch-lectures in America during 1884 and 1885. He is the author of *Natural History*, London, 1852; *Anecdotes of Animal Life*, 1854–55, 2 vols.; *My Feathered Friends*, 1857; *Common Objects of the Seashore*, 1857; *Common Objects of the Country*, 1858; *Illustrated Natural History*, 1856–63, 3 vols.; *Glimpses into Pet-land*, 1863; *Homes without Hands*, 1865; *Bible Animals*, 1869; *Insects at Home*, 1871; *Insects Abroad*, 1874; *Man and Beast*, 1874–75, 2 vols.; *Pet-land Revisited*, 1884; *Old and New Testament Histories for Schools*, 1864; *Nature's Teachings*, 1876; *Graduated Natural-History Readers for Schools*, 5 vols.; *Man and his Handiwork*, ——; *Horse and Man*, 1885, etc. (Most of these works are being continually reprinted, the number of editions not being specified.)

WOODBRIDGE, Samuel Merrill, D.D. (Rutgers College, New Brunswick, N.J., 1857; Union College, Schenectady, N.Y., 1858), **LL.D.** (Rutgers College, 1883), Reformed (Dutch); b. at Greenfield, Mass., April 5, 1819; graduated at the New-York University, 1838, and at the Theological Seminary at New Brunswick, 1841; became pastor at South Brooklyn, N.Y., 1841; Coxsackie, 1850; New Brunswick, N.J., 1852; and professor of ecclesiastical history and church government, and dean of the Theological Seminary of the Reformed Church, New Brunswick, 1857. He is the author of *Analysis of Theology*, New York, 1872, 2d ed. 1882.

WOODFORD, Right Rev. James Russell, D.D. (by Archbishop of Canterbury, 1869), lord bishop of Ely, Church of Scotland; b. at Henley-on-Thames, April 30, 1820; d. at Ely, Oct. 24, 1885. He was late scholar of Pembroke College, Cambridge; graduated B.A. (senior optime and second-class classical tripos) 1842, M.A. 1845; ordained deacon 1843, priest 1845; was second master of Bishop College, Bristol, 1843–45; perpetual curate of St. Saviour's, Coalpit Heath, 1845–48; of St. Mark's, Easton, Bristol, 1848–55; vicar of Kempsford, Gloucester, 1855–68; examining chaplain to the late bishop (Wilberforce) of Oxford and Winchester, 1868–73; vicar of Leeds, 1868–73; select preacher at Cambridge, 1861, 1867, 1873, 1875, 1878; honorary chaplain to the Queen, and honorary canon of Christ Church, 1867; consecrated bishop, 1873. He was the author of *The Church Past and Present* (four lectures), 1852; *Sermons*, London, 1873, 3 vols.; *Six Lectures on the Creed*, 1855; *Occasional Sermons*, 1856-61, 2 series, 2d ed. 1861-65; *Ordination Lectures*, Oxford, 1861; *Christian Sanctity* (four sermons), Cambridge, 1863; *Ordination Sermons*, 1872.

WOODROW, James, Ph.D. (Heidelberg, Germany, 1856), **M.D.** (*hon.*, Medical College, Augusta, Ga., 1861), **D.D.** (Hampden-Sidney College, Prince Edward County, Va., 1871), **LL.D.** (Davidson College, twenty miles from Charlotte, N.C., 1883), Presbyterian (Southern Church); b. at Carlisle, Eng., May 30, 1828; graduated at Jefferson College, Canonsburg, Penn., 1849; studied at Heidelberg, Germany, 1855-56, and elsewhere in Europe, 1856; was professor of natural sciences, Oglethorpe University, near Milledgeville, Ga., 1853-61; in South-Carolina University, whose headquarters are at Columbia, S.C., 1869-72; and in South-Carolina College, Columbia, the chief part of the university, 1880, to the present. In 1861 he became professor of natural science in connection with revelation, in the Presbyterian Theological Seminary at Columbia, S.C.; was removed by board of directors, Dec. 10, 1884, on account of views presented in an address on *Evolution*, delivered in May, 1884; the act not being sustained by the controlling synods, he was officially informed by the board (meanwhile remodelled), Dec. 10, 1885, that he had not been removed, but was still in office. He then resumed his duties as chairman of the faculty and professor. He was ordained in 1860; since 1861 has edited *The Southern Presbyterian Review*, and since 1866 *The Southern Presbyterian*.

WOODRUFF, Frank Edward, Congregationalist; b. at Eden, Vt., March 20, 1855; graduated at the University of Vermont at Burlington, 1875, and at the Union Theological Seminary, New-York City, 1881; was fellow of his class, and as such studied two years in Germany and Greece (Tübingen, Berlin, and Athens); was inaugurated as associate professor of sacred literature in Andover Theological Seminary, Mass., 1883.

WOOLSEY, Theodore Dwight, D.D. (Harvard College, Cambridge, Mass., 1847), **LL.D.** (Wesleyan University, Middletown, Conn., 1845), Congregationalist, son of William W. Woolsey, a prosperous merchant of New-York City, and of Eliza Dwight, sister of President Dwight of Yale College, New Haven, Conn.; b. in New-York City, Oct. 31, 1801; entered Yale College 1816, graduated 1820; for a year (1820-21) studied law in New-York City, without a view to practising it, and then theology at Princeton Theological Seminary, N.J. for nearly two years (1821-23); was a tutor at Yale College for about two years (1823-25); soon afterwards went to Europe, where he spent three years, chiefly in France and Germany. In Germany he studied Greek; at Leipzig under Godfrid Hermann, at Bonn under Welcker, and at Berlin under Boeckh and Bopp. Returning to the United States, he was appointed professor of Greek at Yale College in 1831; and held the office actively until 1846, when he was chosen president of Yale College, which position he continued in for twenty-five years, until 1871, when he resigned his connection with the institution, and withdrew from public life. He was a member of the American Company of Revision of the New Testament, and its chairman (1871-81). He is the author of editions of the Greek text, with English notes, for the use of college students, of the *Alcestis* of Euripides, Cambridge, Mass., 1834; the *Antigone* of Sophocles, 1835; the *Prometheus* of Æschylus, 1837; the *Electra* of Sophocles, 1837; and the *Gorgias* of Plato, 1843; *Introduction to the Study of International Law, designed as an Aid in Teaching and in Historical Studies*, Boston, 1860, 5th ed. enlarged, New York 1879, London 1875, 2d ed. 1879; *Essays on Divorce and Divorce Legislation, with Special Reference to the United States*, New York, 1869, 2d ed. revised 1882; *Religion of the Present and of the Future: Sermons preached chiefly at Yale College*, 1871; *Political Science, or the State, theoretically and practically considered*, 1877, 2 vols., London, 1877; *Communism and Socialism in their History and Theory: A Sketch*, New York, 1880; editor of new editions of Francis Lieber's *On Civil Liberty and Self-Government*, Philadelphia, 1871 (originally Philadelphia, 1853, 2 vols.), and *Manual of Political Ethics*, 1871, 2 vols. (originally Boston, 1838-39, 2 vols.); besides, he is the author of smaller works and of a number of essays and reviews, e.g., in *The North-American*, *Princeton Review*, *The Century*, and especially in *The New Englander*, of which latter for several years after its first appearance (1843) he was one of a committee of publication.

WORCESTER, John, New Church (Swedenborgian); b. in Boston, Feb. 13, 1834; became pastor of the New Church Society at Newtonville, Mass., 1869; instructor in theology in the New Church Theological School, Boston, 1878, and president 1881. He is the author of *A Year's Lessons from the Psalms*, Boston, 1869; *Correspondences of the Bible: the Animals*, 1875, 2d ed. 1884; *A Journey in Palestine*, 1884.

WORDSWORTH, Right Rev. Charles, D.C.L. (Oxford, 1853), bishop of St. Andrew's, Dunkeld, and Dunblane, Episcopal Church in Scotland; b. at Bocking, Eng., Aug. 22, 1806; was a student of Christ Church College, Oxford; took the prize for Latin verse 1827, and for the Latin essay 1831; graduated B.A. (first-class classics) 1830, M.A. 1832; was ordained deacon 1834, priest 1840; was a private tutor for several years, and had under his instruction both Mr. Gladstone and Cardinal Manning; from 1835 to 1845, second master of Winchester College; from 1847 to 1854, warden of Trinity College, Glenalmond, Perthshire; and in 1853 was consecrated bishop. He was a member of New-Testament Company of Bible Revisers. He is the author of *Græcæ gram. rud.*, London, 1839, 19th ed. 1868; *Greek Primer*, 1871, 6th ed. 1878; *Christian Boyhood at a Public School*, 1846, 2 vols.; *Two Judicial Opinions on the Doctrine of the Eucharist*, 1858-61; *Discourse on Scottish Reformation*, 1860, 2d ed. 1863; *On Shakspeare's Knowledge and Use of the Bible*, 1864, 3d ed. 1880; *Catechesis*, 1868; *Outlines of the Christian Ministry*, 1872; *Remarks on Dr. Lightfoot's Essay on the Christian Ministry*, 1879; *Anni Christiani quæ ad clerum pertinent Latinè reddita*, 1880; editor of *Shakspeare's Historical Plays, Roman and English*, 1883, 3 vols. *

WORDSWORTH, Right Rev. Christopher, D.D.

(Cambridge, 1839), D.C.L. (*hon.*, Oxford, 1870), lord bishop of Lincoln, Church of England; b. at Bocking, Oct. 30, 1807; d. at Lincoln, March 21, 1885. He was scholar of Trinity College, Cambridge; chancellor's English medallist for poem, *The Druids*, 1827–28; Porson prizeman, 1828; Browne's medallist, 1827–28; Craven scholar, 1829; graduated B.A. (senior classic) 1830, M.A. 1833; travelled in Greece, 1832–33; was ordained deacon 1833, priest 1835; fellow of Trinity College, Cambridge, 1830–36; public orator, 1836; head master of Harrow School, 1836–44; canon of Westminster, 1844–69; Hulsean lecturer, Cambridge, 1847–48; vicar of Stanford-in-the-Vale, Berkshire, and rural dean, 1850–69; archdeacon of Westminster, 1865–69; consecrated bishop, 1869. He took part in the Old-Catholic Congress held at Cologne, September, 1872. He was the author of *Athens and Attica: Journal of a Residence there*, London, 1836, 4th ed. 1869; *Inscriptiones Pompeianæ: Ancient Writings copied from the Walls of the City of Pompeii*, 1837, 2d ed. 1838; *Greece: Pictorial, Descriptive, and Historical*, 1839, 8th ed. by H. F. Tozer, 1883; *Preces selectæ*, 1841; *The Correspondence of Richard Bentley, D.D., with Notes*, 1842, 2 vols.; *On Church Extension*, *Theophilus Anglicanus; or, Instructions concerning the Church and the Anglican Branch of it, etc.*, 1843, 9th ed. 1865 (French trans., Paris, 1861); *Catechetual Questions*, 1844; *Theocritus* (edited), Cambridge, 1844, 2d ed. 1877; *Discourses on Public Education*, London, 1844; *Diary in France*, 1845, 2d ed. 1846; *Defence of the Queen's Supremacy*, 1846; *Letters to M. Gondon on the Destructive Character of the Church of Rome, both in Religion and Polity*, 1847, 3d ed. 1848; *Sequel to the Previous Letters*, 2 editions, 1848; *Scripture Inspiration; or, On the Canon of Holy Scripture* (Hulsean Lectures for 1847), 1848, 2d ed. 1851; *On the Apocalypse; or, Book of Revelation* (Hulsean Lecture for 1848), 1849, 3d ed. 1852; *Harmony of the Apocalypse*, 2d ed. 1852; *The Apocalypse in Greek, with MSS. Coll., etc.*, 1849; *Manual for Confirmation*, 1849; *Memoirs of William Wordsworth*, 1851, 2 vols.; *S. Hippolytus and the Church of Rome in the Third Century, from the newly discovered "Philosophumena,"* 1853, new edition, 1880; *Notes at Paris*, 1854; *Tour in Italy*, 1863, 2 vols., 2d ed. 1863; *The Greek New Testament, with Prefaces, Introductions, and Notes*, 1856–60, 4 parts, 2d ed. 1872; occasional sermons preached in Westminster Abbey, 1850–68 (*On Baptism, On Calvinism, On Secessions to Rome, Secular Education, Use of Catechisms and Creeds in Education, On an Education Rate, On the History of the Church of Ireland, On National Sins and Judgments, On the Religious Census, On an Increase in the Episcopate, On Tithes, On Church Rates, On Marriage and Divorce, On the New Romish Doctrine of the Immaculate Conception, On Marriage with a Deceased Wife's Sister, On the Doctrine of the Atonement*); *Funeral Sermon on Joshua Watson, Esq., D.C.L.*, *Funeral Sermon on the Rev. Ernest Hawkins*, and other single sermons; *On the Inspiration of the Bible* (five lectures), 1861, 2d ed. 1863; *On the Interpretation of the Old and New Testaments*, 1861, 2d ed. 1863; *The Holy Year; or, Original Hymns for Sundays and Holy Days*, 1862, 5th ed. 1868; *The Old Testament in the Authorized Version, with Notes and Introductions*, 1864–71, 6 vols., 2d ed. 1868–72; *The Church of Ireland: Her History and Claims* (four sermons), 1866, 2d ed. 1867; *Union with Rome: An Essay*, 1st to 5th ed. 1867; *History of the Church of Ireland* (eight sermons), 1869; *The Maccabees and the Church; or, the History of the Maccabees considered with Reference to the Present State of England and the Universities*, 1871, 2d ed. 1876; *On the Procession of the Holy Spirit*, 1872; *On the Cologne Congress of Old Catholics*, 1872; *Fellowships and Endowments*, 1872; *Twelve Addresses at the Visitation of the Diocese and Cathedral of Lincoln*, 1873; *On Cremation; On the Millennium; On the Need of a Revision of the New Lectionary; On Confession and Absolution; On the State of the Soul after Death; Pastoral to the Wesleyans*, 9th ed.; *On the Sale of Church Patronage; Irenicum Wesleyanum*, 1876; *Diocesan Addresses at Visitation*, 1876; *Ethica et Spiritualia (Extracts from the Fathers, etc.)*, 1877; *The Newtonian System: Its Analogy to Christianity*, 1877; *Bishop Sanderson's Lectures on Conscience and Law*, 1877; *Letters to Sir George Prevost, on Sisterhoods and Vows*, 1878; *Miscellanies Literary and Religious*, 1878, 3 vols. (being selections from the bishop's works, with additions); *Ten Visitation Addresses*, 1879; *Translations of the Pastoral Letters of Lambeth Conferences into Greek and Latin, made by Desire of the Presiding Archbishops*, 1868 and 1878; *On the Duration and Degrees of Future Punishments*, 1878, 2d ed. ——; *On the Present Disquietude in the Church*, 1881; *On the New Revised Version*, 1881; *A Church History to the Council of Chalcedon, A.D. 481*, 1881–83, 4 vols. (vol. i., 3d ed. 1883; vol. ii., 2d ed. 1882; vols. iii. and iv., 2d ed. 1885); *Guides and Goads, from the Fathers, etc.*, 1883; *Conjectural Emendations of Passages in Ancient Authors*, 1883.

WORDSWORTH, Right Rev. John, D.D. (Oxford, 1885), lord bishop of Salisbury, Church of England, eldest son of Christopher Wordsworth, bishop of Lincoln; b. in the head master's house, Harrow-on-the-Hill, Middlesex, Eng., Sept. 21, 1843; educated at Ipswich Grammar School, 1854–57; Winchester College, 1857–61; New College, Oxford (scholar), 1861; first class moderations classics, 1863; graduated B.A. (second class classics) 1865, M.A. 1868; chancellor's prize for Latin essay, 1866; Craven scholar, 1867; assistant master at Wellington College, 1866–67; fellow of Brasenose College, Oxford, 1867; tutor of Brasenose College, 1868–83; ordained deacon 1867, priest 1869; prebendary of Lincoln, 1870–83, and examining chaplain to the bishop of Lincoln, 1870–85; proctor of the University of Oxford, 1874; select preacher, 1876; Grinfield lecturer on LXX., 1876; Whitehall preacher, 1879; Bampton lecturer, 1881; first Oriel professor of the interpretation of Holy Scripture (with canonry of Rochester annexed), 1883–85; theological examiner, 1882–83; became bishop of Salisbury, 1885. He was at the Old-Catholic Congress at Cologne with the bishop of Lincoln in 1872, busy collating Latin manuscripts in Italy, France, and Spain, for an edition of the Vulgate New Testament, 1878–83. He is the author of *Lectures introductory to a Study of the Latin Language and Literature*, Oxford, 1870; *Fragments and Specimens of Early Latin*, 1874; *University Sermons on Gospel Subjects*, 1878; *The One Religion: Truth, Holiness, and Peace desired by the Nations and* *revealed by Jesus Christ* (Bampton Lectures), 1881; *The St. Germain St. Matthew* (g_1): *being No. 1 of a Series of Old Latin Biblical Texts*, 1883; articles on *Constantine the Great and his Sons*, and on *The Emperor Julian*, and others in Smith and Wace's *Dictionary of Christian Biography*; various pamphlets and sermons, viz., *Erasmus; sive Thucydidis cum Tacito comparatio* (chancellor's Latin prize essay), 1866; *Keble College and the Present University Crisis*, 1869; *The Church and the Universities: A Letter to C. S. Roundell, M.P., with Postscript*, 1880; *Prayers for Use in College*, 1883; *Love and Discipline: A Memorial Sermon preached at Lincoln after the Funeral of Christopher Wordsworth, Bishop of Lincoln*, 1885 (March); *A Farewell Sermon, on Ps. cii. 25, 28*, Rochester, September, 1885.

WRATISLAW, Albert Henry, Church of England; b. at Rugby, Warwickshire, Nov. 5, 1821; educated at Christ's College, Cambridge; graduated B.A. (twenty-fifth senior optime and third in first class classical tripos) 1844, M.A. 1847; was elected fellow of Christ's College; became tutor; was twice examiner for classical tripos; head master of Felstead Grammar School, 1852–55, and of Bury St. Edmunds Grammar School, 1855–79, when he retired on a pension of two hundred pounds a year; and, in the same year, became vicar of Manorbier. His theology is "Broad Church." He is the author of *Loci Communes, Common Places* (delivered in the chapel of Christ's College, conjointly with Professor Swainson), London, 1848; *Bohemian Poems, Ancient and Modern, translated from the Original Slavonic, with an Introductory Essay*, 1849; *The Queen's Court Manuscript, with other Ancient Bohemian Poems, translated from the Original Slavonic into English Verse*, Cambridge, 1852; *Barabbas the Scapegoat, and other Sermons and Dissertations*, London, 1859; *Notes and Dissertations, principally on Difficulties in the Scriptures of the New Covenant*, 1863; *Baron Wratislaw's Adventures, translated out of the Original Bohemian*, 1865; *Diary of an Embassy from King George of Bohemia to Louis XI. of France in the Year 1464, translated from a Bohemian MS.*, 1871; *Life, Legend, and Canonization of St. John Nepomucen*, 1873; *The Native Literature of Bohemia in the Fourteenth Century* (Ilchester Lectures, 1877, Oxford), 1878; *Biography of John Hus*, 1882.

WRIGHT, Charles Henry Hamilton, Ph.D. (Leipzig, 1875), **D.D.** (Trinity College, Dublin, 1879), Church of Ireland; b. in Dublin, March 11, 1836; educated at Trinity College, Dublin; won first-class Hebrew prize, 1854, 1855, 1856; Arabic prize, 1859; first-class divinity testimonium, 1858; graduated B.A. (respondent) 1857, M.A. 1859, B.D. 1873 (*stipendiis condonatis*); was incorporated at Exeter College, Oxford, as M.A., 1862; Ph.D. at Leipzig (thesis: *Qui de interpretatione librorum Veteris Testamenti historicorum commentariis editis optime meruit*). He became curate of Middleton-Tyas, Yorkshire, 1859; British chaplain at Dresden, 1863; chaplain of Trinity Church, Boulogne-sur-Mer, 1868; incumbent of St. Mary's, Belfast, 1874; incumbent of Bethesda Church, Dublin, 1885. He was Bampton lecturer at Oxford, 1878, and Donnellan lecturer, Dublin, 1880–81. He is a member of the German Oriental Society. He has written *A Grammar of the Modern Irish Language*, designed for the use of the classes in the University of Dublin, Dublin, 1855, 2d ed. revised and enlarged, London, 1860; *The Book of Genesis in Hebrew*, with a critically revised text, various readings, and grammatical and critical notes, London and Edinburgh, 1859; *The Importance of Linguistic Preparation for Missionaries in General*, together with remarks on Christian vernacular literature in Eastern languages, London, Williams and Norgate, 1860 (pamphlet); *The Book of Ruth in Hebrew*, with a critically revised text, various readings, including a new collation of twenty-eight Hebrew MSS. (most of them not previously collated), and a grammatical and critical commentary, to which is appended the Chaldee Targum, with various readings, and a Chaldee glossary, 1864; *The Spiritual Temple of the Spiritual God: being the Substance of Sermons preached in the English Church, Dresden*, 1864; *Bunyan's Allegorical Works, or the Pilgrim's Progress and the Holy War: together with his Grace Abounding, Divine Emblems, and other Poems*, edited with notes original and selected, and a life of Bunyan, 1866; *Ritualism and the Gospel: Thoughts upon St. Paul's Epistle to the Galatians*, with an appendix, 1866; *The Fatherhood of God, and its Relation to the Person and Work of Christ, and the Operations of the Holy Spirit*, Edinburgh, 1867; *The Pentateuch, or the Five Books of Moses in the Authorized Version*, with a critically revised translation, a collation of various readings translated into English, and of various translations, together with a critical and exegetical commentary, for the use of English students of the Bible: *Specimen part containing Gen. i.–iv., with commentary*, pp. viii., 48, London and Edinburgh, 1869; *The Footsteps of Christ, translated from the German of A. Caspers, Church Provost and Chief Pastor at Husum, by Adelaide E. Rodham* (edited), Edinburgh, 1871; *Memoir of John Lovering Cooke, formerly Gunner in the Royal Artillery, and late Lay Agent of the British Sailors' Institute, Boulogne: with a Sketch of the Indian Mutiny of 1857-58, up to the Final Capture of Lucknow*, London, 1873, 2d ed. 1878; *"Born of Water and of the Spirit," no Proof of the Doctrine of Baptismal Regeneration: a Contribution to the Baptismal Controversy, preached before the University of Dublin*, Dublin, 1874 (pamphlet); *The Church of Ireland, and her Claims to the Title, considered in the Light of History and Recent Legislation*, 1877, 2d ed. 1878 (pamphlet); *Religious Life in the German Army during the War of 1870–71*, a lecture and review, London and Edinburgh, Williams and Norgate, 1878 (pamphlet); *Zechariah and his Prophecies considered in relation to Modern Criticism*, with a grammatical and critical commentary and new translation (the Bampton Lectures for 1878), London, 1879 (March), 2d ed. 1879 (June or July); *Dublin University Reform and the Divinity School*, four pamphlets, with a general preface and appendix, Dublin, 1879; *The Divinity School and the Divinity Degrees of the University of Dublin*, 1880 (pamphlet); *The Divinity School of Trinity College, Dublin, and its Proposed Improvement*, submitted to the General Synod of the Church of Ireland, 1884 (pamphlet); *The Book of Koheleth, commonly called Ecclesiastes, considered in Relation to Modern Criticism and to the Doctrines of Modern Pessimism*, with a critical and grammatical commentary and a revised translation (the Donnellan Lectures for 1880–81), London, 1883; *Biblical Essays; or, Exegetical Studies on the Books of Job and Jonah, Ezekiel's Prophecy of Gog and Magog*, St. Peter's "*Spirits in Prison*," *and the Key to the Apocalypse*, Edinburgh, 1885; with numerous other pamphlets and articles, for instance, in *The Nineteenth Century* (for February, 1882), on *The Babylonian Account of the Deluge*, *The Site of Paradise* (October, 1882), *The Jews and the Malicious Charge of Human Sacrifice* (November, 1883).

WRIGHT, George Frederick, F.A.A.S., Congregationalist; b. at Whitehall, N.Y., Jan. 22, 1838; graduated at Oberlin College 1859, and Theological Seminary, Oberlin, O., 1862; was in the Seventh Ohio Volunteer Infantry five months of 1860; became pastor at Bakersfield, Vt., 1862; at Andover, Mass., 1872; professor of New-Testament language and literature in Oberlin Theological Seminary, 1881; was assistant geologist on Pennsylvania survey 1881, and United-States survey since 1884. He is the author of *The Logic of Christian Evidence*, Andover, 1880, 4th ed. 1883; *Studies in Science and Religion*, 1882; *The Relation of Death to Probation*, Boston, 1882, 2d ed. 1883; *The Glacial Boundary in Ohio, Indiana, and Kentucky*, Cleveland, 1884; *The Divine Authority of the Bible*, Boston, 1884; is an editor of the *Bibliotheca Sacra*.

WRIGHT, Milton, D.D. (Westfield College, Ill., 1878), United Brethren in Christ; b. in Rush County, Ind., Nov. 17, 1828; educated at Hartsville College, Ind., 1853; became a member of the White River Conference, Ind., 1853; ordained, 1856; was pastor at Indianapolis, 1855–56; at Andersonville, Ind., 1856-57; missionary in Oregon, where he was pastor at Sublimity and most of the time president of Sublimity College (a denominational institution), 1857–59; in the itinerancy in the White River Conference, 1859–69, during which he was presiding elder (1861–64, 1866–68), and pastor at Hartsville, Ind., and teacher of theology in Hartsville College (1868–69); was editor of *The Religious Telescope* (church organ), Dayton, O., 1869–77 (being elected two terms); bishop (assigned to West Mississippi District), 1877–81; presiding elder in White River Conference, 1881–85 (editor and publisher of *The Richmond Star*, Richmond, Ind., 1883–85); re-elected bishop for the term of four years, and sent to the Pacific Coast District, 1885. His writings are wholly journalistic, except a few tracts.

WRIGHT, Theodore Francis, Swedenborgian; b. at Dorchester (now Boston), Mass., Aug. 3, 1845; graduated at Harvard College 1866, and at New Church Theological School, Boston, 1868; since 1868 has been pastor at Bridgewater, Mass.; since 1879 editor *New Jerusalem Magazine* (monthly), Boston; and since 1884 instructor in homiletics and pastoral care, New Church Theological School. During 1864–65, he was first lieutenant One Hundred and Eighth Regiment United-States colored troops. He is the author of *Life Eternal*, Boston, 1885.

WRIGHT, William, M.A., Ph.D. (*hon.*, Leyden), **LL.D.** (*hon.*, Cambridge, Dublin, Edinburgh, St. Andrew's), layman, Church of England; b. in India, Presidency of Bengal, Jan. 17, 1830; educated at St. Andrew's and Halle; was appointed professor of Arabic in University College, London, 1855; in Trinity College, Dublin, 1856; assistant in department of MSS. in British Museum, 1861; assistant keeper of MSS., 1869; professor of Arabic in the University of Cambridge, 1870. He is a fellow of Queens' College, Cambridge. He was an Old-Testament reviser (1870–85), and is a corresponding or honorary member of many learned and royal societies. He is the author, translator, or editor of *The Travels of Ibn Jubair* (Arabic), Leyden, 1852; *Analectes sur l'histoire et la littérature des Arabes d'Espagne, par al-Makkari*, livres i.–iv., 1855; *The Book of Jonah in Four Oriental Versions, with Glossaries*, London, 1857; *Opuscula Arabica*, Leyden, 1859; *A Grammar of the Arabic Language*, London, 1859–62, 2 vols., 2d ed. 1874–75; *The Kâmil of El-Mubarrad* (Arabic), Leipzig, 1864–82, 11 parts; *Contributions to the Apocryphal Literature of the New Testament* (Syriac and English), London, 1865; *The Homilies of Aphraates* (Syriac), vol. i., 1869; *An Arabic Reading Book*, Part 1, 1870; *Catalogue of the Syriac MSS. in the British Museum*, 1870–72, 3 vols.; *Apocryphal Acts of the Apostles* (Syriac and English), 1871, 2 vols.; *Catalogue of the Ethiopic MSS. in the British Museum*, 1877; *The Chronicle of Joshua the Stylite* (Syriac and English), Cambridge, 1882; *The Book of Kalîlah and Dimnah* (Syriac), Oxford, 1883.

WRONG, George McKinnon, Church of England in Canada; b. at Grovesend, Ontario, Can., June 25, 1860; graduated concurrently at University College and at Wycliffe College, Toronto, 1880; became dean of residence, Wycliffe College, and lecturer in ecclesiastical history and polity, 1883.

WYLIE, James Aitken, LL.D. (Aberdeen, 1856), Free Church; b. at Kirriemuir, Forfarshire, Scotland, Aug. 9, 1808; educated at Marischall College of the University of Aberdeen 1822–25, and at University of St. Andrew's 1826; received his theological training in Original Secession Hall under Rev. Dr. Paxton, Edinburgh, 1827–30; was minister of Original Secession Congregation at Dollar, 1831–46; associated with Hugh Miller in the editorship of *The Witness*, Edinburgh, 1846–56; editor of *Free Church Record*, 1853–60; professor to Protestant Institute of Scotland, Edinburgh, 1860 to date. The Institute is an extra-mural lectureship, founded by the Protestant churches of Scotland, for the indoctrination of students in the distinctive principles of the Roman-Catholic and Protestant theologies. He wrote the Evangelical Alliance's first prize essay on Popery. He has travelled over nearly all Europe, and also Asia Minor, Palestine, and Egypt. In 1868 he was examined before the House of Lords, on the working of canon law with reference to the establishment of the papal hierarchy in Great Britain. In 1881, on the occasion of his jubilee, he received a public testimonial, portrait with three hundred guineas, etc. He is the author of *The Modern Judea compared with Ancient Prophecy*, Glasgow, 1841 (sale twenty thousand copies); *Scenes from the Bible*, 1843 (sale fifteen thousand copies), last ed. 1882; *On Unfulfilled Prophecy*, 1845; *Ruins of Bible Lands: Journeys over the Region of Fulfilled Prophecy*, 1845, 14th ed. 1880; *The Seventh Vial, or Past and Present of Papal Europe*, 1848, 4th ed. 1868; *The Papacy: its History, Dogmas, Genius, and Prospects* (The Evangelical Alliance prize essay), 1851, 4th ed. 1860, German trans., Elberfeld, 1853, 2d ed. 1854; *From the Alps to the Tiber* 1856 (sale two thousand copies); *The Gospel Ministry: Duty and Privilege of Supporting it* (first prize essay), 1857 (sale ten thousand copies); *Wanderings and Musings in the Valley of the Waldenses, Travels, etc.*, 1858; *The Great Exodus; or, the Time of the End*, 1862, 2d ed. 186–; *Rome and Civil Liberty*, 1864 (sale fifteen thousand copies); *The Awakening of Italy and the Crisis of Rome*, 1866 (sale two thousand copies); *The Road to Rome via Oxford, or Ritualism identified with Romanism*, 1868; *Daybreak in Spain: a Sketch of Spain and its New Reformation, a Tour of Two Months*, 1870; *Impending Crisis of the Church and the World*, Edinburgh, 1871; *The History of Protestantism*, London, 1875–77, 3 vols. (sale sixty to eighty thousand copies), Dutch trans. 1876–78, German trans. 18—; *The Jesuits: their Moral Maxims and Plots against Kings*, Edinburgh, 1881; *Visit to the Land of the Pharaohs*, 1882; *Over the Holy Land*, 1883; editor of new edition of the *Scots Worthies*, with supplemental biographies; *Dictionary of the Bible*, 1870, 2 vols.; besides pamphlets on the Popish controversy.

Y.

YERKES, Stephen, D.D. (La Grange College, Tenn., 1857), Presbyterian; b. in Bucks County, Penn., June 27, 1817; graduated at Yale College, 1837; studied theology privately; was pastor and teacher in Baltimore and Harford Counties, Md., 1843-52; professor of ancient languages, Transylvania University, Lexington, Ky., and pastor of Bethel Church, 1852-57; since 1857, professor in Theological Seminary, Danville, Ky. (of Oriental and biblical literature, 1857-69; of biblical literature and exegetical theology since).

YOUNG, Alexander, D.D. (Jefferson College, Canonsburg, Penn., 1856), **LL.D.** (Washington and Jefferson College, Washington, Penn., 1873), United Presbyterian; b. near Glasgow, Scotland, June 4, 1815; graduated from the Western University of Pennsylvania, Pittsburgh, Penn., 1838; professor of Latin and Greek in the same, 1838-40; pastor of Associate Reformed Church at St. Clairsville, O., 1842-58; co-pastor at Monmouth, Ill., 1859-60; sole pastor, 1860-63; was co-pastor of the Second United Presbyterian Church, Monmouth, 1863-66; was sole pastor, 1866-71; was professor in all departments (except history) of the Associate Reformed Theological Seminary, Oxford, O., 1855-58; transferred, with the seminary, to Monmouth, Ill., in the same relations, September, 1858, and so continued until 1864; during this period also professor of Greek and Latin in Monmouth College; professor of apologetics and all departments of theology in the seminary, 1864-76; and of evidences of Christianity, in Monmouth College, 1864-76; of apologetics and pastoral theology in the United Presbyterian Theological Seminary, Allegheny, Penn., 1874 to date, changing chairs with other professors as interest or preference required.

YOUNG, Robert, LL.D., F.E.S.L., layman; b. at Edinburgh, Sept. 10, 1822; received education at private schools, 1827-38; served apprenticeship to the printing-business, 1838-45; became a communicant in 1842; joined the Free Church, and became a sabbath-school teacher, in 1843; commenced bookselling and printing in 1847; married, and went to India as a literary missionary and superintendent of the Mission Press at Surat, in 1856; returned in 1861; conducted "Missionary Institute," 1864-74; visited New York, Boston, Princeton, Philadelphia, Washington, etc., in 1867; carried the *Analytical Concordance* through the press in 1876-79; took special interest in the "Aberdeen" attacks on the Bible, 1875-80, and in "Presbyterian Union," 1884-85. A moderate Calvinist, simple Presbyterian, and strict textual critic and theologian. His works, chronologically arranged, are, *Book of the Precepts; or, the Six Hundred and Thirteen Affirmative or Prohibitive Precepts, collected by Rabbi Moses Ben Maimon,* with a life of Maimonides, edited in the original Hebrew, with a translation; *Chaldee Portions of Daniel (ii. 4-vii. 28) and Ezra (iv. 7-vii. 26) in the Original Chaldee,* with corresponding Greek, Syriac, and (Rabbinical) Hebrew; *Ethics of the Fathers, collected by Nathan the Babylonian, A.D. 200, in the Original Hebrew,* with an English translation, and an introduction to the Talmud; *Hexaglot Pentateuch; or, the Five Books of Moses in the Original Hebrew,* with the corresponding Samaritan text and version, the Chaldee Targum, the Syriac Peshito, and the Arabic of Saadiah Gaon, arranged interlinearly, with comparative tables of alphabets and verb (Gen. i.-v.); *Westminster Assembly's Shorter Catechism,* translated into Arabic, French, Hebrew, Gaelic, Samaritan, Spanish, Syriac, also Dutch, German, Greek, Italian, Latin, and Portuguese; *Christology of the Targums; or, the Doctrine of Messiah, as unfolded in the Ancient Jewish Paraphrases, or Translations of the Sacred Scriptures into the Chaldee Language,* in Hebrew, Chaldee, and English; *Rabbinical Vocabulary, with List of Abbreviations and an Analysis of the Grammar, adapted expressly for the Mishna and the Perushim,* with introduction; *Obadiah's Prophecy against Edom, in the Original Hebrew,* with the corresponding Chaldee, Syriac, and Arabic versions, interlinear; *Paradigms (Complete) of the Verbs, Regular and Irregular, in Hebrew, Chaldee, Samaritan, and Syriac; Root-books of the Hebrew, Chaldee, Samaritan, Syriac, Greek, and Latin Languages,* containing every root in each, in alphabetical order, with English explanations; *Song of a Finlandian Country-Girl,* in Finnish, with translations into Hebrew, Samaritan (ancient and modern), Chaldee, Syriac, and English; *Israelitish Gleaner and Biblical Repository,* containing rare and interesting poems, tales, and other compositions into Hebrew and from it, translations from the Targums, etc. (the above were published in Edinburgh, 1849-56); *Gujarati Grammar and Exercises; or, a New Mode of Learning to Read, Write, or Speak the Gujarati Language,* on the Ollendorffian system, with *Key*; *The First and Second Books of Chronicles, translated into the Gujarati Language, from the Original Hebrew* (these two were published in Surat, 1857-60); *Bible (The Holy), consisting of the Old and New Covenants, translated according to the Letter and Idiom of the Original Languages* (do., 2d ed., revised, larger type); *Hebrew Tenses, illustrated from the Biblical Text, the Cognate Languages, and the Chief Biblical Critics; Chronological Index to the Bible, Old and New Testaments; Variations of the Alexandrian, Vatican, and Sinaitic MSS. of the New Testament; Marginal (Ten Thousand) Readings for the English Testament, in Addition to those given by the Editors of King James's Bible,* being a series of more literal renderings, derived from an examination of the original Scriptures, when compared with the common version; *Concise Critical Comments on the Holy Bible,* being a companion to the new translation of the Old and New Covenants, specially designed for those teaching the word of God, whether preachers, catechists, Scripture-readers, district-visitors, or sabbath-school teachers; *Grammatical Analysis of the Hebrew, Chaldee, and Greek Scriptures,* consisting of the original texts unabridged, the parsing of every word, with all its prefixes and affixes, and a literal translation: *The Twelve Minor Prophets*, complete; *Biblical Notes and Queries regarding Biblical Criticism and Interpretation, Ecclesiastical History, Antiquities, Biography and Bibliography, Ancient and Modern Versions, Progress in Theology, Reviews of Religious Works, etc.; Hebrew and Chaldee Vocabulary*, consisting of every word in the Old-Testament Scriptures, whether noun, verb, or participle: the verbs with their conjugations, and the nouns with their gender, to which is added the number of times in which each word occurs, with the etymological and idiomatic renderings of the new translation; *Introduction to the Hebrew Language, in a Way hitherto unexampled; Biblical Tracts for Every Day in the Year, on the Most Important Facts and Doctrines of Scripture*, illustrated from itself; *Analytical Concordance to the Bible*, on a new plan, with every word in alphabetical order, arranged under its own Hebrew or Greek original, with the literal meaning of each and its pronunciation, exhibiting about 311,000 references, or 118,000 beyond Cruden, marking 30,000 various readings in the Greek New Testament, with the latest information on biblical geography and antiquities of the Palestine Exploration Society, etc., — all designed for the simplest reader of the English Bible; *Appendixes to the Analytical Concordance: I. For Sabbath-school Teachers* (Analytical surveys of [1] all the "Books," [2] all the "Facts," [3] all the "Idioms," of the Bible, [4] Bible Themes, — questions, canonicity, rationalism, etc.). *II. For Divinity Students* (reversed indexes to the Analytical Concordance, forming [1] a Hebrew Lexicon [2] Hebrew tenses illustrated, [3] a Greek Lexicon): with 23 pictorial views of Palestine, 16 Bible maps, and 25 fac-similes of biblical MSS.; *Contributions to a New Revision; or, A Critical Companion to the New Testament*, being a series of notes on the original text, with the view of securing greater uniformity in its English rendering, including the chief alterations of the "Revision" of 1881 and of the American Committee; *Concordance to Eight Thousand Changes of the Revised New Testament; Dictionary and Concordance of Bible Words and Synonymes*, exhibiting the use of above ten thousand Greek and English words occurring in upwards of eighty thousand passages of the New Testament, so as to form a key to the hidden meanings of the Sacred Scripture; *Twofold Concordance to the New Testament*, (1) to the Greek New Testament, exhibiting every root and derivative, with their several prefixes and terminations in all their occurrences, with the Hebrew originals of which they are renderings in the Septuagint; (2) a concordance and dictionary of Bible words and synonymes (being a condensation of the New-Testament part of the English Analytical Concordance); also a concise concordance to eight thousand changes of the "Revised" Testament; *Grammatical Analysis of the Book of Psalms in Hebrew*, the original text unabridged, the parsing of every word, with all its prefixes and affixes, with a literal translation; *Paradigms of the Hebrew Verbs, with the Serviles in Large Open-faced Characters.*

Z.

ZAHN, Theodor, Lic. Theol. (Göttingen, 1867), **D.D** (*hon.*, Göttingen, 1872), German Protestant; b. at Mörs, Rhenish Prussia, Oct. 10, 1838; studied at Basel, Erlangen, and Berlin, 1854–58; became teacher in Neustrelitz gymnasium, 1861; *repetent* at Göttingen 1865, *privat-docent* 1868, professor extraordinary 1871; ordinary professor at Kiel 1877, and at Erlangen 1878. He is the author of *Die Voraussetzungen rechter Weihnachtsfeier*, Berlin, 1865, pp. 48; *Marcellus von Ancyra*, Gotha, 1867; *Hermæ Pastore N. T. illustr.*, Göttingen, 1867, pp. 52; *Der Hirt des Hermas untersucht*, Gotha, 1868; *Ignatius von Antiochien*, 1873; *Constantin der Grosse und die Kirche*, Hannover, 1876, pp. 35; *Ignatii et Polycarpi epistulæ, martyria (Pat. apos. rec. de Gebhardt, Harnack, Zahn)*, Leipzig, 1876; *Weltverkehr u. Kirche während der drei ersten Jahrhunderte*, Hannover, 1877, pp. 50; *Geschichte des Sonntags vornehmlich in der alten Kirche*, 1878, pp. 79 (Norwegian trans., Kristiania 1879, Dutch trans., Amsterdam 1884); *Sclaverei und Christenthum in der alten Welt*, Heidelberg, 1879 (lecture); *Acta Joannis*, Erlangen, 1880; *Forschungen zur Geschichte des neutestamentl. Kanons und der altkirchlichen Literatur*, 1881 sqq.: I. *Tatian's Diatessaron*, 1881; II. *Der Evangeliencommentar d. Theoph. v. Antiochien*, 1883; III. *Supplementum Clementinum*, 1884; *Cyprian v. Antiochien u. die deutsche Faustsage*, 1882; *Die Anbetung Jesu im Zeitalter der Apostel*, Stuttgart, 1885 (lecture); *Missionsmethoden im Zeitalter der Apostel*, Erlangen, 1886 (2 lectures), pp. 48; numerous articles, etc.

ZELLER, Eduard, German Protestant; b. at Kleinbottwar, Würtemberg, Jan. 22, 1814; studied at Tübingen and Berlin; became *privat-docent* of theology at Tübingen, 1840; professor extraordinary at Bern, 1847, ordinary, 1849; of the philosophical faculty, at Marburg 1849, at Heidelberg 1862, and Berlin 1872. He is the author of *Platonische Studien*, 1839; *Geschichte der christlichen Kirche, uebersichtlich dargestellt*, Stuttgart, 1848; *Die Philosophie der Griechen*, Tübingen, 1844–52, 3 vols., 4th ed. 1876–81, 5 vols.; *Das theologische System Zwingli's*, Tübingen, 1853; *Die Apostelgeschichte nach ihrem Inhalt und Ursprung kritisch untersucht*, Stuttgart, 1854; *Vorträge und Abhandlungen*, Tübingen, 1865, 2d ed. Leipzig, 1875, 2d series 1877, 3d series 1884; *Staat und Kirche*, Leipzig, 1873; *Geschichte der deutschen Philosophie seit Leibnitz*, Munich, 1872, 2d ed. 1875; *David Friedrich Strauss in seinem Leben und seinen Schriften*, Bonn, 1874; *Grundriss d. gesch. d. griech. Philosophie*, 1883; 2d ed. 1885 (English trans., *Outlines of the History of Greek Philosophy*, Lond. and N. Y., 1886); *Friedrich d. Gr. als Philosoph*, Berlin, 1886. He is son-in-law of Dr. Baur.

ZEZSCHWITZ, Gerhard von, D.D., Lutheran; b. at Bautzen, July 2, 1825; studied at Leipzig, 1846–50; was university preacher there, 1856; professor extraordinary, 1857–61; honorary professor at Giessen, 1865; ordinary professor at Erlangen, 1866, till his death, July 20, 1886. He published numerous sermons, and *Petri apostoli de Christi ad inferos descensu sententia*, Leipzig, 1857; *Profangräcität und biblischer Sprachgeist*, 1859; *System der christlich kirchlichen Katechetik*, 1 Bd. 1863–72, 2 vols., 2d ed. 1872–74; *Die Katechismen der Waldenser und Böhmischen Brüder, kritische Textausgabe*, Erlangen, 1863; *Ueber die wesentlichen Verfassungsziele der lutherischen Reformation*, Leipzig, 1867 (pp. 64); *System der praktischen Theologie*, 1876–78, 3 parts; *Der Kaisertraum des Mittelalters in seinen religiösen Motiven*, 1877 (pp. 31); *Das Drama vom Ende des römischen Kaisertums und von der Erscheinung des Antichrists. Nach Hdschs. d. 12. Jahrh. in deutsch*, 1878 (pp. 75); *Vom römischen Kaisertum deutscher Nation, ein mittelalterl. Drama*, 1877; *Die Christenlehre im Zusammenhang*, 1880–82, 3 parts, 2d ed 1883–85; *Luthers kleiner Katechismus*, 1880–81, 2 parts; *Lehrbuch der Pädagogik*, 1882; *Luthers Stellung*, Hamburg, 1883 (pp. 26). *

ZIMMER, Friedrich Karl, Ph.D. (Halle, 1877), **Lic. Theol.** (Bonn, 1880), German Protestant; b. at Gardelegen, Prussia, Sept. 22, 1855; educated at Tübingen and Berlin; became *privat-docent* of theology at Bonn 1880, the same at Königsberg, and pastor at Mahusfeld 1883; professor extraordinary, and pastor of the Deaconesses' hospital, Königsberg, 1884. He edited *Halleluja*, 1880–85. He is the author of *J. G. Fichte's Religionsphilosophie*, Berlin, 1878; *Der Spruch vom Jonazeichen*, Hildburghausen, 1881; *Galaterbrief und Apostelgeschichte*, 1882; *Exegetische Probleme des Hebräer und Galaterbriefs*, 1882; *Concordantiæ supplementariæ omnium vocum N. T.*, Gotha, 1882; *Die deutschen evangelischen Kirchengesangvereine der Gegenwart*, Quedlinburg, 1882; *Der Verfall des Kantoren- u. Organistenamtes in der evangelischen Landeskirche, Preussens, seine Ursachen u. Vorschläge zur Besserung*, 1885; several minor articles on church music and exegesis.

ZOECKLER, Otto, Ph.D. (Giessen, 1854), **Lic. Theol.** (do., 1856), **D.D.** (*hon.*, do., 1866), Lutheran; b. at Grünberg, Hesse, May 27, 1833; studied at Giessen, Erlangen, and Berlin, 1851–56; became *privat-docent* at Giessen, 1857; professor extraordinary, 1863; ordinary professor at Greifswald, 1866. He became *consistorialrath* at Greifswald, January, 1885. He edited the *Allgemeine literarische Anzeiger für das Ev. Deutschland*, 1867–74; and since 1882, has edited the *Evangelische Kirchenzeitung* (founded by Hengstenberg); and since 1866, been principal editor of *Der Beweis des Glaubens*. He is the author of *De vi ac notione vocabuli ἐλπίς in N. T.* (inaugural dissertation), Giessen, 1857; *Theologia naturalis: Entwurf einer systematischen Naturtheologie vom offenbarungsgläubigen Standpunkte*, vol. i., Frankfurt-a.-M., 1860; *Kritische Geschichte der Askese*, 1863; *Hieronymus, sein Leben und Wirken aus seinen Schriften dargestellt*, Gotha, 1864; commentary on *Chronicles*, *Job*, *Proverbs*, *Ecclesiastes*, *Canticles*, and *Daniel*, in Lange's *Bibelwerk*, Bielefeld, 1866–72 (translated New York, 1870 sqq.); *Die Urgeschichte der Erde und des Menschen*, Gütersloh, 1868; *Das Kreuz Christi*, 1875 (English trans., *The Cross of Christ*,

London, 1877); *Geschichte der Beziehungen zwischen Theologie und Naturwissenschaft*, 1877–79, 2 vols.; *Die Lehre vom Urstand des Menschen*, 1879; *Gottes Zeugen im Reich der Natur*, 1881, 2 vols. (Norwegian trans., Christiania 1882, English trans. 1886); editor of and contributor to *Handbuch der theologischen Wissenschaften*, Nördlingen, 1883–84, 3 vols., 2d ed. 1884–85, 4 vols.

ZOEPFFEL, Richard Otto, Ph.D., D.D. (both from Göttingen, 1871 and 1878), Protestant theologian (school of Ritschl); b. at Arensburg Livland (Russia), June 14, 1843; studied theology at Dorpat, 1862–68 (with interruptions); history at Göttingen, 1868–70; became *repetent* of theology at Göttingen, 1870; professor extraordinary of theology at Strassburg, 1872; ordinary professor there, 1877. He is the author of *Die Papstwahlen und die mit ihnen im nächsten Zusammenhange stehenden Ceremonien in ihren Entwickelung vom 11. bis zum 14. Jahrhundert*, Göttingen, 1871; (with Holtzmann) *Lexikon für Theologie und Kirchenwesen*, Leipzig, 1882.

ZUNZ, Leopold, Ph.D., Hebrew; b. at Detmold, Germany, Aug. 10, 1794; d. at Berlin, March 21, 1886. He was educated at the University of Berlin; became rabbi to the new synagogue there, 1820, but retired after two years, and started a society for Jewish culture and science, to which Heinrich Heine belonged. But the society, which was nicknamed "Young Jerusalem," although embracing many men of talent, soon broke up, perhaps because of Zunz's radicalism. Many of its members became Christians. From 1824 to 1832, Zunz was director of the New Jewish Congregational School. From 1825 to 1835 he edited the *Spener'sche Zeitung*. From 1835 to 1839, at Prague, he again undertook ministerial functions. From 1839 to 1850 he was director of the Normal Seminary in Berlin. Since 1845 he was a member of the Board of Commissioners for the educational interests of the Jews in Prussia. His long life was one of great literary activity. His works are distinguished by learning and by beauty and clearness of style. Among them may be mentioned, *Etwas über die rabbinische Litteratur*, Berlin, 1818 (which first brought him into notice); *Predigten*, 1823, 2d ed. 1846; *Die gottesdienstlichen Vorträge der Juden, historisch entwickelt*, 1832 (his most valuable book); *Namen der Juden*, Leipzig, 1837; *Zeittafel über die gesammte heilige Schrift*, Berlin, 1839; *Zur Geschichte und Literatur*, Bd. 1., 1845; *Damaskus, ein Wort zu Abwehr*, 2d ed. 1859; *Die synagogale Poesie des Mittelalters*, 1855–59, 2 parts; *Die Vorschriften über Eidesleistigung der Juden*, 1859; *Wahlrede*, 1861; *2. Wahlrede*, 1861; *Politisch und nicht politisch* (lecture), 1862; *Selbstregierung* (lecture), 1864; *Sterbelage*, 1864; *Die geistige Gesundheit* (lecture), 1864; *Die hebräischen Handschriften in Italien*, 1864; *Literaturgeschichte der synagogalen Poesie*, 1865; *Nachtrag dazu*, 1867; *Israels gottesdienstliche Poesie* (lecture), 1870; *Deutsche Briefe*, Leipzig, 1872. *

APPENDIX:

Mostly additions sent by the writers too late for insertion in the proper place. New book-titles follow directly after the authors' names.

ACHELIS, E. C. *Aus dem akademischen Gottesdienst in Marburg, Predigten*, Marburg, 1886.

ACQUOY, John Gerard Richard, D.D. (Leiden, 1857), Dutch Protestant theologian; b. at Amsterdam, Jan. 3, 1829; educated at the University of Amsterdam; became Reformed pastor at Eerbeek 1858, Koog 1861, Bommel 1863; professor of theology at Leiden, 1878; professor of ecclesiastical history, and history of Christian doctrine, in the same, 1881. In 1877 he became a member of the Royal Academy of Sciences. He is the author of *Gerardi Magni epistolæ XIV.* (his D.D. thesis), Amsterdam, 1857; and in Dutch of "Herman de Ruyter, after Published and Unpublished Documents," 1870; *Jan van Venray*, 1873; "The Cloister of Windesheim and its Influence," 1875, 3 vols.; "The History of the Reformed Church of Holland," in preparation.

AHLFELD, J. F. Cf. art. Herzog[2] XVII. 637 sqq.

ALLEN, A. V. G., received the degree of D.D. at Harvard's 250th anniversary, Nov. 8, 1886.

ALEXANDER, Bishop W. *The Divinity of our Lord*, London, 1886.

ALEXANDER, Henry Carrington, D.D. (Hampden-Sidney College, Va., 1869), Presbyterian; b. at Princeton, N.J., Sept. 27, 1835; graduated at the College of New Jersey, Princeton, N.J., 1854, and at the Theological Seminary in that place, 1858; was stated supply of the Eighty-fourth-street Church, New-York City, for six months in 1858; the same in the village church of Charlotte Court-House, Va., from Oct. 1, 1859, to May, 1861, pastor until Jan. 1, 1870; since professor of biblical literature and interpretation of the N. T., Union Theological Seminary, Va. Author of *Life of Joseph Addison Alexander, D.D.*, N.Y., 1870, 2 vols.

ARNOLD, M., resigned his inspectorship, November, 1886.

BAIRD, H. M. *The Huguenots, and Henry of Navarre*, New York, 1886, 2 vols.

BARTLETT, E. C., edited with J. P. Peters, *The Scriptures for Young People*, New York, 1886 sqq. 3 vols.

BARING-GOULD is lord of the Manor of Lew Trenchard and Waddlestone; eldest son of Edward Baring-Gould, J. P. and D. L. for County Devon, representative of the ancient family of Gould of Devon, which has occupied estates in the county since the reign of Henry III. Lew Trenchard became the property of the Goulds in 1625, and has continued in the family since. He is J. P. for County of Devon. To the list of his books add: *The Trials of Jesus*, London, 1886; *Nazareth and Capernaum: Ten Lectures on the Beginning of our Lord's Ministry*, 1886; *Our Parish Church: Twenty Addresses to Children on the Great Truths of the Christian Faith*, 1886.

BAUDISSIN, W. W. F., D.D. (*hon.*, Giessen, 1880).

BAUR, G. A. L., D.D. (*hon.*, ——, 18—); was member of commission for revising Luther's Bible. Add to list of books: *Sechs Tabellen über die israelitische Geschichte*, Giessen, 1848; (edited) *Andreas Kempfer's Selbstbiographie*, Leipzig, 1882; (with Dr. Karl A. Schmid), *Geschichte der Erziehung*, Stuttgart, 1884.

BEECHER, H. W., made a brilliant lecturing tour in England in the summer of 1886, and was offered a public reception by the Common Council of Brooklyn, but declined it (November, 1886).

BEETS, Nicolaas, D.D. (Leiden 1839, Edinburgh 1884), **Phil. Mag.** and **Litt. D.** (Utrecht, 1865), Dutch Protestant, religious poet; b. at Haarlem, Sept. 13, 1814; studied theology at Leiden; became Reformed pastor at Heemstede 1840, at Utrecht 1854; professor of theology at Utrecht, 1875. He is the author in Dutch of *Camera obscura* (under the pseudonyme of Hildebrand), Haarlem, 1839, 16th ed. 1886 (translated into different languages of Europe; the French title is, *Scènes de la vie hollandaise*, Paris, 1856); "Biography of J. H. van der Palm," 1842 (English trans. New York, 1865); "Hours of Devotion," 1848-75, 8 vols. (German select trans. Bonn, 1858); "St. Paul, at the most Important Times of his Life and Activity," 18—, 3d ed. 1859 (German trans. Gotha, 1857, Danish trans. Copenhagen, 1858); "Literary Recreations," 1856, 2d ed. 1873; collected edition of his poems, 1864-85, 4 vols.; "Literary Miscellanies," 1876, 2 vols.; editor of the complete works of Staring and Bogaers (Dutch poets of the nineteenth century), 1862 and 1871 respectively; and of Anna Rœmer Visscher (seventeenth century), 1881; translator into Dutch of *Emblèmes chrétiens* by Georgette de Montenay, lady of honor to Jeanne d'Albret, Queen of Navarre, 18—.

BEHRENDS, A. J. F. *Socialism and Christianity*, New York, 1886.

BELL, Frederik Willem Bernard van, D.D. (Leiden, 1849), Dutch Protestant theologian; b. at Rotterdam in the year 1822; studied at Leiden; became Reformed pastor at Noordwykerhout 1849, at Hoorn 1853, at Amsterdam 1855; professor of theological encyclopædia, interpretation of the Greek Testament, and moral philosophy, at Groningen. He is one of the founders and editors of the *Theologisch Tijdschrift*, Amsterdam and Leiden, 1867 sqq. He is the author of *De patefactionis christianæ indole, e vocabulis φανεροῦν et ἀποκαλύπτειν, in libris Novi Testamenti efficienda* (his D.D. thesis), Leiden, 1849; and in Dutch of "Discourse upon the Character of the Independent Theology," Amsterdam, 1872; "The Science of the Moral Life," 1874; "The Connection of Logic and Ethics," 1877.

BENDER, W., belongs to the left, or radical, wing of the school of Ritschl.

BENRATH, K., D.D. (*hon.*, Jena, 18—).

BENSON, Archbishop. *Communings of a Day held with Masters of Public Schools in the Chapel of Winchester College* (six short addresses), London, 1886.

BERESFORD, Right Hon. and Most Rev. Marcus Gervais, D.D. (Cambridge, 1840), **D.C.L.** (Oxford, 1862), Lord Archbishop of Armagh and Clogher, and Primate of All Ireland, Church of Ireland, a nephew of the first Marquis of Waterford; b. at Kilmore, Ireland, in the year 1801; d. at Armagh, Dec. 26, 1885; educated at Trinity College, Cambridge; graduated B.A. 1824, M.A. 1828; ordained deacon 1824, priest 1825; became rector of Kildallen, 1825; later vicar of Drungand Lara, and also vicar-general of Kilmore and archdeacon of Ardagh; bishop of Kilmore, 1854; translated to Armagh, 1863. *

BERNARD, Hon. and Right Rev. Charles Brodrick, D.D. (Oxford, 1866), lord bishop of Tuam, Killaloe, and Achonry, Church of Ireland, son of the second Earl of Bandon; b. at Bandon (?), Ireland, Jan. 4, 1811; educated at Balliol College, Oxford; graduated B.A. 1832, M.A. 1834, B.D. 1866; was ordained deacon 1835, priest 1836; was vicar of Bantry, 1840–42; rector of Kilbrogan, senior prebendary of Cork, and rural dean, 1842–66; consecrated bishop, 1867. He is the author of occasional sermons and lectures. *

BERSIER, E. *Les Réfugiés français et leurs industries* (lecture), Paris, 1886.

BESTMANN, H. J. *Die evangelischen Missionen und das deutsche Reich* (lecture), Leipzig, 1886.

BEVAN, L. D., was assistant and co-pastor with Rev. Thomas Binney, 1865–66; became pastor at Melbourne, Australia, 1886.

BEYSCHLAG, (Johann Heinrich Christoph) Willibald, D.D. (*hon.*, Königsberg, 1861), United Evangelical; b. at Frankfort-on-the-Main, Sept. 5, 1823; educated at the gymnasium in Frankfort, and at the universities of Bonn and Berlin, 1840–44; became *Vicar* at Coblenz, 1849; *Hülfsamtspfarrer*, also *Religionslehrer* in Trier, 1850; court preacher at Carlsruhe, 1856; ordinary professor of theology at Halle, 1860. He is theologically a pupil of Schleiermacher and Nitzsch, and a leader of the "Middle Party." His principal work is the *Life of Christ*, 2 vols. To the books mentioned on p. 17, add *Zur deutschchristlichen Bildung* (collected popular lectures), Halle, 1880.

BICKERSTETH, E. *The Rock of Ages*, 1858; *The Lord's Supper*, 1881; "*From Year to Year*," *or poems for every Sunday and Holy-day in the Year*, 1883; *Lay Ministration* (a paper), London, 1886.

BLUNT, J. H. *Dictionary of Sects*, etc., new ed. 1886.

BOARDMAN, George Nye, D.D. (Middlebury College, Vt., 1867), Congregationalist; b. at Pittsford, Vt., Dec. 23, 1825; graduated at Middlebury College, Vt., 1847, and at Andover Theological Seminary, Mass., 1852; was resident licentiate, 1852–53; professor of rhetoric and English literature in Middlebury College, 1853–59; pastor of Presbyterian Church at Binghamton, N.Y., 1859–72; since 1872 has been professor of systematic theology in the Chicago Congregational Theological Seminary. He is the author of *The Will, Virtue* (two essays), Chicago, 1882; (with others) *Current Discussions in Theology*, 1883 sqq.

BONAR, H. *Hymns of Faith and Hope*, new ed. 1886.

BONET-MAURY, A. G. C. A., when at Beauvais, built a church. In 1885 he became librarian of the Musée pedagogique, Paris. To list of books add: *L'Empéreur Akbar. Un chapitre de l'histoire de l'Inde au XVI.e siècle, par le Comte F. A. de Noer, traduit de l'allemand, avec une introduction* (by Bonet-Maury), Leiden, 1883–86, 2 vols.

BONNET, J., is a professor in the University of France. His *Olympia Morata* has been translated into several languages, besides the German (Hamburg, 1860); his *Aonio Paleario* into German (Hamburg, 1863), Italian (Florence, 18—); his *Récits*, etc., into German (Berlin, 1864). He edited the admirable *Mémoires* of Louis de Marolles, from the time of the Revocation, Paris, 1882; and a third series of *Récits du seizième siècle*, 1886.

BORDIER, Henri Léonard, Reformed Church of France, layman; b. in Paris, in the year 1817; educated at the École de droit and the École des Chartes in Paris, and licensed in law, and as palæographic archivist in 1840; but has ever since devoted himself to historical studies. He was successively, for a time, assistant to the historian Augustin Thierry; assistant in the Academy of Inscriptions; secretary *par interim* of the École des Chartes; a member of the commission on the departmental archives of the minister of the interior (1846), archivist of the national archives (1850), dismissed on the establishment of the Empire. He was, during the siege of Paris, on the commission upon the papers of the Tuileries; and in 1872 nominated honorary librarian in the department of manuscripts in the National Library. He has been for many years on the committee, of the "Société d'histoire du protestantisme français." He is the author of numerous works, noted for their great accuracy. Among them may be mentioned: various notices in the *Bibliothèque de l'école des Chartes*, Paris, 1841-86: *Histoire générale de tous les dépôts d'archives existant en France*, 1855; *Les églises et monastères de Paris*, 1856; an edition of *Libri miraculorum aliaque opera minora* of Gregory of Tours, Latin text with French translation, 1857-64, 4 vols.; a French translation of the *Historia Francorum* of Gregory of Tours, 1859-61, 2 vols.; (with Ed. Charton) *Histoire de France*, 1859-61; *Les inventaires des archives de l'Empire*, 1867; *Une fabrique de faux autographes*, 1869; *Chansonnier huguenot du seizième siècle*, 1869; *L'Allemagne aux Tuileries, de 1850 à 1870*, 1872; *La Saint Barthélemy et la critique moderne*, Geneva, 1879; *L'école historique de Jérôme Bolsec*, Paris, 1880; *Nicolas Castellin de Tournay, réfugié à Genève (1564-1576)*, 1881; is re-issuing with enlargements and corrections, the brothers Eugène and Émile Haag's *La France protestante* (original ed., Paris, 1848–59, 10 vols.), Paris, 1877 sqq.

BREDENKAMP, C. J. *Der Prophet Jesaia erläutert*, Erlangen, 1886 sq.

BRIGGS, C. A. *Messianic Prophecy*, New York and Edinburgh, 1886.

BRIGHT, W., was educated at Rugby School; ordained deacon 1848, priest 1850; appointed proctor of the chapter in convocation, 1879.

BROOKE, S. A. *The Unity of God and Man, and other Sermons*, London, 1886.

BROWNE, E. H., was educated at Eton. Besides the commentary on *Genesis*, he wrote the *Introduction to the Pentateuch* in the *Speaker's Commentary*.

BRUCE, A. B. *The Miraculous Element in the Gospels*, New York, 1886 (lectures delivered in the Union Theological Seminary, N.Y., on the Ely Foundation).

BRUECKNER, B. B., is Ph.D. and LL.D. as well as D.D. He is *Propst* of St. Nicholas and St. Mary, vice-president of the Berlin *Ober-consistorialrath*, *Mitglied des Staatsrath*, and *Domherr* in Brandenburg. His *Predigten 1853-60*, 5th ed. Leipzig, 1886; *1861-66*, 5th ed. 1886.

BRUSTON, C. A. *Du texte primitif des Psaumes*, 1873; *Études sur l'Apocalypse*, 1884; *Les deux Jehovistes, études sur les sources de l'Histoire sainte*, 1885.

BUCHWALD, G. A. *Landeskirche und Freikirche*, Zwickau, 1886; *Die Lutherfunde der neueren Zeit insbesondere in der zwickauer Ratsschulbibliothek* (lecture), Zwickau, 1886, contributed to *Blätter für Hymnologie*.

BUCKLEY, J. M. *The Land of the Czar and the Nihilist*, Boston, 1886.

BURGON, J. W. The list of Dean Burgon's publications, as given by himself, is as follows: *Mémoire sur les vases Panathaiques par le Chev. Brönsted* (translated), London, 1833; *The Life and Times of Sir Thomas Gresham*, 1839, 2 vols.; *Petra, a Poem*, 1846; *Some Remarks on Art*, 1846; (edited with Rev. H. J. Rose) *Fifty Cottage Prints*, 1851; *Thirty-six Cottage Wall-Prints*, 1853; *The Pictorial Bible*, 1854; *Oxford Reformers*, 1854; *The History of our Lord* (with 72 engravings): *a Plain Commentary on the Four Holy Gospels*, 1855, 8 vols. new ed. 1877, 4 vols., reprinted Philadelphia, 1856 and 1868, 2 vols.; *Ninety Short Sermons, for Family Reading*, 1855, 2 vols.; *Historical Notices of the Colleges of Oxford*, 1857; *One Soweth, and Another Reapeth* (ordination sermon), 1859; *Portrait of a Christian Gentleman: a Memoir of P. F. Tytler, Esq.*, 1859; *Inspiration and Interpretation* (answer to *Essays and Reviews*), 1861; *Letters from Rome to Friends in England*, 1862; *A Treatise on the Pastoral Office*, 1864; *Zaccheus*, 1864; *Work of the Christian Builder tried by Fire*, 1865; *Ninety-one Short Sermons*, 2d series, 1867, 2 vols.; *The Lambeth Conference and the Encyclical*, 1867; *Plea for a Fifth School*, 1868; *Disestablishment, The Nation's Formal Rejection of God and Denial of the Faith*, 1868; *England and Rome: Three Letters to a Pervert*, 1869; *The Roman Council*, 1869; *First and Second Protest against Dr. Temple's Consecration*, 1869; *Protests of the Bishops*, 1870; *Dr. Temple's Explanation examined*, 1870; *The Last 12 Verses of the Gospel according to St. Mark, vindicated against Recent Critical Objectors and established*, 1871; *The Review of a Year*, 1871; *Woman's Place*, 1871; *An Unitarian Reviser of our Authorized Version, Intolerable*, 1872; *The New Lectionary*, 1872; *The Athanasian Creed to be retained in its Integrity, and why*, 1872; *The Oxford Diocesan Conference, and Romanizing within the Church of England* (2 sermons), 1st to 3d ed. 1873; *A Plea for the Study of Divinity in Oxford*, 1875; *Home Missions and Sensational Religion*: also *Humility, Ad Clerum*, 1876; *The New Lectionary examined, with Reasons for its Amendment* (jointly with the Bishop of Lincoln and Dean Goulbourn), 1877; *Nehemiah, a Pattern for Builders*, 1878; *The Servants of Scripture*, 1878; *The Disestablishment of Religion in Oxford, the Betrayal of a Sacred Trust: Words of Warning to the University*, 1880; *Prophecy,—not "Forecast," but (in the words of Bishop Butler) "The History of Events before they come to pass,"* 1880; *Divergent Ritual Practice*, 1881; *Canon Robert Gregory, A Letter of Friendly Remonstrance*, 1st and 2d ed. 1881; *The Revision Revised: Three Articles from the Quarterly Review, with a Reply to Bishop Ellicott's Pamphlet, and a Vindication of the Traditional Reading of 1 Tim. iii. 16*, 1883; *To Educate Young Women like Young Men, and with Young Men, a Thing Inexpedient and Immodest*, 1884; *Poems (1840-78)*, 1885.

CARROLL, Henry King, LL.D. (Syracuse University, N.Y., 1885), Methodist layman; b. at Dennisville, N.J., Nov. 15, 1847; was self-taught; became editor of *The Havre Republican*, Maryland, 1868; assistant editor of *The Methodist*, New York, 1869; of *The Hearth and Home*, New York, 1870; night agent of the New-York Associated Press, 1871; special correspondent of the Boston (Mass.) *Traveller*, 1873; religious editor of the New-York *Independent*, 1876. He was a delegate from the Methodist-Episcopal Church to the Œcumenical Methodist Conference in London, 1881; organizing secretary of the Methodist Centennial Conference, 1884. He was the chief editor of the *Proceedings of the Centennial Methodist Conference*, New York, 1885; is the author of the pamphlets, *World of Missions*, New York, 1882; *Catholic Dogma of Church Authority*, New York, 1884; and is a frequent contributor to the *Methodist Quarterly Review*, New York.

CASPARI, C. P., shared in the new Norwegian translation of the Old Testament, which appeared in 1887.

CASSEL, P. *Kritisches Sendschreiben über die Probebibel*, Berlin, 1885 (Heft I., *Mit e. wissenschaftl. Anmerkung über Hellenismen in den Psalmen*; Heft II., *Messianische Stellen des alten Testaments. Anhängt sind Anmerkungen über Megillath Taanith*); *Aus dem Lande des Sonnenaufgangs*, 1885; *Zoroaster, sein Name und seine Zeit*, 1886 (pp. 24).

CHESTER, Right Rev. William Bennet, D.D. (Trinity College, Dublin, 1883), lord bishop of Killaloe, Church of Ireland; b. at Ballyclough, County Cork, Ireland, in the year 1820; educated at Trinity College, Dublin; graduated B.A. and divinity testimonium (second-class) 1846, M.A. 1856, B.D. 1883; ordained deacon and priest, 1846; became curate of Kilrush, 1846; vicar of Killead 1847, of Killkee 1849; rector of Ballymackey and chancellor of Killaloe, 1855; rector of Nenagh 1859, of Birr 1875 (prebendary of Tipperkevin or canon of St. Patrick's, 1877-84; archdeacon of Killaloe, 1880-84); bishop of Killaloe, Kilfenora, Clonfert, and Kilmacduagh, 1884. *

CHEYNE, T. K. *Job and Solomon; or, the Wisdom of the Old Testament* (an introduction to the criticism and exegesis of *Job, Proverbs, Ecclesiastes*, and *Ecclesiasticus*), 1886. He also contributed to the Queen's Printers' *Teacher's Bible*; and art. *Hittites* in the 9th ed. of the *Encyclopædia Britannica*.

CHURCH, R. W. *Advent Sermons*, London, 1886; *Human Life and its Conditions*, 2d ed. 1886.

CLARKE, J. F. *Vexed Questions in Theology*, 1886: *The Fourth Gospel*, 1886.

COMBA, E. *Vera Narrazione del Massacro di Valtellina di V. Parravicino*, 1886; *Parafrasi sopra l' Ep. di S. Paolo ai Romani di F. Virginio*, 1886. He is editing the *Histoire des Vaudois d'Italie depuis leurs origines jusqu'à nos jours*, 2 vols.

CONDER, Eustace Rogers, D.D. (Edinburgh, 1882), Congregationalist; b. near St. Albans (the ancient Verulam), Eng., April 5, 1820; educated for the Christian ministry at Spring Hill College, Birmingham; entered, 1838; graduated M.A. in philosophy, with gold medal, at the University of London, 1844; became Congregational pastor at Poole, Dorset, 1844; at Leeds (East Parade Congregational Church), 1861. He was chairman of the Congregational Union in 1873. He is "distinctly and strongly evangelical, with high views of authority of Scripture; but of broad sympathies, unpledged to any party formula or narrow creed." He is the author of *Memoir of Josiah Conder* (his father, see *Encyclopædia*, iii. 2590), London, 1856; *Commentary on St. Matthew's Gospel*, 1866; *Sleepy Forest, and other Tales for Children*, 1872; *The Basis of Faith, Critical Survey of Christian Theism* (Congregational lecture for 1877), 1877, 3d ed. 1886; *Outlines of the Life of Christ*, 1881; *Drops and Rocks, and other Talks with the Children*, 1882; a great number of articles in reviews and magazines, lectures, etc.

CORNILL, Carl Heinrich, Lic. Theol. (Marburg, 1880 [?]), **D.D.** (*hon.*, Heidelberg, 1886), German Protestant theologian; b. in Germany, April 26, 1854; pursued his theological studies at Marburg, and other universities; became *privat-docent* of theology at Marburg, 1880 [?]; professor extraordinary at Königsberg, 1886. He is the author of *Jeremia und seine Zeit*, Heidelberg, 1880 (pp. 39); *Der Prophet Ezechiel geschildert*, 1882 (pp. 53); *Das Buch des Propheten Ezechiel* (a critical reconstruction of the Hebrew text), Leipzig, 1886 (pp. xii. 513). *

COTTERILL, H., d. at Edinburgh, Thursday, April 15, 1886.

COULIN, F. *La vocation du chrétien*, Paris, 1870.

CRAMER, Jacobus, D.D. (Utrecht, 1858), Dutch Protestant theologian; b. at Rotterdam, Dec. 24, 1833; educated at Utrecht; became adjunct to the director of the Missionary Society of Rotterdam, 1858; Reformed pastor at Oude Wetering 1859, at Charlois 1862, and at Amsterdam 1866; professor of the history of the Christian religion, early Christian literature, and history of Christian doctrine, at Groningen, 1876, since 1884 at Utrecht. He is an advocate of the evangelical orthodox theology, as appears, amongst other things, from the "Contributions in the Domain of Theology and Philosophy," which he published with G. H. Lamers (Amsterdam, 1867-85, 5 vols.). He is the author of *Specimen historico-dogmaticum de Arianismo* (his D.D. thesis), Utrecht, 1858; and in Dutch of "Christianity and Humanity," Amsterdam, 1871; "Alexander Vinet, considered as a Christian Moralist and Apologist," 1883 (crowned by The Hague Society).

CREIGHTON, M., Hon. D.C.L. (Durham, 1885). In 1885 he was appointed by the Crown, canon of Worcester Cathedral; in 1886 sent by Cambridge University to represent John Harvard's college (Emmanuel), at the 250th anniversary of the founding of Harvard University, on which occasion (Monday, Nov. 8, 1886) he received the degree of LL.D.

CREMER, A. H. *Biblisch.-theologisches Wörterbuch. Suppl. Heft zur 3. Aufl.*, Gotha, 1886 (English trans. of the *Supplement*, Edinburgh, 1886).

CROSBY, H. Full title of his N. T. *Commentary* is, *The New Testament in both Authorized and Revised Versions, carefully annotated*, Boston, 1885.

CROSKERY, T., d. at Londonderry, Oct. 3, 1886.

CULROSS, James, D.D. (St. Andrew's, 1867), Baptist; b. near Blairgowrie, Perthshire, Scotland, in November, 1824; graduated M.A. at the University of St. Andrew's, 1846; engaged in theological studies till 1849; was Baptist pastor at Stirling, 1850-70; Highbury Hill, London, 1870-78; Adelaide Place, Glasgow, 1878-83; was appointed theological tutor by the Baptist Union of Scotland, 1869; since 1883 he has been president of the Bristol Baptist College. He was president of the Union, 1870; vice-president of the Baptist Union of Great Britain and Ireland, 1886. He is the author of *Lazarus revived*, London, 1858, 3d ed. 1863 (incorporated in *The House at Bethany: its Joys and Sorrows, and its Divine Guest* [1876]); *The Missionary Martyr of Delhi*, 1860; *The Divine Compassion, or Jesus showing Mercy*, 1864; *Emmanuel, or the Father revealed in Jesus*, 1868, 2d ed. 1869; *John whom Jesus loved*, 1872, 2d ed. 1878; "*Behold, I stand at the Door, and knock*," 1874, 2d ed. 1877; "*Thy First Love*," *Christ's Message to Ephesus* [1877]; *The Greatness of Little Things* [1879]; *William Carey*, 1881; *The Service of the King*, Edinburgh, 1884; besides small books, and contributions to periodical literature.

CUNITZ, A. E., studied at Strassburg, Göttingen, Berlin, and Paris. Of the *Histoire ecclésiastique*, vols. i., ii., and iii. 1st part, have appeared. He also has written *Histoire critique de l'interprétation du Cantique*, Strassburg, 1834; *Ueber die Amtsbefugnisse der Consistorien in der prot. Kirche Frankreichs*, 1847; and several articles in the *Allg. Lit. Zeitung* of Jena, in the *Revue de théologie* of Strassburg, in Herzog, etc. Died in Strassburg, June 16, 1886.

DALE, R. W., in 1885 was appointed by the Crown a member of a commission for inquiring into the working of the English system of elementary education. He has written *A Preliminary Essay* to a translation of Carl Schmidt's *Social Results of Early Christianity*, London, 1885.

DALTON, H. *Nathanael*, St. Petersburg, 3d ed. 1886; *Immanuel* (trans. into Dutch); *Der verlorne Sohn*, 2d ed. 1884.

D'ALVIELLA, Count E. Goblet. *Harrison contre Spencer* (trans. into English by Prof. E. L. Youmans, as appendix to the reprint of Harrison and Spencer's *The Nature and Reality of Religion*, New York, 1885); *Cours d'introduction à l'histoire générale des religions*, Ghent, 1886; articles in *Revue de l'instruction publique*.

DAVIDSON, R. L., was educated at Harrow.

He was appointed domestic chaplain to the Queen, 1883.

DAVIES, J. L., contributed *Peaks, Passes, and Glaciers*, to *Tracts for Priests and People.*

DEANE, H., was Grinfield lecturer in the University of Oxford, 1884–86. He has also written various sermons and articles.

DEANE, W. J., was educated at Rugby. *Catechism*, 3d ed., 1886.

DECOPPET, Auguste Louis, Reformed Church of France; b. in Paris, Feb. 4, 1836; studied at the preparatory school of theology of Batignolles; became professor of history and French literature in the Royal College of Noorthey, Holland, where the Prince of Orange studied, 1858; determining on a ministerial career, he entered the theological seminary of Montauban, and graduated B.D. 1863; became pastor at Alais 1863; pastor of the Reformed Church of Paris 1869, and is now at the Oratoire. Among his works may be mentioned, *Catéchisme élémentaire*, Paris, 1875; *Paris protestant*, 1876; *Sermons*, 1876; *Sermons pour les enfants*, 3 series, 3d 1880 (translated into Danish, Hungarian, German [Gütersloh, 1883], and English); *Méditations pratiques*, 1881. *

DELITZSCH, Friedrich. *Prolegomena eines neuen hebräisch-aramäischen Wörterbuchs zum Alten Testament*, Leipzig, 1886.

DENISON, Ven. G. A., is brother of the late Lord Ossington, speaker of the House of Commons, 1857–72; of the Bishop of Salisbury, 1837–54; and of Sir William Denison, K.C.B., Governor of Tasmania, Sydney, Madras, 1846–66. The archdeacon, as member of the Lower House of Convocation from revival of Convocation in 1852, was chairman of committees reporting in condemnation of *Essays and Reviews*, and of Bishop Colenso's writings on the Old Testament. The Elementary Education Act conditioned the public grant upon the change of the schools of the Church of England into state schools, and in the attendent controversy he bore a prominent part. In December, 1885, after the general election, he issued a pamphlet, *Mr. Gladstone*, in its 7th thousand, March, 1886.

DERENBOURG, Joseph, Ph.D. (Giessen, 1834); b. at Mayence, Aug. 21, 1811; studied at the Talmudical School and in the gymnasium of Mayence, and at the universities of Giessen and Bonn. He came to Paris in 1839; became a corrector of the press in the National Printing House (1852), especially of Hebrew (1856); professor of rabbinic and Talmudic Hebrew in the University of Paris, 1877. In 1871 he was elected a member of the Academy of Inscriptions and Belles-lettres. He is one of the most frequent contributors to the *Journal scientifique de la théologie juive*, and to the *Revue juive scientifique et pratique*, *Journal asiatique*, *Revue critique;* editor of Lokmann's *Fables*, Paris, 1846; the second edition (with M. Reinaud) of the *Séances de Hariri*, 1847–53; author of *Essai sur l'histoire de la Palestine*, 1867, etc. *

DIECKHOFF, A. W., was professor extraordinary at Göttingen, 1854, before becoming ordinary professor at Rostock, 1860. He has written *Zur Lehre von der Bekehrung und von der Prädestination: Zweite Entgegung auf missourische Ausflüchte*, Rostock, 1886; *Der Ablassstreit, Dogmengeschichtlich dargestellt*, Gotha, 1886.

DITTRICH, F., was professor of moral theology, 1872; of ecclesiastical history, 1873. He has published *Observationes quædam de ordine naturali et morali*, Braunsberg, 1869; *Regesten und Briefe des Cardinals Gasparo Contarini (1483–1542)*, 1881; *Gasparo Contarini, eine Monographie*, 1885. In the *Indice Lectionum Lycei Hosiani Brunsbergensis* he wrote the following articles: *De Socratis sententia, virtutem esse scientiam*, 1868; *Quid e S. Pauli sententia lex mosaica in moribus spectaverit*, 1871; *De Tertulliano christianæ veritatis regulæ contra hæreticorum licentiam vindice*, 1877; *Quæ partes fuerint Petri Pauli Vergerii in colloquio Wormatiensi*, 1879; *Sixti IV. Summi Pontificis ad Paulum III. Op. Pontif. Max. compositionum defensio*, 1883. He edited the *Mittheilungen des ermlaendischen Kunstvereins*, Braunsberg, 1870, 1871, 1875; has also contributed to the *Zeitschrift für Geschichte und Alterthumskunde Ermlands;* to the *Historisches Jahrbuch der Görres-Gesellschaft* (*Die Nuntiaturberichte Giovanni Morone's vom Reichstage zu Regensburg 1541*, 1883); and to the *Beiträge zur Geschichte der katholischen Reformation im ersten Drittel des 16 Jahrhunderts*, in 1884 and 1886.

DIX, M. *The Gospel and Philosophy*, New York, 1886.

DIXON, R. W., is the son of James Dixon, a celebrated Wesleyan preacher. He has written *Lyrical Poems*, Oxford, 1886.

DODS, M., wrote other articles in the *Encyclopædia Britannica*, besides those mentioned; *Parables*, 1st series, 3d ed. 1886.

DOEDES, J. I., teaches also natural theology and textual criticism. Page 56, l. 14, r. *Kerkelijke;* l. 19, supply *de* before *Jesu.*

DONALDSON, J., rector of the University of St. Andrews, 1886.

DORNER, A., studied at Berlin, Tübingen, and Göttingen. He has written, *Ueber die Principien der kantischen Ethik*, Berlin, 1875; *Schelling, zur Erinnerung an seinen hundertjaehrigen Geburtstag*, 1875; *Dem Andenken von I. A. Dorner*, 1885. In *Studien und Kritiken: Hartmann's Philosophie des Unbewussten*, 1881; *Ueber das Wesen der Religion*, 1883; *Das Verhältniss von Kirche und Staat nach Occam*, 1885. In Herzog², *Augustin, Johannes von Damask, Duns Scotus, Dorner.*

DORNER, I. A. Add to his works: *Zum dreihundertjährigen Gedächtniss des Todes Melanchthons*, 1860. The eschatological portion of his *System of Doctrine* was separately edited in English under the title: *Doctrine of the Future State*, with an introduction and notes, by Dr. Newman Smyth, New York, 1883; English trans. of his *Sittenlehre*, by Dr. Mead, *Christian Ethics*, Edinburgh, 1887. His essay *On the Sinless Perfection of Jesus* (1862) was translated into French in the "Revue Chrétienne," and into English by Dr. Henry B. Smith, in the "American Presbyterian Review," New York, 1863. Comp. art. *Dorner*, by his son, in the Appendix vol. of Herzog², xvii. pp. 755–770.

DOUEN, E. O. *Essai historique sur les Églises du département de l'Aisne*, Paris, 1860; besides nearly a hundred contributions in Lichtenberger's *Encyclopédie des sciences religieuses* [forty signed], he published in the *Bulletin de l'histoire du protestantisme* in 1886 a fragment of a partially executed work upon *La Révocation de l'Édit de Nantes à Paris.*

DRUMMOND, Henry, has made scientific expeditions in Europe, America, and Central Africa, and is the author of various scientific papers.

DUCHESNE, L., since 1885 has been "*Maître de conférences d'histoire à l'École des Hautes-Études de la Sorbonne*," Paris.

DUHM, B., D.D. (*hon.*, Basel, 1885).

DUNS, J., became a fellow of the Royal Society of Edinburgh, 1859; wrote *Memoir of Sir James Simpson, Bart., M.D.*, Edinburgh, 1873.

DWIGHT, T., received the degree of LL.D. at the 250th anniversary of Harvard College, Nov. 8, 1886; translated the third edition of Godet on *John*.

DYER, H. *Records of an Active Life*, New York, 1886.

EATON, Samuel John Mills, D.D. (Washington and Jefferson College, Washington, Penn., 1868), Presbyterian; b. at Fairview, Erie County, Penn., April 15, 1820; graduated at Jefferson College, Canonsburg, Penn., 1845; studied at the Western Theological Seminary, Allegheny, Penn., 1846–48; was stated supply and pastor at Franklin, Penn., 1848–82; at Mt. Pleasant, Penn., 1848–55. He was permanent clerk, synod of Allegheny, 1859–70; stated clerk, synod of Erie, 1870–81; has been stated clerk, presbytery of Erie, since 1853; trustee of Washington and Jefferson College, Washington, Penn., since 1879; director of the Western Theological Seminary since 1880. He was a delegate in the Christian Commission, 1864; travelled in the East, 1871. He is the author of *History of Petroleum*, Philadelphia, 1864; *History of the Presbytery of Erie*, New York, 1868; *Ecclesiastical History* (in *Centennial Memorials of Presbyterianism in Western Pennsylvania*, Harrisburg, 1869); *History of Venango County, Penn.*, 1876; *Lakeside*, Pittsburg, 1880; *Memoir of Rev. Cyrus Dickson, D.D.*, New York, 1883; *Jerusalem*, 1883; *Palestine*, 1884; *Lamberton Memorial*, Pittsburg, 1885.

EBRARD, A. *Apologetics: or, The Scientific Vindication of Christianity*, translated by Rev. W. Stuart and Rev. John Macpherson, Edinburgh, 1886, 2 vols.

EDDY, Z., removed to Detroit, Mich., in 1886.

EDEN, R., d. at Inverness, Thursday, Aug. 26, 1886.

EDERSHEIM, A., was the first Jew to carry off a prize at the gymnasium of Vienna. He was educated in Hungary as well as in Austria (Vienna). He wrote articles *Josephus* and *Philo*, in Smith and Wace's *Dictionary of Christian Biography;* and commentary on *Ecclesiasticus*, in the *Bible* (*Speaker's*) *Commentary on the Apocrypha; Israel and Judah, from the Reign of Ahab to the Decline of the Two Kingdoms*, 1886.

EDWARDS', L., collected works were published in Welsh at Wrexham. The most important are, "The Doctrine of the Atonement," and "The Harmony of the Faith."

ELLICOTT, Bishop. *Are We to Modify Fundamental Doctrine?* 2d ed. 1886.

ELLIOTT, C., is a member of the Victoria Institute of London.

EYRE, C., went to Newcastle-on-Tyne, 1843; was canon theologian and vicar-general; is a member of the Order of the Knights of Malta, and also of the Holy Sepulchre.

FAIRCHILD, J. H., was tutor in languages in Oberlin College, 1839–42.

FARRAR, A. S., was select preacher at Oxford, 1885–86; examining chaplain to the Bishop of Peterborough since 1868.

FARRAR, F. W., travelled in the United States in 1885, and lectured on Dante, Browning, and the Talmud; contributed commentary on *Judges* in Bishop Ellicott's *Commentary*, and on *Book of Wisdom* in *Bible* (*Speaker's*) *Commentary on the Apocrypha.*

FAUSSET, A. R., B.D. and **D.D.** (by special grace of the Board of Trinity College and University, Dublin, 1886), became canon of York Minster, 1885.

FERGUSON, Samuel David, D.D. (Theological Seminary, Gambier, O., 1885).

FFOULKES, E. S., was examiner in the Honour School of Theology, Oxford, 1873–75; wrote *Primitive Consecration of the Eucharistic Oblation*, London, 1886; numerous articles on church history and theology in Smith's Dictionaries of *Christian Antiquities* and *Biography*.

FIELD, H. M. *Blood thicker than Water: a few Days among our Southern Brethren*, New York, 1886. Started Nov. 4, 1886, for Spain and Algiers.

FISHER, G. P., received the degree of D.D. at the 250th anniversary of Harvard College, Nov. 8, 1886. Add: *Catholicity* (sermon), 1886.

FLIEDNER, F., edits also *Blätter aus Spanien;* and the periodicals, *Christian Review* (fortnightly) and *Children's Friend* (monthly); has prepared, in Spanish, *Lives of Livingstone, Luther, Dr. Fliedner* (his father), *John Howard, Elizabeth Fry, Hymnbook for Sunday Schools*, and various other books for the Spanish Christian literature.

FLINT, R., was appointed in 1859 to the pastorate of the East Parish, Aberdeen, and in 1861 to that of Kilconquhar, Fife. He is a corresponding member of the Institute of France, and a fellow of the Royal Society of Edinburgh. Author of *Vico*, Edinburgh, 1884.

FOSTER, R. V., was chief editor of the comments on the *International Lessons*, and other Sunday-school literature of the Cumberland Presbyterian Church, from 1880 to 1881; and for three years, since 1877, he was in charge of the belles-lettres department of Cumberland University, at the same time discharging the duties of his theological professorship. — Trinity University is at Tehuacana, Tex.

FRANK, F. H. R. *System of the Christian Certainty*, Eng. trans., Edinburgh, 1886.

FRANKE, A. H., D.D. (Halle, 1885).

FREPPEL, C. E. *St. Irénée*, 3d ed. 1886.

FRICKE, G. A., became *Consistorialrath* in 1882.

FRIEDLIEB, J. H., 2d ed. *Synopsis Evangeliorum*, Regensburg, 1869.

FRIEDRICH, J. Died in summer of 1886.

FRITZSCHE, O. F. *Confessio helvetica posterior*, Zürich, 1839; *Duplex libri* Ἐσθήρ, *textus græca*, 1848; *Specimen ed.-crit. interpr. veter. lat. N. T.*, 1867; *Epistola Clem. ad Jacob. et Rufini interpret.*, 1873.

FUNCKE, O. *Willst du gesund werden?* 4th ed. 1886.

FUNK, F. X. *Kirchengeschichte*, 1886 sqq.

GAMS, Bonifaz, Ph.D. (Tübingen, 1838?), **D.D.** (*hon.*, Tübingen, 18—), Roman Catholic; b. at Mittelbuch, Jan. 23, 1816; studied at Tübingen, where he received the prize of the theological faculty, and the first homiletical prize, 1838; became *vikar* at Aichstetten and Gmünd, 1838; acting preceptor at Horb, 1811; made a scientific journey at the expense of the State, 1842–43; became acting pastor at Wurmlingen, 1844; acting professor at Rottweil, 1844; chief preceptor at Gmünd, 1845; professor of theology at Hildesheim, 1847; novice in the Benedictine Abbey of St. Boniface in Munich 1855, monk there 1856; rose to be superior, but later resigned. He has published *Die sieben Worte Jesu am Kreuze*, Rottenburg, 1845; *Ausgang und Ziel der Geschichte*, Tübingen, 1850; *Johannes der Täufer im Gefängnisse*, 1853; *Die Geschichte der Kirche Jesu Christe im 19. Jahrhundert*, Innsbruck, 1853–58, 3 vols.; *Die 11. Säkularfeier des Martyrtodes des hl. Bonifazius in Fulda und Mainz*, Mainz, 1855; *Margott, die Siege der Kirche im ersten Jahrzehnt des Pontifikats Pius IX.*, Innsbruck 1860, 2d ed. 1860; *Katechetische Reden gehalten in der Basilika zu München*, Regensburg, 1862, 2 vols.; *Organisierung des Peter-Pfennigs*, 1862; *Kirchengeschichte von Spanien*, 1862–76, 4 vols.; *Register zu den historisch-politischen Blättern*, Munich, 1865; *Der Peterspfennig als Stiftung*, Regensburg, 1866; *J. A. Möhler, ein Lebensbild, mit Briefen und kleineren Schriften Möhlers*, 1866; *Das Jahr des Martyrtodes der hl. Apostel Petrus und Paulus*, 1867; *Kirchengeschichte von J. A. Möhler*, 1867–70, 3 vols.; *Series Episcoporum ecclesiæ catholicæ quotquot innotuerunt a B. Petro Ap.*, 1873; 1st supplement to the same, *Hierarchia cathol. Pii IX.*, Münich, 1879; *Der Bonifazius-Verein in Süddeutschland 1850–80*, Paderborn, 1880; *Predigt aus Anlass des Jubiläums*, Munich, 1881; 2d supplement to *Series episcop.*, Regensburg, 1886; numerous reviews and articles in the Tübingen *Quartalschrift*, etc. *

GANDELL, R. His fellowship of Hertford College is unendowed. The edition of Lightfoot's *Horæ* was published by the Clarendon Press, Oxford.

GASS, F. W. J. H. *Optimismus und Pessimismus, der Gang der christlichen Welt- und Lebensansicht*, Berlin, 1876; *Geschichte der christlichen Ethik*, Bd. II. 1886.

GERHART, E. V., was editor of Rauch's *Inner Life of the Christian*, Philadelphia, 1856.

GEROK, Karl, 9th ed. of 2d series of *Palmblätter* is under title, *Auf einsamen Gängen*, Stuttgart, 1885; *Illusionen und Ideale* (lecture), 1st–3d ed. Stuttgart, 1886.

GIBB, John, D.D. (Aberdeen, 1886), Presbyterian; b. at Aberdeen, Scotland, in the year 1835; educated at the University of Aberdeen, at Heidelberg and Berlin, and also at the Divinity Hall of the Free Church in Aberdeen; became colleague of Rev. G. Wisely at Malta, 1866; theological tutor in the College of the Presbyterian Church of England, London, 1868; professor of New-Testament exegesis in the same, 1877. He is the author of the translation of Augustine's *Lectures on the Gospel according to John*, vol. i. (in Clark's series), Edinburgh, 1873; *Biblical Studies, and their Influence upon the Church*, London, 1877; *Gudrun and Other Stories*, 1881 (2d ed. *Gudrun, Beowulf, and the Song of Roland*, 1884); *Luther's Table-Talk* (selected and edited), 1883; articles on theological and historical subjects, in *Contemporary Review, British and Foreign Evangelical Review, British Quarterly Review*, etc.

GLADDEN, W. *Applied Christianity*, Boston, 1886.

GLOAG, P. J. *Introduction to the Catholic Epistles*, Edinburgh, 1886.

GOODWIN, H., D.C.L. (Oxford, 1885), *Creation*, 1886.

GORDON, W. R. *Peter Never in Rome*, New York, 1847; several tracts and sermons on various subjects, 1848–49; *The Iniquity of Secession*, 1862; *The Assassination of President Lincoln*, 1865; *An Answer to the Romish Tract, "Is it Honest"?* 1867; *Controversial Letters in Defence of* [the same], Youngstown, O., 1868.

GREEN, S. G. *What Do I Believe?* 1881; *Christian Ministry to the Young*, 1883.

GREGORY, C. R., travelled during 1885 and 1886 in England, France, and the East, in the interests of biblical textual criticism.

GRUNDEMANN, P. R., has been, since 1882, president of the Missions-Conferenz in the Province of Brandenburg; has written, *Zur Statistik der evangelischen Mission*, Gütersloh, 1886.

GUTHE, H., new ed. *Palästina*, 1886.

HAERING, T. *Die Theologie und der Vorwurf der "doppelten Wahrheit." Rede zum Antritt des akademischen Lehramts an der Universität Zürich*, Zürich, 1886 (pp. 31). He is joint editor of the *Theologische Studien aus Würtemberg*, and belongs to the right or conservative wing of the school of Ritschl.

HALE, E. E. Of Mr. Hale's other works may be mentioned, *The Man Without a Country*, Boston, 1861; *If, Yes, and Perhaps*, 1868; *Ingham Papers*, 1870; *How To Do It*, 1871; *Christmas Eve and Christmas Day*, 1872; *His Level Best, and other stories*, 1872; *Workingmen's Homes*, 1874; *In His Name*, 1874; *Seven Spanish Cities, and the Way to them*, 1883; *Sermons and Easter Poems*, Boston, 1886; (with Susan Hale) *The Story of Spain*, N.Y., 1886 (several editions of each).

HALEY, J. W., is translating Eusebius' *Preparatio Evangelica* from the original Greek, a work which has never yet been accomplished.

HALL, N. His church has a membership of nine hundred, and Sunday schools with six thousand children. The Lincoln Tower is a hundred and twenty feet in height; the spire is formed of red and white stone representing the stars and stripes. It has two class-rooms called "Washington" and "Wilberforce." To his list of works add: *Family Prayers in the Words of Scripture*.

HANNE, J. W., gave public lectures upon history and philosophy, Protestantism, etc., at Brunswick, 1840–50; was pastor in different places of the Kingdom of Hannover, 1851–61.

HARNACK, A. *Codex Rossanensis*, Leipzig, 1880; *Der Ursprung des Lectorats und der anderen niederen Weihen*, Giessen, 1886; *Die Quellen der sogenannten apostolischen Kirchenordnung*, Leipzig, 1886; *Die Apostellehre u. die jüdischen beiden Wege* (enlarged reprint of art. on the subject in the Appendix to Herzog[2]), 1886.

HARNACK, T. *Luther's Theologie*. 2. Abth. *Luther's Lehre von dem Erlöser und der Erlösung*, Erlangen, 1886.

HARPER, W. R., has been since 1885 principal of the schools of the Institute of Hebrew.

HARRISON, Ven. Benjamin, Church of England; b. in England about the year 1810; was a student of Christ Church, Oxford University, graduated B.A. (1st-class classics and 2d-class mathematics) 1830; Ellerton theological prize, and Kennicott Hebrew scholar, 1831; English essay, and Pusey and Ellerton Hebrew scholar, 1832; M.A., 1833; was ordained deacon, 1832; priest, 1833; select preacher at Oxford, 1835–37; domestic chaplain to the archbishop of Canterbury, 1838–48; six preacher in Canterbury Cathedral, 1842-45; became archdeacon of Maidstone with canonry in Canterbury Cathedral, annexed 1845. He was a member of the Old-Testament Company of the Anglo-American Bible-Revision Committee from its organization in 1870. He is the author of *An Historical Inquiry into the True Interpretation of the Rubrics respecting the Sermon and the Communion Service*, London, 1845; *Prophetic Outlines of the Christian Church and the anti-Christian Power, as traced in the Visions of Daniel and St. John* (Warburtonian Lectures), 1849; *Privileges, Duties, and Perils in the English Branch of the Church of Christ at the Present Time* (six sermons preached in Canterbury Cathedral), 1850; and the following charges: *Prospects of Peace for the Church*, 1875; *The Church in its Divine Constitution and Relation with the Civil Power*, 1877; *The More Excellent Way*, 1878; *Memories of Departed Brethren*, 1879, *Church's Work and Wants*, 1881; *Disestablishment and Disendowment*, 1883; *Legacy of Peace*, 1883; *Address to the Archdeaconry of Maidstone*, 1885; *The Continuity of the Church, and its Present Position in England*, 1886. *

HATCH, E. *Individualism and Ecclesiasticism, Their Common Place in the Church of Christ* (sermon), London, 1886.

HAUCK, A. *Die Entstehung des Christustypus in der abendländischen Kunst*, Heidelberg, 1880; *Kirchengeschichte Deutschlands*, 1st part, Leipzig, 1886.

HAURÉAU, J. B. *Hugo de Saint Victor*, 2d ed. 1886.

HAWEIS, H. R., visited America in 1885, and preached at New York and Boston, also before Harvard and Cornell Universities, addressing immense congregations. He also delivered seven lectures at the Lowell Institute, Boston, which drew together the largest audiences ever known to have assembled there. In the same year he visited Philadelphia, Baltimore, and Washington (where he was received by the President of the United States); and, after lecturing at Montreal and Kingston, Canada, returned to London in the spring of 1886. *My Musical Life*, 2d ed. 1886.

HEDGE, F. H., received the degree of LL.D. at Harvard's 250th anniversary, Nov. 8, 1886.

HEIDENHEIM, Moritz, Ph.D. (Giessen, 1851), Anglican theologian; b. at Worms, Sept. 23, 1824; educated at the gymnasium at Worms, and at the universities of Würzburg and Giessen; studied theology subsequently at King's College, London, and was elected associate of the college 1855. He worked for several years in the library of the British Museum, and in the Vatican and other libraries at Rome and elsewhere. He has been since 1864 "English chaplain" of the Anglican Church at Zürich, and *privat-docent* in the theological faculty of the university there. He has published *Deutsche Vierteljahrsschrift für deutsche und englische theologische Forschung und Kritik*, Gotha, 1860–62, and Zürich, 1863–65, 4 vols.; *Bibliotheca Samaritana* (text and annotations), Leipzig, 1884 sqq., 3d part, 1886.

HEINRICI, K. F. G. *Wesen und Aufgabe der evangelisch-theologischen Facultäten*, Marburg, 1885.

HEMAN, C. F. *Die historische und die religiöse Weltstellung des jüdischen Volkes*, 1882.

HERVEY, A. C., D.D. (Oxford, 1885), wrote also on the Pastoral Epistles in the *Pulpit Commentary*.

HESSEY, J. A., was educated at Merchant Taylor's School, London. Author of *Report on "Duties of Archdeacons" to the Lower House of Canterbury Convocation*, London, 1886.

HETTINGER, F. *De theologiæ speculativæ et mysticæ connubio in Dantes Trilogia*, Würzburg, 1882. He was made honorary member of the Louvain theological faculty in 1884.

HEURTLEY, C. A. *Faith and the Creed. Dogmatic teaching of the Church of the Fourth and Fifth Centuries*, Oxford, 1886 (a translation of Augustin's *De Fide et Symbolo*).

HILGENFELD, A., belongs to the school of Baur.

HINCKS, E. A., S.T.D. (Yale, 1885).

HITCHCOCK, R. D., received the degree of LL.D. at Harvard's 250th anniversary, Nov. 8, 1886.

HODGE, Archibald Alexander, died, after a short illness, at Princeton, Nov. 11, 1886, aged sixty-three years. He had a remarkable resemblance to his distinguished father, agreed fully with his system of theology, filled his chair, and was a very popular teacher and preacher. His funeral, Nov. 15, was attended by a large concourse of pupils and friends from near and far.

HOEKSTRA, Sytse, D.D. (Amsterdam, 1857), Dutch Protestant theologian; b. at Wieringewaard, Aug. 20, 1822; studied at the Mennonite Seminary at Amsterdam; pursued a career of great literary activity, writing many books upon practical theology, and contributing to the principal Dutch reviews,—*Jaarbœken voor wetenschapelijke Theologie; Licht, Liefde en Leven*; especially to the *Theologisch Tijdschrift*, Amsterdam, 1867 sqq.; was elected a member of the Royal Academy of Sciences, 1868; had charge of the department of logic in the Amsterdam University, 1876; and has been since 1879 professor of the philosophy of religion in the Municipal University of Amsterdam. He is the author in Dutch of "The Triumph of Love" (expositions of the Canticles), Amsterdam, 1856; "Liberty in Relation to Morality, Conscience, and Sin," 1858; "Principles of the Doctrines of the Ancient Mennonites," 1863; "Psychological Foundation of Religious Faith," 1864; "The Hope of Immortality," 1867; "The Foundation of the Categorical Imperative," 1873. *

HOELEMANN, Herman Gustav, was teacher of religion, and upper teacher (fifth 1835, fourth 1839) in the gymnasium at Zwickau. To the list of his books (p. 101) add, *De interpretatione sacra cum profana feliciter conjungenda*, Leipzig, 1832; *Hebräische Anthologie, mit Commentar und Lexikon*, 1834; *Meschalim solemnibus natal. Dr. Aen. Orthob. Schulzii dicati*, 1839; *Nahum oraculum*, 1842; *Teutoburger Inschriften . . . sammt Erläuterungen und Erweiterungen*, Meissen, 1843; *Bibelstudien*, Leipzig, 1861; *Die Stiftung der Heidenmission auf dem Berge in Galiläa* (sermon), Zwickau, 1865; *Neueste Bibelstudien*, Leipzig, 1875. He edited from 1846–48, the *Sächsisches Volksblatt für die Angelegenheiten des Staates und der Kirche*; founded in 1851, and edited until 1853, the *Sachsisches Kirchen-Schulblatt*; since 1832 has contributed weekly to different periodicals.

HOERSCHELMANN, Ferdinand, D.D. (*hon.*, Erlangen, 18—); became pastor *adjunctus* at Fellin, Livonia, 1855; pastor *ordinarius*, 1861; ordinary professor of practical theology, and university preacher, at Dorpat, 1875. He received the order of St. Stanislaus (2d class) and St. Anna (2d class). Besides books in the Esthonian language, — e.g., *Introduction to the New Testament*, Dorpat, 1866; *Matthias Zell and his Friends*, 1874; *Lectures*, 1875, 3d ed. 1884, — he has published various German addresses, etc.

HOFFMAN, E. A., S.T.D. (Racine College, Racine, Wis., 1883).

HOFSTEDE DE GROOT, Cornelis Philippus, D.D. (Groningen, 1855), Dutch Protestant theologian, son of the succeeding; b. at Groningen, in the year 1829; educated at Groningen; became Reformed pastor at Rottum 1856, at Dwingeloo 1860, at Purmerend 1864, at Kampen 1866; the appointee of the synod of the National Church to be professor of systematic theology, ecclesiastical history of the Dutch Reformed Church, and canon law, in Groningen, 1878; and died there Aug. 11, 1884. He is the author of *Pauli conversis præcipuus theologiæ Paulinæ fons* (his D.D. thesis, Groningen, 1855), and in Dutch of "Letters upon the Bible," Amsterdam, 1860; (with L. van Cleeff) "The Apocryphal Gospels," 1877; the Dutch translation of Wylie's *History of Protestantism*, 1876–78; "One Hundred Years of the History of the Reformation in the Netherlands (1518–1619)," Leiden, 1883.

HOFSTEDE DE GROOT, Petrus, D.D. (Groningen, 1826), Dutch theologian; b. at Leer, in the year 1802; studied at the gymnasium and University of Groningen; became Reformed pastor at Ulrum, 1826; professor of theology at Groningen, and university preacher, 1829; *emeritus*, 1872. He inaugurated the Groningen school of theology, which is the opponent of the so-called "modern theology." In its interest he edited the review, *Waarheid en Liefde*, from 1837 to 1872. He is the author of *Disputatio, qua ep. ad Hebr. cum Paulin. epistolis comparatur*, Utrecht, 1826; *Disputatio de Clemente Al., philos-christ. sive de vi quam philos-gr. imprim. Platonis habuit ad Clem. Al. religionis christ. doctorem informandum* (his D.D. thesis), Groningen, 1826; *Institutiones historiæ ecclesiæ christianæ, in scholarum suarum usum breviter delineatæ*, 1835, 2d ed. 1852; *Institutio theologiæ naturalis*, Utrecht, 1842, 4th ed. 1861; (with L. Pareau) *Encyclopædia theologi christiani*, 1844; in Dutch, "History of the Brothers' Church at Groningen," Groningen, 1832; "The Agitations in the Reformed Church of the Netherlands from 1833 to 1839," 1840 (issued anonymously as from X; German trans. ed. by Gieseler, Hamburg, 1840); "Jesus Christ the Foundation of the Unity of the Christian Church," 1846; "The Divine Education of Humanity up to the Coming of Jesus Christ," 1846, 3 vols., 3d ed. 1st 2 vols. 1855, 2d ed. 3d vol. 1885; "The Groningen Theologians," 1854 (German trans., Gotha, 1863); *Kort overzigt van de leer der zonde* ("Brief Examination of the Doctrine of Sin"), 1856; *Over de evangelisch-catholieke godgeleerdheid als de godgeleerdheid der toekomst* ("On the Evangelical-Catholic Theology as the Theology of the Future"), 1856; "The Nature of the Gospel Ministry," 1858; *De zending, eene voortgaande openbaring van God* ("On Missions as a Progressive Revelation of God"), Rotterdam, 1860; *Mededeelingen omtrent Matthias Claudius* ("Information concerning Matthias Claudius"), Groningen, 1861; *Het evangelie der apostelen tegenover de twijfelingen en de wijsheid der wereld* ("The Apostolic Gospel over against the Doubts and the Wisdom of the World"), The Hague, 1861; *Ary Scheffer*, 1862, 2d ed. 1872 (German trans. 186–, 2d ed. 1870); "Basilides considered as the First Witness in Favor of the Authenticity of the Writings of the New Testament and of the Fourth Gospel," 1866 (German trans., Leipzig, 1867); "The 'Modern Theology' of the Netherlands described according to the Principal Writings of its Most Illustrious Representatives," 1869 (German trans., Bonn, 1870); *Johan Wessel Ganzevoort*, 1871; "The Course of the Schism in the Reformed Church of the Netherlands," 1874; "The Old-Catholic Movement," 1877.

HOLSTEN, K. L. *Die drei ursprünglichen, noch ungeschriebenen Evangelien*, Karlsruhe und Leipzig, 1883; *Die synoptischen Evangelien nach der Form ihres Inhalts*, Heidelberg, 1886; *Ursprung und Wesen der Religion* (lecture), Berlin, 1886. He belongs to the Tübingen school, and closely adheres to Dr. Baur's views on the alleged antagonism between Petrinism and Paulinism.

HOLTZMANN, H. J. *Hist. Krit. Einleitung ins N. T.*, 2d ed. 1886.

HOOD, E. P. *The Vocation of the Preacher*, London, 1886.

HOOP-SCHEFFER, J. G., contributed also to the *Doopsgezinde Bijdragen*, and wrote "A History of Baptism by Immersion," Amsterdam, 1882.

HOOYKAAS, I. *Proeve eener Geschiedenis der Beoefening van de Wijsheid onder de Hebreën*, Leiden, 1862.

HOPKINS, M., received the degree of LL.D. at Harvard's 250th anniversary, Nov. 8, 1886.

HOW, W. W. *Commentary on the Four Gospels*, 18—; *Cambridge Pastoral Lectures*, 1884.

HOWSON, J. S. *The Diaconate of Women in the Anglican Church* (with a short biographical sketch by his son), 1886.

HUMPHRY, W. G. *Occasional Sermons*, London, 1886.

HUNTINGTON, W. R. Joint author of the so-called "Book Annexed."

HURST, J. F., made a tour through Egypt, Syria, and Greece, 1871; made an official tour through India, and the Methodist missions in Europe and Turkey, 1884; edited (in connection with Prof. H. C. Whitney) *Moral Essays of Seneca*, 1877; wrote *Christian Union*, 1880; *The Gospel a Combative Force*, 1884; *Short History of the Early Church*, 1886.

HURTER, H. *Nomenclator*, etc., Innsbruck, 1871–86, 3 vols. He is the son of Antistes Hurter, who joined the Roman-Catholic Church. See *Encyclopædia*, p. 1043.

IMMER, Heinrich Albert, D.D. (Basel, 1860), Swiss Reformed theologian; b. at Unterseen, Aug. 10, 1804; d. at Bern, March 23, 1884. His father was pastor of Unterseen, Canton Bern. There was a clumsiness about him which his father mistook for stupidity, and severely punished. The effect of such treatment was to retard his mental development. He learned bookbindery at Lausanne and Zürich, and began business at Thun; but the reading, in 1834, of Schleiermacher's

Reden über die Religion so powerfully moved him, that he determined to study theology. He entered, after a brilliant examination, the University of Bern in 1835, passed his theological examination in 1838, and continued his studies at Bonn and Berlin 1838–40. He then returned home, became a pastor, and, after ten years' service, became professor extraordinary of theology at Bern 1850, ordinary professor of New-Testament exegesis and of theology there 1856, and so remained until his retirement as professor *emeritus* in 1881. He exerted a great and wide influence. He was the author of *Schleiermacher als religiöser Character* (lecture), Bern, 1859; *Der Unsterblichkeitsglaube im Lichte der Geschichte und der gegenwärtigen Wissenschaft* (lecture), 1868; *Der Conflikt zwischen dem Staatskirchenthum und dem methodistischen Dissenterthum im Jahr 1829 in Bern*, 1870 (pp. 71); *John Bunyan*, Basel, 1871; *Die Geschichtsquellen des Lebens Jesu* (lecture, pp. 29), Leipzig, 1873; *Hermeneutik des neuen Testaments*, Wittenberg, 1873 (English trans. with additional notes, by Prof. A. H. Newman, *Hermeneutics of the New Testament*, Andover, 1877); *Neutestamentliche Theologie*, Bern, 1878. Cf. sketch by R. Rüetschi in Meili's *Theologische Zeitschrift aus der Schweiz*, vol. i. (St. Gallen, 1884), pp. 359–362. *

JACKSON, Sheldon. L. 6, was missionary to the Choctaws in 1858; l. 8, for Crescent r. La Crescent. He was stated clerk of the Synod of Colorado, 1870–81; became superintendent of missions at Sitka, Alaska, 1884; United-States General Agent of Education in Alaska, 1885. Author of *Alaska, and Missions on the North Pacific Coast*, New York, 1880.

JACOBY, C. J. H. *Luthers vorreformatorische Predigt, 1512–1517*, Königsberg, 1883.

JANSSEN, J. *Geschichte des deutschen Volkes*, vol. v. 1st to 12th ed. 1886.

JENNINGS, A. C., became rector of King's Stanley, Gloucestershire, 1886.

JESSUP, H. H. *Women of the Arabs*, New York, 1873; *Syrian Home Life*, 1874.

JOSTES, F. *Die Tepler Bibelübersetzung, eine zweite Kritik*, Münster, 1886. L. 14, r. Germania xxxi. 1–41; 164–204.

JOWETT, B., D.D. (Edinburgh, 18—); elected scholar of Balliol College, Oxford, 1835; published *The Politics of Aristotle, translated into English, with Introduction, Marginal Analysis, Essays, Notes, and Indices*, London, 1885, 2 vols.

KAEHLER, C. M. A. *Die Versöhnung durch Christum*, Halle, 1885 (pp. 42).

KAFTAN, J. W. M., belongs to the conservative wing of the school of Ritschl, and succeeded Dr. Dorner.

KATTENBUSCH, F. W. F. His *Œcumenische Symbole* is not yet ready, nor does he now contemplate so extensive a work as the title sent implies.

KAULEN, F. P., edited the 12th and succeeding editions of C. H. Vosen's *Kurze Anleitung zum Erlernen der hebräischen Sprache* (which is not a translation of the Latin work by the same author), Freiburg, 1874 sqq.

KEIL, J. C. F. The *Einleitung in d. kanon. Schriften des A. T.*, in 2d ed. took in the Apocrypha, and the title was changed to its present form: *Einleitung in die kanonischen und apokryphischen Schriften des Alten Testaments.*

KELLER, L. *Die Waldenser und die deutschen Bibelübersetzungen*, Leipzig, 1886 (pp. 189).

KENNEDY, B. H., fellow of St. John's College, Cambridge, 1828–30; elected fellow, 1885; edited Vergil's Works, with Commentary, 1876.

KESSELRING, H., D.D. (*hon.*, Bern, 1884).

KILLEN, W. D., wrote the continuation (vol. iii). of James Seaton Reid's *History of the Presbyterian Church in Ireland*, Belfast, vol. i. 1834, vol. ii. 1837, vol. iii. 1853, 3d ed. 1867; *The Ignatian Epistles entirely spurious* (a reply to Bp. Lightfoot), Edinburgh, 1886.

KIRKPATRICK, A. F., until 1882, was assistant tutor and junior dean of Trinity College, Cambridge.

KITCHEN, G. W., translated a vol. of *Ranke's History of England* (translated by a company of Oxford scholars), London, 1875, 6 vols.; *A Consuetudinary of the Fourteenth Century for the Refectory of S. Swithin*, Winchester, 1886.

KOENIG, A., has written recensions, apologetical articles in *Mittheilungen aus dem Gebiete des Volksschulwesens*, Osnabrück, 1886; also *Schöpfung und Gotteserkenntniss*, Freiburg, 1885.

KOENIG, J., studied at Freiburg, Tübingen, and Munich; became *repetitor* at Freiburg, 1845. He wrote also *Die Unsterblichkeitsidee im Buche Job*, Freiburg, 1855; and very many articles in different Roman-Catholic periodicals, besides editing the *Freiburger Diöcesan Archiv.*

KOESSING, F. *Der reiche Jüngling*, 1868.

KOESTLIN, J. T., new ed. *Luthers Theologie*, 1863.

KOLDE, Th. *Der Methodismus und seine Bekämpfung* (lecture), Erlangen, 1886.

KRAFFT, W. L., D.D. (Bonn, 1852), travelled with F. A. Strauss (author of *Sinai and Golgotha*) in the East, for the sake of studying biblical antiquities and ancient history (1844); took part in the Evangelical Alliance meeting in New York in 1873; wrote a draught of the Consensus of the Reformed Confessions for the first General Council of the Alliance of Ref. Churches, Edinburgh, 1877 (printed in *Report of Proceedings*, etc., Edinburgh, 1877, pp. 41–48). To the list of his books add, *Carl Küpper, Lebensbild aus der rhein. Kirche*, Bonn, 1860; *Briefe und Documente aus der Zeit der Reformation*, Elberfeld, 1876; *Die deutsche Bibel vor Luther*, Bonn, 1883. Since 1849 he has edited the *Bonner Monatsschrift für die evangel. Kirche der Rheinprovinz u. Westfalen;* and since 1858, *Die Mission unter Israel*, Cologne.

KUENEN, A., is also LL.D. The first chapter (*The Hexateuch*) of the 2d ed. of his *Historisch-kritisch Onderzoek* was translated by Philip H. Wicksteed, with his assistance, and published under title: *An Historico-Critical Enquiry into the Origin and Composition of the Hexateuch*, London, 1886.

KURTZ, J. H. L. 17, after *Begründung* supply *der Einheit u. Echtheit* (*d. Pentateuch*).

LAEMMER, H. *Institutiones des katholischen Kirchenrechts*, Freiburg-im-Br., 1886.

LAGARDE, P. A. de. *Titus bostrenus contra Manichæos syriace*, 1860. L. 31, after *fragmenta* supply *syriace servata quinque.*

LANGE, J. P. These additional titles have been kindly furnished by Miss Lange: *Sendschreiben der evangelischen Freifrau Athanasia an d. Pater Athanasius*, Cologne, 1838; *Kritische Beleuchtung* *der Schrift von Ludwig Feuerbach: Das Wesen des Christenthums*, Heidelberg, 1849; *Die gesetzlich-katholische Kirche als Vorbild der freien evangelisch-katholischen Kirche*, Heidelberg, 1850; *Der Herr ist wahrhaftig auferstanden: die Losung der christlichen Gemeinde unserer Zeit*, Zürich, 1852; *Ueber die geistige Einheit des katholischen Mittelalters* (lecture), Elberfeld, 1858; *Vom Krieg und vom Sieg* (three lectures), Bonn, 1869; *Die Idee der Vollendung des Reiches Gottes und ihre Bedeutung für das historische Christenthum*, Gotha, 1869; *Einheit und Widerstreit der religiös-kirchlichen und der sittlich-humanen Dogmen des Christenthums*, Heidelberg, 1871; *Die protestantische Kirche und der Protestantenverein*, *Epigrammatische Gedichte*, Bonn, 1872; *Moderne Schattenrisse*, Heidelberg 1876, 2d vol., Bonn 1883; *Vom Oelberge, Geistliche Dichtungen*, 2d collection, Bonn, 1880; *Auch in Sachen der rheinischen Mission, ein Wort zur Verwahrung*, Bonn, 1882 (pp. 23); *Wie definirt man die Musik? Eine Kultur- und Kunstfrage*, Bonn, 1882 (pp. 28); *Sendschreiben an den Herrn Pfarrer Julius Thikötter in Bremen in Betreff seiner Darstellung der Theologie Albrecht Ritschls*, 1884 (pp. 22).

LANSDELL, H., distributed in 1878 tracts and Scriptures in Russia, especially in hospitals and prisons. His *Through Siberia* has been translated into German (Jena, 1882, 2 vols.), Swedish, and Danish; his *Russian Central Asia*, into German (Leipzig, 1885, 3 vols.).

LAWSON, A. G., was active on the board of the American Baptist Home Mission Society; edited many of the publications of the National Temperance Society.

LEATHES, S., was in 1885 elected honorary fellow of Jesus College, Cambridge.

LECHLER, G. V., l. 2 fr. bel., r. *sächsischen* for *sächischen*; add: *Urkundenfunde zur Geschichte d. christlichen Altertums*, Leipzig, 1886.

LEGGE, J. *The Travels of Fâ-Hsien*, 1886, has for full title: *Record of Buddhistic Kingdoms: Being an Account by the Chinese Monk, Fâ-Hsien, of his Travels in India and Ceylon (A.D. 399-414) in Search of Buddhist Books of Discipline* (giving a Corean recension of the Chinese text).

LEMME, Ludwig, Lic. Theol. (Göttingen, 1874), **D.D.** (*hon.*, Breslau, 1884), German Protestant; b. at Salzwedel, Aug. 8, 1847; studied at Berlin, 1866-69; was private tutor 1869-72; *Domkandidat* in Berlin, 1872; *Repetent* at Göttingen, 1872-74; *Domhilfsprediger* in Berlin, 1874-76; inspector in the Johanneum at Breslau, 1876-84; and meanwhile *Privatdocent* of theology in the University of Breslau, 1876-81; professor extraordinary 1881-84, ordinary professor of theology at Bonn since 1884. He is a pupil of Dorner, but inclined to the direction given by Richard Rothe. He is the author of *Das Verhältniss der Dogmatik zu Kritik und Auslegung der heiligen Schrift nach Schleiermacher*, Göttingen, 1874; (edited) *Die drei grossen Reformationsschriften Luthers vom Jahre 1520*, Gotha 1875, 2d ed. 1884; *Das Evangelium in Böhmen*, 1877; *Die religionsgeschichtliche Bedeutung des Dekalogs*, Breslau, 1880; *Die Nächstenliebe*, 1881; *Das echte Ermahnungs-schreiben des Apostels Paulus an Timotheus* [2 Tim. i. 1, 2, 10; iv. 6-22], 1882; *Die Sünde wider den heiligen Geist*, 1883; *Ueber die Pflege der Einbildungskraft* (lecture), 1884.

LEO XIII. was arbiter of the dispute between Germany and the Caroline Islands; sent Bismarck, who went half way to Canossa for *political* considerations, the Christ Order (an order of merit for distinguished services to the Roman Church, established by Pope John XXII. in 1317, and never before given to a Protestant); and came out victor for a time in the "Culturkampf" with Germany (1886). His *Latin Poems* were published, Rome, 1886; reprinted with English metrical translation by the Jesuits of Woodstock College, Md., Baltimore, 1886.

LIDDON, H. P., declined bishopric of Edinburgh, 1886.

LIGHTFOOT, J. B., D.D. (Durham, 1879; Edinburgh, 1884).

LINCOLN, H. *Outline Lectures in History of Doctrine*, Boston, 1886.

LINSENMANN, F. X. Add: *Lehrbuch der Moraltheologie*, Freiburg, 1878; *Konrad Summenhart, ein Kulturbild aus den Anfängen der Universität Tübingen*, Tübingen, 1887. Since 1873 he has been joint editor of the *Tübinger Theolog. Quartalschrift*, to which he has been for many years a contributor.

LIPSIUS, R. A., since 1886 has been editor of the *Theologischer Jahresbericht*, founded by Pünjer; *Die Pilatus-Acten*, 2d ed. Kiel, 1886.

LITTLEDALE, R. F. There have been three editions of his commentary on the Psalms.

LOESCHE, G. *Bellarmin's Lehre vom Papst und deren actuelle Bedeutung*, Halle, 1885.

LOMAN, Abraham Dirk, Dutch theologian; b. at The Hague, Sept. 16, 1823; studied at the Athenæum of Amsterdam, the Lutheran Seminary in the same city, and at Heidelberg; became pastor at Maastricht, 1846; then at Deventer, 1849; professor in the Lutheran Seminary, Amsterdam, 1856; of theology in the Municipal University of Amsterdam, 1877! He has written numerous articles in the *Gids* and in the *Theologisch Tijdschrift*, Amsterdam and Leiden, 1861 sqq. (of which he was one of the founders). He is the editor of various hymn-books, old national Dutch songs, and of other musical compositions; and the author of *De germani Theologi humanitate* (his inaugural address), Amsterdam, 1856; and in Dutch of "Why seek the Living among the Dead?" 1862; "The Testimony of the Muratorian Canon" (upon the Gospel of John), 1865; "Protestantism and the Authority of the Church," 1868; "The Gospel of John: its Origin, First Readers, and its Acceptance in Antiquity," 1873.

LOMMATZSCH, Siegfried Otto Nathanael, Lic. Theol., Ph.D. (Berlin, 1860 and 1863), **D.D.** (*hon.*, Berlin, 1883), German Protestant theologian; b. at Berlin, Jan. 21, 1833; studied at the University of Berlin, 1853-59; became *privat-docent* there, 1870; professor extraordinary of theology, 1879. He is a disciple of Carl Immanuel Nitzsch, and Twesten, and an adherent of the so-called "Middle Party." Since 1881 he has been a member of the Royal Commission for the examination of upper-class teachers in evangelical theology. He is the author of *Schleiermacher's Lehre vom Wunder und vom Uebernatürlichen im Zusammenhange seiner Theologie und mit besonderer Berücksichtigung der Reden über die Religion und der Predigten*, Berlin, 1872; *Luther's Lehre vom ethisch-religiösen Standpunkte aus mit besonderer Berücksichtigung seiner Theorie vom Gesetze*, 1879.

LORIMER, George Cheney, D.D. (Bethel College, Russelville, Ky., 186–), Baptist; b. near Edinburgh, Scotland, in the year 1838; came to the United States in the year 1856; studied at Georgetown College, Ky.; was ordained pastor at Harrodsburg, Ky., 1859; from there went to Paducah, Ky., and thence to Louisville, Ky., where he remained eight years; then went to Albany, N.Y., and was there two years; thence to Shawmut-avenue Church, Boston; thence to Tremont Temple Church in the same city; thence to the First Church, Chicago, Ill., and is now pastor of the Michigan-avenue Church of that city. He is the author of *Under the Evergreens; or, a Night with Saint Nicholas*, Boston, 187–; *The Great Conflict: Discourse concerning Baptists and Religious Belief*, 1877; *Isms Old and New: Sermon Series for 1880–81*, 1881; *Jesus the World's Saviour: who He is, why He came, and what He did*, 1883; *Studies in Social Life*, New York, 1886. *

LOWE, W. H., was educated at Durham school; rowed in Cambridge University boat against Oxford, 1868, 1870, 1871; was curate of Fen Ditton, 1873–75; of Milton, 1880–82; in charge of Willingham, 1886; captain of Second Cambridge (University) Rifle Volunteers, 1882–86. He edited *Túzuki i Jahángíri*, 1886.

LUCKOCK, H. M. *The Bishops in the Tower*, London, 1886.

LUTHARDT, C. E., became canon of Meissen, 1870.

LYON, D. G. *Assyrian Manual*, Chicago, 1886.

MABON, A. V. W., was in Hudson County, N.J., superintendent of public schools (1848–55), examiner of all the teachers of public schools (1848–65), and commissioner for the equalization of taxes, 1876–81. The New Durham Church under him (1846–81) was not only prosperous, but the parent of several other churches.

MACDUFF, J. R. *Brighter than the Sun*, 1886; *Morning Family Prayers for a Year*, 1886; *Ripples in the Twilight: Fragments of Sunday Thought and Teaching*, 1886.

McILVAINE, J. H. *The Wisdom of the Apocalypse*, N.Y., 1886.

MACKARNESS, J. F., was educated at Eton.

MACLAGAN, W. D., served in the Indian army 1846–52, and retired as lieutenant.

MACLEAR, G.F., was appointed honorary canon of Canterbury in 1885.

MACMILLAN, H., F.S.A. Scot. (1883). *The Olive Leaf*, London, 1886.

MAGOON, Elias Lyman, D.D. (Rochester University, N.Y., 1853), Baptist; b. at Lebanon, N.H., Oct. 20, 1810; d. in Philadelphia, Penn., Nov. 25, 1886. He was educated at New Hampton Academy (1830–32), Waterville College, Me., now Colby University (1832–36), and at the Newton (Mass.) Theological Institution (1836–39); became pastor of the Second Baptist Church, Richmond, Va., 1839; resigned on account of the division in the denomination on the question of slavery, and became pastor of the Ninth-street Baptist Church, Cincinnati, O., 1845; of the Oliver-street Baptist Church, New York, 1849; of the First Baptist Church, Albany, N.Y., 1857; of the Broad-street Baptist Church, Philadelphia, Penn., 1867. He was apprenticed to the bricklayer's trade in 1826, worked at it until 1830; and by means of it during vacations and at other times supported himself through his academy, college, and seminary life. Because of it he early took interest in ecclesiastical architecture, and gathered in the course of years a large and valuable library upon the subject. He was a man of catholic tastes, wide reading, and great personal charm. A few years before his death he sold for twenty thousand dollars his art collection to Vassar College, of which he was a director, and at the same time presented his Protestant literature collection to Newton (Mass.) Theological Institution, his illustrated art works to Rochester (N.Y.) University, many of his miscellaneous works to Colby University and to Bates College (Maine), a collection of water-colors to the Metropolitan Museum of Art, New-York City, and his Roman-Catholic theological works to Cardinal McCloskey. He is the author of *Orators of the American Revolution*, New York, 1848; *Proverbs for the People*, Boston, 1848; *Living Orators in America*, New York, 1849; *Republican Christianity*, Boston, 1849; *Westward Empire, the Great Drama of Human Progress*, New York, 1856. *

MAHAN, A. *Out of Darkness into Light*, London and Boston, 1875; *Autobiography: Intellectual, Moral, and Spiritual*, London, 1882.

MAIER, A., is commander of the Order of the Zähringen Lion with the Star. He wrote *Historisch-kritische Untersuchungen über den Hebräerbrief*, Freiburg, 1851; *Die Glossolalie des apostolischen Zeitalters*, 1855; *Exegetisch-kritische Untersuchungen über die Christologie*, 1871.

MANN, W. J. *Life of Melchior Mühlenberg*, 1886.

MANNING, H. E. *Petri Privilegium, Miscellanies*, London, 1877, 2 vols.

MARQUIS, David Calhoun, D.D. (Washington and Jefferson College, Washington, Penn., 1875), Presbyterian; b. in Lawrence County, Penn., Nov. 15, 1834; graduated at Jefferson College, Canonsburg, Penn., 1857; taught, 1857–60; studied in Western Theological Seminary, Allegheny, Penn., 1860–62, and in the Theological Seminary of the North-west, Chicago, Ill., 1862–63; became pastor at Decatur, Ill., 1863; of North Church, Chicago, Ill., 1866; of Westminster Church, Baltimore, Md., 1870; of Lafayette-park Church, St. Louis, Mo., 1878; professor of New-Testament literature and exegesis in the Theological Seminary of the North-west (since 1886, McCormick Theological Seminary), Chicago, Ill., 1883. He was moderator of the General Assembly of the Presbyterian Church at Minneapolis, Minn., 1886.

MARTI, Karl, Lic. Theol. (Basel, 1879), Swiss Reformed; b. at Bubendorf, Baselland, Switzerland, April 25, 1855; studied at Basel, Göttingen, and Leipzig; became pastor at Buns, Baselland 1878, at Muttenz 1885; has been *privat-docent* at Basel since 1881. He belongs, in general, to the school of Ritschl. He is the author of the articles "Die Spuren der sog. Grundschrift des Hexateuchs in den vorexilischen Propheten des Alten Testaments," in *Jahrb. für prot. Theol.*, 1880; "Die alten Lauren und Klöster in der Wüste Juda" (on basis of information from Baurath Schick in Jerusalem), in *Zeitsch. d. deutsch. Palestinvereins*, 1880; "Das Thal Zeboim" [1 Sam. xiii. 18], in same, 1884; and minor articles in the Swiss *Kirchenblatt*.

MERRILL, S., has visited Palestine three different times, and has made the largest collection of birds and animals from that country that at present exists. He published *The Site of Calvary*, Jerusalem, 1886.

MERX, E. O. A., Ph.D. (Breslau, Aug. 9, 1861), **Lic. Theol.** (Berlin, 1864), **D.D.** (*hon.*, Jena, 1872); at Tübingen was professor of Semitic languages, at Giessen of Old-Testament exegesis, and now of the same at Heidelberg. To list of books add: *Grammatica syriaca*, vol. i., Halle, 1867; *Vocabulary of the Tigré Language written down by Moritz von Beurmann*, 1868; (with Arnold) the 2d ed. of Tuch's *Commentar über die Genesis*, 1871; *Neusyrisches Lesebuch, Texte im Dialect von Urmia*, Giessen, 1871; *Türkische Sprüchwörter in Deutsche übersetzt*, Venice, 187–; *Zur Religionsphilosophie*, Giessen, 1872; *Die Saadjanische Uebersetzung des Hohen Liedes in's Arabische, nebst andern auf das Hohe Lied bezügl. arab. Texten*, Heidelberg, 1882; *Wissenschaftl. Gutachten über die Stellen aus Sohar und Vital auf die H. Prof. Rohling seine Blutbeschuldigung gründen will*, Vienna, 1885; *Chrestomathia targumica vocalibus babylonicis instructa quam e codd. Mspts. eddidit, lexicon adjecit, Historia artis grammaticæ apud Syros, accedit interpretatio Dionysii Thracis et Severi bar Sihakku grammatica syriaca*, 1887; also articles, e.g., in the transactions of the Fourth Oriental Congress, Florence, 1880; *De Eusebianæ historiæ ecclesiasticæ versionibus syriaca et armenica* (with Professor Wright of Cambridge, he has undertaken a revision of the Syriac text of Eusebius with a translation); in those of the Fifth Congress, Berlin, 1882, *Bemerkungen über die Vocalisation der Targume, mit Anhang über die Tschufutkal'schen Fragmente;* in Uhlig, "G. Dionysii Thracis ars grammatica," Leipzig, 1883, *De versione armenica Dionysii Thracis disputatio;* in "Deutsche morgenl. Zeitschrift," 1885, *Proben der syr. Uebersetzung von Galenus' Schrift über die einfachen Heilmittel;* in "Protestant Kirch. Ztg.," 1885, *Eine mittelalterliche Kritik der Offenbarung*, and *Zum 200 jährigen Geburtstage Sebastian Bach's* ("*Bach als religiöser Componist*").

MESSNER, K. F. H., d. in Berlin, Nov. 7, 1886. The paper he edited was suspended Nov. 13.

MITCHELL, A. F., was moderator of the General Assembly of the Church of Scotland in 1885.

MOELLER, E. W., edited De Wette's commentary on Revelation, Leipzig, 1862.

MOFFAT, J. C. *Comparative Religions* has passed through several editions.

MOMBERT, Jacob Isidor, D.D. (University of Pennsylvania, Philadelphia, 1866), Episcopalian; b. at Cassel, Germany, Nov. 6, 1829; received his first education in the schools there; spent several years in business, which gave him opportunity of an early residence in England; there he passed through college, and after studies continued at Leipzig and Heidelberg, and extensive travels, took orders in the Church of England in 1857; was curate in Quebec, Canada, 1857–59; assistant (1859), and then rector of St. James's Church, Lancaster, Penn., 1860–69; American chaplain, Dresden, Saxony, 1869–75; since which time he has only partially exercised his ministry, having been engrossed with literary labors. Theologically he holds catholic and non-partisan ground, alike remote from the puerilities of mediæval formalism, and the daring negations of the followers of Reuss. His studies have ranged over many fields in theology, philology, philosophy, history, and art. He has written many scholarly articles in different religious periodicals; translated *Tholuck's Commentary on the Psalms* (London 1856, Philadelphia 1857), and the *Commentary on the Catholic Epistles* in the American Lange Series, New York, 1867; edited with prolegomena (containing a Life of Tyndale) and various collations, William Tyndale's *Five Books of Moses* (being a verbatim reprint, copied by his own hand, of the edition of 1530 in the Lenox Library, New York, and compared with Tyndale's Genesis of 1534, and the Pentateuch in the Vulgate, Luther, and Matthew's Bible), New York [1884]; and is the author of the following independent works: *Faith Victorious: Account of the Venerable Dr. Johann Ebel, Late Archdeacon of the Old Town Church of Königsberg, in Prussia*, London and New York, 1882; *Handbook of the English Version of the Bible, with Copious Examples illustrating the Ancestry and Relationship of the Several Versions, and Comparative Tables* [1883]; *Great Lives: A Course of History in Biographies*, Boston, 1886, 2d ed. 1886.

MOORHOUSE, J., was chaplain in ordinary to the Queen, 1874–76.

MORISON, James. *The Extent of the Atonement* has been often reprinted; *Saving Faith*, 9th ed. 1886; *St. Paul's Teaching on Sanctification, a Practical Exposition of Rom. vi.*, 1886.

MORRIS, J. G., was the first editor of *The Lutheran Observer*, Philadelphia, Penn.

MOULTON, W. F., with Milligan, wrote the commentary on John, in Schaff's *Popular Commentary*.

MYRBERG, O. F. L. 19, add after Notes: and Commentary. To list add: in Swedish: "Introduction to Romans," 1868; "Voices from the Holy Scriptures," 1877; "The Epistles translated from the Original," 1883; several pamphlets; founded in 1884, *Bibelforskaren*, a journal for critical and practical Bible studies.

NIELSEN, F. K., was a member of the commission for a new hymn-book for the Danish Church, which appeared in 1885. To list of books (in Danish) add: *The Ethics of Tertullian*, 1879; *Scandinavian Free-Masonry and its History*, 1882; *The Basis of Free-Masonry*, 1883; *Lodge and Church*, 1883 (German translation, Leipzig, 1883); *Essays and Criticisms*, 1884.

NILLES, N. *Selectæ disputationes academicæ juris ecclesiastice*, Innsbruck, 1886 sqq.

NIPPOLD, F. W. F. *Die altkatholische Kirche des Erzbisthums Utrecht*, Heidelberg, 1872; *Die römisch-katholische Kirche im Königreich der Niederlande*, Leipzig, 1877; edited *Christian Carl Josias, Freiherr von Bunsen, Deutsche Ausgabe, durch neue Mittheilungen vermehrt*, 1868–72, 3 vols. Of the *Zur geschichtlichen Würdigung der Religion Jesu*, the 7th part appeared in 1886. The new edition of Hagenbach has been enlarged by him.

OETTINGEN, A. *Was heisst christlich-social? Zeitbetrachtungen*, Leipzig, 1886.

OLTRAMARE, M. J. H., D.D. (Strassburg, 1882).

OORT, H. *The Human Sacrifices in Israel* (Dutch), 1865; his *Gospel and Talmud* was translated with many additions in *The Modern Review*, London, 1883 (July and October); *Atlas for Biblical and Ecclesiastical History*, 1884, etc.

OSGOOD, H., is the author of articles in *The Baptist Review*, and other periodicals.

OVERTON, John Henry, Church of England; canon of Stow Longa in Lincoln Cathedral; was scholar of Lincoln College, Oxford; first class moderations, 1855; B.A., 1858; M.A., 1860; was ordained deacon 1858, priest 1859; was curate of Quedgeley, Gloucestershire, 1858–60; rector of Legbourne, Lincolnshire, 1860–83; since 1879 has been canon of Stow Longa in Lincoln Cathedral; and since 1883 rector of Epworth, Diocese of Lincoln. With Rev. C. J. Abbey he wrote, *The English Church in the Eighteenth Century*, London, 1878, 2 vols.; and separately, *William Law, Nonjuror and Mystic*, 1880; *Life in the English Church, 1660–1714*, 1885; *The Evangelical Revival in the Eighteenth Century*, 1886; and contributed to the *Encyclopædia Britannica* (9th edition) and *The Dictionary of National Biography*. *

OXENHAM, H. N. *Memoir of Lieut. Rudolph De Lisle*, R.N., London, 1886; translated Döllinger's *The Pope and the Council, by Janus*, London, 1869, 3d ed. 1870; *Letters from Rome, by Quirinus*, 1870; edited with introduction, notes, and appendices, *An Eirenicon of the Eighteenth Century*, London, 1870.

PARK, E. A., received the degree of LL.D. at the 250th anniversary of Harvard University, Nov. 8, 1886.

PARRY, E., in 1882 declined election by the Australian bishops, as bishop of Sydney and metropolitan.

PATON, J. B. B.A., 1849.

PAXTON, John R. The "R." is a mere initial.

PAYNE-SMITH, R., wrote commentary on the books of Samuel, in the *Pulpit Commentary*.

PEROWNE, J. J. S., was educated at Norwich Grammar School; was Bell's University scholar, 1842; Crosse Divinity scholar, 1845; prebendary of St. David's Cathedral, 1867–72. He is the author of *Remarks on Dr. Donaldson's "Jashar;" The Church, the Ministry, the Sacraments* (sermons), 1882; *The Athanasian Creed* (a sermon); *Confession in the Church of England* (sermon with appendix); articles on the Pentateuch, Zechariah, etc., in Smith's *Dictionary of the Bible*; articles in the *Contemporary Review, Expositor, Good Words*, etc.; editor of *Rogers on the Thirty-nine Articles* (Parker Society), 1853; *Al-Adjrumiieh* (an Arabic grammar) 18—; *The Remains Literary and Theological of Bishop Thirlwall*, 3 vols.; and *Cambridge Greek Testament for Schools*, 1884 sqq.

PFLEIDERER, O. English translation of *Religionsphilosophie, The Philosophy of Religion on the Basis of its History* (vol. i., Spinoza to Schleiermacher), London, 1886.

PHILPOTT, H., was chancellor of the University of Cambridge in 1847.

PIERCE, H. N., was ordered deacon 1848; ordained priest, 1849; planted the Episcopal Church in Washington County, Tex.; was rector at Matagorda, Tex., 1852–54; took temporary charge of Trinity Church, New Orleans, last half of 1854; rector of St. Paul's, Rahway, N.J., 1855–57; of St. John's, Mobile, Ala., 1857–68; of St. Paul's, Springfield, Ill., 1868–70; consecrated bishop, 1870.

PIERSON, A. T. *The Crisis of Missions*, New York, 1886.

PIGOU, F. Full title of work cited as *Early Communion* is *Early Communion Addresses at Huddersfield, Liverpool, etc.*, London, 1877.

PITRA, J. B., was transferred in 1884 to the see of Porto et Santa Rufina. The second series of the *Spicilegium* is under title *Analecta Sacra Spicilegii Solesmensi*; and the third, *Analecta Novissima*, has already begun.

PLATH, K. H. C. *Fünfzig Jahre Gossnerscher Mission*, Berlin, 1886; *The Subject of Missions considered under Three New Aspects* (the Church and missions; the representation of the science of missions at the universities; commerce and the Church), Eng. trans., Edinburgh, 1873.

PLUMMER, A., was educated at Lancing College, Sussex, 1852–58; wrote on Epistles of St. John, in *Cambridge Greek Testament*, 1886; also *The Church of the Early Fathers*, London, 1887.

PLUMPTRE, E. H. *Lazarus and Other Poems*, 1864, 4th ed. 1884; *Master and Scholar* (poems), 1866, 2d ed. 1884; *Christ and Christendom* (Boyle Lectures), 1867; *Theology and Life* (sermons), 1866, 2d ed. 1884; *Introduction to the New Testament*, 2d ed. 1884; *The Commedia and Canzoniere of Dante Alighieri* (new trans., with life, notes, and portraits), 1887, 2 vols.

PORTER, J. L. *Jerusalem, Bethany, and Bethlehem*, London, 1886. Dr. Porter was missionary in Syria, 1849–59.

PREGER, W. *Die Entfaltung der Idee des Menschen durch die Weltgeschichte*, München, 1870; *Der kirchenpol. Kampf unter Ludwig d. Baier u. sein Einfluss auf d. offentl. Meinung in Deutschland*, 1877; *Die Verträge Ludwigs d. Baiern und Friedrich dem Schönen 1325 u. 1326*, 1883; *Die Politik Johannes XXII. in Bezug auf Italien und Deutschland*, 1885; *Psalmbüchlein Bibl. Psalmen in deutschen Liederweisen*, Rothenburg, 1886; articles on R. Merswin, J. Tauler, Mystische Theologie, in Herzog².

PRESSENSÉ, E., is a corresponding member of the Lowell Institute, Boston, taking the place of Victor Cousin; takes an active part in the French Senate as a liberal; wrote *Variétés morales et politiques*, Paris, 1885.

PRIME, Wendell, D.D. (Union College, Schenectady, N.Y., 1880), Presbyterian, son of the late Samuel Irenæus Prime; b. at Matteawan, N.Y., Aug. 3, 1837; graduated at Columbia College, New-York City, 1856; studied theology for one year in Union Theological Seminary, Hampden Sidney, Va., and for two at Princeton (N.J.) Theological Seminary, where he graduated 1861; was pastor of Westminster Church, Detroit, Mich., 1861–67; of Union Church, Newburgh, N.Y., 1869–75; and since 1876 has been an editor of *The New-York Observer*.

PRINS, J. J., became *emeritus* professor, 1885; wrote *Commentatio de loco difficili, 1 Pet. iii. 18–22, præmio ornata*, 1836; *Specimen de loco Luc. ii. 25–35*, 1836.

PUAUX, F., and **SABATIER, A.** *Études sur la Révocation de l'Édit de Nantes*, Paris, 1886.

PÜNJER, G. C. B. *Grundriss der Religionsphilosophie*, ed. R. A. Lipsius, Braunschweig, 1886.

QUINTARD, C. T., D.D. (Trinity College, Hartford, Conn., 1866).

RAEBIGER, J. F. *Kritische Untersuchungen*, 2d ed. 1886.

RAINY, R., takes a leading part in all the affairs of the Free Church of Scotland.

RAND, W. W. *Dictionary of the Bible* was upon the basis of Edward Robinson's.

RANKE, E. *Specimen codicis Novi Test. Fuldensis*, Marburg, 1860.

REICHEL, C. P., was first senior moderator classics, 1843.

REISCHLE, M. W. T. *Ein Wort zur Controverse über die Mystik in Theologie*, Freiburg, 1886.

REUTER, H. F. *Augustinische Studien*, 1887.

RÉVILLE, A., was pastor at Luneray (Seine Inférieure), 1849-51; the English translation mentioned, l. 11, is of the *Manuel d'instruction Prolégomènes*, 2d ed. 1885; *Les Religions des peuples non civilisés*, Paris, 1883, 2 vols.; *Les Religions du Mexique, de l'Amérique centrale et du Pérou*, 1884. In 1886 he was made president of the *Section des études religieuses*, founded at the École des Hautes Études at the old Sorbonne, by the National Government, and lectures there on the history of doctrines.

REYNOLDS, H. R. *Buddhism and Christianity Compared and Contrasted* ("Present Day Tracts," No. 46) 1886.

RICE, E. W. *Pictorial Commentary on St. Matthew*, 1886.

RIGG, J. H. Full title, l. 32, *The Sabbath and the Sabbath Law before and after Christ.*

RIGGS, E. *Suggested Emendations of the Authorized English Version of the Old Testament*, Andover, 1873; *Suggested Modifications of the Revised Version of the New Testament*, 1883.

ROBERTS, W. C., LL.D. (College of New Jersey, 1886).

ROBINSON, C. S. Name of present church changed in 1886, from "Memorial" to "Madison Avenue." L. 23, after "thousand" add: copies.

ROBINSON, E. G., received the degree of LL.D. at the 250th anniversary of Harvard University, Nov. 8, 1886.

ROBINSON, T. H. In Harrisburg, was pastor of Market-square Church.

RUDIN, E. G. W. N. *Survey of the Scriptural History of the Old Testament* (in Swedish), 1886.

RÜETSCHI, R., is editor of the *Kirchenblatt für die reform-Schweiz.*

RYDBERG, A. V. His "Romantic Stories" and "Freebooter" have been translated into Danish and German; his "Adventures of Little Vigg," into German and French; issued "The Sibylline Books and Voluspa," Stockholm, 1881; "Poems," 1882 (Danish, German, and Polish translations); "The Myth of the Sword of Victory," Copenhagen, 1884; "Investigations in German Mythology," Stockholm, 1886.

RYLE, J. C., was educated at Eton.

SALMON, G., contributed various articles in Smith and Wace's *Dictionary of Christian Biography.*

SAMSON, G. W., issued new edition, with supplements, of his *Divine Law as to Wines*, Philadelphia, 1886; *Guide to Self-Education*, 1886.

SANDAY, W., studied at Balliol College as well as at Corpus Christi College, Oxford.

SAUSSAYE, P. D. C. German translation of *Vier Schetsen* has not yet appeared.

SAVAGE, M. J. *Social Problems*, 1886.

SAYCE, A. H. *Inscriptions of Mal Amir*, etc., 1885; *Assyria: its Princes, Priests, and People*, 1886.

SCHAFF, D. S., was moderator of the Synod of Missouri, 1886.

SCHANZ, P. *Commentar über das Evangelium des Matthaeus*, Freiburg, 1879; *Marcus*, 1881; *Lucas*, Tübingen, 1883; *Johannes*, 1885.

SCHÉELE, K. H. G. German translation of *Church Catechising*, Gotha, 1886; he is editor of the "Review for Christian Faith and Education," Upsala, 1883-86, Visby since 1887.

SCHENCK, W. E., retired from secretaryship in 1886.

SCHERER, E. H. A., since 1849 has been a frequent contributor to the *Revue de théologie*, and since 1861 on the political and literary staff of *Le Temps.* He published *Melanges de critique religieuse*, Geneva, 1860.

SCHICKLER, Fernand de, Baron, French Protestant layman; b. in Paris, Aug. 24, 1835; early distinguished himself, and endeared himself to his co-religionists, by his devotion to the cause of Protestantism in France, which his wealth enabled him materially to aid. He has been since 1865 president of the "Société de l'histoire du protestantisme français;" since 1878, president of the "Société biblique protestante de Paris;" since 1879, member of the Central Council of the Reformed Churches. In 1877 he was president of the liberal delegation of the reformed churches of France. He has contributed to the *Bulletin* of the "Société de l'histoire du protestantisme français;" to the *Journal du protestantisme français;* to the history of the Bible Society of Paris (*Notices biographiques sur les membres du comité biblique*), 1868; to the *Histoire de France dans les archives privées de la Grande-Bretagne*, 1879; to the *Rapport présenté au Jubilé semi-séculaire de la Société pour l'encouragement de l'instruction primaire parmi les protestants de France*, 1880; and has separately published *En Orient*, Paris, 1862; *Notice sur la Société de l' histoire du Protestantisme Français 1852-72*, 1874. *

SCHNEDERMANN, G. H., contributed to Strack and Zöckler's *Kurzgefasst. Kommentar*, Nordlingen, 1886 sqq., the commentaries on Corinthians, Ephesians, Colossians, and Philemon. He succeeded Kaftan in private teaching of dogmatic and New-Testament theology at Basel, 1883.

SCHOLZ, A. *Commentar zum Buch Judith*, 1887.

SCHUETTE, Conrad Hermann Louis, since 1884 editor of *The Columbus (O.) Theological Magazine.*

SCHULTZ, Friedrich Wilhelm, Lic. Theol., Ph.D. (Berlin, 1852 and 1853 respectively), **D.D.** To list add: "Cyrus der Grosse" (in *Theol. Studien u. Kritiken*, 1853, pp. 624 sqq.); "Die innere Bedeutung der alttestam. Feste" (in *Deutsche Zeitschrift* of Schmieder, 1857, Juni- u. Juli-heft); "Ueber die Eintheilung des Decalogs" (in *Luth. Zeitschrift* of Rudelbach and Guericke, 1858, I.); numerous geographical and historical articles in Herzog[2]; the sections on the geography of Palestine, the history and archæology of Israel, and the theology of the Old Testament, in Zöckler's *Handbuch der theologischen Wissenschaften*, Nördlingen, 1882, 2d ed. 1884.

SCHULTZ, H. *Zur Lehre vom h. Abendmahl*, Gotha, 1886. He belongs to the school of Ritschl.

SCHULTZE, L. T., was director of the seminary at Magdeburg, for the training of teachers of religion in the gymnasia. Edited *Libri symbolici eccles. Luth.*, Berlin, 1856; Melanchthon's *Loci præcipui*, 1856; Luther's *Ausführliche Erklärung der Epistel an die Galater*, 1856; author of article *Ueber das Reformatorium vitæ clericorum vom 1494 des Jacobus Philipp von Basel* in *Ztschr. f. kirchl. Wiss.*, 1886.

SCHWANE, J. *Ueber die Verträge*, Münster, 1871, 2d ed. 1872.

SCHWARZ, K. H. W. Eight vols. *Predigten aus der Gegenwart*, Leipzig, 1858–82.

SEEBERG, R. *Zur Geschichte des Begriffs der Kirche*, Dorpat, 1884.

SEELEY, J. R., was bracketed, with three others, first in the first-class in classical tripos.

SEISS, J. A. *Right Life*, Philadelphia, 1886.

SEPP, J. N., D.D. Deposed by Lola Montez, and expelled from Munich, 1847. He was member of the parliaments at Frankfort, Berlin, and Munich. Add to list: *Poems: Marcos Bozzaris*, 1860; *Ludwig Augustus, Koenig von Bayern und das Zeitalter der Wiedergeburt der Künste*, 1869; *Altbayerischer Sagenschatz, zur Bereicherung der indogermanischen Mythologie*, 1876; *Staats-Kirchenzustände in Suddeutschland*, 1878; *Ursprung der Glasmaler-kunst im Kloster Tegernsee*, 1878; *Die Felsenkuppel auf Moria eine Justinianische Sophienkirche*, 1882; *Ein Volk von zehn Millionen, oder der Bayernstamm, Herkunft und Ausbreitung über Oestreich, Kärnthen, Steyermark und Tyrol, Kampfschrift wider Czechen und Magyaren* (a drama), 1st and 2d ed. 1882; *Der Jaegerwirth und die Sendlingerschlacht*, 1882; *Der bayerische Bauernkrieg (1705)*, 1884; *Die göttliche Tragoedie* (Passion-drama for the play at Oberammergau in 1890), 1886.

SEYERLEN, K. R., *repetent* in the theological seminary at Tübingen, 1859–61.

SHAFTESBURY, Earl of, was educated at Harrow School; was an ecclesiastical commissioner from 1841 to 1847. His first public philanthropic effort was in 1833, when he introduced in the House of Commons a bill limiting the hours of children's labor in factories to ten a day. It was defeated; but a Government bill enjoining that with the exception of silk and lace mills, no children under nine were to be employed in the factories, while those under thirteen were to work not more than forty-eight hours a week, and were to receive from their employers at least two hours schooling a week, was carried. But it proved so imperfect and ineffective, that in 1838 he introduced another bill on the subject. This the Government also opposed. The outcome of the agitation was, however, that in 1850 he carried his point; and in 1853 Lord Palmerston gave the measure its present shape, viz., that children between eight and thirteen years of age must not be employed more than six hours and a half daily, or ten hours on alternate days, while those of tender years must do their work between ten and six o'clock. In 1840 he secured a royal commission to inquire into the condition of the children not protected by the Factory Act, e.g., those in mines; and, on the strength of its revelations, introduced two bills in 1842, one removing female children from the mines and collieries, and the other providing for the care and education of children in calico-print works. In 1844 he founded the Ragged School Union in London, which has done so much for the outcast children there. In 1864 he introduced in Parliament measures which ultimately led to the prohibition of chimney-sweeping by boys, and the compulsory employment of machines for the purpose. He was in 1834 one of the founders of the London City Mission; and in 1842, of a society for the construction of model lodging-houses. He was president of the British and Foreign Bible Society from 1851 till his death, as also of the Young Men's Christian Association. He was largely instrumental in reforming the treatment of lunatics. He did much to elevate the costermonger class. But it would be impossible to estimate the good he did in the course of his long and active life. He was connected with nearly three hundred religious societies, and with many other philanthropic institutions. In 1884 the freedom of the City of London was presented to him. The secret of his success was his humble piety. For a full account of his extraordinary usefulness, see EDWIN HODDER: *The Life and Work of the Seventh Earl of Shaftesbury, K.G.*, London, 1886, 3 vols. *

SHORT, C., d. in New-York City, Dec. 24, 1886.

SMYTH, E. C., received the degree of D.D. at the 250th anniversary of Harvard University, Nov. 8, 1886.

SMYTH, N., edited, with introduction and notes, the eschatological portion of Dr. I. A. Dorner's *Theology*, separately in an English translation, *Dorner on the Future State*, New York, 1883.

SPALDING, J. F. For three years his jurisdiction included New Mexico, and for three years more New Mexico and Arizona. He was a member of the House of Deputies of General Convocation in 1865, 1868, and 1871.

SPENCER, Jesse Ames, D.D. (Columbia College, New-York City, 1852), Episcopalian; b. at Hyde Park, Dutchess County, N.Y., June 17, 1816; graduated at Columbia College, New-York City, 1837; studied theology at the (Episcopalian) General Theological Seminary, New-York City; became rector of St. James, Goshen, N.Y., 1840; resigned on account of ill health 1842; went to Europe; on his return taught, and engaged in literary work; travelled in Europe and the East, 1848–49; became professor of Latin and Oriental languages in Burlington College, N.J., 1849; was editor and secretary of the Episcopal Sunday-school Union and Church Book Society, New-York City, 1851–57; declined election as vice-president of Troy University, 1858; was rector of St. Paul's, Flatbush, L.I., 1863–65; professor of Greek, College of the City of New York, 1869–79. He is the author of *Discourses*, New York, 1843; *Egypt and the Holy Land*, 1849; *History of the United States*, 1856–69, 4 vols.; *Greek Praxis*, 1870; *Young Ruler, and Other Discourses*, 1871; edited *The Four Gospels, and Acts of the Apostles, in Greek, with English Notes* (together with the Greek text of the rest of the New Testament), 1847; *Cæsar's Commentaries* (with notes and lexicon), 1848; *Archbishop Trench's Poems*, 1856; *Xenophon's Anabasis* (from MSS. of Prof. A. Crosby), 1875; Arnold's series of Latin and Greek text-books. *

SPITTA, F. A. W. *Festpredigten*, Bonn, 1886.

STEINER, H. *Der Zürcher Professor Joh. Heinrich Hottinger in Heidelberg, 1655–61*, Zürich, 1886.

STEVENS, A., hon. A.M. (Brown University).

STEVENS, W. B., practised as a physician in Savannah, Ga., 1838–43.

STEVENSON, WILLIAM FLEMING, D.D. (University of Edinburgh, 1881); b. in Strabane, County Tyrone, Ireland, Sept. 20, 1832; d. at Rathgar, Dublin, Ireland, Sept. 16, 1886. He was of that Ulster Presbyterian stock, which has given a special character to the northern province of Ireland. He graduated M.A. at the University of Glasgow, and finished his theological studies in Scotland and Germany. Occasional passages in his writings show that while interested in the speculative and critical sides of German theology, it was the warm, spiritual, Christian life of Germany, as displayed in German hymns and missions, which attracted him most. In 1856 he was licensed to preach by the Presbytery of Strabane, became town missionary, and worked in the fever-stricken lanes of the poor part of Belfast. In 1860 he accepted the call of the newly organized Rathgar-road Presbyterian Church, situated in a suburb of Dublin. Mr. Stevenson was the first minister of this church, and it was his first and only regular charge. On the 2d of February, 1862, the present church building was dedicated, Dr. Norman McLeod preaching the opening sermon. Literary work, especially about this time, occupied much of Mr. Stevenson's attention. His contributions to *Good Words*, Dr. McLeod's periodical, were numerous, and dealt largely with the heart-life and practical Christianity of Germany. *Praying and Working*, London, 1862, is of interest to the student of social problems, as well as to the friends of missions. *Lives and Deeds worth knowing*, New York, 1870, composed of collected articles, and published without authority, is not less interesting. *Hymns for Church and Home*, London, 1873, has a scholarly accuracy and thoroughness which make it very valuable to hymnologists.

In 1871 Mr. Stevenson was called to the work which, in some sense, was the most important of his life, for in that year he became co-adjutor with Rev. Dr. James Morgan, the convener of the Assembly's Foreign Mission; and in 1873 he became sole convener, while retaining the pastorate of his church. Successful as a preacher and a pastor, he seemed even better fitted for this new work, which he had assumed with great diffidence. In 1873 he visited America on the occasion of the meeting of the Evangelical Alliance in New York. In 1877 he undertook a journey round the world, in the interests of missions; some papers from his pen appeared on the subject of this journey, in *Good Words*. In 1881 he was unanimously chosen as moderator of the General Assembly of the Presbyterian Church in Ireland, which met in Dublin. Of course many offers came to him from fields of work wider than the comparatively narrow one of Irish Presbyterianism; but he simply could not leave his beloved people. His life had now been carried on for many years, under the highest pressure from his double duties as a pastor, and as an organizer and administrator of mission-work. His death, hastened by overwork, occurred suddenly, painlessly, and almost without warning, from heart-disease, in the full tide of his activity. As a pulpit orator, Dr. Stevenson belonged to the first class. His writings give a good idea of his pulpit style. His broadly tolerant spirit won the victory over even Irish party feeling, which runs almost as high in matters ecclesiastical as political. He was a member of the Senate of the Royal University; and his appointment as chaplain to the vice-regal court, under Lord Aberdeen's administration, was regarded as marking a change in the attitude of the government towards Presbyterianism, as the attendance at his funeral of the clergy and highest dignitaries of the Episcopal and other churches, was regarded as an indication of the beginning of a better relation between the branches of the Church Catholic in Ireland than has existed in the past. ROBERT W. HALL.

STOCKMEYER, I. *Die persönliche Aneignung des in Christo gegebenen Heiles*, 1878.

STOECKER, A., is a member of the Reichstag and of the Prussian Chambers. He combines political with religious activity as a leader of the anti-Semitic movement, and of Christian socialism.

STOKES, G. T. *Ireland and the Celtic Church, a History of Ireland from St. Patrick to the English Conquest in 1172*, London, 1886; *Synopsis of Mediæval History*, 1886.

STORY, R. H., was appointed second clerk of the General Assembly, in succession to Professor Milligan, in May, 1886; and one of her Majesty's chaplains in September, 1886.

STRACK, H. L., "while acknowledging the full right of critical investigation, is convinced that such investigation ought to be combined with reverence for the Holy Scriptures and an earnest Christian faith. That Christ died for us, and rose again, is an irrefutable fact, nay, one inaccessible to criticism." The Kaiser Wilhelm Gymnasium, where he taught in 1872–73, is in Berlin. The title of the monthly *Nathanaël*, which he edits, has been changed, as also its place of publication; it is now called *Nathanaël. Zeitschrift für die Arbeit der evangelischen Kirche an Israel*, Karlsruhe u. Leipzig. He edits, with Professor Zöckler of Greifswald, the *Kurzgefasster Kommentar zu den heiligen Schriften Alten und Neuen Testamentes, sowie zu den Apokryphen*, Nördlingen, 1886 sqq.

STRONG, Josiah, D.D. (Adelbert College of Western Reserve University, Cleveland, O., 1886), Congregationalist; b. at Naperville, Du Page County, Ill., Jan. 19, 1847; graduated at Western Reserve College, Hudson, O., 1869; studied theology at Lane Theological Seminary, Cincinnati, O., 1869–71, but did not graduate because of failure in health; was pastor of a home-missionary church at Cheyenne, Wyoming Territory, 1871–73; of the Western Reserve College Church, Hudson, O., 1873–76, when the college church, having united with the village church, no longer needed a pastor; of the Congregational Church at Sandusky, O., 1876–81; secretary of the Ohio Home Missionary Society, 1881–84; pastor of the Central Congregational Church, Cincinnati, O., 1884–86, when he became general agent of the Evangelical Alliance for the United States of America. He is the author of *Our Country*, published by the American Home Missionary Society, New York, 1885, 6th ed. (26,000th) 1886.

STUART, George Hay, Presbyterian layman; b. at Rose Hall, County Down, Ireland, April 2, 1816; educated at Banbridge, Ireland; took up his residence in Philadelphia in 1831; went into business, became president of the Mechanics' National Bank of that city; afterwards the Merchants' National Bank of Philadelphia was organized for him, and he became its president. He was the president of the United-States Christian Commission during the civil war (see article, "Christian Commission," in *Schaff-Herzog Ency-*

clopædia, i. 449); is president of the Philadelphia branch of the United-States Evangelical Alliance; vice-president of the American Bible Society, of the American Tract Society, of the National Temperance Society; director of City Trusts (which includes Girard College), director of the Equitable Life Assurance Society of New York, director of the Insurance Company of the State of Pennsylvania; was chairman of the first executive committee of the Board of Indian Commissioners, organized under President Grant (serving until the original Board resigned); first president of the Young Men's Christian Association in Philadelphia, and president of three International Conventions of Young Men's Christian Associations; president of the Presbyterian National Convention which met in Philadelphia in 1867, resulting in union of O. S. and N. S. Presbyterian churches; and is prominently connected with other religious and philanthropic associations. See sketch of his life by Rev. Dr. Wylie, in A. S. Billingsby's *From the Flag to the Cross; Scenes and Incidents of Christianity in the War*, Philadelphia, 1872. (Substituted by Mr. Stuart for sketch given on p. 212.)

STUBBS, W. *Seventeen Lectures on the Study of Mediæval and Modern History, and Kindred Subjects*, London, 1886.

SWETE, H. B., was educated at King's College, London; curate of Tor, Torquay, 1869–72.

TALMAGE, Thomas DeWitt, D.D., Presbyterian; b. near Bound Brook, N.J., Jan. 7, 1832; graduated at the University of the City of New York 1853, and at the New Brunswick (Reformed Dutch) Theological Seminary, N.J., 1856; became pastor of the Reformed-Dutch Church at Belleville, N.J., 1856; Syracuse, N.Y., 1859; Second Church, Philadelphia, Penn., 1862; Central Presbyterian Church, Schermerhorn Street, Brooklyn, N.Y., 1869. In 1870 the congregation erected on the same street, near the old site, a new and much larger church, known as the "Tabernacle." It was burnt Dec. 22, 1872; rebuilt, 1873; dedicated Feb. 22, 1874. The new tabernacle seats some five thousand persons; the church has now in 1886 three thousand three hundred and eleven communicants. Dr. Talmage edited *The Christian at Work*, New York, 1873–76; *The Advance* of Chicago, in 1877 and 1878; and now edits *Frank Leslie's Sunday Magazine*. His sermons are published every week in all the countries of Christendom, and translated into Norwegian, Russian, German, French, and Italian. Over six hundred secular and religious papers each week publish them entire, and thousands furnish synopses. Of the volumes made up of his sermons, lectures, essays, etc., may be mentioned, beside foreign publications, seven volumes of sermons, *Crumbs Swept Up*, *Abominations of Modern Society*, *Shots at Targets*, *Around the Tea-Table*, *Night Side of New York*, *Mask Torn Off*, *The Marriage Ring*, *The Battle for Bread*, *Orange-Blossoms Frosted*. (Substituted by Dr. Talmage for the sketch upon p. 214.)

TAYLOR, C., is author of articles in *The Expositor* (*The Didaché, and the Epistle of Barnabas*, June, 1886), *Journal of Philology*, Smith and Wace's *Dict. Christ. Biography*, etc. He came to the United States in 1886 as delegate from Cambridge University to Harvard University, and received from the latter the degree of LL.D. at its 250th anniversary, Nov. 8, 1886.

TAYLOR, M. W. *Life of Amanda Smith*, 1886; *The Negro in Methodism* (preparing).

TAYLOR, W. M. *The Parables of Our Saviour Expounded and Illustrated*, New York, 1886.

THIERSCH, H. W. J. *De Pentateuchi versione Alexandrina libri iii.*, Erlangen, 1841; *Grammatisches Lehrbuch für die ersten Unterricht in die hebräische Sprache*, 1842, 2d ed. under title *Hebräische Grammatik für Anfänger*, 1858; *Einige Worte über die Aechtheit der neutestamentlichen Schriften*, 1846; *De Epistola ad Hebræos commentatio historica*, Marburg, 1848; *De Stephani protomartyris oratione commentatio exegetica*, 1849; *Erinnerungen an E. A. von Schaden*, Frankfurt-a.-M., 1853; *Griechenlands Schicksale*, 1863; *Ueber vernünftige und christliche Erziehung der Kinder*, Basel, 1864; *Friedrich Thierschs Leben*, Leipzig, 1866, 2 vols.; *Melanchthon*, Augsburg, 1877; *John Wesley*, 1879; *Die Physiognomie des Mondes*, Nördlingen, 1879; *Ursprung und Entwicklung der Colonieen in Nord-Amerika, 1496–1776*, Augsburg, 1880; *Ueber Johannes von Müller den Geschichtschreiber, und seinen handschriftlichen Nachlass*, 1881; *Lavater*, 1881; *Edmund Ludlow und seine Unglücksgefährten als Flüchtlinge an dem gastlichen Herde in der Schweiz*, Basel, 1881; *Samuel Gobat*, 1884 (English translation, London, 1884); *Abyssinia* (English translation by Mrs. Sarah M. S. Pereira, London, 1885).

THOMAS, D., helped to secure the first twenty thousand pounds for the University of Wales; delivered an inaugural address on the opening of University College, under the presidency of the lord lieutenant of the county, 1877. The first seven volumes of *The Homilist* were republished 1886. He furnished the homilies, and Dr. Farrar the exegesis, in the commentary on Corinthians, in *The Pulpit Commentary*.

THOMAS, Owen, D.D. (College of New Jersey, Princeton, 1877), Welsh Calvinistic Methodist; b. at Holyhead, Anglesea, North Wales, Dec. 16, 1812; attended the Bala Calvinistic Methodist College from 1838 to October, 1841; then for two sessions the University of Edinburgh, but was unable, owing to circumstances, to finish the curriculum; became minister at Pwllheli, Caernarvonshire, 1844; (of the English Church) at Newtown, Montgomeryshire, 1846; in London, 1850; of the Welsh Presbyterian Church, Prince's Road, Liverpool, 1865. He was moderator of North Wales Association in 1863 and 1882; moderator of General Assembly, 1868; has been repeatedly sent as a deputation to visit the Scotch (Free), Irish, and English Assemblies, as well as to the Council of the Reformed Churches. His father was a stonecutter by trade, and he worked at this trade from his fourteenth to his sixteenth year. He has been for years joint editor of the *Traethyrdydd*, the oldest and ablest Welsh quarterly, and is the author of a large number of articles on theological, philosophical, critical, and historical subjects; many articles in the *Welsh Encyclopædia*; *Life of John Jones* (*Talsarn*) (containing a large account of the Welsh preachers, and theological controversies in Wales), Wrexham, 1874, 2 vols.; and a translation of *Kitto's Pictorial New Testament* into Welsh, with very extensive additions, forming a full commentary on the Epistles to the Galatians, and most of Ephesians, Colossians, and Philippians, and especially of Hebrews (Wrexham, 1885, 2 vols.).

THOROLD, A. W., was canon residentiary of York, 1874–77.

TIELE, C. P. *De godsdienst der liefde* ("The Religion of Love"), Amsterdam, 1868; *Babylonisch-assyrische Geschichte*, vol. i., Gotha, 1886; 2d ed., much enlarged, of French translation of *Geschiedenis van den Godsdienst*, 1886; Danish translation of same, Copenhagen, 1884.

TITCOMB, J. H., resigned his bishopric in consequence of a terrible mountain accident. He is now vicar of St. Peter's, Brockly, London.

TOLLIN, H. G. N. *Die hohenzollernschen Colonisationen*, 1876; *Die magdeburger Wallonen*, 1876; *Die französischen Colonieen in Oranienburg, Köpenick und Rheinsberg*, 1876; *Albrecht von Mainz und Hans von Schenitz*, 1878; *Bürgermeister Aug. Wilh. Franke*, 1884.

TOORENENBERGEN, J. J. van. The first tom. of the *Monumenta*, etc., contains a reprint of the excessively rare *Œconomica Christiana*, whence the *Summe of Holy Scripture* is drawn.

TOWNSEND, L. T. *The Bible and other Ancient Literature in the Nineteenth Century*, 1885; *Pulpit Rhetoric*, 1886.

TRENCH, R. C. *Sermons New and Old*, London and New York, 1886.

TROLLOPE, E., is the son of the late Sir John Trollope, Bart., and brother of the late Lord Kestwen, and was archdeacon of Stow in 1867.

TROUTBECK, J., was educated at Rugby School.

TSCHACKERT, P. [Johannes Briessmann's] *Floscriti*, 1887.

TUCKER, Henry William, Church of England; prebendary of Wenlocksbarn in St. Paul's Cathedral; educated at Magdalen Hall, Oxford; graduated B.A. 1854, M.A. 1859; ordained deacon 1854, priest 1855; was curate of Chantry, Somersetshire, 1854-56; West Buckland, 1856-60; Devoran, Cornwall, 1860–65; assistant secretary of the Society for Promoting Christian Knowledge, 1865–79; since 1875 has been secretary to the Associates of the late Rev. Dr. Bray; since 1879, secretary of the Society for the Propagation of the Gospel in Foreign Parts, and also honorary secretary of the Colonial Bishops' Fund. He is the author of *Under his Banner: Papers on Mission Work of Modern Times*, London, 1872, 7th ed. 1877; *Memoir of the Life and Episcopate of Edward Feild, D.D.* (bishop of Newfoundland), 1878, 4th ed. 1879; *Memoir of the Life and Episcopate of George Augustus Selwyn, D.D.* (bishop of Lichfield), 1878, 2 vols., 4th ed. 1881; *The English Church in Other Lands; or, the Spiritual Expansion of England*, London and New York, 1886.

TUCKER, W. J. One of the founders and editors of *The Andover Review*.

TULLOCH. L. 36, after *Philosophy* add: *in England in the Seventeenth Century*.

TWINING, Kinsley, D.D. (Yale College, New Haven, Conn., 1884), Congregationalist; b. at West Point, N.Y., July 18, 1832; graduated at Yale College 1853, and at Yale Theological Seminary 1856; was resident licentiate at Andover Seminary, 1857; was pastor of the Congregational Church, Hinsdale, Mich., 1857–63; acting pastor of the First Congregational Church, San Francisco, Cal., 1863–64; and then for nearly two years out of ministerial service in poor health; pastor of Prospect-street Congregational Church, Cambridgeport, Mass., 1867–72; of the Union Congregational Church, Providence, R.I., 1872–76; in Europe, 1876–78; became literary editor of the New-York *Independent*, 1880.

TYLER, W. S. *Homer's Iliad, Books xvi.–xxiv.* New York, 1886. He received the degree of LL.D. at Harvard's 250th anniversary, Nov. 8, 1886.

UHLHORN, J. G. W. English translation, by Sophia Taylor, of vol. i., *Die christliche Liebesthätigkeit, Die alte Kirche*, under title, *Christian Charity in the Ancient Church*, Edinburgh, 1883.

VALENTINE, M., LL.D. (Wittenberg College, Springfield, O., 1886).

VAN DYKE, Joseph Smith, D.D. (College of New Jersey, Princeton, N.J., 1884), Presbyterian; b. at Bound Brook, N.J., Nov. 2, 1832; graduated at the College of New Jersey 1857, and at the theological seminary 1861, both in Princeton, N.J.; was tutor of Greek in the college there, 1859–61; pastor of First Presbyterian Church, Bloomsbury, N.J., 1861–69; and since has been pastor of the Second Presbyterian Church, Cranbury, N.J. During 1859 and 1860 he was engaged in lecturing upon education, in conjunction with the superintendent of public schools in New Jersey. He is the author of *Popery the Foe of the Church and of the Republic*, Philadelphia, 1871, 12th thousand, New York, 1886; *The Legal Prohibition of the Liquor Traffic* (Tract No. 174 of the National Temperance Society), New York, 1879; *Through the Prison to the Throne, Illustrations of Life from the Biography of Joseph*, New York, 1881, 5th ed. 1886; *From Gloom to Gladness, Illustrations of Life from the Biography of Esther*, 1883, 3d ed. 1886; *Giving or Entertainment— Which?* (pamphlet recommending giving, in preference to other modes of raising money for church and charitable purposes), 1883, 11th ed. 1886 (ten thousand sold); *Theism and Evolution: an Examination of Modern Speculative Theories as related to Theistic Conceptions of the Universe*, 1886 (April), 2d ed. (October) 1886.

VENABLES, E., wrote article "Monastic Rules and Architecture," in *Dict. Chr. Antiq.*; and articles "Bunyan," "Brevint," "Bullingham," "Cecil (Richard)," etc., in Leslie Stephen's *Dict. Nat. Biog.*

VINCENT, M. R. *Christ as a Teacher*, 1886; *Bible Words* (in preparation).

VOELTER, Daniel Erhardt Johannes, Ph.D., Lic. Theol. (both Tübingen, 1880 and 1883 respectively), Protestant theologian; b. at Esslingen, Würtemberg, Sept. 14, 1855; studied at Tübingen (Evangelical Theological Seminary and University); became *repetent* in the theological seminary there, 1880; *privat-docent* of theology in the university, 1884; ordinary professor of theology in the Lutheran Seminary in Amsterdam, 1885; and since February, 1886, has also held the same position in the University of Amsterdam. He is the author of *Die Entstehung der Apokalypse*, Freiburg, 1882, 2d ed. 1885; *Der Ursprung des Donatismus*, 1883.

VOLCK, W., edited not only the ninth but the tenth and eleventh volumes of Hofmann's *Die h. Schrift N. T.*, Nördlingen, 1883, 1886. In the 10th ed. of Gesenius the title reads: *Hebräisches und aramäisches Handwörterbuch*.

WACE, Henry, was curate of St. Luke's, Borwick Street, London, 1861–63. King's College, of which he is principal, is in London.

WADDINGTON, C., discovered the true date of Polycarp's martyrdom (A.D. 155).

WAGENMANN, J. A., D.D. (1862), editor of the *Jahrbücher f. deutsche Theologie*, 1862–78; wrote articles in Herzog and *Allg. deutsche Biographie.*

WALDENSTRÖM, P. P. "On the Meaning of the Atonement" (*Om försoningens Betydelse*, Stockholm, 1873, reprinted Chicago, Ill., U.S.A.). A sermon preached in 1872 first gave impetus to the theological movement with which he is identified, and the book was written to defend and explain his views which had attracted so much attention. He prefers to put his distinctive teaching thus: *Non per gratiam propter Christo propitiatorem, sed propter gratiam per Christum mediatorem, redemptorem.* He is commonly accused in Sweden of denying the divinity of Christ; but this is a slander, for just the contrary is the case. In his translation of the New Testament, he accepts and defends the reading ὁ μονογενὴς θεός in John i. 18.

WANAMAKER, John, Presbyterian layman; b. in Philadelphia, Penn., in the year 1838; received a common-school education, and early went into business. After being a clerk for a while in the year 1861, he started in the clothing business on his own account. He subsequently enlarged and altered his business, until now he is the owner of one of the largest retail stores in the United States, employs some three thousand persons, and is known throughout the country. He has displayed similar energy in Christian work. He started, in 1858, a Sunday school over a shoemaker's shop in the south-western part of Philadelphia, out of which has grown Bethany Presbyterian Church, with a seating capacity of 1,800, and Bethany Sunday School, numbering in 1886 2971 members. He was one of the founders of the Christian Commission; president of the Young Men's Christian Association of Philadelphia from 1870 to 1883; and has been prominent in many other Christian enterprises. He was chairman of the Bureau of Revenue and of the Press Committee, which did such efficient service in starting the Centennial Exposition in Philadelphia in 1876. Approved by Mr. Wanamaker.

WARFIELD, B. B., has written articles on biblical criticism and the *Didaché*, in "Bibliotheca Sacra," "Presbyterian," "Andover Review," and "Expositor," etc.

WATTS, R., established the Westminster Church in Philadelphia 1852, and was ordained pastor of it 1853; was installed in the Gloucester-street Church, Dublin, 1863.

WEED, Edwin Gardner, D.D. (University of the South, Sewanee, Tenn., 1886), **S.T.D.** (Racine College, Wis., 1886), Episcopalian, bishop of Florida; b. at Savannah, Ga., July 23, 1837; graduated from the General Theological Seminary, New-York City, 1870; became rector of the Church of the Good Shepherd, Summerville, Ga., 1871; bishop, 1886. *

WEISS, Carl Philipp Bernhard, Ph.D. (Jena, 1852), **Lic. Theol.** (Königsberg, 1852), **D.D.** (*hon.*, Königsberg, 1862); studied at Königsberg, Halle, and Berlin, 1844–48; was *Divisionspfarrer* at Königsberg, 1861–63; *Consistorialrath und Mitglied des Consistoriums* at Kiel, 1874–77; *Mitglied des Consistoriums* at Berlin, 1879–80; since 1880, *Ober-Consistorialrath und vortragender Rath im Ministerium der geistlichen u. Unterrichts-Angelegenheiten.* To list of works add: *Lehrbuch der Einleitung in das Neue Testament*, Berlin, 1886. His *Lehrbuch der biblischen Theologie* was translated, Edinburgh, 1882–83, 2 vols. New editions of his commentaries, in the Meyer series, Mark and Luke (1885), John (1886), Romans (1886), Timothy and Titus (1886). Besides books, he has written numerous elaborate articles in *Studien u. Kritiken*, *Jahrbücher f. deutsche Theologie*, etc.

WEISS, Nathanaël, Reformed Church of France; b. at La Croix-aux-Mines, near Saint Die (Vosges), March 27, 1845; studied at the Protestant gymnasium at Strassburg, and finished course of theology with Protestant faculty of that university, 1867; was private tutor in Alsace and Paris, 1867–69; won the Schmutz prize by thesis, *Exposition, comparison et critique du système ecclésiastique de Schleiermacher et de celui de Vinet*, 1868; was Reformed pastor at Glacière, 1869–71; missionary agent of the French Sunday-school Society, 1871–75; pastor of the Reformed Church of Boulogne-sur-Seine since 1875; and is now adjunct librarian of the "Société du protestantisme français." He contributed articles upon Protestant France to Lichtenberger's *Encyclopédie des sciences religieuses*, and edited for the first time, with an introduction and notes, *La sortie de France pour cause de religion, de Daniel Brousson et sa famille, 1685–93*, Paris, 1886. *

WEIZSAECKER, K. *Das Neue Testament übersetzt*, Tübingen, 1875, 2d ed. Freiburg, 1882; *Das apostolische Zeitalter der christlichen Kirche*, Freiburg, 1886.

WELLHAUSEN, J. English translation of *Prolegomena*, with introduction by Prof. W. Robertson Smith, under title *Prolegomena to the History of Israel, with a reprint of the article Israel from the "Encycl Britannica,"* Edinburgh, 1885.

WENDT, H. H., studied at Leipzig and Göttingen, as well as at Tübingen.

WESTCOTT, B. F., was a member of the Royal Commission on ecclesiastical courts, 1881–83; 2d ed. of *General View Hist. Eng. Bible*, 1872; *Christus Consummator: Some Aspects of the Work and Person of Christ in Relation to Modern Thought* (sermons) 1886.

WHEDON, D. D., studied law at Rochester and Rome, N.Y.; became teacher in the Oneida Seminary, 1830. Two additional volumes of his collected writings appeared in 1886. Emory and Henry College is at Emory, Washington Co., Va.

WIKNER, C. P. "Sermons," vols. i., ii., 1877, 1883; "Notion of Quality," 1880.

WILKES, Henry, d. in Montreal, Wednesday, Nov. 17, 1886.

WILKINSON, W. C. *The Baptist Principle*, 1881; *Webster: an Ode*, 1882; *Classic French Course in English*, 1886. He has been several seasons "adjunct lecturer" on English literature in Wellesley College. He is at present (1886) conductor of a department (Pastoral Theology) in *The Homiletic Review.* He has twice travelled in Europe, attending lectures during one winter at the University of Paris, and spending some months in Germany, as well as visiting the chief centres of art in Italy.

WILLIAMS, G., is on the committee of the British and Foreign Bible Society; is ex-president of the Sunday-school Union.

WILLIAMS, William R. Mr. Mornay Williams, his son, sends this additional information: "Dr. Williams had no middle name; the initial 'R' having been assumed by him, in early life, because of the annoying mistakes constantly arising from the simple appellation William Williams. He was ordained and installed as pastor of the Amity Baptist Church on the same evening on which the church itself was recognized, Dec. 17, 1832, remaining pastor to the time of his death, never having had another charge, nor his people another pastor. He was the first secretary of the American Baptist Home Missionary Society (1832); the first secretary, and one of the draughters, of the constitution of the Baptist Ministers' Conference, in January, 1833; for many years a member of the board of trustees of Rochester Theological Seminary, in the formation of which, as also of the University of Rochester (both established in 1850), he was actively concerned. He was also for many years on the publishing committee of the American Tract Society, and in that position corrected the proofs of their foreign publications (viz., French, German, Italian, and Spanish); he was one of the vice-presidents of that society, as also of the American Bible Society. He wrote the introduction to [the American reprint of John] Harris's *Great Commission; or, the Christian Church constituted and charged to convey the Gospel to the World*, Boston, 1842; to that of Miss Grigg's *Jacqueline Pascal, or Convent Life at Port Royal*, New York, 1854; and to [W. W.] Everts's *William Colgate: a Christian Layman*, Philadelphia, 1881. His *Religious Progress*, and *Lectures on the Lord's Prayer*, were both republished in Scotland [in one volume, Edinburgh and London, 1851]."

WILSON, J. L., became secretary *emeritus*, 1885. Died at his home near Marysville, S.C., July 13, 1886.

WISE, D. *Young Knights of the Cross*, New York, 1886.

WITHEROW, T. Italian translation of *Scriptural Baptism*, Florence, 1877.

WITHROW, J. L., preached the opening sermon at the Des Moines meeting of the A. B. C. F. M. in 1886; accepted call to Third Presbyterian Church, Chicago, Ill., 1886.

WOLF, E. J., has published some sermons; is editor of *The Lutheran Quarterly*.

WOODRUFF, F. E., wrote on the Greek Fragment of the Rainer MSS., and a vindication of the genuineness of the Pastoral Epistles, in *The Andover Review*, 1886.

WOOLSEY, T. D., received the degree of **LL.D.** at Harvard's 250th anniversary, Nov. 8, 1886.

WORDSWORTH, C., D.C.L. (*hon.*, Oxford, 1853), **D.D.** (*hon.*, Edinburgh and St. Andrews); *Catechesis*, 4th ed. 1868; *Remarks on Dr. Lightfoot's Essay*, 2d ed. 1884; *Discourse on Scottish Church History*, 1884; *Public Appeals in Behalf of Christian Liberty*, 1886, 2 vols.

WORDSWORTH, J., was exhibitioner of Winchester College. *Portions of St. Mark and St. Matthew from the Bobbio MS. (k), and Other Fragments* (with Dr. Sanday and H. J. White), being No. 2 of a series of Old Latin biblical texts, 1886; "The Corbey St. James (*ff.*)" in *Studia Biblia*, Oxford, 1883; *A Pastoral Letter to the Clergy and Laity of the Diocese of Salisbury*, Salisbury, November, 1885; *Self-Discipline in Charity* (sermon on St. James i. 26, 27, preached in Salisbury Cathedral on May 30, 1886, for the clergy orphan schools), Salisbury, 1886; *Bristol Bishopric Endowment Fund* (sermon on Heb. xiii. 14, preached in Bristol Cathedral, June 27, 1886), Bristol.

WORTHINGTON, George, D.D., LL.D. (both from Hobart College, 1876 and 1885 respectively), Episcopalian, bishop of Nebraska; b. at Lenox, Mass., Oct. 14, 1838; graduated at Hobart College, Geneva, N.Y., 1860, and at the General Theological Seminary, New-York City, 1863; became assistant at St. Paul's Church, Troy, N.Y., 1863; rector of Christ Church, Ballston Spa, N.Y., 1865; rector of St. John's Church, Detroit, Mich., 1868. He was in 1879 twice elected by the clergy bishop of Michigan, but the laity refused to confirm. In 1883 he declined election by the General Convention as missionary bishop of Shanghai. In May, 1884, he was elected bishop of Nebraska, and declined; in November, 1884, was elected a second time, accepted, and was consecrated in St. John's Church, Detroit, Mich., Feb. 24, 1885.

WRIGHT, C. H. H. *The Divinity-school Question*, Dublin, 1886 (pp. 8); *Biblical Essays: or, Exegetical Studies on the Books of Job and Jonah, Ezekiel's Prophecy of Gog and Magog, St. Peter's "Spirits in Prison," and the Key to the Apocalypse*, Edinburgh, 1886.

WRIGHT, W., M.A.

WYLIE, J. H. *History of the Scottish Nation*, 1886, 2 vols.

YOUNG, R. *Materials for Bible Revision* (drawn from the *Analytical Concordance*), 1886.

ZAHN, T. *Hermæ Pastor e N. T. illustr.*, Göttingen, 1867; *Missionsmethoden im Zeitalter der Apostel*, Erlangen, 1886 (two lectures).

ZELLER, E. *Plato's Gastmahl, übersetzt und erläutert*, Marburg, 1857; *Vorträge*, 2d ed. Leipzig 1875, 3d series Leipzig 1884; *Geschichte d. deutsch. Phil.*, 2d ed. 1875; *Grundriss d. Geschichte d. griech. Philosophie*, Leipzig, 1883, 2d edition 1885 (English translation by Sarah Frances Alleyne and Evelyn Abbott, *Outlines of the History of Greek Philosophy*, London and New York, 1886); *Friedrich d. Gr. als Philosoph*, Berlin, 1886.

ZEZSCHWITZ, Gerhard von, was pastor at Grosszschocher near Leipzig, 1852–56; lived at Neuendetteslau without office, 1861–63; lectured at Frankfurt, Basel, and Darmstadt, 1863–65; out of these lectures came *Zur Apologie des Christenthums nach Geschichte und Lehre*, Leipzig, 1866.

ZOECKLER, O., edits, with H. L. Strack, *Kurzgefasster Kommentar zu den heiligen Schriften A. u. N. T.'s nebst den Apokryphen*, Nördlingen, 1886 sqq., 12 vols.

www.ingramcontent.com/pod-product-compliance
Lightning Source LLC
Chambersburg PA
CBHW030345270326
41926CB00009B/962